CONTINUED FROM FRONT FLAP

ous countries. Consequently, the lists published in this volume are the most comprehensive and complete available in English.

This, the first collected edition of the annual book lists published by the Society, is under the distinguished editorship of Professor Rowley. It fulfills a vital need; since many of the post-war issues have long been out of print.

An invaluable source work, *Eleven Years of Bible Bibliography* is a notable contribution to Old Testament studies, and a standard reference work of enduring usefulness.

ELEVEN YEARS
of
BIBLE BIBLIOGRAPHY

ELEVEN YEARS
of
BIBLE BIBLIOGRAPHY

The Book Lists of
The Society for Old Testament Study
1946-56

EDITED BY

H. H. ROWLEY, D.D., THEOL. D., F.B.A.

PROFESSOR OF HEBREW LANGUAGE AND LITERATURE
UNIVERSITY OF MANCHESTER

 # THE FALCON'S WING PRESS

INDIAN HILLS, COLORADO

Manufactured in the United States of America

Library of Congress Catalogue Card Number: 57-7079

PREFACE

BEFORE the Second World War the British Society for Old Testament Study began to issue annually to its members a short list of books bearing on the Old Testament which had appeared during the previous year. This was suspended during the war because we were cut off from access to so much of the literature that was appearing. After the war I was asked to undertake the editorship of the revived Book List, and it immediately assumed larger proportions and became a more comprehensive list.

The notices on the books included are deliberately kept as short as possible, and are designed to indicate to scholars the area with which the book deals and the quality of the book. Full-length reviews would defeat the whole purpose of the List. That it has met a need has been made clear by the wide interest it has aroused, both within the membership of the Society and beyond.

When I undertook the editorship I little realized the burden I was assuming. That burden could not have been carried but for the help of innumerable friends. My correspondence with a very wide circle of Old Testament scholars in more than a score of countries kept me in touch with a large part of the significant literature which was appearing, though despite that help and every effort I could make, it was inevitable that some important books should be missed. Omniscience, even in the limited field of publications bearing on the Old Testament, is not given to man.

For the preparation of the notices I have had the willing help of a large number of members of the Society appointed for the purpose, and have often been able to call on the help of foreign scholars for notices on books which were either not available in England or impossible to obtain in time for inclusion in the next issue. To all who have helped me, either by keeping me in touch with what was appearing or by writing the notices, I offer my thanks.

It has often been suggested that the List should also include brief abstracts of articles in our field. This would have enlarged the List beyond the resources of the Society, and would have required a much larger panel of writers than we had available. That need has now been met on a scale we could not have rivaled by the publication of the *Internationale Zeitschriftenschau für Bibelwissenschaft und Grenzgebiete*. Our more modest Book List has proved of value to librarians in keeping their acquisitions up to date, and has enabled scholars pursuing any particular piece of research to know what books have recently appeared relevant to their study. To have served scholarship in the role of the honey bee, fructifying the work of others, has brought some satisfaction as well as much labour and constant care.

Now that I have handed over the editorship of the Book List to the younger and more vigorous hands of the Rev. G. W. Anderson, I hope that this reissue of the eleven issues I have edited may serve some who have not had access to the separate Lists, most of which have gone quickly out of print. Scholars who would like to receive the annual lists as they appear may secure them from Mr. D. R. Ap-Thomas, Llansadwrn, Anglesey, Wales.

H. H. Rowley

Manchester
England

CONTENTS

1946

This issue of the Book List contains notes on books published since the last issue in 1940, and on some earlier foreign works which were not then available in this country. It has been prepared by a Sub-Committee consisting of Miss B. K. Rattey, Mgr. J. M. T. Barton, Dr. David Daube, Professors G. R. Driver, A. R. Johnson, N. W. Porteous, O. S. Rankin, N. H. Snaith, and H. H. Rowley (Editor). The thanks of the Committee are given to the Rev. J. N. Schofield, who generously consented to prepare a large number of the notices, and to Professors W. Baumgartner, of Basel, Johs. Pedersen, of Copenhagen, and J. van der Ploeg, O.P., of Nijmegen, for notices on a number of continental works—principally works not yet available in this country. The Editor acknowledges with thanks help received from Mr. P. R. Weis, principally in the preparation of the notices on works written in Hebrew.

Every effort has been made to make the List as comprehensive as possible, but there are inevitably gaps, and especially where German books are concerned. The Editor learned of the titles of a number of German works too late to secure notices on them from continental colleagues. It is not always easy to draw the line between works that fall within the sphere of the interest of the Society and those that fall without, and by extending the range to include works with a more remote connexion with the Old Testament a more extensive List could have been prepared. The Editor asks the indulgence of those who would have had a wider net.

Prices of foreign books, where known, are given either in foreign currency or in the English equivalent actually charged.

GENERAL.

DE BOER, P.A.H. (ed. by) : *Oudtestamentische Studiën*, vols. I—III, 1941–43. (Brill, Leiden. £4. 10s. 0d.)

> The first volume is in two parts. The first (1941) contains four articles in English and one in French. Two especially are to be commended. B. D. Eerdmans makes what appears to be a sound suggestion that non-resident Israelites placed some personal object in the Temple precincts so as to secure, though by proxy, the blessings of dwelling in the holy hill. Th. C. Vriezen deals with the diverse comments on Jacob's character in Hosea xii by proposing a dialogue between prophet and people. The second part (1942) is a collection of ten essays on Masoretic Psalms by B. D. Eerdmans. Two are of particular importance ; in the first (" On the road to monotheism "), the theory is propounded that each man has his own particular El, at the head of all of which is the great El of nature, but that (e.g. Psalm cvii) men rebelled against the words of El, and the council of Elyon, and cried to Jahu. In the essay on the Chasidim, he makes these to be a pre-exilic group, and identifies them with the Servant of the Lord.

> The second volume (1943) is a Festschrift to Professor Eerdmans on his 75th birthday. It is prefixed with a list of his fifty-two publications of various types. There are ten contributors, who write in English (three), French (six), and German (one). Each article would merit a place in any collection, but in particular we recommend two of the French articles, one by Th. C. Vriezen on the meaning of the phrase " the image of God " in the Creation story, and the other by M. A. Beek on the relations between Jews in Jerusalem and Egypt in the second century B.C.

> The third volume (1943) is in Dutch and is a study by P. A. H. de Boer entitled *De Voorbede in het Oude Testament* (Intercessory Prayer). There is a short summary in English at the end of the book. The author stresses the importance of the content of these prayers, and points out that earlier prayers are regarded as themselves having effective power (cf. blessings and curses). The prayers deal with the qualities of God, and not the situation of the individual. In later prayers the ethical content has developed, and the argument of the prayer is a confession of guilt.   N.H.S.

BURROWS, E., S.J. : *The Gospel of the Infancy and other Biblical Essays*, edited by E. F. Sutcliffe, S.J. 1941. (Burns, Oates and Washbourne, London.)

> The bulk of the essays here reprinted or printed for the first time are of interest to Old Testament scholars. In his treatment of St. Luke chapters 1 and 2 the author is concerned to show the fundamental parallelism of these chapters with I Samuel 1—3. The most important paper " The Servant of Yahweh in Isaiah : an Interpretation " was read to the Society for Old Testament Study at the winter meeting of 1937, less than a year before Fr. Burrows' lamented and

all-too-early death. The suggested interpretation, as members may recall, is that " the Servant is not Israel nor any of the collectivities or abstractions proposed ; nor precisely any individual ; but the HOUSE OF DAVID ". The other papers (on the interpretation of Psalm 110 ; Sanctifying Grace in the Old Testament ; the Doctrine of the Shekinah and the Theology of the Incarnation ; Speculation on the Doctrine of the Two Adams ; the Name of Jerusalem ; and a Note on Ziqqurats), while always gracefully written and scholarly, are less impressive. J.M.T.B.

COLWELL, E. C. : *The Study of the Bible.* 3rd impression. 1945. (University of Chicago Press.)

> The President of the University of Chicago gives in this little work a fresh and vividly written account of the process of Canonisation which gave us the Bible, of the history of the text and its transmission, of the successive attempts at translation and finishes up with three chapters on interpretation. He advocates, in opposition to what he calls the " modernising " method, the historical method which proceeds by literary and historical criticism, and he defines the ultimate aim of Biblical interpretation as the disclosure of the vital religious life of Israel and the early Christian Church. This indicates the merit and the limitations of the book. N.W.P.

DAVIS, J. D. : *The Westminster Dictionary of the Bible,* 5th Edition, revised and rewritten by H. S. GEHMAN. 1944. (Westminster Press, Philadelphia. $3.50.)

> Brief in compass (less than seven hundred pages, $9'' \times 6''$) this handbook has been brought up-to-date with material from archæological sources (e.g. Lachish Letters, Ras Shamra texts, the John Rylands fragment of the Fourth Gospel, the Chester Beatty papyri), and bears the marks of Gehman's wide reading and industry. Its point of view is dominantly conservative, but it treats other positions with respect, and gives some account of them within the limits of its brief space. H.H.R.

DUGMORE, C. W. (ed. by) : *The Interpretation of the Bible* (Edward Alleyne Lectures, 1943). 1944. (S.P.C.K., London. 6s. 0d.)

> This volume contains a series of six lectures. The first three are mainly historical in character and deal with the view taken of the Bible in the Early Church, in the Middle Ages and in the earlier period of " Protestantism. The last three, by R. H. Lightfoot on the " Critical Approach to the Bible in the Nineteenth Century ", by T. W. Manson on the " Failure of Liberalism to interpret the Bible as the Word of God " and by J. Lowe on the " Recovery of the Theological Interpretation of the Bible ", are of real value for the present day, both for their shrewd appreciation of the modern situation, for their balanced judgment and for their timely words of

warning as to possible dangers. T. W. Manson urges a return to the point at which Liberalism took the wrong turning. The last essay—by the Dean of Christ Church—discusses the tendency to authoritarianism, characteristic of certain continental theologians, and to mystical interpretation, which appeals especially to some Anglican theologians.

N.W.P.

DUSSAUD, R. : *Mélanges Syriens offerts à M. René Dussaud*, vol. 2. 1939. (Geuthner, Paris.)

This second volume presented to M. Dussaud contains fifty-five essays, mainly in French, covering a very wide range ; about twenty are concerned with post-biblical periods but the remainder are of value for Biblical archæology, language, and interpretation. (For Vol. 1 see Book List, 1940.)

J.N.S.

GLANVILLE, S. R. K. (ed. by) : *The Legacy of Egypt*. 1942. (Clarendon Press, Oxford. 10s. 0d.)

While only one chapter of this book directly touches the Old Testament—Oesterley's chapter on " Egypt and Israel "—and nearly half of the book deals with Egypt in post-Old Testament times, it should not be overlooked by the Old Testament scholar. Egypt was so important an element of Israel's *milieu*, that the earlier chapters on her culture and institutions are of value for the appreciation of the background of the Old Testament, while Oesterley's chapter summarizes the historical, religious and literary connexions between Egypt and Israel. H.H.R.

Hebrew Union College Annual XV. 1940. (Cincinnati. $3.00.)

S. H. Blank writes on Deutero-Isaiah, dealing with (1) the monotheistic argument from prophecy, (2) the 'Ebed Yahveh and the prophetic movement. J. Lewy maintains the original identity of Habiru and Hebrews, on the basis of parallels between the habiru servant in texts from Nuzi and the 'ebed 'ibri. J. Morgenstern discusses the historical antecedents of Amos : (1) David and Solomon, (2) the Northern Kingdom to Omri, (3) the reformation in the South, (4) Omri and Ahab, (5) Elijah, (6) Micaiah ben Yimlah, (7) 853—841, (8) Elisha and the prophetic reformation in the North, (9) 841—805, (10) 805 to Amos, (11) the social and religious background of Amos. S. Krauss has some textual remarks on Daniel 8^{5ff}. H. H. Rowley argues that Jewish proselyte baptism probably existed by the beginning of the Christian era ; that it expressed a change of heart and mediated grace ; but that the baptism of John differed from it in being (1) public, (2) symbol of a new life rather than creed, (3) associated with eschatological notions. H. Englander urges that Jacob Meir Tam's merit as a grammarian—triliterality of the Hebrew root—is overrated. D.D.

J. Morgenstern re-interprets and re-dates Psalm **48**, starting from the thesis that vv. 5—8 are an interpolation. J. Bamberger shows that those Aggadists who make Moses receive the entire Torah, written and oral, during his forty days on Mount Sinai are combating Christian and Gnostic ideas. L. Finkelstein argues that early Aggadic material was handed down in five forms : (1) the anecdotal, no part being fixed, the basic idea alone determining tradition, (2) the semi-normative, catchwords being fixed but tradition still being oral, (3) the fully fixed oral norm, (4) the earliest written form, deriving from (2), i.e. with catchwords committed to writing, (5) the written text, emerging either out of (3) or out of (4). A. Guttmann discusses the anonymous Mishnah. John Toland's remarkable attitude to Judaism and the Old Testament is analysed by M. Wiener. A. Sperber holds that the current grammatical theories cannot save Tiberian phonology, a medieval system. He attempts to recover the state prior to Masoretic activities, with revolutionary conclusions : a most interesting article. A. Weiss (in Hebrew) investigates some methods adopted by the compilers of the Mishnah in arranging their material. D.D.

J. and H. Lewy investigate the week and the oldest West-Asiatic calendar. Few of their conclusions are as improbable as the one that the time-unit day arose in view of the coming and going, not of the sun, but of the diurnal winds. J. Morgenstern discusses the Ark, comparing the Arabic Otfe, Markab, Måhmal and Kubbe. H. M. Orlinsky argues that the Ketib *thtw* is but the earlier spelling of *thtyw*—no form *tahtô* existed ; that the Qere *bynyw* is due to an error of the Masoretes—only *bênô* is correct ; that the extraordinary form *b'dynw* is a corruption of '*dynw* ; that the Ketib '*nw* for *we* is a corruption of '*nhnw* and identical with the Mishnic form by mere coincidence ; that the Ketib *z'th* is a corruption of *z't* ; that the yod in '*lyw* and '*lyw* does not go back to the original roots '*ly* and '*ly* ; and that the diphthong *au* is indicated by *yw* only, and not by *wy* as well. A. Sperber outlines the radically new methods he intends to use in establishing a fresh edition of the Hebrew Bible. He considers that the dagesh has outlived its existence, that a single vowel-sign should be substituted for qāmeç and pathaḥ, and one other for çērê and seghôl : conclusions brilliantly advocated and certain to delight undergraduates. A. Cuttmann contends that Akiba's achievement consisted, not in creating an outstanding Mishnah, but in organizing the whole of tradition according to (1) subject-matter—Mishnah, Halakic Midrash, Aggada—and (2) importance for life—Mishnah, Tosefta, Baraita. H. Englander comments upon Rashi's grammatical remarks. S. Atlas (in Hebrew) gives an excellent illustration of the way the Talmud presents a Halakic discussion as a unit even though its earlier portions reflect a state of law quite different from the final. D.D.

J. Morgenstern discusses (1) the Ephod—originally, in his opinion, the tent-sanctuary with its betyls, (2) the Tent of Meeting—borrowed, he says, by Moses from the Kenites but purged of betyls, represented in J as the place of revelation of Yahveh, the universal, heavenly god, while P reverts to the notion of Yahveh's dwelling. H. F. Fischel surveys the Jewish interpretation of the 'Ebed Yahveh passages from Rabbinic times to the nineteenth century. R. Gordis argues that both the conventional and the less conventional Wisdom writings reflect the outlook of the upper classes, later crystallized as Sadduceeism. A. Cronbach summarizes what the various Apocrypha and Pseudepigrapha have to say about (1) poverty and wealth, (2) benevolence, (3) social justice, (4) world peace, (5) the ideal society, with interesting results : e.g. IV Ezra does not list poverty among the miseries heralding the Messiah ; in Wisdom of Solomon, Sodom is arraigned, not as in the Talmud for injustice, but for departure from Wisdom only ; in Judith, Israel's downfall is ascribed to the worship of false gods only, no mention being made of oppression of the poor, emphasized by the prophets ; visiting the poor comes only in the Story of Ahikar, laudations of the poor only in Ecclesiasticus and the Zadokite Fragments. F. Rosenthal argues that yom tob, " day of plenty ", probably acquired the sense of "holiday" in the Maccabean period, when the sacredness of the festivals was not stressed and each could be joyfully celebrated ; he would not, however, rule out the possibility of foreign astrology being responsible, "holiday" going back to "auspicious day ". J. Lewy writes on the old West-Semitic sun-god Hammu, discussing (1) the theophoric name element Hammu, (2) the place name Hamat, (3) Hamat-Soba and Subat-Hamatu, (4) the mountain name Haman, (5) the origin of the Hammu-rapi dynasty—he says it may come from as far west of Babylonia as Coele-Syria, (6) Hammu and Ham—he declares Noah's second son identical with the sun-god, (7) the town names Amedi and Emesa—both, in his view, mean " belonging to Hammu ", and he notes that under Elagabal, descendant of priests of Emesa, the sun cult of Coele-Syria once more became a world religion.   D.D.

LATTEY, C., S.J. : *Back to the Bible.* 1945. (Burns, Oates and Washbourne, London. 5s. 0d.)

This little book, to which the Archbishop of Liverpool con tributes a foreword, discusses in simple language such topics as reason and revelation, the inspiration of the Bible, Adam and Eve, the documentary hypothesis, Wellhausen's historical stages in the history of the " Place of Worship ", the prophets, the Synoptic Gospels, the Fourth Gospel, and St. Paul.   J.M.T.B.

LIEBERMAN, S. : *Greek in Jewish Palestine.* 1942. (Jewish Theological Seminary of America, New York. $3.00.)

The sub-title is " Studies in the Life and Manners of Jewish Palestine in the II–IV Centuries C.E. ", and the following subjects are examined : the Greek of the Rabbis, the Greek of the Synagogue, Gentiles and Semi-proselytes, Pleasures and Fears, Oaths and Vows, Greek and Latin Proverbs in Rabbinic Literature, and Misunderstood Expressions. The author discusses to what extent Hellenistic culture penetrated the various strata of Palestinian Jewry—the educated class of Rabbis, the middle class and the lower class. A good many of his observations, such as those on Greek versions of the Old Testament other than the Septuagint (pp. 47ff.), or on the varying approach of the same preacher to the same text according to the standard of his audience (pp. 161ff.), should be taken note of by students of the New Testament. Occasionally conjectures are presented as certainties. But the author displays an immense learning, also in less familiar sources both Jewish and Gentile ; and he is careful in questions where many others are not, for example, in distinguishing between academic and popular material. This is one of the most interesting recent publications in the field of Rabbinics.

D.D.

MARTIN, H. : *The Meaning of the Old Testament*, 7th Edition, revised. 1946. (S.C.M., London, 2s. 6d.)

In its revised form this non-technical introduction to the Old Testament will renew its usefulness, which has been proved by its many editions. It discusses the Inspiration of the Bible, and then treats of the books of the Old Testament by categories—History, Law, Prophecy, Psalmody, Wisdom, Apocalyptic—offering to the general reader an excellent short exposition of the modern approach. H.H.R.

MERCER, S. A. B. : *The Supremacy of Israel* (Bohlen Lectures 1943). 1945. (Christopher Publishing House, Boston, Mass. $3.00.)

Is a description in four lectures of the civilizations of ancient Egypt and Babylonia told in a homely manner. The influence of these empires on Israel, examples of their literature, accounts of their art, science and industry are presented interestingly and brought under the general theme that in the sphere of religious and moral ideas Israel is supreme. In criticism of Zionism Professor Mercer holds that the glory and supremacy of Israel is menaced by this political aim. One of the most useful parts of the book is the chapter on " The Recovery of Forgotten Empires", which is a short history of archæological research and of the early and later efforts of decipherment of inscriptions. O.S.R.

MILLER, M. S., and J. L. : *Encyclopedia of Bible Life*. 1944. (Harper, New York. $4.95.)

Interesting popular collection of material useful for Bible background. Arranged under twenty-two heads, with good indices, the book can easily be used for reference ; it is simply written by authors with first-hand knowledge of Palestine and with the assistance of competent American scholars and archæologists ; there are useful maps and many illustrations. J.N.S.

7

NÖTSCHER, F. : *Biblische Altertumskunde* (Die H. Schrift des Alten Testaments übersetzt und erklärt, Ergänzungsband III). 1940. (Hanstein, Bonn.)

> This last book of Professor Nòtscher's is intended as a supplementary volume to the *Bonner Bibel* series. This Catholic commentary, as is well known, is one of the same kind as the English *Cambridge Bible* and does not address itself in the first place to professional scholars, but to a much wider public. The *Biblische Altertumskunde* makes no exception to this general rule as its author says in its preface. But this does not alter the fact that it betrays in every chapter the solid scholarship of its author and proves to be a very useful and well-written handbook. In the references at the foot of the pages the author deals with the principal literature, not fully, but competently.
>   J.v.d.P.

PAYNE, E. A. (ed. by) : *Studies in History and Religion, presented to Dr. H. Wheeler Robinson, M.A., on his seventieth birthday.* 1942. (Lutterworth Press, London. 21s. 0d.)

> Contains fourteen essays, of which four are on Old Testament subjects, and the rest on New Testament, Doctrine, Philosophy and History. The Old Testament essays are by G. Henton Davies, on " The Presence of God in Israel"; L. H. Brockington, on " The Correlation of Natural and Spiritual in Prophetic Experience "; J. N. Schofield, on " The Significance of the Prophets for the Dating of Deuteronomy"; and J. B. Middlebrook, on " The Old Testament Pattern of History ". The first is a historical study of the ideas of the various periods ; the second is a psychological study ; the third is a critical study, arguing that Deuteronomy is dependent on Jeremiah, and not *vice versa* ; the fourth is analytical, and it sets the apocalyptists, who are faulty theologians, in sharp contrast to the prophets. The essays are all written by pupils of Wheeler Robinson's, with the exception of one by a colleague.
>   H.H.R.

PHILLIPS, GODFREY E. : *The Old Testament in the World Church.* 1942. (Lutterworth Press, London. 10s. 0d.)

> Mr. Phillips is Professor of Missions at the Selly Oak Colleges, and the book is concerned with the use of the Old Testament on the Mission Fields. He deals first with present problems, and then proceeds to discuss the place of the Old Testament in the history of the Christian Church from the time of Jesus to the present day. He emphasizes the need of each Testament for the interpretation of the other. He concludes with practical suggestions for the necessary use of the Old Testament in Africa, India, and China. Altogether a most valuable piece of research, both in its examination of past and present, and in its constructive approach to the future.
>   N.H.S.

RICHARDSON, A.: *Preface to Bible-Study*. 1943. (S.C.M., London. 5s. 0d.)

An attempt to combine a frank acceptance of the critical approach to the Bible with the belief of the Christian Church that in the Bible God has spoken and still speaks to men. The author is critical of those who think it sufficient to claim that the Bible contains the record of religious experience. He lays great emphasis on the Biblical vocabulary. N.W.P.

ROBERT, A. (ed. by): *Supplément au Dictionnaire de la Bible* (formerly ed. by the late L. Pirot). 1941 Fasc. XVIII Hetzenauer-Images; 1943 Fasc. XIX Images-Inscriptions. (Letouzey et Ané, Paris.)

The appearance, never very rapid, of this useful supplement to Vigouroux's *Dictionnaire* has been notably slowed down by the war. It is to be emphasized that the work is a supplement, not a complete recasting of its predecessor in this field. Among the more notable articles in these two fascicles are the late L. Delaporte's contribution on the Hittites, G. Contenau on the Horites, the late J. B. Frey, formerly secretary of the Biblical Commission, on " Images chez les Juifs ", and " Inscriptions et autres textes concernant l'histoire biblique " for which Charles Jean discusses the Semitic texts and B. Van de Walle those from Egypt. J.M.T.B.

ROBERTSON, E., and WALLENSTEIN, M. (ed. by): *Melilah, a volume of studies I*. 1944. (University Press, Manchester. £1.)

This volume in Modern Hebrew contains a number of essays in the field of Judaica, and the following essays on subjects more closely related to the Old Testament : " The Translation of Jonathan ben Uzziel on the Pentateuch " (W. Gottlieb); " A Summary of Mesopotamian Material concerning the Flood " (T. Fish) ; " Saadia Gaon as Translator and Commentator " (E. Robertson); " The Law and the Prophets " (H. H. Rowley); " The Influence of Deuteronomy on Hosea " (S. Sperber). H.H.R.

SMALLEY, BERYL: *The Study of the Bible in the Middle Ages*. 1941. (Clarendon Press, Oxford. 17s. 6d.)

It would be hard to think of any subject of living interest in which the only textbooks were almost three hundred years old, yet this appears to be the case with medieval exegesis (for which the classic authority is still Richard Simon). Miss Smalley's delightful book is not a history of medieval biblical scholarship ; she merely sets out to show that such a history should be written and to provide some of the materials. The chapters on the Victorines, whose great tradition began in 1110 with the founding of the Abbey of St. Victor in Paris, are especially interesting. Students of scholastic Latin, no less than exegetes, will be delighted to have in an appendix specimens of the great Andrew of St. Victor's highly individual commentaries. It is to be hoped that Miss Smalley will, sooner or later, be persuaded to write that fully documented and reasonably complete history of medieval biblical studies for which her present monograph is so outstanding a preparation. J.M.T.B.

SPARKS, H. F. D. : *The Old Testament in the Christian Church.* 1944. (S.C.M., London. 6s. 0d.)

The book is popular and not academic. The author seeks to answer in plain terms the question " Why should we read the Old Testament at all to-day ? " First he summarizes the attitude of past generations of Christians to the Old Testament. Then he discusses the various ways in which modern discoveries have affected the traditional attitude, and concludes with a chapter on the value of the Old Testament to-day. This, in chief, is that from beginning to end it speaks of a God who lives and works in the world He has created. The book is written from the Anglican point of view, and does not deal with theological questions of interpretation which to some are paramount. N.H.S.

VINCENT, L. H., O.P. (ed. by) : *Mémorial Lagrange.* 1940. (Gabalda, Paris. Fr. 600.)

The memorial volume to the great scholar who was for so many years prior and director of studies at the École Biblique, Jerusalem, contains very little about Père Lagrange himself, apart from Mgr. Chaine's charming account of the Father's " Journée et menus propos ". This is the more understandable as a full appreciation of the work, if not of the life, was published by Bloud and Gay in 1935 under the title : " L'œuvre exégétique et historique du R. P. Lagrange ". Since Lagrange was a scholar of wide range and at the time of his death in March, 1938, had ceased to specialize in the Old Testament for many years, it is not astonishing that the present volume does not contain any outstanding proportion of articles of peculiar interest to an *Alttestamentler*. One may mention the late G. A. Barton's " Danel, a pre-Israelite hero of Galilee ", D. Buzy on the " Song of Songs ", L. Gry on " La ' Mort du Messie ' en IV Esdras, VII, 29 ", A. Roberts, S.S., on " Le Yahwisme de Prov. x 1–xxii, 16, xxv–xxxix ", the late F. Thureau-Dangin on " Le nom du prince de Jérusalem au temps d'el-Amarna ", and Ch. Virolleaud on " Un état de solde provenant d'Ugarit (Ras Shamra)". J.M.T.B.

VOSTÉ, J. M. : *Biblica et Orientalia Rev.mo Patri Iacobo-M. Vosté dicata ob xii lustra aetatis.* 1943. (Pont. Athenæum "Angelicum", Rome.).

This *Festschrift* offered to the present Secretary of the Pontifical Biblical Commission contains twenty contributions (including a bibliography of Père Vosté's very numerous writings) in five languages (Latin, English, French, German and Italian). The subjects are grouped under five headings— Scriptural Introduction, Old Testament, New Testament, History of Exegesis and " Orientalia Christiana ". The Old Testament section comprises articles by G. Boson on " Ras Samra e l'Antico Testamento ", by R. de Vaux, O.P., on " Le schisme religieux de Jéroboam Ier ", by A. Miller, O.S.B., on " Fluchpsalmen und israelitisches Recht ", and by G. M. Behler, O.P., on " Divini amoris suprema revelatio in antiquo foedere data (Osee, cap. II)". J.M.T.B.

WEIR, C. J. MULLO (ed. by) : *Presentation Volume to Williams Barron Stevenson*. (*Studia Semitica et Orientalia II*.) 1945. (Glasgow University Oriental Society.)

A *Festschrift* presented to Emeritus Professor W. B. Stevenson in celebration of his seventy-fifth birthday by members of the Glasgow University Oriental Society. Three of the seven contributions have relevance to the Old Testament, viz. an important study of the Balaam-Balak songs and saga by J. Mauchline, who incidentally argues for Aram as Balaam's place of origin, an essay on the Hurrians by J. Paterson, which contains a comparison of Hurrian and Hebrew legal practice, and, more on the margin, an inquiry into Muhammad's Knowledge of the Old Testament by Richard Bell, a leading Islamic Authority. N.W.P.

WENSINCK, A. J. : *Semietische Studiën uit de Nalatenschap van Prof. Dr. A. J. Wensinck*. 1941. (Sijthoff, Leiden. Fl. 7.75., Bound, Fl. 8.75.)

A posthumous collection of ten papers, of which some have been published earlier. Four are concerned with Islamics, and three have a wider range, while the remaining three are concerned with the Old Testament. Of these the first was published in 1913. It is a commentary on Psalm 91 designed to bring out its use in connection with demonology, and containing some interesting suggestions on textual points. The second is on " The Origin of Yahwism " and it has not hitherto been published. It examines the pre-Mosaic religion and shows why the tradition that Moses introduced Yahwism to Israel is to be trusted ; assembles the evidence for the view that Yahweh was the God of Jethro more fully than is commonly done ; and offers a critical analysis of the place of Kadesh and Sinai in the traditions. Both of these papers are in Dutch. The third is one of three papers in English, and it deals with " The Significance of Ritual in the Religion of Israel". It was first published in 1919, but is-probably little known to English readers. It claims that the prophets have too largely monopolized the attention of scholars, and that for the common people the ritual, which was their only means of approach to God, was the most important side of religion, and it concludes by studying the ritual use of the Psalms, whose chanting is believed to have accompanied ritual acts. While none of these views are unique, the author brings his own contributions to them all. H.H.R.

EDUCATIONAL.

(Books which are primarily written for, or of value to, Schools are included here. In all of the other sections there are additional books useful for pupils or teachers, but with a wider usefulness also.)

BARCLAY, G. : *The Bible Speaks to our Day*. 1944. (S.C.M., London. 2s. 0d.)

This slender volume is likely to be of service to teachers as a basis for discussions with Upper School Forms. Drawing upon both Old Testament and New Testament, the author shows the relevance of the Bible for the needs and circumstances of the present day. B.K.R.

11

BATHO, D. : *Birth of Judaism.* 1945. (S.P.C.K., London. 5s. 0d.)

Notes used in her own work by a most able and scholarly teacher have been expanded to form this book. For Upper School Forms and for Training College Students this survey of Jewish history and religion from Jeremiah to Ezra will be found invaluable. B.K.R.

DAVIES, J. B. THOMSON : *Heralds of God.* 1942. (S.C.M., London. 5s. 0d.)

A readable and interesting presentation of the subject : suitable for Middle School Forms (ages 12–14). B.K.R.

PRITCHARD, N. L. : *The Presentation of the Old Testament.* 1944. (S.P.C.K., London. 3s. 0d.)

A useful book on the method of teaching the Old Testament ; more suitable for Primary School teachers. B.K.R.

A Syllabus of Religious Education for use in Secondary Schools in Scotland (First Year). 1945. (Church of Scotland Publications Department, Edinburgh. 4s. 0d.)

This syllabus will be of real value to teachers of the Old Testament in schools because of the able notes on the Old Testament Lessons prepared by the Rev. D. M. G. Stalker. N.W.P.

TASKER, R. V. G. : *The Old Testament in the New Testament.* (S.C.M., London. 6s. 0d.)

In this volume, the first five chapters of which are based on lectures given to teachers, Professor Tasker has stressed the fact—too long neglected—that the Old Testament is an essential part of God's revelation, and that it is vitally important for a right understanding of the New Testament. The book, which is written with freshness and lucidity, will appeal to teachers and older pupils as well as to the general reader. B.K.R.

ARCHÆOLOGY.

Annual of the American Schools of Oriental Research, vol. xxi–xxii. (1941–43). 1943. (New Haven. $4.00.)

The volume completes Professor W. F. Albright's account of the excavations begun in 1926 at Tell Beit Mirsim (see vols xii, xiii, xvii). The book, which records the Iron Age remains, is written with the author's usual full comparative stratification, and is of importance for the period of the Monarchy. The volume also contains a valuable study of pottery forms by Professors J. L. Kelso and J. P. Thorley, and an account of the soundings at Zâheríyeh in 1932. J.N.S.

Annual of the American Schools of Oriental Research, vol. xxiii (1943–44). 1944. (New Haven. $2.50.)

> Devoted to an account of the Sumerian Literary texts from Nippur, now in the Museum of the Ancient Orient at Istanbul. It is written by S. N. Kramer, Curator of the University Museum at Pennsylvania, with a parallel translation into Turkish of the Preface and Introduction. There are ninety-four plates showing copies of a hundred and sixty-seven of the two thousand texts found in 1889–1900, most of which are still unpublished. J.N.S.

BURROWS, M. *What Mean these Stones*? 1941. (American Schools of Oriental Research, New Haven. $1.25.)

> An excellent, reliable, popular introduction to the study of Biblical archæology with special reference to its value for the understanding of Biblical religion. The book includes Old and New Testament background, has a good chapter on epigraphical remains, is well illustrated, and can be thoroughly recommended. J.N.S.

DUSSAUD, R. : *Découvertes de Ras Shamra et l'Ancien Testament*, 2nd Edition. 1941. (Geuthner, Paris. English price 10s. 6d.)

> The first edition appeared in 1937 before M. Schaeffer's final campaigns in 1938–39 and has here been enlarged and revised. Very close connections between Ras Shamra and the Old Testament are claimed, which, if accepted, will have important bearing on Old Testament exegesis. A full, critical edition of the texts is necessary so that the parallels can be thoroughly tested. J.N.S.

GELB, I. J. : *Hurrians and Subarians*. 1944. (University of Chicago Press. $2.50.)

> An important monograph, which first reviews the history of our knowledge of Hurrians and Subarians, and the theories that were based upon it, and then proceeds to argue that these are two different peoples, and not one, as has been supposed by many. All that is known of each from the various periods is then separately collected. Subarian beginnings are lost in the darkness of the prehistory of Babylonia, but they mainly figure as living in the north between the Tigris, the Zagros Mts. and the Diyala. The Hurrians, however, are invaders who made sporadic appearances very early, but who became more prominent after 1500 B.C., when as illiterate barbarians they drove the Kassites before them into Babylonia. Coming from the neighbourhood of Lake Van, they invaded Mesopotamia and Assyria, and through Syria and Palestine some of them probably reached Egypt as part of the Hyksos invasion. The whole is carefully documented, and it offers a valuable contribution to our knowledge of Israel's milieu. H.H.R.

GLUECK, N. : *The Other Side of Jordan*. 1940. (American Schools of Oriental Research, New Haven. $1.25.)

> Written by an able Jewish archæologist, on the staff of the Hebrew Union College, Cincinnati, the book is a popular, well-illustrated account of the archæological surveys he conducted as Director of the American School at Jerusalem. It contains valuable material for the history and civilization of Trans-Jordan, and is of particular interest as a contribution towards the solution of problems of dating the Exodus.
>
> J.N.S.

GORDON, C. H. : *The Living Past*. 1941. (Day, New York. $2.50.)

> Attempts to present a popular account of the methods and results of archæology. It is plentifully interspersed with amusing autobiographical details, and has useful chapters on seals, the Nuzu tablets, and the Ras Shamra texts and Lachish ostraca.
>
> J.N.S.

GORDON, C. H. : *The Loves and Wars of Anat*. 1943. (University Press, Princeton. $1.50.)

> In the series of Princeton Oriental texts, this book gives a reliable translation of the main poems found at Ras Shamra, with short explanatory notes and a general introduction.
>
> J.N.S.

HEIDEL, A. : *The Babylonian Genesis : the Story of Creation*. 1942. (University of Chicago Press. $1.50.)

> This little book contains all the Sumerian and Accadian legends of creation in translation without the transliterated texts, with a brief introduction on the sources and extremely concise philological notes ; and it is brought to a conclusion with essays on the Greek accounts of these legends and the relationship of them to the stories in the Old Testament. The translation offers a number of new references, based on the slips for the Accadian Dictionary at Chicago, some obviously right but others doubtful ; and the problem of relationship, soberly discussed, reaches the conclusion that the Babylonian and Hebrew authors did not borrow their common matter from the one or the other but owed it to an inheritance " going back to a time when the human race occupied a common home and held a common faith ". At the end of the book are twelve plates of illustrations and a map. The author modestly claims to address only students of the Old Testament ; but the book is extremely well done and, while indispensable to these, will be found useful also by professed Assyriologists.
>
> G.R.D.

INGHOLT, H. : *Rapport Préliminaire sur Sept Campagnes de Fouilles à Hama en Syrie* (1932–38). 1940. (Munksgaard, Copenhagen. Kr. 22.00.)

> A careful, well-documented account of excavations at Hamath in Syria during the final campaigns before 1939. The author, who was leader of the Danish expedition, traces the results back through twelve strata from A.D. 1400 to the fifth millennium B.C. There are many cross-references to biblical parallels and Palestinian archæology.
>
> J.N.S.

DE KONING, J. : *Studiën over de El-Amarnabrieven en het Oude Testament inzonderheid uit historisch Oogpunt.* 1940. (Meinema, Delft.)

A doctoral thesis defended at the Free University in Amsterdam and containing a full account of the Amarna tablets in their bearing on the history of the period of Israelite entry into Egypt and the Exodus. The author does not accept the results of source criticism of the Hexateuch.   J.N.S.

KRAMER, S. N. : *Sumerian Mythology.* American Philosophical Society Memoirs, Vol. XXI. 1944. (Philadelphia. $2.00.)

This is a well-written and interesting account of the growing mass of Sumerian myths, which are now being gradually pieced together from broken and fragmentary tablets scattered over the world, based largely on the author's own researches into this subject. He then gives a popular account of a number of myths of origin, the deluge, the descent into the nether world, and so on, accompanied by long extracts from the best preserved texts. The work will be welcomed by Assyriologists as correcting the hitherto prevalent tendency to ascribe these myths for the most part to Babylonian sources and by Biblical scholars as throwing important light on some of the early stories in the Old Testament.   G.R.D.

KRAMER, S. N. : *Enki and Ninhursag : a Sumerian " Paradise Myth ".* 1945. (Bulletin of the American Schools of Oriental Research, Supplementary Studies No. 1, New Haven. 75 cts.)

Scholars have long recognized that the difficult text which the late Professor Langdon published in 1919 under the title of *Le Poème Sumérien du Paradis du Déluge et de la Chute de l'Homme* had nothing to do with Paradise, the Flood or the Fall of Man ! Dr. Kramer, the eminent Sumerologist, now offers a new transliteration, which can be checked by the three excellent photographs at the end of the volume, and translation with philological and grammatical notes which go far to setting the interpretation of this obscure poem on the right lines. The work is admirably done ; and a series, which begins so auspiciously and promises three such volumes a year for the modest sum of $1.00 a year, deserves all the support that it can get from subscribers.   G.R.D.

DE LANGHE, R. : *Les textes de Ras Shamra-Ugarit et leurs rapports avec le Milieu Biblique de l'Ancien Testament.* 2 vols. 1945. (Duculot, Gembloux.)

A full and independent discussion of all available remains from Ras Shamra, and of the extensive literature already written. The work is in three parts : part one gives a critical and analytical consideration of the texts ; part two discusses the geographical milieu, and part three the profane historical milieu and culminates in a short, cautious and conservative estimate of the Biblical implications. It was begun in 1935 as a thesis for the Catholic University of Louvain.   J.N.S.

McCown, C. C. : *The Ladder of Progress in Palestine.* 1943. (Harper, New York and London. $3.50.)

An excellent handbook of Palestinian archæology, grouped largely round subjects and sites. There are chapters on method, on prè-history, on the development of the alphabet, and on a number of selected sites—Jericho, Tell Beit Mirsim, Beth-shan, Samaria, Jerusalem, Gerasa, and others. A short account of the Lachish Letters figures in the chapter on Border Cities of the Shephelah. The whole is well informed and well illustrated and it forms an excellent introduction to Palestinian archæology—though not comparable with Burrows' *What Mean these Stones ?* for evaluating the significance of the material. H.H.R.

Noth, M. : *Die Welt des Alten Testaments* ; *Einführung in die Grenzgebiete der alttestamentlichen Wissenschaft* (Sammlung Töpelmann, Theolog. Hilfsbücher 5). 1940 (Töpelmann, Berlin.)

I. Geography. II. Archæology of Palestine. III. Elements of ancient oriental history (countries, cultures, writings and inscriptions, languages, nations, states, dates, religions). IV. The text of the Old Testament—A very valuable and reliable handbook. The best part is Section II, where Noth finds himself fully in his element. III is rather scanty, often amounting to no more than a list of names, dates and books, and not very thrilling for students. IV does not come within the scope of the title. W.B.

van den Oudenrijn, M. A. : *Les fouilles de Lākīš et l'étude de l'Ancien Testament.* 1942. (University Press, Fribourg en Suisse.)

Rectoral address at the opening of University year, 1942; and discusses the bearing of the Lachish Letters on textual and literary criticism of the Old Testament. There are fourteen pages of useful notes. J.N.S.

Patton, J. H. : *Canaanite Parallels in the Book of Psalms.* 1944. (The Johns Hopkins Press, Baltimore.)

A comparative study of the Ugaritic texts and the Psalter, designed to bring out the close parallels in vocabulary, literary form, and patterns of thought. Valuable for the expert, but also calculated to stimulate the interest of the intelligent beginner. A useful piece of work, thoroughly well done. Lithoprinted. A.R.J.

Picard, L. : *Structure and Evolution of Palestine.* 1943. (Hebrew University, Jerusalem.)

Geological survey of Palestine written originally for a Middle-East geological congress, and published as Vol. iv of the Bulletin of the Geological Department of the Hebrew University in Jerusalem. Part I describes the geological structure of the country and Part II compares it with neighbouring countries and suggests the lines of evolution. J.N.S.

POIDEBARD, A. : *Tyr, un Grand Port Disparu* ; *recherches aériennes et sous-marines*, 1934-36. 1939. (Geuthner, Paris.)

> Two volumes, one of maps and twenty-nine plates, and the other a careful statement of the results of investigation at the site of Tyre. M. L. Cayeux, from similar work at Delos, discusses the author's findings and adds his conclusions.
>
> J.N.S.

PRITCHARD, J. B. : *Palestine Figurines in relation to certain goddesses known through literature*. 1943. (American Oriental Society, New Haven. $1.75.)

> Volume 24 of the American Oriental Series, lists and discusses two hundred and ninety-four nude, female figurines found in excavations in Palestine, compares them with others found elsewhere in excavations or literature, and deals with the possible identification of them with one of the female deities at Ras Shamra.
>
> J.N.S.

HISTORY.

ENGBERG, R. M. : *The Hyksos Reconsidered*. 1939. (University Press, Chicago.)

> This booklet reviews the evidence for the Hyksos invasion of Egypt and concludes that there was gradual cultural infiltration from the beginning of the nineteenth Dynasty, and that this culture survived long after the end of political domination. It is usually supposed that the Hyksos absorbed the culture of conquered peoples.
>
> J.N.S.

FEIGIN, S. I. : *Some Secrets of the Past (Missitrê he'ābār)*. 1943. (Sepharim, New York.)

> A collection of twenty-six essays in Hebrew, of which all but five have been previously published in English, Hebrew or Yiddish, dealing with Biblical and historical studies, containing many interesting and not a few adventurous suggestions. In Article 7 Feigin advances the view that the possession of the Ark was a primary condition of authority, and supposes that when Shiloh was destroyed the Ark passed over to Benjamin, and when David established his dynasty, it passed over to Judah. In Article 8, on the Defeat of Sennacherib, he supposes that in the original text one hundred and eighty-five men of Sennacherib's army died. In Article 17 he defends the view that Ugaritic is a Canaanite dialect against Goetze's view that it is Amorite. Article 22 deals with the date of the Exodus, which is ascribed to 1379 B.C., after a sojourn in Egypt of one hundred and forty-three years. Article 23 argues that *m* was an old case ending, which survives in a number of forms that have been mistakenly regarded as plurals. These samples from articles both new and old indicate the range of subjects dealt with, and the originality of the author.
>
> H.H.R.

17

JACOBSON, D.: *The Social Background of the Old Testament.* 1942.
(Hebrew Union College Press, Cincinnati. $2.00.)

A straightforward study of the social institutions of the
ancient Semites, with special reference to Israel. Marked by
sound documentation and for the most part commendably
cautious, it may be safely recommended as a useful introduction to the subject.   A.R.J.

MAISLER, B., and BEN SHAMMAI, M. H.: *History of Palestine (Tôledôth
'Ereç Yisrael)* I, *From the Earliest Times to the Israelite Monarchy.*
1938. (Mizpah, Tel Aviv.)

The first volume of a scholarly history of Israel, written
in Hebrew. It pays much attention to archæological material,
with the literature on·which the writers show wide knowledge.
The introductory chapters deal with prehistoric geological
times, and the story is then carried down through the Patriarchal period and the period of the Settlement to the reign
of David. The scope of the work only embraces the political
and social history of Israel, and it deliberately leaves the
religious history out of its purview.   H.H.R.

MONTET, P.: *Le drame d'Avaris : essai sur la pénétration des Sémites
en Égypte.* 1940. (Geuthner, Paris. Fr. 200.)

A reconstruction of the history of Avaris, identified with
Tanis, and based on the author's researches there and at
Byblos. It includes a new discussion of the religious significance of the city, the origin of the Hyksos, and the date of
the Exodus—which is here put at about 1220 B.C.   J.N.S.

SMITH, S.: *Alalakh and Chronology.* 1940. (Luzac, London.)

A short, clear statement of the reasons that led the author
to believe that it is necessary to lower drastically the usually
accepted dates in Babylonian chronology. Partly this change
of dating, accepted by other scholars, is due to evidence from
Sir L. Woolley's excavations at Atshanah, the ancient Alalakh
in Syria.   J.N.S.

SMITH, S.: *Isaiah Chapters xl-lv : Literary Criticism and History.*
(Schweich Lectures 1940). 1944. (O.U.P. 10s. 6d.)

The three lectures comprise seventy-five pages, and are
followed by over a hundred pages of selected bibliography
and notes, textual and exegetical. These latter are particularly valuable and comprehensive. The first lecture
deals with recent criticism of the sixteen Babylonian chapters.
They are a series of prophetic utterances, perhaps book-
speeches, perhaps distributed as fly-sheets (Flugblätter),
during the five years or so ending in 538 B.C. The second
lecture deals with the history of the years 556–539 B.C.,
and entails a certain amount of reconstruction of Babylonian
history. The third lecture seeks direct references in the
prophecies to the history as set forth in the previous lecture.
Dr. Smith sees in the prophet the leader of an underground
movement in support of Cyrus, whom he believed to be the

new king appointed by God, and His vice-regent in Judah. The prophet was arrested and executed (Isaiah liii), but his loyalty to Cyrus secured Cyrus's support for the returning exiles. N.H.S.

STEINDORFF, G., and SEELE, K. C.: *When Egypt ruled the East*. 1942. (University Press, Chicago. $4.00.)

Apart from the introductory and concluding chapters, this book concentrates particularly on the eighteenth Dynasty. It is well written in popular style, well illustrated, and a production which is a delight to handle and read. J.N.S.

WALLIS, L.: *The Bible is Human*. 1942. (Columbia University Press, New York.)

A vigorous, stimulating work by an economist who believes that the Bible must be studied as secular history. There is the same emphasis on social history as in the author's two previous books (*Sociological Study of the Bible*, 1912, and *God and the Social Process*, 1935). It is an interesting mixture of acute observation and unproved theories, and should be read with caution by those untrained in Hebrew and modern biblical scholarship. J.N.S.

WRIGHT, G. E., and FILSON, F. V.: *The Westminster Historical Atlas to the Bible*. 1945. (Westminster Press, Philadelphia. $3.50.)

This work, which has an introductory article by Professor W. F. Albright, is far more than an atlas; it is an excellent production including thirty-three maps in colour and two in black and white; a special article accompanies each map and the work is up to date, accurate, and well written. There are also good indexes. J.N.S.

TEXT AND VERSIONS.

BIRNBAUM, P.: *The Arabic Commentary of Yefet Ben 'Ali the Karaite on the Book of Hosea*. 1942. (The Dropsie College for Hebrew and Cognate Learning, Philadelphia. $1.50.)

An edition of this commentary of the second half of the tenth century, based on a number of manuscripts. In his learned and clear Introduction Dr. Birnbaum contends that, just as Yefet drew on Rabbanite sources though himself a Karaite, his influence on Rabbanite successors such as Abraham ibn Ezra and David Kimhi was enormous. The author argues that the anonymous Arabic translation of the later Prophets contained in the Bodleian Codex Huntington 206 is the work of Yefet. D.D.

BROOKE, A. E., and McLEAN, N.: *The Old Testament in Greek*, Vol. III, Pt. i : Esther, Judith, Tobit. 1940. (Cambridge University Press. 20s. 0d.)

The present fascicule of 144 pages is the beginning of the third volume of the great Greek Old Testament, of which the first part appeared exactly forty years ago; and it is sad that not only Dr. Brooke has now died, but also Mr. Allberry, whom the editors thank in the preface for his help, has been killed in the war. Meanwhile, readers are compelled anxiously to await the announcement, of which the Syndics of the Press give notice at the beginning of the volume, concerning the continuation of the work ; it would be a disastrous blow to Biblical scholarship if the work were now abandoned.

The editors take these three books here as they are found in many manuscripts containing the historical books, so that it is easy to put them before the Sapiential works which they follow in Dr. Swete's small edition. This edition otherwise follows the general plan of the work ; but the editors have had the advantage of seeing the proofs of Sir F. G. Kenyon's edition of the Chester Beatty text of Esther, and they have added the Old-Latin text of Tobit, owing to its importance for the Sinaitic text of this book, at the end of the volume.

G.R.D.

DAICHES, D. : *The King James Version of the English Bible.* 1941. (University Press of Chicago. 15s. 0d.)

Gives, as the sub-title states, an account of the development and sources of the English Bible of 1611 with special reference to the Hebrew Tradition. The author draws a picture of the growth of Hebrew studies in the centuries prior to 1611 in England and of the help which, in this period, Jewish teachers of Hebrew gave Christian scholars here and abroad (Mirandola, Reuchlin) in the acquiring of the language which alone made the translation and interpretation of the Old Testament possible. The knowledge of Hebrew on the part of the individuals who helped in the translation of the Authorised Version is so far as possible assessed. A comparison of English versions up to and including the Authorised Version is made in the light of the Hebrew text of Isaiah and completes a very well written study.

O.S.R.

FRITSCH, C. T. : *The Anti-anthropomorphisms of the Greek Pentateuch.* 1943. (Princeton University Press. $2.00.)

This dissertation, presented for the doctorate of Princeton University, contains a concise but fairly complete collection of the devices adopted by the Septuagint to get rid of or tone down the anthropomorphisms in the Hebrew text of the Pentateuch, classified in eight chapters. The author finds that the Greek translators followed no consistent method in avoiding anthropomorphisms, their thoroughness varies from book to book, and they even in some passages use expressions more anthropomorphic than the Hebrew writers ; and he concludes that the tendency towards anti-anthropomorphisms was not inherent in Judaism itself but was due to Greek influence. The book leaves the impression that its author has not progressed far beyond the point which most scholars had reached by intuition but that, even if he has not said the last word on his subject, he has made a suggestive contribution to it which may inspire future work.

G.R.D.

KÖHLER, L. : *Kleine Lichter : fünfzig Bibelstellen erklärt.* 1945. (Zwingli, Zürich.)

> Professor Köhler here gathers together the notes on a number of difficult words and passages in both Old and New Testaments that he has published, often in local newspapers that are difficult to obtain abroad, over a number of years. Most of his solutions are as neat as they are convincing ; and readers will learn with interest that Solomon ate not " capons " but, like the Romans, " cuckoos ", that the word translated " crane " denotes the " yellow-vested bulbul ", and that salt does not lose its " savour " but its " virtue " through becoming under certain conditions chemically inactive or even a chemical reagent. The small size of this valuable little book is no measure of its value, which is high. G.R.D.

Liber Psalmorum cum Canticis Breviarii Romani. Nova e textibus primigeniis interpretatio latina cum notis criticis et exegeticis, Professorum Pontificii Instituti Biblici edita. 1945. (Pontifical Biblical Institute, Rome. 180 lire.)

> For the proper understanding of the reasons that have prompted the making of this new translation of the Psalter, those interested should consult the authoritative article by Augustine Bea, S.J., in *Biblica,* Vol. 26, fasc. 3, 1945, pp. 203—237. An English translation of this article is to be found in the *Catholic Biblical Quarterly,* Vol. 8, No. 1 (January, 1946), pp. 4—35. It was notorious that St. Jerome's Gallican Psalter was in many places barely intelligible, and that its Latinity was very far from classical. Great credit is due to the translators of the new version (whose names are printed on p. 103 of the CBQ) and not least to His Holiness the Pope, who gave them every encouragement and followed the whole process with intense interest. In the present volume, arranged in the order of the Psalter, there are notes, and corrections of the text are listed in transcription. There is also another edition without notes arranged in the order of the Roman Breviary and adapted for the recitation of the Office. J.M.T.B.

RIESSLER, P. : *Erklärung von Textschwierigkeiten des Alten Testaments.* (Ed. by Dr. F. Stier.) 1939. (Grünewald, Mainz.)

> P. Riessler, Professor of Old Testament at the Catholic Faculty of Theology at Tübingen, died 16.ix.35. His former pupil, and successor to his chair, F. Stier, has edited the last study of his master : an exposition of his ideas on the origin of the masoretical text of the Old Testament. According to Riessler, our present Hebrew text is nothing else than a translation from the Greek (or Latin), whilst this supposed Greek (or Latin) text is again a translation from the Aramaic. The editor, Dr. Stier, warns his readers not to reject this theory precipitately, but this has not prevented it from encountering but criticism. J.v.d.P.

ROBINSON, H. W. (ed. by) : *The Bible in its Ancient and English Versions.* 1940. (Clarendon Press, Oxford. 12s. 6d.)

An important collection of essays on the Hebrew Bible (by the Editor), the Greek Bible (W. F. Howard), the Syriac Bible (T. H. Robinson), the Latin Bible (H. F. D. Sparks), and the English Versions (to Wyclif, Sir William Craigie ; sixteenth century, J. Isaacs ; Authorized Version and after, J. Isaacs ; Revised Version and after, C. J. Cadoux), with a concluding essay by the editor on " The Bible as the Word of God ". The other ancient versions receive but slight incidental mention. While the work is incomplete, therefore, as a manual of the textual criticism of the Old and New Testaments, it assembles a vast amount of valuable material not conveniently assembled elsewhere, and some of the chapters—notably that by Isaacs on the Sixteenth-Century Versions—are brilliantly done.   H.H.R.

ZARB, S. M. : *Il testo Biblico.* 1939. (Pontificio Istituto "Angelicum", Rome. 4s. 0d.)

Contains seven useful but simple lectures on the text and versions of the Bible, though not attempting to offer a manual of textual criticism. The first lecture rapidly reviews ancient and modern versions of the Bible, while the next two deal with the Hebrew text of the Old Testament. A large part of these is occupied with a survey of the surviving non-Biblical texts in Canaanite Hebrew and Aramaic from the pre-Christian period, and there is no discussion of the problems of the Hebrew text, or illustration of the variety of types of error that were liable to arise. The next chapter discusses the original text of the New Testament, and this is followed by chapters dealing with the Septuagint and the Vulgate. Much of the chapter on the Septuagint is taken up with an account of the Letter of Aristeas and the question of its genuineness.   H.H.R.

ZIEGLER, J. (ed. by) : *Isaias.* 1939. (Vandenhoeck and Ruprecht, Göttingen, £2. 2s. 0d.)

This is the fourteenth volume of the great edition of the LXX which the *Societas Litterarum Gottingensis* is issuing, and all will hope that it will not be the last. It contains an elaborate *Einleitung* on pp. 1—121 describing the manuscript sources and discussing the grouping of the manuscripts (Alexandrian text, Hexaplar, Lucian), the *catena* groups, and the later Greek translations (Aquila, Symmachus, Theodotion); and this is followed by pp. 123—370 of the Greek text, to which is attached an elaborate critical apparatus. Here a welcome novelty is introduced, in that the renderings of the later translators are added under the manuscript variant readings. The reader thus has, so to say, Brooke-McLean and Field at hand all at the same time and on one page, which is a great convenience.   G.R.D.

ZORELL, F., S.J.: *Psalterium ex hebraeo latinum*. 1939. (Pontifical Biblical Institute, Rome. English price, 5s. 6d.)

The original edition of this excellent psalter was published in 1928. It has now been re-issued with some corrections and improvements in handy and pocketable form. The merits of the work are already known to serious students of the Psalms—an exceedingly clear translation of the Hebrew in Latin, a summary of the " argument " of each psalm, and a very adequate set of notes. Most of the Semitic words are given in transcription, but there is a lengthy section entitled " Crisis Textus Hebraici " in which, as might be expected, the Hebrew is quoted in its own characters, and other Semitic languages in transcription. J.M.T.B.

LITERARY CRITICISM.

BENTZEN, A.: *Indledning til det Gamle Testamente*, 2 vols. in 3 (continuously numbered pages). 1941. (Gads Förlag, Copenhagen.)

Treats of the critical introduction to the books of the Old Testament, and, more briefly, of the Apocrypha and Pseudepigrapha, of the variety of the forms of Hebrew literature, and of the Canon and Textual Criticism of the Old Testament. Critically Bentzen presents no startling views, but gives evidence of wide reading and sound judgment. The most valuable feature of the work is the large amount of space devoted to the study of the forms of Hebrew literature. The whole provides an excellent presentation of the positions of to-day. H.H.R.

CASSUTO, U.: *The Documentary Hypothesis and the Composition of the Pentateuch*. 1941. (Hebrew University Press, Jerusalem.)

Eight lectures in Hebrew, offering a popular résumé of the author's Italian work *La questione della Genesi*, 1934. Argues that the Divine names cannot be used for literary analysis, but that the choice was determined by the subject matter, and similarly the other pillars of the documentary hypothesis are vain and worthless. The author would have needed far less ingenuity to overthrow his arguments than he has expended on their creation. He observes that the name Yahweh had not been common among Israel while they were in Egypt, in agreement with Exodus 6[2]—which says something quite different, and too embarrassing to Cassuto's hypothesis to be squarely faced. He holds that the Pentateuch was the artistic creation of an author who used various traditions of older origin. H.H.R.

COOK, S. A.: *An Introduction to the Bible*. 1945. (Penguin Books, Harmondsworth. 1s. 0d.)

A marvellous shillingsworth ! In addition to chapters on the English Bible, on the Growth of the Bible, the Language and Ideas of the Bible, the place of Zion in its thought, and some

23

Fundamental Problems of the Bible, there is a brief survey of the world's religions, and two compact chapters summarizing what is usually meant by Introduction. It is incredible that so much information should be compressed within so small a space without forfeit of clarity. Lucidity is not always Cook's *forte*, but there can be no complaint here. In two final chapters the author passes beyond his theme to offer his contribution to the solution of the spiritual problem of our time.

H.H.R.

COPPENS, J. : *Histoire critique des livres de l'Ancien Testament*, 3rd Edition 1942. (de Brouwer, Desclée, Bruges.)

The first edition of this useful manual appeared in the *Nouvelle revue théologique* in 1938, and the second edition (in book form) followed in the course of the same year. The new edition has been entirely reset and a good deal of additional matter, mostly bibliographical, has been added. The author, as his regular bulletins in the *Ephemerides Theologicae Lovanienses* prove, is singularly well-informed about all the fluctuations of Pentateuchal and other Old -Testament criticism, and a great part of the volume is taken up with summaries of other people's opinions. Perhaps the most interesting chapter is that on " Les Directives Ecclésiastiques " which discusses very thoroughly the bearing of the various decrees issued by the Pontifical Biblical Commission between 1905 and the present time. The full text of all the earlier decrees may be found in the *Enchiridion Biblicum*, published by the Vatican Press in 1927. J.M.T.B.
(N.B.—An English translation of the second edition was published in 1942, under the title *The Old Testament and the Critics*, by St. Anthony Guild Press, Patterson, N.J.) H.H.R.

DAVID, M. : *Het Huwelijk van Ruth*. 1941. (Brill, Leiden.)

A brief study of the marriage of Ruth and the implications of the story for the dating of the book. The author thinks that Ruth 1^{11} f shows that the writer of the story failed to distinguish between levirate marriage and marriage with a uterine half-brother, and that therefore he must have lived after the custom of levirate marriage was obsolete. Relevant passages in Jeremiah and Deuteronomy are examined and the conclusion reached that the book is later than Deuteronomy, and therefore from the exilic or post-exilic period. Since no polemic against the marriage regulations of Ezra and Nehemiah is found, David would incline to the exilic period. A useful study, which rather overworks Ruth 1^{11} f.

H.H.R.

ENGNELL, I. : *Gamla Testamentet : en traditionshistorisk inledning*, I. 1945. (Svenska Kyrkans Diakonistyrelses Bokförlag, Stockholm. Kr. 6.75. Bound, Kr. 9.75.)

The first part of a Swedish Introduction to the Old Testament, which is likely to take its place as a work of importance. The present volume deals with the Canon and Text, literary forms, the religious history of Israel, and the Pentateuch. In the last section there is a review of the history of criticism to Wellhausen and since Wellhausen, and the work is of importance as offering a general Introduction from the point of view of the Scandinavian school that rejects the Wellhausen hypothesis. Engnell regards Deuteronomy to 2 Kings as a Deuteronomic history, and Genesis to Numbers as a priestly document, and to this extent works with a generally Wellhausenian scheme. He does not operate with written sources of these, however, so much as with traditions, and these much less clearly defined than the old documentary sources, and following Pedersen he does not attempt to analyse the Passover complex, Ex. 1—15.   H.H.R.

HÖLSCHER, G. : *Die Anfänge der hebräischen Geschichtschreibung.* (Sitzungsberichte der Heidelberger Akademie der Wissenschaften, Phil.-Hist. Klasse, 1941/2, 3. Abh.). 1942. (Winter, Heidelberg.)

The title hardly allows us to recognize that Hölscher presents us with a monograph on the Jahwist, whose writing is analysed and regarded as the relatively uniform and planned work of a historian. Hölscher allows it to extend to I Kings 12^{19} ; like Mowinckel, he takes the so-called J$_2$ in the earliest history to be E. Its compilation took place about 800 B.C. Such historiography—experienced history, in the sharpest contrast to the Canaanite religion—is unique in the ancient East. In spite of its conscious clinging to the older method of approaching the problem, a very valuable work. W.B.

HÖPFL, H., O.S.B. : *Introductio Specialis in Vetus Testamentum,* editio quinta ex integro retractata, quam curaverunt A. Miller, O.S.B., et A. Metzinger, O.S.B. (=*Introductionis in sacros utriusque Testamenti Libros Compendium,* vol. 2). 1946. (Ephemerides Liturgicæ—Editiones Comm. A. Arnodo, Rome.)

Although this book bears still the name of its first author Dom. Höpfl, it has become an entirely new volume of a size twice as big as its predecessor. It gives no new solutions of old problems but deals with them as fully as possible and offers in its notes and references an abundant literature which makes it useful even to those who do not share with its authors the principles of Catholic exegesis. As for this last, the authors have abandoned in several questions (e.g. the historicity of the books of Esther, Tobias, Judith, the authorship of Daniel, etc.) the conservative or ultra-conservative point of view, and we find more moderate opinions. It marks therefore, in more than one respect, the progress of official Catholic Old Testament study.
                                                                       J.v.d.P.

HUMBERT, P. : *Problèmes du livre d'Habacuc.* 1944. (University of Neuchâtel Press. Fr. 12.00.)

A brilliant and detailed, though not wholly convincing, study of the book of Habakkuk, leading to the conclusion that the author was a cultic prophet attached to the Jerusalem temple, who composed the whole book as a liturgy for a service of intercession in 602—601 B.C., and whose originality lay in his synthesis of prophetic thought with the official cultus, and in the idea of using a liturgy to attack the syncretism of Jehoiakim. The whole book is integrated into this liturgy, consisting of a complaint and an oracle, a second complaint and oracle, five imprecations and the concluding prayer in chapter 3, and the oppressor throughout is held to be Jehoiakim. There is a study of every significant word in the book in relation to its other occurrences in the Old Testament, leading to the conclusion that there is nothing which could not come from the end of the seventh century B.C., and much evidence that points to that date.

H.H.R.

IRWIN, W. A. : *The Problem of Ezekiel.* 1943. (University of Chicago Press. $3.00.)

This book, dedicated to T. H. Robinson and to British Old Testament scholars in general, presents what claims to be a scientific method for dealing with the problem of Ezekiel, in contrast to the subjective work of others. In fact, it seems to be as subjective as any. Every interpretation of an oracle is rejected as coming from a later hand, and, after the manner of Hölscher, all that is not poetry is rejected. In the end about one-fifth of the book is attributed to Ezekiel. Almost all the dates in the book are rejected, the whole of chapters 40—48 are rejected, and throughout the remainder isolated verses or sections are rejected with a confidence that the reader may not share.

H.H.R.

KAPELRUD, A. S. : *The Question of Authorship in the Ezra Narrative.* 1944. (Dybwad, Oslo. Kr. 7.00.)

A lexical study of Ezra 7—10 and Nehemiah 8, in relation to the rest of the Old Testament. Wider questions of philology are untouched. Words and phrases are studied in the order of their occurrence, and their affinities with other passages noted, and the conclusion reached that considerations of language and style show that the whole of this section, whether written in the first or the third person, has a common authorship and comes from the Chronicler—though the Chronicler is held to be a circle rather than an individual. Sometimes the author's conclusions outrun his evidence, but much patient and careful work has gone into his book.

H.H.R.

LINDBLOM, J. : *Boken om Job och hans lidande.* 1940. (Gleerups Förlag, Lund. Kr. 8.75, Bound Kr. 11.50.)

Gives in Swedish a comprehensive description of the book of Job and the problems connected with it. The rôle it has played in world literature is illustrated by quotations from Lowth, Humboldt, Herder and others ; it is compared with Hamlet, with Milton's, Klopstock's and Dante's works ; a whole chapter is devoted to a comparison with Goethe's *Faust*, and another treats of its relations with Aeschylus ; its place in Old Testament literature and its relation to Egyptian and Babylonian documents is pointed out.

Lindblom supposes an Edomite original of the tale of Job has been judaized (by the introduction of the figure of Satan), and the original words of the friends have been removed and replaced by the poem that gives the book its real character (cf. infra, on the following work). Lindblom describes the presupposition of the book in the old Israelite view of life and emphasizes that the problem is how to reconcile the justice of God with the actual injustices of the world. Of all these problems he gives a very sound treatment.

J.P.

LINDBLOM, J. : *La composition du livre de Job.* 1945. (Gleerups Förlag, Lund.)

A complex theory of the origin of the book, which finds the prologue and epilogue to be older than the dialogue and themselves to be composite. Lindblom argues that there was first an Edomite form of the prologue and epilogue, which was then expanded by an Israelite writer, who imported Job's wife and the Satan, and substituted a fresh ending. Later the Edomite ending was reimported in an amended form beside its successor. Still later a three-cycle dialogue was substituted for an older dialogue, but the third cycle is now disordered. Then the Elihu speeches were added, and still later chapter 28. The Behemoth and Leviathan poems came next, and yet later 40^{8-14} and 42^{1-6}. The importance of this review of the problems of the book, and of modern literature on it, will be recognized by those who do not share all the details of its theory.

H.H.R.

MESSEL, N. : *Ezechielfragen.* 1945. (Dybwad, Oslo. Kr. 13.00.)

Yet another solution of the problem of Ezekiel. Messel finds a Babylonian background to the book entirely wanting, and instead locates Ezekiel in Palestine *circa* 400 B.C. He places him after the work of Nehemiah, but does not discuss his relation to the work of Ezra. The " exiles " are the returned exiles, the purity of whose religion contrasts with that of those who remained in Palestine. The degraded Levites of chapter 44 are not the country priests, as commonly supposed, but Temple priests in Jerusalem who lacked the purity and monotheism of the returned priests. The book is held to have been much glossed, and Messel offers an analysis of the entire work, in which the glosses are distinguished. The author had had no access to Irwin's solution, of course, and more surprisingly he shows no knowledge of Torrey's theory.

H.H.R.

MORGENSTERN, J. : *Amos Studies*, Parts I, II, and III. Vol. I. 1941. (Hebrew Union College Press, Cincinnati.)

A series of studies reprinted from the Hebrew Union College Annual, and designed as the first half of a complete commentary on the book of Amos. The thesis of the whole work is that Amos delivered a single, unified address at the northern sanctuary of Bethel, and that this took place at daybreak of the autumnal equinox during the feast of Asif in 751 B.C.

Part I deals with the biographical sections (including the visions), Part II presents the argument with regard to date, and Part III gives an excellent survey of the history of Israel from the time of David to that of Amos with a view to placing the prophet's message in its appropriate setting. The main argument, which involves some re-arrangement of the text, is not without its difficulties ; but on the whole this is a refreshingly original piece of work, full of suggestion, and attractively written.   A.R.J.

NOTH, M.   *Ueberlieferungsgeschichtliche Studien I* (Schriften der Königsberger Gelehrten Gesellschaft xviii 2).   **1943.**   (Niemeyer, Halle.)

Investigates, first, the *Deuteronomic* work as to its extent (in Genesis—Numbers not demonstrable, starts only in Deuteronomy), method and leading ideas (the steady apostasy on the soil of Palestine until the downfall ; explanation of the meaning of that history), and finds it the work of a Palestinian private individual.   Similarly the work of the Chronicler : compiled in the third century, special Levitic interests not demonstrable.   In an appendix, P and the redaction of the Pentateuch are dealt with : the Hexateuch sources do not extend beyond Joshua, and even there they cannot be established with certainty ; first of all P, which does not know anything of any tradition of conquest of the land, is missing. A very careful and thorough inquiry, which fills, especially in the first part, an old gap.   W.B.

ÖSTBORN, G. :   *Tora in the Old Testament : a Semantic study*.   1945. (Håkan Ohlssons Boktryckeri, Lund.   English Price, 15s. 0d.)

The volume (written in English) consists first of a discussion of the etymology of the word *tora*.   The original meaning of the root is held to be " show the way, point with the finger ". From this three main meanings evolve for the noun, directive (e.g. oracles and omens), instruction (ethico-religious and worldly), and law (verdict, rule, way).   The author proceeds to examine in turn the work of the various imparters of *tora*, the Deity, king, priest, wise man, prophet.   Comparisons are made with other Semitic religions, but these are illustrative rather than determinative.   The volume is comprehensive, careful, and precise, and is a valuable asset for the study of Hebrew religion and custom.   N.H.S.

PFEIFFER, R. H. :   *Introduction to the Old Testament*.   1941.   (Harper, New York. $4.00.)

A monumental work, on a much larger scale than S. R. Driver's, though addressed to a less exclusively scholarly audience.   It is invaluable for its acquaintance with a vast range of modern work, and its review of the variety of solution offered for the various problems.   It is therefore an indispensable tool, even for those who may at many points disagree with the author's solutions.   The chapters on the Canon, on the Text and Versions, and on the Codes of Law in the Pentateuch (the last of these being much influenced by Alt) are worthy of special mention. Naturally there is some unevenness, but the encyclopædic quality of the book is rarely lacking. In the Pentateuch Pfeiffer finds an Edomite source S, more or less corresponding to Eissfeldt's L, though not wholly coterminous with it. In reaction against recent tendencies, the author dates most of the psalms in the period 400—100 B.C. Job (without the Elihu speeches) is attributed to an Edomite sage *circa* 600 B.C. H.H.R.

POWIS SMITH, J. M. : *The Prophets and their Times*, 2nd Edition, revised by W. A. Irwin. 1941. (University of Chicago Press. $2.50.)

> The revision does more than bring the original work up to date, by references to publications of the sixteen years that separated the two editions. Irwin reverses Smith's judgment on the ecstatic nature of Hebrew prophecy, largely rewrites the chapter on Hosea and almost entirely rewrites the chapter on Ezekiel. On the marriage of Hosea Irwin holds that Gomer was a religious prostitute, and the adulteress of chapter 3 a different woman. He believes that Hosea not only attacked the fertility cult, but had the genius to recognize the truth it contained. His chapter on Ezekiel he describes as " a bare and bald sketch of a great career ", and it is not very satisfying. Its critical views have been subsequently presented and defended in a separate work (see under Irwin : *The Problem of Ezekiel*). On the whole the new parts of the book are not the best parts. H.H.R.

STEINMUELLER, J. E. : *A Companion to Scripture Studies.* Vol. II. *Special Introduction to the Old Testament.* 1942. (Wagner, New York.)

> This textbook of special introduction follows the customary lines and does not seem to be any improvement on various works by Catholic authors in Latin, French and German, notably the late Dom Hildebrand Höpfl's *Introductionis Compendium*. Like Höpfl, Dr. Steinmueller has given much attention to his bibliographies, but he is equally unhelpful as regards the use of them. The main impression given by the work is one of competence ; there is little or no suggestion of brilliance or originality. J.M.T.B.

TORCZYNER, H. : *The Song of Songs.* 1942–43. (Yabneh, Tel Aviv.)

> This book is written in Hebrew. It argues that Canticles is a collection of Songs by poets in connection with various occurrences in Solomon's court. The central figures are a maiden (identified with Abishag) and her northern lover, from whom she was not won by Solomon. Many ingenious detailed suggestions are put forward, e.g. that the doublets in the Song may be due to the King's command to the court singers to treat the themes he proposed, or that Baal-hamon means " The man of capital "—who then surprisingly becomes the tenant farmer. H.H.R.

Torrey, C. C. : *The Apocryphal Literature, A brief Introduction.* 1945. (Yale University Press, New Haven. $3.00.)

This book offers a General Introduction on subjects connected with the Apocrypha and Special Introductions to the individual books. Introductions are also given to two works not hitherto found in collections of the Apocrypha, viz. *The Lives of the Prophets* and *The Testament of Job.* The title *Pseudepigrapha* for some books so described is misleading and should, he says, be discarded and the designation *Apocrypha* should be used to include all the extra-canonical writings. The Christian element in Old Testament Apocrypha is difficult to demonstrate and is not extensive, but is there. The book presents a good survey of the use of the Apocrypha in the Christian Church, their influence and the controversies about them. The author asserts that a concise handbook treating of the Apocrypha supplying the most necessary information and references to guide the student to the most important literature in the case of each book is needed. This handbook will certainly serve as a useful supplement and companion to the introductions in " The Apocrypha and Pseudepigrapha " edited by Dr. Charles. O.S.R.

Weiser, A. : *Einleitung in das Alte Testament.* 1939. (Kohlhammer, Stuttgart.)

Though on a considerably smaller scale than Eissfeldt's great Introduction to the Old Testament, this volume by the Professor of Old Testament in Tübingen which appeared just before the war will be found to have a value of its own. Weiser seeks to combine the history of Hebrew literature from its origins in oral traditions with introduction in the narrower sense of analysis of the individual books, and insists on the importance of correcting the modern tendency initiated by men like Gunkel to concentrate on types of literature reduced to their smallest units by recognizing the presence of large literary structures in the Old Testament and the personal religious experience of the individual writers. Like Eissfeldt, Weiser has sections on the Canon and on the Text and Versions of the Old Testament, but, unlike the former, he does not include an introduction to the Apocrypha and Pseudepigrapha. N.W.P.

EXEGESIS.

Bierberg, R. P. : *Conserva me Domine : Psalm* 16 (15). 1945. (Catholic University of America Press, Washington, D.C.)

This full-length treatment of a psalm of only eleven verses was offered to the theological faculty of the Catholic University of America in part fulfilment of the requirements for the degree of Doctor. Part I of the treatise gives a translation of the psalm, some introductory notes, the text with annotations, and a chapter on the sense of the psalm. Part II contains an exegetical investigation of verses 10 and 11, a summary of modern interpretations, and the evidence for the traditional interpretation. In the controversy about verses 10—11 as to whether these verses merely *admit* of a reference to a future happy immortality or positively *affirm* such a reference, the author is in favour of the second interpretation. J.M.T.B.

BRIERRE-NARBONNE, J. J. : *Le Messie souffrant dans la littérature rabbinique.* (Geuthner, Paris. Fr. 150.)

M. Brierre-Narbonne here continues his studies of Messianic prophecy in the Old Testament and in Rabbinic writings. The first part of the book (93 pp.) contains translations of, and comments on, the germane passages in the Talmuds, the Midrashes, various medieval collections of folklore, and in the Kabbala (Zohar). These are all based on five passages of Scripture, Isaiah liii ; Zechariah ix 9 ; xii 10, 12 ; Psalm xxii ; Psalm lxxxix. The second part (40 pp.) discusses these passages in turn, and deals with the origin of the idea, chiefly whether independently Jewish or partly Christian. The book concludes with the Hebrew text (40 pp.) of the actual passages translated in the first part. " The Catholic reader will recognize a brief exposition of his faith. The Jewish reader will recognize equally the diverse opinions which have a place in the very core of Judaism. Every reader will be struck by the resemblances between the teaching of Church and Synagogue." N.H.S.

CALLAN, C. J., O.P. : *The Psalms translated from the Latin Psalter, in the light of the Hebrew, of the Septuagint, and Pešitta Versions and of the Psalterium juxta Hebraeos of St. Jerome, with Introductions, Critical Notes and Spiritual Reflections.* 1944. (Wagner, New York.)

This is a reproduction in part of a similar book issued some years ago by the two Dominican professors at Maryknoll Missionary Seminary, New York—Frs. C. J. Callan and J. A. McHugh. It is claimed that, apart from the introductions, the bulk of the work is new. The translation is, in this new work, a real translation, not a paraphrase, and the " spiritual reflections ", perhaps the least satisfactory part of the book, were not given in *The Psalms Explained.* It seems a pity that so little attention has been paid to the liturgical aspects and uses of the Psalter which might have been outlined, after the manner of Canon A. Van der Heeren's *Psalmi et Cantica Breviarii Explicata* (1913. Beyaert, Bruges ; 4th Edition 1932). J.M.T.B.

CASSUTO, U. : *From Adam to Noah.* 1944. (Hebrew University Press, Jerusalem.)

A philologico-historical commentary on Genesis 1^1—6^8 written in Hebrew, offering the support of a detailed textual study to the author's general hypothesis on the composition of the chapters. He thinks they rest on different and even conflicting traditions, but that as a literary composition they form a unity. Variation in the use of Divine names

31

and in vocabulary are ascribed to the deliberate choice of a
single author in view of the subject-matter dealt with, and
much emphasis is laid on the prevalence of seven and its
multiples in the artistry of the chapters. The Creation
narrative is held to rest on older poetic compositions.

H.H.R.

CASTELLINO, R. G. : *Le lamentazioni individuali e gli inni in Babilonia
e in Israele.* 1939. (Società Editrice Internazionale, Turin.)

A judicious study of the psalms of individual lament and
hymns of praise in Babylonian and Hebrew literature, with
copious quotations from the relevant passages. In both
halves of the work each literature is first studied by itself
and then the two are compared. Similarities of literary
form, of style and of language, are found without obscuring
the more significant differences of spirit and religious outlook.
Castellino concludes that there was no direct influence of
the Babylonian on the Hebrew poems, but thinks there may
have been indirect influence through Canaanite channels.
These conclusions are not novel, but the work is valuable
for the collection of the evidence on which they rest.

H.H.R.

COHEN, A. : *The Psalms : Hebrew text, English translation and
commentary.* 1945. (Soncino Press, Hindhead. 12s. 6d.)

COHEN, A. : *Proverbs : Hebrew text and English translation, with an
introduction and commentary.* 1945. (Soncino Press. 10s. 0d.)

COHEN, A., GOLDMAN, S., LEHRMAN, S. M., REICHERT, V. E., and
SLOTKI, J. J. : *The Five Megilloth : Hebrew text, English translation and commentary.* 1946. (Soncino Press. 10s. 6d.)

The first three volumes of a Jewish commentary on the Old
Testament, containing the Hebrew and English in parallel
columns, with commentary beneath. There is little discussion
on linguistic or textual points, and emendation of the text
is excluded. The position is generally conservative, but the
editors are acquainted with critical work and take some
account of its positions. No account is taken of Babylonian
or Egyptian literature in dealing with Psalms and Proverbs.
There is a strong interest in the religious teaching, which gives
the books practical value for Jew and Christian, and some
Rabbinical material is embodied. The editors hold that David
inaugurated lyrical poetry, but did not write all the psalms
attributed to him, and that the Psalter was completed in
the period after Ezra and Nehemiah ; that Proverbs was
completed in the same age, but has a Solomonic nucleus,
first edited in the time of Hezekiah ; that the Song of Songs
is of North Palestinian origin, and traces the story of love's
triumphs over the blandishments of a court ; that Lamentations is by Jeremiah ; and that Esther is of uncertain
date, but by a Persian Jew. On Ecclesiastes the editors
are in disagreement, Reichert rejecting and Cohen accepting
the Solomonic authorship. The volumes are beautifully
produced, and offer a welcome presentation of a Jewish point
of view in exegesis. H.H.R.

DANELL, G. A. : *Studies in the Name Israel in the Old Testament.*
1946. (Appelberg, Uppsala.)

A full and careful study of all the occurrences of the name
Israel in the Old Testament, and examination of its significance. The connotation varies between the whole of the
tribes, a major group over against a minor group, the
northern tribes over against Judah, and Judah as the
remnant of the nation. In many cases it is not immediately
obvious which is the precise significance, and so there is
often a careful examination of a passage. The examination
is, broadly speaking, book by book, and the well-documented
studies will be found very valuable, even by those who may
disagree with the interpretation of some of the passages.
Prefixed to these studies is a discussion of the etymology
of the name Israel, which is held to be a divine name, and
equated with Jeshurun and Asher, and a brief discussion
of the origin of the people of Israel and the problems of
their settlement in Canaan.   H.H.R.

DUPONT-SOMMER, A. : *Le quatrième livre des Machabées, Introduction,
Traduction et Notes.*   1939.   (Champion, Paris, English price,
10s. 6d.)

In his introductory matter (particularly his examination of
the philosophic and religious ideas) and the textual notes
he presents us with a very full study of IV Maccabees.
Briefly his view is that IV Maccabees dates from the
beginning of the second century A.D. (117/18) ; that it is
a real synagogue sermon (as against Norden and Schürer,
that it was not preached to hearers but written for readers),
though it is not based on a biblical text but on the philosophic
proposition that the pious reason subdues the passions ;
that it was preached at Antioch where the tombs of the martyrs
of the Maccabean persecution were, on the day commemorating
their martyrdom ; that IV Maccabees draws its historical
data from II Maccabees and oral tradition and not from
Jason of Cyrene's work. The author has much of interest
to say about the association of the martyrs with Antioch,
and he suggests that the Epistle to the Hebrews and the
Epistle of Ignatius which derive from the same period as
IV Maccabees share in the religious thought and atmosphere
which produced the sermon. It is not clear why M. Dupont-
Sommer insists on IV Maccabees having been preached in
a synagogue. If the martyrs' tombs and relics were at
Antioch, the sacred spot where these were was the most
appropriate place for the panegyric.   O.S.R.

GERLEMAN, G. : *Zephanja textkritisch und literarisch untersucht.* 1942.
(Gleerup, Lund.   Kr. 10.)

A valuable and careful comparison of the Hebrew text with
those of the Septuagint, Peshitta and Vulgate versions, and
lesser use of other versions, with a translation of the text
adopted, and chapters on each of the three chief versions

used, followed by a discussion of the date and thought of the book. Gerleman ascribes Deuteronomy to cult-prophetic circles in the Jerusalem Temple. Zephaniah is held to be in general a disciple of Isaiah, who stands over against the Deuteronomic circles, yet not so sharply as might appear. For he too is found to be influenced by the nationalistic ideas of the cultic prophets. The common view that Zephaniah's prophecies were uttered . at the time of the Scythian peril is rejected and declared to be without the slightest foundation.   H.H.R.

HALLER, M., and GALLING, K. : *Die fünf Megilloth.* (Handbuch zum AT, ed. by O. Eissfeldt, I 18). 1940. (Mohr, Tübingen.)

Haller's treatment of Ruth, Canticles, Lamentations and Esther is restrained in textual criticism, strongly interested in literary history and still more in the history of religion. As regards Canticles, he advocates a cult-mythological interpretation : behind the love lyric and the bucolic of the twenty-six songs are real marriage songs of an originally pagan, but long ago assimilated, cult of vegetation and fertility gods, of which we know more to-day especially owing to the Ugaritic texts. The inclusion of Canticles in the Canon does not, of course, become more intelligible on this view ; such mythological elements could well have become part of the ordinary love poetry. As regards Ruth, Haller finds behind the now rural story a cult legend from Bethlehem (Staples), for which the names offer no sufficient support. As to Esther, he accepts Jensen's mythological explanation, in spite of Cosquin and Gunkel ; also what we know of the Babylonian casting of lots (pūru) does not refer to the coronation of the king but to the starting of the Eponymate. The five songs of Lamentations were collected, perhaps composed, for the wailing on the fall of the City. Galling distinguishes in Ecclesiastes thirty-seven proverbs (sentences) and knows well how to determine its position within the whole Wisdom Literature : how much it has taken over, how much it combated or modified. In this way, Ecclesiastes can be understood, without any rearrangements and with a minimum of excisions, as a strongly individual work. Entirely convincing.   W.B.

KISSANE, E. J. : *The Book of Isaiah translated from a critically revised Hebrew text with commentary.* 1941 vol I (i—xxxix) ; 1943 vol. II (xl—lxvi). (Browne and Nolan, Dublin. £1. 1s. 0d. per vol.)

Mgr. Kissane's commentary has been widely acclaimed as the best recent commentary on Isaiah. It provides an adequate introduction to each volume and to the various divisions of the work, a translation, and a detailed commentary. It has, however, been criticized on the grounds that it gives very little of the Hebrew text (and that not always accurately), that the strophic theory accepted by the author is never really defended as a whole (though it

34

appears to be that elaborated by the late Albert Condamin, S.J., in *Poèmes de la Bible* and other works), and that the doctrinal evaluation of several important passages is not so complete as it might be. The commentary is, notwithstanding these reflections, a valuable and a readable one. The author has evidently taken great pains to keep abreast of all the recent literature.   J.M.T.B.

KÜHNER, H. O. : *Zephanja*. (1943. Fr. 3.)

ZIMMERLI, W. : I *Mose* 1—11, *Die Urgeschichte*. (2 parts. 1944. Fr. 7.00 and 6.50.)

BRUNNER, R. : *Ezechiel* (2 parts. 1944. Fr. 8.80 and 7.00). Parts of the series *Prophezei, Schweizerisches Bibelwerk für die Gemeinde*. (Zwingli-Verlag, Zürich.)

I. Kühner's *Zephanja* is a short, well-written exegesis. It is sermonic in character without being prevailingly so and without impairing its exegetic value. It holds close to the text and is a real Bible-study. The doctrinal allusions to Christ, His cross and the atonement effected thereby, which are suggested to the author's mind by the message of Zephaniah, are hardly consistent with the author's admission (p. 29) that these events were not present to the mind of the prophet, but they are understandable from the early Christian viewpoint expressed in I Peter 1 [10-11]. The contents correspond with the purpose of the series (für die Gemeinde) and with the series " Prophezei ", which was the name given to those popular daily scripture-expositions which Zwingli and his associates conducted in Church from the year 1525 onwards.

II. Brunner's *Ezechiel* aims at presenting the theological content of this difficult book so as to meet the requirements of the ordinary congregation. The author therefore does not attempt to solve the literary problems of Ezekiel but he provides a most readable preliminary to more specialized study. The quotations from an earlier Ezekiel-expositor, namely Calvin, lend an additional interest to Brunner's work. Brunner regards " the thirtieth year " (1[1]) as referring to the prophet-priest's age (Numbers 4[30]) ; the Israel of chapters 6—7 as being not the whole nation but the Northern Kingdom that once was ; the hostility and trade-rivalry of Phœnician Tyre over against Jerusalem (26[2f]) as being inspired by anti-Semitism.

III. Zimmerli's *Urgeschichte* (Genesis 1—11) is a work that will be a real acquisition both to the theologian and to the teacher of the history of the religion of Israel. It deals verse by verse with the text, without this interest in detail disturbing the harmonious presentation of the main theme. The language which the author has at his command is a vehicle of great beauty of expression (e.g. on Genesis 3), and while deepening the impression of the religious values of the Genesis narratives he appreciates the results of modern research, linguistic, textual and religious-historical.
                                                                      O.S.R.

LATTEY, C., S.J. : *The Psalter in the Westminster Version of the Sacred Scriptures.* 1945. (Sands, London. 10s. 6d.)

The first book of the Psalter was published in the Westminster Version shortly before the war ; it provided an introduction, a translation printed in the customary fine and large type of the Version, and a full accompaniment of notes. The remaining volumes have been delayed by the war, and, as some consolation in the difficult conditions of the present day, Fr. Lattey has given us an *editio minor* containing the whole of the text, a short introduction and a minimum of notes. The translation seems to be highly successful, thoroughly scholarly, and in a format convenient for the pocket. One may regret the attempt to re-popularize " Jehovah " and the rather lengthy series of errata.

J.M.T.B.

NOORDTZIJ, A. : *Het Boek Levitikus, opnieuw uit den grondtekst vertaald en verklaard.* 1940. (Kok, Kampen.)

A useful brief commentary, based on the author's own translation, in the series *Korte Verklaring der Heilige Schrift met Nieuwe Vertaling.* The introduction contains some original views of the author's. For Noordtzij rejects the Wellhausen view of the origin of the Pentateuch, and instead finds a substantial Mosaic core in the legislation. He recognizes that a number of passages ill fit their present context, and there are many indications of the post-Settlement period. He therefore holds the original book to have gathered a number of later accretions. He is doubtful how far the Holiness Code should be treated as a separate source, and inclines rather to follow Eerdmans. H.H.R.

RIDDERBOS, N. H. : *De " Werkers der Ongerechtigheid " in de individuelle psalmen.* 1939. (Kok, Kampen. 13s. 6d.)

An examination of Mowinckel's theory (Psalmenstudien I, 1921) that the " workers of iniquity " are sorcerers, etc. The book is a thesis for a doctorate in the University of Amsterdam, is written in Dutch with a five-page summary in German. The author discounts Mowinckel's main contention, but allows exorcist references in particular cases. The sickness-prayers are mostly on behalf of the king. The enemies are real, either heathen or within the state. These latter comprise Saul and Absalom, general political opposition, personal hatreds and post-exilic disputes. Mowinckel is right in his insistence on a close primitive connection between Israel and her neighbours. The author's conclusion is that the special revelation to Israel is concerned not so much negatively in correcting these primitive ideas as in positively making known the Nature of Jahweh. A careful study, with eminently reasonable and moderate conclusions.

N.H.S.

SNAITH, N. H. : *Study Notes on Bible Books* : *Notes on the Hebrew Text of 2 Samuel xvi—xix* (1945. 2s. 6d.) ; *Notes on the Hebrew Text of Isaiah xxviii—xxxii* (1945. 2s. 6d.) ; *Notes on the Hebrew Text of Jeremiah iii, vii and xxxi* (1945. 2s. 6d.) ; *Amos, Part I, Introduction* (1945. 2s. 6d.) ; *Amos, Part II, Translation and Notes* (1946. 4s. 0d.) ; *The Book of Jonah* (1945. 2s. 6d.) ; *The Psalms, A Short Introduction* (1945. 2s. 6d.) ; *The Book of Job* (1945. 2s. 6d.) ; *The Hebrew Text of Job i—vi* (1945. 2s. 6d.). (Epworth Press, London.)

These excellent little books are designed primarily for private students. The introduction to Amos is a very good account, not only of the prophet and his message, but of the historical and economic conditions of the eighth century. Similarly the volume on the Psalms is as good a summary of recent work as could be compressed within this compass. That on the book of Job is also a most useful succinct introduction, with chapters on the Satan and the Life after Death. Critically Snaith follows Baumgärtel in the view that the original work consisted of the prologue and epilogue, separated by a single cycle of speeches, Job's monologue (now distributed), and the first Divine speech, with Job's submission. All of these volumes should be widely useful. They are not concerned with the Hebrew text. The remaining volumes consist of short notes on the Hebrew text—which is not itself printed in full, as it is in the S.P.C.K. texts. They all contain the distilled wisdom of the latest commentators.

H.H.R.

TORCZYNER, H. : *The Book of Job Interpreted* (in a Hebrew Commentary). 2 vols. 1941. (Hebrew University Press. Jerusalem.)

Dr. Torczyner here replaces his previous *Buch Hiob* (1920, Vienna) with a fresh reconstruction of the Book of Job. According to him, the poetical parts were composed in Aramaic in the sixth century B.C. by a Judæan exile anxious to glorify the God of Israel in heathen Babylon ; the speeches of Elihu and his friends were composed by Ezekiel, whose prophecies (the reader learns) resemble these in style, notably in their repetition, their pre-occupation with celestial objects and operations, and their freedom from Babylonian mythology ; a translator then turned the whole work into Hebrew, unfortunately throwing it into disorder as the papyrus on which he was working was damaged and defective ; this translator was a disciple of Ezra or a group of scribes of that period ; the Prologue and Epilogue were reflections of but a stage in the development of the story of Job which originally circulated in several forms and which the translator(s) put into its present form ; the original story, which served as a background to the poetic dialogue, described Job's return to a purer and more perfect faith in God, belonged to the Mosaic age, and Job himself was Jobab, king of Edom, who was removed from his throne in favour of Balaam but, on passing God's tests, was restored to it. Incidental remarks by Dr. Torczyner contain the refutation of his own theory, and the work can only be regarded as a curiosity of misapplied learning and ingenuity. G.R.D.

RELIGION AND THEOLOGY
(including the religion of neighbouring peoples).

ALBRIGHT, W. F. : *From the Stone Age to Christianity* : *Monotheism and the Historical Process.* 1940. (The Johns Hopkins Press, Baltimore.)

The aim of this absorbing study is to trace the development of the idea of God from prehistoric antiquity to the time of Christ. In Chapter I the author sketches the principles underlying the use of the archæological data available, and in Chapter II he develops his organismic philosophy of history with its emphasis upon patterns of culture which point to " a macrocosmic thinker who is above these configurations of human societies ". Chapter III offers a masterly survey of what was known down to 1940 of prehistory and the ancient Near East until the Middle Bronze Age, while Chapters IV—VI deal specifically with developments in Israel and Judaism, paying special attention to Israelite origins (and in particular the person and work of Moses, who is regarded in a qualified way as a true " monotheist "), the prophetic reformation, and the emergence of Christianity. The work in enriched by a valuable appendix of notes to the successive chapters ; and the whole forms an extraordinarily erudite publication, far-reaching in its scope and bold in its execution. A stimulating and provocative piece of work, not to be missed.
A.R.J.

ALBRIGHT, W. F. : *Archæology and the Religion of Israel.* 1942. (The Johns Hopkins Press, Baltimore. $2.25.)

Offers a brief discussion of the sources available for an understanding of the religions of the ancient Near East, followed by a more detailed exposition of the findings of archæology in relation to (*a*) the religion of the Canaanites (cf. Ras Shamra), and (*b*) that of Israel down to the 5th century B.C. It thus forms a supplement to the writer's previous work, *From the Stone Age to Christianity* (1940), and is designed to reinforce the author's conclusion that in its main outlines the Old Testament tradition is historically sound, and that from beginning to end ethical monotheism was the distinctive feature of Israel's religion. At the same time these more controversial aspects of the writer's work are kept largely in the background ; and the volume as a whole, being enriched like its predecessor with a valuable collection of notes, is a real boon for the hard-worked student of the Old Testament.
A.R.J.

BALSCHEIT, B. : *Der Gottesbund : Einführung in das Alte Testament.* 1943. (Zwingli-Verlag, Zürich. Fr. 6.80.)

A popular and non-technical Introduction, which assumes without discussing the usual critical findings on questions of authorship and date, and which is more concerned with the purposes for which the books were created in their final form. The primary interest, as the main title indicates, is in the religious meaning of the Old Testament. Balscheit ascribes Deutero-Zechariah to the age of Antiochus Epiphanes, Habakkuk to the Greek period, finds five Servant Songs in Deutero-Isaiah, and thinks the Servant may have been a figure of the past, or Jehoiachin, or the prophet himself, in some degree, though the faith of the Songs found its goal in Christ. While not all his positions will be shared, his wisdom in seeking to rest the religious understanding of the Old Testament on critical foundations is to be commended.

H.H.R.

BALSCHEIT, B., and EICHRODT, W. : *Die soziale Botschaft des Alten Testaments für die Gegenwart*. n.d. (Reinhardt, Basel.)

Contains two essays, on " The social significance and validity of the Old Testament legislation " (Balscheit), and " The social message of the prophets as Word of God for the present day " (Eichrodt).

Three religious beliefs, says Balscheit, underlie Old Testament legislation, viz. : that the Israelite man who is the subject of Old Testament law is a man who has been redeemed by God from Egyptian bondage and from privation of rights ; that God is the patron of the poor, the widow, orphan and stranger ; that the land has been given by God and is not individual property but has been allotted to the tribes and their subdivisions who safeguard both the land and the individual's right. In the light of these principles the author examines various Old Testament enactments. The essay is an illuminating and valuable critical study. The references to the ancient oriental Law-corpora (e.g. Codex Ham.) and to old Swiss and Bavarian laws are of much interest. Eichrodt's essay is a thoughtful investigation. The eschatological character of the prophet's message conditions the description of the message as *social*. The social element in the message is not regarded by the prophets as a means of preventing the doom of the End-time or of establishing a Kingdom of God, for the present time is only a period of grace and the Judgment cannot be averted. The social conduct which the prophets demand is an act of faith, that is of obedience to God's will without enquiry into the results or success of such obedience. Nevertheless, the content of the social teaching of the prophets reveals the economic forces which oppose it and explain it, e.g. acquaintance of the Hebrews with the heathen city-culture, and their contact with the incipient capitalistic economy, which weaken the old Israelite judicial principles and traditions. Finally Eichrodt answers, with much wisdom, the question : " How far may the prophets' social demands be regarded as Word of God for us to-day ? "

O.S.R.

BENTZEN, A. : *Det sakrale kongedømme*. 1945. (Gad, Copenhagen.)

An excellent, up-to-date survey of recent studies of the Psalter in terms of divine kingship, with a critical review of the arguments for and against this theory (especially as developed by the new Swedish school associated with the names of Widengren and Engnell), and a rapid glance at the material available in the psalms themselves. Indispensable for all workers in this field.

A.R.J.

BERGEMA, H. : *De boom des levens in Schrift en historie.* 1938.
(Schipper, Hilversum.)

A study of the conception of the Tree of Life as found
(*a*) in Scripture, and (*b*) in Sumer, Babylon, Assyria, Egypt,
Persia, Judaism, early Christianity, and Islam. Written
from a strongly conservative position which accepts the
historicity of Genesis 2—3, and finds possible reminiscences
of this primitive tradition both in the Bible itself and in the
many non-Biblical sources which the author examines.
Characterized by wide reading, and valuable for its extraordinarily full documentation and many plates.

A.R.J.

BRONGERS, H. A. : *De scheppingstradities bij de profeten.* 1945.
(Paris, Amsterdam.)

The book is a thesis for a doctorate in the University of
Leiden, written in Dutch with a five-page English summary.
It is a study of the way in which the prophets make use of
the creation tradition. There are five chapters, dealing
respectively with Genesis i¹—ii⁴ᵃ, Amos, Isaiah, Jeremiah
and Deutero-Isaiah. Everywhere the creation is subservient
to the main theme of God's work of salvation. The short
sixth chapter is a summary, and there are two short
excursuses, one on the Name Jehovah Sabaoth (because of the
LXX interpretation) and the other on Hebrew cosmology
(because of the relation of Hebrew tradition with Mesopotamia
and Ras Shamra). The two most important matters are the
emphasis on the way in which the Hebrews interwove myth
and history and the excellent discussion of Isaiah xl.

N.H.S.

CLOSEN, G. E., S.J. : *Wege in die Heilige Schrift : theologische
Betrachtungen über religiöse Grundideen des Alten Bundes.* 1939.
(Pustet, Regensburg.)

In this book, the author (who died during the war) tries to
expose to the general reader some of the fundamental religious
ideas of the Old Testament. The " mystery of Scripture ",
he says, " is only accessible to one who is able to say and to
pray : ' I believe in the Holy Scripture ' " (p. 11). The
book deals with a variety of subjects (e.g. the doctrine of
grace in Genesis, the sacrifice of Isaac, the vocation of Isaiah,
the new covenant of Jeremiah xxxi, the Messiah, priest for
ever, De Profundis, etc.) under three headings : " From
the world of the Patriarchs ", " Teaching and life of the
Prophets ", " The songs of the people of God ", with some
appendices. The general tendency is, besides theological,
also somewhat parenetical, which may be one of the causes
that the first impression was soon out of print and that it
has been translated into other languages. The Dutch translation (1945. Bruges, Belgium) had a preface by J. Coppens.

J.v.d.P.

Cook, S. A. : *The Rebirth of Christianity*. 1942. (Penguin Press, London. 1s. 0d.)

> To readers of Professor Cook's previous volumes, in which he deals with the necessity for a new synthesis of Christianity and modern thought, this *multum in parvo* volume needs no introduction. Brilliant, challenging and at times perplexing, it provides much food for thought, not least to the student of the Old Testament. N.W.P.

Cunliffe-Jones, H. : *The Authority of Biblical Revelation*. 1946. (James Clarke, London. 7s. 6d.)

> A plea for the interaction of the historical and the theological in Biblical study. The author is at pains to insist that there must be no turning one's back on the gains won by historical and literary criticism. He claims, however, that for the Christian the Bible is not primarily the record of religious experience but mediates a Word of God which judges experience. Biblical Theology ought to be a Theology of the Word rather than a Theology of Response. The book will undoubtedly provoke fruitful controversy and should be overlooked by no one who is interested in Biblical Theology. There are chapters of importance about the relation of the Testaments. Professor Cuniffe-Jones favours a measure of Christological exegesis of the Old Testament, though he says that all exegesis must start from the meaning of the original author. N.W.P.

Dhorme, E. : *Les religions de Babylonie et d'Assyrie* ; and Dussaud, R. : *Les religions des Hittites et des Hourrites, des Phéniciens et des Syriens* (in one volume). 1945. (Presses Universitaires de France, Paris. Fr. 160.)

> This volume is part 2 in the first section of a series of five sections dealing with world religions under the general title " ' Mana ' : Introduction à l'Histoire des Religions ". M. Dhorme, after a résumé of Mesopotamian history, describes first the idea of God, then the gods of the sky, the earth, the waters, and the under-world. Next, there follow the star-gods, the gods of nature and the national gods. Succeeding chapters describe temple, clergy, cultus, magic, divination and astrology, and finally the myths of various types. After each chapter there is a series of notes with references to the sources where further information is to be found. The second part of the volume, that by M. Dussaud, is note-worthy chiefly for its description of Phœnician religion, based mostly on the Ras Shamra tablets. The volume provides good summaries of the various religions, without encumbering detail, but there is the tendency, common in studies of Mesopotamian religion, to neglect the time factor, and to assume, in respect of both cultus and ideas of gods, that what is true of one place and one time, is true of all places at all times. N.H.S.

DUGMORE, C. W. : *The Influence of the Synagogue upon the Divine Office.* 1944. (Oxford University Press. 10s. 6d.)

> A careful and discriminating study of the extent of early Christian indebtedness to Jewish liturgical forms based on the Genizah text of the *Shemoneh Esreh* (published with a translation in an Appendix, side by side with the modern form) as compared with the earliest known elements of the Christian liturgy. Where materials are scanty conclusions should be cautious, and Dugmore displays this quality. He finds the Synagogue to have influenced the Church in the times and type of its worship, in phraseology and in the subjects of prayer, but is not convinced of any wholesale borrowing.   H.H.R.

DUSSAUD, RENÉ : *Les origines cananéennes du sacrifice israélite,* 2nd Edition. 1941. (Presses Universitaires de France, Paris. English price, 9s. 6d.)

> A reprint of the edition of 1921, with thirty pages of *Nova Addenda* at the end to bring it up to date. These pages are mainly devoted to a treatment of the relevant material from Ras Shamra. One of its sections is devoted to the Passover, which Dussaud would not separate from Unleavened Bread, holding that both belonged together in their origin. He accepts Eissfeldt's view that *molk* was a technical term for a human sacrifice (see Book List for 1935), and holds that the reform of Moses consisted in installing the Canaanite God Yahweh as the tribal God of Israel in place of El, the father of Yahweh. The slender evidence for the last of these views is not presented here.   H.H.R.

EDELKOORT, A. H. : *De Christus-verwachting in het Oude Testament.* 1941. (Veenman & Zonen, Wageningen. Fl. 8.40, Bound, Fl. 9.50.)

> A very large volume on the hope of Christ (this term is deliberately used in preference to Messiah because of its association with the idea of salvation rather than reign) in the Old Testament. All of the eschatological passages of the Old Testament, whether they envisage a personal leader or not, are studied in detail, in the light of all the modern literature that has been devoted to them. The author is in general conservative, especially in his conclusions, but he has written a very scholarly work, of real value for its survey of modern interpretations. The Servant Songs of Deutero-Isaiah (ascribed to the period of the exile in accordance with the normal critical view, and hence showing that Edelkoort's conservatism is relative, and not absolute) are given a messianic interpretation. The author shows greater confidence in deciding which of the psalms studied are pre-exilic and which post-exilic than most would profess to-day.
>
> H.H.R.

EICHRODT, W. : *Theologie des Alten Testaments*. Teil 3 : Gott und Mensch. 1939. (Hinrichs, Leipzig.)

This third volume completes Professor Eichrodt's epoch-making work on Old Testament Theology. (In some editions it is bound up with Teil 2.) In the first section the author refuses to find in the Old Testament evidence for a development from collectivism to individualism (in the proper sense of the latter word) and claims that individuality was given its proper place in Israel even in early times. He then goes on to consider the various elements in Man's relation to God and shows how piety among the Hebrews was related to morality. Concluding sections are devoted to the discussion of the Old Testament teaching about sin and forgiveness and to the hope of immortality, which arose out of the conviction that the relations of the individual to God could not be dissolved by death. N.W.P.

EICHRODT, W. : *Das Menschenverständnis des Alten Testaments*. 1944. (Majer, Basel. Fr. 5.50.)

In this work, which forms a very useful appendix to his *Theologie des Alten Testaments*, Eichrodt develops the view that the basis of the Old Testament view of man is his sense of an absolute obligation to fulfil the will of God. This is shown especially in the distinctive Hebrew conception of law, and here Eichrodt makes effective use of Alt's well-known monograph. He argues that the sense of obligation was deepened and preserved by the prophets, who also, by their conception of history, prevented God's will from being identified with an impersonal, unchanging law. The further fact that for the Hebrews the God who is lawgiver is also creator barred the way to any deification of nature which might have led to self-deification on man's part or to the claim that he was capable of legislating for himself. Eichrodt shows how the belief in God as creator became the basis of a true conception of human community and concludes by considering at length the various difficulties in the way of recognizing absolute obligation due to facts like those of suffering and sin and the secular claims of society.
N.W.P.

EISSFELDT, O. : *Tempel und Kulte syrischer Städte in hellenistisch-römischer Zeit*. (Der Alte Orient, Bd. 40). 1941. (Hinrichs, Leipzig.)

Treats of Gerasa, Baalbek, Palmyra and Dura, dealing in each case with the history of the town, its temples, cults, deities and myths. It is thus, in a certain sense, comparable with Rostovtzeff's *Caravan Cities* ; more precisely, owing to its different aim, a very valuable complement of it : an excellent summary of the archæological and religio-historical researches of the last decade in which the religio-historical research is in some cases also further developed. For the Old Testament, too, the benefit is not small, since the older Phœnician-Syriac religion is visible through the Hellenistic-Roman dress. W.B.

ENGNELL, I. : *Studies in Divine Kingship in the Ancient Near East.*
1943. (Almqvist & Wiksell, Uppsala.)

An examination of the conception of divine kingship and its
associated ritual pattern, as found in ancient Egypt, Sumer
and Accad, Asia Minor, and the West-Semitic world in general.
The work reaches its climax in an elaborate study of the
Ras Shamra texts from this standpoint, and the whole is
intended to serve as background to a detailed
examination of the Old Testament material, and in particular
the Psalter, with a view to establishing the existence of
similar phenomena in ancient Israel. It thus runs on lines
parallel to those associated with the somewhat loosely-
labelled " Myth and Ritual School " in Great Britain, and
altogether is an important study, written with an engaging
confidence, and possessing an excellent bibliography. The
sketch which the author gives of his conclusions with regard
to the Old Testament suggests that the companion volume
is likely to be much more controversial.   A.R.J.

HALDAR, A. : *Associations of Cult Prophets among the Ancient Semites.*
1945. (Almqvist & Wiksell, Uppsala. 16s. 0d.)

An inquiry into the special functions and general organization
of those members of the cultic personnel in the ancient
Semitic world, including pre-Islamic Arabia, who were
concerned with oracular direction in one form or another.
The author pays due regard to the part played in this respect
by the cultic prophet in ancient Israel, although in his
enthusiasm for his subject he sometimes goes a little too far.
A stimulating piece of work, admirably documented, and yet
another indication that the new Swedish school of biblical
scholars, with its dominant interest in comparative religion
from the cultic angle, is a force which no diligent student
of the Bible can afford to neglect.   A.R.J.

HEBERT, A. G. : *The Throne of David.* 1941. (Faber and Faber,
London. 12s. 6d.)

The author is concerned, as the sub-title states, with the
" Fulfilment of the Old Testament in Jesus Christ and His
Church ". The book has a foremost place in the present-day
movement to rehabilitate the Old Testament as an integral
part of the Word of God. The central theme, which gives
a unity to the two Testaments, is the Messianic Hope. Various
themes are in turn discussed (e.g. Israel's Universal Mission,
Law and Sacrifice in Ancient Israel), and the contention is
that the full realization is achieved in the New Israel of
Jesus the Messiah and His Ecclesia. A most valuable book,
but the reader must take particular heed of the author's
own warning that " mystical interpretation " can easily be
dangerous to sound exegesis.   N.H.S.

HEINISCH, P. : *Theologie des Alten Testaments* (= Die H. Schrift des Alten Testaments übersetzt und erklärt, Ergänzungsband I). 1940. (Hanstein, Bonn.)

> In the preface of this work, the author declares that his intention in writing it has been to explain the religious ideas, proposed by the inspired authors of the Old Testament, in their connection with each other, and to construct with these materials a " building ". Anyone who has dealt with the subject knows how difficult, not to say impossible, this task is. The book of Heinisch proves certainly to be very useful, and it is doubtless the best of its kind written by a Catholic author, but the general pattern of it is still too much borrowed from scholastic theology. This applies especially to the first part, dealing with the doctrine of God, in which we find even a paragraph on the " Aseität " (*aseitas*) of God. In this respect the method of Eichrodt was certainly better.
>
> J.v.d.P.

HUMBERT, P. : *La " Terou'a " : analyse d'un rite biblique.* 1946. (University Press, Neuchâtel. Fr. 5.00.)

> A very thorough study of all the passages in which the word *Terū'ā*, and its associated verb are found, with a view to determining its precise range of meaning and how far that range developed within the Old Testament period. Humbert shows that the term denotes a collective and primarily, if not exclusively, vocal sound. It was a cultic war-cry which was also used in the ritual of the enthronement of Yahweh, and in the post-exilic period it became increasingly associated with the Temple cultus. The whole monograph is a model of exact semasiology. H.H.R.

HVIDBERG, F. F. : *Graad og Latter i det Gamle Testamente.* 1938. (Gad, Copenhagen.)

> This study of weeping and laughter in the Old Testament limits its interest to cultic weeping and laughter, whose traces are collected and studied. The first half of the work consists of a study of some of the Ras Shamra texts, which are given in translation. From the cultic drama of the Old Canaanite religion, with its emphasis on fertility and sexual rites, the author proceeds to the study of the Old Testament passages which refer to it, in its double aspect of lament and joy. An able study, which would have gained in usefulness if it had been provided with an index. H.H.R.

HVIDBERG, F. F. : *Den Israelitiske Religions Historie.* 1944. (Munksgaard, Copenhagen. Kr. 7.50.)

> In reaction against recent tendencies to treat of Old Testament Theology, Hvidberg prefers to deal with the history of Israel's religion, and defends his choice. The chapter on pre-Israelite Canaan contains a good deal of material from Ras Shamra, and throughout the book is strong on the Canaanite and popular side of Israel's religion. There are chapters on pre-Mosaic and Mosaic religion, on

the syncretism with Baalism, on the Canaanite-Israelite cultus, on the prophetic reaction, and on " Reform, Exile and Judaism ". It is significant that a single chapter is deemed sufficient to treat of the whole period from the seventh century onwards. The book provides rather the background of Israel's religious history than an adequate account of that history.   H.H.R.

JOHANSSON, N. : *Parakletoi : Vorstellungen von Fürsprechern für die Menschen vor Gott in der alttestamentlichen Religion, im Spätjudentum und Urchristentum.* 1940. (Gleerupska Universitetsbokhandeln, Lund. English price, 16s. 6d.)

As indicated by the sub-title, this is a study of the various types of intercessor between man and God which are to be found in the Old Testament, in later Judaism, and in early Christianity. The writer endeavours to cover every example, both human and divine, his ultimate aim being to seek an elucidation of three major problems, that of the Servant in the so-called Servant Songs, that of the analogous material in the Enoch literature, and that which is raised by the conception (or conceptions) of the intercessor in the New Testament. The author makes things as easy as possible for the reader by quoting the relevant passages at length and, more often than not, offering the original Hebrew, Greek, Syriac, and Ethiopic texts in addition to a translation. While the conclusions drawn will not always command assent, the work may be recommended as a painstaking and useful treatment of the subject.   A.R.J.

JOHNSON, A. R. : *The One and the Many in the Israelite Conception of God.* 1942. (University of Wales Press Board, Cardiff. 2s. 0d.)

A highly suggestive development of the idea of corporate personality and of the various extensions of personality to explain the relation between the human personality and the divine. It is argued that in various passages of Scripture there is an oscillation between the thought of the social unit as an association of individuals and as a corporate personality, and that this explains the otherwise suspicious alternation of singular and plural. There is a very interesting discussion of the word *ruaḥ* conceived as an extension of the personality of God, and this is used to throw light upon references in the Old Testament to'" Sons of God " and to the " Angel of Yahweh ", and finally upon those passages in the Old Testament where the prophet seems to be identified with God.   N.W.P.

JOHNSON, A. R. : *The Cultic Prophet in Ancient Israel.* 1944. (University of Wales Press Board, Cardiff. 3s. 6d.)

This pamphlet of sixty-four pages has been already recognized by Old Testament specialists as of quite unusual importance for the understanding of the Hebrew prophets. It links up with Mowinckel, *Psalmenstudien III* and expands

part of the author's article entitled " The Prophet in Israelite
Worship " which appeared in *The Expository Times*, April,
1936. The thesis is that the prophet, no less than the priest,
was an important cultic official at the Israelite sanctuaries,
above all in the Temple at Jerusalem. As the spokesman
of Yahweh he was expected to give oracles and to divine.
As the representative of the people he was what the author
calls " a specialist in prayer ", " his function was to promote
the *shālōm* or ' welfare ' of the people, whether an individual
or a ' corporate personality ' ". A suggestion of Eissfeldt's
that after the exile the cultic prophets formed Temple choirs
and merged into the other Levitical orders is elaborated
and presented in the most convincing manner. N.W.P.

LANGTON, E. : *Good and Evil Spirits : A study of the Jewish and
Christian Doctrine, its Origin and Development.* 1942. (S.P.C.K.,
London.)

In the foreword to this book Dr. Oesterley commends the
author's work for its wideness of range, its method of
treatment and the sympathetic appreciation of the beliefs
which have been man's heritage throughout the ages. This
volume (to be followed by another developing the same
theme) has for its purpose " to set the whole body of Jewish
and Christian teaching upon the subject of good and evil
spirits against its historical background : to trace each
conception to its source in primitive animism or in the more
developed beliefs of the cultured peoples of the ancient
world ". The student and teacher of the history of religion
will be glad of such clear and succinct studies as here are
offered on a multitude of cognate subjects (the origin of
the belief in the spirit of man, ancestor-worship, animism,
totemism, mana, taboo, demons, place of departed spirits,
survival-beliefs in the Old Testament, Greece, Egypt, Iran,
Babylonia, idea of immortality, etc.). The reader will much
appreciate that the concepts of The Apocryphal literature
and the New Testament on the destiny of the individual,
resurrection, judgment, Messianic Kingdom, Parousia,
Paradise, Gehenna are explored and clarified. The writer
has at his disposal a wide bibliography which he uses without
embarrassment to his style and without falling into the danger
of presenting to the reader more than the latter can do with.
O.S.R.

MORGENSTERN, J. : *The Ark, the Ephod, and the Tent of Meeting.*
1945. (Hebrew Union Press, Cincinnati.)

Reprinted from the Hebrew Union College Annuals xvii, xviii;
it discusses the nature and rôle of the Ark, particularly in
the pre-exilic period and compares Arabic parallel structures.
The author suggests that the Ephod was the generic name
for such tent shrines, and attempts to trace their development. J.N.S.

47

MOWINCKEL, S. : *Die Erkenntnis Gottes bei den Alttestamentlichen Profeten.* 1941. (Grøndahl, Oslo.) (Only now obtainable in the *Norsk Teologisk Tidsskrift for* 1941. About 14s. 0d.).

Like everything which comes from Professor Mowinckel's pen, this essay of sixty-four pages is of outstanding importance and should not be missed by any serious student of Hebrew prophecy. The author is concerned with the theological question of how knowledge of God is possible and with the practical consequences of such knowledge. He begins by examining the meaning of the expression *da'ath 'elohim* in the Old Testament, and indicates its reciprocal character and the way in which it inevitably passes over into action. This knowledge is characteristic of the members of the Covenant People and in the first instance of its leaders. Mowinckel then proceeds to deal with the knowledge of God claimed by the prophets of judgment, a knowledge which comes to them in response to their obedience to the divine call. It implies something of the concentration of ecstasy, but the external symptoms of ecstasy are of little consequence. The prophet possesses his knowledge of God because God's Word comes to existence in him, but this is an event of his normal mental life and may involve the focussing of thoughts he has already entertained, yet with an element of compulsion which leads to a conflict between a moral obligation and a natural reluctance. This special word which a prophet receives communicates a knowledge of God which every Israelite should possess. The prophet is able to recognize it for what it is because he has a criterion in Israel's tradition and because it is in agreement with the chaiacter of God thus known to him, but he is also enabled to advance beyond the knowledge of God possessed by his predecessors. Essentially this knowledge is knowledge of what God wills that men should do. The problem of how all men were eventually to attain to such knowledge was eventually solved by the answer that God would pour out His Spirit upon them. N.W.P.

NOTH, M. : *Die Gesetze im Pentateuch, ihre Voraussetzungen u. ihr Sinn* (Schriften der Königsberger Gelehrten Gesellschaft xvii 2). 1940. (Niemeyer, Halle.)

Starts from the theological question as to how the Old Testament as a whole can be taken as a " law ". All its laws, even Deuteronomy (!) were only seemingly State Laws. In reality they were statutes of a sacral association : in the first place of the amphictyony of the 12 tribes, maintained even after their end in expectation of a forth-coming restoration ; finally, however, understood as a strict unity of divine origin. Clever and stimulating, but also arousing opposition. W.B.

PHYTHIAN-ADAMS, W. J. : *The People and the Presence.* 1942. (O.U.P. 12s. 6d.)

The theme is that the faith and worship of Israel revolved round the belief in the " tabernacling " Presence of God on earth. The later tendency to think of God as dwelling in heaven set up a dualism, resolved only in the Incarnation. In the God-Man the People and the Presence meet in an " At-one-ment ". The Old Testament is dealt with in the first half of the book. The author tends to be conservative in his " Introduction ". On the other hand his thesis involves new facets which make the book of special interest. Chief among these is the contention that the exile and the post-exilic periods enhanced the belief in the earthly Presence of God. A stimulating book. N.H.S.

PEDERSEN, J. : *Israel : Its Life and Culture III—IV*. 1940. (Povl Branner, Copenhagen, and Humphrey Milford, London.)

The original Danish edition of this imposing work was published as long ago as 1934 ; but the present English translation has benefited from the fact that in the meantime the author was able to make certain changes, notably as a result of the discoveries at Ras Shamra. It forms the sequel to *Israel : Its Life and Culture I—II* (1926), in which the author sought to present the typical Israelite conception of man (*a*) as an individual with his own peculiar powers, and (*b*) as compelled to live in community, and therefore in conformity with certain basic principles governing both his own well-being and that of the society of which he forms a part. In this volume the author seeks to describe the way in which Israelite society was organized under the concept of " Holiness " for the preservation of its common life. Part III deals with the implication of " Holiness ", and describes those sacred persons, places, and objects which were thought necessary for its maintenance. Part IV treats of the ritual acts and the sacred seasons by means of which the required " Holiness " might be renewed, and offers in conclusion a short (and, indeed, by contrast a somewhat cursory) sketch of the relations between Israel and Yahweh in their expression on the plane of history. As in the case of *Israel I—II*, the author is inclined to be discursive ; but on the whole the discussion of the conception of " Holiness " and of the significance of the cultus which occupies the greater part of the book reveals the same wealth of learning and the same gift for sympathetic interpretation as made the earlier volume so attractive and valuable. Undoubtedly a work of the first importance. A.R.J.

ROBINSON, H. W. : *Redemption and Revelation in the Actuality of History*. 1942. (Nisbet, London. . 12s. 6d.)

This is the third volume of the late Principal Wheeler Robinson's great trilogy. Like the previous volumes it contains much of interest and value for the student of the Old Testament. The first part deals with history as the revelation of God. In the second part will be found a discussion of the various media characteristic of religions and in particular of the religion of Israel. It is indicated that for four religions, viz. Zoroastrianism, Judaism, Christianity and Islam, the chief medium of contact with God is to be found in the prophetic consciousness. After a discussion of the psychology of prophecy we are given an exposition of the three chief philosophical implicates of the prophetic consciousness, viz. the validity of the value-judgments of morality, the personality of God, and the " actuality " of human history. The concluding part of the book deals with the Christian doctrine of redemption.   N.W.P.

ROBINSON, H. W. : *Inspiration and Revelation in the Old Testament* 1946. (Oxford University Press. 15s. 0d.)

This magnificent posthumous work from the pen of the late Principal Wheeler Robinson will make students of the Old Testament realize afresh how much has been lost by his death. There is here no sign of failing powers but the mature conclusions of a richly endowed mind. The book purports to be prolegomena to the Theology of the Old Testament which Dr. Robinson had planned to write and seeks to give the form of the revelation. The first three parts deal with the fundamental topics of God and Nature, God and Man, God and History. Specially interesting sections deal with Nature-miracles, Hebrew psychology, the vocabulary of time, the prophetic interpretation of history and the Day of Yahweh. The remaining four parts deal with revelation through the Prophet, the Priest and the Sage, and with the response to revelation of the Psalmist. Much of interest will be found about the author's views on the psychology of prophecy, the function of the priest in Israel, the relation of priest and prophet, and the part played by the Wisdom writers in interpreting experience and in facing some of the problems which beset the religious view of the world. Dr. Robinson finds revelation in " the interpretative interplay of event and faith together constituting the religious fact ". There are the data of human life (Nature, Man, and History) interpreted by Prophets, Priests and Sages. Through these data God makes Himself known in a personal relationship to man, the guarantee of the truth of the revelation being of the nature of a value-judgment, which is ultimately what the authority of Church or Bible amounts to.   N.W.P.

ROWLEY, H. H. : *The Relevance of the Bible.* 1941. (James Clarke, London.   6s. 0d.)

In this book Professor Rowley seeks in his usual competent and lucid way to demonstrate the abiding significance of the Bible and especially its relevance to ourselves. He argues that the inspiration of the Bible is to be found in the fact that it contains a record of the religious experience of Israel and of the early Christian Church. Into that experience it is possible for us to enter that we may be able better to face the tasks of our own age. The thesis is exemplified in an interesting study of the prophets, and this is followed by chapters on such topics as the unity of the Bible, the use of the Bible and the Biblical views of God and sin.
                N.W.P.

ROWLEY, H. H. : *The Relevance of Apocalyptic : A Study of Jewish and Christian Apocalypses from Daniel to the Revelation.* 1944. (Lutterworth Press, London. 8s. 6d.)

> Gives an account of the rise of Apocalyptic, introductions to the Apocalypses of the last two centuries B.C. and the first century A.D., and a chapter on the enduring message of this literature. Without going at length into the subject of the marks of Apocalyptic (cf. p. 23n) the author traces the growth of Apocalyptic from the pre-exilic writing prophets, accounts for their different outlook as arising out of internal political changes, shows that Apocalyptic and eschatology are not coterminous in their significance, explains how in the case of Daniel pseudonymity was " born of a living process . . . the precise opposite of deceit ". What is said of Daniel is particularly good. The introductions are short but there are critical notes on a number of interesting points, e.g. the date of Jubilees, the figure of Taxo in *Assumptio Mosis*, etc. The chapter on the enduring message of Apocalyptic is popular, containing some good things. To attempt a book of this small size (168 pages) on Apocalyptic and to succeed so well in describing the nature of its thought and the books which convey it, is a great feat.   O.S.R.

ROWLEY, H. H. : *The Missionary Message of the Old Testament.* 1945. (Carey Press, London. 5s. 0d.)

> A parergon but an interesting and useful one. Professor Rowley follows the missionary strand through the Old Testament from Moses onwards and concludes with a study of the Second Isaiah and in particular of the bearing of the Servant Songs on his theme. There is an exposition of the Servant Songs which represents a certain fusion of the Collective and the Messianic interpretations.   N.W.P.

SCHOFIELD, J. N. : *The Religious Background of the Bible.* 1944. (Nelson, London. 17s. 6d.)

> A companion volume to the author's earlier volume entitled *The Historical Background of the Bible.* The whole stretch of Israel's history (up to and including Early Christianity and its conflict with Judaism) is dealt with in a most interesting and readable manner. Full use is made of the wealth of material furnished by archæology and the science of Comparative Religion. The fact that one is frequently moved to demur to certain of the author's judgments adds to the interest of the book. The book is well illustrated and excellently produced.   N.W.P.

SCOTT, R. B. Y. : *The Relevance of the Prophets.* 1944. (The Macmillan Company, New York. $2.50.)

> A refreshingly original study, more concerned with the function and meaning of prophecy, and the common elements in the teaching of the great prophets (e.g. their " theology ", their attitude to history, etc.), than in the individual prophets themselves. It is noteworthy that in common

51

with recent trends the author recognizes a strong ethical current in Israel prior to Amos, and traces this to the covenant idea within the Mosaic tradition. Definitely not a case of "the mixture as before", but a work which may be warmly recommended as offering sane reading for all who are interested in a theological approach to the Old Testament. Written in a light and attractive style, but obviously the work of one who is a master of his subject.   A.R.J.

RYDER SMITH, C. : *The Bible Doctrine of Salvation, A Study of the Atonement.* 1941. (Epworth Press, London.)

Terms such as *salvation, vicarious, vicarious sufferings, atonement, redemption* are clarified. Lower and higher significances of what is called salvation are defined. The author shows the degree in which the "societary" and covenantal principles worked in such saviour-personalities as Moses and Elijah and the prophets or are expressed in the Old Testament Messianic conceptions and in the Servant Songs. These principles come to a climax in the last Servant Song. Psalm li represents the high point of what the Old Testament has to say about salvation, viewing this as the changing of a bad man into a good man, which is the true definition of salvation. Particularly valuable is the author's examination of the post-exilic sacrificial system in regard to the effecting of salvation. After a very careful, detailed and honest study of the question he concludes that the use of ritual in the Old Testament in relation to the doctrine of salvation is only illustrative, however helpful a right use of ritual may be to those who cry out for a "clean heart" and "a right spirit". Preparatory to treating of "the soteriological teaching of the New Testament, Apocalyptic thought (in which nothing appears as to the salvation of sinners), the topics of mediation and of sin and repentance, as these emerge in Judaism, are discussed. In a chapter on "the Servant", "the Lamb" and "the Shepherd" the author shows that this soteriological imagery of the New Testament is derived from the last Servant Song (Isaiah liii). It is impossible to praise this book too highly.   O.S.R.

SNAITH, N. H. : *The Distinctive Ideas of the Old Testament.* 1944. (Epworth Press, London. 10s. 0d.)

"Thy sons, O Zion, against thy sons, O Greece" would have made an appropriate motto for this most valuable book in which the author elucidates the meaning of certain of the primary religious terms in the Old Testament, such as *qodesh, sedeq, 'ahabah* and *hesed,* and relates them to their New Testament equivalents. In this connection he demonstrates the superior value of the LXX as compared with the Greek of the Papyri and *a fortiori* as compared with Classical Greek, when we are seeking to establish the meaning of the New Testament terms which should thus be linked with the Old Testament terminology lying behind the LXX. For *'ahabah* and *hesed* he suggests the translations "election-love" and "covenant-love".   N.W.P.

STAMM, J. J. : *Erlösen und Vergeben im Alten Testament.* 1940. (Francke, Bern. Fr. 8.00.)

Originally a dissertation for the doctorate of Basel University, this careful study of the words and metaphorical expressions used in the Old Testament to express the ideas of redemption and forgiveness furnishes some interesting results. The words for redemption are of legal origin, but gradually in certain cases the legal sense tends to fall into the background. The expressions for forgiveness on the other hand seem to have originated in the cult. The conception of redemption is essentially Israelite, connected as it is with the covenant relationship between God and Israel. It is important to notice that the ideas of redemption and forgiveness are in the Old Testament expressed in various ways other than by the use of technical terms.   N.W.P.

VANDIER, J. : *La religion égyptienne.* 1944. (Presses Universitaires de France, Paris.)

The first volume of a new series of manuals to appear under the title " Mana ". It contains a short general introduction to the History of Religion by R. Dussaud, and a fine bibliography of the whole subject by H. C. Puech. Then follows Vandier's study of Egyptian religion. The text is free from footnotes, but each chapter is followed by notes on special points. The author finds an incipient monotheism in Egyptian religion, not confined to the reform of Akhnaton. The treatment is in chapters dealing with the gods, theology and legends, funerary rites, divine kingship, the cultus, and magic.   H.H.R.

VISCHER, W. : *Das Christuszeugnis des Alten Testaments.* II. Die früheren Propheten. 1942. (Zollikon, Zürich. English price, 22s. 6d.)

A continuation of Vischer's earlier volume published in 1934 which dealt with the Law, this book seeks, with reference to the historical books, to demonstrate the author's thesis that the Old Testament as a whole is witness to Jesus as Messiah. Vischer belongs to the group of Swiss theological commentators who practise so-called Christological exegesis. Though not opposed in theory to literary and historical criticism, and though frequently most suggestive and stimulating, Vischer will be felt by most readers to be frequently carrying his method of exegesis to unwarranted extremes.   N.W.P.

VRIEZEN, TH. C. : *Hosea : profeet en cultuur.* 1941. (Wolters, Groningen. Fl. 0.80.)

Inaugural lecture on assuming the chair at Groningen. A learned study of the prophet's attitude to contemporary culture, introduced by a review of some earlier revolts against urban culture. Vriezen leaves undiscussed all the critical problems of the book, and concentrates his attention on Hosea as a critic of culture. He denies that he was opposed to culture in itself, or that he cherished the nomadic ideal. His message was fundamentally religious, and was a declaration that loyalty to the will of God and a religiously based loyalty of man to man was a firmer bond of society than culture.   H.H.R.

WENSINCK, A. J., and KRAMERS, J. H. : *Handwörterbuch des Islam.* 1941. (Brill, Leiden. £2. 10s. 0d.)

Consists of a selection of the articles from the *Encyclopædia of Islam*, and its Supplements, and especially those dealing with Islam as a religion. Some of the articles are printed unchanged, some are abridged, some are compiled from material in the Supplements as. well as in the main work, and some are completely new articles. The index at the end enables the reader to tell in a moment to which category any particular article belongs. The original Encyclopædia is out of print in all three editions, and this abridged edition at a mere fraction of the cost should be widely useful.

H.H.R.

WIDENGREN, G. : *Psalm 110 och det sakrala kungadömet i Israel.* 1941. (A.-B. Lundequistska Bokhandeln, Uppsala.)

A short but important monograph on one of the most discussed of the Psalms, designed to bring out its connection with the sacral rôle of the king in the Jerusalem Cultus, and emphasizing its pre-Israelite, and specifically Canaanite, antecedents.   A.R.J.

WIDENGREN, G. : *Religionens värld : Religtonsfenomenologiska Studier och översikter.* 1945. (Svenska Kyrkans Diakonistyrelses Bokförlag, Stockholm. Kr. 14, Bound, Kr. 16.50.)

An important work by a leading member of the Swedish school, covering a wide field, but with bearing on our field at many points. Widengren criticizes the *mana* view, as commonly conceived, holding that it is not impersonal force, but personal. He discusses acutely the concept of holiness, in relation to *tabu*, and proceeds to treat of the high god. He takes an anti-evolutionistic position, and argues for a primitive monotheism which gave place to polytheism through the hypostatization of the separate activities of the high god, who was identified with Heaven, and who manifested himself in the processes of Nature. Myth, ritual, sacrifice—traced primarily to a communion significance—the divine kingship and enthronement rites, death and the relation of spirit and soul, eschatology and apocalyptic, are all in turn studied, and then Gnosticism— treated in the light of Iranian material—the relation of the individual and society, and mysticism. Its positions will not command universal agreement, but its importance will be generally recognized.   H.H.R.

WILDBERGER, H. : *Jahwewort und prophetische Rede bei Jeremia.* 1942. (Zwingli-verlag, Zürich. Fr. 5.20.)

This study is a thesis accepted for a doctorate in Theology in the University of Zürich. It is a detailed examination of the prophetic consciousness, based on the most " unwilling " of all the prophets. Is it possible to distinguish between the veritable Word of God and the prophet's own words ? The basis of the study is a close analysis of the various introductory formulæ to the short pieces of which the book is composed. Each formula has its own significance. The prophet is not only the " funnel ", but the interpreter of the Word of God. The test of the prophet is the essential unity between the Word and the interpretation. N.H.S.

WOLFE, R. E. : *Meet Amos and Hosea.* 1945. (Harper, New York. $2.00.)

A popular presentation of the author's views, which is to be followed by a work addressed more directly to scholars. Amos was " the founder of the social gospel "—if judgment can be equated with gospel—and both Amos and Hosea were martyred. Gomer is acquitted of pre-marital sin, but is held to have fallen to prostitution after marriage, and to have paid the price the law demanded—viz. death. It is a pity to present conclusions of this kind with so much confidence and so little evidence. The oracles of both prophets are translated and placed in their assumed order of utterance, and provided with background and inter-pretation. H.H.R.

WRIGHT, G. E. : *The Challenge of Israel's Faith.* 1944. (University of Chicago Press. $1.50.)

This book is an example of what President Colwell calls the " modernizing " tendency in Biblical interpretation. It is written in the style of a challenge to the purely objective study of the Old Testament and contains a passionate plea that the Bible should be interpreted as the Word of God with a relevance to the successive crises of history, including the history of our own times. Though slight in compass and somewhat sketchy in treatment, Professor Wright's book is of significance for Old Testament Theology. N.W.P.

POST-BIBLICAL JUDAISM.

BAMBERGER, B. J. : *Proselytism in the Talmudic Period.* 1939. (Hebrew Union College Press, Cincinnati.)

BRAUDE, W. G. : *Jewish Proselyting in the First Five Centuries.* 1940. (Brown University, Providence, R.I.)

Both authors conclude that the Rabbis throughout the Talmudic period were very eager for and friendly to converts, the statements usually taken as pointing the other way being either rare exceptions or misunderstood. The material presented—far more fully by Bamberger—is certainly impressive, but they seem slightly to overshoot the mark.

Bamberger inclines to minimize differences. On the omission in the tractate Gerim of the requirement of circumcision he remarks (p. 39) : "no doubt the text is defective". But where the parallel in Bab. Yebamoth, which does mention circumcision, has "we baptize him", Gerim has "they cover him with water as far as the genitals". This, to me, suggests that, in Gerim, baptism is meant to replace circumcision. Braude does not note the version of Gerim at all. Neither discusses such wider problems as the evolution of the Noachic commandments, without a clearer understanding of which we cannot hope really to see through the Rabbinic attitude to proselytism. The books are very readable.　　　　　　　　　　　　　　　　　　　　D.D.

BEEK, M. A. : *Nationale en Transcendente Motieven in de Joodse Apokalyptiek van de laatste Eeuwen voor Christus.* 1941. (Van Gorcum, Assen.)

An Inaugural Lecture delivered in the University of Groningen dealing principally with Daniel, The Testaments of the Twelve Patriarchs, and Enoch, with special reference to the figures of Messiah and Son of Man. The author hazards the view (cf. his *Das Danielbuch,* 1935) that the Aramaic Daniel began to appear at the time when Deutero-Isaiah prophesied.
　　　　　　　　　　　　　　　　　　　　H.H.R.

EPSTEIN, L. M. : *Marriage Laws in the Bible and the Talmud.* 1942. (Harvard University Press, Cambridge, Mass.)

NEUFELD, E. : *Ancient Hebrew Marriage Laws.* 1944. (Longmans, Green & Co., London.)

Two learned works, which happily supplement one another, Epstein's laying the greater emphasis on Talmudic and even post-Talmudic developments (one remembers his earlier *The Jewish Marriage Contract,* 1927, New York), Neufeld on comparison with other Semitic systems, though he, too, takes account of Rabbinic views. Neither book opens up any new approaches—such as are badly needed on matters like the relation between intent and form in the conclusion of marriage—but both are highly useful as painstaking surveys of the present state of research.　　　　　D.D.

FISCH, S. : *Midrash Haggadol on Numbers.* 1940. (Manchester University Press. 30s. 0d.)

An edition based on a Bodleian manuscript (dated 1598), of the Midrash Haggadol on the first five chapters of Numbers. In a commentary Dr. Fisch gives Rabbinic sources and explains difficulties. In the Introduction he discusses the nature of the Midrash and its relation with other Rabbinic writings, extant or lost. He favours the view according to which Abraham, son of Maimonides, wrote the Midrash (Egypt, thirteenth century) ; David al-Adeni, he argues, translated it from Arabic into the Hebrew which we possess (Yemen, fourteenth century). The question whether Midrash draws on the Mekilta de-Rabbi Ismael on Exodus and Sifre on Numbers he answers in the affirmative.

A piece of sound, meticulous scholarship.　　　　　　D.D.

OESTERLEY, W. O. E. : *The Jews and Judaism during the Greek Period: the background of Christianity.* 1941. (S.P.C.K., London. 10s. 6d.)

The prefatory note states that this book is not intended for specialists on the subject. It is a very good and useful introduction on a number of well-selected subjects relative to the title. To name a few for example : " The use of the Scriptures in the New Testament ", " The Apocalyptists ", " Hellenistic Influence upon the Jews ", " The influence of Persian thought and teaching ", " The Messiah ", " Immortality ", " Worship (Temple, synagogue) ", " Angelology ". Most acceptable is the bibliographic direction for further study attached to the subjects discussed.   O.S.R.

SCHOUSBOE, J. : *La secte juive de l'Alliance Nouvelle au pays de Damas et le Christianisme naissant.* 1942. (Munksgaard, Copenhagen.)

A new theory of the so-called Zadokite Work, which holds that it was written *circa* A.D. 70 by followers of John the Baptist, with much anti-Christian polemic. The " Teacher of Righteousness " or " Unique Teacher " is held to be John the Baptist, and the " Man of Insolence " to be Jesus, whose followers are believed to have engaged in bloody persecution of the Baptist's followers. Schousboe identifies the followers of John the Baptist with the Dositheans, and holds that the Baptist took over the leadership of a community which came into existence *circa* 24 B.C. Despite these hazardous views, the book has real value by reason of the material it assembles, and especially for its collection of ancient evidence about the Dositheans.   H.H.R.

SJÖBERG, E. : *Gott und die Sünder im Palästinischen Judentum nach dem Zeugnis der Tannaiten und der apokryphisch-pseudepigraphischen Literatur.* (BWANT 27). 1939. (Kohlhammer, Stuttgart.)

A careful investigation by a Swedish author of one of the basic questions of ancient Jewish theology. The relation of God to man is determined by a balance between justice and mercy. No fixed rule exists for this balance, but God's mercy is greater than His punishment, according to the Tannaites. The covenant of Sinai gave the Israelites an obligation that enabled them to be rewarded for obedience but also to be punished for sin. God shows His mercy t the sinners for the sake of the fathers and of His name, ar the punishment becomes chastisement, not destruction, a at last Israel is saved. As for the heathen, they go to Gehen with their gods, bêcause they have rejected the Torah, God shows His mercy toward them in supporting them this life and in postponing their ordeal. Their conver plays no rôle in Tannaitic literature. Fast, good works charity are not reckoned as expiating in Tannaite but as tokens of conversion, which but opens the w mercy and forgiveness. Sacrifice and other cultic a expiating by the will of God. This very useful boo with a treatment of the Apocrypha and Pseudepi where the same ideas in the main are found.

PHILOLOGY.

BIRKELAND, H. : *Akzent und Vokalismus im Althebräischen.* 1940. (Dybwad, Oslo. Kr. 15.00.)

Cantineau argued in 1931 that the position of the accent in Biblical Hebrew and Aramaic, as recorded in the Massoretic text, is explicable only on the assumption that the system goes back to one in which the accent must have fallen uniformly on the penultimate syllable ; and he supposes this in its turn to have displaced a different system identical with that which is general in Arabic and which he assumes to have been the primitive system not only of the Arabs but generally also of the Semites. Birkeland, while doubting the validity of this conclusion for Aramaic, regards it as absolutely proved for Hebrew, and in the present book he works this theory out by tracing it back from the Tiberian system, through Old-Hebrew into Canaanite. Incidentally, he seeks to show that the fixing of the accent on the penultimate syllable must have preceded the loss of the ultimate short vowel, which is universally admitted to have been present in Hebrew as, for instance, in classical Arabic. Naturally in such an undertaking much must be highly speculative, and the author does not avoid all the pitfalls ; at the same time he makes clear much that has hitherto remained obscure. Students, however, are warned that, interesting as the book is, it makes very hard reading.

G.R.D.

BRØNNO, E. : *Studien über hebräische Morphologie und Vokalismus.* 1943. (Brockhaus, Leipzig.)

A very thorough treatment of the fragments of the Greek transcription of the Hebrew text of eleven psalms belonging to the second column of Origen's Hexapla, which were found on a palimpsest in 1894 by Cardinal Mercati. The fragments contain about 1,000 words and are characterized by the author as the oldest known vocalized Hebrew text of considerable length. His method is to study the material as illustrating an independent tradition in the history of the Hebrew language, beside that of the M.T. This he carries out by giving a whole Hebrew Grammar based on these fragments. One of his results is that Philippi's law is not valid in this tradition. The book is a valuable contribution to the research of the later history of the Hebrew language.

J.P.

DUNAND, M. : *Byblia Grammata, Documents et Recherches sur le Développement de l'Écriture en Phénicie.* 1945. (Beyrouth.)

After an introduction fitting Phœnician archæology into the general background of history, the author has a chapter on potters' marks and so on ; in the following two chapters he publishes or republishes a dozen important inscriptions found in the last fifteen or twenty years at Gebal : first, ten in a pseudo-hieroglyphic script concealing an unknown

58

language and, second, two new Phœnician inscriptions which he assigns to the seventeenth to fifteenth centuries B.C. The former are an interesting puzzle for decipherers, whilst in the latter every letter and word can be read and understood ; and, as they are, too, the earliest Phœnician texts so far discovered, their significance for the history of the alphabet cannot be overrated. The last two chapters are devoted to the problem of the alphabet and in them the author reaches the conclusion that the Phœnician alphabet had as its immediate source the Byblian pseudo-hieroglyphic script of the Gebalites which in its turn owed much to the very strong Egyptian influence to which the archæology of the neighbourhood is witness. The work, which is admirably written and excellently illustrated, is of the greatest importance for the study of Phœnician origins.   G.R.D.

(*Note.*—Prof. E. Dhorme, in a communication to the Académie des Inscriptions on August 2nd, 1946, has succeeded in deciphering the pseudo-hieroglyphic inscriptions, showing that they are in syllabic Phœnician.   H.H.R.)

GORDON, C. H. : *Ugaritic Grammar (Analecta Orientalia 20)*. 1940. (Pontificium Institutum Biblicum, Rome. 140 lire.)

Dr. Gordon's work follows the usual way of grammars, giving both accidence and syntax of the language of the texts from Râs Shamrah in great detail ; the only cause for regret in this part of the work is that the author has not attempted, in spite of the paucity of matter, to set out the various parts of speech in tabular form ; for only so is it easy to gain a clear conception of the construction of a language. In fact, this part of the work is much obscured by a large amount of translation, which, though extremely valuable, is out of place where it is put. There is also an excellent glossary which unfortunately is not by any means complete. The book, however, is a mine of information and contains much fresh matter, and is therefore indispensable to any serious study of these interesting texts.   G.R.D.

HAMMERSHAIMB, E. : *Das Verbum in Dialekt von Ras Schamra*. 1941. (Munksgaard, Copenhagen.)

This study of the Ugaritic verb is an admirable piece of work. The author examines all the forms of the verb, which he sets out in concise tables at the end of the book so that a clear conspectus of them is presented to the reader, and then discusses the uses of the various themes or stems, moods and tenses. He argues for an Aphel or Hiphil (which cannot be decided as no perfect form occurs) beside a Shaphel, and agrees with Gordon against Goetze that there is no present tense corresponding to the Acc. *iqaṭal* but only an imperfect and preterite tense corresponding to the Hebrew *yiqṭōl* in form and use. No student of the important Ugaritic tablets can afford to be without this book, in which the matter is lucidly arranged and the discussions are clearly set out and argued.   G.R.D.

HARRIS, Z. S. : *Development of the Canaanite Dialects*. 1939. (American Oriental Series, vol. 16, New Haven. $2.50.)

The author's purpose is to examine the various dialects grouped as Canaanite (namely Hebrew and Phœnician, but not Aramaic and Amorite, so far as this is known) and spoken in Syro-Palestine between 2000 B.C. and the beginning of the Christian era, seeking to trace the development of each sound and form in the several languages. He divides this group into two sub-groups : the coastal dialects including Phœnician and Ugaritian and the speech of Yâdi, and those of the inland, including the speech of Hamat, Hebrew and Moabite ; and he shows that the changes usually began on the coast and worked their way inwards, although many of the developments failed to penetrate into Palestine. The general conclusions may be accepted as sound, but much of the detail rests on very slight evidence and there is a heavy draft, if not over-draft, on the argument from silence ; there is also an inadequate appreciation of the fact that the script is almost always incapable of accurately representing any given sound, while the evidence of the transliterations of the LXX, though mentioned, is rarely used (for example, the Assyrian *Ausi'* is no evidence of the pronunciation of the Hebrew " Hosea ", as the Accadian syllabary could not represent *ŏ*, while the LXX's two transliterations of this name with *au* and *ŏ* are valid evidence but are not cited) ; and the whole work is made very difficult reading by the use of an esoteric jargon which will be largely unintelligible except to the specialist reader. G.R.D.

JEAN, C. F. : *Grammaire hébraïque élémentaire*. 2nd Edition. 1945. (Letouzey et Ané, Paris. Fr. 120.)

This book is a student's grammar, well arranged and clearly set out. It contains all the usual tables and a good selection of syntactical examples to introduce the learner to the construction of sentences ; and there is also a very brief chrestomathy, consisting of the first three chapters of Genesis with the necessary vocabulary. The Hebrew part is followed by a *précis* of Biblical Aramaic Grammar. Unfortunately, what ought to be a very good little book is marred by an exceptionally large number of misprints and some mistakes which can only be positive errors not of the printer but of the author, which will make it an unsafe guide for the beginner. G.R.D.

LEFEVRE, J. : *Précis de grammaire hébraïque*. 1945. (Firmin-Didot, Paris. Fr. 200.)

This unpretentious work contains an outline of the accidence with a very sketchy account of the syntax of the Hebrew language. There are also a few brief exercises, Biblical sentences in which every word is parsed, inserted in a separate booklet. The book is only intended for beginners, and its lay-out is well adapted to its purpose ; but it is unfortunately not free from misprints which can but lead the learner astray. G.R.D.

ODEBERG, H. : *The Aramaic Portions of Bereshit Rabba, with Grammar of Galilæan Aramaic.* 2 vols. 1939. (Gleerup, Lund. Kr. 12 and 8.)

The first volume contains the text in Hebrew script and in Roman letters on opposite pages, followed by brief notes and a few further extracts from Midrash and Targum in transliteration only. The second volume contains a Grammar based on the texts, including a study of the Syntax. The Grammar is written in English, and all the examples are given in transliteration only. The whole constitutes a very valuable addition to our literature on Aramaic Grammar, though it is a great pity that Hebrew type was not used in the second volume as well as in the first. The transliterations of the first volume could well have been spared in compensation.   H.H.R.

ORAHAM, A. J. : *Dictionary of the Stabilized and Enriched Assyrian Language and English.* 1943. (Assyrian Press of America, Chicago.)

This work, a dictionary of the Syriac dialect spoken by the Assyrians now settled on the River Chabur in North-East Syrian territory, is a labour of love on the part of the author and his wife, who are themselves Christians of Persian origin from a village near Lake Urmia. It contains some twenty-one thousand words printed in the Nestorian script, transliterated into European characters, and provided with English translations and paraphrases ; and the actual printing is the joint labour of husband and wife. It is obviously intended for his compatriots living in the United States of America, which explains the often quite needless explanations of ordinary English words ; for these will without doubt greatly enhance its usefulness to such readers. Whence he has drawn his vast Syriac or, as he sometimes calls it, "Assyriac" vocabulary and how much of it his readers will understand is a matter for speculation ; for he says that three thousand words suffice for ordinary persons of Assyrian birth. In conclusion, this dictionary is not so much a scientific work as a compilation for native speakers of the language settling in the United States of America.
                                                        G.R.D.

ZORELL, F. : *Lexicon Hebraicum et Aramaicum Veteris Testamenti.* Fasc. 1—5. 1946. (Pontificio Istituto Biblico, Rome. £1. 10s. 0d.)

A welcome addition to philological literature. The order of words is not by roots but purely alphabetic, and the language is Latin throughout. Fr. Zorell has done much to bring our dictionaries up to date, but he has perhaps not cast his net wide enough in the vast and growing literature of the subject ; and there are notable omissions not only on this score but also of actual words. The references to the sources whence he derives many of the new suggestions, too, are unfortunately scanty. A welcome feature is the insertion of the vocabulary of Ben Sirach ; but one may regret the absence of that of the inscriptions. The book can, however, be safely and profitably put into the hands of all students of the Biblical text.   G.R.D.

1947

The Book List is prepared by the following Committee :
Miss B. K. Rattey, Mgr. J. M. T. Barton, Dr. David Daube,
Professors G. R. Driver, A. R. Johnson, N. W. Porteous,
O. S. Rankin, Rev. J. N. Schofield, Professors N. H. Snaith
and H. H. Rowley (Editor). This issue contains notes on
books published since the last issue, together with some on
books of the years 1939-1946, on which, for various reasons,
notes could not be obtained in time for the 1946 issue. There
are unfortunately still some gaps which will be filled, if
possible, in the 1948 issue, after which it is hoped that the
Book List will rarely include books published more than
eighteen months before its appearance. The Editor has
again to acknowledge the help received from some scholars
who are not members of the Book List Committee, and
particularly from some continental scholars : Professors
W. Baumgartner of Basel, A. Bentzen of Copenhagen,
P. A. H. de Boer of Leiden, O. Eissfeldt of Halle, E. Hammershaimb of Aarhus, A. Parrot of Paris, F. Stummer of Munich,
Th. C. Vriezen of Groningen, W. C. van Unnik of Utrecht ;
Professor G. W. Anderson of Handsworth, and Mr. P. R.
Weis of Manchester.

Prices of foreign books, where known, are given either
in foreign currency or in the English equivalent actually
charged.

Titles to which an asterisk (*) is prefixed are recom
mended for inclusion in school libraries.

H. H. ROWLEY.

GENERAL

Actes du XXe *Congrès International des Orientalistes.* 1940. (Bureaux du Muséon, Louvain.)

This volume contains short abstracts of all the papers read at the Brussels Conference of 1938. Those which directly concern the Old Testament include Vaccari's on the Pentateuchal question, Sidersky's on the agrarian festivals of the Phoenicians and Hebrews, Zolli's on the psalm of Habakkuk read in connexion with Ikhnaton's reform, papers on the Ras Shamra texts by Aistleitner, de Vaux, Albright, Gaster, Virolleaud and Dussaud, Kappler's on the Göttingen edition of the Septuagint, Birkeland's on the social implications of the Hebrew language, Saydon's on assonance as a device for expressing emphasis, Dennefeld's on the Elihu speeches, Hempel's on the limits of anthropomorphism in the Old Testament, Daiches' on the meaning of ' sacrifices ' in the Psalms, Noth's on the part of tradition in the early history of Israel, Cook's on the bearing on modern thought of the re-discovery of the ancient orient, Rowley's on Israel's sojourn in Egypt, Puukko's on the interpretation of history in the prophets, Morgenstern's on the mythological background of Ps. 82, Vellas' on problems of the Septuagint, Causse's on the myth of the pilgrimage to Jerusalem and its part in the formation of the Jewish church, Eissfeldt's on Cult-topography in Philo of Byblos, and Mayence's on the mosaic in the synagogue of Apamaea. In addition to these, several of the papers read in other sections are of interest to the *Alttestamentler*. Many of the papers have been published *in extenso* elsewhere, and are given in varying degrees of fullness, while Zolli's stands *in extenso* here. H.H.R.

GINZBERG, L. : *Louis Ginzberg Jubilee Volume,* 2 vols. 1945. (American Academy for Jewish Research, New York.)

One of these volumes is in English and the other in Hebrew. The English volume contains the following articles on the Old Testament and related ancient literature : Albright's study of the list of Levitic cities in Josh. xxi and I Chron. vi, reaching the conclusion that the list dates from the early part of Solomon's reign ; Bickerman's discussion of the date of IV Maccabees, which he assigns to *circa* 35 A.D. ; Gandz's on complementary fractions in Bible and Talmud ; Ginsberg's on. psalms and inscriptions of petition and acknowledgement, dealing with the Ben-hadad inscription first published by Dunand in 1941, and other inscriptions in relation to the Psalms ; Gordis's studies in the relationship of Biblical and Rabbinical Hebrew, offering a number of suggestions for the elucidation of O.T. passages ; Marcus's treatment of Jewish and Greek elements in the Septuagint, reaching the conclusion that the LXX represents a *Jewishly* hellenized form of Palestinian culture ; Sperber's specimen of a Targum edition, giving the text of I Sam. xvii, with supralinear pointing and critical apparatus ; Spiegel's essay on Noah, Daniel and Job, treating of the Ras Shamra texts, the Ezekiel references, and the primitive form of the book of Job ; and Torrey's revised view of I Esdras. In the Hebrew volume there is less of direct interest to the *Alttestamentler*, but many of the articles in both volumes, dealing with later Judaism, are of interest and value. The articles noted above make this work one of importance to the Old Testament scholar.   H.H.R.

Hebrew Union College Annual, xix. 1945-6. (Cincinnati. Price : $3.00.)

This annual continues to flourish and to publish important articles in the field of Old Testament and Judaica. This volume contains several valuable articles, of which the following may be noted. S. H. Blank writes on the Dissident Laity in Early Judaism, and argues that in post-exilic times there was not a little opposition to the temple as the sole legitimate sanctuary, and to its sacrificial ritual as acceptable to God ; I. Sonne reconstructs Psalm ii, eliminating all tristichs, and substituting the name of Hezekiah for *hoq Yhwh* in v. 7, and dating the psalm at the time of that king's accession ; J. Goldin discusses the two versions of Abot de R. N. ; E. Werner has a long liturgico-musical study on the Doxology in Synagogue and Church ; J. Lewy has an article running to nearly 90 pages on the Late Assyro-Babylonian cult of the Moon and its culmination in the time of Nabonidus ; and J. Morgenstern discusses Psalms viii and xix A, holding that the former is to be dated not earlier than the 4th cent. B.C., and comes from the same circle as the later of the two strands into which he divides Gen. i, while Psa. xix A is considerably earlier than Psa. viii, but reflects the same strand of the Creation narrative in an earlier stage.   H.H.R.

LEFORT, L. TH. : *Mélanges L. Th. Lefort.* (Le Muséon, vol LIX, 1-4.) 1946. (Louvain.)

This *Festschrift* volume of essays presented to the well-known coptologist Canon L. Th. Lefort, who has been director of *Le Muséon* for a quarter of a century, contains little of direct interest to students of the Old Testament. G. Dossin writes on ' Les deux songes de Gilgamesh,' and N. Schneider on ' Die Ilum-Personennamen der III-Urkunden ' ; R. de Langhe contributes a study of great interest to philologists on 'L 'enclitique cananéenne—*m(a)* ' ; and J. Coppens essays a fruitful, if necessarily tentative, account of ' Les parallèles du Psautier avec les textes de Ras-Shamra-Ougarit.'   J.M.T.B.

(There are 56 papers in all, several of which are on Egyptological subjects not without interest to the Old Testament student, e.g., A. de Buck's on ' La composition littéraire des Enseignements d'Amenemhat,' and P. Gilbert's on ' La composition de l'Ode à la Mort dans le dialogue égyptien du Désespéré.' Of closer interest are the papers of R. M. Tonneau on ' Texte syriaque de la Genèse, l' Héxaéméron ' ; L. Dieu on ' Le texte copte sahidique des Livres de Samuel ' ; P. Lacau on ' Fragments de l'Ascension d'Isaïe en copte ' ; and, still closer, J. van der Ploeg's on ' Le sens du verbe hébreu bārā,' étude sémasiologique.'   H.H.R.)

MERCATI, G. : *Miscellanea Giovanni Mercati*, Studi e Testi 126), vol. VI. (Paleografia-Bibliografia-Varia). 1946. (Bibliotheca Apostolica Vaticana, the Vatican City. Price : Lr. 2,400.)

This final volume of the magnificent series presented to Cardinal Mercati contains only one contribution of direct value to an *Alttestamentler*, but this is an outstanding one. It is ' Die Entstehung des Alphabets : eine kritische Übersicht ' by Augustine Bea, S.J., the rector of the Roman Biblical Institute. Bea divides his study into two parts, of which the first gives a list, accompanied by valuable comments, of the various inscriptions discovered in Sinai, in Southern and Central Palestine, in Phoenicia, and at Ras Shamra. The second part is devoted to a careful estimate of the tendencies of modern critical interpretation of these discoveries. The author makes it clear that the time has not yet come for even a semi-final conclusion on the vexed question of the origin of the alphabet, but as a survey of recent literature, the present essay should be of notable service to all students of the Old Testament.   J.M.T.B.

(*N.B.*—Of the six volumes of this Festschrift, the first contains the Biblical articles. This arrived only in time for inclusion in the supplement to the present Book List. H.H.R.)

PAYNE, E. A. : *Henry Wheeler Robinson*. 1946. (Nisbet, London. Price : 12s. 6d.)

Half the book (there are 212 pages in all) deals with the life of this outstanding Old Testament scholar and teacher, his varied interests, and his solid and enduring contributions to Bible scholarship and to theology generally. The short biography is followed by six hitherto unpublished lectures, of which the last two are of particular interest from the Old Testament point of view. The fifth discusses ' The Principle of Authority in the Christian Religion,' in which the authority of the Bible receives some notice. The last is concerned with ' The Christian Doctrine of Eternal Life,' the first part of which deals with the approach in the Old Testament and in Judaism. There are two passages only in the Old Testament which deal directly with life after death, Isa. xxvi, 19 and Dan. xii, 2. The further development, visible in later Jewish books, is along the ' line of living faith,' and ' not from the mere survival of death in Sheol.'   N.H.S.

PODECHARD, E. : *Mélanges E. Podechard*, with an *avant-propos* by F. Lavallée. 1945. (Facultés Catholiques, Lyon.)

The well-known French Sulpician, Canon Emanuel Podechard, retired from his chair of Old Testament and Eastern languages in 1943 and received the present *Festschrift* from twenty-two of his friends and former colleagues. Only five of the essays are exclusively related to the Old Testament, namely, D. Buzy's plea for abandoning the attempt to detect a pre-established harmony between the findings of prehistory and the first chapters of Genesis ; J. Chaine's study of ' Une réponse du folklore hébreu à la question de l'origine des langues ' in the tower of Babel narrative ; A. Gelin's ' Le passage de la polygamie à la monogamie ' ; L. Gry's ' Manassé dans les légendes midrachiques ' ; and A. Robert's pleasant, if somewhat unconvincing, blend of the literal and the typical senses in his exegesis of Cant. v 1-15 and vii 2-6. Perhaps however, the outstanding contribution is the one entitled : ' L'archéologie et la Bible ' by that most meticulous of all antiquaries, L. H. Vincent, O.P., himself a *lyonnais*, in which he discusses the nature, rôle and method of archaeology, and the assistance it gives in such topics as the site of the Davidic Jerusalem, the dimensions of Solomon's temple, the date of the fall of Jericho, and the bearings of the discoveries at Ur, Kish and Tello upon the Flood-story in Genesis. (He has every reason to query the credentials of the alleged 1932 expedition to Mt. Ararat, as the names of ' Professor Stoneass ' and of the ' Royal Yalevard University ' sufficiently indicate.)

J.M.T.B.

ROBERTSON, E. ; and WALLENSTEIN, M. : *Melilah*, vol. ii. 1946. (University Press, Manchester.)

The second volume of these studies written in Modern Hebrew fully maintains the standard of the first. It contains eighteen articles covering a wide field, of which only those which more closely concern the Old Testament are mentioned here. H. Yalon offers a contribution to Hebrew lexicography, finding *hirdiph* (Jg. xx, 43)=*chase, hidhrikh* (ibid.)=*overtake*, and traces of a root *shanah*=*revolt* in the Old Testament ; N. Morris writes on Discipline in the ancient Hebrew school (a translation of material published in his English book on *The Jewish School*, 1937) ; I. D. Markon describes a unique Leningrad MS. of Daniel Al-Kumisi's commentary on the Minor Prophets, and offers extracts illustrating the exegetical and other value of this work ; Ch. Rabin discusses the ancient Arabic dialects and their relation to Hebrew, arguing against a sharp division between the northern and southern branches of Semitic speech by quoting grammatical data common to Hebrew and some W. Arabic dialects ; while the senior editor, E. Robertson writes on the Priesthood and the Kingdom. This last article is a translation of Dr. Robertson's Tyndale Lecture, which was published in the *Bulletin of the John Rylands Library* in 1944, under the title ' Samuel and Saul.' The remaining articles deal with Midrash and Rabbinics, and with mediaeval and modern Hebrew literature and customs.

P.R.W. and H.H.R.

VAN OVEN, J. C. : *Symbolae ad jus et historiam antiquitatis pertinentes Julio Christiano van Oven dedicatae*. 1946. (Brill, Leiden. Price : £2 4s. 6d.)

The studies in this *Festschrift* cover a wide field, including Greece, Greek and Roman Egypt, Rome and Byzantium, and Western Europe. There are four contributions dealing with Ancient Egypt and the Near East, of which three are written in French and one in Dutch, with an English summary.

À. de Buck writes on Literature and Politics under the Twelfth
Egyptian Dynasty, and argues that the *Teachings of
Amenemhat* was a piece of propaganda on behalf of the first
Pharaoh of the Twelfth Dynasty (cf. also the same writer's
essay in *Mélanges Lefort* on ' La composition littéraire des
Enseignements d'Amenemhat ') ; B. A. van Proosdij writes
on *Šar Mēšarim* as a title of Babylonian kings as legislators,
and shows that the term early acquired the meaning of mercy
as well as justice ; W. F. Leemans discusses the meaning of
the Akkadian term *kidinnu*, which he interprets as a symbol
of divine right, in a paper marked by a prudent reserve ;
and F. M. Th. Böhl writes (in Dutch) on an assignment of debt
from the time of Darius I, written in cuneiform with an
Aramaic endorsement. None of these very directly touches
the Old Testament field, though the first two are not without
interest for the *Alttestamentler*.   H.H.R.

ARCHAEOLOGY

ANDRAE, W. : *Alte Feststrassen im nahen Orient.* (Sendschrift der
   Deutschen Orient-Gesellschaft). 1941. (Hinrichs, Leipzig. Price :
   Rm. 4.80.)

   Deals with the streets, specially designed for festal and
   processional purposes, which have been unearthed either
   deliberately or indirectly by the Deutsche Orient-Gesellschaft
   at Babylon, Assur, Uruk and Hattusa (Boghazköy). With the
   aid of four illustrations in the text and eleven plates all these
   streets, which have left their stamp upon the foregoing places,
   are here clearly set out in respect of their course and its
   equipment, the character and arrangement of their ' stations,'
   and especially their starting-points and termini. The exact
   significance of these archaeological discoveries is not altogether
   certain, but in the nature of the case this is only to be expected.
                                                             O.E.

BÖHL, F. M. TH. : *Het Gilgamesj-epos.* 1941. (Amsterdam.)

   The translation of the Gilgamesh epic of Professor Böhl is
   the first Dutch translation from the original text. By this
   work Böhl therefore has much obliged his countrymen. The
   form of this translation, too, is excellent, being written as
   much as possible in the original metrical verses.

   Besides this poetical translation the book contains a rather
   detailed commentary, very useful not only for the common
   reader, but also for professional students ; the additions and
   corrections of the texts are all duly noted.

   In the Introduction Böhl explains the epic as a tragedy
   depicting the inward purification of the hero, who, guided
   by Shamash, the god of righteousness and truth, turns away
   from the goddess Ishtar, and therefore witnesses the tragic
   death of his friend Enkidu. The epic reveals the hidden
   controversies in the Babylonian religion.   Th.C.V.

CONTENAU, G. : *La divination chez les Assyriens et les Babyloniens*. 1940. (Payot, Paris.)

The author, after a statement of divination from classical ancient times up to our day, studies the Babylonian rules of divination. He successively considers the different means employed by soothsayers : ' oracles, nécromancie, oniromancie, incubation, hépatoscopie.'

Several chapters deal with various omens drawn out from human and animal oddities, from inanimate beings, and finally from the stars. In Babylonia, divination was very nearly a state institution.   A.P.

CONTENAU, G. : *Le Déluge babylonien, Ishtar aux Enfers, la Tour de Babel*. 1941. (Payot, Paris.)

This book is compounded of three essays about Babylonian myths and is meant for the general public. In the first of these, the author sums up the various traditions (Assyro-babylonian, Sumerian) connected with the Flood and included in several episodes of the Gilgamesh epic. The author also shows that the old story sometimes runs parallel with the biblical narration, and he points out some of the archaeological evidences of Ur and Kish. The myth of Ishtar's Descent to the Nether World is located in Mesopotamian religion, this religion being ' naturiste ' in its core. We find in this book the Akkadian version of the texts, but these ought to be completed by S. N. Kramer's works on Sumerian mythology.

The ' Tower of Babel ' chapter is a short statement of the ziqqurat problem, too important a matter to be studied in this superficial way.   A.P.

DALMAN, G. : *Arbeit und Sitte in Palästina*, vol. vi : *Zeltleben, Viehund Milchwirtschaft, Jagd, Fischfang*. 1939. Bertelsmann, Gütersloh. (Schriften des Deutschen Palästina-Instituts, ix.)

The well-known merits of the former volumes are to be found in the present volume, which is especially rich in important Biblical references throughout. It may suffice to mention the nine pages of discussion of *chalab* and *chem'a*. The Appendix contains supplements and corrections to volumes iv and v.   W.B.

FINEGAN, J. : *Light from the Ancient Past*. 1946. (Princeton University Press or Oxford University Press. Price : $6.00 or 25s. 0d.)

The writer attempts the ambitious task of surveying the archaeological background of the Hebrew-Christian Religion from the earliest times until after the end of the Roman period, and he has collected an enormous amount of material.

The book is well written, and has ample notes ; there are 204 illustrations, 6 maps, and 4 plans, and a good general index. It is a very valuable book both for the advanced student and for the beginner because the writer explains his terms and takes little for granted ; he is careful to correlate the finds in different fields, and the short sections make reading easy.

In the main he follows Albright's dating but has not always seen the effect of the late dating of Hammurabi ; there is too occasionally a looseness of expression which may give wrong impressions—the forms of Hebrew poetry are dated from about 500 B.C. The book is however an excellent one and can be highly recommended.   J.N.S.

FRANKFORT, H. & H. A., WILSON, J. A., JACOBSEN, T., IRWIN, W. A. : *The Intellectual Adventure of Ancient Man.* 1946. (University of Chicago Press. Price : $4.00.)

> A series of lectures, originally given as a public course in the Division of the Humanites in the University of Chicago, on the speculative thought of ancient Egypt (Wilson), Mesopotamia (Jacobsen) and the Hebrews (Irwin), with an introduction and conclusion (by the Frankforts) on ' Myth and Reality ' and ' The Emancipation of Thought from Myth.' While there is room for disagreement at certain points, this handsomely produced volume is never dull. In fact, besides being a pleasure to handle, it is both pleasing and stimulating to read, and renders a real service by the way in which it helps the student of the Old Testament to see the thought of ancient Israel against the background provided by that of the ancient Near East as a whole.   A.R.J.

GINSBERG, H. L. : *The Legend of King Keret.* (*Bulletin of the American Schools of Oriental Research* : Supplementary Papers Nos. 2-3). 1946. (New Haven. Price : $1.25.)

> This small but admirable work contains the complete text, transliterated and translated, of the legend of Keret from Ras esh-Shamrah (Ugarit), together with 10 pages of introduction and 16 pages of closely printed philological notes. It thus completes the work begun by the same scholar in his *Kitbe Ugarit* (Jerusalem, 1936) ; for this missed the legend of Keret which had not then been published. The author has taken full account of all previous work on this text and has contributed much from his own resources ; the work therefore greatly advances the interpretation of the story.
> G.R.D.

GLUECK, N. : *The River Jordan.* 1946. (Westminster Press, Philadelphia and Lutterworth Press, London.)

> A much more popularly written book than the author's archaeological survey of Trans-jordan, and of the 268 pages, 113 are full page illustrations. The term ' River Jordan ' is widely interpreted and the pictures include Caesarea on the Mediterranean, and Amman in Trans-jordan ; there is much quotation from the Old Testament, New Testament, Josephus, the Talmud, the early Christian Fathers, and Classical writers.
> The book contains much of interest to Bible students, and the language, as picturesque as the scenes which are described, holds the attention of the general reader. In his desire for a dramatic picture of Abraham's forced march the writer assumes the emergence of the domesticated camel at an earlier date than is generally accepted. He rightly stresses the amazing skill and energy of the Roman settlers, and, against Adam Smith, claims that the Jordan Valley was not an empty wilderness but one of the richest parts of ancient Palestine.   J.N.S.

HEIDEL, A. : *The Gilgamesh Epic and Old Testament Parallels.* 1946. (Chicago and Cambridge. Price : 20s. 0d.)

The present book is parallel to the same scholar's *Babylonian Genesis* (Chicago, 1942). After a general introduction on the legend of Gilgamesh, Dr. Heidel offers a fresh translation of the whole poem, followed by translations of all related texts, not only Sumerian and Accadian but also Greek ; but he does not give the actual text either of the poem itself or of the secondary sources. The last 132 pages are devoted to long discussions of the problems raised by this cycle of legends, namely the Flood and Death and the After-life. The author has had the inestimable advantage of access to the files of the Assyrian Dictionary now in course of compilation in the Oriental Institute of Chicago University and he has made full use of this privilege ; consequently the translations are considerably in advance of anything that has preceded them. The expositions of the views of the Sumerians and Accadians on death and the after-life are rich in references drawn from the same source and will well repay careful study ; but the views on the Hebrew aspect of this problem do not show the same acquaintance with the relevant literature and are in some respects uncritical.
G.R.D.

LABAT, R. : *Le caractère religieux de la royauté assyro-babylonienne.* 1939. (Adrien-Maisonneuve, Paris.)

In view of the increasing interest in the question of divine kingship in the ancient east, this important study of the religious character of the kingship in Assyria and Babylon will be of interest to more than Akkadian scholars. The author shows that as far back as our knowledge goes the kingship had a sacred character in Babylonia, and he studies the accession and funeral rites, as well as the *akitu* festival by which the king's tenure was annually renewed. In that festival the seizing of the hand of the god was less significant, according to M. Labat, than is often supposed, and was not an exclusively royal privilege. The part of the king was to represent the god in the *hieros gamos* that marked the festival and to offer sacrifices. His priestly functions are here fully studied, together with the ways in which he represented the gods amongst men and men before the gods.   H.H.R.

LETTINGA, J. P. : *Overzichten van de Geschiedenis en de Opgravingen in het Nabije Oosten I : rās eš-šamrā en mīnet el-beida'.* (Mede-deelingen en Verhandlingen No. 6 van het Vooraziatisch-egyptisch Gezelschap ' Ex Oriente Lux.') 1942. (Brill, Leiden.)

One cannot imagine a better start for this series of surveys of the history and excavations of the Near East. Everything that needs to be said by way of introduction to Ras Shamra is here said with masterly conciseness, so that the reader of this work will have a real acquaintance with this field. It is divided into six parts : I. General Introduction (A., Discovery of *rās eš-šamrā* ; B., Old Name of *rās eš-šamrā* and *mīnet el-beida* ' ; C., The Languages spoken in Ugarit ; D., Contents

and Date of the discovered Texts) ; II. History of Ugarit ;
III. Survey of the Archaeological Campaigns (1929-1939) ;
IV. Survey of the *rās eš-šamrā* Texts ; V. *rās eš-šamrā* and
the Alphabet ; VI. Select Bibliography. The book deserves
the widest circulation.   O.E.

MARIANI, P. B. : *Danel, ' il patriarca sapiente ' nella Bibbia, nella
tradizione, nella leggenda.* 1945. (Pontificium Athenaeum An-
tonianum, Rome. Price : 7s. 6d.)

An elaborate and detailed study of the references to Danel
in Ezk. xiv 14, 20, xxviii 3, with a full survey of the interpretations placed on them from the patristic period down
to the present time, including Jewish interpretations, and an
examination of the reasons which rule out the identification
of this Danel with the prophet Daniel, followed by a study
of the Danel of the Ras Shamra texts and the theories which
have been erected thereon, and a critical examination of the
reasons which have been proposed for the identification of
this Danel with the Danel of Ezekiel. Two appendices give
(a) Italian renderings of the translations of a part or the
whole of the relevant Ras Shamra texts by Gaster, Aistleitner, Dussaud, Cassuto and Gordon, and (b) a brief survey
of the chief poems contained in the Ras Shamra texts ; while
a postscript is devoted to the examination of an article by
Stocks in ZDMG 1943, on ' Danel, die südbabylonische und
nordpalästinisch-phönikische Überlieferung.' The book is
remarkably cheap, and has a high value if only because it
serves as a compendium of the history of interpretation
of the Biblical and profane texts.   H.H.R.

MONTET, P. : *Tanis, douze années de fouilles dans une capitale oubliée
du delta égyptien.* 1942. (Payot, Paris.)

The excavations pursued in the Delta town are here summed
up. They had important results : the town, its walls, its
temples (Horoun, Anta) are now well known. But most
important of all is the discovery of royal graves belonging
to pharaohs of the twenty-first and twenty-second dynasties
(Osorkon, Psousennès.)

These graves had not been looted and they contained a
magnificent sarcophagus, and precious works of art.   A.P.

OBERMANN, J. : *How Daniel was blessed with a son.* 1946. (American
Oriental Society, Baltimore.)

Dr. Obermann here offers a new interpretation of the second
(really the first) tablet of the Ugaritic legend of Aqhat son
of Dan'el, in the course of which he somewhat boldly restores
fifteen consecutive missing lines from parallel passages. He
regards the story as reflecting a rite of incubation, comparing
it with ' the several pre-natal narratives exant in Scripture
in which virility of an aged husband is restored, infertility
of a barren wife is cured, by divine intervention,' but he
admits that of the two other motifs characterizing the Ugaritic
scene, those of incubation and intercession, only more or less

faint echoes are discernible in the pre-natal narratives of Scripture. Other common points found are the cycle of seven days as a ritual feature and social custom and the duties of children towards their parents. Although however there are a number of acute observations in this study, much is of a speculative nature.　　　　　　　　　　　　　　　　G.R.D.

PARROT, A. : *Archéologie mésopotamienne*. 1946. (Michel, Paris. Price : Fr. 480.)

> An authoritative work by Professor Parrot, who was in charge of the French archaeological mission at Mari. The writer confines his book to the area of the Tigris and Euphrates from the earliest times to the Seleucid era, with the exception of Dura-Europos, Seleucia and Ctesiphon.' The book opens with an interesting account of 35 early travellers, the beginning of discoveries of Assyrian, cuneiform, and Sumerian antiquities, and the commencement of large scale excavations. Chapters are then given to excavations in different regions treated in chronological order. It is an extremely valuable collection of material, and interest is added by the inclusion of biographical information about the travellers and archaeologists who are mentioned. There are bibliographical notes at the end of each chapter, and the book is well illustrated.　　　　　　　　　　　　　　　　J.N.S.

PARROT, A. : *Malédictions et Violations de Tombes*. 1939. (Geuthner, Paris.)

> Contains more than the title would suggest ; the writer describes methods of burial in Mesopotamia, Syria, Phoenicia, Palestine, Trans-jordan, Egypt, Asia Minor, Greece, and Rome and suggests that it is possible to trace evolution.. In each case he quotes and discusses the means taken to protect the tombs, and compares the inscriptions containing curses on those who would violate the tombs with similar curses on treaty breakers and despoilers of statues. The final chapter, 'La " domus aeterna " ' contains a useful discussion of the close connection between the care for the preservation of tombs and a belief in life after death. There are ample notes, bibliography and illustrations.　　　　　　　　　　　　J.N.S.

THOMAS, D. W. : ' *The Prophet* ' *in the Lachish Ostraca*. 1946. (Tyndale Press, London. Price : 2s. 6d.)

> Professor Thomas in this interesting lecture examines the mysterious problem of the ' Prophet ' mentioned in four places in the famous Hebrew potsherds from Lachish, and after a careful discussion of the evidence, concludes that he is not Jeremiah and indeed that ' we do not know who he was.' Incidentally, Professor Thomas draws attention to a fundamental error underlying the attempt to identify the prophet, namely the insistence on ' treating the Ostraca as an interrelated group ' and adds a prudent warning on seeking for some direct contact with the Old Testament in all new archaeological discoveries in Palestine.　　　　　　G.R.D.

Van Praag, A. : *Droit matrimonial assyro-babylonien*. 1945. (Noord-Hollandsche Uitgevers Maatschappij, Amsterdam.)

This exhaustive study of Assyro-Babylonian marriage is based on all the relevant texts and a wide knowledge of the modern literature of the subject ; and indeed possibly too much space is given to setting the views of various scholars over against each other and then rather summarily dismissing the one or the other. On this score the author might with advantage have reduced considerably the bulk of his book ; nonetheless he reaches the eminently reasonable view that marriage was not a marriage by purchase and that the purpose of the written contract was merely evidentiary, that there was no *traditio puellae* in the technical sense and that marriage was effected by the act of consummation.   G.R.D.

HISTORY

Daniel-Rops : *Histoire sainte du peuple de la Bible*. 1946. (Fayard, Paris. Price : Fr. 150.)

This well written, but in general uncritical, history of Israel from Abraham to Jesus, came under the German interdict during the war, and the first edition (1943) was destroyed in consequence. It rests on wide reading, including some areas of the archaeological field, and shows knowledge of critical work on the Old Testament while rarely taking serious account of it. It does however place the writing of the book of Daniel in the 3rd and 2nd centuries B.C., and holds that its stories are not completely historical. Ezra is dated half a century after Nehemiah, though it is stated that they were in any case contemporaries. On the other hand the whole of the book of Isaiah is ascribed to Isaiah on the simple alleged ground that the Biblical Commission had so decided. Jonah is placed in the eighth century B.C. Despite its uncritical treatment of the history and of the religious development of Israel, it will have real value for the general reader to whom it is addressed, if it stirs his interest in the Biblical narratives, and communicates the writer's sense of its living importance.
H.H.R.

Jansen, H. L. : *Die Politik Antiochos des IV*. 1943. (Dybwad, Oslo.)

After treating of the sources that refer to the history of Antiochus IV and of such important events of this history as the campaigns against Egypt, the confiscation of the temple-treasury in Jerusalem, the decrees concerning the religion of the Jews, Jansen endeavours to explain what the motives and reasons of the policy of Antiochus were. The questions the author seeks to answer are : Why did Antiochus go to war with Egypt ? and how can we explain his policy in regard to the Jews and his confiscation of the temple-funds ? We cannot here go into detail but factors upon which the solution of the problem depends are : the hard conditions of peace and taxation laid by the Romans in the time of Antiochus III upon the Seleucid government ; the falling away from the latter of Armenia, Parthia and Elam ; the need of an endeavour to preserve unity in all parts of the kingdom in view of the burden that had to be borne ; the presence in Jerusalem of a strong Egyptian party of anti-Seleucid character, the economic support of which was the temple-treasury ; the Maccabean successes rendered possible by the fact that Antiochus had taken more than half of his troops to Parthia.   O.S.R.

JOHANNESEN, E. : *Studier over Esras og Nehemjas Historie.* 1946. (Gad, Copenhagen.)

The author of these studies was an undergraduate of the University of Copenhagen. The book was written as answer to a prize-question set by the University in 1941. After finishing his studies in 1943 by passing his theological examination in a most distinguished manner, he had planned to carry the work up to date to use it as a thesis for the doctorate. But on the 24th November, 1944, his career was suddenly interrupted : he was murdered by a gang of terrorists in German service. The Theological Faculty resolved to publish the book in the shape in which it had been handed in to the University in 1942, as a memorial.

It is a magnificent example of the mass of knowledge and maturity reached by this young undergraduate (he was born 1918). The book gives a thorough examination of all problems concerning the subject, criticises above all the theory of the late date of Ezra and advocates a return to traditional views in most cases, but not without reserves. Also the intricate textual problems are dealt with resulting in a rejection of the theories preferring III Esdras to the Massoretic Text.
                                                        A.B.

PIRENNE, J. : *Les grands courants de l' Histoire Universelle.* 1. *Des origines à l'Islam.* 1945. (Albin Michel, Paris.)

This is the first volume of an important synthesis ; it deals with the Ancient Orient and in particular with the biblical world. The history of the Hebrews is well outlined and numerous maps help the reader to follow the geographical fluctuations.

The conclusion shows that Israel could very rarely be independent (this happened in Solomon's time) and most of the time was used as a pawn by Egypt, Assyria, Babylonia, and later on, after Alexander the Great, by the Seleucids and the Romans.   A.P.

TEXT AND VERSIONS

ALLGEIER, A. : *Die Psalmen der Vulgata.* 1940. (Schöningh, Paderborn.)

Dr. Allgeier gives not a commentary on the Vulgate Psalter, as might be expected from the title, but discussions of its critical problems. An edition of St. Jerome's famous *Epistula ad Sunniam et Fretelam*, which is inserted, will be welcomed by many scholars. The author maintains the view that the Vulgate Psalter (*Psalterium Gallicanum*) was composed later than the *Psalterium iuxta Hebraeos* and is therefore the latest Psalter-text prepared by St. Jerome.

(I possessed this book, but lost it during the siege of Breslau and have not been able to get access to it in libraries. The publisher informs me that the whole stock of this work was destroyed in an air-raid. I can, therefore, only rely on memory for the writing of this notice.)   F.St.

GERLEMAN, G. : *Studies in the Septuagint.* 1. *Book of Job.* 1946. (Gleerup, Lund.)

> This work is a careful and detailed study of the Septuagintal text of ' Job.' The author's conclusions are that the same translator made the Greek versions of both ' Proverbs and Job,' which are creative works of translation, even though the creation is due to a failure in mastering the difficulties of the original text. He shows also a tendency to reduce and simplify parallel and synonymous clauses or to recast them in such a way that they throw a more direct light on the main theme ; herein he shows a lack of sympathy with the original Hebrew poet. Consequently the translation was intended not for the synagogue but for wide and general use in Alexandrian circles. It was made before the 2nd century B.C. There is also a chapter on the derived Ethiopic version, in which the reader is warned to treat it with great caution, in view of ' the translator's imagination and love of fabulation.'   G.R.D.

GERLEMAN, G. : *Studies in the Septuagint. II Chronicles.* 1946. (Gleerup, Lund.)

> The present work is on the same lines as the author's study of the Greek version of Job. He shows conclusively that the Greek translator of ' Chronicles ' cannot have been Theodotion or even the translator of Ezra-Nehemiah. He was also distinct from the translator of ' Kingdoms ' ; for, in spite of numerous close correspondences, possibly due to a process of harmonization, the differences are too striking and indeed such as to give relief to the individual peculiarities of the translator of ' Chronicles.' He is also familiar with and not infrequently dependent on the Greek version of the Pentateuch, even though some of these resemblances may be due to liturgical usage. The translation further exhibits a strange Hellenistic and Egyptian colouring characteristic of the Ptolemaic courts of the 2nd century B.C. It may therefore be assigned to the early part of that century.   G.R.D.

SCHILDENBERGER, J. *Die altlateinischen Texte des Proverbienbuches untersucht und textgeschichtlich eingegliedert : erster Teil. Die alte afrikanische Textgestalt.* (Texte und Arbeiten, herausegegeben durch die Erzabtei Beuron, I. Abt., 32-33). 1941. (Beuron.)

> The learned Benedictine father gives us the first part of very thorough and exhaustive prolegomena to a future edition of the Old Latin texts of Proverbs. Though he is able to use the rich treasury of Old Latin Bible texts collected by the late Joseph Denk and now completed by the monks of Beuron, his industry and carefulness are not on that account

to be the less appreciated. He begins with Cyprian and ends with Ambrose and some other authors of the fourth century. Manuscript witnesses of the same form of the Old Latin text of Proverbs are the *Vienna fragments* (ed. by A. Vogel, in 1868), the *Glosses of the Valvanera and Madrid Bibles* and the *Quaestiones Salomonis* (Cod. lat. Monacensis 14096). Schildenberger discusses with special thoroughness the text of Cyprian and of the manuscript witnesses—their method of translation and their vocabulary—matters of great interest not only for the history of the Biblical text, but also for Latin philology.

He demonstrates by well-selected examples that the translation is, in general, literal, but that there is a series of passages rendered freely, though even these may be really literal translations based on a Greek text no longer extant. As for the Latinity, I fear that I have helped to mislead the author by my *Einführung in die lateinische Bibel* where I followed Rönsch and Kaulen in asserting that the Latin of the Pre-Vulgate is ' vulgar.' I would now prefer to call the idiom of these texts an ' unliterary form of younger Latinity.' In the literature of the post-Cyprian times Ambrose holds a special place, having the African text but being influenced by the European recension. We await with eagerness the continuation of this careful study, and even more the edition of the text of the Old Latin Proverbs by the Beuron monks.   F.St.

WEBER, R. : *Les anciennes versions latines du deuxième livre des Paralipomènes*. (Collectanea Biblica Latina, vol. VIII.) 1945. (Abbaye St. Jérôme, Rome.   Price :   10s. 0d.)

This work gives in full the Latin text of II Chronicles from the tenth century MS., known as the First Bible of Alcala, at Madrid, which contains the Vulgate text for most books, but a different text for Tobit, Judith, Esther, Maccabees and II Chronicles. In addition we have here all fragments of other non-Vulgate Latin renderings which have survived in patristic quotations or other texts. There is a valuable introduction in which each of the sources drawn on is treated, and relations with the Greek and Hebrew texts examined. The author reaches the conclusion that there were several Latin versions besides the Vulgate, and that the one most widely used, and preserved for us in full, may rest on Theodotion rather than on the LXX. The book is a valuable addition to our materials for textual criticism.   H.H.R.

ZIEGLER, J. : *Duodecim Prophetae*. 1943. (The Göttingen Septuagint, vol. xiii. Vandenhoek & Rupprecht, Göttingen.)

The editor of this latest volume of the Göttingen Septuagint is already well known, and has proved himself through his edition of Isaiah (see *Book List* for 1946). The arrangement is the usual one. After 146 pages of Introduction follows the text with apparatus. The general result is that the translation here keeps more closely to the Hebrew original than in Isaiah. The work is supplemented by Ziegler's article ' Studien zur Verwertung der Septuaginta im Zwölfprophetenbuch,' in ZAW lx, 1944, pp. 107-131, with its critical remarks on Kittel BH³, Oesterley, Meinhold-Lietzmann, Swete, Rahlfs, etc.
                                                                     W.B.

LITERARY CRITICISM

BRINKER, R. : *The Influence of Sanctuaries in Early Israel.* 1946. (Manchester University Press. Price : 21s. 0d.)

Another attempt to produce a more satisfactory synthesis than that associated with the name of Wellhausen. In line with the recent work of Professor Edward Robertson, who writes a commendatory preface, the author finds that the book of Deuteronomy was compiled by Samuel with the help of the early prophetic guilds as the constitution for a united Israel, while P in origin turns out to be no less than the *tôrāh* of the ancient Canaanite sanctuary at Gibeon. The book undoubtedly contains a number of shrewd and pertinent observations ; but on the whole it is a difficult work to appreciate, as the author's canons of criticism often appear to be somewhat different from those employed by the writer of this note. A.R.J.

EISING, H. : *Formgeschichtliche Untersuchung zur Jakobserzählung der Genesis.* 1940. (Lechte, Emsdetten.)

Dr. Eising gives a very. comprehensive examination of the stories of Jacob and Joseph in Genesis according to the so-called ' formgeschichtliche ' method inaugurated by Gunkel and the Danish folklorist Olrik. Eising presents a clear exposition of the method, with interesting personal contributions, e.g., concerning a difference between ' Gattungsgeschichte ' and ' Formgeschichte,' the latter being the most comprehensive category. He brings penetrating analyses of the separate narratives, in many respects a real commentary on the stories, and at last summarizes his results. It is impossible in a brief note to discuss the many single points which may attract attention, and in some places arouse opposition. But the book is one which must be taken into account by everybody working on Genesis. I think it a drawback that the author has not given a more complete investigation of the thesis of literary criticism. He might have spared room for it, perhaps, by more economy of language. A.B.

GORDIS, R. : *The Wisdom of Ecclesiastes.* 1945. (Behrman House, New York.)

A sumptuously produced book containing a new interpretation of Ecclesiastes, together with an excellent original translation into modern English and a handful of notes. The writer is held to have been a disillusioned old man, either a bachelor or childless, a cultured aristocrat of the old school, whose early passion for justice and truth had led him nowhere, and who perceived that the best thing to do in life is to live. With the exception of the concluding verses the book is held to be a unity, using a conventional religious vocabulary and some orthodox maxims, in order to attach the author's sceptical comments to them, and deceiving the Librarian of the Synagogue into the happy mistake of preserving it. It is described as ' one of man's noblest offerings on the altar of truth.' The work is ascribed to the fourth or third century B.C., though on p. 18 it is placed after Ben Sira. H.H.R.

LONGACRE, L. B. : *The Old Testament: its Form and Purpose.* 1945. (Abingdon - Cokesbury Press, New York - Nashville. Price : $2.)

A painstaking and unpretentious effort to provide what the author calls ' a popular synthesis of the results of the Old Testament study that has been carried on since the days of Astruc.' The writer is thus less concerned with the principles underlying the literary analysis of the Old Testament than with the unities which are discernible when this has been carried out ; and he finds these (a) in the editorial standpoints of the Deuteronomists, the Priestly School and the Chronicler, and (b) in the similarity of outlook which may be traced in the work of the more outstanding canonical prophets, the wisdom writers and the psalmists, etc. In addition, the last two chapters represent a commendable attempt to deal with the problems attaching to the interpretation of the Old Testament and the question of its enduring value. The book is a little lacking in balance (the prophets, for example, being treated summarily in less than thirty out of two hundred and sixty four pages), but, on the whole the author's lucid exposition and simple style, coupled with his obvious concern to be of service to the perplexed beginner, should enable it to serve a useful purpose. A.R.J.

EXEGESIS

BENTZEN, A. : *Fortolkning til de gammeltestamentlige Salmer.* 1940. (Gads Forlag, Copenhagen.)

This bulky commentary on the Psalms (691 pp.), which is a sequel to the author's *Indledning til de gammeltestamentlige Salmer* (1932), is a good expression of the method and results of recent Psalm criticism. The fundamental view of Bentzen is largely the same as that of Mowinckel ; still in many details he offers his independent and well-judged view. Nor can a Danish commentary on the Psalms deny its obligation to Buhl, of course, though his commentary on the Psalms (2nd ed. 1918) seems very obsolete now in its fundamental view. Bentzen holds, like Mowinckel, that the Psalms are cultic poems, usually rituals, written by ritual poets, which by no means prevents individual experiences from occasionally breaking through and stamping the Psalms. In the investigation of each psalm Bentzen first deals with the discussion of the kind of the psalm and, if it is possible to say anything about it, its time of composition. In principle, he places the Psalms in the pre-exilic age, unless cogent reasons require otherwise. E.H.

BENTZEN, A. : *Jesaja I-II.* 1943-44. (Gads Forlag, Copenhagen.)
When Bentzen published this work (of which Part II came out before Part I) the need of a Danish commentary on Isaiah had already been felt for some years, that of Buhl being out of print. As was to be expected, Bentzen finds no definite plan of composition in Proto-Isaiah and is also bound to declare a number of sections to be non-Isaianic. It is of interest to note that he regards the Messianic prophecies in chapters ix and xi as genuine. On the other hand, he considers

Deutero-Isaiah (ch. xl-lv) to have been arranged on a definite progressive plan. In Trito-Isaiah (ch. lvi-lxvi) the connection is again looser and not the work of a single man. On the question of the Ebed-Yahweh songs Bentzen holds the view that they deal with the prophet himself, but he goes still further and asserts that Ebed-Yahweh is both Messiah and Israel and Deutero-Isaiah and his circle. The poems express the idea of ' the Imitation of Christ ' in Israel. Many may find it difficult to unite all these viewpoints, but the history of exegesis has shown, on the other hand, how difficult it is to carry through a single conception. As usual, Bentzen's knowledge of literature is excellent ; only during the war he has been cut off from using the recent English and American literature. Nor has he been able to pay regard to the latest commentary on Isaiah by Mowinckel (in vol. III of the Norwegian translation of the O.T. with notes) as it reached him too late. E.H.

BENTZEN, A. : *Prædikerens Bog*. 1942. (Gads Forlag, ·Copenhagen.)
The author remarks in his preface that this commentary on Ecclesiastes is principally meant for undergraduates, but any reader will find that it offers valuable suggestions for advanced students, too. The book is strongly influenced by the conception of Johannes Pedersen, whose lectures on Ecclesiastes the author had heard in his university years (later known from ' Scepticisme israélite,' *Rev. d'Hist. et de Phil. rel.*, 1931).

There is no introduction to the work, as Bentzen has already treated the problems in question in his *Indledning til det Gamle Testamente* (1941.) E.H.

BÖHL, F. M. TH. : *De Psalmen I*. 1946. (Wolters, Groningen. Tekst en Uitleg series.)
This first part of a popular commentary on the book of Psalms contains an Introduction, a translation of Pss. i-xli, notes on these psalms, and a list of over fifty alterations of the M.T. The Introduction (pp. 5-40) offers a conveniently arranged survey, dealing with such questions as canon, composition, classes, liturgical use, foreign influences, age and authorship, musical forms and religious meaning. The author accepts Mowinckel's theory of an annual festive accession to the throne in Israel. On the whole, however, he defends the traditional view. The Introduction and notes put the reader into touch with the latest literature. P.A.H. de B.

CEUPPENS, FR. : *Genèse I-III*. 1946. (Desclée, de Brouwer, Paris.)
A careful and detailed study of these chapters. The author accepts the view that the first account of creation is historical in substance, but artistic in form, and not to be treated in terms of a scientific work. He claims that it is independent of the cosmology of Babylon or any other ancient land, while admitting resemblances. Similarly he holds the Paradise story to be quite independent of the myths of other peoples, and to be historical. Readers who may not accept these positions will yet find much that is of value in this study.
H.H.R.

EDELKOORT, A. H. : *De profeet Zacharia.* 1945. (Baarn).

A popular interpretation of the book of Zechariah. The author thinks the whole book was written by the priest-prophet Zechariah, chaps. i-viii in his youth, 520-518 B.C., and the last chapters in his old age, after 480 B.C. In this last part of the book the prophet finds comfort in the 'eschatological future,' disappointed in the present time. Successively are translated and commented on the visions and the additions thereto, added by the priest-prophet himself, i-vi ; the perorations in vii f. ; the disappointment, x 1-5, xiii 1-6 ; and the eschatological comfort, ix, x, xi, xiii, xii, xiv.

The aim of the author—in every respect praiseworthy—is to give a book of comfort in war time to the Christian reader of the Bible. It is a pity that we do not find a detailed critical defence of Dr. Edelkoort's opinions and often bold guesses.

P.A.H. de B.

EDELKOORT, A. H. : *Stil tot God, de psalmen voorheden.* 1941. (Amsterdam.)

Twenty meditations on Pss. i, iv, viii, xiii, xxiii, xxvii 1-6, xxvii 7-14, xxviii, xxx, xxxii, xxxix, xlvi, xlvii, liv, lvii, lx, lxi, lxii, lxv. This book does not offer an exegetical commentary, but seeks to explain the actual religious meaning of the psalms.

P.A.H. de B.

EERDMANS, B. D. : *The Hebrew Book of Psalms.* 1947. (Brill, Leiden. Oudtestamentische Studiën IV.)

This voluminous commentary on the book of Psalms constitutes a veteran scholar's work with all the marks of a new and fresh approach, bearing witness to the spiritual vitality of its author. In his ' Essays on Masoretic Psalms ' (O.T.S. I, 1942, pp. 1-16, 105-296) some special subjects were discussed —e.g., the Chasidim, the Songs of Ascents—but in this new book the author treats the whole Psalter. We find a new translation of each psalm and in his comment Eerdmans stresses above all his view of the Chasid as a member of an old ·body of defenders of orthodox Jhwhism, ' partisans of Jahu.' He thinks a great number of psalms originate in the pre-exilic circles of Chasidism. In the Introduction are discussed *inter alia* the *Gattungsforschung,* the collection of the psalms, the enemies in the psalms, origin and date, the singers (the Psalms were not written for the temple cult), and a detailed treatment of titles and technical terms. Here we find very interesting solutions of difficult expressions, most of them worthy to be considered.

It is not probable that this commentary will at once convince every scholar by all its new translations and interpretations. But we can be sure that the book through its own independent, and often surprising and instructive approach to so many problems will be used by every student of the psalms who prefers originality to the usual compilations.

P.A.H. de B.

FREY, H. : *Das Buch der Kirche in der Weltwende : die kleinen nachexilischen Propheten, für Freunde und Verächter der Bibel ausgelegt.* (Die Botschaft des Alten Testaments. Erläuterungen alttestamentlicher Schriften. XXIV Band.) 1941. (Calwer Vereinsbuchhandlung, Stuttgart. Price : Rm. 7.)

A translation and exposition of the second half of the ' Minor Prophets ' (excluding Jonah), which is divided into four parts, i.e., I. God's Temple : Haggai i-ii ; Zechariah i-viii. II. God's Family : Malachi i-iv. III. God's Day : Obadiah i ; Joel i-iv. IV. God's King : Zechariah ix-xiv. Despite the evidence which it offers of the author's familiarity with critical problems of an historical kind, the exposition has more of a dogmatic and practical character, since it seeks to unfold ' through a period of two centuries the path followed by the community from which the Christ was to emerge, and within which he was to work, and on whose soil at the Cross the sentence as to the world's fate was to fall.' Indeed that is why the author calls this particular collection of prophetic works ' Das Buch der Kirche in der Weltwende.' Even those to whom this kind of christological (or ' ecclesialogical ') interpretation of the Old Testament does not appeal can learn much from the author's effort to derive a permanent religious content from these texts. O.E.

GRETHER, O. : *Das Deboralied : eine metrische Rekonstruktion.* 1941. (Beiträge zur Förderung christlicher Theologie, xliii, No. 2.)

Useful on account of the complete survey of earlier discussions of the metre, and moderate in its textual criticism. Less cogent are its transpositions (verse 12 to follow verse 8 ; verses 18 and 23 to follow verse 15a ; verse 22 to precede verse 21), and its deletions (verses 9 and 31). Hence the result—strophes of five verses, the odd strophes being double threes and the even double fours—is not beyond doubt. W.B.

HALDAR, A. : *Studies in the book of Nahum.* (Uppsala Universitets Årsskrift 1946 : 7). 1947. (A.B. Lundequistska Bokhandeln, Uppsala. Price : Kr. 7.)

A study of the text and interpretation of Nahum, rejecting the cultic liturgy theory, but ascribing the book to a cultic prophet who engaged in political propaganda against Nineveh largely cast in terms of the mythical-ritual combat of Yahweh with his foes. There is much comparison with Ras Shamra and Mesopotamian material. Haldar rejects metrics as an instrument of textual criticism, denies the existence of a mutilated acrostic in chap. i, and dismisses most of the innumerable emendations proposed. He is restrained in emendation, though often giving to the text a new meaning in harmony with his general view. While he is not always convincing on textual matters, his caution in emendation is to be commended, and his general interpretation of the book may with some reserve be accepted. Similarly caution in the use of metre is wiser than its rejection out of hand as an instrument of criticism. H.H.R.

HAMMERSHAIMB, E. : *Amos*. 1946. (Busck, Copenhagen. Price : Kr. 12.25.)

A judicious little commentary in Danish on the book of Amos, designed for the use of students but dealing with all essential questions of text, grammar and exegesis. Found by the reviewer to be a useful handbook for his own class work.

A.R.J.

MILLER, A., and SCHILDENBERGER, J. : *Die Bücher Tobias, Judith und Esther*. (Die Heilige Schrift des Alten Testaments, ed. by F. Feldmann and H. Herkenne, IV.3.). 1940-41. (Hanstein, Bonn. Price : Rm. 14.20.)

Of the three biblical works treated in this volume Tobit and Judith are dealt with by Miller, and Esther by Schildenberger. The treatment of each book is characteristic of the series, involving an introduction which deals with questions of textual transmission, literary structure, historicity, canonicity and the like, followed by a bibliography, and thereafter a translation into German occupying the upper half of each page with below a verse by verse exposition.

While both introduction and commentary touch upon the more academic issues which arise, they are less concerned with the solution of these problems than with the religious value of the books in question. Thus, while it is true that questions of text are extensively discussed, the translation is based, not upon a text built up on definite critical principles, but upon a kind of *textus receptus* ; and in the case of historical questions, instead of presenting clear alternatives (which, admittedly, is not always easy), the expedient is adopted of saying that narratives of a more poetical kind are often of much greater religious value than those of a strictly historical nature. The conservative view, which maintains the historical character in the strict sense, is abandoned, but the opposite view, that Tobit, Judith and Esther are mere fictions of the writers for parenetical purposes, is also rejected. The two commentators think that there is in these narratives 'a historical nucleus,' which is, however, difficult to determine, but that these books are 'no historical book in the strict sense' (Tob.), 'a parenesis with historical background' (Judith), 'genus of the free-modelled narrative' (Esther). O.E., F.St.

REICHERT, V. E. : *Job, with Hebrew Text and English Translation*. 1946. (Soncino Press, Hindhead.)

This further volume in the Soncino Books of the Bible is to be welcomed for its presentation of a Jewish point of view. The policy of the series precludes textual emendation and critical discussion, since it is designed for general Jewish use. The editor uses both Jewish and Christian commentaries, and in his translation sometimes departs from the standard rabbinical interpretations. The Introduction is very brief, and the editor would apparently have preferred more freedom to discuss questions of integrity. He has to content himself with referring the reader to the works where this is discussed, while he accepts the complete integrity of the work, including chap. xxviii and the Elihu speeches, in his commentary.

Despite the limitations imposed by the series, the commentary should be widely useful to Christian as well as Jewish readers, and not least for the translation it offers. H.H.R.

RUDOLPH, W. : *Jeremia.* (Handbuch zum Alten Testament, ed. by O. Eissfeldt. Erste Reihe, 12). 1947. (Mohr, Tübingen.)

In format the present volume is in keeping with the others which have already been published in this series. In content the book is distinguished by a well-informed and intelligent use of the work of earlier commentators, a thorough and independent treatment of the text, penetrating literary analysis, careful regard for the contemporary conditions, and a forceful and sympathetic exposition of that which is of enduring significance in Jeremiah's message. It is only to be expected that from time to time conclusions reached on textual points should not be such as to command general acceptance, and indeed Rudolph himself now not infrequently departs from the conjectures which he presented a decade and a half ago in Kittel's *Biblia Hebraica.* Much the same holds good with regard to his treatment of the literary analysis of the book, for example the division of the material into three sources A, B and C, which he has adopted in his own way from Mowinckel. However, questions of this kind always arise in cases where the facts admit of different conclusions, and the particular one which is expounded by Rudolph always brings with it an advance in one's understanding of the passage even for someone who may hold a different view. O.E.

SCHULZ, A. : (1) *Psalmenfragen. Mit einem Anhang : Zur Stellung der Beifügung im Hebräischen.* (Alttestamentliche Abhandlungen XIV, 1). 1940. (Aschendorff, Münster i. W.)

(2) *Die Psalmen und die Cantica des Römischen Breviers verdeutscht.* 1939. (Regensburg.)

(3) *Biblisches Lesebuch aus den Alten Testament.* 1940. (Regensburg.)

Dr. Schulz gives in his *Psalmenfragen* a series of critical and exegetical remarks on passages of the Psalms, some after the manner of Dr. Daiches' studies some years ago. New solutions of many a *crux interpretum* are proposed, which may be examined with profit by all commentators. Many of his proposals are likely to be accepted as definitive. It is not possible to discuss details. As the author says in his preface, these are ' chips, so to say ' of his translation of the Psalms published in a beautifully produced booklet mentioned above as No. 2.

Dr. Schulz is known not only as a Biblical scholar, but also as a champion of the worthy and cultured use of his mother-tongue. So we may expect a translation of high merit. Nor are we disappointed. The author knows how to combine faithfulness to the original with modern, idiomatic German expression ; nevertheless, he never lets us forget that we have to do with a sacred text, though he avoids artificial archaisms. This is a high merit in times like the present in which the sense for sacred style is widely lost. The text of the Psalms and the Canticles (i.e., Ex.· xv, 1-18 ; Dt. xxxii, 1-43 ; I Sam. ji, 1-10 ; I Chron. xxix, 10-13 ; Tob. xiii, 1-10 ; Jdth. xvi, 13-17 ; Sir. xxxvi, 1-19 ; Is. xii ; Is. xxxviii, 10-20 ; Is. xlv, 15-25 ; Jer. xxxi, 10-14 ; Dan. iii, 52-57 ; Dan. iii, 57-88, 56 ; Hab. iii ; Lk. i, 46-55 ; Lk. i, 68-79 ; Lk. ii, 29-32) is followed by short explanations.

The *Biblisches Lesebuch* gives selected texts—chiefly, but not exclusively, poetical—of the Old Testament, illustrating the ideas of God, of his relation to the world and to mankind, of the Messiah, of the attitude of man to God and of man to man, of the power of God's grace in man, and some texts of various content such as the blessing of Jacob (Gen. xlix. 1-20) etc. As for the translation, we have only to repeat what has been said above on his translation of the Psalms. Short explanations are added here also.   F.St.

VALVEKENS, P. J. B. : *De Boeken Paralipomenon*. 1942. (Beyaert, Bruges. Price : 9s. 0d.)

This is a very brief commentary on the two books of Chronicles, in the series *Het Oude en het Nieuwe Testament*, edited by J. Th. Beelen. The text stands in Latin and Flemish, in parallel columns, and short comments, of little critical value, stand at the foot. Sometimes attempts are made to harmonize the divergences from the parallel passages in Samuel and Kings ; in the case of the price paid to Ornan for his threshing-floor Chronicles is preferred to Samuel for reasons similar to those which prompted the Chronicler to invent the higher price. A more discriminating assessment of the strength and the weakness of the books of Chronicles would have been more satisfying.   H.H.R.

WUTZ, F. : *Das Hohelied*. 1940. (Kohlhammer, Stuttgart.)

The MS. of this work was already in a fit state for publication at the time of the author's death in March, 1938, and it has been seen through the press by J. Goettsberger without any interference on his part in order (as he himself says at the end of his preface) to present Wutz in his ceaseless activity, penetrating ingenuity, bold gift of synthesis, and conscious independence in the textual and exegetical study of the Old Testament. The book certainly bears witness to his bold gift of synthesis and conscious independence. Like its predecessors, *Die Psalmen textkritisch untersucht* (1925), *Die Transkriptionen · von der Septuaginta bis zu Hieronymus* (1933), *Systematische Wege von der Septuaginta zum hebräischen Urtext* (1937), *Das Buch Job* (1939), it is based upon what is assumed to be a sound method of textual criticism, whereby not a letter of the present text is left unaccounted for, and, through the conjectural introduction of numerous Hebrew vocables which are not otherwise attested, a text is furnished which diverges considerably from that which has come down to us. This in turn yields a highly individual translation of the twelve sections into which the Song of Songs is thought to be divided, and so renders possible an equally peculiar conception of the book as a whole. That is to say, ' it is a question of a continuous dialogue between two young lovers, who are animated just as much by true love as by a refined modesty, and in this true love their common poverty overcomes all obstacles.'   O.E.

RELIGION AND THEOLOGY

ALFRINK, B. J. : *Over ' Typologische ' Exegese van het Oude Testament.* 1945. Dekker and van de Vegt, Nijmegen.)

This interesting treatment of the typical sense as used in Scriptural exegesis was the subject of Alfrink's inaugural address (23rd November, 1945) when he succeeded Paul Heinisch as Old Testament professor in the Catholic University, of Nijmegen. It is a clear and readable account of the various aspects of the *sensus typicus* with a particularly careful study of its employment in the writings of the Fathers. An appendix supplies bibliographical details and numerous quotations from the scholastic writers and from recent papal encyclicals.

J.M.T.B.

ALLIS, O. T. : *Prophecy and the Church.* 1945. (Clarke, London. Price : 15s. 0d.)

The book contains a detailed examination and refutation of the doctrine of Dispensationalism according to which the Christian Church is an interruption of Jewish hopes of the literal fulfilment of prophecy and may at any moment be rapt away to make possible the coming of the Jewish millennium when practically the whole world will be saved by the propagation of a Jewish gospel. The relevance of this book for Christian students of the Old Testament is that it will help them to realise how urgent is the task of facing up to the theological problems of the relation of the Testaments to each other.   N.W.P.

BEEK, M. A. : *Het twistgesprech van de mens met zijn God.* 1946. (Van Gorcum & Co. N. V., Assen. Price : 2s. 9d.)

This is a monograph of 24 pages, and is in Dutch. It is Dr. Beek's inaugural lecture as Professor of Hebrew language and literature in the University of Amsterdam. The author reviews the development of the study of Old Testament religion during the last twenty years, particularly the pronounced swing away from what is similar to Israel's environment to what is distinct from it. There is a controversy between God and man, and this is the theme of the Old Testament, most evident in Jeremiah, and dramatised in Job.   N.H.S.

DE BOER, P. A. H. : *De Boodschap van het Oude Testament.* 2nd ed. 1946. (Van Gorcum, Assen.)

A brief study of the varieties of literature in the Old Testament, and the purpose for which they have been preserved. At the head of each section is a reference to a passage to be read before the section is studied, giving a specimen of the variety treated in the section. Within the section there is no attempt to survey all the passages that belong to it, since the aim is to illustrate rather than to be comprehensive. Simply written for the ordinary reader, it gives within its brief compass some clear idea of the message of the Old Testament for modern readers. Its sections deal with the origins of Israel, her laws (including prophetic law), the hymn of creation, ancient stories, leaders (priests, kings and prophets), psalms and the treatment of suffering (Job and the Servant). There is a short introduction, dealing with the world in which Israel was set, and a table of the important events of her history. H.H.R.

BRILLET, G. : *Isaïe*. (Témoins de Dieu, No. 6). 1945. (Les Éditions du Cerf, Paris. Price : 5s. 6d.)

After a brief survey of the historical background of the work of Isaiah, the author gives a short account of the life and work of the prophet, and a good summary of his message, in which the social and religious aspects are traced to the religious experiences of Isaiah and his essential conception of God. Hence he is presented not as a statesman or a social reformer, but as a Witness of God. There is a good chapter on the literary genius of the prophet and a brief account of the compilation of the book. This is not treated in detail, but it is significant that the study is limited to chapters i-xxxix (a footnote refers the rest to the *book* of Isaiah but not to the *prophet*), while it is recognized that elements in the first part (e.g., xiii, l-xiv, 22 and xxiv-xxvii) cannot be by the prophet.
H.H.R.

BUBER, M. : *Het geloof van Israël* (an article in *De godsdiensten der wereld*, ed. by G. van der Leeuw. 1940. Amsterdam.)

An outline of the history of the religion of the Israelite people, which believes in God as Lord of life and work. Buber begins with the Song of Deborah and treats successively the gathering at Shechem, the events at Mount Sinai, the pre-Sinaitic relation of Israel and Jhwh, the god of the patriarchs, the Exodus as a religious act, divine and human kingship, Jhwh and Baal, sacrifice, righteousness, love, the kingdom of God, the battle against the sanctuary. The author develops the ideas published in his *Königtum Gottes* (2nd ed., 1936). The outline is incomplete and ends with the treatment of Jeremiah's strife. In the second edition of this philosophico-religious work we expect the complete treatment of the subject.
P.A.H. de B.

BURROWS, M. : *An Outline of Biblical Theology*. 1946. (Westminster Press, Philadelphia. Price : $3.50.)

This book offers a compilation of the Biblical teaching contained in both Testaments and is designed above all to provide a basis for sound Biblical preaching. The author's method is historical but he seeks to show that the Bible supplies ' an interpretation and critique of the history from the point of view of the divine will.' He is thus able to use the Bible itself to determine what parts of its contents are of little or no importance to-day. The authority of the Bible is to be found in the self-evidencing power of its truth in human experience. This truth is presented in ancient forms and requires continual reformulation. Its unity is to be found in the general direction of the process which culminated in the revelation of God in Christ. The usual topics of Biblical Theology are dealt with in detail and there are also sections on such topics as public worship, Christian service and moral and social ideals. The book is very fully documented with scriptural references but references to learned publications and even to extra-canonical primary sources are deliberately excluded. N.W.P.

DAUBE, D. : *Studies in Biblical Law*. 1947. (Cambridge University Press. Price : 21s. 0d.)

The author of this book attempts to reconstruct parts of ancient Hebrew law as something distinct from religion, even something earlier than religion ; he then discusses the way in which ancient codes were compiled and amended. He then proceeds to examine the doctrines of redemption, compensation, communal responsibility, and finally that of *summum ius summa iniuria* in relation to the story of Jacob and Esau. Unfortunately the writing is diffuse and the point, if there is one, is often hard to disentangle, and many of the points are extremely far-fetched—for example, that when Rachel gives up Jacob for a night to Leah it is *conductio rei* ; in fact, the whole analogy of Roman law is seriously overdone. Also, the critical analysis of the Hebrew documents is almost totally disregarded. Nonetheless, even though a reader may disagree with both method and conclusions, many incidental suggestions thrown out by the author certainly deserve consideration and may well be right. G.R.D.

*DODD, C. H. : *The Bible To-Day*. 1946. (Cambridge University Press. Price : 7s. 6d.)

The small size of this book is no index of its importance. Like all Professor Dodd's work it is highly stimulating and should be over-looked by no one who is interested in a religious exposition of the Bible relevant to our own day. Emphasis is laid on the People of God as the theme of the Old Testament and this is shown to link up with the emergence of the Christian Church. Helpful things are said about biblical criticism, about the way in which the moral difficulties in the Old Testament should be faced, about the pattern of Israel's history and the prophetic interpretation of it. Much space is, of course, given to the New Testament. The last chapter with its discussion of the way in which the Bible as the record of a history becomes relevant to the need of the individual, becomes in fact the story of ' Everyman,' will be found particularly suggestive. N.W.P.

DUBARLE, A. M. : *Les Sages d' Israël*. 1946. (Les Editions du Cerf, Paris.)

In this excellent work we have discussed the ideas and teaching of the Wisdom Literature of Israel. This includes the two accounts of Creation, Proverbs, Job, Qoheleth, Ben Sira, Wisdom, and a short chapter on the teaching of the Gospel on chance and destiny, happiness, the resurrection and truth. In the middle of the book there is a chapter entitled ' Gleanings ' which deals with Deuteronomy, the Wisdom poem in Baruch, certain Psalms, and the Old Testament conception of Sheol.

Throughout the discussion is thorough and informed. Job xxviii is treated for practical purposes as separate from the rest of the book, and disorder in the third cycle of speeches is recognized. But the Elihu speeches are accepted as integral to the work, and an artistic preparation for Yahweh's speech, which they reinforce. Elihu is said to be unmentioned in the Epilogue because he was implicitly approved. Qoheleth is described as a disconcerting book, which contains the expression of an experience rather than a divine communication. It is held to be a unity, save for the concluding verses and some observations relating to Providence and Judgement, which were added as a corrective by a disciple.   H.H.R.

EDSMAN, C. M. : *The Body and Eternal Life*. 1946. (Horae Soeder-blomianae, Stockholm.)

This is a study (104 pp.) of the history of the interpretation of Isaiah lxvi 7-8 and in particular of that understanding of this passage which sees in it a reference to the resurrection of the body. Added to this is a comparative study of various images and arguments which were employed by apologists of the early Church with the purpose of making the idea of the resurrection of the body credible. The author pursues the latter theme into the sphere of Iranian religion where belief in the resurrection of the body was a fundamental doctrine. The author's problem is introduced by a very interesting citation from Jacob of Serugh (Syriac text with English translation) taken from a treatise not yet published entitled : ' On the Resurrection of the Human Bodies ' by John of Dārā (9th century).   O.S.R.

EERDMANS, B. D. : *The Religion of Israel*. 1947. (Leiden.)

This book may be called a special Introduction to the Old Testament, as well as a history of Israel's religion. After an inquiry into the sources it describes Israel's religious thought from the events at Mount Sinai until the beginnings of Christianity. In addition to the contents of the Dutch edition of 1930—many years out of print—this English revised edition offers a critical examination of some studies published in recent years. It is distinguished for its careful interpretation of many parts of the Hebrew Bible, and for its clear analysis of various books of the Old Testament. In general the author does not follow the systems of others, but takes his own line, known from his detailed studies on the Pentateuch (*Alttestamentliche Studien* i-iv, 1908-12), and other essays, published in various Journals. The book is a valuable contribution to the literature on Israel because of its illuminating exegetical and historical discussions. As a compendium of the results of the work of a lifetime it is a welcome gift, and ripe fruit.   P.A.H. de B.

FREDERIKSSON, H. : *Jahwe als Krieger*. 1945. (Gleerup, Lund.)

A summary of the Old Testament material dealing with Yahweh and warfare. The first part assembles the references to Him as the commander of armies—the hosts of Israel, or foreign powers who were bent to His will, of eschatological hosts, of demons, of heavenly powers, and of the forces of Nature. The second part deals with Yahweh as an individual champion against human or superhuman foes, and of the weapons of His armoury with which metaphor credited Him. There is nothing strikingly new in substance here, but the author is to be thanked for ordering and classifying what the Old Testament has to say on this subject. H.H.R.

HANSON, R. P. C., and HARVEY, B. : *The Loom of God*. 1945. (Association for Promoting Christian Knowledge, Dublin and Belfast. Price : 3s. 6d.)

The sub-title describes this as ' An Introduction to the dogmatic study of the Bible.' Actually it is mainly concerned with the Old Testament. The first part offers a simple account of the modern approach to the Old Testament, and shows that it is in no way hostile to its religious value. There follows the ' thematic study ' in which some of the main ideas of the Old Testament are briefly examined, together with their counterparts in the New. Much is well said, and the whole should be widely useful, though it tends to view the Old Testament too largely from the standpoint of the New, and the reviewer would deprecate the use of the term ' dogmatic study ' of the Bible. H.H.R.

HERNER, S. : *Die Natur im Alten Testament*. (Bulletin de la société royale des lettres de Lund, 1940-1941.) 1941. (Gleerup Förlag, Lund.)

This work deals with the subject under the general headings : Heaven, Earth, Plants and Animals. What the Old Testament has to say on sun, moon and stars ; on water, mountains and stones ; trees and plants ; cattle, wild animals, birds and fish, is here gathered in very convenient form. The author is more concerned with the ideas which the Old Testament writers have of the various natural phenomena than with drawing any critical conclusions, but he sets forth these ideas in a plain and attractive manner. Most interesting is the comparison of the J and P sources in regard to their notions about the animal world. Striking also is it to discover the profundity of the book of Job and its deep divergence in important points from the rest of Old Testament literature in its outlook upon nature. O.S.R.

HERNER, S. : *Sühne und Vergebung in Israel*. 1942. (Gleerup, Lund.)

In this little book Herner assembles the evidence from the whole of the Old Testament concerning the related ideas of expiation and forgiveness, showing how the emphasis shifts from one to the other. In particular he points out how P is dominated by the thought of expiation, the Psalter by that of forgiveness apart from expiation. N.W.P.

JACOB, E. : *La tradition historique en Israël.* 1946. (Faculté de Théologie Protestante, Montpellier. Price : Fr. 120.)

> A most interesting discussion of the historical tradition of the Hebrews in many ways similar to, and to some extent supplementing, Professor North's monograph on the same subject. Considerable space is given to the oral tradition, to the nature of myth—the author insists that myth is based on a historical element and is not the creation of cultic rites—and to the part played by the priests at the sanctuaries, by the prophets and by the court annalists in transmitting the historical tradition. There is a most valuable study of the distinctive Hebrew technique of historical writing.
>
> The various works of historical synthesis are reviewed. In his Section on the Yahwist the author indicates that he inclines to the Volz-Rudolph view of the ' Elohist.' He has interesting things to say about the development of autobiographical writing in prophetic circles and compares this with the memoirs of Ezra and Nehemiah. A really significant book.   N.W.P.

KOHNSTAMM, PH. : *Het Oude Verbond : ein Inleiding in Oud-testamentische Theologie.* 1945. (Ten Have, Amsterdam. Price : 8s. 6d.)

> The author first defends the retention of the Old Testament in the Christian Church, against the neo-Marcionite attitude, and then shows how in various ways the Old Testament was a preparation for the New. He shows briefly how many of the fundamental ideas of the Old Testament are enduringly valid, but tends to view it in an over-teleological way. The reviewer would have seen the former side of this more emphasized and developed. The Old Testament lives in its own right, and not only as a preparation for the New. It should also have been more clearly brought out that for its understanding a historical sense is needed. While Old Testament theology is different from the history of Old Testament religion, it can never be rightly apprehended without a grasp of the latter.   H.H.R.

LAUHA, A. : *Zaphon : Der Norden und die Nordvölker im Alten Testament.* (Annales Academiae Scientiarum Fennicae, B XLIX, 2.) 1943. (Helsinki. Price : About 7s. 6d.)

> Deals with the Old Testament conceptions of the North and the peoples of the North with due regard to etymology, the geographical and historical conditions, the association of the North with the divine Mount of Assembly, and, of course, the recurrent threat of disaster from the North. The author finds that, besides obvious elements of a mythological kind, one should be prepared to recognize the presence of folk memories going back to the collapse of the Hittite Empire and the breakdown of the Aegean civilization c. 1200 B.C. Of limited value, as the author's reading appears to have been restricted in the main to a number of works written in German.   A.R.J.

MÖBIUS, K. : *Die Aktualität der Eschatologie bei den alttestament-lichen Propheten.* 1940. (Steinach.)

> This book is only the first chapter of a dissertation from the University of Jena, accepted 1934. It is a work in the field of Old Testament Theology. The problem of time and eternity is placed in the centre instead of our idea of history. It is impossible to understand the judgment of the prophets on the background of an empirical world ; on the contrary, the world must be regarded from the other side, from the End. A real appreciation cannot be given of the book until it is published in its complete form. A.B.

*NORTH, C. R. : *The Old Testament Interpretation of History.* 1946. (Fernley-Hartley Lecture, The Epworth Press, London. Price : 10s. 6d.)

> The purpose of this able book is indicated in the title and it can be confidently recommended as one of the most stimulating recent discussions of its subject. It falls into two main sections. Firstly, there are a series of chapters dealing seriatim with the interpretation of history in the sagas, by the Prophets, the Deuteronomists, the Priests (e.g., in P and Chronicles-Ezra-Nehemiah) and in Daniel. Secondly, in the three concluding chapters, Professor North discusses a number of relevant topics and this will be found the most original and stimulating part of his book. He argues that the Hebrew conception of divine personality is the necessary basis of ethical monotheism and that the history in which God is the chief actor is itself redemptive and is not just the husk that conceals a redemption which is non-historical. The outstanding miracle of the Old Testament is the prophetic consciousness, defined with Heschel as the divine *pathos.* The main lack in the Old Testament is its lack of an adequate conception of the Holy Spirit. N.W.P.

NYSTRÖM, S. : *Beduinentum und Jahwismus. Eine soziologisch-religionsgeschichtliche Untersuchung zum Alten Testament.* 1946. (Gleerup, Lund. Price : Kr. 10.)

> This comparative study is designed to show, not only that the history of Israel reflects the unceasing conflict between the customs and ideals of the nomadic peoples of Arabia as opposed to the settled population of Palestine, but that the worship of Yahweh introduced a third element which, while preserving many of the social ideals of the desert, was in conscious antagonism to the pride and self-sufficiency of the Bedouin. The work as a whole is interesting and suggestive, but unfortunately it lacks balance. By concentrating upon the data furnished by recent or comparatively recent accounts of the Bedouin (Burckhardt, Doughty, Hartmann, Hess, Jaussen, Musil, Oppenheim et al.) and neglecting the data which is now available for a better understanding of Canaanite culture, the author obviously does less than justice to the latter. A.R.J.

POLLOCK, S. : *Stubborn Soil*. No date given, but published 1946. (Sidgwick & Johnson, London. Price : 12s. 6d.)

The title refers to human experience, as illustrated in three stages by the Wisdom Books of the Old Testament, Proverbs, Ecclesiastes, Job—orthodoxy, the breakdown of orthodoxy, an effort at reconstruction respectively. A good popular account of the teaching of these books, written in a thoroughly lively style. The book is based on critical study, and concludes with the author's own translation, wherein he steers ' between the Scylla of literalism and the Charybdis of paraphrase.' The author is enthusiastic over his theme, and makes the old books speak for to-day. N.H.S.

RIDDERBOS, J. : *Profetie en Ekstase.* 1941. (Aalten.)

In this popular booklet (92 pages) Professor Ridderbos (Theol. Seminary of Kampen) considers the ecstatic phenomena of Old Testamentic prophecy, whose existence he assumes especially in the case of the ' group-prophets ' and of Ezechiel. He warns against the opinion that all effects of the prophets should be explained as ecstatic symptoms. The leading idea of his book is the denial of the view that Israelitic ecstasy was developed from foreign countries and should be considered as ' identity-mysticism.' The ecstatic possibilities of Israel were used by the divine Spirit and produced the holy ecstasy (cf. glossolology in the old Christian Church). He stresses the idea that ecstasy in Israel is a temporary form and not the ' Grunderlebnis ' of prophecy itself (Moses) ; this had its origin in the vocation of God, who presses man into his service, and calls upon his will, instead of effacing it. Th.C.V.

*ROWLEY, H. H. : *The Re-Discovery of the Old Testament*. 1946. (Clarke, London. Price : 10s. 6d.)

Professor Rowley puts his readers still further in his debt by this new volume from his unresting pen. The purpose of this excellent book is to make a contribution to the religious understanding of the Old Testament, while holding fast to the historical view which criticism has made possible. Helpful and balanced chapters deal with the data of archaeology. The importance of Moses as the founder of Israel's religion is emphasised. There is discussion of the problems of the relations between the prophet and the priest and of the attitude of the prophet to sacrifice. Justice is done to the post-exilic age in view of its actual achievement in preserving the prophetic oracles and such books as Job, in making the Psalter its manual of praise, and in creating the Synagogue. Many of the topics of Old Testament theology are discussed illuminatingly. Of particular interest is Professor Rowley's view stated in more than one place of the Servant Songs. His treatment of the relation of the Testaments avoids on the one hand the Scylla of uncontrolled allegorising and on the other the Charybdis of pure historicism. N.W.P.

RYLAARSDAM, J. C. : *Revelation in Jewish Wisdom Literature*. 1946. (University of Chicago Press. Price : $3.00.)

A useful study of the Wisdom Literature—Proverbs, Job, Ecclesiastes, Sirach, Wisdom, Baruch, IV Maccabees, Pirke Aboth—as the vehicle of revelation. The books are not dealt with separately and successively, but each chapter treats of them as a whole. They are first set in the context of ancient oriental Wisdom Literature, and then follow chapters on the Nationalization of Wisdom, the Hope of Wisdom, the Transcendence of Wisdom, and Wisdom and the Spirit. In these the author seeks to unfold the outlook and spirit of Hebrew Wisdom. The canonical material is found to reflect an outlook not integrated with the national religious tradition—witness the omission of the concept of mercy—but later it became completely integrated, when Wisdom was equated with the Law, to the loss of all creative quality. The normal omission of the divine name Yahweh in the dialogue of Job is held to indicate that for the sage Yahweh was still too much of a tribal and national deity to be safely given a place in discussions of universal interest. Slips are surprisingly numerous for a University Press publication, and for some the printer cannot be held responsible.   H.H.R.

SCHMIDT, J. : *Der Ewigkeitsbegriff im Alten Testament*. (Alttestamentliche Abhandlungen XIII, 5.) 1940. (Aschendorff, Münster, i.W. Price : Rm. 10.40.)

The aim of the present book is defined on page 2 as that of examining both linguistically and exegetically the Old Testament terms for eternity with due regard to the Old Testament text, the development of the whole of the Old Testament world, and the literature which has so far appeared on this subject.' It is carried out in four chapters, of which the first deals with ' A Linguistic Examination of the Old Testament Terms for Eternity,' while the second, third and fourth treat of ' God and' Eternity in the Old Testament,' ' Man and Eternity in the Old Testament,' and ' Eschatology and Eternity in the Old Testament.' An epilogue presents a summary of the conclusions, while an index of scripture references and a subject index make possible a rapid appraisal of what is at the reader's disposal. Finally the extensive bibliography, which is prefixed to the study as a whole, makes the reader easily acquainted with such publications as have already appeared on the subject. Although the data sometimes permit a different conclusion from that of the author, nevertheless his book makes a real contribution to the elucidation of the question with which it deals.   O.E.

SCHÖNBÄCHLER, V. : *Die Stellung der Psalmen zum alttestamentlichen Opferkult*. 1941. (Paulusdruckerei, Freiburg. Price : 7s. 6d.)

A dissertation (76 pp.) on the verses in the psalms which deal with sacrifices. The author deals first with the words, those relating to bloodless sacrifices and then those relating to blood sacrifices. He next discusses passages which are clearly in favour of the sacrificial system, and then those which are apparently against. Dealing specially with the latter, he sums up previous opinion both of those who agree that these passages are antagonistic and of those who are of the opposite point of view. His own judgement is that verses apparently antagonistic to the cultus must be read in the light of the rest. They are really favourable, and are attempts to secure a deeper inner meaning and a spiritualising of sacrifice.

N.H.S.

STAMM, J. J. : *Das Leiden des Unschuldigen in Babylon und Israel.* 1946. (Zwingli-Verlag, Zürich. Price : Fr. 5.50.)

A useful study of the respective Babylonian and Hebrew views regarding the suffering of the innocent. The common element is accounted for by the inheritance of Oriental wisdom in both religions, but, whereas in the Babylonian texts examined, the conclusions reached result from the rejection or reacceptance of the authority of a cult-religion, in Hebrew religious experience there was a real encounter with a divine Thou through which faith was re-established at a new level. In Babylon there were substitutionary rites but only at the magical level. In Israel where such rites are few, there is substitution at the moral level recognised as a unique possibility of vicarious suffering in response to the will of God.

N.W.P.

STEIN, B. : *Der Begriff Kebod Jahweh und seine Bedeutung für die alttestamentliche Gotteserkenntnis.* 1939. (Lechte, Emsdetten, i.W. Price : Rm. 12.)

The first three sections deal with the Kebod Yahweh in the historical books, the psalms and the prophets. The fourth and last section presents a summary of the conception as a whole, and here special attention is paid to the task of tracing its connection with the idea of the Kingdom of Yahweh and the Eschatological Hope in addition to a discussion of its relations with the root *kbd*. The content of the conception is defined tentatively as ' The Majesty of the divine King in its manifestation,' and the author seeks to show that this manifestation is primarily experienced in the sphere of God's redemptive activity—righteousness and love—and is only secondarily extended to the world of nature, an assumption which gives cause for reflection. For other reasons too the book will need to be read with caution. The lack in the first place of any historical criticism and in the second place the exaggerated use of modern scholastic subtleties particularly call for adverse criticism. Taking the book as a whole, however, one may say that it represents not only an extensive but a valuable contribution to the clarification of the conception with which it deals ; and in this connection what is specially deserving of notice is the working out of its relation to the idea of the Kingdom of Yahweh, both offering a complete parallel in so far as both are connected with the Eschatological Hope.

O.E.

STEINMANN, J. : *Job*. (Témoins de Dieu, No. 8). 1946. Les Éditions du Cerf, Paris. Price : 5s. 0d.)

A useful study of the book of Job, conceived as a drama. The author's general positions are much influenced by Dhorme's great commentary and by Hölscher. He dates the book of Job in the post-exilic period, on grounds of thought and language, and ascribes to the original writer the Prologue and the Epilogue, held to be written on the basis of an older tradition, and both the Yahweh speeches, but recognizes the Elihu speeches and chapter xxviii to be interpolations. He discusses the theological background of the book and outlines the course of its argument, with copious quotations of the text, and discusses its contribution to thought and faith. While there is little that is original in this study, it is a useful exposé of the message of the book of Job.   H.H.R.

SUTCLIFFE, E. F., S.J. : *The Old Testament and the Future Life*. (The Bellarmine Series, vol. VIII). 1946. (Burns, Oates and Washbourne, London. Price : 16s. 0d.)

Fr. Sutcliffe's latest contribution to the Bellarmine series is based upon a series of lectures delivered at Heythrop in the scholastic year, 1942-3. After two chapters on Egyptian and Babylonian ideas of the future life, there is an introductory chapter on Hebrew ideas on this topic, and next, studies of eschatology in the Pentateuch and Ecclesiasticus. These are followed by two chapters on Sheol and its inhabitants, and later chapters discuss rewards and punishments after death, purgatory or the intermediate state, the resurrection of the body, the constituents of man in Hebrew thought, and, finally, the eschatology of the extra-canonical books pertaining to Old Testament times.

The students for whom the book is primarily designed will unquestionably find much to interest and inform them in the course of its two hundred attractive and well-printed pages. It may, however, be doubted whether the arrangement of the subject is the best or the clearest imaginable, and there are times when, in the exegesis of the most vital passages, wider reference might have been made to the extensive literature, more particularly to the literature of modern times. It is certainly astonishing that in discussing Job no mention is made of the commentaries by Dhorme, Peters, König and Driver-Gray, and that neither Montgomery nor Charles is quoted apropos of Daniel.   J.M.T.B.

ZIMMERLI, W. : *Le prophéte dans l'Ancien Testament et dans l'Islam*. 1945. (La Mission de Bâle, Lausanne. Price : Fr. 1.25.)

In this brief study we are offered a comparison of Muhammad with the Old Testament prophets. Alike they regarded themselves as charged with the message of God, and acted under a sense of divine constraint, and the term prophet is therefore rightly applied to Muhammad. But prophets may be true or false, and the distinction lies in the content of the message.

The essential message of the Old Testament prophets was the demand for obedience to the will of God. They and Muhammad demanded faith, but by faith they meant yielding that obedience, while he meant the acceptance of his teaching. Moreover, power corrupted his prophetic quality. Hence contrast as well as similarity is to be observed.   H.H.R.

POST-BIBLICAL JUDAISM

BUBER, M. : *Mamre : Essays in Religion.* 1946. (Melbourne University Press in association with Oxford University Press. Price : 12s. 6d.)

> A collection of nine essays in an English translation by Greta Hort, all but one of which originally appeared in German in 1933 and 1935. The last four, which take up two-thirds of the book, have Chassidism as their theme ; so that in the main it is the first five essays (on ' The Faith of Judaism,' ' The Two Centres of the Jewish Soul,' ' Imitatio Dei,' ' Biblical Leadership ' and ' Trust ') which must justify the inclusion of this slender volume in a book-list of the Society for the Study of the Old Testament; and this they undoubtedly do. Indeed, the whole book should be found full of suggestion by all who are concerned for the religious value of the Old Testament and its elucidation in terms of revelation, and not least by those whose attitude to Scripture is thoroughly critical.   A.R.J.

DRAZIN, N. : *History of Jewish Education from* 515 *B.C.E. to* 220 *C.E.* 1940. (The Johns Hopkins Press, Baltimore.)

> This is a useful collection of the meagre materials available for the writing of a history of Jewish education. A tradition in Baba Bathra is interpreted to mean that the Men of the Great Assembly founded higher education, Simon ben Shetah founded secondary education, and Joshua ben Gamala founded primary education. Apart from this there is little on the development of education, but there is a good sketch of the educational system found amongst the Jews in the Tannaitic period—its spirit and ideals, its organization, its content and its methods. The chapter on the education of girls and women includes some special pleading, such as the use of Prov. vi 20 to support the view that girls were educated. It is doubtless true that all parents from the time of Adam and Eve have taught their children some things, but that hardly qualifies them for inclusion in the ranks of educators in the technical sense.   H.H.R.

HERFORD, R. T. : *Pirkē Aboth.* 3rd ed., 1945. (Jewish Institute of Religion, New York.)

> The amount of revision given to this edition does not seem to be considerable—the Scripture references on p. 155 have not been corrected—but the Introduction has been rewritten and rearranged. The section on the purpose and significance of Aboth shows most change, though the view that Aboth formed an appendix to the Mishnah, whose study did not at one time extend beyond Nezikin, is maintained here as in the earlier edition. The author says the book ' is the best which I could produce under the conditions of the present

tim ›.' It is, indeed, an excellent edition, with text, translation and notes embodying a vast amount of learning, and written with a sympathy and understanding that could not be surpassed by a Jewish writer.   H.H.R.

HOLSTIJN, H. J. E. W. : *Oden van Salomo, zangen van rust in den Heere*, with an introduction by J. de Zwaan (Leyden). No date (1942). (Ruys, Zutphen.)

In publishing this book the late Rev. Westerman Holstijn did not aim at a contribution towards the solution of the many vexed problems which beset the famous collection of the Odes. He did not even give a literal translation. But wanting to bring out the spiritual meaning of these songs for his compatriots he offers a metrical free version in Dutch accompanied by very short notes. It helps us to understand the spiritual contents rather than the exact wording. This 'translation' is not based upon the edition of Harris-Mingana but upon the Greek reconstruction of Frankenberg (1911). Its chief value consists in conveying the 'atmosphere' of these remarkable hymns ; the scholar will find it of little use.   W. C. van Unnik.

ODEBERG, H. : *Fariséism och Kristendom*. 2nd ed. 1945. (Gleerup Lund. Price : 5s. 6d.)

This is a brief but penetrating and closely-reasoned account of the differences between Pharisaism and Christianity by the Professor of New Testament exegesis at Lund. He maintains that the conflict is often so represented that Pharisaism is made out to have been quite different from what it in fact was, whereas Christianity is described in terms appropriate to the real Pharisaism. It is wrong to describe Pharisaism as casuistry, as concerned with actions rather than character, as an ethical system based on reward and punishment and the conception of human merit, or as a religion of the letter and not the spirit. It was with Pharisaism of the highest type that Jesus and the early Church came into conflict, a Pharisaism not fundamentally different from that reflected in the Rabbinic literature. The essential contrast is found in two opposed estimates of human freedom and human sinfulness. The treatment throughout is most fresh and stimulating.   G.W.A.

ODEBERG, H. : *Fragen von Metatron, Schekina und Memra*. 1942. (Gleerup, Lund.)

A translation of a brief work of unknown authorship, written in Yiddish, with Hebrew and Aramaic quotations, resting on a wide acquaintance with Jewish literature of all periods down to Nahmanides. Its form is that of a catechism, the first nine questions relating to Metatron, the next three to Shekinah, the next two to Memra, while the final question is a general one relating to all three. The answers summarize the statements found in the literature surveyed about Metatron, Shekinah and Memra, and the whole forms a very useful compendium.   H.H.R.

REICKE, BO : *The Jewish 'Damascus Documents' and the New Testament.* 1946. (Wretman, Uppsala.)

A short study of the parallels to the New Testament found in the *Damaskusschrift*—or Zadokite Work as it is often called. There is no discussion of the date of the texts here, though the author indicates his inclination to a date in the second century B.C. His collection of parallels is full and useful. H.H.R.

TORREY, C. C. : *The Lives of the Prophets.* (Journal of Biblical Literature Monograph Series, vol. I.) 1946. (Society of Biblical Literature and Exegesis, Philadelphia. Price : $1.50, Paper : $1.00.)

In his *Aprocryphal Literature* (see *Book List* for 1946) Torrey for the first time gave this little work its full place in such an Introduction. He has now given us for the first time a critical edition of the Greek text, based on the MS. Q, but corrected by reference to the other witnesses and also conjecturally, together with a translation and a short Introduction. The text in no sense offers a collection of biographies of the prophets, but short traditions supplementary to those contained in the Bible. It has long been known, but too long neglected, though Nestle, Hall and Schermann had attempted to rescue it from neglect. Torrey ascribes its composition to the first century, and postulates a Hebrew original. Now that this easily accessible text is available, the work is likely to receive more attention, and the Society of Biblical Literature is to be congratulated on this excellent opening of its Monograph Series, and the veteran Professor Torrey thanked for giving us this edition. H.H.R.

PHILOLOGY

BECKER, J. H. : *Het Begrip Nefesj en het Oude Testament.* 1942. (N. V. Noord-Hollandsche Uitgevers Maatschappij, Amsterdam. Price : About 8s. 0d.)

A detailed examination of all the occurrences of the term *nephesh* in the Old Testament. The different passages are given both in Hebrew and in a Dutch translation ; and, where necessary, they are accompanied by explanatory notes and comments. The passages are classified (with various subdivisions) under five heads, according as the term denotes (i) life, (ii) the seat of the emotions, desire, etc., (iii) the personality as a whole, (iv) a person, or (v) living beings in general. It is unlikely that anyone who has examined the passages in detail for himself will be satisfied with this (or, for that matter, any other) attempt at an exact classification of this somewhat elusive term ; but the work may be warmly welcomed for its useful marshalling of the data. The author is probably right in finding that the original meaning of the term was that of ' breath,' but he is less convincing in his complete rejection of the view that it also admits the meaning ' neck ' or ' throat.' A.R.J.

BLACK, M. : *An Aramaic Approach to the Gospels and Acts*. **1946.**
(Clarendon Press, Oxford.)

This is a first-class work, of importance not only to the
Neutestamentler, but to all students of Aramaic. The survey
of our knowledge of Palestinian Aramaic of the first Century
A.D., with much attention to syntax and vocabulary, poetic
forms and paronomasia, is a most careful and praiseworthy
piece of work. The reconstruction of an Aramaic text from
the Greek, and the conclusions reached in the realm of New
Testament textual criticism and of the study of the Gospel
sources, are matters for the New Testament scholar, and it
is probable that the acuteness and caution of the writer
will be recognized in that quarter. Here it suffices to note
the author's skill and resource as an Aramaic scholar, and
his contribution to the study of the language.   H.H.R.

CARLSON, E. L. : *Elementary Hebrew*. 1945. Central Seminary Press,
Kansas City. Price : $3.50.)

The author of this work sets out to teach Hebrew by the
' deduction method ' ; that is to say, he takes the student
word by word through a number of chapters of Genesis,
writing out each word in Hebrew and English characters and
analysing it, and he adds grammatical remarks after each
verse or group of verses and eventually also exercises. As
no passage is written out straightforward, a Bible is necessary
unless the student is to be hopelessly befogged in a wilderness
of isolated words ; further, the grammatical terms are often
old-fashioned and the explanations by no means always
correct, so that the ordinary student will be well-advised to
follow normal methods of learning the Hebrew language.
                                                      G.R.D.

LE BARON CARRA DE VAUX : *Tableau des racines sémitiques *(arabe-
hébreu) accompagnée de comparaisons*. 2nd ed. 1944. (Maisonneuve,
Paris.)

This work contains a collection of supposed primitive biliteral
roots, alphabetically arranged and compared with the
ex-hypothesi corresponding Indo-European roots. While most
scholars now agree that there is some basis in fact for the
biliteral theory, it is here pushed to extremes ; for example,
the connection between *kerem* ' vineyard,' *hāram* ' devoted,'
charis ' charm ' and *chraomai* ' I use ' seems far-fetched.
Further the author fails to go back to the primitive sense of
many of the roots that he uses and even treats foreign loan-
words as Semitic if he finds them in the Assyrian, Hebrew
or Arabic vocabulary. The work cannot be safely put into
any student's hands.   G.R.D.

FLEISCH, H. : *Les verbes à allongement vocalique interne en sémitique* 1944. (Université de Paris. Price : Fr. 320.)

The object of Professor Fleisch's study is the origin and force of *qâtala* as a stem or theme in Semitic verbs, applying himself principally to Arabic and Ethiopic examples ; there are none in Accadian and very few in Hebrew, while those in Aramaic are practically all due to Hebrew influence. He agrees with Arabic grammarians that the Arabic form was primarily participative, implying ' action with ' but that it thence acquired an emulative force and thence came to denote *action afficiente* or simple action on an object ; this insistence on the object further begat a conative and causative force, whence its common use with denominative verbs in a transitive and even an intransitive sense was derived. Its final use was intensive, to indicate energy or augmentation of application as distinct from intensity of multiplication which *qattala* expressed. As in Ethiopic this form with lengthened vowel has largely lost its force and become a mere variant of the simple stem. Dr. Fleisch concludes that this, the so-called ' third stem,' was a West-Semitic innovation. This may well be right, but one may doubt the author's other conclusions on these grounds : first, that participation may be subsumed under intensity but intensity cannot be subsumed under participation ; second, that participation is not, while intensity is, apparent in every early use of this stem ; and, third, the lengthening of a vowel in the Semitic languages elsewhere represents not participation but intensity. This therefore is most probably the underlying idea of this stem or theme.

G.R.D.

GERLEMAN, G. : *Contributions to the Old Testament Terminology of the Chase.* 1946. (Gleerup, Lund.)

In this brief work, which is an off-print from the *Bulletin de la Société Royale des Lettres de Lund* (vol. IV, pp. 79-90) the author examines the few hunting terms found in the Old Testament ; the subject is small and there is little to be said on it, but the author makes one interesting point that the Hebrew *pahad* is the Latin *formido* ' scare, hunting mark,' namely many-coloured rags and feathers suspended on a cord with the aid of which game were driven in the desired direction, i.e., towards nets or traps or marksmen. G.R.D.

GIERLICH, A. M., O.P. : *Der Lichtgedanke in den Psalmen, eine terminologisch-exegetische Studie.* (*Freiburger Theologische Studien*, Heft 56). 1940. (Herder, Freiburg in Breisgau. Price : Mk. 4.50.)

This dissertation from the Roman Catholic Faculty of Freiburg in Breisgau is an investigation into the idea of ' light ' in the Psalms. It is divided into a *terminological* and an *exegetical* part, the latter examining the contents of the idea of ' light ' in the Psalms. The *first* part examines in the first place the positive ' light termini ' : *light* and related ideas, both simple and complex, both in narrower and wider meaning ; then follows the examination of negative termini : *darkness* and related ideas, in the same manner as the positive ideas ; and lastly positive-negative termini : ' *shadow* ' and related ideas.

The *second part* systematically works out the results of the first part. These are mostly of a statistical kind, to determine the different words used to express the ideas of light, darkness and shadow. The contents of the ideas are summarized as follows : *light* is a creation of God. It is never deified, but is the most impressive revelation of God's glory, the *kabod*. Further the Psalms use the idea of ' light ' as a symbol for natural, spiritual, and eternal life. The symbol ' light ' is never ' mythologized ' and always used only as comparison. It is widened through the light of God's face, used in the Psalter as symbol of God's life-preserving and life-augmenting good will. This simile is also used without any connection with old Oriental myths of the sun, but taken over from the impression of the light of the sun, merely as comparison. The metaphor also comprehends the idea of happiness.

Darkness too is God's work, used by him in his self-revelation. It is the substance of the underworld, but there is no deification or mythologization of darkness. It is symbol of death.

Shadow is only used as symbol in the Psalms, as symbol of different ideas.

Dr. Gierlich's work is very useful as a survey of the Biblical material. But I think that the work cannot be regarded as carried to its end without the background of the Oriental religions.   A.B.

KELLER, C. A. : *Das Wort OTH als ' Offenbarungszeichen Gottes.'* 1946. (Hoenen, Basel.)

This scholarly and important book offers a semantic study of the word *oth* in the Old Testament. The writer's first conclusion is that the direct or indirect author of an *oth* is almost always God and that the word belongs originally to the religious sphere. The various classes of *othoth* are carefully distinguished and examined. Originally the word meant an oracle-sign through which God revealed himself and it always required a word to explain it. In Hebrew prophecy *oth* could mean either a prophetic action or some wonderful act of God which had been foretold and explained in advance. Certain cult institutions, e.g., the mark of Cain, came to be regarded as permanent media of revelation. So with the ' sign on the hand ' (Deut. vi, 8) and religious symbols like the Ark. In the Deuteronomic literature the signs in Egypt became symbols of the uniqueness of God and of his power in electing and preserving his people. In P we have as *othoth* the rainbow, circumcision, the Passover, the Sabbath, etc., which were guarantees of the order of grace under which Israel lived. In a later period the word tended to lose its religious meaning and to be used in purely secular ways.   N.W.P.

Nat, J. : *Hebreeuwsche Grammatica*, 3rd ed., revised by J. J. Koopmans. 1945. (Brill, Leiden. Price : 22s. 0d.)

Nat, J. : *Oefeningen bij de Hebreeuwsche Grammatica*, 2nd ed., revised by J. J. Koopmans. 1945. (Brill, Leiden. Price : 17s. 0d.)

This work is of interest as presenting a different method of learning Hebrew from that used ordinarily in this country. The Grammar is a systematic one, much less full than Gesenius-Kautzsch, but rather fuller on Accidence than Davidson, and shorter on Syntax than Davidson's *Syntax*. The exercises in the accompanying volume do not follow the order of the Grammar at all closely. At the head of each exercise stand the references to the sections of the Grammar on which it is based, chosen from the Accidence and the Syntax, together with a vocabulary whose words are numbered continuously through the book. Any forms required in the exercise based on sections not yet studied have beside them in the vocabulary the reference to the section where they are explained. At the end of the book there are some continuous passages of Hebrew, followed by a supplementary vocabulary, still numbered continuously, which contains the words in these passages and in the Grammar not included in the previous vocabularies. A Hebrew and Dutch index follows, where instead of the meaning of the words being given the number of the word in the numbered vocabularies is found. This method would seem to involve a maximum amount of needless turning of pages, and some disadvantage in the kangaroo use of a systematic grammar. At the same time it is a real advantage for the student to have a systematic grammar in his hand for reference. The two books are excellently printed, and misprints are very rare.

H.H.R.

Ratschow, C. H. : *Werden und Wirken : eine Untersuchung des Wortes hajah als Beitrag zur Wirklichkeltserfassung des Alten Testaments.* (Beihefte zur Zeitschrift für die alttestamentliche Wissenschaft 70). 1941. (Töpelmann, Berlin.)

The author's ultimate aim is an understanding of the course taken by the history of religion in the Old Testament, and what is more an understanding which goes beyond the historical data and can lay claim to presenting its dogmatic and practical significance : hence the sub-title, ' Beitrag zur Wirklichkeitserfassung des Alten Testaments.' In the first place, however, it is an examination of the word *hayah* ; and in this connection its meaning is defined as going beyond that of ' to become ' and ' to be ' and as really signifying ' to be active ' ; hence the main title of the work, ' Werden und Wirken.' Chapter 1 accordingly deals with ' The significance of the Word *hayah*,' and here the examples of this meaning of the word are marshalled for review. This leads to a second chapter on ' The Content of the Word *hayah* ' (A. Personal Activity ; 1. God's Being, 2. God's Aid, etc. : B. Impersonal Activity ; 1. God and Impersonal Power, 2. Curse, etc.), and a third on ' The Use of the Word *hayah*'

(A. In Blessing and Curse ; B. In Miracle Stories ; C. In the Law), in both of which the conclusions of the first chapter find further illustration and corroboration. The fourth and last chapter is a comprehensive study of ' The History of the Word *hayah*.'

Frequently one cannot escape the feeling that the account given of the history of religion in the Old Testament, although on the whole rightly and impressively presented, has not really been reached through the study of *hayah*, but rather that the content of the word as described has been determined by a conception of this history which has been built up on other grounds. One must recognize, however, that the book nevertheless has many a fine observation to offer in its explanation of individual passages and in its general view of the Old Testament.   O.E.

RÜTHY, A. E. : *Die Pflanze und ihre Teile im biblisch-hebräischen Sprachgebrauch.* 1942. (Francke, Berne.)

This is an interesting and useful work which, though confessedly based largely on Löw's *Flora der Juden* and Dalman's *Arbeit und Sitte*, nevertheless contains many acute observations and several new suggestions. Serious students of the Biblical language will have to take it into account in explaining the often vaguely translated names of plants and their parts.
                                                                  G.R.D.

SKOSS S. L. : *The Hebrew-Arabic Dictionary of the Bible known as Kitāb Yāmi' al-Alfaẓ (Agrōn) or David ben Abraham al-Fāsī the Karaite.* Vols. I and II. 1936-45. (Yale and Oxford.)

Dr. Skoss has put all Hebrew and indeed Arabic scholars in his debt by publishing the important dictionary of Al-fāsi in this magnificent form. Although the author lived before the discovery of the triliteral nature of Semitic roots, so that his work is not always easy to use, those who can find their way about it will find much that is curious but much also that is useful in it ; for example, he knows that Aaron made the molten calf not ' with a graving tool ' (R.V.) but ' in a mould ' (Exod. xxxii, 4) ; and he suggests that Jeremiah's mysterious *Peʸrāt* was not the Euphrates but a wady close by Anathoth (Jer. xiii, 4-7), thus anticipating a suggestion made independently by an English and a German scholar in 1880. The edition, which contains not only the Arabic text in Hebrew characters but also a long introduction, has ample tables and indices and, alas! numerous 'corrections,' perhaps inevitable in a mass of intricate printing of this type. The editor is indeed to be congratulated on the completion of an admirable piece of work which will well repay careful study.   G.R.D.

(Unclassified items received too late for classification)

BUBER, M. : *Moses*. 1947. (East and West Library, Oxford. Price : 12s. 6d.)

> Professor Buber here gives us a study of the life and work of Moses resting on the acceptance of the substance of the tradition of the Pentateuch, though with rejection of the detail. The critical principles of the Wellhausen school are dismissed, and while no other principles are formally presented and defended, the author treats as accretion much that he has no use for. Since he neither accepts the traditional view of the authorship and compilation of the Pentateuch nor any of the modern views that have been proposed, it would have avoided the appearance of arbitrariness if he had given a clear statement of his view on this and the reasons which support it. The making of the Golden Calf is accepted as historical, and the Kenite theory of the source of the divine name YHWH is opposed with vigour. Buber follows the view that the meaning of the name is ' Oh He,' While the reviewer would disagree at many points, he welcomes this treatment of Moses as a historical character. The book rests on a very full acquaintance with scholarly literature, as the notes collected at the end of the volume show, and is written in Professor Buber's fascinating style. H.H.R.

DUCROS, P. : *La Bible et la méthode historique*. 1945. Imprimerie Libournaise. Price :- 3s. 6d.

> A brief, but valuable, study of the historical approach to the Bible, with special reference to the Old Testament, showing the service it has rendered to faith, and its implications for the understanding of the inspiration of the Bible. The author studies the relations between the two Testaments, and offers a defence of the Christian retention of the Old Testament, not merely as a preparation for the New, but as integral to the revelation which reached its climax in the New, together with a brief examination of the authority of the Bible. The whole rests on a thoroughly balanced view, which avoids literalism on the one hand and the neo-allegorical method on the other, and which equally avoids an arid rationalism. In the author's view the authority of the Bible is not the authority of a document, but rather the authority of the God who speaks in the Bible through history and through men, and whose word can only be understood when read in the context through which it came, and especially when tested by the revelation in Christ. H.H.R.

*HYATT, J. P. : *Prophetic Religion*. 1947. (Abingdon Cokesbury Press, New York. Price : $1.75.)

> This is an extremely good study of the seven most important canonical prophets from Amos to Deutero-Isaiah, viewed in relation to the ministry of Jesus. There is little that is original in the interpretation or critical views, but we have good surveys of the vitally important experience of the call of these prophets, of their fundamental criticism of life, of

their view of past and future history, of their attitude to the ritual, of their patriotism, and of their view of God and of sin. The reviewer regrets that Moses is denied the title of prophet, and that the prophetic attitude to the cultus ; interpreted quite so negatively. On the marriage of Hosea Hyatt takes the view that Gomer's lapse was post-marital, while on Ezekiel he follows Matthews in a view akin to Herntrich's. The book is well written, well informed, and well fitted to appeal to the wider audience to which it is addressed, and warmly to be commended. H.H.R.

JANSEN, H. L. : *Die Henochgestalt : eine vergleichende religions-geschichtliche Untersuchung.* 1939. (Dybwad, Oslo. Price : Kr. 10.-)

The thesis of this work is that in the figure of Enoch as presented in the Ethiopic Enoch there are both native and foreign elements. The supramundane Enoch is the presentation in Jewish dress of the Babylonian Ea-Oannes, while the earthly Enoch is a prophet and sage who unites in himself the function of an Israelite prophet of judgement and of weal and that of a Chaldaean wise man and apocalyptist. So, too, the Son of Man of the Book of Enoch is identified with Ea-Oannes. In 1 En. lxxi, 14 Jansen is therefore able to retain the text which identifies Enoch with the Son of Man, instead of arbitrarily emending it with Charles. The author does not discuss the date and composition of the book of Enoch, save to observe in passing that the ideas of the section known as the ' Apocalypse of Weeks ' may rest on those of the book of Daniel, of which they seem to be a development, while he appears to find a fundamental unity in the work instead of distributing it amongst several authors. H.H.R.

KRAEMER, R. : *Schöpfer Himmels und der Erden : Ein Buch vom Ursprung, Lauf und Ziel der Welt.* 1944. (Gotthelf-Verlag, Züricn. Price : 12s. 6d.)

In this book it is claimed that the whole Bible is full of the language of ancient oriental myth, in particular the myth of creation with all the complicated motifs associated witn the Zodiac and the heavenly mountain of God. In the Bible we have the answer to the ultimate questions about the meaning and destiny of the world raised by myth which heathen religion failed to give. The error of heathenism was, not that it lived in the thought-world of myth, but that it sought to control the divine powers. The book is interesting and provocative and is worth reading as a daring theological essay. Its weakness is that it is entirely undocumented, that it frequently goes much beyond the evidence and that it treats myth as though it were unified, whereas it actually exhibits extraordinary diversity, changing its form and content according to time and place, and abounds in obscurities. N.W.P.

LAUHA, A. : *Die Geschichtsmotive in den alttestamentlichen Psalmen*, 1945. (Annales Academiae Scientiarum Fennicae, BLVI, 1. Helsinki. Price : 11s. 0d.)

In this work we have a survey of the unmistakable references to history found in the psalms, arranged in the historical order of the events referred to. For the author's purpose history is conceived in a broad sense, to include myth and legend from the Creation, through the story of the Flood and the Patriarchs to the Exodus, Wandering and Settlement, and then on through the period of the monarchy to the Exile. To the post-exilic history he finds few clear and unmistakable references of the same kind, and two pages suffice for their examination. In the earlier part of the book the author endeavours to establish the dependence of the allusions on separate sources of our present Old Testament books, or on the composite form of narratives as they now stand. The whole is a careful piece of work, leading to no startling conclusions, but presenting a very useful survey, that is not without significance for literary criticism, and particularly for Pentateuchal criticism.   H.H.R.

LOUIS, C. : *The Theology of Psalm VIII : A Study of the Traditions of the Text and the Theological Import.* 1946. (Catholic University of America Press, Washington. Price : $2.25.)

This exhaustive study of Psalm viii offers an excellent survey of all the problems associated with the psalm. It presents the text in parallel columns in Hebrew, in the Septuagint, in Jerome's *juxta Hebraeos* version, and in the new Biblical Institute version. There is a careful examination of the text and of all the emendations that have been proposed, followed by the author's literal interpretation of the psalm and a study of its literary characteristics. He then comes to the focus of his interests in the implied theology of the psalm, which is carefully considered both in itself and in its relation to other passages. The concluding chapters deal with the psalm in Apocryphal and Rabbinical literature, in the New Testament, in the Patristic writers, and in later writers, both Catholic and Protestant. On the authorship of the psalm, the writer accepts the Davidic ascription as a working view, though he does not claim that there is any proof of this. Still less, he maintains, is there proof that David could not have written it. He defends the messianic associations of the psalm, though denying that it can be considered a *locus Christologicus* in any strict sense. He shows a wide acquaintance with literature on the psalm, and altogether presents a most valuable study.   H.H.R.

MOWINCKEL, S. : *Zur Frage nach dokumentarischen Quellen in Josua* 13-19. 1946. (Dybwad, Oslo. Price : Kr. 3.00.)

In this short work Mowinckel presents his reasons for rejecting the views of Alt and Noth, which he carefully examines, and argues that the chapters were composed by the author of P on the basis of tradition, and therefore come from the post-exilic period. He holds that in the period of the Judges there was a ten tribe system, and that the twelve tribe system does not antedate the time of David. The character of the lists in these chapters differs from that of administrative lists known from other sources, and in particular Mowinckel finds the treatment of Ephraim and Manasseh reveals the hand of a writer who regarded them as belonging to Samaria and the schismatic Samaritans. He finds that the author was acquainted with Judg. i, but otherwise denies his use of documentary sources. H.H.R.

MERCATI, G. : *Miscellanea Giovanni Mercati*, vol. 1. (Studi e Testi, 121.) (Bibbia-Letteratura Cristiana Antica.) 1946. (Bibliotheca Apostolica Vaticana, Vatican City. Price : Lr. 2,600.)

This volume contains twenty-three articles, covering Biblical and patristic subjects. The principal articles of interest to the Old Testament scholar are by A. Sperber, on ' The Codex Vaticanus,' listing cases where in 2 Sam. LXX[B] represents the Hebrew of the parallel text in Chronicles, cases where LXX[B] has doublets giving the text of Samuel and of Chronicles and a series of duplicated renderings of longer passages ; by R. Weber, on ' Les interpolations du livre de Samuel dans les mss. de la Vulgate,' giving 113 interpolations with MS. evidence and its evaluation, and reaching the conclusion that they are marginal notes later incorporated in the text ; by U. Cassuto, on ' L'ordinamento del libro di Ezechiele,' dealing with the structure and arrangement of the book of Ezekiel ; by F. M. Abel, on ' Simon de la tribu de Bilga,' arguing that, following the O. Lat., in 2 Macc. iii, 4, *Simon of the tribe of Benjamin* should be read *Simon of the priestly class of Bilga* ; by J. M. Vosté, on ' La Pešittā de Mossoul et la revision catholique des anciennes versions orientales de la Bible,' giving a long account of the origin and history of the Mosul edition and the discussion of principles which preceded its appearance. Other articles which touch our field are by A. Vaccari, on ' In margine al commento di Teodoro Mopsuesteno ai Salmi,' and by B. Bischoff, on ' Neue Materialien zum Bestand und zur Geschichte der altlateinischen Bibelübersetzungen.' H.H.R.

RIESENFELD, H. : *Jésus transfiguré*. 1947. (Munksgaard, Copenhagen. Price : Kr. 12.-)

The last third of this book is devoted to the study of the New Testament narratives of the Transfiguration and the analysis of the motifs they contain, while the first two-thirds are devoted to the study of the Old Testament background of these motifs. The author brings much learning and great ingenuity to the study, and relates everything to the Feast of Tabernacles and the enthronement festival, to which an eschatological character belonged from the start. He holds that the old ritual had long disintegrated, but that its ideas lived on and were spiritualized, though they were not always understood by the Evangelists. To the reviewer Divine kingship and its related ideas seen to be pushed rather to extremes and to be given an excessive rôle in the interpretation of the Old Testament. Nevertheless the book is of importance, if only because of its full references to literature, and its author's enthusiasm for his thesis. It is likely to be of more importance for the Old Testament scholar than for his colleague in the New Testament field.　　　H.H.R.

STEINMUELLER, J. E., and SULLIVAN, K. : *A Companion to the Old Testament*. 1946. (Wagner, New York, and Herder, London. Price : $4.50.)

A simple handbook for Catholic readers, dealing briefly with the inspiration of the Old Testament, its canon and text, and archaeology, followed by a brief survey in five chapters of the history covered by the Old Testament in the Roman canon, a single chapter on the prophets, a chapter on Hebrew poetry, largely devoted to its technique and forms, a chapter on the book of Job, and a final chapter on Wisdom. The space devoted to the book of Job seems disproportionate, and there is some lack of balance in the chapter on the prophets, when a single paragraph suffices for their moral and spiritual message and forty pages are devoted to messianic prophecy. The authors curiously state that there are thirty-eight books in the Protestant Old Testament. The Bibliography contains none but Catholic titles, save in the section on archaeology. Despite its limitations, if offers a useful, but uncritical, survey of several sides of Old Testament study, and at several points it has material that is of use to other than Catholic readers.　　　H.H.R.

1948

The Book List is prepared for the Society by the following Committee : Prof. G. W. Anderson, Mgr. J. M. T. Barton, Dr. David Daube, Professors G. R. Driver, A. R. Johnson, N. W. Porteous, O. S. Rankin, Miss B. K. Rattey, Rev. J. N. Schofield, Professors N. H. Snaith and H. H. Rowley (Editor). In addition, Canon H. Danby has kindly supplied some of the notices. The Editor has once more to acknowledge, with thanks, help received from continental scholars, and especially for notes on books which are not available in this country. On this occasion help has been given by Professors W. Baumgartner, O. Eissfeldt and Th. C. Vriezen. Every effort has been made to include notes on wartime publications not included in the 1946 and 1947 Book List, but some books have eluded the Editor and his correspondents, while there are doubtless some whose titles are unknown to him. It is hoped that the three post-war Book Lists will acquaint members reasonably fully with the work which has appeared in our field, and future issues will, with rare exceptions, contain notes only on quite recent books. There must, however, always be some time lag before foreign books are both known and secured in this country. In doubtful cases the Editor has erred on the side of the inclusion of books which are on the fringe of our field, or of secondary importance, as it seemed particularly desirable at a time when books cross frontiers so reluctantly to give the fullest knowledge of what has appeared. It is regretted that the rising cost of printing has necessitated some increase in the price of copies of the Book List beyond the one free copy issued to all members of the Society.

Prices of foreign books, where known, are given either in foreign currency or in the English equivalent actually charged. In some cases variations in exchange would affect the latter to-day.

Titles to which an asterisk (*) is prefixed are recommended for inclusion in school libraries.

H. H. ROWLEY.

GENERAL

AMANN, E. (ed. by) : *Dictionnaire de théologie catholique*. Tome XV, 1. (Tabaraud-Trincarella). 1946. (Letouzey & Ané, Paris. Price : £2 7s. 6d.)

The latest half-volume of this excellent work contains few articles of direct interest to an *Alttestamentler*. There is a short but valuable summary of essential information in the article " Talmud " by the veteran rabbinist, J. Bonsirven. " Testament (ancien et nouveau)" by the editor is mainly an index to other articles such as " Versions de la Sainte Ecriture " (not yet published), " Canon des livres saints " (t. ii, col. 1582-93), and " Marcion " (t. ix, col. 2012 ff). " Théodore de Mopsueste " contains sections on that writer's exegetical methods, scriptural Canon, and doctrine of original sin. It is to be regretted that the article " Théologie " (160 columns) is mainly concerned with the post-Augustinian centuries, presumably because the *Supplément* to the *Dictionnaire de la Bible* must eventually contain a full treatment of Biblical theology. " Thomas d'Aquin," in its scriptural section, the work of C. Spicq, has some interesting details on Aquinas's knowledge, usually quite rudimentary, of the Biblical languages. Apparently he had learnt the Hebrew alphabet, knew something of the metathesis of sibilants, and appreciated in some slight degree the use of the Hebrew tenses. But his etymologies, more often incorrect than exact, are all borrowed. " Tobie " by A. Clamer sets out clearly and unmistakably the objections to the book's historical character, but argues that they are not conclusive against a " noyau historique." The doctrinal content of the book receives full attention. Under " Trente (Concile de)" there is a brief reference to the fourth session (8th April, 1546 : Denzinger-Umberg Enchiridion paragraphs 783-6) on the Canon of Scripture, and the position of the Latin Vulgate.   J.M.T.B.

Bijbelsch Woordenboek. 1941-7. (Romen & Zonen, Roermond. Price : Fl. 18.90.)

The publication of this Bible Dictionary, produced by the co-operation of six Dutch and three Flemish Roman Catholic scholars, was begun during the war and not completed until times were more favourable. It is the first great scholarly work in the Biblical field to be issued by the Dutch Roman Catholics, and it testifies to the growing interest in Bible study amongst Roman Catholic theologians and laymen. In many respects it is an excellent work, clear, well-illustrated, and giving almost all that one could expect in such a work. The Bibliography is full, including work by non-Catholic authors, though there are some gaps. The articles are popularly written, in accordance with the character of the work, and they acquaint the reader with the divergent views on questions where special doctrinal points are not involved, though of course tradition plays its part. On the whole the work can be warmly commended as a well-informed, trustworthy, and in many respects able guide.   Th.C.V.

BRAUN, F. M. : *Les Études Bibliques d'après l'Encyclique de S.S. Pie XII " Divino Afflante Spiritu."* 1946. (Librairie de l'Université, Fribourg, Suisse. Price : 6s. 6d.)

The rector of the University of Fribourg chose for his inaugural address on 15th November, 1946, a subject which gave room for a running commentary on some of the main lessons of the Encyclical *Divino Afflante Spiritu* of 30th September, 1943. The Pope was careful to insist upon the importance of Eastern languages, on the work of textual critics, on the collaboration of the laity in biblical studies, and on the creation of a solidly based biblical theology. On this last point the author draws attention to the Göttingen *Neue Testament Deutsch*, to Gerhard Kittel's *Theologisches Wörterbuch zum Neuen Testament*, to the Basle series of *Abhandlungen*, and to the Neuchâtel *Cahiers théologiques de l'actualite protestante*. The practical side of preparation for preaching the word of God is not forgotten. It may not be out of place to mention a work, here enthusiastically commended, that might otherwise be overlooked.—R. Sugranyes de Franch, *Études sur le droit palestinien à l'époque évangélique* (Fribourg, 1946). J.M.T.B

BRAUN, F. M. : *L'œuvre du Père Lagrange, étude et bibliographie.* 1943. (Editions de l'Imprimerie St. Paul, Fribourg en Suisse.)

This is in no sense a definitive or complete life of the founder of the Dominican school of biblical studies and archaeology in Jerusalem. It is the personal tribute of a devoted disciple, a reminder of some characteristics of Lagrange's life and teaching, and, above all, a tolerably exhaustive bibliography of his writings. The task of cataloguing the 1786 items has not been easy owing to Lagrange's habit of frequently not signing his contributions to the *Revue Biblique* and other periodicals. Even so, as an incomplete record, this digest of one man's literary activity is truly amazing, when it is remembered that many of the entries are long reviews, running in some cases to twenty or thirty pages of the *Revue Biblique*, and that these were usually written in the evenings, when the more important hours for reading, lecturing and writing of books were over ! As M. Chaine has pointed out in his delightful contribution to *Mémorial Lagrange*, the great man was not accessible at all times, his mornings being guarded very strictly against interruptions. But he was far from being a solitary, enjoyed good company and his evening game of chess, and was an intensely lovable and sympathetic character. The bibliography, while in general remarkably accurate, has one amusing little slip under item 966, the well-known Oxford *Studies in the Synoptic Problem*, published in 1911 and reviewed by Lagrange in RB, XX, pp. 454-59. The editor was Dr. William Sanday, Lady Margaret Professor of Divinity, and this group of facts appears in the list (and index) simply as " Lady Margaret "! J.M.T.B.

BRING, R., FRIDRICHSEN, A., LINDROTH, HJ., LINTON, O., NYGREN, A., SJÖBERG, E. : *En bok om Bibeln.* 1947. (Gleerups, Lund.)

This book contains eleven essays by a group of Swedish exegetes and theologians dealing with the significance of the Bible and the relation between the Old and New Testaments in the light of recent critical work and from the point of view of the Lutheran renaissance in Sweden. Only one essay deals exclusively with the Old Testament, that of. E. Sjöberg : ' The History of Israel's Religion and the Revelation of God in the Old Testament '—a sober and judicious survey. Recent developments in the study of the Bible and the modern attitude to it are ably summarized by O. Linton ; and A. Fridrichsen contributes two stimulating papers on ' The Way of the Bible and the Way to the Bible,' and ' Jesus, John and Paul.' Hj. Lindroth and R. Bring represent the interests of the Church historian and the Luther specialist, respectively. A. Nygren's three essays deal with the problems of the relation between the Old and New Testaments, revelation and Scripture, and the critical and devotional uses of the Bible. The book has a quite remarkable unity of outlook, combining insistence on the necessity of a strictly historical study of the Bible with a conviction of its unity. The authors accept with gratitude many of the findings of ' liberal ' scholarship though they depart from its theological position ; and they are as firmly opposed to ' mystical ' interpretation as they are to fundamentalism. All the essays are marked by sane scholarship, lucid argument, and balanced judgement. G.W.A.

(BROCH, O.) : *Festskrift til Professor Olaf Broch på hans 80-Årsgad,* edited by C. S. Stang, E. Krag and A. Gallis! (Avhandlinger utgitt av det Norske Videnskaps-Akademi i Oslo, Hist.-Fil.Kl.) 1947. (Dybwad, Oslo. Price : Kr. 20.00.)

In this collection of linguistic, literary, historical and scientific essays there is but one of interest to the Semitic scholar. This is H. Birkeland's paper on ' The Syriac Phonematic Vowel Systems,' in which he compares the Nestorian and Jacobite vowel systems and tries to get behind them to proto-Aramaic and proto-Semitic. The author modestly confesses that he may have made mistakes, but is seeking a new method of approach to the problems. The paper is very technical, and the subject is one that would better be studied in a wider setting before conclusions about proto-Aramaic and proto-Semitic could be drawn. Moreover we must beware of assuming that a single vowel sign had only a single value for pronunciation. H.H.R.

BROOKS, B. A. : *A Classified Bibliography of the Writings of George Aaron Barton.* (Supplementary Studies, No. 4, of the Bulletin of the American Schools of Oriental Research.) 1947. (New Haven. Price : $0.50.)

This is a useful list of the technical books and articles of the late G. A. Barton—with the exception of encyclopaedia articles—arranged in order of date and also according to their subject matter. It should serve to rescue many of that well-known scholar's articles from neglect, and should prove useful to many research students and scholars.   H.H.R.

COPPENS, J. : *Miscellanées Bibliques*, VII-X (Bulletin d'Histoire et d'Exégèse de l'Ancien Testament, No. 16). 1943. (Bijbelsch Seminarie, Louvain.)

Here are four brief studies dealing with (a) Psa. cx, **7**, where Coppens reads *ḥḥyl bdrk yšt* and finds the sense ' The army stands ready in the way ' ; (b) Gen. iii, 22, which is held to yield the sense ' Behold Adam and whosoever will be born from him will have to experience good and ill ' ; (c) the location of Paradise, which is placed far in the east ; and (d) the number of wonderful trees in the Garden of Eden, where the author rejects the view that the Hebrew for the tree of life is collective. Two of these studies are written in French and two in Flemish.   H.H.R.

COPPENS, J. : *Miscellanées Bibliques* XI-XVII (Bulletin d'Histoire et d'Exégèse de l'Ancien Testament, No. 20). 1947. (Desclée de Brouwer, Bruges. Price : Fr. 10.)

Here are collected two studies adducing Ras Shamra evidence bearing on the interpretation of Psa. cx, **3**, 6b (reading *rabbîm* for *rabbāh*), Psa. lxxxii, 7, and Ex. vii, 19 (where the concluding words are referred to the sap of trees and springs of water) ; a note on Ex. xi, 1 (where *kallāh* is read for *kālāh*, and the sense ' as a bride is sent forth '—cf. *shillûḥîm*—is obtained) ; a criticism of Dubarle's *Les sages d'Israël* (cf. Book List 1947, p.26) in so far as it treats of the Paradise story ; a criticism of some recent British exegetical tendencies, followed by a further warning against the dangers of the allegorical method ; and finally a statement of sound canons of exegesis. H.H.R.

(EISSFELDT, O.) : *Festschrift Otto Eissfeldt zum* 60. *Geburtstage* 1. *September*, 1947, *dargebracht von Freunden und Verehren*, ed. by J. Fück. 1947. (Niemeyer, Halle. Price : Rm. 24.00.)

The fourteen essays in this volume reflect in part the wide range of Professor Eissfeldt's interests and researches. A. Alt reviews the evidence for three sites between Baalbek and Palmyra (Barkusa, Nazala, and Danaba). F. Altheim describes and discusses an inscription found in Afghanistan shortly before the war, of which the script and, in part, the language are Aramaic. W. Baumgartner outlines the problems and material dealt with in the compilation of the Aramaic part of the forthcoming *Lexicon in Veteris Testamenti Libros*. A. Bentzen contributes ' Der Tod des Beters in den Psalmen ' —a brief and pointed comment on the debate between Mowinckel and Widengren. C. Brockelman writes notes on Ugaritic and on Phoenician inscriptions. Topographical and historical questions arising out of Procksch's emendation of Zechariah ix, 1, are investigated in detail by K. Elliger. J. Friedrich discusses Greek and Latin influence in Phoenician and Punic inscriptions. Teachers of Hebrew will find much of interest in J. Fück's ' Gedanken zur Methodik des hebräischen Unterrichts.' M. Haller deals with the relation of act and speech in magic and cult. A. R. Johnson contributes a careful study of the use of *panim* in the Old Testament. P. Kahle's article sums up with lucidity and vigour his views on the principles of Septuagint study. M. Noth argues for the secondary nature of two varying traditions of the site of the crossing of the Red Sea—Lake Sirbonis and the Gulf of Akaba. H. H. Rowley, discussing interpretations of Amos vii, 14f., maintains that the syntactical evidence is inconclusive and that on general grounds the rendering of R.V. is to be preferred. W. Rudolph contributes textcritical notes on Judges. The bibliography of Eissfeldt's works is compiled by R. Sellheim.   G.W.A.

Hebrew Union College Annual, XX. 1947. (Cincinnati. Price : $3.00.)

This volume is dedicated to Morgenstern, who contributes the first article, on Chanukkah. Its immediate antecedent is the Syrian Festival of Baal Shamem, culminating in the New Year's Day ; hence the fire rites. But there is evidence of a festival of seven days, opening with a fast on the 24th of the 9th month, from at least Jeremiah to at least Ezra (Nehemiah ix, 1f., and x, 29-31, belong between Ezra x, 14 and 15, and 16a and b). The 24th became the 25th through a change in the reckoning of the day in the 4th or 3rd century. The relation between Chanukkah and the Asif-Festival and its successor, Sukkot, is investigated ; also the nature of allied festivals such as the Moslem 'Ašûra Day and the Festivals of the Cross and St. Barbara. Syrian influences on the New Testament are suggested.—Taeubler gives an ingenious explanation of Cushan-Rishataim in Judges iii.—Patai uses African installation rites, adopted from the Near East, to throw light on the Bible. From what he says it would follow that the anointing of Saul by Samuel and his confirmation by oracle formed part of one procedure. He might have mentioned that the idea of death and re-birth of the king survived in Pal. Bikkurim 65c.— Landsberger shows that the Mal'ak was wingless, and so was the earliest Christian messenger of God. But the Old Testament knows winged beings between God and man, some with an otherwise human shape. Under Greek influence, this type becomes the winged angel in its later sense. The messenger angel first receives wings in Christian art, ca. 400, but even here there are Jewish adumbrations.—Sonne brilliantly argues that the Dura paintings follow a coherent plan. It rests on the triads Torah, Prophets, Hagiographa and Torah, priesthood, kingdom, the emphasis on the second being anti-Christian. On this basis, he is able to re-interpret the individual panels ; e.g., the execution of Joab stands for the end of Rome. Of particular interest is the discovery of two cycles in each Register, Moses and Jacob in A, Aaron and Samuel in B, historical kingdoms and eschatological kingdom in C.— Guttman discusses the Talmudic attitude to miracles : their influence on law declined because of the Christian danger.— Werner's study on Hellenism and Judaism in early Christian music is fascinating. But is it quite impossible that I Cor. xiv, 34, was directed against Gnostic practices ? There are other interesting contributions, outside the scope of this Book List.
                                                D.D.

*HOOKE, S. H. : *What is the Bible ?* 1948. (S.C.M. Press, London.
Price : 2s. 6d.)

> Much wisdom has been packed into this little book, which
> briefly reviews the character and contents of the Old and New
> Testaments, and shows how intimately they belong together
> and why. The record is first looked at as the deposit of
> experience and then in the concluding chapters as the vehicle
> of revelation given by divine inspiration through fallible
> human personalities. The difficult question of miracle is
> treated in the final chapter, where the Resurrection of Jesus is
> treated as an inner experience rather than an external fact,
> and in the light of this other Biblical miracles interpreted as
> born of the writers' imperfect knowledge of Nature. The
> prophets are perhaps over-assessed and Moses under-assessed.
> Yet as a whole the book is likely to be of the utmost help to
> bewildered and inquiring minds, and should be of particular
> use in schools—and much more widely.   H.H.R.

VAN HOONACKER, A., and COPPENS, J. : *Miscellanées Bibliques*, III-VI.
(Bulletin d'Histoire et d'Exégèse de l'Ancien Testament, No. 12).
1941. (Bijbelsch Seminarie, Louvain.)

> The first of these four short studies is a posthumous publication
> of van Hoonacker's, defending the rendering of Am. vii, 14,
> by the present tense : ' I am not a prophet.' The remaining
> studies are all by Professor Coppens. Of these one deals with
> the pericope Ex. iv, 24-26, where the writer would attach
> the first verse to the preceding narrative and make it refer
> to the threat to Pharaoh, and not to Moses ; the second
> assails the view that work is regarded as cursed in Gen.
> iii, 19 ; while the last deals with the sin in the Garden of
> Eden, examining the views of van Oudenrijn on this subject,
> and offering his own. It deals briefly with the sin, the location
> of the Garden, the tree of life, the serpent, and Adam's rib,
> to some of which questions the author has returned more fully
> in later publications.   H.H.R.

Kernmomenten der antieke beschaving en haar moderne beleving. 1947.
(" Ex Oriente Lux." Leiden.)

> This book is No. 7 of the *memoires* of the Oriental Society
> ' Ex Oriente Lux ' of Leiden, founded in 1933, and it contains
> an account of the work of the Society for the ten years to
> 1943 by A. A. Kampman. The remainder of the volume is a
> symposium on ' nuclear ' periods in ancient near-eastern
> civilization. B. A. van Proosdij contributes an introduction
> on memory and imagination in the growth of ancient history,
> and a general article on the art of story telling in the ancient
> orient. A. de Buck writes an introduction to the Egyptian
> background of the ' Dialogue of the Man Weary of Life.'
> There are two articles on Israel : one by Th. C. Vriezen on the
> conquest of suffering, and the other by I. L. Seeligmann
> on the biblical, hellenistic, and talmudic phases in the growth
> of Jewish historical consciousness. A. A. Kampman also
> writes on Hittite fortifications ; F. M. Th. Böhl on the Gilga-
> mesh epic in old Sumerian ; P. van der Meer on the Agade
> period ; J. H. Kramers on the message of Iran's magi for

east and west ; W. Van Os under the general title of Archaeological Interpretation writes on the doubling of figures in
ancient oriental drawing ; and B. H. Stricker on the Reynst
collection of Egyptian antiquities. The book is well illustrated.

J.N.S.

(LINDBLOM, J.) : *Svensk exegetisk årsbok* XII (Lindblom Festskrift),
ed. by A. Fridrichsen. 1947. (Wretmans Boktryckeri A.-B.,
Uppsala. Price : Kr. 10.00.)

Most of the Old Testament contributions to this Festskrift
deal with (a) Ueberlieferungsgeschichte or (b) divine kingship.
(a) I. Engnell in an essay on prophecy and tradition replies
to Mowinckel's criticism of his position. S. Mowinckel himself
discusses 2 Sam. vii, from the standpoint of the history of
tradition, attacking the attempts at analysis made by literary
critics, and contending that the story is an aetiological legend
(explaining why David did not build the Temple), which arose
in circles connected with the Temple prophets. H. S. Nyberg,
in substantial agreement with Pedersen (*Israel III-IV*) argues
for the unity of Numbers xvi f. (b) A. Bentzen defends the
view that there is a real connexion between the older concept
of kingship and the later idea of the Son of Man. Bo Reicke
expounds Mic. vii, as a liturgical text dealing with the suffering
and restoration of the king, and so seeks to justify its use as a
' messianic ' text. In opposition to the Uppsala school, A.
Lauha of Helsingfors argues that there is a clear difference
between the Old Testament conception of kingship and that
prevalent in the ancient east, since in Israel kingship is
historical, not mythical, in origin, and both kingship and
kings are criticized.

Other subjects are also represented. C. M. Edsman demonstrates the continuity of typological exegesis in Sweden before
and after the Reformation, and discusses recent work on the
' theological ' interpretation of Scripture. G. Gerleman seeks
to show that Ezk. xxxviii f. are dependent on the textual
tradition represented by LXX and Sam. in Num. xxiv, 7.
I. Hylander discusses faith-righteousness in the Old Testament.
E. Sjöberg, in a careful exegetical study, supports the traditional
interpretation of Isa. i, 18. There are also essays by Scandinavian scholars on New Testament subjects, and a bibliography
of Lindblom's writings. All are written in Swedish, Danish,
or Norwegian. There is also a supplement in German by
Bultmann on exegetical problems in 2 Corinthians.

G.W.A.

(LÖW, I.) : *Semitic Studies in Memory of Immanuel Löw*, edited by
A. Scheiber. 1947. (Kertész Könyvnyomda Karcag, Budapest.)

This large Memorial Volume, published by the Alexander
Kohut Memorial Foundation, contains some fifty contributions, several appreciating the personality and work of
Immanuel Löw, and the others ranging over a wide variety
of subjects. Most of the essays are written in Hungarian or
in Hebrew, but there are some in English, French and German.
Of articles directly concerned with the Old Testament there
are four. M. Bernáth writes in Hungarian on ' The conception
of the " Great Beyond " in the Bible,' arguing that while
the Old Testament is in general silent on the question of the

Future Life, since it is concerned with the nation rather than with the individual, Job xxxviii, 17, points to a belief in it ; S. Löwinger writes in Hungarian on ' Nebuchadnezzar's Dream in the Book of Daniel,' suggesting that it represented a review of the Assyrian dynasty of Sargon (gold), Sennacherib (silver), Esarhaddon (bronze), Ashurbanipal (iron) and Shamash-shumukin (clay), and was concerned with the question as to whether Evil-Merodach or Neriglissar should be chosen to succeed Nebuchadnezzar ; R. Patai writes in English on ' Biblical and Rabbinical Data to the " Culture Pattern ",' adducing some Jewish traditions which, though late, he holds to be relevant to support the ideas of the ' Myth and Ritual ' school, while denying that the Israelites identified the king with the god, or that there is evidence that the psalms to which appeal is made were ever used at Sukkoth ; and T. H. Gaster offers ' Some Emendations in the Text of the Bible ' in an essay in which more than a score of passages (more than half in the Psalms) are briefly considered. Several of the essays deal with post-Biblical Judaism, and the whole volume forms a worthy memorial to a distinguished scholar. H.H.R.

(NOTE : For abstracts of the articles by M. Bernáth and S. Löwinger, I am indebted to Mr. P. R. Weis. H.H.R.)

MOWINCKEL, S., and MESSEL, N. : *Det gamle testamente : det senere profeter*. 1944. (H. Aschehoug, Oslo.)

This is vol. III of a Norwegian translation of the Old Testament with introductions and concise commentaries. Vol. 1 (*Loven eller de fem Mosebøker*, by Michelet, Mowinckel and Messel) is dated 1929/30, and vol. II (*De tidligere profeter*, by Michelet and Mowinckel) 1935/6. The purpose of the work is to provide for a wider circle than that of Old Testament specialists a rendering into good modern Norwegian and a scholarly exposition, and to show the relevance and abiding value of the Old Testament from the Christian standpoint. The translation is well set out, the divisions and the analysis of the material clearly indicated, and the poetry is printed as such. Messel is responsible for the work on *Ezekiel*. The remainder of the volume is by Mowinckel. It is difficult briefly to appraise this comprehensive work of more than 800 pages. Of particular interest, however, is the general introduction, in which Mowinckel gives a vigorously written account of the history of the prophetic movement, the teaching of the classical prophets, the rise of apocalyptic, and (from the traditio-historical standpoint) the growth of the prophetic books. Of interest, too, are his remarks on the Christian interpretation of the Old Testament. In the commentaries which are models of brevity, the text is expounded without citation of opposing views. G.W.A.

MURPHY, R. T. : *Père Lagrange and the Scriptures*. 1946. (The Bruce Publishing Company, Milwaukee. Price : $3.75.)

This book is, in great part, the translation of *L'œuvre exégétique et historique du R. P. Lagrange*, a symposium published in 1935 by Bloud and Gay. The work of the great Dominican is divided between five scholars, each a specialist in his own subject, of whom J. Chaine deals with the Old Testament and Semitic studies in general, L. Venard with the New Testament and Christian origins, G. Bardy with the Hellenistic milieu, E. Magnin with the comparative history of religions, and G. Guitton with the influence of Père Lagrange. To these studies the translator has added a short memorial as an old pupil of St. Étienne, in which he pays tribute to Lagrange's versatility, and simple and childlike character. A characteristic photograph serves as frontispiece, and on the cover is a reproduction of the familiar, not altogether legible, signature.   J.M.T.B.

ROBERT, A. (ed. by) : *Supplément au Dictionnaire de la Bible* (formerly edited by the late L. Pirot) Fasc. XX (Inscriptions—Israël). 1947. (Letouzey & Ané, Paris. Price : 8s. 0d.)

This fascicle of about 250 columns of rather small type (which is apt to be wearying to the eyes after prolonged reading) contains some of the most valuable articles so far published in this supplement to the huge *Dictionnaire de la'Bible* formerly edited by the late F. Vigouroux. The article " Inspiration et inerrance " by G. Courtaude, S.J., is a clear, if not very original, statement of the present position in the Catholic schools. " Interprétation (Histoire de l')" has very rightly been handed over to a group of experts. Jewish exegesis is handled by J. Bonsirven, S.J., patristic exegesis by G. Bardy, medieval exegesis in East and West by M. Jugie, A.A., and C. Spicq, O.P., respectively ; the modern period, as regards the Old Testament, by A. Robert. In the last-named section a full column is justly reserved for the great name of Richard Simon, whose pioneer work is very fully discussed in the *Dictionnaire de théologie catholique*, t. XIV, 2, col. 2094—2118. " Isaïe (le livre de)" is the subject of a complete introduction by A. Feuillet, P.S.S. R. de Vaux, O.P., begins what promises to be an important study of " Israël (peuple d')" ; the present fascicle prints no more than a study of the pre-Mosaic period.   J.M.T.B.

WILLOUGHBY, H. R. : *The Study of the Bible To-day and To-morrow.* 1947. (The University of Chicago Press, Chicago. Price : $6.00.)

A collection of twenty-four essays, sponsored by the Chicago Society for Biblical Research and dealing with a wide range of biblical subjects. The essays, many of which are by leading American scholars, are divided into two groups, those which present broad general surveys of certain areas of interest, and those which offer special studies of a number of outstanding questions. As one might expect, the essays vary in quality, but on the whole the level is high ; and it is a special merit of the volume that attention has been given to intertestamental studies and current trends. All in all, therefore, it may be warmly welcomed as one which should be placed in the hands of every potential research student as both a challenge and a guide.   A.R.J.

ARCHAEOLOGY

ADAMS, J. McK. : *Ancient Records and the Bible.* 1946. (Broadman Press, Nashville.)

A useful readable survey of the archaeological evidences in their bearing on the historical narratives of the Old Testament by the late professor of Biblical archaeology in the southern Baptist Theological Seminary, Louisville, Kentucky. Well illustrated and accurate, though with some misprints which should be corrected in another edition. The book suffers from an attempt to correlate too closely external archaeological finds with the Bible in an attempt to prove the integrity of the Biblical narratives, but it is not in any way obscurantist nor does it torture archaeology on a Procrustean bed. It can be confidently recommended as an introduction to the use of archaeology in Biblical study.   J.N.S.

*ALBRIGHT, W. F. : *Archaeology and the Religion of Israel.* 2nd edtion, 1946. (Johns Hopkins Press, Baltimore. $2.25.)

This edition has been photographically reproduced from the first (cf. Book List 1946, p.38), but a large number of changes have been made, though without disturbing the page numbers. About a hundred lines have been re-set and the chronology has been revised and additional dates given.   H.H.R.

Annual of the American Schools of Oriental Research, vol. xxiv (1944-45). 1947. (New Haven.)

This volume is devoted to the 1011 seal impressions on the Nuzi tablets, discovered during the first season of excavations at Yaghlan Tepe, and now housed in the Oriental Institute at Chicago. The author, Dr. Edith Porada, groups the impressions under xxvii heads, describes them, and gives a good photographic representation of each. She then discusses the relation of the material to earlier glyptic groups, the iconography of the seal impressions, and the amount of Mitanni legacy in them. There is an index of the names of the seal-owners and four plates of line drawings, and the whole is produced in the excellent way that characterises all the publications of the American Schools of Oriental Research.   J.N.S.

BÖHL, F. M. TH. : *King Hammurabi of Babylon in the setting of his time.* 1946. (North Holland Publishing Company, Amsterdam. Price : Fl. 1.10.)

This small pamphlet of 28 pages gives an admirable summary of all that is known of Hammurabi, King of Babylon ; for this purpose the author utilizes not only all the old material, including the nine new letters to the well-known governor of Larsa published in 1943, but also the correspondence found at Mâri on the middle Euphrates and now being published by Professor Dossin and the Abbé Jean. The date to which he tentatively assigns Hammurabi is 1704-1662 B.C., the latest yet suggested, while adding the warning that " for the present we shall have to be content with stating that the greater part of the reign of Hammurabi is to be placed after rather than before the year 1700." He also refuses to identify " Amraphel " with Hammurabi of Babylon but, following Gelb, prefers Hammurabi prince of Aleppo, while suggesting that the r may be an error for t in "Amraphel " and that the person meant is *Amût-pî-el* prince of Qaṭnah on the Orontes ; in any case, Abram pursued "Amraphel " not eastwards but northwards (Gen. xiv, 15). This little work is full of interest both to the Assyriologist and to the Biblical scholar who ought by no means to miss it.   G.R.D.

BONKAMP, B. : *Die Bibel im Lichte der Keilschriftforschung.* 1939. (Visarius, Recklinghausen.)

A learned attempt, written from the Catholic standpoint, to demonstrate both the importance of all the cuneiform material (with translations of the most important texts) and, at the same time, the essential independence of the Bible. In part it offers more than the title leads one to expect, in particular the origin of the alphabet and Babylonian cuneiform. In part, however, it offers less in that it breaks off with the Persian period, and leaves the religious texts and myths almost untouched. There is detailed treatment of the Creation, the Flood, the Amarna Age and the royal inscriptions. The author is familiar up to a point with the original material and the relevant literature, but there is a certain lack of philological mastery and historical impartiality, e.g., in his treatment of Belshazzar and Darius the Mede. Further the book is badly arranged and difficult to take in at a glance. Accordingly it can be read with profit, on individual points, but even from its own standpoint it falls considerably short of its target.   W.B.

BRUCE, F. F. : *The Hittites and the Old Testament.* 1947. (Tyndale Press, London. Price : 2s. 6d.)

The Tyndale lecture on the Old Testament for 1947, delivered by the Head of the Department of Biblical Studies at Sheffield University contains a useful review of the Biblical data about the Hittites, and of the history of the re-discovery of the Hittites through Egyptian monuments, Assyrian records, and excavations at Tell el Amarna and Boghaz-köy. There is a short, clearly-written history of the Hittite empire and the neo-Hittite kingdom of Syria based on these new facts. In the light of these discoveries the Biblical data are re-examined and an attempt is made to show reasons why Gen. xxii, need not be regarded as an anachronism, and for the possible identification of Tidal king of Nations (Gen. xiv), with the Hittite king Tudkhalia of c. 1770 B.C. There are three pages of notes and a bibliography.   J.N.S.

CONTENAU, G. : *Manuel d'archéologie orientale*, vol. iv. 1947. (Picard, Paris. Price : £2 15s. 0d.)

This, the fourth volume of Professor Contenau's admirable account of Middle-Eastern archaeology, brings a work begun just twenty years ago fully up to date with ample accounts of all the work done and the objects recovered since the appearance of the last volume in 1931 ; the present volume, therefore, in no way covers again the ground of the preceding three volumes but is a supplement to them, taking up the story where they left it off. It is therefore continued on the same plan and scale as its predecessors, which facilitates reference to previous discussions of a subject. The text is carefully written ; it is mostly descriptive, containing few discussions of views and omitting little if anything of importance. Possibly the chief interest of the work for the ordinary reader is the wealth of illustrations, of which there are 974 in the previous volumes and 337 in the present volume, together with numerous maps. The work will be indispensable to all students of the Middle East and not least of Biblical scholars.   G.R.D.

DALMAN, G. : *Arbeit und Sitte in Palästina. Band VII : Das Haus, Hühnerzucht, Taubenzucht, Bienenzucht.* 1942. (C. Bertelsmann, Gütersloh.)

> The present volume has been seen through the press by L. Rost, who reports that about a third of the eighth and final volume, dealing with domestic life, music and singing, and birth, marriage and death, had already been written up by the author at the time of his death in 1941, and that there is every prospect that it can be completed and edited (no doubt by Rost himself) in keeping with its predecessors in the series. This particular volume needs neither detailed description nor special recommendation ; it is sufficient to say that it is wholly in line with its forerunners, offering a most detailed account of the facts with accompanying illustrations, an equally thorough citation of relevant passages from the Bible, the Talmud, and other ancient literature such as that of Josephus, while only occasional notice is taken of the information yielded by excavations. O.E.

DIRINGER, D. : *The Alphabet. A key to the history of mankind.* 1948. (Hutchinson, London. Price : £2 10s. 0d.)

> Dr. Diringer is already well known to Orientalists and Biblical scholars for his two Italian works entitled *Le iscrizione antico-hebraiche Palestinesi* (1934) and *L'alphabeto nella storia della civiltà* (1937), and this new English book will increase his already deservedly high reputation. It contains concise accounts, to all appearances, of all the scripts and alphabets in the world from the invention of writing to the present day ; it includes some accounts of the Chinese script containing 44,449 symbols in the famous dictionary of K'ang-hsi (A.D. 1662-1722) as well as of that remarkable Indian script which is " often illegible except to the writer." Apart from these vagaries, due importance is given to the Semitic script in its various forms as the parent of most alphabets and to its Greek and Latin offshoots, whence alphabetic writing has been spread over the whole western world. A wealth of historical, often strange and curious, matter in 607 pages is lucidly set forth and the story made fascinating by 256 illustrations inset in the text. All students of civilization will wish and do well to possess themselves of a fascinating book. G.R.D.

DOSSIN, G., and JEAN, C. F. : *Archives Royales de Mari*, I-II. (Textes cunéiformes du Louvre XXII-XXIII) 1941, 1946. (Geuthner, Paris.)

> In these two volumes Prof. Dossin and the Abbé Jean commence the publication of the archives recovered by the French at Mâri on the middle Euphrates, and they here present copies of 280 of the 5,000 letters found in this vast collection of *plusieurs milliers de tablettes* (said to be 20,000) covering a period of fifty-eight years, found at that place. This collection contains the correspondence between Hammurabi, King of Babylon, and Zimrilin, King of Mâri, once his ally and then his enemy ; and the letters so far published are certainly concerned with the encroachments of the

Subaraeans on one side and of Rîm-Sin, King of Larsa, on the other side. They are of the greatest importance not only historically but also linguistically, and their ' Western ' dialect of the Babylonian language is of great interest to Hebraists ; for example *dawidum*, which is used as a title meaning 'chieftain' or 'the like,' throws light on the meaning of ' David,' although this word occurs only as a proper name in the Old Testament. May it not also mean ' chieftain ' on the Moabite Stone ? The copies of the cuneiform text are exemplary, as, one expects from the practised hands of the two editors ; but those who cannot read the cuneiform script will be glad that transliterated texts and translations may be expected to follow each volume in due course.   G.R.D.

EBELING, E. : *Die siebente Tafel des akkadischen Weltschöpfungliedes Enuma Elisch*. (Mitteilungen der Altorientalischen Gesellschaft, XII, 4.) 1939. (Harrassowitz, Leipzig.)

On the basis of a fragment, which was discovered during the excavations at Assur, and fills a great gap in the hitherto extant text, Ebeling is able to present the whole tablet in transcription and translation. Nevertheless it is important to compare the treatment of this section by W. von Soden in *Die Zeitschrift für Assyriologie*, 47 (1942), pp. 8ff.   W.B.

GORDON, C. H. :   *Ugaritic   Handbook*.   1947.   (Pontificium Institutum Biblicum, Rome.)

This new ' Ugaritic Handbook ' expands the author's ' Ugaritic Grammar ' (Rome, 1940) into three parts : I. 'Revised Grammar, Paradigms'; II. ' Texts in Transliteration '; III. ' Comprehensive Glossary '; and will be found indispensable for Ugaritic studies. The first part follows the line of the original work but is considerably enlarged and improved by the addition not only of matter from new texts but also of welcome paradigms. The second part is entirely fresh and will be most welcome to scholars who cannot read the cuneiform text ; for it gives a transliterated text of the whole collection. Thus the Hebraist may be tempted to apply his general knowledge of the Semitic languages to them and to see what he can make of them ; at any rate he will discover many startling echoes of the Old Testament which will explain themselves, even though he may not be able to translate very much in detail. The last volume contains an enlarged vocabulary, apparently complete up to date. In the present state of Ugaritic studies, when so much is uncertain, no scholar will agree with the author on every point, and many will regret the ommission of *'aleph* in the transliteration, but all will be grateful to him for providing them with so much help in this most difficult field of study.   G.R.D.

ILJIN, M. : *Schwarz auf Weiss. Die Entstehung der Schrift*. 1945. (Steinberg, Zürich, Price :   9s. 0d.)

This little book of 170 pages contains a clear but compact account of the developments of writing and the book, from the earliest or most primitive methods of sending a message, through the various systems of pictography down to the modern alphabet, and of the means of writing from tablets and scrolls down to the printed book. The account is generally trustworthy ; but it is surely a lapse to ascribe the decipherment of the hieroglyphic and cuneiform scripts respectively to Champollion and Grotefend, entirely passing over Young, Rawlinson and Hincks. The story is lightly if imaginatively told and is illustrated by a number of black and white sketches which, though at times somewhat fanciful, generally illuminate the point which they are intended to elucidate.   G.R.D.

McCown, C. C. : *Tell En-Nasbeh.* 2 vols. 1947. (Palestine Institute of Pacific School of Religion, Berkeley ; A.S.O.R., New Haven. Price : £4 15s. 0d.)

> Two very important volumes containing the results of the excavations by Frederic Badé between 1926 and 1935. Professor McCown is assisted by Mr. Wampler, who is responsible for the second volume devoted to the pottery, Dr. von Bothmer, Professor Muilenberg and others. Volume I contains a discussion of the identification of the site, chronological problems and data, and materials of cultural significance. The work suffers irreparably from the death of Badé in 1936, and it is difficult to avoid a suspicion that the methods of either the digging or of the recording might have been improved so that the editor, who admittedly ' gave little attention to Tell en Nasbeh,' should not have had to be dependent on innumerable entries in Badé's diaries, which would have meant volumes to his capacious retentive memory but merely suggested to others questions which could not be answered. The method of presentation has resulted in considerable repetition and some lack of co-ordination. The volumes are essential to students of Palestinian archaeology, and though one cannot help feeling disappointed that Badé himself was not able to produce the books, the writers are to be congratulated on their achievement under such severe handicaps ; the volumes are well produced, amply documented, and excellently illustrated.   J.N.S.

van der Meer, P. : *The Ancient Chronology of Western Asia and Egypt.* 1947. (Brill, Leiden.)

> This work, the second volume of a new publication entitled *Documenta et Monumenta Orientis Antiqui,* contains a careful and detailed examination of the inter-relation of the archaeology of the ancient ' Middle East,' including useful synchronistic tables of the cultures and civilizations of this part of the world, the first for pre-historic and protohistoric periods, the second for 2236-1425 B.C., the third for 1425-700 B.C., and the fourth for 700-568 B.C. These are of the greatest use to scholars who may find themselves uncertain about the relation of one culture to another in a different part of the Eastern world. The most interesting point perhaps for the Biblical student is that the author assigns the reign of Hammurabi, the sixth king of the first dynasty of Babylon, to 1711-1660 B.C., the latest date as yet proposed for him ; whether this will be ultimately accepted is another question.
>   G.R.D.

*MOORHOUSE, A. C. : *Writing and the Alphabet*. 1946. (Cobbett Press, London. Price : 7s. 6d.)

This little work gives a brief account of the invention of writing and of various systems of writing in six chapters, the first three devoted to its form and the last three to its use ; and it includes six figures in the text and nine plates. The story is concisely but lucidly told and the illustrations are well chosen both for their intrinsic interest and for the illustration of the text, but they are unfortunately not all very well reproduced. The matter is entirely gathered at second hand, but the author has selected it sensibly and has used it with care and discretion. G.R.D.

VON OPPENHEIM, M. : *Tell Halaf*. 1 : *Die Prähistorischen Funde*, edit. by H. Schmidt. 1942. (deGruyter, Berlin).

This sumptuous production with its many coloured plates is the first of the five volumes which were planned to cover Oppenheim's important excavations at Tell Halaf. It is devoted to the prehistoric finds, and was edited by the Berlin archaeologist Hubert Schmidt, who died in 1933. Oppenheim, who died in 1946, has himself contributed both a foreword and an introduction which serves as a general introduction to the whole work. It is greatly to be hoped that it may prove possible to carry through to completion the important publication which has begun so promisingly with the present volume. O.E.

HISTORY

BRIEM, E. : *Kampen om Palestina genom 5,000 år*. 1943. (Natur och Kultur, Stockholm. Price : Kr. 7.00.)

This is a survey, by the late Professor of the history of religion at Lund, of the history of Palestine from the earliest times till A.D. 1939, ending with a discussion of contemporary political problems. The treatment is clear and interesting and the author has made use both of selections from primary historical sources and of some excellent photographs to illustrate his account. The book is intended for the general reader rather than the specialist. G.W.A.

CHEMINANT, L.: *Le royaume d'Israël*. (Témoins de Dieu, No. 9.) 1947. (Les Editions du Cerf, Paris ; Blackfriars Publications, Oxford. Price : 4s. 0d.)

Here we have a brief survey of the story of the northern kingdom from the Disruption to the Fall of Samaria, viewed as itself a witness of God, with special reference to the prophets, who were the personal witnesses of God. Critical questions are left undiscussed, but the author declares himself in favour of the view that the story of Hosea's matrimonial experiences rests on visions, and not on actual fact. H.H.R.

VAN DEURSEN, A. : *Palestina, het land van de Bijbel*. 1946. (Bosch en Keuning, Baarn.)

A Dutch teacher of Geography, who has occupied himself much with Palestine, here gives a short popular survey of the land from a geographical, geological, climatic and archaeological point of view. The book is written in a somewhat too devotional style, but nevertheless it offers trustworthy guidance to the interested reader. Th.C.V.

DRIOTON, E., and VANDIER, J. : *Les peuples de l'Orient Méditer-*
ranéen. II. *L'Égypte.* 1946. (Presses Universitaires de France,
Paris. Price : 14s. 6d.)

This astonishingly cheap volume of over 700 pages is a re-
issue of the work first published in 1938, with an appendix
bringing up to date the work of Vandier. It has a brief survey
of the religion of Egypt and an annotated and well documented
review of its history, administration and culture from the
earliest times to Alexander the Great. A full Bibliography
stands at the beginning of the volume. For the background
of Egyptian history which the Old Testament scholar must
have it is of the highest value, and while its range means
that no question can be studied in detail, it refers the reader
to the more special discussions of all important questions.
H.H.R.

DUFFY, W. : *The Tribal-historical Theory on the Origin of the Hebrew*
People. 1944. (Catholic University Press, Washington. English
Price : 8s. 6d.)

This is a dissertation of 125 pages, submitted and accepted
for a degree of Doctor of Theology. It is a reassertion of the
traditional view that the accounts of the patriarchs in Genesis
are to be interpreted literally. N.H.S.

FLIGHT, J. W., and FAHS, S. L. : *Moses.* 1947. (Beacon Press,
Boston. $1.00.)

An interesting attempt by a well known Old Testament scholar
to rewrite a Bible story in an authentic and informative way
to appeal to children, and for the use of teachers. Twelve
short simply written chapters tell the story in the writer's
own words, and after each chapter the Bible passage on which
the chapter is based is given from the American Revised
Standard Edition of the Bible. There are attractive illustrations, and a small boy I know read it through at a sitting,
fascinated. There is need for many more such books.
J.N.S.

HELLING, F. : *Die Frühgeschichte des jüdischen Volkes.* 1947. (Vit-
torio Klostermann, Frankfurt am Main.)

This book is a polemic against the history of the religion of
Israel as conceived by the critical historical school, i.e., against
the current modern O.T. criticism. Helling believes that the
Pentateuch is a literary unit belonging to the Mosaic period,
receiving a certain working-over in later times. Without
himself accepting the view that the Pentateuch manifests
itself to be composed of various sources, he uses this theory
against the moderns to show that these ' sources ' all agree
in the description of Israel's early history. The author casts
his darts particularly against the " dogma of primitiveness "
which characterizes the views, e.g., of Gunkel and Gressmann
in regard to the pre-Mosaic period. There was no difference
in patriarchal times in the economy and conditions of the
Hebrews and the Canaanites except that the former were
strangers and sojourners. The Israelites according to Helling
came to Egypt in the time of the friendly Hyksos who were
driven out c.1580. Thutmosis III was the most oppressive
of the Pharaohs. The inscriptions at Serabit, as translated

and explained by Hubert Grimme are used to describe the
religion of Israel in the form it had before Moses appeared as
reformer. The book is a most interesting study and the
bibliography upon which it draws is a valuable feature.

O.S.R.

HOLLEAUX, M. : *Études d'épigraphie et d'histoire grecques.* Vol. III :
Lagides et Séleucides. 1942. (Boccard, Paris.)

This volume consists of a number of collected articles by
Holleaux, published in various Journals over many years.
The essays of most interest to the Biblical student are those
dealing with the death of Antiochus Epiphanes, the date of
the first expedition of Antiochus Magnus into Coele-Syria,
the chronology of the fifth Syrian war, and the interpretation
of the passage of Josephus dealing with the tax farming of
the Tobiad Joseph. Holleaux contests the views that the
Jewish account of the death of Antiochus IV was a fictitious
doublet of that of Antiochus III ; dates the first expedition
of Antiochus III in 222 B.C. (not 221, as Oesterley) ; dates
the battle of Paneion 200 B.C. (not 198 as Oesterley) ; and
disputes the view that the taxes of Palestine were divided
between the Seleucids and Ptolemies, but argues that they
were divided between the Ptolemaic king and queen. Much
acute learning has gone into all the studies, and while none of
the essays is new (some being more than fifty years old),
it is good to have them rescued from their burial in the pages
of journals.

H.H.R.

LEEUWENBURG, L. G. : *Echnaton.* 1946. (N.V. Servire, The Hague.
Price : Fl. 2.90.)

Dr. Leeuwenburg of Leiden, in the series Cultuurhistorische
Monografieën, has contributed a fresh discussion of Echnaton,
the Aton religious reform usually attributed to him, and various
problems raised by the Tell el Amarna letters. After stating
the traditional view he discusses the evidence (cf. A. Erman,
Die Religion der Ägypter, Berlin, 1934) for attributing the
beginnings of the new religious teaching to Amenophis III,
the father of Echnaton. The book is illustrated with reproductions not easily available, but it contains no notes and few
references · the author states that it is a forerunner of a
larger, annotated, and more adequate treatment of the subject.

J.N.S.

SEELE, K. C. : *The Coregency of Ramses II with Seti I and the Date of
the Great Hypostyle Hall at Karnak* (Studies in Ancient Oriental
Civilisation, No. 19). 1940. (University of Chicago Press.)

A careful study of the raised and incised reliefs in the great
Hypostyle Hall, Karnak, the Nubian temple at Beit el-Wali,
the temple at Qurnah, and the temples at Abydos, is used to
substantiate the claim made by Ramses II—disbelieved by
Breasted and others—that during his father's life he was
appointed co-regent. In the dedicatory inscription at Abydos
Ramses quoted his father as saying : ' Crown him as king,
that I may see his beauty while I live with him.' The change
in the official prenomen used by Ramses, the content and the
form of his reliefs, appear to support the truth of this statement. The second pylon at Karnak, the vestibule to the great

hall, was apparently built by Harmhab ; the plan was changed by Ramses I to convert the open court between the second and third pylons into a covered hall with a roof supported by one hundred and thirty-four columns ; the interior decorations were continued by Seti I and completed by his son Ramses II. The book is clearly written, well produced and illustrated.

J.N.S.

TCHERIKOVER, A. : *The Jews in Egypt in the Hellenistic-Roman age, in the light of the papyri.* 1945. (Hebrew University Press Association, Jerusalem.) (In Hebrew.)

The Hebrew University's lecturer in ancient Greek and Roman history here attempts a systematic survey of the scattered details and hints in the papyri referring to Jews. The task is not straightforward since references to Jews are not always explicit and proper names are not in themselves proof of their bearers' Jewishness or non-Jewishness. The high lights in such a study are inevitably the Letter of Claudius on Jewish affairs, and the Acts of the Alexandrian Martyrs and the minutes of the trial of Isidorus and Lampon. But Dr. Tcherikover is also at pains to assemble more humdrum material throwing light on the social and economic conditions of the Egyptian Jews, the history of their settlement in Egypt, their geographical distribution, their occupations (military service is more in evidence than mercantile pursuits), their legal and civic status in Hellenistic and in Roman times, special Jewish taxation, and the rise of anti-semitism among their Greek neighbours ; while a study of the names adopted by the Jews provides a possible index of the degree of their attempts at assimilation. H.D.

WRIGHT, J. S. : *The . Date of Ezra's Coming to Jerusalem.* 1947. (Tyndale Press, London. Price : 2s. 6d.)

In this Tyndale Lecture for 1946 the author examines the grounds on which a number of recent writers have reversed the traditional order of Ezra and Nehemiah, and defends the view that Ezra preceded Nehemiah in the reign of Artaxerxes I. Despite its necessarily brief limits it presents arguments which call for serious consideration. H.H.R.

TEXT AND VERSIONS

AP-THOMAS, D. R. : *A Primer of Old Testament Text Criticism.* 1947. (Epworth Press, London. Price : 3s. 0d.)

This is an invaluable summary of information on the materials for textual criticism and the types of error that have arisen in the text, suitable to be placed in the hands of all students of Hebrew when they first begin to read continuous texts. Students of the New Testament have long had access to such primers, and we have needed such a compendium for the Old Testament, and all teachers of Hebrew will be in Mr. Ap-Thomas's debt for saving much valuable class time by this brief introduction to the principal versions and their use. The author has wisely resisted the temptation to overload his primer, or to enter into discussion on disputed questions. There is a brief chapter on the Canon, which might with advantage be somewhat expanded in a subsequent edition, to yield a primer on Text and Canon. H.H.R.

BEA, A. : *Il Nuovo Salterio Latino.* 2nd ed. 1946. (Pontificio Istituto Biblico, Rome.)
(Also in French) *Le Nouveau Psautier Latin.* 1947. (Desclée, de Brouwer, Paris. Price : 54 francs.)

The French adaptation of this work by the rector of the Biblical Institute in Rome has some small improvements in respect of the second Italian edition, and those who are not at home in Italian will lose nothing by consulting the French. As the publishers claim, the book is not intended to justify, in the strict sense, the decision to make a new Latin rendering of the Psalter. Its aim is to show that the members of the pontifical commission for the new version appreciated the difficulties of their task, took all possible care in their work of translation, and were guided by definite, well-recognized principles in carrying out their duties. The desire for a new version had been freely expressed by many competent authorities, who fully recognized the unsatisfactoriness of the Vulgate Psalter, but not all the suggestions offered could ultimately be adopted, the more so as they were not always mutually consistent. So, for reasons stated in this booklet, a mere revision of the Vulgate text was judged to be insufficient, nor would any mere reprint of St. Jerome's long-antiquated *Psalterium juxta Hebraeos* have been useful or adequate. Many examples are given to illustrate the exact scope of the rendering, the chief fault of which appears to be the translators' frequent lack of appreciation of the " run " of a sentence. The final chapter prints some letters from those who have welcomed the version.   J.M.T.B.

CHURGIN, P. : *The Targum to the Hagiographa.* 1945. (Horeb, New York, Price : 18s. 0d.)

This work contains a detailed examination of the Targumim of those books of the Hagiographa which are provided with them, after a brief introduction on the general question of their origin and date. The conclusion reached is that these Targumim are not a single unified work, but represent various revisions or recensions, none thorough-going and all patch-work, and that no precise date can be assigned to them ; for apart from having grown up gradually, though there was talk of a Targum to the Hagiographa in the Tannaitic period, no citations from it are found even in the Talmud and hardly any in the Midrashim, and its use cannot be definitely proved before the time of the Spanish and French exegetes (for example, Rashi). The arguments are not very clearly presented and are further obscured by being unfortunately presented in modern Hebrew which few non-Jewish scholars read with any ease.   G.R.D.

KAHLE, P. E. : *The Cairo Geniza.* (The Schweich Lectures for 1941.) 1947. (Geoffrey Cumberlege, London. Price : 12s. 6d.)

In these Lectures the author sums up the work of a life-time on the Massoretic tradition. The first Lecture is introductory, giving a general account of the Geniza, and the early visitors to it and the principal works recovered from it, with especial attention to the Zadokite Fragment, a document relating

130

to the Khazars, and Jewish liturgical poetry. The second Lecture
discusses the Massoretic texts ; it establishes the priority of
Ben Asher's over Ben Naphtali's recension and traces back
the vocalization behind that of the Massoretes, who are shown
to owe the conception of vocalization to the professional
readers of the Coran and Arabic scholars. The third Lecture
deals with the main ancient versions of the Old Testament,
showing that our LXX is a Christian recension based on Jewish
Greek ' Targums ' and that the Peshittâ was made for the
Jewish community in Adiabene in the first century A.D.
The importance of this work, its wealth of material and its
originality and freshness of outlook, cannot be overrated,
and it will be indispensable to all students of the Old Testament
whom it ought to stimulate to fresh researches on their own
account into the fascinating fields of study which it opens
up to them.   G.R.D.

Kasowski, C. J. : *Otzar Ha-Targum* (A Concordance to the Targum
of Onkelos). 1940. (Mosad Ha-Rab Kook, Jerusalem.)

The author of two concordances (Mishnah 1927, Tosefta
1933) has produced a third, equally indispensable. The major
part is devoted to the ordinary words. All passages where a
word occurs are listed, wherever possible the Hebrew for which
it stands is prefixed, and in most cases not only the form of
the word itself but also its closest context are quoted. Another
section exhibits the names of persons ; another the names of
God and the words *qodhom* and *memar* ; another pronouns,
particles and numerals ; and yet another gives every form of
every word occurring in the Hebrew Pentateuch and its
rendering in Onkelos. There are prefaces by J. L. Fishman
and Isaac Epstein.

The work follows Berliner's edition of Onkelos (1884) made
on the basis of the Editio Sabioneta 1557. A scholar interested
in variants will not find them in this concordance—but had
they been included, it would no doubt have become too bulky.
P.410, last quotation, read Dt. xxxii, 11 instead of Gn. xxxii,
11.   D.D.

Lisowsky, G. : *Die Transkription der hebräischen Eigennamen des
Pentateuch in der Septuaginta.* 1940. (Dissertation, Basel.)

Presents a list in alphabetic order of all the proper names
in the Pentateuch together with their Greek renderings, and,
by choosing about eighty names which are etymologically
clear or are guaranteed by their frequent appearance, secures
a basis for examining their reproduction in B and the variants,
which is then extended to the remaining names. Despite its
limitation to the Pentateuch, the exclusion of materials from
Hexaplaric and non-Biblical sources, and the lack of a philological treatment, which is reserved for later development,
this is a useful piece of work, thanks to the neatness of its
method and the careful way in which it has been carried
through.   W.B.

McClellan, W. H., S. J., and others : *The Psalms. A Prayer Book. Also the Canticles of the Roman Breviary*. 1945. (Benziger Brothers, New York. Price : $3.85.)

Knox, R. A.: *The Book of Psalms and the Canticles used in the Divine Office*. 1947. (Burns, Oates and Washbourne, London. Price : 12s. 6d.)

> Each of these editions of the Psalter is an attempt to popularize in an English version the new Latin rendering produced by the Pontifical Biblical Institute. The American work is the larger of the two, being printed in bold clear type and containing a " preface, explanatory introductions, verse summaries, reflections and topical guides," in addition to the Latin text and its English translation. There are, however, no footnotes properly so called, whereas the Knox version has a fair number of rubricated notes, which are for the most part translations of the old (unrevised) Vulgate text ! Neither of these versions is at all satisfactory, though the American book is more to be commended as an attempt, often unscholarly and unsuccessful, at a literal translation of the Latin. Knox's version, on the other hand, is more in the nature of an extremely free paraphrase, in which there is every sort of change in the phraseology of the original, and, at times, a reversion to an older and less perfect reading. So, in the Song of Moses in Ex. xv, 1-19, the first verse is correctly rendered by the Jesuit revisers : " . . . . . . equum et currum dejecit in mare," which does not prevent Knox from following the Vulgate with " horse and *rider* hurled into the sea." A detailed appreciation of these books is to be found in the *Catholic Biblical Quarterly*, for July, 1946 (D. J. Unger, O.F.M. Cap.) and January, 1948 (M. J. Gruenthaner, S.J.)   J.M.T.B.

Stegmüller, O. : *Berliner Septuagintafragmente*. (Berliner Klassikertexte aus den Staatlichen Museen zu Berlin, Heft VIII) 1939. (Weidmannsche Verlagsbuchandlung, Berlin.)

> The fragments of the Septuagint belonging to the Berlin Museums, which have already been used in part for editions of the LXX (i.e., from private copies) are here presented in a volume edited with care and thoroughness and containing four plates. The editor's conclusions are summed up at the end under the headings of writing material, format, use of page, size of volume, script, abbreviations, orthography and language, material for the textual critic, together with a list of such names and special words as occur in the fragments and a survey of their distinctive features and range. Altogether a very valuable and useful piece of work.   O.E.

Ziegler, J. : *Die jüngeren griechischen Übersetzungen als Vorlagen der Vulgata in den Prophetischen Schriften*. 1943-44. (Beilage zum Personal-und Vorlesungs-Verzeichnis der Staatl. Akademie zu Braunsberg [Ostpr.].)

> It has been recognized, of course, that Jerome consulted the Greek translations of Aquila, Symmachus and Theodotion in making his Latin translation of the Old Testament ; but in this work Ziegler examines the problem more closely, and sums up his careful investigation as follows : " The many instances which have been advanced at any rate show clearly

how very much Jerome was indebted in his Vulgate to the later translators, particularly Aquila and Symmachus. The introduction into the Vulgate of the Greek renderings of ' The Three ' brings these men closer to us, and at the same time challenges us to investigate and deal carefully with the rest of their readings, so that we may get to know the Vulgate more intimately from this side also. We shall constantly be coming across Aquila, Symmachus and Theodotion here, and we shall recognize and greet them as old acquaintances, although they are clothed in Latin dress."　　　　　O.E.

ZIEGLER, J. : *Textkritische Notizen zu den jüngeren griechischen Übersetzungen des Buches Isaias.* (Vandenhoeck & Ruprecht, Göttingen.)

The editor of Vol. xiv (Isaias) of the Göttingen edition of the Septuagint here presents the fruits of his close study of the book of Isaiah, justifying the readings from Aquila, Theodotion and Symmachus which were admitted into his edition, and examining more closely a number of difficult passages. His study thus forms a valuable supplement to his edition of the text.　　　　　O.E.

ZIEGLER, J. : *Beiträge zum griechischen Dodekapropheton.* 1943. (Vandenhoeck & Ruprecht, Göttingen. Price : Rm. 4.00.)

This brief pamphlet of 67 pages contains concise textual notes on the later Greek versions of the Twelve Prophets, or " inner-Greek " and " inner-Latin " corruptions, and on the Biblical text of Cyril of Alexandria. The author examines minutely and seeks to explain every divergence between the versions and each variant reading in the individual versions and collects Cyril's quotations at the end. The work will not convey much to the ordinary student of the Old Testament, but will have considerable value for the specialist in the texts of the various versions.　　　　　G.R.D.

EXEGESIS

AALDERS, G. CH. : *Het Boek Esther* (Korte Verklaring der Heilige Schrift). 1947. (Kok, Kampen.)

One of the volumes of the popular commentary of the Dutch Gereformeerden, by one of the professors of the Free University in Amsterdam. The introduction and interpretation are of a highly apologetic character. For Professor Aalders only two textual problems remain in the book of Esther, viz., i, 22 and ii, 19. All other questions, historical, ethical and religious, are solved. The book of Esther is not for him a typical Jewish-nationalistic writing, but given by the divine Author of Holy Scripture, who pictures ' a mighty episode of the tremendous struggle between the serpent and the seed of woman, and shows how the seed of woman conquers Satan triumphantly.' ' If the attack had been successful the promise of the conquering seed of woman that was to be born from Abraham would not have been fulfilled.' The historical problem, that Mordecai lived under Xerxes, while belonging to the exiles of 597 B.C., does not exist for Professor Aalders, as he does not relate the subordinate clause in ii, 6 to Mordecai, but to his great-grandfather Kish. The date of the book is held to be not later than the middle of the 4th century B.C.　　　　　Th.C.V.

BÖHL, F. M. TH. : *Psalmen II* (Tekst en Uitleg). 1947. (Wolters, Groningen. Price : Fl. 3.95).

In this volume Professor Böhl continues his work (see Book List 1947, p.18) and gives his commentary on Psa. xlii-lxxxix. Much attention is given to a beautiful translation, which conveys a real impression of Hebrew poetry. Sometimes this involves a free translation, for which on the whole he offers justification. His interpretation stresses the cultic element in the Psalter, but not so strongly as in the first volume. The enthronement festival (xlvii) is more or less accepted as a fact. Böhl also points to the messianic character of some psalms (e.g., Psa. lxxii ; Psa. xlv, is entitled a Messianic Wedding Song). Most psalms are dated in the pre-exilic period, and frequently in the early monarchy. The religious character of the poems is emphasized, and the hope of a future life is found in Psa. xlix and lxxiii. Despite some hesitation on special points of translation and exegesis, this work may be regarded as an enrichment of Dutch literature because of the beauty of its rendering and its thorough treatment.   Th.C.V.

DE BOER, P. A. H. : *Genesis II en III : het veerhaal van den hof in Eden.* 1941. (Brill, Leiden.)

This is an original study of the Paradise story, arguing that the word *tree* is collective, and that we should render *the trees of life*, while ii, 17, does not imply that death is the penalty for man's disobedience in the sense that but for his disobedience he would have been immortal, but that a *penal* death will be his lot. De Boer, however, argues that instead of a penal death man was given penal toil. He ascribes the whole narrative to E rather than to J, and holds the introduction of the name Yahweh to be secondary.   H.H.R.

CAZELLES, H. : *Études sur le Code de l'Alliance.* 1946. (Letouzey et Ané, Paris.)

This is a very important and thoroughgoing study of the Book of the Covenant. The Introduction gives a full survey of all the modern views of the date and origin of the Code, and this is followed by a translation of the text, with textual notes and a very detailed commentary, in which abundant use is made of the material from Ras Shamra and other recent archaeological finds. Following this there is a careful discussion of the forms of the provisions of the Code, of the social background it implies, and of the date and provenance favoured by the author. He finds that it reveals the transition to a settled state, and assigns it to the period of the settlement of the trans-Jordanic tribes in the age of Moses. No student of the Code should miss this study. Written by a lawyer, it shows also the widest acquaintance with all the literature of the subject, as well as a full knowledge of the relevant ancient languages. The Code can rarely have been studied by a better equipped scholar.   H.H.R.

CEUPPENS, F. : *Le Miracle de Josué*. 1944. (Liége. Price : 1s. 6d.)

A lecture published in the Etudes Religieuses series of *La Pensée Catholique*. The author discusses the miracles of Jos. x, 9-14, in the light of Ecclus. xlvi, Josephus, Ant. Jud. V, i, 17, and scientific hypotheses. He reviews the various ways in which Catholic writers have attempted to explain this early poetic statement of ' relativity ' and decides in favour of the belief that the passage faithfully records a historic fall of meteorites followed by a particularly clear night.

J.N.S.

CLAMER, A. (ed. by) : *La Sainte Bible, texte latin et traduction française avec un commentaire exégétique et théologique*. II. *Lévitique, Nombres, Deutéronome*, by A. Clamer, 1946 ; VI. *Les livres sapientiaux*, by H. Renard, D. Buzy, J. Weber, and C. Spicq, 1946 ; VII. *Les Grands Prophètes*, by L. Dennefeld, 1947. (Letouzey et Ané, Paris. Price : About £1 per volume.)

These are three of the more recent volumes of this interesting, if somewhat unequal, attempt at a complete commentary on the Bible. It is to be completed in twelve volumes, of which the majority have now appeared, the chief exceptions being Genesis, Exodus, Acts, and the major Pauline epistles. A memoir of the former editor (L. Pirot) is printed by way of Preface to vol. II.

The present volumes show work competently executed by men who are masters of their subjects, but the proportion of space allotted to commentary varies greatly as between the volumes. The authors of the volumes on the Pentateuch and the Wisdom Literature have been able to comment if not adequately, at least fairly fully, on their respective books of the Bible. It is otherwise with the always careful work of the veteran scholar L. Dennefeld of the Strasbourg Catholic faculty. A commentator who essays to pay some attention to the textual difficulties of the four major prophets (together with Lamentations and Baruch), and has as his first duty the printing of the Vulgate text, accompanied by a French translation, is not likely to be overburdened with space for his ' commentaire exégétique et théologique.' The author is conscious of his lack of elbow-room, but the fault lies with the planners of the series, who should not have attempted to crowd four of the longer works of the Bible within the narrow limits of a single volume.

J.M.T.B.

COHEN, A. (ed. by) : *The Soncino Chumash : the Five Books of Moses with Haphtaroth*. 1947. (Soncino Press, Hindhead. Price : £1 1s. 0d.)

While this volume follows the general plan of the other volumes of the Soncino Books of the Bible, presenting the Hebrew text and the English of the American Jewish translation in parallel columns with commentary below, it differs in that there are no introductions to the books and in that the commentary consists wholly of a digest of comments extracted from the mediaeval rabbinical commentaries of Rashi, ibn Ezra, Rashbam, Nachmanides, Sforno, Kimchi, and Gersonides. All modern sources of knowledge bearing on the text are therefore deliberately excluded. Each section of the Pentateuch is followed by its appropriate Haphtarah, accompanied by translation and notes. Despite its limitations the volume should be of use beyond Jewish circles, its compendium of the classical Jewish comments making readily available to Gentile readers material which has hitherto been accessible only to the specialist—who has not always a Rabbinical Bible at hand. The volume is beautifully printed, and is astonishingly cheap. It is a pity it does not contain an index of the Haphtaroth. The actual compilation of the commentary has been done by H. Freedman (Genesis), J. Rabbinowitz (Exodus), S. M. Lehrman (Leviticus), and S. Fisch (Numbers and Deuteronomy). They have in each case indicated by a symbol the source of the comment given.　　　　　　　　H.H.R.

VAN GELDEREN, C. : *Koningen III* (Korte Verklaring der Heilige Schrift). 1947. (Kok, Kampen.)

This third part of the detailed (in contradiction to the title of the series) commentary on the Books of Kings from the hand of the late Prof. van Gelderen was edited by his successor, Prof. Gispen. It treats 2 Kgs. v-xvii, in a popular way, but dealing thoroughly with all the textual and historical problems. Sometimes the treatment is unduly drawn out, e.g., 2 Kgs. xiii, 21, where the reading *wayyelek* is retained and defended by a whole page of conjecture. Much of the book is worthy of appreciation, and instructive in the field of history ; but sometimes it shows how a commentary should not be written.
　　　　　　　　Th.C.V.

DE GROOT, J. : *De Psalmen*. 1932. (Bosch en Keuning, Baarn.)

In December, 1942, Dutch Old Testament scholarship suffered a severe loss by the sudden death of Prof. J. de Groot, of Utrecht. His last published work was this introduction to the psalms, which had occupied him much during his last few years. It is a popular but very instructive book. Two-thirds of it are devoted to a discussion of the problems arising from the book of Psalms, while at the end a dozen psalms are explained. The work is based on wide scholarship and critical interest, but combines with this a true piety. In some respects the author has been led to somewhat too positive results, e.g., in the chapter on the future life.　　　　　　　　Th.C.V.

HEINISCH, P. : *Probleme der biblischen Urgeschichte*. 1947. (Räber & Cie., Luzern.)

This book is intended to show that, on the basis of Roman Catholic exegesis, the Biblical stories concerning the earliest history of the world and mankind turn out to contradict science only in irrelevant matters, not in matters of doctrine. Heinisch credits the author of those stories not only with the advanced notions of the Roman Catholic religion (e.g., 'in our image' cannot refer to corporeal similarity, only to spiritual, ' thou shalt bruise his heel ' is the *Protoevangelium*), but also with a conscious distinction between these notions, which he did mean to be taken seriously, and others, which he did not (e.g., Ps. civ, with an order of creation different from that of Gen. i, proves that the author of Gen. i, did not regard his order as part of his teaching). Within his system, however, Heinisch is clear and sober ; he rejects the extreme allegorical interpretation of Karl Barth, makes some use of source criticism and compares much non-Israelite material. D.D.

HIPPOLYTUS : *Commentaire sur Daniel*, Greek text with translation by M. Lefévre ; Introduction by G. Bardy. 1947. (Les Editions du Cerf, Paris ; Blackfriars Publications, Oxford. Price : 13s. 0d.)

This is a further volume in the series *Sources Chrétiennes* (see under Origen, below), following Bonwetsch's Greek text with translation facing it. The Introduction gives a short account of the writing of the commentary and a critical appreciation of Hippolytus as a commentator. Useful indexes are added. H.H.R.

LASSEN, A. L. : *The Commentary of Levi ben Gerson (Gersonides) on the Book of Job*. 1946. (Bloch Publishing Company, New York.)

A reliable translation, most welcome to the student of medieval Jewish philosophy and exegesis. As Gersonides's aim is to present his own system (which he finds in Elihu's argument), the Old Testament scholar in the narrow sense may be less interested. There is a useful introduction, summarizing the ideas propounded by Gersonides in his *The Wars of the Lord* ; this work preceded the Commentary, and few fresh ideas are to be found in the latter. The arrangement of the Commentary strikes one as curiously modern. Gersonides goes through each section of Job three times : first he explains the meaning of difficult phrases, next he gives a paraphrase of the section as a whole, and finally he considers the general philosophical principles underlying the section. D.D.

LAURENT, Y. : *Le caractère historique de Gen. II-III dans l'exégèse français au tournant du XIXᵉ siècle*. (Analecta Lovaniensia Biblica et Orientalia, No. 1.) 1947. (Desclée de Brouwer, Bruges. Price : Fr. 20.)

A study of the ideas of Lenormant, Loisy and Lagrange on the historicity of the Paradise story, and of the arguments of the French writers who contested their views. The writer brings out the difference between Lagrange and the others, in that he was primarily interested in what the author intended to teach, and thus distinguished between the form and the essence of the story. The documentation of this study in the footnotes will alone give it high value for future students of these chapters. H.H.R.

LÜTHI, W. : *Die Bauleute Gottes, Nehemia der Prophet im Kampf um den Aufbau der zerstörten Stadt*. 1945. (Verlag Friedrich Reinhardt A.G., Basel.)

This is a book of sermons, thirteen in number, each upon a chapter in Nehemiah. Without giving any minute exegesis such as a commentary might give, these sermons present in relief the salient points in the record of the history of Nehemiah's time. Drawing upon the story of the rebuilding of the walls of Jerusalem by Nehemiah and his men the author shows that in the task of restoring the churches and the Church in the devastated Europe of our day, there are lessons to be learned from that period of poverty, hard work, conflicting interests and opposition in which Nehemiah so courageously fulfilled his purpose and commission. Having as his central theme the thought that Christians are God's workers in the building of the Kingdom of God, the preacher well justifies his method of having a whole chapter rather than a verse as the text for each sermon. Lüthi's writing is very attractive; it has strength and simplicity; it is full of a fine humour and discernment and he has a sense of the realities and possibilities of human nature and of life.   O.S.R.

NÖTSCHER, F. : *Die Psalmen* and *Jeremia und Klagelieder* (Die Heilige Schrift in deutscher Uebersetzung : Echter Bibel). 1947. (Echter Verlag, Würzburg.)

These two volumes, bound in one, are the first and second in the new Echter Bibel, of which Dr. Nötscher is the general editor. Each volume contains a brief introduction of hardly half a dozen papers, followed by a new German translation of the text ; under this is a very concise critical apparatus (in Roman characters) over an exegetical commentary. The translation, in which uncertain words are printed in italic forms and interpolations are marked by square brackets, seems accurate and runs smoothly ; the commentary is simple and to the point. Each volume, which is described as ' Published under Military Control ' receives the *imprimatur* of the Roman Catholic authorities ; the outlook of the editor, therefore, may be described as conservative-critical. The series, if continued on these lines, ought to prove itself useful to a wide circle of general readers but is not likely to contain any startlingly novel views.   G.R.D.

NOORDTZIJ, A. : *Het boek Numeri* (Korte Verklaring der Heilige Schrift). 1941. (Kok, Kampen.)

In a Preface of a highly personal character, the author—the former Professor of Old Testament at Utrecht, deceased during the war in Switzerland—shows that the whole of his scholarly work was directed against Wellhausenism. This commentary betrays this conflict. Professor Noordtzij was convinced that ' as regards the main contents the book of Numbers can easily be explained from Mosaic conditions,' though the book in its present form was perhaps compiled not earlier than the foundation of the monarchy, and some prescriptions are adapted to later circumstances. From this point of view the author discusses the book of Numbers thoroughly, thus yielding a book which has value for scholars of a more critical conviction.   Th.C.V.

ORIGEN : *Homélies sur l'Exode*, translated by P. Fortier ; with Introduction and notes by H. de Lubac. 1947. (Les Éditions du Cerf, Paris ; Blackfriars Publications, Oxford. Fr. 260.)

In the series *Sources Chrétiennes* a number of patristic texts are being published in French translation, some accompanied by the original text, and others, like the present volume, without. There is a good introduction on the exegetical principles of Origen, and the translation is in lucid French. While there is naturally no new contribution to the understanding of the Old Testament, since the work of Origen has long been known and his methods are not those of our day, it is useful to have such texts made accessible in this way in a series comparable with the S.P.C.K. series of texts. H.H.R.

VAN SELMS, A.: *II Kronieken* (Tekst en Uitleg). 1947. (Wolters, Groningen. Price: Fl. 3.95.)

The first part of this commentary on Chronicles appeared in 1939; the delay of this second part was due to the war. Professor van Selms, of Pretoria, gives a rather literal—and sometimes too literal—translation of the Hebrew text, and an exact and fluently written explanation offering much detailed comment. In the discussion of 2 Chron. xxxiv, it is apparent that the author is not convinced that the law-book found in the temple in Josiah's days was the law of Deuteronomy. In other respects, too, the author is over cautious—e.g., in iii, 4, the number 120 is retained. Th.C.V.

TORCZYNER, N. H.: *The Proverbs of Solomon.* 1947. (Yavneh Publishing House, Tel-Aviv.) (In Hebrew.)

Solomon, Professor Torczyner argues, must be given credit for the entire contents of the book; evidence to the contrary rests on mistaken readings. Thus LXX rightly treats Agur (xxx, 1) as a verb, while " Lemuel " (xxxi, 1, 4) is really an Aramaic-form infinitive from *y'l,* " be foolish." Hence xxxi, 1, is to be rendered " Words concerning foolishness in a king," and xxxi, 4, " Kings must not play the fool "; while xxiv, 23, really means "These also (are sayings applicable) to *judges* " (adopting the Arabic force of root *hkm*).

The author again brings to bear his " Old Testament master-key " (that our present books of poems, prophecies and proverbs are no more than anthologies of items lifted from their original contexts, from lost histories which recorded at length the lives and sayings of Israel's worthies), and he seeks to show how reconstituting the missing contexts can throw light on dark places in the Book of Proverbs. Yet it is hard to keep pace with him when he explains the missing sense of Prov. xxvii, 14, by the missing words of the Fable of the Lion in Aḥiḳar (ed. Cowley, 1.110).

Most of the obscurer passages in Proverbs come under Professor Torczyner's treatment, and his adventurousness and philological virtuosity enable him at every turn to enrich and revise the Hebrew vocabulary. Reading him brings prompt reward: his dexterity compels applause—but hardly conviction. H.D.

VAN DER WAETER, D.: *Les Psaumes et les Cantiques du Breviaire Romain.* 1947. (Beyaert, Bruges. Price: Belgian francs 158.5.)

This is a French edition of the Latin text prepared by the Pontifical Biblical Institute. There is a very brief commentary by T. Stallaert, C.SS.R., and the Latin text confronts van der Waeter's rendering. This version has the merit of translating poetry as poetry, though to one familiar with Dhorme's translations in *Le Livre de Job* and other works it does not give the same impression of *netteté.* It would be instructive to compare in detail Ps. lxxiii (Dhorme, op. cit. pp. cxxix ff.) in the two renderings. J.M.T.B.

WEBER, J. J. : *Le Livre de Job. L'Ecclésiaste.* 1947. (Société de Saint Jean l'Évangéliste : Desclée et Cie : Paris. English Price : 6s. 6d.)

The author is the Roman Catholic bishop of Strasbourg, and he has written a popular commentary on these two Wisdom books. He has provided a French translation, based on the Vulgate, but making use of both Hebrew and Septuagint. He dates the original author in the seventh century, a Palestinian of the time of the Judean kindgom. Additions are ch. xxviii, the descriptions of Behemoth and Leviathan, and the Elihu speeches. The book is a discussion on the problem of suffering, proceeding by thesis and antithesis. The notes are useful and generally traditional. Ecclesiastes belongs to the third century. The book is a unity, diverse thoughts at different times, except for the first three and the last six verses which are by a pupil of the author.　N.H.S.

WEISER, A. : *Die Psalmen, Teil* 1. (Das Alte Testament Deutsch, edited by V. Herntrich and A. Weiser, VII. 1.) 1939. (Vandenhoeck & Ruprecht, Göttingen.)

In 1935, Weiser produced a translation and exposition of certain psalms as a supplement to the *Neues Göttinger Bibelwerk, Das Neue Testament Deutsch.* In the meantime, however, the publishers have decided to extend this project and issue a complete translation and exposition of the Old as well as the New Testament, and Weiser's *Ausgewählte Psalmen* of 1935 now appears in this series as *Die Psalmen,* 1, with the promise that the psalms which remain to be treated (rather more than half) will be dealt with in due course. The principles and aims governing the second edition of the book remain the same as for the first. Careful study of the original text and the relevant literature are regarded as axiomatic, but the author passes on only those conclusions which are likely to be of service to the believer or the Church of the present day. "Theological exegesis, building upon earlier expositions of the Psalms, aims at such an unfolding of what is eternally present that the Psalter may be for the reader something more than just a comparatively interesting example of the religious poetry of ancient Israel, in short that it may be a guide for one's own faith and life." This aim is certainly realized.　O.E.

WOLFF, W. : *Jesaja* 53 *im Urchristentum. Die Geschichte der Prophetie "Siehe, es sieget mein Knecht" bis zu Justin.* 1942. (Anstalt Bethel, Bethel bei Bielefeld.)

This work belongs to the province of Church History or Dogmatics rather than that of Old Testament studies, inasmuch as it is concerned for the most part with the way in which Isaiah 53 was understood in primitive Christianity and later Christian writings down to and including Justin, and only by way of introduction pays attention to the interpretation of the chapter in later Judaism and in and of itself. So far as the last point is concerned, Wolff thinks that the interpretation of the Servant of Isaiah 53 in terms of the nation is steadily losing ground, because the indications of " a quite definite personality " are too obvious for them to be overlooked for long. What is more, it is clearly that of Deutero-Isaiah himself. Nevertheless, the description is so varied and intangible that one cannot rest content with this association of the Servant with Deutero-Isaiah, but is driven to the conclusion that in the work of this writer the conception of the Servant of God is meant as prophecy, i.e., that it is a forecast of Jesus Christ.   O.E.

LITERARY CRITICISM AND INTRODUCTION

AUVRAY, P. : *Ezéchiel* (Témoins de Dieu, No. 10). 1947. (Les Éditions du Cerf, Paris ; Blackfriars Publications, Oxford. Price : Fr. 130.) .

> This simple study of the career and message of Ezekiel is based on an original view of the book, for whose justification we must await the commentary on which the author is engaged. He holds that Ezekiel began his ministry in Jerusalem, and prophesied there until the thirteenth year of Jehoiachin's captivity, when he went to Babylonia and there received his second inaugural vision. This stands in chap. i, but it should be transferred to follow chap. xxxiii, and in i, 1, we should read ' in the thirteenth year.' The vision of chap. xxxvii, followed shortly after the second inaugural vision, and chaps. xl-xlviii, are substantially from Ezekiel's hand. The prophet was a fine poet, but normally wrote a diffuse prose, which has been rendered more diffuse by the additions of copyists—though these are not specified in the present work. These critical views are only incidental to the present book, whose purpose is to set forth simply and lucidly the teaching of Ezekiel and to estimate his personality and influence.
>   H.H.R.

BEEK, M. A. : *Amos.* 1947. (" De Tijdstroom," Lochem.)

> In a series entitled ' Introduction to Important Parts of the Bible,' started to promote Bible study in the Christian Church, Professor Beek has written a survey of Amos's preaching in which reference is frequently made to Martin Buber. With the opinion that chaps. i, ii, are meant to be an introduction to the prophecy, and that ' poverty is a highly appreciated ideal in Old Testament piety,' I cannot quite agree. For the rest, we have a useful little book, written in an attractive style.
>   Th.C.V.

BEGRICH, J. : *Studien zu Deuterojesaja.* (Beiträge zur Wissenschaft vom Alten und Neuen Testament, Heft 77) 1938. (W. Kohlhammer, Stuttgart.)

> The author holds that the anonymous prophet whom we know as Deutero-Isaiah made his first appearance about 553-2 B.C., when the revolt of Cyrus against Astyages of Media created a great stir throughout the Near East, and that his activity ceased c.546 B.C. At first in its eschatological period Deutero-Isaiah's message is delivered with the force of a deep conviction, and deals with the pardoning of Israel, the return of the exiles from Babylon, and the gathering of the Diaspora from every land. In this way God's glory is manifested to the whole earth, and all the nations are led to Him.

By 550 B.C., however, it became clear that these lofty hopes were not being fulfilled, but that instead the world was entering a state of peace which made the realization of this eschatological hope unlikely, and so aroused disenchantment and disillusionment amongst those who had been persuaded to indulge in it. However, while this led to the prophet's abandonment of his eschatological views, it also suggested to him a new means of explaining the events of history in terms of Yahweh, and he now interprets Cyrus as the instrument of the divine will. Accordingly during the second period of his ministry, i.e., 550-547 B.C., the figure of Cyrus plays a leading part. The Servant Songs (and Begrich identifies the Servant with Deutero-Isaiah himself) are also shared between these two periods, i.e., (a) xlii, 1-4; xlix, 8-13; xlix, 1-6, xlix, 7; (b) xlii, 5-9; 1, 4-9, and lii, 13—liii, 12, the last passage being held to deal with the prospective martyrdom of the prophet. The author's arguments are always suggestive, and however much one may disagree with his interpretation as a whole, his notes on the text and the literary features of these chapters are always important. O.E.

VAN DEN BORN, A.: *De historische situatie van Ezechiels prophetie*. (Analecta Lovaniensia Biblicà et Orientalia, Fasc. 2). 1947. (Desclée de Brouwer, Bruges.)

This short study is provided with a French summary. The author reviews recent views on Ezekiel and then advances the view that the prophet worked in Jerusalem until 586 B.C., when he went to Babylonia and there continued his work. Apart from a few short glosses, the whole book is accepted as genuine, but with some displacements. The inaugural vision of chapter i, with a few verses from chap. iii, are transferred to follow chap. xxxii, and thus to stand at the beginning of the Babylonian ministry, and chap. xxxvii, 1-14, is brought to follow these transferred verses. The general view is thus closely similar to that of Auvray (see this Book List, p. 31), the only important difference being that the latter assigns chap. xxxiii, to the Palestinian ministry and van den Born assigns it to the Babylonian. The recognition of a Palestinian period of Ezekiel's ministry shows the influence of much recent writing, though the author resists recent tendencies in holding the substantial unity of the book and reducing the work of the glossator to very small proportions. H.H.R.

FOSTER, R. J.: *Psalms and Canticles of the Breviary*. 1947. (The Mercier Press, Cork. Price: 15s. 0d.)

The title of this useful and scholarly work is slightly misleading. There is here no text of the Psalter, and no commentary of the chapter-and-verse variety. The main ideas of each psalm or canticle are explained in the form of a short essay or homily, and the treatment ends with some reflections of a spiritual character. In future editions it might be possible to give the first words of each psalm in Latin or English, since it is far easier to remember psalms by their opening words than to recognize them by their numbers. The order is that of the Breviary Psalter, a point that serves to illustrate the practical nature of the book, which is intended, in the first place, for those who recite the Office of the Latin Church.

J.M.T.B.

GISPEN, W. H.: *Israëls Verhaaldwang*. 1947. (Hummelen, Assen.)

Professor Gispen here maintains that the unity of the Old Testament can be explained from the Semitic love of stories. As a starting-point he takes a rather indefinite idea of a more or less psychological nature : *verhaaldwang*, i.e., the tendency to give everything in a narrative. This constrained Israel to compile large unities of stories, i.e., books. The author applies this principle not only to historical literature, but also to the Psalms and Proverbs, which were written to match the Pentateuch and the Decalogue respectively. In this way Gispen supposes he can take a firm stand against literary criticism with the aid of psychology. While his starting-point is to a certain extent right, and can find support from Pedersen, he appears to draw too sweeping conclusions from it. He supposes that Moses left behind a great number of written sources, from which after his death the Pentateuch was compiled. It is interesting to note that in this respect Gispen comes close to the view of the father of criticism, Astruc, who was, however, more orthodox and closer to tradition than the most anti-critical school can be to-day. Th.C.V.

*HOOKE, S. H.: *In the Beginning* (Clarendon Bible, vol. vi). 1947. (Oxford University Press. Price : 6s. 0d.)

The final volume of the Clarendon Old Testament is intended to give an account of the book of Genesis in the light of generally accepted results of ' higher criticism,' and to indicate some of the directions in which changes are taking place in ' critical orthodoxy.' The book contains a general introduction to Genesis ; a useful chapter on the meaning and function of myth ; and follows through the stories of creation, the flood and the patriarchs ; there are chapters on the early political development of the Hebrews, the religion of the patriarchal period, the religious standpoint of the narrators, and the permanent religious value of Genesis.

A valuable chapter by the late Edwyn Bevan on the religious value of myth in the Old Testament is added, and there is an appendix dividing Genesis between the three main sources J, E, and P. Like all this series the book is well produced and illustrated, but the limitation of the series in size and aim makes it impossible for the writer adequately to document his statements or to discuss the problems which are now being raised so strongly of the relationship between oral and written material in the sources of the Old Testament in general and the Pentateuch in particular. The book is an excellent conclusion to the series. J.N.S.

HOSPERS, J. H. : *De numeruswisseling in het boek Deuteronomium.* 1942. (Dissertation. Utrecht.)

The recently appointed Professor of Semitic Languages at Groningen presented this as his doctoral thesis. In it he tries to explain the variation between plural and singular in Deuteronomy by a theory of three editions through which the book has gone (*Ergänzungs-hypothese*). He distinguishes (1) an edition in the singular (the oldest) ; (2) a re-edition in the plural (pre-exilic), containing (a) chaps. i-vi, ix, 7b-x, 11, xxviii, 69-xxix, 28, (b) some parts of the original law in the plural, and (c) smaller plural additions in the singular text ; (3) a re-edition after the exile, containing only short singular additions (the longest are iv, 29-40, xxx, 1-10). The author follows his own line, starting from the hypothesis that the variation in the numbers betrays a plurality of sources, and that the parts in the same number belong together—except for the short singular additions in the plural parts, which form a third stratum. The author applies his theory too mechanically, or he would not have passed over ix, 22-24, which, although in the plural, distinguishes itself from its plural context, not only by style but by the break between ix, 21 and 25, and moreover çan itself be connected only with ix, 8.

If this is true, we must conclude either that the singular source contains plural passages, or that there are two plural sources.

Other problems are passed without a thorough attempt to solve them and moreover the phenomenological and theological problems are not discussed. It is a great pity that the author did not pay attention to these questions, and so failed to reach a satisfying conclusion. Nevertheless, the accurate survey of the material and the general discussion of the literature will maintain their value.   Th.C.V.

MOWINCKEL, S. : *Prophecy and Tradition : the prophetic books in the light of the study of the growth and history of the tradition.* 1946. (Dybwad, Oslo. Price : Kr. 10.00.)

This is an important study of the place of oral traditon in the transmission of the material in the Old Testament, with especial reference to the prophetic books. It is also a critical examination of the presuppositions of the traditio-historical school, represented by Engnell, and especially of its unwillingness to go behind the tradition to its history. So far from an emphasis on the place of oral tradition dispensing with the work of literary criticism, Mowinckel argues that each reinforces the other, and defends his view by the examination of cases where we can see the development of the tradition within the Old Testament. His criticism of the traditio-historical school is that it is too one-sided in its emphasis on the place of oral tradition, and too neglectful of the history of the tradition, and at the same time too sceptical of the prospects of our knowing anything of the historical basis of the tradition.   H.H.R.

von RAD, G. : *Deuteronomium-Studien*. 1947. (Vandenhoeck und Ruprecht, Göttingen.)

This consists of a collection of acute and stimulating essays on the form-historical character of Deuteronomy and of the Holiness Code, on the ' Name-theology ' of Deuteronomy and the ' Glory-theology ' of the Priestly Code, on the sacred war in Deuteronomy, and the origin and purpose of Deuteronomy, together with a study of the theology of history that marks the Deuteronomic books of Kings. In Deuteronomy von Rad finds older legal provisions taken up into an address to the community, put in Moses' mouth, where they are reinforced and commended. In the Holiness Code, however, we have a Divine speech, of which part is intended to be communicated to the people and part to the priests. The provisions with regard to war in Deuteronomy also show a re-working of older material, and the combined interest in cultic and political questions found here shows that Deuteronomy came from a time of religious and political revival, which the author would place after 701 B.C. Very suggestive are the essays on the theological interest, where von Rad connects the emphasis on the Name of God with the Shechem amphictyony and the Ark, and the emphasis on the Glory of God with the Tent and the Hebron confederacy. In the final essay he stresses the concept of the divine purpose of grace .towards the Davidic house running through the history of the Kingdom.
H.H.R.

*ROBINSON, T. H. : *The Poetry of the Old Testament*. 1947. (Duckworth, London. Price : 6s. 0d.)

Professor Robinson has here given us a companion volume to his earlier *Prophecy and the Prophets in Ancient Israel*, dealing with questions of Introduction and briefly discussing the thought and message of Job, Psalms, Proverbs, Song of Songs and Lamentations. The introductory chapter, on ' Prose and Poetry ' is based on a lecture by Professor E. C. Llewellyn, and while its material is not drawn from the Old Testament it forms an excellent introduction to the subject. The magnificent Bibliography appended to the book was prepared by Professor A. R. Johnson. In the body of the book there is a good chapter on ' The Forms of Hebrew Verse '—a subject in which the author has been interested since he did a doctoral thesis on it nearly thirty-five years ago—and another valuable chapter on isolated poems in the historical books. The chapters on Job present the critically ' orthodox ' view of the composition of the book—they were already printed before Professor Stevenson's Schweich Lectures appeared—and those on the Psalms largely follow Gunkel. It is a pity that Mowinckel is not once mentoned, save in the Bibliography, since his work has had a great influence even where his conclusions are not accepted. On all the books dealt with the more individual views are left aside, and the student who wishes to go on from this excellent general introduction to more advanced and detailed study will find full guidance in the Bibliography.
H.H.R.

STEVENSON, W. B. : *The Poem of Job : a Literary Study, with a New Translation*. 1947. (Oxford University Press, London. Price : 7s. 6d.)

In these Schweich Lectures Professor Stevenson advances a new view of the composition and significance of the book of Job. He holds that the poetic portion of the book is entirely independent of the prose prologue and epilogue, and should be studied by itself without any presuppositions which rest on the prose parts. He then finds that there is no serious evidence that Job's sufferings were due to disease, but rather that they were due to persecution. Job is found to be a rebel against God, whose rebellion was finally overcome, and the friends are seen to have given him counsel which he ought to have heeded. Professor Stevenson's study is preceded by a new translation of the text of the original poetic work, so far as it is possible now to recover it. He finds that a certain amount has been lost from all of the cycles of speeches, and that there is substantial dislocation in the third cycle, and he embodies some reconstruction of the text in his translation. On the other hand he omits altogether chapter xxviii—though holding that it may be from the same hand as the poem of Job—the Elihu speeches, and secondary parts of the divine speeches. An appendix contains notes on the new translation. There is a valuable chapter on ' Rhythm, Assonance, Structure, and Style.' In this the Babylonian Dialogue and a number of other texts are surveyed, and the conclusion is reached that it is impossible that the author of the poem should ever have joined it to the folk-tale, as they are now combined in the Old Testament. The whole work forms a stimulating challenge to commonly accepted views about the book.   H.H.R.

STUMMER, F. : *Geographie des Buches Judith*. (Bibelwissenschaftliche Reihe, Heft 3.) 1947. (Katholisches Bibel-Werk, Stuttgart.)

The various geographical problems which are raised by the Book of Judith are here carefully discussed in sound critical fashion. The study is divided into four parts, " Betulia und Samaria," " Die Reise der Gesandschaft Nabuchodonosors," " Der Machtbereich des Arphaxad," " Der Feldzug des Holofernes " ; and the author's findings are then summed up in a section entitled " Zusammenfassende Würdigung." This is followed by an appendix on " Die geographischen Namen der Vulgatafassung des Buches Judith," which discusses the geography as it is significant for the Vulgate text of the book. Of course this does not help us to arrive at the original text, but it has its value as evidence of what was definitely a later version of the Judith story. So far as the geography of the Greek Book of Judith is concerned, we may say that that is based upon a well-planned scheme by means of which the author wishes to indicate how it came into being, i.e., with the idea of producing something analogous to the Cyropaedia of Xenophon, in which the historical setting is the consciously chosen vehicle of certain specific ideas. Accordingly, if the study has little or no bearing upon the historicity of the Book of Judith, it is all the more important for our understanding of its literary form.   O.E.

DU TOIT, S. : *Bybelse en Babilonies-Assiriese Spreuke*. 1942. (Christelike Uitgeversmaatschappij, Johannesburg, Price : Fl. 5.60.)

Under the supervision of Professor Gemser, of Pretoria, the author—Professor of Theology at Potchefstroom College, South Africa—took his doctor's degree with this thesis. The subject is a comparison of the Babylonian and Assyrian proverbs with the Biblical, leading the author to the conclusion that formally the Old Testament depends on the Babylonian Wisdom literature, but not materially. It is his opinion that on the other hand the latter—at any rate the proverbs of Ahiqar—may be influenced by Israel as a consequence of the exile of northern Israel to Assyria. As an orthodox Reformed theologian, the author considers the Old Testament Wisdom literature to be of the same value as the rest of the Old Testament as regards revelation, and hence that the idea of ' life ' in Proverbs includes a spiritual meaning. Here the results of his research have been definitely influenced by his theological and doctrinal presuppositions. Th.C.V.

VALENTINI, M. : *Il Racconto della Creazione—Filosofia—Storia*. 1946. (Istituto Salesiano, Colle Don Bosco, Asti.)

This is a curious, intensely apologetical little work, written apparently by one who is content to take most of his information on the Bible and science at second-hand. The list of authorities consulted includes a large proportion of popular works, and does not include so fundamental a study as E. C. Messenger's *Evolution and Theology* (Burns, Oates and Washbourne, London, 1940). Some of the diagrams are decidedly ingenious, for example, the two of the *Cosmogonia babilonese* (*sumerica*), one of which is labelled " prima della battaglia " and the other " dopo la battaglia."

For some reason unexplained the only part of the Creation narratives printed in full under the heading " Testo " is that normally assigned to P. J.M.T.B.

RELIGION AND THEOLOGY
(including Religion of Neighbouring Peoples)

ALBRIGHT, W. F. : *From the Stone Age to Christianity*. 2nd edition, 1946. (Johns Hopkins Press, Baltimore. Price : Paper $2.50. Cloth $3.00.)

In this new edition (cf. Book List 1946, p.38) a few corrections have been made and four pages of Addenda have been appended. These contain additional notes on a number of points, of which the most important deal with chronology, ancient cultures, and Albright's reversion to his earlier dating of Ezra towards the end of the reign of Artaxerxes I instead of early in that of Artaxerxes II. Apart from the Addenda the pagination agrees with the first edition. H.H.R.

ALLEN, E. L. : *Prophet and Nation*. 1947. (Nisbet, London. Price : 7s. 6d.)

This is a short but very fresh and attractive study of the conflict of loyalites in which the great prophets found themselves involved, loyalty to their own people and loyalty to the word of Yahweh which they had to proclaim. The prophets selected for the purpose of illustrating the thesis of the book are : Amos, Hosea, Isaiah, Jeremiah, Ezekiel and the second Isaiah. Dr. Allen has a real contribution to make on a number of debatable topics, e.g., on the ' impregnability ' of Jerusalem in 701, which he regards as legend, on the Immanuel prophecy in Isaiah ch. 7, on Ezekiel about whom he is in fundamental agreement with Herntrich—crediting a disciple and redactor with transferring prophecies uttered in Jerusalem to Babylon —and on the Second Isaiah, to whom in a most interesting reconstruction he assigns the Servant Songs.   N.W.P.

*BAKER, G. P. : *The Witness of the Prophets*. 1948. (Abingdon Cokesbury Press, New York. Price : $2.25.)

Here we have a short survey of the witness of seven of the Old Testament prophets—Amos, Hosea, Isaiah, Habakkuk, Jeremiah, Haggai and Zechariah—followed by three chapters on Jesus as the Heir, Prince and Hope of the prophets. The selection of prophets studied is not self-explained, and Deutero-Isaiah's absence is particularly surprising, but the inclusion of Haggai and Zechariah is to be welcomed. There is little that is new in the elements of the prophetic messages unfolded, and indeed there are emphases whose lack of mention is astonishing. For only a selection of the main notes of each prophet's teachings finds mention here, and as a study of the chosen prophets the work is very incomplete. It is written in a fascinating style, however, which will make these prophets live for all readers, and which will impress the selected elements of their messages firmly on the mind as of enduring significance.

It is for this effectiveness of presentation, rather than for originality of content or contribution to scholarship, that the book is to be commended.   H.H.R.

BARTH, CH. : *Die Errettung vom Tode in den individuellen Klage und Dankliedern des Alten Testamentes*. 1947. (Zollikon Verlag, Basel.)

A scholarly and suggestive doctoral thesis from Basel making an important contribution to the elucidation of the meaning of the terms ' life ' and ' death ' in the Old Testament. There are situations in life prior to actual physical death which are described in the Old Testament, and in particular in the psalms indicated by the title, not metaphorically but realistically as implying that a man is already in the realm of death or in its neighbourhood. It is ably argued that here we have cases of *partial* identity. Death, however, as the inevitable close of a full life, is not regarded as an evil. A careful study of those psalms which are supposed to contain references to a future life leads to a negative conclusion. Frequent acknowledgement is made of indebtedness to the pioneer work of Pedersen.   N.W.P.

BERTHOLET, A. : *Der Sinn des kultischen Opfers.* 1942. (de Gruyter, Berlin.)

A convincing demonstration of the way in which many a custom which now appears as a sacrifice was originally something quite different. Offerings to the dead, for example, were simply an extension of the feeding of the living members of the family. In other cases we have to think of a primitive " power " rite, which was based upon the thought of the *mana* inherent in the sacrificial food, the firstling, the blood (human sacrifice !), and so on. It was only later, when it was first linked with a *numen* in terms of a gift, that it became an " offering," and so gave rise to truly religious thinking and could be accompanied by prayer. Equally important for the history of religion and for the study of the Old Testament. W.B.

BONSIRVEN, J. : *Les enseignements de Jésus-Christ.* 1946. (Beauchesne, Paris.)

This recent addition to the *Verbum Salutis* series is mainly of interest to students of the New Testament, who will find in it an almost unsurpassed richness of information and sureness of judgement. The author's rabbinic lore is not fully displayed here ; he is content, often enough, to refer to his classic work in two volumes on *Le Judaïsme Palestinien.* Yet there is one chapter (No. II, Jésus-Christ et Israël) which is of special value to an *Alttestamentler* as a clear discussion of Christ's relation to the Jewish law, with an appendix on His use of the Old Testament. The work as a whole is not always easy reading, but it is one that amply repays the effort to understand its author's meaning. J.M.T.B.

van den BORN, A. : *Profetie Metterdaad.* 1947. (Romen & Zonen, Roermond. Price : Fl. 3.40.)

The author, who took his doctor's degree at Nijmegen, in 1935, with a thesis on prophetic symbolism, renews in this little book his views on the subject. He maintains with more emphasis than before that some symbolic acts are not to be regarded as premeditated, but as being later represented as such. Here the following passages are especially discussed : Hos. i-iii; Jer. xiii, xvi, 1-9 ; Ezek. iv, 4-8, v, 1-4, xxi, 11 f., xxiv, 15-24. The author, who shows the strong influence of Jerome, considers Jer. xiii impossible as a symbolic act from a historical, and Hos. i-iii impossible from a moral, point of view, while Ezek. v, 1-4, xxi, 11 f., would be inconsistent with prophetic dignity. Hos. i-iii, Jer. xvi, 1-9, and Ezek. xxiv, are held to be instances showing that the prophets in retrospect saw their lives in a symbolic light and recognized God's guidance. Dr. van den Born offers an interesting textual analaysis of Ezek. iv and xii, concluding that iv, 12-15, iv, 6 (v, 1-4) and xii, 4-6, 10, 12-15 (cf., xvii, 20f.) are not genuine, while iii, 24-27 and iv, 4f., 7f., are two parallel reports of the same fact. This little book is a valuable study because it draws attention to the varying character of symbolic acts, and helps to solve some problems of the text of Ezekiel. To my mind, however, we are not at liberty to use our moral and aesthetic standards when discussing the question whether the symbolic acts were done on purpose or not. Th.C.V.

CALKINS, R. : *The Modern Message of the Minor Prophets* 1947. (Harper and Brothers, New York—London. Price : $3.00.)

This sympathetic study of the subject by a veteran American preacher follows broadly conventional lines. An appendix in the form of brief exegetical notes adds to its value for the general reader who is prepared to work carefully through the book with the text of the Authorized Version before him.

A.R.J.

CLEMEN, C. : *Die phönikische Religion nach Philo von Byblos.* (Mitteilungen der Vorderasiatisch-Aegyptischen Gesellschaft [E.V.], Band 42, Heft 3.) 1939. (Hinrichs, Leipzig.)

In an introduction the author deals with the way in which the value of Sanchuniathon's Phoenician History, as preserved by Philo of Byblus, has received growing recognition during the passage of the years, and draws attention to the fact that the Ras Shamra texts have thrown quite a new light upon the whole question. The fragments preserved in Philo's treatment of Sanchuniathon's work are then given in the Greek original together with a translation into German ; and this is followed by a triple survey of Phoenician religion as reflected in these fragments, i.e., dealing with the origin of the world, the origin of culture, and the origin of belief in the gods. Although one may be forced to question some of the author's statements, this summary is as valuable as the re-production of the Greek text and its translation into German. O.E.

CONTENAU, G. : *La Magie chez les Assyriens et les Babyloniens.* 1947 (Payot, Paris. Price : 14s. 0d.)

Dr. Contenau, author of numerous works on ancient life in the Middle East, adds a companion volume to his *La Divination chez les Assyriens et les Babyloniens* (Paris, 1940), in the present volume. This contains an exhaustive account of the deities and their mysteries, the practitioners of magic arts and their schools, the application of these practices to such purposes as necromancy, the recovery of health and the effort to win immortality, and as a kind of preventive medicine. The whole account is enriched with full quotations from ancient literature, a number of illustrations both on blocks set in the text (25) and on photographically reproduced plates (8) ; there are, too, full references to the relevant literature and an ample bibliography. The work, though popular in the best sense, will also be of considerable use to specialists.

G.R.D.

COPPENS, J. : *Les Parallèles du Psautier avec les Textes de Ras Shamra-Ugarit.* (Bulletin d'Histoire et d'Exégèse de l'Ancien Testament. No. 18). 1946. (Seminarie Biblique, Louvain.)

This is the valuable paper of Professor Coppens, contributed to the Lefort Festschrift (see Book List, 1947, p.3), which is thus obtainable separately. It was written without access to the work of Patton (see Book List, 1946, p.16), which deals with the same subject. Coppens underlines the importance of the Ras Shamra texts for the interpretation of the Old Testament, but observes that the Bible also throws light on these texts. Without minimizing the points of contact, he finds his study to yield evidence of the originality of Yahwism. H.H.R.

COPPENS, J. : *De Kennis van Goed en Kwaad in het Paradijsverhaal* (Mededeelingen van de Koninklijke Vlaamsche Academie, Klasse der Letteren, vi, 4). 1944. (Standaard-Boekhandel, Antwerp, and W. de Haan, Utrecht.* Price : Fr. 25.)

This is the Flemish study on which was based the paper read by Professor Coppens to the Society for Old Testament Study in September, 1946, and first published subsequently, though dated 1944. It is provided with a French summary, and extensive notes. The author reviews the varied opinions on the meaning of the knowledge of good and evil in this story advanced by earlier scholars, offers a new, annotated translation of the text, and argues for the view that the sin of Adam and Eve was an un-natural revolt against the institution of marriage and its procreative purpose. He thinks the story was directed against the practices of the fertility cult. Much learning and acute reasoning have gone into this study and succeeding students will not want to miss it.   H.H.R.

COPPENS, J. : *La connaissance du Bien et du Mal et le péché du Paradis* (Analecta Lovaniensia Biblica et Orientalia, vol. 3). 1948. (Duculot, Gembloux ; Desclée de Brouwer, Bruges and Paris ; Nauwelaerts, Louvain. Price : Fr. 70 belges.)

Professor Coppens has here published the text of the paper read to the S.O.T.S. in 1946 (15 pages), with 18 pages of notes, 84 pages of Appendices, and full Indexes. It is not just a translation into French of the preceding work (*De Kennis van Goed en Kwaad*), and each contains much that is lacking in the other. The appendices deal with the literary analysis of Gen. ii-iii; the survey of the latest studies (1943-1947) of the subject dealt with in the lecture ; the radical sexual interpretation of Gen. ii-iii; the serpent in the religious symbolism of Palestine, Egypt and Babylon (3 studies) ; and a new interpretation of Gen. iii, 22 (the view given in *Miscellanées Bibliques VII-X*, noted above). There is also a valuable bibliographical appendix on the serpent in ancient art. The whole work is a monument of industry and learning, and it will be invaluable to future students of the pericope. It is dedicated to St. George and the S.O.T.S. in graceful terms that will be deeply appreciated by all members.   H.H.R.

DAHL, NILS A. : *Das Volk Gottes : eine Untersuchung zum Kirchenbewusstsein des Urchristentums.* 1941. (Oslo, Dybwad.)

This exhaustive treatise on ' The people of God ' falls into three main sections (1) The people of God in the Old Testament—a thoroughly satisfactory summary of the evidence bearing on the idea of Israel as the people of God right down to the early Jewish period—(2) The people of God in late Judaism—containing a careful linguistic study of words like *kahal, 'eda, kenishta, ekklesia, sunagoge*, the recognition of changes of emphasis and new forms of the Israel idea, e.g., in Apocalyptic, in contact with the Greek world of philosophy and the mystery religions in Jewish legalism and various sects—(3) The people of God in the New Testament—in the thought of Jesus Himself (Kingdom of God, Son of Man), of the disciples, the early Jewish-Christian community and in Paul. No summary can do justice to the richness of the material provided here nor to the judicious way in which it is presented. This book will long be an indispensable work of reference and is itself a contribution to its subject of outstanding value.   N.W.P.

EISSFELDT, O. : *Geschichtliches und Übergeschichtliches im Alten Testament.* (Theologische Studien und Kritiken, Band 109, Heft 2.) 1947. (Evangelische Verlagsanstalt, Berlin.)

Three simple but suggestive lectures to clergy on the theme, " Volk und ' Kirche ' im Alten Testament." " Ewigkeit im Alten Testament," and " Ist der Gott des Alten Testaments auch der des Neuen Testaments ?" all designed to bring out the genetic relationship between the Old and New Testaments, and all written with an emphasis upon the Christan faith.
                                                                                          A.R.J.

FAUS, W. A. : *The Genius of the Prophets.* 1946. (Abingdon-Cokesbury Press, New York—Nashville. Price : $1.75.)

An exposition of the work of the canonical prophets, with re-current emphasis upon the prophetic psychology as well as the literary form and immediate historical background of their utterances. The writer's approach is balanced and informed, and the book as a whole is written in a simple, straight-forward style which makes it eminently suitable for the intelligent layman. Its major defect is a failure to set the prophets in the general context of Israel's religious tradition, and this is the more remarkable in view of the emphasis laid upon the author's " fresh approach " to the study of the prophets in terms of what is rather awkwardly described as the " life situation " (i.e., *Sitz im Leben*) of their messages. For that matter, however, it is difficult to find any great justification for this claim to be a " fresh approach."
                                                                                          A.R.J.

FRANKFORT, H. : *Kingship and the Gods.* 1948. (The University of Chicago Press, Chicago. Price : $5.00.)

This handsome volume, which is something of a companion piece to *The Intellectual Adventure of Ancient Man* (*vide* the Book List for 1947), is a comprehensive and careful survey of the institution of kingship in ancient Egypt and Mesopotamia. It pays due attention not only to written texts but also to the evidence furnished by contemporary art, and rightly brings out the contrasts as well as the similarities in the two fields of thought. In Egypt, for example, the Pharaoh is " the god incarnate," whereas in Mesopotamia the king, significantly enough, is " the chosen servant of the gods." An epilogue of little more than half a dozen pages offers a comparison with the Hebrew conception of kingship which by contrast is a mere trifling with the question at issue. This is unfortunate, for it mars what is otherwise a most stimulating and important piece of work, which no student of the Old Testament can afford to neglect.   A.R.J.

GALLING, K. : *Das Bild vom Menschen in biblischer Sicht.* 1947. (Kupferberg, Mainz.)

A public lecture, given in the Johannes Gutenberg University of Mainz, briefly reviewing the Old Testament conception of the nature of man and of his need as a sinner, and the New Testament conception of Christ as the response to his need and the goal of manhood. At the end are a number of notes giving useful references to a wide literature.　　H.H.R.

GISPEN, W. H. : *De Levietische Wet op de melaatschheid.* 1945. (Free University, Amsterdam.)

In this Inaurgural Lecture the author discusses the meaning of *sara'at* in the Old Testament in connexion with medical, phenomenological and Jewish theological conceptions, that in various ways give a special religious meaning to the word, seen either as caused by demons or as a punishment from Yahweh (a plague). Gispen holds to the meaning of leprosy, though he acknowledges that the Israelites used the word also for all kinds of analogical phenomena. There follow some remarks about the ceremonial law, while the peroration declares that these must point to Christ, the great Healer of many lepers. In my view this is a somewhat unexpected end to a somewhat unexpected inaugural subject.　　Th.C.V.

HEBERT, A. G. : *The Authority of the Old Testament.* 1947. (Faber and Faber, London. Price : 15s. 0d.)

A challenging and timely book which is in every way an advance on the author's earlier work ' The Throne of David.' He makes a clear break with the doctrine of the inerrancy of Scripture on the one hand and with a fundamentally humanistic liberalism, whether of the Protestant or the Catholic variety, on the other. The Bible must be read as a whole, because it contains the essentially reliable tradition of a history which includes the fulfilment of the Old Dispensation in the New. The word ' homology ' (borrowed from Phythian-Adams) is used to describe the correspondences between the dispensations, what might be called a recurrence of pattern. The rights of Biblical Criticism are fully granted and its results accepted and utilized. A useful distinction is drawn between the theological use of the Old Testament in the New as opposed to the illustrative and allegorical uses. The theological use has reference to real connexions which explain the course which history took. Hebert succeeds in avoiding Vischer's mistake of mis-interpreting what is meant by the contemporaneity of Scripture, and now puts forward a view which in some respects resembles that of C. H. Dodd. Though there will be considerable disagreement on matters of exegetical and other detail on the part of the Old Testament scholar, Hebert's book is not at variance with, but speaking generally, supplements the former's more empirical approach to the original documents.　　N.W.P.

HOLWERDA, B. : *De Priester-Koning in het Oude Testament*. 1946.
(Littooij Azn., Terneuzen. Price : 5s. 0d.)

This inaugural address, after a rapid survey of the wider
Semitic background for the uniting of the function of priest
and king, devotes itself particularly to Ps. cx, and Zech. vi.
The author denies that the priest-king was a feature of Israel's
life, but finds the concept to figure in the eschatological or
messianic hope. Melchizedek and Joshua are found to be
figures of the messianic priest-king, but there is no thorough-
going examination—probably due to the limitations of the
occasion—of the many problems attaching to these two
passages. A concluding section glances at the intertestamental
literature. On the whole this is to be commended rather for
touching a fruitful theme than for dealing with it satisfactorily.
H.H.R.

VAN HOONACKER, A., and COPPENS, J. : *Quelques Notes sur "Absolute
und Relative Wahrheit in der Heiligen Schrift"* (Bulletin d'Histoire
et d'Exégèse de l'Ancien Testament, No. 13). 1941. (Bijbelsch
Seminarie, Louvain.)

Professor Coppens here edits an unpublished paper of the late
Canon van Hoonacker, in which he criticized and answered
Egger's book, whose German title is given in the title of the
paper, and defended the view that the recognition of the
inspiration of the Bible does not preclude the denial of its
complete inerrancy. The work of Egger was aimed at Lagrange
and scholars of his school, and Van Hoonacker defends the
scientific historical method in Biblical study. H.H.R.

HULST, A. R. : *Belijden en loven*. 1948. (Callenbach, Nijkerk.)

In the inaugural address on the occasion of his installation as
Professor of Hebrew and Israelite Archaeology at Utrecht
University, Professor Hulst treated in an outstanding way—
often subscribing to the view of Professor Eerdmans—the
word *toda* in the Old Testament. He argues that originally
toda was a confession of sin combined with a doxology, and it
was offered either as an independent act or in connexion with
a sacrifice. The word can be used as a name for the sacrifice
itself, and on the other hand it can develop to mean the choir
of Levites which has to offer *toda*. In post-exilic literature *toda*
has its own place in the cult beside sacrifice, as is clear from
the book of Chronicles. In Hulst's view this is not a question
of the spiritualization of sacrifice, but a necessary development of the cultic act, in which from the outset both elements,
sacrifice and cultic word, were included. The form and content
of the word *toda* are derived from the Psalms of Praise.
Th.C.V.

JÉQUIER, G. : *Considérations sur les religions égyptiennes*. 1946. (À la
Baconnière à Boudry, Neuchâtel-Suisse. English Price : 15s. 6d.)

A posthumous volume of studies of selected phases of ancient
Egyptian religion, containing a wealth of information, illustrations, and interesting hypotheses. Not all these last will be
accepted, but all are important and are bound to help the
further elucidation of the problems of the origins, developments and equations of Egyptian deities. First, there are

everywhere three stages, fetichism, zoolatry, anthropomorphism, corresponding to the three stages of Egyptian life, nomadic, settled and urban with its domination by the great cities each in turn. For the rest, the author discusses the cults of the cities of Heliopolis, Hermopolis, and of the goddess Hathor. In each case, there are new emphases, particularly in respect of two original deities named Thot, and in connexion with the development of the goddess Hathor.   N.H.S.

KNIGHT, H. : *The Hebrew Prophetic Consciousness.* 1947. (Lutterworth Press, London, Price : 10s 6d.)

A well written, though not fully documented (except as regards Scripture references) contribution to Old Testament Theology. In the first part which deals with history and psychology the thesis of the author is that the Hebrew prophets stood in the direct line of the old diviners in Israel, but that they were profoundly influenced by contact with ecstatic phenomena of foreign provenance which assumed the form they did owing to the psychological assumption that the soul could exist apart from the body. The weakness of this part of the book is that the author uses the word ecstasy in two different senses, and leaves the reader wondering whether ' ecstasy ' of a kind that could be reconciled with Hebrew views of human personality owed anything to ecstasy properly so called. The theological second part of the book is excellent. The author owes something to Heschel and still more to Wheeler Robinson. He is especially interesting in his discussion of revelation and of the relation of time and eternity.

N.W.P.

KOHNSTAMM, PH. : *Staat dan in de Vrijheid. I : Brieven over het O.T.* 1947. (Ten Have, Amsterdam. Price : Fl. 6.90.)

This book was written in the dark years of the war, when the author, a Jewish Christian, had to live in hiding. It contains thirty letters, addressed to his grandchildren, in which he explains the spiritual and eternal values of the Old Testament. The book has an educational rather than a scientific character, but as such it is very valuable. The author accepts the results of criticism, but handles his material as a positive Christian in a generally sound way. This Professor of Natural Philosophy and Education has rendered a real service by this book.

Th.C.V.

DE LANGHE, R. : *Un dieu Yahweh à Ras Shamra ?* (Bulletin d'Histoire et d'Exégèse de l'Ancien Testament, No. 14). 1942. (Bijbelsch Seminarie, Louvain.)

A brief examination of the basis for the view that the divine name Yahweh, in the form Yw, stands in a Ras Shamra text, showing that the context is broken and part of the line is lost. It is, therefore, impossible to determine with any security the significance of these letters, and they provide no sufficient evidence for the worship of Yahweh at Ras Shamra.

H.H.R.

LESTRINGANT, P. : *Essai sur l'Unité de la Révélation Biblique : le problème de l'Unité de l'Évangile et de l'Écriture aux deux premiers siècles.* 1942. (Éditions " Je sers," Paris. Price : 5s. 3d.)

A book by a Roman Catholic (?) scholar which raises, but postpones discussion of, the problem of the relation of the Testaments in view of the moral and intellectual difficulties felt by so many, and confines itself to a careful study of the relevant evidence of the New Testament writers and their successors down to the end of the second century. At the outset the Church has to reconcile its Gospel with a body of Jewish scriptures which it claims as its own. At the end of the period there are two canonical collections of scriptures, the first of which has to be subordinated to the second. In between are the Apologists who use the Old Testament and the Gospel to support each other and Marcion with his denial of the relevance of the Old Testament to the Gospel altogether. At the close comes a detailed examination of the solution offered by Irenaeus.   N.W.P.

MATTHEWS, I. G. : *The Religious Pilgrimage of Israel.* 1947. (Harper and Brothers, New York. Price : $4.00.)

A massive work which seems to sum up the mature results of over twenty years of reading and teaching. There is so much that is first class here that one feels a certain reluctance in drawing attention to parts that are not. The author fails to find any real unity in the religion of Israel though the fact that there is such a unity is impressing itself to-day on an increasing number of scholars. The religion of Israel as a changing social phenomenon, in agreement with Dr. Matthew's admittedly humanistic outlook, is treated as passing through a whole series of different formulations. God is 'a power making for righteousness' which may be identified with man's best self. Elijah is treated as a reactionary who finds God in ' the hushed whisper ' of subtle propaganda and underground plotting accompanied by the dagger stroke, the eighth century prophets are laymen who on the basis of normal intellectual processes (cf. Seierstad) preach social ethics, and Jeremiah is an individualist who responds to the highest he knows and integrates his highest self and Yahweh. In a book of such range it is not surprising that some of the chapters are not up to date. One would like to know whether the paragraph on the Nazarenes on p.255 is to be regarded as an honest attempt at objectivity.   N.W.P.

MAUCHLINE, J. : *God's People Israel.* (Church of Scotland Committee on the Religious Education of Youth.)

In this volume attention has been concentrated upon the history of Israel, and upon the interpretation of that history by men, for whom no historical event was to be regarded as merely contingent or fortuitous. The arrangement of the subject matter is good, and the simple and straight-forward style in which it is written should commend it to teachers of those under fourteen and to Youth Club leaders.   B.K.R.

MINEAR, P. S. : *Eyes of Faith*. 1946. (Westminster Press, Philadelphia ; Lutterworth Press, London. Price : $3.00.)

This book contains much that is good and thought-provoking and it is, therefore, unfortunate, though perhaps unavoidable, that, written as it is in a paradoxical style, it will mystify readers who might otherwise have benefited greatly from what the author has to say and might perhaps have said more briefly and more simply. Dr. Minear's method is doubtless justified by his intention of shocking people out of long established habits of thought which make difficult the appreciation of the Biblical point of view. His debt to Kierkegaard, Buber, Brunner and others will be recognized in what he has to say about the indirect manner of God's communications to man, and an important point is made where he relates the moment of revelation and the content of what is revealed to the tradition which preceded it and to the future which it helps to determine. It may be with some diffidence suggested that a book half the length in plainer language would have been twice as effective.
                                                                        N.W.P.

ORTMANN, H. : *Der Alte und der Neue Bund bei Jeremia*. 1940. (Rudolph Pfau, Berlin.)

This work falls into three parts dealing with (a) the Old Covenant, (b) the New Covenant, and (c) the Covenant People and the Individual. The relation between the Old and the New Covenants is defined as follows : "The contrast between the Old and the New Covenants as conceived by Jeremiah consists in a promise of divine help such as will make possible the fulfilling of its requirements (a failure which was the cause of the nation's shipwreck under the Old Covenant). From the standpoint of the New Testament (i.e., its fulfilment in a quite different sense) both the Old and the New Covenants of the Old Testament are of a piece ; the New Covenant has the appearance of being an extension or final stage of the Old Covenant." Moreover, even the New Covenant, for all its obvious emphasis upon the individual, does not present him as an isolated unit but as a member of society within the nation. For the rest, Jeremiah was able to give such touching expression to the longing for a new covenant embracing the whole people, in which man should have the Law written by God upon the heart, simply because he knew only too well the obstinacy and cunning of his own heart, and so himself longed for a new one. The author makes use of much English as well as German literature on the subject, and in an appendix to his study offers a survey of the views of British scholars.
                                                                        O.E.

PATAI, R. : *Man and Temple*. 1947. (Thomas Nelson and Sons, London. Price : 8s. 6d.)

Dr. Patai is primarily a folklorist and anthropopogist. He discusses in turn the ritual of water-pouring with particular reference to post-exilic Feast of Tabernacles, the symbolism of the Second Temple first in relation to the Mesopotamian Creation myths, and then according to popular imagination, and lastly " from king to Messiah." Such studies have a fascination which is unique, and the volume contains much information not readily accessible. The danger in such studies is that similarities are stressed and differences neglected, and it is much to be doubted whether many of the author's comparisons and explanation are sound.   N.H.S.

PIDOUX, G. : *Le Dieu qui vient.* (No. 17, Cahiers théologiques de l'actualité Protestante.) 1947. (Delachaux et Niestlé, Neuchâtel-Suisse et Paris. Price : 2.75 francs suisses.)

A monograph of 54 pages involving a careful study of the God of the Old Testament as " the God who comes " into this world. He is the God Who has come and Who will come, and the Church is in between these two divine events. The Old Testament is the story of God's intervention on Israel's behalf, with the rescue from Egypt as the great saving act of the past, and His dramatic intervention at the end of time as the final event towards which all things move. All history is therefore, infused with an incomparable urgency. The study has a practical application, emphasising the " Here and Now " of God's saving grace for sinners and condemnation of sin. The author shows that a theology of Crisis can be based on a sound critical study of the Bible and be by no means obscurantist.
                                                    N.H.S.

*POLLOCK, S., and GRANTHAM, W. : *Men of God.* 1947. (Victor Gollancz, London. Price : 8s. 6d.)

A series of six broadcast plays of real merit. The imaginative frame-work of the series and the theme of the sixth play is the story of John the Baptist, and the five earlier prophets presented in dramatic form are Elijah, Amos, Isaiah, Hosea and Jeremiah. What qualifies the book for mention here is the presence in it of an admirable introduction; of interspersed notes and of useful appendices, for all which Mr. Pollock has been responsible. Free handling of the Biblical material is almost always frankly acknowledged and is never seriously misleading. The book can safely be recommended to school teachers.   N.W.P.

*ROBINSON, H. W. : *Two Hebrew Prophets : Studies in Hosea and Ezekiel.* 1948. (Lutterworth Press, London.) Price : 6s. 0d.)

A posthumous publication of two short courses of lectures which are entirely worthy of their late distinguished author and for which thanks are due to their editor. Earlier studies will be recalled by the title of the first : ' The Cross of Hosea.' Dr. Robinson aligns himself firmly with those who regard ch. iii, as an autobiographical sequel to a biographical ch. i. In the second course Ezekiel is credited with successive periods of prophetic activity in Judah and Babylon in agreement with the views of Bertholet published in 1936. Dr. Robinson has wise and valuable things to say about the limitations and merits of Ezekiel's theology.   N.W.P.

SEIERSTAD, I. P. : *Die Offenbarungserlebnisse der Propheten Amos, Jesaja und Jeremia.* (Dybwad, Oslo.)

A very large book to the importance and detail of which justice cannot be done in a brief review. The author is thoroughly conversant with the extensive literature on the subject of the prophetic inspiration—works by Hölscher, Gunkel, Gressmann, Lindblom, Weiser, Cramer, Heschel, Mowinckel, T. H. Robinson, Guillaume and many others—and has something important of his own to say. Is the prophet less a prophet in proportion as the ethical element increases at the expense of the ecstatic ? The problem of his authority and of his sense of a compulsion as resting upon him is discussed. The word of God to the prophet is not something unique out of all relation to the tradition he has inherited (Weiser), neither is it to be identified *simpliciter* with that tradition (Cramer). It is a word which comes to the prophet as something which may be contrary to his own wishes but which he cannot elude, which he could not have inferred from the tradition, yet which can and must be reconciled with it. It must be accepted and assimilated by the total personality of the prophet so that his will and God's will are brought into agreement ; cf. Jeremiah, but also his great predecessors. This book illuminates, and is illuminated by Mowinckel's recent work on the prophets. N.W.P.

SIMPSON, C. A. : *Revelation and Response in the Old Testament.* 1947. (Columbia University Press ; Geoffrey Cumberlege, London Price : 14s. 0d.)

The title of this book is somewhat misleading. It consists of a study of the pre-exilic religion of Israel in terms of the revelation of God through the events of history and the demand through the persons of its prophetic leaders for the response of obedience. Yahwism is held—rightly, in the reviewer's judgement—to have had an urge towards monotheism from its beginnings in Israel. More speculative and questionable is the author's reconstruction of history. He holds that Yahwism began at Sinai before any of the tribes entered Palestine, and that the tribes then separated, some entering Palestine in the thirteenth century, while others went to the region of Kadesh, where Yahwism incorporated the religion of the Kadesh deity of justice, whose Levitic priests led a minority movement in favour of this development. Later a group of Israelites went down to Egypt from Kadesh for a very brief period—insufficient to allow for one born in Egypt to attain manhood before the Exodus—and then escaped. Moses is held not to have entered Egypt, but to have been the priest of Kadesh who received the escaped tribes and interpreted to them the significance of their escape, and who subsequently went to Sinai, though for what purpose is left undisclosed. Neither Moses nor the Joseph tribes can therefore be associated with Egypt. Joshua is held to have been an Amarna age character who antedated the entry of any of the tribes and who was at a much later date fictitiously revived as the supposed leader of a united Israel. The idea of a covenant was taken over at a relatively late date from Shec-hemite Baalism and transferred to Sinai. All of this seems very hazardous, and it is a pity that the fruitful general idea of the book should be so handicapped by its inclusion.   H.H.R.

SJÖBERG, E. : *Der Menschensohn im äthiopischen Henochbuch* (Acta reg. societatis humaniorum litterarum Lundensis XLI). 1946. C.W.K. Gleerup, Lund.)

This is a most valuable study of the section of 1 Enoch known as the Parables (chaps. xxxvii-lxxi), the chief source of our knowledge of Jewish conceptions of the Son of Man at the time of the rise of Christianity. Before sifting out what these conceptions are—the eschatological function of the Son of Man, his pre-existence, suffering, his being concealed, etc.—and weighing their meaning, the preliminary task of literary criticism is undertaken. In this the writer establishes that the Parables are not a Christian work (as Hilgenfeld held), nor are the Son of Man passages Christian interpolations (Bousset and others), nor are xxxvii to lxxi, to be divided into sources (Beer and Charles), but that the chapters as a whole represent an independent literary writing, with very few secondary passages. The date Sjöberg places at some time before A.D. 70, say, the time of the early procurators. A question of much interest is : Is Son of Man a messianic title ? The answer is that the question whether the Son of Man is a current name of the Messiah is wrongly put, since all that can be said is that in the circles to which the apocalyptists and 1 En. belonged it was believed that a heavenly being, a heavenly Man, would judge sinners and redeem the righteous in the end-time. For these apocalyptists the term Son of Man had no other meaning. But if anyone should have claimed to be the chosen redeemer, he could not specify this better than by calling himself the Man, the Son of Man. It is true that in two passages in the Parables the name Messiah is given to the Son of Man but the difference between Son of Man and the Messiah-King of the end-time is apparent and the Son of Man is not described as an earthly Messiah nor as being of the seed of David. On the question of the relationship of the idea of the Son of Man to the non-Jewish oriental conception of the Primeval Man (*Urmensch*), the author affirms the influence of the latter upon Jewish thought. This influence, though responsible for the development of thought upon the Son of Man, is not of a wholesale kind, for similarities in detail are present only in a limited measure and ultimately the Son of Man is a figure of quite a different sort from that of the *Urmensch*. Sjöberg accepts the present difficult text of 1 En. lxxi, 14, which identifies Enoch with the Son of Man. The exegesis which he brings is incapable of relieving the difficulty. The reader may well think that the emendation of the text as found in Charles (Cf. Apoc. and Pseudep. Vol. II) is the only way out of the impasse.   O.S.R.

SNAITH, N. H. : *The Jewish New Year Festival : its Origin and Development.* 1947. (S.P.C.K., London. Price : 13s. 6d.)

This is a brilliant and challenging book, which especially aims to refute Mowinckel's theory of a *Thronbesteigungsfest* in Israel, but which offers much besides. The author argues convincingly that Passover was not a harvest festival or a new year festival, but an apotropaic ritual without any original thanksgiving character. In pre-exilic Israel the New Year festival was in the autumn, and it marked the end of the agricultural year and the beginning of a new year. It therefore offered thanks for the past and prayer for the future, and especially for the hoped for rains. In a careful discussion of the origin of the Sabbath and Hodesh, original views are advanced with strong arguments. Prof. Snaith translates Hodesh ' new month day,' and not ' new moon,' and holds that in pre-exilic times the new month began at full moon, and that Sabbath was the new moon day. Next he argues that the representation of Tishri 10 as New Year's day in Ezek. xl, I, was due to the change of the Calendar to the Mesopotamian system and the difference of 10 days between the lunar and the solar year. Finally he examines some of the arguments which have been advanced in favour of an Israelite festival comparable with the Babylonian. The blowing of the trumpet is held to be associated with the prayers for rain and not with the royal psalms, which were not written until the post-exilic period—as shown by their dependence on Deutero-Isaiah—and were not used in the ritual of New Year's day but were Sabbath psalms. The King motif in the New Year celebration does not go back beyond the second century A.D. On other grounds the influence of the Babylonian *akitu* festival—which is held to have been an annual commemoration festival, and not necessarily a New Year festival, though it became such in Babylon in the sixth century B.C.—is contested, though the author is willing to allow a much greater influence to Canaanite agricultural, in contrast to Babylonian urban, ritual. While many points will be contested, it is certain that this is a book of outstanding importance.

H.H.R.

THAUSING, G. : *Der Auferstehungsgedanke in ägyptischen religiösen Texten*. (Sammlung orientalischer Arbeiten, 16.) 1943. (Harrassowitz, Leipzig.)

This work contains a fairly long introduction dealing with the relevant conceptions and ideas, and this is followed by the texts, i.e., from the Pyramid and Coffin Texts and the Book of the Dead, in translation and accompanied by linguistic and exegetical notes. A welcome addition to the collection of translated texts by G. Roeder and H. Kees, as well as to Kee's *Totenglauben und Jenseitsvorstellungen*.

W.B.

WACH, J. : *Sociology of Religion*. 1947. (International Library of Sociology and Social Reconstruction, London. Price : £1 10s. 0d.)

A comparative study of the relation of religion and society, first published in Chicago in 1944. The author, after a methodological exposition, considers (1) the coincidence of religion and natural group (family cult, local cult, cult by people of the same sex or age), (2) the specifically religious organisation (secret society, founded religion, protests from within a

founded religion), (3) the influence on religion of the stratification of society (occupational differentiation among
primitives, social differentiation in higher civilization), (4)
religion and state, and (5) types of religious authority (founder,
reformer, prophet, seer, magician, diviner, priest, *religiosus*).
There is an enormous amount of material, much of it bearing
on Old Testament questions. The author is extremely cautious.
His conclusion that, on balance, religion has proved an integrating rather than a disruptive force is, therefore, truly
encouraging.   D.D.

WAMBACQ, B. N. : *L'épithète divine Jahvé S^e ba' ôt : étude philologique
historique et exégètique.* 1947. (Desclée, de Brouwer, Paris and
Bruges.)

An elaborate doctoral dissertation reviewing all the theories
of the significance of the term Yahweh Ṣebaoth, and arguing
that while there is no ground for holding that it ever meant
" God of the demons " or " the Warrior God," no single
meaning can be imposed on the term in all its occurrences.
With the developing conception of God there came development in the thought of the " hosts " which he controlled.
At first they were the hosts of the Israelite people, but then
they became the forces of nature and the nations of the
world, while instead of being regarded as the leader and
defender of the Israelite people, Yahweh became thought of
as the vindicator of the moral law by the visitation of his
people. All the occurrences of the term in Old Testament
and LXX are examined, and also all the uses of Ṣaba in the
singular or the plural apart from this divine title ; there are
in addition historical and exegetical sections of the book,
dealing chronologically with the occurrences of the term.
                                                              H.H.R.

POST-BIBLICAL JUDAISM

HERZOG, J. D. : *The Mishnah Berakoth, Peah, Demai.* 1945. (Harry
Fischel Institute, Jerusalem.)

This is the first volume of an edition containing the text,
and an English translation and English commentary by
Herzog : in addition, a selection of variant readings, references
to relevant material, the Hebrew commentary of Obadiah
of Bertinoro (ca.1500) and a Hebrew commentary by members
of the Institute.

Both new commentaries show a profound knowledge of the
traditional Jewish exegesis. For various reasons, far more
space is devoted to Demai than either of the other tractates.
Problems peculiar to modern scholarship are not, however,
considered to any great extent. No mention is made, e.g.,
of Albeck's thesis that the last controversy in Berakoth
VII 5, is an appendix ; yet such points are highly important
for source criticism of the Mishnah.   D.D.

LEVNER, J. B. : *The Legends of Israel*, tr., from the Hebrew by Joel Snowman. 1946. (James Clarke, London. Price : 10s. 6d.)

This is the first volume of a large work by a Russian Jew, who died in 1916, in earlier life a teacher in Odessa, and for his last ten years Crown Rabbi in South Russia. It consists of 207 Jewish legends dealing with the period from the Creation to the Death of Joseph. The sources are the Talmud, the Yalquts, the Midrashs, and Jewish traditional writings generally, and the stories are retold by the author. The book makes the Jewish legends popularly accessible. The occasional Hebrew script is full of errors. N.H.S.

PHILOLOGY AND GRAMMAR

DILLMANN, A. : *Chrestomathia Aethiopica*. Editio stereotypa. Adden da et corrigenda adiecit E. Littmann. 1941. (Keller, Leipzig.)

This well-known work is here reprinted without change save for the addition by Littmann of nine pages devoted to the text, grammar and content of the passages, together with accounts of their origin and translations. These are bound to receive a warm welcome from users of the book. W.B.

JOÜON, P. : *Grammaira de l'Hébreu biblique*. 2nd ed., 1947. (Institut Biblique Pontifical, Rome. Price : £1 12s. 6d.)

The second edition of Fr. Joüon's well-known Hebrew grammar is most welcome, even though a reviewer is bound to express regret that, in consequence of the author's death, it is merely an anastatical reproduction of the first edition ; but the editor, Fr. L. Semkowski, who has also taken upon himself the task of seeing the late Fr. Zorell's *Lexicon Hebraicum et Aramaicum* through the press, has made such corrections of misprints as the process of reproduction allows. This grammar is quite the best in the French language ; the statement of the facts is everywhere lucid and trustworthy even though some of the explanations are out of date (for example, in the retention of the antiquated *inverti* in the description of the consecutive constructions with the verb). None the less, the book is one which every teacher ought to possess and which every student will consult with profit to himself. G.R.D.

ORLINSKY, H. M. : *Notes on the Qal Infinitive Construct and the Verbal Noun in Biblical Hebrew*. 1947. (New Haven, Conn., U.S.A. Price : $0.75.)

This pamphlet, off-print No. 22 of the Publications of the American Oriental Society (vol. lxvii, pp. 107-126), contains a minutely detailed study of the difference in meaning and use between *qĕtol*, which the author regards as the sole infinitive form in Biblical Hebrew, and those suffixed forms with *a* or *i* as their first vowel, which he explains as a quite different type of verbal noun. It is difficult to see the wood for the trees in an article in which notes exceed text on almost every page, and the result seems very much of a distinction without a difference ; in any case the argument is initiated by the author's tacit assumption that the Massoretic vocalization is a trustworthy guide representing the original pronunciation of Hebrew words. G.R.D.

ZOLLI, E. : *Introduzione allo Studio dell 'Ebraico anticotestamentario.*
1947. (Angelo Belardetti, Rome. Price : 6s. 6d.)

> The readers of this small treatise of 123 pages are warned by
> the author that it was not his intention to write one more
> grammar of Old Testament Hebrew. This is, rather, a short
> introduction, intended to prepare the beginner for a more
> extensive treatment of the subject. Within these limits the
> brochure appears to be successful, though the English-
> speaking student of Hebrew will note the absence of any
> exercises in Hebrew composition. A study of many continental
> manuals suggests that there is no equivalent abroad of our
> Davidson-McFadyen with its admirable key to the intricacies
> of the Hebrew prose style. J.M.T.B.

ZORELL, F. : *Lexicon Hebraicum et Aramaicum Veteris Testamenti.*
Fasc. 6, 1947. (Pontificio Istituto Biblico, Rome. Price : 18s. 0d.)

> This new Fascicule of Fr. Zorell's *Lexicon,* already noticed
> on p. 61 of the ' Book List, 1946,' runs from sar to pāśaʿ;
> it is on the same scale and method as the preceding parts
> and contains no new features calling for special notice.
> (Zorell died on 13th December, 1947, the dictionary is being
> finished by the Rev. Père Semkovski.) G.R.D.

1949

This Book List has been prepared by the following Committee appointed by the Society : Prof. G. W. Anderson, Mgr. J. M. T. Barton, Dr. David Daube, Professors G. R. Driver, A. R. Johnson, N. W. Porteous, O. S. Rankin, Miss B. K. Rattey, Professors N. H. Snaith and H. H. Rowley (Editor). The Editor has also to acknowledge with gratitude help received from the following members of the Society : Rev. John Gray, Professors W. D. McHardy and C. R. North, Rev. Bleddyn J. Roberts, Professors T. W. Thacker and D. Winton Thomas ; and from the following continental scholars : Professors A. Lauha and A. F. Puukko, of Helsinki, and Th. C. Vriezen, of Groningen. Every effort has been made to make the List as complete and as up-to-date as possible, though some gaps are inevitable. A few books of which it had been hoped to include notices in the present List have not yet been received and must be held over until the next issue. For the omission of others the Editor has no better excuse to plead than ignorance.

Prices of foreign books, where known, are given either in foreign currency or in the English equivalent actually charged. In some cases variations in exchange would affect the latter to-day.

Titles to which an asterisk (*) is prefixed are recommended for inclusion in school libraries.

H. H. ROWLEY.

MANCHESTER UNIVERSITY.

GENERAL

AMANN, É. (ed. by) : *Dictionnaire de théologie catholique.* Fascs.
CXLVI-CXLVII, Vatican—Violation. 1948. Cols. 2569-3080.
(Letouzey et Ané, Paris. Price : 13s. 6d.)

> The great *Dictionnaire*, which began publication of its first
> numbers in 1902, is now almost complete. Amann, the third
> of its editors and the one who had directed its course since
> Mangenot's death in 1922, himself died on 10th January of
> last year. He had just corrected the proofs of the final article
> (Zwingle). The present fascicules contain no more than one
> article of direct interest to an Alttestamentler—that by Amann
> on " Versions de la Bible " (cols. 2700-2739.) By comparison with
> many of the other articles this is a somewhat slight and
> unoriginal contribution, and in some respects calls for correction
> in the light of Dr. Kahle's recent Schweich lectures. The
> author rightly prefaces his article with the remark that an
> adequate treatment would involve the help of not one but
> several specialists. It is, at least, an honest attempt to face
> all the wider problems in summary fashion.   J.M.T.B.

A Bibliography of Bible Study for Theological Students. 1948. Pp.
vi+86. (Theological Seminary Library, Princeton, N.J. Price :
5s. 0d.)

> With the exception of a few German Grammars and Dic-
> tionaries this Bibliography is confined to works written in
> English, and simply lists the titles of works, with publishers
> and dates, but without comment on their quality. It covers
> both Testaments, and the works are classified. It is much
> more up-to-date than any similar Bibliography, and covers
> both Britsh and American work. While there are inevitably
> gaps, it should be of real service to all interested in Bible
> study, and few readers will fail to find some titles that are new
> to them.   H.H.R.

DE BOER, P. A. H. (ed: by) : *Oudtestamentische Studiën,* Deel V. 1948.
Pp. 218. (Brill, Leiden. English Price : £1 10s. 0d.)

> This is the fifth volume to be published since the war by the
> newly-formed and very active Dutch Old Testament Society.
> It contains 15 separate articles, mostly in English, though
> some are in French, and one is in German. The first three are
> concerned with the spelling and pronunciation of the Sacred
> Name. B. D. Eerdmans argues for Yahu ; G. J. Thierry sees
> a double tradition, Yahweh being the orthodox and Yaho
> the idolatrous unorthodox tradition. B. Alfrink shows how
> the Greek transliteration developed into all sorts of cabalistic
> transformations of the seven vowels of the Greek alphabet.

M. David discusses the laws of the manumission of slaves. Th. C. Vriezen discusses two ancient cruces, one being Ruth iv, 3, this involving the thesis that the right of redemption is kept distinct from the levirate marriage. J. Simons inclines to the northern site for the cities of the plain. Both B. Alfrink and N. H. Ridderbos deal with early ideas of death. M. A. Beek sees no temple prostitution in Amos ii, 6-8, but all of it dealing with the oppression of the helpless. There are two lexicographical notes from J. van der Ploeg. H. A. Brongers deals with the Fear of the Lord on the lines of Otto's *mysterium tremendum et fascinans*. A. H. Edelkoort deals with the two types of prophets as instanced in Micah ii, 6-11, and iii, 5-8. W. H. Gispen shows how the primitive distinction between Clean and Unclean is used to keep Israel the holy people of God. P. A. H. de Boer concludes with a learned essay (including a wealth of work in Semitic philology) on the meaning of *massa* as a prophetic word, meaning the burden of judgement laid upon the prophet.   N.H.S.

BRILLANT, M., and NEDONCELLE, M. (ed. by) : *Apologétique, Nos raisons de croire : Réponses aux objections.* 1948. Pp. viii + 1386, with 96 pages of plates. (Bloud et Gay, Paris. Price : £1 10s. 0d.)

This immense repertoire of apologetic discussions and arguments, first issued in 1937, is, as the editors inform us, in substance identical with the earlier edition. There have, however, been some improvements and additions. Some of the chapters have been rewritten ; others are wholly new. Many of the contributions are not directly related to Old Testament studies. Among those of direct interest one may refer to Magnin's lengthy study of Old Testament religion (pp. 255-327), Tournay's " Comment utiliser l'argument prophétique " (pp. 328-35), and, especially, Coppens' excellent series of replies to difficulties found in the Old Testament books (pp. 977-1029). The last-named article is concerned with objections derived from natural science, those connected with the alleged historical errors in the Bible, those directed against the Old Testament religion and morality, and, finally, those relating to " la Science catholique de l'Ancien Testament " in regard to papal and other ecclesiastical pronouncements in these matters. Under alleged historical errors, Coppens considers in turn the first eleven chapters of Genesis, the knowledge of good and evil in Gen. ii-iii, the nature of the sin committed by Adam and Eve, the longevity of the patriarchs, the flood, the story of Lot's wife, biblical chronology, the fall of Jericho, the stories of Samson, Tobias, and Jonah, and general difficulties arising out of the history of Israel.
                                                                            J.M.T.B.

COPPENS, J. : *Miscellanées Bibliques xviii-xxiii.* (Analecta Lovaniensia Biblica et Orientalia, viii.) 1948. Pp. 48. (Duculot, Gembloux.)

Of the six studies contained in this work five are supplementary to the author's earlier studies on the Paradise story and the sin of Adam and Eve (cf. Book List, 1948, p. 41).

in the first he examines the view of M. Guitton, which has points of similarity with his own, though he was unacquainted with it when he published his earlier study ; in the second he adduces some further patristic views on the sexual character of the sin of Paradise ; in the third he draws attention to Albright's decipherment of the proto-Sinaitic inscriptions and finding of a serpent goddess there ; in the fourth he returns to his rendering of Gen. iii, 22, and considers objections which have been raised against it ; and in the fifth he considers the Philonic and Targumic interpretation of the verse. The last study is a long and detailed review of Vriezen's Introduction noted elsewhere in this List (see p. 36).   H.H.R.

ENGNELL, I., and FRIDRICHSEN, A. (ed. by) : *Svenskt Bibliskt Uppslagsverk* Band I, A-K. 1948. Pp. 1296. (Skolförlaget. Gävle. Price of the whole work ; paper covers, 95 crowns ; cloth, 110 crowns ; half leather, 120 crowns.)

Professors Engnell and Fridrichsen have enlisted the help of a team of very able scholars in the production of this new Swedish Bible Dictionary, which promises, when completed, to be a most valuable work of reference. The shorter articles are written with care and lucidity, and many of them are models of compressed statement. Of the longer articles on Old Testament subjects, special interest attaches to those in which the characteristic views of the Uppsala school find expression, notably Engnell's own contributions on *Gamla Testamentet* and *Gamla Testamentets religion*, in which he states forcibly the general attitude to Old Testament problems adopted by himself and his colleagues. The New Testament articles are also of great interest and outstanding merit, and some of them are particularly rich in theological content. The high level of scholarship is matched by excellence of production. The volume is richly illustrated by carefully chosen photographs which are splendidly reproduced. Altogether this volume is a fine achievement.   G.W.A.

Ex Oriente Lux Jaarbericht No. X (1945-1948). 1948. Pp. 592. (Leiden.)

This substantial volume, mostly in Dutch, embodies four year-books of the Dutch Society for the study of Near-East and Egyptian antiquities. It contains comprehensive summaries of the work done by scholars generally during recent years in the various branches of study in which the society is interested, i.e., all matters concerning the Near East from Mesopotamia to Egypt. Most important from the Old Testament point of view are the summaries dealing with papyrology (since 1941), Old Testament Studies (since 1941), and Peshitta studies (since 1927). There are numerous articles in all the various departments of study. In particular, van der Waerden discusses the Venus Tablets of Ammiṣaduqa, and on the basis of the evidence he produces, he advocates 1727 B.C. as the year of Hammurabi's accession. C. - F. Jean gives transcripts and translations of six letters from Mari. E. Dhorme maintains that the Byblos inscriptions (called pseudo-hieroglyphic by Dunand in 1945) are Phoenician, more primitive than those of Ras Shamra, and proposes a decipherment of three lines. Amongst other articles F. M. Th. Böhl writes at length on " Babylon the Holy City," and J. Simons has a short article in the Palestinian Archaeology section on the three walls of Jerusalem.   N.H.S.

FRIDRICHSEN, A. (ed. by) : *Svensk exegetisk Årsbok XIII* (Pp. 124), with supplement *Symbolae Biblicae Upsalienses XI* (Pp. 98). 1948. (C. O. Ekblad & Co., Västervik ; C. W. K. Gleerup, Lund ; Ejnar Munksgaard, Copenhagen. Price : 8 crowns.)

In the current number of this valuable annual H. Eklund contributes a provocative article on New Testament exegesis and modern thought. The suggestion that the Creation narrative in Genesis i, 1, ii, 4, is a cultic text is carefully examined by H. Ringgren who concludes that it is an anti-cultic revision of the ancient myth of creation. There is a long and judicious review (pp. 32) by H. Birkeland of vol. 1 of A. T. Nikolainen's *Der Auferstehungsglauben in der Bibel*, and a·shorter discussion by A. S. Kapelrud of Ch. Barth's *Die Errettung vom Tode*. Most of the rest of the Årsbok is devoted to reviews by Scandinavian scholars of works on Biblical subjects. The supplement consists of reviews in French and German by non-Scandinavian scholars of books on the New Testament published in Sweden between 1945 and 1948. The volume is an important aperçu of recent work in the Biblical field, particularly in Scandinavia.   G.W.A.

LYONS, W. N., and PARVIS, M. M. : *New Testament Literature : An Annotated Bibliography*. 1948. Pp. xiv + 392. (University of Chicago Press. Price : $4.00.)

This is the first volume of what promises to be an annual series, listing books and articles relating to the New Testament wherever published, with very brief notes on a number of the entries, and references to reviews of the books mentioned. In all there are 3,432 entries, classified and followed by Author Index, Greek Index and Scripture Index. While it is a New Testament Bibliography it contains not a little of importance to the Old Testament scholar, as it includes works dealing with the whole Bible, and with the Versions, and also a valuable section on Judaism. While the annotations are very brief, that is only to be expected in a compilation of such range, and the collectors of the material have put all Biblical scholars in their debt by the immense labours they have undertaken.   H.H.R.

MARCUS, R. : *A Selected Bibliography* (1920-1945) *of the Jews in the Hellenistic-Roman Period*. (Reprinted from the Proceedings of the American Academy for Jewish Research, xvi.) 1947. Pp. 86.

This is a useful addition to our bibliographical material, listing books and articles within its field. There are general works on the Jews and Jewish religion of the period, and on Inter-testamental literature, works on the Jews of Palestine, classified under nine heads for history and ten heads for religion and literature, and works on the Jews of the Diaspora classified under twelve heads in all. There are no notes on any of the works mentioned, but it is of great use to have a classified list of titles covering a quarter of a century's work.

H.H.R.

Orientalia Neerlandica : A Volume of Oriental Studies, published under the auspices of the Netherlands' Oriental Society. 1948. Pp. viii + 498. (Sijthoff, Leiden. Price : Fl. 15.00.)

The publication of this volume of essays on Oriental subjects is issued to celebrate the twenty-fifth anniversary of the Dutch Oriental Society ; and it covers the whole East. Consequently only half a dozen of the studies contained in it will be of interest to students of the Old Testament : Gispen on 'Azazel,' de Boer on Exod. xxi, 7-11, Vriezen on the composition of the Books of Samuel, Simons on Josh. xvi-xvii, Schoneveld on Urim and Tummim (pp. 156-222). All are in English or, if in Dutch, are provided with English summaries ; and all are interesting, even if their conclusions are sometimes reactionary, inconclusive or unconvincing.

G.R.D.

ROBERT, A. (ed. by) : *Dictionnaire de la Bible. Supplément.* Fasc. XXI (Israël—Jésus Christ) Cols. 737-992. Fasc. XXII (Jésus Christ—Judaïsme) Cols. 993-1248. 1948. (Letouzey et Ané, Paris. Price : 7s. 6d., 7s. 0d.)

The article on " Israël " by R. de Vaux, though an able and well-informed synthesis, is not perhaps quite so important as its earlier section in Fascicule XX suggested it would be. It must, of course, be remembered that the articles in the *Supplément* are not intended entirely to replace those of the larger *Dictionnaire.* Gelin's article on " Jérémie " is a good specimen of a compressed introduction to the book and its teaching. Cavallera on " Jerome " (8 columns) may be compared with the 90 columns of Forget's elaborate article in the 8th volume of the *Dictionnaire de théologie catholique.* Perhaps the most remarkable article of any that have recently appeared is that on " Jérusalem " (70 columns) by that veteran archaeologist and supreme authority among living experts, L. H. Vincent of the École biblique et archéologique française. Here will be found much of the matter that has occupied the author's life and work in Palestine since his arrival there in the year 1892, and he is, at the end of a long life, as inspiring, as challenging, and as tenacious of his always well-considered opinions as ever. The question of the third wall of Jerusalem, discussed at length in various articles in the *Revue biblique* for 1908, 1927-8 and 1947, is here summarized magisterially. He is still entirely convinced that the remains explored by Sukenik and Mayer and described by them in their monograph published in 1930, are not to be identified with Agrippa's wall, but are to be connected with the second revolt of Bar-kokhba in A.D. 131-35.

In fascicule XXII one may notice particularly Bonsirven's fine study of " Judaïsme Palestinien au temps de Jésus-Christ."

J.M.T.B.

SEMITICA. (Cahiers publiés par l'Institut d' Études sémitiques de l'Université de Paris. I). 1948. Pp. 86. (Maisonneuve, Paris. Price : £1 1s. 0d.)

> This, the first number of a new venture published under the auspices of the University of Paris, contains seven articles on Sumerian and Accadian, Biblical and Islamic subjects. Biblical scholars will be most interested in Prof. Dupont-Sommer's publication of a new Aramaic document from Saqqarah mentioning a Babylonian invasion of Egypt which may be referred to a date c. 605 B.C. (in which case this document is the oldest known Aramaic papyrus) and a study of the Gezer Calendar by Prof. Février (whose views, however, are not all so novel as they seem to be). Prof. Blachère's study of nafs in the Qur'an, too, is interesting. Altogether, this work, which is not so much a first fascicule of a regular periodical publication as a first instalment of a collection of studies intended to be issued at irregular intervals as material comes to hand or is accumulated, makes a most promising beginning and (except for its price) will be welcomed by all Semitists.   G.R.D.

EDUCATIONAL

*BRAHAM, E. G. : Prophets of Israel. 1948. Pp. 140. (G. Gill & Son, London. Price : 6s. 0d.)

> Teachers will welcome this scholarly and interesting study of the prophets from Amos to Malachi. The author believes that the teaching found in the prophetic literature has no mere transient significance but, because it is a word of God, it has real bearing upon national and individual problems, as well as the social evils of our own day. Unnecessary detail has been avoided and attention concentrated upon the prophet, his circumstances and his message. In the opening chapter the question " What is Prophecy " is dealt with, and in the last the difference in outlook between the philosopher and the prophet is considered : dangerous tendencies in the modern world are shown to be incompatible with the prophets' insistence upon the activity of the Living God and the responsibility of every man to God and to his fellows. An inspiring book written with freshness and lucidity.   B.K.R.

*GOODSPEED, E. J. : How to read the Bible. 1948. Pp. x + 230. (Oxford University Press. Price : 7s. 6d.)

> Instead of the usual historical and critical accounts of the books of the Bible Dr. Goodspeed reviews the main types of literature in the Old Testament, the Apocrypha and the New Testament. The chapter headings indicate his method : e.g., under Popular Religious Poetry he includes a brief account of the Psalms, the Song of the Three Children and the Canticles in St. Luke's Gospel. Other chapters deal with the Poetry of the Prophets, Letters and Epistles, Visions and Revelations and the Literature of Devotion. The author treats the Bible as a living whole, and he hopes that this kind of approach will " help the general reader to find its chief values for himself."

In the last chapter the history of the English Bible is reviewed from Wyclif's first translation (1382) to translations in modern speech, the English R.V. of 1885, and the American Standard version. A useful book of reference for the library of schools and Training Colleges. B.K.R.

*ROBINSON, T. H. : *An Introduction to the Old Testament.* (Merlin Books) 1948. Pp. 190. (Arnold, London. Price : 3s. 0d.)

Within the Bible itself there is visible a long process of development and it is the purpose of the author of this book to trace that development in regard to the O.T.
First the questions " What is the O.T. ?" and " Why should it be studied ?" are answered. The history of Israel from the Exodus to the fall of Jerusalem in 70 A.D. is sketched very briefly, and a valuable section is devoted to describing how the books of the O.T. were written. Finally three chapters are given to an outline of the religion of Israel, special attention being directed to the teaching of the prophets and to the contribution made by the Wisdom writers (" Jewish philosophers ") and by the Apocalyptists in preparation for the fulfilment of the Hope of Israel in Jesus, the Christ.
This little book written in simple and untechnical language is enriched with many illustrations and several maps. It will stimulate interest in the O.T. and reassure ordinary men and women that modern knowledge has in no respect diminished the authority of the O.T. as the Word of God to successive generations of mankind. B.K.R.

ARCHAEOLOGY AND EPIGRAPHY

CHAPIRA, B. : *Les Lettres de Lakiš.* (Extrait de la Revue des Études Sémitiques-Babyloniaca. Fasc. 2, 1942-45.) 1945. Pp. 68. (Geuthner, Paris. Price : 3s. 6d.)

In this study of the Lachish ostraca the author presents the Hebrew texts as read by Torczyner in his 1938 edition and by himself, with commentaries upon them. Some of his readings are antiquated, as might be expected in a work which, though published in 1945, was written in 1939, while others are frequently mere products of a lively imagination. Typical examples of the latter are his filling in of line 3-6 of Ostracon viii so as to produce the date " 28 Nisan of the eleventh year of Zedekiah," and his restoration in Ostracon xvi, line 10 (= Torczyner's line 6) of the Hebrew phrase for " the court of the prison " which is found in Jer. xxxii, 2, etc.—a " discovery " which furnishes, so the author thinks, definite proof that the prophet mentioned in Ostracon iii is none other than Jeremiah. In his interpretation of the texts, which is based upon his belief that they consist of two main groups, one having for its principal theme the prophet, the other the siege of Jerusalem, the author likewise allows his imagination full play. He does not hesitate, for example, on the basis of a single word, to find a connexion between Ostracon iii, lines 19 ff., which contain a warning of some kind from the prophet, and Jeremiah's exhortation to observe the sabbath (Jer. xvii,

19 ff.). Fanciful too is his attempt to show that the proper order of certain chapters in the book of Jeremiah can be restored with the help of these texts. This study is in fact so full of improbabilities that it is of little value to the serious student of these texts.   D.W.T.

Corpus Inscriptionum Semiticarum—Pars prima, inscriptiones phoenicias continens. Tomus III, fasciculus secundus. 1947. Pp. 161-399. (Klincksieck, Paris. Price : approx. £1 19s. 0d.)

This continuation of the famous Corpus is a welcome instalment, and scholars will be glad to know that other fascicules are already in the press or in preparation. The external *format* is the same, except that the wrapper has changed colour and the paper is not so stout and perhaps hardly strong enough for so large a page. The present part continues the publication, in the same style, of the immense number of funerary inscriptions reported from Carthage ; these, of which the last part (issued in 1926) contained 3,914, run on to 5,260, and even so do not bring their collection to completion.
                                                         G.R.D.

DRIVER, G. R. : *Semitic Writing : From Pictograph to Alphabet.* 1948. Pp. 222. (Oxford University Press. Price : £1 5s. 0d.)
In this volume, the Schweich Lectures for 1944, Professor Driver investigates the evolution of the Semitic systems of writing with especial reference to the origin of the alphabet. In the first of the three lectures, on Cuneiform Scripts, he discusses such topics as the use of clay and other writing materials, writing implements, the arrangement of the text, the development from picture to symbol and from words to syllables, scholars and scribes, archives and libraries. The second lecture, on Alphabetic Writing, consists in the main of an examination of ancient Semitic inscriptional material, while the third is on the Origin of the Alphabet. The last is sure to evoke special interest. The close connexion which is found between the Egyptian hieroglyphic system of writing and the Phoenician script is noteworthy, as is the view that the Sinaitic script " was probably not so much ' the missing link ' between Egyptian hieroglyphs and the Phoenician alphabet as one link in a complex chain of development which has not yet been fully unwound." The author's freshness of approach is well illustrated in the sections on the evidential value of the names of the letters, the relation of the form of the letter to its name, the forms and names of the individual letters, and the order of the letters. As for the time and place of the invention of the alphabet, the inventor(s) sprang from one or other of the Semitic peoples which came into contact with the Egyptian between 2500 and 1500 B.C. The first step in the invention was taken in or near Egypt, the invention was developed in Palestine, and perfected on the Phoenician coast. The Greek alphabet emerged, it is believed, about the middle of the ninth century B.C. This volume, replete with information and rich in suggestion, is a work of the highest scholarship, whose value is enhanced by the numerous excellent

drawings, figures and photographic plates, and by the addition of several appendices. With Professor Driver's work and with Dr. Diringer's *The Alphabet* (see "Book List 1948," p. 13) available to them, English readers interested in this field are now uncommonly well provided for. The conclusions reached by the two scholars, it may be added, are sometimes very different.   D.W.T.

EISSFELDT, O. : *Von den Anfängen der phönizischen Epigraphik nach einem bisher unveröffentlichten Brief von Wilhelm Gesenius.* (Hallische Monographien, No. 5.) 1948. Pp. 18. (Max Niemeyer, Halle.)

The English text of the paper which Professor Eissfeldt read to the Society for Old Testament Study in 1947 was published in P.E.Q., 1947, pp. 68 ff. Professor Eissfeldt has now published a German edition enriched with much fuller footnotes. The paper gives the text of the letter of Gesenius, written to E. G. Schultz in Paris and inviting his help on some points in the preparation of his edition of the Phoenician inscriptions then known. The letter is of interest for its revelation of the carefulness of Gesenius and for the persons mentioned—of all of whom Eissfeldt supplies some biographical particulars. In the concluding pages Professor Eissfeldt re-examines the text of the inscriptions referred to in the letter. The concluding part of his paper, offering new support for his view that *molk* was a particular variety of sacrifice, is omitted here.
                                                    H.H.R.

HROZNÝ, B. : *Histoire de l'Asie Antérieure de l'Inde et de la Crète (jusqu'au début du second millénaire).* 1947. Pp. 352. (Payot, Paris. English Price : £1 1s. 0d.)

The author of this book, one of the well-known collection entitled *Bibliothèque Historique*, gives a concise account of the history and civilization of the early Middle East and neighbouring countries down to the end of the Hittite Empire and the coming of the Philistines. While he keeps to the known facts, his story is lucidly and even brilliantly told, but, where historical records fail, imagination is apt to run riot. Hamites and Semites may conceivably have come from the neighbourhood of the Caspian Sea or some Transcaucasian region, but the evidence adduced is barely convincing ; and the suggestion that Sargon of Accad (*c.* 2400 B.C.) reached the Attic silver-mines is a mere, and scarcely probable, guess. Much space is devoted to the author's supposed decipherment, during and just after the war, of the Proto-Indian and Cretan scripts ; but the results as here outlined do not carry conviction. A script possessing 50 signs for variations of *s* and *sh* is not likely to have been an invention of much practical use ! Such a book, then, however interesting and stimulating, must be read with caution.   G.R.D.

DE LANGHE, R. : *De Taal van Ras Sjamra-Ugarit.* 1948. Pp. 34. (Dekker & Van de Vegt, Nijmegen-Utrecht.)

The Ras Shamra Texts, the significance of the contents of which for comparative religion and linguistics of the Near East is universally acknowledged, are generally admitted to be in a Semitic dialect. The exact affinity of this dialect, however, is still far from certainly established. In this paper De Langhe examines this problem afresh. He marshals and surveys documents from Canaan and the immediate neighbourhood from the beginning of the second millennium to the earliest documents of the O.T. including the lists of Palestinian localities in the Egyptian inscriptions of the New Empire. The necessary qualifications are made for differences of time or locality and the essential position of Ugaritic as a Canaanite dialect maintained. This view is supported by the material evidence from R.S. and by the religious position indicated in the texts where Ugarit was culturally and religiously a unit with the rest of Syria and Palestine. The paper is, as all De Langhe's work on Ras Shamra matter, balanced and soundly conservative though too little notice is taken of the considerable Arabic affinities of the Ugaritic dialect and in the survey of the political and cultural contacts of Ugarit surely Noth's vital work on ' Die syrisch-palästinische Bevölkerung ' should have been taken into the reckoning. The conclusion is still far from satisfactory. De Langhe vindicates the place of Ugaritic in the Canaanite group but admits that local variations are natural in this place so far north with contacts with Mesopotamia and the Syrian desert. This latter fact should probably be emphasized. The texts, however, must remain still unhappily the subject of divergent interpretations as long as the linguistic relationship remains no more precisely determined.   J.G.

Megiddo I : Seasons of 1925-34, Strata I-V, by R. S. Lamon and G. M. Shipton. (The University of Chicago Oriental Institute Publications, Vol. XLII.) 1939. Pp. xxviii + 236 and 116 plates interleaved with explanations. *Megiddo II : Seasons of 1935-39*, by G. Loud, 2 vols. text and plates. (The University of Chicago Oriental Institute Publications, Vol. LXII.) 1948. Pp. xxii + 200, and maps and plans, x + 290 plates interleaved with explanations. (The University of Chicago Press, Chicago. Price : £5 10s. 0d. and £8 15s. 0d.)

These three volumes record the results of fourteen years of scientific excavation of Megiddo from 1925 to 1939. Unfortunately the elaborate plans for stratified excavation on a grand scale were not carried out and latterly the sectional method had to be applied. This is reflected in the publication and is somewhat disconcerting. The first volume from the ' veterans ' Lamon and Shipton covers the first nine years of the work and is a report on the four strata (V-II) of the Hebrew period with some reference to the documentary evidence of Scripture for the reign of Solomon. The second volume from Loud, Field Director since 1935, is avowedly more of a catalogue, very full and meticulously drawn up with severely scientific method. The writer, however, presents a succinct and masterly correlation of evidence from different sections according to stratification. The whole work is sumptuously produced and completely equipped with excellent photographs with a complete illustrated index of pottery, and scarabs. Not the least important part of the work are supplements on the coins (Vol. 1) by Newell—which incidentally represent all ruling powers from the Persian period to Ottoman times with the notable exception of the Crusaders —on bone tools from the pre-historic period by Miss Bate and Mrs. Crowfoot, on flints by Miss Joan Crowfoot and a posthumous report of the late J. H. Breasted on an inscription of Ramses VI. The volumes, the third of which consists of indexed illustrations and plans, are indispensable as a work of reference for all who handle archaeological evidence from Palestine.   J.G.

OBERMANN, J. : *Ugaritic Mythology*. 1948. Pp. xxiv + 110. (Yale University Press, New Haven. Price : $2.75.)

The title of this work is somewhat misleading, for it is not by any means the general study which seems to be implied, but rather a preliminary attempt at a fresh analysis of the text 5*AB*. The writer holds that this is yet another version of the building saga which appears so clearly in 2*AB*, and that the leading motif of these texts, as indeed of 3*AB* and 6*AB* (which though fragmentary is clearly parallel in parts to 5*AB*), is a struggle for supremacy between the gods which reflects the architectural innovations introduced with the coming of the age of metallurgy. The work is obviously important, even though cn a preliminary reading one may entertain some doubts as to the validity of the author's general thesis ; and with its careful argumentation it is full of stimulus and suggestion.   A.R.J.

OBERMANN, J. : *Discoveries at Karatepe*. (Supplement to J.A.O.S. No. 19 = A.O.S. Offprint series No. 26.) 1948. Pp. 50 with 7 plates. (New Haven, U.S.A. Price : $1.00.)

This somewhat ambitious title conceals an edition of an important Phoenician inscription of the 9th or 8th century B.C., discovered by a Turkish archaeological expedition in 1946 at Karatepe, an elevated stronghold situated in the mountains N.E. of Adana and not far from Zinjîrlū, where other inscriptions of the same period have been found. Its author is one 'ZTWD king of the DNNYM, who are probably mentioned also on the inscription of KLMW ; for this king complains that a king of the D[N]NYM has overrun his territory. The new inscription is remarkable for the numerous echoes of Biblical phraseology which recur in it. The present work contains a text, with photographs, and a translation of the inscription, and introduction and brief philological notes ; it will be found useful by all who are interested in the subject, but must be read in conjunction with other editions that have already appeared, notably that of Professor A. M. Honeyman (cf. *Muséon* LXI 43-57), since the time for a definitive interpretation of this interesting inscription has not yet come. Apparently, indeed, other fragments completing the text may be expected.   G.R.D.

O'CALLAGHAN, R. T. : *Aram Naharaim : a Contribution to the History of Upper Mesopotamia in the Second Millennium B.C.* (Analecta Orientalia, xxvi.) 1948. Pp. xvi+164, (Pontificium Institutum Biblicum. Rome. Price : Lire 6,800.)

> This is a work of first-class importance resting on a wide knowledge of all the modern literature dealing with the area indicated by the title, and gathering together all that is known of its history down to the end of the second millennium B.C. There is an introductory chapter dealing with the period preceding the second millennium, but the main body of the work deals with that millennium. Major problems, such as the date of Hammurabi and the Subarian question, are discussed in brief but richly documented notes. The chief importance of the work, however, will be found in the light it sheds on the cultural background of the patriarchal age through its judicious use of the Mari and other material, which the author so well controls.　　　H.H.R.

PARROT, A. : *Tello : Vingt Campagnes de Fouilles* (1877-1933). 1948. Pp. 368. (Albin Michel, Paris.)

> In this volume we have an important contribution to the literature on the archaeology of Biblical lands. Tello is the ancient Lagash, and here we have surveyed the fruits of twenty expeditions, in the last of which the author shared. The material finds are dealt with in the order of the historical periods to which they refer, and a classified catalogue of them is provided. The volume is well illustrated, and has an excellent Bibliography. The experience and eminence of Parrot as an archaeologist guarantees the quality and the authority of the work.　　　H.H.R.

RIESENFELD, H. : *The Resurrection in Ezekiel xxxvii, and in the Dura-Europos Paintings* (Uppsala Universitets Årsskrift, 1948, xi). 1948. Pp. 40. (Lundequistska Bokhandeln, Uppsala and Harrassowitz, Leipzig. Price : Kr. 1.50.)

> In this study it is argued that the idea of resurrection in Israel was not a late borrowing from the Persians, but had its roots in ancient Canaanite ritual, especially associated with the great festivals, Passover and Tabernacles. The writer holds that Ezk. xxxvii, has behind it this background, and believes it was read in the Passover liturgy before the Christian era began. Further he thinks it lies behind Matt. xxvii, 51-53. In this connexion he notes that the Dura Europos paintings depict the Mount of Olives as cleft in twain by an earthquake, while the dead are raised here.　　　H.H.R.

SCHAEFFER, C. F. A. : *Stratigraphie Comparée et Chronologie d'Asie Occidentale (III et IIe millénaires)*. Pp. xiv+654. 1948. (Oxford University Press. Price : £4 4s. 0d.)

> A synthesis of archaeological evidence from excavations and soundings in Syria, Palestine, Anatolia, the Caucasus, Persia and Cyprus from 2400 to 1200 B.C. this work has long been desired and we are fortunate in having it produced by the excavator of Ras Shamra, a site well stratified in itself with

immediate contacts with Mesopotamia, Egypt, Anatolia, Cyprus and the Aegean. After an account of the cultural and historical phases of Ugarit follows a summary, discussion and correlation of evidence from other sites. In Palestine in particular Schaeffer finds a correspondence with Ras Shamra in its various phases which all would admit on broad lines but fewer will accept in the detail which the author would urge. He stresses the importance of natural phenomena in the history of the Near East. Three earthquakes at least are assumed to have occurred, *c*. 2400, 2100 and 1365 B.C., which Schaeffer regards as generally affecting the whole Near East, thus affording a means of comparative dating. This evidence, however, is not uniform and is often gained by disputing the findings of excavators in the various fields. The author emphasizes the racial trend from North to South, unduly perhaps, since no notice is taken of the Semitic influx attested in the Egyptian Execratory Texts, nor of the Hebrews nor the Khabiru whose incursions one might naturally associate with the level of destruction which Schaeffer notes everywhere in 1365 B.C. The period *c*. 1220 B.C., so clearly marked in all sites, Schaeffer associates with the Sea-Peoples, never so much as mentioning the Hebrews. One feels throughout that the whole study is too much divorced from the very considerable documentary evidence. In the dating of Khammurabi, for instance, Schaeffer prefers the evidence of seal designs and pottery to the Khorsabad king-lists. In the material evidence cited and discussed there are certain regrettable ommissions. The Hyksos are treated too cavalierly. It is strange to hear him complain of lack of material evidence for the period of their invasion and yet find a total neglect of such sites as Tell Jerisheh, Tell Balata and Tell el Far'a (by Nablus) and no discussion of the distribution of the horse and two-wheeled war-chariot and such architectural features as the glacis fortifications and the palace-fort or bit hillani. In an ample work with useful cross-reference and not unwelcome re-dundancy in the text and a wealth of figures and charts the author has put his abundant evidence before us. In his courageous endeavour to present the situation in perspective he has made his subject vastly more interesting and generally intelligible if often challenging his fellow-workers in their own fields.   J.G.

HISTORY AND GEOGRAPHY

ALTHEIM, F. : *Weltgeschichte Asiens im griechischen Zeitalter.* 2 vols. 1947, 1948. Pp. vi+412, vi+262. (Niemeyer Halle/Saale.)

This work is a useful presentation of the political and cultural aims and achievements of Alexander the Great. Of the Dia-dochi the author devotes a chapter to Antiochus III and Antiochus IV but touches scantily and merely incidentally on Palestine and the Jewish patriots. His main interest lies further East and his theme is the inter-relations of Hellenism and the culture of Persia and latterly of the Parthians. Of chief interest to O.T. scholars is the discussion of evidence from Afghanistan for the diffusion of the Aramaic script in the Persian Empire and two chapters, Part IV, chaps. ii-iii, on Hellenistic and Persian literature as formal prototypes of the Books of Esther, Judith and Tobit, and the Tale of Ahiqar, and of apocalyptic.   J.G.

BELL, H. I. : *Egypt from Alexander the Great to the Arab Conquest : a study in the diffusion and decay of Hellenism.* 1948. Pp. viii+168. (Clarendon Press, Oxford.   Price :   10s. 0d.)

This fascinating little book contains the text of the four Gregynog lectures delivered by the author in the University College of Wales, Aberystwyth, in November, 1946. Each lecture has been made into a chapter. The first is an account of the science of papyrology, which has provided the material for the other three chapters. They deal with Egypt in the Ptolemaic, Roman and Byzantine periods. A useful bibliography is appended. The author has devoted himself to a description of the economic, social and administrative development, and has touched upon political history only when it is necessary for the understanding of his subject. The book is written in a lucid and attractive style. It is intended primarily for the non-specialist and admirably fulfils its purpose. It will be welcomed by all whose field of study impinges upon Graeco-Roman Egypt and the papyri of the period.
                                                                                        T.W.T.

BENDIXON, S. : *Israels historia från äldsta tider till Herodes' tronbestigning,* 2 vols. 1948. Pp. 874. (Sohlmans, Stockholm. Price : Paper covers 28 crowns ;   bound 36 crowns.)

The writer of this work has brought to his task the results of very wide reading, including in his presentation much more about general cultural background and religion than one usually finds in a history. There is in some sections an *embarras de richesse* which makes it hard for the reader to follow the argument. Many unusual views are expressed ; but the author's prejudices are not concealed ; and what might have been stimulating independence remains merely exasperating. If an up-to-date, full-length history of Israel in Swedish is a desideratum, we may be confident that this work will not fill the gap.   G.W.A.

BICKERMAN, E. : *The Maccabees, an Account of their History from the Beginnings to the Fall of the House of the Hasmoneans.* 1947. Pp. 126. (Schocken, New York.   Price : $1.50.)

This book provides a simple undocumented account of the rise of the Hasmoneans and their subsequent history. The author writes interestingly. On p. 85 f. the reader will find a scholarly and valuable sketch of the process of Hellenization in the period described and of the work and influence of the Pharisees. How Judaism saved itself from mummification and was able " to enrich itself with new and foreign ideas " is here freshly and briefly set forth.   O.S.R.

BIKERMAN, E. : *Institutions des Séleucides* (Bibliothèque archéologique et historique, Tome xxvi). 1938. Pp. iv+268. (Geuthner, Paris. Price : Fr. 1050.)

> The author confines himself to a description of those subjects pertaining to Seleucid history which he deems can be dealt with on the basis of sufficient evidence. Therefore he does not touch the question of Seleucid colonization or law but gives an account of such institutions as the kingship, the court, the army, the royal fiscus, the administration, the coinage and the religion of the dynasty. The work affords a mass of well documented info mation from Greek and other sources about a period whose storm and stress are reflected in the fact that of fourteen kings who reigned before the decline of the dynasty, only two died under peaceful circumstances. The writer's account of the themes which he has chosen and of the questions which arise from them will prove valuable to future investigators in this field. In the last chapter, namely on *le culte monarchique*, Bickerman establishes that under the Seleucids there was no state religion ; that each city according to its own will ascribed surnames to the king and rendered him honours, human or divine ; and that it was only under Antiochus III that there appeared an organized dynastic cult. The author curtly and properly dismisses the currently accepted view that the cult of the divine king was instituted by Alexander the Great and his successors in order to consolidate their power. O.S.R.
>
> (Despite its date of publication, this work has been included as it contains material relevant to current issues and has been unaccountably missed in earlier issues of the Book List. H.H.R.)

GORDON, C. H. : *Lands of the Cross and Crescent.* 1948. Pp. 268. (Ventnor Publishers, Inc., Ventnor, N.J., U.S.A. English Price : 19s. 0d.)

> The author has travelled widely, both as archaeologist and soldier. This book is an account of the various countries in which he has travelled. The first ten chapters deal with the countries of the Near East which have been subject to Arab-Muslim influence. The last eight chapters deal with European countries (Italy, Vatican State, Germany, France, British Isles, Sweden), ending with a longer chapter on the author's own country. In each case a certain amount of history is given in a pleasant and informative way, and this is followed by the author's comments on the country and the people as he knew them. His comments on Britain are revealing both of us and of him. N.H.S.

RICCIOTTI, G. : *Histoire d'Israël*, translated by P. Auvray, 2nd ed., 2 vols. 1947-48. Pp. 562, 638. (Picard, Paris. Price : £1 16s. 0d. for 2 vols.)

> The remaining stocks of the first edition of this work were destroyed during the war. A new edition has therefore been prepared by the translator, with the approval of the author. This is not a mere reprint of the former edition, but a revised

edition introducing some changes of substance—e.g., Hammurabi is now brought down to the eighteenth century B.C.—with a fresh selection of illustrations, and printed in larger type. On a number of problems, such as the date of the fall of Jericho, the date of the Exodus, the chronological problems of Ezra-Nehemiah, the author refrains from committing himself, while indicating his view of the balance of probability. The whole forms a valuable survey of the history of Israel from the earliest times to A.D. 135.　　　　　　　H.H.R.

STEINMANN, J. : *David, Roi d'Israël.* (Témoins de Dieu.) 1948. Pp. 108. (Les éditions du Cerf, Paris. Price : 3s. 6d.)

In accordance with the scope of the series, we have here a readable sketch of the life of David for the general reader, without discussions of the problems involved, though resting in the main on sound scholarship. Critical positions are taken for granted, and not argued for. Thus the killing of Goliath is attributed to Elhanan, and it is stated that this was transferred to David in the later account. The author has slipped up in saying that the name of Hebron indicates that it was the city of the Habiru. It is true that many have associated these names philologically, but Ras Shamra evidence seems now definitely to preclude such association. The second part of the book deals with David in later thought, e.g., as psalmist, and with the messianic thought that was linked with his name.

H.H.R.

TEXT AND VERSIONS

Biblia Sacra iuxta latinam Vulgatam versionem ad codicum fidem iussu Pii PP. XII cura et studio monachorum Abbatiae Pontificiae Sancti Hieronymi in urbe Ordinis Sancti Benedicti edita : VII. Liber Verborum Dierum. 1948. Pp. xii+324. (Typis Polyglottis Vaticanis, Rome.)

This seventh volume of the great Benedictine edition of the Vulgate is the third to be published since the outbreak of the war (Samuel having appeared in 1944 and Kings in 1945). It contains the two books of Chronicles, giving a critically established text of the Vulgate and a full critical apparatus.

H.H.R.

VAN DEN BUSSCHE, H. : *Le texte de la prophétie de Nathan sur la dynastie Davidique* (Analecta Lovaniensia et Orientalia, vii.) 1948. Pp. 46. (Duculot, Gembloux. Price : Fr. 30.)

In this study we have a detailed examination of the parallel texts of II Sam. vii and I Chron. xvii, and of Psa. lxxxix. The author considers the stylistic and linguistic variations and also theological variations, and concludes that the Chronicler did not base himself on the present text of II Samuel, but that both rest on an earlier text of II Samuel, and that in some respects the Chronicler more faithfully preserves it. This is true of theological ideas as well as of the other respects, for while in both versions there have been changes affecting the divine name and the messianic character of the passage, they are found even more in II Sam. than in I Chron.　　　　　　　H.H.R.

GERLEMAN, G. : *Synoptic Studies in the Old Testament.* (Lunds Univer-
sitetets Årsskrift, N.F. Avd. I, xliv, 5.) 1948. Pp. 36. (Gleerup,
Lund. Price : Kr. 2.50.)

In this brief, but acute and valuable, study the Hebrew and
Samaritan texts of the Pentateuch are examined, and also
the parallel texts in Samuel-Kings and Chronicles. The author
reaches the conclusion that the Hebrew text of the Pentateuch
has been subjected to a late critical revision, since in the
genealogies the Chronicler's spelling agrees surprisingly often
with that of the Samaritan text against the Hebrew. In
Samuel-Kings and Chronicles the LXX frequently has what
he calls ' diagonal affinity,' the Greek text of the one book
agreeing with the Hebrew of the parallel. It is not surprising
that the Greek of Chronicles should be accommodated to that
of the earlier translated Samuel-Kings, but it is surprising
that that of Samuel-Kings, which is in general literal in its
translation, should be accommodated to that of Chronicles.
Gerleman concludes that the commonly recognized revision
of Proper Names in Samuel-Kings extended also to other
matters, and that while the LXX represented the vulgar
text at the time it was made, agreeing often with that of
Chronicles, it was later critically revised.   H.H.R.

MERCATI, G. : *Il Problema della Colonna II dell'Esaplo.* 1947. Pp.
76. (Città del Vaticano. Price : 5s. 6d.)

In this book, extracted from *Biblica* 28, 1947, Cardinal Mercati
discusses mainly the textual difficulties presented by the
Greek transcription in Column II of Origen's Hexapla,
particularly in the extant fragments of the 10th cent. A.D.
Milan Palimpsest discovered by the Cardinal himself. The
standpoint of the author in the present work is one of extreme
caution. He concludes that there is not sufficient evidence to
presuppose any transcription into Greek before the time of
Origen, even for lectionary purposes. There are serious
deficiencies in the Milan palimpsest, such as the condition of
the MS., the incidence of scribal errors, and discrepancies in the
renderings of a common original form, especially of vowels
and diphthongs.

The book is a mine of information, and is indispensable for
Hexaplaric studies. Moreover the evidence of Col. II will
become increasingly relevant as the Hebrew texts of the
Jerusalem scrolls become available. The findings of Cardinal
Mercati, who is the only person really competent to advise
on the Milan palimpsest, will provide a serious check on any
exuberance which may be shown when, as will inevitably
happen, textual forms in Origen II will be compared with
parallel forms in the scrolls.   B.J.R.

PRIJS, L. : *Jüdische Tradition in der Septuaginta.* 1948. Pp. xxviii+
120. (Brill, Leiden. Price : Fl. 15.00.)

The author of this work has collected a large number of passages
in which the translation of the LXX is at variance with the
MT, but agrees with the interpretation expressed or implicit

in Jewish tradition, Talmudic or Midrashic or even medieval ; and in every passage thus discussed he sets out the Hebrew text and the Greek translation side by side and then discusses them in the light of tradition. Unfortunately he is so deeply bogged in detail that he nowhere makes his ultimate purpose clear ; the introduction is as cumbered with detail as the main body of the text and no formal statement of his conclusions seems ever to be made. Further, he is loth to see the obvious and prefers the obscure or far-fetched ; thus he fails to see that the LXX in translating " Tarshish " by " sea " (Dan. x, 6), are not indulging in Haggadic flights of fancy but simply transliterating the Hebrew word into the nearest possible Greek word. What does emerge from the mass of minute discussion is that Jewish tradition, going far back before Talmud and Midrash, has influenced the Greek translators of the O.T. in many places and is therefore in origin pre-Septuagintal ; but the author can hardly be followed when he goes on to argue that the LXX, when their translation diverges from the MT, do not necessarily render a different Hebrew text if tradition is with them (presumably because Talmud and Midrash in their present form represent substantially the MT) ; for their translation is often utterly inexplicable as a rendering of the MT, even on the methods of ancient translators and homiletic exegetes, and the traditions embodied in Talmud and Midrash, if based on an early non-Massoretic text, may equally often have been subsequently adapted to or harmonized with it. Yet, whatever logical defects may be found in the author's reasoning, his work is a mine of information which is often curious or interesting, even if it adds little to the interpretation of the O.T.   G.R.D.

SEELIGMANN, I. L. : *The Septuagint Version of Isaiah : a discussion of its problems.* (Mededelingen en Verhandelingen No. 9 van het Vooraziatisch-Egyptisch Genootschap " Ex Oriente Lux.") 1948. Pp. xxi+124. (Brill, Leiden. Price : £1 7s. 0d.)

This elaborate study of the Greek version of the Book of Isaiah contains four chapters : I. The text of the Septuagint of Isaiah and its transmission ; II. The technique employed in the translation and its relation to the Hebrew text ; III. Date and historical backbround of the translation ; IV. The translation as a document of Jewish-Alexandrine theology. There is also an excursus on the temple of Onias at Heliopolis. The author's conclusions are that (i) the Greek text has been subjected to many partial or complete revisions, based partly on other Greek versions and partly independent and including adaptations to Christian conceptions ; (ii) it has slight value for the critical study of the Massoretic text and must be used with the greatest caution in attempting to restore the true Hebrew text ; (iii) it contains possible allusions to a state of affairs in the middle of the 2nd century B.C. and indeed is shown by historical and theological allusions to be a product of the Hellenistic age. These conclusions are hardly novel, as the author admits ; but his study is valuable for the care with which they are worked out and for the many incidental observations of great interest which he makes in the course of it.   G.R.D.

AALDERS, G. C. : *Het Boek de Prediker*. 1948. Pp. 262. (Kok, Kampen. Price : Fl. 9.75.)

Dr. Aalder's book is the first part of a newly planned commentary on the O.T. (Commentaar op het Oude Testament), which will be published by the Dutch " Gereformeerde " professors of the Free University of Amsterdam and the Theological Seminary of Kampen (editors : G. C. Aalders, W. H. Gispen and J. Ridderbos) ; it will be a strictly scientific counterpart of the more popular series Korte Verklaring der Heilige Schrift by the same theological schools. This part is a rather broadly elaborated one, and has appeared in a handsome edition.

From the short Introduction we learn that Aalders places Qohelet in the last period of the Persian rule and considers him as a Palestinian (Jerusalemite) Jew. The question of the Hellenistic influence on his teaching is therefore scarcely touched. The book itself may be regarded as a rather well balanced unit (the peroration is by the author too), in which Ecclesiastes demonstrates " that human toil on this earth has no enduring value." Passages such as iii, 18 ff. and xii, 7, are in the opinion of Professor Aalders expressions of the belief in the existence of the soul after death.

The editor himself admits in the Introduction that he has been directed in his exegesis by his reformed belief in the unity of Holy Scripture, and we have no doubts about this.

Th.C.V.

*ALLEMAN, H. C., and FLACK, E. E., ed. by : *Old Testament Commentary*. 1948. Pp. viii+894. (Muhlenberg Press, Philadelphia. Price : $5.00.)

This amazingly cheap one-volume Old Testament commentary is not accompanied by the text of the Bible, and is produced by a team of writers, almost exclusively Lutheran. Amongst the introductory articles is one on ' The Old Testament and Archaeology ' by W. F. Albright, who is by far the most distinguished scholar to contribute to the work. There are twelve other introductory articles, all competently written, and the whole commentary shows a conservative critical approach. The introductions to the individual books are brief, and literary criticism is of secondary interest as compared with the thought and meaning of the Old Testament. In a field of study where disagreements are still so numerous amongst scholars, it is inevitable that such a work will not command acceptance on every question, but it can be commended as a most valuable Vade Mecum, though sometimes not quite up-to-date (e.g., the statement that Astarte, Ashera and Ashteroth are alternative ways of writing the same name).

H.H.R.

La Bible du Centenaire, 4 vols. 1916-1947. Pp. xxii+290, xliv+836, xxxiv+522, viii+440. (Société Biblique de Paris.)

This work began to appear in 1916, though the title-page of no volume is earlier than 1928. The writers of the sections are not indicated on the title-pages, though some of the separate fascicules did bear the writer's names. Ad. Lods took a large share in the enterprise and it must have been gratifying to him to see the last sheets through the press before he died. The work consists of very brief Introductions to the books of the Bible, followed by a new translation sumptuously printed on large pages, with commentary at the foot of the page. The translation is of a critically revised text, whose justification is indicated in a separate apparatus above the commentary ; and the commentary rests on critical scholarship. As this is the only Protestant commentary on the whole Bible written in French, and published during the past half century, it is an important work. It is to be hoped that it may be kept in print for many years, though at the moment sets are said not to be available.   H.H.R.

BLEEKER, L. H. K. : *Hermeneutiek van het Oude Testament.* 1948. Pp. 244. (Bohn, Haarlem. Price : Fl. 15.00.)

A new series of Dutch theological manuals, planned in the beginning of the last war (soon after the German invasion) has only begun to appear since last year. This book on the Hermeneutics of the O.T. is the third part that has come out ; it was written by the late professor of the O.T. at Groningen (died 1944). There are few aspects of the subject which have not been treated thoroughly in this work, though the author occupies himself most extensively with the many attempts at christological and theological interpretation of the O.T. Being convinced of the necessity of a strictly philological approach, in the exegesis of Holy Scripture too, he fights against all forms of exegesis that do not take full account of the wording of the text. In the author's opinion the text of the LXX may to a very high degree be trusted.

In this time, in which too many attempts at new exegetical methods confuse the minds of young students of theology, this book is on the whole a very trustworthy guide which may be warmly recommended.   Th.C.V.

CHAINE, J. : *Le Livre de la Genèse.* 1948. Pp. 526. (Éditions du Cerf, Paris. Price : Fr. 600.)

This is the largest volume so far published in this interesting series, that already includes A. M. Dubarle, *Les Sages d'Israël* and A. Gelin, *Les Idées maîtresses de l'Ancien Testament.* Even so, it is not a detailed study after the manner of S. R. Driver's *The Book of Genesis*, though all the leading questions bearing upon Genesis are treated with reasonable fullness. Perhaps the most disappointing chapter is the very short one on the theology of the book, which studies in turn the doctrine of inspiration and the documentary theory, and the religious teaching of Genesis. On the other hand, the section entitled " L'Historiographie chez les Sémites " usefully gathers together the data given by such articles as that of the Ignazio Guidi in *Revue biblique*, 1906, and by the late A. A. Bevan in *Cambridge Biblical Essays :* the latter essay is not mentioned by name. The translation is a highly literal one, and the partition into sources is shown (as in Driver) by marginal letters (which include the letter x for the whole of xiv, and much of xxxvi !) The theory regarding the sources closely resembles that of the late M. J. Lagrange in *Revue biblique*, 1938.

In a brief memoir of the author (who died on 24th March, 1948), A. Gelin remarks of the present work : " C'est un beau livre." Undoubtedly, this is true, but it is not, I fancy, a very original one. Most students will, however, find much to interest them, and it will serve as a useful introduction to the more advanced commentaries.   J.M.T.B.

COHEN, A., ed. by : *The Twelve Prophets, Hebrew Text, English Translation and Commentary*. (The Soncino Books of the Bible.) 1948. Pp. x+368. (Soncino Press, Bournemouth. Price : 15s. 0d.)

In this volume the usual lines of the series are followed. Each book has a very brief introduction—a maximum of four pages—and the Massoretic text is printed side by side with the American Jewish translation with the notes at the foot of the page. Emendation is eschewed, but critical positions are recorded briefly, and sometimes shared. Jonah is held to be post-exilic, and an allegorical interpretation is left open. The date of Joel is left open, though with leaning towards the traditional date. On the other hand the unity of Zechariah is maintained. Hos. iii is held to be the sequel of chapter i. The commentary is useful without being original, and reflects modern commentaries as well as Rabbinical works. The sections were written by S. M. Lehrman (Hosea, Joel, Amos, Nahum, Habakkuk and Zephaniah), S. Goldman (Obadiah, Jonah and Micah), and E. Cashdan (Haggai, Zechariah and Malachi).   H.H.R.

FOHRER, G. : *Das Buch Hiob*. 1948. Pp. 90. (Im Scherpe-Verlag, Krefeld.)

This small and elegant volume is similar in aim in many respects to the translation by Gustav Hölscher, which has been noticed elsewhere in the Book List. Here is a translation into modern literary German, in well-printed type. The volume is evidently intended to present the Book of Job as a literary work, worthy to hold its own place in the world of letters. The speeches of the prologue and the epilogue are in blank (' free ') verse, and the poetic portions are in blank verse and irregular stanzas. There are no chapter and verse references in the text, but the author has indicated his treatment of the original at the end of the volume. He has transposed 27 short passages (usually a verse or a line), and has omitted a considerable number of other lines, in some cases short passages of two or more verses. There are thirteen passages which he has taken out of the main work and placed together at the end. These include the Elihu speeches, the Leviathan and Behemoth sections, and a number of other Songs. The bibliography is exclusively German.   N.H.S.

GOSLINGA, C. J. : *Samuel I.* 1948. Pp. 356. (Kok, Kampen. Price : Fl. 5.50.)

>The author offers in this book, belonging to the series Korte Verklaring der Heilige Schrift, a rather detailed discussion of the text of I Samuel, from the point of view of the Dutch " Gereformeerden " of the Free University. Dr. Goslinga thinks that I Samuel has been written by an author of the time after the separation of Israel and Judah ; he used several sources, but expecially the written books of Samuel, Nathan and Gad (cf. I Chron. xxix, 29) and some other works. While not denying the existence of some uneven places in the narrative of the Books of Samuel, and admitting some additions of later times too, he nevertheless maintains fully their unity. Th.C.V.

GRANT, R. M. : *The Bible in the Church.* 1948. Pp. x+194. (The Macmillan Company, New York. Price : $2.50.)

>In this small volume of less than two hundred pages the author offers a short history of the different methods which have been employed by Christians in the interpretation of the Bible from the earliest times to the present day, and, what is more, he attempts to draw lessons from the mistakes of the past as a corrective for the future. Within his self-imposed limits he shows on the whole an admirable balance, and the book may be warmly recommended as an excellent brief introduction to a subject which is much to the fore at the present time. It should be added that the author, like the writer of this note, writes from a Protestant standpoint. A.R.J.

*HICKS, J. H. : *The Books of History.* 1947. Pp. 160. (Abingdon-Cokesbury Press, New York and Nashville. Price : 60 cents.)

>Dr. Hicks is Old Testament Professor in the Perkins School of Theology at the Southern Methodist University, Dallas, Texas. There are eight small volumes in the series, designed to encourage the ordinary reader in the study of the Bible. The reader is provided with passages for reading from all the historical books from Joshua to Kings, and including Chronicles and Esther. There is a special and popular introduction to each Bible book, and helpful comments on each reading. The outlook is modern, and the book is to be commended as a successful attempt to enable the ordinary reader to read the Bible intelligently and helpfully. N.H.S.

HÖLSCHER, G. : *Das Gedicht von Hiob und seinen drei Freunden.* 1948. Pp. 126. (Insel-Verlag, Stuttgart.)

>This little volume is an elegant translation into modern German. The prose portions are written in folklore style, and the verse portions in four-line iambic pentameters, this being the best way of conveying the pathos of the original to the German reader. The style of the verse translation is literary. There are seven pages by way of introduction and sixteen pages of popular notes. The reader is referred for technical details to the author's commentary on Job in Eissfeldt's *Kommentar im Handbuch zum Alten Testament* (1937). N.H.S.

LATTEY, C. C. : *The Book of Daniel*. 1948. Pp. lii+144. (Browne and Nolan, Dublin. Price : 12s. 6d.)

This, the latest addition to the volumes of the " Westminster Version " provides a somewhat fuller commentary to the book than has been customary in the earlier numbers. As usual there is an introduction that discusses all the more important problems raised by the book, a translation from the three languages involved, and notes, forming a substantial commentary, printed after the translation. There are indexes of biblical references and of proper names. In a second edition it should be relatively easy to give the chapter and verse references at the head of each page in the notes. The author tells us that he first began to lecture on Daniel in 1912, and that in the interval it has seldom been long absent from his thought and study. He does not consider that " further thought or study would alter materially my view of the book, nor yet that my exposition would gain much by being elaborated in greater detail." He stresses as of special importance the need to " take in account, as it were, three historical planes, that of the persecution of Antiochus IV Epiphanes, and of the first and second comings of Christ, Our Lord." The translation, as might be expected in so ripe a scholar, is beautifully clear and dignified ; there are no unwelcome neologisms, and none of the free paraphrase found so abundantly in the Knox version. The notes contain a wealth of erudition, and the whole book will serve as an ideal introduction to the larger works, notably to Linder's vast *Commentarius in Librum Daniel*, to which reference is frequently made.   J.M.T.B.

LESLIE, E. A. : *The Psalms Translated and Interpreted in the Light of Hebrew Life and Worship*. 1949. Pp. 448. (Abingdon Cokesbury Press, New York and Nashville. Price : $5.00.)

This book is professedly written for ministers, teachers, and Bible students, but there are few who will not profit from its study. While simply written it is an essentially scholarly work. It does not deal with the psalms in the order in which they stand in the Bible, or in the presumed order of their composition (like Buttenwieser's, for instance), but according to their types. It thus reflects the approach and method of Gunkel, though the author by no means slavishly follows Gunkel. He also reflects the influence of Mowinckel at a number of points, and especially in the treatment of the Psalms associated with the New Year Festival. Hans Schmidt also makes his contribution to the volume, especially through his *Gebet der Angeklagten in den Psalmen*, to which a section of the present work is devoted. The commentary is always brief, and is never a verse by verse exposition, while the translation is not justified by text-critical notes, though it rests on a critically emended text. The introduction is briefer than might have been expected, but the volume is to be warmly welcomed as giving a fuller insight into recent continental work on the Psalter than can be found in any other English work.   H.H.R.

Pouget, W., and Guitton, J. : *The Canticle of Canticles,* translated
by J. L. Lilly. 1948. Pp. xii+202. (D. X. McMullen, New York.
Price : $3.00.)

> The commentary of Pouget and Guitton, in the Études
> Bibliques series, which was published in 1934, is here made
> available to English readers. The view taken is that the Song
> is a drama, with three characters and a chorus, and that it
> comes from the post-exilic period, as its language indicates.
> The king is not the Solomon of history, nor is it likely that the
> drama was ever staged. Some of the songs were modelled
> on the wedding songs described by Wetzstein (whose name is
> uniformly given as Wetzheim, following the error of the French
> original). A translation supplied with suitable stage directions
> is given, and brief notes are added. It is also maintained that
> from the start the Song was written with a religious purpose,
> to inculcate moral and spiritual lessons. In the Introduction
> some account is given of Fr. Pouget, who died before the work
> was first published in 1934, and who seems to have been a
> man of singular charm, with the heavy handicap of blindness.
>   H.H.R.

Murphy, R. E. : *A Study of Psalm* 72 (71). 1948. Pp. 144. (The
Catholic University of America Press, Washington. Price : $1.50).

> A detailed study of the Psalm, with translation, commentary,
> and discussion of verbal forms, author and date. Three
> additional chapters provide the more controversial material,
> viz., the " Court Style," the " Messianic Background " and
> " Traditional and Modern Interpretations." The author
> disputes the recent classification of the Psalm as a " Royal
> Psalm " in the *Hofstil* of the Near East rather than as a
> Messianic Psalm. Indeed, he questions whether there exists
> in the Psalter any Psalm which actually complies with the
> *Hofstil* of the Gunkel-Gressmann school of thought. But
> Dr. Murphy's treatment would have been more convincing
> had the case for the Royal Psalms been presented more
> adequately ; in particular one misses observations on the
> very careful conclusions of A. Bentzen in his Danish books
> on the Psalms from 1935 to 1945, and on the iconoclastic
> works of Engnell written in Swedish.   B.J.R.

Nötscher, F. (ed. by) : *Die Heilige Schrift in deutscher Übersetzung,
Echter-Bibel : Das Alte Testament. 1. Die Psalmen* by F. Nötscher.
1947. Pp. 292. (Price : DM. 7.80.) 2. *Jeremias, Klagelieder*
by the same. 1947. Pp. 176+24. (Price : DM. 6.20.) 3. *Das
erste und zweite Buch der Makkabäer* by D. Schötz. 1948. Pp.
112. (Price : DM. 4.60.) 4. *Zwölfprophetenbuch, Kohelet* by F.
Nötscher. 1948. Pp. 188+34. (Price : DM. 6.60.) 5. *Isaias* by
Joseph Ziegler. 1948. Pp. 192. (Price : DM. 6.) 6. *Ezechiel*
by J. Ziegler and *Daniel* by F. Nötscher. 1948. Pp. 148+72.
(Price : DM. 6.60.) (Echter-Verlag, Würzburg.)

> It does not appear necessary to discuss individually the first
> six parts of the new and excellent German translation of the
> Old Testament comprised in the Echter-Bibel. Those who
> know the sound and authoritative work of the general editor

in *Das Buch Jeremias* in the " Bonner Bibel " and Ziegler's earlier volumes on *Die Liebe Gottes bei den Propheten* and on *Isaias*, will have every reason to expect that the translations will be scholarly and that the accompanying commentary will give all that can be provided in so small a space. It is true that both introductions and notes are extremely compressed, and that the amount of space accorded to textual criticism cannot be large. It would be true to say that the translations are rightly judged to be the most important part of the volumes. They will be welcomed by all students, but more especially by beginners who may thus be introduced to the larger and more expansive commentaries. A comparison, at various points, of the present volume on Jeremiah with Nötscher's larger commentary fails to show any substantial change of mind. On the famous verse xxxi, 22, the last member is (as before) provisionally translated : " Das Weib umwirbt den Mann(?)." Jerome's interpretation on messianic lines in terms of Is. vii, 14, is described as " reine Vermutung." An average of two to four pages of introduction to the individual books is short measure indeed, but the authors make the most of their limited space.   J.M.T.B.

POULET, D. : *Tous les hommes sont-ils fils de Noé ?* 1941. Pp. 408. (Catholic University Press, Ottawa. Price : 11s. 0d.)

> The author first offers a commentary on the passages of Genesis recording the Flood Story and then examines three theories : (a) the theory of a universal geographical flood, with the destruction of all living creatures save those in the Ark ; (b) the theory of a universal destruction of man, with the exception of the persons with Noah in the Ark ; (c) the theory that the descendants of Cain escaped the Flood, while the descendants of Seth, with the exception of Noah and those with him, were involved. The author decides in favour of the second of these hypotheses, holding that it avoids the extravagances of the first and the limitations of the third. He seeks to establish it rather by citations from the Fathers and by widespread traditions than by solid arguments. A clearer statement of which of the details of the Biblical story may be accepted without extravagance would have enabled us better to test his view. (A brief presentation of theory (c) may be found in E. F. Sutcliffe, *Who Perished in the Flood ?* 1943. [Catholic Truth Society].)   H.H.R.

RAGAZ, L. : *Die Bibel—Eine Deutung :* Vol. I. *Die Urgeschichte.* 1947. Pp. 262. (Price : Fr. 10.) Vol. II. *Moses.* 1947. Pp. 190. (Price : Fr. 9.) Vol. III. *Die Geschichte Israels.* 1948. Pp. 254. (Price : Fr. 11.50.) Vol. IV. *Die Propheten.* 1949. Pp. 274. (Price : Fr. 11.50.) (Diana Verlag, Zürich.)

> These volumes—to be followed by three others on the N.T.— are patterns of beautifully clear print. The interpretation of the Bible which Ragaz presents, at least in the first three volumes, may be described as a philosophic religious *midrash.* Certain thoughts or topics are discerned as being central and symbolical of fundamental truths—Ur-Data—from the standpoint of the faith that the meaning of history is given by

the purpose of God to found a kingdom of righteousness and truth. The reader gains an impression of the skill with which the author shows the living connexion between conceptions embodied in the early Hebrew legends and those problems which face the moralist and historian of modern times. In drawing out this fact Ragaz makes appreciative allusions to the contribution to thought, history and religion by such men as Marx, Lenin and Trotski, as well as by Kierkegaard, Carlyle, Nietzsche and Tolstoi. The teacher of Scripture and the preacher will find this work to be fresh and frank and helpful so far as the religious message of the Bible is concerned, even though a more strictly critical and less conservative treatment of the development of religious thought in the O.T. could be desired. The writer pictures Moses (Vol. II) as the prototype of the servants of God who in the political and social spheres have promoted God's work. " The figure of Moses is raised in the midst of history as a mountain peak massive solid and dark . . . . enveloped by cloud and mists of myth and saga, but revealed also by them." The great leaders of the proletariat have sprung from the bourgeoisie and Moses had to experience that the proletariat, despite all that may be sacrificed for it, continues, when liberated, to judge according to the class-morality of its oppressors, and has little notion of what true socialism is. In Vol. III which covers the period of the conquest of Canaan, the Judges and the Biblical narrative down to the time of Rehoboam, the author portrays Israel's history as affording a contrast between Jahveh as holy God and Baal as deification of the forces of nature—a contrast between right and violence, between democracy and dictatorship. The struggle reflected in these contrasts is viewed as that tension which underlies all history. Vol. IV (the prophets), without any disparagement of the other volumes, may be regarded by the teacher of the O.T. to have this merit above its predecessors, that it depends less on symbolizing and generalizing. The chapters which follow under the title " The nature and task of prophetism " are extremely well done and useful. Some index should have been provided to each volume. O.S.R.

RINALDI, G. : *Daniele* (La Sacra Bibbia, ed. by S. Garofalo, VIII, 3). 1947. Pp. vi+138 and 8 pages of plates. (Marietti, Turin. Price : 6s. 0d.)

This new series of Italian commentaries calls for a special welcome, inasmuch as the volume on Daniel is stated to be the first attempt of its kind in the language. The volumes provide an Italian translation of the original languages faced by the Clementine Vulgate. The latter is printed in italics except in verses (such as ii, 3), where the Latin notably differs from the original. Unlike some other compressed commentaries, this one has a special division, between translation and commentary, devoted to textual problems, in which useful references are given to such works as Gesenius-Buhl and Palacios : *Grammatica aramaico-biblica* (Rome, 1933). The author has been at pains to give references to fuller commentaries wherever he judges that the reader might wish to pursue that matter further. The question of the book's origin is decided in favour of Danielic authorship for the visions, and the compilation of the work as a whole before Maccabean times. This does not, however, exclude later " manipolazioni " of individual passages. The format of the work shows some of the disadvantages of a double-columned commentary, but the printing, even of the smaller type is extremely clear, and the subject-matter is well arranged.

J.M.T.B.

La Sainte Bible, translated into French under the direction of the École Biblique of Jerusalem : *Les livres des Maccabées*, by F. M. Abel. 1948. Pp. 176. *Aggée, Zacharie, Malachie*, by A. Gelin. 1948. Pp. 76. (Éditions du Cerf, Paris. Price : 6s. 6d., 3s. 0d.)

These first two Old Testament volumes (accompanied by two New Testament volumes) commence the publication of a new translation of the Bible into French from a critically established text, accompanied by brief introductions and very brief notes. The critical justification of the text translated is indicated in an apparatus that stands at the foot of the page between the translation and the notes. I Macc. is dated *circa* 100 B.C., and is held to have been composed in Hebrew. II Macc. is dated 124 B.C., and is considered a substantially reliable historical work. Zechariah is divided between two authors, and chapters ix-xiv, assigned to the end of the fourth century B.C. While critical questions are not discussed at length, the works rest on sound critical study both of text and substance.

H.H.R.

SNAITH, N. H. : *Notes on the Hebrew Text of Gen. I-VIII.* (Study Notes on Bible Books.) 1947. Pp. 54. (Epworth Press, London. Price : 4s. 0d.)

Dr. Snaith continues to supply these useful notes on the Hebrew text, invaluable for students of Hebrew who have to work without a teacher, and also for elementary students who work with a teacher. The notes are confined to grammatical and lexical comments, leaving exegesis to the easily accessible English commentaries, and the abundant references to several grammars greatly increase the value of his books. The present volume shares the merits of its predecessors, and reflects the careful and understanding teacher of Hebrew.

H.H.R.

VELLAS, B. M. : *Hermêneia Palaias Diathêkês* (in Modern Greek). 1. *Amôs*. 1947. Pp. 124. 2. *Osêé*. 1947. Pp. 144. 3. *Michaias—Iôel—Obdiou*. 1948. Pp. 136. ("Astêr" Publishing House, Athens.)

Commentaries in Modern Greek are not in common circulation in Western Europe, and the enterprise of the Astêr firm, joined with the enthusiasm and scholarship of a professor at the University of Athens, has resulted in this very satisfactory beginning of a new series that appears to be worthy of all possible encouragement. Each volume follows the same general lines—a reasonably full introduction, a translation from the Hebrew into literary Modern Greek, a text of the Septuagint at the foot of each section of the modern rendering, and a really detailed and painstaking commentary with an eye to all the best work that has been done in Germany and elsewhere. Dr. Vellas tells us that no such full-length commentary of the Old Testament has existed, either in the past or in modern times, for the use of the Orthodox Church, and it is gratifying that the great expense of such a venture has not proved an obstacle even under present conditions. Not a few observations in the commentaries strike one as rather obvious, but it is difficult to appreciate the degree of preparedness on the part of the students for whom the books are primarily intended. Most of the works cited appear to be German, but there is a fairly full bibliography to each volume. Apropos of prophetic symbolism the author has missed the useful volume *Les Symboles de l'Ancien Testament* by D. Buzy (Gabalda, Paris, 1923). J.M.T.B.

WATERMAN, L. : *The Song of Songs Translated and Interpreted as a Dramatic Poem.* 1948. Pp. x+88. (University of Michigan Press, Ann Arbor. Price : $2.00.)

Professor Waterman here presents the view that the Song rests on a historical basis, and that after the death of David and Adonijah's ill-starred bid for her hand, Abishag refused the advances of Solomon through her loyalty to her rustic lover. He holds that the Song is of northern origin, from a time after the disruption of the kingdom, and that it sang of Solomon's rebuff. Later it was rearranged by a southern editor to conceal this. Waterman therefore restores what he believes to have been its original order. The basic assumption that the heroine was Abishag is justified by a reference to LXX B in Ct. vi, 13, which is scarcely sufficient evidence to sustain the theory. A translation and critical notes follow the discussion of the origin and significance of the book, and these will be found of value even to those who do not accept the theory. H.H.R.

WEISER, A. : *Das Buch der zwölf Kleinen Propheten, I : Die Propheten Hosea, Joel, Amos, Obadja, Jona, Micha* (Das Alte Testament Deutsch, 24). 1949. Pp. viii+262. (Vandenhoeck und Ruprecht, Göttingen. Price : subscr. DM. 9.50., separate, DM. 11.80.)

This is the first volume to appear of the projected series of commentaries edited by Herntrich and Weiser. Among the other contributors will be Eichrodt, Noth and von Rad. The present volume shows the general plan to which all will conform, viz., a sound critical attitude presupposed, a brief historical and literary introduction and a commentary with a strong theological emphasis. A few points of interest may be noticed. Weiser, while recognizing the different literary character of Hosea i and iii, still regards ch. iii, as referring to the sequel of what is related in ch. i. This he regards as demanded by the analogy with Israel. Special emphasis is laid on the visions in the book of Amos which are held to have originally formed a separate booklet which may have been put together by Amos himself after the occurrence of the earthquake. The present form of the Book of Joel is attributed to liturgical requirements and this consideration is invoked elsewhere. Weiser is inclined to accept the authenticity of Micah v and vi and vii, 1-7, but sees in ch. iv (mostly) and vii, 7-20, post-exilic additions. There are no references to other literature and no bibliography.

This series of commentaries promises to provide for the Old Testament something of what the Moffatt Commentaries offer to the English reader in the case of the New Testament.
N.W.P.

*The Westminster Study Edition of The Holy Bible : containing the Old and New Testaments in the Authorized (King James) Version : arranged in Paragraphs and in Verses, together with Introductory Articles and Prefaces, Explanatory Footnotes, a Concordance and Maps. 1948. Pp. xxvi+1376, x + 486 + 103 + 6 + 16 plates. (The Westminster Press, Philadelphia. Price : £2 10s. 0d.)

This sumptuous volume represents what is very nearly the ideal edition of the Authorized Version of the Bible. The text is set forth in attractive form, the prose in natural paragraphs and the poetry printed as such, while most useful headings and sub-headings are given to the various sections. The necessary minimum in the way of notes appears at the foot of the page, being designed to clear up the meaning of difficult passages and to aid the reader in grasping the content of each section. The introductory essays to each Testament and the brief introductions to the separate books are models of succinctness, relevance and informativeness. The one blemish is that the Concordance is printed in such minute type. The sixteen maps at the end are the same as those contained in the Westminster Smaller Bible Atlas. This book should be in every library and many individuals will wish to possess it.
N.W.P.

WILLIAMS, A. : The Common Expositor : An Account of the Commentaries on Genesis, 1527-1633. 1948. Pp. ix+297. (University of North Carolina Press. Price : $4.00.)

A thoroughly scholarly piece of work by a leading authority on Milton. Intended mainly for students of the literature and thought of the 16th and 17th cents., but valuable also for the history of biblical interpretation. The Commentaries were compendia of the theology, science, and political philosophy of their period, and writers like Milton, Ralegh, and Sir Thomas Browne depended much upon them.
C.R.N.

LITERARY CRITICISM AND INTRODUCTION

AALDERS, G. C. : The Problem of the Book of Jonah. 1948. Pp. 30. (Tyndale Press, London. Price : 2s. 0d.)

In this Tyndale Lecture, Professor Aalders treats the book of Jonah from the conservative point of view. He argues that the miraculous element cannot be dismissed, but that the real problem of the book is a different one, and concerns the purpose of the author and the literary genre to which the work belongs.

He sets aside some arguments which have been advanced on both sides as inconclusive, and then studies parables and allegories elsewhere in the Old Testament to justify the conclusion that this book is neither parable nor allegory. That the author intended to write history is then held to be demonstrated, and the claim that the Jews and Jesus believed it to be history is held to demonstrate that it is history. Even the prayer of Jonah is held to be authentic. The author is well acquainted with the literature of the subject of every school, and his work may be read with profit by those who will find his arguments unconvincing. He discreetly omits to consider how far the statements of the book of Jonah on the size and population of Nineveh can claim to be historical.

H.H.R.

BENTZEN, A. : *Introduction to the Old Testament.* I. *The Canon of the Old Testament, the Text of the Old Testament, the Forms of Old Testament Literature.* 1948. Pp. 268. (Gad, Copenhagen. Price : £1 4s. 0d.)

This is the first volume of an English translation of the Danish work which appeared in 1941 (see Book List 1946, p. 23). Yet it is much more than a translation, for the whole has been revised and frequently rewritten, to take account of work which was not available to the author in 1941, or which has been published subsequently. In this volume general questions are dealt with, and the special introduction to the individual books will follow in the next. All of the matters dealt with here are but slightly touched in the usual handbooks (with the exception of Pfeiffer's), and we have long wanted a good introduction to the Text and Canon of the Old Testament. Even more valuable is the study of the literary forms of the Old Testament, which is still more rarely given adequate treatment. The whole rests on wide reading, and is especially valuable for its use of Scandinavian material which is not easily accessible.

H.H.R.

COHEN, J. : *Judaica et Aegyptiaca. De Maccabaeorum Libro III Quaestiones Historicae.* 1941. Pp. 68. (M. de Waal, Groningen. Price : 9s. 6d.)

This work is a dissertation submitted for the degree of doctor in the University of Groningen. The author discusses the historical setting of III Maccabees and various historical problems to which the book gives rise. He is, however, chiefly concerned with its date. After re-examining the evidence he comes to the conclusion that it was written between 88 and 77 B.C. He believes that the writer has wrongly coupled the story of the elephants, which in reality should be attributed to Euergetes II, with Philopator's persecution of the Jews in Egypt.

T.W.T.

EISSFELDT, O. : *Geschichtsschreibung im Alten Testament.* 1948. Pp. 48. (Evangelische Verlaganstalt, Berlin.)

This is a study of the type in which the author excels ; for it is a short but extraordinarily detailed and penetrating survey of recent attempts to determine the first appearance of genuine

historical writing in Israel. For the most part it is concerned
with an analysis and comparison of (a) G. Hölscher's *Die
Anfänge der hebräischen Geschichtsschreibung* (1942), which
treats the work of the Yahwist as the first step in this direction,
and seeks to trace its presence beyond the confines of the
Pentateuch, in fact from Genesis ii, down to I Kings xii,
i.e., as covering the period from the Creation to the disruption
of the Hebrew monarchy in 933 B.C.; and (b) M. Noth's
Überlieferungsgeschichtliche Studien I (1943) in so far as it
deals with the work of the Deuteronomist in Deuteronomy—
II Kings, i.e., covering the period from the sojourn at Sinai
to the pardoning of Jehoiachin in 562 B.C. In Noth's opinion
it is this which is to be regarded as the first real attempt at
a piece of historical writing, the work of the Yahwist, which
is confined to the Pentateuch, being merely that of a collector
of data which already have their peculiar stamp. The author
also makes repeated reference to the important article by G.
von Rad, " Der Anfang der Geschichtsschreibung im Alten
Testament " (*Archiv für Kulturgeschichte* 32 [1944], pp.
1-42), which is designed to show that II Samuel ix-xx, and
I Kings i-ii, regarded as " The Story of David's Succession
to the Throne " is really the earliest example of the type of
writing under discussion.   A.R.J.

GINSBERG, H. L. : *Studies in Daniel*. 1948. Pp. xiv+92. (Jewish
Theological Seminary of America, New York.)

This little book contains a series of original and suggestive
studies on the language and compilation of the book of Daniel.
Not less than six authors are postulated, of whom the author
of Dan. i-vi, lived in the first half of the third century B.C.,
but had his second chapter glossed by an author in the second
half of that century, while Dan. vii-xii, comes from the hand
of at least four writers, all living in the first half of the second
century B.C., the fourth of whom glossed the work of the
other three (unless the glosses are to be attributed to yet other
hands). The whole work is held to have been composed in
Aramaic, and part to have been translated into Hebrew
before 140 B.C. by a translator who sometimes failed to
understand the Aramaic, and the translation was undertaken
with a view to canonicity. The reasons offered to sustain these
views do not seem adequate to their task. There are interesting linguistic and textual notes on some points in the Aramaic
part, and some of the notes on the translation Hebrew are
acute and suggestive, even where the facts may be differently
explained. The writing on the wall is held to have consisted
of three words, which referred to Nebuchadnezzar, Evil-
merodach and Belshazzar. The notes, which are gathered
at the end of the book, are about as voluminous as the text,
and reveal the author's wide acquaintance with the literature.
The work may be commended to the careful study even of those
who may not adopt its positions.   H.H.R.

HOSPERS, J. H. : *Twee problemen betreffende het Aramees van het boek Daniel.* 1948. Pp. 28. (Wolters, Groningen. Price : Fl. 1.00.)

In his inaugural address the new professor of Semitic languages at the University of Groningen examines two problems connected with the Aramaic language of the book of Daniel : (a) the dating and (b) the question why a part of Daniel was written in this language.

After surveying the literature of the last decennia, Dr. Hospers, in close relation to Schaeder, arrives at the conclusion that linguistic criteria do not allow any other conclusion about the dating of the Aramaic of Daniel than that it is younger than the Aramaic of Ezra. Historical grounds enabling the dating of the latter about 450 B.C., the first may be placed *post* 400. On the second question Dr. Hospers follows Zimmerman in his opinion that the Hebrew part of Daniel was translated from the Aramaic. The whole book has been edited by an author of the Maccabean period, who used a number of old Aramaic legends. In the Hebrew edition, which followed some time later, these old Aramaic chapters, being well known in this form, remained untranslated.   Th.C.V.

KAPELRUD, A. S. : *Joel Studies.* (Uppsala Universitets Årsskrift 1948 : 4). 1948. Pp. viii+212. (Lundequistska Bokhandeln, Uppsala and Harrassowitz, Leipzig. Price : 10 Kr.)

This volume (written in English) is important because of the considerable use which is made of the Ras Shamra material. The first 175 pages form a commentary, almost verse by verse, in which, again and again, a new light is given to the exegesis because of the Ras Shamra texts. Kapelrud's own position is that Joel himself was a temple-prophet *c.* 600 B.C. His sayings were handed down by word of mouth in priestly circles and committed to writing perhaps as late as the 4th or 3rd cent. B.C. They suffered few changes because of their firm structure on the basis of the ancient cultic pattern. There are traces of this last everywhere in the book, for Kapelrud is a firm adherent of the modern Scandinavian school, though not so extreme as (say) Engnell. His solution is a modification of Engnell's in vol. I of the new Swedish Biblical Encyclopaedia (Svensk Bibliskt Uppslagsverk, 1948, but Engnell's article on Joel was written in 1944 and Kapelrud had access to it). Engnell makes everything cultic, with even the locusts belonging to the cult-motif. Kapelrud finds a historical basis in the locust-plague and in other references also.

N.H.S.

*MOORE, G. F. : *The Literature of the Old Testament,* revised by L. H. Brockington. (The Home University Library.) 1948. Pp. 232. (Oxford University Press. Price : 5s. 0d.)

This is substantially the work written thirty-five years ago by Moore, with some slight revision by Brockington. An occasional paragraph is slightly modified, or omitted, or added, but in general the work done in the field of Old Testament criticism since the appearance of the first edition is left out of account. The chief exceptions to this are the addition of some paragraphs on the literary forms of the Old Testament, the placing of Nehemiah before Ezra, and the addition of some paragraphs on the Psalter and the Cult, taking account of the work of Mowinckel and Gunkel. A short chapter on the Wisdom Writers is also new.   H.H.R.

PUUKKO, A. F. : *Vanhan Testamentin johdanto-oppi* (=*Introduction to the Old Testament*). 1945. Pp. 286. (Suomalainen Teologinen Kirjallisuusseura [=Finnische Theologische Literaturgesellschaft], Helsinki. Price : 250 Finnmarks.)

This work is an academic textbook for Finnish theological students. Without attempting any surprisingly original solutions, the author presents a thorough-going and reasoned statement of the literary critical research. The more recent point of view of the traditio-historical school, emphasizing the oral transmission of the Old Textament text and the improbability of the usually accepted documentary theory, together with the cultic interpretation of many sections of the Old Testament, are scarcely referred to in this book.
                                                                    A.La.

SIMPSON, C. A. : *The Early Traditions of Israel : a Critical Analysis of the Pre-Deuteronomic Narrative of the Hexateuch.* 1948. Pp. 678. (Blackwell, Oxford. Price : £3 3s. 0d.)

This is an elaborate study of J1, J2 and E, governed by the view that each of these documents can be precisely delimited. There is a useful history of Pentateuchal Criticism, though taking inadequate account of recent work, a study of the J1 document, followed by a complete translation of it, a study of J2 and E. In the case of these latter documents there is no connected translation. An immense amount of work has gone into the making of the volume, though too often it is needlessly subjective. The author sometimes frankly reaches a purely conjectural view, and then uses it as the instrument of his analysis. His historical scepticism is extreme, and the views of his earlier book *Revelation and Response* (see Book List 1948, p. 49), whose justification was looked for in this book, are left with no basis but conjecture.   H.H.R.

*SMITH, C. RYDER : *What is the Old Testament ? An Introductory Study.* Revised edition, 1949. Pp. 232. (Epworth Press, London. Price : 6s. 0d.)

This excellent book, first published in 1931, and revised in 1946 and now reprinted, offers an introduction to the religion of the Old Testament, prefaced by some shorter studies of the geography of Palestine, the history of Israel, the significance of the Higher Criticism, and the attitude of Jesus to the Old Testament. It is not intended for specialists, but will be very useful in mediating the fruits of scholarship to a wider circle.   H.H.R.

VRIEZEN, TH. C. : *Oud-israëlietische Geschriften.* (Servire's Ency-
clopaedie.) 1948. Pp. 252. (Servire, The Hague. Price : Fl.
4.20.)

A brief Old Testament introduction in a series comparable
in size to the Home University Library. Within its brief
compass there are two chapters on the prose and poetic forms
of the literature, short chapters on Text and Canon, and
Introductions to the separate books. Its standpoint is in
general the ' orthodox critical ' one, and it gives little attention
to variations from this view in recent work. Some of the
books receive necessarily brief treatment, but the Pentateuch
receives fuller treatment, and here Professor Vriezen offers
a fresh treatment with a greater measure of originality in
his positions. He makes the fullest use of the space allowed
him, and offers a readable as well as a compressed summary.
                                                                    H.H.R.

*WAND, J. W. C. : *The Authority of the Scriptures.* 1949. Pp. 120.
(Mowbrays, London and Oxford. Price : 5s. 0d.)

The last chapter in this book gives its title to the whole. In
it the Bishop of London offers a short general introduction
to the Bible. He deals with the composition of the Old
Testament, Apocrypha, and New Testament, the formation
of the Canon, Inspiration, Revelation, the interpretation of
the Bible, its character as the Word of God, wise Bible reading,
and the authority of the Bible. To cover such ground in so
small a compass is no mean feat, and all is written with judgement. The reader is warned against allegorical and typological
interpretation of the Old Testament and advised to make the
literal meaning the basis of all interpretation. In the last
chapter in particular much wisdom lies, and a balanced view
is presented.   H.H.R.

WENDEL, C. : *Die griechisch-römische Buchbeschreibung verglichen mit
der des Vorderen Orients* (Hallische Monographien, ed. O. Eissfeldt,
Nr. 3.) 1949. Pp. viii+194. (Halle/Saale.)

The author demonstrates that Greek and Roman scribes,
whilst adopting many details of book-form, dating, catchlines, line-counting titles, colophons, and similar technicalities
from early Mesopotamian and Egyptian inscriptions and
scrolls, adapted them to a framework faithful to their own
" Geist," and thereby produced " ein echt antikes Element."
The book contains a convenient assembly of data, drawn from
a variety of inscriptions ranging from Nineveh to Ugarit,
and from papyrus scrolls, together with a discussion of the
ways by which the traditions of book-form, etc., could have
been transmitted to the Greeks, e.g., Phoenician and
Aramaean. The Semitist will learn little new about his own
Fach, and no doubt, will not always agree with statements
made in the book, e.g., occasional over-simplifications, as in
the treatment of the O.T. on p. 87 f. But there is a very
welcome significance to the book, for it presents the findings
of a Classicist who interprets classical antiquities against a
background of historical minutiae from the earlier, pre-
Ionian Near East.   B.J.R.

WIDENGREN, G. : *Literary and Psychological Aspects of the Hebrew Prophets*. (Uppsala Universitets Årsskrift, 1948 : 10.) 1948. Pp. 140. (Lundequistska Bokhandeln, Uppsala and Harrassowitz, Leipzig. Price : Kr. 6.)

In this important study Widengren examines the evidence for the common assumption that the Qur'an and Islamic traditions were first orally transmitted and only written at a later date, and adduces evidence to show that within the lifetime of Muhammad suras of the Qur'an were written down and other written material existed. Thus written and oral tradition existed side by side. Moreover, there is evidence of interpolation within the lifetime of Muhammad, and even of prose interpolation in poetic passages. All of this is held to be of great significance for the literary criticism of the Old Testament prophets. Moreover, in a sedentary culture which had known the art of writing for many centuries it is antecedently more likely that even at the earlier date of the Hebrew prophets, oracles would be written down. To this is added a study of the evidence of the Old Testament itself for the existence of written poems and records in early times, and of the existence of written portions of prophetic teaching in pre-exilic days. Hence, Widengren concludes, oral and written tradition are not to be treated as mutually exclusive alternatives, but are both to be recognized as playing their part in the literary history of the prophetic books. There follows a study of some aspects of prophetic psychology, to be explained by parapsychology and levitation, leading to the conclusion that the so-called ' writing prophets ' are not to be so sharply distinguished from other prophets as is sometimes done.   H.H.R.

RELIGION AND THEOLOGY

(including the Life and Thought of the Neighbouring Peoples)

BENTZEN, A. : *Messias—Moses redivivus—Menschensohn : Skizzen zum Thema Weissagung und Erfüllung* (Abhandlungen zur Theologie des Alten und Neuen Testaments, Nr. 17). 1948. Pp. 80. (Zwingli-Verlag, Zürich. Price : Fr. 7.)

In this excellent short study the author returns to problems which he has already discussed in earlier books and articles. There are four main sections. The first deals with Psalm ii, and with the place of various other Psalms in the enthronement ritual ; the second discusses whether the term " Messianic " can be appropriately applied to the figure of the king in the Psalms, and the relation of kingship to the idea of the " Urmensch " ; the third examines the concept of the Servant of Yahweh in its relation to the king and the prophet, and to the development of the Messianic hope ; and the fourth surveys the revival of the old myth in terms of the later eschatology. Bentzen regards the " Königsideologie " as too narrow, and prefers to deal with the concept of the " Urmensch," from whom are derived the functions of the king, the priest, and the prophet. There emerge three variations of the Messianic figure : the present Messianic king of the Psalms, the suffering, prophetic figure of the new Moses, and the coming Son of Man of *Daniel*. Without adopting the extreme features of the view once held by Sellin, Bentzen argues that an important element in the conception of the Servant is the thought that he is a new Moses. This book is an important and suggestive contribution to the subject ; and it is also valuable for its acute assessment of the work of other Scandinavian scholars, and, in particular, of the views of the Uppsala school. G.W.A.

De la Bible au Monde Moderne : comptes-rendus de deux conférences oecuméniques ,sur l'autorité de la Bible pour le message social et politique de l'Eglise dans le temps présent. (Études Théologiques et Religieuses XXIIIᵉ Année, Nos. 2-3.) 1948. Pp. 152. (Publication de la Faculté de Théologie Protestante de Montpellier. Price : 8s. 6d.)

This book contains the report of two conferences held in London and at Bossey preparatory to the Amsterdam Conference and with a view to the eventual production of a symposium to be entitled " The Biblical Authority for the Church's Social and Political Message To-day." (A typed copy of this preparatory volume in English has been issued by the Study Department of the World Council of Churches in Geneva.) A number of the papers are of quite unusual interest to the Old Testament exegete and theologian, especially perhaps those by Dodd, Richardson, Barth, Nygren and Eichrodt. The reports of the discussions which followed the papers (see pp. 41-55 and 107-146) make absorbing reading. The volume brings to the light certain fundamental differences of opinion, the disagreement being not always between Continental and Anglo-Saxon. For anyone wishing to understand the current theological debate about the Bible this book is indispensable. The presence of a few more Biblical scholars at these meetings might have been an advantage.   .   N.W.P.

BROWNE, L. : *The Wisdom of Israel, an Anthology.* 1945. Pp. xxxii+ 748. (Random House, New York. Price : £1 2s. 6d.)

This anthology is not a collection of excerpts from what is technically called the wisdom-literature of Israel but is a presentation of the fruits of Israel's teaching and thinking throughout the ages in all the literary forms. Mr. Browne claims for the anthology which he has made that it is apparently the first in the English language to plough a furrow through the entire field of the wisdom of Israel. It is a most delightful book, covering the O.T. and the apocryphal writings, the N.T., and the Talmudic times, right down through the medieval period to modern days. The variety and the representative character of the book's contents are most attractive. Here we have the wisdom of the mystics (the Zohar) and of the rationalists (Maimonides, Spinoza), the thoughts of medieval saints (e.g., Baal Shem) and of the poet (Bialik), Yiddish anecdotes and proverbs, responsa and prayers, the reflections of such men as Asher Ginzberg, Felix Adler, Israel Zangwill,

Ludwig Lewisohn, Jakob Klatzkin and Sholom Asch. But this but represents a portion of the good things which the book offers. The short introductions which Mr. Browne gives to the numerous citations are most instructive and valuable. He who reads this anthology will have a knowledge of the contribution of the Jewish mind far above what is usual.

O.S.R.

DAVID, M. : *Les dieux et le destin en Babylonie*. 1949. Pp. viii+120. (Presses Universitaires de France, Paris. Price : Fr. 180.)

In this small volume, in the series Mythes et Religions, Mme David, who is a former pupil of Hrozný's, and whose book carries a Foreword by her teacher, somewhat oversimplifies Babylonian religion. Selecting Destiny as the keynote of her study, and limiting herself to the classical period of the first Babylonian dynasty, she interprets Babylonian religion. Few religions can be traced to a single idea, and it is particularly doubtful if the Babylonians, who were the heirs of Sumerian culture as well as of Semitic ideas, should have their religion so simplified. Within her self-imposed limitations the authoress writes with skill, and her work rests on sound foundations of learning.

H.H.R.

DE DIETRICH, SUZANNE : *Le Dessein de Dieu*. (Collection l' " Actualité Protestante "). 1945. Pp. 299. (Delachaux et Niestlé, Neuchâtel (Suisse) et Paris. Price : 4.75 fr.)

This book is an example of a post-war attitude to the Bible and method of exegesis which has developed in some continental Protestant circles. Modern criticism is accepted (see the notes at the end), but in the body of the book the author searches for the message of the Bible as a whole without any particular reference to these critical results. It is the old Plan of Salvation come to life again, whereby the mystery of the Cross is found to be hidden from Genesis to Revelation. The book is in three parts with Prologue (The Beginning of the Times) and Epilogue (The new heavens and the new earth). The three parts are entitled 'The Unfolding of the Times,' 'The Accomplishment of the Times,' and ' The Last Times.'

N.H.S.

ELLIGER, K. : *Die Bedeutung der Geschichte Israels für die Kirche Jesu Christi* (Sonderdruck aus " Für Arbeit und Besinnung," Kirchlich-Theologische Halbmonatschrift für Geistliche, 2. Jahrgang, Nr. 1 und 2/3.) 1948. Pp. 16. (Quell-Verlag der Evang. Gesellschaft, Stuttgart.)

The thesis of this small pamphlet is that God and the right relationship of man to God is the meaning and aim of history and, in particular, that the history of the Hebrews recorded in the O.T. is a special revelation of God to the Christian Church. In the N.T. and in Christ Himself we have the continuance of the O.T. revelation and the " perspective centre " from which the events and persons of the O.T. appear as having a special significance for the Israel of the new covenant. " According to God's will, the Word entered into history.

As the Word became flesh in Jesus Christ so also it had become flesh in the whole history of the O.T. Only in, with, and under a history can we have the Word—not in history in general which gives only a general revelation, but in that special history whose records are the O.T. and the N.T." This fact necessitates, according to Elliger the " typical " interpretation of the O.T. by the Christian Church—as we find it, e.g., in I Cor. x, lf.; cf. *typicos* v, 11—but this sort of interpretation has to avoid falling into allegorizing, and above all it must in no way prejudice the historical-critical exegesis undertaken by textual criticism.   O.S.R.

*ELMSLIE, W. A. L. : *How Came Our Faith : a study of the religion of Israel and its significance for the modern world.* 1948. Pp. xii+418. (Cambridge University Press. Price : £1 1s. 0d.)

Into this rich book the author has clearly put the thought of many years. It is intended in the first instance neither for the scholar nor even for the theological student, but for the intelligent layman, but it would be a pity if the others overlooked it. The substance of the Old Testament is presented here with an urgent and even passionate contemporary reference. The volume falls into three sections :—Part I. The Old Testament To-day : Part II. The Religion of the Hebrews : Part III. The Faith of the Prophets. The inclusion of much that is familiar to those who are theologically trained is justified by the type of reader which the book has in view. Of outstanding importance in Part I are the sections on the importance of the Hebrew view of life in Ch. I, the valuable discussion of the nature of Hebrew as a literary medium in Ch. III, and the trenchant and salutary criticism of defective methods of Biblical interpretation in the past and at the present day. Three of the chapters in Part II draw the contrast between the faith which the Hebrews brought into Palestine and the Canaan te faith they found there, treating thereafter of Israel's religious fortunes in Canaan. More might have been said of the cultic side of Israel's religion. In Part III, eight successive chapters give a brilliant treatment of the prophetic succession from Moses to the Second Isaiah. All will not agree with the author's uncompromising views about sacrifice and still fewer with his complete acceptance of Torrey's theory about the Second Isaiah. Concluding chapters consider alternatives to the prophetic faith and its effectiveness as a solution of the problem of life. The book is marked by ethical earnestness and an unusual imaginative quality.
                                                  N.W.P.

FOHRER, G. : *Glaube und Welt im Alten Testament: das Alte Testament und Gegenwartsfragen.* 1948. Pp. 260. (Verlag Joseph Knecht, Carolusdruckerei, Frankfort am Main.)

This is a useful collection of theological essays on various Old Testament topics such as prophecy, guilt and suffering, and various ethical and religious questions concerning the cult, the law and the state. The book is a welcome example of the way in which recent history has brought new life and a fresh sense of reality to the study of the Old Testament. Though not strictly a work of scholarship (there is, for example, no documentation otherwise than by scripture references), the book presupposes the results of scholarship and will be found useful by those who have to present to students the specific teaching of Scripture. The method of the author is as a rule to take a topic and follow it right through the Old Testament illustrating it with plentiful quotations.   N.W.P.

FRANKFORT, H. :   *Ancient Egyptian Religion.* 1948. Pp. xiv+172. (Columbia University Press, New York. Price : 17s. 6d.)

Professor Frankfort approaches Egyptian religion from an entirely new angle. He examines first the Egyptians' conception of the gods and their attributes. Next he studies four aspects of Egyptian life, namely the state, way of life, hope (i.e., death and the survival of the individual after death), and literature and art. He finds that one conviction underlies all Egyptian belief and thought—the universe is static and only what is changeless and permanent is significant. This is a most stimulating book and an important contribution to our understanding of the Egyptian mind. Of special interest to the Old Testament scholar are the chapters on the Egyptian way of life (in which there is a reinterpretation of the Egyptian wisdom literature) and the Egyptian hope.   T.W.T.

GADD, C. J. :   *Ideas of Divine Rule in the Ancient East.* 1948. Pp. viii+102. (Oxford University Press, London. Price : 7s. 6d.)

This work contains the Schweich Lectures for 1945, and the author's aim is to survey the characteristic ideas concerning the relations between the gods and mankind, as these found expression in the theory and practice of the peoples of Western Asia and Egypt down to the time of the Persian Empire. In the nature of the case the treatment is somewhat cursory : but it is by a master of the subject, and, as such, it is always interesting and often suggestive. Indeed the student of the Old Testament who is interested in the problems of divine kingship, prophecy and divination, and the history of social and private morality (to mention some of the more arresting features) will find much food for thought—not least where he is provoked to opposition ! Happily the writer appears to have no particular axe to grind, and he is concerned to point out not only the similarities but also the differences which are to be observed in the different fields ; and, as a result, the reader can hardly fail to be impressed time and again by the uniqueness of Israel's contribution to the religious thought of mankind.   A.R.J.

GASPAR, J. W. :   *Social Ideas in the Wisdom Literature of the Old Testament* (The Catholic University of America, Studies in Sacred Theology, Second series, No. 8). 1947. Pp. xiv+208. (The Catholic University Press, Washington, D.C. Price : 12s. 0d.)

The author's purpose is to give an insight into the character of the social thinking of the sages of Israel and he fulfils this aim by treatment of the topics of marriage, the relations of the father to wife and children, education, its principles and methods, the community and its government. This approach to the Hebrew social ideas, through an examination of what the wisdom-literature has to say about the fundamental events of human life, certainly adopts the right and most fruitful method. Dr. Gaspar makes use of a large and valuable bibliography. His discussion of various scripture passages is interesting. He holds the background of the Song of Songs to be the oriental wedding feast and in this regard he appreciates Wetzstein's report of the custom of the " king's week " as enacted at weddings in Syria. This book is a scholarly piece of research. On pp. 93 f, where the subject of " Mother Earth " is being discussed the reader might have expected a more exhaustive explanation of Psalm cxxxix, 15, than is there offered.   O.S.R.

GELIN, A. : *Les Idées Maîtresses de l'Ancien Testament*. 1948. Pp. 86. (Les Éditions du Cerf, Paris. Price : 5s. 0d.)

This is an attractive little theological study of the Old Testament by a Roman Catholic professor at Lyon, published as the second number in the series *Lectio Divina*. It deals with the revelation of God in the Old Testament, which the author does not wish to separate from man's search for God, with God's redemptive plan exhibited in the Promise to Abraham, in the Covenant, in the Kingdom and its culmination in Christ, special attention being given to the Messianic hope, and finally with the individual and the community and the fundamental matters of retribution, sin and grace. The author recognizes the different spiritual levels in the Old Testament and adopts a moderate historical point of view. There is nothing new in this book but there is some originality in the presentation of familiar material. At the end is a useful bibliography of relevant literature, mainly but not exclusively Catholic.
                                                                            N.W.P.

GORCE, M., and MORTIER, R. (ed. by) : *Histoire générale des religions*. I. *Introduction générale—Les Primitifs—L'ancien Orient—Les Indo-Européens*. 1948. Pp. xx+548. II. *Grèce—Rome*. 1944. Pp. 426. III. *Indo-Iraniens—Judaïsme—Origines chrétiennes—Christianismes orientaux*. 1945. Pp. 486. IV. *Christianisme médiéval—Reforme protestante—Catholicisme moderne—Islam—Extrême-Orient*. 1947. Pp. 556. (Librairie Aristide Quillet, Paris. Price : 4 volumes £12 2s. 6d.)

While the student of the Old Testament can hardly fail to be interested in this work as a whole, his chief interest is likely to be in Volume I with its treatment of the religious beliefs and practices of Egypt (Desroches-Noblecourt), Sumer (Contenau), the Hittites (Delaporte), Phoenicia (Vincent) including the mythological texts of Ugarit (Dussaud), Assyria and Babylon (Langdon) and Israel (Barrois). The last, which covers the whole period of Old Testament literature, follows normal critical lines save for certain necessary reserves due to our increasing knowledge of the general culture of the ancient Near East. Reference must also be made to the short but important section of pre-Islamic Arabia (Ryckmans) in Volume IV, which is cf quite outstanding value. The chief defect of the whole work is a certain lack of proportion in the treatment of the different fields of study, some contributions being comparatively full and others more sketchy. Nevertheless it may be warmly recommended, not least for the numerous illustrations in the text and the many plates, some in colour, which give real distinction to the volumes and make them a pleasure to handle.   A.R.J.

GRANQVIST, HILMA : *Birth and Childhood among the Arabs.* 1947. Pp. 292. (Söderström, Helsingfors. English Price : £1 10s. 0d.)

This book is the result of three years spent in Palestine, mostly in the Arab village of Artas, half-an-hour by foot from Bethlehem. Dr. Granqvist has already written on Arab Marriage customs (2 vols., 1935) and on Arab family life (1939). Further volumes on childhood and education await publication. This Finnish lady, whose name easily became *Sitt Halime* (cf. the Prophet's nurse), deals with pre-natal customs, especially as dealing with cohabitation, conception and pregnancy, with birth and post-natal customs, and all matters concerning young children, including play, education and circumcision. The first 200 pages deal with the actual evidence gained through close contact with the women of the village. The last 90 pages contain parallels from her own observations elsewhere, from other authorities, and particularly from the Bible. These last are most valuable for the better understanding of Hebrew life and custom.   N.H.S.

HENNINGER, J. : *Die Familie bei den heutigen Beduinen Arabiens und seiner Randgebiete : Ein Beitrag zur Frage der ursprünglichen Familienform der Semiten.* (In *International Archiv für Ethnographie*, Band xlii.) 1943. Pp. 188. (E. J. Brill, Leiden. Price of the whole volume : £2 2s. 0d. Also obtainable separately.)

The object of this work is to determine whether the character of modern family life among the Arabs provides any evidence that the Semites originally reckoned kinship through the mother. A detailed account is given of varieties of marriage custom, family life, divorce and widowhood, and the relation of the family to larger social units. The author then considers the alleged survivals of " Mutterrecht," and concludes that though there is some evidence from the southern part of the Arabian peninsula, there are otherwise no cogent indications of that system. Much patient research has gone into this treatise, and the extensive modern literature has been carefully sifted. The work is admirably documented, and there is a very full index.   G.W.A.

JOHNSON, N. B. : *Prayer in the Apocrypha and Pseudepigrapha* (J.B.L. Monograph Series, vol. ii). 1948. Pp. iv+78. (Society of Biblical Literature, Philadelphia. Price : $1.00.)

A useful study of the prayers in the Apocrypha and Pseudepigrapha, arranged according to the purpose of the prayers, followed by a study of the basis of the appeals to God and of the recorded responses they found. A concluding summary reviews the theological implications of the passages studied.
H.H.R.

LANGTON, E. : *Essentials of Demonology*. 1949. Pp. 234. (Epworth Press, London. Price : 15s. 0d.)

This book is concerned with the origin and development of Jewish and Christian ideas concerning demons and evil spirits. It is a thorough and comprehensive account of such beliefs as they appear in Old Testament, New Testament, and in Jewish extra-canonical writings. The relationships with similar ideas in Arabia, Mesopotamia and Persia are discussed. The conclusions are balanced, e.g., Satan is a native Hebrew creation, owing nothing originally to Persian ideas, but influenced in later development by the concept of Ahriman. A valuable book in that it collects material not easily accessible. N.H.S.

LAUHA, A. : *Jumalan soihdun kantajia* (= *God's Torch-Bearers*). 1948. (Agricola-Seura, Helsinki).

This little Finnish book on the personalities of the Old Testament is published for study in Bible-circles, but it is useful for all who wish to get a right understanding of the life and work of the Prophets. Besides the Prophets (Elijah, Amos, Hosea, Isaiah, Jeremiah, Ezekiel, Deutero-Isaiah) we find there a very good character-sketch of Abraham, Moses, Gideon, Samuel, David, Solomon, and Josiah. The historical background of all these personalities is based on the results of the modern scientific investigation on the Old Testament. The scientific view and the popular style are successfully combined in this excellent little book. A.F.P.

MONTGOMERY, J. A. : *The Bible : the Book of God and Man*. 1948. Pp. 108. (Ventnor Publishers, Inc., Ventnor, N.J. Price : $2.75.)

It is very difficult to classify and assess this brief and curiously unsystematic volume. Parts of it are extremely elementary and apparently intended for readers who do not know much about the Bible : other parts are well worth the attention of the more informed reader for their sudden flashes of insight and felicities of expression. The book might not unfairly be styled the *obiter dicta* of a very great scholar whose reputation is so secure that he can afford to write for once just as he pleases, moving at will through familiar fields. The central part of the book consists of a couple of essays on the men and women of the Bible and the Apocrypha. A short chapter entitled ' The Ego of the Psalms ' lays particular emphasis on the ' quiet ' and ' humble of the land ' in the Old Testament period and ' the faithful ' and ' the saints ' in the New as forming the background of Biblical religion. A concluding chapter deals with the revelation of God in Nature.

N.W.P.

MUNK, E. : *La Justice Sociale en Israël*. 1948. Pp. 240. (La Baconnière, Boudry, Neuchâtel. English Price : 8s. 6d.)

The series deals with Judaism and its contribution to the present world situation. Judaism is not a set of religious ideas divorced from real life, but has a political doctrine, a clear-cut conception of economics, and a civil code, all of which are precisely what the modern world needs. It is the basis for that world of peace and happiness which good men desire.

It can resolve the antagonism of Capitalism and Marxism. The volume shows how valuable in these respects is Jewish teaching at its best. The author is a devout continental Jew, well-informed as to the best that Judaism has meant down the Ages, but singularly ill-informed as to Christian doctrine and practice.　　　　　　　　　　　　　　　　　N.H.S.

NIKOLAINEN, A. T. : *Der Auferstehungsglauben in der Bibel und ihrer Umwelt. I. Religionsgeschichtlicher Teil* (Annales Academiae Scientiarum Fennicae, B XLIX, 3.) 1944. Pp. 206. *II. Neutestamentlicher Teil* (Annales Academiae Scientiarum Fennicae, B LIX, 3.) 1946. Pp. 250. (Druckerei—A.G. der Finnischen Literaturgesellschaft, Helsinki. Price : I, 13s. 0d. 11, 16s. 6d.)

In Part I the author considers the evidence for belief in resurrection (by which he means a transformed life after death, thought of in bodily form) in the religions of Egypt, Persia, the eastern and western Semites, and of Hellenistic civilization, in the Old Testament, and in later Jewish thought up to the beginning of the Christian era. He presents a good case for a distinctive development of the belief in the Old Testament, based not on analogy with natural processes, or on belief in the inherent powers of the soul, but on the sovereign power of God and the communion of the believer with Him. Perhaps he is too anxious to produce a tidy scheme ; but he reviews the evidence with care and presents his results clearly. In Part II a large part, but not all, of the New Testament evidence is examined. It is unfortunate that so useful a work is not provided with an index, either of the passages discussed or of the main subjects.　　　　　　　　　　　　　　　G.W.A.

NORTH, C. R. : *The Suffering Servant in Deutero-Isaiah.* 1948. Pp. viii+248. (Oxford University Press. Price : 15s. 0d.)

A thorough, competent and exhaustive study of the whole subject, indispensable to the Old Testament student, and of special interest (because of North's own solution) to the New Testament student. The bibliography is practically complete, with well over 300 items listed. The first part of the book (to p. 116) is a historical survey of solutions hitherto proposed as to the identity of the Servant. The grouping of the discussion is historical : Jewish, early and late ; Christian to 18th century ; Döderlein to Duhm ; Duhm to Mowinckel ; Mowinckel to present-day. Within these groups, the material is grouped according to the categories (individual, collective, etc.,) with which the student is familiar. Next, there are translations of the four Servant-Songs, and in addition of the secondary songs (e.g., xlix, 7-13). Critical notes are given in full, with the Hebrew transliterated. Finally (from p. 139) the author discusses the main problems : The Servant as depicted in the songs (e.g., Is the picture consistent ?) ; The authorship of the Songs ; etc. North's own solution is Messianic, but soteriological rather than political. For the rest, the songs were by Deutero-Isaiah himself, though later than the rest and not all composed at one time. There is a certain fluidity in the prophet's conception.　　　　　　N.H.S.

von OPPENHEIM, F. M. : *Die Beduinen.* Band I : *Die Beduinenstämme in Mesopotamien und Syrien.* 1939. Pp. 386 with plates and maps. Band II : *Die Beduinenstämme in Palästina, Transjordanien, Sinai, Hedjaz.* 1943. Pp. 447 with plates. (Otto Harrassowitz, Leipzig.)

> The complete work will contain five volumes, of which the last will deal with the culture and life of the Bedouin. These two volumes deal with the Bedouin of the north and west. The third will deal with the south and east (Arabia proper, Iraq and Persia). The details of the Arabs of Palestine appear in the first 132 pages of volume two. Some of these tribes have been in Palestine for a thousand years ; others not more than a hundred. The general plan of the volumes is to give the history of the group, and its genealogical tree showing the relation between the various tribes in the group. This is followed by a table listing the various tribes with the name of the sheik, the grazing district, and the strength of the tribe in ' tents.' The volumes will provide a comprehensive and authoritative account of the Bedouin of the Near East.
>
> N.H.S.

*PATERSON, J. : *The Goodly Fellowship of the Prophets.* 1948. Pp. xi+313. (Charles Scribner's Sons, New York. Price : $3.00.)

> A good straightforward account of the prophets and their messages for their times. The author is a Scot who studied under MacFayden and Stevenson, and migrated to Drew, N.J., in 1931. Based on lectures to theological students, ministerial conferences, and Adult Education groups, this book should be useful also in the upper forms of schools.
>
> C.R.N.

PEAKE, A. S. : *The Problem of Suffering in the Old Testament.* New edition. 1947. Pp. xvi+180. (Epworth Press, London. Price : 7s. 6d.)

> Many will welcome this reprint of a well-known work, which has long been out of print, with its illuminating discussion of Habakkuk, Ezekiel, the Servant of Yahweh, Job, the Apocalyptists and Koheleth. While all the work of almost half a century is necessarily ignored in this reprint of a work published in 1904, it still has a real value as a classic discussion of its theme.
>
> H.H.R.

PEDERSEN, J. (ed. by) : *Illustreret Religionshistorie.* 1948. Pp. 714. (G.E.C. Gads Forlag, Copenhagen.)

> This volume takes the place of that published under the same title in 1924 and edited by E. Lehmann. Short accounts are given of the great religions of the world. Judaism and Christianity are deliberately excluded, and there is therefore no account of O.T. religion. Of special interest, however, is Pedersen's brilliant survey of Canaanite religion (19 pp.), almost the whole of which is devoted to the Ras Shamra evidence. Pedersen also contributes a very valuable survey of the origin and development of Islam (74 pp.). C. E. Sander-Hansen deals with Egyptian religion (51 pp.) and O. E. Ravn

with that of the Sumerians, Babylonians and Assyrians (53 pp.). H. S. Nyberg gives an excellent outline of Iranian religion (58 pp.) ; and the veteran M. P. Nilsson describes Greek and Roman religion in a contribution which is as fascinating as it is scholarly (92 pp.). V. Grønbech's article on primitive religion (62 pp.) is largely a reprint of an earlier publication, with an appendix on primitive cult written by T. Kemp in collaboration with Grønbech. There are also articles on Nordic religion (39 pp.) by Grønbech, on the religions of India (143 pp.) by S. Konow and P. Tuxen, and on China and Japan (53 pp.) by B. Karlgren. All the articles are in one or other of the Scandinavian languages. The volume is well indexed and illustrated.   G.W.A.

PUUKKO, A. F. : *Israelin uskonnon historia* (=*History of Israel's Religion*). 1940. Pp. 234. (Otava-Verlag, Helsinki. Price : 150 Finnmarks.)

This work written in Finnish is intended in the first place to serve as a textbook for theological students. Hence it contains little that is strikingly new. Nevertheless it offers an able and solid presentation of the Israelite religion, interpreted in the way which is especially associated with Rudolf Kittel. The history of the Old Testament religion is regarded as a sustained struggle on the part of the great prophets for the clarification of ethical monotheism. On the other hand, the author disregards the most recent trends of research with their cultic perspective and the problems they raise.   A.La.

RINGGREN, H. : *Word and Wisdom : Studies in the Hypostatization of Divine Qualities and Functions in the Ancient Near East.* 1947. Pp. 234. (Lundequistska Bokhandeln, Uppsala.)

In this dissertation we have a very learned study of the hypostatization of divine qualities, in which it is shown that monotheism frequently tends to become polytheism through the hypostatization of functions and qualities of God. The author has a wide linguistic equipment, and pursues his study through Egyptian, Sumero-Accadian, West Semitic and pre-Islamic Arabic sources. His longest chapter is devoted to Wisdom in the Old Testament and in Judaism. While the author displays a strongly anti-evolutionistic outlook, and combats the idea that monotheism evolves out of polytheism, he wisely refrains from making the contrary claim that polytheism can only arise along the lines he studies. He recognizes in religion a tendency towards *Götterspaltung*, but also a tendency towards *Göttervereinigung*. Any simple theory of evolution either to or from monotheism is therefore inadequate. The study is to be commended equally for its learning and its restraint.   H.H.R.

SCHMIDT, M. : *Prophet und Tempel : eine Studie zum Problem der Gottesnahe im Alten Testament.* 1948. Pp. 276. (Zollikon, Zürich. English Price : 19s. 0d.)

The author discusses the experience of the presence of God as portrayed in the canonical prophets. He groups the prophets into five chapters, Amos, Hosea and Isaiah ; Micah and Zephaniah ; Jeremiah ; Ezekiel ; Deutero-Isaiah and the post-exilic prophets. Most interest centres round Isaiah of Jerusalem, Jeremiah, and Ezekiel. There is a development from the primitive notion of the secret presence of God in His Temple to the truer experience of Him in the experience and history of the nation and the individual. The beginning of the development is that the Nearness works out as ines-capable Justice in human affairs, and the end is in the Christian idea of ' Christ-in-us '—' We-in-Christ ' and the Indwelling of the Holy Spirit. There are added an excursus on the Servant of the Lord (Exilic Messiah), forty-five pages of notes, and a short bibliography wholly in German. N.H.S.

SMITH, D. H. : *The Pattern in the Mount : Hebrew Ideals and their Influence on Christianity.* 1948. Pp. 128. (Epworth Press, London. Price : 5s. 0d.)

This little book consists of some lectures given in China— and repeated in Chinese at Cheeloo University, where the reviewer formerly worked—dealing with Old Testament institutions and their Christian counterparts. The institutions studied are the Law, the Sabbath, the Festivals, the Temple, the Synagogue, Priesthood and Prophecy, and the Covenant. It is common to consider the teaching of the Old Testament as the foundation of the New, but less common to turn to the institutions. The author's purpose is to show that in each case there was re-adaptation in the New Testament, and that since the spirit is more important than the form further re-adaptation of the form has followed and may still be effected. H.H.R.

STUMMER, F. : *Gedanken über die Stellung des Hohenpriesters in der alttestamentlichen Gemeinde* (reprinted from *Episcopus, Studien über das Bischofsamt : Festgabe Kardinal Faulhaber*). 1949. Pp. 30. (Gregorius-Verlag vorm. F. Pustet, Regensburg.)

This monograph traces the office of the high priest through Old Testament and Apocrypha. His function is religious, his political power secondary, and unimportant beside that of pre-exilic kings and post-exilic prophets. In pre-exilic times the *kohen gadhol* does not specially stand out from other priests, though he had a special duty. The office itself is nowhere praised, but only particular individuals. Three things make a high priest ; he is called by God ; he has the right to enter the Holy Place ; he brings atonement. He must be ' a blameless man.' There is a straight line from Lev. xvi, through Wisd. xviii, 20-25, to Christ. Christ transfers the office into the heavenly sphere. He is not the expectation, but the fulfilment of the Old Testament high priesthood. A thorough, careful, and moderate piece of work. N.H.S.

Susman, Margarete : *Das Buch Hiob und das Schicksal des jüdischen Volkes.* 2nd ed., 1948. Pp. 220. (Steinberg-Verlag, Zurich. Price : 18s. 0d.)

This book is not intended as a commentary on the Book of Job. It uses certain ideas to be found in, or nowadays read into, that work for illuminating the destiny of the Jewish people—the people whose task it is to live without an outward form, to live a purely human life, and to experience the power, truth and hope of God precisely when delivered up to Satan. The argument is passionate, sincere and interesting ; of a mystical rather than a rational nature ; and at times difficult to follow. The reviewer would be hard put to it, for example, to define the author's views on the relation of Judaism and Christianity.   D.D.

Weinberger, O. : *Die Wirtschaftsphilosophie des Alten Testaments.* 1948. Pp. 142. (Springer-Verlag, Vienna. Price : £1 2s. 0d.)

Wirtschaft is defined as comprising " all those processes and institutions which are directed towards the continual supply of material goods to human beings." The book is concerned with the criticism, from the point of view of the Christian-Catholic faith and ethics, of those laws and practices of an economic character which are found in the O.T. In particular, the standard of criticism of such laws—and of views and systems hostile to them—is provided by the contents of the two papal encyclicals *Rerum Novarum* (1891) and *Quadragesimo Anno* (1931). An instructive section of Dr. Weinberger's work is his account of the teaching of St. Thomas Aquinas on the *lex vetus* and the *lex nova* and on the position of the Church relative to the moral, cultic, and juristic precepts of the O.T.—the ceremonial or cultic law being reckoned as obsolete on the ground that it had announced the coming and suffering Christ and therefore, having performed its purpose, its present observance would be a denial of the fulfilment of messianic prediction. Of much interest are the references throughout to personalities of importance in the history of the immediate past, to the views of theologians (e.g., Max Weber and Harnack), to writers more popularly known, such as Nietzsche, Nordau and Rosenberg, and to thinkers whose names are associated with economic theories and systems.   O.S.R.

Whitfield, G. : *God and Man in the Old Testament.* 1949. Pp. 144. (S.C.M., London. Price : 8s. 6d.)

This is a short introduction to some sides of Old Testament thought, written for non-technical readers, and plentifully interspersed with long quotations of passages of major importance from the Revised Version. While there are no references to modern authors, it clearly rests on acquaintance with standard works and is marked by a historical sense. It deals with the Old Testament thought on the unity of God, on His activity in history, on His character and demand, on His approach to men through personality, and on the relation of the individual to the community and of this life to the hereafter. It is a pity the reader is not referred to books for further study, since it only offers a simple introduction to its themes.　　　　　　　　　　　　　　　　　　　　H.H.R.

POST-BIBLICAL JUDAISM

DAVIES, W. D. : *Paul and Rabbinic Judaism.* 1948. Pp. 376. (S.P.C.K. London. Price : £1 7s. 6d.)

The author's purpose is ' to set certain pivotal aspects of ·Paul's life and thought against the background of the contemporary Rabbinic Judaism.' The book consists of ten chapters. The first upon the Judaism of the Diaspora and of Palestine, and the others upon fundamental concepts, e.g., the old and the new man, the old and the new Torah, the old and the new obedience, the old and the new hope. To make special mention of particular subjects discussed, the topics ' The Flesh and Sin,' ' The First and the Second Adam,' ' Christ the Wisdom of God ' afford scholarly dissertations upon Pauline theological ideas. Professor Davies combats the thesis of Montefiore that Paul's thought must be considered as moulded by the Judaism of the Diaspora and became thus subject to Hellenistic influence. The author urges that Hellenistic influence was not confined to the Diaspora and that Palestine was not closed against this influence. In a discussion whether the contrast ' flesh ' and ' spirit ' in Paul's thought was due to Hellenistic influence, the author holds that the Pauline ' flesh ' is an accentuation of the meaning which this word already has in certain late documents of the Old Testament and that the contrast with ' spirit ' is a natural evolution of the Old Testament anthropology. A reader might here perhaps feel that this natural evolution might have been, and probably was, quickened by the influence of Greek thought. The concept of the first and second Adam (cf. 1 Cor. xv), is debated in connexion with Philo's doctrine of the Heavenly Man described in Gen. i, and of the earthly man of Gen. ii, and in connexion with the Rabbinic doctrine of the unity of all mankind in Adam. The development of the latter idea, it is contended, appears in Paul's teaching that Christians are one ' in Christ ' (the second Adam) and that the Church is the ' body ' of Christ. Further, in reference to the theme of Jesus and the Wisdom of God (1 Cor. i, 24 cf. Col. i, 15 f.), Davies sees the link between Jesus and Wisdom as being, in Paul's mind, the conception of Jesus as the New Law—the Law having been by Judaism equated with Wisdom and regarded as being instrumental in creation. The book is an extremely interesting contribution to the study of Paul's religious thought and will be hailed by N.T. scholars as being such. It exhibits the fruitfulness of viewing the apostle's theological conceptions in the light of the Rabbinic background. Of particular value also is the large bibliography of modern works upon which the writer draws.
　　　　　　　　　　　　　　　　　　　　　　　　　　O.S.R.

SUKENIK, E. L. : *Megilloth Genuzoth*. 1948. Pp. 44. (In Hebrew.)
(Bialik Foundation, Jerusalem. Price : LP. 0.75, *c.* 17s. 6d.)

Professor Sukenik here presents a first glimpse of two of the
recently discovered Hebrew scrolls and MSS. which are deposited in Jerusalem. The treatment is lucid, and the numerous
photographs and facsimiles add considerably to the importance
of the book.

Questions of text and script are discussed in the introduction,
the script being compared with that of the Nash Papyrus
and the Uzziah inscription, both placed by Professor Sukenik
not earlier than the 1st cent. A.D. The contents include :
(a) A scroll entitled ' The War between the Children of Light
and the Children of Darkness,' which describes a warfare
between the Jews, or a Jewish sect, and foreign forces at some
time before 135 B.C. The Damascus Document from the Old-
Cairo Genizah is also discussed in connexion with its contents.
There are two facsimiles and numerous passages of transcribed text. (b) A MS. consisting of three folded sheets with
fragments of 39 songs in the style and language of O.T.
Psalms. They are called ' Songs of Thanksgiving.' The MS.
is in poor condition, but two passages have been excellently
reproduced and transcriptions of many others. Both MSS.
are on parchment. (c) A transcript of chs. xlii f. of the Isaiah
scroll, and some valuable suggestions on the script and text.
These will be better appreciated when photostats of the scroll
become available from America.

The author and publishers are to be congratulated on this
profoundly important publication.   B.J.R.

PHILOLOGY AND GRAMMAR

COHEN, M. : *Essai comparatif sur le vocabulaire et la phonétique du
chamito-sémitique*. (Bibliothèque de l'École des Hautes Études
publiée sous les auspices du Ministère de l'Éducation nationale.
Sciences historiques et philologiques, fascicule 291). 1947. Pp.
xi+248. (Librairie ancienne Honoré Champion, Paris. Price :
14s. 0d.)

The author belongs to those scholars who believe that the
Hamitic and Semitic languages come from a common stock.
For purposes of comparison he divides the Hamitic languages
into three groups—Egyptian, Berber and Cushitic. His book
falls into two parts. The first, occupying 42 pages, is a history
and classified bibliography of comparative Hamito-Semitic
studies. This bibliography extends from the eighteenth
century to the year 1945. It is very full and nothing of importance seems to have been overlooked. It is much more .
than a mere list of titles : it gives a résumé or a description
of the contents of books and articles. The second and larger
part of the book is an attempt to establish phonetic equations
between the four groups of languages. It begins with a long
theoretical and practical introduction to lexicographical and
phonetic comparison, which is followed by a study of 521
sets of equated words. All of them, nouns and verbs, denote
objects and actions of every-day life. They are arranged in

such a way as to show what Hamitic consonants are equivalent to a given Semitic consonant. Consonants are grouped according to their phonetic properties, e.g., dentals and labials, and each group is introduced by prefatory observations. Finally, the author provides full indices of all Semitic and Hamitic words employed in the comparative section. Professor Cohen's book is an indispensable tool for all working in the field of Hamito-Semitic relationships, not least because of its valuable bibliographies. It may also be recommended to those non-specialists who wish to acquaint themselves with what has been accomplished in this branch of comparative studies. T.W.T.

CUNY, A. : *Invitation à l'étude comparative des langues indo-européennes et des langues chamito-sémitiques.* 1946. Pp. 274. (Éditions Bière, Bordeaux. Price : 18s. 9d.)

In this book, which the author modestly entitles an " invitation," are presented the facts in favour of deriving the Indo-European and Hamitic languages from a common ancestor called " nostratique." The first and larger part deals with phonetics, the second with morphology. The author sets forth his material with great clarity and orderliness. The field over which he ranges is so vast that inevitably he must quote from languages of which he has little or no first hand experience. It is therefore not surprising to find that in some cases he has not always consulted the best and most recent authorities and that there are occasional slips and misunderstandings. The results are not convincing. It is on the morphological side that the evidence is weakest and one cannot but feel that many equations in vocabulary are due to chance. Further, so many problems of Semitic and Hamitic grammar still await solution that the time has not yet arrived when comparison with the Indo-European languages can fruitfully be made. Nevertheless this well written book merits the attention of all philologists. T.W.T.

FLEISCH, H. : *Introduction à l'étude des langues sémitiques.* 1947. Pp. 148. (Adrien-Maisonneuve, Paris. Price : approximately 10s. 6d.)

This little book of some 150 pages gives a brief but lucid account of the Semitic languages with a useful map of the Semitic world, showing where the various languages have been or still are spoken. The author, who is not concerned to present anything new, summarizes known facts and views in a way likely to be useful to students beginning the Semitic languages. What is most useful is the bibliographical matter, even though the majority of the works cited are French ; German literature is modestly represented, but English works are rarely mentioned. G.R.D.

HATCH, W. H. P. : *An Album of Dated Syriac Manuscripts.* 1946.
Pp. ix+286, with 200 plates. (Harvard University Press. Price :
$25.00.)

This collection of 200 large and clear plates supersedes all
previous collections of reproductions of specimen pages of
Syriac manuscripts, and by its range and completeness it
provides for the first time the materials for a scientific study
of Syriac palaeography. The facsimiles, all of dated manuscripts, illustrate the development of the different Syriac
scripts from the time of the earliest extant dated codex (A.D.
411) down to the end of the sixteenth century, almost all
the manuscripts which antedate A.D. 1,000 being represented,
and thus they provide materials for determining the period
of undated codices. A useful introduction to the study of the
methods of Syriac scribes is given in sixteen short chapters
with the following titles : Writing Materials ; Pens ; Ink ;
Mode of Writing ; Columns ; Ruling ; Colophon ; Dating ;
Miniatures ; Quires ; Styles of Writing ; Observations on
the Forms of Certain Letters ; Seyâmê, the Single Point,
Qûshshâyâ and Râkkâkâ, *Linea Occultans ;* Punctuation ;
Gershûnî ; Periods in the History of Syriac Handwriting.

W.D.M.

HÖFNER, MARIA : *Altsüdarabische Grammatik.* (Porta Linguarum
Orientalium, vol. xxiv). 1943. Pp. xxiv+194 and 2 plates.
(Harrassowitz, Leipzig.)

This work will fill an important gap in the Semitist's equipment. For grammars of the dialects in which the South
Arabian inscriptions are written he has hitherto been dependent
upon the antiquated essay in F. Hommel's *Chrestomathie*
and Guidi's brief sketch in *Le Muséon* 39. Dr. Höfner's
grammar now provides him with a comprehensive study of
Old South Arabian incorporating the results of recent research.
In the arrangement of her material she has followed the pattern
employed by the *Porta* series — *Schrift* — und *Lautlehre,*
Formenlehre, Syntax. In two respects, however, her book
differs from most of its predecessors in the series. First, a
bibliography and chrestomathy are lacking (these it is hoped
to provide as a separate volume in the series). Second, her
tables of forms and examples are in transcription. The
material is presented with admirable clarity and rules are
amply illustrated. From time to time penetrating observations on general linguistics are appended to a section in
order to throw light on some feature of the language or of
Semitic usage. Amongst these the author's remarks on the
Infinitive may be mentioned as specially worthy of attention.
The peculiarities of the three main dialects of Old South Arabian
are carefully distinguished. Dr. Höfner's book will be welcomed
be all Semitists.

T.W.T.

KELSO, J. L. : *The Ceramic Vocabulary of the Old Testament.*
(B.A.S.O.R., Supplementary Studies 5-6). 1948. Pp. 48 including
2 plates. (New Haven, U.S.A. Price : $1.25.)

The present work is an exhaustive study of all the Hebrew
terms for vessels of earthenware and metal-work, together
with the materials used in their manufacture, in the Old

216

Testament. Such a collection has considerable value in itself but the author's self-confidence is often not balanced by the strength of the evidence. He sets himself the task of identifying, so far as possible, every pot or pan mentioned in the Old Testament with a corresponding piece of pottery found in excavation, taking for this purpose those found at Tall Bêt Mirsim, of which he depicts samples on two plates at the end of the book. For example, he says that *mizrāq* " refers to the large four-handled ring-burnished banquet bowl of Iron II " and identifies it with a specific form found at Tall Bêt Mirsim ; but there is nothing to support this identification, so boldly made, and it is difficult to see how a four-handled bowl can have been used as a drinking bowl (Amos vi, 6). Or how does he know that " the *kaḏ* was shorter than the *nēvel* and had an egg-shaped bottom which made for easier carrying "? Accordingly, while students will find the collection of material helpful, they must treat the deductions drawn from it with the greatest caution.   G.R.D.

KOEHLER, L. : *Lexicon in Veteris Testamenti Libros.* Lief. 1 and 2. 1948. Pp. 64 each. (Brill, Leiden. Price : 4s. 9d. each.)

Here we have the first two fascicules of Professor L. Koehler's long expected and most welcome Hebrew Lexicon, containing 128 pages and reaching *'ēmer* ' twig.' The *format* of the printed page is somewhat smaller than that of the last edition of Buhl's *Handwörterbuch* and the printing more widely spaced ; further, all the explanations are given in both the German and English languages. The space so lost, however, is gained by considerably reducing the matter, especially the references, as given by Buhl ; much of this is no loss. At the same time, every effort has been made to bring the whole work as much as possible up to date and those who have neither time nor opportunity or are too slothful to consult periodical literature will receive many salutary shocks. They will find most, if not all, the new meanings proposed for a number of words duly tabulated and will often have to give up cherished illusions. All users will rejoice that the editor has at length been able, even in these difficult times, to start printing the work to which he has devoted a life-time and will look forward to future fascicules with impatience ; and they will be glad to learn that Professor W. Baumgartner has been engaged to prepare a glossary of the Aramaic portions of the Old Testament as a fitting conclusion.   G.R.D.

KOLARI, E. : *Musikinstrumente und ihre Verwindung im Alten Testament. Eine lexikalische und kulturgeschichtliche Untersuchung.* 1947. Pp. 104. (Helsinki. English Price : 9s. 6d.)

The author of this small work is a worthy recruit to the Finnish school, whose lexicographical studies have done so much to give precision to the interpretation of Accadian words, e.g., of Holma on parts of the body and of Salonen on ships. He discusses every word for a musical instrument in the O.T. in the light of philology and use, examines the references in post-Biblical and modern literature and reaches conclusions which will generally commend themselves to the reader. If these are not always new, the collection of all the relevant material, much of it brought to light since Gressmann's *Musik und Musikinstrumente im Alten Testament* (1903), its collection and examination, are all the same extremely useful. There is an admirable bibliography at the end of the book.

G.R.D.

LEIVESTAD, R: *Guds straffende rettferdighet.* (Tilleggshefte til Norsk Teologisk Tidsskrift, 1946.) 1946. Pp. 130. (Grøndahl, Oslo.)

A very interesting examination of the application of the root SDQ to Yahweh in the O.T., in order to determine whether it ever directly expresses the idea of punishment. The author holds that the root normally denotes the positive, saving activity of Yahweh, but is occasionally used of *iustitia distributiva*. He argues, after a careful survey of the relevant passages, that it is never, save in Zeph. iii, 5, used of divine punishment by the classical prophets of judgement, who, he maintains, did not apply the term to Yahweh in other than its traditional sense. He admits that the idea of punishment is present in Is. v, 16 and x, 22, both of which he treats as late. Leivestad's solutions of some of the textual and exegetical problems involved may not always command agreement ; but the book provides a useful and stimulating survey of the problem. References to the literature of the subject could with advantage have been made more precisely. G.W.A.

RINGGREN, H. : *The Prophetical Conception of Holiness* (Uppsala Universitets Årsskrift, 1948 : 12). Pp. 30. (Lundequistska Bokhandeln, Uppsala and Harrassowitz, Leipzig. Price : Kr. 1.25.)

In this short study the author first examines the fundamental meaning of the root qdš in the light of Hebrew, Aramaic, Ethiopic and Arabic evidence. He is doubtful of the assumption of an original meaning ' to be separated ' or of a primary reference to men and things. On the other hand he does not think a meaning ' to be pure ' can be established. He holds that it referred originally to God, and only secondarily came to be applied to persons and things. It was not, however, ethical in its significance. In relation to God it thought of his transcendence ; in relation to man of ritual rectitude. An ethical meaning can be found in a few O.T. passages, but it was not developed. The relation between the root qdš and the roots hrm, hll and kbd receives some study. The whole forms a useful summary, though the reviewer is still of the opinion that an original meaning ' to be separated ' with reference to man offers the most promising clue for the interpretation of the evidence. H.H.R.

1950

This issue of the Book List has been prepared by the following Committee appointed by the Society : Prof. G. W. Anderson, Mgr. J. M. T. Barton, Dr. D. Daube, Prof. G. R. Driver, Dr. J. Gray, Profs. A. R. Johnson, W. D. McHardy, N. W. Porteous, O. S. Rankin, Miss B. K. Rattey, Mr. B. J. Roberts, Profs. N. H. Snaith, T. W. Thacker, D. Winton Thomas, and H. H. Rowley (Editor). In addition help has been received from the following scholars: Profs. W. Baumgartner (Basel), T. Fish, S. H. Hooke, T. W. Manson, C. R. North, Dr. J. W. Parkes, Profs. T. H. Robinson, A. G. Ulecia (Madrid), Th. C. Vriezen (Gröningen), Dr. M. Wallenstein and Mr. P. R. Weis. For all this help the Editor expresses his gratitude.

Prices of foreign books, where known, are given either in foreign currency, or in the English equivalent actually charged. In many cases the latter would be altered by devaluation, but it was thought better to give even this measure of guidance.

Titles to which an asterisk (*) is prefixed are recommended for inclusion in school libraries.

H. H. ROWLEY.

Manchester University.

GENERAL

BERTHOLET, A. : *Festschrift für Alfred Bertholet zum* 80. *Geburtstag gewidmet von Kollegen und Freunden,* edited by Walter Baumgartner, Otto Eissfeldt, Karl Elliger, Leonhard Rost. 1950. Pp. viii+578. (J. C. B. Mohr, Tübingen. Price : DM. 58.00 ; bound DM. 62.00.)

Nearly all the contributions to this volume deal with O.T. and kindred subjects. Five are linguistic or textual : G. R. Driver contributes philological notes on Canticles and Lamentations ; P. Humbert discusses the uses of the root *qana'* in Hebrew ; P. Kahle writes on the Samaritan pronunciation of Hebrew ; J. A. Bewer supplies textual notes ; and K. Elliger deals with the ' evening wolves ' of Habakkuk i, 8, and Zephaniah iii, 3. Many of the essays deal with the interpretation of O.T. passages : Psalm xciv, 20, is discussed by A. Allgeier ; Isaiah viii, 23-ix, 6, by A. Alt ; Daniel vi, by A. Bentzen ; the community law in Deuteronomy xxiii, by K. Galling ; the relation of Psalm civ, to Egyptian sources by G. Nagel ; Hosea iv, 13 f. by L. Rost ; the relationship of Genesis xiv, and Psalm cx, by H. H. Rowley ; 2 Kings xi, by W. Rudolph ; the second commandment by W. Zimmerli. H. W. Hertzberg deals with the structure of Job. Two essays, those by S. Mowinckel and T. H. Robinson, are devoted to the problems of Hebrew poetic form. W. F. Albright writes on recently discovered · references to Baal-Zephon ; and O. Eissfeldt examines the texts relating to the tribute of Niqmad of Ugarit to Shupiluliuma. In the field of religion and theology, F. M. Th. de Liagre-Böhl discusses the interplay between election and the missionary motive in Israel ; J. Hempel writes on the word of God and fate ; G. von Rad investigates the meaning of righteousness and life in the Psalms ; C. Steuernagel surveys the development of Jewish eschatology ; W. B. Stevenson treats of 'Olah and Zebach sacrifices ; and A. Weiser examines the descriptions of theophanies in the Psalter. More general essays on religion are those by S. A. Cook on the relevance of the science of religion, and by A. Jepsen on the phenomenology of religion. G. van der Leeuw writes on the nature of myth, and R. Mayer on a märchen motif alluded ·to in Bab. Ta'anith 8a. W. Baumgartner investigates the background of the ' dividing sword ' of Odes of Solomon xxviii, 4. M. Noth examines the meaning of ' judge of Israel.' J. Lindblom appraises some recent trends in O.T. research. O. Grether contributes an interesting essay on the teaching of Hebrew. E. Littmann writes on Abyssinian parallels to the Old Testament. G.W.A.

Bič, M. : *Palestina od Pravěku ke Křestanstvi* : *I. Země a lid.* (= *Palestine from Prehistoric Times to Christianity. I. The Land and the People.*) 1948. *II. Kult a náboženenstvi.* ᵥ (= *The Cult and the Religion.*) 1949. Pp. 464, 396. (Husova Československá Evangelická Fakulta Bohoslovecká, Prague.)

Here are two volumes of a large and comprehensive work, of which the third and final volume is in preparation, written in the Czech language, but with a summary in French (which alone the reviewer could read !). The first volume deals with the geography of Palestine and its people from earliest times, together with the relations that subsisted between Israelites and their predecessors after their incursion. The second volume deals with the culture of the Near East in ancient times as the background of Israel's culture and religion, and summarizes the religion and theology of the Old Testament. Both volumes rest on wide scholarly reading, as the Bibliographies testify, and there are many pages of plates in each volume. The author takes his stand on the religious quality of the Old Testament and maintains that it is only to be rightly interpreted in cultic and religious terms.   H.H.R.

DE BOER, P. A. H. (ed. by) : *Oudtestamentische Studiën*, Deel VI. 1949. Pp. 218. (Brill, Leiden. English Price : £1 10s. 0d.)

This volume contains two articles only, both in English. The first (100 pp.) is a continuation of the editor's own studies of the relation of the Masoretic Text of 1 *Samuel* to the text of the ancient versions. The present volume contains notes on chapters xviii-xxxi. The notes are thorough and careful, and form a desirable and indispensable addition to the commentaries. Dr. Kahle's conclusions as to the phonological unification of the Masoretes are accepted, but more stress is laid on the preservative work of the Masoretes in respect of different textual traditions. The second article is the post-humously published study by Professor Eerdmans of the text of *Numbers*. It is in line with his previous work on the Pentateuch, rejecting the four-document theory of the Kuenen-Wellhausen school.   N.H.S.

DE BOER, P. A. H. (ed. by) : *Oudtestamentische Studiën*, Deel VII. 1950. Pp. 272. (E. J. Brill, Leiden. Price ; £1 9s. 6d.)

Rather more than half of this new volume of studies published by the Dutch Old Testament Society consists of a study of the text of Zech. ix-xiv by T. Jansma of Leiden. There are discussions on the ancient versions, their method, characteristics, and relationships. Curiously Kahle's studies on the Masoretic text are not mentioned, whilst his *The Cairo Geniza* is mentioned only in a footnote. The last 82 pages of this textual study contain full and exhaustive linguistic and lexicographical notes on all the ancient versions. G. J. Thierry discusses various Hebraic problems, in particular the origin of the *hiph'il*, which he sees in an interjection *ha-* (' look ').

M. David denies that there is any connection of any kind between the Code of Hammurabi and the laws in Exodus. J. Simons stresses the importance of Manasseh's wall in the topography of Jerusalem, maintaining that ' the second quarter ' was the eastern suburbs contained by this wall. Th.C.Vriezen discusses the ritual of sprinkling (*hizza*), whilst the concluding essay (in French—all the rest are in English) is by J. van der Ploeg, who maintains that the ' poor ' in Israel are not the poverty-stricken, but those who were ' humble before God.' N.H.S.

GOLDMAN, S. : *The Book of Books : an Introduction.* 1948. Pp. xvi+460. (Harpers, New York. Price : $3.75.)

This is the first volume of an ambitious programme which is planned to run into thirteen volumes. The author is a Jewish Rabbi of wide learning, whose acquaintance with general literature reminds one of Moffatt's. After short introductory chapters in which the quality of the Hebrew Bible is assessed, its canon is studied, the history of Biblical criticism is reviewed, and Breasted's views in *The Dawn of Conscience* examined, the bulk of the book is devoted to classified literary quotations containing allusions to, or evaluations of, the Bible. While these are of little value to the Old Testament scholar, the vast labour involved in their collection will serve other readers and earn their gratitude, as well as their admiration. The Old Testament scholar will find most to interest him in the review of Biblical criticism. Here the story is traced to Wellhausen, and then on to Cassuto and Kaufman, and the conclusion is reached that Wellhausen is completely antiquated both in his documentary hypothesis and in his view of history. It is, of course, true that Wellhausen is antiquated—as most of us will be in three-quarters of a century—and no one to-day subscribes to all his views. It is improbable, however, that his literary criticism will be replaced by that of Cassuto. Indeed there are so many aspirants to the place of Wellhausen to-day that it is hard for any to secure a following comparable with his. (See also p. 38 below.) H.H.R.

(GOLDZIHER, I.) : *Ignace Goldziher Memorial Volume.* Part I. Edited by S. Löwinger and J. Somogyi. 1948. Pp. viii+434+44. (Budapest.)

The greater part of the contents of this volume do not fall to be considered here but several of the articles are of interest to Old Testament scholars.

1. E. F. F. Bishop on " Eulogētos "—a study of the use of the words for ' blessed ' as applied to God in the O.T., and N.T. and the Koran. He concludes : " Eulogētos with its cognate words in the Semitic dialects would seem to have had a very wide vogue, used mostly with one or other of the divine names, sometimes as a euphemism for them ; and used in circumstances which betray either a relationship to God as Creator, or in a somewhat nationalistic or warlike context, or when deep personal experience was uppermost in the life of the individual concerned."

2. H. H. Rowley on " The Chronological Order of Ezra and Nehemiah," easily the most important article among those here referred to. A characteristically thorough review of the whole question leading to the judicious conclusion that, while the evidence available does not make absolute demonstration possible, the dating of Ezra's mission in 397 B.C. (i.e. the seventh year of Artaxerxes II), advocated by van Hoonacker, presents the fewest difficulties.

3. Joseph Aistleitner on "The Consonants of Ugaritic." The conclusion is that Ugaritic preserves the distinctions of consonants in Proto-Semitic and stands closest to what is found in North Arabic and South Semitic.

4. Samuel Löwinger on " Nebuchadnezzar's Dream in the Book of Daniel." The suggestion is made that the origin of the dream was Nebuchadnezzar's anxiety over the succession to himself which arose from the reflection that Esarhaddon's act in dividing the Assyrian crown between Assurbanipal and Shamash-Shumukin had weakened the Assyrian Empire. Daniel, speaking for the Jewish exiles, warns Nebuchadnezzar against the danger that would result for his dynasty if he made a similar mistake and divided the Babylonian crown between Evil-Merodach and Nergal-Sharezer.   N.W.P.

brew Union College Annual XXI. 1948. Pp. 602. (Cincinnati. Price : $3.00.)

Morgenstern continues his treatise on Chanukkah, discussing Biblical calendars : pentacontad c., c. in Israel until 899, c. from 899 to 841, c. in Israel and Judah from 841 to 714, Deuteronomic c., summary, c. of Holiness Code, c. of Priestly Code. Blank demonstrates that the pattern of the Jeremianic confessions is prayer and answer, the former being intended, by means of narrative, as a plea for justice and an expression of confidence, to evoke God's favour. The pattern goes back to defence in a law court. If it is connected with a customary cult procedure (Eissfeldt), then the latter itself is juridical in form. The author reaches valuable conclusions as to the meaning of prayer in Jeremiah. Cohon outlines the history of ' original sin.' The Paradise story, paralleled by other myths of man versus a jealous god, is designed to explain labour, pain, etc. (The Greek parallel is perhaps closer than he thinks : Pandora, ' she who gives all,' Eva, ' the mother of all living '; see *Guardian* 1945, p. 262.) The notion of hereditary corruption is absent, sin is voluntary ; and the O.T. never uses this story for its theodicy, nor the N.T. except Paul. It is different in the Secrets of Enoch, and for Paul transmitted sinfulness is essential. In Rabbinism the whole subject is less central. Various views are found—among them the Pauline—but that of sin as each man's action still prevails ; hence the emphasis on repentance. The author surveys the doctrines of Augustine, Pelagius, Thomas, etc. Feigin suggests that in Mekhilta on Ex. xxiii, 14, instead of ' this excludes the strangers, *haggerim*,' we ought to read ' the castrated one, *haggarim* '; *garim* being a *qatil* form, and the meaning to be gathered from other

Semitic languages (he seems to have overlooked Jastrow's translation of Biblical *garam* by ' to strip ') as well as Gen. xlix, 14 (on which see his article in J.N.E.S., 1946, pp. 230 ff.). But may the Midrash not have arrived at the exclusion of strangers by pressing the suffix in *zekhurekha*, ' thy males '? Much in the other contributions is of interest for O.T. scholars. Werner argues that the ratio of the octave interval was known to be 1 : 2 at least 900 years before Pythagoras, in Hittite Mesopotamia. The principle of the octoechos originated in cosmological and calendric speculations. The inscriptions of Ps. vi and xii and the arrangement of cxix may presuppose an eightfold modality. But Jewish musicians, in contrast to Syrian, Byzantine and Roman ones, did not impose this system on their traditional tunes. Liebreich's analysis of *Ubha' leṣiyyon* throws light on the canon in post-Biblical Judaism. For example, several lectionaries open with a verse from Chr., to be followed by verses from Ps. in the Masorah, Chr. forms the beginning of the Hagiographa, and it stresses the Davidic origin of the Temple service. Judah Rosenthal (in Hebrew) introduces and reprints a Cairo Geniza fragment, first published by Schechter, of a poem of 11th cent. Palestine, which, directed against the Karaites, lists Bible difficulties that cannot be solved apart from the oral tradition. He investigates the Talmudic origin of the various points. Schoeps (in German) thinks that some Talmudic legends may refer to Simon Magus. But it is unlikely that *ḥisda'* in Eccl. Rabba on i, 8 stands for *teleia agapē*. Why not simply assume a pun on the two meanings of the word (cp. Siphra on Lev. xx, 17) ? This volume contains an Index to H.U.C.A. I-XX. D.D.

Hebrew Union College Annual XXII. 1949. Pp. 490. (Cincinnati. Price : $3.00.)

Gordis shews that apparent contradictions in Ecclesiastes and Job are to be explained, not by excision and re-arrangement, but by assuming a technique of quotation without quotation marks or other express sign. He adduces Oriental and Rabbinic parallels, and distinguishes various types of quotation, e.g, direct quotation of thoughts of the subject (Gen. xxvi, 7 : *thinking*, lest the men should kill me) or oblique repetition of another's opinion (Job xii, 7 f. : *yet you admonished me*, ask now the beasts). Morgenstern holds that Is. lv, 1-5 dates from the last quarter of 520, the same time as Hag. ii, 10-23. and that like 2 Sam. vii and Ps. lxxii, it refers to Zerubbabel; while Is. lx, 1-3, 5-7 dates from the New Year (autumnal equinox) 516, when the Second Temple was dedicated, and refers to the ceremony of the opening of the eastern gate. He reconstructs in detail the intervening period, Zerubbabel's failure, the religious, anti-nationalistic reaction, the emergence of a conversionist movement. In an excursus he says that the description in John vii, 37, of the last day of Tabernacles as ' the great day ' is a reminiscence, preserved by Galilean sectarians, of the old pentecontad calendar with this day as New Year's Day. Landsberger thinks that ' house of the people ' in Jer. xxxix, 8, denotes the Temple, as suggested by Abravanel. He compares Mandaean usage. The post-exilic expression stresses the entire nation's share in the cult. Later it came to mean ' synagogue.' If this is right, the derivation of the synagogue from the town hall must be abandoned ; it was religious from the outset. Daube argues that the Rabbinic methods of interpretation, including Hillel's seven Middoth, derive from Hellenistic rhetoric. Loewe investigates Jerome's rendering of *'olam*, with instructive results.   D.D.

(HROZNÝ, F.) : *Symbolae ad Studia Orientalia pertinentes Frederico Hrozný dedicatae.* Pars prima, pars secunda. (Archiv Orientální, vol. xvii.) 1949. Pp. 424, 452. (Prague.)

These two volumes, dedicated to the eminent Orientalist Professor Hrozný contain 77 articles, a bibliography of Professor Hrozný's published works filling 20 closely printed pages and his photograph. Many, if not most, of the articles are of great interest, and it is possible here only to give the titles of those likely to be of interest to members of the Society. These are ' Bet'el, le sanctuaire du roi,' by Bič, ' Methods of Bible Criticism,' by Daube, ' Ugaritic and Hebrew Problems,' by Driver, ' Der Stadtname Ninĕwe ' by Jelito, ' Die Megalith-Kultur in Palästina ' by Jirku, ' Der Ursprung des Namens der Ammoniter ' by Stamm, 'Le nom divin El ' by Starcky. Not all these articles are of equal merit or equally convincing, but all are worth reading. There are also not a few contributions on subjects more or less directly bearing on the Old Testament which will repay study.   G.R.D.

LÖWINGER, S., and SCHEIBER, A. (ed. by) : *Genizah Publications, in memory of Prof. Dr. David Kaufman.* Vol. 1. 1949. Pp. xvi+106. (Budapest.)

This volume comprises two sections, the one—the greater—being written in Hebrew and the other in English. The Hebrew section contains the following articles : A Kaliric Piyyut mentioned by Kirkisani—by A. Scheiber ; Notes on Kalir's Piyyutim (an addendum to the above)—by M. Zulay (Jerusalem) ; New Fragments from *Sepher Methibhoth* (drawn from the Kaufman Collection)—by S. Löwinger ; An addendum to Löwinger's article—by S. Liebermann ; A Fragment from the Arabic Translation of the '*Azharah* (a piyyutic composition on the 613 Commandments) : '*Attah Hinhaltah Torah le-'Ammechah*—by I. Hahn ; Fragments from the *Mishneh Torah* by Maimonides (drawn from the Kaufman Collection)—by A. N. Z. Roth ; Piyyut-Compositions for the Week Days (from the Kaufman Collection)—by S. Widder ; A Catologue of the Genizah piyyut-compositions in the Kaufman Collection by M. Zulay. The English section contains, in the words of the compilers (S. Löwinger, A. Scheiber, S. Hahn), a ' Report on the Hebrew MSS. in Hungary with special regard to the

Fragments of the Cairo Genizah.' This report was read to the 21st International Congress of Orientalists, Paris, 1948. The collection contains many valuable fragments in various fields of *Judaica*. For the O.T. scholar, however, the following data may be of special interest. There are in this collection : Several unpublished fragments with Babylonian superlinear vocalization ; A fragment of Nehemiah with Tiberian vocalization which embodies some variant readings ; Fragments of the Bible in ' Shorthand Writing '; A number of fragments from the Targum Onkelos and the Palestinian Targum among which is found a ' superdotted ' Targum fragment and a Hebrew-Aramaic-Arabic Biblical fragment ; A good number of Arabic commentaries, including one by Sa'adiah, on the Bible, and an interesting scroll of parchment of Byzantine origin containing a commentary on Ezekiel and Hosea with well over 40 Greek glosses. A few fragments of Abul-Walid and some unidentified lexicographic material in the collection are also worthy of note.　　　　　　　　　　　　　　　M.W.

ROBERT, A. (ed. by) : *Dictionnaire de la Bible, Supplément*, Fasc. XXIII : *Judaïsme-Justice et Justification*. 1949. Columns 1249-1510. (Letouzey & Ané, Paris. Price : 7s. 9d.)

The fascicles of the *Supplément* to the great *Dictionnaire de la Bible* continue to appear at approximately yearly intervals. The first two volumes (eleven fascicles, A—Exode) were published between 1928 and 1934, and the third volume (Expiation—Herméneutique) was ready by 1938. The war, not unnaturally, slowed down the rate of appearance, and a gap of four years separated fasc. XIX from XX. At the present rate of progress it will be many years before we may hope to see the final article on *Zuzim* or *Zwingli* or perhaps even *Zythum* (this last on the same principle as that which induced the compilers of the original *Dictionnaire* to include an article under the heading *Oie !*) Fortunately, quality has been some compensation for slowness in publishing, and the present fascicle completes Bonsirven's admirable article on *Judaïsme palestinien au temps de Jésus-Christ*, the bibliography to which includes a number of recent works, in addition to those listed in the author's larger work under the same title, published in 1934. One may also call attention to two competent articles entitled *Jugement* by R. Pautrel (for the Old Testament) and D. Mollat (for the New). H. Cazelles writes with his accustomed knowledge and acumen on the book of Judges, and *Justice et Justification* are considered by A. Descamps and L. Cerfaux. At one time a familiar criticism of this work was that it included some articles that amounted to fair-sized treatises (as, for example, Bonnetain on *Grace*, with 618 columns and Médebielle on *Expiation* with 262.) This tendency, in so far as it existed, has been corrected, and Descamps and Cerfaux between them need rather less than a hundred columns for their important and intricate subject-matter.

　　　　　　　　　　　　　　　J.M.T.B.

ROBERT, A., and TRICOT, A. (ed. by) : *Initiation Biblique : Intro-duction à l'étude des Saintes Écritures*, 2nd ed., revised and enlarged. 1948. Pp. xxiv+992, with Tables and 8 maps. (Desclée & Cie., Paris, Tournai and Rome. Price : £1 11s. 0d.)

This useful manual was first published in 1939 (see Book List for 1939, p. 12). The new edition is more than 150 pages larger than the old, and the additions include a new section on the Apocrypha (in the Catholic connotation of that term) of the Old and New Testaments ; a section on the Books of the Old Testament more than double the length of the old one ; a re-written section on the Latin Versions ; a new chapter on Catholic Exegesis to replace the one written by the late L. Pirot ; a section on The Temple from the pen of H. Vincent, added to the chapter on Archaeology ; an enlarged chapter on post-exilic history by J. Bonsirven ; and some expansions of the New Testament sections. All of these add appreciably to the value of this already valuable work, which covers the Inspiration, Literature, Textual Criticism, Inter-pretation, Archaeology, Geography, History, Cultural and Religious Background, and Theology of the Bible, as well as post-Biblical Judaism and Islam. Some gaps which were noted in the first edition still remain—e.g. Customs, Ethics—but the range of its contents is commendably wide. The authors are writers of distinction, well-known for their scholar-ship, and they present a brief but fair summary of other points of view as well as their own. The volume is well indexed and there is valuable bibliographical material at the end of each chapter. H.H.R.

ROWLEY, H. H. (ed. by) : *Studies in Old Testament Prophecy. Pre-sented to Professor Theodore H. Robinson, Litt.D., D.D., D.Th., by The Society for Old Testament Study.* 1950. Pp. xii+206. (T. & T. Clark, Edinburgh. Price : 16s. 0d.)

After considerable delay, 1946-1950, the S.O.T.S. welcomes the arrival of the handsome presentation volume to Professor T. H. Robinson, and seldom has great expectation been more worthily and pleasantly satisfied. The volume leaves nothing to be desired.

The writers were given a wide scope—" anything within the field of prophecy "—and consequently the volume contains a variety of extremely important individual essays. But present throughout, indeed, underlying each contribution, is the realisation that Professor Robinson is honoured in person and in work. Possibly it is this which gives an impression of unity to the volume, with the result that we have more than a mere assemblage of essays, and that, to quote the editor, " a greater measure of unity is given to this volume than is often found in similar volumes of essays."

The contributors are among the world-renowned of O.T. scholars, and each article shows the author at his best. Professor Albright makes abundant use of his encyclopaedic knowledge for a discussion of the Psalm of Habakkuk, the late Professor Lods' article gives a hitherto unedited Mari tablet relating to Semitic prophecy, and Professor Driver deals with " Difficult words " with fascinating clarity. For reasons of space I cannot do more than merely list the other contributors : the late Professor S. A. Cook, Profs. Henton Davies, O. Eissfeldt, A. R. Johnson, C. R. North, J. Pedersen, N. W. Porteous, H. H. Rowley, R. B. Y. Scott, N. H. Snaith. A bibliography of the writings of Professor Robinson, covering forty years of notable contributions, is supplied by Prof. Henton Davies. The editor is Prof. H. H. Rowley, who also writes the Introduction. The publishers are to be thanked for a most presentable production. Naturally, all who are interested in the scholarship of Old Testament Prophecy will procure a copy of this most important book.   B.J.R.

Semitica (Cahiers publiés par l'Institut d'Études Sémitiques de l'Université de Paris), II. 1949. Pp. 74. (Maisonneuve, Paris.)

The present fascicule contains two articles of direct interest to students of the Old Testament, namely those of Professor Dupont-Sommer on the Aramaic ostracon of the Sabbath (one of the collection of some 280 inscribed potsherds from Elephantine collected by the late Professor Clermont-Ganneau and now being edited by Professor Dupont-Sommer) and of Mr. J. Schirmann on the new Hebrew scrolls (in which he translates one of the extracts from the ' Praises of the Lord ' published by Professor Sukenik) ; others of interest to the same students are Mlle. Herdner's on the Ugaritic myth of the marriage of Yarih and Nikkal and of Professor Février on Ba'al Addîr. All, including those that I have not mentioned by name, are of a high standard and will well repay study.
G.R.D.

SPADAFORA, F. : *Ezechiele* (La Sacra Bibbia, ed. by S. Garofalo, XIV/3). 1948. Pp. 358+3 plates. (Marietti, Turin. Price : 850 lire.)

PERRELLA, G. M. : *Introduzione Generale alla Sacra Bibbia* (same series). 1948. Pp. xx+33*+345+20 pp. of plates. (Marietti, Turin. Price : 950 lire.)

These are two later volumes in the series of Italian commentaries that made a beginning with Rinaldi's *Daniele*. Each in its own way seems to be successful and to give good promise for future additions to the commentaries. Spadafora's *Ezechiele* in addition to the Vulgate text and an Italian version, provides a compressed but useful introduction, a division of each page devoted to textual criticism, and a commentary that appears, like the book as a whole, to be based upon the best modern work. Up to the present, as the author alleges, the only modern commentary by a Catholic writer is P. Heinisch, *Das Buch Ezechiel* in the Bonner Bibel, published in 1923, a volume that is not one of the stronger numbers in a generally excellent series. Spadafora's favourites among his predecessors are J. Herrmann in K.A.T. and G. A. Cooke in I.C.C. Perrella died on 18th January, 1946, at the age of 55. His articles in the review *Divus Thomas*, published at Piacenza, were widely read and appreciated. The present posthumous work is perhaps the most remarkable of its kind by a Catholic author that has appeared during the past twenty years. It covers the ordinary introductory treatises (Inspiration ; Canon of Scripture ; Texts and Versions ; and Hermeneutics) in a masterly fashion and the author's knowledge of the literature is almost incredibly detailed. It may well be that this is not an ideal text-book for students making their first acquaintance with the treatises, but it is the sort of book that teachers of experience will be the first to appreciate. J. Vosté, who himself died on 24th February, 1949, contributes a short estimate of the loss that Italian Bible studies have sustained by reason of Perrella's death.   J.M.T.B.

EDUCATIONAL

Evans, C. F. : *The Bible.* (Christian Discussion Groups.) 1948. Pp. viii+62. (S.P.C.K., London. Price : 1s. 3d.)

In this slender volume the author tries to show how the Bible as a whole should be read, if its parts are to be brought together as a unity, and its message to be understood as the revelation of the will of God for man. The question is asked : Does the Bible itself provide a starting point for relating the parts to the whole ? This starting point the author finds in the preaching of the Apostles, from which lines radiate outwards into the N.T. and the O.T. The main principles of the faith and life of Israel are outlined briefly but clearly, the Gospel in the Gospels is shown to be rooted in the O.T., because " the O.T. is a forward looking book and the Gospel only makes sense to those who have an O.T. view of life." Chapters 8-10 deal with Life in the Kingdom, the Kingdom and the Church, the Word of God, Inspiration and Revelation. This is a very valuable little book ; in the hands of a competent teacher it will be useful for Sixth Forms, for Bible Classes, and Youth Fellowships.
                                                                    B.K.R.

Latham, L. C. : *Poets, Wise Men and Seers.* (The Bible and the Christian Faith. Vol. 4. Text book—pp. 226 ; Reference book for teachers—pp. 174. (Ginn, London. Price : 5s. 0d. each.)

Each book of this series consists of two parts : a text book for pupils and a reference book for teachers.   The first ten chapters present individual Psalms and groups of Psalms, which embody different aspects of human experience in man's search for God ;   also included in this section are simple accounts of early Hebrew music and poetic forms, as well as of the steps by which the Psalter assumed its present form. The last chapters deal with the Wisdom literature and with Apocalyptic writings belonging to the closing centuries before Christ. The reference book contains explanatory notes on the Bible passages chosen for study and prefaced to each chapter of the text book, teaching hints, subjects for essays, and lists of books which teachers will find helpful in preparing their lessons. The historical background has been kept in view throughout, but the chief aim has been to awaken interest in the Bible as a whole, and to draw upon both the Old and the New Testaments as containing the revelation of God to men, given " little by little and in different ways." B.K.R.

*REDLICH, E. B. : *The Early Traditions of Genesis.* (The Colet Library of Modern Christian Thought and Teaching, ed. W. R. Matthews, No. 4). 1950. Pp. 128. (Duckworth, London. Price : 6s. 0d.)

> Canon Redlich has written an excellent popular ' introduction ' of the first eleven chapters of Genesis. The orthodox documentary theory (J, E, P) is carefully explained, with J and P printed in parallel columns wherever these sources have been combined. There are drawings to illustrate Hebrew cosmology, and everything is done most carefully to interest and instruct the uninitiated. The volume is useful for schools and the general reader. N.H.S.

*SNAITH, N. H. : *The Jews from Cyrus to Herod.* 1949. Pp. 206. (Gateway Handbooks of Religious Knowledge, Religious Education Press, Wallington. Price : 6s. 0d.)

> The book falls into two sections : the first provides the historical background for the second, in which the development within Judaism from 538 B.C. to A.D. 70 is discussed. In spite of the bewildering complexity of forces, political and religious, which distinguish this period of Jewish history, this narrative is clear, concise and readable. A good time chart and a rather unusual map of the World Empires of the Ancient East are provided. In the second and more important portion of the book (pp. 63-205) the growth of Judaism is considered under such headings as Separatism, the Glorious Future, the Messiah, Life after Death, the Law, Temple and Synagogue. These themes are illustrated from apocryphal and apocalyptic writings, and it is shown that the loyal Jew by steadfast resistance to alien influences preserved the unique treasure of this faith, and so made possible the fulfilment of the hopes of prophets and psalmists. The book will be welcomed by lecturers in training colleges and by teachers whose pupils take advanced courses. B.K.R.

ARCHAEOLOGY AND EPIGRAPHY

ALBRIGHT, W. F. : *The Archaeology of Palestine.* 1949. Pp. 256. (Penguin Books, Harmondsworth. Price : 2s. 6d.)

> This is a valuable accession to the already considerable literature on Palestinian archaeology. The writer gives a lucid description of the science of archaeology as developed to date in Palestine and presents its results in an account of the development of civilization from the Stone Age to the Christian Era. As a scientific archaeologist he sets his subject in a larger field than the Biblical one though he never fails to relate relevant matter to the Sacred Record and devotes two chapters to the Bible and archaeology. A feature of the work is the discussion of certain major problems in detail which is surprising considering the magnitude of the subject and the limited size of the book. We are fortunate in having such a succinct statement by one who is at once an eminent field-archaeologist and a specialist in Biblical and other documentary data. J.G.

CONTENAU, G. : *La Civilisation des Hittites et des Hurrites du Mitanni.*
1948. Pp. 202. (Payot, Paris. Price : 10s. 6d.)

> This is a study of the history and cultural relationship and
> development of the autochthonous Asianic elements in
> Anatolia, North Syria and Upper Mesopotamia and the Indo-
> European invaders who emerge as the Hittites and the
> rulers of the kingdom of Mitanni. Material evidence from
> Anatolia before the invasion is analysed and related to Sumerian
> art and the study closes with a similar relation of Hittite art
> to Aegean culture, a theme which deserves much fuller
> treatment. An appraisal of Hittite and kindred influence in
> Syria and Palestine is also desired. The work is avowedly
> not an exhaustive study but is a highly competent résumé
> of the subject where the essentials are brought sharply into
> focus. A revision of the writer's book of 1934 it has the merit
> of adducing material and documentary evidence from recent
> excavations in the area studied and a special feature is the
> citation of judiciously-chosen documents.   J.G.

CONTENAU, G. : *La Civilisation Phénicienne.* 1949. Pp. 316. (Payot,
Paris. Price : Fr. 870)

> This is a revision of the author's work on Phoenician civilization
> in 1926 (2nd ed. 1928), demanded by the archaeological
> discoveries at Byblos and Ras Shamra, and is a useful con-
> spectus of Phoenician history and culture in its religious,
> artistic and literary aspects, particularly in the first millennium
> B.C. The various funerary inscriptions are cited and the
> origins of the alphabetic script discussed without positive
> conclusion. A tedious description of first millennium tombs
> might have been limited, and the very summary note on coins
> and pottery types is disappointing, while in any account of
> Phoenician civilization the literary material from Ras Shamra
> should be much more extensively used. In this particular the
> author's bibliography—by no means complete, though full—
> is more useful than his text and on this and other aspects of
> his subject is one of the major features of the book.   J.G.

DAVID, M. : *Een Nieuw-Ontdekte Babylonische Wet uit de Tijd voor
Hammurabi.* (Stichting voor Niet-Westers Recht, No. 3.) 1949.
Pp. 28. (Brill, Leiden. Price : Fl. 2.50.)

> A summary of the law-code implied in two tablets in Akkadian
> found by the Iraqi Department of Antiquities at Tell Abu
> Harmal in 1945 and dated to the 20th century B.C. The con-
> tents of the more legible of these copies are analysed in broad
> outline and compared in principle and particulars with parallel
> cases in the Code of Hammurabi, the Middle-Assyrian Code
> and the Pentateuchal system. The correspondence with the
> Hammurabi Code is close but in the notable instance of the
> *lex talionis* the older code admits a modification which con-
> firms the writer's appreciation of the new code—that of
> Eshnunna—as the medium of a critical estimate of the Code
> of Hammurabi.   J.G.

DUSSAUD, R. : *L'Art Phénicien du IIe Millénaire*. 1949. Pp. 112.
(Geuthner, Paris. Price : £1 7s. 0d.)

Yet another contribution to the growing literature on Phoenicia
by M. Dussaud and still fresh and vital. The thesis is the
originality of Phoenician art especially with relation to that of
the Aegean. M. Dussaud uses the material, especially in metal
and ivory, from Byblos and Ras Shamra to demonstrate how
Phoenician craftsmen developed Mesopotamian and Egyptian
themes infusing them with a peculiar native vitality. In his
discussion of the ivories he extends his survey to Palestine
(Megiddo and Tell Duweir), and demonstrates that they are
earlier than those of Nimrud and Khorsabad and that Phoenician art is independent of Assyrian influence. The study is
prefaced by a concise historical survey, and throughout there
are many historical references with characteristic independence
of attitude to critical problems such as that of the Hyksos
and the relationship of Hurrian, Hittite and Assyrian art.
Here one will find much to contest but the whole is a most
stimulating work from a master in the field.   J.G.

GOOSSENS, G. : *Les Substituts Royaux en Babylonie* (Analecta Lovaniensia Biblica et Orientalia, Ser. II, fasc. 13). 1949. Pp. 20. (Nauwelaerts, Louvain ; Duculot, Gembloux ; Desclée de Brouwer,
Bruges-Paris. Price : Fr. 20.)

This is a critical examination of the thesis of Frazer that the
Babylonian rites of the Sacea cited by Berosus were part of
an annual festival involving the interim reign and sacrifice
of the substitute king. A summary review of the development
of the theme by Zimmern, Ebeling, Labat and Frankfort is
given. The writer proceeds to examine the Greek evidence and
finds no single text which proves so much as Frazer claimed.
He goes on to cite Assyrian evidence from the 7th century
referring to Babylonia where the substitution was known in
the 19th century and probably earlier but only in times of
crisis and not seasonally. The human sacrifices of the royal
tombs of Ur are discussed as possible instances but this is
admitted to be no more than a hypothesis. This is an excellent
study by a master of critical method. Its value far exceeds its
volume.   J.G.

GORDON, C. H. : *Ugaritic Literature. A Comprehensive Translation
of the Poetic and Prose Texts*. 1949. Pp. 148. (Pontificio Istituto
Biblico, Rome. Price : $2.00.)

Dr. Gordon completes his work on the Ugaritic language with
this translation of the whole body of published texts, which
will be welcomed by all who have studied them. The author
would be the first to acknowledge that his rendering of many
passages cannot be final ; that would be too much to expect
in any attempt to interpret these extremely difficult texts.
Indeed, the translation occasionally has to leave blank spaces
or simply to transliterate words, even though some of these
are surely susceptible of translation (for example, *msl mt*

' path of death ' and *šḥl mmt* ' plain of death '), and at times
he leaves renderings which make no sense and therefore cannot
be right. Yet these failures of interpretation are commendably
few and for the most part an intelligible version is presented.
The general reader will thus obtain a very fair notion of the
sense of these tablets, while the specialist will find much that
throws new light on difficult or obscure passages ; both have
good reason to be grateful to Dr. Gordon for a useful and
valuable contribution to Ugaritic studies.   G.R.D.

GRDSELOFF, B. : *Une Stèle Scythopolitaine du Roi Séthos Ier*. (Études
Égyptiennes, 2nd fasc.) 1949. Pp. 34. (Le Scribe Égyptien, Cairo.)

A valuable study of the more indistinct stele of Seti I from
Bethshan. The writer describes how he treated and deciphered
the inscription in the Museum of Jerusalem and gives his
reading and translation. The 'Apir-w of the inscription are
located by the writer at Yarmouth which he locates after
Albright at Kawkab el Hawa, North of Bethshan. He does
not definitely commit himself to the view that 'Apir-w=
Hebrews but inclines in that direction. On this subject he
relates the evidence from Bethshan to that of the stele of
Amenhotep II from Memphis, where 'Apir-w captives from
Palestine are mentioned. With the latter he would associate
Jacob, thus authenticating the tradition of Exodus xii, 40,
LXX and Josephus, Ant. II, 15, 2) that the patriarchal period
to the Exodus (dated 1223) occupied 430 years. Here a study
of the tribal genealogies of Scripture might have shaken the
writer's confidence in the passage cited.   J.G.

GYLLENBERG, R. : *Sinuhe och Abraham : Patriarkernas värld i
arkeologisk belysning*. (Lutherska Litteraturstiftelsens Svenska
Publikationer, Nr. 3). 1948. Pp. 48. (Förbundets för Svenskt
Församlingsarbete i Finland r. f. Bokförlag, Helsingfors.)

In this booklet Professor Gyllenberg of Åbo gives a popular
account of some of the most important recent archaeological
discoveries connected with the age of the patriarchs as the
background to an interesting comparison and contrast between
the stories of Sinuhe and Abraham. The presentation is fresh
and interesting, and admirably adapted to the needs of the
general reader, for whom the book is intended.   G.W.A.

JOUGUET, P., VANDIER, J., CONTENAU, G., DHORME, E., AYMARD, A.,
CHAPOUTHIER, F., and GROUSSET, R. : *Les premières civilisations*.
(Peuples et Civilisations, ed. by L. Halphen and P. Sagnac.)
1950. Pp. xii+706+4 maps. (Presses Universitaires de France,
Paris. Price : Fr. 1200.)

This volume replaces one issued in the same collection under
the same title in 1926, and is substantially rewritten by a
team of writers of whom four were not in the original team.
It is comparable in range with H. R. Hall's *Ancient History
of the Near East*, and it aims to give in broad sweep an account
of the history and culture of the ancient Near East from its
beginnings to the end of the sixth century B.C. For the sections

dealing with Egypt, Jouguet and Vandier were responsible ; for those dealing with Asia Minor, Mesopotamia, Syria and Palestine, Contenau and Dhorme were responsible ; for those dealing with Greece, Aymard and Chapouthier ; while Grousset contributed a chapter on Indo-European origins and migrations. The work is written by acknowledged masters, and is abreast of recent discovery and research, while its references to other literature will enable the student to find fuller information than can be given in this general survey. For its modest price it offers a most valuable handbook.   H.H.R.

LARGEMENT, R. : *La Naissance de l'Aurore, Poème mythologique de Ras Shamra-Ugarit.* Analecta Lovaniensia Biblica et Orientalia, Ser. II, Fasc. ii. 1949. Pp. 56. (Duculot, Gembloux & Nauwelaerts, Louvain. Price : Fr. 50.)

This translation and commentary on one of the most problematical texts (SS, Gordon 52) opens with a useful summary of the main interpretations with none of which the writer entirely agrees though he does not closely particularize his points of disagreement. He offers a plausible reconstruction of the final fragmentary passage but does not cite his evidence. The commentary contains much good philological matter and many suggestions which the writer's conservative tendencies have forbidden him to adopt in his translation where there are still many transliterations. The continuous part of the text in the second half of the tablet he takes to be the myth accompanying the rubrics and catchlines in the earlier half. The theme of the myth he regards as the birth and nurture of the gracious gods and their fertilization of the desert where they have built their *'d* (Sanctuary). The strength of this work is the use made of the internal evidence of the texts as a whole and a synthesis of the mythological content where the writer permits himself more speculation than in the translation.
J.G.

LETTINGA, J. P.: *Oegarit.* (Cultuurhistorische monografieën). 1948. Pp. 112. (Servire, The Hague. Price : Fl. 2.90.)

One of a series of monographs on the history of culture, this is a very succinct account of Phoenician culture illustrated by the discoveries of Ras Shamra. The excavation of the site is described season by season with a judicious citation of the most significant features and finds, and a reconstruction of the history of ancient Ugarit along the lines already familiar in Schaeffer's Ugaritica. On the texts a description of the various categories is given with a brief résumé of the contents of the longer texts. Here in general the author follows de Langhe and avoids all controversial issues, a note of which together with an appraisal of the work of American and other continental scholars would have made a good book better. With these reservations this is a most admirable introduction to Ugaritic studies.   J.G.

LLOYD, S. : *Foundations in the Dust : A Story of Mesopotamian Exploration.* 1947. Pp. xii+238. (Oxford University Press. Price : 15s. 0d.)

This work is the story of the exploration of Mesopotamia and a century of excavation in the land, suggested to the author in 1945, by the approaching centenary of Layard's pioneer work in Assyria. It is concerned with personalities and the progress of archaeological methods rather than with material remains except in the broadest sense. Interest throughout is sustained by biographical notes of field archaeologists and travellers, which vividly reflect contemporary conditions, and by the personal observations of the author, who served as Technical Adviser to the Iraqi Department of Antiquities.

J.G.

MURRAY, M. A. : *The Splendour that was Egypt : a general survey of Egyptian culture and civilisation.* 1949. Pp. xxiii+354. (Sidgwick and Jackson, London. Price : £1 10s. 0d.)

Miss Murray's book is uniform with J. C. Stobart's *The Glory that was Greece* and *The Grandeur that was Rome*. Like them it is well produced, profusely illustrated, and a most attractive volume to handle. Unfortunately, however, the prospective reader must beware of its external charm. There are chapters on History, Social Organisations, Religions, Art and Science, Language and Literature, and Sir Flinders Petrie, all of which vary in merit. In particular the chapters on History and Religion should be read with caution ; the system of chronology employed is one which has been rejected by most scholars. In other fields also the author has not always kept abreast of modern scholarship. This is not a book which can be recommended with confidence to the general reader, the class for whom it is intended.

T.W.T.

OBERMANN, J. : *New Discoveries at Karatepe: A Complete Text of the Phoenician Royal Inscription from Cilicia.* (Transactions of the Connecticut Academy of Arts and Sciences, Vol. 38). 1949. Pp. 50+one plate. (Yale University Press. Price : $1.25.)

When in 1948, the author published his edition of the statue inscription discovered at Karatepe (see " Book List 1949," p. 13), the " duplicate " inscription, which was found inscribed on a row of orthostats in the course of excavation, in the autumn of 1947, on the north east slope of the hill of Karatepe, was not available for study. It has since become available, and in this work the text of it is given in transcription, with translation and commentary. The great value of this " duplicate " inscription lies in its completeness. It thus makes possible the restoration of the fragmentary columns i and iv of the statue inscription, and in addition it yields further material for linguistic study. Some interesting suggestions are put forward by the author, for example, that the two inscriptions are not " duplicates " only, but parallel texts, each designed to serve a function of its own, and that the inscription appears to have been composed in quasi-poetical

style and rhythm. On the linguistic side, his theory—new
in this edition—that the Phoenician dialect of Karatepe,
if not Phoenician in general, had a causative participle of
the form *yqtl* is noteworthy. All students of this very important inscription will need to take account of this study of it.
They should not, however, fail to read, side by side with it,
Professor Honeyman's treatment of the inscription in P.E.Q.,
Jan.—Apr., 1949, pp. 21-38.   D.W.T.

PARROT, A. : *Ziggurats et Tour de Babel*. 1949. Pp. 230. (Éditions
Albin Michel, Paris.)

Mesopotamian literary and architectural remains, biblical and
post-biblical literature and commentaries, artistic representations, and modern Christian usage, have presented M. Parrot,
archaeologist and student of religions, with an abundance of
material for his purposes. After a brief introduction surveying
the evidence of travellers, he examines the (surprisingly
limited) Mesopotamian literary evidence. More than half
the book is concerned with the architectural aspect of the
ziggurat and the various judgements of authorities, to which
he adds his own. Old Testament students will note M. Parrot's
study of Gen. xi, 1-9. He sees here an account of a ziggurat,
the *étemenanki* attached to the temple of Marduk at Babylon.
His final chapter is headed ' Le Problème dogmatique de la
Ziggurat.' The Mesopotamian ziggurat is the prototype of
the Biblical Tower of Babel, itself not an archetype, because
late in date. M. Parrot has elsewhere treated of the Mesopotamian concern for life as for *le bien suprême*, and he makes
use of that idea to explain the building of ziggurats in Mesopotamia where life was, in the literal sense, precarious. Hence
the need for a divine patron. Men, says M. Parrot, have
always wished to adore on summits, to raise themselves above
the earth, and to have their life-giving patron in their midst.
The ziggurats, besides being an architectural manifestation
of such desires, were also ladders between gods and men
(cp. Jacob's ladder), put there precisely so that the god might
descend from on high. M. Parrot thinks the third millennium
Mesopotamians anticipated Is. lxiii, 19, and that " gate of
heaven " in Gen. xxviii, 17, helps us to understand the " gate
of God " in Gen. xi, 9. The volume is admirably and fully
illustrated by plates and sketches.   T.F.

PARROT, A. (ed. by) : *Studia Mariana*. (Documenta et Monumenta
Orientis Antiqui, iv.) 1950. Pp. 138+6 plates. (Brill, Leiden.
Price : £2 8s. 6d.)

This work contains eight studies of artistic, religious and
philological material by, amongst other experts, MM. Dossin,
Jean and Parrot. Especially useful are the articles on the
Mari pantheon by Dossin and the Mari proper names by Jean.
A Mari bibliography of 211 items is also included.   T.F.

PERKINS, A. L. : *The Comparative Archaeology of Early Mesopotamia*. (Oriental Institute of the University of Chicago, Studies in ancient Oriental Civilization, No. 25). 1949. Pp. 200+plans and diagrams. University of Chicago Press. Price : $8.00.)

This work, under the inspiration of Frankfort, covers the Late Neolithic and Chalcolithic Ages and is somewhat too severely limited to Mesopotamia. Five main periods are distinguished, the Hassunah and the Halaf Periods in Northern Mesopotamia before the settlement of the South, the Ubaid Period in its phases in the North and the South, the Jemdet Nasr or Warka Period in the South and the Ninevite or Gaura Period in the North. The various archaeological stations are noted in their order of significance and the material evidence from each analysed, the respective levels are then synchronised and in a final summary the extent and possible provenance of each culture is discussed. The relative independence and possible relationship of North and South in the later phases of those prehistoric cultures is discussed and in the main the author would emphasize the former condition. Her case is clearly stated and she shows independence of judgement. The book will be a valuable work of reference subject to modifications when more evidence is forthcoming from the neighbouring areas of Anatolia and Iran.　　　　J.G.

PORADA, E., and BUCHANAN, B. : *A Corpus of Near Eastern Seals in North American Collections, vol. I, The Pierpont Morgan Collection*. 1948. Pp. 188+plates clxxvi. (Pantheon Books Inc. for Bollingen Foundation Inc.)

The first of five volumes to be published under the same editorship, this volume deals with the greatest of North American collections of seals, that of the Pierpont Morgan Library, where all periods are represented from the 4th millennium to the 5th-4th century B.C. One volume consists of impressions beautifully and accurately reproduced in photograph and another is devoted to the description of over 1300 seals and their motifs with a brief historical introduction to the several periods and a note of the distinctive features of the seals of each period. This is an invaluable work of reference though one should desire notes on the provenance of the specimens where that is known.　　　　J.G.

ROWLEY, H. H. : *Recent Discovery and the Patriarchal Age*. 1949. Pp. 38. (Reprinted from the " Bulletin of the John Rylands Library," vol. 32, No. 1, September, 1949, Manchester University Press and The John Rylands Library, Manchester. Price : 2s. 0d.)

This is a concise review of the question of the historicity of the patriarchs and is characterized by a keen sense of essentials and acute criticism. The attitude is conservative and the main thesis is that while the evidence does not demonstrate the individual historicity of the patriarchs it does vindicate the historical verisimilitude of the Scriptural traditions. In this particular the most striking feature is the legal system recovered from Hurrian Nuzu which obviously conditioned

the lives of the Hebrew patriarchs. The writer's discussion
of this aspect of the subject is one of the most valuable features
of his work with which we may mention the discussion of the
date of Hammurabi and the identity of the Khabiru-'Apirw.
No less valuable than the text—and no shorter—are the
footnotes and voluminous bibliography.   J.G.

SAINTE FARE GARNOT, J. : *La Vie Religieuse dans l'Ancienne Égypte*.
1948. Pp. viii+146. (Presses Universitaires de France, Paris.
Price : 4s. 6d.)

In very brief compass the author .presents a useful and
trustworthy picture of the religious thought of ancient Egypt.
He aims to give the non-specialist reader a concise account
of modern work in the field and does not put forward original
views. He belongs to the school which seeks to interpret
Egyptian religion and not merely to describe external phenomena. Each chapter is furnished with an excellent bibliography.   T.W.T.

SCHAEFFER, C. F. A. : *Note sur la Chronologie de la Période de
Transition du Bronze Moyen au Bronze Récent* (1700-1500 *av. notre
Ère*). (Reprinted from Syria, xxv.) 1948. Pp. 14. (Geuthner,
Paris.)

A rejoinder to the charge of R. Weill that archaeologists in
Syria have ignored the close association of Hyksos and XIIth
Dynasty remains. To Weill who would reduce the Second
Intermediate Period of Egyptian History, between the XIIth
and XVIIIth Dynasties, to some 30 years Schaeffer replies
emphatically by citing evidence from the whole archaeological
field of the Near East to demonstrate a cultural hiatus between
c. 1700 and 1500 B.C. which Weill entirely ignores. The writer
thus emphasises one of his main theses in his *Stratigraphie
Comparée . . .* , regarding the invasions of the Hyksos in
Egypt and the Kassites in Mesopotamia as episodes of a
catastrophic disturbance of continental proportions, probably
a natural phenomenon. To its immediate purpose the work
is wholly adequate but one still awaits from the distinguished
excavator of Ras Shamra some analysis and synthesis of the
positive features associated with the Hyksos period along the
lines recently followed by H. Stock.   J.G.

SCHWEITZER, U. : *Löwe und Sphinx im Alten Ägypten* (Ägyptolo-
gische Forschungen, 15). 1948. Pp. 76+xvi pages of plates.
(J. J. Augustin, Glückstadt und Hamburg.)

This work is a study of the lion and the sphinx in Egyptian
art throughout the ages. The treatment is historical, falling
into sections corresponding with the major divisions of Egyptian
history. A mass of material is assembled and dealt with in a
scholarly fashion. This is a book which the Palestinian archaeologist will find useful for purposes of reference and comparison.
                                                    T.W.T.

STOCK, H. : *Studia Aegyptiaca II : Die Erste Zwischenzeit Ägyptens.* (Analecta Orientalia 31). 1949. Pp. xviii+110, pl. xiv+5 maps. (Pontificium Institutum Biblicum, Rome.)

This is a work of first-class importance for the study of the First Intermediate Period of Egyptian history. All the evidence, inscriptional and archaeological, for this obscure and difficult period is carefully considered, and a reconstruction of the history and chronology is offered. An analysis of the decline of the Old Kingdom and the rise of the nobles is followed by a detailed study of the 8th, 9th and 10th Dynasties, the core of the book. Next comes a chapter on the foundation of the Middle Kingdom by the nobles of Thebes. Last is a section devoted to chronology. Dr. Stock has produced a book which will be invaluable not only to Egyptologists but also to all students of the ancient Near East. It should be read in conjunction with Winlock's *The Rise and Fall of the Middle Kingdom in Thebes*, a work not available to the author at the time of writing. T.W.T.

VIROLLEAUD, C. : *Légendes de Babylone et de Canaan.* 1949. Pp. 124 with 22 illustrations in text and 2 maps. (Maisonneuve, Paris. Price : Fr. 220.)

This sketch of the legends of Babylon and Canaan is the first of a new collection of popular handbooks, entitled *L'Orient Ancien Illustré*. It is divided into two parts, the first devoted to Mesopotamian and the second to Ugaritic mythology. The work is brilliant but ill-balanced ; for example, half the first part is taken up with Gilgamesh and the rest of it is all that is left to the remaining myths with only half a page allotted to the Epic of Creation. Again, the account of the Ugaritic mythology is marred by the identification of the land invaded by Keret with the Negeb to the south of Palestine, although this theory has long been universally abandoned. The author, however, to whom the study of these poems owes so great a debt, makes a number of good points, and his brief summary gives a very fair picture of an obscure but interesting subject. G.R.D.

WEILL, R. : *La Cité de David.* 1947. Pp. 132+XLII Planches. (Geuthner, Paris. Price : £2 12s. 6d.)

This is a topographical study, thorough but almost wholly confined to the southern extremity of the Ophel Hill, the section of the author's excavations in 1923-24. A report of these operations is given (c. II), the remainder of the book being devoted to the pre-Israelite fortifications (c. III), the water systems (c. IV), the Roman walls (c. V) and the area of the royal tombs and installations in the vicinity. There is an appendix of useful plans and photographs. The discussion of the water systems is particularly valuable but a much fuller citation of archaeological evidence is desirable in the endeavour to date the various structures. J.G.

WISCHNITZER, RACHEL : *The Messianic Theme in the Paintings of the Dura Synagogue.* 1948. Pp. 135 with 31 pp. of photographic reproductions. (University of Chicago Press, Chicago. Price : $6.00.)

A well-produced and original study of these famous murals, characterized by careful scrutiny and much erudition. An introductory chapter describes the conditions under which Mesopotamian Jews lived during the 3rd century A.D. Mrs. Wischnitzer has provided a full bibliography (8 pages), including full note of previous solutions which have been proposed. The sequence of the registers, of which there are four including the dado, is from the bottom, and within each horizontal row, the scenes are arranged in counterparts converging on the axis of the triptych (above the shrine) and the shrine-niche. The whole thirty panels belong to one Messianic scheme of Return, Restoration and Salvation. The authoress follows Friedmann's suggestion that Messiah ben Joseph was of northern origin (Ephraimite remnant), and herself suggests that these Jews of Dura regarded themselves as descendants of the Ten Tribes. N.H.S.

WOOLLEY, SIR L. : *Middle East Archaeology.* 1949. Pp. 46. (Oxford University Press. Price : 2s. 6d.)

The James Bryce Memorial Lecture, this work is a vindication of the excavation of sites of secondary political significance which yield no spectacular evidence. The writer cites his work at Alalakh-Tell Atshana in North Syria which he chose as a potential source of light on the subject of cultural contacts between the Aegean and Asia. Results of his work are adduced only in so far as they demonstrate the influence of Hittite, Aegean, Mesopotamian and Egypt cultures, for a new appreciation of which in their inter-relation he especially pleads. He touches on the value of archaeology for Old Testament study only on the question of the Hittites in Palestine, a rather unhappy digression, reminiscent of his *Abraham, a Study of Hebrew Origins*. J.G.

HISTORY AND GEOGRAPHY

BELLINGER, A. R. : *The End of the Seleucids.* (Transactions of the Connecticut Academy of Arts and Sciences, Vol. 38.) 1949. Pp. 52 (Yale University Press. Price : $1.25.)

The section of history covered by the Seleucid rulers from the time of Demetrius I Soter (162-150 B.C.) to Philip II (67-66 B.C.) is a complicated and confused record. Up to the time of the death of Antiochus VII Sidetes in 129 B.C. the author of this article, as he tells us, summarizes what is contained in the works of E. R. Bevan (*The House of Seleucus*) and Bouché-Leclercq (*Histoire des Séleucides*), but from this date onwards until the end of the dynasty he concentrates with special care upon the conflicts and intrigues of those who gained or aspired to the power of government in Syria. This short period has also been dealt with in detail in the painstaking work of A. Kuhn (1891). Mr. Bellinger's purpose, however, is to add to this material new evidence, chiefly numismatic, which brings our knowledge of the later Seleucids up to date. The very full historical references here given, the numismatic data, and the excursuses on special points will be found valuable to those who wish to devote themselves to a more thorough study of events, in a period not wholly dull, in the history of Syria in the sixty years before this became, with the arrival of Pompey, a Roman province.   O.S.R.

CHURGIN, P. : *Studies in the Times of the Second Temple* (written in Hebrew). 1949. Pp. 382. (Horeb Foundation, New York. Price : $3.00.)

This work contains studies on the Exilic Spirit, which is held to have prevailed throughout the period, the consciousness of the existence of the Diaspora having been too strong to be suppressed by the Return ; on the Samaritan schism, which is traced particularly to the feeling that the rebuilding of the Temple was premature ; on the Hasmonean Rulers, who are held to have shared the apocalyptic hopes of the period, and whose assumption of the title of king was only for foreign political purposes ; on the Babylonian Diaspora, where the Exilic Spirit showed itself in the prevalence of stories associated with the destruction of the First Temple and the Return, stories which are held to have fallen into oblivion in Palestine with the rebuilding of the Temple and to have been revived only after its destruction ; and on the historiography of the period, where features common to the mentality of the Jews of the Diaspora as distinct from those of Palestinian Jews may be seen by the comparison of 2 Macc. and the works of Philo with the only extant Palestinian historical work, 1 Macc., the former being apologetic and marked by a sense of inferiority, while the latter exhibits a spirit of national pride. The works of Josephus are tendencious, with the exception of *Contra Apionem*, where the author's Palestinian character comes to the fore.   P.R.W.

DANIEL-ROPS : *Israel and the Ancient World : A History of the Israelites, from the Time of Abraham to the Birth of Christ.* 1949. Pp. 322. (Eyre and Spottiswoode, London. Price : 16s. 0d.)

The French original of this book was noticed in the Book List for 1947 (p. 12), where attention was called to its excellent style and eager sense of the value and importance of the Old Testament. For these qualities this English translation is to be welcomed. The English title is also an improvement on the French, since it more clearly indicates what the book contains, while the addition of an index is a further improvement. Though the author is acquainted with a good deal of scholarly work, this is not a contribution to scholarship, but a popularization of some of its fruits. Often, however, it offers an uncritical account that ignores scholarly work. Nor is it true to say that ' the Biblical Commission of the Catholic Church still maintains the attribution of the whole (*sc.* of the book of Isaiah) to the great Prophet ' (p. 193). The French edition bore the *imprimatur* of the Catholic authorities, but the English edition follows the Authorized Version in all quotations and in Proper Names. (See also p. 78 below.)   H.H.R.

DAVIS, W. H., and McDOWELL, E. A. : *A source book of Interbiblical History.* 1948. Pp. 626. (Broadman Press, Nashville. Price : $5.75.)

> The authors, both professors of New Testament Interpretation in the Southern Baptist Theological Seminary, Louisville, Kentucky, offer a very useful book to students of the Bible. Their task has been to gather the historical material which sheds a light on the history of events in the period between O.T. and N.T. The period covered is 400 B.C.—70 A.D. Considerably more than half of the book is taken up with the Roman Period from 47 B.C. The sources from which the illustrative passages are drawn are Josephus, I Maccabees, II Maccabees, Polybius and Livy. This work in its selection of material makes very interesting reading, has a fairly good index and will prove to be of valuable and ready assistance to the reader of secular history and to some extent to those whose interests lie in the field of the history of religion.
>
> O.S.R.

FLIGHT, J. W., and FAHS, SOPHIA L. : *The Drama of Ancient Israel.* 1949. Pp. xvi+202. (Beacon Press, Boston. Price : $2.75.)

> Like the earlier volume on Moses (see Book List, 1948, p. 17) this book is written primarily for children, but will be of use to general readers also. It contains twenty-one stories covering the period from the Amarna Age to Solomon, embodying Biblical and archaeological material, and well illustrated with modern pictures and reproductions of ancient remains. The stories are dramatically told, yet told by a scholar who is well acquainted with modern work as well as with the text of the Bible. It does not aim to offer any contribution to scholarship, but to have more books of this kind in the hands of children and young people would be an immense boon, and would contribute much to awaken interest in the story of the Bible.
>
> H.H.R.

GALLING, K. (with EDEL, E., and RAPP, E. L.) : *Textbuch zur Geschichte Israel.* 1950. Pp. vi+90+four maps. (Mohr, Tübingen. Price : DM. 8.40.)

> A collection of 57 texts analogous to Gressmann's *Altorientalische Texte zum A.T.*, though less full in texts then known and incorporating more recent texts, such as certain of the Lachish Letters and the Samaritan Ostraca, with synagogue and ossuary inscriptions and the Jehoiachin text from Babylon. The collection opens with the Tale of Sinuhe and closes with the synagogue inscription from Chorazin. Egyptian texts are the work of Edel and cuneiform documents of Rapp. These are translated with a rigid economy of pertinent notes and a bibliography of the most significant studies. Canaanite, Hebrew, Aramaic and Greek texts are cited by the editor without translation. The whole is a work for scholars and as such a useful work of reference, though it might have gained by the inclusion of more Phoenician matter and some of the Mari texts at the cost of some of the Greek citations from Josephus.
>
> J.G.

HÖLSCHER, G. *Drei Erdkarten. Ein Beitrag zur Erdkenntnis des hebräischen Altertums.* (Sitzungsberichte der Heidelberger Akademie der Wissenschaften, Philosophisch-historische Klasse. Jahrgang 1944/48. 3. Abhandlung.) 1949. Pp. 74. (Carl Winter, Universitätsverlag, Heidelberg.)

In this brochure the author first surveys the development in range and precision of the geographical knowledge of the Hebrews. He then examines in detail three passages (Genesis ii, 10-14 ; P's table of nations in Genesis x ; and Jubilee's viii-ix), and seeks to reconstruct the kind of map which is implied by each of them. A most fascinating work, and invaluable for the wealth of its references to ancient sources, both classical and oriental, and to modern discussions. G.W.A.

MAY, H. G., McCOWN, C. C. & KATES, J. S. : *A Remapping of the Bible World.* (Nelson's New Bible Maps.) 1949. 44 maps. (Nelson, New York. Price : $1.00.)

This collection of maps is the preliminary to a publication on a larger scale and contains 34 maps on the O.T. and 10 on the N.T., of which 30 are of Palestine at different phases of history and of the narrative. The maps are strictly confined to the illustration of the various sections of Scripture. Thus it is possible at a glance to see the actual horizon of the various authors and often to conjecture fairly the provenance and character of the documents. The sites have been located accurately in the light of recent archaeology and exploration though the scientific objectivity of the Westminster Bible Atlas makes it a much more valuable work. J.G.

OLMSTEAD, A. T. : *History of the Persian Empire (Achaemenid Period).* 1948. Pp. xx+576, with 70 plates. University of Chicago Press, and Cambridge University Press. Price : $10.00.)

This magnificently produced volume gives a good general picture of the Achaemenid period, though it has serious limitations for informed readers. Complex problems are apodictically settled (e.g., pseudo-Smerdis is swept aside as a fiction of Darius's ; the date of Zoroaster is settled in a sentence ; Ezra's mission is terminated in 457 B.C. without discussion) and the style has the flavour of journalism (e.g., the Murashu sons are referred to as ' loan sharks '). Nowhere is there an adequate documentation, and the reader is left without any indication where he will find the evidence for many questionable statements. Despite this, the work provides a lively account of the rise and fall of the Achaemenid empire and of its achievements. H.H.R.

TEXT AND VERSIONS

BEA, A. : *Die neue lateinische Psalmenübersetzung.* 1949. Pp. viii+ 172. (Herder, Freiburg im Breisgau.)

This is in substance a translation into the learned author's native language of the work originally composed in Italian, and perhaps best known to the world of scholarship in general through the medium of the French version, entitled *Le Nouveau*

Psautier Latin, which is, in effect, an improvement on the original. The author rightly leads us to expect still further improvements in the present German edition, and a comparison with the French text shows that a number of additional notes and references may be found here, not to mention in any detail the much increased list of articles and reviews dealing with the new version that have accumulated in the course of the past three years. More recently, it would seem, the chief criticism of the version has been on linguistic grounds. Possessors of the French periodical *La Maison-Dieu* (1946, Cahier 5, pp. 66 ff.) may verify the quotation, given diversely in the French and German editions of Bea, on p. 149, n. 1 and p. 115, n. 195 respectively. Was the Latin *foedus* said to be " connu de la Vulgate " (as in the French) or "inconnu de la Vulgate " (as in the German) ? Actually, as Bea remarks, it occurs more than 200 times ! It is regrettable that Hebrew type has to be banished from this edition, and that even the transcription of Semitic characters is, owing to the absence of the necessary founts of type, not as perfect as it might otherwise be.   J.M.T.B.

The Bible : New Translation in Basic English. 1949. Pp. 910. (Cambridge University Press. Price : 12s. 6d.)

The New Testament section of this able and accomplished work has been before the public for some years, and now, as a prefatory note informs us, the whole Bible (with the exception of the deuterocanonical books) comes to us with the guarantee of two committees, the first of them under the direction of Professor S. H. Hooke, the second formed by the Syndics of the University Press. Basic English, the invention of Mr. C. K. Ogden, has a vocabulary of no more than 850 words, but here is what has been styled Basic plus Supplementary, the latter including 50 special Bible words, and " 100 words listed as giving most help in the reading of English verse." Two points are excellently made by the editors : (1) that " there is no question of the Basic work taking the place of the Authorized Version " or, indeed, of any other version that employs an unrestricted vocabulary, and (2) that " Frequently, the narrow limits of the word-list make it hard to keep the Basic completely parallel with the Hebrew and the Greek." This second point indicates what must appear to the ordinary reader the chief weakness of the version, namely, its comparative poverty in the matter of specific terms and its frequent need to employ circumlocution. On the other hand, to the credit side of the enterprise, it must be freely admitted that the foreigner who is learning English for the first time will readily learn to read *and to pronounce* the 1,000 words, for the most part simple and uncomplicated, of the Basic vocabulary. For English-speaking people it will, as the publishers claim, " offer a valuable corrective to careless and ambiguous use of words, and a check on those devices of rhetoric which hide the plain sense of what is being said."   J.M.T.B.

*The Holy Bible, translated from the Original Languages with Critical
Use of all the Ancient Sources* by Members of the Catholic Biblical
Association of America. *The Book of Genesis.* 1948. Pp. vi+130.
(St. Anthony Guild Press, Paterson, N.J.)

> There is not a great deal to be said about this first number
> of the new translation of the Old Testament undertaken by
> American Catholic scholars. It may be recalled that the New
> Testament had already been completed by the early summer of
> 1941, and it is a little hard to explain the long delay in issuing
> this unpretentious edition of Genesis. It may be compared
> with the German *Echter Bibel* in that the emphasis throughout
> is on the translation, but both introduction and notes have
> here been reduced to a bare minimum. Five pages of textual
> notes at the end of the booklet indicate, very briefly, the
> authorities for and against the readings accepted in the text.
>
> J.M.T.B.

Bover, J. M., and Cantera, F. : *Sagrada Biblia : Versión crítica
sobre los textos hebreo y griego.* 2 vols. 1947. Pp. 8+xxviii+2394.
(Editorial Católica, Madrid.)

> The revival of Biblical studies in Spain has brought a new
> age of translations of the whole original text of the Bible into
> modern Spanish. Within three years two of these versions
> have appeared and the first one exhausted two editions of
> several thousands of copies. A third version will appear very
> soon and a fourth is being prepared.
>
> Professor Cantera, of the " Central University " of Madrid,
> has achieved conscientiously his difficult task of translation
> from the Hebrew. He has thoroughly studied the original
> text, selecting the different readings he has judged to be the
> most apt, and has done this in a capable manner and with
> some success. Moreover he has tried to follow it faithfully and
> intelligently, seeking at the same time an idiomatic Spanish
> style. The version is almost always clear and integral though
> not always fluent. It seems meant to appeal to the general
> public ; yet it has a learned character rather than a popular one.
> The translation of each book is preceded by a useful intro-
> duction, adorned with many archaeological illustrations and
> explained with some footnotes rarely of dogmatic tendency.
> The whole production is really a worthy one in fine paper
> and well bound in cloth.
>
> Particularly interesting is the version of the Book of the
> Ecclesiasticus, done now for the first time from the Hebrew
> fragments into Spanish, and also the Psalms : even if the former
> is too dependent on I. Levi's " L'Ecclésiastique " and the
> latter becomes sometimes a little odd because of the attempt
> to give it not very successful versification.
>
> Cantera's work is not perfect, of course ; but it is well done ;
> nevertheless there is often excessive attachment to the text,
> while at the same time there are some additions, some in-
> exactitudes and a lack of really deep explanatory short notes

(always necessary for readers of the 20th century so far away from the times of the O.T.). These do not detract very much from the warm reception this new translation has received.

A.G.U.

ENGLERT, D. M. C. : *The Peshitto of Second Samuel.* (Journal of Biblical Literature Monograph Series, Vol. 3.) 1949. Pp. vi+102. (Society of Biblical Literature, Philadelphia, Pa. Price : $1.00.)

Studies in the Peshitta are all too few and are therefore the more welcome. The Introduction reviews the published studies on the Syriac version of the various books of the Old Testament, and then the author turns to compare the text of the Codex Ambrosianus with the printed editions and to study the inner-Syriac corruptions. The relation of the Syriac text to the MT is then systematically studied and the results classified, and the relations with other ancient versions examined. No strikingly new conclusions are reached or expected on the nature and affinities of the version. The value of this work lies in its careful collection of evidence. The book was received too late to allow of any extensive checking of its contents, but where the reviewer has tested it, it proved reliable. It is reproduced in typescript, the Hebrew, Greek and Syriac reproducing manuscript insertions. H.H.R.

KATZ, P. : *Philo's Bible. The Aberrant Text of Bible Quotations in some Philonic Writings and its Place in the Textual History of the Greek Bible.* 1950. Pp. xii+162. (University Press, Cambridge. Price : £1 5s. 0d.) (The Kaye Prize Essay for 1947.)

In this detailed and masterly treatment, Dr. Katz elaborates his theory that the Biblical passages and quotations in the Philonic writings which do not conform to the Septuagint are generally taken from a Pentateuch Septuagint recension now lost, and have no real relationship to Philo, because they were later substitutions, particularly in the Lemmata. He urther shows that they have considerable affinity with the recension *R* which Rahlfs identified for the book of Ruth and, to an extent, for the Octateuch. The real quotations of Philo, however, on the whole coincide with the LXX. In this way, Dr. Katz is at cross purposes with Professor Kahle (cf. his Schweich Lectures, 1941, pp. 140-6), whom he blames for having rescued a 1907 thesis by A. Schroeder from a well-deserved oblivion. The Schroeder-Kahle theory, says Katz, fails to distinguish between what is really Philonic and what are secondary additions. It is impossible to deal here with any of the issues raised, but, inasmuch as a knowledge of the Septuagint textual history is vitally important to the O.T. scholar, the present volume demands most careful scrutiny. It is but fair to add, however, that this is not a book for the novice.

B.J.R.

KENYON, Sir Frederic : *Our Bible and the Ancient Manuscripts*. 1948. Pp. xii+266. (Eyre and Spottiswoode, London. Price : 15s. 0d.)

This edition is a reprint of the fourth edition, published in 1939, of a book which has proved its usefulness in its various editions for more than half a century. Its next edition will need to be revised to take account of the Dead Sea Scrolls, which were first known too late to be of use in this edition, even if it had not been a reprint only. There are a number of good illustrations, and the text of the book offers an excellent introduction to the tools used by the textual critic in the field of Old or New Testament.   H.H.R.

KNOX, R. A. : *The Old Testament, newly translated from the Latin Vulgate*. 1949. Vol. I. *Genesis—Esther*. Pp. xii+740. Vol. II. *Job—Machabees*. Pp. 864. (Burns, Oates and Washbourne, London. Price : £1 1s. 0d. each volume.)

This version has already been widely praised for the beauty and sonorousness of its English and not less widely criticized (at any rate by most of its reviewers who are specialists in the Semitic languages) for various failures to appreciate the exact sense of the originals. It is, as any reviewer must note, primarily a translation of the Vulgate Old Testament, but there are quantities of footnotes referring to the Hebrew and Aramaic texts, and the version must be judged in some part by the adequacy of such renderings as alternatives to the Vulgate in translation. Occasionally, too, there is carelessness, as in the footnote to Ecclus. i, 5 (p. 1,002), à propos of the Hebrew original " which has been preserved to us only in small part." On the whole, it may be said that this is a spirited and interesting performance, but that it will certainly not be used by scholars as a standard translation, or as a corrective to earlier renderings. Doubtless it will yield an intelligible sense in many *cruces interpretum*, but the sense will not necessarily be that supplied by the best modern scholarship, which is, like most translations of the Bible, the work of many hands.
                                        J.M.T.B.

ORLINSKY, H. M. : *The Septuagint. The Oldest Translation of the Bible*. 1949. Pp. 20. (Union of American Hebrew Congregations, Cincinnati.)

A simple and readable introduction to the LXX, touching on such topics as the Jews of pre-Christian Egypt, the Letter of Aristeas, the order and titles of the books, MSS. and editions of the version and its importance for the study of the MT. It is natural, though not always felicitous, that the material is presented in a way which subscribes only to the author's own views, and there are serious omissions—particularly surprising is the absence of even a brief discussion of Origen's Hexapla.   B.J.R.

PARET, O. : *Die Bibel : ihre Uberlieferung in Druck und Schrift.* 1949. Pp. viii+84 and 61 plates. (Privileg. Württembergischen Bibelanstatt, Stuttgart. Eng. Price : 15s. 6d.)

Dr. Paret is a classical archaeologist engaged at the Württemburg Museum at Stuttgart, but in this book he presents in outline the story of the Bible text transmission. The strength of the book is in the plates ranging from the Nash Papyrus, extracts from Greek Biblical Papyri, the Great Codices and the Hebrew Bible to facsimiles showing the history of the Latin and German Bibles. The text of the book covers a great number of topics, such as Luther's Bible, the Vulgate, the Greek Old and New Testaments, questions of canon, the Massoretic text and even a brief outline of literary and critical introduction. Reasons of space alone would prevent this treatment from being comprehensive, for the subject is far too vast to be introduced in some 50,000 words. One also feels that there are shortcomings which could have been avoided. The general lay-out is not always satisfactory, and the author too frequently betrays a lack of perspective, e.g., he devotes nearly four precious pages to a repetition of the well-known story of how Tischendorf discovered the Codex Sinaiticus. Furthermore, statements which do not command universal acceptance are given here as facts, e.g., it is said that the term Septuagint was first applied to the whole of the Greek Old Testament by Christians in the 2nd century. Nevertheless, the book is a mine of valuable information, and legitimately demands a place among the introductions to the textual study of the Old and New Testaments. The production is really admirable, as might be expected from the Württemburg Bibelanstalt.   B.J.R.

PAYNE, E. A. : *The Bible in English.* 1949. Pp. 24. (Epworth Press, London. Price : 9d.)

In this short lecture Mr. Payne admirably suveys the English versions of the Bible ' from Bede to Basic,' and offers judicious comment—sometimes his own and sometimes quoted from others. Throughout he is objective and unbiassed. Thus, while he condemns Sir Thomas More's attitude to Tyndale's translation, he acknowledges that Tyndale added to his own difficulties by his tendencious notes, though, since every translation is an interpretation, he was bound to take sides by his translation itself in the burning issues—*c'est le mot juste*—of his day.   H.H.R.

PRICE, I. M. : *The Ancestry of Our English Bible.* Second revised edition by W. A. Irwin and A. P. Wikgren. 1949. Pp. xx+350. (Harper and Brothers, New York. Price : $3.75.)

This book is the second, revised edition of the deservedly popular introduction first published by the late I. M. Price, in 1907, with a first revised edition in 1934, and is now substantially revised by Professors Wikgren and Irwin of Chicago. It is in three parts, the O.T. Hebrew text and ancient versions, the N.T. text, manuscripts and ancient versions, and the history of the English Bible. As a general introduction to the textual study of the Bible it is most valuable, and even at the new rates of exchange, it is not an expensive book for the average British student, for it is essentially a student's manual, and is an admirable companion to *The Bible in its Ancient and English Versions*, edited in 1940, by Principal Wheeler Robinson. The presentation of the various topics is factual and adequate, and issues which are controversial are judiciously left open, though, occasionally, one misses some points which might have been included, e.g., the question of the order of the Hieronymian Psalter translations. The study is comprehensive and up-to-date ; thus, the Jerusalem scrolls are discussed (placed tentatively in the first century A.D.), and the new Benedictine Vulgate ; among recent translations the 1946 *Revised Standard (American) N.T.*, the *Westminster Version of the Sacred Scriptures*, 1948, and the Ronald Knox translation of the Bible, 1948. A frontispiece shows the now well-known two columns of the Jerusalem scrolls (unfortunately printed upside down) ; in the middle of the book there are over 50 well-chosen specimen texts in facsimile ; and finally there is a useful index and bibliography of some 350 items, mainly in English, divided according to topics. B.J.R.

SCHEDL, C. : *Die Psalmen nach dem neuen römischen Psalter übersetzt.* 1946. Pp. x+320. (Verlag Herder, Vienna. Price : S. 30, sfr. 9.60.)

This work by an Austrian Redemptorist gives a translation that appears to be faithful and rhythmically satisfactory. The psalms are here arranged in their numerical order, and there are no footnotes to the text as printed in the body of the work. An appendix contains a few notes of a somewhat un-ambitious kind on each of the psalms concerned for the most part with the subjects of the various psalms, their titles in the Masoretic text, and the more obvious side of their exegesis.

J.M.T.B.

SMIT, J. O. : *De Vulgaat.* 1948. Pp. xvi+296. (Bijbelse Mono-graphieën, J. J. Romen & Zonen, Roermond. Price : Fl. 10.50.)

The author gives in the first part of this book a fine, popularly written, enchanting story of the origin and development of the Vulgate ; the second part deals with the modern Bene-dictine revision of the Vulgate, its necessity, methods and problems (the last illustrated by an exposition on Gen. iii, 15). The second half of the book (pp. 167-282) offers such a fullness of scientific notes that the book is not only a good introduction for the common reader, but an almost inexhaustible *vade mecum* on this subject for scholars too. Many illustrations illumine this valuable work. Th.C.V.

STENNING, J. F.: *The Targum of Isaiah*. 1949. Pp. xxviii+232.
(Clarendon Press, Oxford. Price: £1 10s. 0d.)

This edition of the Targum of Isaiah reproduces the text and
superlinear pointing and gives an English translation of the
Yemenite MS., B.M.Or. 2211, fols. 156a ff., and it adds in an
apparatus criticus the evidence of Codex Reuchlinianus as
edited by Lagarde and of ten other manuscripts. In a brief
introduction the editor discusses the characteristics of the
Targum in sections entitled " Paraphrase," " Haggadic
Influence " and " Textual Variations," this last consisting of
the variations of the Aramaic version from the M.T. tabulated
according to their origin in a different consonantal text, in
mistranslation, or in faulty transcription. A fourth section
treats of variations of punctuation in the manuscripts collated.
Extracts from Targum Jerushalmi, based mainly on Lagarde's
edition, are printed conveniently in an appendix. This work
will be welcomed, especially by teachers of Aramaic, as a
convenient edition of an interesting Targum, and as an
additional source of material for the study of superlinear
pointing. Its main defects are that it does not take cognizance
of the work done in this field during the last forty years nor
is its account of the evidence always accurate and complete.

W.D.M.

SUKENIK, E. L.: *Naḥmu Naḥmu Ammi*. 1948. Pp. 12+frontispiece.
(Bialik Foundation, Jerusalem.) (In Hebrew.)

Professor Sukenik prepared this issue of the text of Is.
xl, in the Jerusalem scrolls—or, as he prefers to have them
called, the Judaean Genizah Scrolls—for presentation to the
first meeting of the Constituent Assembly of the State of
Israel, and the author may well be congratulated on the
coincidence of the manuscript discovery and the political
occasion, for, from the whole of the O.T. no more felicitous
choice could have been made than this chapter !

In a brief introduction the author describes the scroll, indicates its date as before the fall of the Second Temple, but
possibly at the end of the Hasmonean period, and mentions
the generally accepted view of Deutero-Isaianic authorship
of Is. xl ff. The body of the brochure consists of a transcript
of the text of the scroll *vis à vis* the author's copy of the M.T.,
which, incidentally, diverges from the M.T. of B.H.3 in some
places. In footnotes which accompany the text, there are
observations on some 30 readings in the scroll, compared with
the M.T., LXX, Peshitta and Vulgate. Thus Professor Sukenik
follows the same general plan as in *Megillôth Genuzôth*.

The frontispiece is an enlarged print of a facsimile of two
columns of the scroll, containing Is. xxxix-xl. Professor
Sukenik and the Bialik Foundation are again to be congratulated on a very creditable production of first-rate importance.

B.J.R.

EXEGESIS

Abel, F. M. : *Les Livres des Maccabées.* 1949. Pp. lxiv+492. (J. Gabalda et Cie., Paris. Price : 1400 Frs.)

This commentary on I and II Maccabees is a worthy addition to the ' Collection d'Études Bibliques.' The Greek text and a French translation are set out on opposite pages. In the commentary a wide range of learning is brought to bear on the elucidation of the text ; and special questions are handled in eight detached notes. In treating the problems of introduction Abel is pre-eminently fair and judicious in his appraisal of earlier views. Discussion of particular points is impossible here ; but it can be said that immense erudition, sanity, and lucidity are the outstanding characteristics of this superb commentary, and that it will be indispensable for the study of these books and of their period. G.W.A.

Alfrink, B. J. : *Het " Stil Staan" van Zon en Maan in Jos.* 10, 12-15. 1949. Pp. 36. (Dekker & Van der Vegt, Nijmegen.)

A study of the narrative of Joshua's defeat of the Amorite confederacy by Gibeon. The writer summarizes the various explanations of the ' sun-miracle,' As a prelude to his own explanation he gives a careful literary analysis of the passage, distinguishing the prose version which attributes the initiative to Yahweh and the poetic version of the same phenomenon where Joshua is the hero. Analysing the language of the poetic version (c. x, 12-15) he demonstrates by citations from Assyrian and O.T. texts that 'md refers not to an astronomic phenomenon but simply to an atmospheric obscuration which occurred at dawn at the time of full moon and lasted a whole day. This occurring in summer would be particularly ominous and sufficient to cause the panic of the Amorites. This work is a sound corrective to exegesis which is based on external and physical evidence to the exclusion of literary analysis of the text. J.G.

Berberich, M. J. : *Brevierhilfe : Eine Handreichung zum Verständnis der Psalmen und Cantica des Breviers.* 1949. Pp. vi+122. (Verlag Kath. Bibel-Werk, Stuttgart.)

The title of *Psalterium Novum*, which is the only one displayed on the cover of this brochure, is more than a little misleading. This, as the style on the title-page itself might show, is not an edition of the new Latin Psalter, but a series of helps 'to the new Psalter's better understanding. These are arranged in the order of the psalms in the Roman Breviary, and the method followed is the selection of the more important or more difficult phrases in the Latin, these being supplied with a reasonably full midrash in German. One may recall a useful little work on much the same lines, though the Latin words are there arranged in alphabetical order, *Knots Untied in the Latin Psalter* by Rev. F. Pinkman. The present work seems to be entirely suited to its purpose, and has, as foreword, some lines of encouragement from Professor Johann Fischer. J.M.T.B.

BEWER, J. A. : *The Book of the Twelve Prophets. Vol. i, Amos, Hosea and Micah, in the King James Version with Introductions and Critical Notes.* 1949. Pp. 80. *Vol. ii, Zephaniah, Nahum, Habakkuk, Haggai, Zechariah, Obadiah, Malachi, Joel and Jonah.* 1949. Pp. 112. (Harper and Brothers, New York. Price : 2s. 6d. and 4s. 0d.)

These small volumes are the first two issues in a new series which is intended " as an aid to a study of the Book of our Christian religion." The text of the A.V. is printed—prose and poetry being shown as such—with modern punctuation and with quotation marks, and with topical headings and sub-headings. The books are arranged in chronological order, and each is supplied with a short introduction, in which the historical background, the prophetic message, and the main literary problems are outlined, and with full footnotes in explanation of the text. There are also brief general introductions. In accordance with the aim of the series, stress is laid on the permanent value of the prophetic teaching and its connection with ideas in the N.T. The introductory sections are well written and to the point, and the notes contain a great deal of useful information. The volumes should be really helpful to the general reader for whom they are intended. The more expert, however, will feel disposed to think that some of the many alternative readings proposed would be difficult to sustain in the light of recent text-critical and philological research.   D.W.T.

La Sainte Bible, translated into French under the direction of the École Biblique of Jerusalem : *Les livres des Rois,* by R. de Vaux. 1949. Pp. 234. *Ezéchiel,* by P. Auvray. 1949. Pp. 190. (Éditions du Cerf, Paris. Prices : 8s. 0d. each.)

These two volumes follow the two which were published last year (*Maccabées ; Aggée, Zacharie, Malachie*). The translation is from a critical text. At the bottom of each page there are two sets of notes, the first giving evidence for any variation from the Masoretic text, and the second giving brief aids to the proper understanding of the passage concerned. There is a short general introduction, and the translations are divided into paragraphs with sub-titles. The discussion of critical problems is necessarily limited, informative rather than argumentative, and based on sound critical study. The first edition of *Kings* is dated prior to the death of Josiah, and a second edition during the exile after 562 B.C. As for *Ezekiel,* the author inclines to Bertholet's suggestion that the prophet went to Babylon in 587 B.C., but hesitates to commit himself fully. Both books contain useful plans of the Temple, the one of Solomon's and the other of the proposals of Ezek. xl-xlviii. (See also p. 40 below, Pautrel, R.)   N.H.S.

CLAMER, A. (ed. by) : *La Sainte Bible, texte latin et traduction française d'après les textes originaux avec un commentaire exégétique et théologique.* Tome III. *Josué—Juges—Ruth—Samuel—Rois.* 1949. Pp. 828. (Letouzey & Ané, Paris. Price : £1 2s. 0d.)

Of the twelve volumes of this series as first announced in 1934, nearly all have now appeared in print, the only exception being Tome I (Genèse-Exode). The volume on the Psalms by E. Pannier is being re-issued by H. Renard, to accompany the text of the new Latin Psalter of 1945. The present volumes confirm the good opinion one has formed of the general qualities of the series. The authors concerned in Tome III are Gelin for Joshua, Tamisier for Judges and Ruth, and Médebielle for Samuel and Kings. It can be said quite emphatically that this is one of the best volumes in the series, perhaps the best in the Old Testament section, and that, where all the commentaries are good, Médebielle easily gains first prize, as might be expected from the author of *L'expiation dans l'Ancien Testament* (Rome, 1924). It will be appreciated that, as in other volumes of this series, the space available for philological discussion is not great, and the number of lines taken up by the text of the Sixto-Clementine Vulgate may be considered to be disproportionately large.

Tome IV distributes the matter among the following authors : Marchal (Chronicles, 252 pages) ; Médebielle (Ezra-Nehemiah, 128) ; Clamer (Tobit, 93) ; Soubigou (Judith, 92 ; Esther, 116) ; Robin (Job, 169). Perhaps the least adequate of these commentaries in Tome IV is Robin's Job, which appears to suffer from overcompression, and from a certain restraint in the matter of textual correction that was certainly not derived from such earlier and ampler works as those by Dhorme or Peters. The number of pages allotted to this book may well be considered insufficient. A similar remark has to be made about some other numbers of this otherwise excellent series, notably in regard to L. Dennefeld's volume on the major prophets.   J.M.T.B.

ELLIGER, K. : *Das Buch der zwölf Kleinen Propheten.* II. *Die Propheten Nahum, Habakuk, Zephanja, Haggai, Sacharja, Maleachi.* (Das Alte Testament Deutsch, 25.) 1950. Pp. 206. (Vandenhoeck und Ruprecht, Göttingen. Price : subscr. DM. 6.80, separate DM. 8.20.)

The first volume of the Minor Prophets (Hosea-Micah) in this series, by A. Weiser, was reviewed in the Book List for 1949, (p. 30 f.). This second volume follows the general pattern of the series. There is a translation of each book (the Hebrew text being emended where necessary), followed by brief historical and literary introductions, and a commentary whose emphasis is theological. Interesting features are—the rejection of the view that the book of Nahum is a prophetic liturgy, in which the fall of Nineveh is celebrated ; the references to the Samaritans which are found in some parts of Haggai (e.g., ii, 10 ff.) and of Proto- and Deutero-Zechariah (e.g., iv, 6 ff., xi, 4 ff.)—not, however, in vii, 1 ff., the deputation mentioned here coming, so it is thought, not from Bethel, but from

Babylon ; and the use of recent archaeological material, e.g., the Ras. Shamra tablets, and the Habakkuk Commentary discovered near Ain Feshkha. The influence of the commentaries of Sellin and Horst is evident ; yet there is a welcome freshness in the author's treatment, notably of Habakkuk and Deutero-Zechariah. Some recent philological and textual work appears to have been missed, but in general the volume is of high quality, and its value does not by any means lie only on the theological side.   D.W.T.

ENGNELL, I. : *The Call of Isaiah: an Exegetical and Comparative Study.* (Uppsala Universitets Årsskrift, 1949 : 4.) 1949. Pp. 70. (Lundequistska Bokhandeln, Uppsala and Harrassowitz, Leipzig. Price : Kr. 3.)

In this short study Engnell sets out Isaiah vi, in MT, LXX, and Peshitta, and prefixes to his exegetical discussion characteristic comments on textual criticism, philology, form criticism, and tradition history. He argues that the MT of verse 13 is sound, defends the primary character of the positive, ' messianic ' elements in the complex of which the chapter forms a part, and maintains that the kingship ideology and the Annual Festival are of prime importance for the interpretation of the passage. In an additional note and a postscript some observations are offered on Kahle's Schweich Lectures and on criticisms of Engnell's own view (notably those of Widengren—1949, Book List, p. 37) ; and the Jerusalem scrolls are enthusiastically hailed as supporting the author's general position. Not all of his contentions will command general agreement ; but this study provides an interesting sample of Engnell's methods and theories.   G.W.A.

FISCHEL, H. A. : *The First Book of Maccabees with Commentary.* 1948. Pp. 118. (Schocken Books, New York. Price : $1.50.)

The text of this volume (No. 17 in the Schocken Library) is the English translation of 1 Macc. by W. O. E. Oesterley in Charles' Apocrypha and Pseudepigrapha of the Old Testament (Vol. 1). The Commentary supplied by Dr. Fischel is adequate, being adapted to the needs of the general reader who is desirous of appreciating the great story of the Maccabean revolt and the history of the period without being " snowed under " by notes. Dr. Fischel's " Introduction" is a masterly piece of writing, exhibiting a well considered judgement upon the influence of Hellenism upon Judaism. This booklet has as its companion in the same Library (No. 6) E. Bickerman's *The Maccabees*, a modern historical interpretation of the Maccabean age.   O.S.R.

FREY, H. : *Das Buch der Kirche in der Weltwende. Die kleinen nach-exilischen Propheten, für Freunde und Verächter der Bibel ausgelegt.* (Die Botschaft des Alten Testaments. Erläuterungen alttestamentlicher Schriften, Band XXIV). Zweite Auflage, 1948. Pp. 352. (Calwer Verlag, Stuttgart. Price : DM. 8.40.)

The first edition of this work, which appeared in 1941, was reviewed in the Book List for 1947 (p. 20), and the writer of this note cordially agrees with what is said there in assessment of its worth. It is written to help promote a sympathetic understanding of the Old Testament from the standpoint of the Christian faith, and it has evidently met with a welcome (and, within the limits indicated by the previous notice, a justifiably welcome) response. A.R.J.

FREY, H. : *Das Buch der Heimsuchung und des Auszugs.* (Die Botschaft des Alten Testaments, Band V). 1949. Pp. 214. (Calwer, Stuttgart. Price : DM. 6.60.)

> This work on Exodus cc. 1-18 was undertaken by the writer while a prisoner of war. The thesis is that as the narrative of the Exodus was a means of revelation to Israel at every critical phase of her history, it has a peculiar value for the Church in the present crisis. The text in German translation is fully cited and annotated by somewhat pedestrian paraphrase rather than exegesis. There are four main sections distinguished by the writer and concluded by a theological essay. The worth of this work is confined to its homiletic value. J.G.

GEMSER, B. : *De Psalmen III.* 1949. (Tekst en Uitleg, J. B. Wolters, Groningen—Batavia. Price : Fl. 4.50.)

> The publication of this third part completes the commentary on the Psalms in the Dutch series " Tekst en Uitleg." Böhl explained the first 89 Psalms, Gemser (University of Pretoria) deals with Psalms xc-cl. Translation and commentary are first-rate, giving evidence of excellent philological training, literary erudition and theological interest. There are only a very few gaps in the bibliography ; thus we did not find Snaith : *Jewish New Year Festival.* In this respect (the Jewish New Year) the point of view of the author is somewhat hesitating. Th.C.V.

GOLDMAN, S. : *In the Beginning.* 1949. Pp. xiv+892. (Harpers, New York. Price : $5.00.)

> The second volume of Rabbi Goldman's vast undertaking has now appeared (see p. 5 above). This deals with the book of Genesis. It offers first a summary of the contents of the book, and a number of selections from its narratives, followed by chapters on the historical background and authorship, marked by the same conservative outlook as the preceding volume, and further chapters on the style and philosophy of Genesis. Six hundred pages are then devoted to echoes and allusions culled from a wide range of literature, similar to those of the former volume. These again command admiration for the incredible diligence of the author, and form the backbone of the volume. They are followed by about 100 pages of commentary on Genesis, based on the author's summary and selections, and a few pages of notes on the rest of the book. A valuable General Bibliography closes the work. H.H.R.

HERTZBERG, H. W. : *Das Buch Hiob*. 1949. Pp. 174. (J. G. Oncken, Stuttgart. English Price : 9s. 6d.)

As the series title indicates, the volume is designed for the general reader rather than for the scholar. There is a new translation with commentary. Bildad's third speech comprises xxiv, 13-24 ; xxv, 2-6 ; Job's ninth speech is xxvi, 1-4 ; xxvii, 11 f. ; xxvi, 5-14 ; Zophar's third speech is xxvii, 7-10 ; 12-23. Otherwise critical matters are not dealt with, and both Elihu's speeches and chapter xxvii are regarded as integral to the book. The book is treated as a whole, as being the Word of God illustrating God's struggle (Kampf) for man, and Man's struggle against God. N.H.S.

NÖTSCHER, F. (ed. by) : *Die Heilige Schrift in deutscher Übersetzung, Echter Bibel : Das Alte Testament*. 7. *Samuel und Königsbücher* by M. Rehm. 1949. Pp. 124+134. (Price : DM. 7.20.) 8. *Chronik* by M. Rehm and *Sprüche* by V. Hamp. Pp. 144+88. (*Price :* DM. 6.90.) 9. *Genesis* by H. Junker. Pp. 148. (Price : DM. 4.80.) (Echter Verlag, Würzburg.)

This excellent series of translations, accompanied by short introductions and compressed notes, has already made a name for itself outside its country of origin, and there is all possible evidence that the editor has taken pains to choose contributors who are really equal to their task. To write a commentary on any of the books mentioned above in so reduced a format is in itself no small achievement. Given the general purpose of the series, which is evidently intended for readers without specialized knowledge, one cannot in the commentary on Samuel and Kings look for the splendid fullness of S. R. Driver's *Notes on the Hebrew Text of the Books of Samuel* or of C. F. Burney's companion volume on Kings. The volume gives reasonably full notes on the more difficult passages, even if occasionally, as in the translation of 2 Sam. v, 8, one could wish that Rehm had shown rather more courage in the matter of reconstructing the text. To be sure, as Driver comments, " the passage is very difficult, and the text certainly to some extent corrupt," but plausible emendations have been proposed by Vincent, Dhorme, T. H. Robinson and others.

H. Junker's *Genesis* is, as might be expected from so well-known a writer, an accomplished piece of work, though occasionally the translation appears rather too free, as in xxxvii, 3. Is it sufficient to describe Joseph's coat as " ein vornehmes Gewand " and to consign the more literal rendering to a note ?

Rehm's *Chronik* and Hamp's *Sprüche* seem to be entirely adequate. As in the former's *Samuel– und Königsbücher* a textual apparatus of select readings is provided. For some reason unguessed this is entirely lacking in Junker's *Genesis*. (See also p. 78 below.) J.M.T.B.

256

PAUTREL, R. : *La Sainte Bible* (traduite en français sous la direction de l'École Biblique de Jérusalem). *L'Ecclésiaste.* 1948. Pp. 34. (Les Éditions du Cerf, Paris. Price : 2s. 6d.)

This small book consists of 12 pages of introduction, followed by a translation with some textual and other notes.

The introduction contains some good things such as the remark that Qoheleth denies that Providence is a sort of calculating machine performing the function of reckoning life and death, happiness and misfortune in terms of reward and punishment. Qoheleth's writing, the translator says, reveals nothing of the character of Semitic poetry or of Greek prose : nor, except at the beginning and the end of his work does he take any heed of aesthetic refinement. The thought of the book is described as being capable of division into eight propositions. In the translation the following points may be selected as worthy of special notice. " Vanité des vanités " (i. 2) is defined in a note as meaning *déception* and thus this word in the passages that follow is the usual rendering of the Hebrew *hebel* (e.g., ii, 26, c'est une déception et du temps perdu). The poem at the beginning of ch. iii is happily rendered (e.g., Un temps pour tuer, / et un temps pour guérir ; / un temps pour détruire, / et un temps pour bâtir). The *crux interpretum* iii, 11, appears as : " Tout ce qu'il fait convient à son heure, mais devant l'ensemble du temps, on ne saisit pas ce que Dieu fait du début a la fin." (See also p. 35 above, *La Sainte Bible.*)   O.S.R.

POWER, A. D. : *The Proverbs of Solomon.* 1949. Pp. 256. (Longmans, London. Price : 6s. 0d.)

This volume follows the author's earlier translation of *Ecclesiasticus* (1939). The translation is reliable, in good English, reproducing the Authorized Version as far as possible, but making full and balanced use of modern critical study of the text. The variations are generally based on such emendations (after the versions or conjectural) as are to be found in the footnotes of Kittel's *Biblia Hebraica* (3rd ed.), and are dealt with lucidly in 78 pp. of notes. A detailed glossary is added, in which much useful information concerning Proverbs in particular and the whole Bible in general is provided for the general reader.   N.H.S.

VON RAD, G. : *Das erste Buch Mose. Genesis Kapital* 1-12, 9. (Das Alte Testament Deutsch, 2.) 1949. Pp. 136. (Vandenhoeck & Ruprecht, Göttingen. Price : Subscr. DM. 4.50 ; separate DM. 5.40.)

This is the first of three volumes on Genesis, all by the same author, in the new Göttingen commentary on the Old Testament, which is to form a companion-piece to the already well-established New Testament series, *Das Neue Testament Deutsch.* It is thus of a semi-popular character, and the approach is designedly " theological." At the same time, as is clear from the list of distinguished contributors, it is obviously intended that the work shall be governed throughout by a high standard of scholarship. A quarter of the present

volume is devoted to a general introduction to the Book of
Genesis, and in the remainder of the work the early chapters
of Genesis are divided into appropriate sections for translation and comment, the discussion in each case being, for
the most part, of a summary and general character. Broadly
speaking, one may say that the author follows the normal
critical analysis of the records into the J, E and P strands;
and his attitude to the work of the Jahwist, whose creative
activity is especially stressed, is that which he has already
set out in *Das formgeschichtliche Problem des Hexateuchs* (1938)
with its attempt to distinguish early cycles of oral tradition
with close cultic associations. As for the commentary itself
and, indeed, the introductory discussion of the question of
interpretation, the author, as one would expect, has a number
of useful and suggestive comments to make, and even the
specialist may find that it can be read with pleasure and
profit.   A.R.J.

RUDOLPH, W. : *Esra und Nehemia mit 3 Esra.* (Handbuch zum alten
    Testament : Erste Reihe 20. Herausgegeben von Otto Eissfeldt.)
    1949. Pp. 220. (J. C. B. Mohr—Paul Siebeck—Tübingen.)

A careful and thoroughly competent piece of work, as is to be
expected in this series. The composition of the book is to be
dated ca. 400 B.C. The historical background which is assumed
is that after the victory of Cyrus, Sheshbazzar came to Jerusalem executive-komissar to clear things up. Later Zerubbabel
was in control, and encouraged by Haggai and Zechariah,
he rebuilt the Temple in the early years of Darius I. Both
Nehemiah and Ezra belong to the reign of Artaxerxes I.
The former was in Jerusalem from 445-433. During his absence
Ezra came to Jerusalem, and by his ruthless enforcement of
strict Jewish law, created such disorder in the land that he
was recalled. Nehemiah returned ca. 400 B.C. in order to
restore the situation. The author thus follows, in general,
the views of Kosters and Kennett.   N.H.S.

SCHUMPP, M. : *Das Buch Ezechiel* (Herders Bibelkommentar : Die
    Heilige Schrift für das Leben erklärt. Band X/1). 1942. Pp. 236.
    (Herder and Co., Freiburg im Breisgau. Price : 17s. 0d.)

This series, which provides a translation made from the
Hebrew text and commentary, aims at helping the reader to an
understanding of the thought of the books of the O.T., and to
an appreciation of their religious value for the present day.
Ezekiel lived in days similar to ours, when the old world was
crumbling and another coming into existence. He is thus
able to speak with peculiar authority to the world of to-day.
From this general standpoint the author writes impressively
and with sincerity. It is not part of his purpose to discuss
literary problems—he adopts the traditional view as to
authorship—and little attention is paid to textual difficulties. Chapters xl-xlviii are only briefly treated, as their
subject matter has scarcely any bearing on life to-day. A
point of interest is the author's strong repudiation of any
suggestion that the personality of the prophet is to be explained
in terms of abnormal psychology.   D.W.T.

SLOTKI, I. W. : *Isaiah : Hebrew Text and English Translation, with an Introduction and Commentary.* 1949. Soncino Books of the Bible. Pp. xiv+338. (Soncino Press, London and Bournemouth. Price : 12s. 6d.)

> In accordance with the plan of the series we have here the Hebrew text and the American Jewish translation set side by side, with the commentary beneath. Attention is not given to textual or critical questions. In the short introduction the author avoids committing himself on the problems of authorship, simply stating that the Bible critics divide the book amongst various authors while others hold unity of authorship but recognize the same exilic and post-exilic background for the second and third divisions. He gives a short résumé of his views on Hebrew metrics, as presented in various publications. The author breaks with Jewish tradition in finding Cyrus referred to in xli, 2. He groups the four Servant passages together in his interpretation, and finds them to refer to the faithful Remnant of Israel. He is well acquainted with modern critical work, but gives us a welcome Jewish interpretation designed for the layman. Would that Christian commentaries, even designed for the ministry, could appropriately print the Hebrew text !
> H.H.R.

VELLAS, B. M. : *Hermêneia Palaias Diathêkês* (in Modern Greek) **4.** *Jonah-Nahum-Habakkuk-Zephaniah.* 1949. Pp. 144. ("Astêr" Publishing House, Athens.)

> Sufficient has already been said about this useful and interesting series of commentaries, written in Modern Greek for the use of Orthodox theological students. As in the earlier volumes (cf. Book List, 1949, pp. 29-30) there is an introduction to each of the books, a translation from Hebrew into Modern Greek, an accompanying Septuagint text (printed in full, but without the *apparatus criticus* to which the large Cambridge edition, Swete, and Rahlfs have accustomed us), and a full commentary. This last seems, once again, to be almost too exhaustive, the more so in that there is not much directly philological discussion and the Hebrew text is nowhere given. There can, however, be no doubt about the author's wide knowledge of the literature and competence in the handling of it. One can only rejoice that, as this is the first modern commentary of its kind in the Greek language, it should be so entirely adequate and well-documented.
> J.M.T.B.

YOUNG, E. J. : *The Prophecy of Daniel : a Commentary.* 1949. Pp. 330. (Eerdmans, Grand Rapids. $4.50.)

> Here we have a strongly conservative commentary on Daniel, governed by the view that the book came from the pen of Daniel in the sixth century B.C., and that the fourth kingdom of chapters ii and vii is the Roman Empire. Darius the Mede is left unidentified, and the ten horns of the fourth beast of chap. vii are similarly interpreted vaguely of ten unidentified kingdoms. The customary leap in the interpretation

of chap. xi is made, the subject being held to change with verse 36 from Antiochus to Antichrist. The author is widely read, and acknowledges his debt to critical scholars, whose views he is unable to accept. The spirit in which the book is written will give it a value even to those who do not share its approach, and the learning of the author will be acknowledged by those who do not share his conclusions. It may be commended to those who wish to see the change in spirit from a former day, as well as the modifications of the case that can be put up for the traditional view.   H.H.R.

ZER-KABOD, M. : *Ezra and Nehemiah*. 1948. Pp. 196. (Rubin Mass, Jerusalem.)

As a result of recent events, there is in Israel a growing interest in the Books of Ezra and Nehemiah, which the Hebrew work under review is designed to further. It consists of a preface ; an introduction ; the text, pointed, with modern punctuation and without accents ; a Hebrew translation of the Aramaic portions ; a commentary in two parts, one giving the main explanations, the other details ; two appendices, one on Persian history, the other containing four Elephantine papyri in Hebrew translation ; several pictures and maps ; and a bibliography. Dr. Zer-kabod (formerly Ehrenkranz) is very critical of hyper-criticism. He prefers the Massoretic Ezra to the Greek ; he ascribes the Books of Ezra and Nehemiah to two different authors ; he regards Ezra and Nehemiah as contemporaries ; Torrey does not figure in the bibliography. His appreciation of the various stages of ancient Hebrew and his knowledge of the Talmudic sources enable the author to shed fresh light on many important passages and problems. A highly useful publication.   D.D.

LITERARY CRITICISM AND INTRODUCTION

AALDERS, G. CH. : *A Short Introduction to the Pentateuch*. 1949. Pp. 174. (Tyndale Press. Price : 6s. 0d.)

Dr. Aalders confesses that his belief in the divine inspiration and entire trustworthiness of Holy Scripture prevents his reaching any conclusions contrary to its infallibility. This involves, for him, acceptance of everything in the Pentateuch as a record of actual fact. The differences of divine names are no criterion for source-analysis, nor are there any duplicate narratives. The variety of law-codes is not inconsistent with Mosaic authorship. Deuteronomy does distinguish between priests and Levites. Exod. xx, 24, does not imply a plurality of sanctuaries, but only a plurality of altars ! There are some post-Mosaica and a-Mosaica. We cannot therefore say that Moses wrote the Pentateuch just as it stands. But it is essentially his work and the final redaction can be dated between the beginning of the reign of Saul and the first seven years of the reign of David.   C.R.N.

BENTZEN, A. : *Introduction to the Old Testament.* II. *The Books of the Old Testament.* 1949. Pp. 300. (Gad, Copenhagen, and Geoffrey Cumberlege, London. Price : £1 10s. 0d.)

Like volume I (see Book List, 1949, p. 32), this is not a mere translation of the corresponding parts of the Danish original. Many alterations and additions have been made ; and the reader is given a valuable survey of recent discussions, notably of Scandinavian work on the Pentateuch and the prophets, to which the volume is an indispensable guide. In discussing the positions of the Uppsala School Bentzen is neither uncritical nor unsympathetic ; and the book is marked throughout by judicious appraisal of contemporary trends as well as by fair statement of the assured results of earlier work. A very welcome feature is the section on the apocryphal and pseudepigraphical literature. G.W.A.

GRANILD, S. : *Ezrabogens literære Genesis undersøgt med særligt Henblik paa et efterkronistisk Indgreb.* 1949. Pp. 292. (Gad, Copenhagen.)

This work is a dissertation submitted for a doctorate at Aarhus University. In a careful literary and linguistic analysis of the MT. of Ezra-Nehemiah the writer argues that various passages usually attributed to the Chronicler come from the hand of a later editor, who was dependent on the Chronicler but more muddled in his chronology. It was this ' Redactor postchronisticus ' who united Nehemiah's memoirs with sections dealing with the return, the rebuilding, and the work of Ezra, and added other material, including all the Aramaic. The treatment of the complex literary problems is thorough and competent ; and the book is important both for its critical discussion of earlier contributions to the subject (including those of Mowinckel, Kapelrud, Engnell and Johannesen), and also for the contentions made in it. G.W.A.

LODS, A. : *Histoire de la littérature hébraïque et juive des origines à la ruine de l'état juif* (135 après J.-C.) 1950. Pp. 1054. (Payot, Paris. Price : Fr. 2400.)

This massive and masterly posthumous work is unlike other Introductions to Old Testament Literature in that it treats of books or sections of books in the order in which the author believes they were written, and covers the Old Testament, the Apocrypha and Pseudepigrapha, and such writings as the Elephantine Papyri, in a single continuous historical survey. In general Professor Lods follows the critical views of a generation ago, and is uninfluenced by more recent challenges to those positions. In common with a number of recent scholars, however, he pays much attention to the fragments of older literature, especially fragments of poetry, embodied in the Pentateuch and historical books, and one of the best sections of the work deals with these. He provides an excellent survey of the history of Pentateuchal criticism, and of the positions of the Wellhausen school which he follows, and then he treats of the main documents in their appropriate historical place. The various sections of composite books are separately treated at different points, and the absence of an index makes it difficult to locate some of these. It is interesting to note that Gen. xiv is still treated here as a late midrash, and the author is uninfluenced by recent tendencies to regard some of the prophetic books as liturgies. On Ezekiel, however, we find that some recent work has had an influence on Professor Lods, though there is an inadequate survey of recent study. The Holiness Code is assigned to the sixth century, and the Prologue and Epilogue of Job are firmly held to be older than the dialogue. The Song of Songs is a collection of love songs, nuptial and other. There is a short section on the Canon at the end, which is slighter than one might have expected in a work on this scale. Professor A. Parrot has contributed a Preface, and Addenda, dealing with the Dead Sea Scrolls and supplementing the excellent bibliographies that conclude each chapter. Altogether this is an important and valuable legacy which Professor Lods has bequeathed to us, and no Old Testament scholar should be without it. H.H.R.

NOTH, M. : *Überlieferungsgeschichte des Pentateuch*. 1948. Pp. viii+ 288. (W. Kohlhammer, Stuttgart. Price : £1 13s. 6d.)

This work carries forward the investigations begun in the author's *Überlieferungsgeschichtliche Studien I* (Book List, 1946, p. 28), and is a reconstruction of the history of the traditions which lie behind J, E and P in Genesis-Numbers and parts of Deuteronomy xxxi-xxxiv. The narrative of P is accepted as the literary framework of the whole, and J as that of the JE material. J and E are assumed to have a common basis (*Grundlage*) in tradition, designated G. The tradition as a whole is analysed into certain major themes (the Exodus, the entry into Palestine, the promise to the Fathers, direction in the wilderness, revelation at Sinai) to which other narratives and motifs have been added. Noth emphasizes the conception of the unity of Israel which is characteristic of the Pentateuchal tradition, as contrasted with the traditions in Judges. He holds that it must have taken shape fairly soon after the settlement in Palestine ; but he concludes that it does not give reliable evidence for a connected account of the earlier history of the Hebrews. Some of Noth's positions will doubtless be disputed ; but this is a work of outstanding importance. G.W.A.

PFEIFFER, R. H. : *History of New Testament Times with an Introduction to the Apocrypha*. 1949. Pp. xii+562. (Harpers, New York. Price : $4.00.)

Here we have a magnificent companion volume to the author's *Introduction to the Old Testament*, on the same elaborate scale. The first half of the book deals with the history of Palestinian Judaism in its political, religious and literary aspects, together with a chapter on Hellenism, and chapters on the Diaspora and on Alexandrian Jewish literature. The second half consists of chapters on each of the books of the Apocrypha—in the usual Protestant sense of the term. Briefer notes on the Pseudepigrapha as well as other literature will be found in the first part of the book. Throughout the author not alone presents his own views, but surveys the various views that have been put forward, and his work is a magnificent compendium of information on the whole field it covers. It is quite indispensable for workers in this field and is unlikely to be superseded in our generation. There are occasional inaccuracies—such as the statement that the Chigi MS. is our only extant MS. of the LXX of Daniel, and the statement that the Pharisees added the Hagiographa to the Canon in A.D. 90—and it is inevitable that the author's views on disputed questions will not always be shared by the reader ; but the book will take its place at once as a standard, and unrivalled, tool.   H.H.R.

ROBERTSON, E. : *Investigations into the Old Testament Problem : The Results*. 1949. Pp. 28. (The Manchester University Press and the John Rylands Library, Manchester. Price : 2s. 0d.)

In this brochure, reprinted from the *Bulletin of the John Rylands Library*, vol. 32, No. 1, September, 1949, Professor Robertson's main lines of study during recent years converge in an attractive synthesis. Both his researches into the history of the Samaritans and his attack on the Wellhausen reconstruction of the Pentateuch and Historical books of the O.T. convince him that " in order to get a clear picture of conditions in Palestine in the period of the Judges . . . it seems necessary to look beyond Jewish sources to the Samaritan . . . for additional supplementary information." (p. 9.) This he would find in traces (not wholly expunged from the present O.T.) of the Aaronite priesthood of Shechem and the Ephraimite strands in the history of Israel. Many experts will disagree with Professor Robertson's thesis, but it is becoming increasingly appreciated that the part played by the shrines in the transmission, if not the creation of the Jewish tradition should be more closely examined, and the series of Rylands Lectures, to which the present lecture is the " summation of the arguments," will call for serious study when such an examination is undertaken.   B.J.R.

WEISER, A. : *Einleitung in das Alte Testament*. 2nd ed. revised. 1949. Pp. 338. (Vandenhoeck & Ruprecht, Göttingen. Price : £1 10s. 0d.)

The most important change in the new edition of this excellent work (cf. Book List, 1946, p. 30) is the addition of a section dealing with the apocryphal and pseudepigraphical literature. The rest of the book has been revised to take account of the discussions of the last decade ; and the bibliographies have been expanded and brought up to date.   G.W.A.

WINNETT, F. V. : *The Mosaic Tradition*. 1949. Pp. xii+220. (University of Toronto Press and Geoffrey Cumberlege, London.) Price: $3.75 ; £1 8s. 0d.)

In Professor Winnett's view the books of Exodus and Numbers contain a continuous tradition emanating from northern Israel, with occasional annotations from P. He finds no trace of a second ' prophetic ' source, but the whole has undergone two revisions, one in the south soon after the fall of Samaria, which gave rise to the Deuteronomic account, and the second after the exile, when the Jerusalem priesthood (P) attempted to harmonise the two existing forms. He notes the frequent occurrence of the figure ten, and finds a consistent pattern running through the whole original document, of which he gives a translation at the end of the book. In the course of the discussion several geographical and historical questions are treated, though there is comparatively little reference to the light which may be obtained from non-Israelite sources. T.H.R.

LAW, RELIGION AND THEOLOGY
(including the Life and Thought of the Neighbouring Peoples)

ALBRIGHT, W. F. : *Von der Steinzeit zum Christentum*. 1949. Pp. 496. (Francke Verlag, Berne.)

This is a German translation, made by Dr. Irene Lande, of the 1946 edition of *From the Stone Age to Christianity*. The materials from the Addenda pages of the English edition have been incorporated in the work, and the author had also revised the English text throughout before the translation was made and added further references to recent works in the Notes. Professor Baumgartner has also added some references, and an occasional note over his initials. This translation represents an improvement on the English edition, therefore. H.H.R.

BAAB, O. J. : *The Theology of the Old Testament*. 1949. Pp. 288. (Abingdon-Cokesbury Press. Price : $3.50)

This book is based on the conviction that the philosophy of the Old Testament, in spite of the diversity manifest in its writings, possesses an essential unity. This unity is given by the religious experience of the one continuing Hebrew community. The author argues for the uniqueness of Biblical religion and for the validity of its main beliefs. He selects for exposition and discussion the religious ideas which are typical and adequately attested, the main topics dealt with being the ideas of God, man, sin, salvation, the Kingdom of God, of death and the hereafter and of evil. Perhaps the most interesting sections are those dealing with the Kingdom of God and death and the hereafter, and the brief discussion of idolatry. The semantic studies are not as full or well-documented as one might wish. The discussion of certain topics is not quite up-to-date, e.g., the Servant of the Lord and the Messiah, and in general one misses reference to the background of contemporary discussion. The significance is

264

indicated but the subject is dismissed in a couple of pages, in striking contrast to the method adopted by Eichrodt. The book would have been a better one if the author had related the religious ideas even more closely than he has done to the religious life of the community. But he has good things to say and, in spite of a few surprising lapses, the book rewards perusal. The concluding chapter on the validity of Old Testament theology is rather weak in argument. N.W.P.

BARTSCH, H. W. : *Schöpfung und Schuld vor Gott.* Evangelische Zeitstimmen, Heft 18. 1948. Pp. 32. (Reich & Heidrich, Hamburg. Price : DM. 0.50.)

In this monograph the author discusses the six outstanding themes of the first eleven chapters of Genesis : Creation of the world, Creation of man in God's image, the Fall, Cain and Abel, Noah and the Flood, Babel. He interprets the various passages to establish the theme of Man's Fall, and subjection to evil ; together with the promise that a time will come when he will be freed from the power of evil, and this by God's grace. He concludes by quoting Heb. xi, 1 and 1 John v, 4 f. N.H.S.

BEEK, M. A. : *Inleiding in de Joodse apocalyptiek van het Oud- en Nieuw-testamentisch tijdvak.* (Theologia, VI.) 1950. Pp. x+148. (De Erven F. Bohn, Haarlem.)

Professor Beek offers a valuable introduction to the apocalyptic writings of the Old Testament and the following period. His field is less extensive than Pfeiffer's in his *History of New Testament Times*, in that he deals only with apocalyptic works, though wider in that he includes the apocalyptic elements in the Old Testament—Isa. xxiv-xxvii, Joel, Ezekiel, Zechariah and Daniel. Included in the individual notes on the various books is a short note on the Dead Sea Scrolls, under Sukenik's title of *Megilloth Genuzoth*, in which reference to their relevance to the study of the Zadokite Fragments is made. Following the individual introductions there are chapters dealing with broader subjects, such as the sectarian *milieu* of the apocalyptists—where further reference to the Dead Sea Scrolls figures—the conception of history found in these works, and the Son of Man. Gathered at the end of the volume are the notes and a useful bibliography. Altogether this is a valuable and up-to-date, though brief, handbook. H.H.R.

BENTZEN, A., HOLM, S. and Søe, N. H. (ed. by) : *Illustreret Religionsleksikon*, Bind I (A-F). 1949. Pp. 522. (Skandinavisk Bogforlag, Odense.)

This is the first volume of a richly illustrated popular encyclopaedia of religion. The emphasis is confessedly on subjects of current interest. Nevertheless this volume contains many excellent articles on matters Biblical and Semitic. Though the work is in Danish, the contributors include Norwegian and Swedish scholars. The articles are necessarily brief ; but their quality is high, and they are written with commendable clarity. Two further volumes have yet to appear. (See also p. 77 below.) G.W.A.

BERTHOLET, A. : *Die Macht der Schrift in Glauben und Aberglauben.*
1949. Pp. 48. (Abhandlungen der Deutschen Akademie der
Wissenschaften zu Berlin.) (Akademie Verlag, Berlin.)

In this study in comparative religion the writer traces the
development of the conception of the power of the written
expression from the primitive hunter's cave-scrawling of his
desired quarry to letters, words, texts and authoritative
books of Scripture. With a wealth of instances cited from the
religions of the world he discusses the use and efficacy of the
written word and is particularly informative on the subject
of the obligation of man as custodian of sacred scripture.
He emphasises the narrow line of division between faith and
superstition in relation to scripture and illustrates the reaction
against bibliolatry in satire and mysticism. A stimulating
study in a very fruitful field.   J.G.

BIČ, M. : *Stopy po Drobopravectví v Jisráeli* (=*Traces of Haruspicy
in the Old Testament.*) 1947. Starozákonné Studie (=Old Testament Studies), i. Pp. 48. (Nákladem Spolku Posluchačů Husovy
Fakulty v Praze, Prosinec.)

This is part of Professor Bič's doctoral dissertation, written
in 1936, and now published in Czech, with an English summary.
Though the Czech is likely to be inaccessible to most foreign
readers, as it is to the reviewer, the summary will be of value.
The author's thesis is that the word *bōķēr*, usually rendered
morning, originally meant *haruspicy*, and retained that
meaning in some passages. The meaning *morning* he holds to
be secondary. With this word he then connects *bōķēr* in Am.
vii, 14, and then holds that *nōķēd* in Am. i, 1, is related in
significance, perhaps meaning *hepatoscopos*. Still more
hazardous is the view that *maštîn bᵉķîr* in 1 Kings xiv, 10, and
elsewhere, means 'those who were feasting at a haruspicy.'
                                                           H.H.R.

BÖHL, F. M. TH. : *Het probleem van eeuwig leven in de cyclus en het
epos van Gilgamesj.* (Mededelingen van de Koninklijke Vlaamse
Academie voor Wetanschappen, Letteren en Schone Kunsten van
België. Klasse der Letteren, IX, 3.) 1948. Pp. 44. (Standaard-
Boekhandel, Antwerp.)

In 1943, the author of this work published a translation of the
Epic of Gilgamesh into Dutch which was well received and,
indeed, was soon out of print, and the second edition is soon
to be followed by a commentary, complete with introduction,
transcription and translation. The present monograph is thus
the result of intensive study, and its pronouncements must be
taken seriously as the fruit of a ripe judgement. The author
traces the fluctuating fortunes of the epic through some fifteen
centuries from its earlier Sumerian form to its latest Accadian
dress, and finds persistent evidence of a struggle between the
different attitudes to the thought of an afterlife which are
furnished by the fertility cult of Inanna or Ishtar, on the one
hand, and the solar cult of Utu or Shamash on the other.
Students of the Old Testament should take note of this
important monograph, as it provides background for our
own understanding of the ceaseless quest for fuller life which
is so characteristic of Israelite thought.   A.R.J.

BORNKAMM, H.: *Luther und das Alte Testament*. 1948. Pp. vi+234. (J. C. B. Mohr [Paul Siebeck], Tübingen. Price: 16s. 0d.)

In this lucid, factual and fascinating study the author discusses Luther's interpretation of the O.T. under the following headings: the O.T. as the mirror of life, the God of the O.T., the O.T. as Word of God, the unity of the O.T., Luther's translation, the characteristics of Luther's interpretation. According to Bornkamm the key to Luther's treatment is that the O.T., in its every detail, points forward to Christ and Luther's well-known anti-Jewish tendencies practically preclude interest in it as a history of the Jews in any secular sense. Consequently tropology and allegorical interpretation play an important part: Christ is the consummation of the Law, the history of Israel is a reflection of the majesty of God; the unity of the O.T. with the New is particularly evident in Luther's translation where ' the whole conception of the O.T. Godhead is consistently coloured by the N.T.' Undoubtedly this volume will abundantly repay thorough study by those concerned with O.T. theology, but it raises inevitable problems. It cannot but reveal the extent to which historical and literary criticism have placed the study of the O.T. on a totally different plane from that of the Reformers, and one wonders how it will be possible to maintain continuity with Lutheran and Reformation theology and at the same time deal fairly with the established findings of Criticism. The volume closes with a table of Luther's published treatments of O.T. books, with particulars of date and editions.   B.J.R.

BOSON, G.: *I Profeti d'Israele*. 1948. Pp. 164. ('La Scuola' Editrice, Brescia. Price: 180 lire.) In the series *Profili della Storia*, itself a section of the comprehensive *Gli Uomini e la Civiltà*.

A small (6¼ by 4¼ inches) paper-backed Italian textbook for schools. The prophets are dealt with in turn, with short sketches of their character, background, and message. The standpoint is traditional. Obadiah and Joel belong to the 9th century, Jonah to the eighth; there was one Isaiah (740-693 B.C.), and the dates for Daniel are 606-536 B.C. The author is professor of Assyriology and Semitic Languages in the Roman Catholic University of S. Cuore di Milano.
                N.H.S.

BROUWER, C.: *Wachter en herder*. 1949. (H. Veenman en Zonen, Wageningen. Price: Fl. 6.40 sewed; Fl. 8.40 bound.)

This thesis, defended at the University of Utrecht, deals (after some preparatory chapters on the significance of the shepherd—who must be distinguished from the watchman, *šomer*—in the Near East and in the O.T., and on the contents of the preceding prophecies of Zechariah) with the difficult pericopes Zech. xi and xiii, 7-9. The starting point is the unity of Zechariah; ix ff. are from *circa* 480. In chapter xi Dr. Brouwer reads the description of God Himself, who as hypostasis of the divine justice, takes over from the shepherds (the leaders of the people) the task of a watchman (allusion to the exile and return, vv, 7 ff.) ; after the return He does not receive from the leaders a sufficient reward (the reinstitution of the temple) and therefore He rejects his people for a second time, delivering it to bad shepherds (vv, 12 ff.). Chapter xiii, 7-9, on the other hand prophesies the appearance of the good shepherd, who must be identified with the one " whom they have pierced " of xii, 10.

In spite of many good passages in the book, especially on theological questions about the relation of the O.T. and N.T., there is a lack of the necessary exactness in the treatment of the philological difficulties of the text, which makes one distrustful of the results of the inquiry. A summary in one of the world-languages, as has of late years generally been given at the end of Dutch theses, is not added.   Th.C.V.

BUBER, M. : *The Prophetic Faith*. 1949. Pp. 248. (The Macmillan Company, New York. Price : $3.75.)

This volume, which originally appeared in Hebrew and has been translated by C. Witton-Davies, represents the second volume of the projected trilogy of which the first volume was published in German under the title ' Königtum Gottes.' In the interval there has appeared the author's ' Moses ' which covers in detail part of the ground covered in the book now under review. From the Song of Deborah, Professor Buber works back, testing the tradition, to the Mosaic period and, behind it, to that of the Patriarchs. Then, in a series of most interesting and stimulating chapters, he works forwards through Hebrew history, with special reference to the prophetic movement, right down to the time of the second Isaiah. In disagreement with some recent tendencies he accentuates the opposition between prophet and priest. Emphasis is laid on the fact that God's sovereignty was intended to extend over the whole of life and that therefore the prophets scarcely recognized any distinction between the sacred and the secular. There is a penetrating study of baalization with special reference to Hosea. The authenticity of the hopeful conclusions to the Books of Amos and Hosea is defended. " Immanuel " in Isaiah vii, is possibly Hezekiah. The passage common to Isaiah and Micah is credited to Isaiah and regarded as having been borrowed by Micah. Micah, surprisingly, is regarded as having had a more penetrating insight into God's will regarding the Temple than his great contemporary. The Second Isaiah is held to have been a sixth century *limmud* of the First Isaiah and interesting links of thought between them are demonstrated. There were many servants but undoubtedly the Second Isaiah ' recognized his own being as one of the temporal elements in the way of the person for whom the very work of the redemption of the world was reserved.' A brilliant and most provocative book, sometimes obscure, but always interesting. It will be the subject of much controversy.   N.W.P.

Burnaby, J. : *Is the Bible Inspired ?* 1949. Pp. 120. (Duckworth, London. Price : 6s. 0d.)

In this brief book we have a valuable review of the question of the inspiration of the Bible. The traditional view which made God the sole author can no longer be maintained, but the view of Lagrange, that inspiration does not mean more than that the author's mind was illuminated to teach what was true through the medium of ideas which came to him in a natural way, is found to point to a sounder view. This leads to a view of the relativity of authority in the Bible, which in practice is recognized by all. While there is nothing essentially new in its positions, the book should do much to dispel the common assumption that scholarship has rendered obsolete the belief in the inspiration of the Bible. H.H.R.

Caiger, S. L. : *Lives of the Prophets.* 1949. Pp. 334. (S.P.C.K., London. Price : 10s. 6d.)

This book is an expansion of the one published in 1936. It has been supplemented by chapters on Samuel, Elijah and Elisha. It is written in a breezy and confident style but the judicious reader will perhaps not be prepared to take as much for granted regarding the scholarly work underlying the book as the author suggests that he should. This book is scarcely a serious work of scholarship but it may have some value for the general reader. N.W.P.

Cerny, L. : *The Day of Yahweh and some Relevant Problems.* 1948. Pp. viii+120. (Filosofická Fakulta University Karlovy, Prague. Price : Kcs. 95.)

This monograph claims attention as a critical review of modern theories on the origin and history of the conception of the ' Day of Yahweh,' and as a contribution to the subject. The author reviews the theories of Charles, Gunkel and Gressmann, Mowinckel and Morgenstern, and the ' Myth and Ritual ' school, and while rejecting all offers a synthesis which embodies elements from all. He thinks the concept is a fundamentally Israelite one, reached in the context of its own experience and history, though integrating into itself elements taken from mythology and the wider cultic background of contemporary peoples. H.H.R.

Chaine, J. : *Introduction à la lecture des prophètes.* 7th ed., revised. (Études Bibliques.) 1946. Pp. 274+10 plates. (Gabalda, Paris. Price : 4s. 6d.)

This is a useful study of the historical background and message of the prophets, chronologically arranged. It is interesting to observe that while Deutero-Isaiah is ascribed to the eighth century prophet, it is treated separately after Ezekiel. Similarly the visions of Daniel are treated in the setting of the Maccabaean period, though they are ascribed to a sixth century author. Joel and Jonah are both dealt with amongst the post-exilic prophets. The introductory chapter offers an unconvincing division of the prophets into voluntary prophets or nabis, from amongst whom the false prophets were recruited, and prophets by vocation. This division is not alone over-sharp ; it ignores the strange fact that the Bible calls the prophets of vocation by the name which the author would attach only to the voluntary prophets. Nevertheless, the book gives a valuable introduction to the prophets and enables the reader to understand their message in the background of their times.   H.H.R.

COPPENS, J. : *Les harmonies des deux Testaments : essai sur les divers sens des Écritures et sur l'unité de la Révélation.* New edition, revised and enlarged. 1949. (Cahiers de la Nouvelle Revue Théologique, vi.) Pp. 148. (Casterman, Tournai. Belgian Fr. 50.)

This is an important study of the correspondence between the Old and New Testaments, supplied in the footnotes with an amazing volume of reference to modern literature on the subject. While disclaiming the allegorical and typological methods of earlier days, now being revived in some quarters, the author maintains that there is a valid argument from prophecy. No exact correspondence between Old Testament prophecies and New Testament fulfilment is to be found or expected ; nevertheless, there is a broad correspondence between the hope of the Old Testament and its fulfilment in the New that is impressive.   H.H.R.

EBERLE, J. : *Die Bibel im Lichte der Weltgeschichte und Weltliteratur,* ed. by F. König, Band I : *Das Alte Testament.* 1949. Pp. xx+322. (Herder, Vienna.)

Dr. Joseph Eberle was an Austrian journalist, amateur theologian and a profound lover of the Bible. He died in 1947, after some years' suffering in a concentration camp, and this book was largely written during the years of ordeal. Dr. Franz König edits the book, and in a foreword provides an apologia. The main importance of the volume lies in the very large number of apt and generally brief quotations particularly from writings of well-known literary men, where the religious value and beauty of the Bible are extolled. Some O.T. scholars will frequently disagree with the author's own observations ; he has little sympathy with Biblical Criticism, and it is but seldom he shows real insight when dealing with critical problems. But all can profit by a perusal of this book.   B.J.R.

EICHRODT, W. : *Theologie des Alten Testaments.* 2 vols. 1948. Pp. viii+276 ; viii+192. (Evangelische Verlagsanstalt, Berlin.)

Many scholars have been waiting impatiently for the re-issue of this monumental book which has established its place as the most thorough modern treatment of Old Testament Theology. The author is reported to have in preparation a shorter one volume work on the same subject which is likely to be trans-lated into English.   N.W.P.

EPSTEIN, L. M. : *Sex Laws and Customs in Judaism.* 1948. Pp. x+252. (Bloch Publishing Co., New York. Price : $3.50.)

This companion volume to *Marriage Laws in the Bible and the Talmud* (1942) discusses sex relations outside marriage, from the Bible to our time : the moral basis, dress, segregation in public places, private relations, natural and unnatural conduct, purity of mind, harlotry, rape and seduction, adultery, command of jealousy. It is a masterly survey, doing justice both to the different social conditions in different ages and to the interplay between ideal Haggadic standards and legal Halakhic rulings. A number of points receive fresh explanations. The interpretation of Dt. xxii, 20 f. as the counterpart of the law concerning the rebellious son, and the distinction between the legal implications of marriage and betrothal are instances. There is a slight bias towards stressing the saner of the Rabbinic teachings ; and some views are questionable, e.g., that about Ex. xxii, 15 (16) f. and Dt. xxii, 28 f. The author thinks that the two laws were promulgated as one whole. But while it is true that they contemplate the same offence, surely Dt., as often, is later than Ex. and designed to improve upon it. The law in Ex. could be evaded by divorcing the woman soon after marriage ; Dt. puts a stop to that (cp. Dt. xxii, 19, with a similar purpose). Ex. does not fix the price and the woman's father could no doubt make difficulties (cp. Ex. xxi, 22, where ' as the judges determine ' is interpolated, and xxi, 30) ; Dt. demands 50 shekels. Ex. allows the father to keep his daughter ; it is doubtful whether Dt. means to abolish this right—the possibility should not *a priori* be ruled out.

D.D.

FARRER, A. : *A Rebirth of Images.* 1949. Pp. 348. (Dacre Press.)

Apart from its intrinsic interest this book holds an appeal to the members of the S.O.T.S. as the brilliant work of the son of an old and valued member of the Society. Although it belongs in strictness to the field of New Testament studies, yet the one great Christian Apocalypse is so saturated with the Old Testament and with Jewish thought and ritual of the early Christian period that the book cannot fail to be of the greatest interest to Old Testament scholars.

Mr. Farrer has set out to show how the luxuriant imagery of Old Testament apocalyptic with all its intricate symbolism has been fused in the crucible of an intensely Christian and poetic imagination into a great poem. He has broken away from the older source-criticism which reduced the Apocalypse to an unintelligible concatenation of shreds and patches, and demonstrated convincingly the unity of design by which the seven-fold pattern composed of such various elements has been woven into a gorgeous and glowing whole of which the Lamb is the living centre. It is without doubt the most original piece of biblical study that has appeared for many a year.. S.H.H.

FINKELSTEIN, L. : *Ha-Perushim ve-Anshe Keneset Ha-Gedolah* (The Pharisees and the Men of the Great Synagogue). (Texts and Studies of the Jewish Theological Seminary of America, Vol. XV. In Hebrew with a summary in English.) 1950. Pp. xv + 102. (Jewish Theological Seminary of America, New York.)

> This is a bold and far-reaching reconstruction of the social and religious history of the Jews in the Persian and Hellenistic periods, from Ezra to Hillel. The main contentions are that Ezra's reforms were meant to create the nucleus of a Holy Nation and that they did in fact create the Society of Hasideans whose affairs were directed by the so-called ' Great Synagogue,' better understood as the ' Great Court.' For a time the Society enjoyed the support of the High Priest (Simeon II, the Just) and many priests ; and members of the Great Court of the Hasideans were added to the Gerousia. The union broke down after Simeon's death ; and during the troubled times in the first half of the second century B.C. the split became definite and the party-names ' Sadducee ' (adherent of the family of Sadok) and ' Pharisee ' (heretic) appeared. The Pharisees, as continuators of the Society of Hasideans, reorganized themselves on a voluntary basis ; but soon developed inner tensions between pro-priestly and anti-priestly parties, with the result that something resembling ' Government ' and ' Opposition ' arose in the Society. This is reflected in the list of ' Pairs ' at the beginning of *Aboth*. The leader of the stronger party was the *Nasi* or President of the Society as a whole. This is not to be confused with the appointment of Hillel by the Elders of Bathyra, which was an appointment as head of a Temple Commission concerned with Sabbath observance. Hillel held two different *Nasi*-ships.
>
> It may be doubted whether the evidence will warrant the putting of the Sadducee-Pharisee split as early as Finkelstein puts it ; but there can be no doubt at all that we have here some most original, suggestive, and fruitful lines of research.
>
> T.W.M.

FREEDMAN, D. N., and SMART, J. D. : *God has Spoken.* 1949. Pp. 268. (Westminster Press, Philadelphia. Price : $2.00.)

> The sub-title of this book indicates that it is intended to serve as an Introduction to the Old Testament for young people. It rests on critical scholarship, though this is never obtruded, and the primary purpose is to bring out the meaning of the various books of the Old Testament for present-day readers. At the end of each chapter there are suggestions as to how the Biblical book treated can best be read. The title indicates the fundamental point of view of the authors, which is to show that the Old Testament is more than the record of Israelite life and thought. H.H.R.

GASTER, T. H. : *Passover : its History and Traditions.* 1949. Pp. 102. (Henry Schuman, New York. Price : $2.00.)

> A popular account, with suitable reproductions of drawings, etc., of Passover, its origin, development, traditions and customs. The author follows the Frazer folklore tradition in

his explanations, stating his own opinions rather than discussing the problems. The short bibliography is one-sided,
and supports the author's attitude. The original intention
of the rite is to re-cement kinship, both amongst men and with
God. Magical protection rites were introduced, and a supposed
limping dance, which is a mourning rite for the vegetation
god who died six months before and is now rising from the
dead. The miraculous elements in the Exodus-story are
explained from the common mass of folklore. The Hebrews
settled in Goshen during the Hyksos domination ; Seti I
was the Pharoah of the Oppression, and Rameses II of the
Exodus. There are interesting, though short, chapters on the
Passover Seder, the Samaritan Passover, and various Jewish
songs (including Canticles) which are associated with the
festival. N.H.S.

GUITTON, J. : *Le Développement des Idées dans l'Ancien Testament.*
(La Pensée Moderne et le Catholicisme, No. 9.) 1947. Pp. 190.
(Éditions Provençales, Aix-en-Provence. English Price : 7s. 0d.)
The author begins by emphasising the difference between the
ancient oriental mentality and the modern western system.
He traces the development from one to the other from the
Old Testament, through the Apocrypha and on into modern
times. This is worked out on two main themes : God and
Creation, Evil and Retribution. The Babylonian origin of the
flood-story is assumed, and so also is the documentary theory
of the composition of the Pentateuch. Full use is made of the
lateness of the P-creation account. The problem of evil is
traced not as a Protestant would expect through the prophets,
but through Job, Ecclesiastes, Wisdom of Solomon, and 2
Maccabees, so that the final biblical development is Res-
surection of the Body, Immortality of the Soul, Prayers for
the Dead. A short concluding chapter views the problem of
evil in the perspective of Christ. N.H.S.

HARMS, K. : *Die falschen Propheten. Eine biblische Untersuchung.*
1947. Pp. 60. (Vandenhoeck & Ruprecht, Göttingen. Price :
DM. 2.80.)
This work was written by a young scholar in a camp for
prisoners of war in France, and is based by force of circumstance simply upon the text of Luther's Bible and without
access to scholarly works of any kind. One cannot read it
without some awareness of the author's poignant feelings,
and yet for the most part it is an objective study which,
within its limits, is very well done. The writer attempts to
distinguish between the " true " and the " false " prophet in
the broadest sense of the term, paying careful attention to the
grave temptations of the latter, from sheer greed of gain to a
false patriotism, with all that these may involve in confusing
the thought of man with the word of God. A final chapter
also touches upon similar features in the New Testament.
The work may be recommended both for its content and for
its attractive style ; and one cannot but hope that in happier
circumstances the author may be able to make that fuller
contribution to Old Testament studies of which he is clearly
capable. A.R.J.

*Heaton, E. W.: *His Servants the Prophets*. 1949. Pp. 128. (S.C.M. Press Ltd., London. Price : 7s. 6d.)

The author's purpose is to explain in comparatively simple language the part played by the prophets in the course of the biblical revelation. The chapter headings may be quoted as giving sufficient indication of his approach, i.e. : " The Prophetic Writings," " The Vocation of the Prophets," " The Vocation of the People," " Religion and Righteousness," " Faith and Fulfilment." Broadly speaking, he may be said to write from the normal critical standpoint, and it is a merit of the work that he refers the reader carefully and constantly to the biblical text in justification of what he has to say. The value of the book would have been enhanced if he had included a short bibliography for further reading ; but on the whole it may be recommended as being, within its limits, a fresh and somewhat original treatment of what is in danger of becoming a well-worn theme.   A.R.J.

Heidt, W. G. : *Angelology of the Old Testament : a Study in Biblical Theology*. (The Catholic University of America, Studies in Sacred Theology, 2nd series, No. 24.) 1949. Pp. viii+120. (Catholic University of America Press, Washington, D.C. Price : 12s. 0d.)

This is a study of the beliefs about angels reflected in the Old Testament. It begins with a study of the terms used for angels and of their nature and activity in a supramundane world, and then turns to their activities and functions in the world of men. While it is not profound it offers a useful assemblage of Biblical materials. For the chapter dealing with the problem created by the merging of the angel into God in some contexts, the author might with advantage have studied A. R. Johnson's monograph *The One and the Many in the Israelite Conception of God*.   H.H.R.

Hempel, J. : *Worte der Profeten in neuer Uebertragung und mit Erläuterungen*. 1949. Pp. 324. (Alfred Töpelmann, Berlin. Price : 18s. 0d.)

This unpretentious-looking volume has that continuously exciting quality which one has come to associate with Professor Hempel's writings. He has packed into small compass an amazing range of knowledge and interesting comment. A notable feature of the book is the copious quotations from the prophetic writings which are given in a new translation, the literary merit of which is considerable. In particular some of the passages are in a most effective trochaic measure which conveys a sense of the vigour of the original. The author draws freely on the New Testament for parallels to the Old Testament.

The book falls into three main divisions. The first deals with the historical and literary framework and discusses the character and value of the stories about the prophets. The second analyses the nature of the prophet's call and then offers a study of the individual prophets in their historical succession. Some of them like Amos and Hosea are rather briefly treated. Perhaps the highlight of the book is the account of Jeremiah, Ezekiel and the second Isaiah. With the exception of chh. xl-xlviii, the Book of Ezekiel is treated as substantially a unity. The third section discusses the prophetic theology in more systematic fashion under the heads of ethical mono-theism, human morality, the prophetic view of the world and nature including a study of the prophetic view of history and finally the prophetic eschatology. In the discussion of history it is argued that the prophetic faith involved the renunciation of all political calculation. It is quite impossible in a brief notice to do justice to the rich quality of this book.

N.W.P.

HERMANIUK, M. : *La Parabole Evangélique. Enquête exégétique et critique.* (Universitas Catholica Lovaniensis. Dissertationes ad gradum magistri in Facultate Theologica consequendum conscriptae. II, 38.) 1947. Pp. 498. (Desclée, de Brouwer & Cie, Bruges-Paris. Bibliotheca Alfonsiana, Louvain. Price : £1 17s. 6d.)

The reason for including this volume in a Book List of the Society for Old Testament Study is to be found in the fact that the author devotes a quarter of his space to a discussion of the term *māshāl* as found both in the Old Testament and in the rabbinic literature of the Tannaitic period. On the whole the survey of its use and possible meanings is quite well done, and there can be no doubt about the importance of the author's contribution to our understanding of this somewhat enigmatic term, not least in his emphasis upon its early symbolic aspect.

A.R.J.

*HIGGINS, A. J. B. : *The Christian Significance of the Old Testament.* 1949. Pp. 190. (Independent Press, London. Price : 8s. 6d.)

A valuable book, written for the ordinary educated Christian, designed to show why the Old Testament is part of the Christian Scriptures and how it should be understood. The first chapter is devoted to Marcion, whose heresy in its modern form of the neglect of the Old Testament this study is designed to attack. The difficulties of the Old Testament are examined, and it is shown that many of them arise from an outlook which has no valid authority for the Christian— an outlook which indeed was largely outgrown within the Old Testament, and which does not mark the higher levels of Old Testament thought. The forward look of much of the Old Testament is next studied and it is shown how the Church found Christ to respond to this forward look. In particular the missionary call of the Old Testament and the response to that call in the activity of the Church is given the focus of attention. Sound in scholarship, and in judgement—which is the hallmark of scholarship—this little book should be widely useful.

H.H.R.

HOOKE, S. H. : *The Kingdom of God in the Experience of Jesus.*
1949. Pp. 160. (Duckworth, London. Price : 6s. 0d.)

> This is primarily a study of the Synoptic Gospels, abounding
> in illuminating suggestions for the student of the New Testa-
> ment. Its relevance to the Old Testament student is seen in
> its constant references to the background of Old Testament
> thought that lies behind the experiences and sayings of Jesus,
> and also in its two introductory chapters, which deal with early
> ideas of divine kinship, in a wider than Israelite setting, and
> with divine kingship in Hebrew religion. The latter chapter
> deals mainly with the transmutation of the idea of divine
> kingship in Israel under prophetic guidance, as a preparation
> for the conception of the Kingdom of God that is found in the
> New Testament. H.H.R.

JOHNSON, A. R. : *The Vitality of the Individual in the Thought of
Ancient Israel.* 1949. Pp. 108. (University of Wales Press, Cardiff.
Price : 6s. 0d.)

> This monograph is in some respects a sequel to the author's
> earlier one entitled ' The One and the Many in the Israelite
> Conception of God.' It is, however, announced as the first
> of a series. Professor Johnson starts from Pedersen's conception
> of *nephesh* as the complete personality, ' the grasping of a
> totality,' ' a unified, manifestation of vital power ' which
> can act through ' extensions of the personality.' There follows
> a long and careful discussion of the series of terms whose usage
> throws light on the Hebrew view of man. Pride of place goes
> to *nephesh* and special attention is paid to the ebb and flow of
> vitality which is characteristic of it. Other terms discussed are
> *ruah* (which throws further light on the conception of man as a
> psycho-physical organism and leads to the thought of Yahweh
> as the ' Giver of Life ') and the words for ' flesh,' ' head,'
> ' face,' ' palate,' ' tongue,' ' hand,' ' blood,' ' heart,' etc.
> Incidentally the author furnishes a complete refutation of
> Wheeler Robinson's ' diffused consciousness' theory, ex-
> plaining the phenomena which led to it as instances of synec-
> doche. A concluding section deals with the Hebrew conception
> of ' life ' and ' death ' as not always clearly distinguished,
> since by ' life ' is frequently meant life in its fullness and by
> ' death ' any form of weakness. There is close agreement
> here with the conclusions of Ch. Barth's *Die Errettung vom
> Tode.* Professor Johnson's semantic study is indispensable
> to the student of Hebrew thought both for its brilliant insights
> and for its unusually complete documentation. N.W.P.

JUNKER, H. : *Jobs Leid, Streit und Sieg oder Ein Mensch ringt mit dem
Schicksal und mit Gott.* (Die Biblische Schatzkammer.) 1948.
Pp. 86. (Herder, Freiburg im Breisgau.)

> The *Biblische Schatzkammer*, the series to which this book
> belongs, aims at the encouragement of the reading of the
> Bible by giving introductions to Scripture themes. Here, on
> Job's suffering, conflict and victory we have an extremely

able piece of exegesis, written, without obtruding an expert's knowledge, in a beautifully clear style, interesting in its narrative and in the study of an inner struggle of a man with his friends and with God. Dr. Junker's work is intended for a wider circle than that of O.T. scholars, and thus does not embrace in its scope any detailed discussion of the literary problems of Job, but his treatment of difficult passages, for example xix, 25-27, and of the hymn upon Wisdom (ch. xxviii) is a sample as his translation of these and other passages is admirable. In the author's opinion ch. xxviii, which he likens to the song of the chorus in a Greek tragedy, is not an interpolation but fits well into the framework of the book's thought. In view of the excellence of this study in Job, its clarity in dealing with complex elements of emotion, reason and faith, it is disappointing to discover that no indication is given of this book's price. O.S.R.

KNIGHT, G. A. F. : *From Moses to Paul. A Christological Study in the Light of our Hebraic Heritage.* 1949. Pp. 194. (Lutterworth Press, London. Price : 15s. 0d.)

This work is an attempt to bridge the gulf between Judaism and Christianity by showing that the Christian doctrine of the Incarnation in no way conflicts with the monotheistic principle which is inherent in the Jewish faith. The approach is made through a study of Hebrew psychology, and is based primarily upon the work of Johs. Pedersen, H. Wheeler Robinson, W. J. Phythian-Adams and, finally, the writer of this note, whose own approach to this subject in terms of the " extensions " of Yahweh's personality appears to provide the main line of argument. Unfortunately, while the author at times shows evidence of a discerning mind, he has failed to realize that the validity of this approach can only be established, if at all, by long and patient examination of the relevant data in all their detail. As it is, he shows little evidence of having attempted a careful and thorough survey of the original sources ; and even his reading of secondary works is sadly limited. His discussion of what he calls " The Evidence of the Human ' Nephesh '," which is basic to the ensuing argument, is painfully superficial ; and it is repellent to find that thereafter he is able to refer constantly to " the *nephesh* of God " or " the divine *nephesh*." Accordingly, while the author may be commended for his eagerness to be of service as a mediator and for his enthusiasm with regard to the subject, one cannot but deplore the fact that he has ventured to treat so intricate a theme in this immature and, one fears, somewhat misleading way. A.R.J.

KÖHLER, L. : *Theologie des Alten Testaments.* 1949. Pp. xii+252. (Mohr, Tübingen.)

A second edition of this important book for the re-issue of which many who failed to procure the first edition will be grateful. Originally published in 1936. N.W.P.

LANGTON, E. : *Essentials of Demonology. A Study of Jewish and Christian Doctrine : Its Origin and Development.* 1949. Pp. xx+234. (Epworth Press, London. Price : 15s. 0d.)

The author's earlier work *Good and Evil Spirits* was noted in the Book List, for 1946, p. 47. The present work is marked by the same qualities, and it offers an excellent summary of information on the Semitic background of the demonology of the Old Testament, and a survey of the ideas in this field which are to be found in the Old Testament and Rabbinic Literature, together with a study of their relation to Persian ideas. The author has read widely, and while there is little that is original in his views, his assembly of material in this field is most praiseworthy. He is not always abreast of recent knowledge—e.g., the flying serpent ought not to be discussed without reference to Ras Shamra texts (p. 38)— and there are gaps in the bibliography ; but there are few works of which this could not be said. There is a brief Foreword by C. Ryder Smith. H.H.R.

MacLAURIN, E. C. B. : *The Origin of the Hebrew Sacrificial System.* 1948. Pp. 30. (Sydney and Melbourne Publishing Co., Sydney. Price : 2s. 6d.)

The aim of the author of this monograph is to show that blood-sacrifice is an addition to Hebrew religion, and that the prophets were wholly against it. The whole treatment of the subject is unsatisfactory. The selection of the material is arbitrary ; the transliteration of the Hebrew is confusing, and the author's knowledge of the relevant literature limited. N.H.S.

MEIKLEJOHN, W. : *The Prophet of Hope. A Study of the Prophet Jeremiah.* 1949. Pp. 72. (Church of Scotland Publications Department. Price : 1s. 6d.)

Published for the Church of Scotland Youth Committee. Stresses that Jeremiah stood nearer to the problems of to-day than the Victorians did. The main lines of exposition follow Skinner's " Prophecy and Religion." There is a questionnaire for further study. C.R.N.

MENDELSOHN, I. : *Slavery in the ancient Near East.* 1949. Pp. vi+162. (O.U.P., New York. Price : $5.00.)

This small work is divided into three chapters entitled : I Sources of Slavery ; II Legal Status ; III The Economic Role of Slavery. Each chapter is then sub-divided into from 5 to 9 sections. The author has thus gathered together all that is known of Sumerian, Babylonian and Assyrian, as well as Hebrew slavery and presented it in readable form. His treatment of the subject is not profound ; it is a descriptive account of the institution of slavery at once sensible and for the most part trustworthy, even though the author may be thought here and there to err in details of interpretation ; for example, the Babylonian *muškênu(m)* ' villein ' belonging

278

to a temple is translated on p. 56, ' commoner ' and on p. 109, ' share-cropper '; both renderings cannot be, and neither probably is, right. An index of Semitic words, which would have brought this discrepancy to light, would have been very helpful to the student and far more useful than the list of scholars who are advertised by having their views expounded or refuted. There are, however, numerous and useful notes with full references to the texts which the author (very often *in extenso*) cites. Altogether the book is well worth obtaining (for no aspect of the subject seems to be overlooked), even if it is not an inspiring work.   G.R.D.

MOORTGAT, A. : *Tammuz, der Unsterblichkeitsglaube in der altorient-alischen Bildkunst.* 1949. Pp. viii+156, with 62 plates. (Walter de Gruyter & Co., Berlin. Price : DM. 25.)

Archaeology and art-history are very fallible guides to the interpretation of ideas, and even when there is a parallel literary tradition, as with the peoples of the Ancient East, contact between the two forms of expression is not always obvious. This general truth is well exemplified in the book here under notice, which is a thoroughgoing attempt to infer from the artistic products of early Western Asia a widespread underlying belief in ' immortality,' concerning which the texts give certain indications of their own, and to use the two kinds of evidence as mutually explanatory. Such essays as this, congenial as they are to some modes of thought, have an air of constraint, for they seem obliged to prove too much in order to establish something. This is very noticeable in Dr. Moortgat's book, nearly one half of which consists of 62 plates illustrating, together with many figures in the text, most of the best-known monuments, large and small, of the old Western Asiatic world, and the implication that all of these diverse things were variously inspired by one single idea at once provokes incredulity. The author's argument is derived principally from the cylinder-seals ; from certain figures, emblems, and motives which first appear in the last pre-historic period he deduces a doctrine of ' Unsterblichkeit,' the meaning of which, in his sense, is not so much immortality (for of such a notion, in the modern acceptation, there is no evidence) as constant renewal of life. His theme, in short, is the dying god, as the title of ' Tammuz ' implies, but he con-siders that the resurrection of this figure inspired a hope of perpetual life among his worshippers, especially kings, who partook of the divine nature. The belief in this kind of ' immortality ' is followed, in a final chapter, through the art of those whom the author calls ' Bergvölker,' i.e., the peoples of northern Mesopotamia, Anatolia, and Assyria. Strained as much of this appears, and over-simplified to serve a single end, no enquiry is wasted which attempts to penetrate the meaning of an ancient art which sometimes looks out so enigmatically from contexts otherwise better understood. There are many suggestive observations in Dr. Moortgat's book, even for those who are not persuaded by his thesis.
                                                                            C.J.G.

MOWINCKEL, S. : *Jesaja.* 1949. Pp. 162. (Gyldendal Norsk Forlag, Oslo. Price : 8s. 6d.)

> This short study is one of a series of popular handbooks dealing with great religious personalities (*Religionens stormenn*). It is a masterly introduction to the understanding of the prophet's environment and his message. Many passages from the text of Isaiah, in the author's own felicitous rendering, are skilfully introduced, making the book, in parts, almost a running commentary. It is interesting to note that the interpretation of the Immanuel prophecy in Isaiah vii, which is here offered differs both from that given in *Profeten Jesaja* (1925), in that the prophecy is taken as promise and not threat, and also from that in *De senere profeter* (Book List, 1948, p. 9) in that the '*alma* is identified with the queen.
>
> G.W.A.

*NORTH, C. R. : *The Thought of the Old Testament.* 1949. Pp. 62. (Epworth Press, London. Price : 3s. 0d.)

> A characteristically lucid presentation of the thought of the Old Testament reached by making a cross section in the post-Exilic period. It consists of three lectures originally delivered to day-school teachers and it can be warmly commended to a corresponding class of readers. The first chapter deals with the Hebrew concept of God as one who reveals Himself primarily in history and especially in the Covenant. The second chapter deals with the Hebrew view of the world and of man's place in it. The third chapter deals with moral evil and God's ways of dealing with it. Particular attention is paid to the corporate emphasis in Hebrew religion. Professor North is at pains to shows that Old Testament religion was essentially a religion of grace and as such was a foreshadowing of Christianity.
>
> N.W.P.

OBERSTEINER, J. : *Die Christusbotschaft des Alten Testamentes.* 1947. Pp. 254. (Herder, Vienna. Price : S. 30, sfr. 13.50.)

> The author studies about forty Old Testament passages which have been traditionally interpreted by the Church as prophecies of Christ, and argues for the traditional interpretation. He is well acquainted with the writings of scholars who adopt different views, and in his notes gathered at the end of the volume gives many references to them. But he will have none of their ' rationalism.' He holds that the messianic message is adumbrated in the historical books, developed in the Psalms and perfected in the prophets, and maintains that the passages studied are direct prophecies, specific and detailed, of the birth, life and work of Christ. His argument will rarely persuade those who do not accept its conclusions before they read it, or who are unwilling to divorce the passages from their context. H.H.R.

OOSTERHOFF, B. J. : *De Vreze des Heren in het Oude Testament.* 1949. (Kemink en Zoon, N.V. Utrecht.)

> The author examines in this book, a thesis of the University of Utrecht, the terminology on the Fear of God (*jir'at Jahwe* and synonyms) successively in the Pentateuch, the historical

and the prophetic books, the Psalms, the Wisdom literature, Nehemiah and Chronicles. The inquiry lacks in many respects the necessary subtlety of distinction ; thus it does not show that *jir'at Jahwe* more than once has the signification of " religion." Most of all we miss a good survey of the use of the words in the different sources of the O.T. The older literature on this theme is only enumerated, its contents are not critically digested in the author's own examination.

Th.C.V.

VAN DER PLOEG, J. : *Missiegedachten in de H. Schrift.* 1949. Pp. 88. (N. V. Gooi & Sticht, Hilversum.)

The four chapters of this work deal with Missionary Thought in the Old Testament, the Missionary Work and Teaching of Jesus, Apostolic Missionary Teaching, and Paul, the Apostle of the Gentiles. In the chapter dealing with the Old Testament there is a brief survey of the relevant passages of Scripture, and the missionary message is traced back to monotheism, which is ascribed to Moses. This ascription is defended by the question how monotheism came into Israel if not through Moses. While the reviewer finds the seeds of monotheism in the work of Moses, he is doubtful of the ascription of full monotheism to him. He agrees that missionary activity is the corollary of monotheism and that there is an incipient universalism, just as there is an incipient monotheism, long before the explicit monotheism and universalism of Deutero-Isaiah. The treatment throughout is simple and clear, and there are no references to other literature, other than the Bible, or discussion of disputed questions.   H.H.R.

PROCKSCH, O. : *Theologie des Alten Testaments.* 2 Lieferungen. 1949. Pp. 384. (C. Bertelsmann, Gütersloh. Price : £1 1s. 0d.)

This is an important publication and a welcome legacy from a great and influential teacher. The whole work of which only half is yet available, is to fall into two parts, the first dealing with the historical world of Israel in its successive periods, the second a systematic study of the ideas " which lie on the horizon and determine the whole theological position. Introductory sections of a strongly Christological character deal with the theology of history and of the Old Testament and make clear the author's fundamental conviction that it is through Christ that Christians stand in an existential relation to the faith of the Old Testament. From this point of view both the historical and systematic parts of the book are to be written. There is also a useful sketch of the history of Old Testament theology.

The historical part has three sections (i) the early prophetic period (including the patriarchal and the Mosaic), (ii) the period of the monarchy with special reference to the prophets, (iii) the period of the Church-State (not yet complete).

Only a few points of interest out of many can be alluded to. Procksch rejects Noth's view of the Habiru and also the

Kenite hypothesis. He recognizes two original divisions of the Hebrew people, an Israel-Leah group associated with Shechem and a Jacob-Rachel group associated with the southern sanctuaries. Levi is specially linked with Qadesh. To Shiloh we owe the Book of the Covenant and the earliest version of the national ' Sage ' of Israel. Of quite special interest is the section on the Hebrew monarchy—its relation to prophets, priests and people and to the Messianic hope. Emphasis is laid on the prophetic opposition to the priesthood and on the non-political reference of the prophetic message. In Isaiah ch. vii, he translates '*almah* by ' virgin.' Deuteronomy is associated with the circle of Isaiah's disciples and, unlike von Rad, Procksch denies that the Levites had any hand in it. The original form of the Priestly Code is dated before the Exile. At times one has the feeling that dogmatic considerations may have unduly affected the author's judgement. N.W.P.

RABAST, K. : *Das apodiktische Recht im Deuteronomium und im Heiligkeitsgesetz.* 1948. Pp. 48. (Heimatdienstverlag, Berlin-Hermsdorf.)

The author of this small book sees two kinds or law, which he describes respectively as *kasuistisch* and *apodiktisch*, in the Pentateuch ; the former contains the provisions (*mišpāṭîm*) set out in conditional form (e.g., Ex. xxi, 18-19), while the latter contains the rules (*huqqîm*) promulgated in imperative form or as commands (e.g., Ex. xxi, 17). He thinks that the ' casuistic ' law, which uses the same conditional form as the other great collections of Laws in the East (those of the Babylonians and Assyrians as also of the Hittites) and which deals with secular affairs, is the older system and is of non-Israelite origin. He regards the ' apodictic ' law, which is preserved in its purest form in the Book of the Covenant and is often expressed in rhythmical form, as a native Israelite creation ; it is the law, commonly religious in tenour, expounded by the priests at the sanctuaries of Yahweh and may be described as *gottgebunden jahvistisch und volksgebunden israelitisch.* The theory is based on the well-known work of Alt, but carried to excess ; and a good deal of interchange or confusion between the two types of law has to be allowed to make it work, whereby the value of the text is considerably diminished. Further, it is open to the obvious criticism that the origin and nature of a law is less surely discovered from its form than from its content. G.R.D.

VON RAD, G. : *Der Prophet Jona.* 1950. Pp. 16. (Laetare-Verlag, Nürnberg.)

In this short study the author gives a résumé of the book which he considers primarily as a narrative such as the narratives of the earlier prophets but more complex. It is a late document and is the consummation of its particular category of literature. The universality of God's purpose is shown in the setting of the consciousness of spiritual particularism, giving the work great value as a subjective study of Jonah—or Israel. The author points out many elements which combine to enhance the value of such self-analysis, not least that of humour and burlesque tempered with serious criticism subtle though trenchant.   J.G.

REED, W. L. : *The Asherah in the Old Testament.* 1949. Pp. 116. (Texas Christian University, Fort Worth, Texas. Price : 11s. 6d.)

The volume is a reproduction by photographic process from the original typescript. It is an extension of the author's Ph.D. thesis at Yale. The thesis is a careful, thorough, and well-balanced study of all the available evidence in the Old Testament, the Versions, archaeology. The author's conclusion is that the ' wooden-pole ' theory should be abandoned. Asherah is the name of a goddess and also of her image. The struggle against Baalism also involved therefore a fight against the fertility cult of Asherah. The volume contains fifteen reproductions of figures ' erroneously identified as the Asherah,' and a full bibliography.   N.H.S.

Religion och Bibel (Nathan Söderblom-Sällskapets Årsbok) VIII. 1949. Pp. iv+26. (C. W. K. Gleerup, Lund. Price : Kr. 2.)

This issue contains but one article, viz., Engnell's presidential address to the Nathan Söderblom Society. His subject is " The Origin and Development of the Prophetic Movement " ; and he holds that its roots lie in both Israelite and Canaanite life, and deplores attempts to distinguish sharply between seer and nabi, between prophets who were cultic and non-cultic, ecstatic and non-ecstatic, professional and non-professional, gregarious and solitary, particularly when such distinctions are linked with a tidy chronological scheme. The differentia of the true Yahwistic prophet lies not in such distinctions but in his proclamation of the Jerusalemite High God and ' Kingship ideology.' The lecture is to appear in expanded form in English in *Studia Theologica.*   G.W.A.

ROELLENBLECK, E. : *Magna Mater im Alten Testament. Eine psycho-analytische Untersuchung.* 1949. Pp. 190. (Claassen & Roether, Darmstadt. Price : 11s. 6d.)

Happily the prospective reader of this book is warned by the sub-title what he may expect ; for, as Freud himself has shown by his own excursion into the field of Old Testament studies, the attempt to apply modern psycho-analytical theories to the literary remains of more than two millennia ago opens the door to what may well become a riot of subjectivity, which pays little or no regard to the findings of modern critical study concerning the records in question. In this particular work the Hebrews beçome a most lively " corporate " personality. which may be pysycho-analysed with quite entertaining, if equally unconvincing results. Despite its vagaries and excesses, the book has its own peculiar interest ; but it affords little if any help towards a sound and balanced interpretation of the Old Testament.   A.R.J.

ROSENTHAL, J. : *Ḥiwi al-Balkhi : a Comparative Study.* 1949. Pp. iv+60. (Dropsie College, Philadelphia.)

This is a study of a Jewish rationalist, who flourished in Persia in the ninth century A.D., and who wrote a book attacking the Bible and its God by propounding two hundred questions or criticisms. Many of the still familiar difficulties are found here. Like so many moderns of the same type the author failed to realize that his difficulties were valid not against the Bible, but against an untenable view of the Bible. The value of Dr. Rosenthal's study, however, is in the succeeding chapters, in which he traces the origin of Ḥiwi's ideas to Zoroastrian, Islamic and Gnostic sources.   H.H.R.

ROWLEY, H. H. : *The Authority of the Bible.* (Joseph Smith Memorial Lecture.) 1950. Pp. 20. (Overdale College, Selly Oak, Birmingham. Price : 1s. 3d.)

In this pamphlet Professor Rowley deals with a problem of very great importance. He draws a useful distinction between the words authority, inspiration and revelation when applied to the Bible, yet shows that they are intimately connected. In discussing the authority of the Bible he takes pains to guard on the one hand against the false objectivism of bibliolatry and on the other against any mere subjectivism. We cannot fall back upon the authority of the Church or any body of men within the Church.

The Bible itself in both its parts contains impressive evidence of the hand of God. In the Exodus complex in the Old Testament, for example, and in the complex of the Cross of Christ and its sequel in the New Testament we have expectations and events answering to these expectations which are not related causally either forwards or backwards. Similarly with the Messianic and related expectations in the Old Testament and their fulfilment in Christ. It is urged that the hypothesis that all this is the Lord's doing is both reasonable and adequate. Reason does not render faith superfluous but it can demonstrate that faith is intellectually respectable.

N.W.P.

ROY, A. : *La Prière de l'Église.* 1948. Pp. 344. (Beauchesne et ses fils, Paris. English price : 7s. 6d.)

A small (6 by 4½ inches) volume with paper backs, containing a rhythmical translation of the Psalter. The order follows the liturgical usage of the Roman Breviary, but three separate indices are appended, so that any particular psalm can be found without difficulty. The translation is from the Hebrew (the imprimatur is diocesan), but the numeration is that of the Vulgate. A very pleasing and elegant French rendering, with helpful sub-titles to each psalm and occasional footnotes.

N.H.S.

SCHEDL, C. : *Sieben Thesen wider äes Alten Testaments Verächter*.
1948. Pp. 30. (Herder, Vienna. Price : S. 3.80, sfr. 1.60.)

The seven theses briefly discussed in this pamphlet by an
Austrian Redemptorist are that the Old Testament is not old
in the sense of being antiquated ; that it is neither mythical
nor fictional ; that it is the history of God's way with men ;
that it is indeed *Heilsgeschichte* : that it is not to be separated
from the New ; that it is to be essentially distinguished from
Judaism ; and that it is to be acknowledged for what it is by
all Christians. The theses with the author's comments on them
were delivered as an inaugural lecture to the Catholic Faculty
of Vienna University on 15th October, 1947.   J.M.T.B.

SCHEMPP, P. : *Die Geschichte und Predigt vom Sündenfall*. 1946. Pp.
142. (Chr. Kaiser, Munich. Price : 7s. 0d.)

An exegetical interpretation of the Fall and the Expulsion
from Eden. The author finds that this ancient account speaks
' without doubt ' to us in this present time of Christ. We share
the guilt of the ' first Adam,' and our restoration to happiness
is to be found in the promised ' second Adam.' The volume is
continuous, without any divisions into chapters or headings.
                                                    N.H.S.

SMART, W. A. : *Still the Bible Speaks*. 1948. Pp. 172. (Abingdon-
Cokesbury Press, New York, and Nashville. Price : $1.75.)

An extremely suggestive and well-written study of the
abiding worth of the Scriptures. The author considers the
widespread neglect of the Bible to-day, and the interest in it
in some quarters as a literary classic or the approach to it
from the point of view of Functional Religion, and finds these
wholly inadequate. Its centre is not man but God, and while
it is frankly hard to read with understanding, it is supremely
important so to read it. The author follows the revelation
through both Testaments, not neglecting the oft neglected
apocalyptic element. His book rests on modern scholarship,
and is throughout infused with a prophetic quality rather than
coldly academic. It abounds in shrewd and penetrating observations, both on the modern world and on the message of
the Bible.   H.H.R.

SNELL, H. C. : *Ancient Israel : its Story and Meaning*. 1948. Pp.
xvi+302. (H. C. Snell, Institute of Religion, Logan, Utah.)

This is intended as a simple text-book for the student of the
history of Israel, with suggested exercises at the end of each
chapter, and collateral reading hints. The author, who is a
former pupil of Professor Irwin's, is heavily dependent on
Oesterley and Robinson's *History of Israel*, and observes that
' if an historical work could ever be definitive, theirs could
well claim such status.' In the final chapter the author assesses
Israel's meaning for the world. This is in accordance with the
principle which he states in his preface, that we must first
approach the Bible as history and see the process of its revelation through the eyes of those who first received it, before
we can perceive its meaning for us.   H.H.R.

STÜVEN, H. : *Die biblische Schöpfungsgeschichte übersetzt und in ihrer poetischen Urform wiederhergesetellt.* 1949. Pp. 20+36 (tables and notes). (Eilenburg, Leipzig.)

> This monograph is composed of reproductions of typescript and handscript. The author has sought to restore the Creation-story of Gen. i, 1-ii, 4a, to what he believes was its original poetic form of double-stressed lines, with key-words, rhymes, antitheses, and repetitions. Subjective and unconvincing.
>
> N.H.S.

VISCHER, W. : *The Witness of the Old Testament to Christ.* I. *The Pentateuch*, translated by A. B. Crabtree. 1949. Pp. 264. (Lutterworth Press, London. Price : £1 5s. 0d.)

VISCHER, W. : *La Loi ou les Cinq Livres de Moïse*, translated by M. Carrez. 1949. Pp. 356. (Delachaux et Niestlé, Neuchatel and Paris. Price : Swiss Fr. 6.50.)

> These are the English and French translations of the first volume of Vischer's *Christuszeugnis des Alten Testaments* (see Book List, 1946, p. 53, for note on vol. ii). Critical questions are ignored and the New Testament is read into the Old to an excessive degree. While the reviewer maintains a fundamental unity in the Bible and finds a real witness to Christ in the Old Testament, he dissents strongly from Vischer's method and uncritical equations—such as the equation of the stranger who wrestled with Jacob at the Jabbok with Christ. Theology cannot at the same time be based on the Bible and determine its exegesis. H.H.R.

(DE VISSCHER, F.) : *Mélanges Fernand De Visscher*, 2 vols. (Revue Internationale des Droits de l'Antiquité, II and III). 1949. Pp. xlviii+552, and 610. (Office International de Librairie, Brussels. Price : B. Frs. 250 each vol.)

> This work, dedicated to the distinguished Belgian legal historian, contains four articles here to be noticed ; the first three are in French. (1) Demangel discusses stratagems in the Greek religion, e.g., the flowing of water from the mouth of a statue of Asclepios at Epidaurus. (2) Imbert argues that in the three centuries after becoming the state religion, Christianity produced no change in the temporal position of slaves ; but by giving them something like spiritual equality, it did prepare reforms. (3) Verdam points out that, in the Old Testament, the place of communal responsibility is in the field of *fas*, not *ius* ; that the idea of individual responsibility is older than most scholars assume ; and that the story of Joseph contains valuable material. Cp. already Daube, *Studies in Biblical Law*, whom Verdam criticises, often on the basis of mistranslation (e.g., he says, vol. 2, p. 415, that Daube calls Ex. xxi, 31, an empty phrase, while in reality Daube writes that it ' is by no means an empty phrase '). (4) According to Daube, the Bible, except in proper codes, is far more interested in acts done in error than in acts done by accident ; the main reason being the tragic quality of the former, which is absent from the latter. D.D.

VRIEZEN, TH. C.: *Hoofdlijnen der Theologie van Het Oude Testament.*
1950. Pp. 302. (H. Veenman & Zonen, Wageningen.)

On a slightly larger scale than Köhler's *Theologie des Alten Testaments*, this volume by a well-known Dutch scholar is thoroughly up-to-date and is characterized by a very balanced judgement. In the opening sections Vriezen deals in a stimulating manner with the current debate on the nature of Old Testament Theology. He emphasizes the uniqueness of Israel's faith without ignoring the light shed on it by comparative religion. He insists that the governing thought of Christ as the fulfilment of the Old Testament necessitates treating the Old Testament record as that of a historical movement culminating in Christ. History, as the vehicle of revelation, must be taken in all seriousness and it must be frankly recognized that Israel's knowledge of God became broader and deeper as the centuries passed.

In a short but quite excellent historical sketch the author shows a clear sense of the importance of the Mosaic period and the relation of the prophets to it.

Vriezen joins issue with Vischer and Miskotte on the nature of the Bible as the Word of God. He draws the necessary distinction between Christ as the Word made flesh and the Scriptures as the Word of God indirectly and metaphorically. He will not allow Old Testament Theology to be dominated by Christology, as that means imposing a system of thought on the Old Testament and ignoring the difference of the Testaments. Incidentally Vriezen also takes sides against Buber's 'aesthetic' approach to Old Testament Theology.

The main part of the book deals with the content of Old Testament Theology. He states at the outset that the knowledge of God according to the Old Testament is not purely intellectual but is in essence man's fellowship in faith and trust with God. God speaks His word within a relationship which He has created. The main subject matter is dealt with under the headings—God, Men, the Communion of God and Men (ending with a discussion of Hebrew piety as men's response to God exemplified specially by the Psalter), the communion of men with men (ethics) and the relation of God, Man and World to each other. It is worthy of note that in dealing with the last topic Vriezen joins issue with Eichrodt and argues that in the Old Testament view of Creation there is no turning away from an anthropocentric to a cosmic world view. This is a notable book.   N.W.P.

*WOODS, J.: *The Old Testament in the Church.* 1949. Pp. x+150.
(S.P.C.K., London. Price: 9s. 6d.)

The aim of this book is to bring out the significance of the Old Testament for the Christian Church, and to show that while it is not regulative for Christian thinking it is yet not superseded. Despite the number of books recently written with this purpose, this is by no means superfluous. It has a quality of style, at times arresting, which will commend it to the readers for whom it is designed. It makes no claim to original scholarship, but rests on the work of many well-known scholars. It is, indeed, surprising that the author, living in West Africa, should have access to so many first-class books as figure in his Bibliography. But while he uses the fruits of scholarship, his primary interest goes beyond scholarship. At the end of the book there are Notes on the Text and Canon of the Old Testament and on Language. These are necessarily brief, but well-informed. The absence of any reference to the recently discovered Scrolls and Fragments in the section dealing with Hebrew texts is to be accounted for by the fact that the manuscript was sent to the Publisher in 1945, since when the writer has been in Nigeria.   H.H.R.

ZIMMERLI, W. : *Das Menschenbild des Alten Testamentes.* (Theologische Existenz Heute : neue Folge 14). 1949. Pp. 28. (Kaiser, Munich. Price : 2s. 6d.),

This brief but closely packed monograph contains a sketch of an Old Testament anthropology. It is claimed that, in spite of the variety of views about man in the Old Testament, there are a number of constants. The Old Testament betrays the influence of international culture upon its anthropology but stamps it with new meaning. The central thought is that of man's meeting with God in the Exodus and in the subsequent decisions of history. In this encounter God makes His demand for man's obedience. The Old Testament deals not with man as an autonomous being but with man as the being called by and responsible to God. It deals further with the whole man in this world, and permits no escape into mysticism or idealism. It is through Christ who fulfils the Old Testament that Israel's anthropology is relevant to us. In an analysis of the Yahwistic and Priestly anthropologies and that found in Chronicles it is shown that in all alike man is the object of God's mercy and is a being designed for fellowship with his neighbour. Sin is an historical fact but is not part of the definition of man. It is dealt with by God's judgement and mercy.   N.W.P.

POST-BIBLICAL JUDAISM

BAECK, L. : *The Pharisees and Other Essays.* 1947. Pp. viii+164. (Schocken Books, New York. Price : $3.00.)

The essays here collected are : The Pharisees, Tradition in Judaism, Judaism in the Church, Origin of Jewish Mysticism, Greek and Jewish Preaching, Two World Views Compared, The Character of Judaism. While strictly scholarly, they contain a message which ought to reach a wide public. Occasionally recent trends are perhaps not sufficiently considered. Is there nothing in T. W. Manson's derivation of ' Pharisees ' from ' Persians '? Was abstention from writing in the Talmudic age complete ? Is it only Jewish mysticism that began by being transmitted orally ? Can we distinguish sharply between the philosophical creeds, propagated by means of sermons, and the mystery religions, meant for those who could not fathom philosophy and dispensing with sermons ? But these are small points. It is an inspiring book. The translation from the German is nearly always satisfactory.   D.D.

HERSHMAN, A. M. : *The Code of Maimonides, Book Fourteen, The Book of Judges, Translated from the Hebrew* (Yale Juadaica Series, vol. III). 1949. Pp. xxvi+336. (Yale University Press, New Haven ; Geoffrey Cumberlege, London. Price : $5.00 ; £2 0s. 0d.)

A fine translation—and the first complete one—of the 13th book of the Mishneh Torah, divided by Maimonides into five chapters : Sanhedrin, evidence, rebels (validity of precedents, rebellious elder, cursing or striking one's parent, rebellious son), mourning, kings (appointment, duties, wars, Noachian commandments, Messiah). The author makes full use of manuscripts and old editions. In a future edition, however, a list of previous translations of the various parts of this book would be welcome. The re-arrangement of 5.7.11 spoils the meaning ; according to Maimonides, it is not that drafting into the army of a newly married involves transgression of two prohibitions, but that Deut. xxiv, 5, prohibits (1) drafting him into the army (2) imposing on him any other public duty. On pp. xxiii f. may be found a rendering of Maimonides' remarks on Christianity.   D.D.

ISAAC, J. : *Jésus et Israël.* 1948. Pp. 578. (Éditions Albin Michel, Paris. Price : 13s. 6d.)

M. Isaac, a Christian of Jewish origin, attacks anti-Semitism by an examination of the Gospels, in particular of the statements, found therein and elsewhere in the N.T., which have been interpreted as hostile to Judaism in a degree which justifies the hating of the Jew and the holding him responsbile for the death of Christ. The author renders a great service by a valuable study which will repay the student apart altogether from his interest in the author's central purpose. Points both for and against the writer's thesis are fairly set out and fairly met. The book is informative but never dull, historical in outlook and treatment, profoundly reverent, bringing out the high points of Jesus' thought and interpreting it in a most illuminating manner. The chapter entitled " The Gospel in the Synagogue," a comparison of Jesus' utterances (Beatitudes, Lord's Prayer, etc.) with Jewish expressions of prayer, and opening up the question of affinity between Essenism and the teaching of Jesus, is well, if but briefly, done. The extent to which Christianity has its roots in Judaism may have been exaggerated at times by scholars, but the author of *Jésus et Israël* lets us appreciate what the evidence, without being strained, reveals.

About a third of the book is devoted to " Le crime de déicide," the charge which has been levied against Judaism under the shield of what has surely been in the record of history the most fateful generalisation, namely, that " the Jews " nailed Jesus to the cross. The principal affirmations which the writer of this remarkable work would stress are as follows : Christianity was not born at a time when Judaism was in a state of decay. The Judaism of the time was alive and energetic, missionary, and finding expression in a variety of religious tendencies and beliefs. The Jews implicated in the condemnation of Jesus— the High priests and their associates—were the representatives of a narrow class, serviceable to Rome, and detested by the people.   O.S.R.

Jocz, J. : *The Jewish People and Jesus Christ*. 1949. Pp. 446.
S.P.C.K., London. Price : £1 1s. 0d.)

A Jewish Christian here asks himself why the Jews have been
completely estranged from Jesus of Nazareth, himself a Jew,
passionately concerned for the welfare of his people. He
discusses the attitude of Jewry to Jesus Christ, and that of
Christians to Jews, throughout the centuries. The first 70
pages or so attempt to reassess what actually happened in
Palestine at the beginning of this era, whilst a large section
(pp. 201-261) deals with contemporary Jewish Christianity.
The book concludes with 100 pages of notes, and a full
bibliography.   N.H.S.

Rabinowitz, J. J. : *The Code of Maimonides, Book Thirteen, The
Book of Civil Laws. Translated from the Hebrew.* (Yale Judaica
Series, vol. II). 1949. Pp. xxiv+346. (Yale University Press, New
Haven : Geoffrey Cumberlege, London. English Price :
£2 0s. 0d.)

' Judaica Research ' at Yale is planning a translation of the
14 books of the Mishneh Torah, with a critical appraisal of
the Code in a 15th volume. This is the first volume to appear,
a translation of the 13th book, ' Judgments,' divided by
Maimonides into five chapters : hiring, borrowing and de-
positing, creditor and debtor, plaintiff and defendant, inheritance. This part of the Code has never been translated
before and Mr. Rabinowitz is to be congratulated on his
achievement. His rendering is literal enough to reproduce the
exact meaning of the original, and free enough to be intelligible.
Besides the standard edition of Vilna, the translator has
consulted earlier ones of Rome and Constantinople, as well as
manuscripts from Yemen and the Oxford Codex.   D.D.

Schoeps, H. J. : *Aus frühchristliche Zeit : Religionsgeschichtliche
Studien.* 1950. Pp. 320. (Mohr, Tübingen.)

Professor Schoeps has gathered in this book thirteen studies
which he describes as by-products of his study of Ebionism.
He deals with : Historical beginnings according to the Pseudo-
Clementines ; their demonology ; Ebionism, mythology and
midrash in Symmachus ; James the Just ; The charge that
the Jews had murdered their prophets ; the destruction of
the Temple in Jewish religious history ; the election of Israel
in the Haggadah ; Jesus and the Law ; Paul as a rabbinical
exegete (Christ the end of the Law, and Paul's attitude to the
sacrifice of Isaac) ; are there references to Simon Magus in
the Haggadah ? ; Gnostic nihilism ; *restitutio principii* as
critical principle of the *nova lex* of Jesus ; *imitatio Dei* and
Christian discipleship.   J.W.P.

Simon, M. : *Verus Israel.* 1948. Pp. 476. (De Boccard, Paris.
Price : £1 0s. 0d.)

This is an important book, studying the relations between
Jews and Christians during the early Christian centuries,

resting on wide reading of Jewish and Christian sources. After a preliminary study of Palestinian Judaism and the Diaspora in the period following the destruction of the Temple, the Christian positions of the time and the Roman attitude to Judaism and the Church, the author turns to his main study, of the conflict between Synagogue and Church, on both its intellectual and its physical side, and of the contacts between the two faiths through Jewish Christianity. The whole forms a valuable study, infused with sympathy and understanding.

H.H.R.

WALLENSTEIN, M. : *Hymns from the Judean Scrolls.* 1950. Pp. 24. (The University Press, Manchester.)

Dr. Wallenstein was probably the first scholar in this country to write on the scrolls, and Hebraists, with many others, greatly appreciated his early articles on them in the *Manchester Guardian* and the *Jewish Chronicle.* He has now placed us in his debt by the early publication of this brochure, which gives, in the main, a text and translation of two of the ' Hymns of Thanksgiving,' with numerous and very useful notes on word-forms. Two plates from Sukenik's *Megilloth Genuzoth* have been reproduced, and Wallenstein's transcription is independent of that of Sukenik. For better or for worse, no cognizance is taken of the numerous translations of these two songs that have hitherto been published, and the present writer would have welcomed Wallenstein's observations on the suggestion by Tournay, *Rev. Bib.*, April, 1949, that Plate 1 in *Megilloth Genuzoth* also contains part of the Songs of Thanksgiving. The present brochure is, however, a welcome addition to the growing literature on the scrolls.   B.J.R.

PHILOLOGY AND GRAMMAR

Corpus Inscriptionum Semiticarum, Pars II, Tomus III, fasciculus secundus. 1947. Pp. 148. (Paris ; e reipublicae typographeo. Price : Fr. 1600.)

The last sheet of this portion of the great *corpus* was printed in August, 1925, and the first sheet of the new fascicule is dated in December, 1947 ; thus the work is continued after an interval of 22 years. The new part contains Nos. 4238-4620 of the Palmyrene inscriptions known in 1926, and is apparently intended as the conclusion of this volume, as an epilogue and a table of contents is added at the end. No volume of plates has been supplied with this as with the preceding fascicules and nothing is said of one ; but the epilogue contains a notice that photographs of individual inscriptions can be obtained from the *Dépôt des Antiquités*, presumably at Palmyra (Tadmor). This is one of the disadvantages of the present hard times ; another is that the paper is not so good as formerly. The scholarship, however, is of the same high standard as ever.

G.R.D.

DUPONT-SOMMER, A. : *Les Araméens*. (L'Orient Ancien Illustré, No. 2). 1949. Pp. 119. (Maisonneuve, Paris. Price : 5s. 6d.)

Professor Dupont-Sommer presents, in brief compass, an excellent study of the history of the Aramaeans from the fourteenth century B.C., when the "Akhlamu" are mentioned for the first time in extra-Biblical sources, to the final disappearance of the Aramaean states of Mesopotamia and Syria in the ninth and eighth centuries B.C. ; of the Aramaean tribes in Babylonia ; and of the language, art and religion of the Aramaeans. A feature of the work is the frequent citation of original texts—Old Testament, Assyrian, Aramaic—especially of the latter, which are often given in fresh translations made by the author. The book is thoroughly up-to-date, and contains some original suggestions, such as the proposed identification of the mysterious kingdom of Katka, mentioned in an Aramaic inscription from Sudjin, with the kingdom of Kaska referred to in the annals of Tiglath-pileser III. The chapter on the Aramaic language and its expansion, the longest of all, is especially good. There are many useful notes, a map, a bibliography, and sixteen illustrations. There are few studies devoted entirely to the Aramaeans. This one, written by an expert—the first of its kind, it seems, in French—is a valuable addition to them.   D.W.T.

KOEHLER, L. : *Lexicon in Veteris Testamenti Libros*, Lieferungen iii-v. 1949. Pp. 92. (E. J. Brill, Leiden.)

This useful Lexicon continues steadily on its way, growing in usefulness as it proceeds. The present parts run from *ballāhāh* ' sudden terror ' to *ḥippāzôn* ' haste,' and like its predecessors, must be in the hands of all serious students of the Old Testament. The editor makes many new suggestions, philological and lexicographical, in numerous articles, and one worthy of notice is the idea put forward on p. 247 that the consecutive *wāw* was originally *wan-* ; for it may be supported by the fact that the Ugar *w-hn* occurs in an abbreviated form as *wn* 'and lo !' although (so far as I have noted), this is never found in anything like a ' consecutive ' construction. The relevant literature, however, has by no means been exhausted, for example *ḥôzeh* and *ḥāzût* ' part ' are both emended out of existence. Otherwise there is little that can be added to the notices, already published, of the previous parts.   G.R.D.

KRAMERS, J. H. : *De Semietische Talen*. 1949. Pp. 198. (Brill, Leiden. Price : Fl. 5.25.)

The writer sketches a general language-atlas of the Semitic East and selects Akkadian, Canaanite, Syriac, Arabic and Ethiopic as the basis of his comparative study of Semitic grammar. Having inter-related those languages he cites short texts with commentary to demonstrate the specific characteristics as well as the affinities of each. The question of the recovery of a hypothetical Semitic mother-tongue is raised but the conclusion is that in spite of the comparative uniformity of the various dialects we are still far from the recovery of

' Ur-Semitische.' The writer considers the possible connection of Semitic with Hamïtic languages, citing certain common features such as the three-radical consonant word form, the gutturals, the feminine ending in -t and a certain etymological correspondence but his conclusion is that, whatever the contacts, the Semitic tongue was truest to type in the North Syrian desert and crystallized here independently of Egyptian. He considers the possibility that the linear Semitic alphabet developed from Egyptian hieroglyphics but leaves this still an open question. The whole is a clear and concise survey of the field of Semitic linguistics and an excellent introduction to more advanced comparative philology calculated perhaps not so much to satisfy as to stimulate.   J.G.

LANDE, I. : *Formelhafte Wendungen der Umgangssprache im Alten Testament.* 1949. Pp. 124. (E. J. Brill, Leiden. Price : Fl. 7.50.)

A doctoral dissertation in which the author examines formal expressions which arose in daily life among the ancient Hebrews, e.g., expressions used in greeting, address and invitation ; in conversation, to signify " yes " and " no," reference to oneself, or to a third person, and so on ; and expressions used to denote various moods and feelings, such as a wish, approval, etc. Where it is possible to do so, the transference of these expressions into other spheres of language, e.g., prophetic utterance, is investigated. There are many parallels in other Semitic languages to the Hebrew expressions here discussed, but there is only occasional reference to them, since the author's primary purpose is limited to a consideration of their occurrence in Hebrew. Within the limits thus set, the author has written a useful little book. It could well form the basis for the fuller treatment on the Semitic side which the subject deserves.   D.W.T.

MOSCATI, S. : *Storia e Civiltà dei Semiti.* Pp. xvi+246, with 32 plates. 1949. (Laterza e Figli, Bari. Price : Lire 1200.)

A concise, but well-informed and instructive, survey of the history and culture of the several Semitic peoples—including Israel—and of their connexions. There is a selected bibliography, and illustrations, some of which are unusual.

W.Bg.

RABIN, C. : *Hebrew Reader.* 1949. Pp. viii+136. (Lund Humphries, London. Price : 10s. 6d.)

This reader, in the words of its compiler, " is intended as a continuation book for the student already familiar with the elements of Hebrew grammar and its purpose is to prepare him for the reading of fiction, newspapers and serious books." We have here passages drawn mainly from various contemporary authors embodying diversified styles with complete vocabularies and notes, following on the whole the principles laid down by the series of Lund Humphries' Modern Languages Readers. This should prove of great help to the student who wishes to acquire the language by self-tuition. It is a pity that owing to the war (for it was during the war time that the bulk of the extracts of this book were put together) the compiler found it difficult to obtain a better and more representative selection of Modern Hebrew prose. Otherwise he would certainly have substituted something better for the number of too-colloquial extracts found in the book. The scanty material available at the time might also account for the faulty graduation of the texts. It is strange, for instance, to find the " Get Up " by Z. Sternfeld which is somewhat deficient and pale in language followed immediately by Bialik's brilliant and idiom-packed " In the Cheder " (by the way, why not Ḥeder ?) It is hoped that in the second edition of this useful reader such shortcomings, as well as the many misprints and inconsistencies in orthography, will be removed.   M.W.

STEUERNAGEL, C. : *Hebräische Grammatik*. 11th ed. 1948. Pp. x+ 160+154 (in series Porta Linguarum Orientalium.) (Harrassowitz, Leipzig. Price : 16s. 0d.)

> This edition is photographically reproduced from the seventh edition, with minor corrections. The first half of the book consists of a systematic grammar, and the second half of exercises and vocabulary. Its usefulness is proved by the number of editions that have been called for.   H.H.R.

Appendix

BENTZEN, A., HOLM, S., and SØE, N. H. (ed. by) : *Illustretet Religionsleksikon*. Bind II (G-M). 1950. Pp. 636. (Skandinavisk Bogforlag, Odense.)

> The second superbly produced volume of this work (see p. 48 of this issue of the Book List) is now issued, marked with the same qualities as its predecessor.   H.H.R.

BURROWS, M., TREVER, J. C., and BROWNLEE, W. H. : *The Dead Sea Scrolls of St. Mark's Monastery*, Vol. I. *The Isaiah Manuscript and the Habakkuk Commentary*. 1950. Pp. xxiv+61 Plates and Transcriptions. (American Schools of Oriental Research, New Haven. Price : $5.00.)

> This eagerly awaited volume is superbly produced and contains facsimiles of approximately the same size as the original of the whole of the two texts it publishes. Each plate is faced with the transcription of the text. There is a short Introduction by Professor Burrows on the discovery of the texts, adding nothing to what was already known, and proposing a standard nomenclature for all the texts ; a short account of the Isaiah

Scroll by Dr. Trever; an introduction to the Habakkuk Commentary by Dr. Brownlee; and a brief note on the palaeography of the Scrolls by Dr. Trever. The photographs are excellent throughout. There are no comments on the texts or study of its forms or collection of its variations from the Massoretic text. The great service rendered by the American Schools is in making these texts available to scholars everywhere, so that they can now be systematically studied by all. The similar publication of all the other texts at an early date is much to be desired.   H.H.R.

DANIEL-ROPS : *Sacred History: the Civilization of the Old Testament World*, translated by K. Madge. 1949. Pp. xii + 434. (Longmans, Green, New York. Price : $4.50.)

This is the same work as appears under a different title in an edition published in England (see p. 24 of this List). The sub-title appears only on the jacket and not on the title page. In the English edition the translator's name does not stand on the title page. In both cases it is the same translator, though there are many curious slight differences and re-arrangements of the text, so that they represent slightly different recensions of the version. The pagination varies in the two editions.   H.H.R.

NÖTSCHER, F. (ed. by) : *Die Heilige Schrift in deutscher Übersetzung Echter Bibel : Das Alte Testament.* 10. *Esra und Nehemia,* by M. Rehm. Pp. 62. *Das Hohe Lied, Rut und Das Buch der Weisheit,* by J. Fischer. Pp. 32 + 16 + 56. 1950. (Echter Verlag, Würzburg. Price : DM 5.20.)

With astonishing rapidity this commentary continues to appear (cf. p. 39 of this issue of the Book List). Both of the authors of this volume are well known, and both maintain the standard of this series, designed for wide use. Rehm adheres to the traditional dating of Ezra and Nehemiah in the reign of Artaxerxes I. Fischer ascribes the composition of the Song of Songs to the fourth century B.C. The reviewer's only regret is that the translation and commentary on five books should be compressed within little more than 150 pages.

H.H.R.

1951

For the preparation of this issue of the Book List the Editor has had the co-operation of the Members of the Book List Committee, appointed by the Society : Prof. G. W. Anderson, Mgr. J. M. T. Barton, Profs. D. Daube, G. R. Driver, Dr. J. Gray, Profs. A. R. Johnson, W. D. McHardy, N. W. Porteous, O. S. Rankin, Miss B. K. Rattey, Rev. B. J. Roberts, Profs. N. H. Snaith, T. W. Thacker and D. Winton Thomas. In addition he acknowledges with gratitude help received from Mr. D. R. Ap-Thomas, Profs. P. A. H. de Boer, O. Eissfeldt, T. Fish, A. Parrot, E. Robertson, I. L. Seeligmann, Th. C. Vriezen and C. J. Mullo Weir ; also from Mr. S. Roberts, the Deputy Librarian of Manchester University Library. Prices of books, where known, are given either in foreign currency, or in the English equivalent. Titles to which an asterisk (*) is prefixed are recommended for inclusion in school libraries.

The Editor is always glad to have his attention called to new books, and especially foreign books, and expresses his thanks to the innumerable foreign correspondents who serve him and the Society in this way. He regrets that a few books have not been received in time for inclusion in this issue.

H. H. ROWLEY.

MANCHESTER UNIVERSITY.

GENERAL

Vid Åbodomens fot, *1924-1949* : *Festskrift utgiven av Teologiska Fakulteten vid Åbo Akademi.* (Lutherska Litteraturstiftelsens Svenska Publikationer, No. 5.) 1949. Pp. 244. (Förbundet för svenskt församlingsarbete i Finland r.f., Helsingfors.)

This volume, published to celebrate the twenty-fifth anniversary of the founding of the theological faculty in the Swedish Academy (i.e. virtually University) in Åbo, contains eighteen essays by present and former members of the faculty. Only one of these deals directly and exclusively with the Old Testament, that by J. Lindblom. He contributes a useful and balanced survey of recent developments in Old Testament research, which leads up to a reconsideration of the relationship between academic research and the devotional use of the Bible. E. Sjöberg, in a study of the conception of man in the Old Testament, the intertestamental period, and the New Testament, traces the rise of a partially dualistic conception as a preparation for some elements in New Testament teaching. Contemporary tasks and methods in the study of religions are discussed by H. Ringgren in an essay which is of interest both because of its intrinsic merit and because of the intimate relationship in contemporary Swedish research between *Religionswissenschaft* and Old Testament study. J. Sundwall writes on textual criticism and the task of the modern translator of Scripture. G. A. Danell argues that belief in the Virgin Birth of Jesus is presupposed by the general testimony of the main New Testament documents. R. Gyllenberg joins issue with Bultmann on *Entmythologisierung*. The other major theological disciplines are represented in the remaining essays. Not the least interesting chapter is that by R. Gyllenberg on the history of the faculty. G.W.A.

Actes du xxi *Congrès International des Orientalistes.* 1949. Pp. vi + 410. (Société Asiatique, Paris. Price : Fr. 2300.)

In this volume are collected the abstracts of nearly 300 papers presented to the Paris Congress of 1948, of which not a few are of importance to the student of the Old Testament. In many cases the full papers have been published elsewhere, but the summaries are valuable in themselves and generally indicate the place of full publication where possible. Of papers relating to the Old Testament field in some way or other three were devoted to the Mari texts (Jean, Dossin, Kupper), three to important unpublished Egyptian Aramaic texts (Driver, Dupont-Sommer, Kamil), three to questions affecting the development of the alphabet (Albright, Dhorme, Robertson), one to Palmyrene (Starcky), one to an unpublished Phoenician inscription (Leveen), one to Ras Shamra (Herdner), one to Tell ed Duweir (Diringer), four to questions of Semitic grammar and philology (Cantineau, Février, Fleisch, Thomas), one to comparative stratigraphy and chronology (Schaeffer), one to the origin of the Philistines (Georgiev), three to Babylonian law (Szlechter, Goetze, Klíma), one to Hurrians and

298

Indo-Aryans in Mitanni (O'Callaghan), and one to Hebrew MSS in Hungary (Löwinger). Surprisingly few papers dealt with the text or interpretation of the Old Testament itself. Bentzen discussed the ' Old ' and the ' New ' in Deutero-Isaiah, Lévy the repudiation of Vashti, and Trencsényi-Waldapfel the social foundation of the two myths of Adam. It will be seen that many are of importance by reason of the new materials they offer, and others by reason of their new interpretations.   H.H.R.

BENTZEN, A., HOLM, S., and SØE, N. H. (ed. by) : *Illustreret Religions-leksikon*. Bind III (N-Ø). 1950. Pp. 546. (Skandinavisk Bog-forlag, Odense.)

> The final volume of this admirable work of reference is as excellent in quality and attractive in appearance as its two predecessors (see *Book List*, 1950, pp. 48, 77). Among the longer articles related to the Old Testament are those on sacrifice (Offer), covenant (Pagt), prophecy (Profetisme), righteousness (Retfærdighed), the Psalter (Salmerne), synagogue (Synagoge), and the Wisdom Literature (Visdoms-litteraturen). There is appended a most valuable survey of the main articles, classified according to subject, so that the reader who is interested in any particular field can see almost at a glance what the encyclopædia has to offer him. G.W.A.

Bijbelse Encyclopædie, edited by W. H. Gispen, F. W. Grosheide, F. J. Brugel, A. van Deursen. 1950. Pp. 520. (J. H. Kok, N. V., Kampen. Price : Fl. 15.)

> The editors and publisher present in this book a reliable guide for devotional and educational Bible study. It is well up to date in matters of history and archaeology, is very well illustrated, and ridiculously cheap, but has one serious weakness, viz. the almost complete lack of literature mentioned. The question whether the practical aim of the book or the anti-critical point of view of the editors must be considered as the cause of this lack, may be put aside here. As to the contents, this Bible dictionary seems to rest for a great part on John Davis' *The Westminster Dictionary of the Bible*, revised by H. S. Gehman, but it may nevertheless be called independently re-written.   Th.C.V.

DE BOER, P. A. H. (ed. by) : *Oudtestamentische Studiën*. Deel VIII. 1950. Pp. 322. (E. J. Brill, Leiden. Price : Fl. 27.50; subscription price : Fl. 15.00.)

> The volume contains the sixteen papers which were read at the international meeting organized by the Dutch Society for Old Testament Study at Leiden in the summer of 1950. There are four papers in German : M. Noth (Jerusalem and Israelite tradition : the emphasis is to be laid upon the sanctuary and the Ark), A. F. Puukko (The " enemy " in the Psalms), M. A. Beek (The problem of Aramaic ancestors of Deut. xxvi. 5), whilst L. Köhler writes of his work on the new lexicon. A. Vincent writes in French on the Old Testament as a storehouse for the early history of religion. The remaining

papers are in English. N. W. Porteous (Semantics and Old Testament Theology) insists that Knowledge of God depends on faith and obedience. G. Gerleman discusses the Septuagint Proverbs as a Hellenistic document. A. Bentzen maintains that the Book of Amos has a marked liturgical element, and discusses chiefly i. 2-ii. 16. H. H. Rowley goes back to royal cultic rites for the origin of both the Suffering Servant and the Davidic Messiah. M. Burrows describes the recently discovered so-called Sectarian Document of the Dead Sea scrolls, seeing in it a ' discipline manual of Judaean Covenanters'. R. B. Y. Scott deals with Exod. xix. 6 (kingdom of priests), whilst J. Bowman, in a somewhat longer paper, writes of the exegesis of the Pentateuch amongst the Samaritans and the Rabbis. N. H. Tur-Sinai denies that the Psalms have a cultic origin, and holds them to be excerpts from historical books. J. Simons deals with Jerusalem exploration. G. D. Young emphasizes the importance of the Phoenician inscriptions of Karatepe in Cilicia. J. W. Wevers discusses the exegetical principles of the Septuagint Version of I Kings. The whole volume is fruitful of ideas, and enormously varied, as this catalogue shows.
N.H.S.

(CHAINE, J.) : *Mémorial J. Chaine.* 1950. Pp. 406. (Facultés catholiques, Lyon. Price : £1 0s. 6d.)

This impressive memorial volume of an excellent teacher and writer, whose character was even more remarkable than his books and lectures, is, like many things of the kind, something of a mixed bag. Chaine, at the time of his death in 1948, had been a specialist in Old Testament for less than ten years, but he had already contributed his valuable section " L'Ancien Testament : Le Sémitisme," to the 1935 volume on Lagrange. The present volume, in addition to short estimates of Chaine himself by Villepelet and Latreille, and a bibliography of his writings, contains contributions by Barucq on a newly discovered document of the time of Amenophis II ; Delorme on Conversion and Pardon in Ezechiel ; Gelin on the meaning of the word " Israel " in Jer. xxx-xxxi ; de Lubac on Origen's commentary on Jer. xx. 7 ; and Podechard on Ps. lxxxii. Archaeologists will welcome Vincent's article on a large priestly burial-place in Jerusalem. Perhaps the most revealing article is that by J. Guitton, recording his adventures as *officier de liaison* between Bergson and Loisy in 1934. Altogether a readable collection with not a few articles of permanent value.
J.M.T.B.

(COOK, S. A.) : *Essays and studies presented to Stanley Arthur Cook,* edited by D. Winton Thomas. 1950. Pp. 124. (Taylor's Foreign Press, London. Price : £1 5s. 0d.)

This volume contains a select bibliography of the writings of the late Professor S. A. Cook and twelve essays covering most branches of Near Eastern studies. They were written by former colleagues of Professor Cook, members of the Faculty of Divinity and Oriental Languages in the University of Cambridge, to celebrate his 75th birthday. Professor Thomas, the editor, contributes the bibliography, and a valuable study of Ostraca xix-xxi from Tell ed-Duweir. Dr. Elmslie considers the " Prophetic Influences in the Sixth Century B.C." Mr. Schofield studies the meaning of the phrase " All Israel " in the Deuteronomic writers. Dr. Diringer writes on the final phases of the struggle between the earlier and the later Hebrew scripts. Professor Glanville contributes some notes on a demotic papyrus from Thebes (B.M. 10026), showing the importance of demotic material for the study of the earlier periods. Mr. Winckworth offers some notes on a common writing of the plural verb-forms in Neo-Babylonian and Late-Babylonian. Mr. Goodman examines some Nestorian Kephalaia (Or. 319, University Library, Cambridge). Mr. Teicher writes on a conflict in Toledo Jewry in the fourteenth century. Mr. Rosenthal has an essay on Edward Lively, a late sixteenth century professor of Hebrew at Cambridge. Professor Arberry discovers the source of Shahrahstānī's chapter on the manners and customs of the inhabitants of pre-Islamic Arabia. Professor Levy writes on the precepts of a Persian " Solomon," king Anusharvan the Just. Professor Bailey explains the origin of the recently discovered sign for 1000 in the Kharoṣṭhī script.

The editor is to be congratulated on the volume he has given us : the essays, though often very brief, are important and stimulating contributions to their respective subjects. It is a worthy tribute to a great scholar.   T.W.T.

'Ensîklôpēdyâ Mikrā'îth. Encyclopædia Biblica, Thesaurus rerum biblicarum alphabetico ordine digestus edd. Institutum Bialik et Museum Antiquitatum ad Universitatem Hebraicam Hierosolytanam pertinens. Vol. I. 1950. Pp. xxxii + 400 cols. (Bialik Foundation, Jerusalem. Price : I£ 30 for the 5 vols. ; I£ 26 if paid in advance).

This work is the first of five volumes of an Old Testament Encyclopædia in modern Hebrew. The scope of the work comprehends the books of the O.T. and Apocrypha, special attention being paid to the contribution of the ancient Jewish tradition to our understanding of the O.T. ; the philology and the archaeology of the O.T. and the Ancient Near East ; the physical and historical geography of Palestine ; the history of the Jewish people and its material and spiritual culture in the biblical period ; the literary and religious history of the O.T. as compared with the literatures and the religions of the Ancient Near East. The choice of the *lemmata* bears witness to a most welcome breadth of outlook. The editor in chief is Prof. M. D. Cassuto. The list of contributors—all Jewish scholars—includes the names of M. Avi Yonah, S. Bodenheimer, N. Glueck, J. Gutmann, I. Heinemann, B. Maisler, M. Narkiss, M. Schwabe, E. L. Sukenik, N. H. Tur-Sinai, S. Yeivin. The method—according to the foreword —is a historical one ; it aims at the reconstruction of the past without any prejudice or preconceived notions whatsoever. A number of articles (Abraham, Aaron, Names of God, etc.) while taking the books of the Bible as having grown together from a variety of traditions, are consistent in rejecting all forms of the documentary hypothesis ; which involves a certain conservatism of approach. Of course the scope and level of the various contributions differ ; a few are confined to a somewhat detailed, but non-original summary of what is known about the subject dealt with ; in others the ingenuity and gift of combination of the authors produce brilliant and highly original views—perhaps even a little too subjective for an encyclopædia. There are a large number of contributions (especially in the fields of history and geography, e.g. *Palestine, Ugarit, Edom, Ephraim,* etc.) of an almost monographic value which are based on an admirable survey of the present state of research, and then go on to improve its results ; also there are several articles which form a very promising beginning of a Jewish religio-philosophical conception of the Bible. The bibliographical references are very rich and on the whole well-selected. The whole work is beyond doubt a first-class achievement and will stand out as a standard work for many years. The external appearance of the volume and its splendid illustrations (*Ugarit, Ur Kasdim, Palestine*) deserve the highest praise.   I.L.S.

Ex Oriente Lux Jaarbericht No. XI (1949-1950). 1950. Pp. 120+27 plates. (Leiden.)

The Dutch Society for the Study of Near-East and Egyptian antiquities continues to publish its year-books, this time two in one volume. (For the last volume containing four year books, cf. Book List 1949, p. 5). This volume is wholly in Dutch except for a two-page article by E. Laroche on the decipherment of Hittite hieroglyphics, and a short review (Excavations at Baghouz, middle Euphrates). There are articles of varying length on the whole field in which the society is interested. From the Old Testament point of view, the most important articles are five in number. J. van der Ploeg has a long article on the Dead Sea Scrolls, concluding with a welcome and comprehensive bibliography. After an account of the discovery of the rolls, there is a discussion of the date (early), followed by a description and discussion of the various individual rolls. J. Simons gives an account of Palestinian archaeology of the post-war period. J. H. Hospers describes the seal found in the summer of 1949 at ' Amman ; in old Hebrew characters, Adoniner servant of Aminadab, ca. 650 B.C. F.M.Th. de Liagre Böhl discusses the Lawbook of Bilalama king of Eshnunna, and provides a Dutch translation of the text. Mesopotamian archaeology is represented by Th. A. Busink's article on the 6th—16th temples at Eridu.
                                                                        N.H.S.

FINKELSTEIN, L. (ed. by) : *The Jews : their History, Culture and Religion*. 2 vols. 1949. Pp. xxxiv+744, viii+688. (Harper & Brothers, New York. Price : $12.00 per set.)

This work, which consists of 35 articles by different contributors (most but not all Jewish), is intended to provide a compact history of Judaism in all its aspects. It is divided into four parts : History of Judaism and the Jews, The Role of Judaism in Civilisation, The Sociology and Demography of the Jews, and The Jewish Religion. The whole is very well conceived. Throughout particular attention is paid to developments in the U.S.A. Some articles, besides summarizing what is known about the subject, include original observations. Old Testament scholars will be specially interested in The Biblical Period by Albright, The Historical Foundations of Postbiblical Judaism by Bickerman, The Period of the Talmud by Goldin, The Bible as a Cultural Monument by Gordis, The Mystical Element in Judaism by Heschel, Judaism and World Philosophy by Altmann, The Contribution of Judaism to World Ethics by Kaplan, Hellenistic Jewish Literature by Marcus, The Influence of the Bible on English Literature by Daiches, The Influence of the Bible on European Literature by Lehner, and The Jewish Religion by Finkelstein. But many of the other chapters contain sections dealing with Biblical questions. Dr. Finkelstein has left his contributors much freedom : if a message none the less emerges, he says in his Foreword, it is ' inherent in the extraordinary events and insights described.' The result amply justifies the method he has adopted. D.D.

[N.B.—Albright's article can be purchased separately, as a 64 page bound booklet, 50 cents plus postage, from Prof. D. N. Freedman, 57 Belvidere Street, Crafton, Pittsburgh, Pa. H.H.R.]

(HIRSCHLER, P.): *Études Orientales à la Mémoire de Paul Hirschler*, edited by O. Komlós. 1950. Pp. vi+144+12. (Budapest.)

This volume, dedicated to the memory of a great man and fine scholar, contains various notes on Old Testament and allied topics : Does the Torah punish impudence ? by E. Roth ; Tel Abib by Löwinger (who argues that the words in Ezekiel iii. 15 are not a city name but mean ' mound of desolation ') ; Jonah legends by Komlós ; The role of the Tzitzit in agreements by Scheiber ; Josephus on prayer in C. Ap. 2, 197 by Hahn (who concludes that there is cynic influence) ; Défense de la version des Septante contre l'accusation d'apanthropie by Trencsényi-Waldapfel (for whom LXX expresses the idea ' for the 70 nations of the world,' ' oecumenical,' and who refers to the elimination of the ass in texts where Moses appears, Exodus iv. 20, Numbers xvi. 15, and to the substitution of ' I am a servant of the Lord ' for ' I am an Hebrew ' in Jonah i. 19). There are interesting articles on other subjects. The reviewer is glad that Ad-Damiri considers excessive chess-playing a venial sin. DD.

(HROZNÝ, F.) : *Symbolae ad Studia Orientalia pertinentes Frederico Hrozný dedicatae.* Pars tertia. (Archiv Orientální, vol. xviii.) 1950. Pp. 552. (Orientální Ustav, Prague.)

This, the third volume of the *Festschrift* dedicated to the eminent orientalist F. Hrozný, contains 37 articles, of which four in some way or other touch the fringe of the Old Testament. Such are those of Alt (' Menschen ohne Namen '), Baumgartner (' Herodots babylonische und assyrische Nachrichten '), O'Callaghan (' An approach to some religious problems of Karatepe ') and Steele (' An additional fragment of the Lipit-Ishtar Code from Nippur '). The first and the last of these articles are perhaps the most interesting to students of the Old Testament, but the other two are equally important in their way. The present volume which is being followed (it is understood) by a fourth, maintains the high standard set by the preceding two and well repays study.

G.R.D.

(KÖHLER, L.) : *Festschrift für Ludwig Köhler zu dessen 70. Geburtstag.* 1950. Pp. 96. (Nr. 3/4, 20 Jahrgang of the *Schweizerischen Theologischen Umschau.* Büchler & Co., Bern.)

A good photograph of Professor Köhler, and a greeting by Professor W. Baumgartner mingling personal notes with a record of the career and achievements of the recipient, form the setting of this Festschrift to one of the best-loved of O.T. scholars. Nine important articles make the small booklet one of academic distinction, five of them deal with the O.T. A. Alt, ' Syrien und Palästina im Onomastikon des Amenope,' examines the names found in this list first published by A. H. Gardiner in 1947, and sees in them evidence for the reconstruction of Palestinian history *c.* 1100 B.C. O. Eissfeldt, ' Nuaḥ " sich vertragen " ', bases the interpretation on the occurrences of an Accadian cognate in the *Statue of Idri-mi* (text published by Sidney Smith, 1949). V. Maag, ' Jahwäs Heerscharen,' discussing the term Yahweh God of Hosts, concludes that the Hosts are the deposed mythical natureforces of Canaan, and that the title was attributed to Yahweh first in the time of the Judges as ' a weapon in the struggle.' S. Speier deals textually with some Targumic renderings. W. Zimmerli, ' Zur Sprache Tritojesajas,' examines the language here in relationship to that of Dt. Is., but to say he shows that there is no essential dependence despite similarity of diction and some direct quotations is a too drastic oversimplification of the author's stimulating discourse. Four essays are placed in the *Praktisch-theologischer Teil*, though O.T. scholars should be interested in W. Kasser's ' Die Stellung des Dekalogs im kirchlichen Unterricht.'   B.J.R.

(van der Leeuw, G.) : *Pro regno pro sanctuario : een bundel studies en bijdragen van vrienden en vereerders bij de zestigste verjaardag van Prof. Dr. G. van der Leeuw*, edited by W. J. Kooiman and J. M. van Veen. 1950. Pp. xii+638. (G. F. Callenbach, Nijkerk. Price : Fl. 40.00.)

In this handsomely produced volume there are forty-seven essays, covering the whole range of theological disciplines, including even Church Music and hymnology, together with a list of Professor van der Leeuw's published works. The following essays relate to O.T. studies : M. A. Beek, ' Het Boek Tobit en de *Mēt Miṣwāh* ' ; A. de Buck, ' The Fear of Premature Death in Ancient Egypt ' (with a reproduction of texts of three MSS providing the text of Spell 175 in the Book of the Dead) ; L. J. Cazemier, ' Het Begrip Zonde in de Pyramideteksten ' ; J. Coppens, ' Nieuw Licht over de Ebed-Jahweh-Liederen ' (where it is argued that the Servant Songs are best understood in the setting of the Davidic dynasty) ; K. A. H. Hidding, ' Tweeërlei Kennis in het Paradijsverhaal.' Attention should also be drawn to R. Bultmann, ' Ursprung und Sinn der Typologie als hermeneutischer Methode.' Though the essay deals in the first instance with the N.T., the author, with his customary erudition and vision, indicates the points of contact, and of contrast, between typology, eschatologisation of prototypes and allegorisation in the Old Testament. Of articles beyond the field of the Old Testament, that on ' Von Dynamismus zu Personalismus,' by our honorary member A. Bertholet, may be mentioned.   B.J.R.

(Marx, A.) : *The Alexander Marx Jubilee Volume* (in English) and *Sepher Hayyobhel* (in Hebrew), edited by S. Lieberman. 1950. Pp. xxiii+547. (Jewish Theological Seminary of America, New York. Price : cloth bound $25.00, paper bound $18.00.)

Of the many valuable articles the following are of immediate interest : A. English. (1) The Judicial Reform of Jehoshaphat, by Albright : argues in favour of the historicity of 2 Chr. xix. 4 ff. (2) The Transmission of the Septuagint, by Bickerman : points out complications neglected by modern investigators. (3) Judah and the Transjordan States 734-582 B.C., by Ginsberg : holds *inter alia* that Isa. ix. 1-6 is not prophecy but thanksgiving, the saviour being Josiah who reconquered Israelite Transjordan. (4) Democratic Origins in Israel by Gordis : *kāhāl* and *'ēdāh* are not late constructions but from nomadic times denote the commonalty and its assembly. (5) A Supplement to the Standard Hebrew Dictionaries of Abbreviations, by Marcus. (6) A New Bible Translation, by Sperber : a criticism of the Jewish Publication Society's translation of 1917. (7) Habiru-' Ibhrim, by Taeubler : the name signifies ' those at the side(s) of the river.' (8) The Hebrew of the Geniza Sirach, by Torrey : the Geniza Sirach is a medieval translation from the Syriac. (9) The Veracity of Scripture in Philo, Halevi, Maimonides and Spinoza, by Wolfson. B. Hebrew. (1) Halakhoth and Derashoth, by Albeck : discusses the problem how far Rabbinic decisions were derived from exegesis and how far exegesis followed the decisions. (2) Chapters from a MS of Midrash Tehillim, by Arzt : edition of a MS not used by Buber, and reaching from Ps. lxxiv to lxxix. (3) The Halakhoth Peculiar to Jerusalem, by Finkelstein : it was not till shortly before the destruction of the Second Temple that Jerusalem was excepted from the rules applying to walled cities. (4) Midrash Koheleth Zuta, by Greenberg : edition of the first chapter of a MS not used by Buber and containing the whole Midrash. (5) The Holy Spirit in the Middle Ages, by Heschel. (6) The Armies of Bar Kokhba, by Krauss : the men ' with a finger cut off ' were volunteers who had resorted to self-mutilation in order to evade Roman conscription. (7) Early Commentators of the Yerushalmi, by Lieberman. (8) New Fragments from Yerushalmi Pesahim 5-7, by Löwinger : edition of twenty-eight Geniza fragments belonging to the Hungarian Academy. One is glad to learn that most Geniza treasures in Budapest have survived. Lieberman adds some comments. (9) The Synagogue at Caesarea and its Inscriptions, by Schwabe : the synagogue has now been located, and some inscriptions are illuminating, e.g. one which shews that in the 5th and 6th centuries the community used the LXX. (10) The Legend of Isaac's Slaying and Resurrection, by Spiegel.   D.D.

Miscellanea Academica Berolinensia : Gesammelte Abhandlungen zur Feier des 250 jahrigen Bestehens der Deutschen Akademie der Wissenschaften zu Berlin. 2 parts in 3 vols. Vol. i—Pp. 252, vol. ii—Pp. 294, vol. iii—Pp. 448. (Akademie-Verlag, Berlin. Price : DM. 39.00 for Part 1, and DM. 73.50 for Part 2.)

This work contains essays covering the whole field of human knowledge. Part i (=vol. i) is concerned with *Naturwissenschaft*. The first half of part ii (=vol. ii) deals with European studies, ancient'and modern. The second half of part ii (=vol. iii) is mainly devoted to Oriental Studies, the remaining essays being on Classical subjects and papyrology. There are only two essays in the whole work which are of interest to the Old Testament scholar and the semitist. They are in vol. iii. One of these comes from the pen of Eissfeldt and is entitled " Jahwe Zebaoth." The writer investigates the meaning of the epithet and suggests that *s⁽ᵉ⁾ba'ot* means " might, mighty." The other, by Enno Littmann, is a new treatment of the three most important inscriptions discovered in Aksum by the German expedition in 1906 and published in vol. iv of the " Deutsche Aksum-Expedition " (Berlin, 1913).   T.W.T.

(Nötscher, F.): *Alttestamentliche Studien. Friedrich Nötscher Festschrift* edited by H. Junker and J. Botterweck. (Bonner Biblische Beiträge, vol. 1.) 1950. Pp. 292. (Peter Hanstein Verlag, Bonn. Price : £2 3s. 6d.)

This Festschrift, dedicated to one of the leading scholars of Europe, with 23 articles, has no scheme or unity but its value is not thereby impaired because the excellence of the individual papers renders the book beyond reproach. A. Allgeier appeals for a return to hermeneutic in his discussion of the purpose and methods of O.T. Introduction. The Form-critics have very useful material in H. Eising, Theophanies in Daniel against the background of other O.T. theophanies ; J. Fischer, the interpretation and literary character of Gen. vi. 1-4 ; A. Kolping, Content and Form in Gen. ii-iii ; E. Pritsch, the juridical usage of the *shubanti* formula in Old Babylonian. Religio-historical studies are given by G. J. Botterweck, the so-called *batti* report on the slaughter at Kadesh ; V. Christian, the origins of Purim ; J. Coppens, the matrimonial story of Hosea ; M. Noth, traditio-historical observations on the second half of Joshua ; F. Schmidtke, the cosmogony of the Sumerian myth ; J. Ziegler, God's ' aids in the morning.' Lexicography and textual studies are provided by A. Alt, Tents and Huts ; G. R. Driver, Problems of the Hebrew Text and Language ; H. Junker, The Bridegroom of blood (Ex. iv. 24-26) ; F. Stummer, *tukku = adpropinquant* (Vulgate of Dt. xxxiii. 3) ; R. J. Tournay, Notes on Pss. xix. 2-5, lxxi. 15f. The Apocrypha is represented by V. Hamp, The Future and the Beyond in Sirach ; J. Schildenberger, Sirach xlviii. 24f. and the authorship of Is. xl-lxvi. For Islam we have W. Hoenerbach, Isaiah in Tabari ; R. Paret, the meaning of *baqiya* in the Koran ; O. Spies, the Origin of Friday as Day of Worship in Islam. The Dead Sea Scrolls are discussed in two articles, P. E. Kahle, who answers Engnell's views on the Isaiah text ; and K. Schubert, who gives a general review of the contents of the scrolls with very useful bibliography, particularly articles in Jewish journals. Finally, G. J. Botterweck gives a list of Nötscher's writings.　　　　B.J.R.

ROBERT, A. (ed. by) : *Dictionnaire de la Bible, Supplément*, Fasc. **XXIV**. *Kalt-Langdon*. 1950. Columns 1-256. (Letouzey & Ané, Paris. Price : 12s. 6d.)

With the present fascicle the *Supplément* enters upon its fifth volume. Owing, partly, to the disturbing effects of war, its publication has been in progress for twenty-three years and it has all but reached the half-way line in the alphabet. The present issue, valuable as it is in some of its aspects, hardly concerns the Old Testament, except in a small minority of articles, e.g. those of *Kerûb, Kerûbim* by J. Trinquet, which owes a good deal to the important series in the *Revue Biblique* for 1926, by Dhorme and Vincent. The treatment of *Kyrios* by L. Cerfaux of Louvain shows that distinguished writer at his best in a subject that he has already handled in masterly fashion in *Le Muséon* and the *Revue des sciences philosophiques et théologiques*. A Gelin on *Lamentations* is decidedly reserved on the subject of the Jeremian authorship, and points to the change of attitude in the latest edition of Höpfl, *Compendium Introductionis in libros V.T.* There are many short biographies of such worthies as Kautzsch, Kennett, Kittel, Knabenbauer, Koenig (E.), Kuenen, Ladeuze, Lagrange, and Lamy, in addition to the two names given in the heading. One may refer, in passing, to the long and important article on *Kénose* by P. Henry.　　　　J.M.T.B.

Robertson, E., and Wallenstein, M. (ed. by) : *Melilah : A Volume of Studies*, III-IV. 1950. Pp. 352. (Manchester University Press. Price : 30s. 0d.)

A volume in Hebrew. Of the many valuable contributions, the following are of direct interest for students of the O.T. : (1) Variants in Editing by Zuckerbram. on 2 Kings xxiv. 18-xxv. 30, Jer. lii and xxxix. 1-10. (2) Lachish Ostraca by Winton Thomas (translated from the English) (3) The Lost Tribes by Klausner : Scotland Yard might find something about the Stone here. (4) Targums by Kahle (translated). (5) The Samaritan Calendar by Robertson (translated). (6) Remarks on Robertson's article by Akaviah. (7) A Contribution to Hebrew Lexicography by Yalon, on some difficult expressions. (8) Obscure expressions in the Midrash by Wartski, on unusual applications of certain phrases. (9) Development of Language by Martin. (10) Discussions of the Angels with God by the late Marmorstein. (11) Christian Legislation concerning Synagogues by the late Krauss. The Editors are to be congratulated on bringing out a publication of such high standard. D.D.

Simon, H., and Prado, J. : *Praelectiones Biblicae : Vetus Testamentum.* Vol. I : *De Veteris Testamenti Historia*, 5th ed. 1949. Pp. xvi+ 716. (Price : 18s. 0d.) Vol. II. *De Veteris Testamenti Doctrina*, 3rd ed. 1950. Pp. xvi+500. (Price : 15s. 0d.) (*Marietti, Turin.*)

The work of the lamented H. Prado, revised and enlarged by J. Simon, has been a standard textbook for many years, though, by comparison with its present immense proportions, it was originally a slender and insignificant growth. It is part of a five-volume selective commentary and introduction to the whole Bible, and the editor has now provided an ample bibliography, a number of excerpts from the Masoretic text printed in Hebrew type, and a quantity of quotations, mostly in French and German, to illustrate and supplement the Latin of the manual itself. In fact, there are almost too many quotations ; thus, in a comparison of the Mosaic Law and the Code of Hammurabi, nearly two pages of small print are devoted to a series of extracts from H. Cazelles: *Études sur le Code de l'Alliance*.

The tendency of the work is distinctly conservative, but the editor seems to be well aware of less traditional views. His Latin is clear and workmanlike, and there can be no question about the breadth of his erudition or his gift of writing interestingly on a variety of topics. On the whole, this manual is one of the best of its kind. J.M.T.B.

Studia theologica cura ordinum theologorum Scandinavicorum edita. Vol. II, Fasc. i. 1948/9. Pp. 102. Fasc. ii. 1948/50. Pp. 100. (C.W.K. Gleerup, Lund. Price : Kr. 8.00 each part separately ; Kr. 12.00 together.

In Fasc. i, Bo Reicke contributes an important article, ' Die Ta'āmire-Schriften und die Damaskus-Fragmente ' in which he proposes the name ' Ta'āmire MSS ' for the entire collection of Dead Sea Scrolls, and other names for several MSS. He discusses the relation of the dating of the scrolls to that of the Damascus document, and works out the suggestion that the 'House of Absalom' referred to in the Habakkuk Commentary denotes the Tobiads. He also draws attention to the points of contact between the Damascus Document and Ezra-Nehemiah. In a discussion of ' Urmensch und " Königsideologie " ' Mowinckel insists on the distinction between Urmensch (a cosmological concept of Indo-Iranian or Indo-European origin which has no true counterpart in ancient Semitic thought) and the earlier concept of the first created man. He denies any original connexion of kingship or messiahship with the *Urmensch* or with the notion of world epochs. His general arguments lead up to a discussion of passages such as Genesis i-iii, Psalms ii, viii, where Bentzen, Engnell and Widengren have found the *Urmensch* concept. With these interpretations Mowinckel disagrees. A. Bentzen takes up some observations of S. Granild (see *Book List*, 1950, p. 44) on Ezra's personality and argues that his virtues were not merely passive. Also of interest are the articles by R. Bultmann on ' Weissagung und Erfüllung,' and by H. J. Schoeps on ' Ehebewertung und Sexual moral der Späteren Juden-christen.' In Fasc. ii the only contribution of direct interest to the *Alttestamentler* is a note by H. Birkeland arguing that *zeh* in Psalm lxviii. 9 and Judges v. 5 is not to be explained as equivalent to Arabic *du*+Genitive. Important articles are contributed by A. Oepke on Matthew xvi. 17-19, and by H. Mosbech on *Apostolos*.   G.W.A.

Studia theologica cura ordinum theologorum Scandinavicorum edita, Vol. III, Fasc. i. 1949/50. Pp. 110. (C.W.K. Gleerup, Lund. Price : Kr. 8.00 separately.)

Contains two important articles in the O.T. field, both in English. H. Ringgren writes on oral and written transmission in the O.T. He regards them as complementary to each other. The greater part of his paper is devoted to a careful examination of parallel texts (Psalm xviii and 2 Samuel xxii, Psalms xiv and liii, etc.) to discover where variants are slips of the pen and where they result from errors of hearing. A careful and sober treatment of the subject.

H. Birkeland throws down the gauntlet to many of his Scandinavian colleagues in a challenging article, ' The Belief in the Resurrection of the Dead in the Old Testament.' He argues, in general, that comparison of phenomena from different religions tends to obscure the distinctive significance which each had in its original setting, and, in particular, that the origin of the late O.T. and Jewish belief in resurrection is not to be found in the death-and-resurrection motif of fertility religion, but in distinctive elements in Hebrew religion, influenced, in a measure, by Iranian religion.

E. T. Pedersen writes on 'Schöpfung und Geschichte bei Luther ' ; O. Linton on Gal. i, ii and Acts xi, xv ; and J. Munck on ' Paul, the Apostles, and the Twelve.'   G.W.A.

Svensk exegetisk årsbok XIV, edited by G. Lindeskog. 1949. Pp. 172.
(Wretmans Boktryckeri Aktiebolag, Uppsala. Price : Kr. 8.)

Regret that Professor Fridrichsen has had to relinquish the
editorship of this excellent annual will be mingled with good
wishes to Dr. Lindeskog. The above number is of the same
high quality as its predecessors. For readers of this Book
List the most interesting item is undoubtedly the long and
valuable article by E. Sjöberg on the teaching of the pre-
exilic prophets, in which he tries to strike a balance between
" Wellhausenism " and the now familiar contentions of the
Uppsala circle. He discusses the following questions : (a)
Is the prophetic monotheism a new element in Hebrew
religion ? (b) Is the prophetic teaching predominantly ethical
and uncompromisingly anti-cultic ? (c) Were the pre-exilic
prophets exclusively heralds of doom or may we legitimately
find in their teaching a pattern of alternating threat and
promise. In both its documentation and its sober and balanced
judgement the article is altogether admirable. The annual
also contains articles by M. Goguel (on the second generation
of the Christian Church) and I. Arbman (on the use of the
Swedish verb *lata* in the N.T.), reviews of recent literature,
and a bibliography (compiled by Bo Reicke) of books on
biblical subjects published between 1941 and 1946.   G.W.A.

Svensk exegetisk årsbok XV, edited by G. Lindeskog. Pp. 136. With
supplement, *Symbolae Biblicae Upsalienses* 13. Pp. 22. 1950.
(Wretmans Boktryckeri Aktiebolag, Uppsala. Price : Kr. 8.)

K. Stendahl contributes a detailed study of the use of *rapha'*
in the O.T., in which he seeks to show that the primary and
dominating sense is associated not with ordinary healing
but with the myth and ritual of the cultic system. Other
articles deal with missionary preaching in Acts (B. Gärtner),
1 Peter iii. 21 (T. Arvedson), the fish symbol and Christian
baptism (G. Grefbäck), and the Caesarean text (L. O. Almgren).
There are reviews of recent literature, and in the supplement
P. S. Minear writes on the Nativity narratives.   G.W.A.

(De Visscher, F.) ; *Mélanges Fernand De Visscher*, vols. 3 and 4.
(Revue Internationale des Droits de l'Antiquité, IV and V). 1950.
Pp. 594 and 572. (Office Internationale de Librairie, Brussels.
Price : B.Frs. 250 each vol.)

For the first two volumes of this work, see Book List 1950,
p. 69. The present volumes contain four more articles which
may interest students of the O.T. The first is in English, the
other three in French. (1) Leemans discusses rates of interest
in early Babylonia. (2) Szlechter investigates the phrases
qaqqadam kullu and *rêšam kullu :* he concludes that they
express, not the idea of surety, but that of *depositum irregulare*.
(3) Dumezil shews that several classical references to the custom
of doing away with the aged are confirmed by independent
traditions of the peoples in question. (4) Mme. Mohrmann
makes some observations on *rationabilis* as representing
logikos in early Christian literature.   D.D.

EDUCATIONAL

HEBERT, A. G. : *The Bible from Within*. 1950. Pp. 192. (Oxford
University Press. Price : 8s. 6d.)

Believing that information *about* the Bible, however valuable
in itself, is but preliminary to the understanding of its teaching
as a " word of the living God," the author of this book sets
out to see the Bible as a whole " from within." Running
through the Scriptures from first to last is found a continuous
purpose of God worked out in the events of history. Beginning
with the call of Abraham and the Exodus from Egypt, that
purpose reaches its consummation in the coming of Jesus,
the promised Messiah, and the admission of all races into the
New Israel, the Christian Church. Ten of the twelve chapters
of which the book consists are concerned with the O.T., and
portions of the chief books are studied in relation to the period
of history in which the author was writing, not merely to that
which is described. Chapter VIII deals with the Messianic
Hope, and chapter XI, entitled " the time is fulfilled " shows
how the pattern of O.T. teaching about the King, the Kingly
Rule of God, the New Covenant, the Outpouring of the
Spirit and the Coming in of the Gentiles recurs and is transcended in the Gospel. " The O.T. is full of anticipations of
Christ and His cross : its broken lights find their completion
in Him who is the Light of the World." Teachers in Secondary
Schools and students in Training Colleges will find this book
most helpful.   B.K.R.

STALKER, D. M. G. : *Genesis i-xii*. Books of the Bible Series, No. 4.
1950. Pp. 62. (Church of Scotland Youth Committee, Edinburgh.
Price : 1s. 6d.)

This is a valuable booklet for Upper School Discussion Groups,
Bible Classes and Training College students. It is clearly and
interestingly written by an experienced teacher, who is skilled
in driving home the point of a section in a short, forceful
sentence.

While full use is made of modern knowledge of early
Semitic traditions and practices, the author is concerned to
show how fundamental are the differences between the ideas
which were the common property of the Semitic world, and
those were proclaimed by the Hebrew teachers. The primitive stories of origins were by them purged of gross, crude and
unedifying elements, and transformed into wonderful vehicles
conveying spiritual truths. To illustrate this, passages are
quoted from the Babylonian Creation story and from the
Gilgamesh epic. Questions such as what is meant by " the
image of God " in man ? Is the Flood historic ? What is
original sin ? are handled wisely, and the booklet ends
with a quotation which gives the key to its character :
" Genesis strikes the first notes of the Unfinished Symphony
of God's love in redemptive activity in human history."
                                                                  B.K.R.

STEDMAN, A. R. : *The Growth of Hebrew Religion.* 1949. Pp. xii+212. (G. Bell & Sons, London. Price : 3s. 9d.)

This volume is intended primarily for use in Secondary Schools ; it will also be found suitable for some Training Colleges. A general survey is made of Israel's religious history from the primitive beliefs of the patriarchal age to the lofty conception of God and of His moral demands upon man, which characterises the teaching of the prophets. The last chapters (50 pp.) are devoted to the work of Nehemiah and Ezra and to the last years of the Jewish state. Reference is frequently made to standard works on the O.T. and to the generally accepted conclusions of modern scholarship. In view of recent adjustments of the dates of the first Dynasty of Babylon, a general revision of the dates on p. 211 and in the earlier chapters of the book seems advisable.　B.K.R.

A Syllabus of Religious Education for use in Secondary Schools in Scotland (Third Year). 1949. Pp. 192. (Publications Department, Church of Scotland Offices. Price : 4s. 0d.)

This is the third instalment of a scheme for Religious Education in Scotland, which is intended ultimately to cover school life from the Nursery School to the Sixth Form of the Secondary School. The present volume represents a year's course of religious instruction ; it consists of 43 lessons, of which 14 are given to the O.T. The subject matter of these 14 lessons is, first, the entrance into Canaan, and the change which that entailed in the social and religious life of the Hebrews ; secondly, the development of civilization in the Northern Kingdom especially, and the moral problems which arose in consequence of that development. The teaching of the prophets Elijah, Amos, Hosea and—rather strangely—Micah, is dealt with in detail (Lessons 20-27). Valuable notes are provided to help teachers with their work, but they are advised not to adhere too rigidly to every item in the syllabus. This warning is certainly necessary, for some of the lessons contain material enough for two or more, and the capacity of children to profit by a lesson, however excellent, varies considerably, and depends primarily upon the teacher's skill in presentation.　B.K.R.

ARCHAEOLOGY AND EPIGRAPHY

BRONGERS, H. A. : *De literatuur der Babyloniërs en Assyriërs.* Pp. 248. (Servire, The Hague. Price : Fl. 3.50.)

This pocket-book summary well deserves success amongst those for whom the series " Servire's Encyclopædie " is intended, and the bibliography following each chapter will be found useful. There are separate chapters on each of the categories of literature which have come down to us from Assyria and Babylonia.　T.F.

BURROWS, M., TREVER, J. C., and BROWNLEE, W. H. : *The Dead Sea Scrolls of St. Mark's Monastery*, Vol. II, Fascicle 2 : *Plates and Transcription of the Manual of Discipline*. 1951. 11 plates and transcription. (American Schools of Oriental Research, New Haven. Price : 16s. 0d., or £2 for complete vol. when ready.)

> Here is the full text of the Discipline Scroll in Facsimile, faced by transcription as in the earlier volume (see *Book List*, 1950, p. 77). There is no introductory matter or comment, and on that account the present facsimile is numbered 2, though it is the first to appear. The American Schools deserve the gratitude of scholars everywhere for the publication of this text in so excellent a form. A translation is being prepared by Dr. Brownlee, to be published as a Supplementary Study of B.A.S.O.R., and it is hoped later to publish notes, comments and critical studies in Fasc. II or Fasc. III of the present work.
>
> H.H.R.

CAVAIGNAC, E. : *Les Hittites*. 1950. Pp. 126. (Maisonneuve, Paris. Price : Frs. 250.)

> This, the third volume of *L'Orient Ancien Illustré*, is a wholly admirable account of the Hittites. In a slim volume of 126 pages, the author, after a brief account of the epoch-making discoveries of the present century, gives a lucid and straight-forward history of the Hittites from the earliest times till the Graeco-Roman age, interspersed with chapters on religion and law, art and literature, and so on. Their relations, too, with their neighbours are not neglected ; but the problem of the Biblical ' Hittites ' is skipped with the remark that ' many Hittite elements had made their way here and there into Palestine and, when the Israelites had settled themselves in the land of Canaan, the Hittite was a familiar figure to them.' The book is completed with an excellent map of the Hittite world in the 14th century B.C. and twenty-one well-chosen illustrations.
>
> G.R.D.

DOSSIN, G. : *Archives Royales de Mari*. I. *Correspondance de Šamši-Addu*. 1950. Pp. viii+226. (Geuthner, Paris. Price : Frs. 800.)

JEAN, C. F. : *Archives Royales de Mari*. II. *Lettres diverses*. 1950. Pp. iv+234. (Geuthner, Paris. Price : Frs. 1600.)

KUPPER, J. R. : *Archives Royales de Mari*. III. *Correspondance de Kibri-Dagan gouverneur de Terqa*. 1950. Pp. ii+118. (Geuthner, Paris. Price : Frs. 500.)

> With these three volumes the editors of the famous correspondence (said to consist of some 20,000 tablets, of which they have so far published 3 volumes of cuneiform text) commence the immense task of making it accessible to readers who are not professed assyriologists. Here 364 letters are presented with transliteration and translation on opposite pages ; each volume contains also a very brief introduction and philological notes and map. Further, a glossary of the whole correspondence is promised in a final volume, which will be awaited with impatience. The work seems to be thoroughly trust-worthy and will be of the greatest use to students of the O.T. and of the Middle East ; for the texts are of primary importance from both the historical and the linguistic point of view.
>
> G.R.D.

Dupont-Sommer, A. : *Observations sur le Commentaire d'Habacuc découvert près de la Mer Morte.* 1950. Pp. 32. (Maisonneuve, Paris. Price : 3s. 6d.)

In the Dead Sea Commentary on Habakkuk, Professor Dupont-Sommer finds that the comment on ii. 15 refers to the capture of Jerusalem by Pompey on the Day of Atonement in B.C. 63, and that this event provides a *terminus a quo* for the scroll. The *terminus ad quem* is argued from other data in the commentary, based on the previous identification, and is estimated at about B.C. 41. The sect to which the cache belonged is the Damascus Covenanters. The reconstruction is attractively and persuasively presented, and, indeed, it could be regarded as conclusive were it not for the fact that other equally feasible hypotheses have been presented. The paper was read to the Académie des Inscriptions et Belles-Lettres on 26th May, 1950.   B.J.R.

Dupont-Sommer, A. : *Aperçus préliminaires sur les Manuscripts de la Mer Morte.* L'Orient Ancien Illustré, No. 4. 1950. Pp. 126. (A. Maisonneuve, Paris. Price : Frs. 250.)

In this extremely fascinating book—the first discussion of the Dead Sea Scrolls in book form—Professor Dupont-Sommer outlines the story of the discovery and indicates its historical significance. The book was written after the publication of his essay on the Habakkuk Commentary (see preceding note), and alongside this scroll he dates the Manual of Discipline and the Psalms of Thanksgiving. The innumerable Biblical quotations in the latter are, according to Dupont-Sommer, to be interpreted allegorically, as those in Daniel, Enoch and the Testaments of the XII Patriarchs. The Warfare scroll he places in the Hellenistic period, and it is to be regarded not as apocalyptic writing but as an issue of rules of combat, regulating the pious Jews in their conduct of holy (but actual) war. The two Isaiah scrolls he tentatively places in the 1st century B.C. The Sect, which Dupont-Sommer calls the New Alliance, is the same as that of the Damascus Document—to which an interesting chapter is given, and, furthermore, is to be identified with the Essenes because of similarities in the form of the oath, in teaching, customs and organization. Differences between the Essenes and the Sect in such matters as attitude to sacrifice and to pacifism are explained by a change of circumstances and of policy in the course of time. Amongst the most important sources of information about the New Alliance are the Pseudepigrapha, particularly the Testaments of the XII Patriarchs and striking affinities between the scrolls and the New Testament are included in the closing section of the book. The author has little to say for those who oppose a 1st century B.C. dating for the scrolls ; the script, he says, is so unique that it could not have been devised at a later period. B.J.R.

314

LEEMANS, W. F. : *The Old Babylonian Merchant : his business and his social position.* Studia et Documenta ad iura antiqui Orientis pertinentia III. 1950. Pp. xii+138. (Brill, Leiden. Price : Fl. 16.)

The present work gives a full account of the activities of the merchant as traveller and money-lender before and during the Old Babylonian period, his agents and his social position ; and it contains sketches of some of the best known merchants, the merchant guilds and the principal towns in which they were centred. The work is a useful compilation, but the reader ought to be warned that the references cited do not always support the text and that the conclusions do not always flow from the premises, while the argumentation is also at points obscure, possibly because the author is using a foreign language. G.R.D.

MARQUET-KRAUSE, JUDITH : *Les fouilles de 'Ay (et-Tell), 1933-35.* 1949. Pp. 370+100 maps. (Geuthner, Paris : Price : 7.000 frs.)

This is the posthumous publication of the results of the three excavations carried out at et-Tell in 1933, 1934 and 1935. The publishers have put together the three preliminary reports which appeared in *Syria* and have added to it the whole inventory (2681 numbers) illustrated by many photographs. In this work there are the description of the town walls, of the sanctuary built right against the wall, of the palace (in which Albright finds a temple), of the lower town (inhabited in the Bronze and Iron Ages) of the necropolis with abundant and very valuable pottery which can be compared with pieces from numerous other sites in Palestine. It may be noted that the rather unexpected result of the exploration was to show that after a prosperous period (the Bronze Age) the town was deserted and did not come to life again until the Iron Age. It is difficult to reconcile this archaeological statement with the biblical record which explicitly states that the king of the town of Ai was taken by Joshua. A.P.

DEL MEDICO, H. E. : *La Bible Cananéenne découverte dans les textes de Ras Shamra.* 1950. Pp. 240. (Payot, Paris. Price : Frs. 630.)

In this excursion from the author's customary field of Byzantine studies one might have expected evidence of critical study of the acknowledged masters in Ugaritic studies. On the contrary, apparently ignoring any such work, except Virolleaud's transcription and strophic arrangement, he produces ' translations ' which must bewilder all who are familiar with the texts, unsupported as his renderings are by philological notes. He finds abundant historical and geographical correspondence with the O.T. and this he takes to extend to the literary categories of the books of the O.T. ; hence the title of his book. Here he commits himself to the most arresting theories. He treats the AB cycle as historical ' Chronicles of the Reign of the Great King,' neither more nor less than annals ' such as those of the Hittite kings or certain books of the O.T.' Private correspondence is taken as psalms and the text SS is taken as a collection of religious and moral precepts, recalling Leviticus and Proverbs and including practical directions for procreation ! J.G.

Pritchard, J. B. : *Ancient Near-Eastern Texts relating to the Old Testament*. 1950. Pp. xii+526. (Princeton U.P. Price : $15.00.)

This sumptuous volume, which will take the place of the old volume of *Texte* in Gressmann's well-known *Altorientalische Texte und Bilder zum Alten Testament* (1926), even though it is unfortunately not accompanied by a volume of *Bilder*, is edited by Dr. Pritchard in collaboration with a number of well-known Orientalists (Albright, Ginsberg, Goetze, Kramer, Meek, Oppenheim, Pfeiffer, Stephens, Wilson) ; it seems to include translations of all known texts, including the Ugaritic, that have any conceivable bearing on the Old Testament, grouped by subjects and each furnished with a brief introduction and bibliography. There are also useful indices at the end of the volume. The translations, of course, vary with the present state of knowledge of the different languages. Ugaritic and Hittite naturally raise the most queries. The names of the translators are a guarantee of the general accuracy of the work, but old-fashioned and/or erroneous renderings have not been entirely eliminated (for example, a 'mad' rather than a 'savage' dog in the Laws of Eshnunna, 'a slave not his own' for 'so as not to be traced' in the Code of Hammurabi, and 'satiation/intoxication' in the Moabite Stone) ; but such oversights are few and far between and detract but little from the value of an indispensable work.   G.R.D.

Reifenberg, A. : *Ancient Hebrew Seals*. (The East and West Library.) 1950. Pp. 58. (The Horovitz Publishing Co., London. Price : 12s. 6d.)

Within the brief compass of a monograph, the author deals with inscribed seals dating from the period of the Hebrew monarchy. There are short sections—16 pages in all—on the origin, use and purpose of seals ; material and technique ; language and script ; inscriptions ; the origin of Hebrew-Phoenician art, and the style of Hebrew seals. Included in the study are seals, not only from Palestine, but also from neighbouring countries, so that their common cultural background may be more easily appreciated. For the same reason, illustrations of contemporary ivories, etc., are given. The inscriptions on the seals testify, the author claims, to the growing religious consciousness of the Jews—pictorial representation becomes rare in Judah from *c.* 600 B.C. The seals serve too to illustrate the art of the Solomonic temple. A special interest attaches to the author's remarks on the influence of Hebrew-Phoenician art on the art of Greece and the west. The work is unfortunately marred by misprints, and by occasional inconsistencies (e.g. Hoglanijah " J. has redeemed me," p. 15 ; Higlanijah " God exiled me," p. 38), and dubious statements (e.g., that no names with El are found in the Lachish ostraca, p. 16). The chief value of the work lies in the excellent illustrations accompanied by descriptions and notes, which occupy 27 pages. Though almost all the seals dealt with have already been published—references to the literature are given—it is useful to have them brought together as they are here.
                                           D.W.T.

SCHAEFFER, C. F. A. : *Ugaritica II* (Mission de Ras Shamra, Tome V).
1949. Pp. xv+320+pl. xlv. (Geuthner, Paris. Price : £3 7s. 6d.)

This volume continues the publication of the archaeological
objects, other than inscribed tablets found at Ugarit ; it
contains four chapters devoted respectively to the golden
bowl and dish, the personal ornaments—with especial reference
to the *porteurs de torques*, the grand figure of ' Baal of the
lightning,' and the pottery. The stratification is carefully
observed, the text is enriched with a wealth of comparative
matter, and the illustrations are as lavish as they are clear.

G.R.D.

SUKENIK, E. L. : *Megilloth Genuzoth. Seqirah Sheniiah.* 1950. Pp. 92.
(Bialik Institute, Jerusalem. Price : £1 11s. 6d.) Written in
Hebrew.

This is a second survey of the Dead Sea Scrolls, complementary
to the first outline by Professor Sukenik in Megilloth Genuzoth
I, 1948 (cf. *Book List*, 1949, p. 51). Specimen texts are given
from all the hitherto published texts and fragments, including
those given by De Vaux in *Revue Biblique*, October, 1949. There
are, however, two major additions, which appear here for the
first time, namely a portion of the Songs of Thanksgiving and
two columns from the Hebrew University scroll of Isaiah,
bearing the text of xlviii. 17—xlix. 7 and l, 7—li. 8. The
facsimile demonstrates adequately the similarity between the
text-form of the scroll and that of the Massoretes, but also
shows diversity between them in paragraph division. The
portions of the Syrian Isaiah scroll discussed at length in the
book are those published in *B.A.* and *B.A.S.O.R.* and Sukenik's
Nahmu Nahmu Ammi, but one notes again that the
" Massoretic Text " given for comparison does not coincide
with any well-established edition, and consequent confusion
exists in matters of orthography and particularly in *scriptio
plena* and *defectiva*—a fundamentally important aspect of
this study. In the introductory notes Professor Sukenik adds
to his earlier account of how he acquired scrolls from the cache
for the Hebrew University, and discusses anew the question
of what he still calls the Genizah. A very useful table shows a
comparison of scripts in the various scrolls.

In the nature of things, Professor Sukenik's publications of
texts from the scrolls are indispensable for all who seriously
study the Dead Sea Scrolls, and the present issue is no
exception. For that reason, however, one must voice the
regret that, whereas so many of the texts reproduced here were
already available in other publications, the really important
new material is so little by comparison. There is a very real
need for the publication of such texts as the Hebrew University
Isaiah scroll, and the still unpublished parts of the scrolls of
Warfare and of the Songs of Thanksgiving, in order that the
contents of the cache can be surveyed as a whole. The present
publication, however, is of great importance, and the author
and publishers are again to be congratulated on a very fine
production.

B.J.R.

WOOLLEY, C. L. : *Ur of the Chaldees*, 2nd edition. 1950. Pp. 208. (Ernest Benn, London. Price : 10s. 6d.)

A second edition of the author's popular work of 1929. The writer has not substantially altered his text except to indicate in the preface that his dates should be reduced probably by some 200 years. Here he is referring primarily to the period of the First Dynasty which he had dated from c. 3100 B.C. The evidence adduced from excavation in the Khabur basin and at Mari—which the writer does not cite—demand a similar reduction of his dates for Sargon, Naram Sin, the IIIrd Dynasty of Ur and Hammurabi. The work is a very lucid description of archaeological methods and results at Ur.

J.G.

HISTORY AND GEOGRAPHY

AVI YONAH, M. : *Geographiah historith shel Erets Yisrael le-min Shivath Zion we-'ad reshith ha kibush ha-'Aravi* (*Historical geography of the land of Israel from the Restoration to the Arab conquest*). 1949. Pp. viii+208, with 13 maps. (Mossad Bialik, Jerusalem. Price : I £2.000.)

This beautiful volume is divided into three parts. The first one (pp. 9-69) gives a survey of the territorial history of Jewish Palestine during the Persian, Ptolemaic, Seleucid, Hasmonaean, Herodian, and Roman periods. The second (pp. 73-84) consists of a chapter on communications, mainly on Roman road construction in Palestine. The third (pp. 87-177) gives a detailed description of the individual parts of the land—Judaea, Samaria, Galilee, Transjordan north of the Arnon, Peraea, *limes Palestinae*, and the Negeb—and their towns and all that is known about them during the periods under consideration. The very full bibliographic references include the ancient sources Jewish (in Hebrew and other languages), pagan, and Christian and the whole apparatus of modern literature as scattered in books and periodicals. A second revised edition of the book is in the press. Special mention should be made of the two large splendid maps, which have been added separately.

I.L.S.

BITTEL, K. : *Grundzüge der Ver- und Frühgeschichte Kleinasiens*, 2nd edition, 1950. Pp. 136+51 illustrations and 7 maps. (Wasmuth, Tübingen. Price : £1 15s. 6d.)

A very comprehensive survey of the political and cultural development of Anatolia especially valuable from one with so much first-hand experience of Turkey and its field archaeology. The main thesis is that local features predominated in spite of political movements from abroad such as the invasion and establishment of the Hittites and the Persians and the expansion of the Phrygian power. He would subdivide the land into three cultural zones, the West coast, the plateau and the Eastern mountains, characterized respectively by the culture of the Lydian Empire, the Hittite Empire and that of Hurrian Urartu. The attitude is soundly conservative.

318

The evidence of archaeology is fully used but never exceeded and deficiencies frankly admitted. The work is of great value not only for the positive evidence cited but also for the outstanding problems which the author brings to notice. Its chief interest for Old Testament scholarship is that in adducing evidence for the Cimmerian and Scythian invasions it elucidates the background especially of Ezekiel and in illustrating the cultural tolerance of Persia it helps us to understand the circumstances of the Jewish Restoration.

J.G.

BOUVET, M. : *Histoire Biblique.* 1950. Pp. viii+472. (de Gigord, Paris. Price : Frs. 410.)

That this book has been found useful by many readers is proved by the fact that it has gone into its tenth edition. These readers are not scholars, however, and the work can claim no scientific value. It offers an uncritical summary of selected Biblical incidents, and takes little account of any extra-Biblical evidence. The Exodus is placed at the impossible date 1320 B.C. The incidents remembered in the Song of Deborah, probably the most important in the whole period of the Judges, are unmentioned. Even for the general reader it has defects, though such usefulness as it has is only for him.

H.H.R.

BRONGERS, H. A. : *Hammurabi* (Cultuurhistorische Monografieën). 1949. Pp. 146. (Servire, The Hague. Price : Fl. 2.90.)

A study of Hammurabi in the setting of his time—here taken as 1728-1686—prefaced by a description of the land and races of Mesopotamia. The writer emphasizes the policy of Hammurabi to develope the secular influence of the throne independent of the temple, a policy which was destined to failure. He gives a new assessment of the significance of Hammurabi in the contemporary Near East which the new evidence from Mari demands and from an analysis of the code and correspondence of Hammurabi he gives a picture of Mesopotamian life and culture in surprising fullness considering the small bulk of the work.

J.G.

FITZGERALD-LEE, J. : *The Great Migration.* 1951. Pp. 212. (Skeffington, London. Price : 8s. 6d.)

The original volume has been extended by the author's son. The theme of the book is that the Exodus was really from Peru. The Red Sea (*yam suph*) is really the Behring Strait, and the migrants went through on dry feet because the straits were frozen. The name ' Abram ' is derived from the same root as ' Eber.' There are many other original and surprising identifications.

N.H.S.

HEINISCH, P. : *Geschichte des Alten Testamentes*. 1950. Pp. xx+388.
(Hanstein, Bonn. Price : DM. 17.50, or bound DM. 21.)

In this *Ergänzungsband* of the Bonner Bible, the indefatigable
Professor Heinisch reviews the history, religion and culture of
Israel from the earliest times to the Destruction of the Temple.
He begins, as the Bible begins, with the Creation, though he
does not treat the early narratives of Genesis as history.
The work rests on sound scholarship and enormously wide
reading (as is testified by the valuable bibliographies), though
it is at times more conservative than might have been expected.
Thus Daniel is treated as a historical figure of the exilic period.
Account is taken of archaeological evidence on various
questions (e.g. the Johoiachin texts published by Weidner
are mentioned), but less notice is given to this side than might
have been looked for. Thus the account of the capture of Ai
in the book of Joshua is treated as historical without any
reference to the problems which archaeology has raised here.
Here and elsewhere problems are lightly passed over, where
they might have been more frankly faced. While there is
little of original value in the book, it is a useful general survey
with a very wide field of interest, and will be of value to more
advanced students if only for its references to literature.
H.H.R.

HITTI, P. K. : *History of Syria, including Lebanon and Palestine*. 1950.
Pp. xxvi+750. (Macmillan, London. Price : £2 2s. 0d.)

The wide sweep of this book, covering the history of Syria
and Palestine from pre-historic times to the present day,
precludes any detailed treatment. Professor Hitti has given a
good general account, however, in this well-illustrated volume.
To the history of the Hebrews from the Exodus to Alexander
only fifty pages are devoted, and to Herod and his father
only a single page. Here and elsewhere there is remarkable
compression, and throughout a complicated task has been
executed with skill. The Old Testament scholar will not come
to it to learn new facts about his own period of interest, but
he will learn much from the integration of the various periods
into the whole and from the balance he finds here. The work
rests on wide reading and shows acquaintance with modern
archaeological work. H.H.R.

LUSSEAU, H. : *Précis d'Histoire Biblique*, vol. I. 1949. Pp. vi+90.
(de Gigord, Paris. Price : Frs. 140.)

Here is a highly compact and useful, though very conservative,
introduction to Biblical study, covering general questions,
such as inspiration, the Canon, textual criticism and hermeneutics, and the study of the first eleven chapters of Genesis.
In the sections dealing with the Biblical chapters we are
given a brief summary of the contents, a study of the literary
genre, and notes on the historico-doctrinal teaching, with
additional paragraphs on occasion, dealing with such things
as the relations with profane documents and with modern
scientific theory. The general conception is excellent, and we
could do with comparable handbooks in English, even though
not governed by the same point of view. H.H.R.

MEEK, T. J. : *Hebrew Origins*. Revised edition, 1950. Pp. 228. (Harper and Bros., New York. Price : $3.00.)

The first edition of this useful book—the Haskell Lectures for 1933-34—was published in 1936. The present revised edition represents a re-writing of the whole volume in the light of later discoveries and research. The first chapter, on the origin of the Hebrew people, has undergone considerable revision, more especially as a result of the emergence of a more certain chronology of the ancient Near East, and the discovery of new law codes has necessitated much alteration in chapter two, which deals with the origin of Hebrew law. Many changes have been introduced also into the other four chapters, whose subjects are the origin of the Hebrew God, of the Hebrew priesthood, of Hebrew prophecy, and of Hebrew monotheism. The author has paid due attention to the comments of reviewers of the first edition, and has brought up to date the literature cited in the footnotes, which are on a generous scale. While he may have seemed to have spoken in the first edition somewhat disparagingly of the documentary hypothesis of the Hexateuch, he now makes it clear that he does not altogether repudiate the theory. His views in this matter agree almost exactly, so he tells us, with those of Professor Bentzen as expressed in the second volume of his *Introduction to the O.T.*, 1949. A reading of Professor Meek's book inevitably calls to mind Professor Rowley's recently published Schweich Lecture, *From Joseph to Joshua*, which cover some of the same ground. The two works read together provide an interesting study in differing interpretations of the data. Professor Rowley's Lectures, in which some of Professor Meek's views are criticised, appeared too late to be utilised in the revision of *Hebrew Origins*.

D.W.T.

NEEDLER, W. : *Palestine Ancient and Modern* (A handbook and guide to the Palestinian collection of the Royal Ontario Museum). 1949. Pp. 116+comparative chronological chart and 35 plates. (University of Toronto Press. Price : 15s. 6d.)

A description of objects illustrating the main phases in the development of Palestinian culture from the Bronze Age to the present day with succint historical notes at appropriate points throughout. Selecting as she does the main types of objects the writer is able to present her subject in clear perspective. While not pretending to fullness, the work will serve as a useful introduction to Palestinian archaeology and make more intelligible to the general reader a subject which too often bewilders by its technicalities.

J.G.

NOTH, M. : *Geschichte Israels*. 1950. Pp. viii+396. (Vandenhoeck & Ruprecht, Göttingen. Price : DM. 19.80.)

This " Lehrbuch," as Noth describes it, is adequately but not heavily documented. It is in four parts and traces the history to the revolt of Bar-Kochba. The first part deals with origins and takes up nearly one third of the whole. Here the reader is

321

given in an easily assimilable form the results of Noth's researches on *Überlieferungsgeschichte*. His view is that Israelite history, like all history, contains an element of the " unhistorical," and that we must often be content with tradition-history rather than with history proper. His attitude to Moses is less positive than that of most contemporary historians. He is emphatic that there was no " divine-kingship" in Israel. The foundations of the book are firmly grounded in the archaeological and critical researches of the past century, and the general conclusion is that Israelite history has no real parallel elsewhere. Indispensable to all teachers of the subject. C.R.N.

ROWLEY, H. H. : *From Joseph to Joshua : Biblical traditions in the light of archaeology.* 1950. Pp. 200. (Oxford University Press. Price : 12s. 6d.)

The first of these lectures—the Schweich Lectures for 1948—is concerned with the extra-Biblical evidence, the second with the Biblical traditions, while in the third is offered a synthesis which aims at framing, on the basis of the evidence discussed in the first two lectures, a view of the history and chronology of the period which will prove at once self-consistent and satis-fying. Professor Rowley's interest in the subject of these lectures is of long standing, and he has already published a number of studies in connection with it. In this latest and more comprehensive study he has found it necessary to introduce only minor modifications into the views which he has pre-viously propounded. The migration of Abraham for Harran is put at *c.* 1650 B.C. ; Joseph was taken into Egypt in the reign of Ikhnaton, under whom he rose to high office, *c.* 1370 B.C. ; the Descent of the Hebrews into Egypt took place *c.* 1360 B.C. ; Rameses II was the Pharaoh of the Oppression, *c.* 1300 B.C. ; *c.* 1290 B.C. Moses was born, and the Exodus occurred *c.* 1230 B.C. Professor Rowley is at pains to present all the available evidence—which he does with all fairness—and he examines fully the different views which are held concerning it. The skill with which he weaves his way through the notoriously complex archaeological and literary problems involved will evoke general admiration. It hardly needs to be said that his knowledge of the literature is remarkable. The list of works consulted occupies twenty-three pages. The names of some of the many foreign scholars referred to will probably be unfamiliar even to some professional O.T. scholars in this country. They will be grateful for this introduction to them, though their work may not always be easily accessible to them. A useful summary of dates is appended, and there are three indices—subject, author and Biblical. In this volume Professor Rowley brings up to date the work of an earlier Schweich Lecturer of over thirty years ago—C. F. Burney. He has had to take account of the important archaeological evidence which has become available since Burney's day, and he handles it with commendable caution—his discussion of the evidence from Jericho, for example, is sobering. It will be of interest to many that Professor Rowley regards his subject not merely as an academic exercise in history and chronology, but as having an importance also for a proper appreciation of the work of Moses and for a right understanding of the development of Hebrew religion. His book will long have a place among the significant literature of the subject. One lays it aside marvelling not a little at the richness of the fare provided. The voluminous foo. notes are a feast in themselves. D.W.T.

SCHARFF, A. and MOORTGAT, A. : *Ägypten und Vorderasien im Altertum.* 1950. Pp. 536+2 maps. (Weltgeschichte in Einzeldarstellung.) (F. Bruckmann, Munich. Price : DM. 18.)

Alexander Scharff, whose work was unfortunately cut short by his death in 1950, gives the " History of Egypt from the earliest times to the foundation of Alexandria," while Anton Moortgat deals with the " History of the Near East to the Hellenistic period." As Moortgat, unlike Scharff, has to consider several peoples and cultures—Hittites, Sumerians, Akkad, Assyria, Elam, etc.—his chronological table, comprising 14 pages, gives parallel columns in which the kings and the most important events of the individual territories are shown side by side, so that in each case contemporary dates impress themselves upon the eye. Both authors give a select bibliography of the literature relative to their respective parts, Scharff at the beginning of each chapter and Moortgat at the end of his study. Both have most creditably fulfilled their task to write the history of the Egyptian and Near Eastern antiquity in a way both scholarly and useful to a wider public. As both Scharff and Moortgat are particularly interested in archaeology and art, these aspects are especially considered and this increases the value and readability of this book. Finally, it should be mentioned that both authors take account of the fact that the history of Israel is closely intertwined with that of Egypt and the Near East, and thus the book is also of great value to theologians and lovers of the Old Testament. O.E.

TEXT AND VERSIONS

Biblia Sacra iuxta latinam vulgatam versionem ad codicum fidem . . . cura et studia monachorum . . . ordinis Sancti Benedicti edita. Libri Ezrae Tobiae Iudith. 1950. Pp. xii+280. (Rome. Price : $4.00.)

This, the eighth volume of the Benedictine edition of the Vulgate, follows the same plan as its predecessors ; the somewhat mechanical preference of a reading found in two rather than a possibly superior reading found in a single manuscript is still observed, although for various reasons the manuscripts chosen are not necessarily the same as in previous books. The critical apparatus, however, is so full and lucid that the student is in no danger of being misled by this method of establishing the printed text. The paper and format are as sumptuous as those of the preceding volumes, in spite of the difficulties of the times. All concerned deserve the warmest congratulations on a magnificent work which will surely stand the test of time and become indispensable to students ' to generations of generations.' G.R.D.

*BRUCE, F. F. : *The Books and the Parchments. Some Chapters on the Transmission of the Bible.* 1950. Pp. 260. (Pickering & Inglis Ltd., London. Price : 12s. 6d.)

This book is essentially a popularization of an important topic, and, as such, is to be highly commended, particularly on the score of its vigorous and clear presentation. It is one of the most readable books I have seen on the subject. Its range is extremely wide, for it includes the whole Bible and the Apocrypha. Consequently, the treatment might sometimes appear to be uneven, and the choice of topics for special study is not always appropriate. Kahle's theory about the early history of the Versions is given without discussion of any alternatives ; the history of the Vulgate, too, might have indicated the divergence of views which has recently emerged. The book has a useful bibliography of English works for further study.   B.J.R.

COPPENS, J. : *La Critique du Texte Hébreu de l'Ancien Testament.* (Introduction à l'étude historique de l'Ancien Testament, III.) 2e édition augmentée. 1950. Pp. 50. (Publications Universitaires de Louvain ; Desclée de Brouwer, Bruges-Paris ; Pontificio Istituto Biblico, Rome. Price : Belgian Frs. 30.)

The story of O.T. textual criticism from the renaissance to present times is surveyed, marred only by a rather over-simplified account of certain aspects, such as the conflict about Bible Inspiration, and a neglect of recent views on the ' oral transmission ' of the text. The writer deplores, as arbitrary, the tendency to treat the text on the basis of metre, and, again, Riessler's re-translation of a hypothetical Greek text to provide a Hebrew prototype ; but he shows a more favourable attitude to the following four kinds of emendations : 1. diplomatic (comparison of readings from the ancient Versions and of variants within the MT itself) ; 2. conjectural ; 3. lexicographical (the approach of G. R. Driver and Winton Thomas) ; 4. palaeographic (the reconstruction of a pre-Massoretic Hebrew text by means of a transcription of the LXX prototype, in the manner of Wutz's theory). Despite misgivings, Professor Coppens is optimistic about the future of textual emendation, and appeals for a better organised publication of proposed emendations.   B.J.R.

DRIVER, G. R. : *L'Interprétation du texte masorétique à la lumière de la lexicographie hébraïque.* (Analecta Lovaniensia Biblica et Orientalia. Ser. II. Fasc. 18). 1950. Pp. 16. (Offprint of Ephemerides Theologicae Lovanienses, 1950, t. XXVI, pp. 337-353. Publications Universitaires de Louvain ; Desclée de Brouwer, Bruges—Paris. Price : Fr. 25.)

Professor Driver gives in this paper an admirable statement of his approach to O.T. textual and lexicographical study. By means of extremely attractive and telling examples, he demonstrates how the root-forms of Hebrew words should be examined to establish their present forms and meanings, and how these are further elucidated by their renderings (good and bad) in the ancient Versions and by comparison with allied terms in cognate languages. The lecture was delivered at the University of Louvain under the auspices of the British Council.
                                                    B.J.R.

GOLDSCHMIDT, L. : *The Earliest Editions of the Hebrew Bible :* with a *Treatise of the Oldest Manuscripts of the Bible* by P. Kahle. 1950. Pp. 60. (Aldus Book Company, New York. Price : £4 10s. 0d.)

From the scholar's point of view this is a book with a misplaced emphasis. The main emphasis is clearly intended by the publishers to rest on the physical presentation of the text and not on its content. One cannot but feel a pang of regret that the work of two well-known scholars should be treated in this way. De luxe and limited editions do not generally appeal to Old Testament scholars.

The late Dr. Goldschmidt had already published a brochure on Hebrew Incunables before he penned the present article in which he traces the progress of the printing of the Hebrew Bible from the Bologna Psalter of 1477· to the Nuremberg Hexaglot of 1599.

Professor Kahle expounds and expands the views he holds on the real source-text of the Hebrew Bible, views to which he gave expression in the Introduction to Kittel's *Biblia Hebraica*, 3rd edition, 1937. He argues strongly for the Ben Asher text, as found in the manuscript preserved in the Karaite Synagogue of Cairo, in preference to the hitherto accepted and exclusively adopted Ben Chayyim text. A point of particular interest is his argument that the Masoretes broke away from an earlier tradition of *Palestinian* pronunciation of Hebrew, closely resembling the Samaritan, to produce an artificial vocalization of their own creating. " We can clearly recognise that the Masoretes have replaced a pronunciation of Hebrew which they regarded as lax, as inaccurate, by a pronunciation which they believed to be the correct one. They have created an ideal Hebrew . . . . . The authors of Hebrew grammars are generally satisfied when they re-discover the rules according to which the Masoretes reconstructed their ideal Hebrew. They do not see the vicious circle in which they move " (p. 60).   E.R.

LINDHAGEN, C. : *ERGAZESTHAI (Apc.* 18 : 17 *Hes.* 48 : 18. 19). *Die Wurzel SAP im NT und AT. Zwei Beiträge zur Lexicographie der griechischen Bibel.* (Uppsala Universitets Årsskrift 1950 : 5). 1950. Pp. 70. (A. B. Lundequistska Bokhandeln, Uppsala and Otto Harrassowitz, Leipzig. Price : Kr. 3.25.)

This detailed work consists of two independent studies. 1. *ERGAZESTHAI* in Rev. xviii. 17 reflects the sense but not the text of Ezek. xxvii. 29, and means ' those who work the sea ' (cf. RV mgn. in contrast to AV). It has a parallel occurence in LXX of Ezek. xlviii. 18f. 2. The root *SAP* (orig. ' rotten, putrid ') acquires a ' religious ' shade of meaning in N.T., viz., ' useless, evil.' In Greek O.T. both meanings are supported. The LXX[B] reading in Isa. xxviii. 21 indicates ' evil, enmity, anger ' or some such actively destructive sense.
The book has a useful bibliography and index.   B.J.R.

ROBERTS, B. J. : *The Old Testament Text and Versions : The Hebrew Text in Transmission and the History of the Ancient Versions.* 1951. Pp. 326. (University of Wales Press, Cardiff. Price : £1 1s. 0d.)

The need of an up to date book in English showing the profound change that has come about in the sphere of the textual criticism of the O.T.—more particularly as the result of the accession of new manuscript material and new attitudes concerning the use of the versions—has long been felt. This book is accordingly greatly to be welcomed. It aims at providing an introduction to the study of the O.T. text and the versions and a conspectus of views obtaining to-day. Part I deals with the Hebrew Bible—the text before the time of the Massoretes ; the Scribes ; the Massoretes ; Tiberian and post-Tiberian Massoretic work ; pointed manuscripts and printed editions ; and causes of textual corruption and their emendation. In Part II the LXX and other Greek versions are treated—the early history of the LXX ; the Greek translations of the second century A.D. ; the LXX of Origen ; the recensions of the LXX ; the manuscripts and printed editions of the LXX, and its character as a translation. Part III deals with the Samaritan Pentateuch, the Targumim, and the Peshitta ; Part IV with the translations based mainly on the LXX (Coptic, Ethiopic, etc.) ; Part V with the Latin translations ; and Part VI with the Arabic versions. As illustrations of the author's standpoint may be mentioned his view that the Lagardean conception of an early archetype M.T. needs to be modified to-day ; his belief that there was a proto-LXX text-form, and his recognition at the same time of the importance of the contributions of Wutz, Kahle and Sperber to the study of this problem ; and his pleas for a view of the versions which regards them not only for their value for the reconstruction of the Hebrew text, but as having themselves value as interpretations, rather than translations, of the Hebrew text. The place of the Biblical portions of the Dead Sea Scrolls in the history of the transmission of the Hebrew text is introduced into the discussion at all relevant points. The author's accurate scholarship is apparent throughout, and his critical judgements are invariably well considered. Not the least valuable part of the work is the brief conclusion in which the probable lines of future development in this field of study are outlined. The bibliography, which occupies twenty-eight pages, contains much material for further research. D.W.T.

Vetus Latina. Die Rede der altlateinischen Bibel nach Petrus Sabatier neu gesammelt und herausgegeben von der Erzabtei Beuron. I. *Verzeichnis der Sigel.* 1949. Pp. 104. (Herder, Freiburg. Price : 16s. 6d.)

The present volume is the beginning of a great undertaking, a complete revision of the text of the Old Latin version of the Old Testament, based on Sabatier's famous edition. It contains lists of all the known MSS and editions of the Latin fathers, which will be used in the preparation of the work. The lists are long, in fact as nearly complete as human labour can make them, and readers will find difficulty in calling many of the abbreviations to mind, while scholars will be tempted to ask how many of the Fathers quoted, especially the late Fathers, will yield texts of independent or substantial value. However that may be, the work will be awaited with impatience and may be welcomed as an indispensable tool to research ; for the text of the Old Latin version is now so scattered as to be almost useless for practical purposes, while Sabatier's volumes have long been not only out of date but also out of print.   G.R.D.

EXEGESIS AND MODERN TRANSLATIONS

BASIL OF CAESAREA : *Homélies sur l'Hexaéméron*, Greek text with Introduction and translation by S. Giet. 1950. Pp. 540. (Les Éditions du Cerf, Paris. Price : £1 5s. 0d.)

This is a further volume in the series *Sources Chrétiennes* (see *Book List*, 1948, pp. 27f.) in which the Greek text and a lucid French translation stand facing one another, with text-critical and other notes beneath, preceded by an Introduction and a good Bibliography. The Introduction discusses the wide range of secular knowledge displayed in the Homilies and the sources whence Basil derived it. The Homilies are of no critical value to the modern Old Testament scholar, but the patristic interpretations are often of value for the study of the history of interpretation, and many will be glad to have this convenient and beautifully printed edition.   H.H.R.

BEA, A. : *Liber Ecclesiastae qui ab Hebraeis appellatur Qohelet*. 1950. Pp. xii + 30. (Pontifical Biblical Institute, Rome. Price : 460 lire.)

This small and handy edition of Qohelet bears the number 100 as the latest of the " Scripta Pontificii Instituti Biblici." The editor, who is well-known as one of the translators of the new Latin Psalter and as the author of the brochure *Il nuovo Salterio latino*, has here provided a new rendering of the Hebrew text, a short introduction, and a minimum of commentary. There are some interesting remarks in the section " De textu et versionibus " on St. Jerome's three editions of the book ; in the section on the doctrinal teaching of Qohelet it is maintained that he was no sceptic or pessimist or Epicurean, but a man with a firm belief in God, who recognized the limitations of his own knowledge in regard to life's problems and difficulties. In xii. 4c Podechard's reading *wayyiqmal qôl* (et avium *cantus attenuatur*) is accepted as probable, and by way of comment it is noted : " 4cd videntur indicare vocem debilem et raucam senis."   J.M.T.B.

BEWER, J. A. : *The Book of Isaiah* (in Harper's Annotated Bible Series). 2 vols. 1950. Pp. 98, 74. (Harper & Bros., New York. Price : 75 cents each vol. An English edition will be published by Eyre & Spottiswoode, London. Price : 5s. 0d. each vol.)

In this edition the text of the A.V. is printed, but poetic passages are set out in lines and the separate units are marked by headings. The notes are brief, but packed with information, and the volumes should be widely useful. The Introductions are very short. The author follows the usual division of the book into three main units, and finds some later material in the first division. In the second division he adheres to the collective view of the Servant. The third division he attributes to four hands. The scholarship of Professor Bewer is above reproach, and the presentation—especially the lay-out of the text—is excellent. Recent sources of knowledge are drawn on, including the Ras Shamra texts, and all who seek a wealth of reliable information packed into the briefest possible compass, yet clearly and legibly printed, will find it here.

H.H.R.

La Sainte Bible, translated into French under the direction of the École Biblique of Jerusalem : *Le Deutéronome*, by H. Cazelles. 1950. Pp. 142. (Price : 260 Fr.) *Le livre de Josué*, by F. M. Abel. 1950. Pp. 88 with map. (Price : 160 Fr.) *Les Psaumes*, by R. Tournay and R. Schwab. 1950. Pp. 482. (Price : 480 Fr.) *Le livre de Job*, by R. P. Larcher. 1950. Pp. 170. (Price : 320 Fr.) *Le livre de Sagesse* by C. E. Osty. 1950. Pp. 116. (Price : 210 Fr.) (Editions du Cerf, Paris.) Subscription price for the seventeen volumes (eight of them New Testament) which have already appeared in this series is 3,930 Fr.

> For earlier volumes in this series, see *Book List* 1950, pp. **35, 40**. The previous high standard of translation is maintained, and also the same general scheme, the translation in paragraphs with headings, and an introduction, popular rather than technical. An early date is assumed for Deuteronomy, with many redactions, especially large-scale insertions *ca*. 700 B.C. (*vide* Welch and Ricciotti), and a final edition in the time of Ezekiel. Joshua contains stories told to pilgrims at the various shrines. It reflects conditions *ca*. 1,000 B.C. It was the damage caused by the Habiru that made it easy for Joshua to share out the land amongst the tribes. The authors of the volume on the Psalms adhere to the Roman Biblical Commission's decree and do not deny the Davidic authorship of the psalms, but are permitted to assume retouching and modifications. Little use is made of Babylonian material, verbal similarities with the Ugarit texts are noted, but there are no references to modern studies in general. The emphasis is on Types of psalms, but not according to the Gunkel classification. The general unity of Job is maintained, but the Elihu speeches are an insertion. xxvi. 5-14 belongs to Bildad's third speech, and Zophar's third speech is xxvii. 13-23 and xxiv. 18-24. The author was of the 5th cent. B.C. Wisdom was written by an Alexandrine Jew in the first half of the first cent. B.C. It shows strong Hellenistic influence and contains the first clear declaration of the immortality of the soul.
>
> N.H.S.

La Sainte Bible. Version nouvelle d'après les textes originaux par les moines de Maredsous. 1950. Pp. xl + 1482. (Editions de Maredsous. Price : £1 7s. 0d.)

> How many recent, or fairly recent, translations of the Bible into French now exist ? To mention only those by Catholic authors, there is the invaluable, indispensable Crampon, the

excellent renderings in each of the volumes of *La Sainte Bible* as edited by Clamer, the *Bible de Jérusalem*, and the present handsome edition in delightfully clear and legible type, by the monks of the great Belgian abbey of Maredsous. Some years ago, one of these monks, H. Duesberg, published two admirable volumes on *Les Scribes Inspirés* (Desclée, Paris, 1938-9), an introduction to the wisdom literature. He himself translated a great part of three of the books, that is, of Proverbs, Sirach and Wisdom, but for Job and Ecclesiastes he relied " à la manière d'une vulgate " upon the classic renderings of E. Dhorme and E. Podechard in the *Études Bibliques* series. " A quoi bon," he writes, " tenter de faire médiocrement ce qui fut réalisé de manière excellente ?" Now it is in no way astonishing that the present single-volume edition does not make use of Dhorme and Podechard, since this would entail the taking over in their entirety of two copyright editions. But it is rather amazing that Duesberg's own translation is not used in the renderings here given of the three books that he has already, in great part, translated. In any event, the renderings, wherever they have been tested, are extremely competent, though perhaps not quite so smooth to the tongue as the earlier versions just mentioned. The price of this volume, which is equipped with short introductions to the books and a quantity of notes, is about half that of Mgr. Knox's three volumes in English, of which the two Old Testament parts were noticed in last year's Book List.

J.M.T.B.

BUZY, D. : *Le Cantique des Cantiques.* 1950. Pp. 230. (Letouzey et Ané, Paris. Price : Frs. 250.)

This is a reprint of the commentary on the Song of Songs contained in *La Sainte Bible*, edited by Pirot and Clamer (see *Book List*, 1948, p. 25), slightly revised and re-arranged. The Introduction contains an additional page, and the complete French translation precedes the commentary, where both Latin and French renderings are given and followed by the commentary. Moreover, the notes do not stand at the foot of the page but alternate with the text. The Song is described as a ' chef d'oeuvre de poésie pure,' and as the Fourth Gospel of the Old Testament. Its primary and literal sense is said to be the union between Yahweh and Israel. Beyond this it is to be read as a parable, whose details must not, however, be pressed.

H.H.R.

CERFAUX, L., COPPENS, J., GRIBOMONT, J. : *Problèmes et Méthode d'Exégèse Théologique.* (Analecta Lovaniensia Biblica et Orientalia Ser. II., Fasc. 16.) 1950. Pp. 92. (Publications Universitaires de Louvain; Desclée de Brouwer, Bruges-Paris. Price : Belgian Fr. 50.)

The brochure deals with the theological and typological ' interpretation ' of the O.T., and the desire for a fuller appreciation of this approach to O.T. study, by no means confined to the Roman community, has received a considerable stimulus in this excellent series of papers. Two papers are supplied by Professor Coppens ; in the one he gives his general views on the problem of the ' wide ' or ' full ' Biblical interpretation, and in the other a discussion of the *proto-evangelion* in Gen. iii. 15. Father Gribomont discusses further the former point made by Coppens, though not always in agreement with him. Professor Cerfaux has some interesting comments on Apostolic exegesis. In addition, an extensive bibliography of some 160 items is given by Professor Coppens. Every O.T. theologian, whatever his approach, should give serious attention to this book. B.J.R.

CLAMER, A. (ed. by) : *La Sainte Bible, texte latin et traduction française d'après les textes originaux avec un commentaire exégétique et théologique.* Tome V. *Les Psaumes.* 1950. Pp. 776. (Letouzey et Ané, Paris. Price : £1 4s. 6d.)

This is a re-editing of an earlier text and commentary by E. Pannier that appeared before the publication of the new Latin Psalter, prepared by members of the Istituto Biblico in Rome, in 1945. The new edition has been entrusted to H. Renard, doyen of the Lille faculty, and has this advantage over most other editions of the Latin Psalter that it prints both texts (the Gallican and the new rendering) one below the other, the third place in the series being taken by Renard's translation of the new Psalter. This is an astonishingly full commentary, given the scope and purpose of the Clamer Bible, and the fact that room has to be found for no less than three Psalters . The introduction seems to be all that could be required ; a page is devoted to a comparison of all four Latin psalters in their rendering of Ps. iv (i.e. the Roman, the Gallican, St. Jerome's *Psalterium juxta Hebraicam veritatem*, and the Istituto version). If somebody would edit a complete Psalter, giving the text of all four versions, it would be of great value to all students of Biblical Latin. J.M.T.B.

CLAMER, A. (ed. by) : *La Sainte Bible, texte latin et traduction française d'après les textes originaux avec un commentaire exégétique et théologique.* Tome VIII, 2e partie. *Les Livres des Macchabées.* 1951. Pp. 240. (Letouzey & Ané, Paris. Price : 8s. 6d.)

The present commentary on Maccabees I & II, was already complete and had received the censor's *Imprimatur* when the two commentaries by Abel (one in the *Bible de Jérusalem* in July, 1948 ; the other in the *Études Bibliques* in October, 1949) made their appearance in print. We are not told how far M. Grandclaudon, the author of this commentary, was able to make any use of Abel's works, at the stages of revision and correction. It is perhaps not altogether a bad thing that his book should be, at least in great part, an independent work, not over-influenced by Abel's fine achievement. This number appears to be well up to the standard of the Clamer Bible. The introductions are particularly to be commended for their clarity and precision. The theology of the two books is briefly but excellently summarized. J.M.T.B.

COHEN, A. (ed. by) : *The Soncino Books of the Bible. Jeremiah : Hebrew Text and English Translation with an Introduction and Commentary*, by H. Freedman. 1949. Pp. xxiii+369. *Kings*, by I. W. Slotki. 1950. Pp. xiii+337. *Ezekiel*, by S. Fisch. 1950. Pp. xvii+351. *Joshua and Judges*, by H. Freedman and J. J. Slotki. 1950. Pp. xvii+333. (Soncino Press, London and Bournemouth. Price : 12s. 6d. per volume.)

These volumes of the series of the Soncino Books of the Bible have the same general features as the earlier volumes—the Hebrew text and the American Jewish Version in parallel columns, with notes at the foot of the page. The notes are brief and simple, with frequent references to the rabbinical commentators. The Introductions are short and conservative in accordance with the aim of the series. Eight lines suffice to dispose of all the recent variety of views on the authorship and date of Ezekiel, for an account of which the reader is referred to the posthumous book of Wheeler Robinson, *Two Hebrew Prophets*. The introduction to Jeremiah is somewhat fuller and is well planned. On the question of Jeremiah's attitude to sacrifice the author writes : ' To deduce that Jeremiah was antagonistic to the ritual of the Temple is to read into his words a thought which he would have indignantly repudiated.' Dr. Freedman makes much use of Peake, Streane and Binns, but surprisingly does not include Skinner in his Bibliography. The introduction to Kings is particularly short, but the commentary is well designed for the readers it has in mind, and like all the volumes will be of use to the non-Jewish reader, though not for philological, textual or critical matters. Joshua is assigned to a hand contemporary with the events it describes save for obvious anachronisms, such as Josh. xix. 47. The archaeological evidence, such as that relative to the fall of Ai, is ignored in the interests of this theory. On the other hand in the commentary on Judges there is more attention to recent archaeology and, within the limits allowed by the series, a more open approach to the problems. Thus, it is recognized that the chronology of the book is schematic and harmonizing attempts are dismissed. All the volumes are beautifully printed, and are a pleasure to handle.   H.H.R.

ERDMAN, C. R. : *The Book of Genesis : an Exposition.* 1950. Pp. 124. (Revell, New York. Price : $1.50.)

An exposition of the book of Genesis in so few pages is necessarily quite inadequate, and the publisher's ' blurb ' which says it is ' significant, enlightening, historic, prophetic, and throws new light on the origin, character, and destiny of man ' may be described as an over-statement. The author, who is Emeritus Professor of Princeton, deals very briefly, in a running exposition, with the book of Genesis in seven main divisions, linked with the names of Adam, Enoch, Noah, Abraham, Isaac, Jacob and Joseph. He does not touch critical questions, but is only concerned to ask what teaching the compiler of the book of Genesis can be supposed to have intended to set forth in the book we now have. It may be agreed that in the search for the origins of the book scholars often forget its purpose, and it is well to be recalled sometimes to this aspect of our work. Something much fuller than this book is really needed, however, and something which does not so divorce this side of our study from every other side of scholarly work.

H.H.R.

FERNÁNDEZ, A., S. J. : *Comentario a los libros de Esdras y Nehemías.* 1950. Pp. xix+459. (Instituto Francisco Suárez, Madrid. Price: 90 pes.)

In a prefatory note " Al Lector " the author explains that the present commentary, or rather the part relating to Esdras, was sent to Madrid for printing at the beginning of the Spanish Civil War and was destroyed in the course of the fighting. Happily, Fernández decided, after much reflection, to re-write his book, and we now have a most useful and thorough treatment of all the main problems connected with Ezra-Nehemiah, together with a number of excursuses that lighten the commentary and help to clarify the argument. On the question of the chronological order, Fernández considers that the book gives the impression that the author was at pains to arrange the events in the exact order in which they happened. He does not accept the widely held theory that Chronicles and Ezra-Nehemiah formed a single book. The problem of 3 Esdras is fully discussed. It is regrettable that the author has not been able to make use of Professor Rowley's contribution to the Ignace Goldziher Memorial Volume, " The Chronological Order of Ezra and Nehemiah " or of the commentary by Médebielle in the fourth volume of *La Sainte Bible*, edited by Clamer.

J.M.T.B.

FREY, H. : *Das Buch der Anfänge* (Genesis i-xi). 1950. Pp. 170. *Das Buch des Glaubens* (Genesis xii-xxv). 1950. Pp. 208. (Vols. 1 and 2 in *Die Botschaft des Alten Testaments.*) (Calwer Verlag, Stuttgart. Prices : DM. 6.20 and 6.80.)

The first volume deals with Genesis as far as xii. 5 ; the second begins at xii. 1 and continues to xxv. 11. Both volumes concentrate on the ' message,' as the general title indicates. The author is not concerned with critical and literary matters. Both volumes are stories of spiritual pilgrimage : the first from Chaos to Creation, but then from being near to God to being far from Him, thence to alienation, mutiny, and finally to a desire for reconciliation. The second volume is the story of Faith, shown in Abraham's departure from his homeland, in his certainty, in conversation with God (xviii. 1—xx. 18), and at last in fulfilment.

N.H.S.

GISPEN, W. H. : *Het Boek Leviticus.* 1950. Pp. 402. (Kok, Kampen. Price : Fl. 15.25 bound.)

The author, Professor in Hebrew at the Free University in Amsterdam, has taken great pains over an accurate and circumstantial treatment of the third book of the Bible. The book is distinguished by its literal translations and by the mention and discussion of opinions of authors from many centuries. There are naturally passages wherein the desire to conform to the fundamentalist view leads to artifical exegesis, and the writer's ideas on the meaning of sacrifice, the date and historical value of the narratives, the extra-biblical items, etc., are open to criticism. The main value of his comment is, in my opinion, the serious attempt to find a suitable translation for each term of the rather technical language of Leviticus.   P.A.H.deB.

GORDIS, R. : *The Wisdom of Koheleth : A New Translation with a Commentary and an Introductory Essay.* 1950. Pp. xxii+32. (East and West Library, London. Price : 5s. 6d.)

This is a revised edition of the author's *The Wisdom of Ecclesiastes,* 1945 (see *Book List* 1947, p. 16). Many of the changes are merely verbal, but others are more substantial and the Introduction has been in part recast. The positions adopted remain in general the same. The commentary part of the book is slight, and consists of a short introduction to each section of the translation. The view of Gordis is that the book is a unity, the appearance to the contrary being due to the author's habit of quoting a conventional maxim and then commenting on it.   H.H.R.

GREENSTONE, J. H. : *The Holy Scripture with Commentary : Proverbs.* 1950. Pp. xliv+354. (Jewish Publication Society of America, Philadelphia. Price : $3.50.)

This commentary, in the same series as Reider's *Deuteronomy* (see *Book List* 1938, pp. 6 f.) and Greenstone's *Numbers* (see *Book List* 1939, p. 7) is marked by the same features as its predecessors. It is based on sound scholarship, and while it does not obtrude critical questions it takes account of them. It had been hoped to include the Hebrew text in this volume, but this could not be done. The American Jewish Translation is used, and beneath it stands an excellent commentary, in which the fruits of modern study are embodied. The Solomonic authorship of the book is rejected, though Greenstone inclines to accept the view of Sellin that there is a Solomonic basis for the second section (x. 1—xxii. 16). Torczyner's theory of the origin of the book is pronounced attractive, but the author does not commit himself to it. Neither does he commit himself to the connexion of a section with *The Wisdom of Amen-em-ope,* though he records the view and Gressmann's consequent emendation in xxii. 20.   H.H.R.

HERNTRICH, V. : *Der Prophet Jesaja : Kapitel 1-12.* (Das Alte Testament Deutsch, 17.) 1950. Pp. xx+222. (Vandenhoeck and Ruprecht, Göttingen. Price : Subscr. DM. 7.80 ; separate DM. 9.40.)

A useful contribution to the now familiar series of semi-popular theological commentaries on the Old Testament. The exposition sometimes stands in marked contrast to that of the older liberalism ; but, if there is reaction here, it is sound in intention, and the author is often successful in exposing earlier weaknesses. Occasionally he has a peculiarly happy translation to offer, and his treatment of Isaiah's attitude to the cultus and the vexed problem of the Messianic Hope may be singled out as of special interest.   A.R.J.

KETTER, P. : *Die Psalmen, aus dem Urtext übertragen und kurz erläutert.* 4th edition. 1949. Pp. 208. (Kepplerhaus Verlag, Stuttgart. Price : 27s. 6d.)

This pleasant little duodecimo was first published in 1937, and is now re-issued with a text based upon the translation of the Psalms edited by the Pontifical Biblical Institute in 1945. The author has succeeded in making a useful and readable translation, issued in a format that can easily be carried in an ordinary pocket. The disadvantage of so portable an edition is that it is printed in extremely small Gothic type. The Psalms are printed in numerical order, preference being accorded to the numbering of the Hebrew original. There are some compact notes, a scheme for reciting the Psalter as an act of private devotion, and translations of the Canticles used in the Breviary office for Sundays (Benedictus, Magnificat, Nunc Dimittis, and Benedicite). Last of all comes a rendering of the Athanasian Creed, which is recited at the office of Prime on Trinity Sunday and on some other Sundays after Trinity, and after the Epiphany. J.M.T.B.

KNIGHT, G. A. F. : *Ruth and Jonah* (The Torch Bible Commentaries). 1950. Pp. 92. (S.C.M. Press, London. Price : 6s. 0d.)

This is the first Old Testament volume of this series of commentaries, which is designed to emphasize the theological and religious significance of the Bible. The critical positions on date and authorship are taken for granted, but the book is written simply for the general reader with the minimum of the paraphernalia of learning. There are three appendices, dealing with The Modern Approach to the Problem of Jonah, Our Lord's Use of the Book of Jonah, and Some Rabbinical Citations. The author too easily accepts the view that the book of Ruth was written as a reply to Ezra, and fails to observe that Ruth is represented as a proselyte, and that in its most exclusive moments Judaism received proselytes. The problem Ezra was concerned with was quite different. He also over-states the significance of Boaz' marriage of Ruth when he says that this brought Ruth into the redeemed community of Israel. Boaz married Ruth because he was her kinsman, and not because she was an alien, and it is hard to see how Boaz brought her into the Israelite community any more than Mahlon, whose line her child was held to continue. Despite criticism on points of details, however, the book should be useful to the general reader. H.H.R.

LERCH, D. : *Isaaks Opferung christlich gedeutet : eine auslegungsgeschichtliche Untersuchung.* (Beiträge zur historischen Theologie No. 12.) 1950. Pp. xviii+290. (Mohr, Tübingen. Price : DM. 25.60.)

As its title indicates this is a study in the history of interpretation, and particularly of Christian interpretation, of Genesis xxii. The interpretations of the Rabbis, Josephus and Philo are first reviewed, and then those of a large number of Christian interpreters from the second century to the twentieth. At the beginning of each section the sources on which it rests are stated. The whole is done with care and thoroughness, and the work is to be highly commended—though the same cannot be said of some of the interpretations reviewed . H.H.R.

LEUPOLD, H. C. : *Exposition of Daniel.* 1949. Pp. 550. (Wartburg Press, Columbus, Ohio. Price : $5.00.)

This is a conservative commentary by an author who is acquainted with some works of a different character, though far less than E. J. Young (cf. *Book List* 1950, pp. 42 f.), and who is less willing to face difficulties than Young. He identifies the Little Horn of chapter vii with the Pope, but thinks it is vain to try to identify the Ten Horns, and holds that no special significance is to be attached to the Three Horns, and that even the number three is not to be taken literally. He makes the astonishingly inaccurate statement that it is only during the last 20 years that Belshazzar has been discovered in ancient records. He also states that there is no record of the profanation of the Temple vessels by Antiochus (cf. 2 Macc. v. 16). Belshazzar is held to have been a true son of Nebuchadnezzar adopted by Nabonidus, despite the explicit statement of the latter that Belshazzar was the issue of his loins. H.H.R.

NÖTSCHER, F. (ed. by) : *Die Heilige Schrift in deutscher Übersetzung. Echter Bibel : Das Alte Testament.* 11. *Tobias, Judit, Esther* by F. Stummer and *Baruch* by V. Hamp. 1950. Pp. 144. (Price : DM. 4.80). 12. *Josua, Richter* by F. Nötscher. 1950. Pp. 71, 83. (Price : DM. 5.00). (Echter Verlag, Würzburg.)

Little need be said about these excellent translations with short notes and even shorter introductions. They continue to appear with regularity, they are beautifully printed in very legible type, and they are a credit to German Catholic scholarship and enterprise. Stummer's Tobias, rather unaccountably, is based not on the Greek text of Codex Sinaiticus, but on the " Vulgärrezension " that is, the recension found at its best in Codex Vaticanus. The introductions to Esther and Judith are largely concerned with the historical problems raised by these books. Nötscher shows his accustomed skill and mastery of his subject-matter in his editions of Joshua and Judges. In the Song of Deborah (v. 8), the difficult 8b is rendered : " Götter, die niemand fürchtete bisher " with which may be compared the Clamer Bible's correction " On choisissait baals et astartés." J.M.T.B.

PODECHARD, E. : *Le Psautier, Traduction littérale et explication historique : I. Psaumes 1-75.* (Bibliothèque de la faculté catholique de théologie de Lyon, Vol. 3.) 1949. Pp. 330. *Le Psautier, Notes critiques : I. Psaumes 1-75.* (id., Vol. 4.) 1949. Pp. 306. (Facultés catholiques, Lyon. Price : Frs. 600 and 1400.)

The former of these works is the first of two volumes which are to be devoted to a translation and exposition of the Psalms, and in due course these are to be followed by a third volume, which is to take the form of a General Introduction to the Psalter, and will deal accordingly with such subjects as the text and versions, titles, types of psalm, authorship and date, and doctrine. The second of the above works is the first volume of a companion publication, which, in so far as it deals with textual, lexical and grammatical problems which have arisen during the preparation of the foregoing work, is intended primarily for Hebraists. The author does not profess to offer more than a literal translation, and, where possible, the exposition of each psalm takes the form of a statement as to its type and the occasion which called it forth, a summary of its theme, a detailed verse by verse annotation, and, finally, the consideration of its date. The author reveals a reasonably wide knowledge of the work of earlier commentators, Protestant as well as Roman Catholic, and indeed there is little in these volumes to suggest that the author is himself a Roman Catholic. In fact his standpoint with regard to the literary problems of the Old Testament appears to be very much that which has been normative in critical circles during recent decades ; and in keeping with this the author tends to date most of the psalms to the end of the monarchy or the early post-exilic period. Both volumes under review reveal a high general level of competence, and they may be warmly recommended as a valuable contribution to the study of the Psalter.   A.R.J.

RICCIOTTI, G., VACCARI, A. & TRAMONTANO, R. (Translators) : *La Sacra Bibbia, tradotta dei testi originali con note a cura del Pontificio Istituto Biblico di Roma*. III. *I Libri Storici*—2. 1948. Pp. 516. (Adriano Salani, Firenze. Price : 950 lire.)

This is a further volume of the translation of the Bible into Italian, of which venture, it may safely be said, A. Vaccari has been for many years the moving spirit. The present volume includes versions of Chronicles, Ezra-Nehemiah, Tobit, Esther, Judith and Maccabees, and in most of them Vaccari has been partly or wholly responsible for the renderings. Perhaps the most interesting examples of his work are Tobit and Judith. Neither of these books (and this is also true of the version as a whole) follows the Vulgate text ; the former is, we are informed, the first Italian translation of the Codex Sinaiticus recension, of which Simpson wrote in his introduction to Tobit in Charles's *Apocrypha* that it represents " the nearest approach which can be made to the original text, whether the latter first appeared in Greek or in a Semitic language." (Charles, i, p. 175). The text followed in Judith is that of the great uncials (i.e. Swete's text) and of Codex 58, with which the Old Latin and Syriac are in close and striking agreement. This is primarily a translation, not a commentary, but this does not exclude a series of careful and often lengthy notes to the various renderings. There are also six plates and four maps, the latter including one of Jerusalem in the time of Nehemiah and another of Palestine in the second century B.C.   J.M.T.B.

RIGNELL, L. G. : *Die Nachtgesichte des Sacharja : eine exegetische Studie.* 1950. Pp. 268. (C. W. K. Gleerup, Lund. Price : Kr. 10.)

This doctoral dissertation, written by a disciple of Lindblom and Gerleman, is a thorough textual and exegetical study of the visions of Zechariah. The author concludes that MT is substantially sound ; and on the textual side his treatment is very much in the tradition of Nyberg's *Studien zum Hoseabuche* and Gerleman's *Zephanja*. He also holds that the dominant influence on the thought of Zechariah comes from his prophetic predecessors and from the native Hebrew religious tradition, and that there is no ground for assuming borrowing from Babylonian or Persian sources even in the angelology or in the " apocalyptic " tendencies in the book. But no summary of conclusions can adequately represent the value of this sober and scholarly piece of research. It will be indispensable for serious study of Zechariah.   G.W.A.

SNAITH, N. H. : *Notes on the Hebrew Text of Genesis xl-xliv.* 1950. Pp. 86. (Epworth Press, London. Price : 6s. 0d.)

Professor Snaith continues to render great service to elementary students of Hebrew by publishing these Study Notes on Bible Books. The Hebrew text is not published in full, as in the S.P.C.K. series, but every student can get a Hebrew Bible. The notes are excellent, with exact information about every form, and abundant reference to the standard Grammars. Private students will find the book invaluable for helping them to get a working knowledge of Hebrew, and classes working with a teacher should also find it most useful. Dr. Snaith would add to his service if he would provide a vocabulary.   H.H.R.

TEDESCHE, S. : *The First Book of Maccabees : An English Translation,* with Introduction and Commentary by Solomon Zeitlin. 1950. Pp. 292. (Dropsie College, New York. Price : $4.00.)

This is the forerunner in a series under the name of " Jewish Apocryphal Literature " sponsored by The Dropsie College. Each book will contain " the best available ancient language text " as well as an English translation, with introduction, notes and critical apparatus. The Greek text of I Macc. is that of Rahlfs, the suggested changes in this text as reflected in the translation and as commented upon in the notes being the work of Dr. Zeitlin. A short but valuable foreword by A. A. Neuman is followed by a preface and introduction by Dr. Zeitlin on the historical background of 1 Macc. and on the usual literary questions. This is done well although the pages on " religious aspects " must seem to many to display a view of the religious history of Judaism that is too narrow, superficial and naïve. This book is to be welcomed from the point of view of its criticism of the treatment which the apocryphal literature has hitherto received at the hands of Christian scholars, however great has been their contribution to the historical study of Judaism and Christianity. This literature, it is represented, though it owes its preservation to the Church, has shewn in its editing and translation " a lack of comprehension of the Jewish background of the apocryphal works and insufficient understanding of the spirit of Judaism of the period." The revived interest of Judaism in the Apocrypha will, it may well be expected, result in a distinctive contribution to scholarship in this field of study. O.S.R.

THILO, M. : *Das alte Testament ausgelegt für Bibelleser.* Bd. I. *Die fünf Bücher Moses.* 1947. Pp. 508 ; Bd. II. *Josua bis Esther.* 1949. Pp. 520 ; Bd. III. *Die Lehrbücher.* 1950. Pp. 356 ; (Bertelsmann Verlag, Gütersloh. Price : DM. 12 per vol.)

Dr. Thilo seeks to present to the ordinary Bible reader an exegesis that is both plain and scientific. For Job, Eccl., Song he gives his own translation but for the rest of Scripture he employs, in the main, that of Luther. The third volume contains (pp. 229-254) a " history of the East in the biblical period " to keep the reader abreast of modern knowledge of the near East. In this historical sketch the author designates Thutmosis III as the Pharaoh of the oppression and 1447 as the year of the exodus. The volumes are plainly ultra-conservative and although the Lutheran version is at times changed for the better and simplified, and references are made to the *Urtext,* Dr. Thilo appears to be quite satisfied with such a reading as " Küsset den Sohn " (Ps. ii. 12). The explanation of Psalm lxxxii as referring to God's judgement upon human judges is given without any mention of any other interpretation. Some expositions are engaging. The light that was created on the first day of creation (Gen. i. 3) did not proceed from any heavenly body but *besteht aus Lichtwellen* which came from some unknown source (cf. Job xxxviii. 19). The deep sleep which fell upon Adam when Eve was created was a sleep in which Adam dreamed that one of his ribs had been taken from him by the Deity for Eve's fashioning. The plurals *us* and *our* in " Let us make man in our image " are explained as meaning that God consulted with the whole of creation before He created man—an old midrashic view. Though the exegetical value of the volumes would have been greater had the Bible reader been given more of the fruits of biblical literary criticism, the author succeeds in offering a most interesting and readable work in which, as seen in the narrative parts, the text and commentary are woven well together. O.S.R.

VELLAS, B. M. : *Hermêneia Palaias Diathêkês* (in Modern Greek). 5. *Haggai-Zechariah-Malachi.* 1950. Pp. 196. ('Aster' Publishing House, Athens.)

Little need be added to the praise already accorded to this excellent and thoroughly up-to-date commentary in Modern Greek, designed for the better instruction of Orthodox theological students. As usual, after the introduction to each of the books, there follows a Modern Greek translation, made direct from the Hebrew, the Septuagint text (without apparatus) and a very full and lucid commentary. There can be no doubt that such works as those by Sellin and Van Hoonacker have been of great service ; these and other books are fully recorded in the ample bibliographies. There are occasional misprints in proper names, e.g. N. Lagrange (in the bibliography to Zechariah, p. 47) should be M. J. Lagrange; Chapman's article " Zacharias slain between the Temple and the Altar " appeared in *J.T.S.*, not *Z.Th.S.*   J.M.T.B.

WEISER, A. : *Die Psalmen I : Psalm 1-60, II : Psalm 61-150* (Das Alte Testament Deutsch, 14 & 15). 1950. Pp. 564. (Vandenhoeck & Ruprecht, Göttingen. Price : Subscr. DM. 7.80 ; separate : DM. 9.40 each vol.)

> Those who have already learnt to appreciate the author's earlier treatment of a number of the psalms in *Die Psalmen ausgewählt, übersetzt und erklärt* (1935), 2nd edition enlarged (1939), will welcome this further expansion of the original work into an exposition of the whole Psalter for inclusion in what is proving to be a successful series of semi-popular commentaries on the Old Testament. In an excellent Introduction of about fifty pages the author shows that he continues to be an ardent but by no means slavish follower of Gunkel in his delineation of the more important literary types ; but, as in the revised edition of his *Einleitung in das Alte Testament* (*Book List* 1950, p. 46), he also shows himself to be in line with current trends by laying an emphasis upon the part played by the cultus in the fostering of Israel's faith and the shaping of its literary expression, particularly from the standpoint of the covenant relationship between Yahweh and the confederate tribes of Israel, and thus, in the case of the Psalter, breaking with the view that the psalms are wholly or almost wholly the produce of post-exilic Judaism. For the rest, the exposition of the individual psalms follows the lines already laid down in the earlier volume ; and the whole may be said to reflect the balance of judgement and spiritual insight which one has learnt to expect from the author.   A.R.J.

WOLFF, H. W. : *Jesaja 53 im Urchristentum.* 1950. Pp. 160. (Evangelische Verlagsanstalt, Berlin. Price : DM. 6.80.)

> A revised edition of a work noticed by Eissfeldt in the *Book List* 1948. A translation and exposition of Isa. lii. 13-liii. 21 concludes with the question, " Who was the Servant ?"—to which the answer is, " The Servant in Deutero-Isaiah is a prophetic forecast of Jesus Christ." In pre-Christian Judaism references to the passage are few and of uncertain meaning. The N.T. references are examined in detail—a work which needed doing—also those in the sub-apostolic literature down to Justin Martyr. The general conclusion is that it was only with the fulfilment of the prophecy that the passage was understood. Although in the N.T. it is hardly ever quoted, this is precisely because it entered so deeply into the consciousness of Jesus and the apostles. In the sub-apostolic age it is viewed " atomistically " and quoted at length, and the length of the quotation is generally in inverse ratio to the assimilation of its full significance.   C.R.N.

ALLIS, O. T. : *The Unity of Isaiah.* 1950. Pp. 136. (Presbyterian and Reformed Publishing Co., Philadelphia. Price : $2.25.)

The denial of the unity of Isaiah is here said to be due to the modern theory which minimises or rejects the element of prediction. Extreme fundamentalists will welcome this book. Others will be exasperated. The main argument seems to be that since Jews and Christians accepted the unity for twenty-five centuries, then the evidence for the unity must be adequate.   N.H.S.

BIČ, M. : *Palestina od pravěku ke křestanství,* iii. *Řeč a písemnosti.* 1950. Pp. 464. (Husova Československá Evangelická Faculta Bohoslovecká, Prague.)

Professor Bič has now brought his *magnum opus* to a conclusion with a volume devoted to the language and literature of Palestine. He treats of the surviving texts which have come down to us, both in Hebrew and in related languages, and outlines the linguistic history of the land. More particularly, of course, he gives attention to the Old Testament, studying its literary forms, and the history of the text. The ancient versions are discussed, and the care of the Massoretes in later times for the maintenance of the text in the form they gave to it described. An up-to-date work on this scale is found in no other country, and Professor Bič is to be congratulated on its completion. The only regret is that the French summary will be the only part accessible to most foreigners—as it was to the present writer. A number of plates give samples of recovered texts, including Ras Shamra texts, Lachish letters, and the well-known page of the Dead Sea Scrolls containing Isa. xl.   H.H.R.

BIRKELAND, H. : *Jeremia, profet og dikter.* 1950. Pp. 104. (Gyldendal Norsk Forlag, Oslo. Price : 8s. 0d.)

This is a short, popular, and very ably written introduction to Jeremiah, similar in scope to Mowinckel's *Jesaia* in the same series (*Religionens Stormenn,* see *Book List* 1950, p. 63). The four sections into which the book is divided deal respectively with Jeremiah's place in the history of religion, the historical background of his ministry, the outward course of his life, and his work as prophet and poet. The last of these is by far the longest, and the most rewarding ; but the book as a whole abounds in profound insights and illuminating observations. A caustic reference in an appendix to the search for cultic patterns in the prophetic literature is of interest in view of some current trends.   G.W.A.

COPPENS, J. : *A. Van Hoonacker, De Compositione Litteraria et de Origine Mosaica Hexateuchi Disquisitio Historico-Critica.* 1949. Pp. 102. (Paleis der Academiën, Brussels. Price : Belgian Frs. 75.)

It is fortunate that Professor Coppens, the disciple and successor of A. Van Hoonacker, has been able to gather together and supplement some notes on the Hexateuch that escaped the catastrophes that destroyed so many documents in Belgium during the late war. The editor has, in many instances, been forced to use his ingenuity in the work of restoring the text as Van Hoonacker wrote it. It is a short but weighty contribution to Hexateuchal problems, and combines a thoroughgoing belief in the documentary analysis of the books with an acceptance of substantial Mosaic authorship, in a sense explained by the author on pp. 82-85. Two specimen pages of the manuscripts, reproduced in facsimile, give some idea of the task undertaken by Coppens. It is perhaps to be regretted that the introduction to a Latin work was not itself composed in Latin, rather than in Flemish. Every *Alttestamentler* may be presumed to know Latin, but he does not necessarily know Flemish. J.M.T.B.

COPPENS, J. : *Les douze petits prophètes : Breviaire du Prophétisme.* 1950. Pp. 60. (Desclée de Brouwer, Bruges, and Publications Universitaires, Louvain. Price : Belgain Frs. 35.)

The indefatigable Professor Coppens here gives us a series of very brief individual introductions to the Minor Prophets of which he is about to issue a translation with commentary. The chief criticism of the volume is that the introductions are far too brief. A page, or at most two, must suffice for most of the books, together with a brief analysis of the contents of the book. The standpoint throughout is the moderate critical position. Joel is ascribed to the post-exilic age, Jonah is regarded as a late work offering its teaching through the medium of fiction, Zechariah is held to be composite. On the vexed question of Hosea's marriage, Hos. iii is regarded as giving the sequel to what precedes, rather than a parallel account to that of chapter i. H.H.R.

EISSFELDT, O. : *Die ältesten Traditionen Israels : ein kritischer Bericht über C. A. Simpson's The Early Traditions of Israel.* B.Z.A.W. 71. 1950. Pp. 100. (Töpelmann, Berlin. Price : DM. 10.00.)

An extended and on the whole sympathetic review of a work which has so far been rather ill received. For Simpson the development of the Pentateuchal tradition extends over two millennia, and he still attempts—despite current critical trends—to sort out its various elements by means of a complicated series of sigla (J^1, J^2, E, D, P,) together with redactors and textual corrections down to the LXX. Eissfeldt frankly says that many of his historical conjectures will never have any following, but he has nothing but admiration for the courage with which new questions are asked and hypothetical answers suggested. If it be true—as it is true—that to wonder is the beginning of knowledge, Simpson's book, for all its faults, should be a fresh call to the solution of Pentateuchal problems. C.R.N.

GINSBERG, H. L. : *Studies in Koheleth.* 1950. Pp. 46. (The Jewish Theological Seminary of America, New York. Price : $1.50.)

This is a valuable philological study of many obscure passages in the book of Ecclesiastes. The greater part of the work (pp. 16-40) seeks to show that Koheleth is a translation into Hebrew from the Aramaic. This thesis, which was set forth by F. C. Burkitt (*J.T.S.* 1922) without the adducement of what could be reckoned as sufficient or convincing proof, has been much strengthened and elaborated by F. Zimmermann (see articles in *J.B.L.* 1945 ; *J.Q.R.* 1945, 1949). Professor Ginsberg brings to Zimmermann's proofs a certain amount of new material and some new viewpoints. He deems the Aramaic composition to date from the third century and its translation to belong to the Maccabean age. O.S.R.

HOWIE, C. G. : *The Date and Composition of Ezekiel.* (Journal of Biblical Literature Monograph Series, Vol. IV.) 1950. Pp. iv + 122. (Society of Biblical Literature, Philadelphia. Price : $1.50.)

After carefully examining the varying current theories the author adduces sound reasons for placing Ezekiel's entire prophetic activity in Babylonia between 593 and 567 B.C. Reference to walls obviously of mud-brick (in chs. viii, xii, xiii and xxii. 28) are attributed to a Babylonian locale. The East Gate of the ideal Temple (xl. 5ff.) is found to conform with the pattern of ninth century and earlier gateways, hence presumably with that of Solomon's Temple. Aramaisms, which are freshly discussed, are concluded to be few and mostly the errors of copyists. " The thirtieth year " (of Jehoiachin's captivity) in i. 1 is regarded as the date of recording or publishing chs. i-xxiv and it is suggested that xxxiii. 21-22 followed by xxiv. 24 were the original ending of ch. xxiv to which chs. xxv-xxxii were appended, chs. xxxiii-xlviii being also mainly the work of Ezekiel but edited by disciples. Ezekiel, though perhaps not an original poet, is declared to have re-fashioned and re-interpreted older poems together with proverbs, stories and other ancient literary material. A discussion of Ezekiel's psychology leads to a rejection of the theory of schizophrenia : Ezekiel was a mystical day-dreamer but not a psychopath or a clairvoyant. Dr. Howie's stimulating and original views deserve careful study. C.J.M.W.

LEWY, I. : *The Birth of the Bible : a New Approach.* With an Introduction by M. M. Kaplan. 1950. Pp. 254. (Bloch Publishing Co., New York. Price : $3.50.)

Here we have one more of the many new attempts to solve the Pentateuchal problem. The prophet Nathan is held to have been the author of the J document, of Gen. xiv and xlix, of the Balaam story, and of the Court History of David, in their original forms. He is also held to have been the author of the Ethical Decalogue, which modified an older Draconian code, and to have opposed all animal sacrifice. His work was modified by the contemporary priest Abiathar, while the northern Elohist was Elisha, and the southern Elohist, or the priestly narrator, is held to have been Jehoiada. D is declared to have been edited by Elisha for Jehu, while Hezekiah is said to have set up a committee which introduced modifications of the then existing sources. The Priestly Code is associated with the reform of Josiah. It should be added that Samuel is credited with the codification of old laws before the time of Nathan. The author is conscious that he will be criticized for the exaggerated rôle he ascribes to Nathan. He is still more liable to criticism since his method is intuition rather than evidence, both in defining the work of Nathan and in re-writing the story of Cain and Abel, and Gen. xiv and other stories. Nor is any adequate effort made to show from the recorded history that the documents were in existence at the dates to which they are ascribed. H.H.R.

MOWINCKEL, S. : *Den senjødiske salmediktning* (Saertrykk av *Norsk Teologisk Tidsskrift*, 1950, h. 1). 1950. Pp. 46+8. (Grøndahl & Søns Boktrykkeri, Oslo.)

This work, which appears to be a *parergon* to the writer's forthcoming *Offersang og sangoffer*, carries further the investigation carried out by H. Ludin Jansen in his *Die spätjüdische Psalmendichtung*, in which it was argued that later Judaism produced a type of psalm which originated not in the cult but in the wisdom circles. Mowinckel re-examines the material to show more clearly the relation of the later to the earlier Hebrew psalmody, and to define more precisely the *Sitz im Leben* and the purpose of the writings in question. His treatment of these is arranged as follows : Wisdom psalms in the Psalter, psalms in the narrative literature of the inter-testamental period, psalms in Ecclesiasticus and Wisdom, the Psalms of Solomon, early Christian psalmody (arguing that in the early church the psalm returned to its origin, the cult), the psalms of Jewish sects (touching briefly on the Dead Sea Scrolls). A most illuminating discussion, admirably documented.   G.W.A.

NEHER, A. : *Amos : contribution à l'étude du prophétisme.* 1950. Pp. xvi+300. (J. Vrin, Paris. Price : Frs. 960.)

A combination of French and Jewish approaches gives this book a special interest. There has been a delay of more than three years in publication, and recent biblical study is largely neglected. The whole book is accepted as the genuine work of Amos himself. The first section concerns the text, with translation, extensive notes and discussions : first, the biographical material (which includes iii. 3-8), then the discourses, the visions and the conclusion (ix. 7-15). Great stress is laid on the *berith noahidique*, as the basis of both the universalism of Amos ("covenant of brethren" equals general humanitarian ethics) and his particularism (Israel has the Law). The prophet is the man who realises that *his* time is inserted in *all* time. This gives the key to the sections on the prophet's message and the significance of his prophecy. He broke up the Jehu compromise of Church and State. The key to his metaphysic is the Omnipresence of God. There is a long discussion of Amos's historical antecedents, and great emphasis on the political and sociological aspects of his message.   N.H.S.

NIEMEYER, C.TH. : *Het Probleem van de Rangschikking der Psalmen.* 1950. Pp. 166. (Drukkerij " Luctor et Emergo,"Leiden.)

A dissertation on the arrangement of the Psalms, with a brief summary in English, which combined a critical survey of the attempts made to answer the question during the last century and a half with an effort to trace analogies in other composite works outside and inside the Old Testament, i.e. (*a*) the Mishnah and the Koran, and (*b*) the Book of the Covenant, Proverbs xxv-xxix, and the Minor Prophets. The author discovers that classification is based in varying degree on author's names, the names of God, the types of psalm, catchwords, content, similarity of form, size and alliteration ; but his main findings are no more than meet the eye in any simple reading of the Psalter.   A.R.J.

PARMELEE, ALICE : *A Guidebook to the Bible* . 1951. Pp. 184. (English Universities Press Ltd., London. Price : 4s. 6d.) (Teach Yourself Series.)

The volume is a shorter edition of a larger volume published in America under the same title. The section on the Old Testament consists of 86 pages ; that on the New Testament of 49 pages ; whilst the remainder deals with the Bible through the centuries. The whole volume is essentially popular and readable, and, within its limits serves as a good introduction to the general reader. The order in which the Old Testament is discussed is Oral traditions, Abiathar (or Ahimaaz) ' the father of history,' then J and E, followed by Amos, and so forth. Ezekiel went to Babylon in 597 B.C. Ezra is wholly ignored. There is no reference to the latest critical work, and most unfortunately of all, there is no bibliography.   N.H.S.

*PATERSON, J. : *The Praises of Israel : Studies literary and religious in the Psalms.* 1950. Pp. x+256. (Charles Scribner's Sons, New York. Price : $2.75.)

A useful and, for the most part, an agreeable popular introduction to the Psalter which follows closely the lines laid down by Gunkel. It falls into three parts, the first being mainly concerned with the growth of the book and the classification of the psalms according to their literary types, the second offering a brief exposition of a characteristic example of each type, and the third dealing in more general terms with the religious teaching of the Psalter as a whole.   A.R.J.

POWER, A. D. : *Sidelights on the Book of Proverbs.* 1950. Pp. 60. (Longmans, London. Price : 3s. 6d.)

The author of " The Proverbs of Solomon " 1949 (see *Book List*, 1950, p.40) gives us in these " Sidelights " a dozen short chapters which are a pleasant and admirable introduction to the Book of Proverbs and, in general, to oriental maxim writings. " Wisdom and its seven Pillars," " Words and their Ways in Hebrew and in English," " Some Emendations," " Idioms and Figures of Speech," " Proverbs in Early Eastern Literature," " Proverbs in Classical and Other Languages " are some of the subjects treated.   O.S.R.

ROBERTS, B. J. : *Patrymau Llenyddol y Beibl.* 1950. Pp. 124. (Cyfres Pobun, Brython Press, Liverpool. Price : 4s. 0d.)

This book is a double number in the popular Welsh series Cyfres Pobun, designed to bring the latest scientific knowledge in all fields within the reach of the educated layman. In this volume Roberts expounds recent theories of composition with regard to both Old and New Testaments, concentrating—as his title " The Literary Patterns of the Bible " suggests—on *Formgeschichte* and *Gattungsforschung.* He makes good use of Scandinavian as well as of German and English writers on the subject, and shows himself well abreast of current trends. This will be an entirely new angle for most of his readers, but the author pauses to help the uninitiated over many of the hurdles, and his book is a very welcome contribution.

D.R.Ap-T.

ROBERTSON, E. : *The Old Testament Problem.* 1950. Pp. 238. (Manchester University Press. Price : 21s. 0d.)

The volume is a collection of lectures delivered mostly at the John Rylands Library between 1938 and 1946. Professor Robertson has never been satisfied with the Graf-Wellhausen hypothesis, and these lectures contain his alternative. The whole of the Pentateuch is early, and Deuteronomy belongs to the time of Samuel. Its origin is Samuel's attempt at centralisation following the disruption of the Eli priesthood due to a quarrel for precedence between the descendants of Ithamar and those of Eleazar. This is from the Samaritan tradition, and part of Dr. Robertson's theme is that sufficient attention has never been given to the ancient traditions, both Samaritan and Jewish. The whole history of the Jews is the story of repeated attempts at unification, both political and religious. Deuteronomy was perforce abrogated at the time of the disruption of the kingdom, and the two most important attempts to reintroduce it were those by Hezekiah and Josiah.

N.H.S.

ROBERTSON, E. : *The Plot of the Book of Ruth.* 1950. Pp. 12. (Manchester University Press. Price : 2s. 6d.) (Reprint from " Bulletin of the John Rylands Library," Vol. 32, No. 2, March, 1950.)

This 4th century B.C. story has a traditional basis of a widow, bereft of husband and sons, returning home with a Moabite daughter-in-law. The author made use of the Tamar-Judah tale and of Hosea ix. 1. Out of these elements, the author, with great literary skill, has fashioned the first historical novel. There is no question of levirate ' marriage.' Naomi traps Boaz. Her conduct must be judged by the standards of the time. The story is essentially human, perhaps with a spice of naughtiness. The motif is the universal appeal of the weak things of the world confounding the strong.   N.H.S.

*ROWLEY, H. H. : *The Growth of the Old Testament.* 1950. Pp. 192.
(Hutchinson's University Library. Price : 7s. 6d.)

This book admirably meets a real need. It presents the general
positions established by the older generation of critical
scholarship, puts the reader *au fait* with the most significant
recent hypotheses, and gives him discriminating guidance and
a clear perspective among their kaleidoscopic variety. The
treatment is at its best where such aid is most needed, in the
problem of the Pentateuch ; but every part of the book is
rewarding ; and readers will share the author's regret that
lack of space precluded fuller treatment of the forms of O.T.
literature. The compactness, comprehensiveness, and lucidity
of the presentation, and the helpful bibliography make the
book an ideal manual for use with students ; but it will also
be invaluable to many besides beginners. A companion volume
on the apocryphal literature would be equally welcome.
G.W.A.

SELLIN, E. : *Einleitung in das Alte Testament.* 8th ed., edited by L. Rost.
1950. Pp. xvi+198. (Quelle & Meyer, Heidelberg. Price : DM.
9.80.)

This eighth edition of Sellin's *Einleitung*, edited by Rost,
keeps substantially to the form of the third edition, which was
translated into English in 1923. A new section of 15 pages
has been introduced on the literary *Gattungen*. Notice has
been taken throughout of the results of recent study, and
references to the literature have been brought up to date.
Rost explains that conditions since the war have made it
impossible to take into account all that has been written outside
Germany, but there are references to the Dead Sea MSS and
to Scandinavian criticism. The volume is packed with
information and the full table of contents makes the materials
in it easily accessible. C.R.N.

STEINMANN, J. : *Daniel.* 1950. Pp. 182. (Les Éditions du Cerf, Paris.
Price : Frs. 220.)

In this short study, in the series Témoins de Dieu, the reader
is offered an introduction to the book of Daniel and interpretation of its chapters. The first chapter gives the background
of history of the Seleucid period in which the author places the
composition of the book of Daniel . He holds that it may rest
on older written sources, but does not think they can be recovered by any analysis of the text. He follows the view that
the work was originally written wholly in Aramaic, and he
identifies the four kingdoms of chapters ii and vii with the
Babylonian, Median, Persian and Macedonian. While these
positions are not new, they have not been characteristic of
Catholic writers. There is a useful chapter on the deutero-
canonical supplements, and a final chapter on the abiding
message of the book. The volume will be most valuable to
the wide circle for which it is written. H.H.R.

STEINMANN, J. : *Le prophète Isaïe : sa vie, son œuvre et son temps*. (Collection " Lectio divina," No. 5). 1950. Pp. 382. (Éditions du Cerf, Paris. Price : Fr. 530.)

The author presents a study of the life and work of Isaiah, the son of Amoz, against the background of contemporary history. He offers a translation of chapters i-xxxix, based upon a Hebrew text established critically, and a commentary on the separate oracles arranged—necessarily hypothetically—in chronological sequence. The translation is occasionally not as accurate as it could be made in the light of recent lexicographical study. The commentary contains much that is of interest, e.g., the virgin of vii. 14 is identified with Abi, the daughter of Zechariah, one of the friends of the prophet. Especially interesting is chapter 18, which is devoted to the thought of Isaiah. Here the double personality of the prophet —the man of action and the mystic—is well portrayed. If, in a sense, it can be said that Isaiah created nothing—all that he says on the larger themes, such as justice, providence, evil, retribution, had been said before him—yet by his gifts of imagination and expression he gave substance to all previous prophetic teaching. The importance of his con-version for the whole of his subsequent religious life is stressed ; while his teaching on messianism is thought to give him a special claim to greatness. Not the least among the many merits of the book is the way in which it is demonstrated that modern critical study has revealed the prophet as a greater man than ever—as more human, more personal, more real, more heroic— and as a man who has still an urgent message for Christians to-day. Layman and specialist alike will read this book with pleasure and profit.   D.W.T.

YOUNG, E. J. : *An Introduction to the Old Testament*. 1949. Pp. 414. (Eerdmans Publishing Co., Grand Rapids. Price : $5.00.)

The author of this full-scale Introduction is well known as a conservative scholar who is widely read and who is at pains to give his readers a fair account of the views he is unable to share. All of these qualities are well exemplified here. He gives a good account of the history of Pentateuchal criticism, though he rejects its conclusions and holds the Pentateuch to be substantially Mosaic. Similarly Joshua is held to be basically by Joshua, Judges to have been compiled early in the monarchy, and Samuel shortly after the Disruption on the basis of older documents. The complete unity of Isaiah is maintained, while Jeremiah is held to be wholly from Jeremiah. A brief review of recent criticism of Ezekiel is given, but the fundamental integrity and authenticity of the book is maintained. Joel is held to be pre-exilic, Zechariah a unity, the Song of Songs to be by Solomon, Job to be a unity coming from the age of Solomon, and the ascriptions of psalms to David authentic. As a rare departure from tradition the book of Ecclesiastes is assigned to the post-exilic age. Of the conservative books on this subject this is easily the best and the most enlightened in its treatment of others, though it is to be regretted that the author cannot divest himself of the idea that critical scholarship is essentially non-Christian.
                                                        H.H.R.

LAW, RELIGION AND THEOLOGY
(including the Life and Thought of the Neighbouring Peoples)

BRUNNER, E. : *Die christliche Lehre von Schöpfung und Erlösung.*
(Dogmatik, vol. 2). 1950. Pp. viii+456. (Zwingli Verlag, Zürich.
Price : Swiss Fr. 21.50.)

> It is little short of astonishing to find the slight place the
> Old Testament has in this volume, and much to be regretted
> that this is apparently deliberate. Theology is never adequately
> based unless it is based on the Bible, and the Old Testament
> belongs, and always has belonged, to the Christian Bible.
> Brunner sometimes goes out of his way to depreciate the Old
> Testament, but if he had tried to understand it better he
> would have found in it a solid basis for the Christian Doctrine
> of Creation and Redemption. Every Old Testament scholar
> will find this volume disappointing, and it is a pity that at
> a time when there is a growing interest in Biblical Theology,
> and particularly in Old Testament theology, Dogmatic
> Theology should be treated as an almost unrelated discipline.
> H.H.R.

(BRUNNER, E.): *Das Menschenbild im Lichte des Evangeliums.* 1950.
Pp. xv+185. (Zwingli Verlag, Zürich. Price : Fr. 13.50.)

> A symposium by ten scholars from seven different countries
> in honour of the sixtieth birthday of Professor Emil Brunner.
> The only contribution of direct interest to students of the
> Old Testament is that by F. J. Leenhardt on " La situation de
> l'Homme d'après la Genèse," which is a modest attempt to
> expound the story of the Fall as involving, not a change in
> man's creaturely nature, but a rejection of his opportunity
> to share the life of God. A.R.J.

COATES, J. R. (trans.) : *Bible Key Words.* I. *Love*, by G. Quell and E.
Stauffer. 1949. Pp. 76. (Price : 6s. 0d.) II. *The Church*, by
K. L. Schmidt. 1950. Pp. 76. (Price : 6s. 0d.) (Both translations
from *Theologisches Wörterbuch zum Neuen Testament*, edited
G. Kittel.) (Adam & Charles Black, London.)

> These are the first two volumes of a projected series of
> translations of selected articles in Kittel's *Wörterbuch*, a
> notable work which needs no recommendation, the publication
> of which is now happily resumed. The first is the article on
> *agape* (1933 edition). The first chapter is by G. Quell, dealing
> with Love in the Old Testament. The remaining five chapters
> deal with the words for Love in pre-biblical Greek, and trace
> the idea in Judaism, in the words of Jesus, and through into
> the sub-apostolic age. The second volume is the article on
> *ekklesia*, and discusses general Greek usage of the word. It
> deals with New Testament usage, Old Testament and Jewish
> usage, and through into early Catholicism. There is a detailed
> discussion of Matt. xvi. 18 and xviii. 17. Professor Coates
> has made additions to the notes, especially in the first volume,
> and has extended the bibliographies. N.H.S.

COPPENS, J. : *Nieuw licht over de Ebed-Yahweh-Liedern.* 1950. Pp. 16. (Desclée de Brouwer, Bruges. Price : Belgian Frs. 25.)

Starts from three premises which Coppens believes have resulted from recent studies : (1) the prophetic character of the Songs, (2) the individual character of the Servant, (3) the predominantly royal character of the Servant. The Prophet of the exile composed the Songs independently of the rest of his work, and himself disposed them in their present contexts. The original of the first three Songs was Jehoiachin, of the fourth Zedekiah, both kings being considered in and for themselves. In the final redaction all the attention is directed to the future Messianic king, and Jehoiachin and Zedekiah are in some sort degraded to the role of types. There is a summary in French.   C.R.N.

CRESPY, G. : *Le Problème d'une Anthropologie Théologique.* 1950. Pp. 136. (Publication de la Faculté de Théologie Protestante de Montpellier. Price : Fr. 250.)

This book represents a departure from the traditional theological anthropology. The approach to the problem is existential, which means that the Biblical revelation is understood as concerning not the nature but the destiny of man. The discussion will be found of real value by those who are interested in the contemporary effort to arrive at a satisfactory Old Testament theology. The author shows indebtedness to the works of men like Van der Leeuw, Niebuhr, Cullmann, Vischer, and Jacob. The book supplements very usefully Jacob's discussion of the nature of myth in *La Tradition Historique en Israël* in the same series of monographs. The " myths " in Genesis 1-3 are subjected to detailed examination and are shown to be non-speculative in character and to derive their authority for us from the relation in which they stand to the redemption wrought by God through Christ, depicting as they do Man in his need of that redemption.   N.W.P.

DANIÉLOU, J. : *Sacramentum Futuri : Études sur les Origines de la Typologie Biblique.* 1950. Pp. xvi+266. (Beauchesne, Paris. Price : 12s. 0d.)

This study of the history of typology from its beginnings in the Old and New Testaments till the end of the fourth century A. D. is a first-rate work of scholarship. The author distinguishes between the eschatological kind of typology which continues what is found in the Old Testament and the Christological kind which finds its primary fulfilment in Christ (realized eschatology !). Various themes are discussed, those of Adam and Paradise, Noah and the Flood, Isaac (his miraculous birth, his ' sacrifice ' and his marriage), Moses and the Exodus, Joshua. Alongside the Christological typology (cf. Matthew) there is the sacramental (cf. John) which sees the work of Christ continued in the Church. All this the author treats as the common typological tradition of the Church. There is, however, to be found among certain of the Patristic writers, notably Clement of Alexandria, Origen and Gregory of

Nyssa, an allegorical method of interpretation which derives from Philo. The approach here is philosophical and not historical and aims at moral instruction. The Biblical narrative is treated as an allegory of what goes on in the soul of man. This may have its value, but must not be regarded as in any sense exegesis of the text.   N.W.P.

DENTAN, R. C. : *Preface to Old Testament Theology.* (Yale Studies in Religion : No. XIV). 1950. Pp. 74. (Yale University Press, New Haven, and Geoffrey Cumberlege, London. Price : 12s. 6d.)

In the first part of this brief but interesting monograph the author offers a survey of the attempts which have been made during the last century and a half to present a satisfactory interpretation of the Old Testament, while the second part is devoted to a definition of the nature, function, scope and method of an Old Testament Theology. The reader will find himself introduced to all the vexed questions with which any-one who attempts this task must be confronted, but the summary nature of the work means that the introduction does not get beyond the bowing stage. The author himself favours a systematic rather than a chronological approach, and thinks it possible to discover a " normative Old Testament Religion." The reviewer wishes that he could be equally confident on this point, but fears that the author has not given due consideration to the practical difficulties which arise, if one is to do justice to the historical aspect of the problem. However, the work is characterized, for the most part, by a balance of judgement which is highly commendable, and it is a pity that one should have to add that the price which has to be asked in this country for so slender a publication is simply staggering.   A.R.J.

EICHRODT, W. : *Israel in der Weissagung des Alten Testaments.* 1951. Pp. 50. (Gotthelf Verlag, Zürich.)

In many recent theological studies of the O.T. the connexion between prophecy and the N.T. seems to have led the exponents to make use of typology or other methods of exegesis which do not command general acceptance by O.T. students. In this very important lecture, however, Professor Eichrodt has discussed O.T. prophecy from the standpoint that the very fulfilment of it in Jesus imposes certain limitations on the hermeneutics of O.T. prophecy without introducing any such artificial exegesis. O.T. theologians will certainly welcome this very attractive treatment of a fundamentally important topic.
                                                                   B.J.R.

FERM, V. (ed. by) : *Forgotten Religions (including some living primitive religions).* 1950. Pp. xvi+392. (The Philosophical Library, New York. Price : $7.50.)

A collection of twenty essays by seventeen scholars of different nationalities, the scope of which is sufficiently indicated by the title. Students of the Old Testament will be most interested in those on ancient Egypt (Mercer), Sumer (Kramer), Assyria and Babylon (Oppenheim), the Hittites (Güterbock) and the

Canaanites (Gaster). The names of the authors give sufficient indication of the worth of these essays, but in the nature of the case the treatment is apt to be too sketchy to be of great value. The essay by Güterbock, however, is quite outstanding, while that of Gaster is useful as offering a summary statement of the point of view advanced in his major work *Thespis : Ritual, Myth and Drama in the Ancient Near East*. A.R.J.

FRANKFORT, H. : *The Problem of Similarity in Ancient Near Eastern Religions*. 1951. Pp. 24. (Clarendon Press, Oxford. Price : 2s. 0d.)

The Frazer Lecture for 1950 by the author of *Kingship and the Gods* (*Book List* 1948, p. 42). Its chief value for students of the Old Testament lies in the author's return to an attack upon the theory of a myth and ritual pattern common to the religions of the ancient Near East along the lines already laid down in the earlier work. A.R.J.

GASTER, T. H. : *Thespis, Ritual, Myth and Drama in the Ancient Near East*. 1950. Pp. xvi+498. (Henry Schuman, New York. Price : £3 4s. 0d.)

In Part I of this important work the author seeks to reconstruct for the ancient Near East a pattern of seasonal rites (neatly classified into two distinct types as those of Kenosis or " Emptying," i.e. rites of mortification and purgation, and those of Plerosis or " Filling," i.e. rites of invigoration and jubilation), which has left traces of its existence in Canaanite, Hittite and Egyptian mythological texts, in Hebrew hymns and similar liturgical compositions, and in the Homeric hymns and the choral odes of the Bacchae of Euripides, etc. In Part II he offers a translation of relevant Canaanite, Hittite, Egyptian, Hebrew and Greek texts, which in every case save the Egyptian has been made direct from the original ; and an appendix of philological notes on the Canaanite, Hittite and Hebrew texts is added for the benefit of the specialist. Despite the fact that the author has little to say on the Mesopotamian field, the whole thus forms an elaborate and impressive variant of the theory of a myth and ritual pattern common to the ancient Near East which has been put forward so energetically by Professor S. H. Hooke ; and it must be said that, like the latter, it easily lays itself open to the charge of presenting us with an over-simplification of the issue. Nevertheless, while there is much in the work with which one may disagree, both as regards the author's general thesis and with respect to the minutiae of translation and interpretation, the fact remains that his imaginative insight and wide knowledge of folklore make this a work of first-class importance for all students of the Old Testament. Indeed the survey of the Ugaritic material, which occupies two-fifths of the book, would alone make it indispensable for advanced students, while all should take note of the author's treatment of Pss. 29, 47, 48, 65, 74, 76, 89, 93, 96, 97 and 98. A.R.J.

GRANQVIST, HILMA : *Child Problems Among the Arabs : Studies in a Muhammadan Village in Palestine.* 1950. Pp. 336. (Söderström, Helsingfors and Munksgaard, Copenhagen. Price : Kr. 30.)

This is the sequel to the volume noted earlier in the *Book List* (1949, p. 43), and it embodies further material gathered in the same intimate contact with village life. It contains five chapters, dealing with the naming of children, the number of children and child mortality, the welfare of the child, the value of children, and their environment. The whole is of high value, since it rests on the observation of an expert western scholar who by her long residence in an Arab home was able to see its life from within. The student of the Old Testament will find not a little that is of interest to him, despite the fact that the book deals with a modern Arab village. There are, indeed, ten pages of Biblical references to parallels of things contained in this volume and its predecessor. Moreover, there are some pages on the size of Biblical families in which Dr. Granqvist challenges some commonly accepted views.   H.H.R.

GUILLET, J. : *Thèmes Bibliques : Études sur l'expression et le développement de la révélation.* 1950. Pp. 284. (Aubier, Paris. Price : Fr. 495.)

While not professing to offer a complete Biblical Theology, this work offers a series of studies in the field of that theology. A number of themes are selected and traced through the Bible. The selected themes are those associated with the Exodus and Wandering in the Wilderness ; Grace, Justice and Truth ; Sin ; Damnation; Hope (including Life, the possession of the land, the inheritance of the Lord, the Vine) ; and the Breath of the Lord. The treatment is simple rather than profound, but the whole is not without value. It would be easy to add to the themes, and to supplement the literature used.

                                                                                    H.H.R.

HALDAR, A. : *The Notion of the Desert in Sumero-Accadian and West-Semitic Religions.* (Uppsala Universitets Årsskrift, 1950 : 3.) 1950. Pp. 70. (A. B. Lundequistska Bokhandeln, Uppsala & Harrassowitz, Leipzig. Price : Kr. 4.)

This short study is divided into three sections, dealing respectively with Sumero-Accadian, Ugaritic, and Hebrew material. The author investigates the equation of the desert with the underworld and the notion of an exodus into the desert as a *descensus ad inferos.* He finds in all three literatures the recurrent motif of the incursion into the sacred place of demonic adversaries who carry off the god. The result is a variation on the theme of the dying and rising god. As in his *Studies in the book of Nahum* (*Book List* 1947, p. 20), Haldar contends that historical events may frequently have been described in terms of the cultic motifs. His interpretation of the texts cited is sometimes debatable ; and his treatment of O.T. passages will strike many readers as more interesting than cogent.   G.W.A.

HEINISCH, P. : *Theology of the Old Testament.* 1950. Pp. 386. (Liturgical Press, Collegeville, Minn. Price : $5.00.) *Teologia del Vecchio Testamento.* 1950. Pp. xx+448. (Marietti, Turin. Price : 1300 lire.)

The original German edition, published in 1940, of this work by 'P. Heinisch was noticed in the *Book List* for 1946. It is claimed by the American translator (W. Heidt) that the German *Grundschrift* of the English version differs in some particulars from the 1940 German text ; the earlier issue has been thoroughly revised ; two new chapters have been added and one of the old ones omitted ; also, the bibliography has been brought up to date. The Italian rendering (by D. Pintonello) forms part of the new Italian commentary, *La Sacra Bibbia*, edited by S. Garofalo. A comparison of the two versions confirms the impression that the Italian rendering is both more accurate and more elegant than the English. The work itself is, in some respects, less satisfactory as an Old Testament Theology than are the works of Eichrodt and Procksch, to mention no others. J.M.T.B.

HERTZBERG, H. W. : *Werdende Kirche im Alten Testament.* (Theologische Existenz Heute : Neue Folge 20.) 1950. Pp. 24. (Chr. Kaiser Verlag, München. Price : DM. 1.50.)

A brief but interesting treatment of what may be called the ' Church ' theme in the Old Testament. Hertzberg believes that the Old Testament must be open towards the New, just as the New Testament is open towards the Old. He finds early evidence of the theological, as opposed to the biological, interpretation of the people of Israel in the amphictyony of the twelve tribes. There is a valuable discussion of the ' Remnant ' and of words like *'am, 'edhah* and *qahal.* The universalist strain in the Old Testament also comes under consideration. The relation between the testaments is competently handled. N.W.P.

KOCH, R. : *Geist und Messias.* 1950. Pp. xxiv+262. (Herder, Vienna. Price : 16s. 0d.)

An examination of the term *rûach* with special reference to its employment by the prophets to describe the activity of God in the Messianaic Age. The author surveys the various uses of the term as applied (*a*) to wind, breath, man's emotional behaviour and his volitional and intellectual life, and (*b*) to the divine principle of life operative in the individual, the nation and the world at large. In the latter connexion stress is laid upon the charismatic character of the *rûach*, and the author rightly combats the view that the linking of the Spirit of God with man's moral life is foreign to Israelite thought. On the whole this part is quite well done, and there is evidence that the author has read reasonably widely on the subject. In the second and third parts, where the author's allegiance to the Roman Catholic Church is more manifest, he examines the special gifts of the Spirit as they are described in connexion with the Messianic King, the Servant of the Servant Songs, and in the forecasts of the universal outpouring of the Spirit in the Messianic Age. Here the discussion is disappointingly superficial, glossing lightly over the fundamental problems and revealing little awareness of contemporary discussion in this field, a fact which in this particular case can hardly be ascribed to post-war conditions, as the author's studies were pursued in Rome. A.R.J.

LINDHAGEN, C. : *The Servant Motif in the O.T.* 1950. Pp. xvi+336· (Lundequistska Bokhandeln, Uppsala. Price : Kr. 15.)

A doctoral thesis with the sub-title "A Preliminary Study to the ' Ebed-Yahweh Problem ' in Deutero-Isaiah." The author gives an exhaustive analysis of the uses of the root ' *bd* and its derivatives in the O.T. and in the most important Semitic dialects. The servant motif is an expression for the weaker partner's relationship to the stronger in a *berith.* The weaker partner must in everything conform to the will of the stronger : he is his master's servant. The relationship between Yahweh and Israel is based on the conception of election, which for Israel was an election to service. The relationship carries with it the enjoyment of protection and blessing for the servant, though this is of course conditional upon his obedience. This ethical content of service is the result of the O.T. conception of God, " Yahweh as the specially ethical High God." Dr. Lindhagen is in general agreement with the critical position regnant in Uppsala, but a study of this kind lies almost entirely outside the arena of polemics. The translation is excellent and the work is very fully documented. C.R.N.

LJUNGMAN, H. : *Guds barmhärtighet och dom. Fariséernas lära om de två ' måtten.'* 1950. Pp. 190. (C. W. K. Gleerup, Lund. Price : Kr. 9.)

The writer of this work (who is a disciple of H. Odeberg of Lund) discusses Rabbinic teaching concerning the two ' norms ' or ' measures ' of mercy and justice. After a preliminary survey of the general use of the term *middah*, he proceeds to argue that the two ' measures ' are to be understood not as modifying each other but as two sides of the one divine action. Thus he seeks to establish a position different from that commonly accepted, and, in particular, from the treatment given to the subject by E. Sjöberg (*Gott und die Sünder.* See *Book List* 1946, p. 57). The book is not easy reading ; but there is a fourteen-page summary in English. G.W.A.

MANSON, T. W. : *The Son of Man in Daniel, Enoch and the Gospels.* (Reprinted from the ' Bulletin of the John Rylands Library,' Vol. 32, No. 2.) 1950, Pp. 24. (Manchester University Press. Price : 2s. 6d.)

In this lecture Professor Manson returns to a subject with which he had dealt in 1931 in his book, *The Teaching of Jesus.* Of the works which have appeared in the interval he selects for fullest treatment Sjöberg's *Der Menschensohn im äthiopischen Henochbuch* (Lund, 1946). Although he acknowledges the value of this book, he differs from Sjöberg on some fundamental points of interpretation, notably rejecting the conception of the Son of Man as a pre-existent being in favour of a doctrine of the pre-mundane election of the Son of Man. For students of the Old Testament the chief points of interest in this lecture will be the discussion of the Son of Man passages in *Enoch* and the use made of the idea of corporate personality in explaining the term Son of Man in the sayings of Jesus.

W.D.M.

DEL MEDICO, H. E. : *Armées et Finances dans l'Ancien Testament.* (Reprint from L'Ethnographie, No. 42, 1944.) Pp. 54. (Société d'Ethnographie de Paris. Price : 2s. 6d.)

The writer's interpretation of the O.T. is extremely material-istic. He states that the only two factors that influenced men in O.T. times were force inspiring fear and wealth as the guarantee of prosperity. All other ideas of the time were functions of these two forces. The spiritual colouring of the O.T. history is adventitious. He reconstructs the interplay of various military forces in Israel and Judah, the chief of which was ' the chariotry,' ' a state without a country,' which deter-mined the history of the whole Near East, eventually settled in Transjordan, and imposed its rulers on Israel and reduced Judah to vassalage. Of this force Nathan, Elijah and Jonadab were heads. State finance was intimately bound up with the sacrificial system. The many entirely novel views of the writer are too numerous to mention. Apart from Scriptural quotation—quite indiscriminate—he continually cites the evidence of Neo-Hittite texts which he calls ' Hivite ' and claims to have deciphered. On these he never particularizes. Though he cites in one footnote ' the copious bibliography in A. Lods' *Israël . . .* , 1932, and *Les Prophètes d'Israël,* 1935, his work is quite independent.

J.G.

MERCER, S. A. B. : *The Religion of Ancient Egypt.* 1949. Pp. xx+ 460+map. (Luzac, London. Price : £2 10s. 0d.)

The author seeks rather to describe Egyptian religion than to interpret it. First, each of the many gods and goddesses of the Egyptian pantheon is fully discussed, and what is known of their cult and centres of worship is stated. This occupies 15 chapters. Next there are chapters on such topics as " The idea of God," " Worship," " Magic," and " Moral." Much reading and research have gone into the making of this book and the whole is fully documented. Naturally not everyone will agree with many of the author's statements, but he has provided scholars with a very useful handbook which takes into account the most recent discoveries and publications. Old Testament scholars will find it a handy and valuable work of reference.

T.W.T.

MICHAELI, F. : *Dieu à l'image de l'homme.* 1950. Pp. 174. (Delachaux & Niestlé, Neuchatel and Paris. Price : Fr. 6.50.)

> The author's aim is to contribute to the growing interest in the theology of the Old Testament by examining its anthropomorphisms and assessing their value as a necessary factor in God's revelation of Himself to mankind. He begins with a survey of the language employed, paying due regard to the employment of synechdoche, metaphor and similar features, and then seeks to trace the methods which were adopted to modify or spiritualize the cruder forms of expression. Finally the author attempts a comparison with the other religions of antiquity in order to bring out what is distinctive and of lasting value in Israelite thought. The treatment of the different aspects of the study is often too sketchy to be satisfactory, and the author's limited reading of the relevant literature cannot be attributed altogether to post-war conditions. Nevertheless the work may be recommended as a most readable introduction to the subject.   A.R.J.

MOWINCKEL, S. : *Religion og Kultus.* 1950. Pp. 146. (Land og Kirke, Oslo. Price : Kr. 9.60.)

> This is an introductory manual to the study of religion from the phenomenological point of view. There are two interesting features in the treatment of the material. First, it is described and interpreted primarily in relation to the cult. Second, the illustrative examples are in the main (though by no means exclusively) drawn from the Old Testament. This method imposes limitations ; but the gains in concreteness and clarity are considerable ; and Professor Mowinckel steers his course with consummate skill between the Scylla of vague generalization and the Charybdis of repetitious detail. The notes give valuable guidance concerning the relevant literature, and will be particularly serviceable to those who want to keep in touch with recent Scandinavian work on the subject. But for readers in this country the chief importance of the book is the comprehensive presentation which it gives of those views about the nature and development of religion which are presupposed in some of Mowinckel's most significant contributions to Old Testament study.   G.W.A.

MOWINCKEL, S. : *Han som kommer. Messiasforventningen i det Gamle Testament og pa Jesu tid.* 1951. Pp. 293+123. (G. E. C. Gads Forlag, Copenhagen. Price : £2.)

> In this work, written in Norwegian but published in Denmark, Mowinckel gives a detailed survey of the origin, development, and content of the idea of the Messiah, and of its relation to the conception of the Servant on the one hand and of the Son of Man on the other. In his discussion of the character of the Israelite kingship as compared with other ancient oriental monarchies and of the cultic functions of the king, he emphasizes the importance of the distinctive Hebraic religious inheritance with its significant ethical emphasis. He denies that Yahweh was thought of as a dying and rising God, or that

356

there is any cogent evidence of the cultic or mythological identification of the king and the fertility god. This discussion leads up to a consideration of the future hope and the place in it of a kingly figure. In the development from a general future hope to a genuine eschatology the decisive phase is found in Deutero-Isaiah, who presents the drama of restoration in cosmic dimensions. Jewish eschatology is accounted for chiefly in terms of the characteristic content of Israelite religion ; and it is denied that there was a widespread, early oriental eschatology. The Servant is treated as a predominantly prophetic figure, possibly influenced in part by traits from the idea of kingship. From this theme the author turns to the later development of the Messianic idea, with the interplay in it of national, political, and particularistic elements on the one hand, and on the other, superhuman, mythological, and universalistic elements. In the later period he admits influence from the concept of the Son of Man, which (as he has so often insisted in recent years) he regards as in origin foreign to Israel and unrelated to the ' kingship ideology.' The book concludes with a discussion of the place held in the teaching and consciousness of Jesus by the ideas of the Messiah, the Servant, and the Son of Man. In this short note it is impossible to summarize adequately, far less to comment on, the contents of this richly rewarding and stimulating book which is unquestionably of first-rate importance. G.W.A

Noss, J. B. : *Man's Religions*. 1949. Pp. xii+812. (The Macmillan Co., New York. Price : 33s. 6d.)

This book, by a great scholar and able writer, has four parts : on Primitive and Bygone Religions (of the latter, the Egyptian, Babylonian, Greek and Roman are discussed), India (Hinduism, Jainism, Buddhism and Sikhism), the Far East (Taoism, Confucianism and Shinto) and the Near East (Zoroastrianism, Judaism, Christianity and Islam). While the author's sympathies unmistakably lie with Protestantism, his description of other creeds is scrupulously fair. Naturally he cannot go into details, still less into controversies ; the suffering servant is Israel, vicariously redeeming the onlooking Gentiles, Akiba introduced the six heads of the Mishnah, and so on. As he usually follows the soundest of the available theories, however, one is grateful for a continuous story. D.D.

Noth, M. : *Geschichte und Gotteswort im Alten Testament*. (Bonner Akademische Reden, 3.) 1950. Pp. 30. (Scherpe Verlag, Krefeld.) In English : *History and the Word of God in the Old Testament*. 1950. Pp. 12. (Reprinted from the " Bulletin of the John Rylands Library," vol. 32, No. 2, March, 1950. Manchester University Press and The John Rylands Library, Manchester. Price : 2s. 0d.)

In this short, but suggestive, lecture, Professor Noth shows how a comparison between the messengers of God as cited in the Mari texts and the Old Testament prophets reveals a close similarity between the two which cannot be accidental. The character of the prophet as the essential mediator of God's word in the Old Testament has thus a history which lies outside Israel. Is, then, a connection between God's word and the ever changing historical phenomena possible ? Is the claim that the Old Testament gives us the pure word of God untenable, if it is allowed that even the essential elements of it have a history ? Professor Noth replies that these questions are not rightly asked, for, according to the Bible, God manifests himself in history through the agency of characters, such as prophets, and of phenomena, such as institutions like the cult and the kingship, as they occur in history. On the connection between history and the word of God as they appear in the Old Testament his conclusion is that " it cannot be proved that the Old Testament method of divine revelation, which makes use of given historical phenomena, stands higher than other methods." All that we can say is that " it speaks to men in the world in which they actually live : in the world of history." Furthermore, " it could not be proved that the Old Testament and the Bible generally do deal with what is truly divine revelation and with what is truly the Word of God." D.W.T.

PARRINDER, G. : *The Bible and Polygamy*. 1950. Pp. vi + 78. (S.P.C.K., London. Price : 2s. 6d.)

This little book was written in response to a practical need arising from the reluctance of some Africans to accept the view that monogamy should be imposed on African Christians as essential. The author offers an objective study of the teaching and practice of both Testaments, examining the extent of, and the reasons for, polygamy in the Old Testament and the growth of monogamy within the Old Testament period. He argues that within Israel monogamy must always have been more widespread than polygamy, and, except in the case of kings and some other leading persons, where polygamy existed it was often owing to the childlessness of the first wife. Even so its fruits were often evil, and the Bible nowhere holds polygamy before men as an ideal. Levirate marriage is said to rest on the principle that a man's widow is inherited by his agnates, and to have been an important factor in polygamy Actually we have little evidence that levirate marriage was often practised, and where it was there is more insistence on the duty of the levir than on his right over the widow. Moreover, there is no evidence that it normally concerned more than the production of a single child, and so far from the widow being regarded as an inheritance of the kinsman, Ruth's *go'el* complained that the marriage would spoil his inheritance. As a whole this study is valuable and scholarly. H.H.R.

PROCKSCH, O. : *Theologie des Alten Testaments*. 1950. Pp. 788. (C. Bertelsmann, Gütersloh. Price : DM. 26.)

The first two *Lieferungen* of this massive book appeared in 1949 and were reviewed in the 1950 *Book List*. The second two

Lieferungen, which complete the work, contain the concluding pages of the third section of the historical part of the book, followed by a systematic study of the world of thought found in the Old Testament. This systematic part of the book is articulated in the three divisions God and the World, God and People, God and Man. Procksch was a great teacher, if one may judge from this record of his teaching and from the distinction of some of his former pupils. One of them, Eichrodt, owes much to his master, but has treated the problems of Old Testament theology even more thoroughly, and has recognized more clearly the unity of the Old Testament. Procksch suggests as a method of procedure in the Systematic part of his work the grouping of the material on each theme or idea round the personality who is chiefly associated with it. This procedure, however, is not consistently adhered to in practice. N.W.P.

Questioni Bibliche alla luce dell' Enciclica " Divino Afflante Spiritu" Parte I (various authors). 1949. Pp. iv+202. Parte II (by A. Bea) : *Il problema antropologico in Gen. 1-2. Il Transformismo.* 1950. Pp. 68. (Pontifical Biblical Institute, Rome. Price : 1800 lire and 900 lire respectively.)

There has been for a number of years a custom of holding a Biblical Week in the month of September, under the auspices of the Pontifical Biblical Institute in Rome. The present work represents, in both its parts, a very welcome publication of some of the conferences given in 1947 and 1948. All of them were on subjects of great importance ; most of them were concerned with the question of *genres littéraires* (It. i generi litterari) in the Bible. So, in the first part, P. Eufrasio di Cristo Re writes on these *genres* as they are dealt with in the Encyclical of 30th September, 1943 ; G. Castellino on the presence of these *genres* in Gen. i-xi, and F. Salvoni on the *genres* is the historical books of the Old Testament. The latter writer has a further article on the cosmological problem in Gen. i. 1-ii. 4 with special references to the natural sciences ; G. Rinaldi contributes literary observations on Gen. ii-iii, and A. Vaccari discusses the supernatural element in the same chapters. By far the most interesting topic is that handled by A. Bea, in which the arguments for the evolutionary hypothesis, particularly in its bearing on man's origin, are briefly assessed, the conclusion being that the hypothesis is not, as yet, proved, and, if in the future, certainty were to be attained, it would be found possible to find a way " per combinarla con la Sacra Scrittura." The learned writer's serenity and objectivity are well displayed here. It is astonishing that his bibliography makes no reference to the important French work *Origine et Évolution de l'Homme* by G. Goury, of which a revised and enlarged edition appeared in 1948. (Cf. H. Vincent's review in *Revue Biblique*, January, 1950, pp. 130-34.)   J.M.T.B.

RICHARDSON, A. (ed. by) : *A Theological Word Book of the Bible.*
1950. Pp. 290. (S. C. M. Press, London. Price : 25s. 0d.)

It is undoubtedly a sign of the reviving interest in Old
Testament theology that such a book as this was planned.
Among the contributors the reader will recognize names which
inspire confidence. The book contains numerous articles
(e.g. *God, Revelation, Sacrifice, Son of Man*) which are models
of clarity and compression. It is inevitable sometimes that the
Old Testament aspect of a word should be inadequately treated
in cases where the contributor is not an Old Testament
specialist. There is a certain lack of balance in the length of
articles. Surprisingly small space is devoted to *Jesus* and
Christ. The Servant of the Lord is treated far too briefly. There
is nothing on *People of God* or (surprisingly in view of current
discussions) specifically on *King.* There should have been a
separate article on *Creation.* These are just a few points which
struck the reviewer.

It is inevitable, of course, that, as the work is based on the
English Bible, certain key words, which are translated by
more than one English word, are dealt with in widely separated
parts of the book. The treatment of the psychological terms is
confusing and inadequate. *Soul* is dealt with under *Spirit and
Mind.* A comparison here with A. R. Johnson's *The Vitality
of the Individual in the Thought of Ancient Israel* is instructive.
When one considers the psychological connotation that belongs
to them in the Bible, it is odd that the words ' bowels ' and
' reins ' receive no notice at all.

Taken as a whole the book is uneven in quality. It does not,
of course, enter into competition with Kittel's *Theologisches
Wörterbuch zum Neuen Testament* which is in a class by itself.
Taken as a whole, without any reflection on the excellence of
some of the articles, it may be said that the value of this book
to the scholar is limited.　　　　　　　　　　　　N.W.P.

ROWLEY, H. H. : *The Biblical Doctrine of Election.* 1950. Pp. 184.
(Lutterworth Press. Price : 14s. 0d.)

While it may be quite true that, as the author himself
emphasizes, there is little that is new in this book, that does
not mean that it is not a valuable addition to the books on
Old Testament Theology, and will not repay study. Familiar
truths are none the worse of being gathered together and
clearly stated. The book is mainly concerned with providing a
comprehensive account of the theme of Election, the Election
of Israel as a people, of individual Israelites and of non-
Israelites. The treatment of the New Testament material is
on a much smaller scale but the student will find that the
exposition is most helpful. The author has a reasonably
conservative, balanced outlook which will, of course, expose
him to criticism from some quarters. He deliberately confines
himself to the Bible and refrains from entering into later
controversies. The book is magnificently documented and
should stimulate further study.　　　　　　　　　N.W.P.

SCHOEPS, H. J. : *Aus frühchristlicher Zeit : Religionsgeschichtliche Untersuchungen.* 1950. Pp. viii+320. (Mohr, Tübingen. Price : DM. 21.)

Most of this collection of thirteen essays had previously appeared in article form in a variety of journals, but we welcome the book as presenting, in a much more convenient form, Professor Schoeps' recent research into the history and teaching of the Ebionites, a study already outlined in his *Theologie und Geschichte des Judenchristentums*, 1949. The attention of the O.T. student is drawn especially to the third essay in the book, entitled ' Symmachusstudien ' (pp. 82-119). Here the author, accepting the old theory based on Eusebius and Jerome that Symmachus was an Ebionite, discusses three major points. 1. Symmachus introduced into his Greek O.T. numerous Ebionite Theologumena. 2. In his rendering of Hebrew mythological figures, such as Rephaim, Lilith and others, Symmachus makes use of Greek myth. 3. He frequently incorporates Midrashic interpretations in his rendering. In nearly all the instances discussed by Schoeps, it may be noticed that the renderings of Symmachus are, on the one hand, independent of the LXX, and, on the other, followed by the Vulgate. The ' Symmachusstudien ' first appeared in *Coniectanea Neotestamentica* (Uppsala), 1942, and *Biblica* (Rome), 1945, 1948, but were revised before inclusion in the present book.   B.J.R.

SCHRADE, H. : *Der verborgene Gott : Gottesbild und Gottesvorstellung in Israel und im Alten Orient.* 1949. Pp. 316+32 pages of plates. (W. Kohlhammer Verlag, Stuttgart. Price : DM. 13.80.)

This book contains a very thorough and stimulating discussion of the belief in the visibility of God as recorded in the Old Testament. The author starts by setting the problem in the framework of the beliefs about images of the gods in the Ancient Near East. He discusses the purpose and meaning of the statues both of gods and of kings and shows the relation between the representation of the king and the god whose temple he built and whose statue he erected. A very interesting chapter on Ichnaten emphasises that the realism of representations of this king and his family is balanced by the exclusiveness of the relation between this particular family and the symbol of the Sun God.

The main part of the book concerns itself with following the history of the oscillations in Israel's faith between the belief that God was the absolutely hidden God and the belief that the vision of God was possible. The meaning of iconoclastic episodes is discussed. Interesting contrasts are indicated between prophets like Jeremiah, whose conception of God is highly spiritualized, and the Second Isaiah, who comes in a polemic against images, on the one hand and Isaiah, who has a vision in the Temple, and Ezekiel, who has a still more detailed vision by the River Chebar, on the other. It is shown how there is throughout a tension between the mystery of God's being and the possibility of vision of God. Late in the Old Testament period we find the belief that man was made in the image of God definitely formulated, though without any clear indication of exactly what that implied. Right at the end of the development we have in the Book of Daniel the confrontation of God as the Ancient of Days and the One like unto a Son of Man. It is significant that in this same book the end of image worship is indicated in the vision of the giant image which is overthrown and demolished by the stone which grows to the dimensions of a mountain and represents the power of God's kingdom. N.W.P.

VERHOEF, P. A. : *Die vraagstuk van die onvervulde voorsegginge in verband met Jesaja 1-39* (with a summary in English). 1950. Pp. 362. (De Bussy, Amsterdam ; Karpstad, Pretoria.)

The writer stands up for the fundamentalist ideas with regard to the predictions in the first part of the Book of Isaiah. He defends himself against critical views as well as against chiliastic use of unfulfilled predictions. A well written and thorough study of its kind, valuable for those who are interested in views on the character of the Bible reports. P.A.H.deB.

VOS, G. : *Biblical Theology : Old and New Testaments.* 1948. Pp. 454. (Wm. B. Eerdmans Publishing Co., Grand Rapids. Price : $5.00.)

This is a large work on Biblical Theology on strictly conservative lines. Biblical Theology is defined as ' that branch of Exegetical Theology which deals with the process of the self-revelation of God deposited in the Bible.' There is a polemic against rationalism and the application of the Concept of Evolution to the Bible. How little relevant this criticism is to the best of modern Biblical Study can be seen by referring to a book like the one by G. E. Wright reviewed in this Book List. Revelation is regarded as proceeding by Epochs—(1) the Mosaic Epoch leading up to and including Moses, (2) the Prophetic Epoch. Then follows a section on New Testament Theology which deals from the point of view of revelation with the Nativity, with John the Baptist, with the Probation of Jesus and with Jesus' Public Ministry. There seems to be a complete ignoring or rejection of criticism and the discussions are largely an echo of the debates of a couple of generations ago. In the New Testament part it is startling to find that the death and resurrection of Christ play scarcely any part in the exposition, while there is no systematic treatment of the Epistles. One is left wondering if the book is actually only a fragment. N.W.P.

WALLIS, L. : *The Bible and Modern Belief.* 1949. Pp. 176. (Duke University Press, Durham, N.C. Price : $2.50.)

The value of this book is in the strong emphasis which is placed on the division and sharp antagonism between Ephraim and Judah. The post-exilic fiction of the Tabernacle in the Wilderness is wholly anti-Ephraimite propaganda. The conclusion is that religion will thrive to-day when we can adjust the social emphasis of the prophets and of Jesus with the individualistic emphasis of Paul . This will end in the disappearance of communism as a menace to the modern world. N.H.S.

WEBER, O. : *Bibelkunde des Alten Testament.* 2 vols. (6th ed.) 1948. Vol. I. Pp. 272. Vol. II. Pp. 296. (Furche-Verlag, Tübingen. Price : DM. 8.80 per vol.)

> This is a type of book which has been necessitated by the fact that theological students so often came to the University with little knowledge of the Bible. The present work is intended to provide, not introduction to the Old Testament but simply knowledge of its contents. The books of the Old Testament are studied as they now lie before us in the Canon. In the Introduction there is a very interesting discussion of the question of literary authenticity in relation to genuineness in the theological sense. The confusion between these two is shown to rest on a wrong view of inspiration. The Old Testament is fundamentally the product of the Hebrew Community. Volume I surveys the contents of the Pentateuch and the Former Prophets. Volume II has a brief but useful introduction dealing mainly with Hebrew prophecy. It is pointed out that the prophets must be understood in their close relation to the community. There follows a survey of the Latter Prophets and the Writings. N.W.P.

WIDENGREN, G. : *The Ascension of the Apostle and the Heavenly Book (King and Saviour III).* (Uppsala Universitets Årsskrift, 1950 : 7.) 1950. Pp. 118. (Lundequistska Bokhandeln, Uppsala & Harrassowitz, Leipzig. Price : Kr. 8.)

> The greater part of this very erudite study deals with material outside the strictly O.T. field. The author's theme is the recurrence of the idea of a heavenly book or tablets of destiny which the king, or prophet, or apostle receives at his ascension. This idea he traces throughout the pre-Islamic period, from the ancient Mesopotamian culture, through Hebrew and Jewish religion (where he finds it illustrated in narratives about Moses and about the prophets and in the coronation ritual), in Samaritan, Rabbinic, and Mandaean literature, and in Arabic Hermetic writings. The treatment is extremely well documented. It is to be hoped that the author's companion studies will soon be published. G.W.A.

WRIGHT, G. E. : *The Old Testament against its Environment.* (Studies in Biblical Theology, 2.) 1950. Pp. 116. (S. C. M. Press, London. Price : 6s. 0d.)

> The value of this little book is out of all proportion to its size. The author acknowledges indebtedness in particular to Albright, Frankfort and Jacobsen. In the first chapter he deals with what he calls the Israelite ' mutation.' The distinctiveness of Hebrew religion cannot be explained by evolution. It was not designed to produce a life in harmony with nature. It was based on historical events. The problem of life lay in adjustment to the will of God. The religion of Israel breaks with the mythopoeic approach to reality. The nature of Israelite Monotheism is shown to lie in the exclusive exaltation of Jehovah as the one source of power, authority and creativity. We have to recognize here an existential point of view.

In Chapter II the author discusses the tension between God and Nature in Hebrew religion, and the meaning of God's Election of Israel. The Covenant is shown to be not in itself a redemptive act but as the putting in concrete terms of the meaning of the relationship involved in Election. The covenant idea goes back early to the pre-monarchical amphictyony of the twelve tribes. Wright is somewhat sceptical of the cult-drama theory and thinks that the covenant with David was subordinate to the covenant of Sinai and that the Monarchy in Israel did not attain the sanctity we meet elsewhere. The belief that God's will was expressed in the Covenant determined the Hebrew view of society and history. History of the divine activity became revelatory, whereas natural religion works itself out into philosophy and mysticism.

In Chapter III it is shown that magic was incompatible with Israel's religion, that Israelite worship was not motivated by the desire to achieve integration of nature and society. Uneasiness was felt in certain quarters about the sacrificial cult, since personal relation could not be achieved by sacrifice. The prophetic attack on the institutions of kingship and cult in Israel would have been unthinkable in polytheism.

N.W.P.

POST-BIBLICAL JUDAISM

BONSIRVEN, J. : *Il Guidaismo Palestinense al Tempo di Gesu Christo.* Trad. dal francese di Giosuè Marigliano. (La Sacra Bibbia, ed. by S. Garofalo.) 1950. Pp. 188. (Marietti, Turin. Price : 450 lire.)

Le Judaïsme Palestinien au temps de Jésus-Christ, édition abrégée. 1950. Pp. 250. (Beauchesne, Paris. Price : Fr. 525.)

Both these works are, in substance, reproductions in the original language or in an Italian translation, of J. Bonsirven's long and substantial monograph, first published as an article in the *Dictionnaire de la Bible, Supplément,* fascicles XXII and XXIII. This was noticed in the *Book List* for 1949 and 1950. The Italian version claims to be equipped "con ritocchi ed aggiunte," but it is far from easy to discover what these can be, apart from a few additions to the bibliography (such as the Italian version of J. Felten, *Neutestament. Zeitgeschichte*) and a quotation from " un autorevole Rabbino italiano," printed as an addition to note 3, foot of p. 173. To obviate all confusion, it must be insisted that both the article and its reprints are abridgements of Bonsirven's large work in two volumes with a slightly longer title : *Le Judaïsme palestinien au temps de Jésus Christ, sa théologie,* published in 1935 and now, unfortunately, out-of-print. Another work by Bonsirven, *Les idées juives au temps de Notre-Seigneur* (1934), also an abridgement of the larger work, is not identical with the recent publications, though the author in his preface to the present French abridgement warns us that some repetition has proved inevitable. J.M.T.B.

DANBY, H. : *The Code of Maimonides, Book Nine, The Book of Offerings.* *Translated from the Hebrew.* (Yale Judaica Series, vol. IV.) 1950. Pp. xxii+236. (Yale University Press, New Haven. Price : $3.50.)

This is the third volume to appear of a complete translation of Mishneh Torah. The first two were noticed in *Book List* 1950, pp. 72 f. The present volume shows that a translation can be a great work. The introduction explains the arrangement adopted by Maimonides—Passover Offering, Festal Offering, Firstlings, Offerings for Transgressions in Error, Offerings to Complete Atonement after Immersion, Substituted Offering— and his method of systematization by including in a section all relevant material, i.e. even such as occurs outside the corresponding part of the Talmud, and excluding all irrelevant material, i.e. even such as occurs in the corresponding part. The notes at the end contain a wealth of information ; the Talmudic source, if any, of each provision is carefully indicated. The translation itself could not be bettered. It might be worth considering whether those benedictions which are mentioned in Festal Offering 3.4 (and Mishnah Sotah 7.7) but not found in extant synagogue liturgy represent lost versions of the Amidah.   D.D.

FINKELSTEIN, L. : *Introduction to the Treatises Abot and Abot of Rabbi Nathan.* Texts and Studies of The Jewish Theological Seminary of America. Vol. XVI. 1950. Pp. 262+xlviii. (The Jewish Theological Seminary of America, New York.)

A publication of great importance, mainly in Hebrew, but with an excellent summary in English. Professor Finkelstein analyses the five collections of which the treatises are composed. He has many stimulating suggestions, such as that the first chapter of Abot, duly emended, preserves a proclamation by the Men of the Great Synagogue of the 3rd cent. B.C. No doubt there will be controversy. The author inclines to ascribe any illogical sequence to re-arrangement. But e.g. Sanhedrin X. 1-4 (part of which, in his opinion, originally formed the beginning of the proclamation mentioned) may well have been placed after IX from the outset ; for though X. 1-3 has no connection with IX, X. 4 has. Professor Finkelstein argues that the stories of Hillel's proselytes have a Shammaitic colouring in Abot of R.N., which is eliminated in Bab. Shabbath. He might have noted that in Bab. Shabbath Hillel receives them into the faith before teaching them, whereas in A. of R.N. teaching precedes initiation. The question, however, is whether the stricter version is not a relatively late correction of Hillelite tolerance.   D.D.

HEINEMANN, I. : *Darkhê ha-Aggadah (The Methods of the Aggadah).* 1949. Pp. iv+284. (The Hebrew University Press, Jerusalem. Price : I £1.550.)

This is a book of first rate importance. In the religio-ethical teachings of the Jewish sages—from the second century B.C.E. till the sixth century C.E.—there are elements of sound philological exegesis on one side and free creations of fancy on the other. Between, there is an interpretation of Scriptures, which seems to deprive the biblical texts of their plain meaning. The author, a classical philologist, equally versed in Jewish and general philosophy, seeks to trace the psychological origin of this particular kind of exegesis in a trend of organic (not logical) thinking, which e.g. attaches more importance to external analogies than to inward conformity. This organic thinking, on principle, attributed to the word of the Holy Writ a plurality of significations, and created forms of popular literature (resulting from synagogal sermons!) standing between science and art. This psychology forms the background for various phenomena of the Aggadic "non-historiographic historiography" (pp. 15-95) ; so e.g. the inclination to make concrete even theoretical biblical data ; to add details which are missing in the biblical accounts ; to identify obviously non-identical persons and periods ; to anachronize and contemporize biblical events. All these phenomena and others are elucidated more fully by their Hellenistic parallels and contrasts. In a second part (pp. 96-164) the "non-philological philology" is dealt with ; i.e. the exegetical utilization of the individual letters, words and sentences (irrespective of their context) and of whole sections. A final part (pp. 165-195) seeks to define the character of the Aggadah and its place in history. The Aggadah then, forms a continuation of biblical thinking, the differences being determined by the transition of Israel's Prophetic Religion into a Book Religion, and by the changes in the forms of thinking, which involve tendencies to greater abstraction as well as to concreteness. The sections in which the author outlines the position of the Septuagint, certain Apocrypha (ben Sira, Jubilees, the Testaments of the Patriarchs), and Philo, which are on the way between biblical and aggadic thinking, are of quite unusual value, as is the closing research on the question of the seriousness of the Aggadah and its relation to play and wit. Full docmentation (pp. 197-266) and indexes complete the book, which worthily ranks with the standard works in the field of Zunz, Bacher and Aptowitzer.   I.L.S.

JANSMA, T. : *Twee Haggada's uit de Palestijnse Targum van de Penta-teuch.* 1950. Pp. 16. (University Press, Leiden. Price : Fl. 1.00)
    This short monograph was delivered on the occasion of the author's taking up his professorship in the University of Leiden. He deals with the Haggadas on Gen. xliv. 18, 19 and Gen. xxxv. 9, and discusses the relation between what is said in *Bereshith Rabba* and what is contained in the fragments of Targums and in the piyyutim from the Cairo Geniza. N.H.S.

(MARMORSTEIN, A.) : *Studies in Jewish Theology, The Arthur Marmorstein Memorial Volume,* edited by J. Rabbinowitz and M. S. Lew. 1950. Pp. 320+xlvi. (Oxford University Press. Price : 30s. 0d.)
    In the English part are reprinted articles on The Background of the Haggadah, The Unity of God in Rabbinic Literature, The Imitation of God in the Haggadah, The Holy Spirit in

Rabbinic Legend, The Resurrection of the Dead in Rabbinic Theology, Eternal Life in Rabbinic Theology, and Judaism and Christianity in the Third Century ; the articles on Imitation of God and Holy Spirit are translated from the German. The Hebrew part reprints articles on The Immortality of Israel in Rabbinic Literature, Redemption in the Haggadah, and The Historical Value of the Haggadah. In addition, a reader will find a brief appreciation by the editors ; a fine memoir by Emile Marmorstein, one of Dr. Marmorstein's sons : and a most welcome bibliography of Dr. Marmorstein's publications, compiled by E. M. The book is well produced (though there is only an Index to the English part), and the topics chosen should interest a wide public. It is a volume worthy of the memory of ' a man of learning and a man of God.'   D.D.

NEWMAN, J. : *Semikhah*. 1950. Pp. xxiv+174. (Manchester University Press. Price : 18s. 0d.)

The author discusses the origin, history and function of *semikhah* (ordination), the rite by which, in the time of the Sanhedrin, the judge received divine authority. The actual laying on of hands became obsolete before the end of the 3rd century. There was an attempt at revival in the 16th century. Rabbi Newman believes that a Jewish court based on a revived *semikhah* rite would restore the Jewish Law to its rightful place, both within the new state of Israel and throughout Jewry. This careful and pious study in Rabbinics is offered as a contribution to that end.   N.H.S.

WENDEL, C. : *Der Thoraschrein im Altertum*. (Hallische Monographien 15.) 1950. Pp. 44. (Max Niemeyer, Halle. Price : DM. 5.00.)

A well documented history of the form of the receptacle containing the Scrolls since Ezra. Originally they were kept in a chest in a separate little room. The chest was replaced by an ark in imitation of the Seleucid practice of keeping royal ordinances in an ark. As an ark was less easily transportable, it was placed in the actual room of prayer, on a platform. At first it had a triangular roof, but from the end of the 2nd cent. A.D. the rounded roof was adopted from Syriac models, in turn influenced by Mesopotamia.   D.D.

WILDE, R. : *The Treatment of the Jews in the Greek Christian Writers of the First Three Centuries*. (The Catholic University of America Patristic Studies. Vol. LXXXI.) 1949. Pp. xviii+240. (The Catholic University of America Press, Washington, D.C. Price : 21s. 0d.)

The main subject of this book lies outside the field of our interest as a Society. By way of introduction to the main treatment, however, Father Wilde outlines the story of Jewish relations with the Hellenistic world in pre-New Testament times. This outline is, however, sketchy, and one often feels that further elucidation is necessary to make it convincing. Thus, we are told that ' Jewish thinkers never wanted to depart from Jewish orthodoxy.' One wonders.   B.J.R.

ASENSIO, F. : *Misericordia et Veritas, el Ḥèsed y 'Ĕmet divinos, su influjo religioso-social en la historia de Israel.* 1949. Pp. iv+344. (Gregorian University, Rome. Price : 26s. 0d.)

It was a happy idea of the author, who was urged on by his master, Alberto Vaccari, to attempt a full-length study of *hesed* and *'emeth* in all their Old Testament occurrences. As a twelve-page index of closely packed Biblical quotations attests, Asensio has covered the ground very thoroughly and has grouped his findings in six chapters with such titles as the Hebrew terms and their translations : the divine *hesed* as an essential element in the history of Israel, and in public and private prayer ; the divine *'emeth* and the idea of covenant ; some characteristics of the divine *'emeth* (its duration, immensity, protective force, and so forth). It is a pity that so little use has been made of English work, but is only fair to say that (perhaps for a somewhat different reason) Spanish authors are somewhat to seek in the bibliography. It may be reasonably felt that no work on the subject is quite complete without some reference to the writings of Dr. H. Wheeler Robinson. J.M.T.B.

BIRKELAND, H. : *Språk og religion hos jøder og arabere.* (Etnologisk samfunn. Skrifter utgitt ved Nils Lid. Nr. 4.) 1949. Pp. 52. (Olaf Norlis Forlag, Oslo. Price : 4s. 0d.)

In this interesting booklet Birkeland surveys the close relation of Hebrew and Arabic to the historical development of the religions with which they are associated. He shows how in Israel conservative tendencies in religion and language produced not the mere fossilization of ancient usage but the creation of something new; and the survey of the vicissitudes of Hebrew is carried forward to cover the contemporary situation. With the agelong conflict and change in Hebrew language and religion Birkeland contrasts the relatively static character of Islam and Arabic, and considers the challenge to both of modern secular culture. The whole discussion is marked by the freshness and originality which are characteristic of the author's work ; and the importance of the book is greater than its brevity might suggest. It may be noted that Birkeland argues that Hebrew was the language normally used by Jesus. G.W.A.

KOEHLER, L. : *Lexicon in Veteris Testamenti Libros.* Lieferungen vi, vii and viii. 1950. Pp. 64 each. (E. J. Brill, Leiden. Price : Fl. 3 per part.)

These three parts, the latest instalments of Professor Koehler's *Lexicon*, run from *huppîm* to *mᵉhôlah :* it is therefore still hardly yet half-way through the Hebrew part. The work, however, is becoming increasingly useful as a supplement to G.-B. and B.-D.-B., as ancient errors, such as ' the entering in of Hamath ' (s.p. 470), disappear, even though the editor does not seem to have drawn everything into his net ; and a note of the source of, and/or the grounds for, new translations of difficult or obscure words is always desirable for purposes of control. For fresh views are not always correctly reproduced; for example, the present reviewer explains *ḥrp* in Ps. vii. 4 as ' disappointed, frustrated ' not as ' confused,' which denotes something quite different. Different explanations, too, are occasionally given of the same word, for example of *m'd* in Ps. xxxi. 12 on pp. 488-9. The English renderings, too, are often surprising if not misleading (for example, ' fedders,' ' grapes not being sweet,' ' eager after,' ' hoarse throat,' ' earthen bottle,' all on pp. 336-7). None the less, these are small blemishes which the reader can for the most part easily put right for himself, and the work is becoming an indispensable tool for the study of the O.T. 　　　G.R.D.

KOOPMANS, J. J. : *Aramese Grammatica (voor het oud-Testamentisch Aramees) met Woordenlijst.* 1949. Pp. x+128. (Nederlandsch Archaeoloisch-Philologisch Instituut voor het Nabije Oosten, Leiden.)

This grammar of Biblical Aramaic was written to meet the needs of Dutch students. In its general scheme and pattern it conforms as closely as possible with J. Nat's *Hebreeuwsche Grammatica* (Leiden, 1947). It begins with a brief discussion of the Aramaic dialects and a short bibliography of grammatical works. The grammar of Biblical Aramaic is next presented in a way which aims to strike a mean between the " descriptive " and the " explicative " methods. Only 11 pages are devoted to syntax. The work ends with paradigms, a vocabulary of Biblical Aramaic and an index. The book is shockingly produced and it is a disgrace to the institution which sponsored it. The author's typescript with autographed insertions are reproduced, apparently by some duplicating machine, on coarsest paper of the worst kind. Often whole words are illegible : some of the paradigms have come out so badly that they are virtually useless. In so far as it is possible to read and judge the book, the author would appear to have written a competent introduction to Biblical Aramaic, but its value to the students for whom it is intended must be enormously lessened by the faulty and careless way in which it has been produced. 　　　T.W.T.

VON MEYENFELDT, F. H. : *Het hart (leb, lebab) in het Oude Testament* (with a summary in English). 1950. Pp. xvi+226. (Leiden. Price : Fl. 8.)

After a catalogue of the passages in which *leb* occurs and some exegetical observations the writer classified the passages. He distinguishes two main groups, the use of *leb* in connection with man and *leb* not concerning man. He concludes that the word represents the whole person and that it already in the oldest parts of the O.T. often emphasizes the individuality of man. The linguistic parts of this study are not elaborated and the book as a whole remains below the quality of Becker's thesis on *nefesh*, Amsterdam, 1942. 　　　P.A.H.deB.

PRIJS, L. : *Die grammatikalische Terminologie des Abraham Ibn Esra.*
1950. Pp. 152. (Sepher-Verlag, Basel. Price : Swiss Frs. 25.00.)

This work, which was awarded a prize by the University of
Bern, falls into two parts. The first, in the form of an introduction, contains six short sections on various aspects of Ibn
Esra's use of grammatical terms. The second is an alphabetical
list of the grammatical terms themselves. Each term is
explained and fully discussed, and its use is illustrated by
copious examples. The author has produced an excellent
book which will be indispensible to all who are interested in
the beginnings of the study of Hebrew grammar.   T.W.T.

TUR SINAI, N. H. : *Ha-Lashon we ha-Sefer (The Language and the
Book) Fundamental problems in the science of language and its
unfolding in literature.* Vol. II. The Book. 1950. Pp. xii+436.
(Mossad Bialik, Jerusalem. Price : I £2.600.)

One of the noted scholars at the Hebrew University proceeds
to collect in three volumes a large number of papers and essays
(those which already have been published elsewhere in a
wholly new form). This second volume contains contributions
in the field of biblical exegesis, including : What is biblical
literature ? (pp. 3-57) ; Riddles and their vicissitudes in
biblical literature (pp. 58-93) ; Metathesis in the text of the
Bible (pp. 106-149) ; Ancient Jewish lore as revealed in the
origin and the earliest transmission of the Alphabet (pp. 150-
194) and a whole series of papers bearing upon individual books
and passages of the Old Testament, especially Hosea (pp.
304-334), Canticles (pp. 351-388), and Ecclesiastes (pp. 389-
409). The putting together of these essays purposes to show
that the heuristic principle underlying all of them, though
likely only to elucidate many isolated obscure passages,
goes on to offer a new conception of Biblical text-history and
literature as a whole. Thus the fascinating essay on Metathesis,
taking advantage of parallel passages in the Scriptures,
Massoretic variants, the Septuagint, and ancient rabbinic
sources, seeks to establish the occurrence of the phenomenon,
its importance for the handing down of the biblical text, and
the rôle played by it in the earliest Jewish exegesis. The
opening essay evolves in an elaborate form Tur Sinai's theory
on the unity of Biblical literature. The whole of it—our author
maintains—originally consisted of a series of tales on heroes
of the past— kings, prophets, including Moses, etc.—interwoven
with famous sayings, songs, speeches, and laws attributed by
the writers of these stories to those personages. Thus, the
Psalms, Canticles, and also the prophecies in the prophetical
books are pseudepigraphic fragments removed from their
original historiographic framework. Owing to this theory
Tur Sinai finds interrelations between passages in separate
parts of the Bible, which apparently do not show any affinity ;
he holds that a large number of biblical texts have reached us
in a secondary recension ; in many cases he rejects the
hypothesis of different sources in favour of the assumption of

various literary stages of the same kernel. Even where the views of the author are not convincing they are stimulating and rich in luminous details.   I.L.S.

ZORELL, F. : *Lexicon Hebraicum et Aramaicum Veteris Testamenti.* Fasc. 7. 1950. Pp. 72. (Pontificio Istituto Biblico, Rome. Price : $2.00.)

This latest fascicle of Zorell's *Lexicon*, which is being continued by Semkovski, runs from *peša'* to *qiššurîm :* it follows the plan of the preceding parts.   G.R.D.

1952

For the preparation of this issue of the Book List the Editor has had the co-operation of the Members of the Book List Committee, appointed by the Society : Prof. G. W. Anderson, Mgr. J. M. T. Barton, Mrs. Burdess, Profs. D. Daube, G. R. Driver, Dr. J. Gray, Profs. A. R. Johnson, W. D. McHardy, N. W. Porteous, O. S. Rankin, Rev. B. J. Roberts, Profs. N. H. Snaith, T. W. Thacker and D. Winton Thomas. In addition he acknowledges with gratitude help received from Prof. P. A. H. de Boer, Canon H. Danby, Profs. O. Eissfeldt, A. Guillaume, Dr. A. S. Kapelrud, Mr. R Loewe, Profs. I. L. Seeligmann, H. Stock and W. C. van Unnik, Dr. M. Wallenstein and Mr. P. R. Weis; also from Mr. S. Roberts, the Deputy Librarian of Manchester University Library. Prices of books, where known, are given either in foreign currency, or in the English equivalent. Titles to which an asterisk (*) is prefixed are recommended for inclusion in school libraries.

The Editor again expresses his thanks to all who have helped him in the preparation of the List by bringing to his attention the titles of newly published books. That there are still gaps is inevitable ; but they are fewer than they would be but for this service.

H. H. ROWLEY.

MANCHESTER UNIVERSITY.

BEATTY, R. C., HYATT, J. P., SPEARS, M. K. (ed. by) : *Vanderbilt Studies in the Humanities*, vol. 1. 1951. Pp. viii+276. (Vanderbilt University Press, Nashville, Tenn. Price : $3.50.)

> This volume contains fifteen essays ranging over a wide range of subjects. Only two of the essays lie within the range of interest of the *Book List*, viz. those by J. P. Hyatt, on ' The Deuteronomic Edition of Jeremiah', and by S. Sandmel, on ' Judaism, Jesus, and Paul '. Hyatt argues that the Deuteronomic edition of Jeremiah can be isolated from the rest of the book and dated about 550 B.C. It incorporates older material which may be authentic, but it also contains freely composed speeches. Moreover, it presents ideas not always in agreement with Jeremiah's. Sandmel calls for stricter methodology in relation to Judaism, and complains that there is too little discrimination amongst the various strands of Judaism, that too many writers quote from Rabbinic sources without consulting the context of their citations, and that too often Judaism is used as a foil for the New Testament. H.H.R.

DE BOER, P. A. H. (ed. by) : *Oudtestamentische Studiën*, Deel IX. 1951. Pp. 190. (Brill, Leiden. Price : Subscription Fl. 15, separately Fl. 25.)

> The Dutch Old Testament Society continues its publishing activities with zeal and efficiency. This volume contains eight articles, two in English, four in French, and two in German. The English essays are by G. J. Thierry and the editor himself. Thierry discusses various items of Hebrew Grammar and Etymology, generally criticising statements in Köhler's new lexicon. In particular, there is an extended note on the origin of the *waw*-copulative and *waw*-consecutive constructions. De Boer sees an original cultic song in Isa. xxxviii. 9-20, introduced there by the Isaiah-editor. The four French articles are as follows. A. de Buck of Leiden finds the origin of the flower on the high priest's turban to be in the creative, life-giving ideas associated also with flower offerings in Egyptian religion, and as gifts both to the dead and the living. J. van der Ploeg writes on Israelite nobles, and Jean de Savignac of Brussels has a careful and thorough article on Ps. cx as interpreted with reference to Egyptian literature. F. Skierksma of Groningen contributes an analysis on the meaning of Circumcision in Israelite history. M. David has an important article in German on the account of the fixing of the cities of refuge in Josh. xx ; A. R. Hulst of Utrecht discusses the name ' Israel ' in Deuteronomy. N.H.S.

BROWN, F., DRIVER, S. R. and BRIGGS, C. A. : *Hebrew and English Lexicon of the Old Testament*. Reprint. Pp. xx+1126. (Oxford University Press. Price : £5 5s. 0d.)

> This reprint contains many hundreds, possibly several thousands, of corrections of misprints and other small slips

that can be corrected on the sheets ; the *Addenda et Corrigenda* have been revised, small ones being incorporated in the text and others inserted in their place. Further, an asterisk has been inserted in the main text wherever the reader ought to consult them. Finally a note has been added after the Preface announcing the preparation of a supplement on which Prof. Driver, with several colleagues, is engaged and inviting those who use the Dictionary to send him corrections and improvements for future editions. H.H.R.

COPPENS, J. : *Miscellanées Bibliques, xxiv : Où en est le problème du Messianisme ? xxv. L'Unité littéraire de Genèse II-III.* (Analecta Lovaniensia Biblica et Orientalia, Ser. II, Fasc. 21.) 1951. Pp. 22. (Publications Universitaires de Louvain, and Desclée de Brouwer, Bruges and Paris. Price : Fr. 20.)

> The first of the two studies issued here consists of an exposition and critical appreciation of Bentzen's *Messias, Moses redivivus, Menschensohn,* while the second is a defence of the literary unity of the chapters indicated against the views of A. Lefèvre, published in *Recherches de Science Religieuse.* In both studies the characteristic breadth of view and acuteness of perception of Coppens are to be seen. H.H.R.

DHORME, E. : *Recueil Édouard Dhorme : Études Bibliques et Orientales.* 1951. Pp. xvi+816. (Imprimerie Nationale, Paris. Price : Fr. 2500.)

> This is a volume of collected essays by our distinguished Honorary Member, which owes its appearance to the initiative of three of his friends. Many will welcome the republication in a most sumptuous edition of these important essays, several of which are continually referred to by other authors. The wide range of Professor Dhorme's learning is well reflected in the volume. Among the twelve historical essays the three longest may be mentioned, viz. those on the dawn of Babylonian history, on the Amorites, and on Abraham in the setting of history. Among the philological articles it must suffice to mention those on the decipherment of the Ras Shamra texts—whose brilliance will long be remembered— on the decipherment of the pseudo-hieroglyphic texts from Byblos, on the language of Canaan, and on the more recently found Amarna tablets. Amongst those dealing with Semitic religion there are articles dealing with Accadian sacrifice, the religion of the Achaemenids, the idea of the Afterlife in Hebrew religion, primitive Semitic religion, pre-Islamic religion, and the god Dagon. Together these essays constitute a rich volume. H.H.R.

HAAG, H., ed. by (with the collaboration of A. van den Born and others) : *Bibel-Lexikon.* 1. Lieferung. 1951. Pp. xiv+cols. 196. (Benziger Verlag, Einsiedeln, Zürich. Subscription price : Fr. DM 8.80 (which entails the taking of the remaining seven parts, which will appear at three monthly intervals.)

> This work is based on the Dutch *Bijbelsch Woordenboek,* edited by van den Born and issued in 1941. It is more than

a German translation, however. The articles have been revised and the references to literature brought up to date. They are mostly brief articles, with abundant cross references, and the whole is well printed, with a few excellent plates. Adequate account is taken of recent archaeology, and in general the writers show a wide acquaintance with the latest literature, both Catholic and Protestant.   H.H.R.

(HROZNÝ, B.) : *Symbolae ad Studia Orientis pertinentes Frederico Hrozný dedicatae*. Pars quarta, pars quinta. (Archiv Orientální, vol. xviii, Nos. 3 and 4.) 1950. Pp. 452, 388. (Orientální Ustav, Prague. Price : Kčs. 570 per part.)

> With the publication of these two parts, the *Festschrift* dedicated to Professor Hrozný is continued (for Parts I and II, see *Book List*, 1950, p. 8 and for Part III, *Book List*, 1951, p. 9). These two parts contain twenty-one and twenty-six articles respectively (Part V contains also four book reviews). The articles which are most likely to interest Old Testament students are (in Part IV) " Der Hedammu-Mythus, das Judithbuch und ähnliches ", by A. Bentzen ; " Die phönizisch-hethitischen Bilinguen vom Karatepe ", by H. Th. Bossert ; " Étude du texte phénicien des inscriptions de Karatepe ", by A. Dupont-Sommer ; " Three early Hebrew seals ", by D. Diringer—one of them, belonging to the late ninth or early eighth century B.C., and bearing an inscription *l-n-r-y* " (belonging) to Neri ", is published here for the first time ; " Origin and significance of the Magen Dawid ", by H. Lewy—the six-pointed star symbol is thought to be the emblem of the planet Saturn (= Salim), the favourite deity of David and Solomon ; and (in Part V) " The goring ox in Babylonian and Biblical law ", by A. Van Selms—the author concludes that the law about the ox that gored proves that the Book of the Covenant cannot be derived from Babylonian sources. Both parts contain articles on Mesopotamian and Hittite subjects, among which the study of law figures prominently.
>   D.W.T.

(LEBRETON, J.) : *Mélanges Jules Lebreton*, I (= Recherches de Science Religieuse, xxxix, Nos. 2-4). 1951. Pp. 480. (Paris. Price : Fr. 1900.)

> The tribute offered to the well-known Jesuit theologian of the Institut Catholique of Paris contains in its first volume no less than thirty-four articles, but of these no more than six have a direct bearing on Old Testament studies. These are the contributions by A. M. Dubarle on the biblical sources of Mary's title as the second Eve ; a commentary by A. Feuillet on Is. xix. 16-25 under the heading " Un sommet religieux de l'Ancien Testament " ; some considerations by A. Robert of the messianic character of Ps. ii, which lead to the conclusion that the Psalm is directly messianic in its entirety ; a discussion of the Song of Songs by D. Buzy, which seeks to establish that the Song is, as a *mâshâl*, a parable, rather than an allegory ; a note on the angelology of Tobit by R. Pautrel

and M. Lefebvre ; and a study of the personality of Achior in Judith by H. Cazelles. Of the remaining articles in this handsomely produced volume two are concerned with the ancient world, fourteen with the New Testament, and twelve with Christian origins and patristic studies.   J.M.T.B.

NOTE : The second volume (Recherches de Science Religiéuse, xl, Nos. 1-2, 1952, Pp. 480) has now been issued. This contains no articles on the Old Testament, but is devoted to Patristics, Church History and Theology.   H.H.R.

(MEINERTZ, M.) : *Vom Wort des Lebens : Festschrift für Max Meinertz*, ed. by N. Adler. (Neutestamentliche Abhandlungen, 1. Ergänzungs-band.) 1951. Pp. 168. (Aschendorffsche Verlagsbuchhandlung, Münster. Price : unbound DM. 10, bound DM. 12.)

This Festschrift to Professor Meinertz on his seventieth birthday contains ten articles on N.T. subjects, three on O.T. and a list of the recipient's publications. Those dealing with the O.T. are : Othmar Schilling of Mainz discusses Righteous-ness and Love in the O.T., mainly from the standpoint of their relevance to modern social application ; Hermann Eising, Münster, outlines the theological contemplation of history in Wisdom of Solomon, particularly in the two historical retrospects, x. 1-xi. 1 and xi. 2-xix. 22 ; Pierre Benoit of Jerusalem calls for a reconsideration of the ' inspiration ' of the Septuagint, mainly on the basis of the ' additional revelation ' of the LXX over against the Hebrew Bible in such matters as the resurrection of Jesus, the Virgin Birth, and the universal participation in the blessings given through Abraham.   B.J.R.

METZGER, B. M. : *Index of articles on the New Testament and the early Church published in Festschriften*. (Journal of Biblical Literature Monograph Series, vol. v.) 1951. Pp. 182. (Society of Biblical Literature, Philadelphia. Price : $2.00.)

This work contains a list of nearly six hundred *Festschriften* and similar volumes arranged in alphabetical order, well over two thousand separate articles classified under various headings, and an index of the authors of the articles. Though the material has been compiled to serve the needs mainly of scholars in the fields of New Testament and the early Church, some volumes dedicated to Old Testament scholars are included, and many of the articles fall within the Old Testament field.   D.W.T.

(MILLER, A.) : *Miscellanea Biblica et Orientalia R.P. Athanasio Miller oblata*, ed. by A. Metzinger. (Studia Anselmiana 27-28.) 1951. Pp. viii+512. (Orbis Catholicus, Herder, Rome.)

This impressive *Festschrift*, offered to the present Secretary of the Biblical Commission on his 70th birthday, contains in all thirty-five contributions, most of them strictly biblical, by as many authors. Of these, twenty are of special interest to an Alttestamentler and a further four to all students of the Bible. Among the former are papers by Cardinal Tisserant on the patriarchal history, I. O. Smit on Gen. iv. 7, J. M. T. Barton on Archaeology and the Exodus (apropos of H. H. Rowley : *From Joseph to Joshua*), F. M. Abel on the apparition in Jos. v. 13-15 ; and B. J. Alfrink on the Achan story in Jos. vii. J. Schildenberger contributes a lengthy introduction to the Books of Samuel, and P. Salmon discusses the text of Job used by S. Gregory the Great in his *Moralia*. G. Boson suggests a logical arrangement and division of the Psalter, which appears to be an improvement on those of the Bible or the Breviary. A. Colunga discusses Messianism in the Royal psalms, and A. Casamassa has given some aids for the study of S. Hilary's *Tractatus super Psalmos*, while A. Kleinhans writes on Henry of Cossey, a fourteenth century commentator on the Psalms. A. Vaccari determines the reading of the Dead Sea Scrolls in some passages of Isaiah (xxxviii. 21 ff. ; xl. 7 ff. ; xxix. 1 ; xxxiv. 14) and F. Stummer makes some observations on Jer. xii. 1-6. H. Haag discusses Ezekiel's contribution to the theology of Messianism. A. Allgeier furnishes a short introduction accompanying the text of Lucifer of Cagliari on some portions of the Minor Prophets ; the Vulgate is printed in parallel and the LXX below. Among articles of general interest are those by A. Bea on the idea of instrumental causality in the treatise on Biblical inspiration, and by P. Duncker on the Council of Trent's labours in establishing the Canon of Scripture. Altogether, a volume of varied interest with contributions varying in length between the four pages of I. O. Smit and the thirty-eight of Schildenberger.

J.M.T.B.

ROBERT, A. (ed. by) : *Dictionnaire de la Bible, Supplément*, Fasc. xxv. *Langdon-Loi Israélite*. 1952. Cols. 257-512. (Letouzey & Ané, Paris. Price : 17s. 0d.)

Gutta cavat lapidem, non vi sed saepe cadendo. This adage which if not classical in one sense deserves to be in another, may comfort those who reflect that the *Supplément* has reached its silver jubilee year without exhausting the letter L's references. The present fascicle has among its high lights an excellent article on " Langues et écritures sémitiques " in which J. Nougayrol is responsible for the East Semitic group, H. Cazelles and J. G. Février for the North West and A. Ryckmans for the South West. " Organisation lévitique " is discussed by A. Lefèvre and under " Logos " there are four sections, of which two are concerned with " La Parole divine dans l'Ancien Orient " (R. Tournay and A. Barucq) and " La Parole divine dans l'Ancien Testament " (A. Robert). H. Cazelles contributes the first part of an important article on Israelite law. There are the usual brief but valuable biographies dealing with such scholars as P. A. Leander, C. F. Lehmann-Haupt, E. Levesque, M. Lidzbarski, A. Lods and M. Löhr.

J.M.T.B.

Rowley, H. H. (ed. by) : *The Old Testament and Modern Study : A Generation of Discovery and Research.* Essays by Members of the Society for Old Testament Study. 1951. Pp. xxxii+406. (The Clarendon Press, Oxford. Price : 25s. 0d.)

The editor of this substantial volume has assembled twelve contributions by leading Old Testament scholars besides providing by way of introduction a valuable essay on Trends in Old Testament Study. As the sub-title indicates, the purpose of this book is to give a survey of the results of Old Testament scholarship during the past thirty years. Professor Albright writes the first two chapters which deal with the Old Testament and the Archaeology of Palestine and the Old Testament and the Archaeology of the Ancient East. Then follow Professor North on Pentateuchal Criticism, Professor Snaith on the Historical Books, Professor Eissfeldt on the Prophetic Literature, Professor Johnson on the Psalms, Professor Baumgartner on the Wisdom Literature, Professor Winton Thomas on the Textual Criticism of the Old Testament, Professor Honeyman on Semitic Epigraphy and Hebrew Philology, Professor Anderson on Hebrew Religion, and Professor Porteous on Old Testament Theology. The last chapter which is entitled Epilogue : The Old Testament and the Modern World, is by Emeritus Professor T. H. Robinson, the only contributor to the present volume who had written also for the two earlier volumes of essays, *The People and the Book* (1925), and *Record and Revelation* (1938).

As in all such collections, uniformity of view has not been sought. The editor's cautious approach to the question of the dating of the Dead Sea Scroll of Isaiah (p. xxv) may be contrasted with Professor Albright's decided opinion (p. 22). But there is a general uniformity of excellence and reliability and the editor is to be congratulated on his choice of his team. The reviewer has heard a teacher protest that the present work upsets the neat systematic account he had been giving of many Old Testament problems. This is, of course, not a criticism of the book but a measure of its success in depicting the present position of Old Testament studies. All who are interested in the new sources of knowledge, in the changing viewpoint in Old Testament scholarship, and in the varied challenging interpretations which show the vitality of Old Testament studies at present will appreciate the guidance afforded by these authoritative essays. It is a book of which our Society may well be proud.   W.D.M.

Semitica (Cahiers publiés par l'Institut d' Études Sémitiques de l'Université de Paris) III. 1950. Pp. 84. (Maisonneuve, Paris. Price : 16s. 0d.)

The nine articles contained in this issue are all of a high standard. R. Labat edits for the first time an Assyrian text used by exorcists which has some unusual features ; J. Nougayrol discusses a letter of uncertain date from an un-identified king of Sidon to the king of Ugarit ; J. Cantineau examines recent publications on the problem of the nature of the language of Ras Shamra, and re-affirms his view that it is not a dialect of Canaanite, but a new Semitic language ; A. Dupont-Sommer presents a new study of the entire inscription of Yaḥawmilk, king of Byblos, a fragment of which was recently discovered by M. Dunand, and, with R. Boyer, writes on the Hebrew epitaph of Rab Jonah Duran (*ob.* 1625) found at La Martelle (Var) ; J. Starcky publishes a hitherto unedited Palmyrene bas-relief dedicated to the deities Salman and 'Rgy‘, the latter being a new name, meaning perhaps " he who shakes the earth " ; J. G. Février offers a new translation of pages 25ff. of E. L. Sukenik's *Megilloth Genuzoth* (1st ed.), with a discussion of the military manœuvres described therein ; E. Lambert studies the synagogue of Dura-Europos in relation to the problem of the origin of the mosque ; and J. Cantineau, in a second contribution, deals with the way in which the idea of " scheme "—forms like *'af‘al* and *fā‘il*, used in Arabic for colours and the agent respectively— undergoes alteration in the different Semitic languages, and with the morphological consequences which the alteration involves. D.W.T.

Studia theologica cura ordinum theologorum Scandinavicorum edita. Vol. III, Fasc. ii. 1949/51. Pp. 84. (C. W. K. Gleerup, Lund. Price : Kr. 8.00, or Kr. 12.00 annually.)

Three contributions to this fascicle are of direct interest to the *Alttestamentler*. E. Hammershaimb discusses the Immanuel sign in the light of contemporary theories of divine kingship, interpreting the prophecy as one of promise for Judah, and linking it with Is. ix. 1 ff. and xi. 1 ff. In an article entitled ' King Ideology—" Urmensch "—" Troonsbestijgingsfeest " ' Bentzen discusses points raised in recent writing about these subjects and submits a rejoinder to Mowinckel's contentions (see *Book List*, 1951, p. 14). He also contributes a note on ' Sirach, der Chronist, und Nehemia ', dealing with the possibility that Chronicles was combined with the Ezra and Nehemiah material in varying ways before the whole complex reached its canonical form. The remaining articles are : ' " Weg ", " Wanderung " und verwandte Begriffe ' (a discussion of ethical terminology) by G. Wingren ; ' Der fremde Exorcist ' (Mark ix. 38 ff.) by E. Wilhelms ; 'A Problem concerning the word Order in the New Testament ' by A Wifstrand ; a note by C. Spicq on ' anchor ' and ' forerunner ' in Hebrews vi. 19 f. ; and ' Theologie und Geschichte des Judenchristentums ' by W. G. Kümmel. All the contributions are in English, German, or French. G.W.A.

Studia theologica cura ordinum theologorum Scandinavicorum edita. Vol. IV, Fasc. i. 1950/1. Pp. 108. (C. W. K. Gleerup, Lund. Price : Kr. 8.00, or Kr. 12.00 annually.)

The articles in this issue are almost exclusively Biblical, and two of them are of particular interest to students of the O.T. and of Judaism. In ' Cult and Prophetic Words ' A. S. Kapelrud argues (*inter alia*) that allusions in the prophets' teaching to details of cultic practice would readily be understood by their hearers. E. Sjöberg's contribution, ' Widergeburt und Neuschöpfung im palästinischen Judentum ', is a careful and important study of the occurrence of these ideas in rabbinic and pseudepigraphical literature (touching also on the Dead Sea material). Sjöberg shows that the idea of new creation is used in a more varied way in the former than in the latter, and that the idea of new birth was more sparingly and cautiously used. This rewarding article leads up to a brief consideration of the N.T., in which Sjöberg holds that both Jewish and non-Jewish Hellenistic influences have affected the concept of the new birth. G. A. Danell discusses evidence of Paul's knowledge of the tradition about the Virgin Birth. O. Moe writes on ' Das Abendmahl im Hebräerbrief ' (Heb. xiii. 9-16). W. Michaelis deals with a point in Lucan linguistic usage. A. Ehrhardt writes on ' Creatio ex Nihilo '. G.W.A.

Transactions of the Glasgow University Oriental Society, vol. xiii, ed. by C. J. Mullo Weir. 1951. Pp. iv+68. (Glasgow University. Price : 12s. 6d.)

This volume contains a few articles bearing on the Old Testament, together with articles in the field of Arabic and Indian studies. N. W. Porteous writes on 'Aspects of Ancient Commerce ', tracing the beginnings of international commercial law to the Phoenicians and the Babylonians ; D. M. G. Stalker on ' Ezekiel and Jesus ', showing the influence of the prophet on Jesus ; O. S. Rankin on ' Wagenseil and the *Tela ignea Satanae* ', on the missionary polemics of a Christian against the Jews ; C. J. Mullo Weir on ' Problems of Western Asiatic Pre-history ' ; and J. Mauchline on ' Yaḥad and Yaḥdāu in the O.T.', arguing that there are passages where these mean ' alone ' or ' by themselves '. H.H.R.

WASZINK, J. H., VAN UNNIK, W. C., DE BEUS, CH. (ed. by) : *Het Oudste Christendom en de Antieke Cultuur*, 2 vols., 1951. Pp. viii+602, vi+478. (Tjeenk Willink, Haarlem. Price : Fl. 45 for 2 vols.)

This comprehensive work has been prepared by a large team of writers, and it offers a broad survey of Early Christianity in the background of the culture out of which it sprang and in which it lived. The first volume deals with Hellenistic culture and Judaism in the Hellenistic period, while the second deals with the life and thought of Early Christianity to the time of Irenaeus. While it is only the first volume that falls properly within the sphere of interest of this *Book List*, the second will probably also be of the greatest value to many of its readers. The first volume contains an excellent review of the history of Palestine by M. A. Beek, a chapter on Judaism by P. A. H. de Boer—the best in the volume—one on the Diaspora by W. C. van Unnik, one on the Septuagint by W. S. van Leeuwen, together with many others. The chapter on Hellenistic religion is broken amongst several authors, as is that on philosophy. The second volume has chapters on the background of history, on New Testament literature, on John the Baptist and the Mandaeans, on the teaching of Jesus and the Early Church, and on the life and worship of the Early Church, with a final chapter on the post-apostolic age and Gnosticism. At the end of each chapter a short bibliography is given. The whole is a work of high value and of sound scholarship.   H.H.R.

EDUCATIONAL

AVERY, MARGARET : *Teaching Scripture. A Book on Method.* (Gateway Handbooks, No. 4.) 1951. Pp. 190. (Religious Education Press, Wallington. Price : 6s. 0d.)

This is a wise book, written by one who is expert both in the material and in the art of teaching, and who, while fully alive to the fact that teaching is an art of a peculiarly personal kind, modestly and persuasively shares with us the fruits of her own wide experience. She has an inexhaustible understanding of the young and has much that is valuable to say about the selection of material for children of different ages and the need for a discriminating use of Agreed Syllabuses. Indeed for many perhaps not the least valuable parts of this book will be her appraisement of syllabuses, so readily taken as given by the young teacher. The teaching of the Old Testament need not be begun too young, and while in the lower forms interest will naturally centre on incident, the aim will be to get some glimpse of the Old Testament as a whole in the upper classes and particularly some grasp of its theology, so as to bring out its organic relation to the New Testament. She rightly stresses the fact that teaching under an agreed syllabus, though undenominational, must be Christian and cannot avoid being doctrinal. About half the book is on method in the technical sense. While wishing the Scripture lesson to profit from new ways she yet sits lightly to many modern slogans. " There is no special virtue in ' activity ' ; busyness is not necessarily creative " ; " It is better to have no picture at all than an inferior one." There is some avoidable repetition, the diagrams are perhaps of doubtful value and the index is inadequate, but the book is so helpful that it might repay the effort to make one's own.
                                                                M.B.

BRIGGS, G. W., CAIRD, G. B. and MICKLEM, N. : *The Shorter Oxford Bible.* 1951. Pp. xxiv+476. (Oxford University Press, London. Price : 7s. 6d.)

One would wish every child to have a complete and legible Bible, in which he could learn his way about under the guidance of a teacher who knows how to select. So many practical difficulties arise, however, that there is plenty of room for the kind of help which the *Shorter Oxford Bible* offers. The child will much prefer this attractive book, with its carefully selected well set out passages, to the sort of Bible which is usually the alternative ; the teacher will here find much suggestive guidance, and so will the private reader. Even so the book should be used along with a complete Bible, for which it is not a substitute, and indeed, in the absence of an index, it would otherwise be impossible to follow up the many useful cross references.

A great deal is attempted, and it is perhaps the teacher and the private reader, rather than the child, who will profit from the wise editorial help, so masterly in its simplicity and condensation. The approach is modern. The aim is religious and theological. In Jesus " the righteous Remnant of Israel was reduced to one. But by his death he made a New Covenant which made it possible for sinful men . . . to receive the gift of the Holy Spirit." Passages are selected and arranged to bring out this central theme, the book ends with a number of passages intended to show the scriptural basis of the creed, and at every point scholarship is the handmaid of theology. There are two small but clear maps at the end, an outline syllabus for Primary and Secondary schools, and a brief and useful chronological table.   M.B.

BROWNE, L. E. : *From Babylon to Bethlehem. The Story of the Jews for the last five centuries before Christ*, revised and enlarged with the assistance of M. Black. 1951. Pp. 120. (Heffer, Cambridge. Price : 6s. 0d.)

Written in a clear and fresh style this account of the period described will be most acceptable to beginners desirous of a short survey of Jewish history in the last centuries B.C. and, as the book's cover says, will be most useful for the sixth form of schools. The chapter on " Pharisees and Sadducees " makes liberal and welcome use of excerpts from the non-canonical literature. That on " How they built the Temple " is also well done though its explanation of Hag. ii. 12 is rather drastic. The view given of messianic belief is that which the author gives in *The Messianic Hope*, etc.   O.S.R.

FIRTH, CATHERINE B. : *A People of Hope*. (The Bible and the Christian Faith, No. 3.) 1950. Text book : pp. xiv+272, Reference book : xviii+206. (Ginn & Co., London. Price : 6s. 6d. and 7s. 6d.)

A People of Hope attempts to sum up in one simple text book, designed for grammar school children of thirteen or fourteen, the history of Israel from Abraham to the Christian era. The attention given to the patriarchs results in very great condensation towards the end, but it is a delightful book with excellent maps and illustrations and carefully selected biblical passages suggested for reading with each chapter. Abundant use is made of archaeological material, the approach is scholarly and the emphasis right. "A covenant is an agreement between two people so close that the two may be treated as though they were one."

The Reference Book for the teacher which accompanies the text book contains concise and up to date notes on the most varied material, source criticism, archaeology (particularly good), the Messianic hope (less good), notes on books, background of every kind ; suggestions on teaching method and some suggestions for exercises in the modern style. There are also some useful selections from sources, some of them not easily accessible, diagrams and time charts and tables, and details of the illustrations in the text book.

The text book is indexed and it is a pity, in view of its usefulness and its necessarily scrappy character, that the Reference Book is not indexed too.   M.B.

PARMELEE, ALICE : *A Guidebook to the Bible*. 1951. Pp. 174. (The Teach Yourself Books, English Universities Press, London. Price : 6s. 0d.)

This little book is an abridgement of a somewhat larger work already published in America, and is intended for adults, eager but ill-informed and in need of guidance in their approach to the Bible. It is claimed that it is both scholarly and readable. So many matters have to be settled on each page that no one who knows the stuff will agree with all the answers, but it is a brilliant little book and the author certainly succeeds in carrying her learning lightly and bringing to life everything she touches, even J.E.D. and P. We see Abiathar, ' without any models to guide him ', making his contribution to 1 Sam., and we have a close-up of H., busy in his house in Babylonia among·his collection of scrolls. The book is written with contagious enthusiasm and contains some memorable phrases. " History was a kind of sacrament to Israel." " The Euphrates and the Nile flow through the Bible " but " to explain the uniqueness of the Bible we shall have to find what it was that Israel did not share with her neighbours." There is a third section on " the Bible through the centuries ", an appendix of suggested readings from the Bible and a good index.   M.B.

ARCHAEOLOGY AND EPIGRAPHY

ALBRIGHT, W. F. : *Ha-Archaeologia shel Erets Yisrael*, translated by A. Amir, with an appendix on the Dead Sea Scrolls by E. L. Sukenik. 1951. Pp. 260 with illustrations. ('Ain 'Oved, Tel Aviv. Price : I₤ 2.150.)

This is a literal translation of Prof. Albright's *Archaeology of Palestine* (Pelican Books, 1949) into Hebrew, with only a few additions. The Hebrew edition is concluded with a list of 89 unusual Hebrew terms which are found in the translation. This list makes us realize the interesting problem, how far modern Hebrew lends itself to the expression of all shades of meaning and all technical terms of science. (The Hebrew of this book, for that matter, has been the subject of controversy in the Israeli press.) Prof. Sukenik contributes a short chapter on the Dead Sea Scrolls, in which he sticks to his opinion about the dating of all the Scrolls—including the Midrash on Habakkuk !—during the second century B.C.E. (it is interesting to note that Albright's opinion as expressed on p. 202 deviates from this dating !) He also again prints some fragments of the Thanksgiving Psalms and War Scroll, which have already been published in his Megillôth Genûzôth I and II.

I.L.S.

Annual of the American Schools of Oriental Research, vol. xxv-xxviii (1945-49). *Explorations in Eastern Palestine,* IV, Part I : *Text,* Part II : *Pottery Notes and Plates,* by N. Glueck. 1951. Pp. 712. (American Schools of Oriental Research, New Haven. Price : $12.00.)

These two volumes complete the publication of Prof. Glueck's able archaeological survey of Transjordan, and are devoted to Transjordan north of Amman and the Jordan valley. The thesis of the sequence of occupation and recessions of sedentary culture, already formulated by the writer, is, in the main, substantiated. His general position, however, is somewhat modified. He finds that sedentary occupation goes back much earlier than he had at first thought, in fact to the beginning of the Chalcolithic age, and the last phase of the Early Bronze age (just before 2100) is for the most part quite lacking in Gilead and the Jordan valley. In the highlands the Middle Bronze I period is attested but there are almost no traces of subsequent occupation until the Iron age, when there was intense settlement throughout the whole area, especially in the second phase of the Iron age (*c.* 900-600 B.C.). Two interesting aspects of this valuable work are the study of Nabataean and Byzantine remains as far as the Wadi Sirhan and a series of splendid air photographs of the Jordan valley.

J.G.

BOSSERT, TH. : *Altsyrien. Kunst und Handwerk in Cypern, Syrien, Palästina und Arabien von den Anfängen bis zum völligen Aufgehen in der griech.-röm. Kultur.* 1951. Pp. 106+39 maps+1417 plates. (Wasmuth, Tübingen. Price : £2 12s. 6d.)

This work is a very useful collection of plans and reproductions of antiquities from or pertaining to Syria and Palestine and including Cyprus and South Arabia, with maps of the areas studied. The text is practically confined to the bibliography of each illustration. This last feature is useful, especially in respect of the older authorities, though there are few citations of works within the last decade. Consequently there is a tendency to early dating, especially in the Sargonid period and that of the Third Dynasty of Ur. The Sinaitic inscriptions are dated in the 19th or 18th century and the Ahiram inscription in the 13th, while the Middle Bronze building on Gerizim is still termed a sanctuary. *Vice versa,* by citing Watzinger (*Denkmäler . .*) rather than Crowfoot (*Samaria-Sebaste II,* 1938) the writer robs Ahab of the credit of the Samarian ivories.

J.G.

BOWMAN, J. and TALMON, S. : *Samaritan Decalogue Inscriptions.*
(Reprinted from the *Bulletin of the John Rylands Library,*
vol. 33, No. 2, March, 1951.) Pp. 36. (Manchester University
Press and The John Rylands Library, Manchester. Price : 2s. 6d.)

In this work the two authors study together the four extant
Samaritan Decalogue Inscriptions. One,˚ coming probably
from Nablus, was recently " rediscovered " by the authors
among other monumental slabs in Leeds ; another is the
well known inscription in the wall of a minaret attached to
the Chizn Yakub Mosque in Nablus (the authors draw attention
for the first time to the presence in it of what may be a
crusader's mark) ; the third, also found in the vicinity of
Nablus, is in the Palestine Museum ; the fourth, hitherto
unrecorded, was identified at Bir Yakub (Sychar) by Dr.
Bowman in 1950. Good photographs of all four inscriptions
are provided, and transcriptions of the texts are given. Among
the matters discussed are the fluctuations in the text of the
Decalogue handed down in these inscriptions ; the points of
difference between the Samaritan and Massoretic Hebrew
Pentateuchal versions of the Decalogue ; the Samaritan
Pentateuchal versions as compared with the inscriptions ;
the orthography and epigraphy of the inscriptions, and their
date. On this last all important question, the authors believe
that, while the present state of knowledge concerning Samaritan
epigraphy does not allow safe conclusions to be drawn, the
fluctuations of text just referred to may point to a time before
the text of the Samaritan Decalogue had become definitely
fixed. A date in the early Christian centuries is thought
probable, a pre-Origenic date possible. The authors have
brought forward much that is new, and their monograph
carries the study of the Samaritan Decalogue a considerable
stage further.   D.W.T.

DOSSIN, G. : *Archives Royales de Mari IV. Correspondance de Šamši-
Addu.* 1951. Pp. 132 with map. (Imprimerie Nationale, Paris.
Price : Fr. 600.)

The present volume continues the publication of the important
collection of cuneiform tablets from the Middle Euphrates in
transliteration and translation with another 88 letters ; and
it will suffice to say that it maintains the high standard of
excellence of its predecessors. One may hope that the corresponding volume of cuneiform texts will soon appear. G.R.D.

Eretz Israel, Archaeological, Historical and Geographical Studies (in
Hebrew.) Vol. I. 1951. Pp. xii+184. (Israel Exploration Society,
Jerusalem. Price : £3 12s. 6d.)

With this stately volume the Israel Exploration Society
inaugurates a series of yearbooks. The second and third
volumes are already in preparation ; the third will be dedicated
to the memory of Prof. Cassuto. This first volume is dedicated
to Prof. M. Schwabe—Rector of the Hebrew University—
on his sixtieth birthday and it opens with a bibliography of

his writings (138 items). It is impossible to enumerate here all of the twenty-seven studies on philological, geographical, archaeological, and historical questions which follow ; we can mention only a few. M. Stekelis writes on " The Yarmukian culture ". In 1943 remnants of a prehistoric settlement, hitherto unparalleled in the Near East, were found in the triangle bounded by the Jordan and Yarmuk rivers and the Sea of Galilee. Dr. Stekelis, one of the excavators, gives an admirable sketch of the stratigraphic problems and the material civilization. B. Maisler contributes a second preliminary report on his excavations, during the first two seasons, at Tell Qasilê. After having surveyed the stratigraphy he goes on to describe the following periods : Philistine (str. XII-XI) ; post-Philistine—pre-Israelite (rich in pottery X) ; early United Israelite Kingdom (IX) ; Kings of Israel (to this period belong two ostraca VIII-VII) ; Persian (VI), Roman Byzantine (V-II). A. Reifenberg calls attention to the importance of air photographs to distinguish (e.g.) traces of the Christian church and altar on Mt. Gerizim. N. H. Tur-Sinai maintains 'Azazel to be not a demon, but the goat of the wilderness, cf. *'êz* and Accadian *azlû*. U. M. D. Cassuto, in " The rise of historiography in Israel ", traces various marks of an ancient epic in the Biblical story of the Exodus. A. Malamat, " The historical background of two prophecies on the Nations ", finds in Zech. ix. 1-6 an echo of several military expeditions of Sargon II, and in Jer. xlvii of the Scythian looting of Ascalon. Instructive for the method of Flavius Josephus and the texts of which he made use is F. Z. Melamed, " Josephus and Maccabees I : A comparison ". Deserving of special praise is the fine study of A. Schallit, "Alexander Jannaeus's Conquests in Moab " which, tracing the sources of Josephus, *Antiq.*, xii. 397 and xiv. 18 arrives at striking conclusions, as to the Greek Bible translations once current side by side with the Septuagint, and as to the original sources, now lost, on the Hasmonaean period. V. Tscherikover, " Was Jerusalem a Greek *polis* under the Roman Procurators ?" relying mainly on a fresh interpretation of the relevant passages in Josephus, denies that Jerusalem ever was a Greek *polis* in Roman times. M. H. Segal, " Problems of the Dead Sea Scrolls " initiates his researches on the Sect and on the orthography of DSIa which he has in the meantime continued, completed, and revised elsewhere (*Tarbiz* xxii, 1951, pp. 136 ff. ; *J.B.L.*, lxx, 1951, pp. 131 ff.). The production of a volume on such a high level, in regard to both content and form, in the Israel of to-day, is an encouraging and promising performance.   I.L.S.

GROENEWEGEN-FRANKFORT, H. A. : *Arrest and Movement.* 1951. Pp. xxiv+222+xciv plates. (Faber & Faber, London. Price : 50s. 0d.)

This book is a study of the art of Egypt, Mesopotamia and Crete from the standpoint of space and time. Mrs. Frankfort explains many peculiarities in the representational art of these three ancient Near Eastern countries and she has produced a work which is important to the specialist and the general reader alike. It is lavishly illustrated with plates and figures in the text, which enable the reader to follow her arguments with ease.   T.W.T.

HEIDEL, A. : *The Babylonian Genesis*. 1951. Pp. xi+153 with 12 plates and maps. (University Press, Chicago. Price : $3.50.)

This is a new edition of an excellent work, already well known to students both of Assyriology and of the Old Testament. It contains an introduction in which the various problems raised by the ' Epic of Creation ' are thoroughly discussed, an accurate translation, and an exhaustive appendix in which the parallel matter in the Old Testament is fully examined.
                                                                G.R.D.

LACHEMAN, E. R. : *Excavations at Nuzi, V.* (Harvard Semitic Series, vol. XIV.) 1950. Pp. 50+118 plates. (Harvard University Press, and Geoffrey Cumberlege, London. Price : $6.00 or 40s. 0d.)

This volume includes the transliteration of a group of economic and legal contracts supplementing similar documents published in vol. XIII of the same series, together with 265 copies of cuneiform texts from the Royal and Temple archives of Nuzi. Those texts are published for the first time, with the exception of a few which were published in *R.A.*, 36, 1940. The editor appends 10 plates of seals associated with the documents.
                                                                J.G.

MAISLER, B. : *The Excavations at Tell Qasîle : Preliminary Report.* 1951. Pp. 58+22 plates. (Israel Exploration Society, Jerusalem.)

The author presents a collection of reprints from the *Israel Exploration Journal*, vol. I, 1950-51, on the first three seasons' work at Tell Qasîle, North of Tell Aviv. Though not extensive, the excavation has yielded a good stratification from the Early Iron Age to the Arab period. The pottery of the earliest six strata should prove valuable material for a clear understanding of the various phases of the Iron Age, particularly when studied in conjunction with the pottery from Samaria. One questions whether the writer is quite entitled to relate the various periods of the occupation of the site to Hebrew history as closely as he does. Of great interest to O.T. scholars are two inscribed sherds similar to the Samaritan dockets, with which the writer suggests that they are contemporary, and an inscribed Hebrew seal, which he dates in the Persian period. The worth of all three objects, however, is seriously impaired by the fact that they were found on the surface two and three years before excavation began.   J.G.

MOSCATI, S. : *L'epigrafia ebraica antica 1935-1950* (Biblica et Orientalia, N. 15.) 1951. Pp. 124. (Pontificio Istituto Biblico, Rome. Price : L. 4,200.)

The author aims in this work at presenting and evaluating research in the field of ancient Hebrew epigraphy during the period 1935 to 1950. The year 1935 is chosen as the point of departure because in the previous year Dr. Diringer's well known book, *Le iscrizioni antico-ebraiche palestinesi*, appeared. After an introductory chapter on excavations and publications, and on the ancient Hebrew script, the author passes in review recent studies of the Gezer tablet, the ostraca from Samaria, the Siloam inscription, the Ophel ostracon, seals, stamped jar-handles, weights, the ivories from Samaria, and various new inscriptions. A notable omission is any treatment of the Lachish ostraca. The omission is deliberate, for there are already the two editions of Torczyner, and further study of the ostraca is expected in the third official volume of the excavations. The author's critical discussion of such questions as the dating of the documents, their interpretation, character, artistic form, and disputed readings, is marked by careful scholarship and independence of judgement, and his survey, with its valuable bibliographical information, is one which all those interested in this field will wish to possess. It shows how very much alive Hebrew epigraphy is as a subject. Many doubtless will be surprised to discover, for example, how many new readings in the Siloam inscription have been proposed in recent years. The author's caution in the matter of dating, which results largely from his clear recognition of the scantiness of the material available, is frequently noticeable and is a welcome feature of his work. Besides three indices, there are thirty-three pages of plates, and a comparative table of alphabets.   D.W.T.

NEUFELD, E. : *The Hittite Laws, translated into English and Hebrew with Commentary.* 1951. Pp. xii+212 with 50 plates. (Luzac, London. Price : £1 15s. 0d.)

Dr. Neufeld's work is far the best edition of the extremely difficult Hittite Laws that has so far appeared. One can but regret that he has provided a Hebrew translation instead of a transliteration of the Hittite text ; for the photographs, good as they are, are no adequate substitute for a printed text.   G.R.D.

OTTEN, H. : *Mythen vom Gotte Kumarbi. Neue Fragmente* (Deutsche Akademie der Wissenschaften zu Berlin. Institut für Orientforschung. Veröffentlichung Nr. 3). 1951. Pp. 40+11 plates. (Akademie-Verlag, Berlin. Price : DM. 14.25.)

In the twenty-third part of the *Keilschrifturkunden aus Boghazköi*, which appeared in 1943, Otten published amongst other texts several Hittite fragments of the Kumarbi myth. H. G. Güterbock, *Kumarbi : Mythen von churritischen Kronos aus den hethitischen Fragmenten zusammengestellt, übersetzt und erklärt* (Zürich-New York, 1946) arranged these in two groups of myths, the ' Myth of the Kingdom in Heaven ', and the ' Song of Ullikummi '. In the present work Otten publishes 31 new fragments from the Berlin Museum, which make possible a deeper understanding of both myths, and which will also throw new light on the question of the relations between the Hurrian and the Canaanite-Phoenician mythology, and on the dependence of the Greek myth on the Phoenician.   O.E.

PENDLEBURY, J. D. S. : *The City of Akhenaton*. Part III. *The Central City and the Official Quarters*. ((Forty-Fourth Memoir of the Egypt Exploration Society.) 1951. Vol. i. (text) pp. xx+262 ; Vol. ii. (plates) pp. xii+cxii plates. (O.U.P. Price : £8 15s. 0d.)

Mr. Pendlebury, who was Director of the Egypt Exploration Society's excavations at Tell-el-Amarna 1931-37, was killed in Crete in 1941. He had completed his manuscript in 1939, and Professor Fairman, who had assisted him in the excavations during the seasons 1931-36, took over the task of revising and editing that manuscript. This he has done with great care and skill, altering the original as little as possible. The present memoir publishes the results of the excavations at Tell-el-Amarna during the seasons 1926-27 and 1931-36. Mr. Pendlebury describes the archaeological results of the work on the Central City, which includes the Great Temple, the Great Palace and the " Foreign Office ". Professor Fairman contributes a chapter on the inscriptional material discovered. Other writers have also made contributions on various topics. The volume of plates contains not only photographs of all the important objects brought to light and transcriptions and copies of inscriptions, but also plans and reconstructions of the Great Temple and Palace prepared by Mr. Lavers. All who are interested in the religion and history of the Amarna Age will wish to consult these volumes.   T.W.T.

SCHOFIELD, J. N. : *Archaeology and the After-Life*. 1951. Pp. 78. (Lutterworth Press, London. Price : 2s. 6d.)

The author's aim is to harmonize the evidence of archaeology, which in the Palestinian and surrounding area witnesses to funeral and mourning customs which imply a belief in survival after death, with the state of belief that is disclosed in the O.T. literature. He thinks that the disparity between the archaeological and the O.T. fields is only apparent since in the O.T. there is no static uniformity of belief, nor even at any one time one consistently held opinion about death and the hereafter, but that in Israelite history there was at all times as much diversity of belief as exists among men in the world of to-day.   O.S.R.

SCHOTT, S. : *Altägyptische Festdaten*. (Abhandlungen der Mainzer Akademie der Wissenschaften und der Literatur, geistes– und sozialwissenschaftliche Klasse, Jahrgang 1950, Nr. 10.) 1950. Pp. 122+16 tables and 5 plates. (Franz Steiner Verlag, Wiesbaden. Price : DM. 14.00.)

This work contains a collection of Old Egyptian notices on Egyptian calendars, with discussion on them. The collection of dates is complete, and questions about the year and its seasons, astronomical relations and dates, Egyptian chronology and Annals, are discussed. All who are interested in the calendar, or in questions affecting Old Testament chronology, will do well to observe the author's remarkable and useful collections of data, and views based on them.   H.S.

SCHOTT, S. : *Hieroglyphen : Untersuchungen zum Ursprung der Schrift.* (Akademie der Wissenschaften und der Literatur ; Abhandlungen der geistes- und sozialwissenschaftlichen Klasse, 1950, Nr. 24.) 1951. Pp. 156+15 plates. (Franz Steiner Verlag, Wiesbaden. Price : DM. 21.00.)

Professor Schott makes a detailed investigation of the origins and development of the Egyptian hieroglyphic script. He traces the stages by which pictorial symbols passed into the complicated system of writing already in vogue in the Old Kingdom. His work is addressed primarily to Egyptologists and is concerned solely with the Egyptian method of writing. Scholars interested in the wider problem of the origins of writing will, however, find much of value to them in this book. T.W.T.

SHORT, A. R. : *Archaeology Gives Evidence.* 1951. Pp. 64. (Tyndale Press. Price : 2s. 0d.)

This work is a rather cursory and not too original citation of the salient points where archaeology illustrates the O.T. or indicates the historicity and antiquity of the N.T. documents. The writer admits that convinced Christians ' will attach little or no importance to such facts and discoveries ' as he adduces. For such, he declares, ' this attitude is quite right '. But for such as feel disquietude at the discrepancies between the Bible and their secular reading he hopes that what he has written may allay doubts. We welcome his caution that his work has left many questions unanswered. Unfortunately it has also left many debatable propositions unquestioned. Of these may be mentioned Garstang's date of the fall of Bronze Age Jericho and its relation to the Hebrew Invasion, the Hellenistic date of the Dead Sea Scrolls and the Mosaic authorship, in the main, of the Pentateuch, which he takes to rest upon a journal kept by Moses in the desert. J.G.

STARCKY, J. : *Palmyre.* (L'orient ancien illustré, 7.) 1952. Pp. 132 with 11 figures in the text and 14 plates. (Maisonneuve, Paris. Price : Fr. 350.)

This little book gives an admirable account of the ancient city of Palmyra in six chapters ; these, after an introduction dealing with the site and the inscriptions found there, describe the Graeco-Roman town, its rulers, its commerce and the caravans frequenting its mart, its religion and its art. The story is told concisely but with perfect clarity and is enlivened with a considerable number of illustrations which have clearly been carefully chosen and are for the most part excellently reproduced. G.R.D.

VRIEZEN, TH.C. and HOSPERS, J. H. (ed. by) : *Palestine Inscriptions.* (Textus Minores, vol. xvii.) 1951. Pp. 40. (Brill, Leiden. Price : Fl. 2.25.)

This collection of inscriptions has been compiled chiefly as an aid for theological students attending lectures in the University of Groningen. It consists of the best known ancient Phoenician inscriptions—those of Ahiram, Yehimilk, Abibaal, Elibaal and Shefaṭbaal—the Gezer calendar, the inscription of

Mesha, a selection of the ostraca from Samaria, the Siloam inscription, nos. i-iv of the Lachish ostraca, specimens of seal inscriptions, the Uzziah inscription and another Aramaic tomb inscription. All the inscriptions are transcribed into the Hebrew square script, except the last two, for which the square script was originally employed. No translations are offered and there are no plates. Brief notes, mainly on linguistic matters, but containing also bibliographical information, are provided. So far as they go they are helpful. Outmoded readings are, however, sometimes perpetuated, notably in the case of the Lachish ostraca. As a class book the work should prove useful both to teachers and students. The latter especially will welcome the inclusion in it of some inscriptions which may not be very easily accessible to them elsewhere.

D.W.T.

HISTORY AND GEOGRAPHY

ABEL, F. M. : *Histoire de la Palestine depuis la conquête d'Alexandre jusqu'à l'invasion arabe.* I. *De la conquête d'Alexandre jusqu'à la guerre juive.* 1952. Pp. xvi+506. (Gabalda, Paris. Price : Fr. 2600.)

This work may be said to complement and to complete Abel's *Géographie de la Palestine,* and his commentary *Les Livres des Maccabées.* As always with the historical and archaeological work of Vincent and Abel one has the impression that immeasurable competence and complete impartiality have conspired to produce a masterpiece. The present volume is in good part concerned with events already discussed in the very full commentary on Maccabees, and all will appreciate the author's remark that human knowledge would have been most grievously curtailed if these books had not survived. The volume falls naturally into two divisions, i.e. Palestine under Greek rule .until the capture of Jerusalem by Pompey, and the further history of Palestine after it had taken its place in the Roman Empire. It is a historical and political study. For the religious ideas of that period the reader is referred to M. J. Lagrange's *Le Judaïsme avant Jésus-Christ.* One may specially commend this work for the clarity with which the author explains the often detailed and complicated history and the excellent way in which his knowledge of the monuments in and around Palestine helps towards an explanation. It is sober history, not romance, and is not perhaps written in a very adventurous way, but this is only to say that few works in any language can possess the charm and the excitement of the late Dr. Edwyn Bevan's *Jerusalem under the High Priests.* But Abel's book covers a longer period than Bevan's and is likely to be regarded as even more indispensable for all students of the nine centuries under discussion.   J.M.T.B.

ALBRIGHT, W. F. : *The Biblical Period.* Pp. 64. (Blackwell, Oxford. Price : 5s. 0d.)

This valuable extract from Finkelstein's *The Jews* (see *Book List,* 1951, p. 8), offering a broad survey of the history and culture of Israel in the Biblical period, is now available in an English edition. It has been widely used in America amongst students.   H.H.R.

BRANDON, S. G. F. : *The Fall of Jerusalem and the Christian Church.*
1951. Pp. xx+284. (S.P.C.K., London. Price : 30s. 0d.)

The thesis of this very learned book is that all the New Testament documents are tendentious, and that when we get behind
them we find that Jesus was associated with the nationalistic
Zealots, and that His arrest nipped in the bud a political
movement. The Jerusalem Church is found to have lived in
good relations with the Jewish authorities, and to have
supported the Jewish revolt. The story of Acts xv is dismissed,
and the Jerusalem Church and its leaders are held to have
opposed Paul everywhere and to have been against the admission of Gentile Christians. Paul was compelled to bow to
their authority and his arrest is attributed to their subtle
contrivance. With his death their victory was complete,
until the Fall of Jerusalem eliminated them and discredited
them. The first reaction to the new situation is seen in Mark's
Gospel, while the Lukan work rehabilitated Paul. On the
other hand the Gospel of Matthew and the Epistle of James
represent a reaction from Alexandria, where these works are
held to have originated. While this book is obviously addressed primarily to New Testament scholars, its novel view
of the part played in the history of the Church by the Jewish
revolt will interest all who are interested in the history of the
Jews during the Second Commonwealth.   H.H.R.

CORNELIUS, F. : *Geschichte des alten Orients.* (Schaeffers Abriss aus
Kultur und Geschichte, Abt. I Geschichte, 3. Band.) 1950. Pp.
130. (Kohlhammer, Stuttgart and Köln. Price : 10s. 0d.)

This is a very concise synopsis of the ancient history of the
Near East until the end of the Hellenistic period. In the
main the writer is well informed and follows the low system
of dating in the Hammurabi period. There are, however,
certain uncritical features, such as the association of the
Beni-iamini of Mari with the Israelite Benjamin, of the
Hebrews with the Hyksos on the strength of the name Jacob-
har, etc. There are also inaccuracies, such as the notice of
Solomon's stables at *Jericho*, and the deportation of Josiah's
successor to Babylon. Within such limitations, the work
will serve as quite a useful introduction to the general subject
of the ancient history of the Near East or to the history of
any particular period in its general context.   J.G.

*HENREY, K. H. : *An Historical Background to the Old Testament.*
1951. Pp. 134. (United Society for Christian Literature, Lutterworth Press, London. Price : 5s. 0d., limp cloth 4s. 0d.)

The purpose of the book is to show the kind of world which
surrounded the people of the Old Testament. It thus deals
with the surrounding peoples, and only incidentally with
Judah and Israel. The Old Testament narratives are used
extensively, interspersed with short summaries and illustrations. Nearly half the book deals with the period down to
David (something has gone wrong with his dates on p.46),

and very little space is given to the Greek period. The dating is traditional; Abraham, ca. 2,000 B.C. (but ca. 1750 B.C. in table on p. 133); Moses, the end of 13th century; Ezra, ca. 450 B.C. and Nehemiah a little later.   N.H.S.

HESTER, H. I. : *The Heart of Hebrew History : A Study of the Old Testament.* 2nd ed., 1950. Pp. xvi+326. (William Jewell Press, Liberty, Missouri. Price : $3.00.)

This volume has a certain value for elementary pupils as a brief guide to the contents of the Old Testament, though it is not adequate as the College text-book it claims to be. There is little attempt to set Hebrew history in world history, and while there is a chapter on Archaeology and the Bible little account is taken of the work of the last fifty years. Less than forty pages suffice to deal with the history from B.C. 600 to the end of the inter-testamental period, together with all the Biblical writers from Jeremiah on. Moreover, there is scarcely any attempt to deal with the problems that face the student of the Bible. Whatever the nature of the answers offered students of College grade should face them, and not be treated in a way more appropriate for children. As a school-boy, brought up in a conservative tradition and unacquainted with any other, the reviewer would have found this inadequate.   H.H.R.

*MOULD, E. W. K. : *Bible History Digest.* 1950. Pp. 202. (Exposition Press, New York. Price : $3.00.)

Professor Elmer Mould has provided a simply written account of the major historical events from 2000 B.C. to A.D. 100. The book is attractively arranged with modern (but not too modern) captions. There are a number of specially drawn maps. The book is suitable for schools, except that warning is necessary in respect of the treatment of the early post-exilic treatment, where the author departs from the usual chronology. The temple was completed in the second year of Darius II (419 B.C.) ; both Nehemiah and Ezra appeared in Jerusalem in the time of Artaxerxes II.   N.H.S.

OBBINK, H. W. : *Oude Geschiedenis van het Nabije Oosten* (Offprint from Wereldgeschiedenis, Deel I, derde druk). 1951. Pp. 74. (De Haan, Utrecht. Not obtainable separately but only in the whole work, which is published in six volumes. Price : Fl. 15 per volume.)

This is a survey of the main features and phases of the ancient history of the Near East to the end of the Achaemenid period. The writer makes full use of the new archaeological material, which, however, might have been somewhat more fully cited without the danger of obtrusion. We note the lowered dating of the period of Sargon and Naram-Sin and of the Third Dynasty of Ur and of Hammurabi and the 13th century date of the Exodus. Israel is not omitted from the survey and there is a short section on Hebrew prophecy treated along orthodox lines. The whole work is characterized by an admirable sense of perspective.   J.G.

Rᴇʜᴡɪɴᴋᴇʟ, A. M. : *The Flood in the Light of the Bible, Geology, and Archaeology.* 1952. Pp. xxii+372. (Concordia Publishing House, St. Louis.)

The author aims to reconcile the literal reading of the Bible with science. He cites with approval scientific evidence of a very different earth in Eocene and Miocene ages, but rejects geological chronology. He holds that during the 1656 years from the Creation to the Flood the population of the world might have reached as much as eleven thousand million, with a high degree of civilization. Some cosmic event which tilted the world's axis and flooded the entire earth is then held to have taken place so recently as the Biblical chronology of the Flood implies, and Noah is held to have constructed an Ark capable of holding 10,000 railway cattle cars, together with storage capacity for food for all these creatures. The author expresses no sympathy for the slender crew who were each charged with the feeding of more than 1,000 car loads of creatures per day, in addition to a modest amount of cleaning. This would allow perhaps one minute to fetch the food for each car load, estimated by the author to hold the equivalent of 60 to 80 pigs, and to do the necessary cleaning. This sounds exhausting, but by the end of a hundred hour week they would perhaps get used to it. The author dismisses the theory that the animals were fed with ante-diluvian vitamin tablets, but thinks perhaps they may have hibernated for part of the time in the Ark. The book is fantastic in its naïveté, but interesting because of the information it collects. Even the Fundamentalist will say *Non tali auxilio.* H.H.R.

TEXT AND VERSIONS

Biblia Sacra iuxta Latinam Vulgatam Versionem . . . IX. Libri Hester et Job cura et studio Monachorum Abbatiae Pontificiae Sancti Hieronymi in Urbe. 1951. Pp. xii+208. (Typis polyglottis vaticanis, Rome.)

This, the ninth volume of the great Benedictine edition of the Vulgate Old Testament, contains the books of Esther and Job, edited on the same plan as the previous volumes, with the necessary changes in the manuscripts available for these books ; in addition certain fragments of manuscripts and three ancient commentaries have been used in Job. The standard is of the same unvarying excellence. G.R.D.

Eɪssғᴇʟᴅᴛ, O. : *Variae lectiones rotulorum manu scriptorum anno 1947 prope Mare Mortuum repertorum ad Jes 1-66 et Hab 1-2 pertinentes.* 1951. Pp. 8. (Privileg. Württ. Bibelanstalt, Stuttgart. Price : 1s. 3d.)

This contains the variant readings of the Dead Sea Scrolls as given in the new edition of Kittel's *Biblia Hebraica.* Those who have the previous edition will find this convenient and useful. H.H.R.

FISCHER, B. (ed. by) : *Vetus Latina : die Reste der Altlateinischen Bibel.* 1951. Pp. 33*, 151. (Herder, Freiburg. Price : DM. 35.00.)

The introductory fascicle of this important work was noticed last year. In the present part are contained an introduction in which the classification of the sources and the method of the work are set out and Genesis i. 1-ix. 14 (Greek text of the LXX and the Latin text in several recensions, with an immense collection of variant readings). When complete, this monumental work will be invaluable. G.R.D.

GLEAVE, H. C. : *The Ethiopic Version of the Song of Songs.* 1951. Pp. xxxii+42. (Taylor's Foreign Press, London. Price : 17s. 6d.)

This valuable little study is a critical edition of the Ethiopic version of the Song of Songs. An Ethiopic text with a full apparatus criticus and an English translation are given on opposite pages. The Introduction, amongst other things, deals with previous editions, available manuscripts and their classification. The author died at the early age of 28 before completing his work for the printers, and Dr. Rabin generously undertook the task of seeing it through the press. Professor Driver contributes a memoir on the author. It is sad that one who would have contributed so much to the study of the Ethiopic Version, a much neglected field of Biblical research, should not have been spared to produce further studies of this calibre. T.W.T.

KITTEL, R. : *Biblia Hebraica. Editio septima aucta et emendata typis editionis tertiae expressa.* 1951. Pp. liii+1,434, with 2 maps. (Privilegierte Württembergische Bibelanstalt, Stuttgart. Price : £2 5s. 0d.)

The most notable feature of this seventh edition of *Biblia Hebraica* is the inclusion, in a third critical apparatus, of various readings in the 'Ain Feshkha scrolls of Isaiah and Habakkuk. For this purpose Millar Burrows' official edition of the scrolls, published in 1950, has been used. In the foreword the editors emphasize the importance of these readings—most of them are, they believe, of far greater importance than anything offered hitherto in the first and second critical apparatus. Since the large number of variant readings made it impossible to include them all, the selection is restricted in the main to those which are significant from the point of view of interpretation. Readings which are of purely orthographic or grammatical interest are not included. The selection of variants here included—subjective though it must be to some extent, as the editors acknowledge—will be of interest to many. Those who desire a more complete view of the situation as regards variant readings will, however, need to consult, not only the official edition, but also the contributions to the problem which have been made by other scholars. This seventh edition has been much improved by the correction of misprints and of some other technical inaccuracies in printing. D.W.T.

SOISALON-SOININEN, I. : *Die Textformen der Septuaginta-Übersetzung des Richterbuches.* (Annales Academiae Scientiarum Fennicae, B. 72 : 1.) 1951. Pp. 124. (Druckerei-A. G. der Finnischen Literaturgesellschaft, Helsinki. Price : Finn. Mark 400.)

This investigation into the text forms of the LXX translation of the book of Judges is a valuable contribution to LXX study. It consists of six sections. In the first, which is of an introductory character, the author reviews previous research on this subject, and emphasizes the outstanding importance of the work of Otto Pretzl. The second deals with the LXX material and its grouping ; the third with translation technique in the different text forms ; the fourth with the relation of the text forms to the M.T. ; the fifth with their relation to the translations of Aquila, Symmachus and Theodotion ; and the sixth with the origin of the text forms and the significance of their differences for LXX research. These complex problems are discussed most competently, with a wealth of illustrative detail. Three conclusions of general interest may be noted. First, the author agrees with Pretzl that the divergency in the A and B texts—so remarkable in this O.T. book—point to two recensions of one and the same translation, and not, as was declared so impressively long ago by Lagarde and G. F. Moore, to two independent translations of the Hebrew text. Secondly, he differs from Pretzl in holding that all known text forms of Judges are Origenian in character. And thirdly, on the problem of the recovery of the original Greek text, he thinks that, while it may be possible in isolated instances to decide how the pre-Origenian text must have read, the peculiar history of the LXX renders the restoration of the original text form impossible. His study of the syntax of the Greek text of Judges forms a specially important part of his work, and his plea for further studies of a similar kind will, it is to be hoped, evoke response. At some points the readers may feel disposed to question the validity of the author's views—for example, when he postulates, unnecessarily, it would seem, a Hebrew text different from the M.T. behind a Greek rendering. A useful bibliography is appended. D.W.T.

EXEGESIS AND MODERN TRANSLATIONS

AUGÉ, DOM R. : *Jeremias* (Vol. XIV of *La Biblia : Versió dels Textos Originals i Comentari.*) 1950. Pp. 406. (Monastery of Montserrat.)

The Benedictines of the great monastery of Montserrat in Catalonia continue to maintain their very high standard in both scholarship and beauty of production. The present edition of Jeremiah provides a short introduction on the life and activity of the prophet, the text of the Vulgate with an accompanying translation of the Hebrew, and a very full and adequate commentary in which Hebrew type appears with all reasonable frequency. As in all the major commentaries the Massoretic text is often corrected, usually in the light of the versions, and the author is well at home in all, or nearly all, the best work that has appeared in Germany and elsewhere. One misses from the bibliography Rudolph's commentary in the *Handbuch z.A.T.* and A. C. Welch's valuable study *Jeremiah, His Time and His Work*, reissued in 1951. One misses too any comprehensive treatment of the doctrine of Jeremiah. The pages on the relation between the prophet and Deuteronomy reach no very firm conclusion. The commentary appears to be generally wise and sensible in its handling of the many *cruces interpretum*, and perhaps the only serious regret must be that the work is written in Catalan, a language so little known in this country. J.M.T.B.

BEWER, J. A. : *The Book of Jeremiah*, i. *Chapters* 1-25. (Harper's Annotated Bible Series.) 1951. Pp. 80. (Harper & Bros., New York. Price : 75 cents. English edition published by Eyre and Spottiswoode, London. Price : 6s. 0d.)

As in the previous volumes of this very useful series of brief commentaries, there is a short Introduction, followed by the printing of the Authorized Version, beneath which brief but judicious notes stand. It is of the highest value to have simple commentaries of this kind, written for the general reader, prepared by a scholar of the eminence of Professor Bewer. While there is no discussion of issues on which scholars are not agreed, it may be noted that Bewer adopts the view that Jeremiah at first supported Josiah's reform, and also finds the Scythian peril to be the background of the prophet's early work. He also follows the view that Jeremiah held that sacrifice was not only useless, but harmful, and that God had never wanted it. He recognizes that Jeremiah predicted the destruction of the Temple *unless the people repented*, but does not explain why repentance should preserve the Temple, if its whole cultus was both harmful and alien to the will of God.
H.H.R.

[NOTE.—The two volumes on Isaiah (see *Book List*, 1951, p. 32) have now been issued in the English edition. Price : 6s. 0d. per volume.]

La Sainte Bible, translated into French under the direction of the École Biblique of Jerusalem. *La Genèse*, by R. de Vaux. 1951. Pp. 222. (Price: 17s. 3d.) *Le Lévitique*, by H. Cazelles. 1951. Pp. 132. (Price : 6s. 6d.) *Isaïe*, by P. Auvray and J. Steinmann. 1951. Pp. 250. (Price : 12s. 6d.) *Jérémie, Les Lamentations, Le Livre de Baruch*, by A. Gelin. 1951. Pp. 310. (Price : £1 4s. 0d.) *Le Livre de Jonas*, by A. Feuillet. 1951. Pp. 34. (Price : 1s. 6d.) *Le Livre des Proverbes*, by H. Duesberg and P. Auvray. 1951. Pp. 132. (Price : 10s. 6d.) *Le Cantique des Cantiques*, by A. Robert. 1951. Pp. 60. (Price : 5s. 0d.) *Tobie*, by R. Pautrel. 1951. Pp. 54. (Price : 4s. 3d.) (Éditions du Cerf, Paris.)

For notices of previous volumes in this Roman Catholic Series, see *Book List*, 1949, p. 27 and 1950, pp. 35, 40. The same uniform pattern is being followed for the whole series : translation from a critical text ; short foot-notes, both critical and exegetical ; concise introduction and the text in paragraphs with sub-titles. The *Genesis* volume has a general introduction to the Pentateuch, outlining the history of criticism from the 16th century onwards, including the Graf-Wellhausen scheme, and mentioning the latest ' oral-tradition ' theories of the new Scandinavian school. In the introduction to Genesis itself, critical references are therefore absent, but both here and in *Leviticus*, the authors deal with subject matter rather than with critical questions. De Vaux does discuss the material as being ' Yahwist ' traditions, and so forth. In *Leviticus*, the four sections (i-vii, viii-x, xi-xvi, xvii-xxvi) are held to be from different dates. The book is a synthesis, but largely pre-exilic, with post-exilic elements in vii-x, xviii, and xxiv. The editors of *Isaiah* are conditioned by the declaration of the Biblical Commission in 1908, that there is not sufficient evidence to modify the traditional view as to the unity of the book, but they are plainly drawn to the idea of an exilic ' second-Isaiah ', and to immediately post-exilic origin for most of lvi-lxvi. In the *Jeremiah* volume, the work of Baruch and subsequent editors is recognized, and so also is the modern classification of oracles, biography and auto-biography. *Lamentations* are sixth century : *Baruch* is from Maccabaean times and from the Dispersion. *Jonah* is regarded as being post-exilic, the time of the reformers, Ezra and Nehemiah. *Proverbs* is by many authors, there being two Solomonic collections with appendices. The general discussion of the material in the book is helpful, especially the short account of foreign ' Wisdom '. *Canticles* is set out as consisting of a prologue, five poems with a denouement, with viii. 8-end as appendices. The author is in the Hosea-tradition, and his date ca. 500 B.C. The account of the interpretation of the Song is particularly useful. *Tobit* is placed between Job and Esther, between Zechariah and Daniel, and so 4th or 3rd century, later than the Book of Ahikar, and from the Dispersion, probably from Egypt.   N.H.S.

La Sainte Bible de Jérusalem. Le Livre des Juges, Le Livre de Ruth, by A. Vincent. 1952. Pp. 168, with map. (Price : Fr. 510.) *Amos, Osée*, by E. Osty. 1952. Pp. 128. (Price : Fr. 390.) *Michée, Sophonie, Nahum*, by A. George. 1952. Pp. 96. (Price : Fr. 285.) (Éditions du Cerf, Paris.)

These further volumes of this series maintain the level of the preceding volumes. The translation is here, as in the other volumes, the main feature. Beneath the text stand textual notes, and beneath these the very brief exegetical notes. The short introductions to each of the books offer a moderate critical approach. While there is no disposition to reject passages wholesale as secondary, a number of passages are so rejected. The end of Amos is held to be authentic, but Mic. iv. 1-3 is held to be post-exilic, vii. 8-10, 11-13, 14-20, to be exilic, and Zeph. iii. 18b-20 to be exilic. The view that Nahum is a liturgy is rejected. Ruth is ascribed to *circa* 450 B.C., and placed definitely before the period of Nehemiah's activity.

Within the limits of space provided by these volumes they are wholly excellent, both in their judicious introductions and in their translations.   H.H.R.

Bijbel, nieuwe vertaling op last van het Nederlandsch Bijbelgenootschap bewerkt door de daartoe benoemde Commissies. 1951. (N. V. Uitgevers-Maatschappij, Gebr. Zomer & Keuning, Wageningen.)

The generally accepted Dutch translation, the " Staten-vertaling ", dates from 1637, and the need for a better and more up-to-date translation has long been felt in Holland. Several private translations have been published in the last hundred years, but none of them could find a favourable reception in all quarters amongst the non-Roman churches. Since 1926 the work for this long-desired work was undertaken by the Dutch Bible Society which was beyond the suspicions of private opinions. The N.T. part was published in 1939. The Committee for the O.T. continued its work in spite of the difficult conditions during the occupation. At the end of 1951 this O.T. part was finished. The O.T. translation was prepared by a group of the foremost scholars of Holland who notwithstanding all sorts of denominational and other differences worked together in close collaboration. The result has been a translation which could be accepted by all members of the committee, though individually they might have preferred another reading. As far as we have controlled the text this translation is good modern Dutch, not very " free ", but keeping close to the original. It is well abreast of present-day scholarship and may be recommended for consultation by scholars in other countries engaged in similar work.
                                                                W.C.van U.

Cassuto, U. M. D. : *A Commentary on the Book of Exodus* (in Hebrew). 1951. Pp. xii+352. (The Magnes Press of the Hebrew University, Jerusalem. Price : I£ 2.600.)

This commentary was published in November, 1951 ; four weeks afterwards, at the death of the author, it was practically out of print. The design of the commentary is much more concise than that on Genesis (see *Bi. Or.*, June, 1952) a circumstance which is a distinct advantage for the structure of the work. Cassuto sees in the Book of Exodus a composition in three parts, to which he gives instructive titles : I. i-xvii, Bondage and Deliverance ; II. xviii-xxiv, The Teaching and the Commandment ; III. xxv-xl, The Sanctuary and the Worship. The commentary on part I is marked by the emphasis with which the author once more contests the documentary hypothesis. According to him the story of the Exodus is a uniform composition, in many passages of which can be traced the ancient epics which are no longer extant, but which once preceded the descriptions in prose of the same subject. In order to explain and to illustrate the laws in part II, the author makes frequent use of the Ancient Near Eastern Codes of Law (including those of Eshnunna and Lipit Ishtar).

The laws of the Torah must be understood as a confirmation, a revision, or an abrogation of current legal traditions of the Ancient East. The religious character of the laws of the Torah is stressed, as against the legislation by the kings, of which Cassuto—in contradistinction to Noth—finds traces outside the Torah, e.g. 1 Sam. xxx. 24, 59 ; Is. x. 1 ; Jer. xxxiv. 8ff. The explanation of the description of the tabernacle in part III owes its particular character to the continual comparison with cultic architecture and objects in the Ancient Near East, especially those of Ras Shamra, etc. Striking is the explanation of the position of xxxii-xxxiv between the commandments about the construction of the Tabernacle and their execution, as due to their contents : the withdrawal of God's Presence in Israel (xxxiii. 7) as a result of the golden calf, and its renewal by Moses' prayer (xxxiv. 9). The author's exceptional command of the Hebrew language and knowledge of ancient Semitic culture matures numerous original and ingenious observations and interpretations.   I.L.S.

COHEN, A. (ed. by) : *The Soncino Books of the Bible. Samuel : Hebrew Text and English Translation, with an Introduction and Commentary*, by S. Goldman. 1951. Pp. xv+361. *Daniel, Ezra and Nehemiah*, by J. J. Slotki. 1951. Pp. xvii+279. *Chronicles*, by I. W. Slotki. 1951. Pp. xv+361. (Soncino Press, London and Bournemouth. Price : 15s. 0d. per volume).

These volumes complete this series (see *Book List*, 1951, p. 36), and Publisher and General Editor are to be congratulated on the speed with which they have appeared and the high technical qualities of the production. The commentaries are not designed for students or specialists, but for the general reader, and therefore critical questions are but little discussed. The editors are familiar with modern scholarly work, but rarely commit themselves to accept its conclusions. In Dr. I. W. Slotki's words : "Taking account of the latest results of Biblical criticism and modern scholarship while remaining loyal to Jewish tradition was the principle adopted in the preparation of the commentary." There is no discussion of textual problems, and even in 1 Sam. xiv. 41 the reading of the LXX is unmentioned. While Christian scholars must envy the conditions which permit the printing of the Hebrew text for general readers, Jewish scholars may envy the greater freedom which Christian scholars have in facing textual and critical problems in works addressed to the general reader. Within the limitations of the series these volumes should serve a useful purpose amongst Jews and beyond.   H.H.R.

CRICHTON, T. S. : *Deuteronomy*. (Books of the Bible Series, No. 5.) 1951. Pp. 58. (The Church of Scotland Youth Committee, Edinburgh. Price : 1s. 6d.)

A little book for beginners ("It may surprise some to know that this text (vi. 5) is actually in the Old Testament"), which explains in simple language how the great Hebrew conceptions of love towards God and man were applied in a society very different from our own, though with analagous problems. This is well done. Selection and arrangement are good and scholarship, present in the background, does not obtrude, and a balanced judgement on controversial issues, when they are touched, is offered. Occasionally perhaps prejudices emerge, as when the author refers to the " night of legalism " which settled down upon the religion of Israel in the centuries before Christ, and wonders why our Lord had so little to say against sacrificial worship. " Questions for discussion " at the end form a valuable appendix which would appear to be the fruit of much experience with young people.

M.B.

CUNLIFFE-JONES, H. : *Deuteronomy. Introduction and Commentary.* (Torch Bible Commentaries.) 1951. Pp. 192. (Student Christian Movement Press, London. Price : 8s. 6d.)

Principal Cunliffe-Jones approaches the Book of Deuteronomy as a homiletic theologian, and though he accepts many of the generally acknowledged critical findings, he leaves aside problems of exegesis which have been discussed during recent years. His main concern is with the application of the contents of Deuteronomy to present-day moral and religious issues, and his remarks are frequently pertinent and interesting, though not always likely to command universal agreement.

B.J.R.

ELLIGER, K. : *Das Buch der zwölf Kleinen Propheten. II. Die Propheten Nahum, Habakuk, Zephanja, Haggai, Sacharia, Maleachi.* (Das Alte Testament Deutsch, 25.) 2nd ed. 1951. Pp. iv+208. (Vandenhoeck und Ruprecht, Göttingen. Price : Subscr. DM. 8.00, separate DM. 9.60.)

The first edition of this volume was issued so recently as 1950 (see *Book List,* 1950, p. 36). The call for a new edition is evidence of the reception it has had. The author has taken the opportunity to make minor changes in the text, but there have been no major changes. He has, however, been able to incorporate the indication of significant variations in the text of Habakkuk as contained in the Dead Sea Scroll text.

H.H.R.

The First Book of Moses called Genesis—Book of the Origins. Translated by the Commission for the Revision of the Old Testament appointed by the Hungarian Bible Council of the Evangelical Churches. With an introduction by L. M. Pákozdy. 1951. Pp. xxviii+50. (Press Department of the General Convent of the Reformed Church in Hungary, Budapest.)

This is the first instalment of a trial edition of a new Revised Hungarian Old Testament. The commission has succeeded in rendering the *hebraica veritas* in a highly readable Hungarian of a marked literary character albeit by frequent additions of adverbs, prepositions and particles which are not expressed in the Hebrew text. There are also cases of deviation from the M.T., some of which (e.g. xiii. 2, 17; xiv. 21, 24 ; xviii. 6, 16; xxxii. 10-12) do not seem to be justifiable by literary considerations and even disregard the " principle of concordance " by which the Commission endeavoured to abide. The title of the volume is given in Hungarian, Latin, Hebrew and English, while the Introduction is printed in English and German. In this Introduction the principles which govern the translation are set out. At the foot of the page Scripture references are given.   P.R.W.

GORDIS, R. : *Koheleth : The man and his world.* 1951. Pp. 396. (The Jewish Theological Seminary of America, New York. Price : $5.00.)

This volume is No. XIX of *Texts and Studies* of the Jewish Theological Seminary and is a worthy addition to the notable commentaries of Barton, Hertzberg and Galling. The Hebrew text and the English translation are most perspicuously arranged (pp. 136-191) in the various literary units into which it is thought that Koheleth falls. The translation, modern in speech yet moving with dignity, differs in some respects but, on the whole, very little from that given by Gordis in *The Wisdom of Ecclesiastes* (New York, Behrman House, 1945). The writer in *Koheleth—the man and his world* gives us an excellent commentary which endeavours to do justice not only to his own exegesis but to the interpretations given by other exegetes. Of course, after all has been said, there still remains room for difference of opinion, as those who know the Hebrew text of Koheleth may gather from Gordis' translation of iii. 11 as : " Everything He has made proper in its due time and He has also placed the love of the world in men's hearts ". Also whether Gordis' rendering of iv. 5, 6 meets Koheleth's meaning is very doubtful. But it cannot be expected that all the difficulties in Koheleth will ever find a solution which is agreed upon by all. The fifteen chapters of convenient size which the author offers upon the background of Koheleth and on the literary and linguistic questions connected with this book will be appreciated by scholars. Especially chap. vii on the language of Koheleth is welcome. Since the time of Burkitt's suggestion —supported and much strengthened later by Zimmermann and Ginsberg— that Koheleth is a translation from the Aramaic, many have considered that this theory explains Koheleth's textual character. But Gordis argues very convincingly against this and concludes that the book was written in Hebrew by a writer who in daily life used Aramaic freely.   O.S.R.

GUTBROD, K. : *Das Buch vom Lande Gottes (Josua und Richter).* 1951. Pp. 282. (Price : DM. 9.60.)

LAMPARTER, H. : *Das Buch der Anfechtung (Das Buch Hiob).* 1951. Pp. 262. (Price : DM. 12.50.)

KESSLER, W. : *Zwischen Gott und Weltmacht (Das Buch Daniel).* 1950. Pp. 206. (Price : DM. 7.20.) Die Botschaft des Alten Testaments, vols. x, xiii, xxii. (Calwer Verlag, Stuttgart.)

The volumes of this series contain a translation of the text, divided into sections, each followed by a short exposition. This rests on modern scholarship, but does not concern itself with the minutiae of exegesis, but is more concerned to unfold the religious significance of the text. It also offers what is so often demanded to-day in some quarters—a Christian interpretation of the Old Testament. The volumes are not written for academic readers, but should prove widely useful to those for whom they are written, and not least because they bridge the gulf between the scholar and the unlearned readers, and bring scholarship and devotion together.

H.H.R.

HAURET, CH. : *Origines de l'Univers et de l'Homme d'après la Bible* (*Genèse I-III*). 1950. Pp. 258. (Gabalda, Paris. Price : 9s. 0d.)

Here is a valuable running commentary on the first three chapters of the Bible, resting on wide study of modern work, which aims, in the words of Professor Coppens (who contributes an Introduction), to fulfil the difficult and delicate task of remaining faithful to the directives of the Roman Church and also to the progress of science. The author is more concerned that the reader should be aware of some of the many problems that surround these chapters than to offer assured solutions. H.H.R.

HÖLSCHER, G. : *Das Buch Hiob.* (Handbuch zum Alten Testament, I. Reihe, 17.) 2nd ed. 1952. Pp. ii+102. (Mohr, Tübingen. Subscription Price : DM. 6.00 in paper and 8.50 bound ; separately DM. 7.00 or 9.50.)

It is good to know that out-of-print volumes of this series are being revised and reissued. The revision of the present work has brought it abreast of much of the literature that has appeared since the first edition was published, and is found in innumerable little changes and additions. The book is three pages longer than the first edition. All who missed the first edition of this excellent commentary will desire the second ; and some will be glad to have both. H.H.R.

KALT, E. : *Genesis, Exodus, Leviticus.* (Die Heilige Schrift für das Leben erklärt, vol. I. Herders Bibelkommentar.) 1948. Pp. 496. (Herder, Freiburg. Price : 38s. 6d.)

This is the fourteenth volume to be issued, the total number in the series being twenty-one. It is a popular commentary for Roman Catholic readers, and consists of a translation of the Vulgate into German, section by section, with each section followed by a short commentary. The sections roughly follow those demanded by critical literary analysis, but the declaration of the Biblical Commission is followed, by which Moses is regarded as the author. The final editing has been done by Dr. Nikolaus Adler. N.H.S.

LEVENE, A. : *The Early Syrian Fathers on Genesis, from a Syriac Manuscript on the Pentateuch in the Mingana Collection.* 1951. Pp. 354. (Taylor's Foreign Press, London. Price : £1 15s. 0d.)

Dr. Levene prints a facsimile and offers a translation of the first eighteen chapters of a Nestorian manuscript now in the

404

Library of the Selly Oak Colleges, Birmingham. The manuscript contains a compilation from the work of Theodore of Mopsuestia, Ephraim and other writers, and forms an exposition in thirty-four chapters of the Book of Genesis. Dr. Levene prefaces his edition of the text with an account of the manuscript and a study of the types of exegesis represented in it. He adds grammatical and etymological notes, and he compares the contents of his text with parallels from Rabbinic sources. While we welcome this edition of the text and congratulate Dr. Levene on an excellent production, it may be suggested that in the next volume the grammatical and etymological notes, the least successful part of the work, might well be omitted.   W.D.M.

MAAG, V. : *Text, Wortschatz und Begriffswelt des Buches Amos.* 1951. Pp. xvi+254. (Brill, Leiden.)

In this dissertation Professor Maag offers first the text of the Book of Amos so printed as to indicate which words he judges to belong to the original text and which variety of gloss he finds in the remaining words. Following each portion of the text are textual notes, the translation, notes on the translation, and short discussions of the genuineness. All this occupies about one quarter of the volume. About the same space is devoted to a complete vocabulary of the book. A further hundred pages are given to discussion of individual words, while the final section collects groups of words belonging to a single field of ideas, such as words relating to time, place, farming and war, and offers a discussion of some of the leading ideas of Amos. The author shows independence of judgement, and not seldom goes his own way on textual questions (e.g. in viii. 14 he prefers to read *'ashērath* for *'ashmath* rather than find the deity *Ashima* here), and he has many original contributions to philology.   H.H.R.

MONTGOMERY, J. A. : *A Critical and Exegetical Commentary on the Books of Kings,* edited by H. S. Gehman. 1952 (1951 on Title page). Pp. xlviii+576. (T. & T. Clark, Edinburgh. Price : 35s. 0d.)

Our late lamented Honorary Member, Professor Montgomery, completed this work in 1941, but withdrew it later, since publication was delayed by the war, and then died before it could go to press. Professor Gehman undertook the difficult task of editing it and seeing it through the press, bringing its references to literature up to date, and adding from the stores of his own very wide learning. The Introduction is particularly strong in the section dealing with the text and versions, and throughout the commentary much emphasis is laid on this. The pattern of the volume follows that of other volumes in the series, with the exegetical work in larger type and the philological and textual notes in small type at the end of each section. There are special notes on major issues, and to the section on chronology in the Introduction Gehman has added his own chronological tables.

One of the outstanding features of the volume is the wealth of its reference to relevant literature. The transliteration of Hebrew words is not quite uniform, and diacritics are sometimes employed and sometimes not, while Greek accents are only sporadically added. The substance of the commentary and the riches of scholarship that have gone into its preparation make it a worthy member of an important series.

H.H.R.

NÖTSCHER, F. (ed. by) : *Die Heilige Schrift in deutscher Übersetzung, Echter Bibel : Das Alte Testament.* 13. *Job* by H. Junker, and *Sirach* by V. Hamp. 1951. Pp. 104, 146. (Echter Verlag, Würzburg. Price : DM. 7.50.)

This excellent series, of which the first numbers appeared as recently as 1947, is now almost complete in its Old Testament section. Lieferung 14 will be an edition of the Pentateuch by H. Junker and H. Schneider, and the last part will be the table of contents with maps and chronological tables.

The present editions of Job and Sirach reach the same high level of competence and clarity as the earlier volumes, and little need be said about their general contents. Sirach, it may be noted, is equipped with a reasonably full textual apparatus, whereas in Job very few textual corrections are noted at the foot of the text. This is to be explained partly, no doubt, in terms of Junker's opinions on the text of Job, as given in the short introduction to his commentary. It seems that he mistrusts the tendency shown in some modern commentaries to indulge in abundant textual correction and considers that difficulties in the text are to be resolved by interpretation and not by textual emendation.   J.M.T.B.

ORIGEN : *Homélies sur les Nombres*, translated with Introduction by A. Méhat. 1951. Pp. 570. (Les Éditions du Cerf, Paris. Price : 24s. 0d.)

This new volume in the series *Sources Chrétiennes* (see *Book List*, 1945, pp. 27 f., 1951, p. 32) contains only the French translation of Origen, with Introduction, instead of printing also the Greek text as in the volume of Basil of Caesarea. The Introduction examines the exegetical principles of Origen, which are well illustrated in the course of these homilies. The rendering is into very readable French, and there are some footnotes to the translation. While few will wish to revive Origen's exegesis, many will be glad to have access to his work in this convenient form.

H.H.R.

PENNA, A. : *Principi e carattere dell 'Esegesi di S. Gerolamo.* (Scripta Pontificii Instituti Biblici.) 1950. Pp. xvi+236. (Pontificio Istituto Biblico, Rome. Price : 23s. 8d.)

Three years ago, in 1949, Penna published through the firm of Marietti a book of some 450 pages entitled *S. Gerolamo.* It was, first and foremost, a life of S. Jerome, though his exegetical methods were studied briefly in the chapter headed " Il biblista." The present volume is a scholarly and well-documented account of Jerome's hermeneutics, in particular

406

his attitude towards the two chief senses of Scripture (literal and spiritual) and his manner of harmonizing these senses. Two useful sections at the end of the book discuss the actuality of Jerome's hermeneutics and the value of his exegesis. Apropos of Jerome's knowledge of Hebrew, the author considers that some modern writers have been too severe in their judgements, though he admits that nobody would feel bound to defend the derivation of the Latin *nugae* from a Hebrew root!   J.M.T.B.

PRADO, J. : *Biblia y Predicacion.* 2. *Amos el Profeta Pastor.* 1950. Pp. 64. (Price : 1s. 6d.) 3. *Judit.* 1950. Pp. 168. (Price : 2s. 6d.) 4. *Tobias.* 1950. Pp. 208. (Price : 3s. 0d.) (Edit. el Perpetuo Soccorro, Madrid.)

Prado, who is the author of a number of excellent Latin works on the Bible under the general title of *Praelectiones Biblicae* (cf. *Book List*, 1951, p. 13) has here done something to popularize his considerable knowledge of the Old Testament books. One gathers that the first two were broadcast in part or whole in the series " Emisiones Biblicas " from Radio Madrid in the first half of 1944. Each brochure contains an introduction, a version of the biblical text and what is styled a " comentario teológico-popular " which sufficiently explains itself. All three volumes are nicely printed and convey a quantity of information most agreeably. The famous *crux interpretum* of Amos ii. 13 is here rendered : " Pues ved que haré crujir el suelo a vuestros pies, cual crujir hace el carro lleno de haces." One can only wish all success to this excellent venture.
                                                    J.M.T.B.

VON RAD, G. : *Das erste Buch Mose. Genesis Kapitel* 12, 10-25, 18 (Das Alte Testament Deutsch, 3). 1952. Pp. 90. (Vandenhoeck & Ruprecht, Göttingen.)

The second instalment of this commentary on Genesis fully maintains the high standard set in the previous volume. Although the nature of the series precludes detailed discussion of the sources, the results of technical scholarship are presented with great skill and clarity ; and in passages such as xv. 1-6, xviii. 20-23, xxii. 1-19 the author's keen theological insight and gift of concise and telling exposition have full scope.   G.W.A.

STEVENSON, W. B. : *Critical Notes on the Hebrew Text of the Poem of Job.* 1951. Pp. viii+170. (University Press, Aberdeen. Price : 16s. 0d.)

Dr. Stevenson's little work is not so much an original contribution to the study of the Hebrew text of Job as a companion to his Schweich Lectures entitled ' The Poem of Job', delivered in 1943 and published in 1947. There is indeed little if anything that is actually new but the author has cast his net far and wide amongst the commentaries and, even though he seems to have overlooked a certain amount of recent periodical literature, has nevertheless provided a needed and welcome companion to his previous volume.   G.R.D.

THILO, M. : *Das alte Testament ausgelegt für Bibelleser*. Bd. IV. *Die prophetischen Bücher*. 1951. Pp. 488. (Bertelsmann Verlag, Gütersloh. Price : DM. 12.)

In the *Book List*, 1951, p. 43 a description is given of vols. I-III and of the character of this work as a whole. Vol. IV, on the prophetic books, follows the same method as its predecessors, the translation and commentary being concurrent, the style fluent and readable and well adapted to the use of " Bible-readers ". O.S.R.

WEISER, A. : *Das Buch Hiob* (Das Alte Testament Deutsch, 13). 1951. Pp. 268. (Vandenhoeck and Ruprecht, Göttingen. Price : Subscription DM. 9.50 ; separate DM. 10.80.)

This important addition to the literature on Job is intended primarily to grapple with the profound religious argument of the book. Scholars will note with interest the author's judgement on various points of detail in the interpretation and will not hold it against him if, in agreement with the plan of the series, he does not support his conclusions with all the apparatus of learning. There is clear evidence that behind the interpretative judgements lies a scholarship of first rank. One point of special interest is that Dr. Weiser finds in the form of the book not only the literary types of the wisdom literature but also those belonging to the Hebrew cult—the psalms of complaint and thanksgiving, the motif of the divine trial and the oath of purification. Peculiar to itself is its dramatic character which reflects the actual spiritual experience of the author. The book of Job offers not solutions of intellectual problems but the solution *in life* of the problem of human existence. The real problem is not that of the suffering of Job but the problem of God which arises from it. The movement of the book shows Job approaching nearer and nearer to the solution of his personal problem, the deeper he enters into the reality of suffering. The solution, so far as there is one, lies in the personal encounter with God.

Dr. Weiser holds that the actual prologue and epilogue are not to be equated with the so-called *Volksbuch* but were composed for their present position by the author of the poem. The translations he offers are rhythmical in character and form an attractive part of this commentary. N.W.P.

WOLFF, H. W. : *Haggai*. (Biblische Studien, Heft 1.) 1951. Pp. 48. (Buchhandlung des Erziehungsvereins Neukirchen, Kreis Moers. Price : DM. 1.90.)

This is the first of a series of commentaries, promised at the rate of four a year, under the general editorship of O. Weber, H. Gollwitzer and H. J. Kraus. The author has provided a critical, exegetical and homiletical study of the book in the evangelical tradition. The date of the book is given as *ca.* 520 B.C. ; and the dating given in i. 15a is taken to belong to the section ii. 15-19. This is a useful monograph, and in it the prophetic message is plainly set forth, both for the prophet's day and for ours. N.H.S.

LITERARY CRITICISM AND INTRODUCTION
(including History of Interpretation and Special Studies)

ALLIS, O. T. : *The Unity of Isaiah.* 1951. Pp. viii+136. (Tyndale Press, London. Price : 12s. 6d.)

This is an English edition of the work reviewed in the 1951 *Book List*, p. 45. The author finds it much easier to set up skittles and knock them down and suppose that he has smitten the critics hip and thigh than to allow his readers to have any fair view of the critics. The reader is given to understand that those who find a Deutero-Isaiah do so because they have an *a priori* disbelief in predictive prophecy. The author completely ignores the nature of the argument for Deutero-Isaiah, which is that here we do not have a prophet's announcement to an eighth century audience of things that should be in the distant future, but that we have a prophet's assumption that he and his hearers are in a sixth century background. H.H.R.

BOUT, H. : *Het zondebesef in het Boek der Psalmen.* 1952. Pp. viii+192. (Utrecht University. Price : Fl. 8.50.)

This book on the notion of sin in the Psalms deals with the character, the origin, the extent and action, and the removal of sin. The treatment is characterized by an extensive number of quotations of authors and a close affiliation to Calvin's commentary on the Psalms. P.A.H.deB.

BRANNON, C. H. : *An Introduction to the Bible.* 1950. Pp. xii+292. (Graphic Press, Raleigh, N.C. Price : $4.75.)

This very unusual Introduction is by an entomologist, who has studied Greek and Hebrew and who has read much modern literature on the Bible and corresponded widely with leading scholars in Britain and America. What he offers is a series of disconnected notes on special points arranged in order of the text, rather than what is ordinarily understood by an Introduction. A good deal of useful and up-to-date information is assembled, though it is not always quite accurate. Thus on p. 1 it is stated that according to rabbinical tradition ' Ezekiel gave us the Torah '. Sometimes highly disputable statements are made categorically, as when the Pharoah of the Oppression is said to be Amenophis II (p. 22) and the Pharoah of the entry into Palestine Rameses II (p. 38). The Israelites are said to have entered Palestine by arrangement with the Pharaoh as an Egyptian military force. The Suffering Servant of Isa. liii is identified with Jeremiah (p. 96). The *melek* of Judges xvii. 6, xviii. 1 is said to be ' the travelling supervisor of Pharaoh ' (p. 47). The book needs to be read with some discrimination, therefore. H.H.R.

VAN DEN BUSSCHE, H. : *Het Probleem van Kronieken* (Analecta Lovaniensia Biblica et Orientalia, II, 19). 1950. Pp. 26. (Publications Universitaire de Louvain, Louvain. Price : 4s. 0d.)

> This monograph, following earlier studies (see *Book List*, 1949, p. 18), attacks the orthodox Wellhausen school, which holds that Samuel-Kings is more trustworthy, historically and theologically, than Chronicles. The text of Samuel has received more modification than that of Chronicles, mostly because the latter escaped the attention of the Massoretes. The article contains a careful, documented study of the work done on Chronicles particularly in the last thirty years.
> N.H.S.

CHEVERTON, C. F. : *The Old Testament for New Students*. 1951. Pp. 224. (Bethany Press, St. Louis. Price : $3.00.)

> This is a very simple review of the Old Testament, with attention to its message. Critical questions are nowhere directly presented or discussed, but the book rests on critical study, many of whose conclusions are tacitly assumed. There is no attention to archaeology. At the end of each chapter suggestions for ' assignments ', and for discussion are made. But for its very high price it might be recommended for use in schools at some levels.
> H.H.R.

CONTRI, S. : *La Sapienza di Salomone*. 1950. Pp. 28. (Edizioni Criterion, Milan. Price : 11s. 0d.)

> The title of this brochure must not deceive any reader. It is no more than the introduction to a larger work which will contain chapters on the various sapiential works of the Old Testament—Ecclesiastes, Sirach, Song of Songs, Proverbs, and the so-called Wisdom of Solomon and will end with a chapter on scriptural inspiration. The present work does not venture beyond some general ideas on inspiration, the Papal encyclicals, and some references to the purpose of the complete work, which will be (perhaps a trifle ambitiously) to introduce the reader to the Bible by way of the wisdom literature, and to add force to the Catholic position in regard to biblical interpretation.
> J.M.T.B.

COPASS, B. A., and CARLSON, E. L. : *A Study of the Prophet Micah*. 1950. Pp. 170. (Baker Book House, Grand Rapids, Mich. Price : $1.75).

> This study of the prophet Micah attributes the entire book to Micah, with the exception of the oracle duplicated in Isaiah, where judgement is suspended as to whether it is from either or from another. The critical questions which have led to the commonly accepted theory of the composite origin of the book are not considered. There is, however, a useful review of Israelite prophecy down to the eighth century (both Joel and Jonah being here included as earlier than Micah), and a survey of the historical and social background of the work

of Micah. These, together with the interpretation of the message of the prophet, should enable the general reader to understand the meaning of the book of Micah. There is an appendix giving a full translation of the Moabite Stone, and another on Serpent Worship. H.H.R.

*HART, H.ST.J. : *A Foreword to the Old Testament : an Essay of Elementary Introduction.* 1951. Pp. xvi+184. (A. & C. Black, London. Price : 10s. 6d.)

This is an unusual but very valuable book, offering a short introduction to many sides of Old Testament study—geography, history, religion, literature, canon. While it contains *multum in parvo*, it is not a mere *précis*, but is written in a lively style which holds the interest, and enriched with some quotations from uncommon sources. Its scholarship is reliable, and whoever masters its contents will have a comprehensive knowledge about the Bible. If he also follows the author's advice and reads the Biblical passages to which he is referred, he will in addition have a wide acquaintance with the Bible. The book can be unreservedly commended to students at all levels, and to the general reader. H.H.R.

DANELL, G. A. : *Psalm* 139 (Uppsala Universitets Årsskrift 1951 : 1). 1951. Pp. 38. (A. B. Lundequistska Bokhandeln, Uppsala : Otto Harrassowitz, Leipzig. Price : 2 Kr.)

In this typical product of the so-called Uppsala School the author first offers a verse by verse translation of Psalm 139, accompanied by textual, grammatical and lexical notes, and then attempts to deal with the more general question of interpretation and the *Sitz im Leben* of the psalm as a whole. While toying with the thought that the background is that of an ordeal (cf. H. Schmidt, *Das Gebet der Angeklagten im Alten Testament*, 1928), he ultimately places the psalm in a context suggested by Solomon's vigil at Gibeon (1 Kings iii. 5-15), and advances the view that it was used as ' the king's declaration, his profession to Yahweh after his enthronement during the New Year Festival.' Although the reviewer himself takes the view that several of the royal psalms stem from the celebration of the autumnal festival in Jerusalem, the argument in this case seems to be very strained throughout. At the same time it is only right to add that it is presented modestly and with hesitation. A.R.J.

HAR'UBENI, N. *New Light on the Book of Jeremiah* (Published in Hebrew, *'Or Hadash 'al Sepher Yirmeyahu*). 1950. Pp. 150+20 plates. ('Am 'Obhed Publishing House, Tel Aviv.)

The author has made a study of the climatic and agricultural conditions in the neighbourhood of 'Anathoth, and on the basis of these offers his explanations of some of Jeremiah's ideas and metaphors. 'Anathoth is on the border between the agriculture of the hills and the pastoral industry of the wilderness, and its mean rainfall is minimal ; this is held to explain Jeremiah's proclivity to water metaphors and those drawn from loss of direction in the desert. While some of the explanations offered are plausible, a number are too subjective to carry conviction ; and it is unfortunate that the author's photographic evidence, which has been skillfully drawn, has not been reproduced more successfully. In an appendix, useful corroborative material is proffered (independently) for the identification proposed by Clermont-Ganneau and Macalister of Rachel's Tomb with the *Kubur bani 'Isra'il* south of Geba' and Ramah. The author's tendencies are conservative, which induce in him an irritating tendency to see in many of the suggestions of modern editors of Jeremiah (whom he has consulted conscientiously) an almost perverse obtuseness that would have been impossible, he declares, if they had made investigations of the land and its conditions.   R.L.

KRAUS, H. J. : *Die Verkündigung der Weisheit : Eine Auslegung des Kapitels Sprüche* 8. 1951. Pp. 48. (Buchhandlung des Erziehungsvereins Neukirchen, Kreis Moers. Price : DM. 1.90.)

> This is No. 2 in the series *Biblische Studien* which aim at helping the biblical student and the theologian with sound and critical expositions of bible passages. H. J. Kraus' exegesis of Prov. viii is well and interestingly done. In v. 30 he prefers the rendering " da war ich als *Liebling* ihm zur Seite " to Luther's " da war ich der Werkmeister bei ihm."   O.S.R.

LINDBLOM, J. : *The Servant Songs in Deutero-Isaiah. A New Attempt to Solve an Old Problem.* (Lunds Universitets Årsskrift, N. F. Avd. 1. Bd. 47. Nr. 5.) 1951. Pp. 104. (C. W. K. Gleerup, Lund. Price : Kr. 11.00.)

> Professor Lindblom here sets out at length the interpretation of the Servant Songs which he outlined in a paper read to the Society in January, 1950. Holding that the first question to be settled is that of the literary character of the Songs, he argues that they are allegories, and that their interpretation and application are to be found in their immediate contexts. xlii. 1-4 is an imaginative portrait of a vassal of Yahweh, which is applied to Israel in xlii. 5-9. xlix. 1-6 and l. 4-9 are pictures taken from actual experience (that of the prophet himself) and applied in xlix. 7 to Israel and in l. 10f. to two groups among the prophet's hearers. In the fourth Song, lii. 13—liii. 1 contains a divine declaration, applying to the Jewish community the allegorical passage which follows in liii. 2-12 (a prophetic revelation in visionary form), the whole being closely linked in sense to lii. 7-12 and liv. 1-10. In addition to this stimulating treatment of the main problem the book contains chapters on the thought of the Songs in relation to the whole prophecy, on the prophet's use of figurative language, and on the problem of eschatology in Deutero-Isaiah (Lindblom argues that the prophet's view of the future was not in the strict sense eschatological). This monograph deserves careful study, and is a valuable addition to the literature on the Songs and on Deutero-Isaiah.
> G.W.A.

MOWINCKEL, S. : *Offersang og sangoffer. Salmediktning i Bibelen.* 1951.
Pp. 500+164. (Aschehoug & Co. (W. Nygaard), Oslo.)

Professor Mowinckel here presents the results of a lifetime's work on the Psalms in a massive and comprehensive volume to which it is impossible to do anything like justice in a brief note. The whole range of Psalter study is here covered (some themes at greater length than others), often with challenging criticism of Mowinckel's forerunners or of younger scholars, at times with fair-minded concessions to his critics. The starting-point of the treatment is Gunkel's method, with a reaffirmation of Mowinckel's own contention that the Psalter was far more intimately linked with the cult than Gunkel allowed. In the treatment of literary classification there is much that is of interest and importance. In his reconstruction of the cultic background the decisive differences between him and Uppsala are decisively stated. On ' the workers of iniquity ' he repeats his concessions to Birkeland. In a very interesting chapter on poetic form he inclines decidedly to the views of Hölscher as against Sievers. Many fine passages of religious interpretation occur throughout the book, including the discussion of the *differentiae* of Hebrew-Jewish Psalmody. There is a chapter on the Christian use of the Psalms which is the more moving when one realizes that it was originally written during war-time occupation. An immensely valuable book. G.W.A.

NEHER, A. : *Notes sur Qohéléth (L'Ecclésiaste)* : 1951. Pp. 110. (Les Editions de Minuit, Paris. Price : Fr. 210.)

A delightful and informative booklet which enters into the spirit of Qoheleth. The author well describes the thought of this most baffling of the Hebrew sages in a single sentence— " La prudence et l'aventure ont conclu un pacte dans Qohéléth et y marchent de pair." The philosophy of the middle way combining with the trend of irony, pessimism and cynicism to verge toward extremes belongs to the problem which Qoheleth sets its interpreters. M. Neher deftly sketches the conclusions to which, from the early to the latest times, the most notable of the interpreters of Qoheleth have come. With regard to Qoheleth's teaching the writer struggles with the problem of the exact relationship and meaning which the concepts of time contained in *zeman*, *'eth* and *ha-'olam* have in Qoheleth's mind. Whether he has adequately solved this problem must be left to the reader's judgement. The same applies to M. Neher's attempt to explain Qoheleth's philosophy of life, which is grounded on the conviction that " all is vanity " (*hebel*), as having its background and interpretation in what the book of Genesis has to say about Abel (*hebel*) Cain and Seth. O.S.R.

RIDDERBOS, N. H. : *Psalmen en Cultus.* 1950. Pp. 40. (Kok, Kampen.)

In this inaugural lecture Professor Ridderbos examines some of the views of Gunkel and Eerdmans on the psalms. In the course of this examination he contests the view of Eerdmans that there was no connection between the

413

psalms and the cult. Evidence is collected from outside the Psalter to establish the place of psalms in the ritual, or the religious use of song, and a number of psalms are found to support such a view of their origin. Eight pages of notes at the end give reference to much modern literature, including the works of Mowinckel and others, whose views find only incidental mention here.   H.H.R.

RIDGE, F. M. : *The Prophet Amos.* 1951. Pp. 16. (Epworth Press, London. Price : 6d.)

A brief exposition of the significance of Amos for to-day. The background of his own time is but slightly referred to, and a passing allusion suffices for v. 18-24. The authorship of the book is somewhat naïvely attributed to Amos, who is said to have returned to Tekoa to write it. Mr. Ridge's booklet will nevertheless be useful to the general reader, for whom it is written.   H.H.R.

ROBINSON, D. W. B. : *Josiah's Reform and the Book of the Law.* 1951. Pp. 40. (The Tyndale Press, London. Price : 2s. 0d.)

While maintaining that the Lawbook found in the Temple was Deuteronomy, the author argues that the reform of Josiah had begun before the finding of the book. This is supposed somehow to overthrow the critical view of the date of Deuteronomy. Since the reform was associated with Josiah's political revolt, some measure of reform would be inevitable, just as Hezekiah's was. It might even take the form of centralization, as Hezekiah's did, even had the Lawbook not been found. The author holds that Deuteronomy is of Mosaic authorship, and that a copy was deposited in the Temple at its foundation, and probably read to the king every seven years before it was lost at a date which may not have been unduly long before 621 B.C. What he fails to explain is why no centralization of worship was carried out by the kings whom he supposes to have known this law until the time of Hezekiah, when no Lawbook is mentioned, and why Josiah's Passover, celebrated in Jerusalem, was unique since the entry into the land, if it had been known all along that this was how it should be celebrated. While there is much in this booklet with which the reviewer would agree, its conclusion is a complete *non-sequitur*.   H.H.R.

RUBOW, P. V. : *Bibelsk Læsning.* 1951. Pp. 64. (Gyldendalske Boghandel. Nordisk Forlag, Copenhagen. Price : Kr. 8.75.)

The author who is professor of the History of Literature in the University of Copenhagen has also previously written about literary problems in the O.T., especially in the Pentateuch. He has here given a special treatment of Genesis, which he considers to be the work of a single, very skilled, writer, who created the pattern for later writers. Professor Rubow has very caustic remarks about the way in which the commentators usually cut Genesis into small parts which they distribute amongst different " sources ". This book is thus an attempt to see Genesis as a literary unity and it is carried through consistently.   A.S.K.

SMALLEY, BERYL : *The Study of the Bible in the Middle Ages.* 1952.
Pp. xxii+406. (Blackwell, Oxford. Price : 37s. 6d.)

This is a second and much enlarged edition of the work reviewed
in the *Book List*, 1946, p. 9. The revision has not only brought
the book abreast of work that has appeared since the first
edition, but has allowed the expansion of the chapters on
Andrew of St. Victor and on the Friars, and the rewriting of
the Conclusions. The final section of the chapter on Andrew
of St. Victor is devoted to a pupil, Herbert of Bosham, on
whom Mr. Loewe recently read a paper to our Society, and
whose work, in the form of a commentary on the Psalter,
has only come to light in the Library of St. Paul's Cathedral
quite recently. For the new material this edition contains,
and for the reissue of the material of the old edition, this
fascinating study is most warmly to be welcomed, and the
patient research of the authoress has opened new windows
into the world of mediaeval Biblical scholarship. The learning
on which the book rests is immense, and though the price
may seem high in that it is more than double that of the first
edition, the rapid rise in costs and the fact that the book is
lengthened by one third sufficiently account for it. The fact
that it is not just one book amongst many dealing with its
subject, but the only book in English dealing with this field
of study, makes it indispensable to those interested, and its
high excellence makes it well worth its price.   H.H.R.

SNAITH, N. : *Hymns of the Temple.* 1951. Pp. 128. (S. C. M. Press,
Ltd., London. Price : 7s. 6d.)

The author, in his earlier work *Studies in the Psalter* (1934),
has already shown his keen interest in Books II and III of
the Psalms, and he here returns to the subject with what he
describes as " a sort of running commentary " on Pss.
xlii-xliii, xliv, xlvi, l, and lxxiii. The commentary itself is
preceded by a short introduction which deals briefly with the
place of the Psalter in the Bible, its compilation, the poetry
of the psalms, and the recent developments in this field which
are associated with the names of Gunkel and Mowinckel.
In the main part of the book the author often wanders off
into fields which seem only remotely connected with the psalms
under discussion, so that " rambling commentary " would
seem to be a more suitable description. At the same time the
work as a whole is marked by that combination of scholarship
and evangelical fervour which one has learnt to expect of the
author, and it is written throughout in a characteristically
stimulating way. On the other hand the author is not always
a safe guide ; for example, it is a reversal of the facts to say
that the work of Gunkel was a development of earlier work by
Staerk and Kittel (p. 29) and it is an exaggeration to say
that ' Gunkel was ' inclined to date the psalms largely in the
pre-exilic period ' (p. 30).   A.R.J.

STEINMANN, J. : *Les Psaumes*. 1951. Pp. 188. (Gabalda, Paris. Price : Fr. 400.)

This little book has grown out of three lectures delivered at Easter 1951. It contains a simple review of a number of psalms, arranged according to their types, and giving in each case a translation—often based on an emended text—with short observations. The chapters deal with Royal Psalms, Messianic Psalms, Hymns, Psalms of Judgement, Cries of Suffering, the Psalm of Immortality (Psa. xvi), Lamentations and Imprecations, Wisdom Psalms. The final chapter is on the Theology of the Psalms. It is a work of popularization, rather than one offering an independent contribution to scholarship.   H.H.R.

SWEETAPPLE, H. D. S. : *Hebrew Heroes and Patriots*. 1952. Pp. 60. (Church Book Room, London. Price : 2s. 0d.)

This little book is designed to help Clergy and Teachers in the instruction of the young, and it offers a brief survey of the books of Judges and Ruth. Critical and moral problems are passed over without mention, though the author expresses the view that the cruelties, wars of extermination and fratricidal strife of the time were ennobled by the belief that men were doing God service ! This is scarcely the teaching to offer to young or old.   H.H.R.

THIELE, E. R. : *The Mysterious Numbers of the Hebrew Kings*. 1951. Pp. 298. (University of Chicago Press. Price : $6.00.)

The volume is a reconstruction of the dates of the reigns of the Israelite and Judahite kings. The discrepancies of Hebrew chronology for the period of two kingdoms are well-known. The author makes all the reigns fit. He assumes an accession-year system in the south trom Rehoboam to Jehoshaphat, and again from Amaziah to Zedekiah, with a non-accession year system from Jehoram to Joash. In the north, he assumes a non-accession system from Jeroboam to Jehoahaz, and an accession-year system from Jehoash to Hoshea. In addition to this, he assumes three periods of over-lapping reigns in the north and six co-regencies in the south. The results of much painstaking investigation are set out clearly in a number of appendices.   N.H.S.

ULECIA, A. GIL. : *Introducción General a la Sagrada Biblia*. 1950. Pp. xxii+298. (Publicaciones Afebe, Madrid. Price : 60 pesetas.)

This is one of the many excellent publications of the Instituto Central de Cultura Religiosa Superior, and in a remarkably compact and interesting manner covers all the usual questions normally treated in Catholic universities and seminaries under the heading of general introduction to the Bible. There is a preliminary chapter on the names and divisions of the Bible and on the dignity, usefulness and difficulty of Scripture studies. Then follow chapters on the inspiration of the Bible and the Canon of the Old and New Testaments, on the Texts and Versions of Scripture, and on Biblical Hermeneutics.

The discussion of the various topics appears relatively elementary when compared with that in such a work as the *Introductio Generalis in Sacram Scripturam* by B. Gut, published in the Editiones Comm. A. Arnodo, Rome in the same year, but Ulecia's work is far better adapted to the use of the educated laity than any Latin manual could be. It has a further advantage over many books of the kind in that it contains a fair number (fourteen in all) of small but clear photographs of portions of the Lachish letters, the Dead Sea Scrolls, the Nash papyrus, three of the Greek codices, and the Alcala Polyglot. One may fully agree with the judgement of the Archbishop of Saragossa in his preface that the work is " completa, docta y muy apropriada para seglares."

J.M.T.B.

WELCH, A. C. : *Jeremiah : His Time and His Work*. 1951. Pp. viii + 264. (Basil Blackwell, Oxford. Price : 15s. 0d.)

Despite the work which has been done on the subject since this book was first published (Oxford University Press, 1928), it is good to have it reissued and thus made more generally available ; for, if it rarely makes exciting reading, it is marked by robust common sense and should not be neglected by anyone who seeks to understand the prophet and his message. In developing his own treatment of the subject Welch offers much penetrating criticism of the work of earlier scholars ; and in some ways it is in his discussion of such problems (e.g. the attempts to identify the foe from the North) that he is at his best. Indeed it is just here that one finds both the strength and the weakness of the book ; for, valuable and necessary as such discussions are, the author's method tends to obscure the person of the prophet, who never quite comes to life as he does in the well-known work of J. Skinner, *Prophecy and Religion* (Cambridge University Press, 1922), with which it inevitably invites comparison. Nevertheless it is only right to add that here too Welch has much of value to say, notably in his discussion of Jeremiah's inner life, his attitude to Josiah's reform and his sympathetic approach to the exilic community. It is much to be hoped that the reissue of this book will encourage students of the Old Testament to examine afresh the standpoint of a scholar whose work has not, perhaps, received quite the recognition which it deserves.

A.R.J.

LAW, RELIGION AND THEOLOGY

AALDERS, J. G. : *God en Magog in Ezechiël*. 1951. Pp. 176. (Kampen. Price : Fl. 4.90.)

An exegetical treatment of Ezek. xxxviii and xxxix, the fulfilment of the prophecy in the Maccabaean period, and the relation to Rev. xx. 8 and 9. The author thinks the prophecy mainly historically determined. It shows, however, also eschatological features : " Gog from the land of Magog " is in a typological sense the God-opposed world power, as it will reveal itself in the last days. A combination of sound exegetical arguments and speculative ideas. There is a summary in English.

P.A.H.deB.

417

AALEN, S. : *Die Begriffe ' Licht ' und ' Finsternis ' im Alten Testament im Spätjudentum und im Rabbinismus.* (Skrifter utgitt av Det Norske Videnskaps-Akademi i Oslo. II. Hist.-Filos. Klasse. 1951, No. 1). 1951. Pp. 324+26 (Jacob Dybwad, Oslo.)

This learned and detailed investigation was planned as a prolegomenon to an exposition of the concepts of light and darkness in the N.T., but developed into an independent study. As it now stands it falls into three parts, a preliminary section on the O.T., one on the intertestamental literature, and a third on the rabbinic literature and the worship of the Temple and the synagogue. The range of the inquiry is much wider than might at first sight be suggested by the title. From an initial distinction between the literal and derived senses the writer proceeds to a discussion which includes the divisions of time, the calendar, the autumn festival (he denies that it was a New Year festival, and holds that the ' New Year ideology ' emerges only in the rabbinic literature), the festival of *Hanukkah* (which he refuses to connect with a Syrian sun festival), the conception of *kabhodh*, the missionary motive. In this wide-ranging inquiry many questions of contemporary interest are handled with erudition and independence.

G.W.A.

ALBRIGHT, W. F. : *De l'Âge de la Pierre à la Chrétienté : le Monothéisme et son évolution historique,* French Translation by M. Th. Barrelet-Clémentel. 1951. Pp. 304. (Payot, Paris. Price : Fr. 750.)

Professor A. Parrot contributes a brief Introduction to this French translation of Albright's well-known work. All the valuable notes of the English edition have been omitted, and there is no index. Both of these omissions are regrettable. There is added, however, a four-page chronological table which represents the views of Albright in June, 1951. The translation appears to be well done, but this edition is less important than the German (see *Book List,* 1950, p. 47). H.H.R.

ANDERSON, B. W. : *Rediscovering the Bible.* 1951. Pp. xvi+272. (Association Press, New York. Price : $3.50.)

In this book the author essays a brief survey of the religious development recorded in the Bible, and offers answers to such questions as ' In what sense is the Bible the Word of God ?', ' What is the role of the Chosen People in the Bible ?', ' How should we view the miracles of the Old Testament ?', ' What should be our attitude toward the immoralities of the Old Testament ?', ' Is the Christian God truly the God of wrath ?', ' Why do good people suffer ?'—to name only those which deal directly with the Old Testament. The Liberal Protestantism of a generation ago and Fundamentalism are alike rejected, though the author is nearer to the former than to the latter. He is less definite on the positive side than the negative, and gives the impression that whether the Mosaic tradition contains *Geschichte* or not, its importance as *Heilsgeschichte* is unaffected. Nor does he seem to have discovered the significance of sacrifice in the Bible. It is scarcely referred to and does not figure at all in the Index. While the reviewer would often go farther than the author, much is useful in this book. It is dedicated to Professor James Muilenburg, than whom no more inspiring teacher of the Old Testament is to be found across the Atlantic. H.H.R.

ATKINSON, B. F. C. : *The Christian's Use of the Old Testament.* 1952. Pp. 130. (Inter-Varsity Fellowship, London. Price : 6s. 0d.)

This is an excellent little treatment of the enduring value of the Old Testament for the Christian, finding in the basic teachings of the Old Testament the foundation for the Gospel, in its devotional content food for the spirit, in its anticipations the witness to Christ. The author's doctrine of inspiration leads him into some inconsistency, however. He holds that the Mosaic law ' set God's perfect standard before men ' (p. 75), but since we read of Christ's ' removal of certain other ethical imperfections which obtained under the law ' (p. 71), it would appear not to have been perfect. Moreover, since the Bible is said to be unmarred by human fallibility (p. 11), the responsibility for the imperfections is placed squarely on God. The reviewer's more conservative theology is shocked by this. The reviewer regrets also that the author, while disclaiming the desire to cast any reflection on anyone, should grossly misrepresent others by saying that it is prejudice against the supernatural which leads to the placing of Daniel in the second century B.C. (p. 16). Yet these blemishes should not be seen out of proportion in a useful book. H.H.R.

AUVRAY, P., and others : *L'Ancien Testament et les Chrétiens.* 1951. pp. 240. (Les Editions du Cerf, Paris. Price : Fr. 480.)

Thirteen Catholic authors contribute chapters to this collective work, which should be widely useful. Amongst the chapters may be noted those of Auvray, on the technical equipment of the exegete, enabling him to understand the text-critical problems, and the literary and historical context—the latter in the setting of the wider history of the ancient Near East ; of Gelin, on how the people of Israel read the Old Testament ; of Cerfaux, on the exegesis of the Old Testament in the New ; and of Dubarle on the Christian reading of the Old Testament. There are also chapters on Patristic and Mediaeval interpretation, on typology, besides some others. The writers are well-known scholars, and they have produced a valuable little survey. H.H.R.

Bibelsyn. En indførelse i aktuelle bibelproblemer. 1951. Pp. 288. (Nyt Nordisk Forlag. Arnold Busck, Copenhagen. Price : Danish Kr. 14.85.)

In some ways this collection of essays on the authority, unity and interpretation of the Bible invites comparison with the Swedish volume, *En bok om bibeln* (see *Book List*, 1948, p. 4).

It differs markedly from it, however, both in plan and in intention. It is in no sense a synthesis, but aims at expressing clearly and without compromise the divergent attitudes to Scripture which exist in Danish Church life and theology to-day. Exponents of the varying tendencies have contributed articles on each of the main themes. These are : the Word of God and Scripture (Th. Krøgholt, N. H. Søe) ; the historical approach to the Bible (H. Mosbech, S. A. Nielsen, K. Diderichsen) ; Jesus and Paul (T. Wilhjelm, L. Brøndum) ; the Fourth Gospel (K. Olesen-Larsen, R. Prenter) ; the O.T. and the New Covenant (A. Møller, E. Thestrup Pedersen, A. Bentzen) ; Bible, tradition, confession (H. Simonsen, R. Prenter) : the authority and use of the Bible (J. Jensen, C. Bartholdy, J. W. Jacobsen). Of the contributions relating to the O.T. those by E. T. Pedersen and A. Bentzen are the most useful, the former discussing the witness of the O.T. to Christ, the latter dealing with the relation between the two Testaments on lines similar to those suggested in *Messias— Moses redivivus—Menschensohn.* G.W.A.

BOTTERWECK, G. J. : ' *Gott erkennen* ' *im Sprachgebrauch des Alten Testaments* (Bonner Biblische Beiträge 2). 1951. Pp. 104. (Peter Hanstein Verlag G.m.b.H., Bonn. Price : DM. 9.50.)

The reviewer has long felt the desirability of a careful examination of the ideas embraced by such expressions as ' to know God' and ' the knowledge of God' in the Old Testament; and here we have a welcome attempt to go beyond what has been offered hitherto. The author finds its theological foundation in Yahweh's having taken knowledge of Israel as the people who were to be the recipients of His self-revelation, and as a result he discusses the revelation of the divine name, the modes of revelation (quite the weakest part of the book), and the ideas of ' election ' and ' covenant '. This is followed by a survey of the implications of such knowledge of God for morality and religious experience, some attention also being paid to the fulfilment of Yahweh's purposes in the Messianic Age. The work is carefully documented, and the author proceeds along moderately critical lines ; but the treatment as a whole is too summary and too neglectful of the historical factors to be anything like satisfactory. Within its limits, however, it is an attractive piece of work with promise of better things to come ; and it may be cordially recommended as a useful guide to further reading. A.R.J.

BRANDON, S. G. F. : *Time and Mankind : An Historical and Philosophical Study of Mankind's Attitude to the Phenomena of Change.* 1951. Pp. xiv+228. (Hutchinson, London. Price : 18s. 0d.)

The Publisher's ' blurb ' states that this work ' undertakes to survey the attitude of men to Time's enigma from the prehistoric era, through the great cultures of the Ancient Near East, to the formation of the traditional Western view of life. As a result of this survey three distinctive patterns of reaction emerge : a primitive belief that Time's effacing stream can be controlled by ritual magic ; a philosophy of *carpe diem ;* a faith that Time is the field in which God's providence is revealed '. More than a quarter of the book is devoted to the Israelite and Jewish thought, which provides the third of these attitudes. The author is widely learned, and there are abundant notes—gathered at the ends of the chapters—with references to a vast literature, while a considerable bibliography is printed at the end. There are chapters on prehistoric man, on Egypt, Mesopotamia, Greece and Rome, as well as on the Christian view.   H.H.R.

BROWNE, L. E. : *The Messianic Hope in its Historical Setting.* 1951. Pp. 54. (S.P.C.K., London. Price : 3s. 0d.)

These lectures make a good case for holding that in II Isa. the Servant of Yahweh in the Songs is Israel, the nation. Possibly the author might have fulfilled his task more completely had he applied his findings, more specially than he attempts to do, to the exposition of ch. liii. Dr. Browne is confident that in Jer. xxxi. 35-40 " the reference is to the eclipse of the sun " (May, 585 B.C.) that was foretold by Thales and sure that " the correct translation " of Isa. ix. 6 is "A wonderful counsellor, a veritable hero, who will have a long and peaceful life." The conclusion however towards which Professor Browne works is that in Isa. lv. 3-5 we have " the identification of the messianic king with the nation of Israel and also with the Servant of the Lord." These verses are, he says, a key passage, the significance of which has hitherto been missed. But it should have been noticed that Volz also regards these verses as a key passage leading to quite a different interpretation of II Isaiah's thought, in particular to its non-messianic character. Another deduction is based by Dr. Browne on Test. Lev. xviii. 2-9 where quite legitimately he interprets the words " With the Father's voice as from Abraham to Isaac " as referring to Abraham having said in scripture : " God will provide himself with a lamb for a burnt offering, my son ." The author concludes from this, that if God, as the text implies, " is to speak these same words to his son, the Messiah, it must refer to the sacrificial death of the Messiah, linking up again the ideas of the Messiah and the Suffering Servant." But this is surely illogical, for if the lamb prepared for a burnt offering was a substitute for Isaac (regarded as representing the Messiah) then we have what we would expect to find at the date of Test. Lev., say 200 B.C., namely, that the idea of a Suffering Messiah was not yet entertained by Judaism.   O.S.R.

COATES, J. R. : *The Saving History : a Study of Old Testament Crises in relation to modern problems.* 1951. Pp. 96. (Lutterworth Press, London. Price : 3s. 6d.)

A study of the critical moments of Old Testament history, brief but marked by freshness of treatment and real originality. The thesis of the book is that the Old Testament exhibits the catastrophes of Israel's history as creative crises. Each crisis in the history of Israel proceeds through four stages—Problem, Prophet, Revolution, Law. Particular points of interest are the ingenious interpretation of Isaiah vii. 10-16, the view of the prophet as miracle and as a forerunner of Christ, the argument in favour of regarding *Daniel* as part of the wisdom literature and as propaganda for Hebrew humanism as opposed to Greek, and *Job* as a gospel for those under the spell of Greek humanism and as a book designed to answer practical and not speculative questions. N.W.P.

COATES, J. R. (trans.) : *Bible Key Words.* III. *Sin,* by G. Quell, G. Bertram, G. Stählin and W. Grundmann. 1951. Pp. 96. (Price : 7s. 6d.) IV. *Righteousness,* by G. Quell and G. Schrenk. 1951. Pp. 82. (Price : 7s. 6d.) (Both translations from *Theologisches Wörterbuch zum Neuen Testament,* edited by G. Kittel.) (Adam & Charles Black, London.)

For the two previous volumes in this series, see *Book List,* 1951, p. 53. The compass of the volume on *Sin* is indicated by the titles of the various short articles included, each written by one or more of the authors. The articles are entitled : Sin in the Old Testament, including a linguistic study in Hebrew and LXX ; The Doctrine of Sin in the Septugint ; the Jewish Idea of Sin ; Greek Usage in the New Testament ; Sin and Guilt in Classical Greek and Hellenism ; Sin in the New Testament. The volume on *Righteousness* deals first with Justice in the Old Testament, and then in turn with the Greek idea of Justice, the word *dikaios,* the word *dikaiosune,* ending with a discussion of Justification. In both volumes (the originals are dated 1933 and 1935 respectively) there is more emphasis on Greek than on Hebrew. The translator has added notes to the essays and items to the bibliographies to bring the articles up to date. N.H.S.

COPPENS, J. : *Nouvelles Réflexions sur les divers Sens des Saintes Écritures.* (Analecta Lovaniensia Biblica et Orientalia, Ser. II, Fasc. 27.) 1952. Pp. 20. (Publications Universitaires de Louvain, and Desclée de Brouwer, Bruges and Paris. Price : Fr. 20.)

This is a defence of the views of Professor Coppens on Inspiration, defending the view that beyond the literal sense which was present to the mind of the writer there was often a ' sens plénier ', intended by the Holy Spirit but hidden from the writer. H.H.R.

COPPENS, J. : *Un nouvel essai d'Herméneutique biblique.* (Analecta Lovaniensia Biblica et Orientalia, Ser. II, Fasc. 25.) 1951. Pp. 10. (Publications Universitaires de Louvain, and Desclée de Brouwer, Bruges and Paris. Price : Fr. 10.)

This is an extended review of the work of Schildenberger, noticed elsewhere in this issue of the Book List. While Professor Coppens finds much to welcome in the volume he offers criticism at a number of points. H.H.R.

COPPENS, J. : *Le Messianisme israélite selon Alfred Loisy*. (Analecta Lovaniensia Biblica et Orientalia, Ser. II, Fasc. 26.) 1951. Pp. 20. (Publications Universitaires de Louvain and Desclée de Brouwer, Bruges and Paris. Price : Fr. 20.)

This is a brief study of the development of the view of Loisy as shown in early articles and in the successive editions of his *Religion d'Israël*, underlining the decline of his penetration from the standard of his earlier work.   H.H.R.

CROUSE, M. ELIZABETH : *Les Grands Thèmes de la Bible*, with Introduction by J. de la Tardoire. 1951. Pp. xxx+446. (Editions Fischbacher, Paris. Price : 13s. 0d.)

Miss Mary-Elizabeth Crouse, of Philadelphia, U.S.A., who, in 1940, published *The Making of the Book : The Story behind the Bible* (Heffer, Cambridge) here gives an interesting, nontechnical survey of Bible history and religion in which she combines a basically allegorical approach with the generally accepted Higher Critical positions. The framework of the book and its line of development is musical : the Bible is a grand oratorio, with a variety of component parts—preludes, hymns, recitals and such items.   B.J.R.

EICHRODT, W. : *Gottes Ruf im Alten Testament. Die alttestamentliche Botschaft im Lichte des Evangeliums*. 1951. Pp. 128. (Zwingli-Verlag, Zürich. Price : Fr. 5.70.)

Contains five semi-popular expositions of O.T. passages : Psalm xxiv (*Offenbarung*), Genesis xii. 1-3 (*Erwählung*), Isaiah vii. 1-17 (*Glaube*), Jeremiah vii. 1-15 (*Dienst*), Psalm xcvi (*Vollendung*). Each passage is given in the Luther version, with such modifications as are essential. The exegesis is sound and penetrating ; and the application of the biblical message to modern conditions is most effective. In contemporary discussion about the relation of the O.T. and the N.T. few things are more desirable than that principles of interpretation should be exemplified by the treatment of specific passages. Eichrodt has rendered a real service by the publication of these studies in which he writes both as O.T. scholar and as Christian expositor.   G.W.A.

EICHRODT, W. : *Man in the Old Testament* (Studies in Biblical Theology). 1951. Pp. 84. (S.C.M. Press, London. Price : 6s. 0d.)

A most welcome translation of the monograph entitled *Das Menschenverständnis im Alten Testament*, reviewed in the 1946 *Book List* (p. 43) which makes available Dr. Eichrodt's rich and penetrating study to a much wider circle of readers. Exceptionally valuable are its exposition of the fundamental character of Hebrew law and Hebrew institutions. Connected as it is with the sense of absolute obligation, its analysis of the Hebrew view of history and time as contrasted with the Greek tendency to regard human life as capable of being moulded like a work of art, and its profound grappling with the consequences of man's creatureliness which excludes self-deification and is determined by a Thou which makes an absolute claim. Of great theological value is the concluding study of what Dr. Eichrodt calls " the antinomies of the unconditional ought " which urge man forward to his sole and final hope in the forgiving and re-creating mercy of God. An essay which only a master could have written.   N.W.P.

ELLISON, H. L. : *Men Spake from God : Studies in the Hebrew Prophets.* 1952. Pp. 160. (Paternoster Press, London. Price : 10s. 6d.)

This is a conservative introduction to the prophetic books of the Old Testament, with emphasis on the teaching of the prophets. Joel and Jonah are placed first amongst the prophets, though without assurance, and the unity of most of the books is maintained. It is suggested that Deutero-Isaiah, whose exilic background is recognized, was treasured by the disciples of the prophet until the exilic age. The book of Daniel is held to have been worked over in the Maccabaean age. Zech. ix-xi, Zech. xii-xiv, and Malachi are held to be anonymous sections added at the end of the Book of the Twelve. On a number of questions the author has a more open mind than many conservative writers, and his book is one of the best of its kind. Curiously enough, though many critical authors are referred to, Robinson's *Prophecy and the Prophets* is nowhere mentioned.
H.H.R.

GALLING, K. : *Die Krise der Aufklärung in Israel.* 1951. Pp. 24. (Gutenberg, Mainz.)

In this work, his Rektoratsrede at Mainz, Professor Galling would see in Jerusalem in the time of Solomon a counterpart to the wisdom-schools of Egypt. He emphasizes elements in the Hebrew Wisdom Literature which reflect the element of natural history in the recently published Onomasticon of Amenope. Eventually he studies Qoheleth, which he places in the 3rd century. The writer of this book is a bold critic of the current wisdom of the schools, and the apparently redeeming clauses in the final chapter are later additions from two hands of the orthodox schools.   J.G.

HESSE, F. : *Die Fürbitte im Alten Testament.* 1951. Pp. 150. (University of Erlangen Dissertation.)

An inaugural dissertation of the University of Erlangen, this little book presents a thorough and valuable study of the practice of intercession in Israel and of the underlying implications. It supplements Johannson's *Parakletoi* and offers criticism of de Boer's monograph which appeared as vol. III of *Oudtestamentische Studiën.* It argues that de Boer has associated intercession too exclusively with the priesthood and the cult, whereas the original intercessor was the man of God or the prophet and there was a juridical side to his activity. Hesse thinks that intercession comes at the intersection of the cultic and the juridical. He further criticises de Boer for failure to recognize the development in the Old Testament away from religious magic. Hesse's work deals with aspects of intercession excluded from Johannson's work by its scope but limits itself in time to the pre-Christian period. The book is divided into two main sections—Parts I and II Historical, and Parts IV to VI Systematic, with a short section, Part III on terminology, in the middle. Of particular interest, to select just a few points from the wealth of interesting observations, are the distinctions drawn between the removal by intercession of hindrances to the movement of " Heilsgeschichte " and attempts to alter the will of God, the discussion of the reason why certain great prophets ceased to intercede or were forbidden to do so, the explanation given of Jeremiah's prayers for vengeance on his enemies, the recognition of the union of atonement and intercession in the person of the servant (Isaiah 53), the identification of blessing as a form of intercession and the distinction drawn between the prayer for blessing which might be made by anyone and prayer on behalf of the guilty.   N.W.P.

KIDNER, F. D. : *Sacrifice in the Old Testament*. 1952. Pp. 28. (Tyndale Press, London. Price : 2s. 0d.)

In this lecture we have a brief examination of the burnt-offering, the meal-offering, the peace-offering, the sin-offering and the guilt-offering, with an introduction in which it is argued that Israel's sacrificial system was of divine origin and that all the Pentateuchal provisions for sacrifice were communicated to Moses. It is recognized that Israelite sacrifice comes out of a wider background of sacrifice, but it is rightly pointed out that this does not weaken its claim to divine sanction. The prophetic attitude to sacrifice is not considered, but there is a concluding section on the spiritual implications of acceptable sacrifice.   H.H.R.

KRAUS, H. J. : *Die Königsherrschaft Gottes im Alten Testament* (Beiträge zur historischen Theologie 13.) 1951. Pp. xii+156. (Mohr, Tübingen. Price : DM. 15.)

In this well-written monograph the author offers another attempt to solve the problem of the so-called " Enthronement Psalms," specifically Pss. xlvii, xciii, xcvi-xcix. He can discover nothing to justify the theory of an Enthronement Festival in pre-exilic Israel along the line advocated by Mowinckel ; but he finds evidence for a celebration of Yahweh's choice of Zion and the foundation of the Davidic dynasty which is to be associated with the first day of the Feast of Tabernacles in its pre-exilic form. Pss. ii, xxivB, lxxii, lxxxiv, and cxxxii are thought to belong to this celebration, while Pss. lxxviii, lxxxvii, lxxxix and cxxii are cited as offering additional evidence of its existence. During the Exile the faded Messianic hope which had its roots in this festival was revived by Deutero-Isaiah, who, under Babylonian influence, revised it in terms of Yahweh's own Kingship. As a result this conception found a place in the New Year Festival of the post-exilic period, the Enthronement Psalms being hymns which were composed specially for this setting in terms of what may be described as "realized eschatology". In the reviewer's opinion the author shows an uncritical dependence upon Gunkel's theory of the development of the different types of psalm, and, what is worse, pays insufficient attention to the important work by N. H. Snaith, *The Jewish New Year Festival* (*Book List*, 1948, pp. 50 f.). Cf., for example, pp. 118 f. with Snaith, *op. cit.*, pp. 177 ff. On the other hand, he shows an admirable desire to do justice to the distinctive features in Israelite thought within the general culture pattern of the ancient Near East; and, unacceptable as the main thesis may be, the work is to be welcomed as a valuable contribution to current discussion.   A.R.J.

LOCKHART, C. : *Principles of Interpretation*. 2nd ed., reprinted, 1950. Pp. 260. (Central Seminary Press, Kansas City, Kansas. Price : $1.50.)

This little book on the principles of exegesis of the Bible was first published in 1901, and the revised edition appeared thirty-five years ago. Nevertheless it is still of value, and if all interpreters of Scripture would observe its fifteen axioms and fifty-one rules, it would be a distinct gain. A few chosen at random are : Before interpreting a passage, investigate its genuineness ; Before interpreting a passage, determine whether it is literal or figurative ; Before interpreting a passage, determine whether it is prose or poetry ; The simplest and most natural interpretation of a passage must be preferred ; The meaning of a rare word, not decided by usage, should be sought first in the etymology, then in early versions, and lastly in kindred tongues. In each case there is first a discussion of examples and then the formulation of the rule. The whole is simple and intelligible to the general reader, who would, however, scarcely be able to apply some of the rules himself.   H.H.R.

ÖSTBORN, G. : *Cult and Canon, a study in the Canonisation of the Old Testament*. (Uppsala Universitets Årsskrift 1950 : 10). Pp. 130. (Lundequistska Bokhandeln, Uppsala and O. Harrassowitz, Leipzig. Price : Kr. 6.00.)

This study follows on from the author's earlier work, *Tōrā in the Old Testament* (*Book List*, 1946, p. 28). The sub-title indicates the scope and intention of the book. The theme is that the various books of the Old Testament Canon were not chosen because of their inspirational value, but because they constituted the recitations at the divine services. The author seeks to trace throughout an alternation of judgement and salvation, misfortune and good fortune. For instance, Exodus-Deuteronomy is an extension of the cult-story of Exod. i-xv (cf. Pedersen). It is all the story of divine activity. This is true of neighbouring cults. Behind the Israelite—Yahwistic Canon, there is a Canaanite Canon, the fundamental difference being that in the Old Testament, it is Yahweh Himself, and none other, Who is the Saviour.   N.H.S.

PHYTHIAN-ADAMS, W. J. : *With Unveiled Face*. 1952. Pp. vi+72. (Tufton Press, London. Price : 3s. 6d.)

The book is written in the belief that the Bible is the record of a living faith, inspired by God and finding its fulfilment in Jesus Christ. Various themes are traced through the Old Testament and into the New Testament in accordance with this principle—Redemption, Covenant, Inheritance, Son of David, the Angel of the Presence, Servant of God, the Sanctuary, with a short additional note on the Nature of Sin. The sub-title is ' a short course of Bible Study for Christians '. The description is exactly right, and the book is especially valuable for Christian study groups.   N.H.S.

VAN DER PLOEG, J. : *Enkele Beschouwingen over de Theologische Aard en de Methoden der Wetenschap van het Oude Testament.* 1951. Pp. 16. (Dekker & van de Vegt, Nijmegen. Price : Fl. 1.)

This is the inaugural lecture given by van der Ploeg on 12th October, 1951, when he took possession of the chair of Old Testament and Hebrew in the Catholic University of Nijmegen, in succession to B. J. Alfrink, now coadjutor-bishop of Utrecht. The title " Some remarks on the nature of theology and the methods of the science of the Old Testament " promises a far-ranging discussion and, within the limits of eleven pages devoted to the lecture as such, this is provided. He has many wholesome and useful things to say about the rightful place of Biblical study in a theological course and lays emphasis (as does Joüon in his *Grammaire de l'hébreu biblique*) on the philological requirements of Old Testament study. "As regards philology, not only a knowledge of the Biblical languages is requisite. He who would be a good Hebraist, even in the restricted sense of one knowing the Hebrew of the Old Testament, must possess at least working knowledge of the other Semitic languages and of their structure." There are also some good remarks on exegetical method, illustrated by reference to the Dead Sea Scrolls, and on the present state of Old Testament theological study.   J.M.T.B.

VON RAD, G. : *Der Heilige Krieg im Alten Israel* (Abhandlungen zur Theologie des Alten und Neuen Testaments, Nr. 20). 1951. Pp. 84. (Zwingli-Verlag, Zürich. Price : Fr. 7.50.)

This monograph is an expansion of the paper which Professor von Rad read before the Society for Old Testament Study at its Summer Meeting in Bangor in 1949. The author thinks that it is possible to distinguish in the early narratives of the Old Testament a conception of warfare, carried out as a sacral activity in complete dependence upon Yahweh, which specially deserves the designation " Holy War " ; and he seeks to show that this particular conception was relegated to the background with the establishment of the monarchy and only came to the fore again with the appearance of the Deuteronomic School. Professor von Rad never fails to write in an interesting way ; and in view of the circumstances attending the publication of this work and particularly the fact that he has graciously dedicated the monograph to the Society, it would be pleasant to be able to add that he has established his case. However, to one reader at least the author appears to work with too narrow a conception of the sacral aspect of warfare, too rigid a system of classification in dealing with the different types of narrative, and too eclectic a use of the Old Testament literature in general to be at all convincing ; and it is surely an exaggeration to find the origin of Israel's faith in the eager prosecution of such warfare at the time of the settlement.　　　A.R.J.

RICHARDSON, A. and SCHWEITZER, W. (ed. by) : *Biblical Authority for To-day*. 1951. Pp. 348. (S.C.M. Press, London. Price : 18s. 0d.)

This magnificent volume contains a World Council of Churches Symposium on ' The Biblical Authority for the Churches' Social and Political message to-day '. It is divided into four parts. The first part discusses the authority of the Bible from the point of view of seven distinct denominations. In spite of the differences revealed the remarkable fact which emerges is the degree of agreement. The second part deals with biblical theology and ethics to-day, and consists of a survey of the world position by Dr. Wolfgang Schweitzer. Parts III and IV are perhaps the ones which offer most of interest to the Old Testament specialist. In Part III the principles of interpretation are discussed by Dodd, Florovsky, Marsh, Muilenburg and Wright. Dodd's contribution is marked by his usual clarity. Perhaps the most valuable are the last two, especially Wright's discussions of specific illustrations of the Bible's message for the social life on pp. 230 ff. At the end of this section are given the Guiding Principles for the Interpretation of the Bible, as accepted by the Ecumenical study conference at Wadham College, Oxford, 1949 and published in *Interpretation*, October, 1949. Part IV contains some specific applications of these principles. Particular attention should be called to the brilliant essay by Eichrodt on the question of property which likewise appeared in the number of *Interpretation* referred to above.　　　N.W.P.

ROWLEY, H. H. : *Moses and the Decalogue*. (Reprinted from *The Bulletin of the John Rylands Library*, vol. xxxiv, No. 1, Sept., 1951). 1951. Pp. 38. (The John Rylands Library and the Manchester University Press. Price : 2s. 6d.)

An impressive argument is here presented for the Mosaic origin of the Decalogue in an earlier and shorter'form than those found in Exodus xx and Deuteronomy v. Professor Rowley puts forward a strong case for the attractive hypothesis that the Ritual Decalogue of Exodus xxxiv was originally a Kenite Yahwistic code brought into Palestine by the southern tribes, whereas the Ethical Decalogue was associated with the events of the Exodus and the prophetic personality of Moses. He argues cogently against the objections to the

Mosaic origin of the Ethical Decalogue based on (a) the prohibition of image worship, (b) the supposed later origin of the Sabbath Law, (c) the absence of any reference to circumcision. Both the discussion of the relevant problems and the bibliographical material provided in the notes make this study indispensable for future work on the subject.

G.W.A.

ROWLEY, H. H. : *The Meaning of Sacrifice in the Old Testament.* 1950. Pp. 38. (Reprinted from the *Bulletin of the John Rylands Library*, vol. 33, No. 1, September, 1950. Manchester University Press and The John Rylands Library, Manchester. Price : 2s. 6d.)

The author does not admit the thesis that Hebrew sacrifice was wholly Canaanite in origin, though this is true of not a little of it. No simple idea will suffice to explain all the sacrificial ritual : some sacrifices were gifts, some communion, some propitiatory. In popular thought, sacrifices were supposed to be effective in themselves, but the prophets were always fighting this. They were potent only when accompanied by genuine penitence. The monograph concludes with a discussion of the ' sacrifice ' of the Suffering Servant. The term ' to justify ' means ' to have become righteous ', separated from their sins and cleansed in their inner nature. N.H.S.

RYDER SMITH, C. : *The Bible Doctrine of Man.* 1951. Pp. xiv + 274. (The Epworth Press, London. Price : 18s. 6d.)

A great amount of most praiseworthy industry has gone into the making of this book by a veteran scholar who has written numerous books on the teaching of the Bible. It is divided into three parts which deal with the Old Testament in Hebrew, the Old Testament in its Greek form including the Apocrypha and the New Testament. Each part contains two chapters entitled ' What a man is ' and ' What a man ought to be '. The book offers a detailed semantic study of the meaning of the principal terms used in connection with the Biblical anthropology. Parts I and II are of particular interest to Old Testament scholars. It is a little unfortunate that the fact that the author had already published a volume entitled *The Bible Doctrine of Society* and has another in preparation with the title *The Bible Doctrine of Grace* has led him in the present volume to concentrate on Man as an individual. The section of the book on the LXX is a little overweighted with detail and makes heavy reading. The complete absence of notes and references to literature does not mean that the author is not fully aware of other work in this important field. In particular he agrees with recent criticism of Wheeler Robinson's theory of ' Diffused personality '. Of particular interest is Dr. Ryder Smith's discussion of the *imago dei* as being more broadly based than is often supposed, of the emergence among Greek-speaking Jews of a new set of psychological terms and of the ideas of conscience and will. A valuable section deals with the concept of Wisdom in the Apocryphal books of *Sirach* and *Wisdom* and the relation between Wisdom and the Spirit of God. It is made abundantly clear that the almost universal Jewish belief was that man was free to do what he knew he ought to do. ' Ought implies can '. This is not contradicted even by the doctrine of the *Jetser Hara'* expounded in *Second Esdras*.   N.W.P.

SCHILDENBERGER, J. : *Vom Geheimnis des Gotteswortes. Einführung in das Verständnis der Heiligen Schrift.* 1950. Pp. 532. (F. H. Kerle Verlag, Heidelberg. Price : DM. 15.80.)

This voluminous book contains an introduction to the interpretation of the Bible from the Roman Catholic point of view. There is much here that even those who do not share the whole dogmatic standpoint of the writer will find helpful and instructive. What is said about the inerrancy of Scripture will be felt by many to be too a priori in character, but in chapter 5, on the Scriptural mode of expression, especially in the section entitled ' One-sided, generalising and exaggerated mode of speaking ' there is much of interest. It is intriguing to see, for example, the way of handling the literary problems of a book like Joshua. Frank acknowledgment is made of the valuable contributions of non-Catholic scholars to *Gattungsforschung*, but it is claimed—and with this many Protestant scholars would agree—that the further step of determining the religious and distinctively Israelite use to which the literary forms have been put, is still more important. There is the admission too, though it is not underlined, that both the Mosaic Law and the authentic oracles of the prophets may have been supplemented later by those writing in the spirit of Moses, Isaiah, etc.

A very large part of the book is given to the discussion of the literary forms of Scripture and this is done under the headings prophecy, law, history (including the Gospels), descriptions of Nature, lyric (especially the Psalms), Wisdom writing and the apostolic epistles.

Finally the various kinds of spiritual interpretation are expounded, much weight being laid on the interpretations of the Fathers and the Doctors of the Church.

It is good to have this convenient means of ascertaining the contemporary Roman Catholic attitude to a whole range of problems which concern us all.   N.W.P.

TASKER, R. V. G. : *The Biblical Doctrine of the Wrath of God.* 1951. Pp. 48. (The Tyndale Press, London. Price : 2s. 0d.)

This monograph represents the Tyndale Lecture in Biblical Theology for 1951. It is essentially an essay in New Testament Theology—able but perhaps one-sided—its interest for Old Testament scholars being lessened by the fact that, whether legitimately or not, the Old Testament is scarcely allowed to speak for itself. To get a stereoscopic view of the Old Testament one should probably look at it through the eyes of more witnesses than St. Paul and one or two others. The author seems singularly insensitive to the difficulties which beset his interpretation.   N.W.P.

VELLAS, B. M. : *Apanthisma rhētōn tēs Palaias Diathēkēs*. 1951. Pp. 250. (Athens.)

This is a small anthology of texts in the Greek Old Testament, arranged under key words. Passages akin in thought are gathered together under a single word, so that it is not quite the concordance principle which is here used. It is designed primarily for preachers though it will have other uses. It draws on the Apocrypha as well as on the books of the Hebrew Canon.   H.H.R.

VISCHER, W. : *Les Premiers Prophètes*, translated by Pierre Klossowski. 1951. Pp. 618. (Delachaux et Niestlé, Neuchatel and Paris. Price : 16s. 0d.)

This is the French translation of the second volume of Vischer's *Das Christuszeugnis des Alten Testaments* (1942). The German edition of this volume on Joshua-Kings was noticed in the 1946 *Book List*, p. 53. For notices of the French and English editions of the preceding volume, see the 1950 *Book List*, p. 69. The author maintains that the Old Testament as a whole is a witness to Christ, but he ignores critical questions, and reads the New Testament into the Old in a way which will not commend itself to many.   N.H.S.

ZIELHUIS, L. : *Het offermaal in het heidendom en in de Heilige Schrift*. 1951. Pp. 200. (T. Wever, Franeker. Price : 10s. 6d.)

The volume is in two parts, the first dealing with the sacrificial meal of heathenism, and the second with the sacrificial meal of Scripture. There is a nine-page summary in English. The discussion in the first part is governed by the author's assumption of an original monotheism combined with an original state of innocence. In the second part the author neglects altogether the modern critical study of the Bible. The 'Avondmaal' (Lord's Supper) is the climax of sacramental eating, and in it Christ restored this gift to man, as salvation which he could have won before the Fall by eating of the tree of life.   N.H.S.

THE LIFE AND THOUGHT OF THE NEIGHBOURING PEOPLE

CASSUTO, U. M. D. : *The goddess Anath, Canaanite Epics of the Patriarchal Age*. Texts, Hebrew Translation, Commentary and Introduction. 1951. Pp. 110 with plates. (The Bialik Institute, Jerusalem. Price : I₤ 2.400.)

Prof. Cassuto died on 18th December, 1951, in Jerusalem. A few months before his death, he bequeathed us his work on *The goddess Anath*. It was beautifully produced by the Bialik Institute (under the aegis of the Council for the Hebrew language). Its aim is to give the Israeli reader of to-day access to a specimen of ancient Canaanite epics, in transcription and with translation and commentary in modern Hebrew. Besides, the author offers here a condensation and completion of his

431

studies during many years, on the Ugaritic literature and its relation to the Old Testament. The first chapter of the Introduction gives a survey of the Ras Shamra texts, especially of those which were found or published only after H. L. Ginsberg's edition *Kitvê Ugarit*, 1935. A splendid second chapter, dealing with the literary relations between the Ras Shamra texts and the Old Testament, does not emphasize casual resemblances, but systematically analyses all phenomena of language and style which are common to both literatures. The third chapter describes the gods who figure in the epic of Baal and attempts a new reconstruction of the epic of Anath. Then follows the translation of this epic together with a commentary, in a Hebrew of remarkable quality. The author here goes his own way and his explanations often seem more plausible than those of Virolleaud, Aistleitner, and Gordon.   I.L.S.

EISSFELDT, O. : *El im ugaritischem Pantheon.* 1951. Pp. 84 and one plate. (Akademie-Verlag, Berlin. Price : DM. 9.00.)

This small book contains an exhaustive account of *'el* as a common noun and as the name of the supreme god of the pantheon at Ugarit. It is a technical monograph, full of useful suggestions for students of the Ugaritic texts and illustrated by references to other Phoenician and Aramaic texts. A stele carved with the figure of El serves as frontispiece.   G.R.D.

FISH, T. : *Some aspects of kingship in the Sumerian city and kingdom of Ur.* (Reprinted from *Bulletin of the John Rylands Library*, XXXIV.) 1951. Pp. 10. (Manchester University Press, and the John Rylands Library, Manchester. Price : 1s. 0d.)

This small offprint of about half a dozen pages is a useful corrective to the views usually expressed about ' divine kingship ' in the ancient East. The author points out clearly that, although the kings of Ur performed religious acts and were indeed before all else priests, they were in no sense deified ; and this conclusion refutes the assertion that ' the apotheosis of kings clearly replaced in importance the worship of the great gods for three centuries under the kings of Ur and Isin ' (Engnell's *Divine Kingship*, p. 30), at any rate in reference to one of these two states.   G.R.D.

FRANKFORT, H. : *The Birth of Civilization in the Near East.* 1951. Pp. 116. (Williams & Norgate, London. Price : 16s. 0d.)

Professor Frankfort's book contains four chapters which are expansions of lectures which he gave at Indiana University, Bloomington. The first is an introductory essay on the Study of Ancient Civilizations, which is followed by a survey of the Prehistory of the Ancient Near East. His third and fourth chapters are on early Mesopotamian and Egyptian civilization respectively. The author considers the birth of civilization in the Near East from the standpoint of the social and political changes which took place in Mesopotamia and Egypt, an aspect which hitherto has received little attention. In so doing he has made an important contribution to our appreciation of this remote period of Near Eastern history. In an appendix he shows that the two great centres of civilization were in contact with one another towards the end of the fourth millennium, the formative period, and that Egypt was influenced by Mesopotamia. T.W.T.

KAPELRUD, A. S. : *Baal in the Ras Shamra Texts.* 1952. Pp. 156. (Gad, Copenhagen. Price : Kr. 15.00.)

In this valuable study of all the material relating to Baal in the Ras Shamra texts, Dr. Kapelrud published the fruits of studies which were in part carried on in Yale under the guidance of Professors Goetze and Obermann. The author first studies the character of the Baal texts, and concludes that they are ritual texts, finding significance, in the fact that they were found in a temple. He shows that Baal is referred to under other names and that while he is the son of Dagan he is also presented as the son of Il, though not directly called by this name. In this the author finds reflected the probable fact that Baal was a younger god who ousted Il from his place in the pantheon. The family relationships of Baal and his character and task are carefully studied. Fundamentally Dr. Kapelrud finds that the texts reflect cultic acts which they accompanied, whereby the renewal of fertility was annually brought about. Yet at the same time he finds reflected in them the ousting of Il by Baal which can scarcely be thought to have been annually renewed. The work thus offers an important contribution to the debate on the character of these texts. H.H.R.

ROBINSON, T. H. : *A Short Comparative History of Religions.* 2nd ed., 1951. Pp. xii+184. (Duckworth, London. Price : 7s. 6d.)

The first edition of this little book was issued by the Oxford Press twenty-five years ago ; the new edition appears with some revision in Duckworth's Theology Series. The revision will be found particularly in the sections on the lower levels of religion. As is natural in the work of a Semitic scholar the weight of attention is given to the Semitic religions, Judaism, Islam and Christianity. To these religions one third of the book is devoted, whereas Chinese religion gets but three pages. The whole forms a very useful introduction to the subject, and a short Bibliography offers the reader suggestions for further reading. H.H.R.

ROWLEY, H. H. : *Submission in Suffering and other Essays on Eastern Thought.* 1951. Pp. x+170. (University of Wales Press, Cardiff. Price : 12s. 6d.)

This is a remarkable book which only the author could have written. It consists of three studies. In the first Prof. Rowley shows how the Hebrew in both Testaments viewed the problem of the sufferings of the innocent and he carries his researches into the field of the Chinese, Indian, and Arabian religions. The second and third essays deal with the Chinese Sages and the Golden Rule, and the Chinese philosopher Mo Ti. These second and third studies will take most readers into unknown country where they will find much food for thought. The ethical teaching of Confucius often seems to anticipate Jewish and Christian teaching ; but the motive of the love of God is missing, and noble forbearance and active kindness spring from the sage's conviction of his innate superiority. There is something extraordinarily modern in much of the teaching of Mo Ti who seems to have lived *c.* 400 B.C. He taught that a universal love was the cure for man's evils ; the parable of the Good Samaritan would have evoked an immediate response from him. However he seems to have thought that men could be forced to love one another. In China his writings were neglected for centuries. Whatever happened to his writings the reader cannot but feel that he has had a tremendous influence on his countrymen. Of all the religious teachers of China, Mo seems to be the only man with a firm and intelligible belief in God. Prof. Rowley's exposition of these little known Oriental thinkers, as one would expect, is marked by sympathy and clearness.   A.G.

WIDENGREN, G. : *The King and the Tree of Life in Ancient Near Eastern Religion = King and Saviour IV* (Uppsala Universitets Årsskrift 1951 : 4). 1951. Pp. 80. (A. B. Lundequistska Bokhandeln, Uppsala : Otto Harrassowitz, Leipzig & Wiesbaden. Price : 4 Kr.)

In this further contribution to his important series of studies in the sacral kingship of the ancient Near East the author seeks to prove the existence of a close connexion between the Tree of Life, in its cultic form as a symbol of the dying and rising god, and the sacral king as its guardian and waterer, i.e. as a royal " gardener ". He also adduces further evidence in support of the view that the royal sceptre was theoretically a branch of the Tree of Life (or, under Egyptian influence, the Plant of Life), which is then identified, so to speak, with the king. The work again offers evidence of the author's industry in the collection of data which may seem to be of value for comparative purposes ; and, while some of his arguments seem unconvincing (especially when he turns to what he regards as analogous features in the Old Testament), he has a number of instructive and suggestive things to say on a subject which demands the critical attention of all who are interested in biblical interpretation.   A.R.J.

WILSON, J. A. : *The Burden of Egypt.* 1951. Pp. xx + 332. (University of Chicago Press. Price : $6.00.)

As its subtitle indicates, this book is an interpretation of Egyptian culture. Starting from prehistoric times, the author describes and interprets Egyptian civilization, phase by phase, until the conquest by Alexander. Each of his chapters surveys a major period of Egyptian history. He attempts to answer such questions as the endurance of Egyptian culture for 2,000 years, its sudden rise and its ultimate petrifaction and disappearance. He considers the religious, intellectual, and political development of the Egyptians. Profound learning and wide reading have gone into the making of this mature work. The Biblical scholar will find much to interest him in it.

T.W.T.

THE DEAD SEA SCROLLS

BROWNLEE, W. H. : *The Dead Sea Manual of Discipline. Translation and Notes*. (Bulletin of the American Schools of Oriental Research. Supplementary Studies, Nos. 10-12.) 1951. Pp. 60. (New Haven, Conn. Price : $2.00.)

Eleven columns of the Dead Sea scroll, the Manual of Discipline, which were transferred to the A.S.O.R. for publication, are here translated and annotated with a very high degree of efficiency and clarity by Professor Brownlee. The author, who acknowledges help received from other scholars, does not claim that his translation is definitive, but we may add that, alongside of the published facsimiles and transcription of the scroll (cf. *Book List*, 1951, p. 18) the present work is indispensable for the study of this important scroll. In the notes, which amount to well over five hundred in all, the author discusses, among other things, textual matters relating to his rendering, the numerous affinities with other scrolls, the Damascus Document and various books of the Apocrypha, and contacts of text with the Old Testament and of context with the New Testament and with the Essenes. In nine appendices subjects of importance in the scroll are briefly discussed, and a translation is given of one of the songs in the scroll of Hymns (published by Sukenik, *Megillôth Genûzôth* II, plate X). The Editor, Professor W. F. Albright, adds a Postscript on the ' Chronology of the Dead Sea Scrolls '.   B.J.R.

DELCOR, M. : *Les Manuscrits de la Mer Morte. Essai sur Le Midrash d'Habacuc*. (Lectio Divina, 7.) 1951. Pp. 84. (Les Editions du Cerf, Paris. Price : Fr. 300.)

A new translation, with full annotation, forms the body of this work, but on its basis Father Delcor argues that the Wicked Priest is Alexander Jannaeus, and that the Midrash deals with the persecution by him of the Pharisees. Both parties are implicitly referred to in the commentary. Professor Dupont-Sommer's theory is attacked on a number of points : the Kittim cannot be Romans because of the evidence of the Warfare scroll and of 1 Macc. and Jubilees ; the capture of Jerusalem by Pompey on the Day of Atonement is queried. The scrolls are compared with the Psalms of Solomon, and among other interesting points discussed are the plenitude of *matres lectionis*, the *mebaqqer* of the scrolls and *episkopos* in the New Testament. Kahle's argument based on the presence of codex fragments in the cache is refuted by the fact that the fragments are not codices but pieces of leather written on both sides by different hands. In two appendices are a translation of one of the Songs of Thanksgiving and a short bibliography.   B.J.R.

435

DEL MEDICO, H. E. : *Deux Manuscrits Hébreux de la Mer Morte. Essai de Traduction du " Manuel de Discipline " et du " Commentaire d'Habbakuk " avec Notes et Commentaires.* 1951. Pp. 144. (Libraire Orient. Paul Geuthner, Paris. Price : Fr. 700.)

It will be noticed that the facsimile edition of the Dead Sea Manual of Discipline shows a variety of marginal marks, and Dr. del Medico has seen in these an indication of divergent sources which were used for the composition of the Manual. He gives a translation—with notes and discussions—of the document on the basis of three principal divergent sources : the first (Sadokite, *S*) deals with questions of Torah, Priests, etc., the Temple ; the second (Rabbinic, *R*), contains descriptions of the academy and its activities ; the third (Zealot, *Z*), has political, doctrinal and historical details about the Zealots. A fourth (secondary) source is a commentary on Isaiah (*J*), and has affinities with the teaching of ·John the Baptist. In an annotated translation of the Habakkuk Commentary del Medico shows that it deals with events *about* 66 A.D., and contains reminiscences of the eruption of Vesuvius ; it was composed shortly after the fall of Jerusalem.

B.J.R.

DRIVER, G. R. : *The Hebrew Scrolls from the Neighbourhood of Jericho and the Dead Sea.* (Friends of Dr. Williams's Library, Fourth Lecture, 1950.) 1951. Pp. 52. (Oxford University Press. Price : 3s. 6d.)

It is well-known that the redoubtable Professor Driver has consistently argued against a pre-Christian or an early dating for the Dead Sea scrolls, and in the present brochure he gives the fullest statement of his case to date. He challenges the customary use made of evidence supplied by archaeology, even the residual radio-active carbon of the wrapping ; likewise, palaeography and its concomitants—ink, ruling, etc., must, he says, be regarded as inconclusive. Orthographic and linguistic aspects, however, such as the plethora of scriptio plena, the presence of Aramaizing influences, the peculiar suffixal forms, the substitution of synonyms for rare words, indicate a date well into the Christian era. The division of the text in the Isaiah scroll stands in agreement with that of the Great Greek Codices, B, S, A, and is probably contemporary with them. Indeed, Professor Driver argues here that a date towards 500 A.D. may be regarded as a suitable *terminus post quem* for the scrolls.

B.J.R.

DUPONT-SOMMER, A. : *Observations sur le Manuel de Discipline découvert près de la Mer Morte.* 1951. Pp. 32. (Adrien-Maisonneuve, Paris. Price : Fr. 120.)

This is the full text of a communication read to the Académie des Inscriptions et Belles Lettres on 8th June, 1951. It is probably the first monograph on the Manual of Discipline to be published after the appearance of the full Hebrew text in the American facsimile edition. It consists of a study of the beliefs and practices of the sect reflected in the Manual in comparison with those of the Essenes as known to us from ancient sources. Dupont-Sommer finds further support for his theory that the sect consisted of Essenes, and that the Dead Sea Scrolls are of importance for the study of Judaism in the Hasmonaean and Roman periods, and that they throw light on Christian origins.   H.H.R.

DUPONT-SOMMER, A. : *The Dead Sea Scrolls. A Preliminary Survey* (Translated from the French by E. Margaret Rowley). 1952. Pp. 100, with 10 plates and 1 map. (Basil Blackwell, Oxford. Price : 7s. 6d.)

> Miss Rowley has produced an excellent translation of this book, into the text of which a few changes have been introduced. Comparison with the French edition (which was reviewed in the *Book List* for 1951, p. 19) prompts a word of admiration for the quality of the production.   G.W.A.

HABERMANN, A. M. : *'Edah we-'Eduth. Three Scrolls from the Judaean desert. The Legacy of a Community, edited with vocalization, introduction, notes and indices* (in Hebrew). 1952. Pp. vi + 168 with nine plates. (Mahberoth le Sifruth (Central Press), Jerusalem. Price : I£ 3.800.)

> All who are interested in the famous Dead Sea Scrolls owe thanks to Mr. A. M. Habermann, the able librarian of the Schocken Library in Jerusalem, for this handy and very useful small volume. In a general Introduction the writer gives a more popular survey of the questions connected with the manuscripts which, he is inclined to think, were written not later than 80 B.C.E. The Bibliography is unfortunately rather incomplete with regard to publications in languages other than Hebrew ; as to Israeli titles it is of a unique and valuable completeness. Then follow, with special introductions, the texts of DSH, DSD and CDC (in disagreement with the title the latter properly speaking has not been found in the Judaean Desert !). Being well aware of the risks of the matter Habermann ventures to add a vocalization and a punctuation to these texts, an addition which not a little facilitates the reading, even for those who are well versed in reading the unvocalized texts of post-Biblical Hebrew. The value of the notes accompanying the texts is greatly enhanced by the glossary which gives, in the arrangement of a concordance, an index of the terminological vocabulary of the sect, as contained in the above-mentioned texts. This glossary—although not entirely complete—makes possible a fruitful study of the sect, its concepts and its milieu. Some of Habermann's own theories are worth mentioning here. In contradistinction to most Israeli co-workers in this field he denies that *yahad* is the name of the sect ; he holds that it is rather a qualification of a class in it ; a higher degree he sees in the *rabbîm*. He maintains that there is a lacuna between the columns 9 and 10 of DSD. He recognizes in the last leaf of Schechter's text A of CDC a fragment of the *Sêfer ha-Hagû* a book (on the pronunciation of the Tetragrammaton ?) which is mentioned

in CDC and in the still unpublished parts of DSD, as belonging to the scriptures of the sect. His readings of the texts by no means slavishly follow those of former editors and translators and his interpretations too are new in several places. He knows, as he himself modestly puts it, ' that errors will be found in his reading and that . . . improvements will be made '. He brings a number of new suggestions in his additions and corrections. However, his familiarity with post-biblical Hebrew (both Mishnaic and mediaeval) enables him to find many happy and convincing solutions to the difficulties with which these texts abound.   I.L.S.

KAHLE, P. : *Die hebräischen Handschriften aus der Höhle*. 1951. Pp. 92. (W. Kohlhammer Verlag, Stuttgart. Price : £1 1s. 0d.)

The weight of authority which Professor Kahle brings to the study of Hebrew manuscripts lends a special importance to his pronouncements on the 'Ain Feshka scrolls. The lectures which are here printed were delivered by him in several German universities in 1950. They are fully documented, there is a bibliography, an index, and twelve pages of well selected photographs. Only a few indications of the author's views can here be given. The cave from which the manuscripts come was not a Geniza, but a hiding place, in which an extensive library of manuscripts of different dates was concealed, probably in the third century A.D., by the Essenes. The two Isaiah scrolls represent two forms of " vulgar " texts which circulated before the standard text was fixed. Their variant readings are consequently of great importance. In the St. Mark's scroll, Isaiah xxxiv. 17-35, which had been omitted by the scribe, has been inserted in a form which agrees with the M.T. This addition cannot then be earlier than the second century A.D. The orthography of the second Isaiah scroll has been accommodated to that of the M.T., and it too cannot be earlier than the second century. In the St. Mark's scroll there are two types of text, and the special peculiarities of the scroll are to be seen only in the second half. Dupont-Sommer's date—shortly before 40 B.C.—for the composition of the Habakkuk Commentary is probable, but the 'Ain Feshka manuscript is a copy of the work made before A.D. 70. The Leviticus fragments in ancient Hebrew script are definitely of Jewish, not Samaritan, origin, and may be as old as the first century B.C., if not older. The manuscripts are thus all centuries older than anything in the Cairo Geniza. The argument that the jars are decisive for the dating of the manuscripts is brought into question, and due caution is observed in the use of palaeography as a criterion of dating. Among other considerations bearing upon the date of the manuscripts which are discussed are the papyri fragments written on both sides, which are parts of codices, not scrolls ; the fact that no parchment was found in the cave ; and the traces of Estrangelo script which Professor Kahle claims to have detected on a leather fragment. The relation of the Isaiah text to the LXX is shown to be bound up with the attitude taken towards the character and history of the Greek Bible. The significance of the St. Mark's text of Isaiah for the pronunciation of Hebrew is considered at length. Finally, objection is taken to the description of the discoveries as " sectarian "—rather do they witness to the rich possibilities of religious development within Judaism. Since the study of the scrolls proceeds at a great pace, readers may care to be referred to a later contribution on the age of them by Professor Kahle published in *Vetus Testamentum*, i, 1951, pp. 38 ff.   D.W.T.

LAMBERT, G. : *Le Manuel de Discipline du Désert de Juda. Étude Historique et Traduction Intégrale.* (Analecta Lovaniensia Biblica et Orientalia. Ser. II, Fasc. 23.) 1951. Pp. 40. (Publications Universitaires de Louvain.)

> The brochure appeared as an article in *Nouvelle Revue Théologique*, 1951, pp. 938-975. In the introductory section Father Lambert examines the constitution of and the aims ascribed to the ' Community of Alliance ' (he objects to ' New Alliance ' or ' New Covenanters ') in the Manual of Discipline of the Dead Sea scrolls. He then gives a fully annotated translation of the document, which will, undoubtedly, stand comparison with the now growing number of renderings. The author does not advance any theory for an identity of the party with any previously known sect, but in occasional notes he refers to some current views. Linguistic notes, however, are abundantly supplied.   B.J.R.

VERMES, G. : *La Communauté de la Nouvelle Alliance.*

COPPENS, J. : *Les Manuscrits du Désert de Juda.* (Analecta Lovaniensia Biblica et Orientalia, Ser. II, Fasc. 22.) 1951. Pp. 18. (Publications Universitaires de Louvain. Price : Belgian Fr. 20.)

> This publication is an extract from *Ephemerides Lovanienses*, 1951, Vol. XXVII. The cataclysmic fire in the third hymn of the Dead Sea Songs of Thanksgiving brings Father Vermès to consider the scrolls generally against the background of this widespread literary phenomenon, and he sees in the Righteous Teacher a Noah *redivivus*. He finds affinities with numerous apocalyptic writings, e.g. the Life of Adam and Eve, the Sibylline Oracles, and, in Christian writings, 2 Pet. ii. 5, Hermas, Justin, Origen, etc. He also finds an implicit reference to Noah in the Hab. Comm., col. II, 2 ff., where the Wicked Priest did worse than Ham, Noah's son. Historically, Vermès finds the appropriate setting in the period around the burning of Jerusalem and the eruption of Vesuvius, i.e., late first century A.D., and the Habakkuk scroll can be brought down even to the time of Bar Cochba. Professor Coppens, in a very valuable survey of current theories, supports Vermès.   B.J.R.

CHOUCROUN, I. –M.: *Le Judaïsme, doctrines et préceptes.* 1951. Pp. 156. (Presses Universitaires de France, Paris. Price : 8s. 0d.)

Rabbi Choucroun's little book is at once concise and comprehensive and is written in a flowing style, holding the reader's interest. A brief introduction on Judaism from early times up to our day is followed by three chapters on Jewish teaching upon God, man and his destiny, and on Israel and humanity ; then come five chapters on moral questions involving the individual, the family and society ; finally, a short valuable description of the religious practices of Judaism. Highly informative are the author's pages on ' le divorce israélite ', ' la prière et le culte synagogal ' and ' les jours austères '. Upon the subject of the unity of God the writer's account of Hebrew belief in biblical times as being a rigorous monotheism, and of the figure of Satan in the O.T. as being only an allegorical representation, perhaps is the only instance where the Rabbi's religious enthusiasm may be observed to have gone somewhat further than the evidence warrants. The book is No. 26 of the series entitled *Mythes et Religions.*   O.S.R.

FEIGIN, S. I. : *Anshe Sepher, Hoqerim v-Sopherim* (Men of Letters, Scholars, and Writers). 1950. Pp. x+484. (" Ohel " Publication, New York. Price : 28s. 0d.)

This book, which is written in Hebrew, is divided into two main sections, the one called The Scholars' Section, the other The Writers' Section, both of which are divided into various subsections. Of the many interesting articles the essays on Shim'on Bernfeld, David Yellin, Israel Eitan, Naftali Hertz Torczyner, Louis Ginzberg, Heinrich Zimmern, John Merlin Powis Smith and William Foxwell Albright are of direct interest for students of the Old Testament. While dwelling upon the life-story of some of these scholars the author assesses their manifold researches in various branches of Semitic Studies. The publishers are to be congratulated on a fine production.   M.W.

GOLDIN, H. E. : *Hebrew Criminal Law and Procedure : Mishnah, Sanhedrin-Makkot.* 1952. Pp. 308. (Twayne Publishers, New York. Price : $4.75.)

This work, although written by a lawyer with the emphasis on the legal aspect of the two Tractates, both in the elaborate introduction and the explanatory notes accompanying the translation of the Hebrew text, does not become involved in the intricacies and details of legal problems and is, therefore, a suitable introduction for students wishing to acquaint themselves with the major principles of Talmudic criminal jurisprudence and procedure. The volume contains a translation of the tractates Sanhedrin and Makkot, with full notes standing beneath the text.   P.R.W.

HADAS, M. : *Aristeas to Philocrates (Letter of Aristeas)*, edited and translated. 1951. Pp. 234. (Harper & Bros., New York and Hamish Hamilton, London. Price : $4.00 or 28s. 0d.)

This book reproduces H.St.J. Thackeray's Greek text of Aristeas from Swete's *Introduction to the Old Testament in Greek* (Cambridge, 1905) and contains the translation of the letter, the English page by page alongside the Greek. A most useful and full introduction (90 pages) and notes deal critically with the various literary, historical and religious questions which arise from the letter. As was the first volume of the Jewish Apocrypha to be published under the auspices of Dropsie College (viz. 1 Macc., see *Book List*, 1951, p. 42) this edition of Aristeas is a pattern of clarity in form and type. As a commentary and introduction Professor Hadas' work has an advantage over any of the current introductions in that it makes good use of several of the relevant specialised studies upon individual themes which have appeared in the last three decades and recently, such as, *inter alia*, the researches of Février on the date and sources of Aristeas (1925), of Goodenough (1928) on the political philosophy of Hellenistic kingship, of Westermann on Slavery in Ptolemaic Egypt (1929) and of the works of Tarn and Rostovtzeff on the Hellenistic age.   O.S.R.

KLEIN, I. : *The Code of Maimonides, Book Twelve, The Book of Acquisition. Translated from the Hebrew.* (Yale Judaica Series, vol. V.) 1951. Pp. xvi+336 (Yale University Press, New Haven. Price : $5.00.)

This is the fourth volume to be published of the *Mishneh Torah*, Maimonides' systematic presentation of the whole corpus of Judaism (see *Book List*, 1950, pp. 72 f. ; 1951, p. 70). This Book Twelve brings together all the laws dealing with ownership of property : the manner of acquiring real and movable property, securing title to ownerless property, validity of gifts, joint ownership and neighbours' rights and limitations, partners, agents and trustees, and the rules, rights and obligations bearing on slaves. The Introduction is compact even to meagreness. The translation is clear and readable, though forms like " donee ", " vendee " and " transferee " could have been spared ; and references (p. 62) to " barrels ", " casks ", and " bungholes " give a misleading picture of utensils in Roman Palestinian times. The Notes might well have been more generous and the object of closer care. Such comments as (p. 322) " our text reads . . . ", (313) " the Venice edition reads . . ." (there are four Venice editions), (p. 314) " the ordinary editions . . .", suggest a somewhat casual attitude towards the textual evidence ; and several times technical terms from other departments of Jewish law are explained somewhat perfunctorily when a reference ought to have been given to the section of the Code where those terms are expounded at length in their proper context.   H.D.

LAURENTIN, A. : *Le Pneuma dans la Doctrine de Philon.* (Analecta Lovaniensia Biblica et Orientalia, Ser. II, Fasc. 24.) 1951. Pp. 50. (Publications Universitaires de Louvain, and Desclée de Brouwer, Bruges and Paris. Price : Fr. 30.)

A careful study of the meaning of *pneuma* in Philo, reaching the conclusion that there is a fundamental unity of sense in his use of the word, but that this unity is a unity of relation, and that the *pneuma* is always of divine origin.   H.H.R.

LAUTERBACH, J. Z. : *Rabbinic Essays.* 1951. Pp. xvi+570. (Hebrew Union College Press, Cincinnati. Price : $5.00.)

Dr. Lauterbach was one of that diminishing band of Jewish scholars who have combined the traditional Talmudic learning acquired in their youth with habits of modern critical study acquired in their maturity. His main work was in the field of Tannaitic literature (he wrote most of the articles on this subject in the last six volumes of the *Jewish Encyclopedia*) and many of the now prevalent ideas and theories about that literature and Pharisaism owe their formulation to him. He was Professor of Talmud at the Hebrew Union College of Cincinnati from 1911 to 1942, and the present sumptuous volume is a monument raised in his memory by his pupils. A brief Appreciation and a Bibliography of his writings are followed by a reprint of six of the more substantial of his published essays (" The Sadducees and Pharisees ", 1913 ; " The Ethics of the Halakah ", 1913 ; " Midrash and Mishnah ", 1915 ; "A Significant Controversy between the Sadducees and the Pharisees ", 1927 ; " The Pharisees and their Teachings ", 1929 ; " *Tashlik*, a Study in Jewish Ceremonies ", 1936) ; and two unpublished studies : " The Sabbath in Jewish Ritual and Folklore ", and " Jesus in the Talmud ". Regrettably the volume has no index. H.D.

LESLAU, W. : *Falasha Anthology : Translated from Ethiopic sources, with an Introduction.* (Yale Judaica Series, vol. vi.) 1951. Pp. xliii+222. (Yale University Press, New Haven. Price : $4.00.)

In this volume specimens of the literature of the Falasha, a very ancient and isolated Jewish community living in regions north of Lake Tana in Abyssinia, are made available for the first time in an English translation. The works included are *Te'zāza Sanbat* (" The Commandments of the Sabbath "), Abba Elijah, The Book of the Angels, The Apocalypse of Baruch, The Apocalypse of Gorgorios, The Testament of Abraham, The Death of Moses, and Prayers. Each translation is accompanied by an introduction, which contains a synopsis of the work and a discussion of such questions as the sources of it, its character, and its age. Short bibliographies are provided for each work. The general introduction includes sections on the life and customs—both secular and religious—of the Falasha, their literature, and their history and origin. To his treatment of these matters the author brings first hand knowledge of the Falasha—he visited them in 1947—and the work throughout is of high quality. Students of Judaism will find much to interest them in the Falasha form of it, which is, the author believes, primitive, and might date from a time when the Mishnah and Talmud were not yet compiled. That it has some original features is seen, for example, in its concept of the Sabbath, which is viewed as a female figure who is crowned on the Sabbath by angels and goes down to Sheol to deliver sinners from punishment. There are over forty closely printed pages of valuable notes, a select bibliography, a glossary, an index of scriptural and other references, a full general index, and seven illustrations.   D.W.T.

LIEBERMAN, S. : *Hellenism in Jewish Palestine.* Studies in the literary transmission beliefs and manners of Palestine in the I century B.C.E.—IV century C.E. (Texts and Studies of the Jewish Theological Seminary of America, Vol. xviii.) 1950. Pp. xiv+232. (Jewish Theological Seminary of America, New York. Price : $7.00.)

This volume is a sequel to the author's *Greek in Jewish Palestine,* and continues in the path first pointed out by Graetz and Krauss of illustrating rabbinic literature and institutions from patristic literature. Lieberman casts his net wider and utilizes Greek and Roman pagan writers of late antiquity, with valuable results. In a series of profusely documented essays on literature, religious ceremonial, and other public antiquities he demonstrates the unity of the pattern of many institutions of the ancient Mediterranean world. Essays of concern to O.T. scholars deal with *Ķeri* and *Kethib.* Corrections of the *Sopherim,* the *puncta extraordinaria* and critical devices of the MT ; also with rabbinic exegesis and its hermeneutic rules, and the method of the publication of the *Mishnah.* In addition to their own findings the essays (though sometimes discursive) are a useful lesson in methodology, and emphasize our need for scholars who are as at home in Athens, Alexandria, and Rome, as in Jerusalem and Babylon.

R.L.

PFEIFFER, R. H. : *Il Giudaismo nell 'Epoca Neotestamentaria.* 1951. Pp. 120. (Edizioni dell ' Ateneo, Rome. Price : 700 lire.)

Three years ago Professor Pfeiffer was invited by the University of Rome to give a course on Judaism at the beginning of the Christian era, and the lectures were in due season delivered between February and June, 1951. The lecturer was asked to explain the subject of the course in a printed volume, and we have here a brief summary of what was said, as it was found impossible to print the lectures *in extenso.* Naturally, as the author declares, considerable use has been made of his admirable work in English, the *History of New Testament Times, with an Introduction to the Apocrypha* (Harper, New York, 1949) and of a translation of the Jewish apocryphal literature, which is to be published at some future date. Pfeiffer has, however, not been content to summarize his larger work ; he has thought out afresh and worked out again the relevant matter of the *History,* and has brought the bibliography up to date. The introductory chapter on " La sopravvivenza d'Israele " does not appear to be taken from the English work.   J.M.T.B.

SMITH, M. : *Tannaitic Parallels to the Gospels* (Journal of Biblical Literature Monograph Series, Vol. VI). 1951. Pp. 216. (Society of Biblical Literature, Philadelphia. Price : $1.50.)

By the term Tannaitic literature (abbrev. TL) the author means the Mishnah, Tosefta, Mekilta, Sifra, Sifre on Numbers, Sifre Zutta, Sifre on Deut., Midrash Tannaim and some of the oldest prayers (especially the xviii Benedictions) of the Jewish liturgy. Though his comparison of these works with the Gospels has in the main a philological purpose Dr. Smith's book contains a good deal more and will be of the greatest importance to New Testament scholars. He sifts the TL and Gospels for parallels in vocabulary, in idiom, in meaning, in literary form and in types of association, etc. In criticism of the method of scholars who seek to show that the Fourth Gospel has been translated from the Aramaic, Dr. Smith says that the proof of translation must be built not on the difference between John and the synoptics, but on the parallelism between John and Aramaic writings. But since there are no Aramaic works for the period of the Gospels— except perhaps *Megillath Ta'anith*—the parallels in word and idiom, etc. found in the Gospels and TL (the language of which is so close to Aramaic) are of great account. In working out the statistics of the parallels that are discovered Dr. Smith shows that " it is impossible to speak, as Torrey spoke, of the language of the Gospels as a word-for-word translation of a Hebrew or Aramaic text, for it does not contain the expressions which any such translation would necessarily contain." Dr. Smith's work deals with the fundamentals of N.T. criticism, is a very valuable piece of spadework, and an appreciable if brief supplement to the work of Billerbeck and Strack. O.S.R.

SPIRO, A. : *Samaritans, Tobiads and Judahites in Pseudo-Philo—Use and Abuse of the Bible by Polemicists and Doctrinaires.* (Reprinted from the Proceedings of the American Academy for Jewish Research, Vol. XX.) 1951. Pp. 78. (The American Academy for Jewish Research, New York.)

Pseudo-Philo's work on the Biblical Antiquities, a Biblical history from Adam to Saul which was preserved in Latin, was published by Sichardus (1527). Cardinal Pitra (1884) showed that the Latin was a translation from the Greek. An English translation (the *Biblical Antiquities of Philo, etc.*, 1917) has been prepared by M. R. James ; and Guido Kisch has placed in the hands of scholars a critically edited text (1949). In his study of Pseudo-Philo's work which may be as old as the first century A.D., Mr. Spiro gives an excellent account—with valuable notes—of how Pseudo-Philo, emphasizing the destiny of Judah and Jerusalem, combats the claims of Samaritan and Transjordanian schismatics by a polemic which adds to, subtracts from, and otherwise colours the Biblical narrative. Mr. Spiro's study offers a useful contribution to the history of Jewish religious polemic. O.S.R.

VRIEZEN, TH.C. : *Palestina en Israël*. 1951. Pp. 250. (H. Veenman & Zonen, Wagenegen. Price : Fl. 7.90.)

This book is inspired by the personal observations and experience of the writer in Palestine as a student 25 years ago and more recently when he attended the semi-jubilee of the Hebrew University in 1950. He projects modern Palestine and its problems against a wide background of history, culture and religion reaching back to the dawn of the Bronze Age. In this, the more academic part of the work, he is conservative and somewhat superficial. His treatment of Zionism is well-informed, thorough and honest, if occasionally uncharitable to the mandatory power. He does not exonerate the Christian Church from blame in helping to create a Jewish problem. He hopes for the development of a new relationship between Jew and Christian and even ventures to hope that such a relationship may yet be possible among the communities in Palestine itself by some creative spiritual event by which alone the Palestine problem may be solved.　　　　J.G.

WEINGREEN, J. : *The Rabbinic Approach to the Study of the Old Testament*. (Reprinted from the *Bulletin of the John Rylands Library*, xxxiv, No. 1.) 1951. Pp. 28. (The John Rylands Library and Manchester University Press. Price : 2s. 6d.)

In this paper, which was read to the Society for Old Testament Study, Professor Weingreen shows that the preference of the mediaeval commentators for plain interpretations rather than fanciful was dictated by the religious interest of preserving for their own generation many of the results of the older interpretation. The Chronicler could alter his text to bring it into accord with what was thought proper in his day, but after the fixation of the text by the Massoretes this was no longer possible, and hence the way of interpretation alone could be followed. Many illuminating examples are given, and the whole forms a valuable study which Professor Weingreen hopes to expand into a fuller treatment.　　　　H.H.R.

PHILOLOGY AND GRAMMAR

BEN YEHUDA, E. : *Thesaurus totius hebraitatis et veteris et recentioris*. Vol. xiii. 1951. Pp. 6221-6703. (Hemda and Ehud Benyehuda, Jerusalem-Talpiot. Price : £5 19s. 0d.)

The appearance of a new volume of the *Thesaurus* is always an important event in the world of Hebrew scholarship. This volume, which is dedicated to Mr. Harry S. Truman, runs from *qarar* to *raṣuy*. Professor Tur Sinai, Ben Yehuda's successor as editor of the *Thesaurus*, had available the material collected for this volume by his predecessor. The arrangement of the material, however, is his, and he contributes much additional lexicographical and bibliographical matter. The extensive notes for which he is responsible are only one of the impressive features of the work. This volume was prepared in the face of many difficulties arising from the political situation in Israel, and Hebrew scholars everywhere will feel especially grateful on that account to the editor and to all those, including the Government of the State of Israel, who have played a part in the production of it. It is good to know that the material for the last two letters of the alphabet has been safely preserved.   D.W.T.

BIRKELAND, H. : *Lærebok i hebraisk grammatikk*. 1950. Pp. 158. (Grøndahl & Søn, Oslo. Price : 23s. 0d.)

This is a most successful attempt to reduce Hebrew to its simplest terms for beginners. The principles of the language are lucidly and adequately explained and illustrated and 31 pages of paradigms conclude the work. Notes, conspicuous in the text by small type, introduce the student to more specialized questions, where the writer indicates his method of historical philology.   J.G.

BLACK, M. : *Rabbula of Edessa and the Peshitta*. 1951. Pp. 10. (Reprinted from the *Bulletin of the John Rylands Library*, Vol. 33, No. 2, March, 1951.) (Manchester University Press and the John Rylands Library, Manchester. Price : 1s. 0d.)

In this lecture Dr. Black examines the Gospel quotations in Rabbula's Syriac Version of Cyril of Alexandria's *de recta fide*. With Dr. Vööbus of Chicago Lutheran Theological Seminary, he recognizes the presence of Old Syriac readings but, while Vööbus had deduced that Rabbula used some form of the Old Syriac Gospels and had challenged Burkitt's theory of the Rabbulan " authorship " of the Peshitta New Testament, Dr. Black's conclusion is that Rabbula's revision lay somewhere between the Old Syriac and the Syriac Vulgate as we now know it.   W.M.McH.

BLAKE, F. R. : *A Resurvey of the Hebrew Tenses with an appendix : Hebrew influence on Biblical Aramaic*. 1951. Pp. xii+96. (Pontificio Istituto Biblico, Rome. Price : 28s. 0d.)

This sketch of the Hebrew verbal system offers a collection of examples drawn largely from the *Hebrew Tenses* (1892) of the reviewer's father and shows how the old explanation of its peculiarities fails in the light of Prof. H. Bauer's *Die Tempora im Semitischen* (1910) ; and he rightly argues that these peculiarities are due to historical causes. He does not however push his reasoning home ; for example, he does not go so far as to postulate a preterite tense quite distinct from the imperfect tense. The failure is due to disregarding the different accentuation of the varying forms and the comparable idioms in the cognate languages ; and these phenomena, taken together, are crucial for the explanation and understanding of the Hebrew tense system, as shown in the reviewer's *Hebrew Verbal System* (1936). Unfortunately, too, the author uses old terms to describe these phenomena (e.g. " converted perfects " and " imperfects ") which have long been recognized as incorrect and can only mislead the student ; but it is useful to have an explanation, even under an antiquated terminology and without a complete solution of the problems involved, attempted along reasonable lines. No treatment, however, that leaves everything published since the first German war out of account is likely to be found satisfactory.

G.R.D.

BOTTERWECK, G. J. : *Der Triliterismus im Semitischen.* 1951. Pp. 76. (Hanstein, Bonn. Price : DM. 7.50.)

This volume is the third of the admirable *Bonner Biblischer Studien* published under the editorship of Professor F. Nötscher (whose *Festschrift* was the inaugural volume) and Professor K. T. Schäfer. The author devotes the first chapter to the work of previous scholars on the biliteral origin of Semitic roots, examines the growth of triliteral roots with especial reference to selected bases (*GL*, *KL*, *QL* ; *BR*, *PR*), and sets out his conclusion, that certain fundamental acts or actions were originally represented by a pair of consonants whose pronunciation echoed the sounds made in producing them, and that these biconsonantal bases were subsequently triliteralized by the insertion of weak letters by reduplication, or by the addition of formative elements, many of which can be traced elsewhere, e.g. in the pronouns, in the Semitic languages. The author argues his case in a convincing manner and has produced a work well worthy of study by all philologists.

G.R.D.

COHEN, H. M. : *Schets der Ontwikkeling van het Hebreeuws tot moderne Omgangstaal.* 1951. Pp. 120. (Joachimsthal, Amsterdam.)

This work is a doctoral thesis submitted at the University of Amsterdam. Dr. Cohen divides the Hebrew language into five main periods : Biblical, Mishnaic, 500 A.D.—*c.* 1750 A.D., *c.* 1750 A.D.—*c.* 1900 A.D., *c.* 1900 A.D.—the present day. He devotes a chapter to the Hebrew of the first three periods, comparing them and noting their differences. " Modern " Hebrew begins about 1750 A.D. with the Haskala movement ; the Hebrew from this time down to 1900 A.D. is separately described and an account of the chief writers is given. Lastly, the Hebrew of the most recent period is treated. Separate chapters are then devoted to Eliezer ben Yehuda, the Council for the Hebrew language, and Bialik. The book ends with a chapter on the influences to which modern Hebrew has been subjected and a discussion of some aspects of this phase of the language. There is an English summary of each chapter at the end of the book.

The author has given a most interesting and valuable account of the various stages through which the Hebrew language has passed. He rejects Bergsträsser's view that Modern Hebrew is a European language wrapped in a transparent Hebrew garb, and he stresses the historical importance of the revival of Hebrew for the Jewish race.

T.W.T.

DEIMEL, A. : *Šumerisches Lexikon* Tl. IV, Bd. I. *Pantheon Babylonicum* herausgeg. von A. Deimel. Pp. viii+132. Bd. II. *Planetarium Babylonicum* herausgeg. von F. Gössmann. Pp. xvi+226. 1950. (Päpstl. Bibelinst., Rome. Price : £4 2s. 6d.)

These two volumes continue Fr. Deimel's well-known and extremely useful Sumerian lexicon ; and they exemplify the regular marks of all his work, completeness and accuracy, to perfection. The entries in the first are arranged under ideograms given in the cuneiform script, those in the second are transliterated into the European alphabet. The *Pantheon*, which follows Fr. Deimel's *Pantheon Babylonicum* published in 1914, is greatly enriched by new texts published since then and is especially valuable for the revised or corrected readings of many names which the editor has been able to introduce. The *Planetarium* is an attempt to make the matter referring to the stars and planets collected in the *Šumerisches Lexikon* accessible to students not acquainted with the cuneiform script and is the first catalogue devoted especially to this subject ; but it goes far beyond a mere catalogue in the wealth of information which the editor has added to his source-book. Both volumes will be of the greatest service to assyriologists and indeed to other students.   G.R.D.

VAN DORSSEN, J. C. C. : *De Derivata van de Stam 'aman in het Hebreeuwsch van het Oude Testament.* 1951. Pp. xii+140. (Drukkerij Holland N.V., Amsterdam. Price : Fl. 5.90.)

This doctoral dissertation, which carries a brief English summary at the end, sets out the Hebrew text, with translation and brief comment, of every passage in the Old Testament which contains any form, nominal or verbal, connected with the selected root. The author then goes over all his material again to sum up his views as to the particular meaning of each form. He has read widely and has gathered his material assiduously, but his professed purpose to aid the theologian to a deeper understanding needed for its realization a much fuller examination of difficult and disputed texts. Space might have been saved by eliminating the repetition the method entailed.   H.H.R.

FRIEDRICH, J. : *Phönizisch-Punische Grammatik.* (Analecta Orientalia 32.) 1951. Pp. 182. (Pontificium Institutum Biblicum, Rome. Price : £4 6s. 0d.)

This grammar is not intended to supersede Z. S. Harris' *Grammar of the Phoenician Language* (1936), but to be used side by side with it. In two respects especially it differs from Harris' work. In the first place, it takes account of new texts which have been discovered since Harris' grammar appeared, the most important being, of course, the inscriptions found at Karatepe. And secondly, the principles of historical grammar are applied, within the framework of the general development of the language, to the study of individual forms.

The grammar is divided into three parts—*Schrift- und Lautlehre* (pp. 1-43), *Formenlehre* (pp. 44-120), and *Syntax* (pp. 120-152). The extensive use the author makes of the transcriptions of Phoenician words in ancient documents is noteworthy, as is the attention he pays to the representation of vowels in late Punic inscriptions. His examination of the peculiarities of Phoenician syntax is especially valuable as breaking new ground in a hitherto much neglected field of study. Very welcome too is his grammatical and lexicographical sketch of the local dialect of Yaudi in North Syria, which is distinctive enough, he thinks, to merit the special designation " Jaudisch " (pp. 153-162). There are indices of Semitic, Greek, and Latin words, as well as a subject index. Two excellent up-to-date tables, showing the development of Phoenician and Punic scripts, are supplied. This grammar, with its high scholarship and clear presentation of the material, will be indispensable to all students of Semitic languages. Students of Phoenician are indeed fortunate in the appearance of two grammars of the language within the space of fifteen years. Between the grammars of Schröder and Harris there was an interval of nearly seventy years.　　　D.W.T.

GRETHER, O. : *Hebräische Grammatik für den akademischen Unterricht.* 1951. Pp. 478. (Evangelischer Presseverband für Bayern, München. Price : DM. 12.50.)

The grammar opens with a succinct account of the Hebrew language and script, and of the vocalisation and transmission of the M.T. This is followed by some sound practical advice on the learning of Hebrew (the author has the self-taught student partly in mind). Then come the four main parts of the work. The first deals with the structure of the language ; the second is devoted to verbal paradigms and tables of nominal forms ; the third consists of exercises ; and the fourth contains three vocabularies—one which has specific reference to the exercises, a second which goes beyond this specific need, and a third which is a comprehensive vocabulary in alphabetical order. The author's presentation is generally clear and occasionally novel. The treatment is sometimes antiquated—for example, the account given of the " waw consecutive ". But the merits of the work—not the least of which is the demonstration of the earlier stages in the development of grammatical forms—are considerable, and entitle it to be numbered among the more important Hebrew grammars of recent times. It is regrettable that no indices are provided, and still more so that the author's early death did not permit him to see the work through the press.
　　　D.W.T.

HARRIS, R. L. : *Introductory Hebrew Grammar.* 1950. Pp. 90. (Wm. B. Eerdmans Publishing Company, Grand Rapids, Michigan. Price : 20s. 0d.)

This grammar, reproduced by photography from a typed original, consists of twenty lessons (mostly accompanied by exercises), verbal paradigms, a Hebrew-English vocabulary (which includes all the verbs used more than a hundred times in the O.T., and all the nouns used more than two hundred times), and an English-Hebrew vocabulary of the words which occur in the exercises. Features of the method employed are—the learning of the verb by rule rather than by rote ; the recognition of noun forms without a detailed knowledge of noun classes and vowel changes ; the addition, in the vocabularies, of Biblical names and expressions which aim at aiding the memory of the student ; and the reversal of the order of third, second and first person in the verbal paradigms. References are frequently made to the grammar of Gesenius-Kautzsch and occasionally to Bergsträsser's. While there is much in the present work which beginners, for whom it is intended, would find helpful, it suffers, unfortunately, from serious defects. For example, there are numerous instances of wrong vocalisation—some of them quite elementary—and of mis-spellings of consonants ; grammatical forms are often erroneously given ; many of the Hebrew sentences in the exercises are quite un-Hebraic in character ; and there are a number of dubious statements on points of grammar.

D.W.T.

KÖHLER, L. : *Lexicon in Veteris Testamenti Libros.* Lieferungen ix-xi. 1951-52. Pp. 64 each. (Brill, Leiden. Price : 4s. 6d. each.)

These three fascicules of Professor Köhler's Lexicon reach the preposition '*al*, so that it is now more than half done ; each successive fascicule increases the utility of this dictionary, which is fast becoming indispensable to all serious students of the O.T.
G.R.D.

KUKENHEIM, L. : *Contributions à l'histoire de la grammaire grecque, latine et hébraïque à l'époque de la Renaissance.* 1951. Pp. x + 144. (Brill, Leiden. Price : £1 11s. 6d.)

After a brief introductory chapter (pp. 1-6), two thirds (pp. 7-87) of the rest of this book are devoted to a history of Greek and Latin grammarians and another third (pp. 89-113) is occupied with Hebrew grammarians, who primarily if not alone are of interest to students of the Old Testament. The story, which runs from R. Sa'adyah Gaon (A.D. 882-942) to Séb. Munster's *opus grammaticum* (Bâle, 1556) is concisely but clearly told ; the author well brings out each scholar's weak and strong points and fairly estimates his contribution to the study of Hebrew grammar, while showing how that study slowly but surely took shape and how the work of the grammarians of the Renascence came to a clear end in consequence of their having no sense of evolution. The work seems accurate enough ; but the present reviewer can but reflect that the statement that the importance of the chair of Hebrew at Oxford (as also elsewhere) *ne paraît pas avoir été très grande* from the 13th to the 15th century is misleading, since there was no Hebrew professorship at Oxford till 1546. G.R.D.

LEMOINE, E. : *Théorie de l'emphase hébraïque.* 1951. Pp. 66. (Geuthner, Paris. Price : Fr. 350.)

The size of this small, paper-bound, pamphlet is no guide to its importance, which is considerable ; for it contains a completely fresh and suggestive examination of emphasis and determination in the Hebrew language. In the first part the author points out the failure of current views to explain the use of the definite article and then puts forward his own theory, that it is ' le signe de la notation des faits, soit par narration, soit par description, soit par déclaration ', and that its absence is ' le signe de la notation de la pensée, soit par proverbe, soit par réflexion, soit par imagination ' ; it is in fact an emphatic prefix. In the second part the author works out the manner in which emphasis is marked by this prefix in various types of sentence. The whole work deserves very careful study.　　　　　　　　　　　　　　　　　　　　　　G.R.D.

NAKARAI, T. W. : *Biblical Hebrew.* 1951. Pp. 200. (Bookman Associates, New York.)

This grammar, which is intended for beginners, contains the elements of Hebrew grammar and syntax, texts for reading, specimens of Hebrew manuscripts, and an extensive vocabulary, which occupies over seventy pages, and which includes, besides all the words which occur in the grammar and the texts, almost all the words which occur over fifty times in the Hebrew Bible. Among the more unusual features of the work are the transcription of Hebrew sounds into phonetic script, the representation of a long vowel by a colon after it, and the way in which the paradigms are presented—a *Pe Waw* verb appear as *wtl*, an *'Ayin Waw* as *qwl*, etc. The student will find the author a generally reliable guide, and he will derive much help from his book, though he may feel that some of the information provided goes beyond his immediate needs, as, for example, when he is told that the letter *teth* is a " coronal-palato-alveolar emphatic plosive, unvoiced " (p. 2). The relevance of the other Semitic languages for the understanding of Hebrew is indicated from time to time, and there are occasional references to Mishnaic and modern Hebrew. While the reproduction of the texts and the specimens of Hebrew manuscripts leaves something to be desired, the work is well produced. There are surprisingly few misprints.　　　　　　　　　　　　　　　　　　　　　　D.W.T.

REPO, E. : *Der Begriff " Rhema " im Biblisch-Griechischen. Eine traditionsgeschichtliche und semologische Untersuchung. I. "Rhema" in der Septuaginta.* 1951. Pp. 194. (Druckerei-A. G. der Finnischen Literaturgesellschaft, Helsinki.)

This doctoral dissertation is the first part of an inquiry into the occurrence of *rhema* in LXX and N.T. The word occurs much more frequently (in the non-grammatical sense) in the Greek Bible than in contemporary Greek ; and within the Biblical literature there is a remarkable range in the frequency of its occurrence. Repo presents statistics and graphs to show that the frequency is highest in the earliest books to be translated, and in those which emanated from conservative Jewish circles with a predominantly Semitic linguistic background, whereas *logos* is more frequent later and in books where Hellenistic influence is stronger. As a result of his examination of the meaning of Hebrew words from the roots DBR and 'MR and of *rhema* and *logos*, he concludes that *rhema* is the more satisfactory rendering of the Hebrew terms for ' word ', In the discussion of the Hebrew terms no account seems to be taken of the important monograph by Grether. But the work as a whole is illuminating and valuable.   G.W.A.

SELIGSON, MIRIAM : *The Meaning of* nephesh mēth *in the Old Testament* (Studia Orientalia edidit Societas Orientalis Fennica XVI : 2). 1951. Pp. 100. (Societas Orientalis Fennica, Helsinki. Price : 15s. 6d.)

A somewhat sketchy study of the term *nephesh*, which, it is claimed, always has the basic meaning of " potency " and, what is more, a potency which finds expression not only in the activity of living creatures but also in the process of decay observable in the dying and the dead. Accordingly the *nephesh mēth* " is the disease and death demon which is still supposed to hover around the bòdy but which now is called ' the potency in the dead '." In the reviewer's opinion the work represents a Procrustean *tour de force*, which offers little evidence of any appreciation of the finer points of semantic development or the subtleties of idiom ; but, as the author sometimes attempts a criticism of the reviewer's own work in this field, the final verdict must be left to another.
          A.R.J.

TOUZARD, J. : *Grammaire hébraïque abrégée*, New edition by A. Robert. 1949. Pp. viii+114+36. (Gabalda, Paris. Price : Fr. 400.)

This introductory grammar, which carries short exercises, is arranged somewhat differently from that most widely used amongst us. After the general principles the Noun is treated, together with the Numerals, then the Article and Particles, after which the student comes to the Pronouns and the Verb. There is a brief treatment of Syntax, and then one or two models of analysis and annotated passages. The last 36 pages carry the Paradigms, but there is no vocabulary. The whole constitutes a most useful introduction to the language, marred only by a number of misprints. It is unfortunate to have so long an errata sheet in a book designed for beginners. H.H.R.

TUR-SINAI, N. H. : *Ha-Lashon veha-Sepher, Kerech ha-Lashon* (in Hebrew). 1948. Pp. 472, (Bialik Foundation, Jerusalem.)

This book deals with problems of language in general and with Hebrew problems, with special reference to the language of the Bible, in particular. Prof. Torczyner, who has laboured in the field of Hebrew philology for the last forty-five years or so, reprints a number of his researches which appeared in the past in non-Hebrew journals. However, clothed here in a Hebrew attire and embodying a sprinkling of additional material, they have a distinctive flavour and the author as a result sounds more convincing in his arguments. The book includes also some new and partially new researches. The main problems dealt with are those of the Hebrew alphabet, inscriptions, the structure of language, word-phenomena and phrases. The article *MiNZoPHaCH Zophim 'Amarum*, which deals with the history of the final letters in Hebrew, assumes special significance now in view of the recently discovered Judean Scrolls, where the final letters present an intriguing study. The book abounds in original and ingenious ideas which, not necessarily always accepted by the reader, are most suggestive and stimulating.   M.W.

WASH WATTS, J. : *A Survey of Syntax in the Old Testament.* 1951. Pp. x+150. (Broadman Press, Nashville. Price : $3.75.)

The author of this little work seeks a fresh solution of the problems of the verb in the Hebrew language of the Old Testament ; but his theory seems to be descriptive rather than explanatory (like so many scientific theories), insofar as it is clear ; for the argument is not always lucidly expressed, so that the author's reasoning is in places hard to follow. He seems also to pay too little attention to the historical aspect of the problem, which is important to the study of the development of verbal usage. Students of the subject, however, will find that the author drops many hints well worthy of consideration.   G.R.D.

WEGNER, M. : *Die Musikinstrumente des alten Orients.* (Orbis Antiquus, Heft 2.) 1950. Pp. 74. (Aschendorffsche Verlagsbuchhandlung, Münster in Westfalen. Price : 7s. 6d.)

Utilising ancient sources, both archaeological and literary, the author first gives a descriptive survey of the musical instruments in use at different times in Egypt, Mesopotamia, among the Hittites, in Syria, Israel and Greece, and then proceeds to consider the extent to which Greece was dependent for her musical instruments upon the peoples of the ancient Near East. Her dependence, the author holds, has been much exaggerated by some writers. He thinks that in its beginnings Greek music owed little, if anything, to oriental sources. Later on, however, oriental influence is to be expected, and it may be seen more especially on the side of percussion instruments (the xylophone, for example, certainly came into Greece from the east). Some interesting views are expressed on Israelite musical instruments—e.g., the identification of the *shalish* with the sistrum is thought likely ; the list of instruments in Dan. iii contributes nothing to our knowledge of Israelite music ; and the disappearance of the *ḥalil* " pipe " after the Exile and the introduction of the *meṣiltayim* " cymbals " may perhaps point to a preference in the later period for noisy rather than soothing music. The individuality of the Greeks as revealed in their musical instruments ; the importance of musical instruments as illustrating political history ; and the different ends which music served among the peoples of the Near East and among the Greeks—on these, and on other, themes, the author has suggestive comments to make. There are ample notes, a bibliography, nine figures, sixteen pages of plates, and an ingenious chronological table of ancient instruments. The author has assembled a great deal of valuable material—so recent a discovery as the highly interesting representations of musical instruments at Karatepe is included—and he has presented it most attractively and with rare conciseness.   D.W.T.

Young, G. D. : *Grammar of the Hebrew Language.* 1951. Pp. 214. (Zondervan Publishing House, Grand Rapids, Michigan. Price : $4.00.)

The author of this grammar—which is reproduced by photography from typescript—aims at helping students to read and interpret the Hebrew text of the Old Testament with all possible speed. He believes that this end is best achieved if beginners are introduced from the start to actual texts, which should be presented to them in transliteration, and only later in Hebrew script. In order, however, that his grammar may be used also by a wider circle of teachers, he employs both transliteraticn and the Hebrew script. Part 1 of the grammar (pp. 1-81) consists of thirty lessons, the majority of which contain passages from the book of Ruth, with necessary translations ; grammatical notes, and vocabularies. The remainder deal mostly with additional points of grammar and syntax. Part II (pp. 89-202) is devoted to phonology, morphology and syntax. The Hebrew verb, the author holds, is most effectively mastered, not by the memorizing of paradigms, but by the use of analytical charts such as he provides. Full paradigms are, however, also supplied in deference to those who prefer this way of teaching. With regard to the tenses, we read with some surprise that " nothing has yet appeared to replace the conclusions enunciated by Gesenius and (S. R.) Driver " (p. 182). Not only the Semitic languages, including Ugaritic, but also Egyptian, are sometimes called upon to illustrate Hebrew. The author is quite aware that there will be many who will not agree with the method of teaching Hebrew which he advocates, but he assures us that personal experience has shown him the value of it.   D.W.T.

1953

In addition to the members of the Committee, appointed by the Society to prepare this issue of the Book List, I have again had to call on the help of a number of other scholars, both at home and abroad. In some cases this was due to the inaccessibility of a book in this country and the desire to make the List as complete as possible ; in others due to the heavy burdens that were falling on some members of the Committee and their unwillingness to review more books. The names of all the reviewers who have helped me will be found in the key to their initials given overleaf. To all of them I express my thanks. In addition Mr. S. Roberts, the Deputy Librarian of Manchester University Library, has given me help in a number of ways and deserves the thanks of the Society as well as of its Book List Editor. My daughter, Margaret, has prepared all the material for the printer, in addition to much other help in preparing the List.

While the List is incomplete, it is my aim to make it as complete as possible, though this sometimes means the inclusion of notes on books of slight importance to scholars. The notes should enable readers to see for what purposes books are useful. In many cases it has proved impossible to get access to books in time for inclusion in the List, even though they have been published for some time ; in others because of my ignorance of their publication. Amongst the list of titles of books held over only books which have already been received are included. Of these some were published too recently to allow of a review, and others have taken too long to reach my hands. To the members of the Society and the foreign scholars who have notified me of the publication of new books I express my thanks. Omniscience is given to few, and I am not amongst them, and I rely on much help to track down all the books here included.

The difficulty of classifying books is often great, and it would often be easy to justify their inclusion in more than one section. Titles to which an asterisk (*) is prefixed are recommended for inclusion in school libraries. Prices, where known, are given in their original currency or in their English equivalent.

MANCHESTER UNIVERSITY.   H. H. ROWLEY.

Les Actes des Journées Scientifiques d'Orientalisme, 1949. (*Archiv Orientální* xix, Nos. 1-2.) 1951. Pp. 320. (Orientální Ustav, Prague.)

> This issue of *Archiv Orientální* is wholly devoted to the proceedings of the Conference held in Prague in 1949. Besides a wealth of material in Arabic, Turkish, Iranian, Indian and Far Eastern subjects, there are certain communications of more particular interest to O.T. scholars. These include a study by Klima of the pre-Hammurabi legal code from Tell abu Hirmil (pp. 37-59) and an article by Bentzen on latest developments in Pentateuchal studies (pp. 226-232). This article, substantially the same in content as relevant passages in the writer's ' Introduction to the O.T.' II (1949), is largely devoted to a presentation of Engnell's position. Besides reviews of recent books, there are several papers on the course of Oriental studies in Czechoslovakia, Jugoslavia, Holland, Denmark, Finland, and Italy. J.G.

BERTHOLET, A.: *Wörterbuch der Religionen*. (Kröners Taschenausgabe, Band 125.) 1952. Pp. viii+532. (Alfred Kröner Verlag, Stuttgart. Price : £1 9s. 0d.)

> Many people apart from the German-reading public will welcome this extremely useful and comprehensive encyclopædia largely composed by the late Professor Bertholet, one of the most renowned of the S.O.T.S. Honorary Members, and published posthumously. The brief articles, remarkably up-to-date in content, deal with all religions, and in considerable detail with Biblical and Christian items ; and in many places a standard book or two are mentioned as introductory to further reading. New Testament and Church History articles are provided by Professor von Camphausen. B.J.R.

CLARK, K. W. (Director) : *Checklist of Manuscripts in St. Catherine's Monastery, Mount Sinai. Microfilmed for the Library of Congress, 1950.* 1952. Pp. xi+53. (Library of Congress Photoduplication Service, Library of Congress, Washington. Price : 50 cents.)

> In this list of MSS, microfilmed and otherwise photographed at the Mount Sinai Monastery under the auspices of Dr. Kenneth Clark, who also writes the introduction to the list, the following MSS are of special interest for O.T. study :— 140 Greek MSS (*c.* 120 of them Psalters or Commentaries on the Psalms) from the 8th to the 17th centuries ; five Syriac O.T. Lectionaries (10th to 13th centuries) and some 30 Syriac Psalters (12th to 14th centuries) with earlier MSS of Samuel (7th century) and Kings (8th century) ; Georgian (4 MSS), Slavonic (8) and Ethiopic (4) Psalters (mainly 10th century and later) ; 66 Arabic MSS of various O.T. books (9th to 14th centuries), with three Psalters (8th and 9th centuries) in Greek and Arabic. Further important lists of illuminated MSS are given, and a bibliography of " Published Catalogs of Mt. Sinai Manuscripts." B.J.R.

DAICHES, S. : *Bible Studies*. 1950. Pp. x+134. (Goldston, London. Price : 10s. 6d.)

Many members of the Society will remember with affection Dr. Samuel Daiches, who was for many years a member until his death, and whose vigour in discussion was only matched by the gentleness of his spirit. In this volume thirty of his published articles have been gathered together and reissued. Many of them appeared in the Bulletin of the Bible Readers' Union, and a wider circle than the readers of that publication will be glad to have this characteristic collection of his studies. Nearly half of them deal with the meaning of individual words, and the same number with the exegesis of particular passages. Dr. Daiches' views are always original, even where they are not convincing, and his deeply religious character is imposed on all his work. To survey all these papers is here impossible, and it must suffice to select one or two. Dr. Daiches held that *'am hā'āreṣ* means *the representatives of the people*, that the *sacrifices* in the Psalms were not animal but spiritual, that Mic. vi. 8 should be rendered ' The man, i.e. Moses, hath shewed thee what is good,' and that Amen-em-ope used the book of Proverbs and not vice versa. It is a pity there is no indication in the volume of the original date and place of publication of each of the papers.   H.H.R.

DUSSAUD, R. : *L'Œuvre scientifique d'Ernest Renan*. 1951. Pp. 288. (Geuthner, Paris. Price : Fr. 1650.)

A valuable review of the work of Renan in the light of more recent, and especially of present-day, scholarship. While much of the work of Renan dealt with the New Testament and Christian Origins, not a little had to do with the Old Testament and oriental studies. The present volume is of value not only for its objective information about the career and work of Renan, but because the rich stores of Dussaud's learning are also drawn on, and his own views on many questions expressed. The Ras Shamra texts and the Dead Sea Scrolls figure here, and many authors of later date than Renan are referred to.
          H.H.R.

ENGNELL, I., and FRIDRICHSEN, A. (ed. by) : *Svenskt Bibliskt Uppslags-verk*, Band II, L-Ö. 1952. Pp. 1696. (Skolförlaget, Gävle. Price of the whole work : paper covers 95 crowns ; cloth, 110 crowns ; half leather, 120 crowns.)

This volume contains work of as distinguished quality as its predecessor (*Book List*, 1949, p. 5). It has been superbly produced, and is a delight to handle. The many maps, plates, and other illustrations form a valuable adjunct to the articles. Among the latter, many are of outstanding interest and importance for all who want to understand contemporary Scandinavian Biblical scholarship. To name but two, ' Moseböckerna ' and ' Religionsvetenskap ' merit close study. The work is the product of co-operation between an unusually gifted team of scholars ; but students of the Old Testament will be particularly indebted to Professor Engnell, who, both as editor and contributor, has borne a heavy burden, and to whose energy and erudition much is due.   G.W.A.

A Guide to Christian Reading. 1952. Pp. 120. (Inter-Varsity Fellowship, London. Price : 5s. 0d.)

This is 'A classified list of selected books' covering the whole range of religious reading—Bible, Theology, Church History, etc. It is definitely and deliberately selective. The standpoint is conservative evangelical. This involves many omissions in the lists of O.T. books especially. Books dealing with Higher Criticism are, whenever possible, avoided. The N.T. lists are less one-sided, and the rest of the volume is well balanced.
                                                                                    N.H.S.

HAAG, H., ed. by (with the collaboration of A. van den Born and others) : *Bibel-Lexikon*, Parts 2 and 3. 1952. Cols. 197-612. (Benziger Verlag, Einsiedeln, Zürich and Cologne. Subscription price : Swiss Fr./DM. 11.00 per part.)

These two parts of this work (on which see *Book List*, 1952, pp. 4f.) run from *Bibel* to *Gottesknecht* (unfinished), the longest article being on *Bibelübersetzungen* (21 cols.). The articles are all up-to-date, and the references to literature are often particularly valuable. While it is on a much smaller scale than the French *Supplément au Dictionnaire de la Bible*, or than Vigouroux's *Dictionnaire* which preceded it, it offers a very serviceable work of reference, abreast of Catholic and non-Catholic work, and the more valuable in view of the age of the larger works of reference of this kind on which the English student still so much relies. The short article on Ezekiel, for instance, summarizes the great variety of recent views on the book in a way not accessible to the reader of any comparable English work.   H.H.R.

Hebrew Union College Annual XXIII, Part 1. 1950-51. Pp. 710. (Cincinnati. Price : $3.00.)

This impressive volume, which marks the seventy-fifth anniversary of the Hebrew Union College, contains thirty-three articles, written in several languages. Only those which are of special interest to O.T. students are noted here. W. F. Albright studies Ps. lxviii in the light of Ugaritic, and finds that it is a catalogue of lyric poems, consisting of about thirty incipits. S. Mowinckel discusses the traditional form of the poetry of the Psalms and the place of the personal element therein. A number of fresh emendations in the Hebrew text of the Psalms are proposed by H. L. Ginsberg. T. J. Meek examines some of the emendations in Deutero-Isaiah proposed by Torrey, and concludes that they are to be rejected, as also is Torrey's dating of the prophet in the Persian period. Isaiah lxiii. 7-14, together with Ps. cvi, is dated by J. Morgenstern *c.* 460 B.C. H. H. Rowley restates the case for the unity of the book of Daniel. The curse, blasphemy, the spell and the oath in the O.T. are explored by S. H. Blank, with special emphasis on the effective power of the spoken word. C. H. Gordon writes on belt-wrestling, both as a sport and as an ordeal in court, in the O.T. and elsewhere. R. Marcus suggests that at some points Ringgren's views on Biblical hypostases of Wisdom need to be revised, and that there are other and larger questions which relate to the problem of hypostases which need to be considered. The orthography and pronunciation of the Tiberian Massora are discussed by L. Koehler. N. Glueck gives an account of some Biblical sites in the Jordan valley. I. Sonne presents the text, with a translation and commentary, of a column of the Hodayoth (Plate X in E. L. Sukenik's Megilloth Genuzoth, 1st. ed.), and thinks that the author of it, who is attacking heretics, moved in the world of Jewish Gnostics in the second century A.D. J. Lewy masses evidence for the belief that Mount Tabor was named after a god Tabor " The Metal-worker." F. Rosenthal investigates the root ṣdḳ with a view to discovering how in post-Biblical Hebrew ṣedaḳa came to mean " charity." And finally, R. Dussaud emphasizes the inadequacy of the literary-critical approach to the study of the religion of the O.T. ; the history of religions, combined with recent discoveries, calls for a fresh outlook on the problems involved.   D.W.T.

Hebrew Union College Annual, Vol. XXIII, Pt. 2. 1950/51. Pp. 678+ 94. (Cincinnati.)

This, the second volume of the impressive *Festschrift* to the 75th anniversary of Hebrew Union College, is of varied interest. It contains in all 32 articles, but of these no more than two have a direct bearing on Old Testament studies. M. Vogelstein, in ' Nebuchadnezzar's Reconquest of Phoenicia and Palestine and the Oracles of Ezekiel ', seeks to prove that Nebuchadnezzar's famous thirteen years' siege of Tyre, which he dates 598-586, was followed by a second siege, hitherto unknown, by the same king in the year 572, which resulted in the capitulation of Tyre in 570 or 569. Comte du Mesnil du Buissoh, in ' Les Dieux et les Déesses en Forme de Vase dans l'Antiquité Orientale ', shows that cultic vases were not only believed to be animated by the deity but that popular belief sometimes confused these vases with the deity itself. Of the other articles three deal with post-Biblical Judaism, whereas the remainder are concerned with the history, homiletics, liturgy, music, art and social and economic questions of medieval and modern Judaism.   P.R.W.

Internationale Zeitschriftenschau für Bibelwissenschaft und Grenzgebiete, 1951-52, Heft 1. 1952. Pp. 196. (Katholisches Bibelwerk, Stuttgart. Subscription : 25s. 0d.)

This bibliographical publication is of the greatest value, particularly to supplement the *Book List*. It lists the titles of articles in the Biblical field—in many cases adding a short abstract—in a classified arrangement. The work has been done by a group of scholars, Protestant as well as Catholic, and the number of the journals and series whose articles are indexed runs to no less than 393. Altogether there are 1391 articles listed in this issue. To any scholar engaged in research this will be an indispensable tool. In the body of the work references are given by the number of the journal in the Key which stands at the beginning. So long as the Key is repeated in each issue, the slight inconvenience will be justified by the saving of type. A number of slips and misprints have been noticed, and an occasional misclassification ; but these will be a source of peril only to those who lift their references without verification ! The price is remarkably low.   H.H.R.

Jaarbericht Ex Oriente Lux, No. 12, 1951-52. 1952. Pp. 144+30 plates and 1 map. (Society Ex Oriente Lux, Leiden.)

Most of this issue is taken up with articles dealing with contacts between the Benelux lands and the Near East from the time of the Crusades on. J. van der Ploeg has a short article on his visit to Transjordan in 1949 and 1950, and a longer article on the Dead Sea Scrolls. In the latter article a large number of publications which have appeared since his earlier article are reviewed, and there is a valuable bibliography at the end. Professor van der Ploeg has made important contributions to the study of the Scrolls, and his acquaintance with the vast literature about them is almost complete. In addition there is an article on the Code of Lipit-Ishtar, and articles dealing with Egypt and Iran. Lists of the publications of G. van der Leeuw and J. H. Kramers are also given.   H.H.R.

Joy, C. R. : *A Concordance of Subjects.* 1952. Pp. xii+480. (A. & C. Black, London. Price : 25s. 0d.)

This is a valuable supplement to the ordinary type of Concordance, in which texts are arranged under the words which they contain. Here they are arranged under key-words which indicate their ideas, though the key-word may not be itself found in the text. The claim that this is a new type of Concordance is not strictly accurate. The reviewer has for many years used a similar work, on a much smaller scale, which by 1883 had reached its one hundred and forty-third thousand. In the present work the Scripture verses are cited, and many cross references are given. It should be widely useful, and not least to scholars.   H.H.R.

(Lohmeyer, E.) : *In Memoriam Ernst Lohmeyer,* ed. by W. Schmauch. 1951. Pp. 376. (Evangelisches Verlagswerk GmbH., Stuttgart. Price : 33s. 6d.)

Several of the contributions in this memorial volume to a distinguished New Testament scholar have a bearing upon the Old Testament, and two at least are directly concerned with it, i.e. " Das Volksbegehren ", by Martin Buber (pp.

53-66), which deals with Israel's request for a king in 1 Samuel viii, and was to have been published as the first chapter of *Der Gesalbte = Das Kommende II* , and "Alttestamentliche Wurzeln der ersten Auferstehung" by Leonhard Rost (pp. 67-72), which is a suggestive if short discussion of the Old Testament antecedents to Revelation xx. 3-6, notably Daniel xii. 2f., Isa. xxvi. 19f. (in conjunction with lxvi. 22f.), and Ezekiel xxxiv. 23f., xxxvii. 24.   A.R.J.

(MARGOLIS, M. L.) : *Max Leopold Margolis, Scholar and Teacher*, ed. by R. Gordis. 1952. Pp. 124. (Alumni Association, Dropsie College for Hebrew and Cognate Learning, Philadelphia. Price : $2.50.)

Twenty years after the death of a scholar who is described as " the greatest Jewish master of Biblical learning yet arisen in America", some of his pupils, now themselves mature and well-known scholars, have produced this volume as a tribute to his memory. R. Gordis writes an appreciation of the life and career of M. L. Margolis. The contributions of Margolis to Biblical and Rabbinic studies, to Semitic studies, to the study of the Septuagint and to the history and philosophy of Judaism are discussed by F. Zimmermann, E. A. Speiser, H. M. Orlinsky and J. Bloch. J. Reider's full and classified bibliography of Margolis' writings completes an interesting and useful book.   W.D.M.

MARTIN-ACHARD, R. (ed. by) : *État présent des Études Vétérotestamentaires = Études théologiques et religieuses*, xxvii (1952), No. 3. Pp. 84. (Montpellier. Price : Fr. 300.)

This particular issue of *Études théologiques et religieuses* marks the first step in an attempt which is being made by a number of Old Testament specialists in France and Switzerland to bridge the gulf between the expert in this field and the average Protestant pastor. It contains the following articles : " Pour comprendre l'Ancien Testament " (Aubert), an attempt to illustrate the difficulty of conveying Israelite thought in translation by a survey of the use of the term *dābhār* in its relation to Yahweh ; " La philologie sémitique et l'Ancien Testament " (Michaud) ; " Les manuscrits hébreux de la Mer Morte " (Jacob) ; " La critique actuelle et les problèmes que pose la Genèse " (Nagel), with special reference to the work of Chaine and de Vaux ; " Récentes introductions à l'Ancien Testament " (Goy), a survey of the work of Pfeiffer, Bentzen, Weiser, Sellin-Rost and Lods ; " L'espérance messianique d'Israël " (Pidoux), a review of Mowinckel's *Han som kommer ;* and " Où en est la typologie de l'Ancien Testament ?", an assessment of recent discussion of the typology of the Old Testament with due recognition of its historical aspects. All these articles have some sound comments to offer and, despite what is said about their primary purpose, may be read with profit by the expert.   A.R.J.

*MILLER, MADELEINE S. and J. L. : *Harper's Bible Dictionary*. 1952. Pp. xii+852+16 maps. (Harper & Bros., New York. Price : $7.95, thumb indexed $8.75.)

This excellent and up-to-date Bible Dictionary will be widely useful, especially because of its emobodiment of the work of recent archaeology. There are articles on Ras Shamra and on the Dead Sea Scrolls—including mention of part of the 1952 finds—and the list of archaeological sites examined, with the names of the excavators and the principal finds (pp. 33 ff.) is particularly valuable. Some of the articles are by Edwin Lewis, R. H. Pfeiffer, and J. A. Bewer, while A. P. Wikgren and F. C. Grant contributed charts. The chronology adopted throughout is Albright's, and he and G. E. Wright were frequently consulted by the authors, in addition to a number of other well-known scholars. The authors are, however, alone responsible for most of the articles. The volume is excellently illustrated and the maps of the *Westminster Historical Atlas* have been reproduced at the end. An enormous amount of work has gone into the preparation of the book, which should be in every School Library, and which will supplement the older works for busy clergy and ministers. Its reduced scale as compared with Hastings's *D.B.*, will limit its value for scholars, especially on literary critical matters, but it will often be consulted with advantage and with much saving of time.   H.H.R.

Orientalia suecana I, Fasc. 1/2, ed. by Erik Gren. 1952. Pp. 94. (Almqvist & Wiksells Boktryckeri Aktiebolag, Uppsala. Subscription price : Kr. 20.)

This new periodical is evidence (if such were needed) of the enthusiasm and learning with which oriental studies are pursued in Sweden ; and the contents of the first double fascicle are not only varied, but of high quality and importance. T. Säve-Söderbergh, writing on ' The '*prw* as Vintagers in Egypt ' makes a contribution to the '*prw*-Habiru question, based in part on hitherto unpublished Egyptian material. I. Engnell presents the first part of a study entitled ' *Pæsah-Maṣṣōt* and the Problem of " Patternism " ' ', in which he lists and briefly characterizes the Biblical sources for the festival, and proceeds to a discussion of the details found in Ex. xii. 1ff., contrasting the spring festival (as a more disintegrated example of the old cultic pattern) with the feast of Tabernacles. A. Haldar discusses the wall painting from court 106 of the palace of Mari, which he interprets in terms of the New Year Festival. Other articles are : ' Buntkeramik in Anatolien', by H. H. v. der Osten ; ' Mithra en vieux-perse', by S. Wikander ; and ' Xosrau Anōšurvān, les Hephtalites et les peuples turcs ', by G. Widengren.   G.W.A.

(N.B. Fasc. 3/4 consists of a single article which lies outside our field.   H.H.R.)

(Press, I.) : *Yerushalayim*, ed. by M. Ish-Shalom, M. Benayahu and A. Shohet. 1953. Pp. 326. (Rabbi Kook Foundation, Jerusalem. Price : I. £2.800.)

This Hebrew volume, dedicated to I. Press by the *Lema'an Yerushalayim* Association, on the occasion of his 75th birthday, contains twenty articles (including a Bibliography of the writings of I. Press) all of which have some bearing on Jerusalem—ancient and modern. The articles of special interest to Biblical scholars are : ' The Military Campaign of Amenhotep in the Land of Canaan ', by B. Mazar-Maisler, ' Geographical Names in Eretz-Israel according to Phoenician Inscriptions ', by N. Slouschz, ' The Chronological Order of the Yannai Coins ', by B. Kanael, ' The Wall of Agrippa's and Titus's Siege ', by M. Avi-Yona, ' Josephus's views on the Future of Israel and its Land ', by A. Shohet.   M.W.

Reallexikon für Antike und Christentum : Sachwörterbuch zur Auseinandersetzung des Christentums mit der Antiken Welt, ed. by Th. Klauser, together with F. J. Dölger, H. Lietzmann, J. H. Waszink, and L. Wenger. Lieferungen 9 and 10. 1951-52. Pp. 80 each. (Hiersemann Verlag, Stuttgart. Price : DM. 11.– and 12.50.)

The first seven parts of this work appeared during the War, 1941-45. The eighth, which completed the first volume (pp. viii+640 ; price : DM. 90.–), appeared in 1950. It is now expected that the remaining parts will appear without undue delay. The aim of the work is to survey the pre-Christian and Christian periods of antiquity, with recognition of their continuity and their difference. It includes within its scope not only the Greek and Roman worlds, but also Egypt, the Near East, and Iran, down to about A.D. 600. It is thus of importance to the Old Testament scholar, as well as to the New Testament scholar and the Church historian. The most important article in the two latest issues, from the point of view of the *Alttestamentler*, is Stummer's 55 page article on Circumcision.   O.E.

(Robinson, D. M.) : *Studies Presented to David Moore Robinson on his Seventieth Birthday*, vol. i. 1951. Pp. lx+876+111 plates and about 100 figs. in the text. (Washington University, St. Louis, Missouri. Price : $25.00.)

This stately quarto volume (to be followed by another, even more substantial, one) contains more than a hundred contributions from leading archaeologists and classical scholars in all parts of the world. Few of the papers are below the high standard set by the editor, George E. Mylonas. Besides the papers there are biographical and bibliographical sections. While only a few of the contributions bear directly on the O.T., many touch indirectly on it : e.g., V. Gordon Childe on the " Significance of the Sling ", the late J. D. S. Pendlebury on " Egypt and the Aegean ", W. F. Albright on the Wen-Amun Report, S. N. Kramer on the Sumerian school system, George Lippold on " Heilende Schlange ".   W.F.A.

Studia theologica cura ordinum theologorum Scandinavicorum edita, Vol.
IV, Fasc. ii. 1950/52. Pp. 80. (C. W. K. Gleerup, Lund. Price :
Kr. 8.00, or Kr. 12.00 annually.)

A Bentzen contributes to this fascicle an article, ' Der böse
Fürst ', in which he investigates the background of a tale by
H. C. Andersen, tracing part of the history of the ancient royal
ideology and the recurring protests against it. ' The
Restoration of Col. II of the Habakkuk Commentary of the
Dead Sea Scrolls ' by E. Sjöberg is a careful study based on a
smaller estimate of the missing portion of the MS. than is
suggested by the plates in the American edition. G. Lindeskog
contributes a New Testament article : ' Logia-Studien.'
G.W.A.

Studia theologica cura ordinum theologorum Scandinavicorum edita, Vol.
V, Fasc. i. 1951/52. Pp. 64. (C. W. K. Gleerup, Lund. Price :
Kr. 8.00, or Kr. 12.00 annually.)

None of the articles in this fascicle bears directly on the O.T.
Jørgen Pedersen writes on ' L'Intellectus fidei et la notion
de théologie chez saint Bonaventure '. N. A. Dahl contributes
two notes on Romans v, and T. Arvedson comments on Phil.
ii. 6 and Mt. x. 39. B. Noack discusses the quotation in Eph.
v. 4. G.W.A.

Studia theologica cura ordinum theologorum Scandinavicorum edita. Vol.
V, Fasc. ii. 1951/52. Pp. 106. (C. W. K. Gleerup, Lund. Price :
Kr. 8.00 or Kr. 12.00 annually.)

This fascicle is dedicated to Professor Fridrichsen (the first
editor of the periodical) on the occasion of his 65th birthday.
It begins with a long and important discussion by Mowinckel
of Pedersen's view that Exodus i-xv contains the cultic legend
of the Passover festival. He argues that the chapters form an
integral part of an historical work, that they contain much
more than the material of a cultic legend, that Pedersen's
arguments against documentary analysis are inconclusive, that
two literary sources are to be found in the chapters, and that
literary criticism and the traditio-historical approach are both
necessary in studying the pericope. A. Kuschke contributes a
study of Old Testament ethics (particularly comparing the
Wisdom and Prophetic literature), in the light of an earlier
article by Wingren. J. Munck examines an ossuary inscription
published by Sukenik. The other articles are on New Testament subjects : E. Sjöberg on Matt. vi. 12ff. ; P. Seidelin
on the sign of Jonah ; N. A. Dahl on the parables of growth.
G.W.A.

Svensk exegetisk årsbok, XVI, ed. by G. Lindeskog. 1951/52. Pp. 100.
With supplement : *Symbolae Biblicae Upsalienses* 14. 1952. Pp.
100. (Wretmans Boktryckeri Aktiebolag, Uppsala. Price : 15s. 6d.)

One article in this number is of special and direct interest to
the *Alttestamentler*. In a fresh and stimulating contribution
G. A. Danell raises again the question whether Amos really

was a nabi, and concludes that Amos says ' I am not ', but implies ' I am a nabi *extra ordinem.*' L. Wikström offers a convenient historical survey of the uses of the term ' myth ', relating primarily to contemporary discussion of the New Testament. R. Gyllenberg writes on the introductory greetings in the Pauline epistles, and H. Riesenfeld on Christian worship in the light of the New Testament. The important supplement by Bo Reicke on the Dead Sea Scrolls is noticed separately (see p. 72).   G.W.A.

VACCARI, A. : *Scritti di Erudizione e di Filologia.* Vol. 1. *Filologia Biblica e Patristica.* 1952. Pp. xlvi+392. (Edizioni di Storia e Letteratura, Rome. Price : L. 4000.)

This is the first volume of the *Festschrift* prepared in honour of Vaccari's fortieth year of teaching in Rome, which is, at the same time, his sixtieth year as a member of the Society of Jesus. Apart from a short introduction by G. de Luca, it is made up entirely of select items from the 374 entries in the jubilarian's bibliography and, with one exception, all the fifteen papers have been already published. The exception is the admirable and conspicuously erudite discussion of the psalters of Jerome and Augustine, of which only a few pages have hitherto seen the light. Among the older papers, those of most interest to an *Alttestamentler* are the ones on the fortunes of the Letter of Aristeas in Italy, leading up to an appraisement of R. Tramontano's superb edition ; on Hebrew Messianism and Vergil's Fourth Eclogue (in which the reference to Lagrange at p. 70, n. 1 should be *Revue biblique,* 1922, pp. 552ff.) ; on Hesychius of Jerusalem and his commentary on Leviticus ; on the genuine commentary on the Psalter of Remigius of Auxerre ; and on the Antiochene text of the Psalms in the fourth century. In fine, a volume of varied interest and one that by its fine printing and admirable learning will give pleasure to all friends of the Biblical Institute and of its senior professor.   J.M.T.B.

WEIGLE, L. A. (ed. by) : *An Introduction to the Revised Standard Version of the Old Testament.* 1952. Pp. 92. (Thomas Nelson & Sons, New York. Price : 5s. 0d.)

This brief but extremely important introduction gives an account of the stewardship of those scholars in America who produced the *Revised Standard Version of the Old Testament* which was completed this year, and will be read with the greatest interest and with considerable profit by all who wish to know about the background and the performance of that work. Though the brochure is a symposium contributed by twelve of the surviving members of the O.T. Committee, and represents the specialist interests of the authors, the dominating and unifying *motif*, the R.S.V., is never forgotten. The work cannot be too warmly recommended. The contents are :— Preface to the R.S.V. of the O.T. ; Method and Procedure of the Revision (W. A. Irwin) ; The Authorized Revisions of the

King James Version (G. Dahl) ; The Hebrew Text and Ancient VSS of the O.T. (H. M. Orlinsky) ; The Language of the O.T. (W. F. Albright) ; The Geography of the O.T. and the R.S.V. (H. G. May) ; Archaeology and the Translation of the O.T. (J. P. Hyatt) ; The Style and Vocabulary of the R.S.V. (Millar Burrows) ; The Poetry of the O.T. (J. Muilenburg) ; The Wisdom Literature of the O.T. (L. Waterman) ; Preaching Values of the R.S.V.—the Prophets (W. L. Sperry) ; The Use of the O.T. in Worship (F. James) ; Some misleading Words in the King James Version ; The Revision Committee and the Advisory Board.

B.J.R.

(WEIL, G. E.) : *Gotthold E. Weil Jubilee Volume.* 1952. Pp. 108+XII. (The Magnes Press, The Hebrew University, Jerusalem.)

' On 13th May, 1952, the School of Oriental Studies of the Hebrew University celebrated the 70th anniversary of its Nestor, Prof. Gotthold E. Weil, and decided to commemorate this event by a Jubilee Volume '. It is a beautifully produced volume, containing seventeen articles contributed by pupils and colleagues of Professor Weil. To Biblical scholars ' Mas ' Obhedh (Corvée) ' by A. Biram and ' Some Ideas of the Place of Ugaritic among the Semitic Languages ' by N. H. Tur-Sinai are of interest. Both of these articles will, according to a statement on p. VII, appear in full English translation elsewhere.

M.W.

EDUCATIONAL

City of Norwich Education Committee Agreed Syllabus of Religious Instruction. 1951. Pp. viii+104. (Fletcher & Son, Ltd., Norwich. Obtainable from the Director of Education, Education Office, Norwich. Price : 8s. 6d.)

The authors of this syllabus acknowledge their indebtedness to the Cambridgeshire, Surrey, and Sunderland Agreed Syllabuses in particular and justifiably claim for their own production the merits of compactness and brevity. Only one extended note is included, on Worship and the School. Apart from incidental stories the Old Testament is not introduced into the syllabus until the fourth year of the Junior School, and then the emphasis is on the prophets and their teaching. At the Secondary School stage the theme of the Old Testament teaching is God's revelation and man's response to it, and the course is carefully planned. The syllabus is of particular value for the fourth and fifth years of the Secondary School ; the theme for the fifth year is the unity of the Bible, and this section contains useful diagrams and notes.

L.A.P.

MORSLEY, H. V. : *Junior Bible Archaeology.* 1952. Pp. 100. (Epworth Press, London. Price : 6s. 6d.)

This book is written in a simple style adapted to children of Secondary School age. A short introduction on " scientific digging " is followed by some account of the excavations of

Woolley at Ur and of Layard at Calah, by a graphic description of the Pyramids, by short descriptions of the fall of Jericho, Hezekiah's tunnel, excavations at Lachish, etc., and finally by short chapters on cuneiform writing, hieroglyphics and alphabetic writing. Some pages make interesting reading but the book is disjointed and scrappy and occasionally inaccurate and misleading. There are no maps or illustrations though the text refers to a picture that was evidently intended to accompany it.

L.A.P.

Teachers' Notes on the Syllabus of Religious Education for use in Primary Schools in Scotland. 1952. Pp. 120. (Church of Scotland Offices, Edinburgh. Price : 4s. 0d.)

A Syllabus of Religious Education for use in Secondary Schools in Scotland, Fourth Year. 1951. Pp. 156. (Church of Scotland Offices, Edinburgh. Price : 6s. 0d.)

The Cheshire Agreed Syllabus of Religious Instruction. 1952. Pp. xiv+202. (University of London Press, London.• Price : 8s. 6d.)

A Scripture Course for Friends' Schools. 1952. Pp. 20. (Bannisdale Press, London. Price : 1s. 6d.)

Many Agreed Syllabuses have come into being since the Education Act of 1944, made their use in the state schools obligatory and a change of approach is now discernible. The pioneers, very conscious of the religious controversy which had bedevilled R.I. in the schools for long enough, and walking warily, rejoiced to find so much common ground. But a generation had grown up, often ill-taught and out of touch with organised Christianity, and syllabuses, admirable as evidence of a more constructive approach, were found to be very far removed from those destined to use them. So the newer syllabuses aim at teaching the teacher, difficult though it is to help him to a more mature and theological approach while at the same time grading the material, with much inevitable repetition for the different age groups.

The Teachers' Notes on the Syllabus of Religious Education for use in Primary Schools in Scotland has been prepared with the help of experienced teachers. The Person of Jesus is the focal point and the material is divided into what Jesus did, stories he told, and stories which he heard as a boy. Excellent introductory and background notes are given and, in the later sections, some suggestions as to treatment and aim. There is little extra-biblical material but David Livingstone, Mary Slessor and William Quarrier find a place among the " Friends of Jesus "

A Syllabus of Religious Education for use in Secondary Schools in Scotland, (Fourth Year), also a teachers' handbook, runs from Isaiah of Jerusalem to Nehemiah ; the New Testament covers St. Matthew. The notes are brief, scholarly and most helpful.

The Cheshire Agreed Syllabus of Religious Instruction is a mine of information and helpful suggestion; it has a valuable bibliography and is very modern in its general approach. It covers the whole age range from Nursery to school leaving age, hopefully placed at 16-17, and it is intended that " no boy or girl shall go out into the world without a knowledge of the Christian faith, its origin, development and meaning, and its abiding value as a way of life ". It is very much alive to the part played by the teacher. Much extra-biblical material (historical, biographical, missionary, doctrinal) is suggested, opening up possibilities to the intelligent teacher, and much of it refreshingly relevant to modern life. In our field some of the information is perhaps over-confident. Abraham is placed about 2100 B.C. ; a new book of the law was composed in the Southern Kingdom in the early seventh century . . . It has a very necessary index and two interesting appendices on Church history in Cheshire, and Cheshire schools.

The little *Scripture Course for Friends' Schools* is an outline which combines religious warmth with great intellectual honesty. If there is a gap between Paul and George Fox which gives it something of a sectarian flavour this syllabus has a quality which suggests how desirable it is that R.I. should be the integration of the young into a way of life which is there. The Agreed Syllabus, however good, and though it is so very much better than nothing at all, starts at a, now unavoidable, disadvantage and calls for the most enlightened and devoted work on the part of the teacher.   M.B.

ARCHAEOLOGY AND EPIGRAPHY

BARROIS, A.-G. : *Manuel d'Archéologie Biblique*, vol. II. 1953. Pp. xii+520. (Picard, Paris. Price : Fr. 2.250.)

The first volume of this work appeared in 1939 (see *Book List*, 1939, p. 3), and the second has been eagerly awaited these many years. It deals with the family, political institutions, law and the administration of justice, war, the arts, economics, burial, cultic centres and rites (both non-Israelite and Israelite). The whole work is of the highest importance, and it rests on up-to-date scholarship and is finely illustrated. No Old Testament scholar should be without it, and it is hard to single out any section for special mention. That on the family and that on the development of the art of writing, widely different from one another, are both excellent, and the tables of signs will be found very valuable, while the section on non-Israelite religion contains a good summary of Ras Shamra material. Alt's theory on the God of the patriarchs is rejected as ' gratuitous ', and the theory that connects the sabbath with Babylonian *šapattum* or with the full moon is rejected.   H.H.R.

BOULTON, W. H. : *Archaeology Explains*. 1952. Pp. 96. (Epworth Press, London. Price : 6s. 0d.)

The purpose of this work is to demonstrate how archaeology has elucidated details of the Bible record, the historicity of which is thereby enhanced. There is however, a tendency to selection of such instances and less objective interest in the archaeology of the ancient Near East than is desired even in a work where the Bible is the primary interest. On details the writer is generally well-informed, though there is an obvious reliance on a limited number of secondary authorities and general rather than specialized studies. There are also certain inaccuracies (e.g. Hazael's ivories were not from Carchemish but from Arslan Tash). There is also a tendency to ignore outstanding problems. Hammurabi, for instance, is dated ' somewhere about the time of Abraham ' but there is no attempt to utilize the Mari, Khorsabad, and Babylonian material to fix his date. The Mari excavations, in fact, are never mentioned and Ras Shamra only once cited for evidence of Horites in Syria. This little book, with its apposite archaeological illustrations from Genesis to Revelation would be quite a useful Bible class handbook. J.G.

CHILDE, V. G. : *New Light on the Most Ancient East*. 1952. Pp. 256+XXXIX pl. (Routledge and Kegan Paul, London. Price : 28s. 0d.)

In the third edition of his study of the archaeology of the ancient Near East Professor Childe limits himself, as he had previously done, to the formative period from the Neolithic revolution to the culmination of the urban civilization of Egypt, Sumer and the Indus towards the end of the 3rd millennium. Though the attention of the writer is focussed on those centres of riverine culture, the really new element in his work is an appraisal of the mass of new material from the intervening areas of Iran, Upper Mesopotamia, and Syria-Palestine. The new edition by its fuller documentation will be welcomed by specialists, though the general reader will perhaps regret that the broad features, so conspicuous in the earlier editions, are somewhat obscured by the additional details. J.G.

Corpus Inscriptionum Semiticarum, Pars II, tomus iii : Tabulae, fasciculus I. 1951. (e Reipublicae Typographeo, Paris. Price : 36s. 0d.)

The present fascicle contains 33 plates illustrating the Aramaic texts in the corresponding fascicle of the *Corpus*, all beautifully reproduced and well maintaining the high standard of excellence set by previous volumes of this publication. G.R.D.

DOSSIN, G. : *Archives Royales de Mari. V. Correspondance de Iasmaḫ-Addu*. 1952. Pp. iii+141. (Imprimerie Nationale, Paris. Price : 19s. 6d.)

This, the fifth volume of this important volume of texts, contains another 88 letters transliterated and translated with the masterly skill which Professor Dossin is showing in all his work. It contains also useful summaries of the contents of each letter at the beginning and brief philological notes at the end, both equally well done and equally welcome. The texts are all of the first importance for both historians and philologists and will amply repay careful study. The volume exactly follows its predecessors in form, and its successors will be eagerly awaited. G.R.D.

DOSSIN, G. : *Musée du Louvre. Textes cunéiformes, Tome XXV. Archives royales de Mari IV.* 1951. Plates lxxx. (Geuthner, Paris. Price : Frs. 2250.)

This is the fourth volume of the famous correspondence from Mari on the Middle Euphrates and the second containing letters of Šamši-Addu, king of Assyria. The copies maintain the high standard of excellence which this well-known series has always shown. G.R.D.

EISSFELDT, O. : *Sanchunjaton von Berut und Ilumilku von Ugarit.* 1952. Pp. 74. (Max Niemeyer Verlag, Halle. Price : 15s. 0d.)

In this monograph Professor Eissfeldt examines carefully, on the one hand, the late and contradictory accounts of Eusebius, Porphyry and Philo concerning Sanchuniathon, and, on the other hand, the contemporary and clear evidence from Ras Shamra concerning Ilumilku. His aim is to obtain as clear a picture as possible of the two men, and to show how the information from Ras Shamra concerning Ilumilku makes it possible to pierce the shadows which surround the figure of Sanchuniathon and to see him more distinctly as the person he was. Ilumilku is seen to have been both scribe and author, a man highly regarded in his own country, and in touch with professional colleagues abroad. Sanchuniathon, it is suggested, may be viewed in a similar light. He may be regarded as a learned man, well known both in Beirut and further afield, a man who enjoyed the same kind of international renown as did Ethan the Ezrahite and the other wise men referred to in 1 Kings v. 11. D.W.T.

EISSFELDT, O. : *Taautos und Sanchunjaton.* 1952. Pp. 70. (Akademie-Verlag, Berlin. Price : 10s. 0d.)

In the first part of this work the author discusses the origin and nature of Taautos, who is referred to several times by Philo Byblius. In one group of passages he is spoken of as a man, in another as a god. Both groups agree, however, in attributing to him the invention of the alphabet and other signs, a fact which suggests that underlying his name is a word meaning " sign ". The name is accordingly to be connected with the root *t'h* " mark ". A fuller form, perhaps *ba'al* or *'el ta'awat* " lord " or " god of the sign ", may have become shortened to *ta'awat*. It is possible that Taautos, whose name and form may be a specifically Phoenician creation, may have been known as early as the period of the Ras Shamra texts. In the second part of the work, which is

470

devoted to a discussion of the Sanchuniathon problem, it is emphasized that the extracts from Philo's Phoenician history preserved by Eusebius contain elements which could have been taken from an older Phoenician *Vorlage* ; and that the Ras Shamra texts and the Hittite mythological texts from Boghazköy—the date of both sets of documents is *c.* 1400 B.C.—show points of contact with Philo's Phoenician history, and so may prove to be of importance for the solution of the Sanchuniathon problem. The case for the view that Sanchuniathon wrote a history of his land and people in Beirut *c.* 1400 B.C. is held to be much stronger to-day than heretofore. The extent to which the fragments of Philo's history may go back to Sanchuniathon's work remains, however, difficult to determine in detail. D.W.T.

FAKHRY, A. and RYCKMANS, G. : *An Archaeological Journey to Yemen,* 3 parts. 1951-52. Pp. xvi+188, xii+96, x+XCII plates. (Government Press, Cairo.)

The writer presents an account of his visit to San'a and certain sites in the vicinity, notably Ma'in and Marib (Part I). His activity was limited yet he contrived to make useful notes and to take a whole volume of photographs (Part III) including nine of the famous dam and related inscriptions. In Part II G. Ryckmans transcribes and translates 132 inscriptions of various length with commentary. As these exclude inscriptions from the sites already published, this is an indication of the amount of epigraphic material extant in South Arabia. Ryckmans also adds a short note on Sabaean history and religion as an appendix to the first part. J.G.

GORDON, C. H. : *Introduction to Old Testament Times.* 1952. Pp. viii+312. (Ventnor Publishers, Ventnor, N.J. Price : $4.75.)

This is a good popular survey of the history of Israel in the Old Testament period, in the setting of the known culture and history of the ancient Near East. After a short chapter of Prolegomena on sources and method and another on the early Biblical narratives and their essential significance, there are chapters on Egypt, Mesopotamia, Ugarit and Homer before the Patriarchal Age is reached. Later there is a chapter on Karatepe. For the rest the history of Israel is reviewed but with extra-Biblical materials as well as the Old Testament constantly in mind. It is inevitable that in a book of this character much debated problems are apodictically settled. On the other hand the reader will gather a great deal of information not readily accessible in works on this scale. In no other comparable book will he find the Karatepe discoveries laid under contribution, and the chapter on Homer will be an illuminating surprise to many readers. Few readers will fail to glean fresh knowledge or to profit by the study of this book. H.H.R.

GORDON, C. H. : *Smith College Tablets—110 Cuneiform Texts Selected from the College Collection.* (Smith College Studies in History, Vol. XXXVIII.) 1952. Pp. vi+38+cxx plates. (Smith College, Northampton, Mass. Price : $2.00.)

> The 110 tablets now in the Smith College, Northampton, Mass., U.S.A., are of various dates, from pre-Ur III to Achaemenian times. They are all from Lower Mesopotamia and, with the exception of one religious text, they are mostly administrative records and contracts. In themselves they are not exceptional, but they add details to what we know already, and thus help to build up the complete picture of the social life of the times in which they were written. Professor Gordon is to be thanked for publishing all the texts in copy, giving a summary of their contents, and setting them briefly in their historical context. Those who are not Assyriologists will find his description of " Contents and Problems " useful. A very good book within its limits.   T.F.

GURNEY, O. R. : *The Hittites.* 1952. Pp. 240. (Pelican Books, London. Price : 3s. 6d.)

> This is an excellent summary of what is known of the Hittites from excavations in their Anatolian homeland and from their records. For citations from the latter the work is particularly valuable. After a summary of the history of Hittitology the writer traces the history of the Hittites from their appearance in Anatolia to the destruction of their Empire at the end of the Bronze Age. He deals with their vassal states which survived this catastrophe in North Syria and the Tauric foothills. He also discusses the question of Achaeoi-Akhiyawa and of Hittites in Palestine, the latter, however, without arriving at any convincing conclusion. Social, legal, and military institutions, religion, warfare, art, language, and literature are discussed. In the last department we are shown the development from the recording of annals to the writing of history and are introduced to Hittite mythology which, the writer suggests, may be associated rather with the native subjects than the ruling caste of the Hittites.   J.G.

KENYON, KATHLEEN M. : *Beginning in Archaeology.* 1952. Pp. 204. (Phoenix House, London. Price : 12s. 6d.)

> In a masterly presentation of the practical problems and a description of the modern methods of archaeology, Miss Kenyon has given the fruits of her wide experience in various fields in Britain and the Near East and also in the class-room. After a concise account of the growth and diffusion of early cultures westwards from the Near East from the pre-historic period to the Iron Age, the various fields are delimited in Britain, Europe, the Near, Middle and Far East, and even America. The technique of field work, including excavation, surveying, recording, treatment of objects, photography, surface exploration, and aerial survey is most thoroughly described. This little work, lucid, concise, and bearing the stamp of genuine authority in every statement, will command the respect of all interested in archaeology from the established authority to the first beginner.   J.G.

KRAMER, S. N. : *Enmerkar and the Lord of Aratta : a Sumerian Epic Tale of Iraq and Iran.* 1952. Pp. 56+XXVIII pl. (The University Museum of Pennsylvania, Philadelphia. Price : $1.00.)

This epic fragment, on twenty tablets and fragments from the early excavations at Nippur and now in the Museum of the Ancient Orient in Istambul and the University Museum, Pennsylvania, is the largest of this *genre* of Sumerian literature yet discovered. A transliteration is given with translation and commentary and a brief introduction. Photographs and transcriptions are given in the plates. The writer dates the tablets *c.* 1700 B.C. but maintains that the tradition goes back much earlier. He suggests that the events depicted fell in the beginning of the 3rd millennium. If that is correct, the significance of the text is that it demonstrates economic and cultural contacts between Sumer and Iran in the proto-dynastic period, which archaeology had already indicated. The text indicates that not only were such contacts closer than archaeologists had imagined, but that this relationship might amount to political domination by such a city-state as Erech.

J.G.

LAROCHE, E. : *Recueil d'onomastique hittite.* 1952. Pp. 154. (Librairie C. Klincksiek, Paris. Price : Fr. 1080.)

Professor Laroche has combed all the published Hittite texts, cuneiform and hieroglyphic, in order to collect and study Hittite personal names. His work falls into three parts. First, he provides a catalogue of the names sub-divided into those which occur in the Boghazköy texts, those which occur in other Hittite cuneiform texts and those from hieroglyphic sources : he gives full references to the published literature for each name. In the second part he studies the origin and types of the names, and in the third part he analyses their structure. The result is a work of the greatest importance for Indo-European philologists. It is hardly less important for the student of the history of the ancient Near East, in that it provides him with an index of all persons mentioned in the Hittite texts so far published.   T.W.T.

MALAMAT, A. : *The Aramaeans in Aram Naharaim and the Rise of their States.* (In Hebrew.) 1952. Pp. 76. (Israel Exploration Society, Jerusalem.)

This is a doctoral dissertation prepared with the guidance of B. Maisler. The study, as the title suggests, is somewhat too severely limited to the area of the Euphrates and beyond to be of great significance for Old Testament study. The emergence of the Aramaeans in the politics of the Near East is traced in Assyrian records from the beginning of the 12th century. The work is well documented and the Assyrian sources critically examined, though the writer is less concerned with the internal political development and culture of the Aramaic states than with their geographical distribution and their chronology. This is the real strength of the work. A section on Tell Halaf in the period of Kapara shows that the writer is conversant with the situation in Syria and with recent archaeological research there. The only point at which the work impinges directly on O.T. study is an appendix on Israel and Aram Şobah, which the writer locates on the Euphrates in the region occupied later by Bit Adini. In marked contrast with the critical handling of the Assyrian evidence is the unquestioning acceptance of the Biblical statement of the campaigns of Saul against the Aramaeans.

(with acknowledgements to M.W.)   J.G.

MOSCATI, S. : *L'Oriente Antico.* 1952. Pp. 120, with 30 pages of plates. (Vallardi, Milan. Price : 2,000 lire.)

This work forms part of *Storia Universale,* which is being published under the direction of Professor E. Pontieri, of the University of Naples. There are five main chapters, (i) Introductory (geography, peoples, chronology, the beginnings of history), (ii) *c.* 2600-2000 B.C. (Sumerians and Semites in Mesopotamia ; Egypt), (iii) *c.* 2000-1550 B.C. (Amorites ; Hammurabi ; Egypt), (iv) *c.* 1550 to the twelfth century B.C. (Egypt ; Hittites ; Hurrians ; Cassites ; Assyrians ; Semites in Syria and Palestine), (v) From the twelfth century to 332 B.C. (New Assyrian empire ; Aramaeans ; Hebrews, Chaldaeans ; Egypt ; Persia). In accordance with the general plan of the book, the political history of the people is first presented and this is followed by accounts of their religion, literature, art, and other aspects of their life and thought. The more important documents and monuments receive attention, and the insertion of the sections relating to Egypt, which are written by Dr. S. Bosticco, at appropriate places— a somewhat unusual but attractive arrangement—is designed to indicate Egypt's role in the contemporary historical situation. The bibliographies are ample, up to date, and conveniently arranged, and the five chronological tables, corresponding to the five main chapters, are set out so as to furnish a synoptic view of the history. The plates, which have been well selected, add greatly to the interest and usefulness of the work. There is a good map, and a full index of names is supplied. Students who wish to be introduced, by way of broad outlines, to the study of the ancient east will find the book reliable, instructive, and, despite the great amount of material which has had to be compressed, readable. D.W.T.

PARROT, A. : *Découvertes des Mondes Ensevelis.* 1952. Pp. 150. (Delachaux and Niestlé, Neuchâtel and Paris. Price : Swiss Fr. 7.80 ; subscription price : Swiss Fr. 7.00.)

This is a general conspectus of Near Eastern archaeology by the excavator of Mari. With illustrations from his personal experience in Mesopotamia he describes the technique and problems of archaeology and devotes a chapter to the history of the science in Western Asia. He next gives the broad outlines of the history of the region with citation of relevant archaeological evidence through a period of five millennia until the late Roman period. He concludes with a somewhat sketchy but eminently sane account of the bearing of archaeology upon the Bible.   J.G.

PARROT, A. : *Déluge et l'Arche de Noé*. (Cahiers d'Archéologie Biblique I). 1952. Pp. 62. (Delachaux and Niestlé, Neuchâtel and Paris. Price : Swiss Fr. 3.90 ; subscription price : Swiss Fr. 3.50.)

This is a summary review of the Biblical narratives and of the various Mesopotamian traditions of the Flood together with a review of the archaeological evidence which has been claimed for this phenomenon. The work closes with a brief account of the role played by the Ark in Christian exegesis and art. The author speaks with the authentic voice of one of the foremost archaeologists and his review of the archaeological evidence of ' Flood ' strata in various Mesopotamian sites is particularly valuable.   J.G.

SIMONS, J. : *Jerusalem in the Old Testament*. 1952. Pp. xiv+518+ 33 plates. (Brill, Leiden. Price : Fl. 80.00.)

The writer presents a most thorough topographical study of ancient Jerusalem, characterized by a meticulous survey and criticism of the archaeological research of the site and, *pari passu*, of the ancient documents, particularly Josephus, Nehemiah, and the relevant parts of Jeremiah. He is appreciative particularly of the work of Weill in the extreme South of the city of David on the south-east hill, but he fairly and fully represents the work of others. He maintains that the south-west hill was occupied in pre-Israelite times and was incorporated into the capital city, probably by Solomon. This, however, he demonstrates from documentary evidence rather than from the excavations of Bliss on the south-west hill and Johns in the Citadel. He devotes an illuminating chapter to Jerusalem as indicated in Nehemiah. This source, he admits, is vital, but not independently of other sources and archaeology. In the vexed questions of the 2nd and 3rd—Agrippa's—walls he may be said to be conservative, tracing the former from the Citadel eastwards, then northwards to the fortress Antonia, northwest of the Temple area, and taking the latter to follow generally the line of the modern (Turkish) wall of the Old City. He appreciates the importance of Hamilton's recent soundings outside this wall, but considers them on too small a scale to decide such a difficult problem and finds Hamilton's report too difficult to admit of unequivocal judgement. He agrees with Vincent on the poor quality of the more northerly wall discovered by Robinson and later investigated by Sukenik and Mayer, but has no decided views on its origin. The work is sumptuously produced with abundance of plates and plans, though somewhat marred by minor technical errors. These, however, are far outweighed by the outstanding merit of the book, which is a real classic in its subject.   J.G.

VANDIER, J. : *Manuel d'archéologie égyptienne. Tome premier : Les époques de formation.* 1952. Pp. viii+1044. (Editions A. et J. Picard, Paris. Price : Fr. 4300.)

The first volume of this work is issued in two parts. The first part deals with the prehistoric period and the second with the first three dynasties. The work is a detailed study of all the various types of objects which excavations have revealed, and it is richly illustrated with drawings, plans and charts. When completed it will be a reference work of the greatest importance to all Near Eastern archaeologists, whatever their speciality.   T.W.T.

WOOLLEY, SIR LEONARD : *A Forgotten Kingdom.* 1953. Pp. 200+24 plates. (Penguin Books, Harmondsworth. Price : 2s. 6d.)

This is a popular account of the author's excavation of ancient Alalakh in the basin of the Lower Orontes. The site was chosen because of its situation on the ancient trade route from Mesopotamia to the timber-bearing Amanus and to the sea, and because of its secondary importance, which adapted it to play an assimilative role, thus faithfully reflecting the successive cultures of the Near East. The work is a good description of archæological method and emphasizes the influence of the various cultures of Mesopotamia in North Syria. Besides the evidence that is adduced for social and political conditions in Syria and in patriarchal times, Old Testament students will be particularly interested in the study of the inscription of Idri-mi, where the author accepts the ' *apiru* as Hebrews, and in an elaboration of his view that Khirbet Kerak ware is associated with a Caucasian people who settled first in North Syria and then were displaced, some to Anatolia and some to Palestine, whence the ' Hittites ' of Hebron in the time of Abraham.   J.G.

HISTORY AND GEOGRAPHY

ABEL, F. M. : *Histoire de la Palestine depuis la conquête d'Alexandre jusqu'à l'invasion arabe.* II. *De la Guerre Juive à l'invasion arabe.* 1952. Pp. x+406. (Gabalda, Paris. Price : Fr. 2200.)

The first volume of this important work was noticed in the *Book List* for 1952. It is not, as has already been stated, a history of religious ideas (for which one is referred to other works), but it is a historical and political study which, in the present volume, deals with a period less well known to most students of Holy Scripture than the subject-matter of the earlier volume. This volume opens with a chapter on the organization of the Jewish resistance movement by the extremists and on the campaign of Vespasian and Titus in Peraea, Idumaea and Judaea. There follows a rather compressed account of the siege of Jerusalem ; in the absence of a map of Jerusalem and its environs this becomes more than ordinarily difficult to follow. Later chapters study the periods from the reign of Vespasian to the death of Trajan, under the reigns of Hadrian and the Antonines, under Septimius Severus and Caracalla, and under the Syrian dynasty. The remaining chapters of the second part deal with the years from the accession of Maximinus the Thracian until the portion of Constantine's reign that precedes the foundation of Constantinople.

The third and last part has seven chapters covering the years 325-640 (from the time of the Council of Nicaea down to the conquest of Palestine by the Arabs). Of special interest are the three concerned with the Constantinian dynasty, ending with the death of Julian in 363 ; the reign of Justinian ; and the successive stages of the Arab conquest. The great defects of this sober and scholarly work are that it fails to provide adequate maps and that, in two volumes of more than nine hundred pages in all, covering a total period of nine hundred years, no space has been found for a general index.

J.M.T.B.

AUERBACH, E. : *Moses.* 1953. Pp. 244. (Ruys, Amsterdam. Price : Fl. 15.0.)

In this book, written in German, Dr. Auerbach offers a critical survey of the life and work of Moses. His conclusions are that Moses is a historical character and a Levite. Historical substance is found in the story of his stay in Midian and of his leading of Israel out of Egypt. The goal of the Exodus is held to have been Kadesh, and the plan to conquer Canaan is found to be a later idea that came into being in Kadesh. The divine name Yahweh is held to have been first made known to Moses. The Decalogue is attributed to Moses, and the twelve tribes of the Sinai Covenant are held to be not the same as the later twelve sons of Jacob. To Moses is attributed monotheism, and an essentially ethical religion. Chronological problems are not discussed, and there is no attempt to set Moses in world history. Despite this weakness in a biographical work—understandable, indeed, in view of the vexed nature of the problems—the work is of some importance. Its generally conservative conclusions do not rest on an unwillingness to face critical problems, and on a number of issues views which are not conservative are expressed.

H.H.R.

BARON, S. W. : *A Social and Religious History of the Jews*, Vol. I, Ancient Times, Parts 1 and 2. Second ed., rev. and enlarged. 1952. Pp. xii+416, vi+494. (Columbia University Press, New York and Geoffrey Cumberlege, London. Price : $12.50 or £4 2s. 0d.)

These are the first two volumes of a work which will run to seven volumes, and they cover the period down to Talmudic times. They rest on very profound learning, and the references to literature in the voluminous notes are so rich as to be worth the price of the volumes in themselves. These notes are gathered at the end of each volume, and occupy a quarter of the total pages. Mosaic monotheism is maintained, and the Decalogue is attributed to Moses. The period of the Judges is passed over lightly, and the eighth and seventh century prophets have less space than they would normally be given in Christian works, while the Suffering Servant has a single paragraph and a footnote. On the other hand there is an excellent treatment of the Diaspora. The second of these two volumes deals with the post-Christian period. There is a chapter, entitled " The Great Schism ", on the effects of the rise of Christianity on Judaism, and a valuable treatment of the world of the Talmud and of Talmudic law and religion. Everywhere the author's control of literature, including the most recent, is remarkable, especially when the vast range of his subject is considered, and he shows a penetration which makes his work throughout one of great importance. H.H.R.

BUYSSCHAERT, G. : *Israël et le Judaïsme dans le Cadre de l'ancient Orient.* 1953. Pp. 392+2 maps. (Editions Beyaert, Bruges. Price : Belgian Fr. 165.)

This work contains a short account of Egypt and the Semitic World as the setting for the review of the Old Testament. There is a brief summary of the sites excavated in Palestine, and frequent comparison between Biblical and non-Biblical texts. Abraham is made contemporary with Hammurabi in the 18th century B.C., and the Exodus placed at about 1250. Ezekiel is given a ministry in Jerusalem before his deportation to Babylonia, while Ezra is placed after Nehemiah in the reign of Artaxerxes II. Deutero-Isaiah is accepted as addressed to the Exiles, and Trito-Isaiah as an appendix. Daniel is treated after Ezra and Nehemiah, as a work written for the consolation of the Jews in difficult times, applying to Maccabean times ancient prophecies of Daniel's. There are brief notes on some of the pseudepigraphical books, and a short account of the Jewish parties on the eve of the Christian era, where the book ends. The whole covers a wide range and forms a very useful handbook. It is much to be regretted that the author did not live to see his work through the press.
H.H.R.

FERNÁNDEZ, A. : *Geografía Bíblica (El País de Jesús).* 1951. Pp. xviii+138 (with two folding maps). (Editorial Vilamala, Madrid.)

The author who has been preparing a full geography of Palestine for some years past has had the excellent idea of producing a small popular book, which will be found useful by the " público de mediana cultura " and will provide a " geography without tears ". The work is divided between three types of geography—physical, political and historico-topographical, and is printed clearly with a number of excellent illustrations from photographs. The one on p. 88, showing the source at Ain-Fara is explained in a footnote as the probable site of the burial by Jeremiah of his girdle (xiii. 1ff.). Surely it would be better to warn the reader that it is even more probable that the action was entirely symbolic, calling for no geographical identifications ! The maps are excellently drawn, but it was perhaps a mistake to mix Spanish and Arabic designations. At any rate those readers who are not Spaniards might fail to recognize Bethlehem under the style of Belén, and would prefer the Hebrew or the Arabic form. J.M.T.B.

*FISON, J. E. : *Understanding the Old Testament : The way of Holiness*
1952. Pp. 208. (Oxford University Press. Price : 8s. 6d.)

The Old Testament is here introduced to the general reader
in a series of short chapters, twenty in all, each dealing with a
place, event or person within the main sequence of Israel's
history. The language is simple and direct and due regard is
paid to the results of literary criticism, but the more serious
reader may at times feel that the attempt to speak of the Old
Testament in modern idiom is overstrained. The sub-title,
the Way of Holiness, demands a more dignified treatment
than some chapters offer. Nevertheless the book can be
warmly recommended for use in the upper forms of schools
and for group discussions. L.H.B.

HEINISCH, P. : *History of the Old Testament*, E. Tr. by W. Heidt.
1952. Pp. xviii+492. (Liturgical Press, Collegeville, Minnesota.
Price : $6.50.)

The German text of this volume was reviewed in the *Book
List* for 1951, p. 25. The English translation includes some
revised passages (embodying, e.g., reference to the Dead Sea
Scrolls), and there are illustrations (which one reader could
have spared), together with some notes thereon. The History
is a good general account of the whole period from the Creation
to the Destruction of the Second Temple, with some attention
to the religion and culture. It rests on up-to-date scholarship
and very wide reading, and the bibliographical material is
excellent. The standpoint is conservative. The early narratives
of Genesis are not treated as history, but the patriarchal
stories and the Exodus narrative are held to have historical
substance. More surprisingly Daniel is treated as a historical
person of the sixth century B.C. Ezra is held to have preceded
Nehemiah, and Ezekiel is presented as prophesying only in
Babylonia. The translation is fluent, and the book is well
produced, save that the notes are all printed at the end.
H.H.R.

SCHMIDTKE, F. : *Der Aufbau der babylonischen Chronologie.* 1952. Pp.
104, with 4 Tafeln. (Aschendorff, Münster-i.-W. Price : DM. 6.50.)

This brief work in the first chapter discusses the sources of
Babylonian chronology and its problems, and in the second
sets out the lists of Babylonian and Assyrian kings with their
dates ; the author assigns Hammurabi, following the king-
list A+B, to 1730-1688 B.C. Appendices contain WB. 44,
the king-lists of Larsa, Babylon and Khorsabad, the Synchronistic History and the Babylonian Chronicle, all in transliteration, and the Ptolemaic Canon. The work will be found
trustworthy and useful by all students of Babylonian and
Assyrian history. G.R.D.

VELIKOVSKY, I. : *Ages in Chaos*. 1952. Pp. xxiv+350 with 9 plates and 2 end maps. (Doubleday & Co., New York. Price : $4.50.)

The main thesis of the author is that somehow six hundred years of Egyptian history have been duplicated in all our history books, and that what is normally regarded as having happened in Egypt between 1780 and 1360 or so really happened between, say, 1500 and 850. Thus among other shocks to the orthodox, the Exodus coincided with the Hyksos *invasion*, Hatshepsut was the Queen of Sheba, the Amarna Letters were written by Jehoshaphat and Ahab. Some of the parallels the author quotes in support of his thesis are certainly very remarkable, though many of his equations make one gasp ; but we must wait for the promised second volume to see what Velikovsky will do with the now superfluous second half millennium of Egyptian history. In view of his high regard for Assyrian chronology (p. 99 f.), it would have been advisable to have included an explanation of the widely accepted synchronism of Akhnaton (now *ca.* 850 by Velikovsky's dating) with Asshuruballit I (*ca.* 1350). The reviewer found the argument strongest where his own knowledge was weakest.

D.R.Ap-T.

TEXT AND VERSIONS

FISCHEL, W. J. : *The Bible in Persian Translation*. 1952. (Reprinted from *Harvard Theological Review*.) Pp. 46. (Luzac, London. Price : 6s. 6d.)

A valuable account of the many translations of the Bible into Persian, both before the time of Jacob ben Tavus—whose translation of the Pentateuch stands in Walton's Polyglott in Persian script instead of the translator's Hebrew script—and since. The work of Vecchietti in collecting manuscripts and in transcribing the text is outlined, and also the part played by Akbar the Great and Nādir Shah in causing translations to be made. While there is no discussion of the quality and worth of the translations, much little-known information is gathered here.

H.H.R.

*MAY, H. G. : *Our English Bible in the Making*. 1952. Pp. 154. (Westminster Press, Philadelphia. Price : $2.75.)

Professor May was a prominent member of the Committee which prepared the 1952 Revised Standard Version of the Bible in America, and in the present book he has a very interesting story to tell about its activities. This story, however, is not given undue prominence, for it has been fitted into a setting which covers the whole history of Bible translation from ' The Bible in Greek ' to the twenty or so English translations of the present century, with brief discussions of 'A Half-century of Discovery '—inscriptions, the Dead Sea Scrolls, the Cairo Genizah, N.T. papyri, and the ' International New Testament Manuscripts Project '; and a host of other topics. I cannot think of a better introduction for senior School and junior University students and Sunday School teachers, especially in America.

B.J.R.

POPE, H. : *English Versions of the Bible*, ed. by S. Bullough. 1952. Pp. xii+788. (B. Herder, London. Price : £3 15s. 0d.)

This is an immense work that has been many years in the making and that its author did not live to complete. It is designed as a history of all versions in English that have been made in these islands and in all other lands of English speech, and its five main parts deal respectively with Anglo-Saxon and Early English (which includes Middle English) manuscript versions, early printed editions, the Rheims-Douay and the Authorised Versions, Catholic Versions since Rheims-Douay, and Protestant versions since the Authorised. The appendices include reprints of the prefaces to the Rheims New Testament of 1582 and the Douay Old Testament of 1609, and a list of private versions published between the Authorised and the Revised versions. There is a very full bibliography running to thirty-two pages, and a supplement on American editions of the Catholic Bible. A good deal of the cataloguing of long-defunct editions may seem to be superfluous and to add unnecessarily to the cost, but, by way of compensation, there has been a praiseworthy and well-rewarded effort to be as complete as possible. The least satisfactory chapters are those on the pre-Wycliffite and Wycliffite versions, where there is need for a full discussion of Gasquet's theory set out in *The Old English Bible* and of M. Deanesly's reply to it in *The Lollard Bible*.   J.M.T.B.

RYPINS, S. : *The Book of Thirty Centuries : An Introduction to Modern Study of the Bible.* 1951. Pp. xviii+420. (Macmillan, New York, and London. Price : $7.00, or 52s. 6d.)

This is a remarkable book, remarkable because it is written by a professor of English, who has read widely in the Biblical field and who has familiarized himself with the Hebrew language and with the problems of textual criticism. Much more space is devoted to the Old Testament than to the New, and one suspects that the author found the problems of the former the more fascinating. Most of the work is taken up with the nature and transmission of the text, and with ancient and modern translations, and a great deal of information is here assembled which will be of value to every reader. Every Hebrew word is transliterated, and but for its very high price the book could be recommended for inclusion in every school library. The final chapter attempts the difficult task of giving a review of the Higher Criticism of both Testaments in 65 pages. As an introduction to Lower Criticism and Higher Criticism it is over-weighted on the side of the former, while there are other sides of modern study which are not dealt with at all. It represents, nevertheless, a great achievement and readers of every level will use it with profit. At the end of the book are some valuable tables.   H.H.R.

481

Vetus Latina. Die Reste der altlateinischen Bibel nach Petrus Sabatier neu gesammelt und herausgegeben von der Erzabtei Beuron. 2. *Genesis.* 2te Lief. 1952. Pp. 129-288. (Herder, Freiburg. Price : DM. 29.75.)

The second fascicle of the second volume of the new edition of the Old-Latin Bible, which contains Gen. ix. 14—xxvii. 23, continues this important work in precisely the same manner as in the preceding chapters. The next part is expected to appear in the coming autumn.   G.R.D.

VÖÖBUS, A. : *Die Spuren eines älteren äthiopischen Evangelien-textes im Lichte der literarischen Monumente.* (Papers of the Estonian Theological Society in Exile, No. 2.) 1951. Pp. 40. (Estonian Theological Society in Exile, Stockholm.)

This paper is concerned to show from a study of Gospel citations in monastic writings of the 14th—15th centuries that behind the much-revised Ethiopic ' vulgate ' is a version made from the Old Syriac. Dr. Vööbus offers also a recon-struction of the history of the Church in Abyssinia which is important for the study of the history of a neglected version of the Bible.   W.D.M.

WALLENSTEIN, M. : *The Piyyuṭ, with special reference to the textual study of the Old Testament.* (Reprinted from *Bulletin of the John Rylands Library,* vol. 34, No. 2, March, 1952.) 1952. Pp. 8. (Manchester University Press and The John Rylands Library, Manchester. Price : 1s. 6d.)

In this article the author draws attention to a source of study for the textual criticism of the Hebrew Bible which has hitherto been little utilised, viz. payyeṭanic literature, i.e. synagogal poetry. He gives a general account of this literature, with special reference to the period beginning with Yannai, of Palestine, about the seventh century, and the period of the Jewish poets of Spain, which begins about the tenth century. In particular he examines in some detail the Qerobhah type of piyyuṭim, which is the first in order of time, and which contains a larger number of Biblical verses than is usually the case with other types of piyyuṭim. As a rule these verses follow the M.T., but there are exceptions. In the examples which are given, Yannai's text sometimes agrees with the LXX and other ancient versions, and sometimes, so it would seem, in the case of Isaiah, with the St. Mark's scroll, against the M.T. Interesting though these variants are, the all important question is the significance of them. Into this question the author does not enter here, but he intends to return to it. The possibility that some of the variants may be due to copyists' errors must, as he says, be allowed for. Orthographical considerations too are involved. Only when these, and perhaps other, problems have been investigated, will it be possible to assess the contribution which payyetanic literature may have to make to textual criticism.   D.W.T.

WÜRTHWEIN, E. : *Der Text des Alten Testaments. Eine Einführung in die Biblia Hebraica von Rudolf Kittel.* 1952. Pp. 176. (Privileg. Württ. Bibelanstalt, Stuttgart. Price : DM. 5.20.)

> This is an extremely valuable handbook which every student should acquire for guidance in the use of the third and subsequent editions of *Kittel's Biblia Hebraica.* The story of the Massoretic text and the Versions is simply though adequately related from the standpoint of the *Sigla et Compendia* in the Prolegomena to *BH*, the sigla being appropriately introduced in the margins. If the narrative be felt to mirror too rigidly the theories of Professor Kahle, that is understandable because of the part played by this scholar in the production of *BH* : furthermore, especially in the discussion of the Septuagint, the writer states quite clearly that other interpretations are possible. The brief treatment of the Vulgate, and the dismissal of the Benedictine edition with a bare mention reflects the *apparatus criticus* of the edition ; on the other hand, the Dead Sea Scrolls figure quite prominently. An admirable feature of the book is a collection of 40 plates, with brief discussions : they include prints which cover the whole range of inscriptions and manuscripts relevant to O.T. textual study. A brief bibliography and index are added. The production of the work leaves nothing to be desired. B.J.R.

ZIEGLER, J. : *Der Bibeltext im Daniel-Kommentar des Hippolyt von Rom.* (Nachrichten der Akademie der Wissenschaften in Göttingen. 1. Phil.-Hist. Klasse, Nr. 8.) 1952. Pp. 36. (Vandenhoeck and Ruprecht, Göttingen. Price : DM. 3.50.)

> The importance of Hippolytus' *Commentary on Daniel* (*c.* 200 A.D.) and his slightly earlier *De Antichristo* has long been recognised for the study of the Theodotionic text of Daniel, and in the present brochure Dr. Ziegler, in his usual thorough and scholarly way, has given a detailed analysis of the text-forms. He gives all the necessary information about editions of the work, their manuscript bases, the quoted passages and their relationship to the Codices. Along with providing support for B, which is to be expected, the readings reflect Q and min. 230, which belongs to the same family as Q. In some variants, however, Ziegler adduces evidence for a Greek rendering no longer extant. B.J.R.

EXEGESIS AND MODERN TRANSLATIONS

ALFRINK, B. J. : *Josue.* (De Boeken van het Oude Testament : Deel III, Book I.) 1952. Pp. 122. (J. J. Romen & Zonen, Roermond en Maaseik. Price : Fl. 4.27.)

> The series will be in twelve parts, extending to nearly 5,000 pages, and is by a group of Roman Catholic scholars under the general editorship of Professors Grossouw, van der Ploeg, and van Dodewaard, with Dr. van den Born as secretary.

Each volume will contain an introduction followed by the author's own translation and exegesis of the original text. Mgr. Alfrink holds that the author of Joshua used five sources : ii. l-vi. 25, the story of Jordon and Jericho with occasional aetiological emphasis ; the Ai story ; two poetic quotations ; a list of west-of-Jordon kings (xii. 9-24) ; the story of the overrunning of southern Judah (x. 28-39). There are notes on the style of the author who is responsible for considerable portions of chapters i-xii, as well as in his editing of the G-document on which most of chapters xiii-xxiv is based. The exegesis, which occupies the lower half of each page, is clear and helpful.   N.H.S.

ALLIS, O. T. : *God Spake by Moses*. 1951. Pp. 160. (Marshall, Morgan and Scott, London. Price : 9s. 6d.)

A running commentary on the Pentateuch, presupposing Mosaic authorship, though ' how much of it he received by direct revelation, how much by inheritance, we do not know '. Higher Criticism is either ignored or cavalierly dismissed, but considerable space is devoted to such matters as the refuting of theories put forward by British-Israel. There are some useful homiletic suggestions in the book.   B.J.R.

BEA, A. : *Canticum Canticorum Salomonis quod hebraice dicitur Šîr Haššîrîm, nova e textu primogenio interpretatio latina cum textu masoretico ac notis criticis et exegeticis*. 1953. Pp. vi+66. (Pontifical Biblical Institute, Rome.)

This handy and useful little edition of the Song of Songs provides, as the title-page shows, the Massoretic text, a new Latin translation, and a variety of notes. There is also a valuable introduction of over twenty pages giving all reasonable guidance on such topics as the interpretation of the book, the literary form and arrangement, the authorship and date, the text and versions, and the history of the book's interpretation. On this last point Bea remarks very justly : '' Cantici interpretum ingens est numerus ''. He himself favours the so-called *interpretatio figurata* which considers that the literal sense is uniquely the metaphorical sense, but not with the implication that all the details are to be interpreted allegorically. Rather, he would prefer to interpret them parabolically and the essence of his system is expressed in the sentence : '' Sponsa Cantici est populus Dei, ab eo specialiter electus et variis viis ac rationibus ad perfectam cum Deo unionem amoris perductum '', (p. 7). He rejects emphatically any view that denies the literary unity of the work. J.M.T.B.

BENTZEN, A. : *Daniel* (Eissfeldt's Handbuch zum Alten Testament, erste Reihe xix.) Zweite, verbesserte Auflage. 1952. Pp. 88 (Mohr, Tübingen. Price : DM. 6.10.)

This is the second edition of what is recognized as one of the finest modern commentaries on *Daniel*. The first edition was noticed briefly in the 1937 *Book List*. The book is essentially the same as formerly but it is considerably increased in size (88 pages as compared with 54). There are interesting additions in the Introduction—a paragraph on the place of *Daniel* in the Canon, the relation of Daniel to Ezek. xiv and xxviii, and to Danel of the Ras Shamra myth much more fully dealt with, the dating of the book calculated more exactly as 166 or 165 B.C., a new suggestion that *Daniel* was originally circulated in fragments in different languages, Hebrew and Aramaic—cf. the Greek of the additions—what we have now being a patchwork reconstruction and yet essentially a unity, the suggestion that the original LXX represents a version corresponding more closely to the contemporary struggle and perhaps deriving from oral tradition, a paragraph on the form-criticism of the book.

Very full account has been taken of recent literature and this appears both in the critical notes and in the exposition. Extra references are added and sometimes whole new paragraphs appear. Two recent commentaries which are frequently referred to are that of Young (conservative) and Steinmann (French Catholic).

This new edition quite definitely replaces the first edition for all who wish to keep up to date with the study of the book of Daniel.   N.W.P.

BEWER, J. A. : *The Book of Jeremiah*, ii. *Chapters* 26-52. (Harper's Annotated Bible Series.) 1952. Pp. 88. (Harper & Bros., New York, and Eyre and Spottiswoode, London. Price : 75 cents or 6s. 0d.)

Professor Bewer is bringing out these volumes in rapid succession, and continues to pack a great deal into a small space. A surprising amount of textual criticism is included in the notes, considering the limited space, and while discussion of issues cannot be offered it will be a gain to every reader to have the judgement of a scholar of Bewer's eminence on all the problems associated with the book of Jeremiah. It may be noted that he retains xxxi. 31-34 for Jeremiah, but rejects 29 f. as showing the influence of Ezekiel. Most of xlvi-xlix is held to be Jeremianic, but l-li are rejected as exilic.   H.H.R.

The Holy Bible. Revised Standard Version, Containing the Old and New Testaments, Translated from the Original Tongues, Being the Version Set Forth A.D. 1611, Revised A.D. 1881-1885 and A.D. 1901, Compared with the Most Ancient Authorities and Revised 1952. Pp. 1290. (Nelson, Edinburgh. Price : 30s. 0d.)

By far the greater part of the changes in this Revision were mandatory and almost mechanical—the removal of all Elizabethan words and usages not familiar to the present-day American ; yet (deliberately according to a statement by Dean Weigle, Chairman of the Revision Commission) reversion to the simplicity of the King James' Version away from the 1881, 1901 revision, was attempted when possible ; and this may account for the preservation, especially in more familiar passages, of much of the A.V. rhythm and felicities (e.g. in Ps. xxiii. 6 RSV keeps " mercy " for *hesed* instead of its more usual rendering " steadfast love " ; and even Is. liii can be read in the Revision without discomfort). The other feature of this Revision, and the one which mainly interests the Old Testament student, is the degree of venturesomeness in revising the underlying Hebrew text. The Revisers allowed themselves (a) to adopt (tacitly) vowelling other than that of the M.T., (b) to change the consonantal text on the authority of early versions, (c) to change traditional renderings in the light of new knowledge provided by archaeology and the cognate languages, and (d) to repair the text conjecturally. Subjective judgement comes into play in all four of these processes and the Revisers are open to criticism from many sides ; but generally the Revisers have tended in the direction of caution. They accept, for example, the stock conjectures " kiss his feet " in Ps. ii. 11, " Rimmon " in Is. x. 27, and even Cheyne's " lamentations " for M.T.'s " ships " in Is. xliii. 14 ; they admit the *pim* (surely misspelt : the middle yodh is more likely to be consonantal) in 1 Sam. xiii. 21 ; but they prefer " young lions " to " unbelievers " in Ps. xxxiv. 10, and " fist " to " shovel " in Ex. xxi. 18 ; and in Ex. xxii. 5 they keep the traditional " cause to be eaten " instead of (as in BDB and Driver in *Camb. Bib.*) " cause to be burnt ".

H.D.

The Holy Bible translated from the Original Languages with Critical Use of all the Ancient Sources, by Members of the Catholic Biblical Association of America. Vol. I. *Genesis to Ruth.* 1952. Pp. 664. (St. Anthony Guild Press, Paterson, N.J.)

The members of the Catholic Biblical Association of America have already edited a complete New Testament and the Old Testament books of Genesis and the Psalter. The present volume, giving the entire text of eight books, is one that, as the title-page alleges, has made full use of all the ancient versions in controlling the Massoretic text, and prints at the end of the volume about nineteen pages of closely-set corrections, some of them lengthy. So, for example, in Judges xx. 30-35 (part of the account of the Benjamite war) the text is largely rewritten or rearranged. The translation, as a work of literature, does not seem to be quite in the front rank, but there is plenty of evidence that no pains have been spared to achieve a readable and accurate rendering. It should be borne in mind that, whereas the New Testament section of this version was made on the basis of the Vulgate, the whole of the Old Testament will, as in the present volume, be translated from the Hebrew, Aramaic and Greek originals.

J.M.T.B.

La Sainte Bible de Jérusalem. L'Exode, by B. Couroyer. 1952. Pp. 182, with map. (Price : 12s. 0d.) *Les Nombres*, by H. Cazelles. 1952. Pp. 158 with map. (Price : 10s. 0d.) *Judith, Esther*, by R. P. Barucq. 1952. Pp. 130. (Price : 8s. 6d.) (Editions du Cerf, Paris.)

For previous volumes in the series, see *Book Lists*, 1949, p. 27 ; 1950, pp. 25, 40 ; 1951, p. 33 ; 1952, pp. 27, 28. The pattern and standard of the previous volumes is maintained. The larger part is devoted to the translation, with technical and exegetical notes as necessary. In each case there is a short introduction, where the emphasis is on doctrine rather than on authorship and date. In the Exodus volume the existence of the various strands is recognized, and indicated where helpful. The later date (Ramses II, Meneptah) is taken for the Exodus. The Numbers volume is more conservative, and the Mosaic authorship is stressed with redactions. The date for *Judith* is given as 200 B.C., or 103-76 B.C. or 70 B.C., and for *Esther*, between the 4th and 1st centuries B.C., but probably *ca.* 140 B.C. In these two volumes especially the emphasis is on teaching and doctrine.　　　　　　　N.H.S.

La Sainte Bible de Jérusalem. Esdras, Néhémie, by A. Gelin. 1953. Pp. 124. (Editions du Cerf, Paris. Price : Fr. 390).

This further volume of the same series as the preceding has appeared while this issue of the *Book List* has been in the press. The Introduction places the work of the Chronicler between 350 and 300 B.C., and on the vexed question of the date of the mission of Ezra and of Nehemiah places Ezra's arrival in Jerusalem between the first and second visits of Nehemiah. Thus Ezra's work is held to have commenced in 427(?)-426(?) and Nehemiah's second visit to have taken place before 424. As always in this series the translation is of first importance ; the commentary is brief, but judicious and reliable.　　　　　　　H.H.R.

BÜCKERS, H. : *Die Bücher der Chronik.* (Die Heilige Schrift für das Leben erklärt, Band IV/I. Herders Bibelkommentar.) 1952. Pp. xii+380. (Herder, Freiburg. Price : DM. 17.50.)

A new volume in this well-known series, in which an expository exegesis follows each section of the text freshly translated from Kittel's BH. Literary and textual notes are not included, but a number of emendations are accepted. The unity of authorship throughout the Chronistic work, except for glosses, is maintained, and composition tentatively assigned to 300-250 B.C. · *Kings* and *Chronicles* are considered to have drawn independently from a common source. Opinions will differ as to the precise degree of credibility to be attached to some of the Chronicler's unsupported statements, and Bückers recognizes, but tends to minimize, many of the difficulties. It is however a careful and sincere commentary of value to scholars as well as to the ordinary Bible reader.

　　　　　　　D.R.Ap-T.

BUTTRICK, G. A. (ed. by) : *Interpreter's Bible*, Vol. I. (General and Old Testament Articles, Genesis, Exodus.) 1952. Pp. xxx+1100. (Abingdon-Cokesbury Press, New York, Nashville. Price : £3 10s. 0d.)

This first major Bible commentary both exegetical and expository for many years in English will consist of six volumes on each Testament. (Those subscribing to the series will receive the last volume containing *James-Revelation* and the Indexes free.) The twenty-two general articles (eleven specifically O.T.) have references to a wide range of literature and append selected bibliographies (except that by G. A. Barrois on Chronology Metrology and Numismatics). In the actual commentaries there is an Introduction to the book, again with select bibliography, and then each passage of Scripture is quoted according to the King James and the American Revised Standard Versions in parallel columns at the head of the page ; below that comes the exegesis, and last the exposition, all clearly distinguishable. For *Genesis* the main Introduction and the Exegesis are by C. A. Simpson, who also contributes the general article on The Growth of the Hexateuch. The Exposition is by W. R. Bowie. For *Exodus* the authors are J. Coert Rylaarsdam and J. Edgar Park respectively. Rylaarsdam takes much more account of oral tradition than does Simpson, but neither gives the attention we should expect to the views of the " Scandinavian school ". There are a number of maps in black and white ; and the coloured end papers give really excellent representations of the physical contours of the Near East nexus (front) and the land of Palestine (back). Among British contributors may be mentioned H. H. Farmer, N. H. Snaith and T. H. Robinson ; others are to follow. This volume can be highly recommended ; technically also it is an outstanding production and very good value. D.R.Ap-T.

A Catholic Commentary on Holy Scripture, ed. by B. Orchard, E. F. Sutcliffe, R. C. Fuller, and R. Russell. 1953. Pp. xvi+1312. (Nelson, Edinburgh. Price : £4 4s. 0d.)

This large and learned work may be regarded as the most impressive result, so far, of the fresh encouragement and impetus given to Roman Catholic biblical studies by the recent pronouncements of the Pope himself and of the Pontifical Biblical Commission. Over forty scholars have contributed to the volume ; and they have succeeded in compressing a vast deal of factual information and doctrinal instruction into the available space. Articles of general introduction take up some 300 pages, the commentaries, with their special introductions, about 900 pages. The indexes, general and geographical, take 87 pages and there are 16 pages of good clear maps. The New Testament is more fully treated than the Old. The general articles cover a wide field including some matters of special interest to Roman Catholics, e.g. the replies of the Biblical Commission, the position of the Mother of Jesus in the Bible, and the history of Rheims-Douay Version. Bible students generally will look with keen interest to see how far the new volume is able to take up and use critical conclusions (and hypotheses) about biblical problems. The general impression made by the writers is one of cautious advance and of readiness to leave the way open for further investigation. The work as a whole should be of great use to both Catholics and Protestants. T.W.M.

CLARKE, W. K. L. : *Concise Bible Commentary*. 1952. Pp. 996. (S.P.C.K. London. Price : 30s. 0d.)

Here is an up-to-date and comprehensive commentary on the whole of the Bible and the Apocrypha. It is popular, for the general reader, but also scholarly. It is much to be commended, and within the limits imposed by space, it is thoroughly admirable. There are twenty-nine general articles, nearly half of them dealing with the Old Testament. At the end of the book, there is a glossary, suggested courses for study, and a short account of some extra-canonical books. Critically, the author follows the generally accepted modern positions, including the later of the two dates usually canvassed for the Exodus, the 397 B.C. date for Ezra. Note is taken of the Dead Sea scrolls and the Ugaritic material. A very satisfactory piece of work and a monument of industry. N.H.S.

GAROFALO, S. (ed. by) : *La Sacra Bibbia. Il Libro dei Re,* by S. Garofalo. 1951. Pp. x+296. (Price : 950 lire.) *Geremia*, by A. Penna. 1952. Pp. 442+9 pp. of plates. (Price : 1700 lire.) (Marietti, Turin and Rome.)

These two recent additions to the series entitled *La Sacra Bibbia* are most welcome, and there is every prospect that the commentaries will rank as some of the best ever published in Italy in recent times. As usual a good deal of space is required for the printing of the Sixto-Clementine version, which faces an Italian translation based on the original text. In both commentaries much attention is given to textual corrections, and the notes in the lower part of each page are normally full and adequate. Garofalo's commentary on Kings suffers from having slightly antedated the appearance of Montgomery's I.C.C. volume, and from his having been unable to make use of E. Thiele's monograph on *The Mysterious Numbers of the Hebrew Kings*, which would have been of marked assistance in the section headed " Cronologia ". Conversely, Penna's *Geremia* appears to have missed little or nothing of any importance, and may on various grounds be considered to be the more thorough and original work. His acquaintance with all the best that has been written on Jeremiah (and this edition includes Lamentations and the Letter of Jeremiah) is exceptionally wide. Like most modern writers on that prophet he is especially indebted to such names as Volz, Skinner, Rudolph and Nötscher (whose commentary in the " Bonner Bibel " is rightly described as the most exhaustive Catholic book of Jeremiah that has appeared). Altogether this is a rich and satisfying piece of work, and a worthy successor to its author's excellent Hieronymean studies.

J.M.T.B.

GISPEN, W. H. : *De Spreuken van Salomo*, Deel I. (Korte Verklaring der Heilige Schrift.) 1952. Pp. 284. (J. H. Kok, Kampen. Price : 13s. 0d.)

This volume deals with the first fifteen chapters of Proverbs. It contains a short introduction, and then there follows the commentary proper. This is composed of short sections in the new translation which is a feature of the series, with each piece of text followed by a commentary which goes into considerable detail. The critical position is that Solomon was the author of a great deal of the book, but that it is a collection of collections. Mention is made of the great antiquity of similar collections in the Near East, going as far back as 2450 B.C.   N.H.S.

HERTZBERG, H. W. : *Der Erste Jesaja, übersetzt und ausgelegt—* zweite völlig neuarbeitete Auflage. 1952. Pp. 156. (J. G. Oncken Verlag, Kassel.)

This translation and exposition of First Isaiah belongs to the series ' Bibelhilfe für die Gemeinde ' to which a number of scholars contribute and which is.edited by Dr. Erich Stange. Professor Hertzberg has given an excellent translation of First Isaiah. The chapters follow in the order that is given them in the Bible without any attempt to group them in their historical sequence, except that the vision and call of Isaiah (chap. vi) is placed at the beginning. In its first edition in 1936 the translation was not complete. This defect has now been rectified. Textual notes relative to variations from the massoretic text, etc., are relegated to an appendix and the most important variations witnessed to by the Dead Sea Scroll of Isaiah are indicated by the abbreviation T.M. (Totes Meer). The notes which concern the exposition are given at the end of the sections dealt with. In Professor Hertzberg's work we are fortunate in having the literary units in Isaiah's prophecies clearly defined and accompanied by an exegesis which takes account of the historical situations to which the prophet's oracles belong or may belong. Not only the so-called " Bible reader " but the preacher and teacher have here a work of the greatest value. There is a useful *Übersicht* of the content and topics of Isaiah's teaching at the end of the book. The *Bemerkungen zum Urtext* ought to be in a little larger print.   O.S.R.

KISSANE, E. J. : *The Book of Psalms*, Vol. I. 1953. Pp. xlviii+320. (Browne and Nolan, Dublin. Price : 30s. 0d.)

The lay-out of this commentary is similar to that of the author's commentary on Isaiah. To each Psalm there is a brief introduction, dealing with its subject, structure, contents, and sometimes its date or messianic character. Then follows the author's translation of the text from the Hebrew, with appended notes on any textual changes adopted, and then the commentary. Moderate recourse is had to emendation, sometimes on the basis of ancient versions, and sometimes conjectural (as in ii. 11f., where Bertholet's emendation is followed). A number of the psalms are accepted as genuinely Davidic, but Psa. li is assigned to the exilic period. The Introduction is, naturally, to the entire Psalter, but the commentary includes the first two books of the Psalter only. The Introduction is brief, and the classification of the psalms adopted is Prayers for deliverance from trouble, Prayers for deliverance from enemies, Psalms of confidence, Psalms of thanksgiving, Didactic psalms, and Prophetical psalms. The headings of the psalms are held to indicate sometimes the collection from which they were taken, sometimes their character, sometimes their liturgical purpose, and sometimes their musical accompaniment. The volume forms a welcome addition to the rapidly growing literature on the Psalter.

H.H.R.

NORTH, C. R. : *Isaiah* 40-55. (The Torch Bible Commentaries.) 1952. Pp. 150. (S.C.M. Press. Price : 8s. 6d.)

This is a brief but excellent commentary on the Second Isaiah by the leading British authority on the subject and it will adorn the series to which it belongs. In the Introduction a judicious selection is given of the information which it is essential that the general reader should have. The views of C. C. Torrey are passed over in silence. The verse by verse exposition is a model of relevance and succinctness. Indeed it is just because Dr. North has such a complete mastery of the literature of the subject and of the problems at issue that he is able to be lucid in his exposition. Theological difficulties are faced honestly and profoundly (see e.g. the comment on xlii. 13ff.). The quality of this little book serves to fan the hope that the same author will one day give us a full-scale treatment of the same subject.   N.W.P.

NÖTSCHER, F. (ed. by) : *Die Heilige Schrift in deutscher Übersetzung, Echter Bibel : Das Alte Testament.* 14. *Exodus, Leviticus and Numbers* by H. Schneider, and *Deuteronomy* by H. Junker. 1952. Pp. 90, 64, 94 and 104. (Echter Verlag, Würzburg. Price : DM. 11.40.)

The appearance of four books of the Pentateuch (Exodus-Deuteronomy) in a single volume brings to an end the Old Testament section of the excellent and popular *Echter Bibel*. It will be recalled that Junker's commentary on Genesis appeared in this series in 1949, and was noticed in the *Book List* for 1950. A table of contents to the whole series, together with maps and chronological tables, is promised for the immediate future.

There is not a great deal to be said about the present volume, in which Junker has only one book to comment on as compared with Schneider's three, and this for the second time, as an earlier commentary on Deuteronomy from his pen appeared in the Bonner Bibel as long ago as 1933. As might be expected in so essentially popular a commentary the introductions and notes tend to be kept very short, and it may be regretted that so little space is given to textual criticism. From this standpoint the series compares unfavourably with some of the volumes of the French series *La Sainte Bible*, while it may be freely allowed that the material production is superior and the print far less trying to the eyes. J.M.T.B.

Nötscher, F. (ed. by) : *Die Heilige Schrift in deutscher Übersetzung, Echter Bibel : Das Alte Testament.* 15. *Register*, by the Editor. 1953. Pp. 154+2 maps. (Echter Verlag, Würzburg.)

The index volume has appeared while this List has been in the hands of the Printer. In addition to a good subject index it contains a chapter on chronology, and one on weights and measures. In its preparation the Editor has had the help of Fischer, Rehm, Schneider and Schötz, in addition to that of three members of the Bonn Seminar. The speed with which the whole commentary has been prepared is amazing, and this index will add much to the usefulness of the work. H.H.R.

van der Ploeg, J. : *Spreuken.* (De Boeken van het Oude Testament : Deel VIII, Book 1.) 1952. Pp. 108. (J. J. Romen & Zonen, Roermond en Maaseik. Price : Fl. 3.72.)

For details of the whole series see the notice of a companion volume by Mgr. Alfrink on Joshua (p. 30). The introduction is short. In it the editor discusses the various sections of the book, two Solomonic collections, one from the 8th century, and the rest of unknown authorship. There is a discussion of the relation of the LXX text to the Hebrew text, and a useful account of the origin of Hebrew Wisdom. In the exegetical notes particular attention is paid to the personification of Wisdom in chapter viii. The fullest use is made throughout of modern scholarship, both Protestant and Catholic. N.H.S.

Power, A. D. : *Ecclesiastes or The Preacher, a new translation, with introduction, notes, glossary and index.* 1952. Pp. 156. (Longmans Green and Co., London. Price : 8s. 6d.)

In his introduction the author describes his intention as being to state the more important conclusions at which the principal authorities on the book of Ecclesiastes have arrived. In facing the questions which a study of Ecclesiastes raises he refrains from arguing too much in favour of any one opinion but leaves the reader to make his own choice. Thus Mr. Power's small book does not offer any full-scale discussion of the problems which Ecclesiastes presents nor does it endeavour after completeness in details such as we have in the larger commentaries, but we have from his pen certain views and aspects, together with notes and a glossary which are interesting and informative. In the translation the reader's eye will catch at a glance such renderings as : "And there is nothing completely new under the sun " (i. 9) ; " I tried exciting my appetite with wine (but behaving reasonably) and fastening on folly " (ii. 3) ; " he hath given ignorance to them so that no man can fathom the work which God worketh from first to last " (iii. 11). O.S.R.

Puukko, A. F. : *Raamatun selitysteos*. 1. *Viisi Mooseksen kirjaa*. (=A Commentary on the Holy Bible. 1. The Pentateuch.) 1952. Pp. 316. (Werner Söderström Oy, Helsinki-Porvoo. Price : Fmk 1000.)

Professor Puukko has the merit of bringing the results of research on the Bible to profit the practical work of the Church. He is one of the leading scholars who gave the Finnish people and Church an excellent new translation of the Bible in 1938. In 1946 he published an extensive study on the history of the Finnish translations of the Scriptures. In recent years he has devoted his time to the preparation of a large Finnish commentary on the Bible to contain five parts (four on the O.T. and one on the N.T.). The first volume of the series, the commentary on the Pentateuch, has now appeared, and the manuscript for the remaining volumes is almost finished. In form the book resembles the well-known *Bibelwerk* by Kautzsch-Bertholet. The Biblical text, in the new official translation, is at the top of the page, and the explanations below. The latter deal mainly with the history, culture and religion, geography, archaeology, etc. The work of Professor Puukko is based on moderate literary criticism, as represented by his late teacher Rudolf Kittel. The latest views on the history of tradition and the significance of the cult for O.T. religion have no obvious influence on his interpretation. His book is, however, an excellent guide to the O.T. Its style is clear and easily readable, in spite of its scientific accuracy.

A.La.

Rabast, K. : *Die Genesis*, Vol. 1. 1951. Pp. 204. (Evangelische Verlagsanstalt, Berlin. Price : DM. 9.00.)

Dr. Rabast, who is Pfarrer of the Martin Luther Church in Dresden, has a thoroughgoing contempt for Source Criticism of the Pentateuch, and thinks the ' Redactor ' is far too stupid a fellow ever to have existed. Consequently, in this commentary on Genesis, of which the present volume dealing with chs. i-xi is the first of two, Dr. Rabast presupposes the unity of the Book, with Moses as the author. In the Introduction he deals briefly, in the orthodox fashion, with the textual transmission of Genesis, but in two other sections which deal with the Sources and the Author, he is critical and iconoclastic without being very original. In the body of the book, the translation and text-division reflect the writer's scheme, and each section is supplied with grammatical and exegetical discussions, and, notably, metrical divisions for numerous passages. Despite his standpoint, the writer bases his argument from time to time on remarks by Noth, Eichrodt and others of the ' critical ' persuasion, and his bibliography is extensive and useful. In his homiletic discourses Dr. Rabast is sometimes alarming, as, e.g., when he attributes, apropos of Gen. xi, the loss of the ship Titanic to blasphemy on board.

B.J R.

(N.B. Dr. Rabast died on 17th April, 1952, at the early age of forty-one. H.H.R.)

Das Alte Testament, translated by E. Henne, 2 vols. 1952. Pp. 1144 and 1192. (Schöningh, Paderborn. Price : DM. 12 per volume.)

This is the 9th edition (first published 1934, 1935) of a Catholic translation of the Old Testament into German. It is based on the Hebrew text, divided into paragraphs with the poetry printed in verse form and is very pleasant to read and handle. The translator has prefaced each book by a short note on its origin and has supplied footnotes to the more important passages. Both translation and notes show the author to be well abreast of modern scholarship (see Gen. iii. 8, 1 Kings xix. 12) but the translation shows some slight changes from the Hebrew in the interests of harmony (Exod. xxxiii. 18, 19) and some reminiscences of the Vulgate (Ps. xxiii. 5). L.H.B.

VELLAS, B. M. : *Ekklêsiastika Anagnôsmata tês Palaias Diathêkês*. I. *Eklektoi Psalmoi* (*Eisagôge—Keimenon—Hermêneia*). 1951. Pp. 230. (Athens.)

Vellas, whose excellent commentaries on the Minor Prophets are already known to readers in this country, has now edited a selection from the Psalter, preceded by an introduction on the forms of Hebrew poetry and on the Psalter in general. Altogether some forty psalms are printed, all according to the Septuagint and, in contrast with the author's earlier exegetical works, there is no continuous translation into Modern Greek. In every case the text is explained very fully and with numerous references to the Greek Fathers and to the most recent works of scholarship, both Eastern and Western. It may perhaps be mentioned, for the sake of Western scholars, that the numbering of the Psalms is Septuagintal, and not Massoretic. In a number of instances the names of Western scholars and their works are misspelt. For the modern attitude towards the interpretation of the Psalter, readers are referred to A. R. Johnson's essay in *The Old Testament and Modern Study*. J.M.T.B.

WEISER, A. : *Der Prophet Jeremia : Kap. i-xxv. 13.* (Das Alte Testament Deutsch, 20.) 1952. Pp. 228. (Vandenhoeck & Ruprecht, Göttingen. Price : 12s. 6d.)

This volume contains translation and exegesis only. The introductory chapter with its considered judgements on prophet and book is promised in the second volume, not yet to hand. Once more, as in his previous volume in this series (*Das Buch Hiob*, *Book List* 1952, p. 37), Dr. Weiser offers attractive rhythmical translations, here of the oracles only. Once more also, effective use is made of the modern cult approach. For example, the vision of the seething cauldron is not political so much as cultic, an example of the frequent theme of God's sending foreign armies in judgement. The rough outline in chapter i receives its fulfilment in Nebuchadrezzar's capture of the city. We look forward to the second volume with pleasurable anticipation. N.H.S.

ZIEGLER, J. : *Ezechiel*. (The Göttingen Septuagint, vol. XVI, i.) 1952. Pp. 330. (Vandenhoeck & Ruprecht, Göttingen. Price : DM. 41.80 unbound, DM. 45.80 bound.)

The present volume begins with a careful and trustworthy introduction dealing with the Greek manuscripts (papyri included) and patristic citations, the derived ancient versions, the ' families ' of the Greek witnesses to the text and the three recensions and the *catenae*, the late Greek versions and the orthography (pp. 1-89) ; after this introductory matter it contains the Greek text (pp. 91-330). The first *apparatus criticus* sets out the main variant readings from the manuscripts and other sources ; the second, printed beneath it, presents the Hexaplar translations, which are thus conveniently recorded in close connection with the Septuagintal tradition. The work will be an indispensable tool of Biblical research. G.R.D.

ZOLLI, E. : *Il Salterio : Nuova Traduzione e Commento*. 1951. Pp. 236. (Edizione Viola, Milan. Price : 550 lire.)

This work of a renowned Italian scholar is, as he tells us, the result of sixty-three years acquaintance with the Psalter and forty years spent in its close study. The publisher in a note facing the title-page informs us that the work may be considered " sotto tutti gli aspetti originalissimo " and, while the superlative may be judged to be excessive, there is no doubt that the result of so much labour is generally satisfactory and interesting. There is not a great deal of textual emendation, at any rate of the conjectural variety. On the other hand, Zolli has thrown light on a number of difficult passages with the help of his profound knowledge of Hebrew and of comparative lexicography. Some of his suggestions are really helpful ; others, it must be admitted, are much less convincing, but all are worthy of study. A number of doctrinal and liturgical notes add to the value of a volume which has been published at a very moderate price and so put at the service of a large circle of readers. J.M.T.B.

LITERARY CRITICISM AND INTRODUCTION
(including History of Interpretation and Special Studies)

BENTZEN, A. : *Introduction to the Old Testament*, 2nd edition, with corrections and a supplement. 1952. Pp. 264+252+30. (G. E. C. Gad, Copenhagen, and Geoffrey Cumberlege, London. Price : £4.)

The new edition of this valuable and comprehensive Introduction will be warmly welcomed. The original two volumes (see *Book List*, 1949, p. 32, and 1950, p. 44) are now bound in one. Many minor changes and additions have been made in the text ; and the whole work is brought still more up-to-date by a thirty-page appendix. G.W.A.

BROWNE, L. E. : *Ezekiel and Alexander*. 1952. Pp. 34. (S.P.C.K., London. Price : 3s. 6d.)

Here is another attempt to solve the riddle of Ezekiel. The author's theme is that the book is a pseudograph belonging to the period of Alexander the Great. The exile is the Caspian exile of *ca*. 344 B.C., and all the smaller date-figures are from that datum. Thus the inaugural vision (5th year) is 339 B.C. Some of the dates fit very well into this scheme, particularly the oracle against Tyre in chapter xxvi (eleventh year, 333/2 B.C.). The other series of dates (25th year, 27th, 30th) are reckoned from the accession of Artaxerxes III. Professor Browne's suggestions are less satisfactory here, and perhaps he would have done better to have abandoned chapters xl-xlviii as integral to the book. At the least, the author has produced a theory which deserves careful and respectful attention. He may prove in the end to have done much more than this.   N.H.S.

CHIVERS, K. : *Does Genesis make Sense ?* 1952. Pp. 110. (S.P.C.K., London. Price : 3s. 6d.)

This little book, written in a colloquial style, offers the reader a brief introduction to the literary criticism of Genesis and a short account of its historical and religious value. Then follows a series of notes on the text of Genesis, insufficient to deserve the name of commentary, and with headings to the sections that read like newspaper headlines. A rapid survey of the history of interpretation follows, together with a statement of the enduring value of the book. The author has skilfully compressed much within his few pages, but might with advantage have maintained more dignity of style.   H.H.R.

COPPENS, J. : *La Prophétie de la 'Almah* (Analecta Lovaniensia Biblica et Orientalia, 2nd series, No. 35.) 1952. Pp. 34. (Publications Universitaires de Louvain, and Desclée de Brouwer, Bruges and Paris. Price : Belgian Fr. 25.)

In this study Canon Coppens reviews recent exegesis of the Immanuel prophecy, and more especially the work of some Catholic writers, and argues for the literal messianic view of the prophecy. His very extensive bibliographical control is apparent here, as in all that he writes, and it is certain that his hope that his work will be of service to colleagues ' moins bien documentés ' is sure to be realized. That the view he adopts does not solve all problems he frankly acknowledges, and in particular he confesses that the chronological difficulty ' n'est peut-être pas entièrement dissipée '. He concludes by disclaiming the idea that he will convince all his readers, but says that if his study provokes a convincing reply he will be well repaid.   H.H.R.

FOHRER, G. : *Die Hauptprobleme des Buches Ezechiel.* (Beihefte zur Zeitschrift für alttestamentliche Wissenschaft, 72.) 1952. Pp. 288. (Alfred Töpelmann, Berlin. Price : DM. 28.00.)

> The traditional view of the Book of the Prophet Ezekiel has still its adherents. The prophet went into exile in Babylonia with the first deportation in 598 B.C. He began to preach in 593, and his last words were in 571. His message was at first unconditional disaster, then conditional prosperity, and lastly, certain prosperity. The book as a whole is from an Ezekiel of the early exile. He was an ecstatic. There is a minimum of redaction, and numerous glosses of every type, mostly half-verses and rarely extending for more than two or three verses. The most extensive glosses are in chapters xvi, xxviii, xxxviii, and in the concluding nine chapters.   N.H.S.

*FORD, D. W. C. : *A Key to Genesis.* 1951. Pp. x+72. (S.P.C.K. London. Price : 3s. 6d.)

> This excellent little book offers to modern readers a brief exposition of the enduring message of the book of Genesis when read as a book of religion, and not of science or history in the strict sense of the word. The various sections into which the book of Genesis falls are taken in turn and the teaching embodied in them summarized effectively. It should be of value in schools as well as for the general reader.
>   H.H.R.

GELIN, A. : *Jérémie.* (Témoins de Dieu, 13.) 1952. Pp. 198. (Les Editions du Cerf, Paris. Price : 6s. 6d.)

> A very readable and helpful study of Jeremiah, the man and his message, with full reproductions of many passages from the book, taken from the new French translation by the ' School of Jerusalem' (*La Sainte Bible, Book List,* 1952, p. 27). The author himself was responsible for the translation of ' Jeremiah ', and this book is the first of a trilogy. Full use is made of all modern studies in this biography of the prophet.   N.H.S.

HÖLSCHER, G. : *Geschichtsschreibung in Israel. Untersuchungen zum Jahvisten und Elohisten.* 1952. Pp. 412. (Acta Reg. Soc. Hum. Litt. Lundensis, L. Gleerup, Lund. Price : Sw. Kr. 45.)

> This work (completed in 1948) is a recapitulation and continuation of Hölscher's *Die Anfänge der hebräischen Geschichtsschreibung,* 1941/2 (see *Book List,* 1946, p. 25), including now the Elohistic source. It is out and out literary criticism. The first section treats of J, the second of E, and the third distils and separates the literary sources J and E from Genesis to Kings. Hölscher still regards J as a homogeneous history extending from Creation to the death of Solomon, written in Judah/Jerusalem during the reign of Joash. The author used mainly oral material, supplementing occasionally with his own reconstruction of events. Hölscher still regards J_2 as the early part of E, to whom he would also assign much of the pre-Patriarchal material usually assigned to J, and whose

history of the nation continues down to 2 Kings xxv. **30**. E was acquainted with J, but also with additional oral and written material. He, too, was a southerner—either Micaiah ben Gemariah (Jer. xxxvi. 11) or some other contemporary relative of Gedaliah and descendant of Shaphan the scribe. As a historian E is inferior to J, aiming more at a theologically sound, and edificatory, interpretation of history. E's history has received additions from the hands of E_2 before J and $\underline{E}$ were amalgamated. This book is a must for those who can still find some good in the literary approach to Old Testament literature. D.R.Ap-T.

KERRIGAN, A. : *St. Cyril of Alexandria : Interpreter of the Old Testament.* (Analecta Biblica, 2.) 1952. Pp. xl+488. (Pontifical Biblical Institute, Rome.)

In this large and learned work the exegetical principles of Cyril are studied and illustrated, and their relations with the principles of other patristic interpreters are examined. The author complains that too little attention is paid to the exegesis of the Fathers, and by this dissertation, which was prepared under the direction of Father Vaccari, he offers a contribution towards the filling of the gap. Beyond this, however, the study is relevant to recent discussions of exegetical principles and method, to which reference is frequently made. Cyril rarely speaks of the allegorical sense, but distinguishes a literal and a spiritual sense, and these are carefully analysed. As an essay in the history of exegesis this work deserves the highest praise. H.H.R.

DE LEEUW, V. : *De Koninklijke Verklaring van de Ebed-Jahweh-Zangen.* (Analecta Lovaniensia Biblica et Orientalia, 2nd series, No. 33.) 1952. Pp. 28. (Publications Universitaires de Louvain, and Desclée de Brouwer, Bruges and Paris. Price : Belgian Fr. 25.)

In this study, written in Dutch but with a short French summary, the author argues that the Servant in the Servant Songs is conceived in royal, rather than in prophetic, terms. He examines all the phraseology with royal associations relating to the person or the work of the Servant, and also observes that the literary context of the Songs is based on psalms concerned with the enthronement of Yahweh. These in turn recall the Babylonian Marduk liturgies. Hence he argues that just as Marduk had a royal representative on earth, so the Servant is conceived of as Yahweh's representative. H.H.R.

LINDER, S. : *Palästinische Volksgesänge aufgezeichnet und gesammelt. Aus dem Nachlass herausgegeben und mit Anmerkungen versehen von Helmer Ringgren. I. Mit einem Beitrag vom Herausgeber : Die Volksdichtung und das Hohe Lied.* (Uppsala Universitets Årsskrift 1952 : 5.) 1952. Pp. 110. (Lundequistska Bokhandeln, Uppsala, and Harrassowitz, Wiesbaden. Price : 10 Swedish crowns.)

While on a visit to Palestine in 1912, the late Professor Linder collected Arabic *Volksgesänge* which he hoped ultimately to publish. Through the *pietas* of Dr. Ringgren, a third of the total is now made available in this work. The songs are arranged in six groups according to subject : circumcision, love and marriage, death and mourning, entreaties for rain, songs of work, and a miscellaneous group. The Arabic is printed in transliteration, with a German rendering opposite. Material left by Linder has been incorporated in the notes. It was Linder's conviction that modern Palestinian songs of this type provided illuminating parallels with the Song of Songs. In the essay which is appended to the collection. Ringgren assembles many such parallels culled from Linder, Dalman, Stephan and others, and discusses the dual relationship of the Biblical text to the ancient Tammuz cult and the modern *Volksgesänge*. This little work is a fitting memorial of a great lover of the Holy Land, who himself published all too little.

G.W.A.

*MURRAY, A. V. : *How to Know your Bible : A Guide to Biblical Study*. 1952. Pp. 185 + 7 maps. (Allen and Unwin, London. Price : 12s. 6d.)

This excellent book is intended to be used with the text of the Bible. It gives particular attention to a large selection of the books of the Bible, and offers a brief introduction to the historical setting and background, and an analysis of the contents designed to enable the reader to understand the significance of the various sections. Nine representative books are first taken and studied in the following order : Amos, Hosea, Isaiah, Micah, Deuteronomy, Philippians, Acts, Galatians, Mark. There follows a general survey of the Old Testament and then of the New. No one who uses the book as it is meant to be used can fail to gain an intelligent understanding of the contents and meaning of the Bible. Questionable statements are occasionally made, such as the illustration of the variety of the Bible by the remark ' It is as if the first 66 volumes of Everyman's Library were all bound together in one book ' (p. 25). The Servant Songs of Deutero-Isaiah are delimited as xlii. 1-7, xliii. 1-13, xliv. 1, 21-23, xlix. 1-13, l. 4-9, lii. 13-liii. 12, and the Servant is interpreted as Israel in every age collectively and individually considered (p. 118).

H.H.R.

NOTH, M. : *Die Welt des Alten Testaments. Einführung in die Grenzgebiete der alttestamentlichen Wissenschaft*, 2nd ed. (Sammlung Töpelmann, 2. Reihe : Theologischer Hilfsbücher, Bd. 3.) 1953. Pp. xvi + 314. (Verlag Alfred Töpelmann, Berlin.)

This book is the second edition of the work which first appeared in 1940 (cf. *Book List*, 1946, p. 16). The topics and the order of the material are the same as in the former, but there has been considerable modification, and notice is taken of the many important subjects which have appeared during the past twelve years. The four main sections are geographical history, archaeology, history of the Near East, O.T. text and versions. Each section is, necessarily, self-contained, and though the book consequently lacks unity, it is a positive encyclopædia of information, up-to-date and reliable, and altogether a remarkable achievement in condensation. There is a fourfold index, 4 plates, a synoptic table of main events in Near East history ; bibliographies and explanatory illustrations are interspersed within the book. It is quite indispensable for a general introduction to O.T. study.

B.J.R.

PETERS, N. and DÉCARREAUX, J. : *Notre Bible, Source de Vie : Introduction à la lecture de la Bible.* 2nd ed., 1950. Pp. 280. (Editions Beyaert, Bruges. Price : Belgian Fr. 78.00.)

This book is designed for the general reader, and it emphasizes the spiritual and devotional value of the Bible. It starts from the encyclical *Divino afflante Spiritu,* and in the first part presents the Catholic view that the reading of the Bible is not necessary but useful, provided it is controlled by the Church. This does not mean the absence of freedom in the interpretation of the Bible, but a disciplined freedom. There follows a section on the Bible and Culture, in which the literary forms of the Bible are described. Next, and at greater length, comes a study of the religious light given in the various parts of the Bible, and its relation to theology and law. The concluding sections, which deal with the power of the Bible to nourish the spirit and to minister consolation, are particularly valuable to the general reader. Here such unusual aspects as the prayers of the Bible, the Bible in the liturgy, the Bible as a book of optimism and of joy, are unfolded. While not written for scholars it is the work of scholars, and much is well, and even movingly, said.   H.H.R.

PFEIFFER, R. H. : *Introduction to the Old Testament.* 1952 (undated). Pp. xii+910. (A. & C. Black, London. Price : £1 10s. 0d.)

The first edition of this work was noted in the *Book List,* 1946, pp. 28f. A corrected edition, with bibliographies brought up-to-date, appeared in America two years later, and of this edition a British issue has now been released for the first time, and at a very modest price for so large and important a volume. It is superfluous to praise this work, which is indispensable to every serious student of the Old Testament, not only for its presentation of Pfeiffer's own views, but for its encyclopædic learning and for its survey of the views of others on every problem with which it deals. There are long sections on the Canon and Text of the Old Testament, in addition to a thorough treatment of all the critical problems of date and authorship attaching to each of its books. Pfeiffer is himself largely unaffected by some of the movements in recent scholarship, particularly those which react against the literary criticism of the Pentateuch, and incline to the pre-exilic dating of many of the psalms, though his acquaintance with the work of almost every school is phenomenal. Of the Scandinavian school of Uppsala, however, he takes little account, and neither Nyberg nor Engnell figures in his Index. There is one reference to Widengren (whose name is given incorrectly). It should be added that the vastness of the work is not indicated by the number of its pages. Often a vast amount of information is compressed within a few pages. A good example of this is in the three pages devoted to the Servant of the Lord, where a considerable literature is surveyed and classified.   H.H.R.

von Rad, G. : *Studies in Deuteronomy*. (Studies in Biblical Theology, No. 9.) 1953. Pp. 96. (S.C.M. Press, London. Price : 7s. 0d.)

This is a translation by David Stalker of the author's *Deuteronomium-Studien* (2nd ed.), 1948 (see *Book List*, 1948, p. 35), with a Scripture reference table added. It will be an advantage to many to have it in an English translation which is generally good and pliable. The author rejects the originality of the demand for centralization, and attributes the book to country Levite circles who would restore the tradition of the old Yahweh amphictyony of Shechem. There is an interesting comparison between some aspects of Deuteronomic and Priestly theology, and the chapter on the theological basis of the book of Kings is excellent. The author now has an expanded treatment of the Holy War elsewhere (see *Book List*, 1952, p. 56). This booklet contains very much that is fresh and attractive, but it is not definitive.   D.R.Ap-T.

Steinmann, J. : *Le Prophète Jérémie : sa vie, son œuvre et son temps.* (Lectio Divina, 9.) 1952. Pp. 328. (Les Editions du Cerf, Paris. Price : Fr. 885.)

Here is an up-to-date work, after the style of Skinner's and G. A. Smith's, giving a running account of the life and times of Jeremiah, into which are fitted translations of much of the book of Jeremiah, arranged according to the author's view of their probable dating. Thus chap. xviii is brought into association with Jeremiah's call. Extracts from the Lachish Letters and the Jehoiachin Tablets are given in translation, and passages from Zephaniah, Nahum and Habakkuk are included. Brief textual notes accompany the translations (drawing on DSH in the case of Habakkuk). The acrostic in Nahum i is translated into a corresponding French acrostic. The author excuses himself from dealing similarly with Ezekiel, as he proposes to devote a separate work to him, and with Deuteronomy, as it would require too much space. What he does give makes a very good book.
                                                      H.H.R.

Terrien, S. : *The Psalms and their Meaning for To-day*. 1952. Pp. 278. (Bobbs-Merrill, Indianapolis and New York. Price : $3.00.)

This most attractively written book is designed for the general reader rather than the scholar. It rests fundamentally on a study of the *Gattungen* of the Psalms, after the manner of Gunkel, and consists of a study of a number of the more familiar psalms, arranged in the order of their types. There is a short Introduction on ' The Origin of the Psalms ', and the psalms then chosen for treatment are xxix, viii, xix, civ (Hymns of Praise), cxiv, xlvi, xlvii, cx (Hymns sung to the Lord of History), cxxii, xv, xxiv, lxxxiv (Hymns sung to the Lord of Zion), lxxx, cxxxvii, xc (Prayers in time of Crisis), xlii, xliii, xxii (Personal Supplications), li, cxxx (Penitential Prayers), cxxiv, cvii, lxv, ciii (Songs of Faith), xxvii, cxxi, xxiii (Psalms of Trust), cxxix, lxxiii (Psalms of Wisdom). There is a final chapter on the meaning of the psalms for to-day. The whole forms an excellent introduction to the Psalter in the light of modern study.   H.H.R.

TRAINA, R. A. : *Methodical Bible Study*. 1952. Pp. x + 270. (The Author, 73 College Place, Ridgefield Park, N.J. Price : $3.95.)

This is a study of hermeneutical method, designed for users of the English Bible, and especially for preachers. Emphasis is laid on accurate observation of the contents of the text as the basis of interpretation, which is reached by a series of ' interpretive questions '. Rather heavy weather is made of elementary English grammar, and the analysis of method seems to be over-systematized and elaborate. The only example of the application of the method given is Psa. xxiii, on which 52 observations and corresponding questions are given—some of them glimpses of the obvious. The author warns against approaching the Bible with any pre-conceived ideas, dogmatic or other, or forcing of the text to subserve the reader's purpose. Mythological, allegorical, typological, and literal interpretations are alike deprecated, and many first class books are recommended to the reader. Its chief value is as a collection of elementary rules for preachers.
                                                                                                     H.H.R.

LAW, RELIGION AND THEOLOGY

ANDERSON, G. W. : *The Prophetic Gospel. Studies in the Servant Songs*. (Manuals of Fellowship. Third Series, No. 3.) 1952. Pp. 32. (The Epworth Press, London. Price : 1s. 0d.)

A very readable and helpful homiletic discourse on the Servant Songs of Deutero-Isaiah, showing an admirable fusion of competent O.T. scholarship and sincere evangelical purpose. The author follows Mowinckel in regarding Song 3 as consisting of Is. 50, 4-11.   B.J.R.

BAUMGÄRTEL, F. : *Verheissung : Zur Frage des Evangelischen Verständnisses des Alten Testaments*. 1952. Pp. 164. (C. Bertelsmann, Gütersloh. Price : DM. 7.00.)

This is an important theological study of the meaning of the New Testament word ' promise ' (Epaggelia) to which, though there is no actual Old Testament equivalent, a number of Old Testament expressions can be recognized as corresponding, provided we make due allowance for the fundamental differences between the Testaments. Baumgärtel holds that there has been a serious confusion of thought between the expressions ' promise ' and ' prophecy '. The relation between the Old and New Testaments should be thought of as fundamentally that between *promise* (not prophecy) and fulfilment. The New Testament view that in Christ and the Church prophecy was fulfilled is to be regarded as of temporary significance. Biblical criticism has made this kind of interpretation of the Old Testament impossible for us. Furthermore it is unnecessary : to the Christian the whole Old Testament as it is in all its incompleteness is completed in Christ. The promise in the Old Testament appears as God's claim upon Israel (' I am the Lord thy God '), a claim which is made actual in Christ. The book contains some very interesting criticism of scholars like Vischer, Eichrodt and Bultmann and in particular a discussion of the papers of Zimmerli and von Rad in *Evangelische Theologie*, 1952, Heft 1/2 reviewed in this *Book List*. In particular Baumgärtel offers criticism of von Rad's advocacy of *Heilsgeschichte* on the ground of its ambiguous relation to actual history, and of Typology on the ground of its irrelevance to the real business of Biblical exposition. N.W.P.

BOMAN, T. : *Das Hebräische Denken im Vergleich mit dem Griechischen*. 1952. Pp. 186. (Vandenhoeck and Ruprecht, Göttingen. Price : DM. 9.80.)

This book contains a valuable discussion of the character of Hebrew thought as compared with Greek and covers a wide field. The two modes of thinking are represented as complementary rather than as radically opposed to each other. It is argued that the contrast is often wrongly represented as one between Hebrew thought as dynamic and Greek thought as static, whereas the latter is really to be characterised in more positive fashion as laying the emphasis on harmony. In the same way we are told that it is untrue to say that in the Hebrew view God is active while in the Greek view he is not. The book contains a valuable discussion of the meaning of the verb *hāyā* in Hebrew, also of the meaning of *dābhār* and *logos* as representing different ways of conceiving the meaning of *word*. The Hebrew collective, it is maintained, is prior to the *nomen unitatis* and serves the same purpose as the Platonic idea, though it was given to the Hebrew by his very language, whereas Plato had to struggle painfully to achieve the abstraction.

A comparison is drawn between the Greek interest in the outward appearance of things and people and the Hebrew interest in the way in which things are made and the Hebrew tendency to describe qualities of people rather than physical appearance. Of considerable originality is the author's explanation of the descriptive similes employed in the Song of Songs. This leads on to a valuable section on anthropomorphisms. A later section compares the Hebrew and Greek views of time and space and there is some criticism of

Cullmann's theory. In a discussion of symbolism and instrumentalism it is argued that God not only controls events but seeks to reveal his nature. Both the Hebrew view of things as instruments and the Greek view of things as symbols are necessary. The Greek type of thought is essentially logical, whereas the Hebrew is psychological. The Hebrew thinker is peculiarly well fitted to investigate the problems of history and morality.

The author joins issue with Pedersen who regards Hebrew thinking as pre-logical and primitive, arguing that, though different in its way of apprehending reality, it is on a level with Greek thinking. Neither mode of thinking in fact can be dispensed with.   N.W.P.

BUBER, M. : *Right and Wrong : An Interpretation of Some Psalms.* 1952. Pp. 62. (S.C.M. Press, London. Price : 6s. 0d.)

In a foreword to this work, which is presented in a smooth and pleasing translation by R. Gregor Smith, the author explains that the interpretation which he here offers of Psalms xii, xiv, lxxxii, lxxiii and i (in that order) " is intended to make clear what they have to say to us about the difference between mere conscious being and true existence as the nearness of God. It may therefore be described as an essay in existential exegesis." If the prospective reader bears this in mind and looks for no more than some general comments along these lines, he may not be so disappointed as was the reviewer, who must reluctantly confess that for the most part he found the studies in this slender volume far too vague and indeterminate to be particularly helpful.   A.R.J.

COATES, J. R. (trans.) : *Bible Key Words.* V. *Gnosis,* by R. Bultmann. 1952. Pp. xiii+67. (Price : 7s. 6d.) VI. *Apostleship,* by K. H. Rengstorf. 1952. Pp. xii+76. (Price : 7s. 6d.) (Both translations from *Theologisches Wörterbuch zum Neuen Testament,* edited by G. Kittel.) (Adam & Charles Black, London.)

For previous volumes in the series see *Book Lists,* 1951, p. 53 ; 1952, p. 51. These two volumes naturally deal chiefly with non-Old Testament material. After dealing with the idea of Gnosis in Greek literature and amongst the Gnostics themselves, the author deals with Hebrew and Septuagint usage. In the O.T., knowledge means perception accompanied by emotion, or rather by a movement of the will. In LXX it is a challenge to man which may lead to salvation. There are sections on Jewish and early Christian usage, and a valuable note on compounds of the Greek verb. The volume on Apostleship has no section specifically on the Hebrew O.T., and so far as this Book List is concerned, deals with the Rabbinic *shaliach.*   N.H.S.

COPPENS, J. : *Vom Christlichen Verständnis des Alten Testaments.*
(Folia Lovaniensia, Fasc. 3-4.) 1952. Pp. 100. (Publications
Universitaires de Louvain, Desclée de Brouwer, Bruges and Paris ;
Herder, Freiburg-im-Breisgau. Price : Belgian Fr. 50.)

This interesting little book falls into three parts, an essay
on the Christian understanding of the Old Testament, a
bibliographical supplement to previous works of the author, in
particular his *Les Harmonies des Deux Testaments* (1943),
and a very welcome exhaustive bibliography of his own
amazingly voluminous literary output. The essay commences
with a brief account of the remarkable revival of Biblical
Studies in recent years in the Roman Catholic Church.
Professor Coppens expresses friendly criticism of certain
developments, viz. the advocacy of ' spiritual ' interpretation
by de Lubac, which he fears might lead to occasionalism, and
of typological interpretation by Daniélou, which on the whole
he rejects in favour of the literal meaning. Then follows
criticism of Bultmann's view of Christian typology according
to which there is a complete renewal of the Old Testament,
or rather the supersession of the Old Testament excludes the
fulfilment of Old Testament prophecies. In opposition to this
Professor Coppens maintains that there is actual fulfilment
in a sufficient number of crucial cases, e.g. in the case of
Genesis iii. 15, Psalm cx. 3, Isaiah vii. 14, Isaiah lii. 13-liii.
12, Daniel vii. 13-14. The essay concludes with a discussion
of what Professor Coppens calls *Vollsinn* (Full interpretation)
of Scripture. He recognizes its value as a completion of the
literal interpretation *per analogiam fidei* as compared with
typology which departs from the literal meaning. Such
interpretation, however, is the task of the theologian, not of
the expositor. N.W.P.

DE LA CROIX, P.-M. : *L'ancien Testament : source de vie spirituelle.*
1952. Pp. 930. (Les Études Carmelitaines chez Desclée de Brouwer,
Paris. Price : 34s. 0d.)

This volume is an example of Roman Catholic piety at its
best. To the author, the whole of the Bible (Old Testament,
Apocrypha, New Testament) speaks unfailingly of Christ.
It is a study of the way in which a man may find union with
God, Who is Father, Saviour, Husband. The Old Testament
portrays God Himself, His dealings with the soul of man,
His ways with man, all to lead us to that union with God
which is the life of the soul that is fixed in God, issuing in
His service and praise. N.H.S.

DÉMAN, P. (and BLOCH, R.) : *La Catéchèse Chrétienne et le Peuple de
la Bible.* (Cahiers Sioniens, Special number, 1952, 3/4.) Pp. 220.
(Paris. Price : Fr. 450.)

The author asserts that current *exposés scolaires* used in
French-speaking Catholic schools, by their omissions, wrong
emphases, and even errors, convey to the young a very
imperfect, and often an erroneous impression of the Jews,
their history and, especially, their unique place in God's

dispensation. The indictment is made in all charity and on the basis of all available evidence. Side by side with what is not there, or what ought not to be there, the author indicates the essentials of the full Catholic teaching. The book covers Judaism in the O.T., between the Testaments, and in the N.T. Non-Catholics, whose concern is the teaching of Scripture to the young, will find much that is interesting, and may be useful, in this unique contribution to Jewish-Christian understanding.   T.F.

DODD, C. H. : *The Old Testament in the New.* 1952. Pp. 22. (University of London, Athlone Press. Price : 2s. 0d.) ; *According to the Scriptures.* 1952. Pp. 146. (Nisbet, London. Price : 10s. 6d.)

The first book is a single Ethel M. Wood lecture delivered in March 1952, the second is a revised form of a course of Stone Lectures delivered in March 1950 ; both deal with much the same subject, but on different scales. Dodd examines the Old Testament passages quoted in the New Testament, and finds that they come mainly from particular portions of the Prophets and Psalms, the quotation being intended to call to mind the whole context. There seems to be a general agreement as to the scope and treatment of these passages, though Dodd now denies the existence of any written collection of Proof Texts at this date. The New Testament writers preserve a historical sense in their use of Old Testament material, and their principles and methods are still valid and necessary for Christian theology to-day.   D.R.Ap-T.

DRIVER, G. R. and MILES, J. C. : *The Babylonian Laws*, Vol. I. *Legal Commentary*. 1952. Pp. xxxii+518. (Clarendon Press, Oxford. Price : £2 10s. 0d.)

The authors of *Assyrian Laws* (1935) have produced another excellent book, a detailed analysis of the Code of Hammurabi, supported by a wealth of learning and, in the main, displaying an admirable soundness of judgement. When the second volume, which is to contain a transliterated text and a translation with philological notes and a glossary, has appeared, we shall possess a standard work on Babylonian law in English not parallelled in any other language. The methods used are not invariably up-to-date. The authors are no doubt right in denying any influence of CH on the Mishpaṭim. When, however, they base this conclusion on such arguments as that the Hebrew legislation concerning ' the goring ox ' is more primitive than the Babylonian (pp. 443f.), they are guilty of over-simplification. For one thing, while in some respects the Mishpatim are more primitive (e.g. unlike CH, they lay down that an ox killing a person must be stoned), in others they are more advanced (e.g. unlike CH, they deal not only with an ox killing a person but also with one man's ox killing another man's ox—a case of damage to property). The portion showing a more advanced character may indeed be an addition to the original Mishpaṭim (see the reviewer's *Studies in Bibl. Law*, 1947, pp. 86ff.) ; but it does require consideration. For another thing, the mere fact that a law is more primitive than another does not prove its independence. It is sufficient to remember what happened to Roman law when it was adopted by the Germanic tribes that settled in the Western empire. The reviewer is very pleased to note that the authors (p. 317) share his view (*Studies*, pp. 124ff.) that the ' *go'el* of the blood ', by killing the wrongdoer, restores the original proportion of power between the families involved ; and that the translation ' avenger of blood ' is misleading.

D.D.

EDLUND, C. : *Das Auge der Einfalt. Eine Untersuchung zu MATTH. 6, 22-23 und LUK.* 11, 34-35. (Acta seminarii neotestamentici Upsaliensis edenda curavit A. Fridrichsen, XIX.) Pp. 122. (Munksgaard, Copenhagen, and Gleerup, Lund. Price : 16s. 3d.)

Though primarily a study in the theology and exegesis of the New Testament, this work also has a particular interest for the student of the Old Testament and the intertestamental period. Of the five chapters, one is devoted to a very useful survey of the use of the root TMM in the Old Testament as expressing the ancient Israelite ideal of piety. In another, the intertestamental developments are outlined, and there is an illuminating study of the use of *haplotes* in the Testaments of the XII Patriarchs. These discussions prepare the way for the treatment of the logion and of its place in New Testament teaching. A sound, scholarly piece of work. G.W.A.

Evangelische Theologie. 1952. Heft 1/2. July/August. Pp. 104. (Chr. Kaiser Verlag, München. Price : DM. 3.00.)

It seems desirable to draw the attention of readers of the *Book List* to this important double number of *Evangelische Theologie.* The articles it contains are the work of a distinguished group of German scholars who are planning the Old Testament part of a new series of Biblical Commentaries. The commentaries, which are to be on a generous scale, will aim at being thoroughly scientific and, at the same time, serviceable to students and preachers for their theological and homiletical work. The preparatory articles here offered are as follows : (a) a short sermon on Ruth i, by G. von Rad ; (b) a discussion by M. Noth (who is to be general editor of the commentaries) of the way in which the Old Testament can be actualized in preaching, the suggestion being that, just as there was recital of the acts and commands of God in Old Israel, so this recital in all its variety of witness can be made its own by the Christian Church ; (c) a discussion by von Rad of the Old Testament *kerygma* or *Heilsgeschichte* which he interprets typologically, typology being regarded as interpretation which goes beyond the strictly historical meaning which applies to the acts of God in the Old Testament as a whole and which recognizes the limitations of the Old Testament which are removed in Christ ; (d) a study by W. Zimmerli of the related conceptions Promise and Fulfilment in which particular emphasis is laid on the role of prophecy in Israel ;

(e) a penetrating discussion by H. J. Kraus comparing Jewish and Christian exposition of the Old Testament with special reference to the views of Martin Buber ; (f) a specimen exposition of Hosea ii. 1-3 by H. W. Wolff in which typological exegesis is practised and is differentiated from both allegorical and existential.   N.W.P.

FRIEDRICH, G. (ed. by) : *Theologisches Wörterbuch zum Neuen Testament* (begun under the editorship of G. Kittel), Band V, Lief. 9-11. 1952. Pp. 513-704. (Kohlhammer, Stuttgart. Subscription price : DM. 4.60 per Lieferung.)

The *Book List* did not include mention of the pre-war volumes of this great work, and has not noted the post-war issues. The fourth volume was completed during the war and the fifth started. Since the war the first four volumes have been reprinted and the fifth continued. The 1952 issues carry the work from *ouranos* to *pais Theou* (incomplete). Many of the articles are long and important, and since account is taken of the Old Testament they are often of great value to the *Alttestamentler*. The longest article in these issues, as well as the most important for Old Testament students is the incomplete article on the Servant of God, the Old Testament section of which is by Zimmerli. Here and elsewhere the rich documentation makes the work quite indispensable. H.H.R.

FROST, S. B. : *Old Testament Apocalyptic : Its Origins and Growth*. 1952. Pp. xiv+270. (The Epworth Press, London. Price : 22s. 6d.)

The main thesis of this work is that the eschatology of the Old Testament is to be traced in origin to the Hebrews themselves and not to any extraneous source, that after the Exile it was increasingly expressed in mythological terms, and that apocalyptic is the direct result of this fusing of eschatology and myth. On the whole it is a pity that the author was not content to limit himself at this stage to, say, the development of eschatology ; for his treatment of the vast subject which he has chosen is really too sketchy to be satisfactory. This is the impression created at the outset by his treatment of the formal characteristics and general content of apocalyptic, and unfortunately it is confirmed by further reading. It is also unfortunate that the work bears other marks of hasty composition ; and, while this finds some explanation in the preface, it is none the less to be deplored. On the other hand, it is clear that we have here an author who can think for himself and is able to present his argument in an enlightening way and with a happy turn of phrase. It is greatly to be hoped that he will continue his work in this field ; for he has much to say that is helpful and suggestive. He is, of course, working along sound lines when he thinks in terms of the fusion of eschatology and myth, although the reviewer would date this much earlier than the author does.   A.R.J.

GELIN, A. : *Problèmes d'Ancien Testament*. 1952. Pp. 112. (Emmanuel Vitte, Paris. Price : 5s. 9d.)

In the first of the four sections of this book the author compares the situation in 1893, when the encyclical *Providentissimus Deus* was issued, and that in 1943, when the encyclical *Divino Afflante Spiritu*, which came as ' a breath of fresh air, of ozone after the storm ', was issued, and examines some current attitudes. He rejects typology and allegory, and offers some sound pedagogical principles for the teaching of Scripture, and emphasizes the necessity to consider every passage in relation to its literary form. In the second section he considers the problem of the Bible and Science, and maintains that they belong to different planes, and that each order of knowledge must enjoy its own proper autonomy. In the third he examines the ethical difficulties of the Old Testament, and argues that the individual problem must be examined in the light of the whole, and that, viewed in its totality, the Old Testament has a profoundly moral character. In the final section he deals with the relation of the Bible to the community from which it came and which it served to nurture and guide. H.H.R.

DE GROOT, J. and HULST, A. R. : *Macht en Wil*. 1952. Pp. 354. (G. F. Callenbach, Nijkerk. Price : Fl. 15.00.)

We have here a useful theological, biblical study of the nature and purposes of God. The book was planned and begun by Dr. de Groot, and, after his death in 1942, completed by Dr. Hulst. The text of the book is the opening sentence of the Schema : ' Jahwe, our God ; Jahwe is One ', and these two phrases form the titles of the two sections of the book. In the first section, we have three sub-titles : What God is, What God does, What God demands. These involve discussions of His names, His attributes and the forms in which He is envisaged. Next, we have God as acting in history and in creation. Lastly, He demands fear, trust, obedience, worship in the cultus, and loyalty from His elect people. The second part of the book is a study of the historical development of monotheism in Israel. N.H.S.

HAY, W. C. : *The Wideness of God's Mercy : a Study in the book of Jonah*. 1952. Pp. 32. (The Church of Scotland Educational Department. Price : 1s. 0d.)

This booklet, published for the Church of Scotland's Youth Committee, tells the story of the book of Jonah sympathetically, describes the evil of a narrow race-consciousness and contrasts this with the larger and beneficial outlook brought to mankind by the belief in God as the Father and Lover of all races and individuals. The book, particularly in the chapter entitled " conclusion ", achieves its aim of being instructive for young people. O.S.R.

IRWIN, W. A. : *The Old Testament : Keystone of Human Culture.*
1952. Pp. xiv + 294. (Henry Schuman, New York. Price : $4.00.)

This work is an expansion of the author's important contribution to the symposium *The Intellectual Adventure of
Ancient Man* (*Book List*, 1947, p. 8) ; and its theme, which is
presented in a characteristically vivid and arresting way, is
the Hebrew contribution to man's thought concerning himself
and the world in which he lives. For the most part the treatment of the conception of God and man and their mutual
relationship follows familiar lines, although it is good to find
that the author can be lyrical about the great canonical prophets without neglecting the work of their less spectacular
colleagues amongst the writers of the Wisdom literature. For
the rest, the chapters on the theory of law and the interplay
of nature and history in Hebrew thinking seem to the reviewer
outstanding in their balance and suggestiveness. Indeed the
whole work provides what should be a useful corrective to the
current exaggeration of the part played by ' event ' in the
revelation to Israel ; and the reviewer would add by way of
incentive that in the circumstances it is a great pity that
the author has not gathered up his occasional comments
upon this subject and fused them into a fuller treatment of
what is an important and urgent question.   A.R.J.

JUNG, C. G. : *Antwort auf Hiob.* 1952. Pp. 172. (Rascher Verlag,
Zürich. Price : DM. 11.80.)

This book may be described as a revival of Gnosticism and
Marcionism in the mind of a modern psychiatrist whose
outlook is determined by the sceptical tendencies of empirical
psychology and by a highly individual eclectic mysticism.
The starting point of his speculations is the Book of Job in
which he sees the emergence of an enlightened spiritual
human personality capable of judging his divine tormentor
who is an a-moral, unconscious, force partially controlled by
the evil power of Satan. Satan's control, however, is checked
by that of ' Sophia ' under the influence of which God decides
to become man and answer Job's challenge—an answer given
in the suffering of Christ where God suffers what He has
caused Job to suffer. How far removed the author is from
the essence of Christian philosophy is shown by his fundamental
presupposition that the affirmations of Christianity, as of
other religions, are myths, not in the sense of fictions, but as
ever recurrent pointers to archetypes in the inscrutable
Absolute. The same heterodoxy appears in his elaborate study
of the Book of Revelation which he regards as proceeding
from an irruption of the dark, irrational forces of the unconscious and as symbolizing the numinous, incalculable
aspect of the godhead. The metaphysical dualism thus
postulated will be overcome by the progressive spiritualisation
of humanity and the attainment of the perfect man through
the reconciliation of opposites. In this connexion the author
assigns the highest importance to the recent papal definition
of the Assumption of Mary and shows that it meets humanity's
longing for peace and harmonization in the inner depths of

being. It was the papal declaration which prompted him to write this essay in esoteric symbology.　　　　　H.K.

KRAUS, H.-J. : *Prophetie und Politik*. (Theologische Existenz Heute— Neue Folge 36.) 1952. Pp. 88. (Chr. Kaiser Verlag, München. Price : DM. 3.90.)

An interesting study of an important theme. Israel is a people chosen and saved by God. The covenant relationship, though historically mediated, is constantly renewed, especially in the holy war and through the charismatic leader. The development of the monarchy was an act of rebellion against the sovereignty of God, the evils of which became apparent under Solomon. The state as an expression of the human desire for security and self-determination stands over against the Divine claim for unconditioned loyalty, trust and obedience. The prophets of the state cult give sanctions to the royal policies ; the ' great prophets ' continually challenge these, while directing the attention of Israel to the new order when again the sole sovereignty of God will be acknowledged. The concluding chapter indicates the function of the Church. This is confessedly only a sketch of a highly important subject, but it indicates some useful lines of investigation. A.S.H.

KRUSE, H. : *Ethos Victoriae in Vetere Testamento*. 1951. Pp. xii+38. (Rome.)

This short monograph is an extract from a longer work which the author has prepared on the ethics of war in the Old Testament, and it describes the attitude towards those whom they had defeated in battle which was adopted by or prescribed for the Israelites as compared with other peoples of the ancient Near East, particularly the Assyrians. The author has a number of interesting comments to make on the problems raised by the notion of a just war and the indiscriminate punishment of the vanquished, and the value of the work is enhanced by a bibliography which will prove of real service to anyone who wishes to pursue the whole subject in greater detail.　　　　　A.R.J.

LINDBLOM, J. : *Israels religion i gammaltestamentlig tid*, 2nd revised ed. 1953. Pp. 274. (Svenska Kyrkans Diakonistyrelses Bokförlag, Stockholm. Price : 20 Swed. crowns.)

The first edition of this work appeared in 1936, and has rendered excellent service in Scandinavia as a text-book for students. In the new edition the general plan of the book is unaltered ; but both the text and the bibliographical notes have been brought up-to-date, and considerable parts of the book have been thoroughly revised. The presentation is admirably lucid and fair. The author does not try to fit the evidence into any neat evolutionary scheme, but emphasizes the disturbing and creative influence of the great crises and leading personalities. He shows us the Old Testament in its ancient setting, yet brings out its distinctive religious characteristics. In these days of widely divergent theories it is an enviable achievement to have produced an account of Israel's religion which is at once so reliable and so readable. G.W.A.

LOYD, P.: *Readings on the Psalms*. 1953. Pp. 124. (A. R. Mowbray, London. Price : 5s. 0d.)

The late Bishop of St. Albans planned a devotional diary which should cover a whole year. He died before his task was half complete. This volume is a shortened edition of what Bishop Loyd had written before his death. The volume contains ninety-four extracts from the Prayer Book Psalter, extending as far as Ps. lxvi. Each section consists of two or three verses from the psalm (with R. V. notes at the bottom where helpful), a meditation, and a prayer. The volume fulfils its purpose beyond question, and is of great assistance in the development of Mental Prayer.   N.H.S.

MACE, D. R. : *Hebrew Marriage : a sociological study*. 1953. Pp. xvi+272. (Epworth Press, London. Price : 21s. 0d.)

The author collected most of the material for this work between 1935 and 1942, and seldom shows acquaintance with more recent work. He does not refer to the works of Neufeld and Epstein, and in his discussion of the patriarchal narratives shows no knowledge of the significant finds of the last twenty to twenty-five years. His access to foreign work is limited (the title of Wellhausen's *Reste arabischen Heidentums* is uniformly wrongly given), and the notes and transliterations show some raggedness (*'am* is always wrongly given and there is much lack of uniformity). Despite all this, we have here a useful survey of Old Testament practice and teaching, resting on fairly wide reading of English discussions, covering the whole field of sexual relations. Dr. Mace contests the view that there are traces of the matriarchate in the Bible, and holds that Hebrew marriage was always fundamentally monogamous. He studies marital and extra-marital relations, levirate marriage and divorce. For a wide circle his book will fill the serious gap which the ' blurb ' declares to exist in the literature, but it will not be found to make any important original contribution to the study of the subject.   H.H.R.

MANSON, T. W. : *The Old Testament in the Teaching of Jesus* (Reprinted from the *Bulletin of the John Rylands Library*, vol. 34, No. 2, March 1952.) Pp. 24. (Manchester University Press and the John Rylands Library, Manchester. Price : 2s. 6d.)

The purpose of this lecture is given as an examination of " the way in which appeal is made to the Old Testament in the teaching of Jesus ". The bulk of it is devoted to a thorough study of the textual evidence. It emerges that Mark in recording Jesus' quotations from the Old Testament tends to agree with the Hebrew or the Targum against the LXX. Matthew and Luke show some tendency in the same direction. In some cases it seems probable that later scribes have accommodated the text of the quotations to the LXX. Dr. Manson further indicates that the texts quoted in Matthew as having been fulfilled seem to come from a collection of

Testimonia probably originating in Palestinian Jewish Christian circles. The voice at the baptism (though the Western text follows the LXX), the answers to the temptations and the cry of dereliction seem on the whole to point to Palestinian tradition. The evidence of the Fourth Gospel points to Hebrew and Aramaic sources for the quotations. In conclusion Dr. Manson suggests that an examination of the use made of the quotations by Jesus Himself justifies the conclusion that His " treatment of the Old Testament is based on two things : a profound understanding of the essential teaching of the Hebrew Scriptures and a sure judgement of his own contemporary situation." N.W.P.

MARSH, J. : *The Fulness of Time.* 1952. Pp. x+190. (Nisbet, London. Price : 15s. 0d.)

This book is the child of a marriage between an Idealist philosophy of Time and a Reformed biblical theology. As such it seems to be healthy and full of promise, and nowise to suffer from its mixed parentage ; in fact it embodies a very valuable contribution to the modern, more positive, constructive, application of the Bible's teaching to human life and experience to-day. It can be highly recommended on that score. The theology is Reformed, brought " up-to-date " by an acceptance of the normal critical standpoint with regard to matters of biblical " introduction ", and an emphasis on the paramount importance of the Exodus for an understanding not only of the thought of the Old Testament, but apparently also for that of Jesus in the New. D.R.Ap-T.

MAY, W. J. : *Human Nature in the Bible : a Modern Commentary on the Old Testament Story.* 1952. Pp. 96. (Epworth Press, London. Price : 6s. 0d.)

This is a popular account of much of the Old Testament, concentrating mainly on the narrative portions, which are sometimes vividly retold. It provides useful material for simple expository talks. G.W.A.

MURTONEN, A. : *The Appearance of the Name YHWH outside Israel* (Studia Orientalia, edidit Societas Orientalis Fennica, xvi, 3). 1951. Pp. 12. (Helsinki. Price : 1s. 9d.)

In this brief study the author examines the possible appearances of the name YHWH, and especially in the composition of Proper Names, outside the Bible. He accepts too readily the alleged occurrence in Ugaritic and generally offers little discussion of the data. Nor does he appear to have had access to published discussions, such as de Langhe's discussion of the point just mentioned (see *Book List*, 1948, p. 45). He is unaware of the alleged occurrence of the name in an Edomite text (cf. Grdseloff, *B.E.H.J.*, i, 1946, pp. 81ff.). On the whole question dealt with in this study cf. E. Dhorme, *Revue de l'histoire des religions*, cxli, 1952, pp. 1-18. H.H.R.

MURTONEN, A. : *A philological and literary treatise on the Old Testament Divine Names* (Studia Orientalia, edidit Societas Orientalis Fennica, xvii, 1). 1952. Pp. 106+map. (Helsinki. Price : $1.75.)

> This monograph contains an elaborate examination of the Hebrew divine names. The author's conclusions are that *'ēl* is a proper name meaning ' great, strong, without like, and to whom man can, does, and must trust himself ', from a root philologically irrecoverable, that *'eloªh* is in origin a vocative form derived from this name, and that *Yahweh* is derived from a root *hww* ' spoke ' (cp. Ugar. *hwt* ' speech, word ') and so means ' Commander ' as in *Yahweh Sabaoth*— ' Commander of the Hosts '. Whatever may be thought of the conclusions drawn by the author from his arguments, many of these are so speculative as to make the conclusion highly uncertain ; but the collection of material is of the highest value.   G.R.D.

ÖSTBORN, G. : *Yahweh's Words and Deeds. A Preliminary Study into the Old Testament Presentation of History.* (Uppsala Universitets Årsskrift, 1951 : 7.) 1951. Pp. 76. (Lundequistska Bokhandeln, Uppsala, and Harrassowitz, Wiesbaden. Price : 6s. 0d.)

> In this brief survey the author considers in turn the presentation of history in Genesis-Numbers, Deuteronomy-Kings, the work of the Chronicler, the Latter Prophets, and Apocalyptic. As the title indicates, he draws attention to the close link between the words (both prediction and command) and the deeds of Yahweh. He maintains that throughout the Old Testament history is conceived of as a succession of cyclic epochs, analogous to the cyclic processes of nature, and developing as a sequence of covenantal relationships broken and then restored. He holds that this cyclic conception has close affiliations with the cult, and that it is not incompatible with the teleological view of history, the successive periods being comprehended in a larger, inclusive unity. It appears that this study is the precursor of a larger work. There is certainly room for expansion of the themes here touched upon. But, as it stands, the essay is slight, and rather one-sided. The English style is awkward, and, at times, obscure.
>   G.W.A.

PRADO, J. : *Biblia, Paz y Eucaristía.* 1952. Pp. 140. (Ed. El Perpetuo Socorro, Madrid.)

> This is the fifth number of Prado's useful little series with the general title of " Biblia y Predicacion ". It has as subtitle, not printed on the title-page, " La prehistoria biblica ", and this is the real subject of the booklet, while the title itself is largely to be explained by the fact that the book was written as an act of homage on the occasion of the 35th International Eucharistic Congress at Barcelona in May, 1952. The Biblical prehistory is discussed, very briefly, in seven chapters dealing in turn with the earthly paradise, original sin, the *Protevangelium*, the history of Cain and Abel, the corruption that caused the flood, God's covenant with

Noah, and the tower of Babel. All these themes have been already treated at far greater length in the author's *Prae-lectiones Biblicae* (*Vetus Testamentum,* I) (Madrid, 1949).

J.M.T.B.

QUELL, G. : *Wahre und falsche Propheten : Versuch einer Inter-pretation.* 1952. Pp. 218. (C. Bertelsmann Verlag, Gütersloh. Price : DM. 17.00.)

The problem of true and false prophets and prophecy is here subjected to a penetrating re-examination, at once challenging in its frank treatment of what seems an insoluble problem and in its more positive approach through the channels of faith. Broadly speaking, the author admits the failure of most of the criteria of true and false in prophecy for we always come up against one or other of two imponderables, the person of the prophet and the fact of God's revelation through prophets. The problem is seen to be essentially religious rather than theological. The claim to divine authority has to be believed and trusted in, but cannot be proved, because, as Quell says : " Prophetie ist nicht von Menschen, und was von Menschen ist, ist nicht Prophetie " (p. 190). At heart the essence of prophecy is that it reveals the *wonder* of God. This book is a welcome addition to the literature on prophecy.   L.H.B.

REHM, M. : *Das Bild Gottes im Alten Testament.* 1951. Pp. 96. (Echter Verlag, Würzburg. Price : DM. 3.80.)

This is a popular account of the Israelite conception of God written from sixteen different angles, the most outstanding examples being the sections on the divine names, and the holiness, righteousness and kindness, as well as love, of God. If it contains little that is new and suffers somewhat from over-simplification, it is written for the most part with discernment. To the reviewer its chief defect is to be found in the fact that, while the author is not unaware of the historical factors in the expression of Israel's faith, his method is too analytical to do full justice to his theme ; and the result is that, while the reader is enabled to get some idea as to how the Israelites pictured God, he is not given a sufficiently clear picture as to how they found Him actually to be. Even so, this is an attractive little book, in which the author shows an acquain-tance with the work of Protestant as well as Roman Catholic writers.   A.R.J.

ROWLEY, H. H. : *The Servant of the Lord and Other Essays on the Old Testament.* 1952. Pp. xii+328. (Lutterworth Press, London. Price : 25s. 0d.)

In this volume, which is inscribed to our Society, Professor Rowley has reprinted seven studies which have previously appeared in various learned journals. The titles are : ' The Suffering Servant and the Davidic Messiah ', ' The Nature of Old Testament Prophecy in the Light of Recent Study ', ' The Chronological Order of Ezra and Nehemiah ', ' The

Marriage of Ruth ', ' The Interpretation of the Song of Songs ',
' The Unity of the Book of Daniel', ' Recent Discovery and
the Patriarchal Age'. All have been revised, and the references
to the literature have been brought up-to-date. To these
papers there is prefixed a discussion of the problem of the
Suffering Servant in the light of the debate of the last thirty
years. This contains a most valuable survey of the great mass
of relevant literature, and a restatement of the writer's own
position. While sympathetic to some forms of individual
interpretation, he holds that in the thought of the prophet
the collective aspect was retained, not outgrown, and that
the Christian fulfilment of the Servant's mission is not only
individual in Jesus, but collective in the Church. As a guide
to the literature of each problem handled, and for the lucid
exposition of the issues at stake, this volume, it need hardly
be said, will be quite indispensable to all serious students of
the Old Testament.   G.W.A.

RUST, E. C. : *Nature and Man in Biblical Thought.* 1953. Pp.
x+318. (Lutterworth Press, London. Price : 31s. 6d.)

This essay in Biblical Theology by a member of our Society
is to be warmly welcomed. The author is not primarily a
specialist in either Old or New Testament, but a theologian.
He is acquainted with a great deal of the recent literature
on the Old Testament, though his acquaintance with the
Scandinavian school is slight and mainly indirect, and a
number of non-Scandinavian monographs on aspects of his
subject are not referred to. The emphasis on Biblical thought
is in refreshing contrast to Brunner's neglect of the Old
Testament (*cf. Book List*, 1951, p. 53) ; for the Old Testament
is here treated as a significant part of the Biblical revelation.
The author discusses the Biblical doctrine of Creation, the
Hebrew conception of the nature of Man, and mediating
conceptions in the Old Testament and in Judaism, before
passing over to the New Testament. The whole forms a
significant and valuable study, to swell the number of recent
monographs in the field of Biblical, or Old Testament, Theology.
                                                            H.H.R.

SCHILLING, O. : *Der Jenseitsgedanke im Alten Testament : Seine
Entfaltung und deren Triebkräfte.* 1951. Pp. viii+136. (Rheingold
Verlag, Mainz. Price : 22s. 0d.)

This may be warmly welcomed as a careful attempt to trace
the development of the belief in an after-life within the pages
of the Old Testament. The author draws upon Protestant
as well as Roman Catholic writers ; and despite a certain
conservatism with regard to the literary history of the Old
Testament, which enables him to discover, for example, the
hope of a resurrection of the individual in the message of
Isaiah, he has a number of interesting and original suggestions
to make, even though his argument occasionally appears a
little forced. At the same time there are some surprising gaps
in his reading ; and, while he makes it clear that war conditions
must account for some of them, they hardly justify the

absence of any reference to the important work of, say, W. O. E. Oesterley, H. Wheeler Robinson and J. Pedersen, much of which has a direct bearing upon the author's theme.

A.R.J.

SMITH, C. RYDER : *The Bible Doctrine of Sin and of the Ways of God with Sinners*. 1953. Pp. viii+222. (Epworth Press, London. Price : 20s. 0d.)

Dr. Ryder Smith continues to issue his valuable studies in the field of Biblical Theology. The present work is divided into three parts, the first dealing with the Old Testament, the second with the Greek Old Testament and the Apocrypha (with an appendix on 2 Esdras), and the third with the New Testament. The chapter headings in each of these three sections are the same, so that the reader has the feeling of going ' round and round the garden '. They deal with ante-cedent ideas about God, with the doctrine of sin (with a careful examination of terms and metaphors, and of what to-day is called corporate sin, as well as individual sin, a discussion of the nature of sinfulness and the seriousness of sin), and with God's two ways with sinners (punishment and plea). Throughout there is an abundance of reference to Scripture passages, and as a study of the contents of the Bible on this subject the book will be of value to every reader. There is little reference to other literature about the Bible.

H.H.R.

WATERMAN, L. : *The Religion of Jesus*. 1952. Pp. 252. (Harper & Bros., New York. Price : $3.00.)

This Book List is concerned only with the first fifty-five pages, which contain a rapid, selective summary of Hebrew-Jewish religion down to the time of Christ. There is no mention of the Exodus, and one reference to Moses as the pseudo-author of an apocalypse. Hosea was the first great figure. He was mainly responsible for the prophetic stream of development which reached its Old Testament climax in Jonah. It was ethical, anti-ritualistic, non-nationalistic, non-messianic. God's favour depends on man's doing justice on earth, and there is no formal organisation, no priesthood, no hierarchy. The aim of the book is, in the words of the blurb, " to lead away from the theological Christ to the great ethical figure of the man Jesus." Christianity went astray when it departed from the ethical teaching of Jesus, who was in this full prophetic stream. At-one-ment with man will lead us to at-one-ment with God.

N.H.S.

VAN DER WEIJDEN, A. H. : *Die " Gerechtigkeit " in den Psalmen*. 1952. Pp. xvi+252. Nijmegen, Holland. Price : Fl. 9.75.)

This is a straightforward, factual examination of the meaning of the terms ' righteous ', ' righteousness ' as it may be determined by actual usage within the Psalms. The author has not only surveyed these two terms, but has also included a study of related words and ideas, both in regard to men's behaviour among themselves and to God's exercise of righteousness.

L.H.B.

WELCH, A. C. : *Kings and Prophets of Israel*, ed. by N. W. Porteous, with a memoir of (the author's) life by G. S. Gunn. 1952. Pp. 264. (Lutterworth Press, London. Price : 18s. 0d.)

From the manuscript material left by Professor Welch six studies have been selected for publication in this book : ' Moses in the Old Testament Tradition ', ' Saul ', ' David ', 'Amos ', ' Hosea ', ' Isaiah '. The last three invite comparison with chapters iv, v, and vi of Welch's Kerr Lectures, and contain, as the editor observes, a more mature treatment of these prophets. They are also, perhaps, the most rewarding part of the present volume. But the whole is of uncommon quality. The technical details of scholarship are not discussed ; but the Biblical material is presented and interpreted with a rare blend of independent judgement and spiritual insight. Again and again one is reminded of A. B. Davidson ; and that ought to be praise enough for any essay in Biblical exposition. Readers will be grateful for the admirable memoir by Dr. Gunn, and for the care with which the volume has been edited. Though most of the material in the book must have been put together nearly a generation ago, there is surprisingly little which sounds out of date ; and it may be safely predicted that a generation hence these studies will still be fresh and rewarding.   G.W.A.

WILLIAMS, R. R. : *The Perfect Law of Liberty*. 1952. Pp. 70. (A. R. Mowbray, London. Price : 3s. 6d.)

The author is Principal of St. John's College, Durham. The volume is an interpretation of Ps. 119. Each stanza of this acrostic psalm is given in the Prayer Book Version with a parallel column of textual notes, and preceded by a title. There is an introduction, dealing chiefly with Coverdale's work as a translator, with an appendix on the liturgical use of the psalms. The volume is useful for devotional study, especially to members of the Anglican communion. N.H.S.

WRIGHT, G. E. : *God Who Acts : Biblical Theology*. (Studies in Biblical Theology, 8.) 1952. Pp. 132. (S.C.M. Press. Price : 8s. 0d.)

Readers of Professor Wright's earlier contribution to the same series, viz. *The Old Testament against its Environment*, will turn eagerly to this new work and will find a great deal to interest them. The author's theme is that Biblical Theology, instead of offering a systematization of religious ideas should consist of a recital of the acts of God as recounted in the *Heilsgeschichte* of the Old Testament and in the *kerygma* of the New Testament. He indicates his approval of the conclusions of Noth and von Rad who have drawn attention to the cult-recital at the Israelite Shrines and regard the Deuteronomic History as a development of this. What may be called the *kerygma* of the Old Testament must be taken seriously as that of which in Christ we have the fulfilment. Old Testament anthropology is concerned with man as a responsible being set in community, capable of receiving God's revelation and responding to it. This is the meaning of the *imago Dei*.

Professor Wright suggests a possible ' lay-out of Biblical Theology ' (He avoids speaking of Old Testament theology as a separate discipline) thus :

(1) The acts of God especially in the Election of Israel and setting up of the Covenant people.

(2) The doctrines of Creation and Revelation.

(3) The life of man, sin, death, judgement on society, eschatology, the work of Christ, the Kingdom, the Second Advent and the Resurrection.

(4) The worship and service of God.

Professor Wright admits a certain difficulty in placing the Wisdom Books within his scheme.

He concludes with an acute criticism of Bultmann's ' Demythologising ' of the New Testament, which is thoroughly relevant to the argument of the book.　　　　N.W.P.

YOUNG, E. J. : *Isaiah 53 : a Devotional and Expository Study*. 1952. Pp. 94. (Eerdmans, Grand Rapids. Price : $1.50.)

This little book is by one who is firmly convinced of the unity of Isaiah, and of the messianic reference of the chapter studied as a specific prophecy of the work of Christ. The author is well acquainted with the work of critical scholars, whom he treats with courtesy and fairness even where he parts company with them decisively, and the work of Uppsala is as familiar to him as that of older writers. Yet his book is written for simple readers and it offers a verse by verse commentary that is at once exegetical and devotional, without being homiletical. He is conservative in his attitude to the text, and while he attaches much importance to the agreement of the Dead Sea Scroll St. Mark's Isaiah text with MT he would appear to attach less to its disagreements.　　　　H.H.R.

YOUNG, E. J. : *My Servants the Prophets*. 1952. Pp. 232. (Eerdmans, Grand Rapids, Mich. Price : $3.00.)

The author of this volume, who is a well-known and well informed conservative scholar, here studies the origin and nature of Old Testament prophecy. After a review of recent theory on the book of Deuteronomy he declares for the Mosaic authorship, and then has chapters on—*inter alia*—Moses, the terminology of prophecy, the schools of the prophets, the prophets and the cultus, true and false prophets. In the course of the book there are extended examinations of the views of A. R. Johnson, Haldar, Mowinckel, Engnell, Widengren, and others. Essentially the author's argument is that while false prophecy in Israel is not to be distinguished outwardly from true prophecy, the one has nothing to do with the other. False prophecy came from the background of Canaanite and Near Eastern prophecy, while true prophecy was a divine institution through Moses. The sharpness of this antithesis is less easy to maintain than to announce, especially as Young welcomes the softening of the antagonism between prophet and priest in recent study. The emphasis on the predictive element in prophecy—with, curiously, less ample treatment of messianic prophecy than might have been expected—and on prophecy as the organ of revelation would be shared by many who travel on a different road. The critical discussion of recent theories by a conservative scholar, whose enlightenment is revealed in the manner of his introduction of these theories to his readers, is to be welcomed. The reviewer often disagrees with the argument even where he agrees with the conclusion. H.H.R.

THE LIFE AND THOUGHT OF THE NEIGHBOURING PEOPLE

ANTHES, R. : *Die Maat des Echnaton von Amarna.* (Supplement to the Journal of the American Oriental Society, No. 14.) 1952. Pp. 36. (American Oriental Society, Baltimore. Price : $1.00.)

Dr. Anthes here makes a careful study of the use of the word " maat ", conventionally rendered " truth ", in the inscriptions of the Amarna period. He suggests that the concept of " maat " in the Amarna age differs from that of the earlier period in that it is more strongly centred in the person of the king. T.W.T.

BONNET, H. : *Reallexikon der ägyptischen Religionsgeschichte.* 1952. Pp. xvi+884. (Walter de Gruyter, Berlin. Price : DM. 92.00.)

This dictionary of the ancient Egyptian religion is a valuable addition to the literature of the subject, replacing Lanzone's long since antiquated *Dizionario di mitologia egizia.* There are articles on a wide variety of topics concerned with the religious life of the Egyptians, each furnished with a brief bibliography. They give the results of modern scholarship in a concise and clear form. Professor Bonnet's book, the product of many years' reading, will be an indispensable work of reference to Egyptologists and Old Testament scholars alike, but its high price will prevent most scholars from purchasing it for their private libraries. T.W.T.

BOTTÉRO, J. : *La Religion Babylonienne.* 1952. Pp. 150. (Presses Universitaires de France, Paris. Price : 300 Fr.)

In this very concise and competent study of Babylonian religion the author describes and discusses the religious sentiment, the theology of God, Man, and the Universe, and the cult, divination, etc. of ancient Mesopotamia. His main thesis is that the substratum of religion was Sumerian polytheism, the deification of numerous natural phenomena all localized, but that this was infused by the Semites with a new spirit, the profound consciousness of Divine transcendence. Thus the Semites systematized the pantheon and saw in Divine providence a reflection of their own monarchic system. A chapter is added on the survival of Babylonian philosophy and its influence on Greek philosophy. In his study of a most complex problem the author throughout tends to over-simplification, due, perhaps, to the limited scope of the work.

J.G.

Černý, J. : *Ancient Egyptian Religion*. 1952. Pp. xii+160. (Hutchin-son's University Library, London. Price : 8s. 6d.)

Professor Černý has produced a work of the greatest value to all who wish to understand Egyptian religion. He has con-densed the results of recent research in this field, and presented them in a manner which the layman can understand. Behind everything that he writes is a profound knowledge of the Egyptian texts and the Egyptian language. His book is the best of its kind available to English readers and should be on the shelves of every Old Testament scholar. T.W.T.

Finegan, J. : *The Archeology of World Religions*. 1952. Pp. xl+600, with 260 photographs on plates outside the text and 9 maps in the text. (Princeton University Press, Princeton, N.J. and Geoffrey Cumberlege, London. Price : $10.00 and 63s. 0d.)

The author of *Light from the Ancient Past*, which has had an extraordinarily favourable reception in America, follows it up with a corresponding volume in the same format devoted to the archæological background of Primitivism, Zoroas-trianism, Hinduism, Jainism, Buddhism, Confucianism, Taoism, Shinto, Islam, and Sikhism. The work has been carefully done and follows the best authorities. Nothing like it can be found anywhere. W.F.A.

Hooke, S. H. : *Babylonian and Assyrian Religion*. 1953. Pp. xii+128. (Hutchinson, London. Price : 8s. 6d.)

This little book contains a succinct but trustworthy account of the religion of the Babylonians and Assyrians. The successive chapters deal with sources of information, cultural background, pantheon, temples, rites and mythology, religion and life, divination, the gods and the moral government of the world ; and the appendix contains a translation of a few selected documents. The work is admirably conceived and packed with information and will undoubtedly be of great use to students not only of Babylonian and Assyrian but also of Hebrew religion. G.R.D.

Roeder, G. : *Volksglaube im Pharaonenreich*. 1952. Pp. 274. (W. Spemann Verlag, Stuttgart. Price : DM. 17.80.)

This is a popular introduction to Egyptian religion by a veteran German Egyptologist. A long chapter devoted to a regional study of religious beliefs is valuable and instructive. Old Testament scholars will find the chapters on piety in daily life and the influence of Egyptian religion on the neighbouring peoples of interest.   T.W.T.

WEISINGER, H. : *Tragedy and the Paradox of the Fortunate Fall.* 1953. Pp. 306. (Routledge & Kegan Paul, London. Price : 21s. 0d.)

The strange title of this book conceals its real nature : it is in fact an essay in the field of the comparative study of religion. The author, who is an Associate Professor of English in the University of Michigan, attempts to explain the origin and nature of tragedy in the light of the ' Myth and Ritual ' thesis : to him ' Tragedy . . . represents the highest stage in the development of the myth and ritual pattern as regards the method by which its ends are secured '. The ' paradox of the fortunate fall ' (cf. the theme of *felix culpa* in patristic thought) he sees as ' summing up in brief the essence of the myth and ritual of the ancient Near East, sharper in its formulation, more ideological, yet, at the same time, carrying with it the emotional aura of the myth and ritual pattern '. In working out his thesis the author bases himself upon the studies of S. H. Hooke, T. H. Gaster, I. Engnell, G. Widengren and E. O. James ; he is aware that the ' Myth and Ritual ' thesis has been publicly criticised, but he makes no attempt to refute that criticism in justification of his own position. What is claimed to be evidence in support of his case is culled from the literatures of Egypt, Mesopotamia, Canaan, Israel, the Hittites, Greece and Christianity but the material is taken at second-hand and in a most uncritical manner. Accordingly, although the book is well documented and equipped with an extensive bibliography, its chief significance is as a monument to the influence of the ' Myth and Ritual ' school. S.G.F.B.

WHITE, J. E. : *Ancient Egypt.* 1952. Pp. xii + 218. (Allan Wingate, London. Price : 21s. 0d.)

The author of this work, which is addressed to the general public, intended it " to serve as a clear and comprehensive introduction to Egyptology ". He has indeed produced a useful little book, which is packed with information, derived on the whole from reliable sources and presented in an attractive manner. It is illustrated with 48 well chosen photographs. His approach is original. After a chapter on the Nile and the geography of Egypt, he deals with the various grades of ancient Egyptian society ; the Pharaoh, the priest, the aristocrat, the architect, the craftsman, and the commoner. Lastly he provides three chapters on the history of Egypt.   T.W.T.

THE DEAD SEA SCROLLS

BARDTKE, H. : *Die Handschriftenfunde am Toten Meer. Mit einer kurzen Einführung in die Text—und Kanonsgeschichte des Alten Testaments.* 1952. Pp. vi+176. (Evangelische Haupt-Bibelgesellschaft, Berlin. Price : DM. 8.50.)

After a brief glance at the history of the text and canon of the New Testament and a fuller treatment of the text and canon of the Old Testament, the author outlines the story of the discovery of the Scrolls and discusses their age and genuineness. The Biblical texts, both of the larger MSS and the known fragments, and the non-Biblical texts are then considered separately and in detail. The concluding section refers to the 1952 discoveries and adopts de Vaux's revised dating of the deposit in the cave. There is also a bibliography. Although intended for the general reader, the work has also something to offer to the scholar, especially in its translations of the non-Biblical texts so far published in part or in whole. For the historical setting of the Essene group reflected in them, and especially in the Manual of Discipline, Bardtke goes back to the end of the 3rd cent. or the beginning of the 2nd cent. B.C., and places the migration to Damascus even earlier than Rowley (in *Analecta Lovaniensia,* see below, p. 73), and offers detailed reasons for his view.   O.E.

BIRNBAUM, S. A. : *The Qumrân (Dead Sea) Scrolls and Palæography* (Bulletin of the American Schools of Oriental Research. Supplementary Studies Nos. 13-14.) 1952. Pp. 52. (American Schools of Oriental Research, New Haven. Price : $1.50.)

Dr. Birnbaum is primarily, if not exclusively, a Hebrew palæographer, and students of the DS scrolls are greatly indebted to him for his early and helpful contributions to the question of dating the scrolls on a palæographical basis. Not all scholars, however, have accepted his conclusions, some have simply repudiated them while others argue that the paucity of comparable material for dating considerably reduces the importance of palæography for dating the scrolls. In the present pamphlet Dr. Birnbaum inveighs against some of these scholars, notably Kahle, Teicher, Lehmann and Lacheman : nor does the fact that no two of them agree together reduce the fury of Birnbaum's attack. Much important information emerges from the polemics, and for this we are grateful. And particularly we owe a great deal to Birnbaum—and the publishers—for eighteen admirable tables which indicate the stature of the author as a palæographer. These figures will be useful whatever the outcome of ' the battle of the scrolls ' may be.   B.J.R.

DUPONT-SOMMER, A. : *Nouveaux Aperçus sur les Manuscrits de la Mer Morte.* (L'Orient Ancien illustré, No. 5.) 1953. Pp. 222. (A. Maisonneuve, Paris.)

In this volume Professor Dupont-Sommer gives some account of finds which have been made since his former book was written (including a summary in the appendix of the article which de Vaux has now published in the January issue of the *Revue Biblique*, telling of finds more recent than those reported to the Paris Academy in April, 1952), and a defence of his views against some of the criticisms which have been made, together with an examination of materials from the first find which have been published since his earlier book appeared. There is thus an account of the excavations at Khirbet Qumran, a full defence of his identification of the Kittim with the Romans, and a much fuller treatment of the people from whom the scrolls came—identified still with the Essenes—than was possible before, when only parts of the Manual of Discipline had been published. There is also a chapter on the Testaments of the Twelve Patriarchs and the Scrolls, with special reference to the Teacher of Righteousness in the Testament of Levi. Zoroastrian influence on the community of the Covenanters is maintained, and the author defends himself against strictures on his earlier statements on the relations between the Teacher of Righteousness and Jesus, by writers who have not always noted the precision of his choice of words. This book is thus an important contribution to the continuing debate on the Scrolls.   H.H.R.

EDELKOORT, A. H. : *De Handschriften van de Dode Zee.* 1952. Pp. 168. (Bosch & Keuning, Baarn. Price : Fl. 6.80.)

Professor Edelkoort has given a longer and more general introduction to the Scrolls than has hitherto appeared, and the book is most welcome as a comprehensive, well-balanced and interesting exposition, despite the fact that it is in parts inevitably dated because of discoveries and discussions published whilst the book was in the press. DSIa is given a setting in the story of the textual transmission as a pre-Massoretic text-form of the 2nd cent. B.C. DSH is newly translated, and regarded as a Midrash whose exact date cannot be determined, but which fits in well with the late Maccabean period. DSD, also translated, is discussed in connection with CDC, and a series of 18 points is given in favour of associating the party with the Essenes, though other possible names are mentioned. DSW, DST and the remaining fragments are less thoroughly outlined, though, again, we are indebted to the author for valuable translations. In fact, in its translations of the Scrolls, the book is an important one. A short postscript refers to the Khirbet Qumrân excavations, but the general bibliography is disappointing.   B.J.R.

JANSSENS, H. F. : *Vocabulaire du " Manuel de Discipline ".* 1952. Pp. ii + 36. (Brussels. Obtainable from the Author, Rue du Château 13, Termonde, Belgium.)

This useful alphabetic tabulation of DSD vocabulary will be of considerable service to those interested in the lexicography of the Scrolls. It is a preliminary work, but, without minimizing its value, one cannot but regret the absence of one or· two features, e.g. there is no definition and no attempt to distinguish between nuances of certain words and phrases.
                   B.J.R.

Reicke, B. : *Handskrifterna fran Qumrân (eller 'Ain Feschcha)* I-III. (Symbolae Biblicae Upsalienses XIV.) 1952. Pp. 100. (Wretmans Boktryckeri, Uppsala.)

This book is printed as a supplement to *Svensk exegetisk årsbok* XVI (see p. 11), but may also be bought separately. In it Docent Reicke gives a general account, for the benefit of Swedish readers, and particularly of New Testament students, of some of the main facts and problems connected with the Dead Sea Scrolls. In Part I he enumerates and describes the MSS, and touches briefly on the problem of dating. Part II contains a translation of DSH (with concise notes on doubtful readings and the like), followed by a discussion of the historical background. Discarding his original view Reicke now inclines to a date between 90 and 80 B.C. for the historical allusions in this document, and sees in the Wicked Priest the Hasmonaean dynasty in general and Alexander Jannaeus in particular. Of the Teacher of Righteousness he says that he cannot be identified with any definite person in the period in question. Part III consists almost entirely of a rendering of DSD (again, concisely annotated), followed by a succinct statement of the affinities and importance of the document.   G.W.A.

Roberts, B. J. : *Some observations on the Damascus Document and the Dead Sea Scrolls.* (Reprinted from *Bulletin of the John Rylands Library*, vol. 34, No. 2, March 1952.) 1952. Pp. 22. (Manchester University Press and The John Rylands Library, Manchester. Price : 2s. 6d.)

The author's aim is to consider some issues common to both the Dead Sea Scrolls and the *Damascus Document*, and to suggest conclusions concerning the character and beliefs of the New Covenanters, the term he adopts for the sect from which both sets of documents emanate. The author shares with some other scholars the view that the literature of the New Covenanters reveals a pattern or method of exegesis which was in common vogue among them. For a clearer understanding of the exegesis, a discussion of the word *pesher*, as it occurs in Daniel, and more especially in the *Habakkuk Commentary*, is necessary, and this is provided. The *Habakkuk Commentary*, the author believes, belongs to a literary *genre* which makes it impossible to identify the historical allusions in it. While it adds little to what is already known about the content of apocalyptic thought, it bears important testimony to the quality of apocalyptic round about the beginning of the Christian era. Three characteristic terms, each with its apocalyptic nuance, in the *Damascus Document*, are examined, and more clearly defined, viz., qeṣ " period ", goral " lot " and *raze* " secrets ". It is recognized that the proposed identification of the sect with the Essenes has much in its favour, but it is regarded as not free from difficulty. The part played by Zadok and his followers in opposition to orthodox Judaism is thought to be a fruitful line of approach to this problem. All that can be said at this stage about the sect, however, is that it was a " Bible party ", an apocalyptic group awaiting the fulfilment of the word of God. Features which are similar in these documents and in the N.T. are noted, but the author makes it clear that these similarities do not point to the association of the New Covenanters with the early Christians, much less to their identification with them.

D.W.T.

ROWLEY, H. H. : *The Covenanters of Damascus and the Dead Sea Scrolls*. (Reprinted from *Bulletin of the John Rylands Library*, vol. 35, No. 1, Sept. 1952.) 1952. Pp. 46. (Manchester University Press and The John Rylands Library, Manchester. Price : 3s. 0d.)

This lecture to the John Rylands Library preceded Professor Rowley's Louvain lectures on which his book, reviewed below, was based ; nevertheless, in many ways the lecture is complementary to the book. Particularly is the question of the date of the Sect, and its historical setting in the Maccabaean period more fully discussed. Other points outlined in greater detail here are the relationship of the scrolls with the Cairo Genizah *Zadokite Work*, and various problems arising from the attitude of some scholars to the study of the scrolls. The lucidity of the argument, the full annotation and the copious bibliographical references are, as always in Professor Rowley's works, extremely valuable.

B.J.R.

ROWLEY, H. H. : *The Internal Dating of the Dead Sea Scrolls*. (Analecta Lovaniensia Biblica et Orientalia. Ser. II. Fasc. 30.) 1952. Pp. 22. (Publications Universitaires de Louvain ; Desclée de Brouwer, Bruges-Paris. Price : Fr. 25.)

Professor Rowley, in this typically balanced and exhaustive discussion of a most controversial topic, critically examines the theories of Delcor, Segal, Dupont-Sommer, Teicher and Eisler, together with the mention of other writers, and thinks that Dupont-Sommer has ' rightly perceived the date of the rise of the sect ', namely, the Maccabaean Age, though he does not accept that authority's identifications. He proceeds to offer the following identifications : the Teacher of Righteousness with Onias, the Wicked Priest with Menelaus, the Man of Scorn and of Untruth with Antiochus, the House of Absalom with the Tobiads, the sect of the Scrolls with some of the earlier supporters of Judas, who are ' either an early group out of which Essenes and others may have grown, or the Essenes in a much earlier stage of their existence than we find reflected in Josephus '.

B.J.R.

ROWLEY, H. H. : *The Zadokite Fragments and the Dead Sea Scrolls*. 1952. Pp. xiv+134. (Basil Blackwell, Oxford. Price : 16s. 0d.)

This book cannot be too highly recommended for use both by the specialist and the general student of the scrolls : nowhere has the reviewer seen the peculiar talents of Professor Rowley as a scholar exercised to greater advantage. It is the author's singular achievement that he has reduced the bewildering variety of views and theories into a consistent and lucid pattern, and given a judicious analysis of the more important discussions. For this, the specialist will be at least as grateful as the general reader. The abundant annotation, with trenchant observations and full references to publications, is indispensable for future work, and the bibliography, covering thirty-six pages, contains almost all published works to date. Professor Rowley's main interest lies in the question of dating the composition of the scrolls and the Zadokite Fragments ; and he argues with cogency for the Maccabaean period. He rightly insists, however, that the general problem of the scrolls includes other, quite independent, questions, such as when were the present scrolls copied, when were they deposited in the cache, and the relevance of the scrolls for the study of the Karaite movement in the Middle Ages. There are indexes of subjects and authors, and two pages of ' additional notes ' mention some of the work done on the scrolls during the printing of the book.   B.J.R.

ZEITLIN, S. : *The Zadokite Fragments : Facsimile of the Manuscripts in the Cairo Genizah Collection in the Possession of the University Library, Cambridge, England, with an Introduction.* (The Jewish Quarterly Review Monograph Series, No. 1.) 1952. Pp. 32+20 plates. (The Dropsie College for Hebrew and Cognate Learning, Philadelphia. Price : $2.00.)

By this first number the J.Q.R. Monograph Series makes a most worthy *début* with the publication for the first time in facsimile of the whole of the extant Zadokite Fragments, better known as the Damascus Document. The two MSS have been in the University Library of Cambridge for the past half-century, but hitherto students have depended in the main on Schechter's transcription (1910) and the much better edition of the text by Rost (1933—this latter, surprisingly, is not mentioned by Dr. Zeitlin in his introductory notes.) The present facsimile edition is well produced, though there are occasional parts of the text which are more easily decipherable in the photostats. In the Introduction Dr. Zeitlin argues vehemently for a medieval dating for the Fragments, which, he says, are to be ascribed to the Karaites ; furthermore, ' the text was written in very poor, ungrammatical Hebrew by a Karaite who has insufficient knowledge of the Hebrew language.'   B.J.R.

POST-BIBLICAL JUDAISM

BLACKMAN, P. : *Mishnayoth* (in six volumes). Vol. I. *Order Zeraim.* Vol. II. *Order Moed.* Pointed Hebrew text, Introductions, Translation, Notes, Supplements (Flora, Biographies), Indexes. 1951, 1952. Pp. 542 and 574. (Mishna Press, London. Price : £2 2s. 0d. each.)

This is a bold and useful—and likewise generous—publishing venture and well satisfies the purpose which it sets before itself ; and it is greatly to be hoped that the remaining four volumes will not fail to appear in due course. The edition seeks to make the Mishnah's contents accessible and comprehensible to the Jewish reader who may, or may not, have any knowledge of Hebrew, and its *kashruth* is fully certified. The text follows the ordinary Mishnayoth editions, and alongside is a literal rendering in English and a concise commentary. Each tractate has a short introduction and each volume is lavishly equipped with useful appendixes. The translation prefers literalness to clarity (cf. Suk. 1 : 7, " One loosens them and one is removed between every two . . . R. Meir says, One takes out every alternate one "), and can even present the term " holyday-day " as a translation of *yom tobh*. The edition does not attempt to meet any exacting claims of scholarship. Impressive though the Editor's interest is in natural history (he gives six lines to the botanical definition of apple, and nine lines to the dandelion), he still allows the oecologically impossible weasel (it should be " rat ") to run about among the wine-cellars of Sharon ; the reader is not bothered with snags in text or interpretation, and no use seems to have been made of J. N. Epstein's great *Introduction to the Text of the Mishnah* (1948) as a guide to variant readings.   H.D.

DAVIES, W. D. : *Torah in the Messianic Age and/or the Age to Come.* (Journal of Biblical Literature : Monograph Series, Vol. VII.) 1952. Pp. 100. (Society of Biblical Literature, Philadelphia. Price : $1.50.)

Dr. Davies seeks to find out whether in Jewish thought before and during Gospel times the belief existed that the status of the Law would change with the coming of the Messianic Age. The answer, he considers, " would illumine for us the impact of the Gospel on the Torah, and thus best enlighten us on the various attitudes within the Early Church towards Judaism and also within Judaism towards the Church ". He examines the Old Testament evidence—particularly Jer. xxxi. 31-34, and the Servant Poems, and those other passages which speak directly or inferentially of the more perfect time when man shall have God's law in his heart. Dr. Davies then explores the Apocrypha and the Zadokite Document. In the end he can only endorse G. F. Moore's conclusion (*Judaism*, I, 271) that not only would the Torah remain a force in the Messianic Age but would be " better studied and better observed than ever before ". The rabbinical sources are then consulted, but they provide slippery footing and offer no forward steps in the inquiry. For any positive conclusion Dr. Davies is thrown back on the New Testament : " We may with some confidence assert that the Gospel of Matthew regards the words of Jesus as a New Torah . . . the words of Jesus ' fulfilled ' the Law and the Prophets, they were the Torah of the Messiah."
                                                                        H.D.

GUTKIND, E. : *Choose Life : the Biblical Call to Revolt.* 1952. Pp. viii+312. (Schuman, New York. Price : $4.00.)

The only reason for the inclusion of this book here is to warn members that despite its sub-title it is not a book about the Bible, but a prophetic message to the Jews to realise that Israel is not a religion or a nation, but a people called to unite for the coming ' global showdown ', in which the present confusions may be transcended in a new era of *shalom,* and in which the Jews are destined to play the central part.
H.H.R.

HERBERG, W. : *Judaism and Modern Man.* 1952. Pp. 312. (Farrar, Strauss and Young, New York. Price : $3.75.)

This is perhaps the most profoundly theological study of Judaism which has come from a contemporary and orthodox Jewish writer. Though the discussion of the modern world draws somewhat heavily on Christian authors such as Niebuhr and Tillich, and passes too lightly over Jewish insights, the first sections, dealing with the theology and religion of Judaism in the Old Testament are admirable ; as is the closing section on the mystery of Israel. J.W.P.

HERTZ, J. H. : *Sayings of the Fathers,* with an Introduction and Commentary. 1952. Pp. 96. (East and West Library, London. Price : 10s. 6d.)

Abhoth, though the least characteristic tractate in the Mishnah, is yet the most frequently published, and it can claim to be among the most translated items in world literature. The English version given here proves, however, not to be a new translation : it has been tacitly reproduced from the translation in *The Authorised Daily Jewish Prayer Book* (1891) by S. Singer. It has been ' touched up ' occasionally, presumably by the late Chief Rabbi. Thus Hillel's familiar saying, ' The more women, the more witchcraft ' (so Singer), becomes ' The more *wives,* the more witchcraft '—and so Dr. Hertz points out, Hillel is seen discountenancing polygamy a thousand years before it was formally banned by Western Jewry ; and the older (literal) rendering, ' nor can an ignorant man be pious ', is modified to ' be truly pious '. The Commentary is straightforward, with only the immediate needs of the English reader in mind. Problems are passed over ; e.g. nothing is said (p. 49) of the variant ' The world is judged by grace, and not according to works ', where more printed editions have ' . . . yet all is according to the amount of work'. The familiar title ' Ethics of the Fathers ' is, Dr. Hertz points out, misleading ; we have here not an ethical treatise but casual *obiter dicta,* of which the majority are haggadic sayings in praise of Torah. The book has an ornate exterior and no Index. H.D.

KADUSHIN, M. : *The Rabbinic Mind.* 1952. Pp. xviii+394. (Bloch Publishing Co., New York. Price : $5.00.)

Rabbinic thought and teaching has always, from medieval days onwards, failed to respond to attempts to reduce it to dogmatic essentials or any philosophic scheme. It is by nature a free and indigenous growth from the Bible, trimmed to no logical or doctrinal pattern, with no eye to the approval of such things as oecumenical councils. This, as Schechter once pointed out, has its advantages : it enabled the Rabbis " to enunciate religious ideas without spinning them out into creedal principles ; to present aspects of a subject which may well be modified or qualified by other aspects of that subject ". But, asks Mr. Kadushin, " has it no integrating principle at all ?" His answer is that rabbinic teaching rests on a series •of " value concepts " (e.g. God's justice, God's love, Torah, and Israel), themselves undefined and supplemented by groups of " sub-concepts " (e.g. the Kingdom of Heaven, the ṣaddiḳ, and the hasid). Though not subjected to definition these are given form through the media of Haggadah and Halakah : thus Haggadah allows the value-concept to be applied in all varieties of situation, to become vivid, regardless of consistency ; while Halakah " prescribed ways for the concretization of the concepts in day-by-day living ". H.D.

MENOUD, P.-H. : *L'Église naissante et le Judaïsme* (= *Études Théologiques et Religieuses*, xxvii, 1952, No. 1). 1952. Pp. 52. (Faculté de Théologie Protestante, Montpellier. Price : Fr. 200.)

A single monograph occupies the whole of this issue, as has happened in some other cases with this journal. It is devoted to some aspects of the tension between the infant Church and Judaism. Starting from the polarity of Pauline and Johannine thought, in which love for Israel and condemnation of Israel figure alike, the author shows that the anti-Jewish sentiment of the New Testament is not anti-semitism, but is fundamentally theological. Passing to the study of the theological conflict he underlines the fact that Judaism preserved the old, while Christianity, though basing itself on the old, offered what was a new religion, distinct from the old, whose authority yet derived from the old. Hence the two faiths which had so much to bind them together became involved in conflict which reached also the political sphere. H.H.R.

NEMOY, L. : *Karaite Anthology. Excerpts from the Early Literature.* Translated from Arabic, Aramaic, and Hebrew sources, with notes. (Yale Judaica Series, Vol. VII.) 1952. Pp. xxvi+412. (Yale University Press, New Haven ; Geoffrey Cumberlege, Oxford University Press, London. Price : $6.00 ; English price : 40s. 0d.)

Though many of the important Karaite texts have been published and a very few translated into English, only a few essays and dictionary articles on the Karaites are easily available to non-technical students. The present volume is therefore a desirable supplement to the usual works of reference. After an outline of the history of the Karaites

Mr. Nemoy gives extracts from fourteen writers, from Anan in the 8th century to Bashyatchi in the 15th, prefacing each with a biographical note, and concluding the selection with the marriage ritual and a few other shorter liturgical extracts. The range of subjects is narrow—chiefly law, biblical exegesis and anti-Rabbanite controversy, with only occasional excursions into history and poetry. Like the other volumes of the series the editorial work is highly polished ; so it is a shock to meet such a rendering as " The choice is up to her " (p. 29) and to find the Palestine town of Ramleh located on the banks of the Jordan (p. 335). The famous passage from al-Kirkisani which figured prominently in the early controversy about the Zadokite Fragments, is quoted (p. 50), but without comment.   H.D.

THIEBERGER, F. : *Die Glaubenstufen des Judentums.* (Sammlung Völkerglaube.) 1952. Pp. 208. (W. Spemann Verlag, Stuttgart. Price : DM. 11.80.)

The author of this interesting if controversial book is a disciple of Martin Buber ; and he adopts his teacher's metaphysical and religious standpoints, without apparent modification, for an interpretation of O.T. religious history. Dr. Thieberger is familiar with the main trends in analytical O.T. study, and introduces many of its findings into his review ; more notice could have' been taken, however, of a modified Form-criticism which would have fitted in very well with the author's standpoint. Monotheism was always incipient in Jewish religion, and is its major contribution. Up to the close of the exile it developed, partly by absorbing from neighbouring cults, and found its expression in Torah and Temple. The effect of the exile was to produce a theocracy (not a hierocracy), with the Torah as basis for a Judaism that neither king nor priest could disturb. The next stages were the canon and the expansion of the Torah in the Oral Law. Finally a mystical stage was developed by the Rabbis and by Philo. The book closes with notes on four plates which are interspersed in the text, a brief bibliography and an index. It is as an interesting synthesis, a ' running commentary ' on a philosophical postulate that the book is to be welcomed ; there are possibly too many novel theories to make it a useful popular introduction to the topic.   B.J.R.

WEIS, P. R. : *Mishnah Horayoth.* 1952. Pp. xxxvii+111 and a chart of sources. (University Press, Manchester. Price : 25s. 0d.)

This is an extremely valuable analysis of the sources of the Mishnic tractate Horayoth. An extensive comparison of parallels to be found in Rabbinic literature enables Rabbi Weis to establish the authorship of many paragraphs of the tractate. In other cases, what has come to be known as the logico-juridical method is used with great skill. Moreover, Rabbi Weis rightly argues that where Tannaites of a certain period differ as to the meaning of a decision, the basic decision must date at least from the preceding generation. Careful attention is paid to a restoration of the genuine text. The result is a history of the tractate which forms a notable contribution to our knowledge. Professor E. Robertson has provided a fine translation and written an illuminating foreword. The only criticism one would submit is that the tractate is called ' abstruse '. This is an old prejudice ; but as the reviewer tried to show (*The Guardian*, 1941, pp. 393, 406), Horayoth contains the most fertile ideas about the problem of rulings which are at the same time erroneous and authoritative.   D.D.

PHILOLOGY AND GRAMMAR

AL-YASIN, IZZ-AL-DIN : *The lexical relation between Ugaritic and Arabic.* (Shelton College Semitic Monograph Series I.) 1952. Pp. 188. (Shelton College, New York. Price : $2.00.)

A new series of Semitic monographs, issued under the auspices of Shelton College, begins with this typescript study of the Ugaritic language in the light of the Arabic dictionary. The author has made a useful contribution to the study of the Ugaritic texts, which, although it is one-sided in that every-thing possible is explained in the light of one and that the latest of the Semitic languages as known to us through its literatures, none the less adds not a little to our knowledge. Some of his interpretations deserve careful attention, even though others can hardly be right. The general conclusion is that the Ugaritic language is neither exclusively Canaanite nor exclusively North-Arabic, but that its precise position within the Semitic family remains to be determined.

G.R.D.

BEER, G. : *Hebräische Grammatik*, 2nd ed., revised by R. Meyer, Vol. 1. (Sammlung Göschen, 763/763a.) 1952. Pp. 158. (Walter de Gruyter, Berlin. Price : DM. 4.80.)

This first volume of the second edition of Beer's Hebrew grammar in the well-known series of German primers deals with the orthography, phonetics and morphology of Hebrew. The approach is historical and comparative. Full use is made of Ugaritic, which is cited whenever possible. The author has compressed a mass of information and suggestions into this excellent little book. It is warmly recommended to all interested in the history of the Hebrew language. T.W.T.

BEN-YEHUDA, E. : *Thesaurus Totius Hebraitatis et Veteris et Recentioris.* Vol. XIV. 1952-3. Pp. xx+468. (Hemda and Ehud Benyehuda, Talpiot, Jerusalem. Price : £6 10s. 0d.)

This volume of Ben-Yehuda's dictionary, edited by Professor Tur-Sinai, comprises the words from *rizzuy* to *shallekheth*. The author aimed to give in this volume, as he aspired to give in its thirteen companion volumes, all the words found in the various forms of Hebrew literature—from the Bible to the last Hebrew word coined by the author and his contemporaries in the various Hebrew publications of their time. Each word is translated into German, French and English and is fully defined in Hebrew, the definition being substantiated by a great number of appropriate quotations drawn from a variety of Hebrew sources. To take meaning I of the first word of this volume as an example : *rizzuy*. This piel verbal noun which derives from the Biblical *rẓh*, ' be pleased with ', ' accept favourably ', has here the meaning of ' appeasing ', ' winning favour '. In support of this meaning twenty-eight quotations from eighteen famous post-Biblical authorities are given, amongst whom are : Talmud Babli, RaSHi, Rabbi Abraham bar Hiyya Hannasi', Responsa, Geonica, Rabbi I. Abrabanel. From the payyetanic literature we have among others quotations from Yosi ben Yosi, Yannai, Meshullam b. Kelonimos and Shelomoh Hakkatan. There is also a good number of lexicographical notes. Professor Tur-Sinai has added numerous quotations from sources not examined by Ben-Yehuda as well as many valuable philological and bibliographical notes, and he is to be congratulated on his scholarly work. One, however, wonders whether he made full use of the linguistic material embodied in the Judaean Scrolls of which he makes mention in his additional ' List of Books '. Expressions like *u-bhirki'a* (or *u-bhirko'a*), *yabbasha* and *'esh 'okheleth be-khol sho'obhehem* (or *sho'abhehem*), which occur in the hymns of the Scrolls, could have been profitably included in the notes of pp. 6736-6739 and pp. 6788-6790, 6792 respectively. Hebrew scholars all over the world are eagerly awaiting the last two volumes, the one containing *shll-ttrn* and the other supplementary material the early appearance of which was promised by Ben-Yehuda's son, Ehud, in his introductory note to vol. XIV.　　M.W.

CHOMSKY, W. : *David Ḳimḥi's Hebrew Grammar (Mikhlol) systematically presented and critically annotated.* 1952. Pp. xxiv+428. (Bloch Publishing Co., New York. Price : $7.50.)

The first part of this book was published nearly twenty years ago. It is now republished and completed on the initiative and through the generosity of some of Dr. Chomsky's friends who have deserved well of scholars. Ḳimḥi's work is not translated in the order of his own text, but in systematic arrangement which makes it simpler for modern students to use. Dr. Chomsky has added notes which sometimes trace Ḳimḥi's ideas to their sources, and sometimes give the background of mediaeval controversy, and at other times supply references to modern grammatical works. It is interesting to find that traces of the passive of Ḳal were recognized by ibn Janah, though until quite modern times they did not figure in our grammars. Ḳimḥi's own work is interesting, but with Dr. Chomsky's notes it is a mine of information for scholars.　　　　　　　　　　　　　　　　　H.H.R.

CROSS, F. M. and FREEDMAN, D. N. : *Early Hebrew Orthography. A study of the epigraphic evidence.* 1952. Pp. 78. (American Oriental Society, New Haven. Price : $2.50.)

> The purpose of this study is to show that the Aramaeans, who took over the Phoenician script between the 12th and 10th centuries B.C., were responsible for introducting *matres lectionis c.* 900 B.C. and that the Hebrews adopted them *c.* 900-850 B.C. ; the practice of using them in medial positions came about as a subsequent extension of the principle of the representation of final vowels by them. These suggestions are plausibly argued and may be substantially correct ; but the evidence is often very slight, being based on inscriptions which are few and far between and often very brief, so that examples of crucial forms do not always appear in them. The authors also occasionally make dubious assertions or overlook inconvenient evidence (for instance, the Ugaritic texts have shown that ' *hê* ' *locale* is distinct from the termination of the accusative case). G.R.D.

HOROWITZ, M. : *Précis de grammaire hébraïque.* 1951. Pp. 110. (Union des Hébraisants, Paris. Price : 10s. 3d.)

> The " Union des hébraisants de France " engages in a variety of activities which aim at the furtherance of the study of Hebrew. In pursuance of this aim the author of this grammar has written several works designed to help students to acquire a knowledge of the language. The present volume, which completes his series of such works, is intended for use by those who already possess a sound foundation of the language. It consists of eight main sections, which deal in turn with phonetics, nouns, adjectives, pronouns, numerals, verbs, particles and prepositions. The inclusion of much that belongs to post-Biblical and modern Hebrew makes the grammar of limited value for students of O.T. Hebrew. The wider circle of Hebrew students to whom it is addressed should, however, find much in it to help them. The presentation is clear, much use being made of tables, and in general it is accurate, though the vocalisation of Hebrew words is not infrequently faulty. Among the more unusual features of the work is the addition throughout of Hebrew grammatical terms. D.W.T.

JANSMA, T. : *A Selection from the Acts of Judas Thomas.* (Semitic Study Series, N.S., No. 1.) 1952. Pp. x + 46. (Brill, Leiden. Price : Fl. 4.75.)

> The text in this Selection consists of a shortened version of four Acts and includes the Hymn of the Soul (pp. 35-40). It is based on the edition of Wright, and readings from MSS published by Mrs. Lewis and P. Bedjan are given in an apparatus. Professor Jansma has rendered a service to Syriac studies by producing this handy and beautifully printed manual for class reading. W.D.M.

KÖBERT, R. : *Textus et Paradigmata Syriaca*. 1952. Pp. 106. (Pontificium Institutum Biblicum, Rome. Price : L.900.)

A new Syriac chrestomathy is a boon to the beginner, and the selection of texts here gathered together will be widely useful. Ezra vii. 12-26 is given in Aramaic and Syriac on opposite pages, and then an excellent selection of Old Testament, New Testament and extra-Biblical Syriac texts. There are about forty pages of extra-Biblical texts. The New Testament selections are confined to the Gospels, while the Old Testament texts include passages from Genesis and the Psalter, together with the Servant Songs from Isaiah. Prefixed to the texts are tables of noun and verb formations. The whole is photographically reproduced from the careful and clear handwriting of R. Wessely. A vocabulary would have added greatly to the value of the work, since few beginners can afford a Syriac lexicon.   H.H.R.

KOEHLER, L. : *Lexicon in Veteris Testamenti Libros*. Lief. XII-XV. 1952. Pp. 705-960. (Brill, Leiden. Price : 4s. 6d. each part.)

This year has brought four more parts of Professor Koehler's invaluable *Lexicon*, containing nearly 260 pages and running from *'al* to *shehîn :* and at this rate the Hebrew part ought to be finished in the course of the coming year. Even though the author may have missed a few things in articles or commentaries, these parts, like their predecessors, will be indispensable to all students of the Old Testament, whose dictionaries are sadly out of date.   G.R.D.

MARGALIT, D. : *Lashon u-Rephu'ah Ba-TeNaKH*. 1950. Pp. 166. (W'adhath ha-Yobhel shel 'irgun Roph'e Ḳuppath Ḥolim 'Ammamith, Tel-Aviv.)

For the benefit of the Biblical scholar this volume may be divided into two main sections, the one containing researches in Biblical medical terms and the other in general Hebrew (mainly Biblical) word-phenomena and phrases. In both sections full account is taken of colloquial Arabic. In the first section the author identifies *negha' ṣara'ath* (Lev. xiii. 3) with syphilis ; *basar* (12 times in Lev. xiii) with the sexual organ of either male or female. Further, *zobho* (Lev. xv. 2) he takes to refer to gonorrhoea. From the many matters discussed by the author in the second section only one will be mentioned. The author takes many instances of the word *mah* which occur in the O.T. to mean, as in colloquial Arabic, ' no ', ' not '. Of the 47 passages quoted in support of this meaning the passage from 1 Kings xii. 17, where *mah* is to be found as parallel to *we-lo*, is perhaps the soundest. Moreover, the Targum renders here *mah* as *leth*.   M.W.

NYBERG, H. S. : *Hebreisk Grammatik*. 1952. Pp. xvi+332. (Almqvist & Wiksells Skolböcker, Hugo Gebers Förlag, Uppsala. Price : Kr. 45.00.)

This book has been written as ' an elementary grammar intended for beginners, but also to provide a deeper insight into the language for more advanced students '. It follows the pattern of G.-K., however, rather than McFadyen-Davidson or Weingreen. Nyberg does not set out to treat the language of the O.T. exhaustively, but concentrates more especially on the classical Hebrew prose of Genesis, Judges, and Samuel, with less reference to Kings and Ex.-Deut., and less still to the prophetical and poetical books. The detailed Contents Table supplies the lack of a subject index, but it is regrettable that no Scripture reference index is provided.

Only Massoretic Hebrew is treated, and its value as fairly correctly expressing the pronunciation of the living language is unrepentantly upheld. Nyberg has paid special attention to his sketch of the syntax which occupies the smaller second part of the volume, since he regards G.-K. as very much out of date, and feels that there is a definite lack of anything more modern and reliable.

An independent study and carefully considered appraisal of the data are evident throughout, and will make this a useful handbook even for those whose knowledge of Swedish is only slight.   D.R.Ap-T.

SELLERS, O. R. and VOIGT, E. E. : *Biblical Hebrew for Beginners*, 2nd ed., 7th printing. 1951. Pp. 60. (Blessing Book Stores, Inc., Chicago. Price : $1.50.)

This manual, composed by two teachers of theology, is intended primarily for use in class, and not for self-instruction. It consists of forty one hour lessons, which contain vocabularies, sections of grammar, and reading and writing exercises. Some of the exercises are printed from type, others are reproduced from handwriting. There are in addition comprehensive vocabularies, tables of nouns and of the suffixes, and verbal paradigms. The work was first printed in 1941, but it has been in use in mimeographed form since 1927. The authors testify that it has proved useful in helping many a beginner to acquire the elements of the language. That this is so may well be believed, for the information imparted is concerned with essential knowledge, is clearly presented, and is in general reliable. Some things in it, however, need correction—for example, errors in the vocalization of Hebrew words, and the regular use of the negative *lo'* with the participle. Some of the Hebrew sentences in the exercises, too, have an English rather than an Hebraic ring.   D.W.T.

STRACK, H. L. and JEPSEN, A. : *Hebräische Grammatik mit Übungsbuch :* 15th edition (Clavis Linguarum Semiticarum, edidit H. L. Strack, Part 1). 1952. Pp. xii + 266. (C. H. Beck, Munich. Price : DM. 16.00.)

This is the fifteenth edition of the well-known Hebrew Grammar of the late Dr. H. L. Strack, completely revised if not rewritten by Dr. A. Jepsen. The work, which more or less follows the traditional lines laid down by scholars of the last hundred years for grammars intended for beginners, will be as useful as the preceding editions for such persons. The presentation is clear, the fount good and the paper as fair as can be expected at the present time.   G.R.D.

ZORELL, F. : *Lexicon Hebraicum et Aramaicum veteris Testamenti*, Fasc. 8. 1952. Pp. 64. (Pontificium Institutum Biblicum, Rome. Price : 11s. 6d.)

The present fascicule runs from *qešeṭ* ' bow ' to *šārap* 'burnt' and so brings the late Dr. Zorell's lexicon near to the end of the Hebrew part. The work runs very much on traditional lines, but the careful reader will find a certain number of new suggestions which deserve consideration.   G.R.D.

1954

I have once more to thank all those who have collaborated with me in the preparation of this Book List. There are first of all the members of the panel appointed by the Society to write the notices. In addition I have had to call on the services of some others, both in England and abroad, for occasional help, and to these I am especially grateful. Further, Mr. S. Roberts, Deputy Librarian of Manchester University Library, and Mr. L. Galpin, a member of the staff of the same library, have helped me in a variety of ways, and especially with the published prices of a number of the books. Wherever it is known, the price has been added, but for various reasons this has not always been possible.

I have not been able to get access to some of the books I should have liked to include, and the incompleteness of the Book List is greater than I desired. I can only assure the members of the Society that I have endeavoured to make it as complete and as up-to-date as possible. For the notices on Israeli books I am largely indebted to Dr. I. L. Seeligmann. Israeli publishers, with very rare exceptions, are unwilling to send review copies of their books, and efforts to buy their books in this country are often unsuccessful.

The placing of books in the appropriate sections is sometimes arbitrary, since they could be assigned to more than one with reasonable justification. For any errors I have made in this or in other respects, I offer my apologies. Titles to which an asterisk (*) is prefixed are recommended for inclusion in school libraries.

MANCHESTER UNIVERSITY.   H. H. ROWLEY.

GENERAL

(ALT, A.) : *Geschichte und Altes Testament.* (Beiträge zur historischen
 Theologie, No. 16.) 1953. Pp. 224. (Mohr, Tübingen. Price :
 DM. 36, or bound, DM. 39.60.)

> Members of the Society will be interested in this Festschrift
> presented to our latest Honorary Member, Professor Alt,
> on his seventieth birthday. It consists of ten essays and a
> bibliography of his writings. All the essays are in German
> with the exception of Albright's on Dedan, in which it is
> argued that the name as the designation of a tribe is a thousand
> years older than the earliest Biblical allusion. Eissfeldt writes
> on Psalm lxxx, arguing for a probable date between 727 and
> 724 B.C. Elliger examines in detail part of Ezekiel's description
> of the Temple, and essays a plan, while Rost examines the
> passage treating of Noah as a vinegrower (Gen. ix. 18 ff.).
> Baumgärtel writes on the study of the Old Testament in the
> light of the New, repudiating typology but insisting that the
> meaning of the Old Testament as *Heilsgeschichte* cannot be
> fully perceived without the New Testament. Zimmerli has
> the second longest essay on ' Ich bin Jahwe ', while the
> longest is by Edel on some correspondence of Rameses II
> dealing with his matrimonial alliances. Noth has a study of
> Proper Names in Mari and Israel, and Galling deals with the
> god Carmel (on whom Eissfeldt also has a study noted elsewhere
> in this *Book List*). While some of these go beyond the
> boundaries of the Old Testament all are of interest to Old
> Testament students. Von Rad's study lies more within the
> field of the New Testament, and is devoted to the *Vorgeschichte*
> of the form of 1 Cor. xiii. 4-7, with particular reference to the
> *Testaments*. The bibliography was prepared by K. H. Mann.
>
> H.H.R.

DE BOER, P. A. H. (ed. by) : *Oudtestamentische Studiën*, Deel X.
 1954. Pp. 256. (Brill, Leiden. Price : (Subscription) Fl. 17.50,
 (separately) Fl. 29.00.)

> The Dutch Old Testament Society has added another volume
> to this series after an interval of rather more than two years.
> This volume contains three articles in English and three in
> French. First, those in English. L. A. Snijders of Zwolle
> contributes a long and detailed study of the word *zār*. The
> article occupies rather more than half the volume. The
> English is not always easy to understand. There are six
> occurrences of a root *zwr-zrr* (*squeeze*), but the writer is mainly
> concerned with the true *zwr* root (*deviate, go away from, be
> far from*). In the main the contrast is between *zārim* and
> ' holy '. This contrast governs the use of the word as describing
> foreign nations, strange gods, non-priestly Israelites, and even
> the instances in Proverbs. The discussion of the relation
> between *zār* and *nokri* (unknown) is of especial value. J. Simons
> of Leiden has a thirty-page article on the structure and
> meaning of the Table of Nations in Gen. x. There are three
> blocks : Egyptian, Fertile Crescent, outer belt. Put is Libya.
> Chr. H. W. Brekelmans of Oudenbosch denies that Ex. xviii

supports the theory of the Kenite origin of Yahwism. Lastly, the three French articles. J. van der Ploeg discusses the origin and nature of the *šoter*. The name was introduced in the time of the kingdoms. They were secondary officials in general. A. van den Born of Achterveld discusses certain place names : Magog, Gibeah and Gibeon. Finally, the editor deals with the meaning of the root *qwh*. The article is notable for its full use of the renderings of the ancient versions. He finds, behind the alleged three distinct roots, a common fundamental idea of ' cohesion, consistency, firmness '.

N.H.S.

BÖHL, F. M. TH. DE LIAGRE : *Opera minora : Studies en bijdragen op assyriologisch en oudtestamentisch terrein.* 1953. Pp. xvi+570. (J. B. Wolters, Groningen. Price : Kr. 30.00.)

This handsome volume is an unusual kind of Festschrift, presented to the distinguished Leiden orientalist. It contains twenty-seven of his own occasional publications (with some revision), seven in Dutch, nineteen in German, and one in English, some of which have previously been noticed in earlier issues of this *Book List*. Professor Beek contributes a brief biographical introduction ; and there is a well-arranged bibliography of Professor Böhl's works. The Old Testament essays reprinted are : ' Het ontstaan en de geschiedkundige waarde van Oudtestamentische verhalen ', ' Wortspiele im Alten Testament ', ' Das Zeitalter Abrahams ', ' Priester und Prophet ', ' Prophetentum und stellvertretendes Leiden in Assyrien und Israel ', ' Missions– und Erwählungsgedanke in Alt-Israel ', ' Die Juden im Urteil der griechischen und römischen Schriftsteller ' ; and the Assyriological part of the collection is also full of valuable material for the Alttestamentler, e.g., the essay on the New Year festival in Babylon and Israel, and the study of Hammurabi and his time. Altogether a most valuable collection.

G.W.A.

(DOLD, A.) : *Colligere Fragmenta : Festschrift Alban Dold zum 70. Geburtstag,* ed. by B. Fisher and V. Fiala. (Beiheft, Texte u. Arbeiten.) 1952. Pp. xx+296. (Erzabtei, Beuron in Hohenzollern. Price : 50s. 0d.)

It is only fitting that a special Beiheft should celebrate the long association of Dold, a Beuron Benedictine, with the series to which he has contributed so many volumes, beginning with the first of all in 1917. This volume, to which thirty scholars have contributed, does not contain a large number of papers that would specially interest an *Alttestamentler*. There is, however, a valuable study of the Septuagintal text used by Jerome in his incomplete commentary on Jeremiah. This is by J. Ziegler, the editor of the great Göttingen Septuagint, and emphasizes as specially significant a long list of special readings that cannot be traced to any existing Greek translation and appear to be the commentator's own free rendering. M. Stenzel writes on the Vulgate text of Habakkuk, and A. Vaccari, in a stimulating paper on the variants " ipse " or " ipsa " in the Latin of Gen. iii. 15, stresses the need of keeping

an eye on the commentaries of ancient writers if one wishes
to be certain of their choice of text. F. Stummer comments
on the difficult Latin reading of Sir. xxi. 10 : '' Via peccantium
complanata lapidibus,'' and refers to the German proverb,
familiar in its English form : '' Der Weg zur Hölle ist mit
guten Vorsätzen gepflastert.'' R. Weber discusses the faulty
reading in Ps. lxxviii. (MT. lxxix.) 10 : '' Vindica sanguinem
servorum tuorum qui effusus est.'' J. Eschweiler's attractive
article on the illustrated psalter preserved at Stuttgart
has unfortunately lost a page or so owing to an error in
printing. Three of the 318 illustrations are reproduced by way
of pictorial supplement to the text.   J.M.T.B.

(Dornseiff, F.) : *Festschrift Franz Dornseiff*, ed. by H. Kusch. 1953.
   Pp. 384.   (Veb Bibliographisches Institut, Leipzig.   Price :
   DM. 20.00.)

   In this Festschrift to celebrate the 65th birthday of the
   Leipzig scholar, Professor Franz Dornseiff, four articles concern
   the Bible student ; M. Lambertz on the genealogies of Mt. i.
   and Lk. iii. ; H. Sasse, ' Sacra Scriptura '—Augustine's
   teaching on Inspiration ; E. Seidl on legal phraseology of the
   ancient Egyptians, mainly court and civil law ; and H.
   Bardtke on paragraph division in DSIa. The last-mentioned
   is the only one with direct interest in the Old Testament.
   The author examines seriatim the paragraphs in the scroll,
   comparing them with those of *BH* 2 *and* 3, a few Genizah
   fragments, *Codex Petropolitanus*, the three Great Codices of
   LXX (*S*, *B* and *A*) and the Ambrosian Peshiṭta. He concludes
   that two-thirds of the open paragraphs in the scroll belong
   to the tradition found elsewhere, but *c.* 120 closed paragraphs
   reflect a now extinct tradition and/or the theological needs
   of the sect. The Massoretic order shows a tendency to combine
   the shorter paragraphs of the pre-Jamnia text-forms. It is
   to be noted, however, that DSIb and a vast number of Genizah
   fragments of Isaiah were not available for comparison.

                                                     B.J.R.

'*Ensîklôpēdyâ Miḳrā'îth*.   *Encyclopaedia Biblica, Thesaurus rerum
   biblicarum alphabetico ordine digestus* edd. Institutum Bialik et
   Museum Antiquitatum ad Universitatem Hebraicam Hierosolytanam pertinenes. Vol. II. 1954. Pp. xxx+cols. 952. (Bialik
   Foundation, Jerusalem.)

   More than three years after the publication of the first volume
   of the fine Biblical Encyclopaedia in Hebrew, there appears
   the second one. It contains the letters *Beth* up to *Zain*
   inclusive, and it is even more bulky than the first one. For a
   general characterization the reader may be referred to the
   notice on Vol. I in this *Book List* (1951, pp. 6 f.). Since the
   publication of Vol. I two members of the Editorial Board,
   Professors Cassuto and Sukenik, have passed away. Of the
   fifty-four contributors to this volume more than twenty are
   new, among them W. F. Albright (*Byblos*), H. Frankfort
   (*Religions of the Ancient Near East*), H. L. Ginsberg (*Daniel*),
   L. Oppenheim (*Babel*).

Whoever writes a note of a few lines on a book like this must of necessity fail to do justice to a large number of shorter and 'longer articles which form a veritable storehouse of information, based on the latest research (*Hellenism*) and into which have been worked many wholly original views (*Gath-Gittaim, Chronicles*). Once more the remarkable breadth of outlook has to be praised.

The contents of this volume are particularly varied. The lack of unity in approach is even more noticeable than is generally the case in an Encyclopaedia. Cassuto contributed twenty-five items, inter alia *Genesis, Leviticus, Numbers, Deuteronomy*. As a matter of fact one reads here in concise form the conservative and slightly apologetic Introduction to the Pentateuch which the author had in mind, but which it was not granted him to write. The extended article *Religion of Israel* has been done by J. Kaufmann, entirely according to the spirit of his *magnum opus* enlarged by a few paragraphs on the exilic and post-exilic periods. To the same field belong the items : *Election, World-picture, Knowledge of God, Anthropomorphism, Divine Revelation*. By far the most voluminous article is that on *Building* (1) materials and technique, (2) dwelling houses, (3) fortification from before the Hyksos up to the post-exilic period, by S. Yeivin who has also contributed many interesting historical and geographical articles (*Benjamin, Gad, Dan, Zebulun, David*). The general impression is that the archaeological, geographical and historical questions have been very thoroughly dealt with, even more so than the literary ones. Perhaps this impression is partly due to the splendid illustrations which are not only extremely well-produced (*Babel, Beth Sh'an, Byblos, Tel Halaf, Hellenism*) but also chosen with exceptional taste and at times of a surprising originality (*Pectoralia, Cattle*). I.L.S.

FRIEDRICH, G. (ed. by) : *Theologisches Wörterbuch zum Neuen Testament* (begun by G. Kittel). Lieferungen 12 and 13. 1953. Pp. 64 per part. (W.Kohlhammer, Stuttgart. Subscription Price : DM. 4.60 per part.)

> Lieferung 12 (pp. 705-768) contains the New Testament part of the article *pais Theou* by Jeremias, the article *parabolē*, which has a discussion by Hauck of *māshāl* in the Old Testament and Judaism and of *parabolē* in the LXX, and the article *paradeisos* by Jeremias.

> Lieferung 13 (pp. 769-832) contains the article *parakaleō* and *paraklēsis* by Stählin which includes sections by other authors on various Old Testament matters, and the article *parthenos* by Delling which has a balanced discussion of Isaiah vii. 14. N.W.P.

HAAG, H., ed. by (with the collaboration of A. van den Born and others) : *Bibel-Lexikon*, Part 4. 1953. Cols. 613-868. (Benziger Verlag, Einsiedeln, Zürich and Cologne. Subscription price : Swiss Fr./DM. 11.00 per part.)

> The subjects in this fourth issue run from ' Gottesknecht ' to ' Judas-kommunion '. Continuing a long and informative

article on the Suffering Servant from the previous issue by J. Fischer, the volume contains articles on Isaiah, Jeremiah, the Jahwist, Jesus Christ, the Johannine literature and Jericho and Jerusalem, the last two incorporating the latest results of archaeological research. The articles are well documented to date and the archaeological articles well illustrated. J.G.

HAAG, H., ed. by (with the collaboration of A. van den Born and others) : *Bibel-Lexikon*, 5. Lieferung. 1954. Cols. 869-1092. (Benziger Verlag, Einsiedeln, Zürich and Cologne. Price : Fr./DM. 11.00.)

This excellent brief Bible Dictionary has not appeared at the rate that was first planned, but the present issue brings the work half way to its conclusion. The articles in this part run from *Jude* to *Matthäusevangelium*. The information in all is up-to-date, though necessarily very compressed. It is a pity that we have no comparable handbook in English that can be called up-to-date. H.H.R.

Hebrew Union College Annual XXIV. 1952-53. Pp. 274+84. (Cincinnati. Price : $3.00.)

This volume, which is dedicated to Leo Baeck on the occasion of his eightieth birthday, contains several articles—there are ten in all—which are of interest to O.T. students. J. Morgenstern holds that Is. lv. 6-13 and lviii. 1-12 were addresses delivered in some synagogue on some Yom Kippur. The former passage belongs to the first half of the fourth century B.C., and the latter to the last half, perhaps the last quarter, of the same century. The evolution of Yom Kippur, within which each of these two passages may be precisely fixed, is carefully traced, with special reference to Lev. xvi, the primary stratum of which is dated in the third quarter of the fifth century B.C., and to Num. xxix. 7-11 and Lev. xxiii. 26-32. Interesting textual and philological notes are contributed by J. Reider and M. Tsevat. B. Maisler thinks that Harosheth of the Peoples was the name of an entire region or district closely related to Galilee of the Peoples, and not of a town in south western Galilee (el-Hâriṭîyye or Tell ' Amr). Harosheth was originally an appellative referring to the hilly and wooded (Heb, *horesh* " wood ") country of northern Palestine. H. A. Fine examines the chronological sequence of the legal and business documents of the Middle-Assyrian period. Not the least valuable feature of the volume is the index to volumes i-xxiii of the *Annual* which is provided. D.W.T.

HOLWERDA, B. (the late) : .... *Begonnen hebbende van Mozes* ... 1953. Pp. 118. (D. H. Littooij, Terneuzen. Price : Fl. 6.00.)

Professor Holwerda died whilst still in his thirties, a grand man and a true scholar. His brother has edited this volume of his literary remains, and we welcome it for Professor Holwerda's sake, and for its own sake. The volume consists of four studies, all in Dutch. The first is his 1949 rectorial address, entitled ' The place which the Lord shall choose '. He does not find any reference here to the centralization of the cult in the time of Josiah. The second study is an exegesis of Amos iii. 3-8, and this is followed by studies on ' The Priest-king in the Old Testament ' and ' The holy-history (Heils-historie) in preaching '. The author's attitude is conservative, but by no means obscurantist.

N.H.S.

(KAPLAN, M. M.) : *Mordecai M. Kaplan Jubilee Volume*, ed by M. Davis. Two parts. 1953. Pp. viii+550 (English Section), Pp. x+ 288 (Hebrew Section). (The Jewish Theological Seminary of America, New York. Price : $25.00.)

Twenty-four authors in the English section, and seventeen in the Hebrew, have gathered together in this congratulatory homage to Prof. M. M. Kaplan of the Jewish Theological Seminary of America, on the occasion of his seventieth birthday. Biblical studies are well represented. R. Gordis offers in the English section a complete translation of the Song of Songs, with philological notes and an introduction in which he discusses previous interpretations and submits his own. He argues that the book is not a literary unity, but an anthology of secular lyrical songs which express ' a wide gamut of the emotions ' of love, or are connected with wedding ceremonies and married life. They are separated in age as widely as the tenth century B.C. (chap. iii refers to King Solomon's marriage) and the Persian Period. The departures from MT are few, mostly a matter of punctuation or a change of a single letter. More often a new meaning is given to Hebrew words as, for example, in i. 4b, which is translated : ' We shall inhale thy love rather than wine ; As fine wine do they love thee '. In vi. 12 Tur-Sinai's emendation is accepted with a slight modification, and in viii. 2, *telammedeni* is replaced by *we'el heder horathi*. No reference is made to the interesting study by W. Heffening, ' Zur Geschichte der Hochzeitsgebräuche im Islam ' in *Beiträge zur Arabistik, Semitistik und Islam-wissenschaft*, ed. by R. Hartmann and H. Scheel, Leipzig, 1944. H. L. Ginsberg offers in *Gleanings in First Isaiah* emendations, new interpretations and reconstructions of MT, and discusses the dependence of Zeph. ii. 4-11 on Is. xi. 14. N. Glueck contends that Deut. xxiii. 8-9 express the univer-salistic sentiments of Trito-Isaiah in ' purposed contrast ' to verses 2-7 ; but suggests at the same time that ' Edomites and Egyptians ' may refer to ' Judaized Idumaeans ' and ' such Jews as those at Elephantine ' respectively. Leo. L. Honor deals rather perfunctorily with *The Role of Memory in Biblical History* ; and I. Efros explains in *Prophecy, Wisdom and Apocalypse* how the line of development from rational transcendentalization of God to mystical unity with the Deity is reflected in the emergence of Wisdom and Apocalytic literature. Boaz Cohen discusses the *Letter and Spirit in Jewish and Roman Law* with special reference to Paul. J. Gordin offers an English translation of the First Chapter of '*Abhoth de R. Nathan*. In the Hebrew section, J. Klausner suggests that Jeremiah is not mentioned in

' Kings ' because their author, writing *c.* 560 B.C., considered the prophet a Quisling and traitor to the national cause. J. Schaechter from Israel submits symptomatically that the right approach to the study of the Bible is that of the ' existentialist ' inspired by Kierkegaard. N. H. Tur-Sinai (Torczyner) explains difficult phrases in '*Abhoth de R. Nathan* and throws light on the term *parush* (Pharisee).

J.L.T.

LOTH, B. and MICHEL, A. : *Dictionnaire de Théologie Catholique : Tables Générales.* Fasc. ii : Arbitrage—Cajétan. 1953. Cols. 241-496. (Letouzey & Ané, Paris. Price : 22s. 3d.)

Now that the great *Dictionnaire de théologie catholique* has been, for some years, complete in its fifteen volumes, it has proved an excellent idea to provide tables that give references to the parts of the work that deal with various aspects of the same subject. Thus the article in these tables entitled "Augustin" spreads its references, additional bibliography and other information over nearly sixteen columns of small type. The opportunity has also been taken to supplement the earlier articles which, as so many of them are not less than fifty years old, are often more than a little out of date. The present fascicle does not contain many headings of interest to students of the Old Testament, who may, however, usefully consult the following articles : Arbres, Arche d'alliance, Assyro-Babylonien, Astarté, Astres, Astruc, Baal, Babylone (et la Bible), Balaam, Baruch and Cabale.   J.M.T.B.

(MORGENSTERN, J.) : *An Index to Biblical Passages cited in the Writings of Julian Morgenstern.* 1953. Pp. viii+136. (Hebrew Union College, Cincinnati, and Jewish Institute of Religion, New York.)

The greater part of the writings of Dr. Morgenstern have appeared without index, since they are published in journals, even though they are sometimes reprinted in book form (as his *Amos Studies*). Many of his articles are longer than some books, and as deserving of index to enable scholars to locate the many original ideas which Dr. Morgenstern has propounded. In 1937 an Index to the Scriptural references in his writings was prepared by two of his students and published by the Hebrew Union College. This covered 36 articles and books, and it has been of frequent use to the present writer. Now an enlarged edition, covering 68 publications has been issued by the Trustees, the index to the publications which have appeared since the first edition being separately given after the re-production of the pages of the former issue. It would be a very great boon if a subject index of his writings could also be prepared to complete the usefulness of this Index. H.H.R.

(PEDERSEN, J.) : *Studia orientalia Ioanni Pedersen septuagenario a.d. VII Id. Nov. anno MCMLIII a collegis discipulis amicis dicata.* 1953. Pp. xx+390. (Einar Munksgaard, Copenhagen. Price : Kr. 40.)

The essays in this volume cover an unusually wide field in oriental subjects and also in the history of religion. It must suffice here to mention those which have direct or incidental reference to Old Testament or Semitic studies. A. Alt discusses the meaning of the Ugaritic term *skn*. The late A. Bentzen writes on the canonization of Canticles. R. Edelmann contributes a note on the Arabic versions of the Pentateuch. O. Eissfeldt sums up the evidence for the significance of the sea in the Bible. I. Engnell considers the possible cultic background of a phrase in Ps. i. A. Goetze discusses negatives in Ugaritic. E. Hammershaimb writes on Ezekiel's view of the monarchy. H. Ingholt discusses views on the meaning of the surname Iscariot, and offers a new suggestion. T. Jacobsen writes on the textile industry at Ur under Ibbī-Sîn. P. Kahle communicates information about the Samaritan Abisha' scroll. J. Laessøe considers the relation of literacy and oral tradition in Mesopotamia. F. Løkkegaard debates problems relating to Ugaritic religion. S. Mowinckel examines the metre and text of Ps. viii. E. Nielsen discusses the place of ox and ass in Hebrew life and religion. S. Pallis surveys the history of Babylon from 538 to 93 B.C. H. H. Rowley (in a contribution which expresses the honour in which Professor Pedersen is held in our Society) re-examines the evidence for the family and tribe of Menelaus, and the nature of the abomination of desolation. G. Widengren discusses ritual emasculation in Semitic religion. The essays are all in English, French, or German ; and the volume is a fitting tribute to the range of Professor Pedersen's learning and influence.   G.W.A.

ROBERT, A. (ed. by) : *Dictionnaire de la Bible : Supplément* fasc. xxvi. (Loi Israélite—Mandéisme). 1953. Cols. 513-768. (Letouzey & Ané, Paris. Price : 22s. 3d.)

Unlike the fascicle immediately preceding it, the present, most recent, addition to the *Supplément* is not strong in articles of interest to an *Alttestamentler*. H. Cazelles concludes his useful summary on Israelite Law, but, as it happens, some part of this is concerned with the Law as found in the New Testament ; A. Lefèvre contributes a short introduction to First and Second Maccabees ; R. de Vaux writes on Macpelah (with special reference to the later history of the Haram at Hebron) and on Mambre ; and R. Pautrel devotes about seven columns to the problems of the book of Malachi. There is also a long article, divided between three authors, under the general heading of " Magie ", in which Sumero-Accadian magic is discussed by J. Largement, Egyptian magic by A. Massart, and magic in the Bible by A. Lefèvre. R. T. O'Callaghan's immensely learned article (cols. 627-704) on the Madaba mosaic, should also be mentioned. For some people the most stimulating contribution will be J. Bonsirven's fourteen-column study of the character and work of Alfred Loisy, who died at a great age in 1940, and is now largely forgotten.   J.M.T.B.

(SCHMITZ, O.) : *Verbum Dei Manet in Aeternum : Eine Festschrift für Prof. D. Otto Schmitz*, ed. by W. Foerster. 1953. Pp. 148. (Luther Verlag, Witten-Ruhr. Price : DM. 4.80.)

Two of the eleven contributors have written on the Old Testament. ' Der Begriff '' Geschichte '' bei Deuterojesaja ' is by Karl Elliger. The kernel of this article is that ' *ēṣāh, 'ōraḥ mišpāṭ* and *derek tebûnôt* (Isa. xl. 13 f.) all refer not to the Creation but to History as a divine teleological process. Johannes Herrmann, ' '' und wenn es köstlich gewesen ist '' : Eine Untersuchung zu Ps. 90, 10 ' is more a disquisition on the implications of Luther's rendering than on the M.T. The remaining papers in this Festschrift are on New Testament subjects.   D.R.Ap-T.

(SCHREINER, H.) : *Dienst unter dem Wort : eine Festgabe für Professor D. Dr. Helmuth Schreiner zum* 60. *Geburtstag.* 1953. Pp. 350. (C. Bertelsmann, Gütersloh. Price : DM. 9.50.)

This volume contains a large number of essays on various subjects presented to the professor of Practical Theology in the University of Münster. Those of particular interest to students of the Old Testament are as follows : ' Der 103. Psalm ' by Joh. Herrmann ; ' Dämonie und Krankheit im Lichte der Erlösung ' by Paul Jacobs ; ' Die Botschaft des Alten Testaments ' by Alfred Jepsen ; ' Das Menschenbild des Alten Testaments ' by Wilhelm Rudolph.   N.W.P.

Semitica (Cahiers publiés par l'Institut d'Études Sémitiques de l'Université de Paris) IV. 1951-1952. Pp. 94. (Maisonneuve, Paris. Price : Fr. 760.)

Of the ten articles contained in this issue, those which will most interest students of the Old Testament are A. Caqot's discussion of an Aramaic inscription from Hatra, which provides the first epigraphic evidence for a goddess *Šgl*, whose connection with the Hebrew *šēgāl* remains, however, obscure ; J. Cantineau's proposed solutions to a number of problems concerning comparative phonetics and phonology in Semitic ; and A. Dupont-Sommer's treatment of the relationship between the *Testament of Levi* (xvii-xviii) and the sect known from the Zadokite fragments and the Dead Sea manuscripts— the '' seven priests '' in ch. xvii refer ·to the Hasmonean dynasty from Judas to Aristobulus II ; the crime and the punishment for it in the same chapter are the persecution of the Master of Justice by Aristobulus II and the capture of Jerusalem by Pompey in 63 B.C. respectively ; and the '' new priest '' in ch. xviii is the Master of Justice himself, who after his death inaugurates the messianic priesthood. Of the other articles mention may be made of J. M. Sola Sole's study of two neo-Punic inscriptions from Ibiza, one of which contains the first known reference to a deity Rešeph Melqarth, and of G. Boyer's discussion of the method employed by jurists in the working out and exposition of their subject in ancient Mesopotamia.   D.W.T.

(STARR, J.) : *The Joshua Starr Memorial Volume : Studies in History and Philology.* (Jewish Social Studies, Publications No. 5.) 1953. Pp. viii+262. (Conference on Jewish Relations, New York. Price : $5.00.)

> Joshua Starr died by his own decision at the age of 42 in 1949. He had already published a long series of books, pamphlets, articles and reviews, which are listed in a Bibliography in the present volume. His friends have commemorated his life and work by a volume of studies which contains nineteen essays, in addition to a short obituary article. Only three of the articles are in the field of Old Testament studies, and none of these is directly on the Old Testament itself. Cyrus Gordon offers a study of ' Stratification of Society in Hammurabi's Code ' ; Joseph Finkel 'An Interpretation of **an** Ugaritic Viticultural Poem ', in which an example of *double entendre* is found in some difficult lines near the beginning of SS, from which the author proceeds to the examination of some examples or near-examples in the Old Testament ; and Ralph Marcus offers an original theory as the origin of ' The Name *Makkabaios* ' which he connects with the noun *miḳwah* = *source of hope.* The remaining articles touch a wide range of subjects, some Islamic but most dealing with aspects of later Jewish history. H.H.R.

Studia theologica cura ordinum theologorum Scandinavicorum edita, Vol. VI, Fasc. i. 1952/53. Pp. 78. (C. W. K. Gleerup, Lund. Price : Kr. 8, or Kr. 12 annually.)

> The only O.T. article in this fascicle is an important study by the young Danish scholar E. Nielsen of the problem of the righteous and the wicked in Habakkuk. He argues that the book (which he treats as a unity) has a cultic background but also a specific historical reference to the deposition and deportation of Jehoahaz (*haṣṣaddiḳ,* the righteous, legitimate ruler) and the accession of Jehoiakim, the usurper (*harasha'*). The remaining articles are : a linguistic examination by B. Reicke of Col. ii. 23 ; a discussion of *panegyris* in Heb. xii. 22 by C. Spicq ; and an interpretation of Kierkegaard's *The Works of Love* by V. Lindström. G.W.A.

Studia theologica cura ordinum theologorum Scandinavicorum edita, Vol. VI, Fasc. ii. 1952/53. Pp. 100. (Gleerup, Lund. Price : Swedish crowns 8.)

> In the sole Old Testament article in this fascicle J. Lindblom returns to the question, ' Gibt es eine Eschatologie bei den alttestamentlichen Propheten ?' He maintains that there is ; though not in the same sense as in Jewish and Christian apocalyptic and Christian theology. It is characterized not by the thought of the end of the world or of history, but by that of a new age. In this sense he traces the eschatology of a universal judgement back to Isaiah, and that of national restoration to Hosea. He finds the eschatology of universal restoration for the most part in passages of exilic or post-exilic date, with Deutero-Isaiah as its clearest exponent. L. Richter

writes on Karl Jaspers and Christian theology ; A. Ehrhardt on ' Let the dead bury their dead '; and W. Nauck on the use of ' salt ' as a metaphor in the New Testament. G.W.A.

Supplements to Vetus Testamentum. Vol. i. Congress Volume, Copenhagen 1953. 1953. Pp. xvi+230. (Brill, Leiden. Price : Fr. 18.)

This important volume, which contains the papers written for the first Congress of the International Organization of O.T. Scholars, held in Copenhagen in August, 1953, is at the same time a Memorial to Professor Aage Bentzen. A short *In Memoriam* is contributed by E. Hammershaimb, and there is a bibliography of Professor Bentzen's writings, and also a photograph of him.

E. Auerbach stresses the importance of recognizing that a large part of the O.T. has been worked over, and that it is all too easy to build up a picture of Israel's history on the basis of this working over, when it is the traditions and accounts in the more original sources which should claim first attention. M. Bič regards the book of Obadiah as a liturgical enthronement oracle, earlier than Amos, in which Edom represents the primaeval enemy who is slain by Yahweh. G. R. Driver takes up the question of the debt which Hebrew poetic diction may owe to Aramaic, and discusses, with numerous illustrations, the difficult problem of determining what may properly be termed "Aramaisms" in the O.T. A. Dupont-Sommer surveys the new material, notably from Ur, Mari and Ras Shamra, which is available for the study of the beginnings of the history of the Aramaeans, which can now be traced back as far as the beginning of the second millennium B.C. B. Gemser shows that motive clauses (e.g., in Ex. xx. 7, xxii. 20, Lev. xxiv. 22) are a peculiarity of O.T. Law, and touches on the connection between wisdom and legal practice. A. R. Johnson suggests that the primary meaning of *ga'al* is " cover, protect ", to which use should also be traced back *ga'al* denoting " defilement ". J. Lindblom argues that Gen. xlix was composed by a prophet during the period David was king in Judah and resided in Hebron ; the meaning of verse 10 is that the kingdom established in Judah through the election of David will be extended to comprise the northern tribes, of which Shiloh is the representative.

S. Mowinckel holds that Taxo (the Latin form of the Greek *taxon* " the Orderer ") in *Ass. Mos.* ix. is a translation of the Hebrew *mehoqeq*, the word which is used of the leader of the sect of the Damascus Covenanters, within whose circle the *Ass. Mos.* originated. J. Muilenburg contributes a general survey, with many examples, of the phenomenon of repetition in ancient Hebrew literature as a major feature of Hebrew rhetoric and style. A. Parrot shows how fresh light has been thrown on a number of O.T. passages (e.g., Ex. xx. 24 ff., Jud. vi. 25, 1 Sam. vii. 6) by the excavation of altars and temples at Mari. G. von Rad illustrates how the Joseph stories reflect an ideal of education which was in vogue in the days of the early monarchy and which is met with in the book of Proverbs and in Egyptian wisdom literature. T. H. Robinson surveys the more important contributions which have been made to the study of Hebrew poetic form, with particular reference to the principles laid down by Lowth. I. L. Seeligmann points out that, if the Midrashim are examined critically, their contribution to O.T. study is seen to be considerable ; they contain, for example, ancient traditions of which the O.T. knows nothing. R. de Vaux, who contributes some reflections on the state of Pentateuchal criticism to-day, upholds the documentary theory in its essentials, but less positively and with some reservations.

Th.C. Vriezen thinks that the term eschatology can rightly be applied to the prophetic expectation of salvation, and he makes suggestions as to the main periods which must be distinguished if the data regarding eschatology are to be surveyed soundly and objectively.   D.W.T.

Svensk Exegetisk Arsbok, XVII, ed. by G. Lindeskog. 1952. Pp. 164. (Wretmans Boktryckeri A.-B., Uppsala. Price : Kr. 10.)

This issue was dedicated to the late Professor Fridrichsen (founder and first editor of the periodical) on the occasion of his sixty-fifth birthday. Publication has been delayed ; and some material has had to be held over for inclusion in the next issue. Only one contribution deals directly with the O.T., that by H. Ringgren on ' the cup of wrath '. This is an interesting study of the relevant material in the O.T. in the light of external parallels, leading to these conclusions : that intoxication is a chaos-*motif* belonging to the New Year festival and the Tammuz cult, and associated with the humiliation of the king and with judgement upon enemies ; and that the allied idea of the cup of destiny may reflect ritual practice in connexion with the fixing of the fate. The remaining articles are on N.T. subjects : E. Sjöberg on Mt. vi. 22 f. ; E. Percy on the Messianic secret in Mark ; B. Reicke on Jesus and the Jews in Mark ; G. Lindeskog on the development of terminology in the N.T. ; H. Riesenfeld on the *pericope de adultera* in early Christian tradition ; H. Sahlin on Chassidism and the N.T. portrait of Christ. There is also a survey by the editor of recent work on the N.T., and a note by J. Lindblom on the work of the Swedish Theological Institute in Jerusalem.   G.W.A.

Talenta Quinque : Commentationes in honorem Ilmari Salomies, Eino Sormunen, E. G. Gulin, Rafael Gyllenberg, G. O. Rosenqvist. 1953. (Otava, Helsinki.)

This *Festschrift* dedicated to the five bishops or professors of theology mentioned in the title, who all of them celebrated their 60th birthday in 1953, contains articles in Finnish and Swedish from all branches of theology. The O.T. articles are five : A. Lauha writes on the role of the cult in modern O.T. research ; J. Lindblom on history and eschatology in the prophets ; A. F. Puukko has called his contribution ' Where was Paradise situated ?' ; H. Ringgren comments on the Benediction of Num. vi, and I. Soisalon-Soininen has a brief article on the language of the LXX.   H.R.

THOMSEN, P. : *Die Palästina-Literatur : eine internationale Biblio-graphie in systematischer Ordnung mit Autoren– und Sachregister*, Vol. vi, Lieferung 1. 1953. Pp. xvi+288. (Akademie Verlag, Berlin. Price : DM. 28.40.)

> After a long interval this invaluable Bibliography has resumed its survey of books and articles dealing with the Holy Land. Volume vi will deal with the literature of the years 1935-44, and this first part deals with general and historical publications, leaving archaeology, geography, topography, and present-day Palestine to be dealt with in subsequent issues. The material has been assembled by Dr. Peter Thomsen, who compiled the previous volumes, but the work has been seen through the press by F. Maass and L. Rost, who will now take over the continuation of this bibliography. Not only are books and articles bearing on the study of Palestinian life and culture from the earliest times included here, but copious references to reviews of the books which are listed. As a bibliographical tool this work is indispensable to all scholars in our field, as its predecessors have been. To the patient labours of Dr. Thomsen through so many years his colleagues owe a heavy debt, and to his successors in this arduous task they accord a welcome.   H.H.R.

TOGAN, Z. V. (ed. by) : *Proceedings of the Twenty-second Congress of Orientalists.* Vol. i. 1953. Pp. 234. (Osman Yalçin Matbaasi, Istanbul. Price : $5.00.)

> This volume, which is illustrated, gives general information concerning the activities of the Congress of Orientalists which was held at Istanbul in 1951. It contains lists of committees, delegates and members ; accounts of the meetings held, both general and sectional, with brief summaries of papers read ; the resolutions which were approved; and descriptions of the excursions and exhibitions which were arranged in connection with the Congress. It can be obtained from Teknik Kitabevi, Mimar Vedat Sok. Nr. 19, Sirkeci, Istanbul, or from E. J. Brill, Leiden. Vol. ii, which will contain the actual texts or summaries of the communications accepted, will be published later.   D.W.T.

Transactions of the Glasgow University Oriental Society, vol. xiv, Years 1950-52, edited by C. J. Mullo Weir. 1953. Pp. iv+68. (Glasgow University. Price : 12s. 6d.)

> This volume contains seven papers and some brief com-munications. J. Bowman presents the theory that a lost astrological work of Apollonius of Tyana has been preserved in Arabic. W. I. Jones describes and discusses a South Arabian inscription found near Muqairas in the East Aden Protectorate. H. C. Thomson carefully examines the meaning of 'āshām in the Old Testament and finds that in its ritual use it carries the idea of substitution, and especially in Isa. liii. 10. J. Wood offers an interesting study of a Syriac MS in the BM., described by W. Wright as ' a sort of Syriac Masora '. J. Paterson writes

on the psalms and the cult, dealing more particularly with some views of von Rad and Weiser. J. Gray examines some Ras Shamra texts dealing with the conflict of the god with the unruly waters as the background of some Biblical references. In one of the communications A. C. Kennedy advances the theory that the Phoenicians already used the letters of the alphabet as numerals before the Greeks borrowed them and that the Greeks used them as numerals before they used them for spelling words. This theory seems very doubtful indeed. The remaining papers lie outside the scope of the *Book List*.

H.H.R.

EDUCATIONAL

CLELAND, W. P. : *The Cross-roads of History*. (Pathfinder Series, No. 1.) 1950. Pp. 96. (Religious Education Press, Wallington, Surrey. Price : Boards 4s., Limp Cloth : 3s.)

> This volume is written by a Senior Secondary School teacher of considerable practical experience. Strictly it is a background book for the New Testament, but it contains many details of Old Testament developments, historical and religious, and is highly to be recommended for use in middle forms of Grammar Schools and upper classes in Secondary Modern Schools.
>
> N.H.S.

HUMPHREYS, AGNES : *From Abraham to Solomon*. 1954. Pp. 140. (S.C.M. Press, London. Price : 6s. 0d.)

> This little book, written by a teacher of Scripture, is designed for lower forms. It selects some of the salient incidents of the Biblical story and either recounts them simply or presents them in brief plays for the children to act. Each lesson is followed by well-chosen questions, designed to bring out the purpose and meaning of the story, or to encourage the children to get into the spirit of the story by themselves writing short plays. The authoress is acquainted with modern work, but the main emphasis is on the contents of the Bible. There are occasional anachronisms, as when Abraham desires his descendants to be true ' sons of Israel ', but the book seems to be excellently designed for its purpose. H.H.R.

THOMSON, R. W. : *How the English Bible Grew*. 1953. Pp. 64. (Religious Education Press, Wallington, Surrey. Price : 2s. 6d.)

> This is the fourth volume of a useful series of school text-books devoted to the story of Christianity in England. This story of the chief English versions of the Bible, from Caedmon to the American Standard Revised Version, is told in eight chapters, simply and briefly, yet with sufficient detail and human interest to hold the attention of any intelligent child in a Modern Secondary School. The book is well written and well produced. L.A.P.

ARCHAEOLOGY AND EPIGRAPHY

*ALBRIGHT, W. F. : *Archaeology and the Religion of Israel*. 3rd ed. 1953. Pp. xii+246. (Johns Hopkins Press, Baltimore, and Geoffrey Cumberlege, London. Price : $3.50 or 28s. 0d.)

> This third edition of Professor Albright's well-known work (on which cf. *Book List*, 1946, p. 38, 1948, p. 11), has been photographically reproduced from the second, but seventy-four additional notes have been added at the end, adding greatly to its value and supplying references to much recent literature. Unfortunately it has not been possible to supply references to these additional notes in the Index. No living scholar can write on this subject with wider knowledge than Professor Albright, or with more authority.   H.H.R.

BRAIDWOOD, R. J. : *The Near East and the Foundations for Civilization*. 1952. Pp. 44. (Eugene, Oregon. Price : 8s. 0d.)

> In the Condon Lectures Professor Braidwood presents a synthesis of his researches in the archaeology of pre- and proto-historic Iraq and the adjoining area. Those familiar with this early stage of archaeology will be interested to note departures from orthodox theories. The domestication of plants and animals, for instance, is stated to be due not to concentration in oases and river valleys as the result of desiccation at the end of the Pleistocene age. Newer evidence is said to indicate a rise rather than a decrease in rainfall. The Persian Gulf, again, did not once extend as far North as Baghdad but has both advanced and receded periodically. He follows Redfield as against Childe in believing that technology and economics were secondary to social development in determining cultural progress. It is to be somewhat regretted that the writer did not integrate his evidence with that now available for neolithic sites in Palestine and Egypt.
>   J.G.

DUNAND, M. : *De L'Amanus au Sinai, Sites et Monuments*, with Preface by M. Chiha. 1953. Pp. 240+Map. (Imprimerie Catholique, Beyrouth.)

> Well written, beautifully illustrated and excellently produced account of the lands of Syria and Palestine and their ancient monuments. It provides a good introduction to the country for those who have not visited it and a useful pleasant reminder for those who have.   J.N.S.

FIGULLA, H. H. and MARTIN, W. J. : *Ur Excavation Texts V* (Letters and Documents of the Old Babylonian Period). 1953. Pp. 80 and CXLII Pl. (British Museum and University Museum, University of Pennsylvania. Price : 84s. 0d.)

> This volume includes 883 texts from the Old Babylonian period at Ur. These comprise private letters, legal and economic documents relative to daily life in Mesopotamia, and five royal documents. Each tablet is carefully transcribed and the contents summarized. The work is prefaced by a very useful classified catalogue of the tablets and their provenance in the excavations and their present location is also noted.
>   J.G.

HARDING, G. L. : *Four Tomb Groups from Jordan*. (Palestine Exploration Fund Annual VI.) 1953. Pp. xii + 76 + 7 Plates. (P.E.F., London. Price : 15s. 0d.)

Lankester Harding here describes the finding of four tombs, at El Husn, Amman, Madeba and Amman respectively, together with their contents. The plates at the end illustrate the contents, and there are several hundred drawings of objects, particularly of pottery, given in the book. B. S. J. Isserlin writes notes on the finds in the first three groups, and Miss O. Tufnell on those in the fourth, which is the tomb of Adoni Nur. It is believed that this is the first time it has been possible to assign a tomb found on either side of the Jordan to a definite person. Adoni Nur's seal describes him as ' servant of Ammi Nadab '. This is believed to be the person named in Ashurbanipal's lists as ruler of Amman. In this case he was a contemporary of Manasseh and the date can be closely determined. Three seals found in this tomb are commented on by G. R. Driver. (Adoni Nur's name is misspelt in the transcription of his seal.) The bowls in this tomb are said to be of better quality than any products of Judah throughout the monarchy. The other tombs are of the Early Bronze, Middle Bronze and Early Iron ages, and have yielded no inscribed objects. H.H.R.

KAPELRUD, A. S. : *Ras Sjamra-funnene og det Gamle Testament.* 1953. Pp. 96. (J. G. Tanum, Oslo. Price : Norwegian Kr. 5.50.)

An excellent, brief, up-to-date account in Norwegian of the Ras Shamra discoveries, intended primarily for the non-specialist. The greater part of the book is devoted to the religious content of the texts, and particularly to the evidence about Baal and El. (Kapelrud differs from Eissfeldt in holding that, at the period from which the texts come, El had lost something of the leading position which he had previously held in the pantheon.) The whole presentation is admirably clear ; and the comparison with the O.T. material is balanced and suggestive. The book is a revised form of lectures delivered in the University of Oslo in 1951. G.W.A.

LAMING, A. (ed. by) : *La Découverte du Passé.* 1952. Pp. 258. (Picard, Paris. Price : Fr. 1900.)

This is an account of recent progress in archaeological method valuable at once for the beginner and for the more experienced field archaeologist in so far as a team of specialists describe such recent developments as aerial reconnaissance, electromagnetic detection, dating fossilized bones by fluoride content, and radiocarbon dating. In articles on new methods of studying pottery, metals, and prehistoric flora and fauna we are made aware of the increasing dependence of the field archaeologist on the laboratory work of the scientist. J.G.

MONTET, P. : *Les Énigmes de Tanis*. 1952. Pp. 170. (Payot, Paris. Price : Fr. 700.)

The author presents a comprehensive account of the latest developments in the excavation of Ṣan el Ḥagar arranged according to the various features examined, e.g. temple precincts of the Pharaohs from the XIXth to the XXIst Dynasties, buildings, tombs, foundation-deposits, and gods. One of the main problems is set by the re-use of older materials, statues not excepted. The work is of first-rate value for field archaeologists. For O.T. scholarship there is practically nothing of direct interest except a short résumé of the evidence that Ṣan el Ḥagar is the old Hyksos capital Avaris, Pi-Ramses (Ramses of Exodus), and later Tanis-Zoan. J.G.

MOORHOUSE, A. C. : *The Triumph of the Alphabet. A History of Writing*. 1953. Pp. xiii+223. (Henry Schuman, New York. Price : $3.50.)

Mr. Moorhouse has provided a concise account of the origin and development of writing, intended for those with no previous acquaintance with the subject. He deals in a number of chapters with its form, the decipherment of unknown languages, pre-alphabetic and alphabetic scripts, the extension of the alphabet, the function and influence of writing, and the spread of literacy. The author cannot have knowledge at first hand of all the subjects treated but he seems, where a reviewer can check him, to be substantially right, even though occasional slips (e.g. in the discussion of the Semitic alphabet) or omissions (e.g. the names of Bauer and Dhorme in connection with the decipherment of the Ugaritic script) of slight importance can be detected ; and some chapters, notably those of general import, are somewhat scrappy. The book, however, may be safely recommended to teachers and others who want a clear introduction to a fascinating subject. G.R.D.

The New Nippur Excavations. 1951. (Bulletin of University Museum, Pennsylvania.) Pp. 40. (University Museum, University of Pennsylvania, Philadelphia.)

In this bulletin D. McCown presents a broad sketch of a season's work at Nippur, specifically on the temple of Enlil (five levels) and on the Scribal Quarter. He is apparently endeavouring to interest a wide public both in this bulletin and in the forthcoming official publication, ' a new type of archaeological book, not, as in the past, one written by specialists for other specialists.' . . . . but ' the story of man's growth at Nippur so that all may look into the past to understand the present better.' F. R. Steele writes of cuneiform tablets and their significance in general and on the season's find at Nippur in particular (' nearly 800 fragments covering a span of over 2000 years '). He summarily classifies these according to date and subject-matter. S. N. Kramer translates and comments upon a Sumerian hymn to Nanshe as illustrating the ancient Sumerian conception of social justice, another Sumerian tablet describing the young scribe's training and exercise, and another reporting a murder-trial about 1850 B.C.

J.G.

NORTH, R. : *Stratigraphia Palestinae*. 1954. Pp. 54. (Pontificium Institutum Biblicum, Rome. Price : Lire 250.)

This, the author's lectures (in Latin) on Palestinian archaeology in the Pontificial Biblical Institute, is an excellent summary of the subject to date and a useful introduction to the technicalities thereof. He broadly and clearly characterizes the various strata from the Arab Period (including the Crusades) to the Palaeolithic Age, selecting type sites for more detailed study. Controversy is always avoided, though the writer is always aware of all controversial issues and the relevant bibliography. There is for all periods a good selective bibliography including recent publications and older works which tend now to be overlooked.

J.G.

PARROT, A. : *Archéologie Mésopotamienne*. Vol. 2. 1953. Pp. 470. (Michel, Paris. Price : Fr. 1380.)

A very useful and compact account of the technique and problems of Mesopotamian archaeology in the series *Sciences d'Aujourd'hui* edited by André George. It is well illustrated and has a good selected bibliography. The first 100 pages contain an account of the organization and conduct of an expedition, and the remainder of the book gives a full account of the stratification at Assyrian sites and discusses problems of chronology and the reasons for accepting the chronology proposed by S. Smith in 1940. The first volume of this work was noticed in the *Book List* 1947, p. 11.

J.N.S.

PARROT, A. : *La Tour de Babel*. (Cahiers d'Archéologie Biblique Vol. 2). 1953. Pp. 58. (Price : Swiss Fr. 3.75.)

Ninive et l'Ancien Testament. (Cahiers d'Archéologie Biblique Vol. 3). 1953. Pp. 76. (Price : Swiss Fr. 4.00.) (Delachaux and Niestlé, Neuchâtel and Paris.)

The former of these works consists of four chapters presenting the written evidence from inscriptions, the O.T., and travellers ; the evidence from archaeology ; representation in art ; the religious and theological significance of the tower story. The second book gives an account of the excavations at Nineveh; Assyrian inscriptions and O.T. evidence ; the fall of Nineveh ; and a comparative chronological table from Tiglath-pileser I to the end of the Assyrian Empire. Both books are excellent small volumes from one who is both a good archaeologist and an O.T. scholar ; they are also well illustrated. J.N.S.

SELLERS, O. R. and BARAMKI, D.C. : *A Roman-Byzantine Burial Cave in Northern Palestine* (B.A.S.O.R. Supplementary Studies, Nos. 15-16). 1953. Pp. 56. (A.S.O.R., Newhaven, Conn. Price : $1.50.)

An account of two weeks' excavation by the American School in Jerusalem· in January, 1949, of a cave with three burial chambers at Silet edh-Dhabr near Samaria. Each chamber had 10 horizontal burial shafts, and in the cave itself were seven silos. Sherds, lamps, coins, bone and metal objects from the 1st. to 7th. cent. A.D. and a pagan Roman limestone bust are described ; 25 pages are given to a study of lamps.

J.N.S.

TUFNELL, OLGA : *Lachish III : The Iron Age.* 2 vols. 1953. Pp. 438 (vol. 1). Pp. 8+130 plates (vol. 2). (O.U.P. Price : 168s. 0d.)

Two previous volumes have been issued in 1938 and 1940 and there is a concluding volume to come on the Bronze Age finds. This volume deals mainly with the Iron Age from 1200 B.C. to the conquest by Alexander. It is divided into four parts— History and Archaeology ; The City ; The Cemeteries ; The Objects. There is an excellent bibliography of the Lachish Ostraca ; also a chapter by Dr. Diringer on Early Hebrew Inscriptions and another by Dr. Margaret Murray on Hiero-glyphic and Ornamental Seals. The volume provides a very important contribution to the whole field of Palestinian archaeology and is a worthy tribute to the encouragement given to Biblical research by the late Sir Charles Marston.

J.N.S.

VINCENT, L. H. and STEVE, A. M. : *Jérusalem de l'Ancien Testament.* 1st part. *Archéologie de la Ville.* 1954. Pp. xii+372. (Gabalda, Paris. Price : with a separate album of 100 plates, 210s. 0d.)

This magnificent volume, representing a great part of the life-work of one who has spent sixty-three years in the study of Palestinian archaeology, is the continuation of a slim work, the first fascicle of *Jérusalem antique*, that made its appearance in 1912 and was devoted to the topography of Jerusalem. In this later volume there is no direct return to topography. The subject throughout is archaeology, and this is the first of two volumes. It is concerned with the archaeology of the city properly so-called, and the second volume will be the long-awaited treatment of the Haram. There are thirteen chapters in the present volume. The first provides a general discussion on the site, with special reference to the accounts found in Josephus. The second deals with the expansion of the city and the existing walls. Chapters III-V discuss, in turn, the three ancient walls, and Ch. VI, mordantly entitled "Autour d'un rempart mouvant," says all that need be said about recent attempts to find substitutes for the ordinarily accepted line of the third wall (that of Herod Agrippa I). Chapters VII and VIII deal, respectively, with the fortresses of the Acra and of the Antonia. Apropos of the second, Vincent still identifies the court of the Antonia with the *praetorium* of Pilate, a position that has been severely criticized by P. Benoit in his article : " Prétoire, Lithostroton et Gabbatha " (*Revue Biblique*, Oct., 1952, pp. 531-550). Ch. IX, on Palaces, includes pages on Herod's palace, the Hasmonean palace, and the three palaces associated with the royal family of Adiabene. Ch. X is concerned with the walls of Jerusalem as described by Nehemiah. Chapters XI and XII, on the water system of ancient Jerusalem, repeat in some measure Ch. IV, II of *Jérusalem antique*, on the Ophel tunnel and its identification with the *şinnor*. Lastly, chapter XIII, on the cemeteries, has sections on the royal tombs, on the necropolis in the royal period, on the monuments of the Kedron valley, and on the tomb of Helen of Adiabene, misnamed by de Saulcy " The Tomb of the Kings ". The plates, as always, are a joy. J.M.T.B.

HISTORY AND GEOGRAPHY

ALT, A. : *Kleine Schriften zur Geschichte des Volkes Israel*, Vol. 1. 1953. Pp. xii + 358. (C. H. Beck, München. Price : DM. 26 bound.)

This first volume of collected essays covers aspects of Israel's history from the earliest times up to and including the period of the settlement. All but two of the studies have already appeared in journals, several of them being very well known, and they are now happily published in more accessible form. Together they make important contributions to our knowledge of the beginnings of Israel. The range of the author's knowledge and interest is indicated by the titles : Der Gott der Väter ; Die Wallfahrt von Sichem nach Bethel ; Die Landnahme der Israeliten in Palästina ; Erwägungen über die Landnahme der Israeliten in Palästina ; Josua ; Das system der Stammesgrenzen im Buche Josua ; Emiter und Moabiter ; Ägyptische Tempel in Palästina und die Landnahme der Philister ; Syrien und Palästina im Onomastikon des Amenope ; Zur Geschichte von Beth-sean 1500-1000 v. Chr. ; Megiddo im Übergang vom Kanaanäischen zum Israelitischen Zeitalter ; Meros ; Die Ursprünge des Israelitischen Rechts; Das Verbot des Diebstahls im Dekalog ; Zur Talions-formal ; Gedanken über das Königtum Jahwes. Their value is increased by the full use that is made, not only of the Old Testament itself, but also of inscriptions and other archaeological material with which the author is well acquainted. The penetrating scholarship behind the essays makes them useful prolegomena to the study of Israel's history. L.H.B.

ALT, A. : *Kleine Schriften zur Geschichte des Volkes Israel*, Vol. 2. 1953. Pp. 476. (C. H. Beck, München.)

The essays collected in this second volume cover a range of topics from the history of Israel during the Monarchy and the post-Exilic Period. Some are geographical studies, the extent of David's kingdom, the divisions of Solomon's time, the territorial significance of Sennacherib's invasion, the districts of Judaea in the time of Josiah, the Judaean and Samaritan border, problems of Galilean geography. Others are ethnographical, such as the part played by Samaria in the beginnings of Judaism, Israel's neighbours in Nehemiah's time. Two of the essays, that on the place of origin of Deuteronomy, and that on Fortesses and Levitical cities in Judaea are printed for the first time. In the essay on Deuteronomy Alt argues for a northern provenance sometime between 722 and 621. L.H.B.

KAUFMANN, Y. : *The Biblical Account of the Conquest of Palestine,* translated from Hebrew by M. Dagut. 1953. Pp. viii+98. (Magnes Press, Jerusalem.)

In this work Professor Kaufmann offers a critical examination of current views, and especially of the views of Alt and Noth, and to a lesser degree of Mowinckel. He will have none of the theory of a Deuteronomistic Historical Work, and claims that Joshua and Judges present an unreal, utopian view of the land of Israel which is very early. The utopian view on which they are based preceded the Conquest. The stories of conquest are all ancient, and Judges is held to be a continuation of the book of Joshua. The date of the compilation of the book of Joshua is placed at about the time of Dan's migration to the north. The translator has done his work well, and the English reads smoothly, if vigorously. The reviewer is doubtful if the literary-critical view here presented will win wide acceptance, though there are many acute observations which deserve to be considered. H.H.R.

ORLINSKY, H. M. : *Ancient Israel.* 1954. Pp. xiv+194. (Cornell University Press, Ithaca, N.Y. Price : $1.75 paper ; $2.50 cloth.)

This is a brief sketch of the History of Israel down to the Persian period by a well-known scholar, who is widely acquainted with modern work but who writes simply and without elaborate documentation. At the end there is a good bibliography, both for more general readers who desire to pursue the study further, and for more advanced readers. Five maps are interspersed in the volume. The whole is excellently balanced and it offers a reliable summary. H.H.R.

PRESS, I. : *A Topographical-historical Encyclopaedia of Palestine.* (In Hebrew, title and preface also in English.) 3 vols. 1946, 1948, 1952. Pp. xc+176, x+266, xxxii+234. (Rubin Mass, Jerusalem.)

This book provides evidence of the lively and enthusiastic interest displayed in the young State of Israel in the topography of the country. In it I. Press, one of the oldest of the experts in Palestinology, attempts quite on his own to compose a topographical encyclopaedia for all the hundreds of years of Israel's history. The book is of value for the scholar as well as for the educated reader, though it is for the second category in particular that the Introduction is intended. This covers a very wide scope. It contains (1) a short but inclusive summary of the history of Palestine from the Stone Age up to the close of the British Mandate, (2) a very valuable and instructive survey (based on the comparison of sources) on the changes in the boundaries of the country throughout the ages and finally (3) an explanation of geographical terms from all the different periods (Hebrew, Greek, Roman and Arabic) with their origin and character and the conclusions to be drawn from them.

The same combination of historical data and actual fact characterises the many entries in the body of the work. The third volume, which appeared after the establishment of the State of Israel, devotes special attention to the recent development of the country. So far three volumes have been published containing all the material from the letter *Aleph* to the letter *Samekh* inclusive. In the final work of five volumes (all of which have been completed in manuscript) there will be a total of about 8,000 entries among which the newly established Kibbuzim and villages will appear side by side with the names known to us from the Bible, Josephus, Christian and Arab sources. Under every entry the writer provides a summary of the philological, historical, and geographical problems centred around the name, accompanied always by a survey of the research into the problem. Whenever possible the entry concludes with a complete list of references for the appearance of the name in the early sources and in the writings of the Middle Ages. The writer does not confine himself to stating the opinions of other scholars. Not infrequently he expresses his own views on the identification of places and other similar subjects.

It is obvious, of course, that such an inclusive work by a single author, even though started upon several years ago and corrected, revised, and improved from time to time, cannot always penetrate to the depths of the critical problems and consider them in all their details. In the Biblical field, for instance, the writer does not always successfully cover all the material and the literature in its many branches. Nevertheless this is a useful and efficient encyclopaedia and the maps and photographs included enhance its value.

I.L.S.

REIFENBERG, A. : *Israel's History in Coins from the Maccabees to the Roman Conquest.* 1953. Pp. 46 (of which over twenty are plates). (East & West Library, Horovitz Ltd., London. Price : 10s. 6d.)

Here Dr. Reifenberg, the well known authority on Ancient Jewish Coins presents enlarged and useful photographs of many familiar Jewish, and of a few Roman, coins of historical interest. He ranges from John Hyrcanus to the suppression by Hadrian of the Second Revolt. A brief essay precedes the plates. It is perhaps always doubtful how far it is any use for the specialist to take the public into his confidence even in books written expressly for their benefit. Nevertheless one could wish that the author had allowed his public to know how very doubtful and speculative are some of the identifications of objects exhibited on Jewish coins, and, above all, had devoted some of the large areas of empty space to a better system of defining the illustrated coins (for which the rubric on page 19 is inadequate) with cross references for all the Jewish coins either to his own *Ancient Jewish Coins* (second ed. Jerusalem 1947) or to the London catalogue of Hill. On p. 10, fourth line from end, for *fig.* 6 read *fig.* 9. Whatever the legend on the reverse of the coin, presumably a denarius(?), illustrated as figures 30 and 31, it has not been accurately transcribed, and a more representative coin would be more suitable for a popular book. The reason for the position of the Short Chronology on pp. 44, 45 is perhaps only known to the publisher. The statement in it under A.D. 97 about Nerva and the Jewish tax is misleading.   H.St.J.H.

VILNAY, Z. : *Ha'arez Bammiqra* (in Hebrew). 1954. Pp. 60. (Tur-Israel, Jerusalem.)

This book, written by a scholar who has literally " walked through the land in the length of it and in the breadth of it ", comprises a comprehensive description of Palestine in the Biblical era. Passages of the Bible in which names of places occur are reproduced in full, to which are added copious notes seeking to identify these names. Here use is made of their Arabic equivalents as well as of archaeological data. The author avails himself also of the various translations of the Bible, amongst them being the LXX, Vulgate, the Peshiṭta and the Targums. Talmudical material is also drawn upon. The book is well produced and includes 79 maps and illustrations. We are promised another book—*Madhrikh 'Erez Isra'el*—in which a detailed bibliography bearing on the present work will be given.   M.W.

TEXT AND VERSIONS

AIURA, T. : *A Study of the Old Testament Quotations in First Clement.* (Annual Studies, vol. 1 ; Department of Theology Series, No. 1.) 1953. Pp. 16. (Kwansei Gakuin University, Nishinomiya-shi, Japan.)

Here is the first fruits of a new venture in Japan, and especially welcome on that ground alone. This monograph by Dr. Aiura is a textual study with the exegesis of the quotations and Clement's use of them reserved for a further study. After a short summary of previous work by Hatch and Swete, the author proceeds. Clement quotes the Psalms most often, beyond doubt he used the Septuagint, Codex A, always as proof texts and often allegorically. Two special points emerge. He omits the last three verses of Ps. li (M.T.) ; Dr. Aiura inclines to the belief that these verses were not in Clement's text. Also, the quotation from Ezek. xviii, 30 is strangely distorted : have we here evidence of the ' two books ' which Josephus mentions ? The scope of the monograph is limited, but we welcome it as the forerunner of other studies to come.
N.H.S.

Biblia Sacra iuxta Latinam Vulgatam Versionen ad codicum fidei . . edita.
X. Liber Psalmorum ex recensione St. Hieronymi cum Praefationibus et Epistula ad Sunniam et Fretelam. 1953. Pp. xvi+300. (Romae typis polyglottis Vaticanis. Price : Lire 4,000.)

This tenth volume of the Vulgate Old Testament, the work of the monks of St. Jerome's Monastery in Rome, may be said, with all due qualifications, to be one of the less interesting volumes of the series. It is prepared with great care and, as usual, gives a wonderful conspectus of the intricate manuscript tradition, but (an important factor for those accustomed to use the Gallican Psalter in the Sixto-Clementine edition) it contains remarkably few (if any) significant variants, and the collation of about a hundred pages with the breviary text of this Psalter goes to show that, in all but a few instances, the texts are all but identical. In some of the earlier volumes one has detected some interesting variants, duly marked with a double " sword " sign wherever the archetype is corrupt and has demanded correction from later MSS, but here there are certainly not more than half a dozen, and none of these can be said to be exciting. In Ps. xxxiv. 26 (*Judica Domine, nocentes me,* at p. 103) "magna" is accepted with the Hebrew LXX and SC against " maligna " in many other codices, and in Ps. xxxvi. 14 (*Noli aemulari* at p. 106) "deiciant" is restored with the LXX and the *Psalterium Romanum* against " decipiant " of the archetype, here clearly in error. Among other variants noted are (Ps. xvii. 18, at p. 70) " confirmati " for the Sixto-Clementine's " confortati ", and (Ps. xxvii. 3, at p. 88) " perdideris " for the S-C. " perdas ". There are, of course, numerous minute variants in spelling and in minor words such as conjunctions, but, on the whole, the main value of this edition is that it gives the textual evidence for a Psalter that, until recently, was almost everywhere used in the Latin rite, though, since 1945, it has been in some measure supplanted by the new edition prepared by the Biblical Institute and authorized for use in public and private recitation.

J.M.T.B.

CLARK, K. W. (Director) : *Checklist of Manuscripts in the Libraries of the Greek and Armenian Patriarchates in Jerusalem. Microfilmed for the Library of Congress,* 1949-50. 1953. Pp. xi+44. (Photo-duplication Service, Library of Congress, Washington. Price : 50 cents.)

This is a companion to the *Checklist of Manuscripts in St. Catherine's Monastery, Mount Sinai,* noticed in the *Book List* (1953), p. 3. As in the earlier list, many of the MSS recorded as available on microfilm are biblical or contain commentaries on Scripture, and the languages represented include Greek, Arabic, Syriac, Georgian, Slavonic, Ethiopic, Latin, Armenian, Persian, Turkish and Russian. Many illuminations from MSS are also entered in the list, a generous selection of them being recorded on 4 x 5 in. film. Re-productions of the 1030 MSS and 1187 illuminations thus photographically copied by the American School of Oriental Research may be purchased from the Photoduplication Service of the Library of Congress, and a debt of gratitude is owed to those who have made accessible this valuable source-material, and particularly to Dr. Clark, director of the photographic expedition, who has now with the help of Mrs. Clark produced this useful index of the material.

W.D.M.

The Second Book of Moses called Exodus—Book of the Migration. 1953. Pp. xxviii + 54. *The Third Book of Moses called Leviticus—Book of the Levites.* 1953. Pp. ii + 40. translated by the Commission for the Revision of the Old Testament, appointed by the Hungarian Bible Council of the Evangelical Churches. (Press Department of the General Convent of the Reformed Church in Hungary, Budapest.)

This second instalment of the trial edition of a new Revised Hungarian Old Testament maintains the pattern and standard of the first (see *Book List*, 1952, p. 31). The Exodus volume has an introduction repeated in English and German, in which the editor, Prof. Pákozdy, illustrates by examples the method adopted in the translation, the design of the explanatory notes and the scope of the reference system. P.R.W.

GARD, D. H. : *The Exegetical Method of the Greek Translator of the Book of Job.* (J. B. L. Monograph Series, No. viii.) 1952. Pp. vi + 108. (Society of Biblical Literature, Philadelphia, Pa. Price : $1.50.)

In this lithoprinted volume a disciple of H. S. Gehman undertakes a study of the LXX deviations from the M.T. in the book of Job, with a view to discovering how far they rest on a divergent text and how far they arise from principles of interpretation. He gives a large number of classified examples, quoting the Hebrew and the Greek text, and leading to the conclusion that for theological and pietistic reasons expressions which were not regarded as edifying were toned down, while anthropomorphisms were frequently avoided—though not systematically eliminated—and anything that appeared to detract from the character of God was modified. In addition, the author finds that many of the omissions from the Greek text as compared with the Hebrew may be explained as due to the same causes. He is persuaded that the Vorlage which lies behind the LXX differed but little from the M.T. H.H.R.

Hebrew Bible : Jerusalem edition. Corrected on the basis of the Masora of Ben Asher by Moshe David Cassuto. 1953. Pp. 1444. (Magnes Press : Jerusalem.)

This edition of the Hebrew Bible is tragedy almost unrelieved. It is not a newly printed edition, but a photographic reproduction of the 1908 Ginsburg Bible, with corrections made on the basis of notes left by the late Professor Cassuto. It is regrettable that his name is associated with the way in which this has been done, because it can scarcely be thought that he would have approved of the procedure of the publishers. The choice of the Ginsburg text is strange, because he was scarcely *persona grata* with orthodox Jewry, and further his edition suffers from a fundamental weakness in that he was influenced by the number of manuscripts which supported any particular variant, irrespective of their relative value. This weakness therefore tends to be perpetuated in the present edition. Further confusion is caused by the fact that Cassuto made his notes on the basis of the Letteris edition. The technical work of publishing is also unfortunate. The pages contain an irregular number of lines to the page, varying from 27 to 29, and where there are the same number of lines on opposite pages, there is often one line overlapping at the top of one page, and another line overlapping at the bottom of the opposite page. On pp. 626-7 the overlap amounts to $2\frac{1}{2}$ lines, and on these particular pages the lines are not horizontal, a feature which occurs with lamentable frequency. This lack of care makes the volume itself look strange, hurried and undignified. In addition the binding is weak : my copy has already come to pieces. There are new mistakes in lines which have been reset. The small circles which indicate the footnotes in the Ginsburg edition have been erased, but sometimes a vowel has gone as well. It is a great pity that the publishers have destroyed the effectiveness of Cassuto's work by their subsequent policy.

N.H.S.

ROBINSON, H. W. (ed. by) : *The Bible in its Ancient and English Versions.* 2nd ed. 1954. Pp. viii + 350. (Oxford University Press. Price : 21s. 0d.)

This new edition of a work first published in 1940 (cf. *Book List*, 1946, p. 22) is reprinted lithographically from the original edition, but with the addition of a ten page appendix on the Dead Sea Scrolls by W. D. McHardy, and with the revision of the bibliography at the end, and eight plates of illustrations. It is curious that the Index has not been revised to include references to the appendix. In the appendix Professor McHardy has given a short account of the finds in the neighbourhood of the Dead Sea, so far as they were known at the time of his writing, together with a rapid survey of the variety of views on them which have been advanced. Professor McHardy advises caution in accepting any of the views, whether on the date of the documents, the date of the deposit in the cave, or the nature of the sect. H.H.R.

SCARPAT, G. : *Il Liber Psalmorum e il Psalterium Gallicanum.* 1950. Pp. 46. (Editrice Libraria " Paideia ", Arona. Price : 4s. 0d.)

The publication in 1945, of the new version of the Psalms made by the Professors of the Roman Biblical Institute has stimulated many students to assess the comparative value of that work when tested, line by line, with the Gallican Psalter, hitherto in use for many centuries in most churches and communities of the Latin Rite. In this booklet the author makes a careful comparison, wholly from the point of view of language, between the two versions, with some help from Zorell's *Psalterium ex hebraico Latinum*, first issued in 1929 (2nd ed., revised 1939). By way of appendix the first sixteen verses of Ps. xxxiv (Heb. xxxv) are printed according to the new version and the Gallicanum. J.M.T.B.

SOISALON-SOININEN, I. : *Vanhan Testamentin alkuteksti* (Suomen Eksegeettisen Seuran julkaisuja 10). 1953. Pp. 92. (Otava, Helsinki.)

This is a very good introduction to the problems concerning "the original text of the O.T." The author sets out with a description of the printed editions and the extant manuscripts and works his way back to the work of the Massoretes and the pre-massoretic text, which is treated with special reference to the Septuagint problem and the Dead Sea scrolls. Different opinions are discussed with sound judgement. Against Kahle the author holds that the variations of the LXX text are due to a rather free transmission of one single translation. The massoretic text is considered to be the best text available to us, although it is not altogether free from minor errors.

H.R.

Vetus Latina. Die Reste der altlateinischen Bibel—herausg. von der Erzabtei Beuron. Vol. II, Fasc. iii. 1953. Pp. 289-448. (Herder, Freiburg. Price : DM. 30.)

The present fascicle of the magnificent edition of the Old Latin version of the Old Testament being edited by the monks of Beuron contains Genesis xxvii. 23—xliii. 22 and exhibits the same admirable qualities as the preceding fascicles.

G.R.D.

WEBER, R. : *Le Psautier Romain et les autres anciens Psautiers Latins :* Edition critique. (Collectanea Biblica, Vol. x.) 1953. Pp. xxiv+ 410. (Abbaye Saint-Jérome, Via de Torre Rossa, Rome. Price : Lire 2,500.)

Weber, who edited in this series of Collectanea in 1945 the Old Latin of II Chronicles, has here produced the first critical edition of the so-called Roman Psalter, which is still in use for the recitation of the Office in St. Peter's, Rome. Until recent times it was commonly alleged that this was St. Jerome's first revision of the Old Latin, but, as a result of the work of the late Donatien de Bruyne, this view is now contested, though, as Weber remarks, the fact that Jerome certainly knew and used this Psalter renders de Bruyne's arguments somewhat less forceful. Here we have more than the text of the Psalterium Romanum, since the editor has very usefully provided in a right-hand column accompanying the main text the variants of the other Old Latin psalters, notably the Milanese and the Mozarabic. The final pages (359-410) offer, as did Allgeier's excellent *Altlateinischen Psalterien*, an *index verborum* intended to serve as a sort of concordance to assist the comparison of the various texts. The printing is a beautiful example of the work of the Vatican Press. J.M.T.B.

BALDI, D. : *Giosuè* (La Sacra Bibbia, ed. by S. Garofalo). 1952. Pp. xiv+178 (with 7 maps and 5 pages of photographs). (Marietti, Turin. Price : Lire 950.)

> Another of the smaller commentaries in the *Sacra Bibbia* series is interesting, first and foremost, because it makes full use of Abel's second volume of *La Géographie de la Palestine* to establish more securely than was always possible in the past the situation and characteristics of the numerous place-names furnished by the book of Joshua. True, this is not the first work of a semi-popular character to show dependence upon Abel. The French commentary by A. Gelin in t. III of *La Sainte Bible*, edited by Pirot and Clamer is equally indebted to Abel, and is, in general, similar in character to Baldi's work, though it lacks the full geographical index, which is so commendable a feature of the Italian volume. This index gives, in three columns, first the biblical name, then the references to the text, and, finally, the modern Arab name, where this can be identified. The first column contains approximately 440 place-names, and is quite invaluable for any student of Joshua. The introductory pages, which discuss the literary and critical problems concerning the book, and its historical and religious value, are not greatly different in their content and findings from those in the French commentary.
>
> J.M.T.B.

La Sainte Bible de Jérusalem. Les Livres de Samuel, by R. de Vaux. 1953. Pp. 240. (Price : Fr. 660.) *Habaquq, Abdias, Joël*, by J. Trinquet. 1953. Pp. 92. (Price : Fr. 270.) *L'Ecclésiastique*, by J. Duesberg and P. Auvray. 1953. Pp. 218. (Price : Fr. 600.) (Les Éditions du Cerf, Paris.)

> For previous volumes in the series, see *Book Lists*, 1949, p. 27 ; 1950, pp. 25, 40 ; 1951, p. 33 ; 1952, pp. 27, 28 ; 1953, p. 34. As before, the commentary is brief and useful, whilst the translation is careful and distinctly helpful. The two strands in 1 Samuel are recognised, and they may be documents or traditions, but they certainly show the ' constants ' of Pentateuchal analysis. The long history which begins with 2 Sam. ix is by an eye-witness, probably either Ahimaaz or Abiathar. The date of the earlier strands is the first hundred years of the monarchy, but the final editing is under Deutero-nomic influence, though this is less marked than in Judges and Kings. Habakkuk is dated just after 600 B.C. ; the origin may well be liturgical, and the author inclines to the authenticity of the last chapter. The introduction to this book is particularly up-to-date, and full reference is made to the Dead Sea scrolls. Obadiah is composite. Vv. 1-7, 10-14, 15cd belong to 550-450 B.C., and the rest ca. 450 B.C. Joel has two distinct elements, both between 400 and 350 B.C. As for Ecclesiasticus, the author himself was at work ca. 190 B.C., and his grandson, the translator, was active ca. 117 B.C. The discussions of the contents of the book and their influence is compact and good.
>
> N.H.S.

BONKAMP, B. : *Die Psalmen nach dem hebräischen Grundtext.* 1949.
Pp. 634. (Wilhelm Visarius, Freiburg i. Br. Price : DM. 28.)

The introduction is almost entirely occupied with a discussion
of the ' Davidic ' psalms and a defence of the rejection of
most of them from the Davidic age. The translation is based
on the Massoretic text, emended where felt by the translator
to be necessary. The translation reads well and deviations
from the Hebrew are indicated in footnotes. After each
psalm there follows a commentary in essay form.

The author's main interest would seem to have been to attempt
to determine the historical background of individual psalms
and to allocate as many as possible to the time of Josiah and
the finding of the Book of Deuteronomy. He ascribes Ps.
xviii to Josiah, xix, xx, xxi to Hilkiah the priest, and
lxxii to the priest Uriah who lived in the time of Ahaz. Where
background and authorship are determined the commentary
on the psalm is of full length, but in other cases the commentary
is often little more than a paraphrase of the psalm, xxiii
is a notable example.

Fuller recognition should have been paid to the work of other
scholars.   L.H.B.

BÜCKERS, H. : *Die Bücher Esdras, Nehemias, Tobias, Judith und
Esther.* (Die Heilige Schrift für das Leben erklärt, Band IV/2.
Herders Bibelkommentar.) 1953. Pp. viii+400. (Herder, Freiburg.
Price : DM.21.)

This expository commentary follows the plan of the same
author's previous volume on Chronicles (see *Book List*, 1953),
though the requirements of sound historical judgement are
less easy to reconcile with the conclusions necessitated by
the author's confession. *Ezra-Nehemiah* is given a consistently
high historical rating ; *Esther* suffers from a few ' kleinen
Unebenheiten und Übertreibungen '. *Tobit* is an ' Idealbild '
of a biblical family, but has an historical kernel ; and so has
Judith, which is tentatively assigned to the reign of Artaxerxes
III. The exposition is generally sound and helpful.

D.R.Ap-T.

BULLOUGH, S. : *Obadiah, Micah, Zephaniah, Haggai and Zechariah.*
(The Westminster Version of the Sacred Scriptures.) 1953. Pp.
lxx+132. (St. Catherine Press, London. Price : 18s. 0d.)

After some years' interval, a further volume of the Westminster
Version, edited by Father Lattey, has made its welcome
appearance. The Introduction consists of a brief note on
Hebrew Metrical Forms, another on the principles of textual
criticism adopted in the volume, a bibliographical note, and
the separate introductions to each of the five Minor Prophets
treated here. The book of Micah is held to be a unity, and—
more surprisingly—similarly with the book of Zechariah.
Micah is credited with the authorship of the poem which
stands also in Isaiah ii. The new translation of the text of
the five books then follows. Here there is no indication to
the reader when the Hebrew is being emended, either on

the basis of the versions or conjecturally. The notes on the five books are collected together at the end of the volume. These show acquaintance with a good deal of modern work, including Professor G. R. Driver's scattered notes, and will be found very useful. The commentary is of the verse by verse kind, the divisions of the books being indicated by headings inserted in the translation.   H.H.R.

BUTTRICK, G. A. (ed. by) :   *The Interpreter's Bible, Volume II* (*Leviticus-Samuel*). 1953. Pp. 1176. (Abingdon-Cokesbury Press, New York and Nashville. Price : **$8.75.**)

The plan of the Interpreter's Bible is now well-known. The present volume maintains the high standard of those which have preceded it. The work on *Leviticus* by Nathaniel Micklem is concerned less with a literary study of the book than with its significance for the development of Hebrew worship, and shows insight and understanding. John Marsh gives a brief introduction to, and a competent exegesis of, *Numbers*, while G. E. Wright's introduction to *Deuteronomy* is very well written and emphasizes the value of it as an exposition of the faith of Israel. Wright associates the code of Deuteronomy with the reformation of Josiah, believes that " the Deutero-nomic tradition stems ultimately from the Shechem sanctuary " and says that " it is not improbable that the book rests on the tradition of an actual address of Moses before his death." In his work on *Joshua*, John Bright accepts the view of Noth that the book is to be regarded as part of the Deuteronomy-Kings literary complex and not to be interpreted in terms of a Hexateuchal problem. He takes full account of recent in-vestigation and of archaeological evidences, as is done by Jacob M. Myers in his treatment of *Judges*, which is recognized to be a compilation from old literary sources and from oral traditions, with a Deuteronomic editing. The small amount of space available for the Book of *Ruth* is competently used by Louise Pettibone Smith, and the volume concludes with the careful and scholarly work of George B. Caird on *Samuel*.
                                                                J.M.

CLAMER, A. (ed. by) : *La Sainte Bible, texte latin et traduction française d'après les textes originaux avec un commentaire exégétique et théolo-gique.* Tome I, 1re partie. *Genèse*. 1953. Pp. 530. (Letouzey & Ané, Paris. Price : Fr. 1225.)

Other volumes of this series have already been noticed in the *Book Lists* for 1948, 1950 and 1951. This volume is by the general editor himself. The French translation is based upon the Masoretic text but incorporates such improvements as the editor thinks desirable. The brief textual notes justify these renderings and are very much to the point. The volume begins with a general introduction to the whole of the Penta-teuch giving a competent survey of Pentateuchal criticism and taking note of the Scandinavian approach to the problem and also of the modern tendency to divide J into earlier and later strata. J is ascribed to the time of Solomon and E to some time between Elijah and the written prophets. The editor's own point of view stands out clearly in his assessment of the historical and religious value of the Pentateuch. There then follows an introduction to the Book of Genesis very largely rehearsing what has already been said and applying it to Genesis. The Patriarchal narratives are to be read as the stories of individuals. Gen. xiv is described as " une des plus anciennes traditions que nous ait conservées la Genèse " (p. 261).

In matters of exegesis also the conservative and spiritual approach shows itself clearly. Man in the image of God (i. 26) is not to be interpreted by v.3 (Seth in the image of Adam) but in a spiritual sense : " c'est donc par l'intelligence, l'autorité, la domination que l'homme créé à l'image de Dieu lui ressemblera " (p. 113). In general, the commentary is full and critical and seems likely to take its place as one of the best in the series to which it belongs.

L.H.B.

DAVIDSON, F., STIBBS, A. M. and KEVAN, E. F., (ed. by) : *The New Bible Commentary*. 1953. Pp. 1200. (The Inter-Varsity Fellowship, London. Price : 35s. 0d.)

This commentary is obviously designed, in the main, for readers who have no knowledge of the Biblical languages, and no awareness of the purposes of Biblical scholarship. It is unfortunate, however, that some of the contributors themselves appear to be unaware of scholarly work that has been done over the last 25 years. There are notable exceptions ; e.g., the commentary on Judges (F. F. Bruce), where textual difficulties are recognized and the reader is helped with good emendations. Bruce has also a brief, but useful, article on the Poetry of the Old Testament, The Fourfold Gospel (in which there is an admirable article on the Synoptic Problem), Acts of the Apostles, and Thessalonians. The scholarly treatment of Proverbs, Ezekiel and Hosea may also be noted. Elsewhere difficulties are recognized, but, apparently in the interests of a preconceived theory, ' explained away ', as in the argument for the unity of Isaiah (W. Fitch) and Zechariah (G. N. M. Collins). Jonah (D. W. B. Robinson) is dated 793-753 B.C. and is a factual record, the material in chap. i. being derived mainly from the sailors. The introduction to the Psalter (L. S. M'Caw) shows a knowledge of recent study, but no use is made of this in the commentary. There appears some inconsistency in condemning ' the so-called documentary theory ' in an article which speaks of pre-Mosaic ' Documents ', ' small additions and perhaps slight emendations ', and dates the Pentateuch in the early days of the Monarchy (G. Ch. Aalders). The commentary on Genesis contains useful homiletical material (E. F. Kevan), but no justification is offered for identifying the angel in Gen. xviii with the Second Person of the Trinity. Daniel (E. J. Young) ' is a product of the Exile and was written by Daniel himself ' and ' while there is nothing in the Aramaic usage of Daniel which in itself would preclude Danielic authorship . . . it is quite possible that the Aramaic . . . is simply a working-over or modernising ' of the original. Chapter v is ' noteworthy for its accuracy '. The article on Revelation and Inspiration (D. Lamont), though brief, is admirable for its insight and devotional spirit.   A.S.H.

DEDEN, D. : *De Kleine Profeten : Osee, Joel, Amos, Abdias, Jonas, Micheas.* (De Boeken van het Oude Testament : Deel XII, Boek I-VI.) 1953. Pp. 234. (J. J. Romen & Zonen, Roermond en Maaseik. Price : Fl. 8.70.)

The series is in twelve sections and will extend to nearly 5,000 pages. It is by a group of Dutch Roman Catholic scholars (see *Book List*, 1953, p. 30). Each of the six books here treated has an introduction, the editor's own translation, his exegesis with a summary of accepted emendations to the text. Dr. Deden follows the main lines of the more liberal Roman scholars. Hosea's activity was between 750 and 737 B.C. The woman of the first three chapters is Gomer throughout, and the chapters are an allegory of God's dealings with Israel. The author allows a late date of Joel, arguing from dependence and style. Amos dates from the time of Jeroboam II, Obadiah ca. 586 B.C., Jonah is a story of the 5th century directed against the exclusiveness of Ezra-Nehemiah. Micah is eighth century, but from ch iv. onwards, the sections are difficult to date and must each be considered separately.   N.H.S.

DITTMANN, W. : *Die Auslegung der Urgeschichte (Genesis 1-3) im Neuen Testament.* Microfilm. 1953. Pp. xvi + 256. (Vandenhoeck and Ruprecht, Göttingen. Price : DM. 16.50.)

The first 89 pages of this study are of interest to Old Testament scholars : they set out in comparatively full detail the manner in which Philo, Josephus and the early Rabbinic authorities read and understood the first three chapters of Genesis. It is rightly held that the interpretation current in contemporary Judaism was the basis for the use made of the creation story in the New Testament. The author devotes much of this early part to Philo and has a useful discussion of the tension between Hebrew and Greek in Philo's exposition. He also shows in a masterly way the difficulties which contemporary Rabbinism faced in their exegesis. (The film is somewhat marred by typing errors and cramped Greek manuscript.)   L.H.B.

FREY, H. : *Das Buch der Gegenwart Gottes unter seiner Gemeinde. Kapitel 25-40 des zweiten Buches Mose.* (Die Botschaft des Alten Testaments. Erläuterungen alttestamentlicher Schriften. 6, 11.) 1953. Pp. 200. (Calwer Verlag, Stuttgart. Price : DM. 9.80.)

The book forms the second part of the discussion of chs. xix-xl of Exodus by the same author and contains his comments on the last fifteen chapters of the book in the symbolic-allegorical-typological manner which is now becoming fairly well established. Though the Higher-critical position is not referred to, some of its main findings seem to satisfy the author, for, e.g., he finds that chs. xxv-xxxi, xxxii-xxxiv, and xxxv-xl are sufficiently distinctive to deserve special treatment. Occasional notice is taken of standard commentaries, such as Holzinger, Beer, von Rad ; and the Massoretic text is sometimes emended for translation according to the Versions. The weight of the interpretation attaches to the symbolic meaning of the text ; in the first instance the historical symbolism is described, and this, in turn, becomes a basis for theological and Christological allusions. In the main, these turn on such items as the Kingship of God, His plan of salvation, the response of the community, Christ as fulfilment of the cultic offices and their various symbolisms. Though the book suffers from the very obvious dangers which always accompany typology, there are a number of very interesting and shrewd observations which are worth while pondering over. B.J.R.

GALBIATI, E. and PIAZZA, A. : *Pagine difficili del Antico Testamento.* 2nd ed., 1952. Pp. 346. (Bevilacqua & Solari, Genoa. Price : Lire 700.)

This is an attempt to survey, largely from an apologetic point-of-view, passages and topics in the Bible that are, for one reason or another, specially thorny. The authors provide, under eleven main divisions, a discussion of the existence of literary types (Fr. *genres littéraires*) in the Bible ; historicity and the *genres :* the biblical account of creation and science ; original sin ; the exegesis of Genesis i-iii. and ecclesiastical tradition ; the Old Testament and pre-history ; the Old Testament and history ; miracles in the Old Testament ; morality and the Old Testament ; and (finally) messianism. Adequate references are made to existing literature, and the whole work appears to be competent and well-informed. J.M.T.B.

VAN GELDEREN, C. and GISPEN, W. H. : *Hosea* (Commentaar op het Oude Testament.) 1953. Pp. 426. (J. H. Kok, Kampen. Price : Fl. 15.75.)

When Professor van Gelderen, of the Free University of Amsterdam, died suddenly in 1945, Professor Gispen completed two commentaries which he left unfinished. One was the third part of a commentary on Kings, which was published in 1947, (*Book List*, 1948, p. 26). The other is a comprehensive commentary on Hosea, completed as long ago as 1950, but now published. It is part of a series under the general editorship of Professors Aalders, Gispen and Ridderbos. The point of view of the authors is conservative, and they are firmly against literary criticism. Emendations to the text are accepted where they are essential, but the authors maintain the whole book to be by Hosea, and to suggest anything else is *puur willekeur* (arbitrariness). Nevertheless, the discussions are full and detailed, the translations are scholarly and accurate, and the linguistic scholarship leaves nothing to be desired. N.H.S.

GOSLINGA, C. J. : *Het Boek der Richteren, Ruth.* Deel I : *Richteren, i-xii.* 1951. Pp. 202. Deel II : *Richteren, xiii-xxi : Ruth.* 1952. Pp. 168. (Kok, Kampen. Prices : Fl. 4.95 and Fl. 4.75.)

For details of the series of which these two volumes (second printing) form a part, see note on Dr. Noordtzij's Ezra-Nehemiah (p. 39). As in the other volumes of the series, there is a new translation, section by section with substantial comments interspaced. The critical position is conservative, and the date of the entrance into Canaan is taken to be 1387 B.C. Fifty pages of the second volume are devoted to the Book of Ruth, which is allocated to the time of the kingdoms. It is not a work of fiction, neither is it a mixture of truth and invention. N.H.S.

†VOR DER HAKE, J. A. (ed. by) : *Commentaar op de Heilige Schrift.* Fascs. 1-13. 1952. Pp. 64 per fasc. (Uitgeverij H. J. Paris, Amsterdam. Price : Fl. 3.00 per fasc.)

This is a one-volume Commentary on the Bible for Dutch readers, having much the same scope as several well-known one-volume Commentaries in English. The first hundred pages or so contain introductory articles on the Bible in general and the O.T. in particular ; then come commentaries on the individual books of the O.T. The O.T. part of the work is now complete, ending on p. 763. The fact that the fourteen contributors include such scholars as Vriezen, Edelkoort, Böhl and Gemser (and De Zwaan and Van Unnik for the N.T.) guarantees the standard of the work. It is intended chiefly for the Christian laity of the Netherlands, and it seems admirably suited to its purpose. F.F.B.

HANSON, A. and M. : *The Book of Job.* (Torch Bible Commentaries.) 1953. Pp. 118. (S.C.M. Press, London. Price : 7s. 6d.)

This is the ninth volume of the series, and the general pattern is followed with introduction and commentary. There is more emphasis on the theme than on critical questions, though these latter are outlined adequately. The critical position is normal. The writer takes over the ancient legend of Job, rewrites the story in traditional folklore style, and adds his own poetic work. The Elihu speeches, the Wisdom chapter, and the two beasts of chapter xl and xli are later interpolations. The theme is the problem of innocent suffering, but more especially the status of man before God. This is seen to be justification by faith and not self-vindication, and thus the link with the New Testament receives additional emphasis. The authors are on the staff of the Andhra Union Theological College, Dornakal, and are to be congratulated on what will prove to be one of the best volumes in the series. N.H.S.

HERTZBERG, H. W. : *Die Bücher Josua, Richter, Ruth.* (Das Alte Testament Deutsch, 9.) 1953. Pp. 284. (Vandenhoeck & Ruprecht, Göttingen. Price : DM. 9.40 ; bound : 11.40.)

For previous volumes in this series, see *Book List*, 1952, p. 37 and *Book List*, 1953, p. 41. The introduction is kept down to a minimum, so that as much space as possible is devoted to interpretation and exegesis. The Joshua literary problem is dealt with on the basis of the work of Alt and Noth. Judges is in a Deuteronomic setting, and Ruth is ' neighbour ' to Jonah. N.H.S.

KASHER, M. M. : *Encyclopedia of Biblical Interpretation. Genesis :* vol. 1. (Translated under the editorship of Rabbi Dr. H. Freedman.) 1953. Pp. xxi+262. (American Biblical Encyclopedia Society, New York. Price : $6.50.)

Rabbi Menahem Kasher has compiled, in Hebrew, a massive collection of Rabbinical sayings on the Torah (*Torah Shelemah*) which is in process of publication, and the present *Encyclopedia*, of which vol. 1 goes as far as Gen. vi. 8, is an anthology in English of the Hebrew version, translated by a number of Jewish scholars. The text of Genesis, taken as a rule from the AJV, is accompanied by a brief commentary by Kasher, and the ' sayings ' are arranged according to subject matter to accompany the verses. The series must be really invaluable to Jews, and to the non-Jew it is of considerable interest, for not only is it good to know what the Sages of Israel had to say about various passages, but also it is important that we thereby discover something of the general Rabbinic approach to Scripture. An Appendix to the volume, contributed by the author and others, contains four excursuses on the following topics : the concept of time in Biblical and Post-Biblical Literature ; the atom in Jewish sources ; creation and the theory of evolution ; creation and human brotherhood ; but they might appear to many readers to be somewhat ingenuous. There is a useful list of 'sources of the commentary' at the end of the book, giving the full name, date, and chief characteristic of the authors quoted. B.J.R.

KETTER, P. : *Die Königsbücher.* (Die Heilige Schrift für das Leben erklärt. Band III/2. Herders Bibelkommentar.) 1953. Pp. x+334. (Herder, Freiburg. Price : DM. 17.50.)

This sequel to the same author's volume on *Samuel* (1940) was ready for print before his death in 1950, and follows broadly the same plan as others in the series. A paragraphed translation from the Hebrew is followed by mainly exegetical comment based on careful scholarship. The book is not as homiletic in tone as some in the same series, but should fulfil its object admirably. D.R.Ap-T.

LAETSCH, T. : *Jeremiah (Bible Commentary)*. 1952. Pp. 412. (Concordia Publishing House, Saint Louis, Missouri. Price : $5.00.)

The book gives a translation, grammatical notes and a running commentary on Jeremiah. It is conservative in its treatment, although not belligerently so. The literary unity of the book is assumed rather than discussed, and rarely are the textual difficulties recognised. The grammatical notes are almost useless, and at times misleading to anyone who reads Jeremiah in Hebrew ; and it is difficult to imagine that they can have value to one who reads only the English text. Where the text is most difficult, no comment is given, e.g. ii. 34 ; v. 26 ; x. 17, etc. A commentary which proposes to ignore such points should not appear to offer grammatical notes. Sometimes the exegetical comments seem pointless, e.g. xxx. 24, ' The end is in Biblical language the opposite of the beginning.' Once these serious limitations of the commentary are recognised it may be possible to appreciate its warm piety. Even here, however, it would surely have proved helpful for the ordinary reader of the Bible to have been told something more of the great Biblical words, Covenant, hesed, righteousness, knowledge. Surely also it would be better to recognise boldly, rather than to ignore, the religious difficulties of such passages as iv. 10 ; xviii. 21-23 ; xlviii. 10 b. A.S.H.

LOEWE, R. : *Herbert of Bosham's Commentary on Jerome's Hebrew Psalter*. (Offprint from Biblica xxxiv.) 1953. Pp. 94. (Pontificio Istituto Biblico, Rome.)

The Commentary was found in St. Paul's Cathedral Library, and Miss Smalley has already noted its importance in *Recherches de Théologie*, xviii, 1951. A study of the commentary shows that Herbert was acquainted with Aramaic, and was perhaps the most competent Hebraist of the Western Church from the time of Jerome to the late 15th century. He had access to Jewish sources, especially Rashi and apparently the Targum, in his studies of the text. In another article (*Transactions of the Jewish Historical Society of England*, xvii, 1953, ' The Mediaeval Christian Hebraists of England '), Mr. Loewe says of him, ' The Rabbinate clearly lost an ornament when Providence decreed that Herbert of Bosham should be born to be a light unto the gentiles.'

In discussing the Commentary, detailed examination is given to the Prologue and Psalms xcix and xc. These are quoted in full, and the discussion which follows indicates especially Herbert's dependence on Jewish sources. A.S.H.

NELIS, J. T. : *Daniel*. (De Boeken van het Oude Testament : Deel XI, Book II.) 1954. Pp. 134. (Romen & Zonen, Roermond en Maaseik. Price : Fl. 5.78, or by subscription Fl. 5.10.)

This is the latest volume in the series by the group of Dutch Roman Catholic scholars who have been active under the general editorship of Professors Grossouw, van der Ploeg, and van Dodewaard. It conforms to the general pattern detailed elsewhere. There are fourteen pages of introduction, ending with a useful list of the dates of Babylonian, Median, Persian Seleucid and Ptolemaic kings. The four kingdoms are Assyria. Media, Persia and Macedon. The author summarizes previous discussions concerning the two sections of Daniel (i-vi and vii-xii) and concerning the two languages. He concludes with Dr. Rowley's suggestions of a progressive publication of stories in Aramaic, the later of which were translated into Hebrew for the more educated, with finally the introduction similarly translated. In the discussion of section I (Chs. i-vi), the chief feature is the possible connection with the Dan-El of the Ras Shamra tablets. In the discussion of section II, we find an account of the development and meaning of Apocalyptic, closing with a study of the message of the book, the new age involving the triumph of the Most High God over ' Satan ' of the second century B.C.   N.H.S.

NOORDTZIJ, A. : *De Boeken Ezra en Nehemia.* 1951. Pp. 279. (Kok, Kampen. Price : Fl. 5.90.)

This volume (a second printing) by Dr. Noordtzij is one of a series of short Bible commentaries (Korte Verklaring der Heilige Schrift) published by the Dutch Reformed professors of the Free University of Amsterdam and the Kampen Theological Seminary. The exegesis is therefore governed by the belief in the unity of the Bible. The series is a popular parallel to a more technical series under the same general editorship, of which the first volume (Leviticus) appeared in 1948, (See *Book List*, 1949, p. 21). For the popular commentary on Leviticus in the present series, see *Book List*, 1951, p. 37, and for the first volume on Proverbs, see *Book List*, 1953, p. 37. Here also the editor has provided a new translation, section by section, with each section followed by a useful commentary in which due weight is given to the historical setting. Dr. Noordtzij takes the view that Ezra's arrival in Jerusalem is to be dated 458/7 B.C., and Nehemiah's 445/4 B.C. The argument here is not as full as it might be, and van Hoonacker's theory of a 398 B.C. date for Ezra is rejected to a large extent on the unlikelihood of Ezra having visited Jerusalem during Nehemiah's first visit, an item of the original theory which has long since been abandoned by advocates of the later date.   N.H.S.

NOTH, M. : *Das Buch Josua,* 2nd edition, 1953. (Handbuch zum Alten Testament, 7.) Pp. 152. (Mohr, Tübingen. Price : DM. 13.00, Bound, DM. 15.50.)

The first edition was noted in the *Book List*, 1938, p. 6. This second edition has been expanded, and, in parts, modified especially in the light of Noth's *Überlieferungsgeschlichtlichen Studien* I (1943) and *Überlieferungsgeschichte des Pentateuch* (1948) ; it is dedicated to ' Harold H. Rowley . . . . in Dankbarkeit und Verehrung '.

The historical and geographical notes are but little affected by the progress of knowledge in the intervening period : the two maps are re-produced with the addition of two locations and one alteration in Map I. The changes in the 2nd edition are mainly in terms of literary criticism. Thus the treatment of xiii-xxi. 42 remains substantially the same as that of the first edition.

Joshua is essentially a Deuteronomic work from beginning to end. There are some additions reflecting the style and interests of the Priestly writer, but they are merely additions. The Deuteronomic work proceeded in two stages. The book was a part of a great Deuteronomic history and is not continuous with the Pentateuchal narratives. Use has been made of aetiological traditions and war stories which were gathered at the sanctuaries, especially Gilgal, were originally local in interest and not temporally related, but were made to refer to all Israel under the leadership of Joshua. The material in this fixed form was used by the Deuteronomist.

The same difference in type indicates the basic material of the book and the secondary material ; and the alterations are considerable. Some passages receive greater attention, e.g. v. 13-15. In the account of Jericho and Ai, use has been made of von Rad's *Der Heilige Krieg im alten Israel*. A criticism must be offered about the way in which the running commentary is separated from the text. Thus, the comments on x. 1-43 follow at the end of x. 43 for some seven pages. Yet on each alternate page appears some part of the text of xi. 1-xii. 6, and even the right hand side has the heading appropriate to the text and not to the commentary. The book is obviously of the greatest importance. A.S.H.

VAN DER PLOEG, J. : *Prediker*. (De Boeken van het Oude Testament ; Deel VIII, Book II.). 1953. Pp. 72. (J. J. Romen & Zonen, Roermond en Maaseik. Price : Fl. 3.06 ; Subscription price : Fl. 2.70.)

This commentary follows the general pattern of the series, with introduction, the author's own translation and exegesis of the text. The standard is well maintained, both in translation and exegesis. The editor dates Ecclesiastes in the third century B.C. Passing reference is made to Greek philosophical writings, but no emphasis is laid upon them. The original pessimism is relieved by pious interpolations. It is natural, since the series is a Roman Catholic venture, that more attention is paid to Roman than to Protestant writers. N.H.S.

PRIERO, G. : *Tobia* (La Sacra Bibbia, ed. by S. Garofalo). 1953. Pp. 148. (Marietti, Turin. Price : Lire 650.)

This, though one of the smaller commentaries in the series, is an excellent example of the work at its best. As might be expected, the element of textual reconstruction is prominent, and the decision was taken to follow the readings of the Vatican MSS, examined directly in the light of the two uncials (B and A) that represent it. The critical apparatus is, however, on a generous scale, while falling far short of the very full discussion provided by D. C. Simpson in his edition of Tobit for Charles's *Apocrypha*. The version differs from that provided by A. Vaccari for his rendering in *La Sacra Bibbia* (III, *Libri storici* 2. pp. 231-67) which, rightly described as " condotto con mano maestra ", follows the Sinaitic recension. For the Vulgate text the editor has wisely decided to stress the relation between this and the Old Latin by marking readings proper to the Vulgate in italics. The introduction contains useful chapters on the original language of Tobit and the principal versions, as well as a discussion of the book's historicity, which, after weighing the various opinions, concludes that it is historical in its main lines. A short section on the liturgical use of the book points to the extensive citation of Tobit in the service-books of the Western Rite, no information being given about the Eastern churches. The commentary, if compressed, is well informed and helpful.

J.M.T.B.

PUUKKO, A. F. : *Raamatun selitysteos*. II. *Vanhan Testamentin historiakirjat* (=A Commentary on the Bible. II. The historical books of the O.T.) 1953. Pp. 394. (Werner Söderström Oy, Helsinki-Porvoo.)

This commentary series, of which the first volume was mentioned in this *Book List*, 1953, p. 40, is intended for the general reader. It gives the text in the new Finnish translation at the top of each page with a running commentary below. In accordance with the general scope of the work, textual problems are rarely discussed, the explanations being mainly geographical, archaeological and historical. The author's purpose is above all to explain the facts, not to give a theological interpretation of the text. His attitude towards the texts is that of literary criticism, and questions of history of tradition are not touched upon. The archaeological evidence might perhaps have been utilized a little more, but as a whole the work gives much useful information to those who want substantial knowledge of the facts and places mentioned in the historical books of the O.T.

H.R.

VON RAD, G. : *Das Erste Buch Mose, Genesis Kapitel 25, 19-50, 26.* (Das Alte Testament Deutsch, Vol. 4.) 1953. Pp. 164. (Vandenhoeck & Ruprecht, Göttingen. Price : DM. 5.40, or Subscription price : DM. 4.50.)

This concludes the translation and commentary of the book of Genesis in this series. The earlier parts have been noticed in previous *Book Lists* (1950, p. 40 ; 1952, p. 36). J.N.S.

RICHARDSON, A. : *Genesis I-XI. Introduction and Commentary.*
(Torch Bible Commentaries.) 1953. Pp. 134. (S.C.M. Press. Ltd.,
London. Price : 7s. 6d.)

> This book admirably fulfils the aim of its series, to bring out
> the theological value of the text for the present day reader.
> There is always the danger of re-opening the door to ob-
> scurantism when we " discover " in the O.T. our own developed
> theology, with supporting quotations from the N.T., but
> Richardson is conspicuously fair to his text while, at the
> same time, making the book feel actual throughout. Ten
> short chapters of general introduction to the book take up
> thirty pages, and the commentary proper treats the text in
> twelve sections. D.R.Ap-T.

RIDDERBOS, J. : *De Kleine Profeten.* Deel I : *Hosea, Joel, Amos.*
1952. Pp. 260. Deel II : *Obadja tot Zephanja.* 1949. Pp. 201.
(Kok, Kampen. Price : Fl. 5.90 each.)

> For details of the series of which these two volumes (second
> printing) form a part, see note on Dr. Noordtzij's *Ezra-
> Nehemiah* (p. 39). The position is orthodox throughout.
> Hosea is dated ca. 740 B.C. The problem of the relation to
> each other of chapters i-iii is solved on the basis of saying
> that the first chapter is realistic, the second figurative, and
> the third visionary. Chapters i-iii date from the time of
> Jeroboam II ; iv-vi. 3 from soon after the fall of the House
> of Jehu ; vi. 4-xi. 11 from Pekah to king Hoshea. The editor
> dates the first section of Joel during the time of Joash, with
> chapter iii as probably a later addition. Amos was active at
> approximately the same time as Hosea, but probably a little
> earlier. In the second volume, Obadiah is ca. 586 B.C. The
> editor finds the idea that the Book of Jonah is a fictitious
> narrative in all ways going against the grain. He emphasizes
> Jonah as a type of Christ. A large part of the volume is
> devoted to Micah, to whom the whole of the book is assigned,
> with chapters iii-v later than vi-vii. Nahum is associated
> with the fall of Nineveh (612 B.C.), Habakkuk with the first
> days following 586 B.C., and Zephaniah with the Scythian
> invasion early in the reign of Josiah. N.H.S.

RINALDI, G. : *Le Lamentazioni.* 1953. Pp. 56. (Marietti, Turin.
Price : Lire 200.)

> Not a great deal is to be said about this pleasant little edition
> of Lamentations, which provides a very brief introduction,
> a translation based on the Hebrew, some summaries of the
> content of the chapters, and a compressed commentary.
> The author, who has already made similar renderings of Daniel,
> the Minor Prophets and the books of Maccabees, dedicates it
> to his students of the University of the Sacred Heart, Milan,
> who have taught him so much by their enquiries. Three pages
> of " Note critiche e filologiche " discuss the variant readings
> of the versions. J.M.T.B.

ROBINSON, T. H., and HORST, F. : *Die Zwölf Kleinen Propheten*.
(Handbuch zum Alten Testament, I. Reihe, 14.) 2nd ed. 1954.
Pp. x+276. (Mohr, Tübingen. Price : DM. 19.80 unbound,
22.60 bound.)

> This second edition of the commentary on the Minor Prophets
> in Eissfeldt's Handbuch contains only a few pages more than
> the previous edition, and the translation is reproduced un-
> changed. Nevertheless there has been a substantial revision,
> more particularly in the philological and textual notes, and
> some modifications in the translation have been inserted in
> the notes. Needless to say DSH has been used for the com-
> mentary on Habakkuk. Moreover throughout the work the
> bibliographies have been brought up to date. Owners of the
> earlier edition should not count this edition a superfluity,
> for it is an indispensable tool for the study of the Minor
> Prophets.   H.H.R.

SCHNEIDER, H. : *Das Buch Daniel. Das Buch der Klagelieder. Das
Buch Baruch*. (Herder's Bibelkommentar, IX, 2.) 1954. Pp.
x+166. (Herder, Freiburg im Breisgau. Price : DM. 9.00, or
11.50 bound ; by subscription DM. 7.40 or 9.80 bound.)

> The usual features of this series are found here. There is a new
> translation, followed by a short commentary designed less for
> scholars than for the general reader. The introductions to
> the books are very brief and do not enter into critical questions.
> In the commentary on Daniel it is recognized that the climax
> of several chapters fell primarily in the time of Antiochus IV,
> but by compenetration they are held to have also a fulfilment
> not yet realized.   In chapter ii, the four kingdoms are
> Nebuchadnezzar, Belshazzar, the Medo-Persian, the Macedonian;
> while in chapter vii we are offered the Neo-Babylonian, the
> Medo-Persian, Alexander, and the Macedonian. Darius the
> Mede is identified with Astyages. The deuterocanonical parts
> of the book are naturally included, as this is a Roman Catholic
> commentary.   The poems of Lamentations are thought
> perhaps to derive from Jeremiah. As with other volumes of
> this series, the commentary should prove useful to the readers
> for whom it is designed. Its author is clearly acquainted with
> scholarly work, but is never unmindful of his readers.
>   H.H.R.

SIMON, U. E. : *A Theology of Salvation : a commentary on Isaiah
xl-lv*. 1953. Pp. x+266. (S.P.C.K., London. Price : 25s. 0d.)

> This unusual and controversial commentary on the Second
> Isaiah is written in a style reminiscent of Barth's Commentary
> on the Epistle to the Romans and from a standpoint similar
> to C. C. Torrey's. Like Torrey, and by the use of similar
> critical methods, the author dissociates the prophecy from
> its traditional connection with Cyrus. Unlike Torrey, however,
> he interprets ' the Man from the East ' not as Abraham but
> as the Messiah whose portrait is eventually painted as the
> Suffering Servant, Israel being called upon to celebrate the
> Servant's future appearance and atoning death here and now

in proleptic Messianic feasts. Babylon is interpreted typologically of the powers of this world which are hostile to God and the prophecy is held to be, through and through, non-exclusive and universalist. In line with recent critical opinion the Second Isaiah is regarded as a member of the Isaianic prophetical school and it is suggested that his work issued in the formation of *ḥaburoth* which carried on the Messianic expectations of the great prophet. While it is admitted that the myth and ritual pattern of oriental religion is reflected in the language of the prophecy, it is cogently argued that a clear differentiation is intended between the cyclic rituals of the dying god cults and the historical salvation which Yaḥweh is bringing about through His Messiah.

There is much in the exegetical detail of this book, not to speak of its literary-historical thesis, about which there will be keen controversy. Whatever the issue of such controversy may be, it should be recognised that Mr. Simon's commentary shares with Torrey's great work a deep religious seriousness and represents a vital contribution to Biblical Theology. The insight shown in the following quotation is worth pondering : " God's Being . . . . cannot be known at all unless he communicates himself to man in acts of judging love. Messianic Salvation he appoints as the only valid plane on which theological understanding can operate." N.W.P.

UBACH, B. : *La Biblia, versió dels textos originals i commentari.* Vol. V. *I i II de Samuel.* 1952. Pp. 344. (Monastery of Montserrat. Price : $7.00.)

The great Montserrat edition of the Bible, in which the Vulgate text is printed with a translation and a commentary in Catalan, pursues its course. It is, as usual, splendidly printed, and it is to be emphasized that the version is based on the Hebrew text, which is freely corrected wherever the editor considers this to be necessary. The commentary is always full and adequate, and on matters of special difficulty (such as the meaning of *ṣinnor* in 2 Sam. v. 8) reference is made to Vincent, Desnoyers and other authorities. It is to be hoped that sooner or later, an *editio minor* will be produced for the benefit of those who would like to have the Catalan translation in a less expensive form. J.M.T.B.

LITERARY CRITICISM AND INTRODUCTION
(including History of Interpretation, Canon, and Special Studies)

AALDERS, G.CH. : *Oud-Testamentische Kanoniek.* 1952. Pp. 416. (Kok, Kampen. Price : Fl. 18.50.)

This very well produced Introduction to the O.T., in Dutch, is written from Aalders's well-known standpoint of the inerrancy of Scripture, &c. After a prefatory chapter on his own aims and methods, the author provides one chapter on the canon of the O.T., and then deals with the books individually and as canonical groups, bibliographies being appended in each case.

The books of Isaiah and Zechariah are literary units ; the Pentateuch, though mainly Mosaic, was put together by someone later than Moses but there are no doublets or strands of narrative in it.

Though the arguments are so often headed into the dogmatically necessary pigeon-hole, the book is valuable for its presentation of all that can reasonably be adduced as argument for the author's views, and also for its wide acquaintance with, and quotation of, the relevant literature of all schools. Authors with whom Aalders disagrees are always treated with courtesy.

D.R.Ap-T.

BEEK, M. A. : *Wegen en Voetsporen van het Oude Testament.* 1953. Pp. 388. (W. Gaade N. V., Delft. Price : Fl. 9.60.)

This attractively printed and bound volume is designed to act as an ' Open Sesame ' to the Old Testament. It is a popular introduction in Dutch, well-bound and printed, with forty pages of photographic illustrations, ranging from Egyptian frescoes to the Dead Sea Scrolls, the cave, the jars, and the Isaiah roll. The book is in eighty-six sections, each section dealt with in a lively and interesting way. For example, the book of Ruth is dealt with as a novelette, and Saul's concubine, Rizpah, is described as Israel's Antigone.   N.H.S.

BOCCACCIO, P. and BERARDI, G. : *Servus Jahweh.* 1950. Pp. 32. (Catholic Book Agency, Rome. Price : Lire 300.)

This booklet is a modern " Walton's Polyglott " for the Servant Songs, printing the M.T. and the corresponding LXX, Peshiṭṭa, Vulgate, Targum Jonathan, and versions in seven modern languages. It will be useful for students who do not wish to go beyond the vulgar text of each version. The textual notes provided at the end are very short and in Italian. The variants of Aquila, Theodotion and Symmachus are given, however, and the main variations of A, S, and B are recorded for the LXX. The New Testament citations of the Songs are also listed. The printing has been carefully done, and all texts are vocalized.   D.R.Ap-T.

BRUNO, A. : *Jesaja : Eine rhythmische und textkritische Untersuchung.* 1953. Pp. 254.
Die Bücher Genesis-Exodus : Eine rhythmische Untersuchung. 1953. Pp. 328. (Almqvist & Wiksells, Stockholm. Price : Swedish Kr. 30.00 each.)

Dr. Arvid Bruno, former principal of one of the colleges of Sigtuna in Sweden, now about 75 years old, has with admirable energy continued to devote close attention to the rhythmic-metrical problems of the O.T., earlier demonstrated in his works *Der Rhythmus der alttestamentlichen Dichtung* (1930) and *Das hebräische Epos* (1935). The two new books form the first parts of a larger work comprising " most of the

582

books of the O.T. ", evidently to appear successively and rapidly. (Next announced is the Book of Jeremiah.)

The author's admittedly bad literary-critical starting point of the thirties in matters of textual criticism has now, he tells us, been radically changed owing to the principles laid down by H. S. Nyberg in his *Studien zum Hoseabuche* (1935), thanks to which " ein Wanderer in unsicherem Moorland plötzlich festen Boden unter den Füssen fühlte " (*Isa.*, p. 10). Undoubtedly this means a great improvement, as is to be seen from the vigorous reduction of emendations. But there are still too many of them *metri causa*, and as Dr. Bruno himself admits he really breaks in a definite way the text-critical principles of Nyberg, sacrificing them on the altar of metrics. In these matters the author is endowed with a very special understanding thanks to which he is able to feel and reproduce as poetry also the epic parts of Gen. and Exod. Thus he gives a poetic-rhythmical translation in German of the whole of Gen. except Chs. v, x, and xxxvi, and of Exod. except the law material.

Dr. Bruno's conception of the metrical principles is hardly inferior to that of many others but probably few will follow him in their application. In the work on Isa. there is a short commentary (pp. 243-354), in the work on Gen.-Exod. a shorter one (pp. 312-327), both consisting chiefly of metrical and text-critical discussions. Recent literature is seldom referred to, and it may be more than a coincidence that the reader meets with misprints like Burrow, (*Isa.*, p. 10), and Eissenfeldt, (ib., p. 256). While feeling the greatest admiration for the author's scholarly fervour and with full understanding for what his researches mean to himself as the elixir of life, the reviewer is sorry to be constrained to state that, owing to the subjectivity of the attitude (more or less inherent in the metrical method itself) Dr. Bruno's in themselves very interesting metrical researches are not of the importance for textual criticism which he himself—like most metrical specialists—opines. (Dr. Bruno's books are dealt with in detail by the reviewer, in English, in the next volume of the *Svensk Exegetisk Årsbok*, to appear at the end of 1954.) I.E.

CHOURAQUI, A. : *Le Cantique des Cantiques*. 1953. Pp. 112. (Desclée de Brouwer, Bruges. Price : Belgian Fr. 45.)

This French translation of the Song of Songs is by a Jewish scholar, A. Chouraqui, with an introduction by a Catholic scholar, R. P. Lucien. The latter is concerned to encourage readers to accept the book as allegory and urges that it gives utterance to " the pre-eminence of the love of God for his people and the joy of the latter in knowing that it is beloved of God " (p. 25). The translation is straightforward and betrays nothing of the allegorical interpretation. L.H.B.

COPPENS, J. : *Chronique d'Ancien Testament. Le problème de l'Hexateuque.* (Analecta Lovaniensia Biblica et Orientalia, 2nd series, No. 38.) 1953. Pp. 21. (Publications Universitaires de Louvain, and Desclée de Brouwer, Bruges and Paris. Price : Belgian Fr. 30.)

> In this study we are given a review of recent Pentateuchal Criticism and its continuation into Joshua-Judges, a good deal of which has been critical of the evolutionary hypotheses of the Wellhausen school. It is observed that much recent Catholic scholarship, in its examination of the Pentateuch, is akin to the views of van Hoonacker. A distinction is drawn between the historical and the literary problems. To Moses must be attributed the monotheistic faith, the revelation of the Divine Name and the Decalogue. Literary analysis will distinguish the familiar strata, and they are seen as amplifications of the initial legislation of Moses, the Decalogue. The first four books should be considered apart from Deuteronomy—Judges. The nucleus of the Tetrateuch has been amplified in priestly circles down to post-exilic times. The date of the Deuteronomic work is difficult to assess, although it appears to have been known in the 7th century B.C. One result of recent study is to make evident the greatness of Moses as the dominating influence in all the strata, although not the actual writer of the whole Pentateuch.
>
> The material is presented with a clarity of expression and a precision which characterises the work of Canon Coppens.
>
> A.S.H.

CRIPPS, R. S. : *Two British Interpreters of the Old Testament : Robert Lowth* (1710-1787) *and Samuel Lee* (1783-1852). (Reprinted from the Bulletin of the John Rylands Library, vol. 35, No. 2, March, 1953.) 1953. Pp. 20. (Manchester University Press and The John Rylands Library, Manchester. Price : 2s. 0d.)

> Mr. Cripps began the reading upon which this paper is based with a concern for the application of Old Testament studies to contemporary needs and problems. The resultant study introduces the subject by showing how Lowth in the 18th. century and Lee in the 19th. sought to apply their critical work on the Old Testament to the life of their times. The paper does much more than this, however, for it gives much biographical detail concerning the two scholars and interesting examples of their exegetical and textual work. The paper is here printed as it was read with the result that the reader sometimes misses the full force of what Mr. Cripps has to say. A little careful rewording would have been an advantage.
>
> L.H.B.

DANIEL, R. T. : *How to Study the Psalms : Based on an Exposition of Twelve Favorite Psalms.* 1953. Pp. 272. (Revell, Westwood, N.J. Price : $3.00.)

> Dr. Daniel, who is an Associate Member of our Society, offers to Ministers and general readers a simple devotional and exegetical treatment of Psalms i, viii, xv, xix, xxiii, xxxii, xl, xlvi, li, xc, xci, and ciii. No questions of reading are

discussed and the English Version is the unquestioned basis of the exposition. The commentary is verse by verse, and there is an Introduction on Hebrew Poetry and a concluding chapter on the teachings of the selected psalms. Psalm xix is held to be a unity and Psalm li to be a Davidic psalm later adapted for use in worship. Psalm xc is held to reflect the experiences of the Hebrews near the end of the wilderness wanderings, while Psalm xlvi is held to spring from the deliverance from Sennacherib. Dr. Daniel takes no account of recent work which concentrates on the cultic background and uses of the psalms.

H.H.R.

DIEM, H. : *Das Problem des Schriftkanons*. (Theol. Studien herausg. von Karl Barth. Heft 32.) 1952. Pp. 24. (Evangelischer Verlag A. G., Zollikon, Zürich. Price : Swiss Fr. 2.10.)

This lecture confines itself to the theological problem of the authority of the canon of scripture for the Protestant Christian. The O.T. is nowhere specifically discussed. Diem would base the claim to canonicity for any passage on the general testimony of the rest of scripture, the possibility of preaching it, and the consensus of the church.

D.R.Ap-T.

EHRENBERG, H. : *Hiob der Existentialist*. 1952. Pp. 70. (Lambert Schneider, Heidelberg. Price : DM. 3.50.)

This is not so much a study of the book of Job, as a representation of the teaching of the book in existentialist terms to meet the condition of 19th. and 20th. century man. The existentialism is not that of Heidegger or Sartre, but approximates to that of Marcel. It is presented in two parts, Dialogues 1 and 2, and 3-5. The climax of Job is seen to be chapter xix. Elihu is accorded a considerable importance. The book is offered under the conviction that ' unsere Zeit ist Hiob-reif geworden.' The Dramatis Personae are : Job, Everyman (the older generation, ' ohne einen endgiltigen geistigen Charakter '), the Reader (present-day youth ' mit dem unbestechlichen Willen zur Entschiedenheit '), and the spirit of Elihu. The voice of God is heard, or half-heard, through Job.

A.S.H.

FEUILLET, A. : *Le Cantique des Cantiques : étude de théologie biblique et réflexions sur une méthode d'exégèse*. (Collection " Lectio divina ". No. 10.) 1953. Pp. 258. (Editions du Cerf, Paris. Price : Fr. 580.)

The chief aim of this work is to draw attention to what the author believes to be one of the greatest revelations of divine love in the Bible, and also to justify the method of parallelisms —literary, historical and theological—for exegetical purposes. The prophetic figure of the marriage of Yahweh and Israel is in the forefront of the discussion, and an important place is given to indications as to the mentality of the post-exilic Jewish community which are to be found in contemporary prophetical writings. The author's conclusion is that the Song can only be rightly understood if it is interpreted allegorically. His work owes much to A. Robert's *Le Cantique des Cantiques* (1951). The Song, which is thought to be a literary unity, consisting of five distinct poems (i.5-ii.7, ii. 8-iii. 5, iii. 6-v. 1, v. 2-vi. 3, vi. 4-viii. 3) is assigned to the middle of the fifth century B.C. It tells of Yahweh's love for his wife Israel, of her faithlessness, of her suffering in exile, and of her restoration. The mentality of the author of the Song was that of the prophets, and he was well versed in prophetical literature. Without the prophets, more especially the Second Isaiah, the Song cannot be understood. Examples of the author's interpretations are—in i. 5 the wife, Israel, is " black " because she laboured in exile beneath the burning sun (cp. Lam. iv. 7f.) ; in i. 6 " my mother's children " are the Chaldaeans, and " mine own vineyard " is Palestine ; in ii. 15 " the little foxes " are the enemies of Israel in Palestine, viz., the Samaritans, Ammonites, etc. ; iii. 6 relates to the arrival at Jerusalem of a company of returning exiles in 538 B.C. (cp. Is. lii. 8f.) ; and in iv. 8 " the lions' dens " and " the mountains of the leopards " denote the captivity (cp. Jer. iv. 7, v. 6, l. 17). D.W.T.

GOITEIN, S. D. : *Two Essays on the Book of Jeremiah* (*Shtē massoth al sēpher Yirmiyyah*). (' Iyyunim for teachers series, 13.) 1953. Pp. 39. (Department of Youth 'Aliyah, Education Department, Jerusalem.)

These two essays are intended for the upper forms of schools, and will therefore perhaps interest teachers of Scripture. In the first, entitled *The Arraignment of Jeremiah*, Prof. Goitein makes the point that Jeremiah recognised the jurisdiction of his judges, and that there is no trace in chap. xxvi of the idea, prominent in later Judaism, Christianity, and Islam, that to do a prophet to death is more reprehensible than the murder of a common man (p. 13). The second essay discusses *Jeremiah's Attitude to Babylon*. The Hebrew is lucid, but the intending reader will be spared the waste of some energy and time if he is warned to make a mark that line 2 on p. 6 should in fact be line 2 on p. 7. R.J.L.

GORDIS, R. : *The Song of Songs : a Study, Modern Translation and Commentary*. (Texts and Studies of the Jewish Theological Seminary of America, No. 20.) 1954. Pp. xii+108. (Jewish Theological Seminary of America, New York. Price : $2.50.)

The major part of this work consists of a new translation of the Song of Songs, each separate poem, according to the translator's division of the book, being given a separate short introduction. The translation is preceded by a brief but valuable Introduction to the whole book, and followed by notes. In the notes a knowledge of Hebrew is presupposed, and Hebrew type is freely used. The Introduction offers a rapid sketch of the history of interpretation, with special reference to the cultic theory, which is rejected, and the

literal interpretation as a collection of love songs, which
is adopted by the author. Dr. Gordis thinks that iii. 6-11
is a royal wedding song going back to the reign of Solomon.
He denies any unity of authorship or date in the collection,
and maintains that it contains material which spans five
centuries. The whole forms a valuable commentary which
will be studied with profit by future students, whatever their
view of the date and authorship, or literary *genre*, of this
most disputed book.   H.H.R.

JEPSEN, A. : *Die Quellen des Königsbuches*. 1953. Pp. 118+2.
(Niemeyer, Halle. Price : DM. 12.30.)

This is a new attempt to analyse the material of the book of
Kings into sources and redactional material, and to distinguish
the purposes which governed the minds of the authors and
redactors. Part I is devoted to analysis ; Part II to a consideration of the sources and redactions ; and Part III to an
estimation of the distinctive character of Israelite historiography. At the end of the book, two pages are added, setting
out the results of the analysis in schematic form.

The early sources are seen to be : a synchronistic chronicle
of the kings of Israel and Judah (S), and annals of these
kings (A). These have been edited by priests of the Jerusalem
shrine, early in the exilic period, preparing for a return from
Exile (R.I) ; then by the ' nebiistic ' or deuteronomic school
(R.II), which interprets Israel's history in terms of the
Exodus tradition. The origin of this work is found in the
Benjamite clan, in Palestine, during the Exile. The third
redaction is of Levitical origin (R.III) ; it is not considerable,
but is to be found especially in 1 Kings xii. 31-xiii. 34 ; 2
Kings xvii. 24-33, 41 ; xiii. 16-20. This redaction comes from
the late 6th century. While the analysis may seem over-nice
at times, it is a valuable contribution to the study of Kings.
The closing section, with its comparison of Israelite and
contemporary historiography, makes clear the distinctive
quality of the Old Testament material, where alone there is an
attempt to see the inner relationship of events in terms of the
revelation committed to Israel. This feature marks both the
early sources and the later redactions.   A.S.H.

KORNFELD, W. : *Studien zum Heiligkeitsgesetz*. 1952. Pp. 158.
(Herder, Vienna. Price : S. 53.)

The first half of this work is a study of the Code of Holiness
along the lines of the now familiar " formgeschichtliche "
approach to the legal codes of the Old Testament. The second
half is devoted to the content and social context of those
laws which deal with breach of marriage and proscribed
sexual relations, and, in the nature of the case, is of a more
anthropological character. The author pays due attention
throughout to the comparative material which is available,
in particular, from the ancient Near East, and on the whole
he offers in this monograph a selection from his studies in
this field which is of so constructive a kind that one is led
to hope that still more may find its way into print.   A.R.J.

KUHL, C. : *Die Entstehung des Alten Testaments.* (Sammlung Dalp, Band 26.) 1953. Pp. 408. (Francke Verlag, Bern, and Lehnen Verlag, München. Price : Swiss Fr. 10.80.)

This introduction to the O.T. is written in such a way that non-Hebraists may read easily. The opening chapter discusses the authority, Canon, criticism and literary character of the O.T. and the subsequent chapters discuss the several books in the order of the Hebrew Bible. The critical and historical problems are honestly faced and discussed, with full re-cognition of recent literature, and throughout the book the author has maintained a high level of religious understanding. The notes, which are assembled at the end of the book (pp. 341-386) contain a full bibliography and enable the author to dispense with references to modern scholars in the body of the book.　　　　　　　　　　　　　　　　　　L.H.B.

MARGOLIS, M. L. : *La Formation de la Bible Hébraïque,* French Tr. by M. Liber. 1953. Pp. 100.) Libraire d'Amerique et d'Orient, Adrien-Maisonneuve, Paris. Price : Fr. 360.)

An authorized translation of the well-known and highly commendable little handbook, *The Hebrew Scriptures in the Making* by the late Septuagint expert, Professor Margolis, which was first published in 1922, and reprinted in 1943 and 1948. The translation is clear and readable, and even the absence of an index, as is supplied in the original, is not embarrassing. In a short preface the translator narrates the story of the book's first appearance, and tells something of the author's eminence.

As the book seems to have escaped notice in the *Book List*, a brief indication of its contents may be made here. It is an intro-ductory study to the tri-partite Hebrew canon. The orthodox (' traditional ') view is outlined, as is also the Critical (' untraditional '), and the author's standpoint, not altogether coinciding with either, is that all three sections grew contem-poraneously but independently. The exclusion of Apocrypha represents the supremacy of Pharisaism.　　　　　　B.J.R.

MORIARTY, F. L. : *Foreword to the Old Testament Books.* 1954. Pp. x+115+3 Maps. (Weston College Press, Weston, Mass. Price : $1.00.)

This is an excellent brief Introduction, written by a Roman Catholic, and therefore including the Deutero-canonical books. Its standpoint is cautiously critical. Daniel is dated in the second century. Deutero-Isaiah and Trito-Isaiah are recognized, but the whole of Isaiah i-xxxix appear to be attributed to Isaiah. The four main Pentateuchal sources are recognized. Ruth is dated in the seventh century, and the Chronicler about 400 B.C. There is no indication that the book of Job contains secondary elements. Several pages at the end contain a Glossary of terms which are explained for the reader.　　　　　　　　　　　　　　　　　　H.H.R.

NIELSEN, E. : *Oral Tradition : a Modern Problem in Old Testament Introduction*, with a Foreword by H. H. Rowley. (Studies in Biblical Theology, No. 11.) 1954. Pp. 102. (S.C.M. Press, London. Price : 7s. 0d.)

This eminently useful little book by a young Danish scholar is an expanded version of three articles which appeared in *Dansk Teologisk Tidsskrift*. It is probably the best introduction (from the traditio-historical side) to the much-debated subject with which it deals. The book begins with an admirable survey of recent literature, showing how the Scandinavian traditio-historical approach differs from earlier estimates of oral tradition. The writer then discusses the general character of oral tradition in the ancient world, and the interplay between oral and written tradition. In the third chapter he investigates the evidence for the use of both methods in ancient Israel. Finally he considers the bearing of *Jeremiah* xxxvi on the whole question, and applies the method to *Micah* iv, v, and *Genesis* vi-ix. The furnishing of such actual examples of the method is one of the chief merits of this study. Notice is also taken (*passim*) of some of the criticisms which have been made of the theories here supported. More might perhaps have been said on this head ; and an additional chapter, summing up and answering such objections, would have enhanced the value of this commendable work.   G.W.A.

NOTH, M. : *Das Geschichtsverständnis der alttestamentlichen Apokalyptik.* (Arbeitsgemeinschaft für Forschung des Landes Nordrhein-Westfalen. Heft 21.) 1954. Pp. 26. (Westdeutscher Verlag, Köln und Opladen. Price : DM. 2.20.)

This brief study is concerned with the interpretation of the vision of the statue in Daniel ii and that of the four beasts in Daniel vii. The four metals of the former, which originally signified four world epochs, and the four grotesque beasts of the latter, which to some extent have their counterparts in the plastic art and in the murals of ancient Mesopotamia, were by the second century B.C. well-known traditional symbols, and are used by the writer of these visions to represent a cycle of four (*die runde Vierzahl*) kingdoms, which are spoken of, sometimes as successive, and sometimes as contemporaneous, a cycle which is about to be completed in his day, because the time allotted to the fourth, Greece, is now short and God's rule is about to be established. Noth seeks to show that Old Testament Apocalyptic used traditional symbols but emptied them of their original significance, and that it interprets history, not " as a movement advancing steadily to a climax ", but " as a series of changeful manifestations of power until God intervenes ". What gives to world history, according to Old Testament Apocalyptic, its final unity and its meaning, is its opposition to God's rule.
                                                                                        J.M.

*Paterson, J. : *The Book that is Alive : Studies on the Old Testament Life and Thought as set forth by the Hebrew Sages.* 1954. Pp. xii + 196. (Scribner, New York. Price : $3.50.)

Professor Paterson's books on the prophets and the psalms have now been followed by an equally good book on the Wisdom literature, written for a wide circle of readers. There is an introductory chapter on the vitality that marks Hebrew thought and speech, and another on the growth of the Canon. The books of Proverbs, Job and Ecclesiastes are then treated, rather in a general expository way than along lines of Higher Criticism, though the whole rests on sound scholarly work. There is a chapter on the didactic psalms, dealing especially with the growth of faith in a worthwhile afterlife. The treatment of the varieties of fool in Proverbs is particularly good, and the whole book is well written.   H.H.R.

Rendtorff, R. : *Die Gesetze in der Priesterschrift. Eine gattungs-geschichtliche Untersuchung.* (Forschungen zur Religion und Literatur des Alten und Neuen Testaments. N.F. 44. Heft. Der ganzen Reihe, 62. Heft.) 1954. Pp. vi + 80. (Vandenhoeck & Ruprecht, Göttingen. Price : DM. 6.80.)

This short but thorough-going and useful analysis of parts of the Priestly Code on form-critical lines is in keeping with the basic principles of this approach as laid down by Alt, von Rad and Rabast, and by way of a qualified amplification of Begrich's thesis in *Werden und Wesen.* The analysis is limited in the first instance to Lev. vi-vii, xi-xv, and then extended to some Law-writing interspersed in P narrative material, Ex. xii, Lev. xvi, Num. v, vi, xix. Rendtorff's conclusions are that Begrich's Priestly *Da'at* (instructions regarding the cult) contains a sub-section which deals with ritual and which is intended for public recital. The actual *Da'at*, he continues, reflects in its literary forms, those processes by which it may be possible to reconstruct their evolution, and the author thinks that in this way a new approach is opened out for the study of cult and ritual in the Pentateuch. As a *Vorarbeit* to this end, the present volume is distinctly promising. The book closes with a bibliography, and a short slip containing errata is included.

B.J.R.

*Robinson, T. H. : *The Old Testament : A Conspectus.* (The Colet Library of Modern Christian Thought and Teaching.) 1953. Pp. 168. (Duckworth, London. Price : 8s. 6d.)

True to its name, it gives a rapid survey of the contents of the Old Testament by one who is well fitted to do so with authority. Indications of date, authorship and historical setting are given as the summary proceeds. Brevity has meant that sometimes, as with Joel, books receive scantier treatment than they deserve.   L.H.B.

Rowley, H. H. : *The Book of Ezekiel in Modern Study*. (Reprinted from *Bulletin of the John Rylands Library*, vol. 36, No. 1, September, 1953.) Pp. 46. (Manchester University Press and The John Rylands Library, Manchester. Price : 3s. 6d.)

This article concentrates on three interrelated questions : the unity of the book of Ezekiel, the date of its composition, and the place where the prophet exercised his ministry. After a detailed survey and judicious appraisal of answers which have been given to these questions during this century, and more particularly since the publication of Hölscher's work on Ezekiel in 1924, Rowley gives his own reasoned conclusion that the contents of the book are in the main from Ezekiel himself (secondary elements being relatively few), that Ezekiel's prophetic ministry was carried on wholly in Babylon in the years preceding and following the fall of Jerusalem, and that his oracles were compiled and edited, as were the three other great prophetic collections, in the fifth or fourth century B.C. Due weight is given to the strong impression of a single personality throughout the book, and there are some interesting remarks on the prophet's psychology. Over and above the value of the text of the article itself, tribute must be paid to the bibliographical value of the characteristically wealthy documentation presented in the footnotes.

F.F.B.

Snaith, N. H. : *Mercy and Sacrifice : A Study of the Book of Hosea*. 1953. Pp. 126. (S.C.M. Press, London. Price : 7s. 6d.)

In this characteristic study of Hosea Dr. Snaith expresses decided views on a number of much discussed issues. He thinks it probable that Hosea was the first of the canonical prophets, slightly antedating Amos. He also thinks he was the first non-cultic and non-ecstatic prophet, who spoke by direct Divine inspiration. It is very doubtful if these clear-cut lines of division can be made. On the marriage of Hosea he holds that Gomer was a pure woman at the time of her marriage who afterwards sank, and chapter iii he holds to be a late inauthentic composition which may be ignored in the discussion of the question (on p. 29 there is a curious inversion in the passage dealing with the prophetic literary types). He favours the extreme school on the prophetic attitude to sacrifice, though he allows that Hosea may not have condemned it absolutely. Although the reviewer is less certain on all these questions he finds Dr. Snaith's book to be important and valuable, and to contain many good things, and to offer a welcome exposition of the prophetic view of the essence of religion. The selective inclusion of Proper Names in the Index does not seem to follow any principle. H.H.R.

Steinmann, J. : *Le Prophète Ézéchiel et les débuts de l'exil*. (Lectio Divina, No. 13.) 1953. Pp. 324. (Les Éditions du Cerf, Paris. Price : Fr. 870.)

Here we are given a translation of the whole book of Ezekiel, but completely rearranged, partly in accordance with the chronological order of the prophecies, and partly (as in the cases of prophetic symbolism) by some other principle. The author follows in the main Bertholet's view of the prophet's career, though he does not argue the case for this. He thinks he prophesied in Palestine until 585 and then in Babylonia. In a brief introduction recent views on Ezekiel are incompletely and rather cursorily surveyed. Brief textual notes justify textual emendations and a short paragraph of commentary follows each translated passage. The following passages are classed as secondary oracles : xxvii. 3a, 9b-25, xxxi. 10-18, xxxii. 28-32, xxiv. 19-23, xxvi. 19-21, xxviii. 20-23, xxix. 9b-16, xxx. 1-19, xxxii. 9-16, xxxvi. 13f., 37 f., xxviii. 24, 25 f., xxix. 21, xxxiv. 25-30, xvi. 44-62, xliii. 10-17, 18-27, xl. 38-43, xliv. 26-31, xlv. 18-20, xlvi. 1-3, 8-10, xlvii. 22 f., and the Gog oracles, while x. 6-17, 20-22 is held to be the work of an editor. The book is believed to have been prepared in part during the period of the exile, but to have been subsequently added to. There are two useful chapters on Ezekiel as man, prophet, author and poet, and as priest and theologian.   H.H.R.

WESTERMANN, C. : *Das Loben Gottes in den Psalmen*. 1953. Pp. 124. (Evangelische Verlagsanstalt, Berlin. Price : DM. 6.50.)

The greater part of this work is devoted to an analysis of the literary forms of the Psalms (complete with tables) of so painstaking a kind that one is left regretting that so much industry should yield so little that seems rewarding to the patient reader. The author's main thesis appears to be that the *Sitz im Leben* of the Psalms as literary types must be found in some vague urge to praise God for the experience of His intervention in history, and that any further attempt to define the *Sitz im Leben* with greater precision (e.g. in terms of the cultus) is comparatively worthless. This may help one to read the Psalter more devotionally ; but to the reviewer, who wishes that he could say that he himself was so helped, it seems to be a counsel of despair for those who seek to read the Psalter with increased understanding.   A.R.J.

YOUNG, E. J. : *An Introduction to the Old Testament*. 1953. Pp. 414. (Tyndale Press, London. Price : 18s. 6d.)

The fourth printing of this book (whose first edition was reviewed in the *Book List*, 1951, p. 52), has now been marketed in an English edition at a substantially lower price than its American counterpart. The author's learning is considerable, and he has a wide acquaintance with views which he does not share. He is always courteous, and usually fair, to those with whom he disagrees. His own positions are conservative in the extreme. Esther is regarded as strictly historical, and the Song of Songs is held to be of Solomonic authorship. Even the ascriptions of psalms to David are held to be authentic. While the reviewer differs widely from the author's positions, he regards this as the best conservative Introduction now available in English.   H.H.R.

ASENSIO, F. : *Yahweh y su Pueblo : contenido teológico en la historia biblica de la elección.* (Analecta Gregoriana, Vol. lviii, sect. A, No. 8.) 1953. Pp. 254. (Gregorian University, Rome. Price : 26s. 0d.)

> The author rightly asserts in his preface that the history of the chosen nation presents many facets, and some of these are considered in the present treatise. After a first chapter on the passage from universalism to election, further chapters consider divine election in the patriarchal history and in the Mosaic dispensation. A fourth chapter is concerned with the various aspects of the presence of Yahweh, and a fifth studies Yahweh, the land and the people of the land. A final chapter entitled " Trayectoria de una formula " treats of the continuity of the election principle, the Messianic aspect, the restoration of the elect people after the exile, and the prophetic succession that ends with Zechariah. The bibliography seems to be reasonably full ; some use is made of Rowley's *Biblical Doctrine of Election*. A good deal of Hebrew type is used for quotations and key-words ; it is unfortunate that the pointing is not invariably very clear. The book is an admirably lucid statement by a scholar whose *Misericordia et Veritas* has already proved his competence in such studies.   J.M.T.B.

BRIGHT, J. : *The Kingdom of God : The Biblical Concept and its Meaning for the Church.* 1953. Pp. 288. (Abingdon-Cokesbury Press, New York and Nashville. Price : $3.75.)

> The author is Professor of Hebrew at Union Theological Seminary, Richmond, Va., and a former pupil of W. F. Albright, to whom the book is dedicated and the influence of whose teaching is evident. The development of the idea of the kingdom of God is traced throughout the O.T. from Moses onwards, with emphasis on the Davidic achievement and expectation, the Isaianic remnant, Jeremiah's new covenant and supremely on the Servant of Yahweh. Bright regards the ' fluid ' interpretation of the Servant passages as the only one that does justice to the evidence, and finds their fulfilment in Jesus and the Church. His book is not intended to be a contribution to O.T. scholarship, although it is soundly based on such scholarship ; he addresses himself in the main to the Christian Church to-day, with more particular reference to the religious situation in America. In this regard he shows himself a true son of the prophets. Among points of O.T. interest are his tracing Israel's monotheism, with the covenant-idea, the decalogue and aniconic worship, back to Moses ; his view that Isa. xl-lxvi is substantially a unity (Isa. lxi. 1-3 ; lxii. 1, 6 f., are reckoned along with the Servant songs) ; his identification (following Gressmann) of the four beasts of Dan. vii. 3 ff. with the four parts into which Alexander's empire was divided. The reviewer notes with sympathy that Bright confesses himself unable to keep his mind made upon the chronological relation of Ezra and Nehemiah.   F.F.B.

BUCK, F. : *Die Liebe Gottes beim Propheten Osee.* 1953. Pp. vi+86. Tipografia Pio X, Rome. Price : Lire 900.)

This pamphlet contains two revised chapters of a doctoral dissertation submitted to the Biblical Faculty of the Pontifical Institute. An Index of Contents to the complete dissertation is provided, by which it appears that there are seven chapters in all, together with an introduction and an epilogue. The two chapters here printed deal respectively with ' The Presentation of the Marriage-Relationship between Yahweh and Israel ' and ' The Qualities of God's Love according to Hosea '. Fr. Buck (rightly) takes quite literally the account of Hosea's marriage to Gomer and her unfaithfulness to him—an experience which gave him an unprecedented insight into the love of God for His people. Certain limitations in Hosea's viewpoint are admitted—e.g. he does not envisage God's love for the individual or His love for other nations than Israel. But Fr. Buck insists that Hosea is distinctively and pre-eminently a preacher of Yahweh's love—a love which is not exhausted in the divine election but persists even when the elect are unfaithful and will not be content short of ultimate redemption. Even the wrath and judgement of Yahweh subserve the final purposes of His love.   F.F.B.

CARPENTER, S. C. : *Priest and Prophet.* 1953. Pp. 16. (S.P.C.K., London. Price : 2s. 0d.)

As a popular lecture which purports to examine the functions of priest and prophet in the Old Testament and relate them to those of the Christian ministry to-day, this pamphlet will probably enable the reader to while away a few minutes quite pleasantly ; but its value for students of the Old Testament may be gauged by the claim that " our scholars now place the prophets in close association with the cultus. And that not only ' the other prophets ', but the reform-prophets."
            A.R.J.

CHURCH, BROOKE P. : *The Private Lives of the Prophets and the Times in Which They Lived.* 1953. Pp. 246. (Rinehart & Company, New York. Price : $3.00.)

The book seeks to present in popular and ' acceptable ' form, the teaching of the prophets Amos, Hosea, Isaiah, Jeremiah, Ezekiel (Ezekial in the publisher's ' blurb '), Second Isaiah, together with details, largely imaginary, of their private lives. The standpoint of the authoress will be recognised from the statement that the prophets ' did not look into the future. They were preachers and reformers . . . . men like you and me, the " commentators " of antiquity '. After a brief survey of the prophetic movement from Moses' day, in which anything remotely supernatural is explained away, each of the prophets is discussed at some length. The ' sermons ' of Amos are concerned with Justice, not Mercy. ' If Amos had a family, one imagines that it was run on the lines of a Puritan household of the 17th century. Certainly a man with a one-track mind and no sense of humour would not make a genial husband and father.' Hosea ' added to Yahweh the quality of love,' and ' preferred to stay at home, perhaps to read a book or study.' The crisis in Jeremiah's life is associated with a tragic love affair from which he never recovered; the violent prayers of ix. 18 ff., and xii. 1 ff. were the immediate outcome. Deutero-Isaiah is dated 425-400 B.C., and the prophet produced his 27 philosophical poems ' in a garden or on a roof ' in Judaea. He was the spokesman of a group which ' met and talked over the great questions of the day.'

The question remains : How could such men as are described in this book have been in any way responsible for the stimulus and strength which the people of God have received from them down to the present day?   A.S.H.

CLOSEN, G. E. : *Clefs pour la Sainte Écriture*, French Tr. by R. Avice, with a Foreword by J. Décarreaux. 1954. Pp. 312. (Beyaert, Bruges. Price : Belgian Fr. 115.)

> The German text of this book was issued in 1939 and reviewed in the *Book List*, in 1946 (p. 40). It consists of 22 chapters in which Old Testament passages are examined. The author is acquainted with the work of scholarship, but he writes for a wide public, with a practical and theological aim. The book falls into three sections dealing with the world of the patriarchs, some passages in the prophets, and a number of psalms. Throughout the author is concerned to show how the Old Testament points on to the New, and his choice of passages is determined by this interest—e.g. the sacrifice of Isaac, the Servant Songs, the New Covenant, the Messianic psalms, the Son of Man in Daniel. The author is conservative critically, especially on the date of Daniel, but his primary interest is not critical but expository.   H.H.R.

CRIADO, R. : *La investigación sobre el valor del nombre divino en el Antiguo Testamento*. (Estudios Ecclesiasticos, Vol. 26.) 1952. Pp. 313-352 and 435-452. (Reprinted from Estudios Ecclesiasticos, Madrid.)

> The present brochure of some sixty pages in all is not, it must be emphasized, a full-sized treatise on the meaning or import of the divine name in the Old Testament. It is no more than the introduction to the author's thesis on this subject, and is in the main a summary of the positions adopted by the scholars who have preceded Criado in discussing this important matter. His own views are reserved for treatment in the thesis proper. From this introductory section one can gather that, in the author's opinion, O. Grether in his *Name und Wort Gottes im Alten Testament* has given us " la más penetrante monografía sobre *sem Yahve* " (p. 435), and that W. Eichrodt may be regarded as Grether's " continuator " (" Eichrodt resume confuerza propia los resultades de Grether . . " (p. 446)). Criado seems to have taken pains to state fairly the views of those whose works he summarizes, but his own philological and doctrinal handling of the issues will be better seen in the major part of the thesis, which is still, apparently, unpublished.
>   J.M.T.B.

DAVIES, G. HENTON : *The Approach to the Old Testament.* 1953. Pp. 24. (Carey Kingsgate Press, London. Price : 1s. 6d.)

This is Professor Henton Davies's Inaugural Lecture, delivered in May in the University of Durham. It suggests that the true approach to the Old Testament must always include a recognition of the total context of the life of the people of God to whom these words were given. The location of Palestine brought Israel within the political movements, culture and religion of many peoples and empires and much was assimilated. Yet there is also a distinctive quality which arises from Israel's monotheistic faith and sense of history. Finally, the Old Testament must be interpreted in the light of its fulfilment in the New. Throughout the Bible the theme of ' the Tabernacling Presence ' claims man's worship.

A.S.H.

DRONKERT, K. : *De Molochdienst in het Oude Testament* (with a summary in English). 1953. Pp. 150. (Drukkerij " Luctor et Emergo ", Leiden. Price : Fl. 7.50.)

This work offers a full study of the Old Testament and external evidence on the worship of ' Moloch ', defending the traditional view that Moloch is the name of a deity, and in particular rejecting the view of Eissfeldt. The author is apparently unaware of Eissfeldt's paper read to our Society, and published in *PEQ* in 1947, or some of his statements would have been modified. He defends the MT pointing on the ground that it finds support in the LXX and in Acts vii. 43, though it is hard to see how MT can be a Proper Name, since it has the definite article. While its conclusions are sometimes less secure than the author appears to suppose, his work has real value for its assembly and discussion of the evidence, and future students of the question will be glad to make use of it.

H.H.R.

EHRLICH, E. L. : *Der Traum im Alten Testament.* (Beihefte zur Zeitschrift für die Alttestamentliche Wissenschaft, 73.) 1953. Pp. viii+180. (Alfred Töpelmann, Berlin. Price : DM. 20.00.)

The reader is here offered an examination of all those passages in the Old Testament which have a bearing on the subject of dreams, the material being dealt with in terms of incubation, dreams which need to be interpreted, dreams which convey a direct message from God, dreams as a medium of revelation, the use of dreams in similes, and, finally, the deliberate rejection of dreams as a valid means of revelation. The author pays due attention to questions of literary criticism, and adds, for full measure, reproductions of the Old Testament narratives in the work of Josephus, the Midrashim and the Koran. He also includes a certain amount of comparative material of varying worth from the cultures of the ancient world, the so-called " primitives " of our own day, general folklore and modern psychology. The chief value of the work, however, is to be found in the careful way in which the author has marshalled the Old Testament data.

A.R.J.

EICHRODT, W. : *Krisis der Gemeinschaft in Israel.* Rektoratsrede gehalten an der Jahresfeier der Universität Basel am 27. November, 1953. (Basler Universitätsreden 33. Heft.) 1953. Pp. 22. (Verlag Helbing & Lichtenhahn, Basel. Price : Swiss Fr. 2.50.)

> This lecture by one of the world's leading scholars in the field of O.T. Theology will receive careful study and would be still more welcome in an expanded form. Very briefly the thesis is that Ezekiel was not a rabid individualist but called individuals into a new community based on a law whose sanction is in the hearts and minds of men. Chapters xl—xlviii, and also the humanly restored Davidic kingdom, are regarded as the work of an epigone.　　　　　　　　　　　D.R.Ap-T.

EISSFELDT, O. : *Der Gott Karmel.* (Sitzungsb. d. deutschen Akademie d. Wissenschaften, Berlin.) 1953. Pp. 48, Ill. 9 on Pl. VI+sketch-map of Syria/Palestine. (Akademie-Verlag, Berlin. Price : DM. 4.)

> This monograph on the existence and identity of a god Carmel worshipped on Mt. Carmel apparently had its origin in the discovery described by Avi-Yonah (*Israel Exploration Journal*, ii, 1952), of a stone foot dedicated to Zeus Heliopoleites Carmelos. It covers therefore some of the same ground as Galling's contribution to the Alt Festschrift, which is briefly reviewed in a postscript. Most of Eissfeldt's arguments appear to be incontrovertible in the light of the supporting evidence adduced ; he also maintains the substantial unity of 1 Kgs. xvi. 29-xix. 18 against both Alt and Gunkel. In Elijah's day he considers it probable that the god Carmel was identified with the Tyrian Baal-Shamem, or possibly Melcart.
> 　　　　　　　　　　　　　　　　　　　　　D.R.Ap-T.

ELLISON, H. L. : *The Centrality of the Messianic Idea for the Old Testament.* 1953. Pp. 24.

WENHAM, J. W. : *Our Lord's View of the Old Testament.* 1953. Pp. 32.

MURRAY, J. : *The Covenant of Grace.* 1954. Pp. 32. (Tyndale Press, London. Price : 1s. 6d. each.)

> These are the Tyndale Lectures for 1953 on the Old Testament, the New Testament and Biblical Theology respectively. While Mr. Ellison's is a relatively slight treatment of its theme, due to the conditions of its delivery, it rests on a good acquaintance with modern literature, and treats of the main messianic categories of the Old Testament. It is supplied with notes at the end and references to a number of works. Mr. Wenham's lecture shows that Jesus treated the Old Testament stories as history, and that he accepted the Old Testament as authoritative and inspired. That inspiration is described as verbal, but the lecturer did not deal with the contradictions in the Old Testament, presumably because they did not arise in the references of Jesus. But they are of importance for the conclusions the lecturer wished his hearers to draw. Mr. Murray's lecture is an excellent, though necessarily brief, study of the meaning of ' covenant ' in the Old Testament

and in the New, both of covenant as between man and man and covenant as between God and man. This lecture has some footnotes and references to literature. It is a pity that the Tyndale lectures do not provide for some much more profound and fundamental treatment of these great subjects. H.H.R.

ELLUL, J. : *L'Homme et l'Argent* (*Nova et Vetera*). 1954. Pp. 220. (Delachaux et Niestlé, Neuchâtel. Price : Swiss Fr. 5.50.)

About one fifth of this book is devoted to the subject of wealth in the Old Testament, and it is argued that whereas riches are regarded as a blessing—in contrast to the New Testament where riches are condemned and personified as Mammon and set over against God—the rich stand often condemned. Some righteous rich figure in the Old Testament, such as Abraham, Solomon and Job, but the temptations of riches are perceived and men who fall into them are denounced. The author is concerned primarily with the world of to-day and the teaching on money which should be given to children.

H.H.R.

ELWERT, M. : *Die Grundhaltung des Frommen gegen Gott, nach den Zeugnissen des Alten Testaments*. Microfilm. 1952. Pp. vii + 166. (Vandenhoeck and Ruprecht, Göttingen. Price : DM. 10.40.)

Discusses the attitude of men to God ; their faith built upon experience of God's Grace, their fear, humility, obedience, trust and prayerful dependence. The foreword says that the book is an expanded form of a prize essay written first in 1936-37 and this is borne out by its form and style. There seems to have been a long interval between writing and publication : the bibliography has a note to the effect that it was prepared before the publication (in 1939) of Teil 3 of Eichrodt's *Theologie des Alten Testaments*. (The typescript shows many corrections and other blemishes.)

L.H.B.

FOHRER, G. : *Die symbolischen Handlungen der Propheten*. 1953. Pp. 107. (Zwingli-Verlag, Zürich. Price : Swiss Fr. 12.00.)

This is an examination of prophetic symbolism in the light of magic and symbolic acts in the religion of other ancient peoples. In the first part of the book the author examines each recorded symbol individually and adduces parallels to it from non-Israelite religions. Some of the parallels appear rather far-fetched and seem to have little or no bearing on the Biblical act. The author then goes on to discuss whether the symbols were actually performed by the prophets, and then, assuming that to be so, whether the prophet was fully conscious as he performed them. The answer in both cases is affirmative, and the book closes with an assessment of the relation of the prophetic symbols to the written words of the prophets on the one hand, and to the power of God on the other. We may be grateful to Fohrer for the material he has here brought together, but could wish that more constructive use had been made of it to demonstrate the uniqueness of the prophetic life and acts. L.H.B.

FRIDRICHSEN, A. (and other members of Uppsala University) : *The Root of the Vine : Essays in Biblical Theology*, with an Introduction by A. G. Hebert. 1953. Pp. 160. (Dacre Press, Westminster. Price : 16s. 0d.)

This work contains the following essays, some at least of which have appeared elsewhere (in whole or in part) in Swedish : ' The Theology of Creation in the Old and New Testaments ' (G. Lindeskog) ; ' The Idea of God's People in the Bible ' (G. A. Danell) ; ' Jesus, St. John and St. Paul ' (A. Fridrichsen) ; ' The Called and the Chosen ' (K. Stendahl) ; ' The New Exodus of Salvation according to St. Paul ' (H. Sahlin) ; ' The Ministry in the New Testament ' (H. Riesenfeld) ; 'A Synopsis of Early Christian Preaching ' (B. Reicke). The volume provides a useful and illuminating sample of the work done by the late Professor Fridrichsen and the circle of younger scholars who owe so much to his inspiration. Though the essays are chiefly on the New Testament, the typological approach involves considerable discussion of the Old Testament material, on which the contributions of Lindeskog and Danell bear most directly. G.W.A.

GELIN, A. : *Les Pauvres de Yahvé*. (Témoins de Dieu, No. 14.) 1953. Pp. 182. (Les Éditions du Cerf, Paris. Price : Fr. 300.)

In the first chapter the author looks at the Old Testament attitude to poverty, which regards it as something improper among the people of God, though the poor may be condemned with the wicked. The oppression of the poor by the rich, however, is an offence against Yahweh. Then the poor in the literature from Zephaniah to the Psalmists are studied, leading on to the consideration of the poor as a spiritual community of righteous persons. This leads on to the poor in the inter-testamental literature, and in particular in the Qumran scrolls, and then on to the New Testament. A short chapter is devoted to the Messiah of the ' poor ', found in Isa. liii and in some psalms. The whole forms a useful, if brief, summary. H.H.R.

GISPEN, W. H. : *De Christus in het Oude Testament* (Exegetica : Oude- en Nieuw-testamentische Studiën, 1.) 1952. Pp. 60+4. (van Keulen, Delft. Price : Fl. 3.50.)

This, the first of a new series of monographs on biblical subjects, is an examination, from a conservative standpoint, of the relation between the Old and New Testaments. The writer discusses the meaning of the imposition of hands in ritual practice, the various types of sacrifice, the fourth Servant Song, the idea of the presence of God with men, and certain passages in Proverbs, Psalms, and the narrative books. In varying ways, the work of Christ is found to be fore-shadowed in these passages. Account is taken of recent non-fundamentalist work on the same theme ; but the choice of passages and the approach to them represent the author's own standpoint, which many will find difficult to accept. G.W.A.

GROSS, H. : *Weltherrschaft als religiöse Idee im Alten Testament.*
(Bonner Biblische Beiträge, No. 6.) 1953. Pp. 158. (Hanstein,
Bonn. Price : DM. 18.00.)

> In this careful and well-documented study the author examines
> the idea of world dominion in the Old Testament and its
> relation to foreign influence. He rejects the idea that it is a
> late or borrowed notion, and finds that it is religiously born
> in Israel. Its foundation is in the thought of God as Lord and
> Judge of the world, and as the final Controller of the destinies
> of men, Whose lordship may be exercised through His people
> or through His representative—the king or the Messiah,
> whether the latter be thought of as David redivivus, the
> Suffering Servant, or the Son of Man. There was always a
> tension in thought between the world that is and the ideal
> world that is to be, and the roots of eschatology are therefore
> held to have been early. Innumerable much-debated points
> arise in the course of the discussion, and the volume offers a
> valuable contribution to the debate.   H.H.R.

HÜBSCHER, A. : *Die grosse Weissagung.* 1952. Pp. 256. (Heimeran
Verlag, Munich. Price : DM. 14.50.)

> This work traces the prophecy of a *Heilszeit* under a great
> and just Prince, following war and other trouble, from Biblical
> times to the present time, with the citation of the most im-
> portant texts and 26 pages of notes. The Biblical beginnings
> are seen too simply and uniformly, but the value of the
> treatment of the further development is greatly enhanced by
> the rich documentation.   W.B.

JOHNSON, D. : *The Christian and His Bible.* 1953. Pp. 144. (Inter-
Varsity Fellowship. Price : 6s. 0d.)

> A vigorous statement of his position by an uncompromising
> fundamentalist which will appeal to those who share his point
> of view and will be interesting to those who wish to understand
> it. This *Book List* is not the place for theological controversy
> but it may be pointed out that the author is scarcely just to
> many Biblical critics when he attributes their opposition to
> his view of inspiration to their ' philosophical viewpoint and
> pre-supposition—whether it be a Hegelian philosophy of
> history or evolutionary materialism in one of its several forms '.
> He is less than charitable when he speaks of ' close practical
> association between a true acceptance of the Bible and (a
> man's) ethical attainment ' and somewhat disingenuous when
> he refers to ' small discrepancies of detail in the Old Testament'.
> The ' Brief History of the Documentary Theory of the Penta-
> teuch ', which is acknowledged to be a summary of a book
> by E. J. Young and is given in an appendix, does not suggest
> any very profound or accurate acquaintance with the diffi-
> culties which Mr. Johnson dismisses so lightly. But at least
> he virtually gives away much of his case on pp. 101-2 where
> he alludes to moral difficulties. Dr. W. J. Martin's inter-
> pretation of Exodus vi. 3, referred to on p. 92, while ingenious,
> is unnatural and improbable. Mr. Johnson has interesting

things to say in defence of the view that revelation is given to us in the form of propositions which can be used as proof-texts for Biblical Theology. He makes no real attempt, however, to meet the objections to this view. N.W.P.

KNIGHT, G. A. F. : *A Biblical Approach to the Trinity.* (Scottish Journal of Theology Occasional Papers No. 1.) 1953. Pp. 78. (Oliver and Boyd, Edinburgh and London. Price : 6s.)

This is the first of a new series, and it will certainly stir up theological thought. The theme is that the true theology of the Old Testament has been buried for centuries because the categories of the theologians have been Greek rather than Hebrew. If God chose Israel, He also chose their thought-forms and their language. It is strange that none of the great classical statements of the Faith have included the declaration that God is love. Plurality in unity is at the basis of Hebrew thought. God's " Glory " is to God what man's body is to man. The body and the soul are not antagonistic. Both are the man, either together or singly. There is an anthropomorphism which is sound, and in this the author finds the Old Testament basis of the Christian doctrine of the Trinity. Curiously, Dr. Aubrey Johnson's monograph, *The One and the Many in the Israelite Conception of God* is not mentioned (1946 *Book List*, p. 46). N.H.S.

KÖHLER, L. : *Der Hebräische Mensch.* 1953. Pp. 182. (Mohr, Tübingen. Price : DM. 9.00.)

This delightful and inimitable little book is one of the best things which Professor Köhler has given us. It is in form a series of lectures delivered in Tübingen on the Hebrew man and represents an attempt to discover what he looked like, how he lived his daily life and what he thought and felt about it all. The evidence of archaeology is used to supplement that of the Old Testament itself and the whole book sparkles with flashes of insight. The author has an eye which sees unexpected things and enables others to see and enjoy them too. One learns, for example, that what is usually called leprosy in the Old Testament is not leprosy, what is the effect on the Hebrew of the fact that he was likely to become a great-grandfather at a comparatively early age (!), what a Hebrew childhood was like and how boys were educated in the school of life. There is an extremely interesting account of the *sod*, which was the men's forum for talk and discussion, and of the way in which proverbial literature developed from such talk. The fear of the uncanny in Hebrew life is discussed. It is shown how strong a hold tradition had and yet how on occasion a Hebrew could take an individual line and stand quite alone. At the end there is an important discussion of the way in which Israel's reverence for tradition enabled its distinctive life to survive foreign influence.

For good measure an appendix to the volume gives a welcome reprint of Professor Köhler's notable lecture ' Die Hebräische Rechtsgemeinde ' originally delivered in 1931. N.W.P.

KÖHLER, L. : *Theologie des Alten Testaments.* 1953. Pp. xi+256. (Mohr, Tübingen. Price : DM. 16.00.)

A third edition of one of the outstanding Old Testament Theologies of recent times. The book is substantially the same as the first edition, but the opportunity has been taken to introduce changes here and there and especially in the notes where references will be found to recent literature. N.W.P.

KRAUS, H. J. : *Gottesdienst in Israel : Studien zur Geschichte des Laubhüttenfestes* (Beiträge zur evangelischen Theologie 19). 1954. Pp. 132. (Chr. Kaiser Verlag, München. Price : DM. 8.25.)

The greater part of this work represents an attempt to trace the history of the Feast of Tabernacles from early times down to the post-exilic period. The important " formgeschichtliche " studies of Alt, von Rad and Noth enable the author to emphasize in this connexion the cultic setting of the Sinaitic tradition as preserved in the formal and seasonal worship of the Israelite confederation of twelve tribes, and this in turn provides the setting for a restatement of Kraus's own theory of the subsequent history of this festival in association with the Jerusalem Temple as given in his monograph, *Die Königsherrschaft Gottes im Alten Testament (Book List,* 1952, pp. 54 f.). The last few pages of the work contain some rather sketchy notes on the relation of the canonical prophets to the cultus and the distinctive elements in Old Testament worship, particularly its emphasis on God's activity in history. Like its predecessor, this monograph is written in an attractive style which holds the attention of the reader, and it may be welcomed, not merely for the author's racy presentation of his own views (which remain untenable so far as the reviewer is concerned), but also for the part which it may play for the beginner as a simple introduction to the views of the above-mentioned scholars. A.R.J.

KÜHNER, H. O. : *Ein Gang durchs Alte Testament.* (Schriften für Gemeindeglieder.) 1953. Pp. 48. (Zwingli Verlag, Zürich. Price : Swiss Fr. 2.80.)

A rapid sketch in five chapters of what a Christian should expect to find in the Old Testament and of the bearing it has on his Christian faith. The intention of the booklet is to show that the Old Testament is relevant for the ordinary Christian as well as the theological student. The treatment is too slight to be critically thoroughgoing and has led inevitably to generalizations such as this : " Das Opfer ist ein Gnadengeschenk Gottes an den Menschen und nicht umgekehrt " (p. 38). L.H.B.

LINDESKOG, G. : *Studien zum Neutestamentlichen Schöpfungsgedanken,* Vol. 1. 1952. Pp. 302. (A. B. Lundequistska Bokhandeln, Uppsala, and Otto Harrassowitz, Wiesbaden. Price : Swedish Kr. 22.00.)

A little over half of this first volume is of special interest to Old Testament scholars. 83 pages are devoted to the Old Testament, 50 to the Apocrypha and Pseudepigrapha and 27 to Philo. The review of Old Testament ideas naturally anticipates what is going to be discussed in the later parts concerning the New Testament. Within the limits thus set the review is useful and suggestive. A distinction is drawn between the mythological idea of creation found in isolated references and allusions and the monotheistic conception with its two classic statements in Genesis i. and ii. Emphasis is laid on the idea of the creative word, the place of man in the created order, the election of Israel and the expectation of a new creation. The work on the intertestamental period is somewhat less satisfactory, probably on account of the large area to be covered. In the main the author has collected quotations which continue the line of thought set out in his Old Testament survey.   L.H.B.

LLOYD-JONES, D. M. : *From Fear to Faith*. 1953. Pp. 76. (Inter-Varsity Fellowship, London. Price : 2s. 6d.)

These " Studies in the Book of Habakkuk " (as the sub-title says), by a well-known London preacher, appear to be a series of sermons recast in literary form, and are examples of a kind of expository preaching which ought to be commoner than it is. Dr. Lloyd-Jones (who has not a little of the true prophetic genius himself) views Habakkuk against his contemporary background towards the end of the seventh century B.C., and then applies his message effectively to the present generation in the western world. When, on p. 42, he rightly mentions *fore-telling* as an essential element in Biblical prophecy, he adds " The critics, again, object to that "; he means, of course, *some* critics.   F.F.B.

MATTUCK, I. I. : *The Thought of the Prophets*. 1953. Pp. 176. (George Allen and Unwin, London. Price : 9s. 6d.)

This volume is one of a series, *Ethical and Religious Classics of East and West*, designed, according to the General Introduction, " to place the chief ethical and religious master-pieces . . . within easy reach of the intelligent reader who is not necessarily an expert." Rabbi Mattuck has written a book on the prophets that achieves this end. In a series of 12 short chapters he reviews the thought of the prophets bringing out their moral emphasis, their concern for God's full control of history and their insistence that a full personal and communal life depends upon communion with God. The studies are based on a thorough knowledge of the contents of the prophetic writings and a full appreciation of modern criticism. The book is well suited for study group or Bible class work.   L.H.B.

MONRO, MARGARET R. : *Thinking about Genesis*. 1953. Pp. xxviii + 222. (Longmans, Green & Co., London. Price : 11s. 0d.)

The authoress of this book is a convert to Catholicism, who writes with an understandable enthusiasm for the superiority of Catholic scholarship, though this is a little inappropriate in a day when there is more co-operation in Biblical studies than formerly. She rejects the ' critical ' view of the Pentateuch, after a very superficial examination, but commends the view of Engnell, and appears to suggest that this is the Catholic *tertium quid*, which is neither fundamentalism nor critical orthodoxy. This appropriation of a view with an admittedly Protestant paternity is paralleled by the proud claim of Catholic paternity, in Astruc and Simon, for the view which is rejected as an unsatisfactory Protestant view. All this is regrettable propaganda. There is much in the book, however, which is admirable to instruct simple readers in the religious and moral values of the early stories in Genesis, and to illustrate the way in which archaeology has shown how the patriarchal stories fit well into the known background of the times in which they are set.   H.H.R.

MOWINCKEL, S. : *Religion und Kultus*, German Tr. by Albrecht Schauer. 1953. Pp. 164. (Vandenhoeck & Ruprecht, Göttingen. Price : DM. 9.80.)

> The Norwegian edition of this book appeared in 1950 (see *Book List*, 1951, p. 61). Many minor changes and additions have been made in this German translation, particularly in the first half of the book. The section on uncleanness, sin, and purification has been transferred to follow the discussion of the creative drama of the cult. A section on religious experience has been inserted near the end. There are some additional references and other modifications in the notes ; and a very brief general bibliography is appended. It is thus an improved form of this excellent manual which is now made available for a wider circle of readers.   G.W.A.

MOWINCKEL, S. : *Zum israelitischen Neujahr und zur Deutung der Thronbesteigungspsalmen*. (Avhandlinger utgitt av Det Norske Videnskaps-Akademi i Oslo. II. Hist.-Filos. Klasse 1952. No. 2.) 1952. Pp. 68. (Jacob Dybwad, Oslo. Price : Kr. 6.00.)

> In this important publication the author replies to a number of criticisms of his interpretation of Israel's autumnal festival as celebrated in Jerusalem in terms of Yahweh's annual enthronement as King, particularly (a) Aalen's denial that the Old Testament offers any evidence for the idea of a New Year, in *Die Begriffe ' Licht' und ' Finsternis ' im Alten Testament, im Spätjudentum und im Rabbinismus*, 1951 (*Book List*, 1952, p. 47), and (b) Snaith's attempt to prove that the Enthronement Psalms were primarily psalms for the Sabbath, in *Studies in the Psalter*, 1934 (*Book List*, 1935, p. 11), and in *The Jewish New Year Festival*, 1947, (*Book List*, 1948, pp. 50 f.).   A.R.J.

MULDER, E. S. : *Die Teologie van die Jesaja-Apokalipse*. 1954. Pp. viii+126. (J. B. Wolters, Groningen & Djakarta.)

> This study of Is. xxiv-xxvii, written in Afrikaans by a pupil of Gemser and Vriezen, was presented for the theological doctorate at Groningen University. More than half the

dissertation is devoted to a translation of these four chapters, with verse-by-verse notes on language, text and exegesis. Dr. Mulder draws on the latest sources of information, such as DSIa for the text and Ugaritic for the language and imagery. Then comes a comparative study of the vocabulary and style of the four chapters (which are considered to form a literary unit). The apocalyptist—a member of the circle of Isaiah's disciples (which must have persisted for centuries)— was acquainted with all the other component parts of our book of Isaiah. The " city of chaos " is Dibon of Moab ; in making Moab the typical enemy of Yahweh and His people the apocalyptist stands in long line of tradition which can be traced from the Balaam oracles through Jeremiah to Daniel and Ben Sira. He himself flourished c. 270 B.C., shortly before the closing of the prophetic canon, when prophecy was passing over to apocalyptic. Special attention is paid to the themes of resurrection and judgement in the apocalypse. In xxvi. 19 we have the completely new conception of a resurrection of individuals from death ; the background of this conception is found in some of the most distinctive elements of Hebrew revelation (e.g. the doctrine of God as the living God, the expectation of His coming kingdom, and the ideas of covenant and election). The doctrine of divine judgement takes a variety of forms, representing various strands of O.T. thought : " the eschatology of the apocalypse shows the transition from ' actualizing ' to ' dualistic ' eschatology " (p. 121).

F.F.B.

PATTERSON, C. H. : *The Philosophy of the Old Testament.* 1953. Pp. 558. (The Ronald Press Company, New York. Price : $5.00.)

This book from the pen of the professor of philosophy of the university of Nebraska is clearly written and well documented. By the term ' Philosophy ' the author has in mind the world-view that is implied in the different O.T. writings since each has its own understanding of the nature of the universe. In fact, however, as he says in the preface, what he attempts to do is to present the significant ideas expressed by the various O.T. writers. Occasionally a manifestly philosophic interest shines through with welcome light as when in dealing with Deutero-Isaiah (xlvi. 8-9) the relation of the divine foreknowledge to human freedom is discussed and the prophet's assertion that Yahweh knows what will happen in human affairs is equated with belief in the individual's moral responsibility. Dr. Patterson presents us with a useful preliminary study of the history of the religion of Israel as well as with a modern critical study of the biblical books such as the general Introductions to the O.T. provide. There is an excellent chapter on the methods of the study of the O.T. where the authoritative, the allegorical, the so-called detached and finally the scientific method are discussed and evaluated. The work of the great pioneers of O.T. investigation is most interestingly told. A description of the Canaanite background

of the religion of Israel and of the inner and outer trans-
formation of the life of the Hebrews worked by their passing
from the nomadic to the agricultural mode of existence,
provides very competently what the student of Hebrew
literature requires to know of Hebrew beginnings. A useful
chapter follows on the early laws of the Hebrews. In the
section dealing with the prophetic books we note that the
works of Jeremiah, Ezekiel and Deutero-Isaiah together with
the problems which, under modern research, these books
have raised receive remarkably clear and, within limits,
thorough treatment. The writer gives very acceptable
descriptions of the historical situations in which the prophetic
works arose. Considerable scope (40 pages) is given to an
account of the apocryphal and pseudepigraphical books.

O.S.R.

PIDOUX, G. : *L'Homme dans l'Ancien Testament.* 1953. Pp. 76.
(Delachaux & Niestlé, Neuchatel and Paris. Price : Swiss Fr. 4.)

This booklet is No. 32 in the publishers' series of *Cahiers
Théologiques :* the author holds a chair in Lausanne University.
Here we have a useful introduction to Old Testament anthropology based largely on the works of Pedersen, Wheeler
Robinson, and Aubrey Johnson. Five chapters deal respectively with (1) ' The fundamental ideas : soul, flesh,
spirit '; (2) ' Man's body '; (3) ' Thought '; (4) ' Life '; (5)
' Man's world '. In a short epilogue the author insists that,
while some aspects of Hebrew anthropology may be considered
outmoded nowadays, its monistic interpretation of the human
personality has as its corollary a sense of moral responsibility
which men to-day sorely need to regain.   F.F.B.

VAN DER PLOEG, J. : *De Kerk en Israël.* 1954. Pp. 80. (N.V. Gooi
& Sticht, Hilversum.)

In this book on the relation between the Christian Church
and Israel the Nijmegen professor deals for the most part
with questions which do not fall within the limits cf Old
Testament studies. The first chapter, however, contains a
brief discussion of the meaning and purpose of God's electing
the people of Israel and entering into covenant-relation with
them.   F.F.B.

RIGAUX, B. (ed. by) : *L'Attente du Messie.* 1954. Pp. 190. (Desclée de
Brouwer, Paris. Price : 23s. 6d.)

This symposium on the messianic hope, by participators in
the fourth session of Journées Bibliques de Louvain, has a
special interest for our Society in that the volume is presented
to Professor Coppens, whose portrait appears as a frontispiece.
Three out of the nine essays are by Professor Coppens himself ;
other contributors (apart from the editor) are L. Cerfaux,
R. de Langhe, V. de Leeuw, A. Descamps and J. Giblet.
The Bishop of Namur contributes a foreword. Of special
interest for O.T. students are Coppens's short reviews of the

thesis of Mowinckel's *Han Som Kommer* and his study of the Immanuel prophecy of Isa. vii. 14-16; De Leeuw's essay on the Servant of Yahweh, in whom he sees a royal rather than a prophetic figure; and Giblet's essay on the idea of a prophet-Messiah, in which he pays special attention to the rôle of the Teacher of Righteousness among the New Covenanters. The essays go some way in the direction of prolegomena to a Biblical theology of messianism. While the royal and prophetic elements in the messianic hope are studied, it would have been good had something been included on the priestly element. On p. 161 reference is made to Torrey's work on the Aramaic substratum of the gospels as having been done " en Angleterre "; unfortunately for us, England must decline this honour.   F.F.B.

Rowley, H. H. :   *The Unity of the Bible.* 1953. Pp. x+202. (Carey Kingsgate Press Ltd., London. Price : 15s. 0d.)

Professor Rowley's latest book presents in published form the W. T. Whitley Lectures delivered at Regent's Park and Rawdon Colleges, and the Julius Brown Gay Lectures delivered at the Southern Baptist Seminary, Louisville, Kentucky, in 1951 and 1952. The exposition of his subject proceeds from a consideration of ' Unity in Diversity ', ' The Law and the Prophets ', and ' God and Man ', to ' The Fulfilment of Promise ', ' The Cross ', and ' The Christian Sacraments '. The last three chapters are perhaps the most important part of the book ; they show that the author, in addition to being a front-rank O.T. scholar, is no mean Christian theologian. It is the first three chapters, however, that come properly within the purview of our Society. The O.T. is approached and interpreted theologically, but along more satisfactory lines than the allegorical and typological methods of Vischer, Hebert and Phythian-Adams. We are already familiar with Rowley's views on the authority of Biblical revelation, the principle of divine election, the Mosaic origin of the decalogue, the prophetic attitude to sacrifice, the mission of the Suffering Servant, the indispensable character of the O.T. as part of the Christian canon, and so forth ; these are developed here in a consecutive and integrated fashion so as to lead on to their N.T. consummation. The treatment has in view a wider circle of readers than Rowley's more technical studies ; but the book is provided with the scholarly apparatus of up-to-date bibliographical and other notes which we have come to expect from him.   F.F.B.

Sauber, K. R. :   *Die Abstraktion im Israelitischen Recht.* (Inaugural-dissertation der Juristischen Fakultät der Friedrich-Alexanders-Universität zu Erlangen.) (Microfilm made from typescript.) 1950. Pp. 51+iv. (Vandenhoeck & Ruprecht, Göttingen. Price : DM. 6.20.)

The author contends that the ' casuistically ' formulated provisions of the O.T. (' if ' followed by detailed facts, and the legal consequences in the main clause), like the Code of

607

Hammurabi, the Assyrian and the Hittite collections, are generalized decisions of cases that actually occurred. The generalization involves little abstraction, the facts still including much that is inessential. The nucleus of these ' casuistic ' provisions was borrowed from neighbouring civilizations. The native law of Israel, on the other hand, i.e. the apodictically formulated and the priestly provisions, shows a higher degree of abstraction than any other Oriental legal system. Many of the apodictic provisions originally were moral norms. Moral norms and priestly regulations are of a general character everywhere, but it was only in Israel, with its all-pervasive religion, that they were made part of the law in the proper sense. Only the bipartite apodictic provisions (facts followed by *môth yûmāth*) are narrow ; they were judgements of the court of the Israelite amphictyonies. This is a work of exceptional promise ; its author is endowed with a powerful intellect, fine scholarship, a wealth of ideas and excellent judgement. To M. David's argument that the parallels between the ' casuistic ' Mishpatim and the Code of Hammurabi point neither to borrowing nor to a common source because similar social conditions produce similar law, Dr. Sauber replies that borrowing also takes place primarily where conditions are similar ; the possibility of dependence, therefore, cannot be ruled out on this ground.

D.D.

SCHMITT, E. : *Leben in den Weisheitsbüchern Job, Sprüche und Jesus Sirach.* (Freiburger Theologische Studien, LXVI. Heft.) 1954. Pp. xvi+208. (Herder, Freiburg. Price : DM. 12.50.)

The significance of the idea of life in the Wisdom literature makes this an important study. The early pages are devoted to a study of the key words, live, life, breath, spirit, *nephesh*, heart, flesh, days and duration. This is followed by a chapter on the O.T. conception of life and its dependence on the ' living ' God. The rest of the book discusses the ways in which the Wisdom Books develop and intensify the general conception of life ; in doing this the author notes the different metaphors that are used and the variety of ideas that go hand in hand with ' life '. Of special interest is the conclusion that in at least two of the three books there may be found a belief in eternal life, notably in Prov. iii. 18, the ' tree of life ' passage, (pp. 91f.) and Job xix. 25 ff. (pp. 173 ff.). L.H.B.

SEYNAEVE, J. : *Cardinal Newman's Doctrine of Holy Scripture according to his published works and previously unedited manuscripts.* (Universitas Catholica Lovaniensis. Dissertationes ad gradum magistri in Facultata Theologica vel in Facultate Juris Canonici consequendum conscriptae.) 1953. Pp. xxviii+408+160*. (Blackwell, Oxford. Price : 63s. 0d. (paper covers) ; 70s. 0d. (cloth)).

This work is a study of Newman's scriptural teaching as a whole, and, of the hitherto unpublished manuscripts printed in the appendix to the book, perhaps the most interesting is a twenty-five page treatise " On the Connection in Doctrine and Statement of the Books of the Apocrypha with the New Testament ", which belongs to some unknown date in his Anglican period. Seynaeve in the main body of the work is chiefly concerned with Newman's teaching on the inspiration of Scripture and on the science of hermeneutics. There is an illuminating introductory chapter on the historical and doctrinal setting of Newman's biblical doctrine. Then follow the four chapters of the first part (Inspiration) which discuss respectively the problem of inspiration in Newman's life and work ; his teaching as an Anglican ; his teaching as found in some newly published papers written between 1861 and 1863 ; and his teaching as it appears in the two articles (published respectively, both in 1884, in the *Nineteenth Century* and in a brochure issued by Burns & Oates), which belong to the last decade of his long life. The second part (Hermeneutics) has likewise four chapters, which deal with his first principles as an exegete ; the unity of the " divine economy " and the harmony between the Old and the New Testaments ; the different meanings (or senses) of Holy Scripture ; and the ideal of the Christian exegete. This is a really fine piece of work and, apart from the detailed treatment of inspiration and hermeneutics, is a much-needed guide to Newman's biblical writings as a whole. The author's courageous decision to prepare his book in English has been fully justified. Though Newman's work has been frequently translated, nothing can take the place of his own sensitive and matchless English, on which an American Free Churchman has written : " He is like the best French prose writers in expressing his thought with such naturalness and apparent ease that, without thinking of style, we receive exactly the impression which he means to convey" (W. J. Long, *English Literature*, p. 557).

J.M.T.B.

SPADAFORA, F. : *Collettivismo e Individualismo nel Vecchio Testamento*. (Quaderni Esegetici, 2.) 1953. Pp. xxiv+398. (Istituto Padano di Arti Graficke, Rovigo. Price : Lire 2,000.)

The author of this competent and rewarding book is already well known to readers of Italian works on Holy Scripture by reason of his commentary on Ezekiel in the *Sacra Bibbia* series edited by S. Garofalo. (Cf. *Book List*, 1950, p. 11.) He himself is the editor of the *Quaderni Esegetici* in which this volume is published. The main purpose of the work is to supply an answer to the question : Is it true, as some critics claim, that the religion of Israel was collectivist) in so far as the relation to Yahweh was that of a community as a whole) in pre-exilic times and became individualistic after the exile ? Spadafora's answer is a most decided negative, since, on his showing, both the collectivist and the individualist aspects of religion are found through Israel's history. Whatever view may be taken of the merits of his case, there can be no mistaking the thorough and rigorous examination that he makes of the available evidence. His main chapters are concerned with the principle of solidarity as it is found throughout the Old Testament ; with collectivism in the

Old Testament (with special emphasis on the Sinaitic pact) ; and with individual religion in the same books. A final chapter studies the teaching of Jeremiah and Ezekiel on these points. It is a little disconcerting that foreign works are sometimes quoted in the original languages, but more often translated, on which issue it may be noted that the Roman Biblical Institute requires a sufficient knowledge of English, French and German as a necessary qualification for all its graduates. The bibliography is extensive, but a number of English and some German works (e.g. Procksch : *Theologie des A.T.*) seem to have escaped the author's notice.   J.M.T.B.

TRESMONTANT, C. : *Essai sur la pensée hébraïque* (Lectio Divina 12). 1953. Pp. 172. (Les Éditions du Cerf, Paris. Price : Fr. 450.)

Although the author of this monograph on Hebrew thinking makes it clear that he is writing from a Roman Catholic standpoint, it has much in common with recent Protestant work in the same field ; and to anyone who appreciates the way in which the Bible is dominated by the thought of man's ceaseless struggle for " life ", it is no matter for surprise that this work has been influenced in large measure by the thought of Bergson. The writer makes skilful use of Greek forms of thought to point the contrast with what the Bible has to say about the act of creation, the creative activity of time, the use of symbolism, the Hebrew conception of man with its avoidance of dichotomy, the distinctive conception of rûach, the practical implication of intelligence which is so characteristic of the Old Testament, and the emphasis on the intellectual aspect of faith which comes to the fore in the New Testament ; and if the reader who is interested in the Bible as Scripture bears in mind that this is an essay of a tentative kind, and that as a result he should not be too impatient of generalizations based on a somewhat indiscriminate use of the Biblical data, he will find much here to arouse his interest and, indeed, guide his own thinking along constructive lines.   A.R.J.

VOLLBORN, V. : *Studien zum Zeitverständnis des Alten Testaments.* (Microfilm made from typescript.) 1951. Pp. 272. (Vandenhoeck and Ruprecht, Göttingen. Price : DM. 16.40.)

This discussion of the Hebrew understanding of time and its significance for exegesis opens with a factual examination of the words for time. Much the same conclusions are arrived at as those of Orelli and emphasis is given to the fact that the Hebrews were interested only in the content of time, especially in relation to the present. This latter fact, namely, the representation of any event in time as though it were here and now, a fact of present time, is expanded in the remainder of the book (pp. 138-272).

To illustrate his point the author draws mainly on the Book of Deuteronomy and shows how the Israelites of a subsequent generation are spoken to as though it were they whom God had delivered from Egypt, tested in the desert and led into

Canaan. Use is also made of Hertzberg's work on the ' Nach-
geschichte ' of Old Testament literature. The book ends with
an affirmation that God is outside the time sequence and can
gather all events into a timeless unity.

There are one or two omissions of important passages in the
examination of the words for time, but perhaps the least
convincing part of the book is the application of the thesis
to the Hebrew tense system. Philological arguments are here
left completely aside and the tense usage is regarded as
dependent on the conception of time as of something relevant
only for the present.   L.H.B.

VRIEZEN, TH.C. : *Die Erwählung Israels nach dem Alten Testament.*
(Abhandlungen zur Theologie des Alten und Neuen Testaments,
No. 24.) 1953. Pp. 116. (Zwingli-Verlag, Zürich. Price : Swiss Fr.
12.50.)

An interesting short study of a central theme. After a preliminary discussion of the theological importance of the
subject to-day, the author examines the various uses of the
root BHR, and offers an exegetical discussion of the relevant
passages. By avoiding the wider sense often given to the
doctrine, and by confining himself largely to the idea of choice,
he presents election as ' a Deuteronomic theologoumenon ',
which is given wider and deeper application in Isaiah xl-lxvi
in relation to the love of God, and in the later literature is
modified in the direction of BDL. Two chapters are devoted
to the relation of election to allied ideas, and to the thought
of the divine rejection. Valuable for its discussion of the Old
Testament material, and for the theological relation between
the two Testaments.   G.W.A.

WEBER, M. : *Ancient Judaism,* translated and edited by H. H. Gerth
and D. Martindale. 1952. Pp. xxviii+484. (Free Press, Glencoe,
Ill., and Allen & Unwin, London. Price : $6.00 or 45s. 0d.)

As the publishers state, this book is not a history of the Jews
in the ordinary sense, but ' the incredible mind of Max Weber
focused on the source of a history '. The author died in 1920,
and now at length his work has appeared in English. Its main
interest is in the social, cultural and religious ideas and practices
of Israel. This does not mean, however, that it is in any
sense a Theology of the Old Testament. Some of its chapters
are on themes dealt with in Pedersen's *Israel,* though they are
very differently treated and the plan of the book as a whole
is quite other. Whereas Pedersen tried to get into the soul
of Israel and see her institutions and practices with her eyes,
Weber looks from afar on them. He is the acute observer,
rather than the sympathetic exponent we find in Pedersen.
Nevertheless, as a penetrating study of many sides of Israelite
thought and practice his book will have a lasting value. The
social structure and laws of Israel, her priesthood, cult and
ethics, and her relations with the surrounding peoples and
cultures are all studied. Naturally no use has been made of
the great expansion of our knowledge since Weber died.
There is a supplement on the Pharisees and on the Essenes,
who are so much discussed to-day.   H.H.R.

611

WELCH, A. C. : *Prophet and Priest in Old Israel.* 1953. Pp. 160. (Basil Blackwell, Oxford. Price : 10s. 6d.)

This is a reprint of the book published in 1936, cf. *Book List*, 1937, p. 13. It presents the inter-relation of prophetic word and priestly cultus and ritual and protests against the too violent opposition which earlier scholars had thought to find between prophet and priest. It is no disparagement of the book to say that much that would have appeared new in 1936, would now be accepted without question. Had the book been written to-day, more attention would have been given to the ' cult prophets ', and the argument would have been strengthened. The book is the product of fine scholarship and of a spirit sensitive to the life of the worshipping community. It should be read by all theological students and by those who are teaching Scripture in schools. A.S.H.

YERKES, R. K. : *Sacrifice in Greek and Roman Religions and early Judaism.* (The Hale Lectures.) 1952. Pp. 268. (Scribner, New York, and Black, London. Price : $3.50 or 18s. 0d.)

The cover designates this book as setting forth the meaning of sacrifice in the ancient religions that formed the milieu in which Christianity had its rise and as being " the most thorough contribution available on the subject ". This claim is certainly substantiated. These Hale Lectures of Dr. Yerkes are a most patient, valuable and welcome investigation of a theme of high importance, and of not a little misunderstanding, in the history of religion. This book demands in its unhurried analysis of terms and of patterns of the sacrificial cult in Greek, Roman and Jewish religious practice the reader's undivided attention which it amply rewards. Dr. Yerkes provides in ch. viii a useful examination of rites in which an animal was wholly eaten by the worshippers, namely, the Athenian Bouphonia, the Magnesian Bull festival, an Arabian rite which continued until historic times, a Moslem parallel and finally the Jewish Passover. We thus have a fairly wide field for comparing conceptions of sacrifice in one of its aspects viz. that of the common meal. Of the Passover (p. 86) the author says that this feast like other feasts of its kind " probably antedated any concept of personal deity ". In a chapter on the " Greek Thusia—Greek cults and Greek Religion " the lecturer shows that the ritual pattern, well established before the days of Homer, was preserved through many centuries, becoming common to the different city-states. The student will especially appreciate the care with which the religious vocabulary associated with sacrifice is treated and subjected as far as possible to definition e.g. *thusia, thuein, eucharistia, hiereuein, hilaskesthai, atonement, kipper* (purification), *kippur,* etc. etc. Some views of the author may here briefly be noted. The act of the killing of the victim is not part of the sacrifice proper but was the last act of the preparation for the sacrifice (cf. p. 135). Sacrifices are not for the removal of sin, cultic or moral. " He who is ' in sin ' cannot sacrifice : he is taboo until he is properly purified, usually by a blood rite of some kind which removes his sins ". The author is forced later, or would appear to be forced, to modify this view somewhat when he proceeds to consider the *chattāth* and *'āshām* offerings, which are not merely purificatory rites removing dis-qualifications such as unwitting error and taboo but involve the burning of parts of the victim upon the altar, that is, they have the character also of being sacrifices.   O.S.R.

THE LIFE AND THOUGHT OF THE NEIGHBOURING PEOPLE

BELL, H. IDRIS : *Cults and Creeds in Graeco-Roman Egypt.* (Liverpool Monographs in Archaeology and Oriental Studies.) 1953. Pp. 117. (University Press, Liverpool. Price : 15s. 0d.)

While the last two of the four Forwood Lectures for 1952 demand less notice here as they discuss the preparation for Christianity in Egypt and the Christian triumph, the other two are of importance for Old Testament studies because they deal with the pagan religions represented in Ptolemaic Egypt and with the Jewish communities there and the relations between the Jews and the other inhabitants of the country. This well-documented book provides a useful and illuminating survey, which is especially valuable because the evidence adduced is based mainly on papyri selected and interpreted by a leading papyrologist.   W.D.M.

BERGMANN, E. : *Codex Hammurabi.* Textus primigenius, 3rd ed. 1953. Pp. 52. (Pontificio Istituto Biblico, Rome. Price : 20s. 0d.)

This is a fresh edition of Dr. Deimel's well known autographed copy of the text of the Code of Hammurabi, copied for scholastic purposes. The somewhat unsatisfactory drawing of the sun-god Shamash receiving the homage of Hammurabi has been omitted from the beginning, and copies of the text of four new fragments (K 10,778, Rm. 2,388, T 8,321, BE 35,271) are added ; but the tablet in the Museum at Istanbul (Ni. 2,553 + 2,565) does not yet appear. The addition of the conventional number of the sections between the columns of the text is also a gain, which all students of the Code will appreciate.   G.R.D.

BERTHOLET, A. : *Grundformen der Erscheinungswelt der Gottesverehrung.* 1953. Pp. 68. (J. C. B. Mohr (Paul Siebeck), Tübingen, Price : DM. 3.40.)

The late Professor Bertholet, a distinguished Honorary Member of the Society, left behind, partly prepared for publication, the text of a lecture delivered before the University of Basel ; the task of preparation has been completed by his friend, Professor J. Hempel. It would appear that Professor Bertholet had intended to make the published version of his lecture into a kind of *Wegweiser* to the well-known *Lehrbuch der Religionsgeschichte* and *Religionsgeschichtlichen Lesebuch*, which he had edited and to which he had contributed. To the *Alttestamentler* the present work will be chiefly useful as a brief compendium of comparative material illustrating the main aspects of religious phenomenology. An evolutionary pattern is tacitly assumed in the presentation of this material, so that the origins of religion appear to lie in a primitive concept of dynamism and in the basic thesis of R. Otto's *Das Heilige* and therefrom develop the practices and institutions characteristic of religious cultus. There is nothing notably new in this survey, although the attention of English-speaking students may be drawn to the interesting instances of divination taken from the *Handwörterbuch des Deutschen Aberglaubens* (Berlin, 1927 ff.) ; there are also some strange omissions, e.g. no reference is made to the now comparatively abundant evidence of the religious beliefs of Palaeolithic Man, and the question of ritual as a basic factor in the generation of religious concept is not discussed.　　　　　　　　　　　　　　　　S.G.F.B.

*CONTENAU, G. : *Everyday Life in Babylon and Assyria,* translated by K. R. and A. R. Maxwell-Hyslop. 1954. Pp. xvi+324. (Arnold, London. Price : 25s. 0d.)

The author, who is a well-known orientalist, author of the extensive *Manuel d'archéologie orientale,* and innumerable other works, gives here an excellent account of Mesopotamian civilization in the period 700-530 B.C. This limited period is chosen because adequate sources of knowledge for this period exist, and it has a unity which does not belong to the whole period of known Babylonian and Assyrian history. The life of the home and of business, food and fashion, and a variety of other details, the life of the king, the thought and religion of the people, are all treated here in a lively and interesting way that will enlighten the non-specialist. The translation is most readable, and the translators have gone to a lot of trouble to supply it with an abundance of illustrations. While, as the translators note, there will not be agreement on all points amongst scholars, the book will serve an excellent purpose in making these ancient peoples live in a real way for its readers, who will gain much background knowledge for the study of the Bible. There is also a useful bibliography.　　　　　　　　　　　　　　　　　　H.H.R.

FALKENSTEIN, A. and VON SODEN, W. : *Sumerische und Akkadische Hymnen und Gebete.* 1953. Pp. 424 and 12 Plates. (Artemis Verlag, Zürich and Stuttgart. Price : Swiss Fr. 17.50.)

We are indebted to the two best German-speaking Sumerian and Akkadian scholars for this rich and fine selection, which includes many little known texts of the lyrical prayers of Mesopotamia. It contains a reliable translation of the several poems, with short notes, and an excellent literary-historical introduction, which discusses the various *Gattungen,* the language, style, arrangement, religious content, and the relation to the Hebrew psalms. The work is invaluable to the Old Testament scholar.　　　　　　　　　　　　　　W.B.

HALDAR, A. : *Det babyloniska skapelseeposet enûma eliš översatt och förklarat.* 1952. Pp. 90+12 plates. (Hugo Geber's Förlag, Stockholm. Price : 23s. 6d.)

Dr. Haldar has done Swedish readers a service by providing the first complete translation into their language of the Babylonian Creation Epic. In a brief introduction, he describes the texts and editions, summarizes the contents of the epic, and gives some account of its religious significance. The translation itself is clearly set out ; but the reader would have been helped still further if the lines had been numbered. There are twenty pages of concise, up-to-date comments on the text, and a good selection of illustrations. The work is based on first-hand examination of the British Museum tablets.
G.W.A.

HINTZE, F. : *Mitteilungen des Instituts für Orientforschung* (Deutsche Akademie der Wissenschaften zu Berlin) I, Heft 1. 1953. Pp. 188. (Akademie-Verlag, Berlin. Price : DM. 18.)

These " communications " which are to appear yearly in one volume consisting of up to four parts deal with the whole Orient, i.e. beside the Near East also Central and East Asia. In the sphere of the Near East the present number contains, in addition to four articles on Egyptology, three essays, namely : Franz Köcher, ' Der babylonische Göttertypentext ' (pp. 57-107 : Copy of the Berlin tablet VAT 15,606+13,991+13,992+13,995+14,358 with Transcription, translation and comments on the " Göttertypentext " offered in this tablet and other fragments) ; Gerhard Rudolf Meyer, ' Zwei neue Kizzuwatna-Verträge ' (pp. 108-124 : Transcription, translation and comments on the Akkadian text supplemented by two newly found fragments. KUB XXXIV, No. 1 and the appreciation of the Hittite Berlin Text published by H. Otten in KUB XXXVI Bo. 9,251) ; Heinrich Otten, ' Ein kanaanäischer Mythus aus Bogazköy ' (pp. 125-150 : The Berlin Hittite texts Bo. 1,556, Bo. 2,567 and Bo. 3,273, which were published in KUB XXXVI, call the divinities Elkunirsa= 'el qoneh 'eres, and Asertu='ašera, and show thereby the influence of Canaanite mythology upon the Hittites).
O.E.

KEES, H. : *Das Priestertum im ägyptischen Staat vom neuen Reich bis zur Spätzeit.* (Probleme der Ägyptologie Vol. 1.) 1953. Pp. xii+324. (Brill, Leiden and Cologne. Price : Fl. 35.)

This book deals with the organisation and structure of the Egyptian priesthood from Dyn. XVIII onwards. The history of many of the great priestly families is also traced. The author has produced a work of great value to students of Egyptian history and religion. The genealogies and lists will be specially helpful.
T.W.T.

KIENITZ, F. K. : *Die politische Geschichte Ägyptens vom 7. bis zum 4. Jahrhundert vor der Zeitwende*. 1953. Pp. xii+233. (Akademie-Verlag, Berlin. Price : DM. 27.00.)

> This period of Egyptian history is of special interest to Old Testament scholars and in Dr. Kienitz's book they will now have a thoroughly reliable and able summary of the results of modern research and archaeological discoveries in Egypt. It may be warmly recommended. T.W.T.

LEIPOLDT, J. & MORENZ, S. : *Heilige Schriften : Betrachtungen zur Religionsgeschichte der antiken Mittelmeerwelt*. 1953. Pp. 218 and 13 Plates. (Harrassowitz, Leipzig. Price : DM. 11.)

> The joint authors offer here a historical sketch of the origin and development of that section of East-Mediterranean literature which reckoned as ' Holy Writ '. Egypt, Israel, Greece, also Christianity and Islam are included.

> Among the subjects dealt with are bibliolatry, public and private reading, and problems of translation and translators (LXX especially). There seems to be little startlingly new, but the material is attractively presented with subject and citation indexes and an appendix of thirteen monochrome plates. D.R.Ap-T.

MERCER, S. A. B. : *The Pyramid Texts in Translation and Commentary*. 4 vols. 1952. Pp. xiv+320, ii+528, ii+428, iv+328+6 plates and 1 map. (Longmans, Green and Co., New York, London and Toronto. Price : 240s. 0d.)

> This is a work of outstanding importance for students of the religions of the Ancient Near East. For the first time all Pyramid Texts so far discovered have been translated into a modern language and a full commentary on them provided. Hitherto we have had to rely on the inadequate French translations of Speleers (published over 20 years ago and which could not therefore contain the new texts from the pyramids of Neit and Pepi II) and upon the brilliant, but incompleted, *Übersetzung und Kommentar zu den altägyptischen Pyramidentexten* by Sethe. The first volume of Professor Mercer's work comprises the translation of the texts, the second and third contain the analysis and commentary. The fourth volume contains 26 excursuses and the indexes. These excursuses are by Professor Mercer himself and seven other American, French, German and Belgian experts on Egyptian religion.

> The archaic language and orthography of the Pyramid Texts make them the most difficult of all Egyptian Texts to translate and understand, and inevitably no egyptologist would find himself in complete agreement with the author's renderings and comments. But whatever minor inaccuracies there may be in the translation, the non-specialist will get an excellent idea of the style and content of this important body of texts.

We owe a deep debt of gratitude to the veteran Canadian egyptologist for what he has given us and for his courage in tackling so immense an undertaking. He modestly claims no more for his work that that it should be an interim translation and commentary. T.W.T.

MOSCATI, S. : *Geschichte und Kultur der semitischen Völker, Eine Einführung.* 1953. Pp. 214+32 plates and 4 maps. (W. Kohlhammer Verlag, Stuttgart. Price : DM. 4.80.)

This is a translation into German of Professor Moscati's *Storia e Civiltà dei Semiti,* which was published in 1949 (it received a brief notice in the *Book List,* 1950, p. 76). It is, however, much more than merely a translation. It may indeed justly be regarded as a new work. It brings up to date the account of ancient Semitic civilisation which was given in the earlier volume. It includes, for example, references to more recent discoveries, such as those at 'Ain Feshkha, Karatepe, Eziongeber and Sakkara ; the section on the O.T. has been expanded ; the bibliography has been revised ; and a largely different selection of plates has been made. The book, which is intended as an introductory manual, contains a wealth of interesting information, accurately presented, concerning the history of the Semites, their language, literatures, religions, laws and art. Careful scholarship has gone into the writing of it, and the layman, for whom it is written, will find that it will serve him well. D.W.T.

VAN SELMS, A. : *Marriage and Family Life in Ugaritic Literature.* (Pretoria Oriental Series, vol. 1.) 1954. Pp. 164. (Luzac, London. Price : 20s. 0d.)

This is a careful study of marriage, the family, death and inheritance at Ugarit, mainly as reflected in the epic texts, in the light of a wide acquaintance with the voluminous literature on the Ugaritic texts, and issued under all reserve, since it rests largely on the inference that current customs are projected into the stories of the gods. A number of customs which do not figure elsewhere in our surviving literature of the ancient Near East are found here, and the author reaches the conclusion that two different forms of marriage, an older and a younger, are reflected here. He is never dogmatic on disputed points, and in his text or in the extensive footnotes indicates with fairness views other than those which he follows. H.H.R.

WIDENGREN, G. : *Religionens värld. Religionsfenomenologiska studier och översikter.* (Second, revised, and enlarged edition.) 1953. Pp. 534. (Svenska Kyrkans Diakonistyrelses Bokförlag, Stockholm. Price : Paper covers, Sw. crowns 25 ; bound Sw. crowns 29.)

The first edition of this book appeared in 1945 (see *Book List,* 1946). The plan of the present edition differs little from it ; but the author has made a large number of minor additions and modifications (chiefly in references to literature), and has inserted one or two longer sections, thus adding to the value of a very stimulating work. G.W.A.

THE DEAD SEA SCROLLS

COPPENS, J. : *Les Documents du Désert de Juda et les Origines du Christianisme*. (Analecta Lovaniensia Biblica et Orientalia. Sér. 11, fasc. 39.) 1953. Pp. 18. (Extrait des *Cahiers du Libre Examen,* 1953, Pp. 23-39. Price : Belgian Fr. 20.)

Professor Coppens reviews the similarities between the Dead Sea Scrolls and the New Testament, and finds them, on the whole, spurious. Points of contact are not with Jesus and the Kerygma but with Pauline and Johannine writings, and even here there are no traces of mutual dependence but both reflect the use of the Old Testament and certain Apocryphal writings. Coincidences are fortuitous, and of secondary importance, for they indicate nothing more than two parallel and roughly comtemporary movements, and in all essential matters each goes its own way. B.J.R.

ELLIGER, K. : *Studien zum Habakuk-Kommentar vom Toten Meer*. (Beiträge zur historischen Theologie, 15.) 1953. Pp. xiii+302+ supplement, (J. C. B. Mohr (Paul Siebeck), Tübingen. Price : DM. 39.60.)

Professor Elliger, who wrote the commentary on Habakkuk in the *Alte Testament Deutsch* series, has followed it up with a detailed and comprehensive treatment of the Habakkuk scroll—the first full discussion of any of the Dead Sea scrolls to be published. The text of the scroll, including conjectural reconstructions of cols. I and II and other lacunae, is examined for its relationship to the MT of Habakkuk, and its contributions to the study of orthography and pronunciation. The language and style of the interpretation, and the hermeneutics are discussed in detail, and the whole scroll is translated and annotated. Two final chapters deal with the historical background and theological content, and an appendix raises the issues of more recent publications. The bibliography of some 100 items lists the works which deal particularly with DSH, and the supplement gives a Hebrew transcript of the text, which, apart from conjectural reconstructions, diverges from that of Brownlee in as many as 15 places, not always, however, convincingly. The reviewer will not be misunderstood when he says that the outcome of this massive work is not sensational, for its value lies in its detailed scrutiny of the text, its competent survey of current debates, its lucid presentation of problems, and its balanced, sensible conclusions. B.J.R.

VAN 'T LAND, F. A. W., and VAN DER WOUDE, A. S. : *De Habakuk-rol van 'Ain Fašha*, with a Foreword by Th.C. Vriezen. (Semietische Teksten met Vertaling, No. 1.) 1954. Pp. 32. (Van Gorcum, Assen. Price : Fl. 1.90.)

With this little publication a new series under the editorship of Professors Hospers and Vriezen makes its beginning. It contains no general introduction to the Scroll, but has the printed Hebrew text and the Dutch translation on opposite pages, with brief notes on both pages beneath. The authors have used all the major discussions of this scroll, but have prepared an edition designed for the use of students. The notes are linguistic and textual, and do not discuss questions of historical interpretation, or the date of the work. The Kittim are identified with the Romans, but there is no attempt to identify the Teacher of Righteousness, or other persons referred to, but on the much discussed XI 6, the view of Dupont-Sommer is followed, but with a query. The whole is excellently suited to the readers for whom it is designed.

H.H.R.

ROBERTS, B. J. : *The Dead Sea Scrolls and the Old Testament Scriptures*. (Reprinted from *Bulletin of the John Rylands Library*, vol. 36, No. 1, September, 1953.) Pp. 22. (Manchester University Press and The John Rylands Library, Manchester. Price : 2s. 6d.)

The author deals with two subjects : (1) the Biblical exegesis favoured by the " New Covenanters "; (2) the character of their Biblical text. Their exegesis is quite different from the *pilpulism* of the Mishna and the allegorizing method of Philo ; it presents closer affinities with the New Testament use of the Old Testament, which has been studied afresh of late by T. W. Manson and C. H. Dodd. It is, moreover, characteristically apocalyptic exegesis (found, for example, in Daniel), in which earlier prophetic oracles (whether " unfulfilled " or already fulfilled) are interpreted as having explicit reference to persons and events in the apocalyptist's own day. Roberts is reserved about the historic occasion of the sectarian works found among the Scrolls ; but when he says that the case for identifying the sect with Essenes, Ebionites, Karaites or Sadducees " can be presented more or less plausibly ", it might be added that the case for some of these identifications is much less plausible than for others. That they were an apocalyptic sect, however, radically divergent from orthodox Judaism, is shown by their acceptance of the Pseudepigrapha. As for their Biblical texts, these (despite " freak readings " in DSIa) are evidence for a pre-Massoretic Hebrew text in substantial agreement with our MT. " The text which we know as the Massoretic is probably very much older than the Massoretic period, and was accepted by Palestinian Jews of all shades of belief and custom ".

F.F.B.

VERMÈS, G. : *Les Manuscrits du Désert de Juda*. 1953. Pp. 216. (Desclée & Cie, Tournai. Price : Fr. 600.)

Father Vermès surveys with notable success the vast field of study presented by the Dead Sea (or, now, Qumrân) scrolls, and the more recent discoveries connected with them. In Part 1 of the book, over eighty literary documents are classified according to content, provenance, ownership, and, where available, edition. The story of the various discoveries, and problems related to the age of the manuscripts are outlined.

Various theories concerning the date and identity of the party are carefully discussed, and the author presents his own conclusions, that they were Essenes in the Early Roman period, with readiness for possible objections. Some of the main religious and theological aspects are presented, though in this part of the work less notice is taken of the available discussions and divergent views. Part 2 of the book provides annotated translation of all published texts, including the Damascus Document, and, in an appendix, two Murabba'at documents, with commentaries. The bibliography, conveniently sub-divided into sections on editions, translations, introductions, archaeology, philology, historical and literary studies, doctrinal problems, is mainly helpful for items of French and Jewish provenance.   B.J.R.

APOCRYPHA AND POST-BIBLICAL JUDAISM

ALBECK, H. : *The six Divisions of the Mishnah*, vocalized by H. Yalon : Seder Mo'ed, 1952, pp. xxviii+516 ; Seder Nezîqîn, 1953, pp. viii+506. (Mossad Bialik, Jerusalem, and Dvir, Tel Aviv.)

Bialik, the greatest poet of the Hebrew Revival, threw open the treasure house of Jewish legend to his people in his Anthology on the Aggadah. It was also a constant dream of his to make the treasures of the Halakah available as well, in a popular edition of the Mishnah with a short commentary, but before his death in 1934 only one small volume was issued—Seder Zeraim. Now after years of preparation, Bialik's programme is being carried out, but in a form far superior to the humble beginnings envisaged by its author. The publication of eight volumes is contemplated in the course of four years. One volume will be devoted to each of the six divisions of the Mishnah, one will be an introduction covering the history of Oral Tradition and of the formation of the Mishnah, and the final volume will deal with all the *Realia* which appear in the Mishnah or the existence of which the Mishnah tacitly assumes.

A unique value—especially to the Biblical scholar and to the research student in Semitic Languages—attaches to this edition due to the entirely new vocalization of the text by H. Yalon, the distinguished grammarian and philologist. From the eighteenth century until to-day the vocalization of the Mishnah and of Hebrew liturgical texts has always been done on the basis of the rules formulated by the Massoretes of Tiberias in connection with the text of the Bible. Nevertheless, there were always those who claimed that the grammar and pronunciation of the Hebrew of the Mishnah are in no way based upon the rules formulated by the Tiberias Massoretes for Biblical Hebrew and many texts discovered in the Cairo Genizah have lent added support to this view. In this edition Yalon has attempted to vocalize the Mishnah according to the original pronunciation of Rabbinical Hebrew. In this undertaking he has drawn on two sources : (1) Traditions in the reading of the Mishnah which have survived with most

extraordinary persistence in various Jewish congregations—
Ashkenazic, Sephardic, Yemenite, Babylonian, Moroccan and
others (the question here is whether Yalon has taken sufficiently
into account the corrupting influence on the various congregations in their readings of the Mishnah, of the accepted
pronunication of the Hebrew spoken by them to-day). (2) a
careful comparison of ancient manuscripts and printed texts.
The results of Yalon's work give evidence of considerable
thought and independence of judgement. In certain cases
he has been able to arrive at a decision in accordance with a
consistent system but in others the extremely varied nature
of the material and the difficulties of coming to a conclusion
have obliged him to be more eclectic.

As to the Commentary : each tractate is preceded by a survey
of all the Biblical references involved and then comes an
introduction to the subject matters of the tractate and its
principal problems. The commentary itself falls into two
divisions. Under the text of the Mishnah (the careful punctuation of which is almost a commentary in itself) is printed a
short explanation. It is obvious that much work has been
put into this but it is faithful in spirit to the classic commentaries and follows in their steps. (In this section of his
work Prof. Albeck has been able to use drafts, made by his
assistants.) In addition to this each volume is provided with
an inclusive appendix (in Seder Mo'ed 111 pages, in Seder
Nezîqîn 102, in close print) in which Albeck dwells particularly
on critical problems and controversial points. Both commentary and appendix reveal a masterly command both of
Talmudic sources of all kinds (the Apocryphal books, Philo,
Josephus, etc. included) as well as the extensive research,
mediaeval and modern, in these fields.   I.L.S.

ALLON, G. : *History of the Jews in Palestine during the Mishnaic-
Talmudic period* (in Hebrew). 1953. Pp. xii+382. (Ha-Qibbuz
ha-meuḥad, Tel Aviv.)

The book contains the lectures on the Early Talmudic period
given by the late G. Allon in the Hebrew University. This
first volume covers the period from the destruction of the
Second Temple (70 C.E.) to the eve of the revolt of Bar
Kochba (132 C.E.). The author, highly gifted both as a scholar
and as an academic teacher, passed away in 1950 in his 49th
year. The lectures have been reconstructed partly from
Allon's own notes and partly from those of his students. It is
obvious that the book has not taken the form that the author
himself would have chosen for it. The concentration of the
material, the titles of chapters, the place references show a
certain lack of accuracy and even the quotations and the
statements of facts are not entirely free from mistakes.

Nevertheless, despite its imperfections of form, this book
which was awarded the State of Israel Prize for Humanities
for 1953 makes a very deep impression. In the Introduction
the writer expresses his view that the destruction of the State
and of the Second Temple does not constitute the direct

opening of the period of the Diaspora. Instead Allon sees the Talmudic period as a period of transition both from the point of view of the position of the country during those hundreds of years and also from the point of view of the degree of autonomy, which the Jewish people enjoyed at the time. (In view of the reservations with which this theory has met in some Israeli reviews, the present reviewer would like to express his concurrence with Allon's opinion. He believes that the thousand years between 586 B.C.E. up to approximately 500 C.E. comprise one long united period in the history of the Jewish people, a period of the unfolding of four great transitory processes.)

The arrangement of the materials in the lectures themselves is partly on a chronological, partly on a topical basis. Rabbi Jochanan ben Zakkai and Rabbi Gamaliel II stand out as central figures. The various chapters deal among other things with the effects of the destruction of the Temple on the national conscience, the position of Judaea in the Roman Empire, Roman military and civil rule, density of population and emigration, branches of agriculture and their products, industry and trade, forms of autonomy and internal rule, the Sanhedrin (its nature and legislative authority), the Halakah as the expression of national life as well as its inspiration, Judaism making its stand against rising Christianity, the situation in the country and the state of mind of the people on the eve of the Bar Kochba revolt.

The book abounds in brilliant and original views and even those to whom these views are not always acceptable cannot but feel a sincere admiration for the writer's masterly control of the sources (as well as the researches on the subjects dealt with) and for his genius in bringing together slight data scattered throughout the wide literature of the time, Talmudic, classical and Christian, inscriptions, papyri and archaeological discoveries. He has a special talent for hearing in the sayings of the Aggadah and Halakah echoes of the life of the time, national, social, and spiritual, but it is in his ability to identify himself heart and soul with the world he is describing that he is particularly gifted.

This book, therefore, represents an achievement of exceptionally high value and the loss of its author is much to be lamented.

I.L.S.

The Apocrypha (King James Version), with an Introduction by R. H. Pfeiffer. 1954. Pp. xl+296. (Harpers, New York. Price : $2.)

This edition of the Apocrypha in the Authorized Version has a very useful Introduction by Professor Pfeiffer, which is packed with information, not a little of which is not easily accessible elsewhere. There is first of all a general section, giving in brief the history of the Apocrypha in the Canon, and then a short special introduction to each of the books. Many who would not tackle so large a book as Pfeiffer's *History of New Testament Times* will find much instruction here.

H.H.R.

BLACKMAN, P. : *Mishnayoth*. Vol. III. *Order Nashim*. Pointed Hebrew text, Introductions, Translations, Notes, Supplement, Appendix, Indexes. 1953. Pp. 518. (Mishna Press, London. Price : 40s. 0d.)

The third volume of this edition and translation of the *Mishnah* follows the pattern of the previous two (see *Book List*, 1953, p. 74). The translation, excessively literal and inelegant, is not always accurate. *Nedarim* I, 3 : *'imra'* is ' ram ', not ' lamb ' or ' sheep ' ; ' book-case ' for *tebhah* (*Ned* V, 5) is odd ; and in *Kethuboth* IX, 1 ; " If this be so, why did he state to her in writing ' I will have no claim whatever to thy property ', so that if she sold it or gave it away her act should be valid ?" the question-mark should come (here and in the Hebrew text) after the word ' property '. J.L.T.

BLOCH, J. : *On the Apocalyptic in Judaism*. (Jewish Quarterly Review Monograph Series, Number II.) 1953. Pp. 154. (Dropsie College, Philadelphia. Price : $2.75.)

This is a study of the rise and development of Jewish apocalyptic writings, their influence upon other forms of literature, their main conceptions and place in Judaism. The author gives a well balanced and just appreciation of apocalyptic, safeguard-ing it against one-sided views and short-sighted judgements which would restrict or unduly minimize the influence of its thought. It is clearly indicated that within Judaism there were circles that could not be expected to be entirely sym-pathetic to apocalyptic works. The Pharisees had reason to fear that the empty and even dangerous dreams of such works might jeopardise the political future of the Jewish community in its relationship to the Roman Power. The editor of the Mishna who has omitted from it all reference to apocalyptic ideas except in a very small passage in a single tractate may be suspected of having been unsusceptible to the religious notions to which he pays so little attention. Besides this, after the two great disastrous wars of 61-70 and 132-135 (Bar Kokba) had extinguished every hope of freedom in Judaism, that literature, wherein the political-religious hopes of Israel had attained its highest expression, virtually came to an abrupt end. Many apocalyptic works no doubt disappeared from this date. But to write the word *finis* over this whole school of thought and writing would be definitely to misread the evidence. It is here that the value of Mr. Bloch's work is to be perceived. The influence of apocalyptic did not come to an end. Its fruits were yet to be gathered ; for in an abundant literature throughout three centuries it had left a legacy to posterity. The author shows how apocalyptic conceptions survive not only in the Church Fathers but also in the early writings of rabbis and how from Haggadic sources the men who compiled the Talmud and Midrashim brought together the apocalyptic teachings of the sages. Also the under-current of this type of thought is apparent in much of medieval Jewish theology and kabbalistic teachings. The conceptions of the apocalyptic literature are not described or discussed in any systematic fashion but the author illumines some of them with useful comments. The book is well printed and its thought and style clear. O.S.R.

BONSIRVEN, J. : *La Bible Apocryphe, en Marge de L'Ancien Testament.* (Textes pour l'Histoire Sacrée.) 1953. Pp. 336. (Librairie Arthème Fayard, Paris. Price : Fr. 500.)

> Contains extracts from the books which are collected in Charles's volume of Pseudepigrapha with the exception of The Martyrdom of Isaiah, Pirke Aboth and Ahiqar and the addition of The Ascension of Isaiah and the sectarian documents from the Dead Sea Scrolls. Each extract is prefaced by brief remarks concerning date and origin and where passages are omitted a précis is given. The translation into French is sometimes the editor's own and sometimes taken from established French translations. L.H.B.

DANCY, J. C. : *A Commentary on I Maccabees.* 1954. Pp. viii +206+1 Map. (Blackwell, Oxford. Price : 18s. 0d.)

> This volume contains a full Introduction with a bibliography (pp. 1-54), followed by a commentary which assumes that the student has the R.V. open before him. Two line maps are provided : the Near East in Hellenistic times, and Palestine in the 2nd century B.C. The work shows wide reading of the relevant literature, coupled with close study of the text and an independent judgement. The commentary is terse and selective : no space is occupied in explaining the obvious ; and genuine difficulties are fairly tackled. Though the commentary is primarily on I Macc., the relevant passages from II Macc. are regularly cited, and, where necessary, commented on. Considerable use is made of the evidence of coins. The commentator has had in mind the needs of students, who have to " do " I Macc. for examination purposes ; to them it will be a present help. And students of longer standing and maturer years will consult it with profit. T.W.M.

HADAS, M. : *The Third and Fourth Books of the Maccabees.* 1953. Pp. 248. (Harper & Brothers, New York, for Dropsie College, Philadelphia. Price : $4.00.)

> Professor Moses Hadas has translated and edited Third and Fourth Maccabees, to form the third volume in the *Jewish Apocryphal Literature* series, sponsored by Dropsie College. Like its predecessors, the volume is well bound and excellently presented. It contains a full introduction to each book, and the Greek Text (after Rahlfs) and the editor's new translation on opposite pages, with careful and informative footnotes where necessary. Third Maccabees is dated 25-24 B.C., when a new crisis occurred in the civic status of Egyptian Jewry. The writer was a Jew of Alexandria who followed the pattern of Greek romance with perhaps a substratum of truth in his story of a census of two centuries before his time. Possibly the book is intended as a corrective of the Esther story.

624

The date of Fourth Maccabees is given as the reign of Caligula (37-41 A.D.). The writer was thoroughly Hellenistic in literary style and thought, so that the book had a great vogue among early Christian writers. The theme of the book is The Sovereignty of Reason, a title given to the work in early days, and the martyrdom of the heroes is treated as an illustration of this theme. The homiletical value of the book was recognised in early Christian times, and the present volume enhances its value in this respect. N.H.S.

HOENIG, S. B. : *The Great Sanhedrin*. 1953. Pp. xviii+310. (Bloch Publishing Co., New York. Price : $5.00.)

There is assembled here a useful mass of material from Greek, as well as Jewish sources, relative to the study of the Sanhedrin. According to Hoenig the Sanhedrin was established in 141 B.C., the year in which the independence of the Jewish nation was proclaimed and the priesthood conferred upon Simon. Simon the Just is identified with Simon the Hasmonean. The two leaders of the Sanhedrin, the Nasi and the Ab Bet Din, are said to be the leaders of the two parties in the Sanhedrin, conservative and liberal (not Sadducee and Pharisee). Rabbinic sources are freely used. The terms Great Sanhedrin and Bet Din ha-Gadol are used indiscriminately and the reader has to make a quick mental equation at each change. It is difficult, at times, to understand exactly what the author does think about the functions of the Sanhedrin. On page 23 we read : " the Bet Din ha-Gadol possessed functions of a religious and judicial nature. It devoted itself purely to interpreting the Law " and on page 85 : " The Great Sanhedrin was more legislative than judicial. Nevertheless its main function was to probe into the constitutionality of the law ". L.H.B.

DE JONGE, M. : *The Testaments of the Twelve Patriarchs*, with an introduction by T. W. Manson. 1953. Pp. 184. (Van Gorcum, Assen, and Manchester University Press. Price : 18s. 0d.)

This Dutch dissertation challenges current views on the *Testaments* very radically. It maintains, after a careful study of the evidence, that there is no adequate reason to suppose that the Testaments are a Jewish work with Christian interpolations. Instead, the author argues that they are a Christian work, which made use of older Jewish material. He would date the work about A.D. 200, and thinks it is of importance for the understanding of Christian thought at that time. The report that fragments of the Testaments have been found at Qumran (cf. *B.A.S.O.R.*, February, 1953, p. 2) does not augur well for the theory, though until we know more of the texts found and the evidences of the date of deposit that accompanied them, it would be premature to pronounce judgement. It may well be that Dr. de Jonge's arguments will be used to throw light on the Qumran finds. His work is in any case careful and thorough, and Professor Manson declares it the best introduction to the study of the *Testaments*. H.H.R.

MANSON, T. W. : *The Servant-Messiah : a Study of the Public Ministry of Jesus*. 1953. Pp. 104. (Cambridge University Press. Price : 10s. 6d.)

The importance of this book is not to be measured by its size and anyone concerned about the subject with which it deals would be well advised to read it. The larger part of the book discusses matters which are not the special interest of this *Book List*. It is otherwise with the first chapter which seeks to describe the Messianic hope as Jews entertained it about the beginning of the Christian era, ' the hope of restoring on a higher level the unity of national life which had been broken at the Exile.' Dr. Manson points for evidence to the apocalypses and to the first chapter of St. Luke's Gospel. His enquiry leads him to discuss the origin of the sects of the Sadducees and the Pharisees, the Messianic expectation of the latter being expressed very fully in the Psalms of Solomon. There is a most useful comparison of the characteristics and tenets of the two sects and, contrary to the view usually held, it is suggested that the name Sadducee has nothing to do with Zadok—the Sadducees emerge in history only after there were hardly any Zadokite priests and in any case the Sadducees were not all priests—but represents a semitizing of the Greek *sundikoi*, while the name Pharisee was a nickname meaning ' Persians ', applied to the sect because of the alleged Zoroastrian origin of some of its beliefs, which was later ' furnished with an edifying etymology ' and interpreted as ' separated '. The second chapter gives a very penetrating account of the ministry of John the Baptist who struck a deadly blow against the Messianic expectation with which large elements in Judaism reached the beginning of the new era.   N.W.P.

MARCUS, R. : *Philo Supplement* (to Loeb Classical Library) : I. *Questions and Answers on Genesis* : II. *Questions and Answers on Exodus*, translated from the ancient Armenian version of the original Greek. 1953. Pp. 552 and 308. (W. Heinemann Ltd., London, and Harvard University Press, Cambridge, Mass. Price : 15s. 0d. or $3.00 each.)

Philo's writings which have been divided into ten volumes in the ' Loeb Classical Library ' edition now receive two supplementary volumes translating the author's work on Genesis and Exodus. All but a small portion of the Greek original has been lost and it is from the Armenian version that the Jewish philosopher's comments on the first two books of the Law have been re-discovered. This version appears to have been made in the fifth century and it is mainly upon three MSS. of this, all of the 13th century, that Dr. Marcus bases his translation, also making use of Aucher's Latin translation of the Armenian version (1826). In his preface the translator commends the Armenian language as felicitous in reproduction of the Greek idiom and states that the Armenian version has shown itself accurate in those places where it can be checked. In the ' Questions and Answers ' the reader is given a very clear view of Philo's method of interpreting scripture, proceeding from the literal to forms of the allegorical. Of much theological interest is his note on Gen. ii. 7 contrasting the ' moulded ' man with the man made " in accordance with the image of God " (Gen. i. 26). Vol. II on Exodus has a most useful index which gives the passages where every significant term occurs and the content of meaning given to it. O.S.R.

SEGAL, M. H. : *Sefer ben Sira ha-Shalem* (The complete Book of Ben Sira), with Introduction, Commentary, and Indices, illustrated with facsimiles (in Hebrew). 1953. Pp. xvi+72+374. (Mossad Bialik, Jerusalem.)

This is a valuable work of high quality into which Prof. M. H. Segal has incorporated the results of several years of research. His interest in Ben Sira is concentrated mainly in the Hebrew remnants of the book. True, he includes his commentary on the remaining chapters as well, but those appear in the form of his own reconstruction (based on the Greek version and occasionally on the Syriac) of the supposedly original Hebrew text of those parts.

The detailed Introduction is notable for the care shown in the construction and classification. It is divided into seven chapters comprising 93 sections. The first chapter is concerned with the personality of Ben Sira and the period in which he lived. Here Segal gives reasons for his acceptance of the view of Jewish tradition that Ben Sira's name was Simon. In the second chapter, dealing with the work itself, Segal divides the book on a new basis (differing from the classification of Smend and Peters) into eight pericopes. The chapters of the book, which are numbered here according to the Hebrew manuscripts instead of according to the Greek, are also divided into verses anew, in keeping with the form of the Biblical proverb. The third chapter is devoted to the form of Ben Sira's writings. The section on the language is interesting, but in the sections on the style there is a notable drawback in the complete failure to consider the modern approach of *Formgeschichte*. The first chapter considers the teachings of Ben Sira. The writer gives a good account of Ben Sira's ethical and religious outlook, though it would have been desirable here to dwell more carefully on the problem of the Hellenistic elements which seem to have found expression in Ben Sira's views despite himself. The fifth chapter dealing with the history of the book is an important one. It is rich in material from the quotations from Ben Sira in the Talmud and the Midrashim. A finer differentiation between the different formulas of introduction of these quotations, between the liberal reproductions and freer renderings, might have offered a better understanding of the semi-canonical character of the book. Segal has an interesting theory that the Amoraim in Babylon in the fifth century made use of a collection of extracts from Ben Sira together with other books. In the sixth chapter an account of the discovering of the Hebrew fragments of the book is accompanied by a detailed description

and study of the five Hebrew manuscripts. (The fixing of
their dates by Dr. S. Birnbaum is printed in the list of
corrections and additions.) Chapter seven gives a consideration of the Hebrew, Greek and Syriac versions and is an
interesting study in the comparative criticism of texts.

In the Commentary the book is divided into its organic
sections. Immediately after each section appear textual
corrections and a detailed philological Commentary. The
Commentary has its own value, quite independent of the
Commentaries already in existence. It is rather a pity however
that the writer, though not entirely neglecting the ideas
expressed, is after all more concerned to explain section and
verse than to provide a historical conception of the topics
of the text.   I.L.S.

STEINMANN, J.: *Lecture de Judith*. 1953. Pp. 136. (Gabalda, Paris.
Price : Fr. 300.)

This is a delightful little volume of notes in exposition of the
book of Judith. Judith is not an historical romance, M.
Steinmann points out, for a romance of this sort must be
careful to recognise certain facts of history while Judith
presents a tissue of anachronisms that must be deliberate.
The events it describes have been placed by critics at various
periods between 650 B.C. and A.D. 118 but the writing's orbit
of thought is apocalyptic and its vision is *au-dessus du temps*.
Its geography also, to which Scripture has contributed place-
names, is largely fanciful. The most important city from
the point of view of the narrative is Bethulia but it is quite
unknown outside the book. What complex of ideas this city
represents in the mind of the author must be left to M.
Steinmann's readers to consider. The story of Judith moves
on to its climax, the victory of the God of Israel over the
"Assyrian" armies. The divine victory initiated by Judith
is depicted with worthy reserve and restraint. It was no
moral objection arising from the assassination of Holophernes
which excluded Judith from the canon of scripture but,
according to M. Steinmann, the book's almost evangelical
universalism which praises the conversion of Achior the
Ammonite and his admission to the congregation of Israel.
                                                        O.S.R.

VAILLANT, A.: *Le Livre des Secrets d'Hénoch : Texte Slave et Traduction
Française*. (Textes publiés par l'Institut d' Études slaves, IV.)
1952. Pp. xxvi+128. (Institut d'Études Slaves, Paris. Price :
Fr. 1,630.)

A fresh critical investigation of the *Book of the Secrets of Enoch*
by an expert in Slavonic studies has long been urgently
needed, for the pioneer (and unfinished) work of Sokolov and
the German and English editions of Bonwetsch and Morfill
(on which Charles's editions were based) leave much to be
desired in the way of critical scholarship. In his now published
Lektüre on II Enoch, M. A. Vaillant, *Directeur d'Études* of the
École Pratique des Hautes Études, has produced a new edition

of the Slavonic text (based, however, on already published MSS.), with introduction, parallel French translation and copious textual and philological notes. The results, if not unfamiliar to Slavonic experts, spring a complete surprise on the student of apocalyptic literature who knows no Slavonic and who has been brought up on the views of R. H. Charles. In spite of the authority of Sokolov and Morfill (and the consentient opinion of Charles) to the contrary, M. Vaillant comes to the same conclusion as Nathaniel Schmidt that the shorter form of the book is alone ancient (the longer ' original ' version is in fact the product of the fantasy of 15th and 16th century Slavonic redactors). The short 10th century apocalypse has preserved a lost ancient *Christian* Book of Enoch known to Origen (hitherto no one has doubted that we had to do with a Jewish apocalypse). II Enoch represented a Jewish-Christian (and Hellenistic) development of the ancient Jewish Enoch tradition. (I Enoch) (its eight beatitudes are suspiciously Mt.'s, and its rewriting of the legend of the miraculous birth of Noah in I Enoch owes not a little to the Christian birth-stories). M. Vaillant has confined his task mainly to placing a critical text with notes and a literal translation at the disposal of the experts in apocalyptic literature : but he has committed himself at the same time to a judgement of the essential character of the original work on which expert opinion may be found to differ (like much in the older ' Jewish ' Enoch some may feel that we have to do with a typical product of a syncretistic Enoch ' cult ', Jewish inspired, but possibly borrowing from Christian—as from other—traditions). M.Bl.

PHILOLOGY AND GRAMMAR

DRIVER, G. R. : *Aramaic Documents of the Fifth Century B.C. Transcribed and edited with Translation and Notes, with help from a Typescript by E. Mittwoch, W. B. Henning, H. J. Polotsky, and F. Rosenthal.* 1954. Pp. xii+60, with 24 plates. (Geoffrey Cumberlege, Clarendon Press, Oxford. Price : 84s. 0d.)

The Aramaic leather documents, from an unknown Egyptian site, which are published in this beautifully produced folio volume for the first time, formed part of the archives of 'Aršam, who was satrap of Egypt in the reign of Darius II. This 'Aršam is to be identified with 'Aršam mentioned in Neo-Babylonian texts, and also with the person of the same name in the Elephantine papyri. The Greek historians Ctesias and Polyaenus also refer to him. None of the documents is dated, but the editor concludes that they were written during the three years 411/10-408 B.C. They were written during 'Aršam's absence from Egypt, and were dispatched either from Susa or Babylon. They consist of instructions issued by 'Aršam and other Persian officers of high rank to subordinate Persian administrative officers in Egypt, and they deal in the main with the administration of the domain-lands in Egypt held by highly placed Persian officers and with the difficulties arising out of the mutual relations of the local officers of the administration to one another and to the subject population. Three letters are of a different character. One is concerned with a commission for a sculptor to make equestrian statues ; another contains instructions for expediting an officer on a journey and supplying him with provisions ; while the third conveys thanks for the dispatch of a cloak and some hides. Thirteen complete letters are included in the volume, with fragments of a number of others. A historical introduction deals with the discovery of the letters, writing on leather, the contents of the collection (the leather bag in which the documents were found is unique), the subject matter of the letters, their order, date, place of origin and language, the persons mentioned in them, and offices in the Persian administration. An appendix is devoted to the Neo-Babylonian, Elephantine, and Greek testimony concerning 'Aršam, and a glossary of Aramaic words is supplied. A wealth of most valuable philological and linguistic material is contained in the notes, and the plates are magnificent, the degree of legibility achieved by the infra-red process of photography being truly remarkable. The publication of this editio princeps is a highly important event in the history of Aramaic studies. Its excellence marks it out as a major work of scholarship, upon which all future study of these texts must be based.   D.W.T.

JENNI, E. : *Das Wort 'ōlām im Alten Testament.* 1953. Pp. 88. (Alfred Töpelmann, Berlin. Price : Swiss Fr. 3.00 from the author, Kirchweg 9, Binningen, Switzerland.)

This is a reproduction of the author's article under the same title in *Zeitschrift für die Alttestamentliche Wissenschaft* lxiv (1952), and lxv (1953). It offers a careful survey of the use of the term 'ōlām in the Old Testament with due regard to its etymology and the comparative material in the epigraphic texts ; and if it contains little that is new, it is a welcome thing to have one's general impressions confirmed by a painstaking study of this kind. Altogether the work may be regarded as a useful contribution to current discussion of the treatment of time in the Bible.   A.R.J.

KÖHLER, L. and BAUMGARTNER, W. : *Lexicon in Veteris Testamenti Libros* (fasc. XV—XVIII). 1953. Pp. 897-1,138+lxviii. (Brill, Leiden. Price : 5s. 6d. each part, except the last, which is 13s. 6d., with binding case.)

It is a pleasure to welcome another four parts of this dictionary issued during the current year and bringing the whole work to completion ; thus making it indispensable to all serious study of the Old Testament. The Aramaic portion, which is by Baumgartner, is equally well done with the Hebrew part, and both authors have done a real service to scholarship.   G.R.D.

KRAELING, E. G. : *The Brooklyn Museum Aramaic Papyri : New Documents of the Fifth Century B.C. from the Jewish Colony at Elephantine.* 1953. Pp. xvi+320+plates. (Yale University Press, New Haven for The Brooklyn Museum, and Geoffrey Cumberlege, London. Price : $10.00 or 80s. 0d.)

Here is published for the first time a collection of Aramaic papyri acquired by the Egyptologist, C. E. Wilbour, in 1893 but unknown until it was bequeathed by Wilbour's daughter to Brooklyn Museum in 1947. It consists of nine complete rolls, eight of which preserved their original cords and seals, besides a large number of fragments. They are now published as seventeen texts, transcribed into square characters, each text being furnished with an introduction, a translation and full notes. Twenty-three excellent plates are given and there are indexes of words and proper names. The editor prefixes a valuable introduction consisting of ten chapters in which he discusses various themes arising from previous recoveries of Egyptian Aramaic documents and shows the bearing of the newly published texts on such problems as the location of the Jewish Temple at Elephantine. All students of the Old Testament ought to have access to this important and handsome publication, and it is to be hoped that Dr. Kraeling will put us further in his debt by producing an edition of his texts suitable for classroom use.   W.D.M.

KUTSCHER, E. J. : *Meḥqarim ba-'Aramith ha-Gelilith* (in Hebrew, with English Summary). 1952. Pp. 68. (Reprinted from *Tarbiz*, vol. XXI-XXIII, Jerusalem.)

This collection of articles deals with problems of Galilean Aramaic, namely with the Aramaic parts of the Yerushalmi, the various Midrashim, Targ. " Jonathan ", etc. G. Dalman's *Grammatik des jüd.-pal. Aramäisch* is now somewhat out of date and embodies some shortcomings, the chief amongst them being the faulty texts he has made use of—texts on which various Babylonian linguistic forms have been grafted by European Jews who were mainly acquainted with the Babylonian Talmud and with the Targ. Onkelos on the Pentateuch. The pruning of some of these graftings is attempted by the author who makes use in the main of Cairo Genizah MSS. In the last section, which has a bearing on the Judean Scrolls, the variations in the pharyngals in the Galilean Aramaic during the first centuries C.E. are dealt with.   M.W.

MOLDENKE, H. N. and A. L. : *Plants of the Bible.* 1952. Pp. 328. (Chronica Botanica Company, Waltham, Mass. Price : 60s. 0d.)

This volume, written by the Curator and Administrator of The Herbarium, New York Botanical Garden, with the assistance of his wife, is intended as a résumé of present day knowledge of the botany of the Bible (O.T., N.T., Apocrypha). The main part of it consists of a discussion of 231 different botanical terms to which reference is made in the Bible. Myths, superstitions and legends about the plants in question find a place in it. There is a bibliography of 605 items, an index of all Biblical verses referred to, and a very full general index. Numerous illustrations and plates are provided. Many interesting identifications are proposed—e.g., *beka'im* in 2 Sam. v. 23f. are Euphrates aspens; *ḥarul* in Zeph. ii. 9 and Job xxx. 7 is possibly the acanthus plant, but in Prov. xxiv. 31 it is the charlock; and *tappuaḥ* is the apricot. On a large part of this work only a botanist can pass judgement. O.T. students, however, will not infrequently be astonished at what they read. For example, of the Ussher chronology, which is here adopted for the dating of Biblical occurrences, it is said—" we realize that modern Biblical scholars do not place complete reliance on this old chronology "; the M.T. " may have been written between the 6th and 8th centuries A.D. ", after which time " it was copied and re-copied by lonely monks "; and the Vulgate is " thought to date to the second century ". Such statements would seem to suggest that, while the volume is one which the O.T. student who is curious about Biblical botany will wish to consult, he will do well to use it with care.   D.W.T.

Rosch-Pinnah, E. : *Hebräisch ein uraltes Hieroglyphensystem.* N.D. Pp. xii+200. (Verlag Transocean and Palestine Ltd., Tel-Aviv. Price : 40s. 0d.)

This book is not worthy of serious attention. Starting from the fact that the Hebrew letters are derived from representations of objects, the author seeks to explain Hebrew words in the light of the original forms of the letters that compose them. Thus the word spelt *'aleph mêm* comes to mean " mother " because it is the mother who gives water (*mêm*) to the ox (*'aleph*), and *.'b* means " father " because it is the father to whom the ox (*'aleph*) and the house (*bêth*) belong !   T.W.T.

Rossell, W. H. : *A Handbook of Aramaic Magical Texts.* (Shelton Semitic Series, No. 2.) 1953. Pp. 154. (Silver Book Shop, Astoria 6, New Jersey, U.S.A. Price : $3.00.)

This Handbook contains a convenient selection, numbering 30, of Aramaic magic bowls from Iraq, with a sketch of their grammar and a glossary. Students of this somewhat recondite subject will find it a trustworthy guide ; but a regret may be expressed that no single bowl is reproduced in facsimile (which can now be easily done by means of a Görtz-lens) to give readers a sample of the script. The book is in typescript, excellently executed and mechanically reproduced ; and the pages are bound together by metallic clips.   G.R.D.

Roussel, L. : *La racine sémantique vue de l'hébreu.* 1953. Pp. 62. (Presses Universitaires de France, Paris. Price : Fr. 250.)

This work is a brief catalogue of Hebrew roots drawn up to show that this was originally bi-consonantal, a fact that has been long recognized. The work is, however, amateurish ; the author uses a new system of transliteration which can only madden the reader, no reference is made to the handful of primitive roots (describing human relationships and various natural objects) which really provide the proof of this fact, and a number of words appear, like members of a stage-army, in several different categories. 								G.R.D.

SEGAL, J. B. : *The Diacritical Point and the Accents in Syriac.* (London Oriental Series, vol. 2.) 1953. Pp. 180. (G. Cumberlege, O.U.P., London. Price : 45s. 0d.)

In this work Dr. Segal, lecturer in Modern Hebrew at the School of Oriental and African Studies, devotes, after a general introduction, four chapters to the study of the diacritical point up to the thirteenth cent., and four to the study of the accents in Syriac up to the same period. There is an appendix of vowel diagrams, and five plates with descriptions are added. A useful bibliography and five indexes complete the work. This forms an admirable collection of material gleaned from manuscripts and native grammarians and treated in a scholarly manner, and, although the subject will not attract many students, the teacher of Syriac will do well to have this work available for reference. 								W.D.M.

SNIJDERS, L. A. : *The Meaning of zār in the Old Testament.* 1953. Pp. viii+154. (Brill, Leiden.)

This is a doctoral dissertation by a pupil of Professor de Boer, which is reprinted in *Oudtestamentische Studiën*, vol. x, and reviewed elsewhere in this issue of the *Book List* (p. 3). A few errata which remain uncorrected in *O.T.S.* are here corrected in an errata slip. 								H.H.R.

1955

This is the tenth issue of the Book List for which I have been responsible. Without the co-operation of many people, in addition to the panel of reviewers appointed by the Society, it would be impossible to make it so widely inclusive. Professors Baumgartner, de Boer, Eissfeldt, Muilenburg, Ringgren, and Weingreen and Abbé Delcor have helped me by writing notices, and many others have helped me with the prices of books. Wherever possible these have been added, in original currency normally.

It will be noted that more Israeli books are noticed in this issue. I have to acknowledge the much greater co-operation I have had from Israeli publishers, and the great improvement in facilities for obtaining their publications. Members who have difficulty in obtaining these books should write to G. Cornfeld, Esq., " Sifrei Israel," 78, Achad-Haam St., Tel-Aviv, Israel.

Owing to my absence in America in February and March, the material had to be sent to the Printer earlier than usual this year. This has inevitably meant that more books have had to be held over than would otherwise have been the case, though I acknowledge with gratitude the help I have had from the Printer by the inclusion of a number of late notices at the proof stage.

Titles to which an asterisk (*) is prefixed are recommended for inclusion in school libraries.

MANCHESTER UNIVERSITY.   H. H. ROWLEY.

(ALT, A.) : *Festschrift Albrecht Alt*. (Wissenschaftliche Zeitschrift der Karl-Marx-Universität Leipzig ; Gesellschafts- und Sprach-wissenschaftliche Reihe, 3. Jahrgang, 1953/54.) Pp. 178.

This Festschrift contains eighteen essays in honour of Albrecht Alt and a Bibliography of his published work. The essays range from Archaeology to Church History and the Study of Religions. No attempt was made to get a unified theme. About half of them are devoted to the Old Testament or associated studies. Mention may be made of the following essays : R. Meyer, ' Die Bedeutung der linearen Vokalisation für die hebräische Sprachgeschichte ' ; J. Herz, ' Formges-chichtliche Untersuchungen zum Problem des Hiobbuches ' ; F. Maass, ' Zur Psychologischen Sonderung der Ekstase ' : and beyond the limits of the Old Testament, E. Sommerlath, ' Glaube und Illusion,' and E. Lauch, ' Etwas vom Codex Sinaiticus.' L.H.B.

(ASSAF, S.) : *Sēfer Assāf* (A collection of studies presented to Rabbi Prof. S. Assaf on the occasion of his 60th birthday, by his friends, colleagues and pupils), edited by M. D. Cassuto, J. Klausner and J. Guttmann. 1953. Pp. 528. (Rabbi Kook Foundation, Jerusalem. Price : 26s. 0d.)

Besides an appreciation of the Jubilant by J. Klausner and a bibliographical list of his writings by J. Raphael, this all-Hebrew volume contains 35 articles. Only those, however, pertaining to the Biblical and the relatively early post-Biblical Jewish period can be referred to here. B. Maisler identified Gimti of El-Amarna 290 : 8-11 with Gath (1 Sam. vii. 10-14) and Gittim (2 Ki. xii. 18) and with Rās Abū Hamīd S.S.E. of Ramla. M. H. Segal 'The Marriage of a High-Priest's Son to the Daughter of Sanballat and the Building of the Temple of Gerizim ' considers Neh. xiii. 28-30 a concise summary of the events described in Josephus, *Ant*. xi. 302-345. J. J. Rabinowitz discovers Jewish influence in some Baby-lonian contract formulas of the Persian period. P. Dickstein finds the Jewish attitude towards marriage expressed in the tendency to regard it as part of public rather than of civil law. B. Cohen reveals the points of contact between Jewish and Roman laws of *usus fructus*. Z. Ben Hayyim ascribes the non-Tiberian vocalization of the suffixes *k, t, h*, to Aramaic influence. J. Guttmann considers Messianism as the crucial factor in the origin of the Trajanic up-risings. A. A. Finkelstein finds Shammaitic influences in *Sifrē* Dt., and holds that the latter was edited by the School of R. Eliezer. M. Margolius places " Sēder Eliyyāhū " in the second half of the 3rd century C.E. A. A. Neuman assigns the original Josippon to the first centuries C.E., showing that it has drawn from sources earlier than Josephus and the Apocrypha. Finally, G. Sholem, discussing the early Cabbalistic associations of physiognomy and chiromancy, publishes a text the beginning of which he believes to contain parallels to the opening passage of the *Manual of Discipline*. P.R.W.

(BAECK, L.) : *Essays presented to Leo Baeck on the occasion of his eightieth birthday.* 1954. Pp. xii+212. (East & West Library, London. Price : 20s. 0d.)

> Several of the essays in this tribute to a distinguished representative of modern Jewry offer something of interest to students of the Old Testament, the most notable being ' Samuel und die Lade ' by Martin Buber, a further section from the author's manuscript of *Der Gesalbte=Das Kommende II* (cf. *Book List*, 1953, pp. 7 f.) ; ' Zwei durch Humanisten besorgte, dem Papst gewidmete Ausgaben der hebräischen Bibel ' by Paul Kahle, who discusses the manuscripts underlying two important critical editions of the Hebrew text of the Old Testament, i.e., that which was prepared by Felix Pratensis for the first Rabbinic Bible published by Daniel Bomberg and that which is printed in the Complutensian Polyglot ; and ' The Universalism of Amos ' by Julian Morgenstern, a study of Amos's place in what the author describes in familar evolutionary terms as ' the advance from nationalism to a thorough-going universalism in the religion of Israel.'   A.R.J.

BIČ, M. and SOUČEK, J. B. (ed. by) : *Biblická Konkordance*, Part i. A-Bezbožný. 1954. Pp. 80. (Artia Ltd., 30, Smečky, Prague. Price : Kčs 10.50 or U.S. $1.10 per part.)

> This is the first part of a comprehensive Concordance to the Czech Bible, prepared by the Professors of the Evangelical Faculty in Prague. At the head of each entry the various Hebrew and Greek words corresponding to the Czech word are given in transliteration, and numbers then indicate which word corresponds to which references (as in Hatch-Redpath). Here, however, in Old Testament references the corresponding words in both the Hebrew and the LXX are indicated. A Hebrew and Greek index will be published on the completion of the work, which is expected to run to about 960 pages. The reviewer understands no Czech, but envies the Czech reader a concordance which gives him more information than can be found in any other one concordance known to the present writer.   H.H.R.

Bijbels Woordenboek. 2nd ed. Part 1, Aalmoes-Egypte. 1954. Cols. 416. (Romen & Zonen, Roermond. Price : Fl. 10.75, or by subscription before the appearance of Part 2, Fl. 9.50.)

> The first edition of this one volume Bible Dictionary in Dutch by Catholic scholars was noticed in the *Book List*, 1948, p. 2. The new edition is considerably revised or rewritten, with a new team of authors on the title page, including A. van den Born, J. Coppens, J. de Fraine, W. Grossouw, and J. van der Ploeg, with the collaboration of a number of other Dutch and Belgian Catholic scholars. Maps are redrawn and bibliographies revised and brought up to date, and some new articles have been added (e.g., one on the École Biblique). The work is substantially longer than the earlier edition, which covered the same range of articles in 351 columns. The new article

on the Day of Yahweh is three times the length of the old article. The new edition is therefore in no sense superfluous for the owner of the old, and is of much value to those who would keep abreast of the very active work of Catholic Biblical scholars.   H.H.R.

(Byvanck, A. W.) : *Varia Historica aangeboden aan Prof. Dr. A. W. Byvanck*. 1954. Pp. x+286. (Van Gorcum & Co., Assen. Price : Fl. 15.)

Of the eighteen essays presented to Byvanck in this *Festschrift* on his seventieth birthday by the Historical Circle of Leiden, three are of interest to O.T. students—those by A. de Buck on " The Hebrews in Egypt "; by J. M. A. Janssen on " Pharaoh Bocchoris " and by F. M. Th. de Liagre Böhl on " The Chaldean Dynasty." De Buck regards the equation Khapiru=*'apiru*= Hebrews as quite probable, and concludes that the Exodus took place shortly before Merneptah's fifth year, but that some *'apiru* remained behind in Egypt. Janssen reviews all the extant evidence bearing on Bocchoris (*bzk-n-rn.f*) and dates him, with E. Meyer, 720-715 B.C. Böhl surveys the history of Babylon from 626 to 539 B.C. in the light of present archaeological knowledge.   F.F.B.

Coppens, J. : *L'Efflorescence des Études Bibliques sur le Vieux Continent*. (Analecta Lovaniensia Biblica et Orientalia, 2nd series, No. 43.) 1954. Pp. 20. (Publications Universitaires de Louvain, and Desclée de Brouwer, Bruges and Paris. Price : Belgian Fr. 10.)

In this paper Canon Coppens briefly surveys the recent outburst of Biblical study in Catholic circles in various countries, especially since the issue of the Encyclical *Divino afflante Spiritu*. Few non-Catholics are aware how remarkable and how widespread is this outburst, though a good deal of it has been noticed in the pages of the *Book List*. This well-documented study directs attention to one of the most significant recent developments in our field. Canon Coppens makes a passing reference to our Society and the part it has played in reviving interest in the Old Testament.   H.H.R.

(Dinaburg, B. Z.) : *Sepher Dinaburg* (in Hebrew), ed. by I. Baer, J. Guttmann and M. Schwabe. 1949. Pp. 448. (Kirjath Sepher, Jerusalem.)

This volume in honour of Ben-Zion Dinaburg (now the Minister of Education in Israel) on the occasion of the completion of 30 years of his researches, contains 29 studies on Judaica, ancient and modern. Of direct interest to O.T. scholars are the following articles : 1. M. Z. (H.) Segal who conjectures that the Book of Joshua is not the result of a mosaic of various pieces but contains three editions. The first (chapters i-xii, xxiv) tells about Joshua and his activities ; the second augments the first, adding chapters xiii-xix, xxiii which deal with the division of Palestine amongst the tribes. The third edition, which incorporates the second edition, and contains chs. xx-xxi and xxii. 9-34, adds details concerning the Priests and the Levites, etc. A fuller treatment by Segal of this subject is to be found in his book *Mebho' ha-Miqra' I*. 2. E. Z. Melammed is concerned with 2 Samuel xxii and its parallel in Ps. xviii. He conclues that in Ps. we have deviations from the original calculated mainly to improve metre and rhythm so as to adapt it for recitation. This may have been done by David in his latter days or by the Levitical Singers of the First Temple. 3. S. Yeivin, who treats of the date of Deut., conjectures that Deut. was mainly composed in the time of Solomon or immediately after his death and originated from the circle of priests and prophets of the family of Eli who were critical of Solomon's activities. 4. Tur-Sinai, who writes on Hosea's life as a symbol of the relationship between Israel and God, intersperses his article with many ingenious and at times daring textual emendations. Of less direct interest to the Biblical scholar are the articles by M. D. A. Cassuto, " Zeus Demarus in the Ugaritic texts "; J. Guttmann, " Enslavement on account of debt according to Jewish Law "; A. Cherikover, " The ideological background of the Epistle of Aristeas." The articles " The Find of Tyrian Shekels in the grounds of the Hebrew University on Mount Scopus," by the late E. L. Sukenik ; " Poor Jews in Ancient Rome," by J. Levi ; and "A Greek Epigram found on a grave in Palestine " by M. Schwabe, may also be of some interest to the Biblical scholar.   M.W.

'ELKOSHI, G. (ed. by) : *Biblical Anthology* (in Hebrew). 1954. Pp. xx+506. (Devir Publication, Tel-Aviv, Israel.)

In this book are collected 170 Hebrew compositions on Biblical themes written by over 70 outstanding Modern Hebrew poets, dramatists, short-story tellers and essayists who lived in the last few centuries. The compositions are arranged in sections under the following headings :—1. The Book of Books (which mainly consists of essays) ; 2. The Story of the Creation and Early Generations ; 3. Patriarchs and Matriarchs ; 4. In Egypt and in the Wilderness ; 5. The Conquest and the Era of the Judges ; 6. Kings and Prophets ; 7. The Exile into Babylon and the Return unto Zion ; 8. Miscellany.
The purpose of this anthology is to stimulate a greater love for the Bible, giving artistic pieces woven round Biblical subjects. It incidentally shows that Modern Hebrew literature is not an altogether brand-new creation, being a lawful offspring of the Book of Books by which it is directly and indirectly influenced in contents as well as—in a number of respects—in form and style.   M.W.

FRIEDRICH, G. (ed. by) : *Theologisches Wörterbuch zum Neuen Testament* (begun by G. Kittel). Band V. Lieferung 14. 1953. Lieferungen 15 and 16 and Band VI, Lieferung 1. 1954. Pp. 64 per part. (W. Kohlhammer, Stuttgart. Subscription Price : DM. 4.60 per part.)

Lieferung 14 (pp. 833-896) contains the article on *paroikos*, *paroikia, paroikeo*, of which the Old Testament part dealing with *ger* and *tôšabh* and the section on Philo and Josephus arc by K. L. and M. A. Schmidt, the article on *parousia* and *pareimi* by Oepke which is important for the Messianic expectation, the article on *parrhesia* by Schlier, the article on *pas, hapas* by Bertram which deals with the conception of the universe in the Old Testament and the conception of universalism, and the beginning of the article on *pascha*.

Lieferung 15 (pp. 897-960) continues the article on *pascha* by Jeremias (Section on LXX and Judaism) and contains the article on *pascha* and related words by Michaelis which gives very useful cross-references for the Old Testament conception of suffering, and the beginning of the article on *pater* and related words by Schrenk and Quell, which has an important Old Testament section and a useful bibliography on pp. 946-8. Lieferung 16 (pp. 961-1032) continues the article on *pater* with at the end a short section by K. L. and M. A. Schmidt on various terms expressing ' hardening of the heart.' Band VI. Lieferung 1 (pp. 1-64) contains the article on *peira* by Seesemann with sections on ' temptation ' in the Old Testament and in Judaism, the article on *penes* by Hauck with sections on ' poverty ' in the Old Testament, the LXX and Philo, and the article on *pentecoste* by Lohse with treatment of the Feast of Weeks in the Old Testament and Judaism.

N.W.P.

HAAG, H. (ed. by ; with the collaboration of A. van den Born and others) : *Bibel-Lexikon*. Part 6. 1954. Cols. 1093-1316. (Benziger Verlag, Einsiedeln, Zürich and Cologne. Subscription price : Fr./DM. 11.00 per part.)

> The articles run from the completion of *Matthäusevangelium* to the beginning of *Personennamen*. Most of the articles are unsigned, but a few of the longer ones are signed, e.g., *Messiaserwartung* (18 columns) by Schildenberger, *Moses* (8 columns) by Cazelles and van den Born, *Offenbarung* (6 columns) by Grossouw, *Palästina* (8 columns) by Stummer, *Pentateuch* (13 columns) by Cazelles. The bibliographies are up-to-date and contain many English items. The article on *Moloch* (by Kornfeld) states, but rejects, Eissfeldt's view, but does not mention Dronkert's monograph (see *Book List*, 1954, p. 59). Moses is credited with substantial monotheism, but not with its formal profession. There are some pages of excellent plates.   H.H.R.

HAHN, H. F. : *Old Testament in Modern Research*. 1954. Pp. xii + 268. (Muhlenberg Press, Philadelphia. Price : $4.00.)

> This is a first-class survey of many sides of modern work on the Old Testament, which should be in the hands of all serious students in this field. In many ways it supplements *The Old Testament and Modern Study*, since it covers a longer period and makes a quite different approach to the subject. In other ways it may be supplemented by our volume, since it omits aspects of modern study there included. It surveys the rise of literary criticism and the Pentateuchal criticism of the last generation, but says less of the other books of the Old

Testament. It then studies the anthropological approach, the *religionsgeschichtliche* approach, Form Criticism, and the sociological, archaeological and theological approaches. The author shows a wide acquaintance with the literature, and offers a well documented study, from which every reader will profit. Throughout it is completely objective, and unmarked by any bias. Indeed there is too little critical appraisal of the positions reviewed. Philology and textual criticism are left unsurveyed, but the book is quite remarkable in the amount it includes. H.H.R.

Hebrew Union College Annual XXV. 1954. Pp. 400+34. (Cincinnati. Price: $3.00.)

This volume contains sixteen articles, five of which are directly concerned with the O.T. S. H. Blank suggests that the second *ne'um Yahweh* in Is. lii. 5 is to be traced to *-ni* in *yehalleluni* (read for *yehalleluni*) which was mistakenly regarded as an abbreviation ; the later history of the text and its significance is also discussed. R. Gordis writes at length on Hosea's marriage and message. Gomer was called " a woman of harlotry," not because she personally violated her marriage vow, but because she was implicated in the sinfulness of the nation (cf. i. 2c)—thus she serves as a symbol of the adultery of Israel, as do her children also. The two similar accounts (in chs. i and ii, which date from the period before B.C. 743, and in ch. iii) represent two interpretations by the prophet of the same experience, but at different periods in his career and from varying viewpoints ; the differences between the two accounts find a natural explanation in the chaotic conditions of the closing years of the northern kingdom which coincided with Hosea's prophetic activity. L. J. Liebreich studies the position of ch. vi in the book of Isaiah, and finds that it forms a suitable conclusion to the chapters before it (special attention is paid to its relationship to ch. v), and an equally suitable introduction to the chapters which follow. J. Morgenstern, in a long article, examines a number of passages in Amos and Is. xxxiv-xxxv, xl-lxvi, and finds support for his threefold hypothesis that in the earliest Hebrew manuscripts of poetic writings, metrical units were written upon separate lines ; that often, through deterioration of manuscripts at their left hand edges, words were lost at the ends of lines ; and that it is frequently possible, through the application of the principles of metre, parallelism, and chiasmus, to recover the missing word or words. H. M. Orlinsky offers a detailed study of the last two clauses of Is. xxxiv. 16 and the first two clauses of xl. 12, and concludes that in both cases the St. Mark's Isaiah scroll represents a corrupt text. E. Werner's contribution on the origin of psalmody contains much that will interest students of the O.T. and the ancient Near East. The articles by H. A. Fine on Middle-Assyrian chronology and religion, and by J. Lewy on the problems inherent in section seventy of the Bisutun inscription may also be mentioned. D.W.T.

(HEIM, K.) : *Theologie als Glaubenswagnis. Festschrift zum* 80.
Geburtstag von Karl Heim. 1954. Pp. 224. (Furche-Verlag,
Hamburg. Price : DM. 10.80.)

This Festschrift contains three articles on the Old Testament.
K. Elliger writes on ' Ich bin der Herr—euer Gott' arguing
that of the two formulas ' I am the Lord ' and ' I am the
Lord your God,' which occasionally occur already in ancient
times but are most frequently represented in H, P, Ezk. and
Dt. Is., the first emphasizes God's holy and jealous being and
demands man's obedience, while the second reminds of God's
merciful acts and calls on man to be grateful. A. Weiser
discusses ' Das Gotteswort für Baruch Jer. 45 und die soge-
nannte Baruchbiographie.' Baruch who, after recording the
threats contained in the original scroll, expressed anxiety
regarding his personal fate, is rebuked and consoled by
Jeremiah. The report on this, Jer. xlv, owes its present place
not to an editor, but to Baruch himself. By the chronologically
incorrect joining of this report to the history of Jeremiah's
sufferings, xxxvii-xliv, he wanted to show that for him as well
as for Jeremiah the vocation of being a prophet and personal
suffering belong together, in accordance with God's inscrutable
will. E. Würthwein writes on ' Jesaja 7, 1-9. Ein Beitrag zum
Thema : Prophetie und Politik,' and maintains that Isaiah's
' If you do not believe, you will not endure,' does not by any
means require the absolute renunciation of the employment
of human means of power but represents a warning directed
to the people and to the king to remain conscious of the
uniqueness bestowed on Israel by the Covenant of Sinai and
the election of the House of David and to refrain from alliances
with foreign and pagan peoples. The other articles in this
Festschrift deal with the New Testament, Systematic and
Practical Theology, and Missions.   O.E.

Internationale Zeitschriftenschau für Bibelwissenschaft und Grenzgebiete,
1951-52, Heft 2. 1954. Pp. xii+228. (Patmos Verlag, Düsseldorf.
Price : DM. 22, or $5.40.)

The second part of this first volume of this *Zeitschriftenschau*
(see *Book List*, 1953, pp. 6 f.) contains 1205 entries, prefaced
by a list of 417 journals which have been used. Almost all
the items give a brief summary of the contents of the article,
and the whole is an indispensable tool for the serious scholar.
Members of our Society have often asked for articles, as well
as books, to be surveyed in the *Book List*. This would be
quite impossible on anything like this scale, for a variety of
reasons. The present issue has been prepared by a very large
international team of scholars. It covers the whole Biblical
field, including the New Testament, and every side of Biblical
study is brought within its purview. The entries are all
classified, and precise details of each article are given, but
the reference to the place where each appeared is by the
number of the Journal in the list at the beginning, and not by
name. It is to be hoped that the time lag of publication of
this survey will soon be shortened.   H.H.R.

Journal of the Manchester University Egyptian and Oriental Society.
No. xxv (1947-1953). 1954. Pp. 38. (Manchester University Press.
Price : 8s. 6d.)

After the appearance of volume xxiv, which covered the years 1942-45, the publication of this journal was discontinued. It has now been resumed under the general editorship of Professor T. Fish. This present volume contains six articles, and a list of lectures which were given to the Society in the years when no journal was published (1946-53). Two only of the articles bear directly on the O.T. J. Gray's " The wrath of God in Canaanite and Hebrew literature " is a study of part of one of the Ras Shamra texts ('*nt* II in C. H. Gordon's *Ugaritic Handbook*, 1947, p. 187), which, it is argued, is related to the cycle of the seasons. Some otherwise obscure conceptions in the O.T. are elucidated, notably that of *zebaḥ Yahweh* in Zeph. i. 7 ff., Is. xxxiv. 6 ff. ; and Ezek. xxxix. 17 ff. Is. lxiii. 1 ff. too is redolent of "Anath's blood-bath," though the independence of O.T. thought here is emphasized. Full philological notes are supplied. A. Rowe, in a brief article, notes some of the more interesting discoveries made at Samaria. He refers, for example, to the alabaster jar presented to Omri by Osorkon II ; to the use of Egyptian hieratic numerals on Israelite ostraca ; and to winged scarab-beetles on the face of clay letter-sealings, which are of the same kind as those found in some of the so-called " Jewish Royal Pottery Stamps." M. Wallenstein writes on a piyyuṭ from the Cairo Genizah. P. R. Weis discusses the plucking of the corn in Matt. xii. 1-8 and parallel passages, and C. F. Beckingham's article is concerned with the Red Sea in the sixteenth century. The remaining contribution is by Professor J. Robson, who writes on the Arabic word *ghinā'* " singing."

D.W.T.

LOTH, B. and MICHEL, A. : *Dictionnaire de Théologie Catholique : Tables Générales*. Fasc. iii. Cajétan—Concordats. 1954. Cols. 497-752. (Letouzey & Ané, Paris. Price : Fr. 980.)

This third fascicule of the vast index to the even vaster *Dictionnaire* contains references to many things but not, as it happens, to any great number of articles bearing on the Old Testament. Among the few that need to be mentioned are those under the headings " Canon des Livres Saints " (in which A. Gelin has some remarks on recent work on the Canon), and " Cantique des Cantiques " (which comprises the same author's summary of opinions about the exegesis, on which there is still very much less agreement than there is about the date). Much information on Old Testament subjects may be found in the long section (columns 655-750) on " Conciles." (Cf. e.g., under "Concile de Trent," col. 675, the references to " Canon des Écritures et traditions.") J.M.T.B.

(NYBERG, H. S.) : *Donum natalicium H. S. Nyberg oblatum*. 1954. Pp. 218. (Almqvist & Wiksell, Uppsala. Price : Sw. Kr. 40.)

The twenty-one essays in this *Festschrift*, in English, French, and German, are mostly about Iranian or Semitic subjects.

Five of them deal directly with the Old Testament. In 'Wort und Realität,' G. Gerleman discusses the *Dinglichkeit* of Hebrew words, and gives a foretaste of his promised syntactical and semasiological treatise. P. Kahle contributes 'The Ben Asher Text of the Hebrew Bible,' arguing against Cassuto's use of the Cairo Codex of Moshe b. Asher as a source for the Ben Asher text. O. Löfgren offers some general observations on the pre-Massoretic text of the Old Testament, and outlines the preliminary results of his own examination of DSIa. S. Mowinckel discusses the reference in Numbers xiii. 22 to the founding of Hebron in the light of other evidence, and concludes that Hebron was a military stronghold of the Hyksos. H. H. Rowley examines critically M. B. Rowton's theory of a double Exodus, and rebuts Rowton's criticisms of his own theory.   G.W.A.

(PYATT, C. L.) : *To Do and to Teach : Essays in Honour of Charles Lynn Pyatt.* 1953. Pp. viii+186. (College of the Bible, Lexington. Price : $5.00.)

In this Festschrift there are five articles bearing on the Old Testament. Sheldon Blank writes on Ps. lxxiii. in which he finds no reference to the Afterlife and where he emends the crucial verse 24 to give ' By thy counsel thou leadest me, keeping me near '. J. P. Hyatt writes on ' The God of Love in the Old Testament,' and insists that the love of God figures much more in the Old Testament than is commonly supposed. Julian Morgenstern examines Isa. xlii. 10-13, and holds that these verses are an intrusion into the text from some other source, and that they are a fragment of a psalm which was composed between 516 and 485 B.C. T. W. Nakarai writes ' Some Notes on the Grammar of Biblical Hebrew,' offering a number of corrections of erroneous and questionable statements found in the current grammars. Finally, O. R. Sellars discusses ' Problems in the Story of Cain.' *Inter alia* he renders Gen. iv. 1 ' I, as well as Yahweh, have produced a man,' and in iv. 5 he finds reference to Cain's embarrassment, and not his anger. The remaining papers deal with theological education and with the life and work of Dr. Pyatt. H.H.R.

Reallexikon für Antike und Christentum : Sachwörterbuch zur Auseinandersetzung des Christentums mit der Antiken Welt, ed. by Th. Klauser, together with F. J. Dölger, H. Lietzmann, J. H. Waszink, and L. Wenger. Lieferungen 11-16. 1952-1954. Pp. 80 each. (Hiersemann Verlag, Stuttgart. Price : DM. 12 each Lief.)

The first ten parts of this *Reallexikon* were noticed in the *Book List,* 1953, p. 10. Since then six further issues have appeared, completing the second volume, which began with the ninth. The articles of most interest to Old Testament scholars found in parts 11-16 are : ' Bileam,' by H. Karpp (cols. 362-373) ; ' Buch II (heilig, kultisch)', by S. Morenz and J. Leipoldt (cols. 688-717) ; ' Cappadocia ' by E. Kirsten (cols. 861-891) ; ' Chaldäer ' by W. J. W. Koster (cols. 1006-1021) ; ' Chaos ' by J. Ternus (cols. 1031-1040) ; ' Christus I (Messias) ' by O. Eissfeldt (cols. 1250-1257).   O.E.

ROBERT, A. (ed. by) : *Dictionnaire de la Bible. Supplément.* Fasc. xxvii (Mandéisme—Médiation). 1954. Cols. 769-1024. (Letouzey & Ané, Paris. Price : Fr. 980.)

This is a valuable number of the supplement to Vigouroux's great Bible dictionary. The work has been in progress for some twenty-eight years and several volumes still remain to be completed. In the present fascicle J. Schmitt concludes his article on Mandaism, and two Louvain Benedictines (C. Van Puyvelde and B. Botte) divide the treatment of Biblical manuscripts as between the Old and the New Testaments. The bibliography of the Scrolls literature is not very complete, and contains no work published since 1952. The article on Mari, as might be expected, is by that veteran authority, Ch. F. Jean. Marriage is discussed, as regards the Old Testament, by W. Kornfeld of the Vienna faculty, and includes a section on marriage customs among the nations surrounding Israel. A Gelin writes, a trifle summarily, on medicine in the Bible, and E. Cavaignac on Medes and Persians. The final article of this part, on Mediation, is divided among four authors, of whom R. Largement deals with Assyria and Babylon, P. d'Audibert-Caille de Bourguet, with Egypt, A. Robert with the Old Testament, and C. Spicq, with the New Testament. There are short biographies of Mandelkern, J. E. Mangenot, G. Margoliouth, M. L. Margolis, K. Marti, F. Martin, G. Maspéro, L. Méchineau, and A. Médebielle. J.M.T.B.

ROBERTSON, E. AND WALLENSTEIN, M. (ed. by) : *Melilah, A Volume of Studies V.* 1955. Pp. xviii+264. (Manchester University Press. Price : 30s. 0d.)

Five of the seventeen articles have a direct or indirect bearing on the Old Testament. J. Gray discusses Arabic affinities with the dialect of Ras Shamra. His suggestions help to understand a number of passages in the Legend of King Keret and the Tale of Aqhat, which hitherto remained obscure. Whether similarities in morphology, vocabulary or grammar are sufficient to establish a direct relationship between Ugaritic and Arabic can not be decided, as our knowledge of Semitic languages, contemporary to the Ras Shamra dialect, is limited. E. Robertson continues his studies on Old Testament problems with an article on the Disruption of Israel's monarchy. The political and religious antagonism between Judah and Ephraim is traced through the early stages of their history. The origin of the bulk of Deuteronomy is placed in the time of Samuel. A. Rubinstein's essay on Luzzatto's Commentary on Isaiah in the Light of DSIa is of some interest for the history of exegesis, though anticipation of some of the readings of the Dead Sea Scrolls is not a specific feature of Luzzatto's commentary. R. Edelmann describes a fourteenth century Ms. in the Royal Library of Copenhagen, which contains an Arabic version of the Pentateuch. He maintains that Arabic characters indicate Christian (Syriac), Samaritan, or Karaite use and adaptations. Saadya's Arabic version, as current among Jews, was written in Hebrew characters. H. H. Rowley contributes an article on The Origin of the Dead Sea Scrolls. It is a succinct summary of his book The Zadokite Fragments and the Dead Sea Scrolls. The Habakkuk Commentary, the Zadokite Fragments and the Milḥemeth Text are assumed to point to the second pre-Christian century. One might argue, however, that references to the strict observance of the Sabbath, the detestation of idolatry and even the law against marrying one's niece are not conclusive as internal evidence for such a date.

The other articles contain valuable contributions to post-Biblical Hebrew literature. It is good to know that Melilah continues to appear.   S.S.

THOMSEN, P. : *Die Palästina-Literatur : eine internationale Biblio-graphie in systematischer Ordnung mit Autoren- und Sachregister.* Vol. vi, Lieferung 2. 1954. Pp. 289-576. (Akademie Verlag, Berlin. Price : DM. 28.)

> The first Lieferung of this volume was noticed in the *Book List*, 1954, p. 15. Dr. Peter Thomsen died on 26th April, 1954, and this part, like its predecessor, has been seen through the press by F. Maass and L. Rost. It contains nearly 4,000 items, dealing with History, Archaeology, Historical Geography and Topography, and with Geography, which appeared during the years 1935-1939 (the first Lieferung gave the years as 1935-1944). Books and articles, and also reviews in important journals, are listed here, and the value of the work to those engaged on research scarcely needs to be emphasized. An enormous amount of work has gone into its preparation. H.H.R.

(UBACH, B.) : *Miscellanea Biblica B. Ubach*, ed. R. M. Diaz. (Scripta et Documenta, 1.) 1953. Pp. 474. (Monastery of Montserrat. Price : Pes. 250.)

> In this substantial volume, published in honour of Dom Bonaventura Ubach, there are thirty articles, both on the O.T. and related subjects and on the N.T. N. Schneider gives an account of the religious surroundings of Abraham in Mesopotamia in the light of available epigraphic evidence. J. Schildenberger examines Gen. xxxii. 23-33, and considers such problems as the literary analysis of the section, how the narrative bears on Jacob and the higher aspects of O.T. religion, whether or not it fits in with the Jacob narrative (more particularly with the narrative of the meeting of Jacob and Esau), and the proper names which occur in the section. W. F. Albright offers some general observations about the early history of the Ammonites, and discusses some recently discovered inscriptions, chiefly on seals. L. H. Vincent writes, with illustrations, on the *mekônôth* (1 Kings vii. 27 ff.) in the light of the bronze objects discovered at Megiddo and in Cyprus. The *mekônôth* were essentially practical appliances—water from " the sea of brass " was distributed in them to different parts of the sacred court. P. Salmon lists in groups some of the new readings in the text of Job in the current Benedictine edition of the Vulgate, and emphasizes the

importance for textual criticism of the fact that the greater number of them agree with the N.T. A. Miller argues that there are psalms which refer directly to the Messiah, rather than to a person as a pattern of the Messiah ; Ps. cx is taken as an example and discussed. A. Robert recognizes the contribution made to O.T. exegesis by representatives of the " Form-geschichtlicheschule," but finds certain weaknesses in their work—in the archaeological and philosophico-religious spheres, as well as in a lack of appreciation of the specific character and considerable rôle of the Yahwistic traditions. M. Delcor attempts to explain the text of Hab. iii as it stands. The psalm furnishes several definite references to Yahweh's exploits at the time of the Exodus, and there is no need to have recourse to the literatures of neighbouring peoples to explain it. It is a historical psalm, and its place after the first two chapters is its proper one. F. M. Abel writes on " the tombs of the kings " in Jerusalem. Four articles, written in Spanish, may be mentioned—on the origin of the Codex Ottobonianus of the Vulgate, by T. Ayuso Marazuela ; on Hepher (1 Kings iv. 10) Migron (Is. x. 28), and the great high place at Gibeon (1 Kings iii. 4), by A. Fernández ; on the musical terms in the titles of the Psalms, by J. Enciso Viana ; and on the literary genre of 2 Maccabees, by P. Bellet.

D.W.T.

EDUCATIONAL

A Bibliography for the Use of Teachers of Religious Knowledge. Compiled by the Institute of Christian Education at Home and Overseas. 1954. Pp. 56. (Religious Education Press, Wallington, Surrey. Price : 2s. 6d.)

This is the welcome fourth, revised edition of a bibliography compiled to meet the need of teachers of Christian knowledge in every type of school. The comprehensive sectional classification includes General Bible Study, including Geography and Archaeology, General Old Testament, Old Testament Periods, and the Comparative study of Religion. Books are also classified by eight index numbers and to many entries are added brief, discriminating notes. Only books in English and in print are included. This revision will add to the usefulness of a bibliography that has already proved its value to teachers of Religious Knowledge. L.A.P.

BROADIE, E. : *The Chosen Nation : Book One : Founders and Leaders.* 1954. Pp. 128. (Religious Education Press, Wallington, Surrey. Price : Boards 5s. 0d. ; Limp 4s. 0d.)

This book, which has a commendatory foreword by Professor H. H. Rowley, is the first of a new " Pathfinder Series," designed to meet the needs of teachers and pupils in the middle forms of Grammar Schools and the upper classes of Secondary Modern Schools, by illustrating the historical, geographical and biographical background of the Bible. The story is carried from Abraham to David in twenty-three short chapters, each followed by a number of exercises. No attention is given to chronology, it was evidently considered undesirable to make any explicit reference to the traditional documentary analysis of the Pentateuch, and only a few passing references are made to archæology. Much that is generally regarded as legend is presented as history. The attempts at rationalisation will not always command assent, e.g., the events of the Exodus are explained in terms of the volcanic eruption of Mount Sinai, and the views expressed are sometimes questionable, e.g., that in the time of David the Israelites did not think Jahweh was very much concerned with the behaviour, whether good or bad, of ordinary men and women. The book is well produced and cheaply priced, is well adapted to the needs of its readers, and will prove useful in the hands of a specialist teacher.

L.A.P.

BULL, N. J. : *The Rise of the Prophets. Lessons on Secondary Sections of the Agreed Syllabuses.* 1954. Pp. 208. (The Religious Education Press, Wallington, Surrey. Price : 7s. 6d.)

This book is an acceptable guide for teachers in Modern Secondary Schools and will be widely welcomed. Its ten chapters deal with the story of the Old Testament prophets from Elijah to Jeremiah, each chapter being divided into three sections, one expository, one headed " Teaching Notes," and one containing suggestions for practical class work and questions for discussion. The text contains numerous quotations from the Agreed Syllabuses, but the page references to sixteen of these syllabuses at the end of each chapter seem unnecessary. A generally conservative standpoint and over-simplification are to be expected in an elementary text-book, but uncritical readers may be misled by the implied condemnation of the priestly element in Israelite religion and by the comparison of the progressive revelation of God through the prophets with a staircase, each step rising from and depending on what had gone before.   L.A.P.

KING, F. W. : *Pipe-line of Power : A Graphic History of the Jews.* 1954. Pp. 96. (Religious Education Press, Wallington, Surrey. Price : 4s. 0d.)

A brief and breezy textbook for the Sec. Mod. School. The symbolism is ingenious and possibly helpful to those whose reading is confined to ' comics '; though it might be confusing. There are occasional inaccuracies, but the approach is enlightened and the balance sound, and in class the author probably gauged the mentality and humour of his children. The printed word does not always capture these contacts, but he has tried hard to make it interesting and to provoke thought, and has found room for quite a lot of facts amid so much jolly padding.   M.B.

MATHEWS, H. F. : *Bible Cavalcade.* 1954. Pp. 184. (Epworth Press, London. Price : 10s. 6d.)

This book, intended for the upper forms of schools, seeks to present a quick-moving picture of the chief figures of Biblical history in the light of their historical background. It is successful in doing this, is up-to-date, and suffers only from its very brief compass, 175 pages only of subject matter, which has occasioned many gaps.   L.H.B.

ARCHAEOLOGY AND EPIGRAPHY

ALBRIGHT, W. F. : *The Bible after twenty years of Archeology* (1932-1952). 1954. Pp. 18. (Biblical Colloquium, Pittsburgh, Pennsylvania. Price : $0.75.)

How Professor Albright contrives to write with freshness and interest on this subject so many times is a source of constant wonder. The present booklet is reprinted from *Religion in Life*, together with four pages of valuable notes of considerable bibliographical interest. The principal subjects dealt with are the Mari and Ugaritic texts, the Lachish letters and the new Aramaic texts from Egypt, the Dead Sea Scrolls and the Gnostic and Manichean texts. A great many other matters of archaeological interest are referred to, and the whole is packed with information. Naturally many of Albright's well-known views are presented here, such as the view that the Song of Miriam in its entirety goes back to the time of Moses, and the claim that ' no arguments have been brought against early Israelite monotheism that would not apply equally well (with appropriate changes in specific evidence) to postexilic Judaism.' H.H.R.

DRIVER, G. R. : *Semitic Writing : From Pictograph to Alphabet*. Revised edition. 1954. Pp. 238. (Oxford University Press. Price : 21s. 0d.)

This revised edition of Professor Driver's Schweich Lectures (the first edition was reviewed in the *Book List*, 1949, p. 10) contains such small corrections as could be made in the sheets, and also a number of "Additions and Corrections," occupying sixteen pages, in which all the fresh matter which has come to the author's notice in the last three years is collected. An illustration of the important new tablet giving the order of the Ugaritic alphabet is included. D.W.T.

EHRICH, R. W. (ed. by) : *Relative Chronologies in Old World Archaeology*. 1954. Pp. xiv+154. (University of Chicago Press, and Cambridge University Press. Price : $2.50 or 19s. 0d.)

This book contains the results of a symposium on " The Integration of Relative Chronologies in Old World Archaeology " held in Philadelphia at the 51st Annual Meeting of the American Anthropological Association. As the papers were limited to half-an-hour in length, they are necessarily very condensed, but the whole collection with its comparative tables accompanied by explanatory comments will provide an invaluable handbook for field-archaeologists and all students of the archaeology of the ancient Near East. The object of the symposium was to establish " an interlocking network of chronological relationships, so that, as any particular stratum or period should be definitively and accurately dated, the corresponding periods or cross-dated complexes of neighbouring areas would also fall into their proper places in terms of absolute chronology." Most of the papers are followed by comparative tables, illustrations of pottery and other artefacts, and useful bibliographies. The area surveyed includes China. S.H.H.

FRIEDRICH, J. : *Entzifferung verschollener Schriften und Sprachen.* (Verständliche Wissenschaft, Geisteswissenschaftliche Abteilung No. 51.) 1954. Pp. 148+73 illustrations+1 map. (Springer-Verlag, Berlin-Göttingen-Heidelberg. Price : DM. 7.80.)

> One of the greatest experts in this field discusses in a concise and clear manner method (differentiation between combinative and etymological procedure) and results in connection with the major decipherments in the world of the ancient East, discussing at the same time the languages and scripts hitherto undeciphered. He is sceptical towards Dhorme's attempt at the proto-Byblos script and makes no mention of Albright's attempt at the Sinaitic script. Ventris's decipherment of the Cretan script was not yet at his disposal. W.B.

JEAN, C. F. : *Six Campagnes de Fouilles à Mari*, 1933-1939. (Cahiers de la Nouvelle Revue Théologique IX.) 1952. Pp. 56. (Casterman, Paris. Price : Belgian Fr. 24.)

> Professor Jean presents a synthesis of the results of A. Parrot's excavation of Mari on the mid-Euphrates and of research on the texts from the site, which number over 20,000. The work is well-balanced, though, naturally, for a reconstruction of historical, social, and religious conditions of the Amorite period (1900 B.C.) the author relies on the texts. Such a succinct statement of the contents of these by one of the editors on the eve of the resumption of the post-war excavation of Mari has an obvious value. J.G.

PARROT, A. : *Mari. Documentation photographique de la mission archéologique de Mari.* (Collection des ides photographiques No. 7.) 1953. Pp. viii+80 pages of plates+12 pages of plans and tables of plates. (Éditions ides et calendes, Neuchatel et Paris. Price : Swiss Fr. 24.45.)

> This is a collection of 132 superbly reproduced plates and three temple/palace plans, depicting the excavations and objects found at Mari. Parrot—he who says ' Mari ' must also say ' Parrot '—contributes a thousand-word introduction in French, with English and German translations appended. The plates are furnished with a trilingual index providing identification and short archaeological notes. This album would be a lovely present—not least for the art lover. D.R.Ap-T.

PARROT, A. : *Le Temple de Jérusalem.* (Cahiers d'Archéologie Biblique No. 5.) 1954. Pp. 94. (Delachaux et Niestlé, Neuchatel and Paris. Price : Swiss Fr. 4.50.)

> This is a useful compendious account of Solomon's, Ezekiel's, and Herod's Temples. The well-known author, the excavator of Mari, has packed an enormous mass of information into a very small compass, and it is to be hoped that the volume will be translated, like its predecessor *Ninive et l'Ancien Testament.* The book is amply illustrated with plates, plans, and text illustrations.

It is a little strange that the author should have omitted all reference to the *Palestine Exploration Quarterly*, although that journal has for many years published authoritative discussions of matters relating to the archaeology of the Temple. For example, no reference is made to the late Professor J. L. Myres' important article on King Solomon's Temple in the *PEQ* for 1948, in which he put forward cogent objections to the view that Jachin and Boaz were independent columns standing on each side of the entrance to the Temple. No mention, either, is made of F. J. Hollis's careful study *The Archaeology of Herod's Temple* (1934, Dent). S.H.H.

PRITCHARD, J. B. : *The Ancient Near East in Pictures relating to the Old Testament.* 1955 (date on title page 1954). Pp. xviii+352. (Princeton University Press, and Geoffrey Cumberlege, London. Price : $20 or £8.)

This is the long awaited companion volume of plates to accompany *Ancient Near Eastern Texts*, which appeared in 1950 (see *Book List*, 1951, p. 21). It contains 769 excellently produced plates, 4 Maps, a complete catalogue of all the illustrations, with short notes on each and bibliographical references, together with a short Introduction. The wide selection of the illustrations, and their careful classification give a very high value to this book, which should soon be a regularly used tool in every classroom where the Old Testament is taught. Every side of life in the world in which Israel lived, in so far as archaeology has recovered it for us, is here illustrated. The work is thoroughly up-to-date, and Professor Pritchard deserves the highest praise for the immense amount of careful scholarship which has gone into its preparation. H.H.R.

WOOLLEY, SIR L. : *Digging up the Past.* 1954. 2nd ed. Pp. 126+32 plates. (Ernest Benn, London. Price : 10s. 6d.)

The first edition of this useful little book was published in 1930, and it still retains its value as a clear and vivid exposition by an expert of the principles and methods of field archaeology. The author's object is to explain to the layman the kind of work that the field archaeologist does and why he does it. What is meant by digging up the past is admirably summed up in the words : "Anybody can dig up things ; but it is only by observation and interpretation that we can dig up the past." S.H.H.

WOOLLEY, SIR L. : *Dead Towns and Living Men.* 1954. Pp. 220. (Lutterworth Press, London. Price : 17s. 6d.)

This is a revised and enlarged edition of a work which first appeared in 1920. It took shape originally as a diversion for the author and his friends when they were prisoners of war in Turkey in 1916. It is less concerned with archaeology and its results than with the local setting of the work and its personal aspects. In his relish for the picaresque and his influence over as notable a galaxy of lovable rascals as the Near East has produced Sir Leonard Woolley appears as a

T. E. Lawrence only a little more subdued. What a team the pair must have made at Carchemish, the scene of most of the book ! The book is one which will be valued by all who have personal knowledge of the Near East and ought to be read by all who intend to dig there.   J.G.

HISTORY AND GEOGRAPHY

ADEMOLLO, E. : *Patriarchi e Guerrieri*. 1953. Pp. 146. (Vita e Pensiero, Milan. Price : Lire 400.)

The main theme of this book is the Exodus, which the writer dates in the reign of Amenhotep IV (Akhnaten). He arrives at this date by working back from the date of the building of the Temple (1 Kings vi. 1) on the assumption that the Biblical year was one of ten months. A work which relies so much on figures ought certainly to reckon with Professor Rowley's *From Joseph to Joshua*, but this is only one of the many significant omissions in a work which is very poorly documented.
J.G.

AKAVIA, A. A. : *The Calendar and its Use for Chronological Purposes* (in Hebrew). 1953. Pp. 182. (Magnes Press, Jerusalem.)

This book, unique in Hebrew literature of modern times, deals with the technical chronology and includes a Jewish-Christian-Moslem Calendar from the Creation to the year 6000 A.M. A full discussion is given about the Hebrew intercalation of which the author is perhaps the greatest authority alive. There is also a discussion on the Christian and Moslem calendars. From the many other systems of the calendar only the more important ones and those which have a bearing on the Jewish chronology are dealt with. There are two special chapters containing a goodly number of tables which will prove very helpful in comparing the various systems of calendars. The Biblical scholar will find special interest in the chapter entitled *The Chronology of the Ancient History of Israel*.   M.W.

ALT, A. : *Die Herkunft der Hyksos in neuer Sicht*. 1954. Pp. 40. (Akademie-Verlag, Berlin. Price : DM. 2.)

Professor Alt re-examines the problem of the Hyksos in the light of the new evidence afforded by the cuneiform tablets from Mari, Chagar Bazar, and Alalakh, and by fresh data from the Execration texts. He puts forward convincing arguments for rejecting the earlier and commonly held view that the Hyksos invasion and conquest of Egypt was a mass movement of a non-Semitic racial group with an admixture of Semitic elements, proceeding from some ill-defined district to the north-east of Syria. He proceeds to argue from the picture of the political situation disclosed by the new evidence that the starting-point of the movement lay in the southern parts of Syria, in Phoenicia, and in Palestine (p. 20), and was composed of Hurrian elements with a ' thin upper layer ' of Semitic leadership. The beginning of the movement coincided with the break-up of the united Egyptian monarchy at the

end of the 18th century, and was a process of gradual in-
filtration. The final impetus was given by the entry on the
scene from the north-east of an Aryan element with the new
decisive weapon of chariotry. The monograph is an important
addition to the already voluminous literature on the problem
of the Hyksos.   S.H.H.

ALT, A. : *Der Stadtstaat Samaria.* (Berichte über die Verhandlungen
der Sächsischen Akademie der Wissenschaften zu Leipzig. Philo-
logisch-historische Klasse. Band 101. Heft 5.) 1954. Pp. 64.
(Akademie-Verlage, Berlin. Price : DM. 3.)

In this valuable monograph Professor Albrecht Alt, with his
customary acuteness and erudition, propounds the interesting
theory that Omri bought from its Canaanite owner the hill of
Samaria, and founded there, on a site which lay in Canaanite
territory, and which had no previous associations with Hebrew
history or religion, a city-state inhabited by a population which
was largely Canaanite. Until the overthrow of the Omri
dynasty by Jehu, a kind of dual kingship existed in Israel :
in Samaria Omri and his successor reigned in a capital which
was their own property by right of inheritance, while at the
same time reigning in Jezreel as kings by the Hebrew principle
of charismatic election. Professor Alt's analysis of the Old
Testament evidence, and his skilful use of the supporting
archaeological evidence, together constitute a story of a
curious episode in the history of Israel which is more interesting
than the latest crime thriller.   S.H.H.

CARLIER, A. : *La Chronologie des rois de Juda et d'Israël.* 1953. Pp.
88+synchronising date table for 940-580 B.C. Litho Ms., unbound.
(55, rue de Varennes, Paris VIIe. Price : Fr. 1,000.)

This ingenious work was begun when the author's normal
pre-occupation with the historical monuments of France was
interrupted—it is to be hoped, only temporarily—by the war.
By a complicated system of pre-reigns, retrospective reigns,
and co-regencies the author seeks to reconcile the conflicting
data of the M.T., but his results are not as plausible as, *e.g.*,
those of Thiele. As an instance, Carlier is forced to deny the
cogency of Ahab's name on Shalmaneser's Black Obelisk.
Other biblical chronologists are scarcely mentioned.
                                                        D.R.Ap-T.

GAROFALO, S. : *I patriarchi della Bibbia* (*Storia Biblica*). 1954. Pp.
226. (Edizioni Radio Italiana. Price : Lire 750.)

The aim of this volume—the substance of a series of talks
given over the Italian radio—is to re-tell, according to the
letter and spirit of the Bible, and in popular form, the story
of the patriarchs and the world in which they lived. There
are three chapters—"Abraham : the great adventure,"
" Isaac and his sons," and " Joseph, the dreamer." The story
is told with considerable artistry. Quotations from the Bible
are generously and skilfully interspersed in the text. The
number of plates—there are six—could with advantage have
been increased.   D.W.T.

GROLLENBERG, L. H. : *Atlas van de Bijbel*. 1954. Pp. 158. (Elsevier, Amsterdam and Brussels. Price,: Fl. 29.50.)

This sumptuous work has been produced by the Dutch Dominican scholar in collaboration with the Biblical geographer A. van Deursen. It immediately challenges comparison with the *Westminster Historical Atlas to the Bible*, which it resembles in general appearance and design. Grollenberg's work is the larger of the two, and this is mainly due to the much greater number of photographic plates (408 as against the *Westminster Atlas's* 77) which illustrate his pages. The maps (37 in number, including those on the end-papers) are supplied with elucidatory legends in unobtrusive red print which does not interfere with the reader's appreciation of the physical and political features. The text (in Dutch) provides a sketch of Biblical history, critically and archaeologically up-to-date, from patriarchal times to the coming of Christ. It is a most useful handbook to Biblical study, and its usefulness would be enhanced if it appeared in an English edition.   F.F.B.

KLAUSNER, J. : *History of the Second Temple*, in five volumes (in Hebrew). 1954. Pp. 324, 278, 280, 310, 336. ('Aḥi'asaph, Jerusalem. Price : 88s. 0d.)

In this fourth edition of the five volumes, a period close upon 700 years is dealt with. We have here a great mine of information not only concerning the Jews of that period but also other peoples with whom the Jews came into contact and by whose cultures and religions they were influenced. The author is at pains, however, to explain at every turn of his work why the Jewish people, though scanty in numbers, did not assimilate with surrounding peoples.

The first volume deals with the last period of the First Temple, drawing, as one would expect, its material from Biblical sources. The second volume is mainly based on Greek sources, on the Apocrypha and on finds in Aramaic, and describes the transition period between the Biblical epoch and that of the Hasmoneans. The third volume contains in the main the material included in *Historiyyah Isra'elith II*, which appeared over thirty years ago. In it Klausner enlarges on the achievements of the Hasmoneans and on the great influence they have exercised on the generations that followed them. Klausner, who investigated this period for forty years, is convinced that it is not a mere episode in the history of the Jews. The fourth volume, which includes mainly the material found in *Historiyyah Isra'elith III*, begins with Herod and concludes with Agrippa I. Unlike Wellhausen, Minkin and others who speak about Herod in favourable terms, Klausner, although giving credit where it is due, draws here a different picture. The chapters in this vol. which deal with Jesus are not a mere abridgment of Klausner's book *Yeshu Hanoẓri* (translated into English by the late Prof. Danby) ; they contain a number of new features. The fifth volume is concerned mainly with The Great Jewish Rebellion which brought about the destruction of the Second Temple. A period of 29 years is given here in great detail. The causes of the rebellion, its personalities and the philosophies of the various Sects as well as the political, economic and spiritual struggles between the various strata of the community are here well set forth.

The pictures drawn in this brilliant work of Klausner are not altogether those one is accustomed to see in history books written in the West about this period. The approach is different, as are the examination and the assessment of the sources. Here Jewish national sentiments are naturally throbbing fast, and although one would like to question some of the theories put forth by Klausner one cannot help accepting many of them owing to their being substantiated by a wealth of data, mostly hitherto untapped.

In an addendum to the fifth volume Klausner gives briefly his opinion about the origin and the date of the controversial newly found Judean Scrolls. Unlike Josephus, who enlarges on the Three Sects only, treating lightly the Sicarii and the Zealots and describing them as mere rebels and robbers, Klausner accords them special and not unfavourable treatment. He puts emphasis on the distinction between the Zealots and the Sicarii, the first being organized in A.D. 6 and the second in the years 52-66. While the Zealots may be described as the warlike party among the Pharisees the Sicarii were the warlike party among the Essenes. Both sects, however, although otherwise adhering to different philosophies were inspired by the Messianic idea in their fight against the Romans. The name Sicarii is one given to this group of fighters by their enemies. The Sicarii rejected this derogatory title and called themselves *Serekh Hayyaḥad*, and it was they who produced the documents found in the Judean Wilderness. The *Milḥemeth* text is not Apocalyptical, containing as it does a detailed programme of a real war planned against the enemy. Between 50-67 there were in Juda many wicked priests. A poem denouncing the House of Ḥanan is found in the Talmud. The " Wicked Priest " mentioned in *Pesher Habakkuk* may well be the one who was cruelly murdered by the " Edomites," i.e., Ḥanan b. Ḥanan, " whom God has delivered into the hand of his enemies to be tortured because of his sin (against) the Teacher of Righteousness " who was none other than Shime'on Bar Giyyora, the leader of the Sicarii.   M.W.

MALAMAT, A. : *Kibbush Ha'areẓ Bime Yehoshua'*. (in Hebrew), 2nd edition. 1954. Pp. 28. (Jewish Agency, Jerusalem).

This pamphlet, intended mainly for the teacher, deals with the conquest of Palestine by Joshua. Special attention is paid here to military-topographical aspects. Sources used for this study include Biblical inscriptions and archaeological finds. A short bibliography, in Hebrew, English, French and German, concludes the pamphlet.   M.W.

NORTH, R. : *Geographia exegetica*. 1953. Pp. 70+4 maps. (Pontifical Biblical Institute, Rome. Price : Lire 450.)

Those who journey through Palestine have often to complain of the size and weight of the various guidebooks, but here is a guide that weighs only a few ounces and can be carried easily in a coat-pocket. It has the advantage over many guides that it is entirely up-to-date and has been planned throughout with scholarly accuracy. In it may be found a highly compressed, but reasonably complete, survey of the historical geography of Palestine from the section (4) headed " Primitivi habitantes Canaan " down to the last section (25) " Palaestina arabo-hebraea." There are also introductory sections on Palestinian cartography, the geology, and the climate, flora, and river-system. It may be hoped that the author may be persuaded to translate his excellent booklet into English.   J.M.T.B.

NOTH, M. : *Geschichte Israels* (Zweite, verbesserte Auflage). 1954. Pp. 436. (Vandenhoeck & Ruprecht, Göttingen. Price : DM. 16.80.)

For the first edition of this work, see *Book List*, 1951, pp. 26 f. No substantial change has been made at any point ; and the general character of the book remains the same. But an index of Biblical quotations has been added, the bibliography has been expanded, and a large number of minor modifications and additional references to literature have been made in the text and the notes, thus enhancing the usefulness of this superb history.   G.W.A.

NOTH, M. : *Histoire d'Israël*. 1954. Pp. 472. (Payot, Paris. Price : Fr. 1,700.)

This French edition appears to be a half-way house between the first and second German editions, incorporating some, but by no means all of the changes in the latter. It would be an impertinence in the reviewer to comment on the stylistic adequacy of the rendering ; nor can he claim to have checked every sentence against the original. But some slips seem to have escaped notice : e.g., *L'Ouest* for *Osten* (p. 23) ; and n. 4 to p. 34, which appears slightly to misrepresent the German.
                                                              G.W.A.

*ORLINSKY, H. M. : *Ancient Israel*. 1954. Pp. xiv+194. (Cornell University Press, Ithaca, N.Y. and Geoffrey Cumberlege, London. Price : $1.75 paper ; $2.50 cloth, or 20s. 0d.)

This excellent little handbook, outlining the History of Israel to the Persian period, which was reviewed in the 1954, *Book List* (p. 23), is now available through the Oxford University Press, and may be warmly commended for wide circulation.   H.H.R.

RICCIOTTI, G.: *Geschichte Israels*, German Tr., by K. Faschian, Vol. I.
1953. Pp. 576+2 Maps. (Wiener Dom Verlag, Vienna. Price:
S. 98.)

The first volume of Ricciotti's well-known *History of Israel*
appeared in Italian in 1932, and in French in 1939 (see *Book
List*, 1939, p. 9). A second French edition appeared in 1947
(see *Book List*, 1949, pp. 17 f.), and this embodied some substantial revision. In the meantime it has appeared in Spanish
and Dutch (neither seen by the reviewer) and it has reached a
fourth Italian edition. The present translation is made from
this, but also owes something to the second French edition.
The work is well illustrated, and the author is familiar with
recent work, both archaeological and critical, and it is not
surprising that a work which is both scholarly and popular
has achieved so wide a circulation. It offers a useful handbook,
marked by caution on some of the most keenly debated
problems, such as the date of the fall of Jericho and of the
Exodus.   H.H.R.

SEMIRIN, S.: *Yoshiyahu uthequfatho* (in Hebrew), with a foreword by
Professor J. Klausner. 1952. Pp. 120. (Mosad Bialik, Jerusalem.
Price: 12s. 0d.)

The book deals with King Josiah and his period. Hence the
discussion on the date of Deuteronomy plays an important
part in it. Semirin argues for tendencies towards the centralization of worship at least from the time of the Judges
onwards. There were main sanctuaries in Shiloh, Nob, and
Gibeon before the Temple in Jerusalem existed. Hosea,
Amos, Asa and Hezekiah fought against idolatry connected
with the *bamoth* before the time of Josiah. Where the arguments
against Wellhausen are not new, other scholars are duly
acknowledged, though David Hoffmann, Menes and H. M.
Wiener could have been consulted with profit.

A detailed analysis of all relevant biblical and extra-biblical
texts shows that Josiah—not least for political reasons—
began with the abolition of the *bamoth* long before the ' *Torah* '
was found. The bulk of Deuteronomy is traced back to the
time of the undivided monarchy. Apart from the considerable
merits of the book as a whole, the re-opening of the discussion
on Deuteronomy and on the historical value of Chronicles
calls for special attention, even if certain questions such as the
position of the Levites in Deuteronomy are not dealt with.
The book was published after the death of its author.   S.S.

TREVER, J. C.: *Cradle of Our Faith*. 1954. Pp. xiv+86. (Newsfoto
Publishing Co., San Angelo, Texas. Price: $3.75.)

A series of coloured photographs accompanied by a short
descriptive text which serves to link them up with the main
outlines of Biblical history from the time of Abraham to the
spread of the Christian faith. The primary aim of the book
appears to be that of encouraging the reading of the Bible
by the general public; but members of the Society should
find that these pleasant photographs will add colour in the
fullest sense to their study of the sacred text.   A.R.J.

VALJAVEC, F. (ed. by) : *Historia Mundi : Ein Handbuch der Welt-geschichte*, vol. II : *Grundlagen und Entfaltung der ältesten Hoch-kulturen*. 1953. Pp. 656. (Leo Lehnen Verlag, Munich. Price : DM. 28.80, or by subscription, DM. 25.00.)

A year after the appearance of the first volume of the monumental *Historia Mundi* (to be completed in ten volumes), the second has followed. This deals with the transition from pre-history to history, the history of Asia from its beginnings to the first millennium B.C., and that of the much later cultures of the Americas to the beginning of the second millennium A.D. The main part of the volume deals with the cultures of Egypt (by R. Anthes), Babylonia and Assyria (by A. Moortgat and G. Furlani), Syria and Palestine (by W. F. Albright), Israel (by W. Eichrodt), Asia Minor (by Sir J. L. Myres), Ancient India (by C. von Fürer-Haimendorf and E. Wald-schmidt), Ancient China (by W. Eberhard), and Ancient America (by H. Trimborn). Although not all the contributions reach the same standard, all offer reliable information on their allotted field, and introduce the reader to little known spheres, besides directing him to further literature. Students of the Old Testament will no doubt turn first to the substantial con-tributions of Anthes, Moortgat, Furlani, Albright, Eichrodt and Myres, but they should also pay attention to the others, the more so as these often reveal connections with the Near East which would usually escape attention.   O.E.

WALLIS, L. : *Young People's Hebrew History*. 1953. Pp. x+118, including index. (Philosophical Library, New York. Price : $2.50.)

The Young People of the title are those in the Training Colleges and Universities of the U.S.A., where there is " an academic ban against Hebrew History." The treatment of history in this book rests on the assumption that all history and sociological processes are the products of evolutionary forces. There is no room for the supernatural, and if it appears in the Old Testament, it must be explained away, or ignored. " Hebrew History was, to a large extent, a series of reactions against economic injustice." The prophets " philosophize the struggle in terms of a war between Yahweh and Baal." The book is warmly commended by leading Old Testament scholars, but the reviewer finds both its underlying assumptions and many of its incidental judgements quite unconvincing.
                                                        A.S.H.

WOLFF, H. W. : *Eine Handbreit Erde, Tagebuch eine Palästina-Reise*. 1954. Pp. 132, with illustrations and map. (Luther Verlag, Witten-Ruhr. Price : DM. 3.50.)

This unpretentious little book is exactly what its title says, a travel-diary of a journey made by a pious German to Palestine in modern times. The author, perhaps a little naïvely, contends that we need some slight knowledge of the Holy Land to enable us to understand the inconceivable reality that it is upon this terrestrial globe that God spoke, became incarnate and suffered.

The diary relates the day to day experiences of the pilgrim as he moves in buses, trains, ships, and expensive motor-cars from one locality of Bible story to the next, always ready, Bible in hand, with the appropriate incident or quotation. Almost his last visit is to the site of Ugarit, the scene of the now famous excavations at Ras Shamra. Here a public official remarked to him, " In Ugarit we can see that the Syrians knew God centuries before the Jews," upon which the author comments, " In truth Ugarit teaches us how different is the God of Israel, the God of the Bible, from the god of the Canaanites."   S.H.H.

TEXT AND VERSIONS

AYUSO MARAZUELA, T. : *La Vetus Latina Hispana*. I. *Prolegomenos*. 1953. Pp. 596. (Consejo Superior de Investigaciones Cientificos, Madrid. Price : Pes. 580.)

This really superbly produced quarto, printed throughout in types that are a joy to middle-aged eyes, is the work of the Canon Lectoral of the Saragossa chapter, and is introduced at some length by the Bishop of Madrid-Alcala. Those who are accustomed to skip introductions of this type will, until they reach page 330 of the text, be in some doubt as to the real purpose of the book. It is, in effect, the result of an investigation that has been spurred on by patriotism, since Dr. Ayuso is convinced (and will supply the proofs in the succeeding volumes) that he has identified a genuine Spanish *Vetus Latina*, which does not coincide with the African or the Itala versions, and is a distinct version in its own right. Meanwhile, one finds here an immense bibliography, some of it not too closely connected with the Old Latin versions, a lengthy treatment of the Old Latin in general, a special introduction to the problem of the *Vetus Latina Hispana*, a study of the Old Latin interpolations in the Vulgate and of the Mozarabic Liturgy, some full appendices and many pages devoted to a series of indexes. It is all rather overwhelming, and we may join the author in his prayer : *Quiera Dios ayudarnos hasta el fin para llevarla a féliz termino*.   J.M.T.B.

BARDTKE, H. : *Hebräische Konsonantentexte aus biblischem und ausserbiblischem Schrifttum für Übungszwecke ausgewählt*. 1954. Pp. xviii+80. (Otto Harrassowitz, Leipzig. Price : DM. 4.80.)

The author has selected 96 pieces, Biblical and non-Biblical, for practice in the reading and vocalisation of unpointed Hebrew texts. Easier pieces come first, more difficult ones follow. Fifty-five of the pieces are from the Old Testament, almost all the books being represented. Then come in turn inscriptions discovered in Palestine—at Gezer, Siloam, Tell Qasileh, Samaria and Lachish ; selections from Ben Sira, the Dead Sea scrolls, and the Damascus Fragments, together with documents from the Wadi Murabba'at (letter of Simeon bar Cochba ; a legal document of the second century ; and a phylactery text) ; and selections from Hebrew translations, medieval and modern, from Greek and Latin (e.g., from the books of Tobit, Judith, 1 and 2 Maccabees). As an aid to the reader, the texts have been edited to some extent, for example, by the introduction into them of material from the apparatus criticus of BH⁷. Bibliographical notes accompany the non-Biblical pieces, and a vocabulary, which is aimed especially at helping the student in the reading of non-Biblical texts, is added. The book is well planned, and should prove most useful to students, to whom the author offers some good advice in their reading of unvocalised texts. The inclusion of some texts which are as yet not easily accessible to students adds much to the interest and value of the work.   D.W.T.

HAUPTMANN, O. H. (ed by) : *Escorial Bible* I.j.4, Vol. I. *The Pentateuch.* 1953. Pp. xii+320. (Pennsylvania University Press, Philadelphia, and Geoffery Cumberlege, London. Price : 40s. 0d.)

The Escorial Bible is an interesting example of a medieval Spanish translation, which has been assigned to the fourteenth century, though the present editor argues for a somewhat later dating in the first third, or even early in the second third, of the fifteenth century. One feature to be noted is that, if Hauptmann's arguments are accepted, the translation was based largely upon the Hebrew original with some help from the Vulgate. It must be allowed that not all the proofs submitted in favour of this thesis are equally convincing. For example, only two instances are given under " (2) translation of words omitted by the Vulgate " and these are *la faz* in verses 2 and 20 of Gen. i, and of *Dios* in verses 4, 5, 11, 17 of the same chapter. But the Vulgate reads *super faciem abyssi* in verse 2, and the omission of the divine name in four out of twenty possible occurrences is not a significant variation. It is a pity also that the bibliography contains so many works that have been virtually superseded. So the only edition of the Vulgate cited is a Madrid edition of 1799, Dalman's *Aramäisch-Neuhebräisches Wörterbuch* is used in the 1901 edition, and the only Hebrew grammar employed is now thirty-five years old.   J.M.T.B.

DE SAINTE-MARIE, H. : *Sancti Hieronymi Psalterium iuxta Hebraeos. Édition critique. Collectanea Biblica Latina : vol. XI.* 1954. Pp. lxxii+262. (Libreria Vaticana, Citta del Vaticano : Price : Lire 2,500.)

This full critical edition of the *Psalterium iuxta Hebraeos* contains a long introduction discussing the manuscripts and the history of the text with their grouping in families, the medieval recensions, the indirect evidence for the text, the work of St. Jerome on the Psalter, and the modern editions of this version. Everything is lucidly set out and concisely discussed. The text is well and clearly printed, and a detailed *apparatus criticus* accompanies it ; an exhaustive *index verborum* (from which only a few pronouns and particles are omitted) and a table of manuscripts completes this admirable work. An idea of the extent of the present work can be obtained by considering that of Lagarde and Harden, while the former

used 4 manuscripts and 5 previous editions and the latter
(who is highly praised) examined 15 and used 9 manuscripts
and cited other witnesses to the text, the present editor has
consulted 85 manuscripts, of which he employs 9, and some
10 previous editions. This work, which promises to become
the definitive edition, is beyond all praise.   G.R.D.

SCHNEIDER, H. : *Der Text der Gutenbergbibel zu ihrem 500 jährigen
Jubiläum untersucht.* (Bonner Biblische Beiträge, No. 7.) 1954.
Pp. 120. (Hanstein, Bonn. Price : DM. 13.20, or bound DM. 17.)

Professor Schneider renders a service to Roman Catholics and
Protestants alike by this very careful and thorough examination of the textual history of the Gutenberg Bible. This
Bible was the first major production of the printing press
in the western world, it is the parent of well nigh every printed
text of the Latin Bible since that time, and its first edition is
scrupulously included in the register of the new Benedictine
Vulgate. It is the pre-1455 history of the Latin transmission,
however, that holds the main attention of the author, and the
survey, though not producing anything remarkably new, is
clear and balanced. Extant manuscripts in the Mainz district
are described ; the story of the expansion of the Paris text
in the Rhineland is traced ; the relation of the Gutenberg
Bible with other text-forms examined ; and the work of
correctors estimated. All this is eminently well done, but
readers of the last chapter, which claims to be a concluding
survey, might feel that the obvious special pleading possibly
detracts from the value of the whole work as a scientific
inquiry.   B.J.R.

*Vetus Latina. Die Reste der altlateinischen Bibel nach Petrus Sabatier
neu gesammelt und herausgegeben von der Erzabtei Beuron.* 2.
Genesis. Lief. 4. Gen. 43, 22—Schluss. 1954. Pp. 449-576.
(Verlag Herder, Freiburg. Subscription Price : DM. 24.55.)

The present fascicle completes the second part of this magnificent edition of the Old Latin Bible. Genesis is now complete,
and readers can gain a fair picture of the scope of the undertaking. At the end are 50 pages of *Nachträge und Berichtigungen*
and *Register*, together with a title-page for the volume. The
editor, Fr. B. Fischer, may be congratulated on a monumental
work which will completely supersede that of Sabatier and
will surely be a *ktēma eis aei* in every theological library.
          G.R.D.

ZIEGLER, J. : *Septuaginta. Vetus Testamentum Graecum auctoritate
Societatis Litterarum Gottingensis editum XVI/ii : Susanna, Daniel,
Bel et Draco :* 1954. Pp. 224. (Vandenhoeck & Ruprecht,
Göttingen. Price : DM. 28. [Bound DM. 32].)

The long-awaited volume of the Septuagint containing Daniel,
Susanna and Bel and the Dragon, follows the plan of its
predecessors : it contains a long introduction (pp. 1-79) giving
a detailed account of the manuscripts on which the Greek
text is based, their peculiarities and their groupings; later
Greek translations, the patristic evidence, and the connected

ancient Versions (Old-Latin, Coptic, Syriac, Ethiopic, Arabic, Armenian). The variant readings from all these sources are duly set out in the critical notes beneath the text (pp. 80-223). The work, so far as a cursory glance can be trusted, is impeccably accurate and will be an indispensable tool for the study of these books.   G.R.D.

EXEGESIS AND MODERN TRANSLATIONS

BARON, D. : *The Servant of Jehovah*. 1954. Pp. xiv+158. (Marshall, Morgan & Scott, London and Edinburgh. Price : 8s. 6d.)

This is an examination of Isaiah lii. 13—liii. 12 in the light of its fulfilment in the life, death and resurrection of Jesus Christ. In this passage, together with xlii. 1-9, xlix. 1-7, l. 4-11, and lxi, the Servant is to be distinguished from Israel, although the collective interpretation is admitted for the remaining prophecies in Isaiah xl—lxvi.

The book opens with a consideration of various non-Messianic interpretations of Isaiah liii, individual and collective, and these are repudiated. (All such interpretations by Christian scholars are labelled ' rationalistic '.) Then follows an exposition of the passage. The Hebrew text is used, but the A.V. translation is generally accepted. Verses 1-9 are interpreted as the lament and confession of penitent Israel. The treatment is informed with a warm devotional and evangelistic spirit ; but its discussion of the Hebrew vocabulary and grammar is dominated by the author's theology. The book was originally published in 1922.   A.S.H.

BEASLEY, W. J. : *Creation's Amazing Architect*. 1955. Pp. 158. (Marshall, Morgan and Scott, London. Price : 8s. 6d.)

The thesis of this interestingly written and attractively illustrated book is that there is a parallelism, too close and detailed to be accidental, between the geological record and the sequence of creative events described in Genesis i and Job xxxviii. The author, who is President of the Australian Institute of Archaeology, makes no claim to expert knowledge either of Hebrew or of geology, but he has had recourse to good authorities in both fields, and the accuracy of his Old Testament translations is attested in a foreword by Prof. M. D. Goldman of Melbourne University.   F.F.B.

BÉGUERIE, PH., LECLERCQ, J. and STEINMANN, J. : *Études sur les prophètes d'Israël*. (Lectio Divina 14.) 1954. Pp. 174. (Les Éditions du Cerf, Paris. Price : Fr. 480.)

The reader is here offered a series of simple, straightforward expositions of the account of Isaiah's call (Béguerie), the psalm of Habakkuk (id.), the book of Nahum (Leclercq), the ' confessions ' of Jeremiah (id.) and the book of Joel (Steinmann). If they yield little that is new, they take note of and indeed have been largely inspired by recent studies in these fields, and due attention is also paid to the comparative material from the ancient Near East, particularly that which is afforded by the discoveries at Ras Shamra.   A.R.J.

BEWER, J. A. : *The Book of Ezekiel*. (Harper's Annotated Bible, Nos. 8 and 9.) 2 vols. 1954. Pp. 72, 84. (Harper, New York and Eyre and Spottiswoode, London. Price : $0.75 or 6s. 0d. each vol.)

These two books continue the series of annotations on the Authorized Version already noted in previous Book Lists. They follow the same pattern of treatment ; an introduction and then the A.V. text set out in prose and verse, with notes at the foot of the page. The traditional view is followed that Ezekiel prophesied in Babylon, being transported to Jerusalem in trance state to witness what went on there. Attention is drawn, both in the introduction and the notes, to duplicate passages, repetitions, and (chiefly in chs. xl-xlviii) secondary material. It is assumed that, although some of this material may be the prophet's own alternative drafts, much of it is the work of subsequent editors. The notes are concise and to the point but are necessarily brief and encumbered with inevitable and frequent improvements on the translation of the A.V. The books may be warmly recommended for those who wish to understand the Book of Ezekiel without resort to the larger commentaries.   L.H.B.

La Sacra Bibbia tradotta dai testi originali con note e cura del Pontificio Istituto Biblico di Roma. Vol. VI. I Profeti—I. Isaia-Geremia. 1953. Pp. 410. (Salani, Florence. Price : Lire 1,200.)

It is not necessary, at this time of day, to say much about the excellent Italian translation of the Bible by Vaccari and other professors of the Biblical Institute in Rome. A notice of one of the earlier volumes may be seen in the *Book List*, for 1951 (p. 41). The present volume is a rendering in limpid and accurate Italian of Isaiah, Jeremiah, Lamentations, and Baruch. There are abundant notes, several illustrations, and a critical appendix showing the readings adopted in the text. One minor criticism might well be that the notes to the text make no reference to this appendix. It might be possible in future editions to mark the variants with an asterisk at the side of the translation.   J.M.T.B.

La Sainte Bible de Jérusalem. Les Livres des Chroniques, by H. Cazelles. 1954. Pp. 246. (Price: Fr. 675.) *Daniel*, by P. J. de Menasce. 1954. Pp. 98. (Price : Fr. 285.) (Les Éditions du Cerf, Paris.)

The volumes follow the pattern already familiar, see *Book List*, 1954, p. 30 and earlier *Book Lists*. In respect of both books the normal modern view is in the main followed. The Chronicler was a pupil of Ezra. He used the biblical sources, the original sources which he regularly mentions, and possibly traditional oracles. He was interested in the origin and development of the church-state of his day, and represents the post-exilic development of the prophetic ideal of a religious, believing community. In the second volume, the setting is the Maccabaean revolt. The author spoke Aramaic but wrote the beginning and the end in Hebrew to secure acceptance. The Aramaic is nearer to extant fifth century Aramaic than to that of the Targums. The editor withholds judgement on the puzzle of the identity of Darius the Mede.   N.H.S.

VAN DEN BORN, A. : *Ezechiël uit de grondtekst vertaald en uitgelegd.* 1954. Pp. 288. (Romen & Zonen, Roermond & Masseik. Price : Fl. 10.80.)

This volume on Ezekiel forms Part XI, Book I, of *De Boeken van het Oude Testament*, a series of O.T. commentaries by Catholic scholars of the Netherlands and Belgium. Van den Born has already contributed to the abundant recent literature on Ezekiel, but here he departs from his former view, that Ezekiel's ministry was exercised in Jerusalem until the end of Zedekiah's reign, and in Babylonia only after that date. This view, he says, does not solve all the problems ; and he is now willing to consider the possibility that the main part of the book is a pseudepigraph of the Ezra-Nehemiah period, worked over and amplified by a glossator, presumably of the Greek period, since " he is probably also the author of chapters xxxviii f., . . . which point to the time of Alexander the Great." The original text of chapters xl-xlviii has been so thoroughly edited that it is impossible completely to distinguish their earlier from their later elements, but those parts are in line with the original prophecy which envisage the new age in terms of a re-distribution of the promised land among those brought back from Israel's dispersion, with Yahweh dwelling in their midst in a new temple. The new temple is intended to be understood literally and not symbolically, but our author is not convinced by the Bertholet-Galling argument that its description reflects personal acquaintance with Solomon's temple. Whatever may be thought of his literary analysis, Van den Born has given us a valuable and important book.

F.F.B.

BRUNO, A. : *Jeremia : eine rhythmische Untersuchung.* 1954. Pp. 284. (Almqvist & Wiksell, Stockholm. Price : Swedish Kr. 25.)

This work follows the same general pattern as the author's earlier volumes on Genesis-Exodus, and Isaiah (see *Book List*, 1954, pp. 45 f.). A German rendering of the text of Jeremiah is set out in strophic form, the whole being divided into three main sections : i-xxii ; xxiii-xlv ; xlvi-lii, the first and third being predominantly ' lyric,' and the second ' epic.' The metrical and textual comments are relatively brief, for the author assumes the general contentions of the earlier volumes. Much labour has gone into the work ; and a summary judgement (which is all that can be offered in a brief notice) may well seem unfair. But the present reviewer remains unconvinced by the author's general approach.   G.W.A.

BRUNO, A. : *Die Psalmen : eine rhythmische und textkritische Untersuchung.* 1954. Pp. 282. (Almqvist & Wiksell, Stockholm. Price : Swedish Kr. 25.)

It is scarcely necessary to add to what has been said about Dr. Bruno's earlier volumes. Even if his rhythmical principles did not seem artificial in themselves, the many changes of text to which he is driven would tell against their validity.

G.W.A.

BUTTRICK, G. A. (ed. by) : *Interpreter's Bible*, Vol. III (Kings— Job). 1954. Pp. 1,198. (Abingdon-Cokesbury Press, New York and Nashville. Price : $8.75.)

Vol. III, which has 11 maps, will enhance the reputation of the series. The Introduction and Exegesis to 1 and 2 Kings are by N. H. Snaith, to 1 and 2 Chronicles by W. A. L. Elmslie, to Ezra and Nehemiah by R. A. Bowman, to Esther by B. W. Anderson, and to Job by S. Terrien. In addition there are the usual expositions of the books by other writers, save in the case of Chronicles.

Snaith shows the influence of the original Deut. compiler c. 610 B.C. and of the later editor c. 550 upon the traditions of Kings, and full account is taken of LXX variants. Elmslie deals frankly with the difficulties and phantasies of the Chronicler, but sympathetically with the Chronicler's purpose and his quasi ' ecumenical mind.' Whereas Elmslie dates the Chronicler to the late 5th Cent., and does not think that he is the editor of Ezra and Nehemiah, Bowman dates the Chronicler as editor of Ezra and Nehemiah to about 350, dating Ezra to 398, whereas Elmslie puts Nehemiah at 384 and Ezra shortly afterwards. The Esther articles are helpful. Terrien interprets Job as a lyrical meditation with a dramatis personæ. He emphasizes a strophic arrangement in the poem, thinks c. xxviii is by the poet, but attributes Elihu's speeches to a lesser poet, though they are a ' gradual ' to the theophany. Noteworthy is Terrien's claim that the ' enigma of suffering is not the central concern of the poet,' and he points to a more theocentric interpretation of the book.   G.H.D.

CASSUTO, M. D. (ed. by) : *Sifre Ha-Miqra* (in Hebrew), with a commentary by A. S. Hartom. *Isaiah*, pp. 194 ; *Jeremiah*, pp. 166 ; *Ezekiel*, pp. 158 ; *Minor Prophets*, pp. 190 ; *Psalms*, pp. 304 ; *Proverbs*, pp. 106 ; *Job*, pp. 148. 1954 (the commentaries on the Prophets and Psalms are reprints from earlier editions which appeared in 1952 and 1953). (Yavneh Publishing House, Tel Aviv.)

The series incorporates the main results of modern biblical scholarship, including the regard for metrical forms, philological, geographical and archaeological details. A brief ' introduction ' precedes each book and each psalm. References are made to the Dead Sea Scrolls to explain the many peculiar spellings in the Book of Ezekiel. The Ras Shamra texts are adduced to further the understanding of remnants of Canaanite mythological conceptions in the Psalms and in the Book of Job. In this and in the occasional slight variants from Manuscript copies of the Massoretic Text, the scholarly hand of the late Professor Cassuto appears to have left its mark. As in the Jerusalem Bible, however, no disciplined co-ordination of efforts has been achieved. No attempt has been made to explain to the reader some of the guiding exegetical principles. In the introduction to Isaiah, e.g., the views of modern scholars on Deutero- and Trito-Isaiah are mentioned. In Professor Hartom's notes on chapters xl, xliv and xlv the impression is given, that the unity of the whole book is suggested. We also miss a bibliography and references to the ancient versions. Textual emendations are not discussed.

Nevertheless the series should prove useful for the general reader, especially in view of valuable suggestions from medieval Jewish commentators. The Hebrew notes are pointed. S.S.

Enchiridion Biblicum : Documenta ecclesiastica Sacram Scripturam spectantia, auctoritate Pontificiae Commissionis de Re Biblica edita. 2nd ed. 1954. Pp. xvi+280. (Arnodo, Rome. Price : 18s. 0d. cloth ; or 11s. 0d. paper.)

This, the second edition of the invaluable *Enchiridion Biblicum*, which was first published in 1927, gives a remarkably useful collection of documents ranging from the Muratorian fragment down to the document, issued on 9th June, 1953, expressing the Biblical Commission's disapproval of Bernhard Bonkamp's work *Die Psalmen* (for details of which, see *Book List*, 1954, p. 31). The documents are printed in various languages, Latin for the most part, but the Secretary's letter to Cardinal Suhard on the problems of the Pentateuch (16th January, 1948), is in French, and the letter of 20th August, 1941, to the Ordinaries of the Italian dioceses, on an anonymous Italian work, is in Italian. There is an appendix on the new regulations for proceeding to the degrees in Holy Scripture, issued on 6th July, 1942. This second edition is in a smaller and neater format, and more elegantly printed than the first edition. On the other hand, the price has been raised quite sensationally. J.M.T.B.

GALLING, K. : *Die Bücher der Chronik, Esra, Nehemia*. (Das Alte Testament Deutsch, 12.) 1954. Pp. 256. (Vandenhoeck und Ruprecht, Göttingen. Price : DM. 8.20, or bound 10.60 ; by subscription, DM. 7.00 or 9.00.)

The volumes in this series follow one another quickly, and both editors and publishers are to be congratulated on their speed and efficiency. This volume consists of eleven pages of introduction, with the rest text and commentary. Professor Galling accepts the idea of two Chroniclers, one of whom was active about 300 B.C. and the other in the time of Antiochus III (the Great). He mentions specially the year 197 B.C., when, according to Josephus, Antiochus issued an edict concerning the restoration of the Jewish temple. This second Chronicler was responsible for additions and especially for a dislocation of the original order (cf. the study of S. Granild, *Book List*, 1950, p. 44). The Nehemiah Memoirs belong to the period 445-430 B.C., and the Ezra Memoirs cannot be earlier than c. 400 B.C. Ezra's visit belongs to the last years of Artaxerxes I or the first years of Artaxerxes II, but on p. 14, the author mentions the latter alternative only. The whole volume is well up to the standard we have grown to expect both of the author himself and of the series. N.H.S.

GAROFALO, S. (ed. by) : *La Sacra Bibbia. Libri dei Maccabei*, by A. Penna. 1953. Pp. 268+1 map+11 pages of plates. (Price : Lire 1,100.) *I Profeti Minori*, by G. Rinaldi. 1953. Pp. 218+7 pages of plates. (Price : Lire 950.) *Baruch*, by A. Penna. 1953. Pp. 60. (Price : Lire 250.) (Marietti, Turin and Rome.)

It is unnecessary to say much about this useful and competent series, which, as usual, prints an Italian translation to face the Vulgate Latin. A select apparatus is printed below both the Vulgate text and the translation. Penna in his edition of Maccabees leans fairly heavily on Abel and the earlier works, but has his own clear and informed way of expressing his meaning, and has evidently made the best use of his authorities. The introduction is particularly good, and its handling of the theological implications of 2 Macc. xii. 38 ff., is judicious. The volume on the Minor Prophets is made up of a general introduction to the prophetic literature and an exegetical commentary on Amos. It is disappointing that Rinaldi has, apparently, been able to make no use of R. S. Cripps's commentary, shortly to be reissued. The few pages on Baruch are perhaps too short measure, but, here again, Penna is able to make a real contribution in his introductory pages on the authorship of the book.   J.M.T.B.

HEGERMANN, H. : *Jesaja 53 in Hexapla, Targum und Peschitta* (Beiträge zur Förderung christlicher Theologie, 56. Band.) 1954. Pp. 128. (Bertelsmann, Gütersloh. Price : DM. 27.)

Gives comprehensive materials for the interpretation of Isa. lii. 13-liii. 12 in Judaism immediately before and during the early Christian era. The secondary Greek versions (Aquila, Symmachus, and Theodotion), together with LXX, Targum and Peshitta, are printed in parallel columns in much the same way as Origen's Hexapla, so that detailed verse-comparisons of them can be made. The conclusion is that all the documents examined understood the Servant as the Messiah. Yet the N.T. shows clearly that Isa. 53 had little influence upon Jewish messianic expectations in general, except, perhaps, in the circle of John the Baptist.   C.R.N.

KISSANE, E. J. : *The Book of Psalms*, Vol. II. 1954. Pp. vi+336. (Browne and Nolan, Dublin. Price : 30s. 0d.)

There is little to add to what was said with regard to the first volume of this commentary on the Psalter (*Book List*, 1953, pp. 37 f.). The exposition of the individual psalms is somewhat summary, and the advanced student may well feel dissatisfied with the tendency to glide over controversial points ; but on the whole it should serve a useful purpose as an introduction to the study of the Psalms, especially for those who have some knowledge of Hebrew.   A.R.J.

KNIGHT, G. A. F. : *Esther, Song of Songs, Lamentations* (The Torch Bible Commentaries.) 1955. Pp. 140. (S.C.M. Press, London. Price : 7s. 6d.)

The author approaches each of these three books with a question. Of *Esther* he asks whether " it adds to our knowledge of the mighty acts of God for the salvation of the world in and through his chosen instrument and people." *The Song of Songs* he introduces with the question " What is its theological meaning ?" and of *Lamentations* he asks how it may be so interpreted as to foreshadow the Cross. Within the limits thus set the commentary is a useful survey of these three books with common-sense explanations of some of the more out of the way words and passages.

But one wonders if these are the right questions to begin with when one opens these books. There would be less danger of distortion of fact if they were asked at the end of the commentary rather than at its beginning. L.H.B.

LESLIE, E. A. : *The Intimate Papers of Jeremiah.* 1953. Pp. 40. (Boston University Press, Boston, Mass.)

This is the fifth Boston University Lecture. It is in paper covers, and is a preliminary study for the later and larger volume (see immediately below), in which the material is embodied. As a short study and account of the prophet's work, the lecture is much to be commended. N.H.S.

LESLIE, E. A. : *Jeremiah—Chronologically arranged, translated, and interpreted.* 1954. Pp. 350. (Abingdon Press, New York and Nashville, Tenn. Price : $4.75.)

The aim of the volume is to ' make the entire book of Jeremiah an intelligible, interesting and inspiring experience.' Professor Elmer Leslie has entirely succeeded. He has provided his own translation. There are eight sections dating from 626-586 B.C., together with a section devoted to supplements and adaptations for the Diaspora (587-200 B.C.) and a chapter on the abiding values in Jeremiah. The book is everywhere dependent on a thorough knowledge of the Hebrew text, full account is taken of the latest work on Jeremiah, but all is so written that the non-Hebraist can reap the fullest advantage. It is a good book for students and preachers. N.H.S.

MOWINCKEL, S. : *Der achtundsechzigste Psalm.* (Avhandlinger utgitt av Det Norske Videnskaps-Akademi i Oslo. II. Hist.—Filos. Klasse 1953. No. 1.) 1953. Pp. 78. (Dybwad, Oslo. Price : Kr. 7.50.)

A detailed exposition of Psalm 68, complete with a transliterated text and translation into German, which seems to have been designed primarily as a defence of the unity of the psalm in opposition to Albright's view that it consists of a series of *incipits*. In Mowinckel's opinion the psalm in its present form was connected with the Enthronement Festival of Yahweh in the Jerusalem Temple, although in origin it may well go back to the time of Saul. As usual Mowinckel presents his argument in a vivid and arresting way, and the present writer finds much in this monograph with which he readily agrees. In so far as the work is intended as a refutation of Albright's theory, however, the author seems to have weakened his case by resorting to a somewhat arbitrary emendation of the text on metrical grounds. A.R.J.

NICHOL, F. D. (ed. by) : *The Seventh-Day Adventist Bible Commentary*.
Vols. 1 and II. 1953, 1954. Pp. 1,120, 1,040. (Review and Herald
Publishing Association, Washington, D.C. Price : $10, per vol.)

These are the first two volumes of a major commentary, to be
completed in seven volumes, prepared by a team of Seventh-
day Adventist writers, including some well-known names,
such as E. R. Thiele, S. H. Horn, LeRoy E. Froom. Its point
of view is very conservative and literalistic. The Mosaic
authorship of the Pentateuch is maintained, and the story of a
world-wide Flood is accepted. Any evolutionary theory is
vigorously resisted. The seven days of creation are believed to
have consisted of twenty-four hours each. Harmonization of
Biblical disagreements is effected by various shifts. Thus
Exod. xii. 40 is harmonized with Gal. iii. 17 by the argument
that ' Egypt ' in the former text includes Canaan. 2 Sam.
xxiv. 1 is harmonized with 1 Chron. xxi. 1 by the view that
in the former case ' he moved ' means ' he did not prevent
Satan from moving.' It would be a mistake, however, to dismiss
this commentary as useless or unscholarly. Some of the
general articles will be read with profit by those who do not
share their viewpoint, and the verse by verse commentary
is full and, of course, much is not marked by the special point
of view of the sponsors of the publication. The general articles
are long, and are not all collected at the beginning of the
first volume. Nine stand in the first volume and three in
the second. There are useful articles on the historical background of the Patriarchal age and on daily life in that age.
Chronology is given special attention, and here the fifteenth
century date of the Exodus is adopted. There is an article on
the Names of God in the Old Testament, and one on the
Hebrew Calendar. The writers are familiar with the work of
modern archaeology, and altogether represent a scholarly
conservatism, which will enable their work to be consulted
with profit at many points.   H.H.R.

NICHOL, F. D. (ed. by) : *The Seventh-Day Adventist Bible Commentary*.
Vol. 3. 1 *Chronicles to Song of Solomon*. 1954. Pp. 1,166. (Review
and Herald Publishing Association, Washington, D.C. Price : $10.)

The third volume of this commentary by a team of Seventh
Day Adventist writers has appeared while the *Book List* has
been in the hand of the Printer. Like its predecessors it reflects
a rigidly conservative point of view. The book of Esther is
treated as history, and Ecclesiastes and the Song of Songs are
both attributed to Solomon. The editors hold that ' there
remains much to support the tradition ' that ascribes the book
of Job to Moses. The contributors are well acquainted with
modern work, and the commentary is up-to-date in its
information. Driver's *Aramaic Documents* and Kraeling's
Brooklyn Aramaic Papyri are used. There are careful notes
on a number of questions, such as the chronological order of
Ezra and Nehemiah—where the traditional order is maintained. Four good general articles are found in this volume,
dealing with poetic forms in Hebrew, musical instruments in

the Bible, the historical background of the period 586 to 400 B.C., and the chronology of the exile and restoration. The usefulness of the commentary is by no means limited to the readers who share its positions. It is to be regretted that there is no indication as to which contributor wrote which parts of the work. H.H.R.

The Fourth Book of Moses called Numbers—The Enumeration of Israel. 1954. Pp. 42. *The Fifth Book of Moses called Deuteronomy.* 1954. Pp. 42. Translated by the Commission for the Revision of the Old Testament, appointed by the Hungarian Bible Council of the Evangelical Church. References and explanatory notes by L. Tóth, assisted by J. Deák. (Press Department of the General Convent of the Reformed Church in Hungary, Budapest.)

These are the fourth and fifth instalments of the new Hungarian Bible, which was reviewed in the *Book List*, 1952, p. 31, and 1954, p. 27. Lay-out and scope are the same as in the previous three parts. The Editors are to be congratulated on the speed with which this publication is proceeding. P.R.W.

PODECHARD, E. : *Le Psautier, Traduction littérale, explication historique et notes critiques : II. Psaumes* 76-100 *et* 110. 1954. Pp. 184. (Facultés Catholiques, Lyon. Price : Fr. 800.)

This volume continues that noted in the 1951 *Book List*. It begins with a memorial note, mainly bibliographical, on M. Podechard who died in 1951. There is a translation of each Psalm followed first by exegetical and historical notes and then by more critical textual notes. In his handling of the material the author is fettered neither by traditional or current interpretation nor by ecclesiastical tradition (Catholic). He is unwilling to recognize any enthronement element in *Yahweh malak* and translates by " Iahvé règne " (xciii. 1, xcvi. 10, xcix. 1) because Yahweh is king for all time (xciii. 2). Psalm cx is interpreted as a celebration of David's installation as both king and priest after the capture cf Jerusalem and the establishment of his court therein. L.H.B.

PUUKKO, A. F. : *Raamatun selitysteos.* III. *Vanhan Testamentin opetuskirjat* (=A commentary on the Bible. III. The Wisdom Literature of the O.T.) 1954. Pp. 256. (Werner Söderström Oy, Helsinki-Porvoo.)

This volume of Prof. Puukko's Bible commentary comprises the books of Job, Psalms, Proverbs, Ecclesiastes, and Canticles. It is arranged on the same plan as the previous volumes (see *Book List*, 1953, p. 40, 1954, p. 41) with the text at the top of each page and a brief, popular commentary below. The author's stand-point is rather conservative. The cultic setting of the psalms is not denied, but the theories of Mowinckel are not even mentioned, and the so-called enthronement psalms are considered to be eschatological. The possibility of Davidic origin is admitted in some cases, but many psalms are dated in post-exilic times. Non-Biblical parallels are occasionally mentioned, but the main stress is laid on the religious ideas.

The book of Canticles is a collection of wedding songs, but the modern cultic interpretation is mentioned in a brief sentence of two lines.

The author received the first printed copies of the book a few days before his death in December, 1954, but the fourth volume, comprising the prophetical books, is ready in manuscript, and it is hoped that it can be published posthumously.

H.R.

RIDDERBOS, N. H. : *Beschouwingen over Genesis I.* 1954. Pp. 42. (Bureau van de Vrije Universiteit te Amsterdam. Price : Fl. 0.75.)

This report, by the successor to G. C. Aalders in the Chair of Old Testament at the Free University of Amsterdam, considers the attitude which may be taken to Gen. i. 1—ii. 4a by a modern scholar who belongs to a strongly conservative tradition. Ridderbos, who is in no sense an obscurantist, considers the subject-matter from the viewpoint of literary criticism, natural science and theology, and concludes that the " days " of this narrative are to be taken neither as days of twenty-four hours nor as longer or shorter periods, but provide a simple framework for the essential revelation.

F.F.B.

SNAITH, N. H. : *Notes on the Hebrew Text of* 1 *Kings xvii-xix, and xxi-xxii.* 1954. Pp. 110. (Epworth Press, London. Price : 10s. 6d.)

A further volume of notes by Dr. Snaith on the Hebrew Text designed especially for those who study by themselves. The notes are so straightforward that a beginner with only a smattering of Hebrew could use them. They are mainly grammatical with full references to the Hebrew Grammars in common use. Textual notes are given where necessary to elucidate the meaning of the Hebrew. A vocabulary to the chapters annotated is given at the end of the book and greatly increases its usefulness.

L.H.B.

STIER, F. : *Das Buch Ijjob : Hebräisch und Deutsch.* 1954. Pp. 352. (Kösel Verlag, Munich. Price : DM. 25.)

The first 214 pages of this study of the Book of Job are taken up with text. The Hebrew text on the left hand page is faced by the German translation on the right hand page. The Hebrew text is that of Kittel's *Biblia Hebraica,* is unpointed and set out in lines and verses. There are, however, a number of omissions and additions made by the author and indicated by square brackets. The translation is a literal rendering of the Hebrew, as the author understands it, but incorporates the textual emendations which are set out in the notes. Following the text there is a discussion of the purpose and interpretation of the book. This follows generally accepted lines ; the prologue and epilogue are regarded as integral parts of the book and the seeming irrelevance of the restoration of Job's fortune is explained on the basis of xlii. 10 where

Job's continued willingness to serve God disinterestedly is
shown in his prayer for his friends. The chapter on Wisdom
is thought to be original but is perhaps a kind of author's
aside to his readers, a suggestion which the author also makes
about some of the material in the speeches. The Elihu speeches
are considered to be a very early interpolation in the interests
of theological exposition. The book ends with notes on the
text in which many useful suggestions are embedded.

L.H.B.

UBACH, B. : *La Biblia illustració pels Monjos de Montserrat*. Vol. xxv.
No. 3. Numbers—Deuteronomy. 1954. Pp. 332 (including maps
and reproductions of photographs). (Monastery of Montserrat.
Price : Pes. 350.)

This is, in all probability, the finest collection of illustrations
to the books of Numbers and Deuteronomy that exists. The
Biblical text, in the Catalan translation of the Benedictines of
Montserrat, is given, in a series of selections, so as to face
each page of maps or photographic illustrations. Many customs
of the modern Arabs of the lands lying between Sinai and
Canaan are carefully recorded in photographs taken on the
spot, and there are also a large number of excellent views of
the landscapes in the desert of Sin, Cades, the land of Moab,
and elsewhere. The panoramic view of the promised land from
Pisgah is something to be studied and admired, as is the
other folding plate showing the region around Cades. One
may sincerely hope that this admirable series may be continued, and may have texts and comments in languages more
generally known than Catalan.   J.M.T.B.

UBACH, B. : *La Biblia, versió dels textos originals i comentari pels
Monjos de Montserrat*. Josué—Jutges—Rut. 1953. Pp. 374.
(Monastery of Montserrat. Price : Pes. 150.)

The Catalan Bible of Montserrat is enriched by this volume,
which follows the general plan of the series. It may suffice to
mention here a few points on which the author's views are of
particular interest. He rejects the Wellhausen view that the
book of Joshua closes the Hexateuch, and notes the important
work of Alt and Noth. He says the latter's work would have
received an enthusiastic welcome, if he had not reduced the
figure of Joshua almost to nothing. On the capture of Ai the
author follows H. Vincent in holding that the ancient ruin was
temporarily re-occupied by the Canaanites. On the composition
of the book of Judges he holds that the compiler combined and
retouched northern and southern traditions, and attributed
to all Israel incidents that concerned particular tribes only.
A later author is held to have added the notices on the Minor
Judges, the Abimelech story, the two appendices, and the
first Introduction. The Catalan translation of the delightful
book of Ruth, with which this volume closes, seems to the
reviewer quite remarkable. Throughout the volume the
author's long years of work in Palestine are reflected in the
abundant and valuable topographical and geographical notes.

M.D.

WEISER, A. : *Der Prophet Jeremia : Kap. xxv. 15-lii. 34.* (Das Alte Testament Deutsch, 21.) 1955. Pp. 260. (Vandenhoeck & Ruprecht, Göttingen.)

The first part of this commentary on Jeremiah appeared in 1952 (*Book List*, 1953, p. 41). The same characteristics appear here: rhythmical translations of the oracles, and effective use of the modern cult approach. The promised general articles appear at the end of this second volume, and occupy the last thirty-four pages. There is an article on the historical background, another on his life and work, and one on Jeremiah's place and influence in Old Testament religion. The last of the four sections concerns Introduction. The chief points here are the expansions in chs. xxvi-xxxvi ; xxxvii-xlv is from Baruch, setting forth Jeremiah's message after his death ; xlvi-li are threats against foreign powers in the exile period ; lii is a subsequent addition from 2 Kings similar to the addition in Isaiah xxxvi-xxxix. N.H.S.

YOUNG, E. J. : *The Messianic Prophecies of Daniel.* (Exegetica, Series I, Part VI.) 1954. Pp. 80. (Uitgeverij Van Keulen, Delft. Price : Fl. 3.95 separately ; Fl. 2.75 to subscribers to the series. Also published by Eerdmans Publishing Co., Michigan, U.S.A., bound. Price : $1.50.)

This contribution (in English) to the Dutch series *Exegetica* is based on the positions laid down in the author's *The Prophecy of Daniel* (reviewed in the *Book List*, 1950) : Daniel is an authentic prophecy of the 6th century B.C. and the four kingdoms of chs. ii and vii are the Babylonian, Medo-Persian, Greco-Macedonian and Roman Empires respectively. (When the author says that, so far as he is aware, there are no present-day " scholarly advocates " of the view that the fourth kingdom corresponds to Alexander's successors, he strangely overlooks Fr. Lattey's identification of it with the Seleucids, although he mentions Lattey's commentary and wrote while Lattey was still alive.) The stone of ii. 34 is the kingdom of the Messiah (and a kingdom presupposes a king); so is the fifth kingdom of ch. vii (but in ch. vii the personal Messiah—the Son of Man—comes more to the fore than in ch. ii). The prophecy of the seventy heptads (ix. 24-27) is also interpreted messianically and seen to be fulfilled in Jesus, who makes the covenant of grace effective with " the many " (cf. Isa. liii. 11 f.) and by his death causes sacrifice and oblation to cease (in the sense set forth in the Epistle to the Hebrew). Like all the author's works, this is marked by strong conservatism, sound scholarship, and charity towards those of opposing views.

F.F.B.

LITERARY CRITICISM AND INTRODUCTION
(including History of Interpretation, Canon, and Special Studies)

CASSUTO, U. : *The Documentary Hypothesis and the Composition of the Pentateuch*, pp. 90 ; *From Adam to Noah*, pp. xv+212 ; *From Noah to Abraham*, pp. 252 ; *A Commentary on The Book of Exodus*, pp. x+352. (in Hebrew.) 1953. (Magnes Press, Jerusalem.)

> This new edition of the four books (see *Book List*, 1946, pp. 23, 31 and *Book List*, 1952, pp. 29-30) contains no new material. At the end of *From Noah to Abraham*, however, comes part of an uncompleted fifth book entitled *Abraham and the Promised Land*—in essence a commentary on the section of *Lekh Lekha* (Gen. xii-xviii), comprising pp. 199-251. In his introduction we see again Cassuto arguing firmly against the documentary hypothesis and showing the unity of the section. As to the narratives of the Torah on Abraham it is shown that the cultural, social, ethnographical and linguistic backgrounds of the stories told in Genesis about Abraham tally well with the recent finds attributed to the first half of the second millennium in the Ancient East. The commentary reaches chapter xiii. 5, stopping at the fifth word.   M.W.

GALLUS, T. : *Interpretatio Mariologica Protoevangelii Posttridentina usque ad definitionem dogmaticam Immaculatae Conceptionis. Pars posterior (1661-1854).* 1954. Pp. xxxviii+384. (Edizioni di storia e letteratura, Rome. Price : Lire 4,000.)

> This, as the title indicates, is the second and final volume of what a Scottish reviewer has aptly termed " this historical study of exegetical analysis." As in the earlier volume, extracts, very often of several pages in length, are given from a large number of authors who have decided for or against the Marian interpretation of Gen. iii. 14-15. Very little in the way of introduction or footnotes is supplied, but, at the end of each section, and in the final summary at the close of this second volume (" Conclusio generalis de tota periodo posttridentina "), statistics show the balance of opinions and the names associated with the various groups. In all (cf. pp. 323 ff.) extracts are given from 574 authors, of whom 490 are Catholics. By far the greater number of the Catholic authors (425 or 86%) explain the text in a mariological sense ; the remaining 14% either give the text inadequate consideration or expound it simply in terms of philology. A supplement might well have been added to show the method of discussion after the definition by Pius IX, but, in fact, the volume comes to an end with the various *schemata* prepared for the Bull *Ineffabilis Deus* of 8th December, 1854.   J.M.T.B.

HAELVOET, M. : *La Théophanie du Sinai*. (Analecta Lovaniensia Biblica et Orientalia, 2nd Series, No. 39.) 1953. Pp. 28. (Publications Universitaires de Louvain, and Desclée de Brouwer, Bruges and Paris. Price : Belgian Fr. 30.)

> The author here attempts a literary analysis of the narrative of the theophany in Exod. xix-xxiv along fresh lines. He holds

that an original account, preserved in parts of xix, xx and xxiv, has been expanded by some elements of independent ancient tradition, some based on Deuteronomy, and some of priestly and ritual origin. He holds that the common analysis into J and E elements fails to solve the real difficulties of the section.   H.H.R.

HARKNESS, G. : *Towards Understanding the Bible*. 1954.   Pp. 138. (Charles Scribner's Sons, New York.   Price : $2.50.)

The book is directed to the " ordinary person." It is admittedly dependent on larger works of scholarship. There are five chapters : 1. The Bible as the Word of God, in which Divine Revelaticn and Inspiration are presented in relation to human fallibility. 2. The World of the Bible, in which the physical, social and religious setting of the Biblical material is described. 3. How the Old Testament was written. 4. How the New Testament was written. 5. The great ideas of the Bible. The material is presented from a moderate and devout liberal point of view.

Some of the comments are possibly misleading : the judges are described as a series of warlords, who seized power to become local despots ; the stories of Genesis are derived from traditions transmitted by women at the well and men around the campfires ; the epilogue to Job is from some later writer who missed the whole point of the book. The book ends with a bibliography (2 pages) and an index (4 pages).   A.S.H.

*HERKLOTS, H. G. : *Back to the Bible. A Literary Pilgrimage*. 1954. Pp. 174+8 Plates. (E. Benn, Ltd., London.   Price :   12s. 6d.)

It is difficult to provide either new or interesting reading in tracing the literary history of the Bible ; here is a praise-worthy attempt. The author, Vicar of Doncaster, denies personal expertise in the subject matter, but shows a good acquaintance with the work of acknowledged experts, and has a gift for lucid exposition allied to a happy faculty for intro-ducing the concrete illustration and personal anecdote that keep the mind alert. The main emphasis is on the New Testament, but it includes a section on the Dead Sea scrolls.
                                                                        D.R.Ap-T.

HOLWERDA, B. : *Dictaten*.   Deel I :   *Historia Revelationis Veteris Testamenti*. Eerste Aflevering. 1954.   Pp. 156. (Brill, Leiden. Price :   Fl. 10.)

This first instalment of a posthumous collection of lectures by Professor B. Holwerda, of Kampen Theological Seminary, deals with Gen. xxv. 19-xxxv. 29, the *toledot yiṣhaq*. Un-fortunately the work on the History of Revelation in the Old Testament, of which this section was intended to form part, remains unfinished. Holwerda understands *toledot yiṣhaq* as " the offspring of Isaac "; the chapters of Genesis which are introduced by this caption deal with the history of Esau and Jacob rather than with that of Isaac himself. Similarly *toledot haššmayim weha'areṣ* in Gen. ii. 4a introduces the narrative of ii. 4b-iv. 26, which records the sequel to the creation story of i. 1-ii. 3. From this it will be seen that Holwerda rejected the ordinary critical analysis of Genesis ; in fact he deplored it (his attitude appears also in his refusal to treat chapter xxvi as a duplicate of chapter xx). His interest, however, in this work is theological. He considers the birth-oracle in Gen. xxv. 23, where he finds the principles of the Biblical doctrine of election, and he traces their development in the following chapters. Indeed the principles of the covenant and of divine election are implicit in the very use of the *toledot* passages as the frame-work of Genesis. Orthodox Dutch Calvinist though he is, he considers that Old Testament exegesis has been adversely influenced by over-concentration on systematic theology, in consequence of which some readers cannot see the word election without thinking of predestination to eternal salvation or doom. He shows remarkably wide and up-to-date familiarity with the contributions of other O.T. scholars. F.F.B.

ROBINSON, T. H. : *Job and his Friends.* 1954. Pp. 126. (S.C.M., London. Price : 7s. 6d.)

Dr. Robinson gives here an excellent general account of the book of Job and its message. He deals with the origin and unity of the book, but also with the course of the argument between Job and his friends and with the purpose which inspired its composition. On the critical questions Dr. Robinson is in agreement with many modern scholars, and he makes little reference to divergent views. The chief value of his book lies in its exposition of the theme of Job. H.H.R.

*ROBINSON, T. H. : *Prophecy and the Prophets in Ancient Israel.* (Studies in Theology, No. 28.) 2nd ed. 1953. Pp. 210. (Duckworth, London. Price : 8s. 0d.)

The new edition of this widely used work will be very welcome. No substantial change has been made in the text except in the chapter on Ezekiel which has been almost completely re-written in the light of recent discussion : but the substantial integrity of the book, and the traditional views of its date and provenance are assumed. A supplementary bibliography has also been added. G.W.A.

STEINMANN, J. : *Les plus anciennes Traditions du Pentateuque.* 1954. Pp. 214. (J. Gabalda et Cie, Paris. Price : Fr. 420.)

The argument of this book is that Moses not only established a legal system for Israel, but also set it in a background of cosmic and national history. Two achievements, in particular, are therefore attributed to Moses, first the crystallization of the incipient monotheism of the Patriarchs, and second the assembly, but not necessarily the writing down, of the nucleus of the Pentateuch, the Book of the Covenant, the Decalogues, and such parts of the Yahwistic narrative as deal with events prior to the time of Moses The legislation is said to have been delivered to Moses at three places : the ritual decalogue and kindred laws at Sinai, the *mishpatim* at Kadesh and the more severe laws against idolatry at Mt. Nebo. This is a suggestive study, although much of it is necessarily based on surmise.

L.H.B.

TATFORD, F. A. : *The Climax of the Ages : Studies in the Prophecy of Daniel*, with an Appendix by F. F. Bruce. 1953. Pp. 270. (Marshall, Morgan & Scott, London. Price : 15s. 0d.)

This is a very conservative verse-by-verse commentary on Daniel by one who is imperfectly acquainted with scholarly work, and who is content to quote Pusey for the statement that ' the character . . . of its Chaldee excludes any later period ' than the sixth century B.C. It may be gently suggested to the author that we have much more knowledge of Aramaic to-day than was available to Pusey. S. R. Driver and the critics generally are dismissed with the simple statement that their case is without substance. The only part of the book which will interest readers of the *Book List* is Bruce's appendix, in which it is argued that Dan. i. 1 and Jer. xlvi. 1 may be reconciled by the supposition that the one reckoned on the post-dating system and the other did not. Mr. Bruce is familiar with scholarly work, including the most recent, and whether his solution is accepted or not, his essay will be read with respect. H.H.R.

TORREY, C. C. : *The Chronicler's History of Israel. Chronicles-Ezra-Nehemiah Restored to Its Original Form.* 1954. Pp. xxxiv+208. (Yale University Press, New Haven, and Geoffrey Cumberlege, London. Price : $5.00 or 40s. 0d.)

Professor Torrey outlines his well-known theory about the literary complex, Chron.-Neh., arguing that they are uniform and fairly consistently developed, but altogether fiction, and produced in the middle third century B.C. Readers are reminded of many details in Professor Torrey's discussions, and these often deserve very serious consideration even when his general theory is found to be untenable. The body of the present book is devoted to the Hebrew text—reproducing Baer's edition, without the accents—with the addition of two passages from Esdras which the author argues have been omitted from the traditional text. They are 1 Esd. i. 21f. which he inserts in 2 Chron. xxxv. 20, and 1 Esd. iv. 47b-56, iv. 62—v. 6, which are added to Ezra i. The English rendering in the AV is given for 2 Chron. xxxv to the end of Nehemiah. The Society would wish to greet Professor Torrey on having passed his ninety-first birthday. B.J.R.

UNGER, D. J. : *The First-Gospel* (*Genesis* 3 : 15). (Franciscan Institute Publications, Theological series No. 3.) 1954. Pp. xii+362. (Franciscan Institute, St. Bonaventure, N.Y. Price : $4.50.)

This is a painstaking, laborious, very fully documented study of Genesis iii. 15 and its bearing upon the dogma of the Immaculate Conception. The author, already known for his translation of the papal documents *Ineffabilis Deus* and *Ad diem illum*, has now made a thorough examination of all the arguments for and against the mariological interpretation, and has severely criticized the method and scholarship of the Benedictine writer L. Drewniak, *Die Mariologische Deutung von Gen. 3, 15 in der Väterzeit* (Breslau, 1934). Unger in his first section, on introductory problems, discusses the senses of Scripture and the genuine reading and explanation of Gen. iii. 14-15. In the second section, a series of chapters surveys authentic documents, ancient Christian tradition, scriptural parallels, theological reasons, and the witness of the Church's liturgy. Perhaps the most interesting section is the bibliographical appendix, giving a complete but not exhaustive list of 352 works, written between 1840 and 1952, with summaries of all the works. Like the giant work of Passaglia, Unger's book may be described as *valde eruditum, sed sua mole lectorem opprimens !*   J.M.T.B.

YOUNG, E. J. : *Studies in Isaiah.* 1954. Pp. 208. (Eerdmans, Grand Rapids, Mich., and Tyndale Press, London. Price : $2.50 or 12s. 6d.)

> Professor Young is well-known as an enlightened conservative writer on the Old Testament, the tenacity of whose adherence to conservative views is only matched by the catholicity and range of his reading and his general fairness to those who differ from him. These qualities are well exemplified in the present volume, which consists of articles which have appeared in the *Westminster Theological Journal*. The first study, which appeared in three articles, is a review of the study of Isaiah over the last century, and it will be found of high value to all interested in this prophet. As an essay in the history of interpretation it deserves very high praise. It occupies about half the volume. Next in length is the study of the Immanuel Prophecy. Two essays are devoted to the Servant, and one defends the rendering 'sprinkle' in Isa. lii. 15. All are well documented studies of high value to scholars of every shool, and the book is marred by only one major defect, in that it is provided with no index.   H.H.R.

LAW, RELIGION AND THEOLOGY

VON ALLMEN, J. –J. (ed. by) : *Vocabulaire Biblique.* 1954. Pp. 314. (Delachaux et Niestlé, Neuchatel and Paris. Price : Fr. 17, or bound Fr. 21.)

> This very useful volume may be regarded as a French counterpart on a somewhat larger scale of *A Theological Word Book of the Bible*, edited by Alan Richardson and published in this country in 1950. Intentionally popular in character and designed primarily for Protestant laymen, though it is hoped that it will prove of interest also to those outside the Church and even to Roman Catholics, this Biblical Vocabulary has behind it serious scholarship. There are distinguished names, French and Swiss, among the contributors, among which British Old Testament scholars will recognize among others

those of Jacob and Pidoux to whom the preparation of important articles has been entrusted. It is interesting to compare Jacob's article on ' God ' with Rankin's article on the same theme in the English volume which has greater theological content. Surprisingly there is only one article by Cullmann. There will be differences of opinion as to the selection of terms for discussion. To some extent the French and English volumes supplement each other. Within the limits set there seems to be much that is interesting and useful in this venture by our French colleagues.   N.W.P.

BENTZEN, A. : *King and Messiah.* (Lutterworth Studies in Church and Bible, No. 2.) 1955. Pp. 112. (Lutterworth Press, London. Price : 10s.6d.)

Shortly before his death, Bentzen prepared an English rendering of his *Messias—Moses redivivus—Menschensohn* (see *Book List*, 1949, p. 37), which has now been published under the above title. References to literature have been brought up to date ; and, although the general plan of the book is not substantially modified, and the author's main contentions remain the same, the argument has been expanded, and, in places, clarified. The improvement in the contents of this important study is matched by the excellence of the format, on which the publishers are to be congratulated. G.W.A.

BERNINI, G. : *Le Preghiere Penitenziali del Salterio : Contributo alla Teologia dell' A.T.* (Analecta Gregoriana, Vol. lxii, sect. A., No. 9.) 1953. Pp. xxiii+322. (Gregorian University, Rome. Price : 28s. 0d.)

In his introduction the author rightly calls attention to the promising reflorescence (*rifioritura*) among Catholics of doctrinal studies designed to make a real contribution to Biblical theology. If, as he writes, complete works covering the whole ground do not abound *nel campo cattolico* (he wrote before the appearance of Van Imschoot's first volume), there are a number of monographs of recent date that discuss particular aspects of Biblical theology or religion. The present excellent study is devoted to the penitential prayers and hymns of the Psalter, in which the first part gives an exegesis of all the psalms in this grouping ; the second deals with the theological presuppositions of these psalms, notably with sin, whether considered in itself or in relation to the divine attributes ; and the third with the effects of penitential prayer, in particular with the forgiveness of sins. A final part considers very briefly the theological and ascetical value of pentitential prayer.

The bibliography, though it gives an appearance of completeness, is notable for some omissions, e.g., Podechard's two volumes on *Le Psautier* (cf. *Book List*, 1951, pp. 40f.) are not listed, though they appeared in 1949. There are, as so often in such works, errors in the spelling of proper names, e.g., Boylon, Dohrme, Gazelles, Van Imschood, etc.   J.M.T.B.

BRUCE, F. F. : *The Sure Mercies of David*. (The Annual Lecture of the Evangelical Library.) 1954. Pp. 24. Price : 1s. 6d.)

The lecture is described as a Study in the Fulfilment of Messianic Prophecy. It sees in the words of Isa. lv. 3 (quoted in Acts xiii. 34) the link between the Davidic line and the Servant of the Lord. Isa. xl-lv are recognised as exilic, and the Servant, originally Israel, becomes an individual who in his own person realized the ideal Israel. Davidic Messiah and Servant become one in Jesus of Nazareth.   A.S.H.

BUESS, E. : *Die Geschichte des mythischen Erkennens. Wider sein Missverständnis in der " Entmythologisierung."* (Forschungen zur Geschichte und Lehren des Protestantismus, herausgegeben von E. Wolf, X, No. 4.) 1953. Pp. 228. (Chr. Kaiser Verlag, München. Price : DM. 10, or bound, DM. 12.50.)

The first three chapters, ' Mythisches Erkennen als Erkenntnis des Unerkennbaren und Unaussprechlichen,' belong—aside from the question of demythologization—to the best that has been written during the last decades on myth. The fourth chapter aims at tracing the uniqueness of the Biblical ' Gotteserkenntnis ' in its combination of omnipotence, justice and love, but it is written from a bird's eye view and too summarily to enable one really to see this hidden core of the Bible in all its parts, even in the most difficult mythical sections, such as Gen. vi. 1-4. Thus the problem still remains for the time being.   W.B.

CAMPBELL, R. : *Israel and the New Covenant*. 1954. Pp. 326. (Presbyterian and Reformed Publishing Company, Philadelphia, Pa. Price : $3.75.)

The author of this work is a successful Canadian businessman. He has devoted many years to an independent study of the covenants of the Old and New Testaments, and is concerned to show their bearing upon the life of the Church to-day. He has read widely and discerningly in the relevant literature and has even ranged into the wide area of homiletical literature, on the one hand, and contemporary interpretations of history, on the other. His point of view is conservative throughout, and his treatment of the biblical sources is uncritical. While he makes much of prediction, he appreciates the dynamic vitality of the prophetic writers and the creative fashion in which their words are appropriated by others. The book is exceptionally well ordered and articulated. The thirty-five chapters are divided into six main divisions : our Hebrew-Christian heritage ; problems of interpretation ; " all things new " ; promise and prophecy ; the new and better covenant ; and war, victory, and peace. While the interpretation is in general quite literalistic, there are sections where the writer has a vivid sense of the symbolism of biblical categories. Everywhere he is interested in showing how Old Testament motifs emerge into the New and how they are there transformed.   J.Mu.

COPPENS, J. : *Le messianisme israélite d'après Paul de Broglie.*
(Analecta Lovaniensia Biblica et Orientalia, 2nd Series, No. 42.)
1953. Pp. 26. (Presses Universitaires de Louvain, and Desclée
de Brouwer, Bruges and Paris. Price : Belgian Fr. 30.)

In this essay, Canon Coppens, who has published earlier studies
of the views of Pascal and Loisy on the same subject, surveys
the ideas of Broglie as set forth in an essay he published in
1895 and in lectures delivered earlier, but published
posthumously. Broglie argued for an inner harmony between
the two Testaments and defended the view that the New
Testament responds to the hope and promise of the Old.
Canon Coppens adds a section on recent ideas on the same
subject, including a long footnote supplementing his own
study of Isa. vii. 14.   H.H.R.

DHEILLY, J. : *Le Peuple de l'Ancienne Alliance.* 1954. Pp. 486.
(Éditions de l'école, 11 rue de Sèvres, Paris. Price : Fr. 480.)

The volume is in stiff paper covers with numerous illustrations,
admirably arranged and produced, except for the MS. facsimile
on p. 354, which has been printed upside down. It is an
official Roman Catholic production for teaching the Old
Testament in second-class French schools. From the Roman
Catholic point of view, the book is excellently well done.
The Abbé Dheilly never loses sight of his holy purpose, and
regularly the explanations are interlocked with Roman
doctrine and references to the Roman liturgy. Little notice
is taken of modern literary study, except in such cases as
Isa. xl-lxvi, where a modern dating is useful and necessary
for the understanding of the message. The book is plainly
arranged, paragraph by paragraph, with numerous and
adequate sub-titles. In technique and lay-out it is a model
for those who would write school-books.   N.H.S.

DE FRAINE, J. : *L'Aspect religieux de la royauté israélite.* (Analecta
Biblica 3.) 1954. Pp. xl+425. (Pontificio Istituto Biblico, Rome.
Price : Lire 5,000.)

This work is yet another product of the current interest in
the theory of kingship as found in the pages of the Old Testament. For the most part it is devoted to the history and
interpretation of kingship in Mesopotamia and in ancient
Israel, special attention being paid to the question of divine
kingship, the cultic role of the king, and his significance as
the guardian or saviour of his people. In surveying the
material the author engages in a running polemic against what
he sometimes describes as the Anglo-Scandinavian School, and
it is just here that the basic weakness of the book is to be
found ; for the author's method involves him in misleading
generalizations with regard to this somewhat fictitious body,
and, what is more, the writers to whom he refers may be cited
without due regard to the context of their remarks and,
indeed, even quoted inaccurately. On the other hand, the
work has considerable value as a source-book for the comparative material from Mesopotamia and as a warning against

too hasty conclusions with regard to some of the Old Testament data ; and to this extent, at least, it may be recommended as a useful contribution to the discussion.   A.R.J.

FRANKEN, H. J. : *The Mystical Communion with Jhwh in the Book of Psalms.* 1954. Pp. viii+98. (Brill, Leiden. Price : Fl. 8.)

The argument of this monograph is based on the assumption that ' we think it justified to speak of the restriction of the personality in the case of magical influences, whereas we speak of the extension of the personality in the case of mystical bents ' (p. 1). Chapter I is devoted to the question of magic and mysticism in the Old Testament. Chapter II deals with what the author regards as the Hebrew terminology relevant to his main thesis. Chapter III discusses the general background of Israelite religion with special emphasis upon the *berit* as having ' provided the distinctive character of mystical trends in the Old Testament ' (p. 63). In Chapter IV the reader is offered an exposition of Psalms xvi, xviii, xxv, xxvii, xxxi, xxxvi and lxiii from this standpoint. While the author's discussion of the terminology may be read with profit, the main lines of his argument are marred by a tendency to make easy assumptions and questionable generalisations ; so that the work as a whole, while suggestive and not without value, is far too sketchy to be satisfactory.   A.R.J.

GOTTWALD, N. K. : *Studies in the Book of Lamentations.* (Studies in Biblical Theology, No. 14.) 1954. Pp. 122. (S.C.M. Press, London. Price : 8s. 0d.)

This book represents a most valuable addition to the literature on Old Testament Theology. It is prefaced by a new translation of Lamentations. Previous studies of the book have too often stopped short after discussion of critical questions instead of going on to theological appraisal. The author argues that, while not the work of Jeremiah, Lamentations comes from the Exilic period, the first four chapters at least being by a single poet. Their acrostic form is explained, not only as an *aide memoire*, but as offering ' a literary form corresponding to the completeness of grief, responsibility and hope.' The mixture of literary types, communal and individual lament and funeral song, is justified as suitable to the purpose of the poet. Lamentations reflects the intensification of the problem of suffering due to the events of history and has contributed to the picture of the Servant in 2 Isaiah. The use in the poems of the category of tragic reversal and the further reversal from despair to hope is illustrated and it is shown that Lamentations exemplifies the ' acceptance of the prophetic interpretation of national tragedy ' which ' deserves to be regarded as the greatest single spiritual achievement of the exile.' We find in the book both the theology of doom and the theology of hope. Further we find a ' fusion of prophetic faith and cultic recitation which represents a union of the priestly and prophetic aspects of Judaism.'   N.W.P.

HARTLICH, C. and SACHS, W. : *Der Ursprung des Mythosbegriffes in der modernen Bibelwissenschaft.* 1952. Pp. 192. (J. C. B. Mohr, Tübingen. Price : DM. 9.80.)

The authors of this work have made a valuable contribution to current discussion of the part to be assigned to the concept of ' myth ' in Biblical exegesis by tracing the use of this term from its adoption, under the influence of C. G. Heyne, by J. G. Eichhorn and J. Ph. Gabler to its employment by W. M. L. de Wette and, finally, D. F. Strauss. The survey of the emergent differences of opinion as regards the content of the term, the problem of the historical factor and the question of ultimate truth is well done, and the work as a whole, which is furnished with a most helpful index, may be warmly recommended as a real stimulus to thought.
A.R.J.

HEMPEL, J. : *Glaube, Mythos und Geschichte im Alten Testament.* 1954. Pp. 62. (Verlag Alfred Töpelmann, Berlin. Price : DM. 6.80.)

The question of the possible relation of myth to history and its value as a means of conveying religious truth, which has come so much to the fore once again in recent years, is here discussed with special reference to the Old Testament. The author finds a process of ' Entmythologisierung ' already at work behind the Old Testament material, which is studied in terms of (a) cosmogonic myth, with due recognition of its employment for eschatological purposes ; (b) soteriological myth, with special attention to the question of sacral kingship, the conception of the Suffering Servant and the new material offered by the Dead Sea scrolls ; and (c) the type of myth used to describe theophanies and similar accounts of divine revelation. The whole forms a clearly written, interesting and constructive piece of work.
A.R.J.

HESSE, F. : *Das Verstockungsproblem im Alten Testament.* (Beihefte zur Zeitschrift für die Alttestamentliche Wissenschaft, No. 74.) 1955. Pp. viii+108. (Verlag Töpelmann, Berlin. Price : DM. 18.00.)

This is a careful and methodical study of the place occupied in Old Testament thought and in the religion of Israel by that trait of character described as hard of heart, stiff-necked or stubborn. The author notes that it is often caused directly by God in his anger and in the interests of ultimate salvation. He notes different points of view about it in the prophets. Isaiah, for instance, looks upon hardness of heart as a sign of God's rejection of those who fail to turn to him, but Jeremiah regards it as the cause of God's rejection.
L.H.B.

VAN IMSCHOOT, P. : *Théologie de l'Ancien Testament.* Tome I. *Dieu.* (Bibliothèque de Théologie. Série III. Théologie Biblique, Vol. 2.) 1954. Pp. 274. (Desclée & Cie, Tournai. Price : Belgian Fr. 140.)

This is the first volume of a very learned and useful Roman Catholic Theology of the Old Testament. So far as the plan of the work is disclosed it seems to offer a combination of the divisions adopted by Köhler and Eichrodt respectively. Köhler supplied the main dogmatic division into theology, anthropology and soteriology, while part of Eichrodt's scheme is introduced in Vol. I under the headings ' God and the World,' ' God and His people.'

Chapter I contains a scholarly enumeration of the divine names, of anthropomorphisms, and of the divine attributes and emotions. Chapter II discusses creation, providence, miracle, angels and demons. Chapter III treats of the various media of revelation, including a careful study of Hebrew prophecy which shows a balanced judgment on the question of the prophetic ecstasy, and sections on the Word, the Name, and Glory, the Face of Yahweh and on hypostases. The opening section on the concept of revelation in the Old Testament is confined to enumeration of the Hebrew terms used. Chapter IV deals with the Covenant and the Election of Israel.

A brief introductory section of the book discusses the object and method of Old Testament Theology, but, though a number of important articles on the subject are promisingly listed at the beginning, there is disappointingly little evidence that the author has reflected on the problems raised in them. There is no real advance here. The value of the book, which is considerable, will be found in the large amount of carefully digested material it offers, in its careful documentation and in its bibliographies. The latter, however, show strange omissions. In the bibliography on prophecy there is no mention of the names of Haldar, Johnson and Welch, while T. H. Robinson's most important treatment of Hebrew Prophecy has escaped notice. The author, however, has been working under difficulties and there is much in this book to be grateful for.   N.W.P.

VAN LEEUWEN, C. : *Le Développement du sens social en Israël*. 1954. Pp. 248. (Van Gorcum, Assen.)

Here is careful and thorough Amsterdam dissertation, accompanied by a bibliography of more than 150 items, dealing with the oft discussed question of the poor in Israel. After a study of all the terms used for the poor, we have a study of the teaching of every part of the Old Testament, designed to protect them against exploitation, and to commend them to charity. A chapter is devoted to the relation between the poor and the pious, and another to the social background of the Wisdom literature, while a final chapter deals with the poor in the messianic age. The work is marked by comprehensiveness and balance, rather than by novelty of conclusion. While poverty may bring refinement of spirit, it is never to be regarded with complacency, but is always an evil to be fought, and especially when it is brought about by the hand of circumstance or exploitation.   H.H.R.

MENDENHALL, G. E. : *Law and Covenant in Israel and the Ancient Near East*. 1955. Pp. 50. (Biblical Colloquium, Pittsburgh, Pennsylvania. Price : $1.00.)

Here two articles from *The Biblical Archaeologist* are reprinted, the first dealing with Ancient Oriental and Biblical Law, and the second with Covenant Forms in Israelite Traditions. Both parts are well documented surveys, gathering together no small amount of material on the general subject with which they deal. In the second part the Israelite covenant forms are brought into close association with Hittite forms, and here is the most challenging part of Professor Mendenhall's thesis. He argues that in early Israelite law the sanctions were religious rather than resting on the power of the state, and that the religious covenants of Israel were modelled on the secular covenants of Hittite Kings. With the fall of Shiloh and the establishment of the monarchy came the breakdown of the covenant form. The whole is a stimulating study, though the reviewer is not convinced that there is any direct reliance on Hittite influence, or that for the pattern of covenant in response to service there is any necessity to look beyond the experience of deliverance from Egypt.

H.H.R.

*NEIL, W. : *The Rediscovery of the Bible*. 1954. Pp. 256. (Hodder & Stoughton, London. Price : 12s. 6d.)

The warm commendation given to this book by the Dean of St. Paul's is richly deserved. It contains a good survey of the assured results of the best biblical scholarship in non-technical language together with a presentation of the biblical insights, thus clearly seen, so that the relevance of the Bible to twentieth century man is cogently demonstrated. Thus it makes clear to the reader with an open mind, be he sceptic or believer, the concern of the Bible to present God in His relations with ourselves. The failure of the ultra-conservative and of the liberal in Biblical studies is recognised ; the modern critical position is fairly presented, with a sober assessment of the results of archaeology. The second half of the book (The Emergent Picture), presents the main biblical themes both historically and theologically ; it is never forgotten that the Bible is a book which challenges its readers to decision.

The book, is, in its correct sense, popular. At the end of each chapter are suggestions for further reading. It will be helpful to teachers of Vth and VIth forms, to students in Training Colleges, to students at the beginning of their theological course, and should be made known to students of all disciplines. It will be useful to all who engage in the teaching work of the Church.

A.S.H.

NORTH, R. : *Sociology of the Biblical Jubilee*. (Analecta Biblica 4.) 1954. Pp. xlvi+246. (Pontifical Biblical Institute, Rome. Price : Lire 3,900 or $6.50.)

An exegetical study of Leviticus xxv, in which the author deals at length with the sociological background of the jubilee law in Israel and the Near East with special reference to slavery, ownership of property and bankruptcy. The author is thus more concerned with the literal meaning of this chapter than with the question of its Messianic interpretation, but in the concluding pages of the work he holds that it may be interpreted thus in a typical sense. The study as a whole shows evidence of wide reading, and there is a useful bibliography. Indeed much of the value of this work is to be found in its introduction to and discussion of the views of other writers on this and related subjects. A.R.J.

ÖSTERLOH, E., and ENGELLAND, H. (ed. by) : *Biblisch-Theologisches Handwörterbuch zur Lutherbibel und neueren Übersetzungen.* 1954. Pp. 748. (Vandenhoeck & Ruprecht, Göttingen. Price : 79s. 0d.)

This is a Bible dictionary on a much more massive scale than the French *Vocabulaire Biblique* reviewed elsewhere in this number of the *Book List*. It is intended for lay people in the Church and will be found of interest as illustrating theological trends in Lutheran Bible exposition to-day. Österloh, one of the editors, seems to have undertaken a large number of the more important Old Testament articles. The interest of the volume for scholars is lessened by the fact that among the forty-seven contributors appear none of the German Old Testament scholars whose names are familiar in this country and this is the more regrettable in view of the notable theological trend in much of the best Old Testament scholarship in Germany to-day. Much, however, that is offered here is sound and will be found useful and stimulating by those for whom the book is intended. N.W.P.

Première Rencontre Biblique. 1954. Pp. 158. (Centre de Liaison et de Documentation Bibliques, Lille. Price : Fr. 200.)

This is a report of papers read at Paris in September, 1953, and of the discussion that followed, at a Conference held under the general title *L'Église et le Message de la Bible.* The papers that will most interest members of the Society are by J. Gelineau on the problem of preparing a satisfactory translation of the Psalms for liturgical use and by L. Cerfaux on the theme that was chosen for the main theme of the Conference. A. Gelin reviewed the present state of the Biblical revival that followed the Papal Encyclical of 1943, and his paper was supplemented by reports of Catholic activity in this field in many countries—including the Far East—but curiously not in Britain or the United States. Non-Catholic work is not envisaged or referred to. H.H.R.

RINGGREN, H. : *Messias konungen.* 1954. Pp. 88. (J. A. Lindblads Förlag, Uppsala. Price : Swedish kr. 3.50.)

This little book gives an interesting, non-technical presentation, with ample illustrations from the text of Scripture, of recent work on the O.T. roots of the Messianic hope and of its bearing on Christian exposition of the O.T. In the royal psalms, the conception of kingship provides the content of the later Messianic hope. In the prophecies of the coming king, that conception is projected into the future. In the Servant Songs (the first three are taken as xlii. 1-7 ; xlix. 1-9 ; l. 4-11), the conception reappears, blended in the Fourth Song (where the author finds echoes of the ritual of the Day of Atonement) with ideas from the Tammuz liturgies. What Engnell has called the 'Ebed Yahweh psalms are cautiously expounded as possible further evidence of the king's part in the cult as the Suffering Servant. The author suggests, in the light of this, that in the Servant Songs the poet finds in this royal ideology the meaning of Israel's suffering and destiny, yet looks forward to a coming, individual Servant-Messiah. The book is written with admirable clarity and moderation.

G.W.A.

Roth, L. : *God and Man in the Old Testament.* 1955. Pp. 168. (Allen & Unwin, London, and Macmillan Co., New York. Price : 10s. 0d.)

This is an anthology of Old Testament passages, varying in length from half verses to whole chapters. The material is presented in fourteen sections, each briefly introduced by a few sentences of explanation, and the whole by a foreword. The book forms one of the "Ethical and Religious Classics of East and West." The text used is that of the Revised Version with a few exceptions. The selection and manner of presentation is wholly admirable, representing not merely individual piety, but the strong faith in which the Jewish Community and the Christian church have been nourished. It is reasonable to suppose that many who are unfamiliar with the Old Testament will find this an attractive introduction, and the modern Marcionite will have to think again about his neglect and disparagement of these Scriptures. A.S.H.

Ryser, F. : *Le Veau d'Or : Le problème de l'Image de Dieu d'après Exode* 32. (Les Cahiers du Renouveau, No. X.) 1954. Pp. 40. (Geneva. Price : Sw. Fr. 2.10.)

This booklet offers a christological exposition of Exod. 32 in which every detail is made to prefigure some Christian fact or event : the tables of stone represent the body of Christ engraved with the word of God ; their breaking his crucifixion ; the rally of Levites to God through Moses the coming of the true church to God through Christ. There seems no end to these anticipations ; the wonder is that a single chapter can hold so many. L.H.B.

Schroeder, F. J. : *Père Lagrange and Biblical Inspiration.* (Studies in Sacred Theology, 2nd Series, No. 80.) 1954. Pp. xii+48. (Catholic University of America Press, Washington. Price : $0.75.)

This is a short abstract of a doctoral dissertation, in which the work of Lagrange is first set briefly in the background of the trends and controversies of his time, and then his view of Inspiration unfolded. By this view, in which a literal and a spiritual sense are distinguished, but which rejects the theory of a *sensus plenior*, Lagrange sought to open the way for scientific Biblical study within the Church to which he belonged. Though this movement was checked for a time, it prepared the way for the larger freedom that Church now allows. In this summary there is little that is strikingly new, but perhaps the full dissertation better brings out the greatness of Lagrange. The slightness of the treatment here contrasts with the fullness of Seynaeve's treatment of Newman's doctrine of inspiration (see *Book List*, 1954, pp. 71 f.), though we are told that in the judgement of some Lagrange was the greatest Catholic Biblical scholar since Jerome.   H.H.R.

VRIEZEN, TH. C. : *Hoofdlijnen der Theologie van Het Oude Testament.* 2nd ed. 1954. Pp. 400. (Veenman & Zonen, Wageningen. Price : Fl. 19.25, or bound 21.60.)

This new edition of Vriezen's work represents a very substantial revision and expansion of it. The length is increased by 100 pages, and a glance at the Index will show how considerable has been the change and how much recent literature has been taken into account. A Scripture Index has been added to the work, and bibliographical lists have been appended to many of the chapters. The welcome accorded to the first edition in the *Book List* (1950, p. 70) may be repeated with more emphasis as this enlarged and improved edition makes its appearance. The general lay out of the book is unchanged, but everywhere there is modification and development, and no owner of the first edition should think the second is a superfluity.   H.H.R.

WESTERMANN, C. : *Das Loben Gottes in den Psalmen.*

In the 1954, *Book List*, p. 55, C. Westermann : *Das Loben Gottes in den Psalmen*, 1953, was reviewed. The Publishers for the Eastern Zone are Evangelische Verlagsanstalt, Berlin, as there stated, but for the Western Zone the Publishers are Vandenhoeck and Ruprecht, Göttingen, and the price DM. 7.80.

WRIGHT, G. E. : *The Biblical Doctrine of Man in Society.* (Ecumenical Biblical Studies No. 2, published for the Study Department World Council of Churches.) 1954. Pp. 176. (S.C.M. Press. Price : 7s. 0d.)

Professor Wright has written this little book on the basis of the discussions of one of the Ecumenical Study Groups which prepared the way for the Evanston Conference. The book deals with the relation between the individual and community in Biblical thought and, modest in size as it is, it offers a contribution to the study of Biblical Theology which deserves to be read and re-read and should be missed by no one who is concerned about the subject. Those who know the writer's earlier *God Who Acts* will recognize here an important supplementation of his thought in his linking of the *kerygma* with the ongoing life of the community. Profound things are said about individualism, responsibility, man's relation to nature and to society and many other related topics. There will be noticed an interesting convergence of various lines of investigation associated with such names as Noth and von Rad, Frankfort, Pedersen, Eichrodt, Dodd, Albright and Mendenhall, names which guarantee the up-to-date-ness of the discussion. This book will be a much needed corrective to the excessively typological interpretation of the Bible which is fashionable in some quarters.   N.W.P.

ZIMMERLI, W..: *Erkenntnis Gottes nach dem Buche Ezechiel. Eine theologische Studie.* (Abhandlungen zur Theologie des Alten und Neuen Testaments, No. 27.) 1954. Pp. 76. (Zwingli-Verlag, Zürich. Price : DM. 8.50.)

This excellent short study is a careful investigation of the antecedents and theological implications of the formula ' and you shall know that I am Yahweh,' which occurs so often in Ezekiel. The instances, elsewhere in the Old Testament, of varying forms of the phrase are collected and classified. The author shows its association with the assessing of evidence in human relationships, and, in the sphere of religion, with the request for a sign. He emphasizes the character of *Erkenntnis*, not as theoretical knowledge imparted by instruction, but as resulting from the action of God. Taking up the results of his essay in the Alt-Festschrift on the phrase ' I am Yahweh ' (with its original setting in the theophanies and in the declaration of the terms of the Covenant), he shows how, when this is the content of the *Erkenntnis*, the evidential effect of a momentary or incidental sign is replaced by *etwas bleibend Gültiges*. This short treatise is closely packed, and rich in suggestion. Its importance is not limited to the book of Ezekiel or to the formula with which it deals.   G.W.A.

ZOLLI, E. : *L'Ebraismo.* (Universale Studium 22.) 1953. Pp. 152. (Editrice Studium, Rome. Price : Lire 200.)

In this small book the author attempts a popular survey of the spiritual life of Israel from the earliest times up to the present day. The first eight chapters deal with the origins of the Hebrews, the age of the patriarchs, the Covenant and the Law, prophetism and prophets, prayer, the hope of Israel, historiography and the history of Israel, and the God of Israel. In the eight chapters that follow are traced the main outlines of the history and the intellectual and spiritual life of the Jews from A.D. 70 to the founding of the modern state of Israel (the final chapter deals with contemporary Jewish literature). Each chapter has its own brief bibliography (a good many misprints occur in them). The author writes interestingly and with simplicity of language, and, within the limits set, he has carried out his task with considerable success.
                                                              D.W.T.

Bottéro, J. and Finet, A. : *Archives royales de Mari XV. Répertoire analytique.* 1954. Pp. viii+348+map. (Imprimerie Nationale, Paris. Price : Fr. 2,500.)

> This work contains full sections on the palaeography and syllabary, list of scribal errors, an index of proper names and a glossary, as well as an analytical table of the subject-matter, of the first five volumes of the texts from Mari, with many corrections of the original transliterations and translations. So far as a reviewer can see without checking innumerable details, the work is as accurate as it is exhaustive and will be absolutely indispensable for the study of these texts. It will also be of great interest to students of the Hebrew language, since the dialect of Mari approaches that of the western Semites in many respects. G.R.D.

van Dijk, J. J. A. : *La sagesse suméro-accadienne. Recherches sur les genres littéraires des textes sapientiaux.* 1953. Pp. vii+146. (Brill, Leiden. Price : Fl. 15.00.)

> This dissertation for the doctorate gives a clear survey of the Sumerian wisdom-literature in brief compass. Sections of the introduction are devoted to an account of the various *genres* of this literature and the conception of wisdom enshrined in it. The main body of the text then follows with seven chapters containing typical examples of each class, with transliterated text and translation of the most important specimens of each type ; these are very well done, being accurate in themselves and furnished with brief but adequate notes. Altogether, the book forms an admirable introduction to this difficult branch of Sumerian literature, while at the same time offering evidence of the great progress made in Sumerian studies in recent years. G.R.D.

Fairman, H. W. : *Worship and Festivals in an Egyptian Temple.* 1954. Pp. 40. (Manchester University Press. Price : 3s. 6d.)

> This is the expanded form of a lecture given by Professor Fairman in the John Rylands Library on 13th January, 1954. Its subject is one that Professor Fairman has made especially his own, Egyptian religion in the Ptolemaic period. We are here given a full and fascinating account of the history of the great Ptolemaic Temple of Horus at Edfu, and of its daily worship together with an account of some of the great annual festivals which were celebrated in the temple. Particularly interesting is Professor Fairman's account and interpretation of the Festival of the Sacred Marriage. Of this he remarks, " It is the perfect Egyptian example of the anthropologist's ideal pattern of sacred marriage, linked with harvest rites and the cult of the ancestors." This is the more significant in view of the late Professor Frankfort's denial, in his Frazer lecture, that the sacred marriage found a place in Egyptian ritual. Considering the well-known conservatism of Egyptian religion, it is unlikely that this ritual was merely a late introduction peculiar to the Ptolemaic period. S.H.H.

HROZNÝ, B. : *Ancient History of Western Asia, India and Crete.* Translated by J. Procházka. 1953. Pp. xvi+260. (Philosophical Library Inc., New York, and Artia, Prague. Price : $12.00 or 96s. 0d.)

In the Epilogue to his book the distinguished Hittite scholar says that in it he has endeavoured to summarize the results of his life's work in the history and languages of the ancient Orient. It is a work of popularization in the best sense, lavishly illustrated, and admirably produced. The translation is clear, and the book should provide an excellent popular guide to the archaeology of the ancient East, including the civilizations of the Indus. The bibliography includes no works published later than 1938 ; hence no mention is made of the decipherment of the Cretan script linear B by Vestris and Chadwick, as announced last year in the Bulletin of Hellenic Studies. Professor Hrozný claims to have deciphered both the Proto-Indian and the Cretan scripts himself during the second World War, but this claim remains unsubstantiated as yet.   S.H.H.

KUPPER, J. R. : *Archives Royales de Mari, VI. Correspondance de Bahdi-lim.* 1954. Pp. ii+124. (Imprimerie Nationale, Paris. Price : Fr. 1,750.)

The present volume, the sixth instalment of this important publication, contains another 80 letters (those published in the recently issued *Textes Cunéiformes du Louvre* XXVII) transliterated and translated, with brief philological notes at the end of the book. The standard of excellence falls no whit behind that of the previous five volumes.   G.R.D.

MOSCATI, S. : *Oriente in nuova luce.* 1954. Pp. 180. (G. C. Sansoni, Florence. Price : Lire 600.)

This volume contains eight essays which aim at showing how recent discoveries have revolutionized the knowledge of the Near East. The first gives an account of some of these discoveries. The next two deal with Ugarit and its myths and legends. The fourth and fifth treat of Israel as a nation and of her religion, and of the significance of ancient inscriptions for the study of Israelite civilization. The last three are devoted to the Arabian field ... to Arabia Felix, the crisis of the Arab empire, and the Islamic sources of the Divine Comedy. The ground covered in the first five essays is mostly familiar to the Old Testament student, but the author shows, as in his previous works (see *Book List*, 1950, p. 76, and 1954, p. 80) an uncommon capacity for lighting upon the essential and for telling the story in his own way. He can pose, too, interesting questions. For example, when is an inscription properly called " Hebrew "? And why were ostraca used rather than papyrus at Samaria and Lachish ? The author is acquainted with the most recent literature, and his book may be warmly commended, to scholars as well as laymen, as an informative and reliable survey.   D.W.T.

SMICK, E. B : *A Cylinder of Nebuchadrezzar II*, . . with an introduction by C. H. Gordon. 1953. Pp. iv+20. (Silver Book Shop, 31-46 30th St., Astoria 6, N.Y. Price : $0.75.)

This typescript edition of a cylinder of Nebuchadrezzar II adds little to our knowledge of the history of that king ; for, although it is not an exact duplicate of any one of the numerous texts published in Langdon's *Neubabylonische Königsinschriften* (Leipzig, 1912), the more or less stereotyped formulae which compose it can be illustrated somewhere from that collection. It fills, however, some gaps in one of Langdon's texts, which he has only imperfectly restored (pp. 78-80, no. 3). Its chief merit, perhaps, is that, unlike most texts of this period which have been edited for the use of students in a script so minute that the struggling beginner and the ageing professor find them equally difficult to read, this is copied in a clear bold script which is a delight to the eyes. It is accompanied by a useful syllabary and glossary, which unfortunately lacks references and in which one or two entries may require reconsideration. G.R.D.

VON SODEN, W. : *Herrscher im Alten Orient*. 1954. Pp. 152, with 40 illustrations and 1 map. (Springer Verlag, Berlin. Price : DM. 7.80.)

The merits of this small book are out of all proportion to its size. The author gives a succint sketch of all the principal rulers in the *Zweistromland* from the earliest time down to the fall of Babylon, from Urukagina of Lagash (*c.* 2370 B.C.) to Nabû-na'id (555-539 B.C.). The achievements and character, so far as they can be extracted from the somewhat bald and formal records of the Sumerians, Assyrians and Babylonians, are clearly outlined, interspersed with notes on religion, literature and art ; the whole account is meticulously accurate and trustworthy and is enlivened by many shrewd remarks. The subject, however, somewhat belies the title, since *Alter Orient* is interpreted in the sense in which Assyriologists are accustomed to use it. G.R.D.

STRICKER, B. H. : *De grote zeeslang*. (Mededelingen en Verhandelingen van het Voor-Aziatisch-Egyptisch genootschap " Ex oriente lux," No. 10.) 1953. Pp. 28+8 figures. (Brill, Leiden. Price : Fl. 3.50.)

A thorough treatment of the Egyptian speculative idol of the serpent biting its tail, the Ouroboros. Dr. Stricker's description of the images and his interpretation of symbols and texts, especially of a passage of Horapollo in the Hieroglyphica, lead to an identification of the serpent as the cosmic foe of the Sun-god. The author does not restrict himself to Egyptian material, however. He deals with data from the literature of the other peoples of the ancient Near East, including Biblical material (Job, Isaiah, Psalms), post-biblical texts (Midrashim, Gemara, Pseudepigraphical Books), a magical papyrus, recently acquired in Leiden, and writings of the Gnostics. The quotations, notes and figures enhance the value of this monograph. The Dutch text is followed by a summary in English. P.A.H.deB.

VERCOUTTER, J. : *Essai sur les relations entre Égyptiens et Préhellènes* (L'Orient Ancien Illustré, 6.) 1953. Pp. 178. (Maisonneuve, Paris. Price : Fr. 480.)

In the vexed question of the inter-relations between Egypt and Minoan Crete the writer is very sceptical about a primary Egyptian or African stimulus in early Cretan culture. This is not to be discerned until the end of the Early Bronze Age. At this time, however, Egyptians and Cretans were in contact and this relationship continued throughout the Middle Kingdom and New Empire. During this period the author maintains that the mediators of this cultural influence were Cretan or Mycenaean merchants who supplied Egypt with commodities she lacked via the Syrian ports. This is a sound thesis well supported by archaeological evidence.   J.G.

WILSON, J. A., SPEISER, E. A., GÜTERBOCK, H. G., MENDELSOHN, I., INGALLS, D. H. H., and BODDE, D. : *Authority and Law in the Ancient Orient.* (Supplement to the J.A.O.S. No. 17.) 1954. Pp. 56. (American Oriental Society, Baltimore 1, Md., U.S.A. Price : $1.00.)

The six papers here published deal with the problem of authority in law in the principal countries of the ancient East (Egypt, Mesopotamia, Hittite kingdom, Canaan and Israel, India, China), of which the first four will be of most interest to students of the Old Testament. The essays discuss the problem of the relation of the king, divine or not, to law on the one side and to his nobles or council on the other side ; interesting points are made, but the treatment is uneven and the matter in places thin and even uncertain.   G.R.D.

THE DEAD SEA SCROLLS

BARDTKE, H. : *Die Handschriftenfunde am Toten Meer. Mit einer kurzen Einführung in die Text—und Kanonsgeschichte des Alten Testaments.* 2nd ed. 1953. Pp. vi+176. (Evangelische Haupt-Bibelgesellschaft, Berlin. Price : DM. 8.50.)

This valuable introduction to the Qumrân Scrolls is virtually a reprint of the first edition (1952, cf. *Book List* for 1953, p. 70). Developments which could not have been included in the first edition are very briefly discussed in four pages at the end of the book, where the text of the first edition has been wholly changed with the exception of the last paragraph of all. One additional plate, a plan of the cemetery at Qumrân, is given. Professor Bardtke intends dealing with these finds, and with the still incompletely published scrolls, in a later volume.   B.J.R.

COPPENS, J. : *Où en est le Problème des Manuscrits de Qumrân ?* (Analecta Lovaniensia Biblica et Orientalia, Ser. II. Fasc. 44.) 1954. Pp. 14 (Desclée de Brouwer, Bruges-Paris. Price : Belgian Fr. 10.)

Professor Coppens, continuing his cautionary attitude already expressed in *Les Documents du Désert de Juda et les Origines du Christianisme* (cf. *Book List*, 1954, p. 81) re-emphasises the dangers of oversimplifying the issues raised by the scrolls. Since the discovery of Khirbet Qumrân and Murabba'at he would allow that the sect of the scrolls is in some ways connected with the Essenes, but only vaguely, and divergences are numerous. There is obvious syncretism in the former sect : the practice of prayer to the sun, the adoption of a special calendar, the cult of the letter *nun*, relations with Pytha-goreanism, these and other points require reconsideration, for they cannot easily be reconciled with the rigorous adherence to a strict legalism which is attested in the scrolls. Do we know enough about the history of contemporary movements such as that of John the Baptist? What about the Karaites? On the other hand, must the *terminus post quem* be the late Hellenistic period? These and other pertinent questions are raised. The author's discussion of *nun* is particularly en-lightening. B.J.R.

DETAYE, C. : *Le Cadre historique du Midrash d'Habacuc*. (Analecta Lovaniensia Biblica et Orientalia, 2nd series, No. 46.) 1954. Pp. 22. (Publications Universitaires de Louvain, and Desclée de Brouwer, Bruges and Paris. Price : Belgian Fr. 25.)

This short study follows Dupont-Sommer in many of its arguments, but sets the historical background somewhat earlier than he does. Whereas Dupont-Sommer placed it after the entry of the Romans into Palestine, Detaye places it before that entry. He identifies the Kittim with the Romans, arguing, *inter alia*, that the fact that they are said to have come from the isles of the sea shows that they could not be the Seleucids. Yet 1 Macc. vi. 29 states that the soldiers of Antiochus came from the isles of the sea. No attempt is made to identify the Teacher of Righteousness, the view of Dupont-Sommer and Goossens being here rejected. Alexander Jannaeus is held to be one of the wicked priests. H.H.R.

DUPONT-SOMMER, A. : *The Jewish Sect of Qumran and the Essenes : New Studies on the Dead Sea Scrolls*, translated by R. D. Barnett. 1954. Pp. xii+196. (Vallentine, Mitchell & Co. Ltd., London. Price : 10s. 6d.)

The original French version of this book appeared in 1953, and was reviewed for the *Book List* (cf. 1953, pp. 70 f.) by H. H. Rowley. There remains only to add some brief comments that the translation is worthy of this important book and renders it in a most readable form. Among more detailed points it may be noted that the map on the frontispiece gives the cave locations more fully than in the original ; the plates in the two versions are different ; the Postscript in the English book is about a year later than in the French and modified accordingly ; and finally that the English version has indexes. More serious is the fact that the lengthy quotations from the Testament of Levi, Philo and Josephus are given in French in Professor Dupont-Sommer's own translation, whereas the English rendering is taken from Charles, Colson and Whiston respectively. B.J.R.

KATZ, B. : *Gilluy Sodh ha-Megilloth ha-Genuzoth bi-Me'arath Yeriḥo*, (in Hebrew). 1950. Pp. 72. (N. Tvarski, Tel-Aviv.)

This small study which deals with the Judean Scrolls consists of an introduction; various pieces of the Scrolls as given in Sukenik's *Megilloth Genuzoth*, Second Survey; and some notes. The author, one has to admit, expresses rather strange views concerning the Scrolls—views based in the main on his book *Perushim Zedhuqim Qanna'im we-Noẓrim*. In his view the Teacher of Righteousness is Zadok the Pharisee, friend of Juda the Galilean. The Man of Falsehood is one of the disciples of Hillel. The House of Absalom is the household of Aba Sha'ul b. Botnith. Katz substantiates his assertions by using arguments which are not always convincing. M.W.

MARTIN, W. J. : *The Dead Sea Scroll of Isaiah*. The Sixth Campbell Morgan Memorial Lecture. 1954. Pp. 22. (The Bookroom, Westminster Chapel, London. Price : 1s. 6d.)

This semi-popular lecture by the Rankin lecturer in Hebrew in the University of Liverpool, deals with the text of the Isaiah scroll as evidence for the early (pre-Christian) scribal and textual transmission of the Old Testament. Textual variants indicate various types of corruption, including line omission : the nature of the text witnesses to the essential similarity of the text in pre-Massoretic times to the later transmission. There are details in the paper at which one might cavil, but the general treatment is instructive and interesting. B.J.R.

MICHEL, A. : *Le Maître de Justice d'après les documents de la Mer Morte, la littérature apocryphe et rabbinique*. 1954. Pp. xxiv+336. (Maison Aubanel Père, Avignon. Price : Fr. 900.)

This is an elaborate study, primarily of the *Habakkuk Commentary*, but with reference also to the other literature of the Qumran sect and to some of the already known works of the intertestamental period. The author examines three of the many views as to the background and date of the Commentary : the theory of the Maccabaean age, the theory of the time of Alexander Jannaeus, and the theory of the time of Pompey. He adopts the first of these and defends it against objections, while also raising objections against the others. He has a chapter on the Kittim, in which he opposes the identification with the Romans, one on the Man of the Lie, one on the House of Absalom, one on the Wicked Priest, and one on the Teacher of Righteousness. On some of these questions—notably on the House of Absalom and the Wicked Priest—he differs from the present writer, but in general his positions are similar to the reviewer's, though presented with far greater fullness and with a wealth of additional arguments. It should be added that his work was independent of the reviewer's, of which he had not heard until Professor Dhorme drew his attention to it after his work was in draft. H.H.R.

Molin, G. : *Die Söhne des Lichtes : Zeit und Stellung der Handschriften vom Toten Meer*. 1952. Pp. 248. (Verlag Herold, Vienna and Munich. Price : DM. 82, or bound DM. 98.)

A very useful handbook of the published material of the Dead Sea Scrolls, divided into three parts. Part I contains the translation and annotation of the texts. Part II discusses questions of date and the characteristics of the sect and their literature ; and Part III, consisting of appendixes, gives more detailed discussion of such topics as the date of the scrolls, their relation to the Damascus Document, Essenism, and New Testament and Apocalyptic Writing. Among the author's conclusions are : the Lev. fragments belong to the fourth and third centuries B.C. ; Warfare, Manual of Discipline and DSIa between 150 and 75 B.C. ; Habakkuk and Thanksgiving somewhat later, and the original of the Damascus Document in 64-63 B.C. ; the commentaries reflect the struggle against Alexander Jannaeus, who might, indeed, be none other than the Wicked Priest himself ; Warfare is not an actual account of a battle but ' an eschatological slaughter '; the whole theology of the scrolls is highly eschatological, and the sect is either the Essenes or very close relatives. The book closes with an index and a map. B.J.R.

Moscati, S. : *I Manoscritti Ebraici del Deserto di Giuda*. (Pubblicazioni dell'Istituto per L'Oriente, No. 51.) 1955. Pp. 50. (Istituto per L'Oriente, Viale D. Lubin, 2, Rome. Price : Lire 1,000.)

The book contains an outline of the scrolls under the following points : (a) The story of the discovery of the Qumrân scrolls, the examination of the caves, Khirbet Qumran, Wadi Murabba'at, Khirbet Mird is given in outline : (b) The texts, with details of publication, nature of the Biblical texts, the Manual of Discipline, Songs of Thanksgiving, Warfare, Habakkuk Commentary (sic), and ' historical texts ' (of Wadi Murabba'at) with translation of parts : (c) The Community of the New Alliance, with a study of the Damascus Document, the dating of the scrolls, the identity of the sect with the Essenes. In an appendix some recent views on the scrolls are briefly discussed. The annotation shows that the author is familiar with some of the more significant discussions, and his purpose is to outline the main positions already presented rather than to suggest any new hypothêsis. B.J.R.

Rabin, C. : *The Zadokite Documents : I. The Admonition. II. The Laws*. 1953. Pp. xvi+96. (Clarendon Press, Oxford. Price : 21s. 0d.)

This edition and translation of the Damascus Documents is of the greatest importance not only for the study of the Documents themselves but also for their contribution to the Qumran scrolls generally. The text of the edition is based on later and better photographs of the originals than were earlier editions, and some unexplainable errors in the earlier editions have now been eliminated. The translation is certainly competent, though it sometimes suffers because of the author's own set purpose, which is ' literalness rather than elegance.' The *apparatus criticus* might have been fuller, but the annotations, mainly philological, contain abundant references to contemporary writings and to the work of modern scholars. Three indexes give parallel passages in O.T., contemporary writings and the Qumran scrolls. It is seldom that the editor's readings could be seriously challenged, but it is debatable whether he is justified in giving a conflate text from the two MSS A and B in the sections where both are extant. True, sigla are used to indicate the texts of A and B respectively but it is still uncertain, despite Dr. Rabin's ' conviction,' that only one archetype is to be presupposed for the two MSS, even if the present form corresponds to it. On the other hand, it would appear to the present reviewer that Dr. Rabin's division of the text into two separate Documents, Admonition and Laws, is sensible and desirable. The book is admirably produced.   B.J.R.

SUKEṆIK, E. L. : *'Ôṣar ham-Meghillôth hag-Genûzôth she-bîdhê ha-Ûnîbhersîṭâh ha-'Ibhrîth.* 1954. Pp. 40+58 plates with corresponding pages of transcription, and numerous illustrations. (Mosad Bialik and the Hebrew University, Jerusalem. Price : 70s. 0d.)

This long awaited volume is a sheer delight, and will give new stimulus to the study of the Dead Sea Scrolls. The plates are, with some exceptions, finely prepared on loose sheets, while the transcriptions are printed in the volume following the Introduction. The whole is enclosed in a case, after the manner of Sachau's *Aramäische Papyrus.* Professor Sukenik died before this edition was completed, and his photograph stands as a frontispiece. The Introduction to the texts in Modern Hebrew is from his pen, but there are no notes on the texts themselves, so that the edition is comparable with those issued by the American Schools. The chapters of the Isaiah MS B are given in fifteen plates, the text of the Battle Scroll in nineteen plates, and the Hymns in twenty-four plates. Professor Sukenik's son has in the press an elaborate edition of the Battle Scroll, with full notes and discussion of all the problems which it raises. Meanwhile scholars everywhere will be glad to have access to the full known text of these Scrolls, and will be grateful for the excellence of most of the facsimiles and the fine way in which the texts are issued. A new outburst of activity on the Dead Sea Scrolls front of scholarship will soon be experienced.   H.H.R.

APOCRYPHA AND POST-BIBLICAL JUDAISM

BIETENHARD, H. : *Die himmlische Welt im Urchristentum und Spätjudentum.* 1951. Pp. vi+296. (J. C. B. Mohr, (Paul Siebeck) Tübingen. Price : DM. 24.)

This book offers a comprehensive treatment of Jewish and early Christian ideas, beliefs and speculations about the heavenly world. We are led by an experienced guide through the somewhat bewildering maze of late Jewish apocalyptic and mystical cosmology to a consideration of ' heavenly signs ' at the Parousia, the Throne of God and the Merkabbah mysticism, Enoch and Metatron and angelology, Paradise, the earthly and the heavenly Jerusalem, etc., etc. The book provides extensive background for the New Testament student and in a concluding *Zusammenfassung* Dr. Bietenhard discusses the place of such ideas in the New Testament as compared with Jewish sources. M.Bl.

BIRKELAND, H. : *The Language of Jesus.* (Avhandlinger utgitt av Det Norske Videnskaps-Akademi i Oslo, II. Hist.-Filos. Klasse, 1954, No. 1.) 1954. Pp. 40. (Jacob Dybwad, Oslo. Price : Kr. 4.50.)

The author here argues that Hebrew continued to be the language of the lower classes in Palestine down to the Christian era, while the upper classes spoke Aramaic, and the learned understood both. Hence, he maintains, Jesus normally spoke Hebrew. The argument that the Aramaic sayings preserved in the New Testament show that He spoke Aramaic is turned by the claim that these show that only exceptionally did He use Aramaic. H.H.R.

BRAND, J. : *Kele ha-ḥeres besifruth ha-talmudh.* (In Hebrew.) 1953. Pp. 634. (Mosad Karav Kook, Jerusalem.)

This special study on *Ceramics in Talmudic Literature* will become an indispensible reference book for rabbinic scholars. Formerly, identification of objects was based on the explanatory remarks of the Geonim, on medieval lexicographers, and on modern etymological studies. Dr. Brand stresses the necessity of examining the earliest sources and of allowing for the development of technical terminology. By detailed evaluation of the vast source material and by the use of methods, now commonly employed in Classical Archaeology, he is able to trace a good deal of Hebrew or Aramaic terms which were later replaced by Greek or Latin ones. Whereas Benzinger could still consider the faith of Israel as a cause of her artistic inability, the nomenclature of 126 ceramic vessels in Talmudic Literature alone testifies to a richness of types even greater than that of ancient Greece and Rome.
Alttestamentler too will profit from the discussion of more than 35 relevant Biblical terms. Indices and drawings enhance the value of the book. It is to be regretted, however, that the English Introduction is inadequate, and that so many misprints have been allowed to stay. There is hardly any reference to the New Testament and to the Apocrypha. S.S.

DALBERT, P. : *Die Theologie der hellenistisch-jüdischen Missionsliteratur unter Ausschluss vom Philo und Josephus.* (Theologische Forschung, No. 4.) 1954. Pp. 148. (Herbert Reich Evangelischer Verlag, Hamburg-Volksdorf. Price : DM. 9.80.)

From this survey of Hellenistic-Jewish Mission literature Philo and Josephus are omitted, since they have been adequately studied elsewhere, and the books of Maccabees, since they are judged to lie outside the scope of the present work. It is therefore limited to the study of the following authors, so far as their works have come down to us : Demetrius, Philo the Elder, Eupolemus, Artapanus, Ezekiel the Tragedian, Pseudo-Hecataeus, Aristeas, the authors of the Wisdom of Solomon and the Letter of Aristeas, Aristobulus, and the author of the Sibylline Oracles. The study is introduced by an account of the rise of the Diaspora and its relations with the world in which it lived, and of the roots of the idea of the Mission of Israel which is found in these works. A careful account of the various works, often surviving only in fragments, is given and the final section summarises their teaching under the headings of monotheism, revelation, and the election of Israel. As an essay on rarely studied aspects of Jewish thought in the Hellenistic age this work may be warmly welcomed.

H.H.R.

DANBY, H. : *The Code of Maimonides, Book Ten, The Book of Cleanness, Translated from the Hebrew* (Yale Judaica Series, vol. VIII). 1954. Pp. xlvi + 646. (Yale University Press, New Haven and Geoffrey Cumberlege, London. Price : $7.50 and 60s. 0d.)

The author of the standard translations of the Mishnah and the section of Mishneh Torah about offerings has left us an equally perfect translation of by far the most difficult part of Maimonides's Code. The Rabbinic rules concerning cleanness are not explicable by rational considerations. Consequently, interpretation of one rule in the light of others—relatively easy in the case of a rational system—requires here extraordinary knowledge and judgement. Danby possessed both. His results may be safely relied on. This volume supplies an indispensable basis for further inquiry not only to such as have no access to the original but also to accomplished Hebraists.

The problems calling for investigation, or renewed investigation, are numerous indeed ; several are indicated by Danby himself. Why did Maimonides expound so carefully a branch of the Law largely inapplicable by his time ? What place did he assign to it in the history, religion and morality of Judaism ? What relation did he assume between intent and physical act ? How far did he succeed in bringing order into the material, by formulating principles and adopting a plausible arrangement ? How far did he advance beyond his commentary on the Mishnah ? Did he apply his medical training to some questions ? What is the background of the definitions of various terms given by him ? It is to be hoped that the last work of the great Oxford scholar will stimulate discussions of such topics, some of them—as Danby no doubt felt— of more than academic interest.

Professor Obermann writes a valuable Foreword, and there is a frontispiece showing Herbert Danby. May a reviewer be permitted to call him an *'ohebh yiśra'el* ?   D.D.

DENTAN, R. C. : *The Apocrypha, Bridge of the Testaments.* 1954.
Pp. vi+122. (Seabury Press, Greenwich, Conn. Price : $2.25.)

The dust cover somewhat surprisingly states that this book is
by the Author of " The Holy Scriptures." The writer is known
to members of our Society by the more modest achievement
of the authorship of his *Preface to Old Testament Theology*.
In the present work he offers a simple account of the books
of the Apocrypha, designed to awaken the general reader to a
sense of the value of these books. There is a short account of
the place of the Apocrypha in the Bible and a chapter on the
historical background of the period between the Testaments,
and then the books of the Apocrypha are treated in the order
of their difficulty, rather than in the order they have in
published editions, or the order of their composition so far as
it may be determined. There is little discussion of questions
of date, integrity and original language, though a Chronological
table at the end indicates the writer's views on such questions.
The main emphasis is on an analysis of their contents and
religious value. All is interestingly written, and the book
should be widely useful.   H.H.R.

DOEVE, J. W. : *Jewish Hermeneutics in the Synoptic Gospels and Acts.*
1954. Pp. 232. (Van Gorcum & Co., Assen, Holland. Price : Fl.
11.50.)

The chief value of this dissertation lies mainly in its bibliographical sketch and attempted assessment of ' rabbinical '
work on the N.T. from John Lightfoot to Billerbeck together
with its analysis of methods of Scriptural exegesis practised
by the Tannaites. Contending views of the value of all such
studies for the elucidation of the N.T. are discussed : the
writer concludes that *rabbinica* do provide a serviceable
instrument for N.T. investigation, especially the rabbinical
use of Scripture. He seeks to show that the same kind of
exegesis is employed in more than one N.T. passage ; thus (he
argues) behind the closely related ideas of kingdom of God
and Son of Man lies a ' rabbinical ' exegesis of Dan. vii. 13,
14, etc. The importance of the O.T. element in the N.T. is
being increasingly recognized : Dr. Doeve's arguments,
however, for the use of rabbinical methods in the extremely
difficult passages he selects fall somewhat short of being
convincing.   M.Bl.

DUPONT, J. : *L'Utilisation apologétique de l'Ancien Testament dans les
Discours des Actes.* (Analecta Lovaniensia Biblica et Orientalia,
2nd Series, No. 40.) 1953. Pp. 42. (Presses Universitaires de
Louvain, and Desclée de Brouwer, Bruges and Paris. Price :
Belgian Fr. 40.)

The author examines the use of the Old Testament, book by
book, in the Acts of the Apostles, and reaches the conclusion
that the speech in Acts ii was produced in the study, and that
evidences of redaction are not wanting in other speeches ;
also that the Bible used by the author of Acts was the LXX,
and that the argument sometimes rests on a double meaning
of a Greek word.   H.H.R.

Rowley, H. H. : *The Relevance of Apocalyptic.*

The second edition of this work, published by the Lutterworth Press in 1947 (the first edition was reviewed in the *Book List*, 1946, p. 51), has been reprinted and issued in the United States by Harper, New York. Price : $2.75.

Schunck, K.-D. : *Die Quellen des I und II Makkabäerbuches.* 1954. Pp. 136. (Niemeyer, Halle/Saale. Price : DM. 8.30.)

This doctoral dissertation (Greifswald, 1953), offers a full and well-documented survey of the work done on this complex and difficult problem in recent years. A clue to the separation of sources in I Macc. is found in the dating of events : all dates giving the year only and using the Autumn of 312 B.C. as the beginning of the Seleucid era belong to a Seleucid source ; those which give fuller details and reckon from the spring of 312 belong to a Jewish source or sources. The Jewish sources are more complex. Four are distinguished apart from official documents, poetical pieces, and editorial matter. A full analysis of these is given (pp. 64-66). The possibility is entertained that the author of the source dealing with Judas Maccabaeus may have been the Jewish historian Eupolemos. The Jonathan and Simon sources are closely connected with the official records of the High-priesthood. II Macc. uses the Autumn of 312 as the Seleucid epoch. It is possible that it used the same Seleucid source that is used in I Macc. The book is based on an epitome of Jason's history (end of second century B.C.). The epitome was made before 60 B.C. and was worked over by the author of II Macc. about the beginning of the Christian era.

There is a full discussion of the notorious discrepancy in order between I and II Macc. regarding the death of Antiochus IV, the rededication of the Temple and the first campaign of Lysias. Schunck offers a very ingenious and attractive solution of the problem, including a restoration of the correct order of events (p. 115). On p. 126 there is a diagram showing the author's allocation of the material to sources not only for Macc. but also for the works of Josephus.

It is a careful and thorough study, packed with information, and presenting a well-argued case for the views which the author adopts.   T.W.M.

Tedesche, S. and Zeitlin, S. : *The Second Book of Maccabees.* 1954. Pp. xvi.+272. (Harper, New York, and Hamish Hamilton, London. Price : $4.00, or 32s. 0d.)

Here is a further welcome volume in the series of Jewish Apocryphal Literature being issued by the Dropsie College. Tedesche is responsible for the translation, which stands opposite the Greek text, after the manner of the Loeb editions of classical texts, while Zeitlin is responsible for the Introduction and the notes. The Introduction is a long one, running to 97 pages, and it sometimes parts company with current views. Zeitlin holds that the Epitomist worked in Antioch

701

in the time of Agrippa I. He gives a good account of the historical background of the period covered by the work, marked by orginal views at a number of points, and has a good section on the religion of the book. Altogether this is a valuable edition, with a contribution of its own to the study of 2 Maccabees.   H.H.R.

WEIS, P. R. : *Midrashic Selections, with Introduction and Notes.* (Semitic Study Series, New Series, No. 2.) 1955. Pp. xviii+54. (Brill, Leiden. Price : Fl. 5.20.)

> This is a small book, consisting of texts taken from Genesis Rabba Chs. xlix-lx, with an introduction and notes. The texts, which are printed in clear type, serve as characteristic samples of Midrashic interpretation. In the introduction Mr. Weis classifies, under descriptive headings, types of exegetical difficulties posed by the Midrashic approach to O.T. texts as well as patterns of Midrashic solutions. He supplies cross references, from the text to the introductory notes and from these to the text. Thus the reader is enabled to understand the nature of the passage he is studying by referring to the notes indicated, while his study of the Midrashic system presented in the introduction gains much from the illustrations afforded by the references to the text. This book fulfils its purpose of being a concise, but instructive, introduction to the study of Midrashic literature.   J.W.

YEIVIN, S. : *Milḥemet Bar Kŏkba* (with appendices, notes, diagrams and photographs). 2nd edition revised. 1952. Pp. 264. (Bialik Foundation, Jerusalem. Price : 18s. 0d.)

> The lay-out of the book is governed by the general thesis that the effects of the unsuccessful revolt of the year 70 were only temporary and the combats confined to a relatively small number of localities, while the Last Revolt involved the whole of the country including Eastern Trans-Jordan with more permanent consequences. Ch. I constitutes a criticism of Josephus's account of the massacre and destruction of the year 70 and reviews the effects of Roman rule up to the year 117. Chs. II-III deal with the personalities of the two principal characters, Hadrian and Bar Kŏkba, whereas the revolt itself is dealt with in chs. IV-V. The scanty evidence of the literary sources, and the numismatic and archaeological indications are combined and, by logical, strategic, and topographical deductions, built up into a chronological sequence of the various phases of the revolt. The epilogue in ch. VI is followed by five appendices, notes and indices. The author does not claim to have offered more than a working hypothesis. This caution is not out of place in a field where so few of the sources considered can be said with certainty to belong to the period in question. This does not detract, however, from the value of the book as the most up-to-date monograph on the subject.   P.R.W.

PHILOLOGY AND GRAMMAR

AISTLEITNER, J. : *Untersuchungen zur Grammatik des Ugaritischen.*
1954. Pp. 188. (Akademie-Verlag, Berlin. Price : DM. 15.)

> These *Untersuchungen* in fact constitute a complete grammar
> of the Ugaritic dialect, arranged according to the usual
> scheme, with a complete list of all the verbal forms and a
> *Formen-index*, including all other parts of speech with them,
> which is almost a glossary : for, although the words are not
> here translated *seriatim*, almost every one is explained under
> one or other of the references. The main part of the book is
> further enriched with many fresh translations, which will
> be of the greatest use to all interpreters of these difficult texts.
>
> G.R.D.

BLACK, M. : *An Aramaic Approach to the Gospels and Acts.* 2nd ed.
1954. Pp. viii+304. (Clarendon Press, Oxford. Price : 25s. 0d.)

> The first edition of this work was noticed in the *Book List*,
> 1947, p. 38. A number of changes have been introduced into
> the text, without disturbance of the pagination, and thirty-
> four pages of Supplementary Notes have been added. Several
> of these notes are of considerable length and of importance.
> In addition there are two new Appendices, one on the Un-
> published Work of A. J. Wensinck, and the other on the
> Aramaic Liturgical Poetry of the Jews (Piyyuṭim). This new
> edition is not, therefore, a mere reprint of the former, but
> contains a substantial amount of new work. It is not alone
> of value to New Testament scholars, but to all students of
> Aramaic. H.H.R.

BLACK, M. : *A Christian Palestinian Syriac Horologion.* (Texts and
Studies, New Series, No. 1.) 1954. Pp. 458+4 plates. (C.U.P.
Price : 70s. 0d.)

> This is an edition of the text of the Berlin MS. Or. Oct. 1019,
> written in Jerusalem and dated A.D. 1187/1188.
> The late Palestinian script is transcribed here into Estrangela,
> and Principal Black has added a translation and a valuable
> introduction. While a warm welcome must greet the pub-
> lication of a Palestinian Syriac MS. of about 200 folios, the
> main interest of the work for the Old Testament student will
> lie in the numerous Biblical texts, chiefly Psalms, here made
> available for the first time and furnished by the editor with
> full critical notes. W.D.M.

FUNDAMINSKY, S. : *A New Hebrew Grammar : Complete Course for
Teachers and Students with Vocabularies and Exercises.* 1954.
Pp. 361. (Jewish Publication Committee, The Narod Press, London.
Price : 22s. 6d.)

> This grammar is the fruit of long years of practical experience
> in teaching Hebrew. Part 1 (chs. i-x) is devoted to phonology

and orthography, Part II (chs. xi-xliii) to etymology and syntax. The grammar includes, besides Biblical Hebrew, some of the more important Mishnaic and later developments of the language. For the student who wishes to begin learning Biblical Hebrew, this " complete course " offers too much, and he will do well to come on to it only when he already possesses a good grounding in Biblical Hebrew, and is in a position more easily to distinguish between classical and later usage. Otherwise he may learn bad habits from the start. The author has a wide acquaintance with Hebrew, and his treatment of some topics, e.g., phonetics, is both fresh and helpful. Sometimes, however, antiquated views are perpetuated, e.g., on *waw* consecutive. A somewhat puzzling feature is the frequency with which the subject is placed first and the verb second in the Hebrew exercises. A fairly large number of misprints have escaped detection. D.W.T.

GELB, I. J. : *A Study of Writing. The Foundations of Grammatology*. 1952. Pp. xvi+296. (Routledge & Kegan Paul, London, and Chicago University Press. Price : 25s. 0d. and $5.00.)

The author of this book discusses the origin and development of writing in eleven chapters on writing as a system of signs, the forerunners of writing, word-syllabic systems, syllabic writings, the alphabet, the evolution of writing, modern writing among primitive peoples, monogenesis or polygenesis of writing, writing and civilization, the future of writing, terminology of writing ; and he adds an extensive bibliography, notes and index. There are also 95 illustrations and a chart showing the genealogy of the various systems of writing which have been invented. Much that he says is interesting and suggestive, but some of the notions which he proposes, *e.g.*, that the Semitic alphabets are not really alphabets but syllabaries, seem highly disputable ; and his arguments are not made easier by a certain obscurity of form and the use of strange terms in setting them out. G.R.D.

GEMSER, B. : *Hebreeuse Spraakkuns*. 1953. Pp. xii+364. (J. L. van Schaik, Pretoria. Price : 37s. 6d.)

In addition to its intrinsic worth, special interest attaches to this book because it is the first Introduction to Hebrew in the Afrikaans tongue. The material is arranged so as to provide a two years' course. In the first year the student is introduced briefly to the Hebrew language, script and phonology, and then goes through the morphology as far as the regular verbs. In the second year (which, like the first, comprises thirty lessons), he goes on to the irregular verbs, syntax and prosody. Each lesson is provided with useful exercises, and the student begins the study of parts of Genesis before the end of the first year. Over 70 pages of paradigms and vocabularies are provided at the end of the volume. Afrikaans-speaking students who use this work may consider themselves fortunate as compared with their English-speaking colleagues who still make shift with Davidson. F.F.B.

JEAN, C. F. : *Dictionnaire des inscriptions sémitiques de l'Ouest.* Livr. 1-2. 1954. Pp. xvi+128. (Brill, Leiden. Price : Fl. 10 each.)

Hard upon Prof. L. Köhler's *Lexicon* comes this new dictionary, designed to include all the words in West-Semitic texts, outside the Bible, of every period ; it runs from ' to *kšr* in these first two fascicles and will consist of six fascicles of the same size when complete. The conception is most welcome, since such a dictionary fills in a serious gap in the equipment of a Semitic scholar ; how far its execution will be adequate is another matter. Already there are signs of weakness, e.g., words inadequately treated (such as *'tr*) or wrongly explained (such as *'ṛṣt* and *gdlt*), words (for example *'ṛdb* and *ḫbr*) and references (as under *'tm* and *gdlt*) omitted. The time, however, has not yet come fully to evaluate this new work ; but all Semitic students will congratulate the author on his courage in attempting such a task and will offer him their best wishes for its fulfilment.   G.R.D.

MOSCATI, S. : *Preistoria e storia del consonantismo ebraico antico.* (Atti della Accademia Nazionale dei Lincei anno CCCLI-1954 : Classe di Scienze morali, storiche e filologiche, Serie viii, Vol. 5, Fasc. 8.) 1954. Pp. 385-445. (Accademia Nazionale dei Lincei, Rome. Price : Lire 650.)

MOSCATI, S. *Il sistema consonantico delle lingue semitiche.* 1954. Pp. 76. (Pontificio Istituto Biblico, Rome. Price : Lire 600.)

The five main sections of the first named work deal respectively with the consonantal system of the Massoretes, of proto-Semitic, of north western Semitic in the second, and first, millennium B.C., and with the pre-Massoretic consonantal system. None of the primitive Semitic phonemes are thought definitely to have fallen out of use completely in the north western Semitic area until towards the middle of the second millennium B.C. In this millennium the interdentals began to fall out of use, and *ś* continued in use only in some localities. In the first millennium B.C. Canaanite exhibits the completion of the reduction of the interdentals, as well as the falling out of use of the velar fricatives, and the coalescence of *ś* and *š*, with dialectical exceptions. The first millennium A.D. saw a phonetic reduction of the gutturals, which the Massoretes restored. In addition, they made a systematic distinction between *s*, *ś* and *š*, and introduced and systematised the distinction in the pronunciation of the *begadkephath* letters. The author's views are in many respects different from those of earlier scholars, and will command serious consideration. His monograph is informative, and he argues his case methodically ; and—a welcome characteristic—he has a sober recognition of the difficulties inherent in the use of the material available.

Professor Moscati's second work, which is an introductory course to the study of the consonantal system of the Semitic languages, consists of three main chapters—on the material, the classification of the proto-Semitic consonants, and the evolution of the system of Semitic consonants. Much of what is to be found in the first work is repeated here, but there are additions, for example, helpful diagrams illustrating the consonantal system of the chief Semitic languages, and a much fuller bibliography. These two works provide the student with a valuable supplement to the work of Brockelmann and others.　　　　　　　　　　　　　　　　　　　　　　　　D.W.T.

NASCIMBENE, R. : *Lezioni di ebraico e lingue semitiche comparate.* Pp. viii + 152. (Litografia Cucchi, Pavia. Price : Lire 1800.)

These " Lessons," which, it seems, were given by the author in the academic year 1944-45, and which are here reproduced by a lithographic process, consist of two main parts. Part I deals with the Hebrew language (writing, phonetics, morphology) ; Part II contains a selection of Semitic texts—Assyrian, Babylonian, Canaanite (Tell el-Amarna glosses, Phoenician, Punic, Hebrew), Aramaic, Syriac, North and South Arabic, and Ethiopic. The author intends to deal with Ugaritic in another course. There is a Hebrew-English vocabulary, as well as various tables and a short supplement containing mainly additional Hebrew texts. While there is much in this work which will be helpful to the student, perhaps its most noteworthy, and useful, characteristic is the way in which it enables him from the beginning to study the fundamentals of Hebrew against the background of comparative Semitic linguistics, and so to obtain in the early stages of his study an idea of the historical development of the language. D.W.T.

OOSTERHOFF, B. J. : *Israëlitische Persoonsnamen.* (Exegetica, Series I, Part IV.) 1954. Pp. 80. (Uitgeverij Van Keulen, Delft. Price : Fl. 3.95 separately ; Fl. 2.75 to subscribers to the series.)

This study restricts itself to the chief types of Israelite personal names found in O.T., excluding non-Hebrew names borne by a few Israelites such as Moses, Aaron, Phinehas, Esther and Mordecai. The author deals first with non-theophoric names (including animal-names, plant-names, and names derived from special circumstances, such as those of the patriarchs), and then with theophoric names (classifying them according as they are compounded with *'el, šaddai, ṣur, Yahweh, ba'al, melek, 'adon, 'ab, 'aḥ, 'am,* or are abbreviated from theophoric names). He does not regard Isaac, Jacob, etc., as shortened forms of theophoric names (*yiṣḥaq-'el, ya'aqob-'el,* etc.). David, a non-theophoric name, is taken to mean " darling " or " beloved," and not associated with the Mari term *dawidum* (" leader "). A final chapter considers the religious significance of the theophoric names. At the end there are useful tables of theophoric names, whether complete or abbreviated, and an index of all the names mentioned.　　　　　　　　　　　　　　F.F.B.

PALACIOS, L. : *Grammatica Aramaico-Biblica ad usum scholarum exercitiis, textibus et vocabulario ornata.* 2nd ed. 1953. Pp. x + 138. (Desclée & Co., Rome. Price : Lire 1800.)

The first edition of this excellent class text-book of Biblical Aramaic appeared in 1935. It has now been reprinted with the correction of some of the relatively few misprints it contained—alas ! not quite all—and with the addition of an appendix containing the text (with translation, brief notes, and vocabulary) of a few non-Biblical passages. These include the Bar-rekub inscription, an Elephantine letter, part of the Palmyrene Tariff, some verses from the Samaritan Targum, and some from the Targum of Onkelos. The body of the book contains an outline of Biblical Aramaic grammar, including syntax, with paradigms, followed by the text of the Aramaic portions of the Old Testament, with brief notes and a vocabulary. In the paradigms an asterisk marks forms which are not actually found in the Biblical passages, but which are supplied for completeness.   H.H.R.

PALACIOS, L. : *Grammatica Syriaca*. 2nd ed. 1954. Pp. xvi+272. (Desclée & Co., Rome. Price : Lire 3000 or bound 3800.)

This is an improved edition prepared by Dom. V. Camps of a work which appeared first in 1931. Phonology, morphology and syntax are dealt with clearly and quite fully in Latin. Numerous exercises for translation from Syriac and a chresto-mathy comprising twelve passages from the Bible and other sources are given. At the end the verb is set out in paradigms, which would be even more useful for beginners if Quššaya and Rukkaka were always indicated. Those who teach Syriac in this country may hesitate to adopt as their only text-book a work written in Latin, but they will find here much material they can make use of in class.   W.D.M.

SCHWARZENBACH, A. : *Die geographische Terminologie im Hebräischen des Alten Testaments*. 1954. Pp. xii+212. (Brill, Leiden. Price : Fl. 21.)

This Zürich dissertation from the school of Ludwig Koehler examines all terms for mountains, valleys, water, cultivated areas, desert, types of soil, etc., adding a concordance of their corresponding terms in the LXX, the Targumim and the Peshiṭta. Useful also are the lists of the new meanings of words (p. 157), of names of places, territories, mountains and rivers (pp. 201 ff.), and of suggested emendations (p. 158.)
                                    W.B.

THACKER, T. W. : *The Relationship of the Semitic and Egyptian Verbal Systems*. 1954. Pp. xxvi+342. (Geoffrey Cumberlege, Oxford. Price : 42s. 0d.)

In this work the author studies one aspect of the problem of the relationship between the Semitic and Egyptian languages. The two parts of the book are devoted, first, to the study of the material which aids the recovery of the vocalization of Egyptian verb-forms (relevant Semitic comparisons are included), and secondly, to a comparison of the Semitic and Egyptian verbal systems. The Egyptian system is not, the author argues, basically non-Semitic with a Semitic super-structure, nor is it basically Semitic with a non-Semitic superstructure. Most probably the Semitic and Egyptian systems are offshoots of the same parent system. They parted at an early and incomplete stage of development, and continued their growth each along its own lines. In addition to an assessment of the relationship of the two systems, a number of suggestions on the Semitic and Egyptian verb, especially the latter, are put forward. For example, it is suggested that the infinitive absolute is the most ancient verb-form possessed by the Semitic dialects. The author of this work, who is among those comparatively few who move easily both in Egyptian and in the Semitic languages, writes as an expert for experts. Only one who, like himself, is an Egyptologist as well as a Semitist, is in a position to appraise adequately the merits of his work. The Semitist will, however, wish to pay tribute to the high quality of the scholarship displayed throughout, and all users of the book will appreciate especially the well ordered arrangement of the material which, in all its technicality, is discussed. This is an indispensable book for serious students of the subject. Its appropriate place on the shelf is between Professor G. R. Driver's *Problems of the Hebrew Verbal System* and Sir Alan Gardiner's *Egyptian Grammar*, to both of which the author acknowledges a special debt.   D.W.T.

ZORELL, F. : *Lexicon Hebraicum et Aramaicum Veteris Testamenti*, fasc. 9. 1954. Pp. 809-912. (Pontificio Istituto Biblico, Rome. Price : Lire 1200.)

> This, the last fascicle of Zorell's Hebrew lexicon, runs from *śrp* ' burnt ' to *ttgr* ' merchandise ' ; thus only one or two Hebrew words and the Aramaic parts are required to bring the work to conclusion. This dictionary follows conservative lines but contains a certain number of novel interpretations which have not yet appeared elsewhere ; but it is especially valuable for its contribution towards the task of bringing references to contemporary literature more or less up to date and for including the words in the Hebrew text of Ben Sira.
>   G.R.D.

1956

This is the eleventh and last issue of the Book List for which I shall be responsible. I should like to express my thanks to the members of the Society for the freedom they have given me for its preparation, and many friends for the help they have consistently given me through the years in a variety of ways. On some the burden of writing notices has fallen very heavily, and they have given their help unstintingly. Through the years the panel of reviewers has been steadily increased to lessen this burden to some extent, and I have always had some help from non-members of this panel. In the preparation of the present issue I acknowledge the help of Professors Baumgartner, Manson and Robinson, and Drs. Ullendorff, Wiesenberg and Zuntz.

The prices of books are given where known, either in the original currency, or, where this is impossible, in English currency. Often this is the most difficult item to obtain, and I am grateful to members of the Manchester University Library staff and to others for help received in this respect.

Another point of difficulty occurs in the case of books which are published both in England and America. Where both publishers are known to me, they are both given. Often part of the information is not available, or one edition appears at a considerable interval after the other, and in such cases it is not given. Happily the Publishers increasingly co-operate by supplying the needed information. Titles to which an asterisk (*) is prefixed are recommended for inclusion in school libraries.

To the Printer I would also express my deep gratitude. For ten years he has helped me in every possible way, and he and I alone know how much the Society owes to him.

Finally, I would offer my best wishes to my successor, Professor G. W. Anderson, and bespeak for him the utmost support that can be given him.

MANCHESTER UNIVERSITY.   H. H. ROWLEY.

GENERAL

The Bible Today : Historical, Social and Literary Aspects of the Old and New Testaments. Described by Christian Scholars. 1955. Pp. xvi+208. (Eyre and Spottiswoode, for *The Times*, London, and Harper, New York. Price : 25s. 0d. or $5.00.)

The Times has done good service to Biblical studies in bringing together, first as a Supplement and now as a book, a notable collection of essays on the Bible. The team of twenty-nine writers are all Christian scholars and experts in their own field. Eight of the essays are devoted to the Old Testament and offer brief but informative surveys of the present state of knowledge in such matters as language, archaeology, text, literary growth and the threefold division of the Canon. The rest of the essays deal with the Apocrypha, the New Testament, the successive English versions, and the place of the Bible in English life. L.H.B.

BIČ, M. and SOUČEK, J. B. (ed. by) : *Biblická Konkordance*. Parts 2-6. Bezbožný-Hora l. 1954 (part 2), 1955. Pp. 80 each part. (Edice Kalich, Prague—agents Artia Ltd., 30 Smečky, Prague. Price : Kˇs. 10.50 or U.S. $1.10 per part.)

This Concordance, whose character was indicated in *Book List*, 1955, p. 4, continues to appear at regular intervals. When it is completed it will give Czech readers—amongst whom the present writer is not included—a working tool which cannot be equalled for the range of its usefulness in any other language. H.H.R.

Bijbels Woordenboek. 2nd ed. Part 2, Egypte-Isaak. 1955. Cols. 417-768+16 Plates. (Romen en Zonen, Roermond. Price : Fl. 10.75.)

The first issue of this new edition, revised and enlarged, and often completely rewritten, was noticed in the *Book List*, 1955, pp. 4f. More than thirty scholars have collaborated in the preparation of the work, many of them well-known Catholic scholars, and it is thoroughly reliable and up-to-date. (The reviewer has noticed one error concerning his own views in the article on ' Esdras.') Most of the articles are brief, but some are substantial. Brief bibliographies are given at the end of most of the articles, and these include the most recent work. Under ' Essenen,' the authors reserve judgement as to whether the Qumran sect belongs here. On much discussed questions, such as the book of Ezekiel and the Song of Songs, the authors present an objective review of the views that are held. Altogether this is one of the best short Bible Dictionaries available in any language. H.H.R.

FRIEDRICH, G. (ed. by) : *Theologisches Wörterbuch zum Neuen Testament* (begun by G. Kittel). Band VI. Lieferungen 2, 3, and 4. 1955. Pp. 64 per part. (Kohlhammer, Stuttgart. Price : DM. 4.60. per part, by subscription.)

Lieferung 2 (pp. 65-126) continues the article on *peristera*, *trugōn* by Greeven and deals with circumcision in the Old Testament and in Judaism in an article by Meyer. Lieferung 3 (pp. 129-192) after some articles of lesser interest to Old Testament scholars contains the beginning of the extremely valuable article on *pisteuō, pistis, pistos*, etc., by Bultmann which includes an important study of the relevant Hebrew words by Weiser. This article is continued in Lieferung 4 which also has an article on *planaō*, etc., by Braun.

Weiser in the section referred to above has an important discussion of the root *'mn*. He argues that, while not so common as certain other roots, its more formal character enabled it to acquire a fuller meaning. It was used to express the reciprocal relationship between God and man and especially the covenant relationship. The word was developed theologically above all by Isaiah. In the Old Testament faith was brought into relation with human history but this insight was largely lost in Judaism. N.W.P.

HAAG, H. (ed. by, with the collaboration of A. van den Born and others) : *Bibel-Lexikon*. Part 7. 1955. Cols. 1317-1508. (Benziger Verlag, Einsiedeln, Zürich and Cologne. Subscription price : Fr./DM. 11.00 per part.)

This excellent handbook continues its course, the present issue running from the completion of *Personennamen* to *Sichem*. The longest signed articles in this part are on *Poesie*, by the late A. Robert, on *Prophet, Prophetismus*, and *Reich Gottes*, all by P. van Imschoot, and on *Rechtfertigung*, by W. Grossouw. As in the previous issues the writers of both signed and unsigned articles offer succinct and scholarly notes, followed by up-to-date bibliographies. There are occasional slips, as in the title of A. R. Johnson's book at the end of the article on *Seele*, (and in the Publisher's attribution on the back cover of the notice in the 1952 Book List to Professor Henton Davies). All in all, this will be a reliable one-volume Bible Dictionary, which will be consulted with profit alongside the larger, and older, dictionaries. H.H.R.

Hebrew Union College Annual, Vol. XXVI. 1955. Pp. 570+74 (in Hebrew)+index. (Hebrew Union College, Cincinnati. Price : $3.00.)

This volume of fifteen articles (two in Hebrew) will take a worthy place in this series of annuals. First J. Morgenstern elicits and expounds a Decalogue in Leviticus xix and links it with the dedication of the 2nd Temple in 516. Next comes Sheldon Blank's study in the Biblical pattern of ' Self-Pity.'

C. H. Gordon provides in ' Homer and the Bible ' an exceptionally interesting study in East Mediterranean Literature in the wake of the Amarna age, to illustrate the thesis that Greek and Hebrew civilizations are parallel products. E. Neufeld investigates the O.T. laws against loans at interest in the light of their cultural background, and much material is gathered here. Other articles include a solution of an Ugaritic mathematical conundrum ; a long and complete study of the evidence concerning Abraham which also sets forth Philo's place in Judaism ; an estimate of the " numinous " element in different forms of the Kedushah ; a portrayal of the Unity of God in the light of various theological contexts, and an illustrated article on marriage contracts. This rewarding volume offers finally and most acceptably an index of the contents of Vols. 1-25. G.H.D.

Internationale Zeitschriftenschau für Bibelwissenschaft und Grenzgebiete,
II, 1953-54, Heft 1-2. 1955. Pp. xii+248. (Patmos Verlag, Düsseldorf. Price : DM. 34.)

This issue continues the important service to scholarship begun by the first volume. It contains the titles of 1,547 articles bearing on the Bible, which have appeared in the 393 periodicals under survey. Almost every entry contains a summary of the article concerned. An international team of more than fifty scholars has co-operated in its preparation, and their service to scholarship is beyond all praise. The entries are classified according to subject, and there is an author index. No one who is interested in research on any Biblical subject can afford to neglect this tool. H.H.R.

Jaarbericht Ex Oriente Lux, No. 13, 1953-54. 1954. Pp. 144+32 plates+ 2 tables+2 maps. (Society Ex Oriente Lux, Leiden. Price : Fl. 25.00 ; by subscription Fl. 15.00.)

There is a supplementary list of the writings of B. S. Kristensen, and a two-page memorial of Henri Frankfort. The volume contains summaries of archaeological research in the Near East : in Egypt and the Sudan from 1946 to 1953, of the Hittite kingdom from 1950 to 1953, and in Iran from 1935 with special attention to Persepolis. There are full bibliographies throughout and the numerous plates are very helpful. In particular there is an account of the recent work at Jericho dealing especially with ancient caves at Palegaura. A long and informative article deals with the Temple of Enlil in the third stratum at Nippur. N.H.S.

LOTH, B. and MICHEL, A. : *Dictionnaire de Théologie Catholique. Tables Générales.* Fasc. iv. *Concordats—Dissimulation.* 1955. Cols. 753-1008. (Letouzey & Ané, Paris. Price : 22s. 3d.)

This great index to the vast *Dictionnaire* is becoming quite indispensable, the more so as some of the earlier articles in the main work are in much need of the additional bibliographies and other details supplied by the *Tables*. The articles of interest to an *Alttestamentler* are not numerous, but in the present fascicle they include all the references to such topics as " Creation " (with its subordinate subject " Conservation," " Cosmogonie " and " Concordisme,") " Critique Biblique," " Daniel," " David," " Décalogue " (already indexed under " Commandements de Dieu,") " Démon," " Deutéronome," and, above all, " Dieu " (under which may be found a useful " Note sur la révélation de Dieu dans la Bible "). There are short biographies of scholars such as Condamin, Coppens, Cornelius a Lapide (i.e., Cornelis Van der Steen), Cornely, Cornill, Delitzsch (Franz and Friedrich), Dennefeld, and Dillmann. J.M.T.B.

(MOWINCKEL, S.) : *Interpretationes ad Vetus Testamentum Pertinentes Sigmundo Mowinckel Septuagenario Missae = Norsk Teologisk Tidsskrift*, 56, 1955, Heft. 1-2. 1955. Pp. 184. (Forlaget Land Og Kirke, Oslo.)

This Festschrift contains fifteen articles. W. F. Albright offers a postscript to his study of Psalm lxviii (*HUCA* XXIII, 1-39), with a note on some Canaanite parallels to Psalm cxxxiv. 3, and A. Alt, discussing Micah ii. 1-5, sees the Davidic line involved in the fall of Jerusalem and considers Micah's expectation to be of a new ruler who will arise out of Bethlehem and of a new freedom which will come to Judah. H. Birkeland uses DSI evidence to show that Hebrew is a *Mischsprache* in which the effects of various linguistic waves of influence can be traced, and O. Eissfeldt engages in a study of the literary composition of the Pseudo-Philo's *Book of Biblical Antiquities* for the value it may have for the literary analysis of the Pentateuch and of the historical books of the Old Testament. R. Gyllenberg writing on " Kultus und Offenbarung," expounds the importance of the modern emphasis on the cult in Old Testament study, while A. R. Johnson examines the meaning of Ḥesed and Ḥāsîd, contending that, while the former may often be rendered as ' loyalty ' or better, ' devotion,' it has sometimes associated with it overtones of ' compassion ' or ' sympathy.' A. S. Kapelrud discusses the circumstances of the sacrifice of the seven members of the house of Saul (2 Sam. xxi. 1-14.) J. Pedersen's article is concerned with the interpretation of the tempter in the narrative of the Fall in the book of Genesis, while J. Lindblom discusses Isaiah xxviii. 16, arguing that the corner-stone symbolizes faith in Yahweh and the building itself the true religion of Yahweh which is the people's only refuge. P. Humbert offers three interesting notes on Genesis i ; C. R. North argues against Torrey and Simon for the exilic date of Deutero-Isaiah, whose expectation was eschatological and is to be mythologically interpreted ; and E. Sjöberg, on the basis of Justin's Dialogue with Trypho, discusses the expectation which was held by the Jews c. 200 A.D. concerning the un-recognized and suffering Messiah. M. Noth examines the

meaning of the designation " the saints of the Most High "
in Daniel vii in an endeavour to decide whether or not the
reference is to heavenly beings and to an eschatological
kingdom. Finally, F. Hvidberg examines Isaiah vi. 13 in
the light of the text in DSIa and concludes that the reference
is not to the stump of a tree but to maṣṣēbōth which will be
swept away in the day of judgement; and N. A. Dahl presents
the view that the baptism of John the Baptist is to be seen
as a preparatory eschatological initiation.   J.M.

NOBER, P. : *Verbum Domini : Indices Voluminum* 15 (1935)—30 (1952).
  1955. Pp. vi+110. (Pontificium Institutum Biblicum, Rome.
  Price : Lire, 900.)

Father Nober, who compiles the invaluable Elenchus Biblio-
graphicus in *Biblica*, has rendered a further service by compiling
a composite index of these volumes of *Verbum Domini*, which
will be of value to scholars as a help to locate articles and
reviews which have appeared in that periodical. It is by such
an index as this that articles are rescued from being buried in
journals and brought to the service of scholarship. There is
an index of articles under authors, and of books reviewed, as
well as a text index, and an index of Hebrew and Greek words
and of some technical terms in Biblical study.   H.H.R.

RIESENFELD, H. (ed. by) : *Svensk Exegetisk Årsbok*, xviii-xix. (1953-54).
  1955. Pp. 220. (Gleerup, Lund. Price : Sw. Kr. 10.)

Two *in memoriam* articles are included in this double volume :
one for Professor Fridrichsen, the first editor ; the other for
Professor Rudberg, an honorary member of the *Uppsala
Exegetiska Sällskap*. A. S. Kapelrud discusses the relation
of the prophets to Israelite law, and concludes that they were
indebted to a legal and ethical tradition derived from Canaan
and not from the desert. C. Lindhagen contributes a fully
documented survey of Swedish views of the Servant of the
Lord since 1800. Principal M. Black examines the theological
conceptions of the Dead Sea Scrolls. B. Gärtner finds in the
Targum on Psalm cxviii. 22-29, evidence that *ṭalya'* was used
as a Messianic title in the double sense *pais* (*doulos*) and *amnos*.
E. Beijer writes on H. Windisch as a New Testament scholar,
H. Riesenfeld on the composition of Mark, and K. Stendahl
on the Law as *paidagogos*. Recent works on Old Testament
subjects are reviewed by I. Engnell.

The editorship of this valuable annual has now passed from
Dr. Lindeskog to Professor Riesenfeld. Readers of the *Book
List* may also be interested to know that membership of the
Uppsala Exegetiska Sällskap is now open to non-Scandinavians,
and that articles in the main international languages are
included in the Årsbok.   G.W.A.

714

RINALDI, G. (ed. by) : *Secoli sul Mondo*. 1955. Pp. 570. (Marietti, Turin. Price : Lire 2,700.)

This volume with its curious and enigmatic title may be said to correspond roughly to the French work (now translated) *Initiation biblique* and, even less exactly, to *The Old Testament and Modern Study*. It is, in fact, a symposium to which some thirty writers have contributed. Of these the majority are Italian, and a small minority French or Belgian. No German or English scholar has been called upon for a contribution. There are four main divisions, dealing respectively with the origins of humanity and the various races ; with Israel in its history and in its archaeological remains ; with the Biblical languages and the psalms, the prophets, and the wisdom literature in general ; and, finally, with the New Testament history and literature. As in most symposia, the articles vary considerably in value. Among the better articles are those by P. Colella on the law of Moses and the legal systems of the ancient east, by J. de Fraine on Israel in its history, and by G. Castellino on poetry and religion in the psalms. It is unfortunate that the only contribution by a woman (Signorina A. T. Serventi) on the Biblical languages, is unequal and sketchy. Exactly seventeen lines are devoted to Aramaic. The bibliographies are relatively full, and are among the more useful features of the work, which is well bound and attractively printed and produced.　　　　　　　　　　　　　　J.M.T.B.

ROBERT, A. (ed. by) : *Dictionnaire de la Bible. Supplément*. Fasc. xxviii. (Médiation-Midrash). 1955. Cols. 1025-1280. (Letouzey & Ané, Paris. Price : 22s. 6d.)

Robert's name appears for the last time as the actual editor of the *Supplément*, on the title-page of this fascicle. He died on 28th May, of last year, and has been replaced by H. Cazelles. This is an excellent number, and contains articles on ' Médiation (dans le N.T.)' by C. Spicq ; on ' Megiddo ' (a welcome complement to the late L. Hennequin's survey in t.iii. cols. 426-33) by A. M. Steve ; on ' Mésopotamie,' in which the history is treated by E. Cavaignac and the religion by R. Follet ; on ' Messianisme ' by A. Gelin, whose concise account may be compared with L. Dennefeld's more ample article in the *Dict. de théologie catholique :* and on ' Métrologie biblique ' by J. Trinquet. Trinquet has unfortunately overlooked the publication in *VT* of Dr. Scott's paper to the Society's Durham meeting in 1950. There are short biographies of J. Meinhold, A. Merk (the Jesuit editor of a Greek New Testament, not to be confused with Adalbert Merx, the rabbinical authority), and E. Meyer.　　　　　　　　　　　　　　J.M.T.B.

ROBERT, A. and TRICOT, A. (ed. by) : *Initiation Biblique : Introduction à l'étude des Saintes Écritures*. 3rd ed., revised and enlarged. 1954. Pp. xxvi+1082+4 charts+8 maps. (Desclée & Cie, Tournai. Price : Fr. 1880, or bound Fr. 2200.)

The first edition appeared in 1939 (*Book List*, 1939, p. 12) and the second in 1948 (*Book List*, 1950, p. 10). There are about 100 more pages in this edition than in the second. The major additions are a new chapter by P. Benoit on Inspiration, sections on the prophetical books by A. Gelin and on the Wisdom books by A. Tricot, and chapters on The Apostolic Age (A. Tricot), The Bible and Theology (Paul Henry), *La pastorale biblique* (Th. Maertens) and The Bible and the liturgy (L. Bouyer). Much of the volume has been reset and partially rewritten. The new material from the Dead Sea caves has been used, and in particular a fuller treatment has been included of the principles and applications of Form Criticism. The book is by Roman Catholics and for Roman Catholics, but a fair summary is given of points of view other than their own. The volume is well-indexed and the range is wide. There are bibliographies at the end of each chapter, predominantly Roman Catholic, but the best known books by Protestants are included. It is a most useful and comprehensive manual.   N.H.S.

(Rowley, H. H.) : *Wisdom in Israel and in the Ancient Near East*, Essays presented to H. H. Rowley, ed. by M. Noth and D. W. Thomas. (Supplements to *Vetus Testamentum*, vol. III.) 1955. Pp. xx+302. (Brill, Leiden. Price : Fl. 32, or by subscription Fl. 25.)

The 22 contributions to this Festschrift for Professor H. H. Rowley represent Old Testament scholarship from 12 countries ranging from Finland to S. Africa, Belgium to the U.S.A. Four of the studies deal with extra-Israelite Wisdom, of which one, " Man and his God " (S. N. Kramer) includes 4 plates, a transliteration and translation of a Sumerian text from the early 2nd millennium B.C. The studies are variously comparative, literary, semantic, philological, exegetical and theological, and are of such a quality as to make this a most important contribution to Old Testament study. The book begins with a ' Select Bibliography of the Writings of H. H. Rowley ' (G. Henton Davies). The editors must be warmly congratulated on gathering together so distinguished a team of contributors.   A.S.H.

XIV Semana Biblica Española (21-26 Sept., 1953). 1954. Pp. xxiv+ 458. (Instituto F. Suarez, Madrid.)

This volume, which has a preface addressed to the members of the Semana Biblica by Mgr. L. Eino Garay, Patriarch of the West Indies and Bishop of Madrid-Alcalá, contains seventeen conferences, some of them of interest to the *Alttestamentler*. The ' Reign of God in the Old Testament ' by M. G. Cordero, ' The Theology of History in the Old Testament ' by R. Criado, and what is styled 'A New Theory on the Sources of Genesis ' by J. Ramos (who criticizes Chaine for distinguishing J and E and elects to regard them as one document) are the chief contributions of this kind. There are also several articles on biblical inspiration, and one on the *sensus plenior*. On the

716

whole, this is not one of the more important volumes of its kind, though it is encouraging to find that a work of this size can be published within a few months of the conference that led up to it.   J.M.T.B.

Semitica (Cahiers publiés par l'Institut d'Études Sémitiques de l'Université de Paris). V. 1955. Pp. 106. (A. Maisonneuve, Paris. Price : Fr. 800.)

This issue contains ten articles. A Caquot finds an astrological origin for the symbolism of the first three beasts mentioned in Dan. vii.—they derive from the circle of twelve animal figures which the Greeks called *dodecaoros:* each beast represents a constellation which has under its control the territories of the empires conjured up by the vision. I. Lévy presents a long and penetrating study of the relationship of 1 and 2 Maccabees, both to each other and to the enigmatic Hebrew work, *Sarbeth Sabanaiel*, of which Origen speaks. A. Dupont-Sommer argues further his identification of the " chief of the kings of Yâwân " in the Zadokite Fragments with Pompey, and of the Kittim with the Romans. To the occurrences in the Habakkuk Commentary, Ben Sira, and the N.T., of the expression " body of flesh," M. Philonenko now adds Enoch cii. 5. M. Testuz publishes two fragments of manuscripts from the Dead Sea. The first contains part of Hos. xiii. 15 and xiv. 1, 3-6, and the second, in Aramaic, belongs to an unidentified work. J. Cantineau, following H. Birkeland, holds the view that Hebrew, albeit strongly Aramaized in some respects, lived on as a spoken language among the ordinary people of Palestine at least until the middle of the second century A.D. J. –G. Février contributes two articles—on a Neo-Punic epitaph (1st century B.C.) of 'Adiyat, priestess and chief singer, and on the different meanings of *'lt* in Phoenician and Punic. M. Sznycer discusses some of the ostraca, probably used as labels in wine stores, found by Russian archaeologists at Nisa. The texts of sixteen of the ostraca are given, with translations, and in some cases notes are added. The language in which they are written is probably Aramaic, and they belong to the first century B.C. J. David-Weill records some better readings in the Arabic papyrus published by him in *Semitica* IV (1951· 52, pp. 67 ff.).   D.W.T.

Studia theologica cura ordinum theologorum Scandinavicorum edita, Vol. VIII, Fasc. i. 1954/55. Pp. 76. Fasc. ii. 1954/55. Pp. 96. (Gleerup, Lund. Price : by subscription Sw. Kr. 12, or Sw. Kr. 8 each.)

In Fasc. i. B. Gärtner discusses the hermeneutic methods of the Habakkuk commentary in relation to the first Gospel, examining suggestions recently made by K. Stendahl. J. Muilenburg reconsiders the evidence for the site of Mizpah in the light of a recent study by Alt, and restates substantially his own former case for the identification with Tell en-Nasbeh. F. Løkkegaard offers ' Some Comments on the Sanchuniaton Tradition,' arguing that it originated between the 8th and

4th centuries B.C. H. J. Schoeps contributes ' Die ebionitische Wahrheit des Christentums.'

In Fasc. ii. E. Nielsen discusses the incident of the burying of the foreign gods in Genesis xxxv. 1-4, adducing parallels from Egypt and Mesopotamia. A. Murtonen briefly considers Old Testament chronology, suggesting influence from eschatological speculation. Other articles are : L. Pinomas, ' Schöpfung und Offenbarung bei Luther ' ; F. Refoulé, ' Situation des pécheurs dans l'Eglise d'après saint Augustin ' ; L. Spicq, ' L'étreinte de la Charité ' ; P. Winter, ' The Treatment of His Sources by the Third Evangelist in Luke XXI-XXIV.'

G.W.A.

Mullo Weir, C. J. (ed. by) : *Transactions of Glasgow University Oriental Society*, xv. (1953-54). 1955. Pp. iv+84. (Oriental Society, The University, Glasgow. Price : 15s. 0d.)

This volume contains three articles of interest to the student of the Old Testament. The Editor writes on the fourteen occurrences in MT. of 3rd. sing. fem. perf. forms in *-āth* or *-ath*, and maintains that they are all spurious. R. A. Barclay connects the Tetragrammaton with the oriental cry *om*, which figures in the familiar formula of Buddhist prayer. W. Cosser argues that in Proverbs, Job and Ecclesiastes the word *life* means *full life* and that it includes fullness of life hereafter as well as here. Of the remaining articles four are on Islamic and Arabic subjects, one of them examining Azad's view that the Dhu 'l-Qarnain of the Qur'an is Cyrus. An Edinburgh India Society Supplement contains one article. There is also a short communication by J. Bowman, arguing that the phylacteries of Matt. xxiii. 5 were Samaritan phylacteries or *kemē'im*. The volume contains also an index of the whole fifteen volumes so far published. H.H.R.

EDUCATIONAL

Youngman, B. : *Patriarchs, Judges and Kings*. (Background to the Bible, 1.) 1955. Pp. 92+2 maps. (Hulton Press, Ltd., London. Price : 5s. 0d., limp ; 6s. 0d. boards.)

This is the first of a series of four books, of which two will be devoted to the Old Testament period, illustrating the geographical, social and religious background of the Bible. The text, which is addressed to the pupils themselves, is suitable for study in the upper forms of Secondary Schools, and is intended to be read in conjunction with specified passages from the Bible. It is divided into sixteen chapters, each relating to one or more of the Biblical heroes, from Abraham to Solomon. The information given is usually reliable, and the book is well written, well produced and modestly priced. The illustrations and maps, particularly the many excellent photographs, are of great value. This book should appeal not only to the more intelligent pupils but also to their teachers and to students in Training Colleges. L.A.P.

ARCHAEOLOGY AND EPIGRAPHY

ALBRIGHT, W. F. : *L'Archéologie de la Palestine*, trans. from English by R. Alapetite. 1955. Pp. 296+30 plates. (Les Editions du Cerf, Paris. Price : Fr. 1080.)

> A translation, by R. Alapetite, of the revised Pelican edition of *The Archaeology of Palestine* (1954) with the additions inserted in their appropriate places instead of at the end of chapters.　　　　　　　　　　　　　　　　　　　　　J.N.S.

AVIGAD, N. : *Ancient Monuments in the Kidron Valley* (in Hebrew). 1954. Pp. xii+143+v. (Bialik Institute, Jerusalem.)

> This fine volume, sumptuously provided with drawings and plates, gives a detailed account of the ancient Jewish tombs of the " Valley of Jehoshaphat." The site, which is outside the boundaries of the State of Israel, was investigated by the author in the years 1945-7, but owing to the disturbed conditions later prevailing in Palestine a small part of the survey could not be brought to a conclusion.

> The tombs may be classified chronologically :

> (1) Siloam tombs dating from the time of the First Temple. This group contains the . . . ? . . yahu inscription (hitherto undeciphered) for which the first reading is proposed in the present volume as well as the 'tomb of Pharaoh's Daughter.' The architectural features of the latter monument are strongly reminiscent of Egyptian burial-chambers.

> (2) Tombs from the period of the Second Temple are principally represented by rock-hewn monuments in the characteristic style of the Hellenistic-Roman period, including the ' tomb of Zachariah ' (in the form of an Egyptian chapel), 'Absalom's Tomb' (a curious mixture of Ionic, Doric, etc., styles), and the ' Tomb of Jehoshaphat ' (subterranean passages).

> The author was well advised in presenting most of the architectural terms in their original Greek or Latin forms (p. 143). The work makes a notable contribution to the history of Jewish sepulchral art.　　　　　　　　　　　　　　　　E.U.

AVI-YONAH, M. and YEIVIN, S. with STEKELIS, M. : *The Antiquities of Israel* (in Hebrew). (Publications of the Ancient East Research Association.) 1955. Pp. xii+344+37 plates. (Hakibutz Hameuchad Publishing House, Ltd., Tel-Aviv.)

> This is the first volume of a projected work of 3 volumes on the Archaeology of Palestine primarily intended for students with no previous acquaintance with the subject. Its first part contains a general introduction : the definition of Archaeology ; an outline of archaeological research, in the world generally and in Palestine in particular, from its inception till the present ; and a description of the historical and

chronological problems involved and of the methods employed by excavators. Its second part deals with archaeological discoveries under 3 headings : buildings generally, places of worship and fortresses. The period under survey stretches from pre-historic beginnings to the Byzantine epoch. Conspicuous by its absence is the Temple of Jerusalem. One cannot but agree with the authors that the building of Solomon, our deficient knowledge of which is entirely based on literary and not on archaeological remains, is outside the scope of their work. The same is, however, hardly the case with Herod's Temple. The appended 99 Plates, an additional 155 illustrations scattered through the text, and 2 maps, greatly enhance the usefulness of the work. E.W.

La Bible et l'Orient. Travaux du premier congrès d'archéologie et orientalisme bibliques (23-25 *Avril*, 1954). (Cahiers de la Revue d'histoire et de philosophie religieuses, No. 34. = R.H.P.R., 35, No. 1, 1955.). 1955. Pp. 146. (Presses Universitaires de France, Paris. Price : Fr. 500.)

Members of the Society will be interested to learn of the holding in April, 1954, of the first French inter-confessional congress dealing primarily with the impact of archaeology on biblical studies. The thirteen interesting and, in some cases, original papers which are printed here together with a précis of the subsequent discussion, were read by or for : M. Lambert (Some literary themes common to Sumerian and the Bible), E. Szlechter (The loan in the O.T. and in the pre-Hammurabic codes of Mesopotamia), Ed. Jacob (History and historians in the O.T.), E. Drioton (The date of the exodus, with notes on some recently found instances of '*Aperiu* in Egyptian texts), H. Cazelles (Geographical indications in the Exodus story), A. Parrot (two papers, The Dead Sea Scrolls from the archaeological standpoint, and Mari and the O.T.), H. Michaud (The name Qumran), A. Dupont-Sommer (The problem of foreign influences on the Jewish sect of Qumran), G. Vermès (à propos of the biblical commentaries found at Qumran), J. Daniélou (The community of Qumran and the organization of the Early Church), Ch. F. Jean (Personal names in the Mari letters and the earliest texts of the Pentateuch), E. Dhorme (The Hebrew text of the O.T.). As might be expected these days, the Dead Sea Scrolls figure most prominently, but the other papers also repay careful reading. Pastor Fabre must have been gratified at the success of this congress which he first mooted and then organized. D.R.Ap-T.

HORN, S. H. : *Light from the Dust Heaps*. 1955. Pp. 96. (Review and Herald, Washington, D.C.)

This work is generally well-informed on the results of archaeology though the fundamentalist standpoint is maintained by a selective use of the data. The theme of the book is 'Archaeological discoveries not only have produced evidence revealing the accuracy of the historical events narrated in the Bible, but also have brought to light ancient manuscripts of the New and Old Testament that have demonstrated that the Bible text as we have it to-day has not been changed or tampered with since the time it came from the hands of its authors.'   J.G.

KELSO, J. L. and BARAMKI, D. C. : *Excavations at New Testament Jericho and Khirbet en-Nitla*, with Supplementary Material by W. F. Albright, A. Jeffery, and C. U. Wolf. (Annual of the American Schools of Oriental Research, xxix-xxx. for 1949-51.) 1955. Pp. x+60+40 plates. (A.S.O.R., New Haven, Conn. Price : $6.00.)

This volume contains a report on the excavations at both places mentioned in the title, with a chapter on the ceramic finds, and one on the masonry and plaster of New Testament Jericho. C. U. Wolf has a chapter arguing that Khirbet en-Nitla is not the Byzantine Gilgal, though it was this traditional identification which led Dr. Kelso to excavate the site. The only inscriptional finds were one containing a Qur'anic text in Arabic at Jericho and two mosaics in Latin at Khirbet en-Nitla. These are discussed by A. Jeffery and W. F. Albright. The former is dated in the tenth century, which Kelso regards as very late, and is of interest because it follows the normal tradition of the text, though the scribe has made some slips. The full text is transcribed in one of the Plates. The other Plates illustrate the work on the site and the ceramic finds. It may be added that Albright believes that one of the Mosaics contains a quotation from a sacred poem, which cannot, however, be identified.   H.H.R.

*PARROT, A. : *Discovering Buried Worlds*, translated from the French by E. Hudson. 1955. Pp. 128. (S.C.M. Press, London. Price : 7s. 6d.)

This work comprises a description of the methods and progress of Near Eastern archaeology chiefly in Mesopotamia, a very broad outline of 'Five Thousand Years of Civilization' and a final very sketchy chapter on the ' Biblical Past and Oriental Background.' It is essentially an introduction to Near Eastern archaeology with limitations which will make it of more practical value to Bible classes and lay study groups than to those more advanced in this field.   J.G.

*PARROT, A. : *The Flood and Noah's Ark*, trans. by E. Hudson. (Studies in Biblical Archaeology, No. 1.) 1955. Pp. 76. (S.C.M. Press, London. Price : 7s. 6d.)

M. Parrot presents a useful adduction of documentary and archaeological evidence for a flood tradition. While the latter evidence shows that great floods were a recurrent phenomenon in Mesopotamia the writer believes that the Biblical and Mesopotamian traditions point back to one great Deluge. The peculiar Hebrew interpretation of the tradition is duly noted.

                                                                            J.G.

PARROT, A. : *Samarie, capitale du Royaume d'Israël.* (Cahiers d' archéologie biblique 7.) 1955. Pp. 118. (Delachaux et Niestlé, Neuchâtel. Price : Swiss Fr. 520.)

> Professor Parrot continues to produce his useful series of popular manuals of biblical archaeology, several of which have already been translated into English. The latest of the series is an interesting and reliable account of the rise and fortunes of the city which the founder of the Omri dynasty built for himself upon ' the horn of a son of oil,' and established as the permanent capital of the northern Kingdom. The history of the city is covered from its founding up to the time of Herod the Great. The chapter on *Israelite Samaria in the Light of Archaeology* is an excellent and authoritative summary of the results of the excavation of the site of Samaria during the last half-century. The illustrations are excellent and the bibliography up to date, even including Professor Rowley's monograph on *Sanballat and the Samaritan Temple* which only appeared in September, 1955. This is so far the best of an excellent series, and it is to be hoped that it will soon be translated into English. S.H.H.

*PARROT, A. : *The Tower of Babel*, trans. by E. Hudson. (Studies in Biblical Archaeology, No. 2.) 1955. Pp. 76. (S.C.M. Press, London. Price : 7s. 6d.)

> M. Parrot relates the Biblical ' tower of Babel ' to the *ziggurats* or staged towers familiar in Mesopotamian archaeology. Various types and examples are described, the plans and details from archaeological reports being particularly valuable. On archaeological and philological grounds—both sound— M. Parrot takes exception to the Biblical interpretation of the building of the tower of Babel as a case of human presumption. Rather does it symbolize man's appeal to God. J.G.

SCHAEFFER, C. F.-A. (ed. by) : *Mission de Ras Shamra VI : Le Palais Royal d'Ugarit. Textes accadiens et Hourrites des Archives Est, Ouest, et Centrales*, by J. Nougayrol, G. Boyer, and E. Laroche. 2 vols. 1955. Pp. xliv+350+17 plates, and 109 plates. (Klincksieck, Paris. Price : Fr. 6.400 the set.)

> It is now 17 years since Professor Schaeffer published the 3rd volume of the Mission de Ras Shamra, and 27 years since the epoch-making excavations at Ras Shamra began. The present volume, devoted entirely to the Accadian and Hurrian cuneiform texts from the royal archives, shows that after the devoted labours of M. Schaeffer and a brilliant band of collaborators, both in the field and in the work of decipherment, for a quarter of a century, the riches of this astonishing site are very far from being exhausted.

> In his introduction Professor Schaeffer announces that Professor Virolleaud, who has hitherto been responsible for the editing of all the cuneiform material, now wishes to devote

himself entirely to the study of the alphabetic cuneiform texts, and that M. Nougayrol will henceforth be responsible for the Accadian material. Hence this volume, which is mainly occupied with the cuneiform texts from the West, East, and Central archives of the royal palace, is almost entirely the work of M. Nougayrol, and it would be impossible to speak too highly of the skill and scholarship with which he has carried out the laborious task of transcribing and translating the very large number of Accadian texts which this volume contains. The Hurrian texts have been admirably edited by M. Laroche, and M. Boyer has contributed a valuable essay on the place of the Ugaritic texts in the history of ancient oriental law. This great volume will be a mine of precious material for orientalists for many years to come. Happy the scholar who can afford to possess it. S.H.H.

WOOLLEY, L. : *Alalakh. An Account of the Excavations at Tell Atchana in the Hatay*, 1937-1949, with section by C. J. Gadd. (Reports of the Research Committee of the Society of Antiquaries of London, No. xviii.) 1955. Pp. xii+412+81 figures+131 plates. (Society of Antiquaries, London. Price : 147s. 0d.)

This exhaustive account of the excavations at Alalakh between Antioch and Aleppo follows the usual form of archaeological reports ; it contains 12 chapters, each dealing with one or more phases of the work and the objects recovered in the course of it (periods ; temples ; defensive buildings ; private houses ; graves ; architecture with the frescoes ; sculpture and terracottas ; seals, beads and amulets, spindle-whorls ; objects of gold and silver and tools ; ivories and vessels of stone, glazed ware and glass ; pottery ; chronology ; residual catalogue). The reports are clear and as concise as possible and lavishly illustrated with line-drawings and photographs. The whole work is a model of its kind. G.R.D.

HISTORY AND GEOGRAPHY

BAER, Y. F. : *Israel Among the Nations*. (In Hebrew.) 1955. Pp. 144. (Bialik Institute, Jerusalem.)

This work, written by a distinguished historian, embodies lectures delivered to students of *Limmudhay Hayesodh* (of the nature of a B.A. General Course) at the Hebrew University of Jerusalem. It deals mainly with the history of the Jews in the period of the Second Temple, or, as the author prefers to call it, the Mishnaic Period in which he would find the key to the understanding of the whole of Jewish history. Modern historical works, it is argued, depend too much on the evidence given by Josephus—evidence which sheds light on the external political events, but little (and at that somewhat distorted !) on the *internal* history of the Jews. This is rectified by the author who assesses the history of the Jews mainly in accordance with its inner traditions and tendencies. One awaits the more exhaustive treatment of all the problems involved as promised by the author. M.W.

DENTAN, R. C. (ed. by) : *The Idea of History in the Ancient Near East.* (American Oriental Series, vol. 38.) 1955. Pp. x+376. (Yale University Press, and G. Cumberlege, London. Price : $5.00 and 40s. 0d.)

This is a happily conceived and excellently executed symposium on a most interesting subject. The nine contributors are all well-known American scholars, each a specialist in his own branch of Near Eastern studies, and all the essays contain valuable suggestions and points of view. One could have wished that the plan of the book included an essay on Hittite historiography, especially in view of Güterbock's suggestion that Israelite recorders of history may have owed something to the example set by Hittite chroniclers. It is also noteworthy that the only contributor who discusses with any fullness the concept of Time in relation to his part of the field is Professor Dinkler in his lecture on the Idea of History in Early Christianity, although Professor Millar Burrows does point out in passing that Israel had abandoned the cyclic conception of history prevalent elsewhere in the ancient Near East. The book will be found of great value to students of the Old Testament background. S.H.H.

GROLLENBERG, L. H. : *Atlas de la Bible,* with Preface by R. de. Vaux. Translated from the Dutch by R. Beaupère. 1955. Pp. 158+37 maps+408 photos. (Elsevier, Paris-Bruxelles-Amsterdam. Price : French Fr. 3,500.)

This Atlas, which appeared first in Dutch (see *Book List,* 1955, p. 21) has now been translated into French, and provided with a Foreword by Père de Vaux. The maps and illustrations are laid out as in the Dutch edition, but the names on the maps and the lightly printed notes which add so much to the usefulness have been put into French. Beside the letterpress numbers in the margins refer the reader to the illustrations which are relevant to each section. The 408 illustrations give a particular value to the work. Many of them are the author's own photographs, and as de Vaux says in his Foreword, they live and speak. They carry the reader back into the past and enable him to enter into the spirit of ancient times and to understand the life and culture of the people of the Bible lands. H.H.R.

KITCHEN, J. H. : *Holy Fields. An Introduction to the Historical Geography of the Holy Land.* 1955. Pp. 160+10 maps. (Paternoster Press, London. Price : 10s. 6d.)

This book admittedly owes much to Sir George Adam Smith's *The Historical Geography of the Holy Land,* but it is on a much smaller scale. The author makes judicious use of the relevant archaeological material to put into their setting some of the incidents recorded in the Old Testament, but he makes some incidental statements which will make informed readers arch their eyebrows, as when he says that the Hittites for a period of a thousand years (before 700 B.C.) " formed an impenetrable barrier between East and West," or that, on the occasion of the flood recorded in the book of Genesis, the down-flowing waters of the Tigris and the Euphrates " were met and dammed back by tidal waves from the sea." Such statements show that while this popularly written book may be read with profit, it should be read with discretion.   J.M.

LEMAIRE, P. and BALDI, D. : *Atlante Storico della Bibbia*. 1955. Pp. x+322+56+13 maps. (Marietti, Turin. Price : Lire 12,000.)

This finely produced work aims at providing the user with a means whereby he may be able, easily and quickly, to acquaint himself with the history and geography of Bible lands against a background of modern excavation and research. It contains, besides clearly printed maps, also plans, chronological tables, numerous photographs, and twenty chapters of text. Three of the chapters are of an introductory character ; in fourteen of them the history from the patriarchal period to the hegemony of Rome is outlined ; and the three remaining chapters deal with the life of Jesus, the Apostolic Age, and Jerusalem. Geographical names are transcribed in such a way that the maps will serve all editions of the atlas in other languages. The indices, which occupy nearly sixty pages, form an important part of the work. There is no bibliography, but authorities are referred to in the body of the text. The authors have a long familiarity with many of the places they describe, and they have given an account of the general story of the ancient Near East, to which Israel and the Old Testament belonged, which is scholarly, readable, informative, and up to date. The well chosen photographs, excellently reproduced, do much to bring this ancient world before the student as a living reality. The price of the work is high, but it offers a great deal. As a well presented historicio-geographical synthesis it deserves warm praise.   D.W.T.

NIELSEN, E. : *Shechem : A Traditio-Historical Investigation*. 1955. Pp. 384. (Gad, Copenhagen. Price : 30s. 0d., bound 35s. 0d.)

For those who are interested in the methods of the Scandinavian traditio-historical school of Old Testament scholarship this book will provide an excellent example of how this new type of criticism works. Dr. Nielsen has already given us an introduction to the methods of the school in his book *Oral Tradition*, and has now followed it up by a full-dress study, in excellent English, of all the Old Testament traditions relating to the important city of Shechem. Each passage with any bearing on the history of Shechem is first subjected to a careful textual critical analysis ; then the findings of the ' orthodox ' literary critics are examined and generally shown to be either misleading or unnecessary ; and finally the traditio-historical method is applied, often with very interesting results, to the relevant passages. The book is an important one, and will give those English scholars who are not familiar with the Scandinavian languages a good idea of the value and limitations of the new method as a tool for Old Testament study. S.H.H.

RICCIOTTI, G. : *The History of Israel*, translated by C. della Penta and R. T. A. Murphy. 2 vols. 1955. Pp. xiv+430, xii+476. (Bruce Publishing Co., Milwaukee. Price : $15 the set.)

The translator's Preface opens with the curiously inaccurate statement that the Italian original of this work was first published some fifteen years ago. The reviewer has possessed it for more than twenty-one years, the second edition of vol. 1 being dated 1934. It has since appeared in further Italian editions and in various other European languages (see *Book List*, 1955, p. 24). The appearance of an English edition is to be warmly welcomed. The bibliographical notes of the original have been omitted, but some additional notes giving references to recent English work have been added, and there has been some revision and addition (including some paragraphs on Qumran and Murabba'at, vol. i, pp. 83 ff.). Like the original, the work is well illustrated, and it offers a scholarly but cautious, and generally conservative, account of the history of Israel. On a number of disputed questions the author is content to state the varying views objectively and fairly. On the question of the relation of Nehemiah's work to Ezra's he favours the view that Nehemiah preceded Ezra, though this is presented as on balance probable, rather than certain. H.H.R.

ROWLEY, H. H. : *Nehemiah's Mission and its Background.* (Reprinted from *Bulletin of the John Rylands Library*, xxxvii. No. 2, March, 1955.) 1955. Pp. 34. (John Rylands Library, Manchester, and Manchester University Press. Price : 3s. 6d.)

This characteristically careful study follows and develops some aspects of the author's essay in *The Servant of the Lord* (1952), pp. 129-186. Nehemiah's work was that of rebuilding the walls of Jerusalem during the reign of Artaxerxes I, after a recent unofficial attempt had been frustrated. The work of Ezra took place in the reign of Artaxerxes II. Special attention is paid to Ezra iv. The work of other scholars is analysed with customary fairness. A.S.H.

ROWLEY, H. H. : *Sanballat and the Samaritan Temple.* (Reprinted from *Bulletin of the John Rylands Library*, xxxviii. No. 1, September, 1955.) 1955. Pp. 34. (John Rylands Library, Manchester and Manchester University Press. Price : 3s. 6d.)

The account of Sanballat in Josephus is judged to be unhistorical, and there is no reliable evidence for the dating of the Samaritan Temple ; neither does the date of that Temple decide the date of the Samaritan Schism. The date of the schism is probably mid-4th century B.C., and the building of the temple almost certainly earlier. The Pentateuch must have been completed and accepted before the schism. A.S.H.

GOODING, D. W. : *Recensions of the Septuagint Pentateuch.* (The Tyndale Old Testament Lecture, 1954). 1955. Pp. 24. (The Tyndale Press, London. Price : 1s. 6d.)

> The author finds that there are traces of a ' widespread revision ' for the alignment of the Greek with the Hebrew text ' that was independent of Origen, and probably ante-dated him ' ; indeed it may have been incorporated (without asterisks) in the Hexaplaric recension itself. It is moreover possible to distinguish the attitude adopted in various manu-scripts towards the revision : thus, B and a number of codices are opposed to it whereas A, papyrus 963 and others adopt its readings. The treatment deals mainly with Deuteronomy, but refers also to the remainder of the Pentateuch. Detailed analyses of eight examples illuminate the author's methodology as well as his results, and form a convincing conclusion to a penetrating and highly suggestive essay in the use of variants for the history of LXX transmission.   B.J.R.

KOOLE, J. L. : *Het Probleem van de Canonisatie van het Oude Testament.* 1955. Pp. 30. (Kok, Kampen. Price : Fl. 1.25.)

> For his inaugural lecture on entering the Chair of Old Testa-ment in Kampen Theological Seminary (18th Jan., 1955), Professor Koole chose to deal with the canonization of the Old Testament books. He can find no point at which the O.T. canon was decisively defined, in whole or in part—either at Jamnia or in the time of Ezra. The books were not canonized so that they might be distinguished from apocalyptic literature (in that case, why should Daniel have been canonized ?), nor can popularity or synagogue use have been *criteria canonicitatis.* The decisive quality which entitled a book to canonical status was divine inspiration, and instead of finding a definitive occasion when a binding decision on canonicity was made, Professor Koole traces a process of recognition of inspired scriptures back from the second century B.C. to the times of David and Samuel, notable landmarks on the way being the work of Ezra and Nehemiah and the discovery of the law-book in Josiah's reign. Among his teachers of Old Testament, to whom he acknowledges his indebtedness, our members will recognize the names of Bertholet, Rost and Sellin.   F.F.B.

LISOWSKY, G. : *Konkordanz zum Hebräischen Alten Testament.* Unter verantwortlicher Mitwirkung von L. Rost. Lieferungen 1 and 2. 1955, 1956 (Lief 2.) Pp. 128 each Lief. (Privileg. Württ. Bibelan-stalt, Stuttgart. Price : DM. 2.60 each.)

> A cheap and practical hand-concordance not printed but duplicated from a legible handwriting ; the text is that of BH³ vocalized. Only the verbs and nouns are completely worked out—all other words are also presented with German-English-Latin translation ; the verbs within the individual

root forms are arranged according to the sequence of the Books, while the nouns are arranged according to their function as subject, object or otherwise. Where necessary the subject is made recognizable by a brief note. The whole layout is brilliantly conceived and executed most carefully by G. Lisowsky. The work, which involved a tremendous effort and the price for which has been kept as low as possible, will be available in a complete form in 12 parts including the Aramaic parts and proper names, by the end of 1957. Although intended primarily for students and clergy, it should prove itself also as a complementary work beside Mandelkern's concordance.   W.Bg.

PRICE, I. M. : *The Ancestry of our English Bible*. 3rd revised edition by W. A. Irwin and A. P. Wikgren. 1956. Pp. xx + 364. (Harper, New York. Price : $4.00.)

> The second revised edition of this work was noticed in the *Book List*, 1950, pp. 31 f. This new edition embodies some minor changes, and continues the account of the Revised Standard Version, and, in addition, has an Appendix on the Dead Sea Scrolls. These had been referred to briefly in the text of the previous edition, but here there is a fuller survey of the views which have been advanced since the scrolls came to light, and a brief account of the finds so far announced, to the date of going to press. This valuable handbook, which offers a short general introduction to the text and versions of the Bible, with special reference to English editions, down to the latest, is suitable for wide circulation. That it has gone through sixteen printings in its various editions is the best testimony to the usefulness it has been found to have.
>   H.H.R.

SCHWARZ, W. : *Principles and Problems of Biblical Translation : some Reformation Controversies and their Background*. With an Introductory Note by C. H. Dodd. 1955. Pp. xvi + 226. (Cambridge University Press. Price : 25s. 0d.)

> This is not, as a superficial glance at its title might suggest, a guide to the modern translator; it is a historical study of theories which have guided translators in the past. There is, of course, the influence of tradition ; a version which has held a commanding position for centuries will not be readily set aside. But new renderings are always possible, sometimes imperative, and translators have, in fact, adopted one or other of two main principles which may be called the Philological and the Inspirational.
>
> As the sub-title suggests, Dr. Schwarz gives most of his attention to the first half of the sixteenth century. The great examples of the Philological school are Reuchlin and Erasmus, both of whom did their work before the Council of Trent dogmatically asserted the plenary inspiration of the Vulgate.

They believed it to be the duty of the translator to reproduce and transmit, as nearly as possible, the exact sense of the words used in the original, thus providing material for exegesis and a system of doctrine. Luther, on the other hand, while accepting the necessity for some standard of philological accuracy, insisted that a translation must conform to a theological pattern whether it be one laid down by ecclesiastical authority or one derived from key phrases and passages in Scripture itself. For this last purpose the direct co-operation of the Holy Spirit is indispensable.

The controversy between Reuchlin and Erasmus on the one side and Luther on the other has its roots in the ancient past. The Inspiration theory goes back to Philo (for the LXX Pentateuch) and Augustine ; the ancient champion of the philological view was Jerome ; the position of all three is discussed. Dr. Schwarz has written an interesting, scholarly, and instructive book, with good indexes and well documented. But an English reader might like to have heard more of Wicliff and Tyndale. T.H.R.

The Septuagint Bible, The translation of Charles Thomson as edited, revised and enlarged by C. A. Muses. 1954. Pp. xxvi+1426. (Falcon's Wing Press, Indian Hills, Colorado. Price : $6.50.)

Charles Thomson's translation was made from an edition of the Sixtine Text and was published in 1808. A revision had become timely. Dr. Muses has done his work well, and, with the help of the printers, has produced a presentable and easily handled edition. It will be of great value for the general reader without ready knowledge of Greek and also of use to the scholar for quick and easy reference. It presents, in translation, the text of *Codex Vaticanus* supplemented, where necessary, from the Sinaitic and Alexandrine codices.

Like all translations, it has to be used with caution ; occasionally the meaning is distorted by paraphrase (e.g., Isa. xi. 3), or by too rigid adherence to the meaning of the Hebrew text (e.g., Psa. lxxx. 2) or by maintaining the classical meaning of Greek words which had suffered change before coming into the LXX (e.g., Exod. xxiv. 11). However, as a translation, it is altogether a handy volume. L.H.B.

EXEGESIS AND MODERN TRANSLATIONS

AALDERS, G. C. : *Ezechiël verklaard*. I. Chs. i-xxiv. 1955. Pp. 400. (Kok, Kampen. Price : 34s. 6d.)

The Emeritus Professor of Old Testament in the Free University of Amsterdam gives us in this (the first of two volumes on Ezekiel) a further contribution to the series " Commentaar op het Oude Testament " of which he is joint-editor along with W. H. Gispen and J. Ridderbos. The commentary is detailed ; the linguistic scholarship is particularly impressive. One may gather that G. R. Driver's articles on Ezekiel in the 1954 volume of *Biblica* did not appear in time for the commentator to make use of them. The text is not printed *in extenso* either in Hebrew or in Dutch, but a Dutch rendering is provided for those passages whose translation demands special attention. In matters of criticism we find the enlightened and uncompromising conservatism which we expect from writers of the *Gereformeerd* school. With regard to Ezekiel, however, this outlook does not involve such a difference of opinion between Aalders and more liberal scholars as it does in some other parts of the Old Testament. The authenticity of the whole book is maintained ; the Massoretic text is held not to be so corrupt as many scholars think, although in certain places the need for emendation is accepted. In the Introduction (which covers the whole book) the vision of the new commonwealth is viewed as a prophetic picture, drawn on Old Testament lines, of the spiritual temple and worship of the New Testament. F.F.B.

BAVINCK, J. H. and EDELKOORT, A. H. (ed. by) : *Bijbel in de Nieuwe Vertaling van het Nederlands Bijbelgenootschap met verklarende Kanttekeningen. Genesis—Numeri.* 1954. Pp. 362. *Job—Hooglied.* 1952. Pp. 450. (Bosch & Keuning, Baarn. Price : per volume, Fl. 17.50, by subscription, Fl. 15.00.)

These are two volumes of an edition of the Bible in the new Dutch translation of the Netherlands Bible Society, supplied with simple annotations for the general reader and a brief introduction to each book. Edelkoort is general editor of the O.T. section, and he has contributed the introductions and notes on Genesis, Numbers and Psalms. A little attention is paid to criticism (e.g., in the introduction to Genesis the criteria for source analysis of the Pentateuch are mentioned but the classical four-document hypothesis " belongs to a by-gone period ") ; but for the most part the comments ignore it and concentrate on elucidating the sense of the Dutch text. The first section of Genesis (" The Creation ") runs from i. 1 to ii. 7 ; the rubric of ii. 4a is the superscription to the paragraph ii. 4b-7, which " reaches its end and goal in the creation of man." The title " David's " at the head of Ps. xxiv " emphasizes that the entrance celebrated in vs. 7-10 is made into the city of Jerusalem, and not into the Temple, which was not yet built in David's time." On " to my lord " in Ps. cx. 1 there is a note: " David, if he is the poet, certainly does not address his son Solomon thus. He rightly gives this title to the Messiah, who indeed was no other than the revelation of God in human form." F.F.B.

BEWER, J. A. : *The Book of Daniel.* (Harper's Annotated Bible Series, No. 12.) 1955. Pp. 38. (Harper & Bros., New York, and Eyre and Spottiswoode, London. Price : $0.75 or 6s. 0d.)

This volume has been published posthumously, and may prove to be the last of the series from the pen of Professor

Bewer. Like its predecessors it contains a brief Introduction, the text of A.V. and very brief comments. The book of Daniel is held to be a unity, coming from the Maccabaean period, and the rival modern views are left without mention. It offers an excellent brief guide to the book on this interpretation.

H.H.R.

La Sacra Bibbia tradotta dai testi originali con note a cura del Pontificio Istituto Biblico di 'Roma. Vol. VII. *I Profeti*—2. *Ezechiele— Daniele—Minori.* 1955. Pp. 440. (A. Salani, Florence. Price : Lire 1200.)

This is the second and last volume of this excellent translation to be devoted to the prophetic literature. The first, containing Isaiah and Jeremiah, was reviewed in the *Book List* for 1955, p. 30. Unlike the first volume, which was wholly the work of Vaccari, this second volume is the work of four translators, of whom Tondelli deals with Ezekiel, Rinaldi with Daniel, Vaccari with the series Amos-Zephaniah, and Bernini with Haggai-Malachi. As in the earlier volumes the introductions are extremely short, but the notes are often full, even though they usually fail to indicate the grounds for any correction of the text. Vaccari in his edition of Amos translates that *crux interpretum* ch. ii. 13 : " Ecco io vi faccio di sotto in- cagliare come s'incaglia un carro ricolmo di covoni." Here the important word (*incagliare*) has a common nautical sense, equivalent to *dare a secco* and meaning " to go aground." Here, it is evidently intended in the sense of " to bring to a standstill." The note explains that this rendering is based on the context and on the use of the cognate Arabic verb.

J.M.T.B.

The Holy Bible translated from the Original Languages with Critical Use of all the Ancient Sources, by Members of the Catholic Biblical Association of America. Vol. III. *The Sapiential Books (Job to Sirach).* 1955. Pp. viii+712. (St. Anthony Guild Press, Paterson, N.J. Price : $5.00.)

Vol. I of this work (*Genesis to Ruth*) was noticed in the *Book List,* 1953, p. 33. The present volume contains Job, Psalms, Proverbs, Ecclesiastes, Canticles, Wisdom and Sirach. The same critical principles are followed in this, as in the first, volume. The basic text used for the Psalms is, however, not the Massoretic, but the Hebrew text underlying the new Latin Psalter (2nd ed. 1945) ; and the translation of Sirach, though based on the original Hebrew text as far as it is pre- served, and corrected from the ancient versions, is often interpreted in the light of the Greek text. A short introduction precedes each book, and brief, but informative, notes ac- company the translation. The textual notes, which cover fifty closely printed pages, indicate that considerable care has been taken to provide an accurate translation. Yet there are many passages where a fuller acquaintance with recent philological work would have resulted in a different, and superior, translation. The translation too is sometimes less elegant than it might be. The volume, is, however, a substantial work of critical scholarship which the student of these Wisdom books will find it worthwhile to consult. D.W.T.

La Sainte Bible, translated into French under the direction of the École Biblique of Jerusalem : *Les Psaumes*, by R. Tournay and R. Schwab : 2nd ed., assisted by J. Gelineau and Th.-G. Chifflot. 1955. Pp. 520. (Les Éditions du Cerf, Paris. Price : Fr. 1,200.)

The first edition was reviewed in the 1951 Book List, p. 33. There are 77 pages of introduction. David did not write all the psalms attributed to him, any more than Solomon wrote Ecclesiastes, the Song or Wisdom. There are discussions of the liturgical use of the Psalter among the Hebrews and in the Roman Church, of Hebrew poetry, and of the general teaching of the Psalms. Great attention is paid to the classification of the psalms after the pattern set by Gunkel. The general style of previous volumes is maintained. The footnotes are particularly noteworthy for their references to other passages of Scripture. N.H.S.

La Sainte Bible traduite en français sous la direction de l'École Biblique de Jérusalem. 1956. Pp. xvi+1670+8 Maps. (Les Éditions du Cerf, Paris. Price : Fr. 1800 in cloth, available also in other bindings.)

The separate Old Testament volumes of what is known as the ' Jerusalem Bible ' have been noted in the *Book List* as they have appeared. Their main feature has been a series of very attractive new translations of the Hebrew text, accompanied by brief textual and exegetical notes. These translations, together with the corresponding translations of the New Testament books, have now been issued in a single volume, available in various bindings, but with some curtailment of the notes. Only by reference to the page facing the title-page is it possible to learn the names of the particular scholars who have been responsible for particular books. The direction of the work has been in the hands of a committee set up by the great Dominican school in Jerusalem, with Father de Vaux at its head, and the work is throughout sound in scholarship and graceful in style—if a foreigner may venture to express a judgement on style. The print is small but legible, and there are two columns on the page, save for Job, Psalms, Proverbs, Canticles, Ecclesiasticus, and Lamentations. The whole forms a handy volume of high value, which will be found of constant use not only to French readers. H.H.R.

VAN DEN BORN, A. : *Samuël uit de Grondtekst vertaald en uitgelegd.* 1956. Pp. 230. (Romen & Zonen, Roermond en Maaseik. Price : Fl. 9.86, by subscription Fl. 8.70.)

This is Part IV, Book 1, of the Dutch Catholic series *De Boeken van het Oude Testament.* Van den Born recognizes

732

that the books of Samuel narrate the happenings of one of the
most important periods of Israel's history : they are concerned especially to record the establishment of two dynasties
—the royal house of David, replacing that of Saul, and the
priestly house of Zadok, replacing that of Eli (cf. 1 Sam. ii.
35). The numerous duplicates in 1 Sam. i. 1-2 Sam. viii. 18
are explained not in terms of two sources but in terms of a
large number of ancient independent traditions from various
circles, which were brought into a continuous narrative,
together with the family history of David (2 Sam. ix-xx),
shortly before the captivity. The Deuteronomic redactor,
it is held, has contributed much less to Samuel than to Judges
or Kings ; for example, the anti-monarchical strata in the
account of the founding of the kingdom should not be ascribed
to his hand. The description of royal despotism in 1 Sam. x.
11-18 must be modelled on a later king than Solomon. The
possibility is recognized that Elhanan (the slayer of Goliath
in 2 Sam. xxi. 19) may have been another name of David's.
In 2 Sam. i. 21 the emendation *sede hare mawet* (" fields of the
hills of death ") is preferred to Ginsberg's " upsurging of the
Deep." The whole commentary is marked by the sound
scholarship which we have come to expect from this series
in general and van den Born's contributions in particular.

F.F.B.

BRUNO, A. : *Die Bücher Samuel : eine rhythmische Untersuchung.* 1955.
Pp. 304. *Die Bücher Könige : eine rhythmische Untersuchung.*
1955. Pp. 300. (Almqvist & Wiksell, Stockholm. Price : Swed.
Kr. 25 each.)

These volumes conform to the pattern of Dr. Bruno's earlier
works (see *Book List*, 1954, pp. 45 f., and 1955, pp. 31 f.).
The Hebrew text is rendered into German, and arranged in
lines and strophes, according to Dr. Bruno's rhythmical
principles. Remarkably little has to be left out as not con-
forming to this scheme. In addition to the rhythmical analyses,
there are some textual notes of a rather sketchy kind.

G.W.A.

BUTTRICK, G. A. (ed. by) : *Interpreter's Bible*, Vol. IV. *Psalms, Proverbs.*
1955. Pp. x+958. (Abingdon-Cokesbury Press, New York and
Nashville, and Nelson, Edinburgh. Price : $8.75, or 67s. 6d.)

W. S. McCullough writes a brief though fairly comprehensive
introduction on the usual topics of Psalm introduction, and
comments on 45 Psalms. W. R. Taylor comments on 105
Psalms. Both acknowledge their indebtedness to Gunkel, and
often follow his classification of the psalms. McCullough
rejects any idea of a New Year Festival, but Taylor favours a
post-exilic New Year festival with pre-exilic antecedents.
McCullough is cautious in dating the Psalms, but Taylor
comes down heavily for the post-exilic period. Both writers
show good knowledge of recent commentators, but neither
has really come to grips with, or made any real attempt to

apply, Mowinckel's conception of " cultic reality." The result is that the exegesis is normally conventional. Three further authors write the homilies.

C. T. Fritsch contributes a good article on Proverbs. His introduction assesses Israel's Wisdom in its international context, but perhaps not so adequately in its context in Israel (cf. i. 7 ad loc.). He is also to be praised for his commentary, for he carefully defines the parallelism of each verse, and builds his exegesis on the meaning of the Hebrew text before him. R. W. Schloerb gives the exposition.   G.H.D.

CASTELLINO, G. : *Libro dei Salmi.* (*La Sacra Bibbia* ed. S. Garofalo.) 1955. Pp. xii+912. (Marietti, Turin. Price : Lire 3800.)

The series of commentaries in the *Sacra Bibbia* series continues to make good progress, and the present volume by the lecturer in Assyriology in the State University in Rome is one of the most successful of them all. The author explains that it differs from the earlier volumes in two important respects. First, the psalms are here printed not in their numerical order or in the order of occurrence in the Roman Breviary, but in an order which takes account of their *genere litterario* and groups them in eleven categories, such as psalms of confidence, canticles of thanksgiving, hymns, royal psalms, and so forth. Secondly, the decision has been taken to separate the direct commentary on the text from the textual and linguistic study of the readings proposed in the translation. The latter (i.e., the textual and linguistic study) occupies no more than sixty pages and follows the numerical order. Castellino claims, no doubt justifiably, that this is the first fully critical study of the psalter to appear in Italian. There can be no doubt that the work has been admirably done, and that the author has fully controlled all the literature available at the time of writing. It is regrettable that neither Kissane's two volumes nor the second volume of Podechard were at hand at the time of going to press.   J.M.T.B.

CRIPPS, R. S. : *A Critical and Exegetical Commentary on the Book of Amos.* 2nd ed. 1955. Pp. xlii+366. (S.P.C.K., London. Price : 25s. 0d.)

This commentary, first published in 1929, has been found useful by many students, and the author, who died while this new edition was still in proof, has added substantially to its usefulness by bringing it up-to-date. There is a completely new preface of twenty-three pages, divided into six sections which deal respectively with archaeology, the date of the prophet's activity, the transmission of the book, the prophets and the cult, the translation and text, together with Hebrew poetry, and exegesis and application. On two central matters the author does not feel that work which has been done in the intervening years since his commentary first appeared obliges him to abandon his previous views. Amos is still placed in 742-741 B.C., or at earliest in 744-743 B.C. ; and the prophets are still thought to have been not opposed to sacrifice as such. References to recent writings are abundant in the preface ; a bibliography of commentaries on Amos published since 1929 is added ; and a few alterations have been incorporated in the text of the commentary itself within the limitations of the photographic method employed. D.W.T.

*DAVIES, G. H. and RICHARDSON, A. (ed. by) : *The Teachers' Commentary*. Revised Edition. 1955. Pp. xvi+572+16 plates. (S.C.M., London. Price : 21s. 0d.)

While the plan of the earlier editions of this commentary remains, most of the material is new, and the new material well reflects the development of Biblical study since 1932. It is no adverse criticism of the commentary to say that one would often wish for fuller treatment of various subjects and passages, for it is designedly related to passages appearing in the Agreed Syllabuses. Guidance for further reading is given both in the excellent General Bibliography, bibliographies on the Old and New Testaments, and those attached to articles and books of the Bible. Detailed comment on the individual articles is impossible in this note, but a word of special gratitude must be expressed for the clarity of the articles on Archaeology (G. E. Wright), History (H. H. Rowley), Literature (G. H. Davies), Religion of Israel (T. H. Robinson), and Theology of the Old Testament (H. W. Robinson—retained from previous editions). Sometimes (notably in I and II Kings—G. Ll. Jones) useful advice is given on teaching method. The 16 Maps at the end are taken from the Westminster Smaller Bible Atlas. The Commentary is a notable contribution to the teaching of Religious Knowledge in schools. A.S.H.

FOHRER, G. and GALLING, K. : *Ezechiel*. 1. (Handbuch zum Alten Testament, 1/13.) 1955. Pp. xxxvi+264. (Mohr, Tübingen. Price : DM. 20.80, or bound 23.50.)

Unlike recent volumes in this series, this commentary is not a revision of an earlier edition, but a new work. As the author himself remarks, it differs from its predecessor by Bertholet (1936) as radically as the latter did from Bertholet's earlier commentary (1897). A comparatively small number of short passages are regarded as not from Ezekiel. Following the lines of his earlier work (see *Book List*, 1953, p. 44), Fohrer finds it unnecessary to discard the traditional account of the date and milieu of Ezekiel's ministry. Both for its sober thoroughness and for its appraisal of recent work, this commentary is absolutely indispensable for serious study of Ezekiel. Galling's contribution, on xl-xlii., xliii. 10-27 (not xliii. 10-17, as in the 1936 work) has also been rewritten. G.W.A.

DE FRAINE, J. : *Rechters-Ruth, uit de grondtekst vertaald en uitgelegd.*
1956. Pp. 162. (J. J. Romen & Zonen, Roermond & Maaseik.
Price : Fl. 6.97, by subscription, Fl. 6.15.)

This volume forms Part III, Book 2, of the Dutch Catholic
series *De Boeken van het Oude Testament.* In accordance with
the general plan, de Fraine presents a new translation of
Judges and Ruth, and supplies his translations with introductions and commentaries. Full account is taken of recent work
on the two books, and copious use is made of older standard
commentaries, such as those of Moore and Burney on Judges.
De Fraine's own conclusions are generally conservative. He
inclines to discern behind the canonical Judges two successive
redactions, which were combined by a third " inspired redactor,"
not necessarily later than the exile. The events with which
Judges deals are dated within the period c. 1200-1040 B.C.
He draws upon Alt and Noth in his account of the historical
situation of that period. His conservatism appears, e.g., in
his agreement with Sayce that the capture of Jerusalem in
Jud. i. 8, " refers to the conquest of the territory of the
city-state of Jerusalem except for the fortress of Zion which
remained Jebusite," and in his reluctance to regard Jephthah's
argument of ch. xi. 14 ff. as directed against Moab rather than
Ammon (in spite of the mention of Chemosh in verse 24).
The book of Ruth (for whose historicity he argues) has as its
chief aim the praise of *pietas,* as shown by God to His people,
by Ruth to Naomi, and by Boaz to his family obligation. De
Fraine seems to regard a pre-Deuteronomic date as most likely
for it.   F.F.B.

GORDIS, R. : *Koheleth : The Man and his World.* (Texts and Studies
of the Jewish Theological Seminary of America, vol. xix.) 2nd ed.,
1955. Pp. xii+404. (Bloch Publishing Co., New York. Price :
$5.00.)

The first edition of this work was published in 1951 (see *Book
List,* 1952, p. 32), and it offered a full and valuable commentary, with careful discussion of all the major questions
which have gathered round this book. The second edition
is a reprint of the first, together with some supplementary
pages which add to its value. There are some additional
notes on the text—about a score in all—together with three
short special notes. The first of these offers further arguments
against the theory of an Aramaic origin for the book, the
second a rather general statement on the principles of scholarly
research as applied to the book of Koheleth, and the third a
criticism of Dahood's theory of a Phoenician background of
the book. Some additional bibliographical entries and corrigenda end the volume, which should not be missed by any
engaged on the study of Koheleth.   H.H.R.

*HEATON, E. W. : *The Book of Daniel.* (The Torch Bible Commentaries.) 1956. Pp. 252. (S.C.M., London. Price : 12s. 6d.)

Here is an excellent and up-to-date short commentary on the book of Daniel, well designed for the wide circle of readers for whom the Torch Bible is published. Almost half the volume is devoted to the Introduction, which offers a good survey of the many-sided problem of this book. It includes a section on the value of the Dead Sea Scrolls for its study, but it appeared too early to note the possible significance of the newly opened Aramaic scroll for the study of the Aramaic of Daniel. The commentary is brief, and the author's point of view throughout is the common critical view that the book was composed in the Maccabaean age, but used older traditional stories for its purpose. Since the author recognizes that the majority of scholars today divide the book amongst two or more authors, he might have given his readers more information on their views.   H.H.R.

The Book of Joshua, The Book of Judges and the Book of Ruth. 1955. Pp. 64. *The First and Second Books of Samuel.* 1955. Pp. 96. Translated by the Commission for the Revision of the Old Testament, appointed by the Hungarian Bible Council of the Evangelical Churches. (Press Department of the General Convent of the Reformed Church in Hungary, Budapest.)

In these parts of the new Hungarian Bible, especially in the Books of Samuel, the application of the principles adopted by the Commission as mentioned in the Foreword to the Genesis volume is conspicuous. Particularly the elasticity assumed for the conjunctive and consecutive *waws* giving them frequently adverbial force, helps not only to give more logical coherence to the narratives but also to overcome exegetical and constructional difficulties. The short explanatory notes on the place names take full account of the latest researches in this field and the reference system not only justifies the translation adopted but amounts veritably to a concise commentary.   P.R.W.

KRAELING, E. G. : *The Old Testament since the Reformation.* (Lutterworth Library, Vol. XLVII.) 1955. Pp. 320. (Lutterworth Press, London. Price : 27s. 6d.)

It is a good thing for Christian students of the Old Testament to be shown (or, perhaps, be reminded) that the problem of interpreting the Hebrew Scriptures and determining their relationship to the New Testament and their value for the Christian Church is nothing new, even though the issues may have changed somewhat with the development of literary criticism and the advance in knowledge represented by the natural sciences. This book, with its survey of the relevant discussion in Protestant circles from the time of Luther to the present day, will not only enable the beginner to bring the various aspects of the problem into focus, but will also serve to draw the attention of more advanced students to authors whose work, though still valuable, is liable to be overlooked. To the writer of this note the space allotted to some of the thinkers under review seems strangely out of proportion, but all the important issues are brought to light, and ample guidance is given to anyone who may wish to pursue the subject for himself. Indeed, if the final pages leave the reader saying to himself " So what ?", this is probably no less than the author intended. In short, this is a challenging book ; and it is challenging in a most helpful way.   A.R.J.

KRAMER, K. F. : *Numeri und Deuteronomium.* (Herders Bibelkommentar : Die Heilige Schrift für das Leben erklärt, Band II/1.) 1955. Pp. xiv+612. (Verlag Herder, Freiburg. Price : DM. 26, bound DM. 30, or by subscription DM. 22, bound DM. 26.)

This volume follows the general policy of others in the series. There is a new translation from the Vulgate into German, accompanied by an ample exposition and application. Critical questions are not elaborated, but where they are touched on the treatment is conservative. Thus the material in the Deuteronomic speeches is Mosaic, although Moses is not the author of the book in its present form. The census-figures in Numbers are artificial, it is remarked in passing, but the twofold census supplies a text for emphasizing the Christian importance of the family. The commentary aims throughout at the edification (in the proper sense of the word) of the Catholic laity.   F.F.B.

MOWINCKEL, S. : *Det Gamle Testamente IV. Skriftene.* 1. *Del.* 1955. Pp. 478. (H. Aschehoug & Co., (W. Nygaard), Oslo.)

A general characterization of the work of which this is a part was given in the *Book List* for 1948 (p. 9). The present volume, which contains Psalms, Job, and Proverbs, follows the same general lines : brief introductions, the Hebrew text rendered into Norwegian (printed as poetry), and concise expositions. Textual notes are printed separately at the end of the volume. The whole work is a masterpiece of compression, and is also lucid and interesting.   G.W.A.

NICHOL, F. D. (ed. by) : *The Seventh-Day Adventist Bible Commentary.* Vol. 4. *Isaiah* to *Malachi.* 1955. Pp. 1184. (Review and Herald Publishing Association, Washington, D.C. Price : $10.00.)

This volume contains three general articles at the beginning, one indicating the view of the chronology of the prophets taken here, one on the role of Israel in Old Testament prophecy, and one on the history of the interpretation of the book of Daniel, summarizing the massive four-volume work of Le Roy Froom on this subject, and indicating the Seventh-Day Adventist view on this book. Briefly this may be said to be the acceptance of the sixth century date, and the relating of the prophecies to the modern world, with an anti-papal interest.

Each of the books has a brief introduction, and throughout the writers—never identifiable for the individual books—show much modern knowledge. The unity of Isaiah is maintained, but in Isa. vii. 14 the rendering ' virgin ' is repudiated after careful and informed consideration. Jonah is held to be historical, and the prophet is placed early in the eighth century B.C. Joel is placed in the seventh century, but in a tentative sort of way ; similarly Obadiah is assigned to a late date, but without final commitment. Lamentations is accepted as Jeremianic. As is perhaps to be expected, the commentary on Daniel gets 140 pages, as against 175 for Ezekiel, 200 for Jeremiah, and 260 for Isaiah. While this is frankly a denominational commentary, presenting the particular views of its sponsoring body, and is governed by a rigidly conservative outlook wherever its special views are not at stake, it is not to be confused with the uninformed conservatism too often found elsewhere. H.H.R.

NÖTSCHER, F. (ed. by) : *Das Heilige Schrift in deutscher Übersetzung Echter Bibel : Das Alte Testament*, 1. *Genesis—Rut.* 1955. Pp. 720+1 map. (Echter-Verlag, Würzburg. Price : DM. 32, by subscription, DM. 28.00.)

This second edition of the new Echter Bibel consists of the re-issue in one volume of commentaries on the first eight books of the Old Testament published separately between 1949 and 1952. The separate books are by H. Junker (Genesis : *Book List*, 1950, p. 39 and Deuteronomy : *Book List*, 1953, p. 38), H. Schneider (Exodus, Leviticus, Numbers : *Book List*, 1953, p. 38), F. Nötscher (Joshua, Judges : *Book List*, 1951, p. 40) and J. Fischer (Ruth). There is a short introduction to the Pentateuch by Dr. Junker. The point of view is conservative, following the 1906 declaration of the Roman Bible Commission. The translation everywhere is good, the textual critical notes are at a minimum but are fuller where there is greater need (e.g., Judges v), and the exegetical notes are reasonably full, considering the necessity of the reduced format. The general purpose of the series is to provide helpful material for non-technical readers, particularly Roman Catholics, and this purpose is well fulfilled. N.H.S.

PIATTI, E. : *Il Libro dei Salmi, Collana Biblica*, No. 11. 1954. Pp. 480. (Edizioni Paoline, Rome. Price : Lire 1,200.)

The author of this translation of the psalms has already written several works on his favourite system of Hebrew metre, and is preparing a book with the title *La Poesia Biblica. La natura, le legge, i paradigmi*. Actually his system is sufficiently indicated in the title of an article that appeared in *Biblica* for 1950 : *I Carmi alfabetici della Bibbia, chiave della metrica ebraica?* Piatti makes a vigorous effort in the present work to imitate so far as may be, the Hebrew metre in his Italian version. He is convinced that a good translation, which preserves something of the metre of the original, makes an elaborate commentary superfluous. There are a few pages of notes on the text by way of appendix. J.M.T.B.

ROUSSEL, L. : *Le Livre de Josué*, chapitres 1-12. (Publications de la Faculté des Lettres de l'Université de Montpellier, VIII.) 1955. Pp. 144. (Presses Universitaires de France, Paris : Imprimerie Barnier, Nimes. Price : Fr. 700.)

The volume deals with the invasion of Canaan. The whole book is treated verse by verse, first a transliteration of the Hebrew, then a translation, and finally comments. The comments are careful and detailed, with every kind of point discussed with the utmost care, whether from the grammatical, lexicographical or literary point of view. The comments are notes rather than sustained discussions, and this makes the volume very useful to a student working by himself, especially if he is a beginner. N.H.S.

RUDOLPH, W. : *Chronikbücher* (Handbuch zum alten Testament, 21. Herausgegeben von O. Eissfeldt.) 1955. Pp. xxvi+338. (J. C. B. Mohr—Paul Siebeck, Tübingen. Price : DM. 24.40 or bound DM. 27.40.)

Professor Rudolph here continues his work on the writings of the Chronicler. (For his commentary on Ezra and Nehemiah, see *Book List*, 1950, p. 41.) We have learned to expect thoroughly competent and valuable work from both author and series, and again we are far from being disappointed. The Chronicler's work is the spear-head of an attack on the pretensions of the Samaritans, ' the first apology of Judaism.' The date is the first ten years of the 4th century B.C. The work has been interpolated by a later editor, notably in the whole of 1 Chr. iii, most of iv and v and vi, the composite psalm in xvi, the whole of xxiii : 3—xxvii, together with other sections, mostly short. These interpolations make the Levitical emphasis the work of a later editor and not of the Chronicler himself. The main original emphasis is the glory of the Davidic kingdom and of the theocratic state, centred in the Jerusalem Temple and its ritual and praise of God. The critical notes are full and detailed., N.H.S.

VELLAS, B. M. : *Eklektoi Psalmoi : Eisagoge, Keimenon, Hermeneia*. (Ekklesiastika Anagnosmata tes Palaias Diathekes, I.) 2nd ed. 1955. Pp. 376. (Athens.)

The first edition of this work was noticed in the 1953 *Book List*. Forty-five psalms are printed in the Septuagint text, and each is followed by a commentary in Modern Greek in which Vellas quotes copiously from the exegesis of the Greek Fathers, and also makes frequent reference to the work of contemporary scholars. On the opening words of Ps. xlv. 6 (xliv. 7 in the LXX numeration which Vellas naturally follows), three alternative interpretations are listed ; Vellas prefers that which takes the king to be addressed explicitly as " God," because he is either identified with the Messiah or viewed as a type of the Messiah. Deification of an ordinary king is totally excluded.

The introduction includes a general introduction to Hebrew poetry, a special introduction to the Psalms (with particular reference to their ecclesiastical use), and a short bibliography.

F.F.B.

WEISER, A. : *Die Psalmen I : Psalm* 1-60 *: Die Psalmen II : Psalm* 61-150. (*Das Alte Testament Deutsch*, 14 and 15.) 1955. Pp. 298 and 286. (Vandenhoeck & Ruprecht, Göttingen. Price : DM. 10.60 each.)

The first edition (1950) of these two volumes was noticed in the *Book List*, 1951, p. 44. The present edition has been reset, but the text itself is substantially the same. The additional twenty pages are due mostly to the footnotes which have been added, referring to books and articles which have appeared since the first edition was published. The two important features are the author's long discussion of literary types of psalms and his emphasis on the use of the psalms in connexion with the covenant and the high feasts. This is one of the most successful books in a successful series. N.H.S.

WIESMANN, H. (ed. KOESTER, W.) : *Die Klagelieder, übersetzt und erklärt.* 1954. Pp. xiv+276. (Hochschule Sankt Georgen, Frankfurt. Price : DM. 25.)

This full-length commentary, in duplicated form, is by a Roman Catholic scholar who had published a number of articles on the book of Lamentations before his death in 1948. It consists of an introduction, translation, exposition, and textual and philological notes. The author believes that the five poems to be found in the Lamentations form a unified whole, based upon a definite plan, and that Jeremiah composed them all. The date of the poems is thus somewhere between 586 B.C. and Jeremiah's death, c. 575-570, though a date as late as the latter need not be supposed. The poems were composed in Palestine or Egypt, perhaps in both countries, probably for a solemn occasion of mourning for the national disaster of 586 B.C. Their chief aim is to lead those who had suffered in this disaster to an understanding of the rulership of God, and to a mode of behaviour consistent with it, so that God's former favour to his people might be restored. The author's advocacy of the traditional authorship of the poems will limit the appeal of his book. He has, however, provided a reliable and readable translation, and his notes, which take particular account of the readings of the ancient versions, contain much useful material, as well as some interesting suggestions. Particularly valuable is his treatment of the religious contents of the poems. D.W.T.

ZIMMERLI, W. : *Ezechiel*, Lief. 1 and 2. (Biblischer Kommentar : Altes Testament, XIII, 1 and 2. General Editor, M. Noth.) 1955. Pp. 80. (Verlag der Buchhandlung des Erziehungsvereins, Neukirchen Kr. Moers. Price : DM. 7.00 each Lief., or by subscription DM. 5.85.)

The names of the General Editor of this new commentary series and of his colleagues are sufficient indication that its quality will be high. This first sample reinforces that impression, and shows that the work has been planned on a massive scale. The entire series will run to some 120 *Lieferungen*, and is expected to take several years to complete. The present issues cover 6 chapters. They contain : (a) bibliographical references (limited to the passage in question) ; (b) a German rendering of the text ; (c) detailed notes on textual and linguistic points ; (d) a full, general discussion of the structure and exegesis of the passage. The general introduction to Ezekiel will appear after the exegesis of the whole book. As a result of a careful, form-critical examination of the passage, and a consideration of the call of Moses, Isaiah, and Jeremiah, and the vision of Micaiah (1 Kings xxii), the author concludes that the throne-vision and the account of the call which follows it form a structural unity, though expanded by editorial additions. Its original form was composed by Ezekiel himself in exile.

Critical comment must be reserved until the commentary as a whole (and particularly the introduction) has appeared. But the patient and thorough treatment which has been given to these opening chapters justifies the expectation that this will prove to be a masterly commentary.   G.W.A.

LITERARY CRITICISM AND INTRODUCTION
(History of Interpretation, Canon, and Special Studies)

BOISSET, J. (ed. by) : *Le Problème Biblique dans le Protestantisme.* (Les Problèmes de la Pensée Chrétienne, 7.) 1955. Pp. 168. (Presses Universitaires de France, Paris. Price : Fr. 500.)

The seven essays of this volume (by M. Goguel, P. Lestringant, E. Jacob, H. Strohl, W. Eichrodt, O. Cullmann and F. Leenhardt) discuss, from different angles, the problems which the Protestant church has had to face and must still face through its possession of Scriptures comprising Old and New Testaments and through the variety of exegetical method which it has known since the Reformation or to which it has become heir. There is some overlapping among the essays but this in no way detracts from the value of this fresh discussion of the relation between Old Testament and New, Law and Gospel, promise and fulfilment, history and faith, historical and typological exegesis.

Old Testament scholars will find special interest in three of the essays. Eichrodt writes penetratingly on the relation between Old and New Testaments, stresses the need for recognizing that the history is written by men of faith in the salvation of God and draws attention to the fact that both Testaments present the kingdom of God as a main theme. Lestringant discusses the unity of the Bible and Jacob the Canonical authority of the Old Testament.

It is clear that both historian and theologian must study the Bible in their own way but must be able to relate their work to each other's. L.H.B.

BROWN, R. E. : *The Sensus Plenior of Sacred Scripture*. 1955. Pp. xiv + 162. (St. Mary's University, Baltimore. Price : $2.00.)

In recent years there has been much discussion of the principles of interpretation of the Bible, and the term *sensus plenior* has come to be used to denote a meaning which goes beyond the literal meaning, while being quite distinct from allegory or typology. The author here reviews the ancient and modern principles of interpretation, and shows that while the term *sensus plenior* is recent, the principle had been earlier recognized. He examines the arguments which have been raised against it, and defends it against them. One of the foremost exponents of the *sensus plenior* is our own Honorary Member, Canon Coppens. This dissertation is a valuable study of the various theories of hermeneutics, and the author's restraint in finding the *sensus plenior*, as shown in his criteria for recognizing where it may legitimately be found, contrasts with the tendency in some quarters to revive allegory and typology, whereby anything may mean anything. H.H.R.

CLEAVER, H. : *An Approach to the Old Testament*. 1955. Pp. viii + 212. (Epworth Press, London. ` Price : 10s. 6d.)

A text-book written for Methodist local preachers on trial and designed to cover their examination requirements. Twelve chapters cover the history, religion and literature of the Old Testament. Controversial matters are not discussed nor differing opinions mentioned, and no references are made to other books on the Old Testament. J.N.S.

GRELOT, P. : *Introduction aux Livres Saints*. (Notre Foi et Notre Vie, No. ix.) 1954. Pp. viii + 230. (Librairie Classique E. Belin, Paris. Price : Fr. 4.50, bound Fr. 5.80.)

This volume contains a very brief Introduction to the Old and New Testaments (about three quarters being devoted to the Old), designed to help the teacher of Scripture in schools. It covers history, religion and literature, and compresses within its relatively few pages the substance of a great deal of modern scholarly work on the Bible. The list of books suggested at the end for further reading consists exclusively of French Catholic works. H.H.R.

LEWY, I. : *The Growth of the Pentateuch*, with an Introduction by R. H. Pfeiffer. 1955. Pp. 288. (Bookman Associates, New York. Price : $4.50.)

The author offers this book as a systematic attempt to replace the Wellhausen view by a better. He opens by declaring that Hilkiah was the author of a seventh century Priestly Code. For this theory intuition suffices, and evidence is dispensed with. Deuteronomy is divided into an ED and a JD. The author of the former is stated to be Elisha, while the latter is attributed to the time of Hezekiah. Elisha's authorship of ED is established by the observation that it speaks of " cattle and sheep " and not " sheep and cattle." Its author was therefore a cattle breeder. Elisha was a rich cattle breeder, *Ergo* he composed ED ! We are told that Deuteronomy could not have been written in the time of Manasseh as an underground reform programme, or it would surely have been known to the priests and prophets, whereas 2 Kings xxii says it was unknown. It is therefore concluded that it was prepared by a " royal commission " under Hezekiah, consisting of officials, priests, and prophets ! It is unnecessary to pursue the author's fancies any further. The shades of Wellhausen will not be unduly disturbed. But it will be a puzzle to some readers why Professor Pfeiffer should characterize this as an ' important book.' H.H.R.

MALAMAT, A. : *Jeremiah, Chapter I*. (In Hebrew.) 1955. Pp. 64. (Jewish Agency, Jerusalem.)

This short study, intended mainly for the teacher, explains the first chapter of Jeremiah, dwelling largely, as one would expect, on problems connected with the call of the prophet and other prophetic phenomena. It also contains philological and archaeological, as well as bibliographical, remarks. M.W.

MARTIN, W. J. : *Stylistic Criteria and the Analysis of the Pentateuch*. 1955. Pp. 24. (Tyndale Press, London. Price : 1s. 6d.)

The author of this short study thinks that criticism of the Pentateuch has taken a wrong direction and that we should read it (but he limits himself practically to the Book of Genesis) as a literary unit. He claims that because attempts to analyse ancient documents in other languages, notably the work of Homer, have signally failed we must lay aside any such attempt on Scripture.

He suggests that documentary analysis began because of a mistranslation of Exod. vi. 2 which he would render : " I suffered myself to appear to Abraham, to Isaac, and to Jacob, as El-Shaddai, for did I not let myself be known to them by my name YHWH ?" Dr. Martin does not, however, follow this up by examining the actual use of the divine name. Again he mentions the possibility that what are apparently two accounts may be due to a device called ' rhetorical amplification '; he does not adduce any example of this but goes on to instance mistranslation (e.g., a perfect instead of a pluperfect in Gen. xxxv. 15) as a further reason for positing two accounts. L.H.B.

VAN DER MERWE, B. J. : *Pentateuchtradisies in die Prediking van Deuterojesaja.* 1955. Pp. xii+280. (J. B. Wolters, Groningen. Price : Fl. 12.)

This Afrikaans thesis was presented for the doctorate in theology of the University of Groningen. The author examines five bodies of Pentateuchal tradition in Isa. xl-lv—those relating to the creation, to the Garden of Eden, to the Flood, to the patriarchs, and to Moses and his time. He finds that Deutero-Isaiah exhibits a marked independence in his treatment of these traditions, which cannot be accounted for altogether by the consideration that the Pentateuch did not receive its final form until after his time. The brief references which he makes to the traditions suggest that they were well-known to his audience ; he uses them, however, with a theocentric and contemporary emphasis ; as God has acted in the past, he can and will act in the present. The Pentateuch traditions, in fact, are invoked as illustrations of the prophet's call : " Behold your God !" F.F.B.

MÖLLER, H. : *Sinn und Aufbau des Buches Hiob.* 1955. Pp. 124. (Evangelische Verlagsanstalt, Berlin. Price : DM. 4.20.)

This monograph by a Lutheran pastor is based on a thorough examination of the relevant literature from Merx and Budde through to the most recent studies. This is plain both from the excellent bibliography and the discussions in the text. The author discusses the relation between the prose and the poetry, and then proceeds to the significance of the various sections of the book of Job, both as isolated units and as parts of the whole. There was one author of the Book of Job but he does not keep to one consistent point of view. Elihu is no mere babbler, but has a definite contribution. The book is more scholarly than the blurb suggests, where the emphasis is laid on evangelical doctrines. These doctrines are to be found, but the basis of the discussion is scholarly and technical.
N.H.S.

MYERS, J. M. : *The Linguistic and Literary Form of the Book of Ruth.* 1955. Pp. x+70. (Brill, Leiden. Price : Fl. 10.)

The thesis of the author is that the book of Ruth was handed down orally for centuries in poetic form, but first had written form in the post-exilic period, when it was given mainly prose form, and the language was slightly modified. The mixture of archaic and late spellings, some syntactical constructions and some links of vocabulary with poetic passages elsewhere are studied, and the text is then printed with alleged poetic passages set out as poetry, and a translation with the same arrangement appended. That several of the speeches are in poetic form has been recognized by other scholars, and is not unusual, but it is hard not to feel that the poetic elements have been unduly added to, or to see why a book that had been orally transmitted in poetry for hundreds of years should not be written down in poetry. The author cites the *Chanson de Roland* as a parallel, but surely that was written down in verse. He also cites Judges iv and v, where again something quite different happened. Although the main thesis is not convincing, there is much useful material gathered here.   H.H.R.

STEINMANN, J. : *Ainsi Parlait Qohélèt.* (Témoins de Dieu, 15.) 1955. Pp. 136. (Éditions du Cerf, Paris. Price : Fr. 240.)

> The little books which compose this series are all well written and essentially readable. This volume maintains the standard. Qoheleth is the chief of the assembly (*qahal*) of sages. The date of the book is roughly 250 B.C. and it is the distilled essence of the master's words published by a pupil in aramaized Hebrew. He is neither hellenist nor prophet, though he welcomed the relics of Greek philosophy and was open to the best wisdom of the Nile and the Euphrates. Many aspects of his work and thought are examined—his aim, the monotony of the world, the ups and downs of life, the bankruptcy of wisdom and the dawn of joy. The total impression on the reader is that Qoheleth has something to say to the 20th century equally as to his own, because of his hard-headed, sceptical approach, uninfluenced by sentiment and romance.
> N.H.S.

LAW, RELIGION AND THEOLOGY

BAMBERGER, B. J. : *The Bible : A Modern Jewish Approach.* (Hillel Little Books, Vol. 2.) 1955. Pp. x+96. (B'nai B'rith Hillel Foundations, New York. Price : $1.50.)

> Dr. Bamberger is Rabbi of the West End Synagogue of New York City and has served as President of the Synagogue Council of America. This small book is an excellent presentation of the claims of the relevance of the Old Testament to the modern world. The author shows how modern archaeological research and critical scholarship have both enhanced the value of the Bible. He points out fairly both the insights which make the Old Testament unique and the deficiencies with which the new scholarship can effectively deal. The three concluding chapters are essentially constructive ; they demonstrate the Old Testament teaching as to the way of life, how the Old Testament is the Word of God, and the theme of the Chosen People.   N.H.S.

BIRKELAND, H. : *The Evildoers in the Book of Psalms*. (Avhandlinger utgitt av det Norske Videnskaps-Akademi i Oslo. II. Hist.-Filos. Klasse, 1955, No. 2.) 1955. Pp. 96. (J. Dybwad, Oslo.)

The author of this monograph here returns to the theme of *Die Feinde des Individuums in der israelitischen Psalmen-literatur* (1933), and seeks to show that the " evildoers " in the Psalms are to be regarded as foreigners or, in so far as Israelites may be included, those of the psalmist's fellow-countrymen who co-operate with the nation's enemies. This thesis is then used as a means of tracing the effect upon Israel's social ideology as the nation came to suffer bitterly from its contacts with foreign peoples ; and this in turn leads to a discussion of the issues of nationalism and univer-salism with special reference to the Psalms which celebrate the Kingship of Yahweh and the ideology of the New Year Festival. Professor Birkeland has no difficulty in showing that, as in the case of communal laments and the royal psalms, the enemies in some of the individual psalms of lamentation are foreigners ; but, despite what he says to the contrary, the present writer cannot see that this is any sufficient proof that they are such in every instance. Nevertheless, while the author again seems to overstate what is otherwise a good case, no serious student of the Psalter can afford to neglect this work, especially as it also contains a number of judicious comments on the question of cultic and other social " patterns."

A.R.J.

BIRKELAND, H. : *Myt och historia i Psaltaren* (Swedish translation by C. M. Edsman from the author's Norwegian MS.). 1955. Pp. 46. (Svenska Kyrkans Diakonistyrelses Bokförlag, Stockholm. Price : Sw. Kr. 2.)

This is a popular summary of the conclusions reached by the author in his larger work, *The Evildoers in the Book of Psalms*. Birkeland emphasizes the national character of the Psalter, contrasting it in this with the teaching of the great prophets. Although he makes extensive use of the cultic interpretation of the Psalms, and holds that most of them were connected with the autumn festival, he claims that in Israel fertility and creation were themes of subordinate importance in that festival : Yahweh's enthronement marked His victory, not over mythological adversaries, but over the actual enemies of Israel, who are, nevertheless, sometimes described in mytho-logical terms. While Birkeland's contentions offer a corrective to certain extreme views now current, the reviewer (who, at the time of writing, has not had the opportunity of consulting Birkeland's larger work) feels that there is some danger that the corrective may itself be taken to extremes. But Birkeland's forthright discussion is very refreshing. G.W.A.

747

Blank, S. H. : "*Of a Truth the Lord Hath Sent Me.*" An Inquiry into the Source of the Prophet's Authority. (Goldenson Lecture for 1955.) 1955. Pp. 18. (Hebrew Union College Press, Cincinnati.)

For the first of the newly instituted Samuel H. Goldenson Lectures Professor Blank selected the subject of prophetic authority, with special reference to the experience of Jeremiah. How did Jeremiah endeavour to convince his hearers (and, on occasion, reassure himself) that he was truly a prophet of Yahweh ? Six arguments are considered : (a) the verification of his prophecies by the event, (b) the prophet's immediate awareness of the voice of God, (c) the unpopularity of his message and the trouble into which it led him, (d) the fact that his message was contrary to his own wishes and was uttered by him only under an irresistible compulsion, (e) its consistency with previous prophecy, (f) its consistency with the known character of God. Jeremiah's experience points the way to the case for the authority of Scripture as a whole, and to the goal of our contemporary quest for religious certainty. Jews and Christians alike will welcome this moving and thought-provoking study.   F.F.B.

de Boer, P. A. H. : *Gods Beloften over Land en Volk in het Oude Testament.* (Libertatis ergo 4.) 1955. Pp. 60. (W. Gaade, Delft, Price : Fl. 225.)

This little book is a contribution to *Libertatis Ergo*, a liberal Protestant series of popular monographs. The author traces the idea of God's promises concerning the land and people of Israel through the Old Testament to the New—and still farther, to the *Urbs Syon aurea* of medieval Christian hymnody and to the influence of the idea on modern Zionism. Special attention is paid to two moments in the O.T. development of the idea—the patriarchal and the Mosaic. The God (or Gods) of the patriarchs and the God who manifested his redemptive power at the Exodus were originally distinct and only later identified (Ex. iii. 14). De Boer therefore deprecates the use of the term ' God of Abraham, Isaac and Jacob ' as a designation of the God of the whole Bible. " It is not without cause that Jesus is placed in the line of Moses, *Moses redivivus*, the deliverer from slavery and inaugurator of a new life, the brotherhood of men and fellowship with God, the marks of the kingdom whose king is God."   F.F.B.

Bonhoeffer, D. : *Schöpfung und Fall : Theologische Auslegung von Genesis* 1-3. 1955. Pp. 120. (Chr. Kaiser Verlag, München. Price : DM. 4.80.)

There have in recent years been important treatments of the early chapters in Genesis, one by von Rad in his commentary and the special study of Genesis i-xi by Zimmerli. Bonhoeffer's little book, though not the work of an Old Testament scholar, reveals remarkable insight, and is in places profoundly moving. It will be felt, however, that he frequently passes beyond the limits of exegesis proper, as for example, in his discussion of the two trees in the Garden, and sometimes, too, the explanations given are unduly subtle and paradoxical. As a contribution to the modern theological debate the book is worthy of close study.   N.W.P.

BRIGHT, J. : *The Kingdom of God in Bible and Church*. 1955. Pp. 292. (Lutterworth Press, London. Price : 30s. 0d.)

This book was published in America in 1953, under a slightly different title (see *Book List*, 1954, p. 56), after winning the Abingdon-Cokesbury prize of $7,500. It is to be hoped that its appearance in an English edition will greatly increase its circulation in Britain, where its fine scholarship and balanced judgement will find recognition and appreciation. The author is one of the ablest members of the group of American scholars known as the Colloquium, and by this broad review of Old Testament thought, with the focus of its interest in the idea of the Kingdom of God, he has stepped into the front rank amongst American Old Testament scholars. The English edition has been reset, and as the book contains four pages more than the American edition, published references to the one edition may not always correspond with the other.
                                                           H.H.R.

BRUCE, F. F. : *The Christian Approach to the Old Testament*. 1955. Pp. 20. (Inter-Varsity Fellowship, London. Price : 6d.)

Professor Bruce finds the Christian approach to the Old Testament in the view that our Lord himself regarded the O.T. as the preparation for the Gospel. The O.T. contains a saving history which is a record both of God's redemptive revelation through His deeds and words, and also of man's response in words and deeds. The booklet is a useful summary of the double theme, for that theme leads to Christ as our Apostle and High Priest.   G.H.D.

CHARY, TH. : *Les Prophètes et le culte à partir de l'exil*. (Bibliothèque de Théologie, Série III. Théologie Biblique 3.) 1955. Pp. x+314. (Desclée et Cie, Tournai. Price : Belgian Fr. 150.)

The earlier part of this monograph is devoted to a comparison of Ezekiel's Temple with that of Solomon as described in the book of Kings, that implied by the P Code, and that of the Chronicler ; and this is followed by a study of Deutero-Isaiah, Trito-Isaiah, Haggai and Zechariah, Malachi, Joel, Deutero-Zechariah and Daniel with a view to determining the attitude to the cultus which is reflected in these works. The author finds that following the Exile there was a real attempt to introduce a new spirit into the formal worship of the Jerusalem Temple, although this was marred by a restriction of outlook which failed to do justice to the universalism of Deutero-Isaiah. The whole forms a careful study, which pays due regard to the dating of the literature on freely critical lines ; and *inter alia* it serves to show once again that we must beware of hasty generalizations as to what constitutes a typical prophet and what is the attitude of such a prophet to the cultus.   A.R.J.

CHASE, MARY E. : *Life and Language in the Old Testament.* 1955. Pp. 202. (Norton, New York. Price : $3.00.)

Professor Chase's earlier book along similar lines, *The Bible and the Common Reader* became popular by reason of its warmth and charm, and the same virtues will no doubt sell this book as well. The present reader enjoyed it, and easily perused it at a single sitting. It is refreshing to read ' shop ' untrammelled by the usual jargon, but rather to be reminded how the Iliad and the Odyssey can be contrasted with the Old Testament and even to come across the names of T. S. Eliot and Dylan Thomas. There are some acute observations on the psychological nuances of some O.T. terms, but there are also some frightening naïvetés, such as, e.g., that the O.T. is one of ' the great monuments . . . of any literature, not because of its material, but rather because of the manner in which the material is presented.' Another submission, in keeping with it, is that ' the one translation closest in the *tone* and the *spirit* of its language to its Great Original is the King James version.' The next best, apparently, is the Jewish translation, *The Holy Scriptures*, 1917.   B.J.R.

COPPENS, J. : *De Messiaanse Verwachting in het Psalmboek.* (Klasse der Letteren XVII, No. 5.) 1955. Pp. 36. (Paleis der Academiën, Brussels.)

This offprint from the *Mededelingen van de koninklijke Vlaamse Academie voor Wetenschappen, Letteren en Schone Kunsten van België* presents a study of the messianic hope in the Psalter, with special reference to Pss. lxxii, cx and ii. A fresh translation of these three psalms is given in Flemish. Coppens denies that the expectation of an eschatological Messiah is found in these or other psalms. We have, on the one hand, a series of psalms which celebrate the future advent of the divine kingdom without any reference to a Messiah ; we have, on the other hand, portrayals of an ideal king, but he is not the Messiah in the proper eschatological sense to which Coppens would confine the term. In this he differs from the ideal king of Isa. ix. 6 f., xi. 1-10, etc., who is definitely eschatological. If some passages from the " royal psalms " have been interpreted Christologically in the N.T. and the Fathers, that will have been in a typological and " plenary " sense. There is a comprehensive bibliography of relevant literature covering the period 1855-1955.   F.F.B.

DELLA CROCE, P. M. : *L'antico Testamento, Sorgente di Vita Spirituale.* 1954. Pp. 796. (Ancora, Milan. Price : Lire 2,000 or 25s. 0d.)

This large work, containing something like a quarter of a million words, appears to be an accurate rendering of the original French book with the title *L'Ancien Testament, Source de la Vie Spirituelle* (cf. *Book List*, 1953, p. 52). It is made up of three parts, namely, " God and the Soul," which deals with divine revelation, the human soul, and the union with God through love ; " Divine Love," studied under the headings Father, Saviour and Spouse ; and " the Ways of God," treating of faith, wisdom, and the purifications in the spiritual life that lead to the transforming union. The text of the Bible is quoted frequently, and often at great length. On the whole, the book would have been more successful if the subject-matter had been set out more concisely. J.M.T.B.

DRONKERT, K. : *Het Mensenoffer in de Oud-Testamentische Wereld.* 1955. Pp. 192. (Bosch & Keuning, Baarn. Price : Fl. 5.40.)

This work on human sacrifice in the O.T. world is a popular recasting of the author's doctoral dissertation *De Molochdienst in het Oude Testament* (see *Book List*, 1954, p. 59). He gives a useful review of the instances of human sacrifice in the O.T., and of others which have been explained in terms of human sacrifice, but wrongly, in his judgement. Thus he argues against the view that the narrative of Hiel the Bethelite (1 Kings xvi. 34) implies foundation-sacrifices. The narrative of Abraham and Isaac in Gen. xxii is an example of " divine pedagogy." It is probably because he has the general Christian public in view that he labours (superfluously, we should think) to prove that Jephthah really did sacrifice his daughter as a burnt-offering instead of heeding the prohibition of Lev. xviii. 21 or profiting by the provision of Lev. xxvii. 1 ff. These laws, being Mosaic, he holds, were in existence in Jephthah's day, but he would not have been familiar with them because of his largely Canaanite upbringing. Mesha's son (2 Kings iii. 27) was at least thirty years old, we are told, but we are offered no specific evidence on the point. There are three appendices—one on Eissfeldt's theory about Moloch, one on child-sacrifice among the Carthaginians, and one in which the massacre of human beings under the *herem* is sharply distinguished from human sacrifice. F.F.B.

EDELKOORT, A. H. : *De Profeet Samuel.* 1955. Pp. 192. (Bosch & Keuning, Baarn. Price : Fl. 5.40.)

This is the published form of a series of lectures which the author gave to a group of ministers in Utrecht University in 1953. The book is in effect an exposition of 1 Sam. i-xv, presented in such a way as to bring out the significance of Samuel's personality and achievement in the setting of his times. Edelkoort draws upon the latest linguistic and historical information, and uses the findings of textual and literary criticism, while maintaining an element of practical religious application throughout. His study appears admirably suited to the kind of public to which it was originally given in lecture-form—a public consisting of those who, without being specialists in the academic sense, have an intelligent and practical interest in Biblical exposition. Such questions as the prophetic office and the nature of kingship in the ancient Near East are treated lucidly. It is thanks to Samuel, the author thinks, that the king in Israel was never treated as a divine person and was never allowed to become a complete despot. Samuel's prophetic ministry was marked by three new features : he prophesied woe as well as blessing ; he prophesied of individuals as well as of nations ; he insisted that sacrificial worship was no substitute for heart-devotion. His name is interpreted (with the aid of Akkadian) as meaning ' child of God ' ; his temperament is classified as ' genuinely choleric.'

F.F.B.

GELIN, A. : *The Key Concepts of the Old Testament*, trans. by G. R. Lamb. 1955. Pp. 94. (Sheed & Ward, London. Price : 6s. 0d.)

This is a translation of *Les Idées Maîtresses de l'Ancien Testament*, 1948, published by Les Éditions du Cerf, Paris, as the second volume of the series *Lectio Divina* (See *Book List*, 1949, p. 42). The author, a Roman Catholic professor at Lyons, deals with God's plan of self-revelation and human redemption, culminating in Christ. Special emphasis is laid on the development of the idea of Messiah. The concluding section deals with Personal Salvation, and here the main theme is the idea of retribution, at first collective, and then personal. The difficulties associated with personal retribution in this world lead to belief in a life hereafter. The material is familiar, but the presentation is fresh and stimulating. The bibliography of the French edition has been omitted. N.H.S.

GRELOT, P. : *Pages Bibliques*. (Notre Foi et Notre Vie, No. viii.) 1954. Pp. 386. (Librairie Classique E. Belin, Paris. Price : Fr. 600, bound 725.)

This consists of a series of selected passages from the Bible accompanied by very brief notes, designed to give a general conspectus of the contents of the Bible. It is concerned almost exclusively with the Old Testament (including the Apocrypha), and in general it accepts critical datings (e.g., Deuteronomy follows the eighth century prophets. P follows Jeremiah but curiously precedes Ezekiel and Deutero-Isaiah, Ruth and Jonah follow Trito-Isaiah, while Joel follows Malachi, and Daniel follows Ben Sira). The selected psalms are scattered in various places. The volume contains a number of illustrations, often from archaeological sources. H.H.R.

JACOB, E. : *Théologie de l'Ancien Testament.* (Manuels et Précis de Théologie.) 1955. Pp. 288. (Delachaux et Niestlé, Neuchâtel. Price : Fr. 1100.)

Jacob follows the order of presentation of Köhler rather than that of Eichrodt, viz., theology, anthropology and soteriology. In an introductory section he traces the discipline of Old Testament theology back to the Yahwist and the Deuteronomist, emphasizes that the New Testament can properly be regarded as a° theology of the Old, since it sets forth Jesus Christ as the Messiah, and traces briefly the history of Old Testament theology up to its modern renaissance ; and he adds an interesting section on the relation of his subject to other branches of Old Testament study, such as history, literary analysis and archaeology.

The first section of the book deals with the nature of God ; for Jacob the dominant truth is that God is alive. Resting on that pivotal point, he proceeds to discuss the divine names, the relation of Yahweh to other gods, the heavenly powers, and the manifestations (angel, face, glory and name) and the attributes of God. The second section is concerned with God's activity ; He is the Creator and the sovereign Lord of history. There follows in logical sequence a study of the nature and destiny of man and of the persons and the related institutions whose function it is to maintain the bond of the creature to the Creator. The final section, while succinctly written, is unexpectedly short, especially in the chapter which deals with sin and redemption. The value of the book is enhanced by the ' Indications bibliographiques ' which are given at the head of the chapters and also of the main chapter divisions. J.M.

JAMES, E. O. : *The Nature and Function of Priesthood : A Comparative and Anthropological Study.* 1956 (1955 on back of title-page). Pp. 336. (Thames and Hudson, London. Price : 25s. 0d.)

In the already considerable list of books to his credit this is perhaps the most important which Professor James has yet produced. It is no small achievement for a scholar who is also a priest in the Anglican Church to have succeeded in dealing objectively with a subject round which so much emotion has gathered. Since Milton wrote, " New Presbyter is but old Priest writ large," the winds of controversy have never ceased to blow about the claims of the priesthood. Professor James has approached the subject entirely from the anthropological and *religionsgeschichtlich* point of view. He begins with a careful discussion and description of the early magico-religious activities of the priest and medicine-man, where his wide knowledge of Comparative Religion enables him to speak with authority. He goes on to discuss the more developed forms of the priesthood in the ancient civilizations of Egypt and Mesopotamia. There is a valuable study of the relations between prophet and priest, and between kingship and priesthood. The recent work done on the subject of cultic associations of prophets has received due notice. Priesthood and sacrifice, the thorny subject of absolution, the priest as the guardian of both secular and sacred learning, all these subjects are illuminated by Professor James's ample learning. The only important omissions noted in the very full bibliographies appended to each chapter are Professor G. R. Driver's study of the Code of Hammurabi, and Thureau-Dangin's *Rituels Accadiens* which contains much valuable information about the functions of the priesthood in ancient Babylon. This is a book of the greatest value to the student of the history of religion.   S.H.H.

JENNI, E. : *Die theologische Begründung des Sabbatgebotes im Alten Testament.* (Theologische Studien, ed. K. Barth, 46.) 1956. Pp. 40. (Evangelischer Verlag, Zollikon-Zürich. Price : Fr. 3.60.)

This is a careful study of the Sabbath commandment in its presumed Mosaic orginal form, and of the ' motive clauses ' attached to it by the deuteronomic and priestly schools respectively. Sabbath may have had an earlier history, but the Mosaic commandment emphasizes, not so much the prohibition of work, as its relationship to the Saviour and Covenant God. The deuteronomic active clause emphasizes the *heilsgeschichtliche* quality of the Sabbath. The priestly school sees in the Sabbath the goal of Creation and a sacrament in which ultimately all mankind must share. The fulfilment is not in the Christian Sunday, but in the work of Christ.
A.S.H.

JOHNSON, A. R. : *Sacral Kingship in Ancient Israel.* 1955. Pp. viii+ 156. (University of Wales Press, Cardiff. Price : 12s. 6d.)

After a series of valuable monographs on what may be called Biblical anthropology, Professor Johnson has returned to the theme of the essay which he contributed to *The Labyrinth* more than twenty years ago, entitled ' The Rôle of the King in the Jerusalem Cultus.' Although the lapse of time and prolonged study have produced certain modifications in the position there taken up, it is interesting and encouraging to find that the central elements of his exposition persist, with important developments. The book is in the main a minute and careful study of all the psalms which have any bearing on the subject of sacral kingship in Israel. The most noteworthy development is that the author gives a much greater prominence to the eschatological interpretation of the psalms as opposed to the historical. This is Professor Johnson's most important book hitherto, and is characterized by that combination of brilliance and painstaking scholarship which we have come to expect from him.   S.H.H.

KEVAN, E. F. : *The Evangelical Doctrine of Law.* (Tyndale Biblical Theology Lecture.) 1955. Pp. 28. (Tyndale Press, London. Price : 1s. 6d.)

Principal Kevan discusses the nature, the function, the abuse, the termination and the use of law. His clear statement enriched by many apt quotations is praiseworthy because it brings the idea of law within the orbit of grace. On the other hand I miss (a) the attempt to relate the idea of law to the idea of the ' living ' God ; (b) the treatment of the various O.T. terms for law (those for sin are given) ; (c) any real appreciation of the value and purpose of cultic law as *Heils-gesetz,* for evangelical and cultic are not exclusive terms. What the author has written he has written well, but there are some things which ought not to have been excluded even in 24 pages. G.H.D.

KLAUSNER, J. : *The Messianic Idea in Israel,* trans. by W. F. Stine-spring. 1955. Pp. xvi+544. (Macmillan Co., New York and Allen & Unwin, London. Price : $7.50 and 25s. 0d.)

Those who have read the two previous books by Professor Klausner, *Jesus of Nazareth,* and *From Jesus to Paul,* will welcome the appearance of the third volume of the trilogy, competently translated by Professor Stinespring, the translator of the second volume of the series. The veteran scholar covers a vast range of Jewish literature from the earliest beginnings of Hebrew writing up to the completion of the Mishnah. The part of the book which will be specially useful to those who are not skilled in the intricacies of Talmudic literature is the third section which deals with the Messianic idea in the period of the Tannaim. Not all scholars will agree with Klausner's insistence on the absolute originality of the Israelite Messianic conception, and his denial that anything resembling it is to be found in any of the early Near Eastern religions. The appendix on The Jewish and the Christian Messiah is of considerable interest. S.H.H.

Moïse, L'Homme de l'Alliance. (Numéro special, Nos. 2, 3, 4, de 1954 des *Cahiers Sioniens.*) 1955. Pp. 406. (Desclée et Cie, Tournai.)

This is a study of Moses, the man behind the traditions, and the portrait of him presented in the Scriptures, and in Jewish, Christian and Muslim thought. It follows a similar study of Abraham, *Abraham père des croyants (Cahiers Sioniens,* 1951). Whatever further traditions and speculations are associated with Moses in later tradition, certain constant features remain : founder and deliverer of the people of God, lawgiver, and above all, mediator of the Covenant relationship. The presentation of the biblical material follows the pattern accepted by conservative critical study ; the post-biblical material is ably summarized and well documented. It is a gathering together of information, much of which from the post-biblical period would not otherwise be readily accessible. One can recognise also an irenical purpose in this study of one who stands at the beginning of, and is reverenced by, the three traditions. A.S.H.

MORRIS, L. : *The Apostolic Preaching of the Cross.* 1955. Pp. 296. (Tyndale Press, London. Price : 15s. 0d.)

The claim of this work to a place in this Book List is that it deals with the meaning of a number of Old Testament terms. It consists of an examination of a large number of New Testament terms used in the interpretation of the death of Christ, in relation to the meaning of the corresponding terms in the Old Testament, as well as their use in Septuagint and New Testament Greek. The meaning of various terms for ' redemption,' of ' covenant,' of the ' blood,' and of terms for ' propitiation ' and ' justification,' is discussed. Too much ground is covered for any thoroughgoing study of these terms, or for any original contribution to be made to their understanding ; and the author is not widely acquainted with the literature in which they are discussed. He does, however, mediate to his readers much generally sound information on the meaning and use of the terms. H.H.R.

NAPIER, B. D. : *From Faith to Faith : Essays on Old Testament Literature.* 1955. Pp. xxii+224. (Harper, New York. Price : $3.00.)

This book is by one who was brought up to sing ' I believe that the Bible is true, though the critics have torn it apart,' and who still holds that faith, though he now adopts critical techniques. Like many other authors today, he is concerned to show that there is a fundamental unity running through the faith of Israel, despite the diversity of sources drawn on in the compilation of individual books, and despite the long religious history recorded in the Old Testament. His method is to select examples of certain types of literature and to show by a brief exposition that they are born of a faith which is at bottom one. The types he uses are Myth, Legend, History, Prophecy, and Law. Genesis provides the material for the first two, the reigns of David and Solomon for the third, some prophecies of Proto-Isaiah for the fourth, while the last deals more generally with the Codes. It is surprising that any exposition of the faith of Israel should omit Moses, or that any account of the categories of its literature should omit the Psalms or the Wisdom Literature, while prophecy might have been more widely represented. Nevertheless, Dr. Napier's book will serve a real purpose in making widely known one of the major trends in the study of the Old Testament today. H.H.R.

NEHER, A. : *L'Essence du Prophétisme.* 1955. Pp. 360. (Presses Universitaires de France, Paris. Price : Fr. 900.)

What gives this book its special value is the fact that the author, who is careful to point out that he writes from a purely Jewish standpoint, has sought to study the subject of Hebrew prophecy against the wider background of (a) the phenomena of prophecy in the ancient Near East generally, and (b) such characteristic categories of Hebrew religious thought as are indicated by the terms *rûaḥ*, *dābār* and *bᵉrît*, and, equally important for the author's argument (cf. *Book List*, 1951, p. 48), the Hebrew concept of time. For the rest, the reader is offered a short history of Hebrew prophecy from the time of Abraham to that of Deutero-Isaiah, an examination of certain outstanding themes in the work of the canonical prophets (e.g., the symbolism of the marital relationship and its bearing on such notions as those of the *bᵉrît*, *ḥesed* and *ḥāsîd*), and, finally, an examination of the prophet's relations with his fellow-members in society and the effect of his call on his own personal life. If the treatment of the subject as a whole is somewhat sketchy, it is nevertheless admirably suggestive and very attractively written ; and it has the special merit of dealing with a well-worn theme in a refreshingly different way. A.R.J.

POLACK, A. N. : *Ha-Tenak Wehattenū'ōt Hassosī'aliyōt Bā'ammīm.* 1954. Pp. 308. (Ayyanot, Tel-Aviv.)

The author of this all-Hebrew book traces the Old Testament influences on the world social movements from the time following Alexander's conquests, when the " City of God " of the Psalms was contrasted with Plato's Republic in the Hellenistic world, to modern Social Zionism which aimed more at restoring the Biblical " Land " than its ethics and morals. These influences were manifold and expressed themselves in different ways : the Biblical idea of the brotherhood of man on the Stoics ; its social legislation on the whole on the Neo-Platonists ; the Nazirite and the communal life of the " Sons of the Prophets " as lived by the Essenes on the monastic movements culminating with Chrysostom. Its anti-feudalism roused the early Crusaders and led to the Carmelite movement on the one hand, and caused numerous revolts among the Russian peasants between the 17th and 19th centuries on the other ; its idea of social justice was a driving force in the Reformation and, finally, the enthusiastic description of the settlement in Palestine after the Exodus as well as after the Babylonian Exile and the Old Testament sympathy for agriculture in general was an encouragement for many efforts at colonization from the first Puritan settlers in America to the Mormons. The author deals with the subject from the point of view of the history of Socialism. The Biblical student nevertheless, may perhaps find interest in the introductory chapter (pp. 4-43) where the social values of the Old Testament are assessed in terms of modern social economics. P.R.W.

RAMM, B. : *The Christian View of Science and Scripture.* 1955. Pp. 256. (Paternoster Press, London, by arrangement with Eerdmans Press. Price : 12s. 6d.)

Dr. Ramm's book is written from what is usually termed the conservative standpoint, but he himself distinguishes between the hyper-orthodox and the orthodox, his own association being with the latter. His analysis of the conflict between science and religion in the last hundred years is well done. His general attitude with regard to scriptural passages in which the question of ' scientific accuracy ' is raised is that he believes in the full inspiration of the Scriptures but recognizes latitude of interpretation. The language of the Bible " with reference to natural matters " is popular, not scientific, it is phenomenal (i.e., concerned with appearances) and reflects the culture of the times in which it was used by the various writers. With regard to the Creation-Evolution conflict of ideas, he is not wholly on the one side or the other, but propounds the view of " progressive creationism." This book will not receive whole-hearted commendation from conservatives or moderns ; that is equivalent to saying that it has something to say to both.   J.M.

RIDDERBOS, N. H. : *Israëls Profetie en "Profetie" buiten Israël.* (Exegetica, Series II, Part 1.) 1955. Pp. 62. (Uitgeverij Van Keulen, Delft. Price : Fl. 3.50 separately ; Fl. 2.75 to subscribers to the series.)

The author gives a comparative study of Old Testament prophecy and parallel non-Israelite manifestations in the Ancient Near East. He adduces non-Israelite examples from Syria and Palestine, from Phoenicia and Ugarit, from Mari and other parts of Mesopotamia, and from Egypt. He recognizes the similarities between some of these manifestations (especially the *muḥḥûm* or *maḥḥûm* of Mari) and prophetic activity in the Old Testament, although he points out that nothing in the non-Israelite world can be compared with the preaching of an Isaiah or a Jeremiah. The possibility is admitted that Israel's forefathers were familiar with certain phenomena which Yahweh later adapted to his service. The fact that Ridderbos is a scholar of the most orthodox Reformed tradition adds weight to his warning against a " cheap apologetic " ; he illustrates what he means by an extended critique of E. J. Young's *My Servants the Prophets*, where the arguments for the dissimilarity between Israelite and non-Israelite prophecy seem to him to be unduly strained. On the other hand he takes issue with Noth for overlooking essential differences. For his own part, he maintains that the essential differentiation lies in an act of faith on the part of those who, like himself, hold that Old Testament prophecy was unique because it was an instrument of the one true God.   F.F.B.

ROBINSON, H. WHEELER : *The Cross in the Old Testament*. 1955.
Pp. 192. (S.C.M., London. Price : 10s. 6d.)

The three monographs, *The Cross of Job* (1938 revision of 1916
edition), *The Cross of the Servant* (1926), and *The Cross of
Jeremiah* (1925), without the bibliographies and questions
for discussion, are republished in this volume. These scholarly
and deeply religious interpretations of suffering in the Old
Testament are of permanent worth and the publishers are to
be congratulated on making them once more available.

A.S.H.

ROTH, L. and ELMSLIE, W. A. L. : *The Significance of Biblical Prophecy
for our Time*. (Rabbi Mattuck Memorial Pamphlet, No. 1.) 1955.
Pp. 20. (London Society of Jews and Christians. Price : 2s. 0d.)

These two scholars, speaking from their Jewish and Christian
standpoints respectively, both agree in showing that the
significance of the prophets for our time lies in their spiritual
authority, but the one emphasizes the moral content and
the other the religious content which looked ahead towards,
and was fulfilled in,· Jesus.

L.H.B.

ROUBOS, K. : *Profetie en Cultus in Israël*. 1956. Pp. 132. (Veenman &
Zonen, Wageningen. Price : Fl. 8.50.)

This doctoral dissertation by a pupil of Edelkoort's consists of
an exegetical examination of passages in the five great pre-
exilic prophets bearing on the relation between the prophet
and the cult in Israel. These and other " classical " prophets,
he concludes, were not cultic functionaries ; on the other
hand, they did not condemn the cult as such, but actually
took part in it. The point of cleavage between them and the
popular religion with regard to the cult was that they looked
upon Yahweh as Owner of the temple, whereas popular
religion viewed him as Occupant of the temple; through this
latter viewpoint the temple became a talisman by means of
which the people imagined they could control Yahweh. The
word of Yahweh spoken by the prophets breaks through this
deadly illusion.

F.F.B.

VAN RULER, A. A. : *Die Christliche Kirche und das Alte Testament*.
(Beiträge zur evangelische Theologie, Band 23.) 1955. Pp. 92.
(Chr. Kaiser Verlag, München. Price : DM. 5.40.)

What is the proper place and the right use of the Old Testament
in the life and theology of the Church ? It is to these questions
that Professor van Ruler of Utrecht addresses himself. He
first notes various attitudes to the Old Testament. These
range from the valuation of it as (1) worthless, through (5)
an estimate of it as *selbständige Quelle für Gottes erkenntnis
und Frömmigkeit* (for which the only two British scholars
referred to, H. W. Robinson and H. H. Rowley, are quoted as
examples) to (10) the understanding of it as *Heilsgeschichte*.

It is in terms of this last standpoint that the book is concerned. The chapters will indicate the movement of thought : I. The Old Testament as such and its exegesis ; II. Is the Christ already manifest in the Old Testament itself ? III. The necessity of the Old Testament for the Christian Church. Allegorization is unacceptable, but there is room for a restrained Typology. It is the same God who speaks in the Old as in the New Testament, but it is the Gospel which gives the real criterion of worth and the true hermeneutic key for interpretation. A reader might feel some disappointment in the comparatively rare use of the great Old Testament insights into the divine Purpose and Character and human nature. The book might be said to offer a theological basis for Old Testament study in the light of present-day scholarship.

A.S.H.

SANDERS, J. A. : *Suffering as Divine Discipline in the Old Testament and Post-Biblical Judaism*. (Colgate Rochester Divinity School Bulletin, XXVIII, special issue.) 1955. Pp. vi+136. (Colgate Rochester Divinity School, New York. Price : $1.50.)

The author is Assistant Professor of Old Testament Interpretation at the Colgate Rochester Divinity School. This volume is in the first place a study of the Hebrew root *yasar*, to which is added the root *yakah*. All the occurrences of these roots are tabulated and carefully analysed. Then there follows a study of Jeremiah from the concept of *musar*, because the author believes that this is where one should begin for a complete biblical study of this word. The value of suffering as divine discipline is next traced under two heads : personal experience and observance of the suffering of others. The subject is then discussed as it is found in the Jewish Midrashes, the Mishna and the Talmud. The volume is a careful and detailed study of the material. N.H.S.

SCHREY, H. H., WALZ, H. H., and WHITEHOUSE, W. A. : *The Biblical Doctrine of Justice and Law*. (Ecumenical Biblical Studies, No. 3.) 1955. Pp. 208. (S.C.M. Press, London. Price : 8s. 6d.)

This book, published also in German by Gotthelf Verlag, Zürich, under the title *Gerechtigkeit in biblischer Sicht*, is an important examination of the fundamental problems of the relations between law and justice, followed by a study of the Biblical view of righteousness as a quality of God and as His gift to His elect people, leading in turn to an examination of the proper attitude of the people of God to contemporary human justice and temporal authorities. The authors hold that the time is not yet ripe for the production of a full-scale theology of law, but maintain that God's Word comes through the Bible to persuade the Church, and through it the world, that what is wrong is being put right in this world through the Spirit. While only one section of the book deals directly with the Old Testament, for that section it deserves a place in this *Book List*. H.H.R.

SMAL, P. J. N. : *Die Universalisme in die Psalms.* 1956. Pp. 236. (Kok, Kampen.)

This Afrikaans thesis was presented to the Free University of Amsterdam for the doctorate in theology. Special attention is paid to between 50 and 60 psalms. The universalism of the Psalter is seen against its particularism ; the latter appears in the emphasis on the covenant made by Yahweh with the people, land, sanctuary and king of Israel. But a universalist outlook is implied in the emphasis on Yahweh—the one, transcendent God—as Creator, Owner, Sustainer of the universe, as King and Judge of the world. It comes to clear expression in those places where the nations are called upon to take note of the mighty acts of Yahweh and pay him their homage (cf. Pss. xxii. 27 f. ; lxviii. 29 ff. ; lxxxvi. 4, etc.). The author agrees with his promoter, N. H. Ridderbos, that Ps. cx is the only psalm which is " messianic " in the direct sense.   F.F.B.

SORG, R. : *Hesed and Hasid in the Psalms.* 1953. Pp. 64. (Pio Decimo Press, St. Louis, Mo. Price : $1.25.)

The author of this little book does not attempt to translate the word *hesed*, whose various translations in the New Latin version he records, but examines the elements which enter into the concept, as they appear from its differing contexts. There is a chapter on ' Cursing in the Psalms,' defending the relevant passages as mild compared with the New Testament, and a brief chapter on the ' Mysticism of the Psalms.' Finally there is a complete list of all the passages in translation where *hesed* or *hasid* occur in the Psalms. The book is intended to be popular and not scientific, and is without any critical discussion. It will be found serviceable to readers who are not equipped for the more learned studies, but is of slight value to more scholarly readers.   H.H.R.

STEINMANN, J. : *Le Livre de Job.* (Lectio Divina 16.) 1955. Pp. 390. (Les Éditions du Cerf, Paris. Price : Fr. 990.)

As one has learnt to expect from the author, we have here a piece of work, which, if it offers nothing startlingly new, is a competent and straightforward introduction to the book of Job. Part I, in which the author dates the original form of the book to the first half of the fourth century B.C., serves as a general introduction, and deals with the cultural background, the problem of suffering in the thought of the ancient Near East as well as that of Greece, and the connexion in thought and literary expression between the book of Job and other parts of the Old Testament. Part II offers, for the most part, a translation of what is regarded as the original work, accompanied by brief textual notes and a running commentary ; and this is followed by a similar treatment of such additional matter as the Elihu speeches and the poem on Wisdom. An interesting discussion of exegetical and other glosses adds to the value of this section. Part III deals *inter alia* with the characters in the drama and the general argument of the book, while Part IV touches lightly on some of the ways in which the book has been interpreted from the time of Gregory the Great down to the present day.　　A.R.J.

SUTCLIFFE, E. F. : *Providence and Suffering in the Old and New Testaments.* 1955. Pp. viii+175. (Nelsons Ltd., Edinburgh. Price : 15s. 0d.)

This is an interesting and competent study of its theme. The opening two chapters deal with the views held by other religions, especially by the Babylonians. It is argued that it is unlikely that a Babylonian Fall story will ever be found ; it would be inconsistent with what we know. In the discussion of Israel's beliefs, a proper balance is struck between individual and corporate responsibility. On p. 57 there should have been a reference to the evidence from Nuzu. On pp. 74-76 there are good remarks on one-sided and hyperbolic Biblical statements. Throughout there appears evidence of cautious textual and literary criticism. One may perhaps be allowed to express dissent from the view expressed on pp. 99-100 that certain of the extremer statement of Ecclesiastes " are not just the human reflections of a Jewish thinker but reflections which God Almighty through inspiration wished to be communicated in the first instance to the Jewish people and to find a place in their Canon of Sacred Scripture. There is consequently nothing in them of unauthorised or indiscreet criticism. They were inspired for a purpose, which seems to have been, as suggested, to raise the minds of the chosen people to higher thoughts of God's manner of apportioning rewards and punishments." The truth in these words might have been better put.　　N.W.P.

TSEVAT, M. : *A Study of the Language of the Biblical Psalms.* (Journal of Biblical Literature Monograph Series, Volume IX.) 1955. Pp. viii+154. (Society of Biblical Literature, Philadelphia. Price : $1.50, or $1.00 for members.)

The author of this unusual type of monograph, which is lithoprinted, seeks to examine the Old Testament psalms (defined as any address to God in metrical form and therefore not to be restricted to the Psalter) from the standpoint of the words, grammatical forms, and phrases, which may be regarded as idiomatic in this connexion when compared with the language of the remaining Biblical literature. By means of a further comparison with (a) similar features in what survives of other Semitic dialects closely related to Hebrew, particularly Ugaritic, and (b) the books of Chronicles, the author concludes that psalmody was an element in Israel's religious life from the time of the Settlement, and that, so far as the Hebrew Scriptures are concerned, the *terminus ante quem* of the psalms is the fifth century B.C. The argument is developed along purely statistical lines, and the monograph as a whole is a monument of industry ; but one cannot help questioning the validity of the author's claims for this kind of statistical approach to the study of the Old Testament, when the surviving literature available for comparison is so limited.

A.R.J.

VELLAS, B. M. : *The Earthquake in the Old Testament* (in modern Greek). 2nd ed. 1955. Pp. 18+German résumé of 2 pp. (Athens.)

This little treatise on earthquakes in the Old Testament first appeared in 1943, in a *Festschrift* for Professor N. Kretikos. The recent earthquakes in Greece led to a request for its reprinting. Vellas distinguishes between literal earthquakes (among which he reckons the phenomena of Gen. xix. 24 ; Ex. xix. 18 ; 1 Sam. xiv. 15 ; Amos i. 1 (cf. Zech. xiv. 5)) and the use of earthquake terminology to describe theophanies and the like. Of special importance is the use of such terminology in an eschatological setting ; e.g., in Isa. xxiv. 18-20, where the earth is destroyed by a great earthquake, to make way for a new creation. Earthquakes, whether literal or figurative, proceed from God ; they are expressions of His judgement, and are designed to lead to repentance. A brief summary of the argument in German is appended to the Greek treatise.

F.F.B.

VISCHER, W. : *Die Immanuel–Botschaft im Rahmen des königlichen Zionsfestes.* (Theologische Studien, 45.) 1955. Pp. 56. (Evangelischer Verlag, Zollikon-Zürich. Price : Fr. 4.70.)

This important study, No. 45 of *Theologische Studien*, is a terminological investigation into Isaiah vi. 1-ix. 6, to show that the Immanuel prophecies are closely related to certain specified texts belonging to the Jerusalem and Davidic version of the royal ritual of enthronement. The apostasy of Ahaz in the Syro-Ephraimitic crisis led Isaiah to re-affirm the Davidic theme, enshrined in the cult, in the form of the Immanuel prophecies. In the first instance these prophecies relate to their contemporary crisis in a polarity of divine discipline and fidelity to the Davidic house, but they are also a Christological token. Though not all the sections are equally convincing and the Christological conclusion is difficult, the main exegetical theme is probably sound.

G.H.D.

VISCHER, W. : *Das Kerygma des Alten Testaments.* (Kirchliche Zeitfragen, 36.) 1955. Pp. 24. (Zwingli-Verlag, Zürich. Price : Swiss Fr. 1.50.)

The author believes that this Kerygma, often cultic, is present throughout the entire O.T. but especially in Is. xl-lv. There he finds it in the principal features of that prophet's teaching and in the motifs of the procession, the law court and, of course, the Servant. There is also an Auto-kerygma. The reviewer agrees that the servant of the 4th Song is God, though he cannot agree with the Christology of the last two pages. The pamphlet, though brief, is brilliant and warmly commended.

G.H.D.

WIDENGREN, G. : *Sakrales Königtum im Alten Testament und im Judentum.* (Franz Delitzsch-Vorlesungen, 1952.) 1955. Pp. 128. (Kohlhammer Verlag, Stuttgart. Price : DM. 10.80.)

> Professor G. Widengren's many contributions in the fields of Old Testament study and comparative religion are marked by such wide reading and originality of thought as to ensure a warm welcome for anything more that he may have to say on these subjects. The present work is fully up to standard, and it is of special importance because it gives us a fuller discussion of the conception of sacral kingship discernible in the Old Testament and related literature than we have had hitherto from any member of the so-called Uppsala School. The aspects of the subject which are here treated are the king's responsibility for the organization of worship ; his function as high-priest, a guardian of *tôrāh*, and one endowed with divine wisdom ; his rôle at the Feast of Tabernacles as suggested by the Samaritan liturgies ; a reconstruction of the enthronement ritual ; an excursus on 2 Sam. vii ; and, of special importance, another on the Israelite New Year Festival. While the present writer is most grateful for his monograph because of the stimulus of its thought, he is uneasy about many of the author's conclusions ; and, broadly speaking, this uneasiness arises from what appears to be a tendency (a) to lift passages from their context and bring them together somewhat uncritically, and (b) to take the language of the Old Testament too literally and with insufficient regard to the peculiarities of idiom and the use of metaphor. This is particularly noticeable, for example, in the argument which Professor Widengren advances to show that Yahweh was thought of as a dying and rising god.   A.R.J.

WRIGHT, J. : *What is Man ? A Christian Assessment of the Powers and Functions of Human Personality.* 1955. Pp. 192. (Paternoster Press, London. Price : 10s. 6d.)

> This book, which is popularly written, covers a wide range but has little particular relevance for Old Testament study. Its concern is a Christian assessment of the powers and functions of human personality, and the author includes in his survey the work of philosopher, biologist and psychologist, as well as the testimony of mystic, spiritualist and exponent of the occult. There is a brief section on the biblical doctrine of man ; the full inspiration and accuracy of the Bible is accepted by the author on the ground that that was the attitude of Jesus Himself.   J.M.

WIERSINGA, H. A. : *Zendingsperspectief in het Oude Testament.* 1955. Pp. 180. (Bosch & Keuning, Baarn. Price : Fl. 5.40.)

> This work reviews the missionary emphasis of the O.T. from the standpoint of a thoroughgoing conservatism in Biblical

criticism. God's interest in the Gentiles is traced from the book of Genesis, where He creates the world of mankind, makes His covenant with the sons of Noah, and promises Abraham that in him ' shall all the families of the earth be blessed,' to Malachi, who describes Yahweh's name as ' great among the Gentiles.' Not only is the missionary outlook of many of the prophets demonstrated ; Daniel, too, ' was a great missionary in the strictest sense of the word ' (cf. his faithful preaching to Nebuchadnezzar in ch. iv), and it is suggested that the magi from the east (Matt. ii) may have owed something of their knowledge of the expected king of the Jews to the tradition of Daniel's preaching in Mesopotamia. The exclusive policy of Zerubbabel, Ezra and Nehemiah was not anti-missionary in intention ; on the contrary, Noordtzij is quoted with approval : ' Without the rejection of *this* people of the land (Ezra iv. 4, etc.), the blessing of *all* peoples would have been rendered impossible.' The book ends with some remarks on the missionary significance of the Jewish diaspora in the light of early Christian evangelization.

F.F.B.

WISKERKE, J. R. : *Volk van Gods Keuze*, with an Introduction by H. J. Schilder. 1955. Pp. 192. (Oosterbaan & Le Cointre, Goes. Price : Fl. 5.50.)

The author of this work on the ' people of God's choice,' a minister in the conservative *Gereformeerde Kerken* of the Netherlands, finds that many theologians of his own school have been too preoccupied with the dogmatic formulations of divine election and reprobation to view the subject of election in its Biblical proportions. He pays tribute to the ' inspiring and stimulating ' works of Rowley and Vriezen, but finds that the former, by his emphasis on election to service, attenuates the Biblical doctrine till it approximates the ' liberal Anglo-Saxon " Social Gospel " ' (believe it or not !), while the latter is unduly influenced by Barthianism. Wiskerke links election closely with the history of salvation and with the idea of the covenant. The pattern election-rejection-re-election is traced throughout the Bible, re-election being bound up with the remnant-doctrine, which receives a Christian reinterpretation from Paul in Romans xi. The first election is related to the Old covenant, re-election to the new ; they correspond to Calvin's ' general ' and ' special ' election res-pectively. Wiskerke, though an orthodox Calvinist, finds ground for criticism in Calvin's exegesis of Jer. xxxi. 31 ff. If his own exposition of re-election after rejection appears to contradict the Canons of Dort, he points out, this is because he uses the term ' rejection ' in a different sense from that of Dort. This is a careful, well-documented piece of work.

F.F.B.

BOTTÉRO, J. : *Le Problème des Ḫabiru à la 4ᵉ rencontre assyriologique internationale*. (Cahiers de la Société Asiatique XII.) 1954. Pp. xxxviii+208. (Imprimerie Nationale, Paris.)

The fourth meeting of an association known as the *Groupe François Thureau-Dangin*, decided to take the problem of the Ḫabiru as the subject for discussion. The organization of the meeting was in the capable hands of M. J. Bottéro, who has brought together in this volume all the texts discussed and all the contributions made by the eminent assyriologists who took part in the meeting. The result is a work of the utmost value for all students of this most intriguing problem. We now have available for the first time all the texts which refer to the Ḫabiru, in the original languages, with translation and critical notes. The care and skill with which M. Bottéro has assembled this mass of material, arranged it, and contributed a valuable conclusion summing up the results of the discussion, cannot be too highly praised. S.H.H.

DRIVER, G. R. and MILES, J. C. (ed. by) : *The Babylonian Laws, Vol. II.*, edited with Translation and Commentary, Transliterated Text, Philological Notes, Glossary. 1955. Pp. viii+426. (Clarendon Press, Oxford. Price : 63s. 0d.)

This volume, a product of consummate scholarship, contains not only the Code of Hammurabi but also the Babylonian laws extant on clay-tablets : Lipit-Ishtar's law, laws from *ana ittishu*, Susian land-law, Old-Babylonian seisachtheia, and Neo-Babylonian laws. The transliterated text and the translation are conveniently set out on opposite pages. They are followed by an extensive philological commentary (the legal commentary occupying volume I) and a complete glossary with the various meanings of each word carefully distinguished. Naturally one can think of a point to add here and there ; and the subtler historical nuances of legal terminology are not always noticed. With the use of *ashshatu*, we may now compare Ugarit *atht*, ' woman,' ' married woman ' (van Selms, *Marriage and Family Life in Ugaritic Literature*, 1954, 62). The word *shalamu*, in the sense of 'to make good,' is confined to restitution in kind : Code paras, 125, 138 (in the glossary misprinted 139), 149, 156, 172 (misprinted 176), 267. It never denotes, say, payment of silver for an object. The reviewer has shewn (*Studies in Biblical Law*, 1947, 134 ff.) that the same is true of *shillem* in the Old Testament, with the exception of Exod. xxi. 34, where the clause ' he shall give money unto the owner of them ' is interpolated. The Babylonian word is actually narrower than the Biblical. The latter may signify simple restitution—an ox for an ox, repayment of a loan— or multiple—five oxen for one. The former is applied only to simple restitution. The Aramaic papyri, incidentally, in their use of *shallem*, are in step with the Babylonian and Biblical terminology : restitution in kind.

There is no doubt, however, that this is and will remain the standard work in its field. D.D.

DUSSAUD, R. : *La Pénétration des Arabes en Syrie avant l'Islam.* (Institut français d'archéologie de Beyrouth, Bibliothèque archéologique et historique, lix.) 1955. Pp. 230. (Geuthner, Paris. Price : Fr. 3,000.)

The writer describes the nature and extent of Arab settlement of Syria and Mesopotamia from Nabataean times until the Moslem invasions and uses the results of his survey to demonstrate the nature and extent of the impingement of desert peoples upon the sown land in earlier periods. This includes the Hebrew settlement which M. Dussaud dates in the 15th century, (citing Prof. Rowley as an authority !). His views of the historical relevance of the Ras Shamra text Krt with his celebrated ' Negebite theory ' and his view of the mention of Asher and Zebulun in that text are retained. This failure to meet serious criticisms of such sweeping assumptions is a serious fault of this work. In the Christian period, however, the survey of the desert marches is welcome and valuable.
J.G.

DUSSAUD, R. : *Prélydiens, Hittites et Achéens.* 1953. Pp. 186. (P. Geuthner, Paris. Price : Fr. 1350.)

This is a review of the ethnography of Anatolia in the light of recent archaeology. Its value for Old Testament study is mainly peripheral though it is useful to have M. Dussaud's succinct statement of his opinions on such matters as Akhiyawa (the Achaeans of mainland Greece), the archaeology of Hittite sites, the Assyrian colonies in Cappadocia, the Hyksos (Semites according to M. Dussaud), and the ' Sea Peoples.' On the subject of Genesis x the writer insists that the association of Lud (Lydia) and the Semites denotes commercial relations. The book ought to be read in conjunction with Schaeffer's *Stratigraphie Comparée et Chronologie d'Asie Occidentale.*
J.G.

GRAY, J. : *The Krt Text in the Literature of Ras Shamra : A Social Myth of Ancient Canaan.* (Documenta et Monumenta Orientis Antiqui, V.) 1955. Pp. x+66. (Brill, Leiden. Price : Fl. 10.)

This fresh attempt to interpret the poem of Keret contains a brief introduction and then the text transliterated and translated in parallel columns, followed by philological notes and a selected bibliography. The editor regards the poem as social propaganda, intended " to articulate and so conserve features thought to be vital to social life, as the nature-myths accompanied the ritual which reassured men of the permanence and regularity of the natural order." The transliteration seems to be accurate ; the translation, especially when it diverges from that of Ginsberg, is sometimes unhappy (e.g., III iii. 35-6), nor does it always make sense (e.g., I i. 33, ii. 189, III vi. 18a, 49). The notes are useful but must be used with

767

caution ; for the laws governing the mutation of sounds are often flouted. The interpretation, however, of these difficult documents is full of difficulty and every fresh attempt, such as the present, is welcome ; neither philological nor grammatical rules are yet fully established, and the translation of numerous words and phrases is still highly precarious.

G.R.D.

GREENBERG, M. : *The Hab/piru.* (American Oriental Series, Vol. 39.) 1955. Pp. xiv+96. (American Oriental Society, New Haven. Price : $3.50.)

This is a valuable collection of all the known material relating to the much discussed problem of the Habiru. The author acknowledges his indebtedness to a number of American scholars who are well-known specialists in cuneiform and Hittite studies and in Egyptology. The first 12 pages are devoted to the history of the problem from the discovery of the Tell el-Amarna tablets up to the most recent discoveries. The next section of the book, from p. 15 to p. 58, contains 166 texts from many sources, Sumerian, Akkadian, Nuzi, Tell el-Amarna, Boghazköi, Ugarit, and others. The texts are given in transcription and translation, and some of them are hitherto unpublished. The third section, from p. 61 to p. 82, contains an analysis of the sources by their groups. In this section the author has attempted to draw out the information furnished by the various sources concerning the social or political status of the Habiru, and their ethnic composition and origins. The final section is devoted to the author's conclusions. While the experts may raise questions as to the accuracy of some of the translations, there is no doubt that this is a most important piece of scholarship, and it will be invaluable to all students of this intriguing problem. The book contains a complete bibliography of all that has been written on the subject, and I cannot detect any omissions.

S.H.H.

MENDELSOHN, I. (ed by) : *Religions of the Ancient Near East. Sumero-Akkadian Religious Texts and Ugaritic Epics.* 1955. Pp. xxx+284. (Liberal Arts Press, New York. Price : $1.75 paper, $3.00 cloth.)

This is the fourth volume in a series called *The Library of Religion* whose aim is to provide for the general reader a series of readings in the sacred scriptures and basic writings of the world's religions, past and present. The volume under review contains Sumero-Akkadian religious texts and Ugaritic epics. The author, already known for a valuable study of slavery in the ancient Near East, has written a short introduction to the selection of texts which constitutes the main body of the book. The translations of the texts, with the exception of the *Shurpu* and *Maqlu* texts which have been translated by the editor, have been taken from Pritchard's *Ancient Near Eastern Texts Relating to the Old Testament.* The editor has rendered a great service to all who are interested in the early religions of the ancient Near East by making available in a reliable translation and in a cheap and handy form the most important myth and ritual texts of Mesopotamia and Syria. Ginsberg's translation of the Ugaritic texts, which is that given in Pritchard, often presents considerable divergences from Gordon's translation, and students need to be reminded that the meaning of these difficult but fascinating texts is still too uncertain to allow of their use without considerable caution. The ritual for the making of the sacred *lilissu*-drum, given in Thureau-Dangin's *Rituels accadiens* would have been a welcome addition to the excellent selection which the editor has given us.   S.H.H.

MOSCATI, S. : *Geschichte und Kultur der semitischen Völker, Eine Einführung.* 2nd ed. 1955. Pp. 218+32 plates+4 maps. (W. Kohlhammer Verlag, Stuttgart. Price : DM. 4.80.) *Histoire et civilisation des peuples sémitiques* (Bibliothèque Historique). 1955. Pp. 238+4 maps. (Payot, Paris. Price : Fr. 850.)

In the second German edition of Professor Moscati's introductory manual the main structure of the first German edition (noticed in the *Book List*, 1954, p. 80) has been retained, but several changes have been introduced. Most noteworthy is the attention which is paid to matters which have assumed prominence in the last two years or so, such as the excavations at Nimrud, Mari and Ugarit, the law-code of Ur-Nammu, the Dead Sea scrolls, the origin of the Aramaeans, the Aramaic documents on leather, and research in Arabia. The section on the Ethiopians has been extended somewhat, and a number of additions have been made to the bibliography. Compared with the original edition in Italian and the first edition in German, the French edition contains some modifications and additions. The four maps are once again included, but the plates and the index which appear in the Italian and German editions are omitted. Their omission is much to be regretted in a book which is designed primarily for the layman, and which is likely to enjoy a wide circulation.   D.W.T.

PHILLIPS, W. : *Qataban and Sheba.* 1955. Pp. xvi+362 (English ed. 336). (Harcourt, Brace & Co., New York, and V. Gollancz, London. Price : $5.00 or 21s. 0d.)

This is a general account—somewhat circumstantial and ingenuous—of the activities of the American Foundation for the Study of Man by the leader of the expeditions. The Biblical student will be impressed with the enormous amount of material, especially epigraphic, which was gathered in the kingdoms of Qataban and Sheba and the manuscript material microfilmed in the monastery of St. Catherine's in Sinai. General and particularly specialist interest will demand the publication of details in an authoritative report by archaeological and epigraphic experts on the large staff of these expeditions unprecedented in finance and equipment. J.G.

Pope, M. L. : *El in the Ugaritic Texts*. (Supplements to *Vetus Testamentum*, Vol. II.) 1955. Pp. x+116. (Brill, Leiden. Price : Fl. 14, to subscribers Fl. 11.)

> The work here noticed is an exhaustive study of the name and style, attributes, position and abode, of El the supreme god at Ugarit, arranged in seven chapters. The chapter on the name ' El ' is inconclusive and therefore disappointing ; and the author does not consider the possibility that it may have had an onomatopoeic origin. Contrariwise, that on El's abode is most interesting and indeed convincing ; this is put at Aphek (Joshua xiii. 4), the Afca about 23 miles to the N.E. of Beirut, midway between Gebal (Byblos) and Baalbeq (Hierapolis), at the source of the Nahr Ibrahim near its supposed subterranean junction with the waters of el Yammuneh. There is also an excellent chapter on El's rank and significance, in which Eissfeldt's view of El as a ' high god ' is vigorously combatted ; and this ' removes the ground from under him . . . ' as the ' object of any serious monotheistic movement.' All in all, the book is an excellent study of the problem which the author has set himself to examine, and it contains many admirable suggestions which will call for careful consideration as the Ugaritic texts are intensively cultivated. G.R.D.

Pritchard, J. B. (ed. by) : *Ancient Near Eastern Texts relating to the Old Testament*. 2nd ed. 1955. Pp. xxii+544. (Princeton University Press, and G. Cumberlege, London. Price : $17.50 or 140s. 0d.)

> This indispensable work, whose first edition was reviewed in the *Book List*, 1951, p. 21, now appears in a revised and enlarged edition, which adds still more to its usefulness. Corrections of errors and misprints have been made, and bibliographical material has been brought up to date. In addition a number of Canaanite texts have been translated by Franz Rosenthal (including the Azitawadda text from Karatepe and several early Aramaic texts from North Syria, the Marseilles Tariff, the Treaty between *Ktk* and Arpad, and some sepulchral inscriptions), several South Arabian inscriptions have been translated by A. Jamme, and some new Akkadian texts have been translated by E. A. Speiser. These additions are all welcome and valuable, and owners of the first edition of the work can get the additions separately for $1.00. Professor Pritchard and his team of fellow-workers have earned the gratitude of scholars everywhere by making available in this convenient, though expensive, form this fine and up-to-date collection of texts. H.H.R.

van Raalte, J. : *De Schrijfkunst in de Bijbellanden*. 1955. Pp. 160. (Bosch & Keuning, Baarn. Price : Fl. 5.90.)

> This popular account of the rise and development of the art of writing in Bible lands, the author tells us, was begun in

the unpromising environment of Buchenwald concentration camp. Since then he has brought his knowledge up to date by reference to the writings of Diringer, Driver, Gelb and others. The main scripts of Near Eastern antiquity are described and some account is given of the history of their decipherment. The recent decipherment of the Minoan script is not mentioned. Van Raalte writes with strong religious convictions : writing in general and the invention of the alphabet in particular should be seen as a gift from God, designed for the recording of His revelation in a form which the ordinary man could read.   F.F.B.

THE DEAD SEA SCROLLS

BARTHÉLEMY, D. and MILIK, J. T. : *Discoveries in the Judaean Desert. I. Qumran Cave I.* 1955. Pp. xii + 166 + 37 plates. (G. Cumberlege, Oxford University Press, London. Price : 63s. 0d.)

The work is issued by the Jordan Department of Antiquities, École Biblique et Archéologique Française, and the Palestine Archaeological Museum, and, in addition to treatises by the editors, contains contributions by Lankester Harding (the discovery), Père de Vaux (ceramics), Mrs. G. M. Crowfoot (linen textiles), J. Plenderleith (unwrapping). There are seventy fragments of text given in transcript and facsimile, divided into Biblical and non-Biblical, edited by Barthélemy and Milik respectively, and accompanied by useful annotations and discussions. The indexes are adequate and ten illustrations are included in the text. The presentation is superb, and the volume obviously forms an extremely valuable addition to the publications containing the texts of the scrolls. It is the first of a series, and subsequent volumes will include máterial from the other caves, and also from other sources such as Khirbet Qumran, Murabba'at and Mird.   B.J.R.

BOCCACCIO, P. and BERARDI, G. : *Interpretatio Habacuc (Pesher Habaqquq). Transcriptio et Versio Latina.* 1955. Pp. 26. (Pontificium Seminarium Picenum, Fani. Price : Lire 650.)

The text has been edited by permission of the American Schools of Oriental Research, and in many details it is an improvement on the transcription published in the first instance by ASOR, though it is right to add that the majority of divergences are concerned with the reading of *waw* and *yodh*. The present edition, however, is rather confused by the introduction into the text of the transcription, albeit interlineally, of emendations proposed by the editors; and the objection is greater because textual additions in the manuscript itself are also made interlineally. The annotation is terse, clear and helpful, and the translation is most useful. Various identifications of persons and events are very briefly indicated, and a bibliography of seven items includes the work of Segert but not Elliger's.   B.J.R.

BURROWS, M. : *The Dead Sea Scrolls.* 1955. Pp. xvi+436+10 plates. (The Viking Press, New York, and Secker & Warburg, London. Price : $6.50.)

Of the great number of works on the Scrolls which have appeared in the last nine years, this is the most comprehensive as well as the most readable. It is written mainly, if one may say so, for the non-professional student by a scholar of repute who has followed the finds closely since they were first made known to the outer world by the late Prof. Sukenik and by Dr. Trever and Dr. Brownlee of the American School of Oriental Research—the School which had the author as its Director at that time. Having read and scrutinized almost every study written on the Scrolls in the major European languages and to a somewhat lesser degree in Modern Hebrew, the author very aptly wove the results of these studies into the general fabric of his work. The first part of the book deals in great detail with the first discoveries and the excitement and controversy which they have aroused, and in less detail, with the later discoveries as known at the time of putting the book together. In other parts of the book the familiar subjects related to the Scrolls are discussed, the author, perhaps wisely at this stage when hundreds of fragments of the Qumran Caves are still awaiting decipherment, not always committing himself to definite views. The last part of the book gives translations of the Damascus Document ; the Habakkuk Commentary ; the Manual of Discipline ; and sections from the War Scroll as well as from the Hymns. In order not to increase unduly the size of the book neither an apparatus criticus nor indexes of any kind are given. The book, however, contains a fairly extensive bibliography as well as some photographs and maps bearing on the Scrolls.

M.W.

*ROWLEY, H. H. : *The Dead Sea Scrolls and their Significance.* (Two Broadcast talks in the B.B.C. Third Programme.) 1955. Pp. 24. (Independent Press, London. Price : 2s. 0d.)

In the first of the two talks, printed here practically as actually broadcast, the story of the later phases of the discoveries in the Qumran caves, Murabba'at and Mird, is outlined, and in the second the author gives his views on the significance of the scrolls, their dating and the identification of the sect. With the qualities which generally accompany Professor Rowley's writings, clarity, fairness and interest, this booklet can be recommended to all who would know something about the scrolls.

B.J.R.

SCOTT, R. B. Y. : *Treasure from Judaean Caves : The Story of the Dead Sea Scrolls.* 1955. Pp. x+44+4 plates. (United Church Publishing House, Toronto.)

Originally broadcast by the Canadian Broadcasting Corporation, this account of the Scrolls should find a ready market among the interested laity, for it is a coherent, clear and interesting account. It touches on some points not hitherto well-known, e.g., ' two manuscripts of Exodus which follow the Samaritan text, and copies of Samuel . . . which are much closer to the old Greek . . . ' The writer thinks that it is ' at least possible ' that John the Baptist ' had been a member of the Qumran community.' B.J.R.

SUKENIK, E. L. (ed. by) : *The Dead Sea Scrolls of the Hebrew University.* 1955. Pp. 40+58 plates of transcription, with corresponding separate leaves of facsimile. (Magnes Press, Jerusalem. Price : 70s. 0d.)

The book is practically identical with the Hebrew edition (cf. *Book List*, 1955, p. 64) : the main differences are—apart, of course, from the fact that the Hebrew has been translated— that the errata slip of the latter has been dispensed with and the corrections duly entered in the text (correctly even where the errata slip is incorrect !) ; variation in the order and numeration of manuscript photographs (as distinct from facsimiles), which is unfortunate and is bound to lead to confusion in references ; and the interesting item of in- formation that the collotype plates of facsimiles were printed in the Cotswolds. B.J.R.

VINCENT, A. : *Les manuscrits hébreux du Désert de Juda.* (Textes pour l'Histoire Sacrée.) 1955. Pp. 282. (Fayard, Paris. Price : Fr. 700.)

After a brief account of the discoveries at Qumran, Murabba'at and El Mird, the author offers an account of the principal texts known at the time of writing (before the full text of the Hebrew University scrolls was available), with a translation of the non-Biblical texts, including the Zadokite Fragments found in the Cairo Geniza. The rendering given of this last is a draft translation by Abbé Michel which was not intended for publication without further revision. Professor Vincent reviews the main theories as to the age and provenance of the Qumran texts, and favours the second century date for the Teacher of Righteousness and the Essene character of the sect. The deposit of the manuscripts in the caves is placed shortly before the fall of Jerusalem in A.D. 70, in accordance with what seems the inescapable evidence provided by the excavation of the monastery. H.H.R.

WALLENSTEIN, M. : *A Striking Hymn from the Dead Sea Scrolls.* (Reprinted from *Bulletin of the John Rylands Library*, xxxviii, No. 1, September, '1955.) 1955. Pp. 26. (John Rylands Library, Manchester, and Manchester University Press. Price : 3s. 6d.)

The author has specialized in the Hymns or Songs of Thanks- giving of the Qumrân Scrolls, and has already published editions and translations of some of the Songs, in *Hymns from the Judean Scrolls*, 1950 (cf. *Book List*, 1950.) In the present work he deals with a lengthy song of some eighty lines, con- tained in three fragments published in facsimile in Sukenik's *'Ôṣar ham-Meghillôth* (Plates 39-41) and reproduced here in reduced size. The treatment consists of a transcription (pointed) and translation, both copiously annotated, and forms a very important contribution to the textual study of the scrolls. B.J.R.

WILSON, E. : *The Scrolls from the Dead Sea*. 1955. Pp. 160. (Allen, London. Price : 10s. 6d.)

The great merit of this book is the vigorous and pleasing way in which it is written. It tells the story of the discovery, and very vividly describes some of the personalities engaged on the scrolls—Father de Vaux, Dupont-Sommer and others. It succeeds in presenting the background of the sect (the Essenes), and, without trying to avoid controversy, raises important issues connected with the relevance of the scrolls for the New Testament and the transmission of the Hebrew text of the Old Testament. But the author fails to do anything like justice to work already accomplished by scholarship, and the book cannot be recommended without reserve because it lacks balance in perspective and contains far too many inaccuracies. B.J.R.

YADIN, Y. : *The Scroll of the War of the Sons of Light against the Sons of Darkness* (in Modern Hebrew.) 1955. Pp. xviii + 398 + vi. (Bialik Foundation ; Jerusalem. Price : 52s. 6d.)

This masterly work, written by both a talented soldier and scholar, comprises two main parts, the one an introduction, arranged according to subjects irrespective of the order of their appearance in the scroll and the second a copiously annotated text to which are added, wherever possible, suggested restorations of the numerous missing parts. It also contains twenty drawings, illuminating subjects related to the war described in the scroll as well as the diverse weapons mentioned therein. The introduction, which occupies the greater part of the book, deals with the contents and the aim of the scroll ; the plan of the war ; the system of the standards of the ' Congregation ' ; the mobilization rules ; the trumpets and the various weapons of war to be used ; the tactics employed by the various units of the warriors ; customs and rituals of the ' Congregation ' ; angelology according to the Scrolls with special reference to the War Scroll.

Examining the authorship of the scroll, it is stated that while there is no decisive proof that it was composed by the Essenes, there is likewise nothing to disprove it. The date of its composition as well as the date of its writing and the time of its hiding in the cave are also discussed. It is suggested with commendable caution that it was composed after the Roman conquest, but before the end of the reign of Herod. It is again cautiously suggested that the copy most likely was made in the second half of the first century B.C. or in the first half of the first century C.E. and that its concealment took place at the beginning of the first century B.C. as a *terminus post quem* and 70 C.E. as *terminus ante quem*. The last chapter gives the principal characteristic expressions which are common to the Scrolls in general. The book concludes with five useful indexes. M.W.

APOCRYPHA AND POST-BIBLICAL JUDAISM

van Andel, C. P. : *De Structuur van de Henoch-Traditie en het Nieuwe Testament.* (Studia Theologica Trajectina, 2.) 1955. Pp. x+132. (Drukkerij Kemink en Zoon, Utrecht. Price : Fl. 10.)

This dissertation, presented to the University of Utrecht, considers 1 Enoch section by section (beginning with chapters xci-civ, cvi-cvii, known separately in Christian antiquity as " The Epistle of Enoch " and entitled by Van Andel " The Wisdom of Enoch ") in order to discover the life-setting, *halakhah* and soteriology implied by each section, and the extent to which life and thought in each tend to centre around a particular figure. The conclusion, supported by parallel studies in other literature of the same general period (particularly Jubilees, the Testaments of the XII Patriarchs, or rather their pre-Christian sources, and the Zadokite-Qumran literature), is that the various sections of 1 Enoch represent successive stages in the development of a religious sect (identical with or related to the Qumran sect), whose life and thought centre with increasing clearness round a dominant figure, whose personality is fused with that of the antediluvian Enoch. The parallel with the Qumran " Teacher of Righteousness " is plain, except that he is not identified with a primaeval character. The resemblance of all this to New Testament Christianity, says Van Andel, is purely formal. In the circle which produced the Enoch literature, the Teacher who realizes the Enoch-ideal is a product of the community ; in Christianity it is Jesus who creates the church.

There is an English summary of the argument on pp. 114-127.
F.F.B.

Baron, S. W. and Blau, J. L. (ed. by) : *Judaism : Postbiblical and Talmudic Period.* (The Library of Religion, vol. iii.) 1954. Pp. xxvi+246. (Liberal Arts Press, New York. Price : $1.75 in paper, $3.00 in cloth.)

The series to which this work belongs offers 'A series of readings in the Sacred Scriptures and Basic Writings of the World's Religions.' Hence, after a short Introduction giving the setting for the quotations, we have a series of extracts from published translations of some of the intertestamental works, Philo, Josephus, works dealing with sectarian movements—including that from which the Dead Sea Scrolls emanated—and passages from the Tannaim and the Amoraim. The whole forms a handy compendium of Jewish orthodox and sectarian teaching, dealing with a variety of subjects, which should be widely useful. H.H.R.

BONSIRVEN, J. : *Textes Rabbiniques des deux premiers siècles Chrétiens,* pour servir à l'intelligence du Nouveau Testament. 1955. Pp. xii+804.ʹ (Pontificio Instituto Biblico, Rome. Price : Lire 4,500 or $7.50, or bound Lire 5,400 or $9.00.)

The library shelf that holds Billerbeck and Moore should certainly make room for this work by Bonsirven. Its main purpose is to let the normative Rabbinic Judaism of New Testament times give an account of itself in its own way and its own words. Philo and Josephus are left out : there is no room ; and, in any case, their works are readily available elsewhere. The same holds of the Apocrypha and Pseudepigrapha. Even when the work is confined to the Rabbinical material, it is still necessary to be selective ; so the final redaction of the Mishnah is taken as the *terminus post quem* now. Within the period the attempt is made to give all that is necessary to have a well-rounded, well-defined picture of the Palestinian background of the New Testament. The materials provided include examples of very early Jewish prayers, the oldest Biblical exegesis represented by *Mekhilta, Sifra,* and *Sifre,* and the earliest codification of the Oral Law represented by the Mishnah, the Tannaitic comments preserved in the Talmuds, the Baraitoth, and relevant extracts from the Tosephta. The Mishnaic material is either translated in full or summarized : the only tractate not represented seems to be *Mo'ed Qatan.* Fully translated portions are in plain type ; summaries are enclosed in [ ] ; and the occasional explanatory words and phrases are printed in italics and put in ( ) in the text. There are three valuable indexes : the first analytical, giving references for all the main topics dealt with in the text, the second of Old Testament texts discussed by the Rabbis, the third of New Testament passages which can be illuminated from the text. There is also a dated list of the Rabbis of the period. Altogether a very useful and convenient book for study and reference.   T.W.M.

BÜCHLER, A. : *Studies in Jewish History. The Büchler Memorial Volume,* ed. by J. Rabbinowitz and I. Brodie. 1956. Pp. xxx+ 280+(viii+78 in Hebrew.) (G. Cumberlege, O.U.P., London. Price : 50s. 0d.)

This handsomely produced book takes the place of a Festschrift that was planned some twenty years ago but, for various reasons, never completed. The eleven essays (eight in English, three in Hebrew) are all by Büchler himself, and they provide a characteristic cross-section of his scholarly work over something like half-a-century. They are mainly concerned with aspects of Jewish life, worship, and history in Palestine towards the end of the pre-Christian period and in the first three centuries of our era. The topics chosen are highly specialized and the treatment most erudite. The essays will thus have their special interest and importance for students of Judaism in this period ; but there are ample gleanings for workers in the Old and New Testament fields. The essays in English have all been translated from German or French : the translations read well, though one is brought up with something of a start by the quaint expression " heathen Christian " which appears several times in the essay on " the Minim of Sepphoris and Tiberias in the second and third centuries."

In addition to the essays there is a brief sketch of Büchler's life and a generous appreciation of the man and his work by Rabbi I. Epstein, a bibliography of Büchler's works, and, as frontispiece to the volume, a portrait of the man himself.

T.W.M.

DAUBE, D. : *The New Testament and Rabbinic Judaism.* 1956. Pp. xviii+460. (Athlone Press, London. Price : 45s. 0d.)

Here we have a new example of the range of Dr. Daube's learning, as well as of its surprising detail. In these Jordan Lectures he sets the New Testament against its Rabbinic background in such a way as to illuminate countless incidents and sayings. He draws not only on orthodox Judaism, but on sectarian Judaism, as it appears in the literature of the Qumran sect and other surviving works, and illuminates the particular nuance of many New Testament Greek words. In the opening section he underlines New Testament links with a number of the Messianic Types in the Old Testament, and then offers some valuable form-critical studies of legislative and other passages, and finally gives examples of a wide range of concepts and conventions on which light can be shed. In a number of cases he argues back on the ground of very slight hints to assumed earlier traditions and interpretations, so that, as might be expected, all are not equally convincing. Nevertheless, the whole forms an important study by one who is equally at home in the literature of Judaism and in the New Testament. H.H.R.

DAVIES, W. D. : *Paul and Rabbinic Judaism : Some Rabbinic Elements in Pauline Theology.* 2nd ed. 1955. Pp. viii+392. (S.P.C.K., London. Price : 18s. 6d.)

The first edition of this book was reviewed in *Book List*, 1949, p. 50. The 2nd edition does not substantially differ from the earlier except in the Additional Notes, pp. 352-366, where opportunity is taken to refer to further literature bearing on the subject matter. Particular reference is made to the Dead Sea Scrolls, a study of which serves to confirm some of the author's expositions of Pauline words and phrases.

A.S.H.

EPSTEIN, J. N. and MELAMED, E. Z. : *Mekhilta d' Rabbi Šim'on b.Jochai.* 1955. Pp. lviii+304. (Mekize Nirdamim, Jerusalem.)

That besides the Mekhilta on Exodus which originated with the School of R. Ishmael there existed another Tannaitic Midrash on Exodus which was usually called Mekhilta of R. Simeon b.Johai (i.e., of the School of R. Akiba) was known from quotations by ancient authors. These had been collected by Friedmann in his edition of Mekhilta. Towards the end of the last century, when the Yemenite Midrash Haggadol was made available to European scholars, J. Levy discovered in it these quotations and in a well-known treatise of his published in 1889 he showed that the mediaeval compiler of this Midrashic work excerpted most of the Mekhilta of R. Simeon. D. Hoffmann, who in 1888 in his *Zur Einleitung in die halachischen Midraschim* established distinguishing criteria between the Midrashim of the School of R. Ishmael and those of the School of R. Akiba, set to work to reconstruct the Mekhilta of R. Simeon on the basis of the Midrash Haggadol by applying these criteria and published his results in a series of articles in *Happeles* 1901-4. Meanwhile Schechter discovered among the Geniza fragments 12 MS. leaves from various parts of the Mekhilta of R. Simeon (about 1/15th of the whole work) which largely confirmed Hoffmann's reconstruction. In 1905 Hoffmann published a reconstructed Mekhilta of R. Simeon on the basis of all the available material. Since that time many additional fragments have been discovered so that out of the 224 pages of the present edition 164 are based on MSS. This in itself, besides the critical apparatus based on 4 MSS. of Midrash Haggadol would render the present work the standard text of the Mekhilta of R. Simeon. There is also a large introduction which includes a discussion on the origin of this Mekhilta by Epstein and chapters dealing with its terminology and its MSS. by Melamed who also provided 9 valuable indices.

P.R.W.

GINSBURG, C. D. : *The Essenes. Their History and Doctrines. The Kabbalah. Its Doctrines, Development and Literature.* Two Essays. 1955. Pp. 246. (Routledge & Kegan Paul, London. Price : 12s. 6d.)

The flyleaf states that of these two essays that on the Kabbalah was first published in 1863 and on the Essenes in 1864 ; and the blurb seems to connect the reappearance of both just now with the ' recent discoveries in the Dead Sea.' The essay on the Essenes is worth perusal, and the Rabbinic references in the annotation and a survey of observations on the Essenes by scholars from the 16th century to the late 19th add to its usefulness.

B.J.R.

GOLDIN, J. : *The Fathers according to Rabbi Nathan,* translated from the Hebrew. (Yale Judaica Series, X.) 1955. Pp. xxvi+278. (Yale University Press and G. Cumberlege, London. Price : $4.75 and 38s. 0d.)

That this work, Aboth of R. Nathan, which is so closely associated with the Mishnaic Tractate Aboth, the Talmudic work best known to the general public, should not have been translated into English until now, may have been due to the fact that translators generally chose either Midrashic or Mishnaic-Talmudic literature, whereas the present work is a Midrash on Mishnah Aboth. Yet, it is because of this uniqueness of utilising Midrash in the service of " wisdom " that this classical work is of special interest to scholars, and again it is its emphasis on wisdom that should make it appeal to the general public for whom this translation is designed. The translation is lucid and idiomatic. It is based on Recension A in Schechter's edition, omitting, however, the brackets which indicate Schechter's additions, a procedure which may be justified in a work designed for the general reader. The notes, however, are copious and not without interest for the scholar as well.

P.R.W.

GORDON, C. H. : *Ugaritic Manual.* (Analecta Orientalia 35.) 1955. Pp. xvi+362. (Pontificium Institutum Biblicum, Rome. Price : Lire 9900, $16.50.)

Professor Gordon continues to merit the gratitude and respect of all interested in Ugaritic studies. In revising his Ugaritic Handbook (see *Book List*, 1948) he has not seriously altered any of his major conclusions. His view still stands that Ugaritic is an independent West-Semitic language whose deviations from other West-Semitic languages are accounted for by the antiquity of Ugaritic and the geographical position of Ugarit in North Syria. The most significant feature of the new book is the inclusion of a cuneiform chrestomathy of 15 pages from the literary texts and a fuller citation of roots from cognate Semitic languages and from Egyptian. The short texts in alphabetic cuneiform from the post-war excavations published in 1951 are also included and there is a useful bibliography. The work will prove eminently suitable for study in seminars.

J.G.

HELFGOTT, B. W. : *The Doctrine of Election in Tannaitic Literature.* 1955 (date on title-page 1954). Pp. xii+210. (Columbia University Press, and G. Cumberlege, London. Price : $3.50 or 28s. 0d.)

This work starts from the challenge thrown down to the Jewish people by the early Christians, when they claimed that they, and not the Jews were the true Israel, the rightful heirs of Abraham. This claim was most specifically set out by St. Paul, particularly in Galatians and Romans. The purpose of the present study is ' to determine the effect of the Christian challenge to the Jewish concept of election in the early Tannaitic period and the reaction on the part of Rabbinic thinking towards that challenge.' The aim is expository rather than judicial, even though the author makes no secret about where his own loyalties lie. He has collected a large body of relevant material and sets it out methodically in chronological order. He gives full documentation for the evidence

779

cited and states the Rabbinic side of the argument with moderation and restraint. It is probably not his fault, but that of his materials, that the total result of the investigation tends to be a catalogue of the views of individual Rabbis, rather than a systematic statement of a single offical Rabbinic doctrine of election. The authorities cited are at one in maintaining against all comers the fact of Israel's election : what is not so clear is the precise doctrinal significance of the fact. None the less it is very useful to have this theological anthology.

Occasionally the author's English is a little puzzling ; and it comes as a shock to read (p. 88) that ' Me-asha ' is ' the Greek for Moses.'

T.W.M.

KLEIN, H. : *The Code of Maimonides, Book Eleven, The Book of Torts, Translated from the Hebrew.* (Yale Judaica Series, Vol. IX.) 1955. Pp. xviii+300. (Yale University Press, New Haven and G. Cumberlege, London. Price : $6.00 or 48s. 0d.)

This is a very able translation of that part of Maimonides's Code which deals with damage to property, theft, robbery, lost property, wounding and homicide. There are few passages the rendering of which is open to serious doubt. In II 1.3 (p. 60 and p. 247, note) it is hardly credible that ' without the owner's knowledge ' should mean ' the owner being unable to identify the offender ' ; and to interpret ' an armed brigand ' as ' an armed brigand keeping his identity secret ' is to read a great deal into the text. The volume will be of particular importance for lawyers. But there are many points of wider interest, for example V 1.9 (pp. 196 f. and p. 274, note), the rule about saving the life of the mother at the cost of that of an unborn child.

D.D.

LIEBERMAN, S. : *Tosefta Ki-Fshuṭah.* A Comprehensive commentary on the Tosefta. *Order Zeraʻim,* Parts 1-2. 1955. Pp. xxviii+872. *The Tosefta, according to Codex Vienna, with variants from Codex Erfurt, Genizah MSS. and Editio Princeps (Venice* 1521) together with references to Parallel Passages in Talmudic Literature. 1955. Pp. xx+294+2 plates. (Jewish Theological Seminary of America, New York. Price : $15.00 for the 3 volumes.)

The study of the Tosefta is fraught with both textual and explanatory difficulties. Unlike the Mishna which became the official text of study in the Babylonian and Palestinian Colleges soon after its promulgation, its complementary work, the Tosefta, was discussed in the Talmud only when relevant to the understanding of the Mishna. In post-Talmudic times when the Mishna was studied on the basis of the Talmud the Tosefta was rarely resorted to. The case was somewhat different with Mishnaic Tractates without Talmud, but these, again, were not studied extensively as they did not usually form part of the curriculum. Thus it came about that the Tosefta has neither a good explanatory nor a strong textual tradition. Prof. Lieberman, who had already earned the gratitude of Tosefta students by his monumental work Tosefeth Rishonim in which he collected all Tosefta references in ancient sources, has in his present works advanced our knowledge both as regards the text and the interpretation of the Tosefta. They consist of (a) a critical edition of the text based mainly on the same two MSS. as Zuckermandel's edition but executed with greater accuracy, (b) a short commentary on the Tosefta and (c) a comprehensive commentary embodying the material collected in the aforementioned Tosefeth Rishonim as well as the views of later authorities and enriched by the author's own comments. There can be no doubt that henceforward serious Tosefta study will not be undertaken without reference to these outstanding works.   P.R.W.

LISOWSKY, G. : *Jadajim (Hände). Text, Übersetzung und Erklärung nebst einem textkritischen Anhang.* (Die Mischna, ed. Rengstorf-Rost.) 1956. Pp. vi+100. (Töpelmann, Berlin. Price : DM. 18.)

Professors Rengstorf and Rost are to be congratulated on their success in resuming the publication of the important *Giessen Mishna* which had lapsed for 20 years. The scope of the present Tractate and its layout conform on the whole to those of its 24 predecessors in the series. The introduction includes sections on the place of the Tractate within the Mishnah, the basic principles it presupposes, historical consideration of its main theme ' washing of the hands,' chronological and biographical notes on the Teachers mentioned in it, its composition and relation to the corresponding Tractate of Tosefta. The text chosen is that of MS. Kaufmann and the readings of 5 other MSS. are given in an appendix. The editors' policy of giving adequate consideration to Jewish tradition has been generally followed by the author in his explanatory notes. Jewish commentators are usually quoted but not accepted uncritically. There are cases where the criticism rests on false premises (e.g., I 1a[2] and I 1b[1] rest on incorrect reading of Tosefta and the linguistic remark in the latter note has no support in Mishnaic Hebrew) but these are to be preferred to those where the ancient commentators are passed by in silence. There are also instances where the note consists of a novel interpretation without reference to the traditional explanation which seems to be followed in the translation (cf. e.g., 1 2d[1]). The author has also occasionally yielded to the temptation to add his novel interpretation to the translation. This may be justified in cases where a literal translation is impossible (cf. the especially attractive reconstruction in I 3d) but not in others (e.g., II 1a or even the beginning of II 4a). The author has taken account of the works of modern scholars relevant to his subject and has given due consideration to the philological and historical problems involved. The work rightly takes its place in the series and will be of interest to all students of Judaism.   P.R.W.

SCHILLING, O. : *Das Buch Jesus Sirach.* (Herders Bibelkommentar, VII/2.) 1956. Pp. xii+218. (Herder, Freiburg. Price : DM. 12, cloth DM. 14.60, or by subscription DM.10, cloth DM. 12.50.)

This belongs to the series entitled *Die Heilige Schrift für das Leben erklärt,* for the characteristics of which reference may be permitted to the 1955 *Book List,* p. 43. It is one of a series intended for popular use, and this unfortunately seems to mean that no problem can be discussed very thoroughly. By comparison Spicq's commentary in the sixth volume of *La Sainte Bible* (ed. Pirot & Clamer ; see *Book List,* 1948, p. 25) is an altogether fuller and more satisfactory study. After the briefest of introductions, in which the author decides for Ptolemy VII as the king Euergetes of the prologue, there follows a clear and readable translation with a brief commentary on the more important verses. Textual questions hardly enter into the author's plan. There are excursuses on such topics as wisdom in Sirach, social life, old age and youth, life and death, the Marian application of wisdom, and the writing of history. One may specially praise the fine clear type and the all-but-unsoilable character of the binding.

J.M.T.B.

PHILOLOGY AND GRAMMAR

BEER, G. : *Hebräische Grammatik,* 2nd edition, revised by R. Meyer, Vol. II. 1955. Pp. 196+20. (Walter de Gruyter, Berlin. Price : DM. 4.80.)

The first volume of this second edition of Beer's Hebrew grammar was briefly reviewed in the *Book List,* 1953, p. 79. The second volume is devoted to the verb, the particles, and to the syntax of the noun and the verb, and there is an appendix of over thirty pages of tables of nominal and verbal forms. The historical and comparative approach which characterized the first volume is carried through into the second, with the same full use made of Ugaritic and the Dead Sea scrolls. The volume is " pocket-size," and it is inevitable that, within so brief a compass, some things should not receive the discussion they deserve (e.g., *waw* consecutive). It contains, however, a large—surprisingly large—amount of important matter. Well printed, handy in form, and reasonably priced, this grammar should be in the possession of all students of the historical development of the Hebrew language.

D.W.T.

BEN-ḤAYYĪM, Z. : *Studies in the Traditions of the Hebrew Language.* 1954. Pp. 150. (Instituto "Arias Montano," Madrid-Barcelona. Price : 21s. 0d.)

This work falls into three parts. The first discusses certain pronominal suffixes and affixes, notably *-kā/-āk* in nouns and *-tā/-t* in verbs, as vocalized in the Massoretic text, and the problems raised by the traditional vocalization ; the second contains some observations on the pronunciation of certain peculiar forms found in the scrolls from the Dead Sea ; and the third examines the importance of the Samaritan pronunciation for that of the Biblical language. The author makes a number of acute suggestions and reaches some conclusions that, however startling they may appear at first sight to be, will require careful examination ; but it is a weakness of his method that, while taking the Aramaic evidence into consideration, he pays little if any attention to the (supposed but often highly probable) proto-Semitic forms which lie behind those found in the historical languages.

G.R.D.

COHEN, M. : *Cinquante Années de Recherches.* 1955. Pp. xvi+388. (Imprimerie Nationale, Paris. Price : Fr. 2.400.)

This volume, published by his friends, is a tribute to the versatility and learning of Marcel Cohen, one of the most remarkable scholars of our day whose name is firmly established in at least three different spheres : as a general linguist, as an Hamito-Semitist and *éthiopisant* in particular, and as a student of French. The present work contains a full bibliography (up to April, 1955), in order of subjects, running to some 1,400 entries (including reviews and notices), the re-issue of some articles now rather inaccessible, and a few hitherto unpublished writings.

The Old Testament scholar will be specially interested in Cohen's *Le système verbal sémitique et l'expression du temps* (Paris 1924), successor in many ways to S. R. Driver's and H. Bauer's works and forerunner, to some extent, of G. R. Driver's book on this subject. The author's *Le parler arabe des juifs d'Alger* (Paris, 1912) and his copious and monumental Ethiopian writings contain much that is at least of peripheral interest to the Hebraist. Those scholars who seek a connexion between Egyptian (and Hamitic in general) and Semitic will find much valuable material in the *Essai comparatif sur le vocabulaire et la phonétique du chamito-sémitique* (Paris, 1947), and students of the alphabet have in Cohen's *L'écriture* (1953) an outline of the invention of writing and its development.

E.U.

FUNDAMINSKY, S. : *A New Hebrew Grammar : First Course for Schools and Learners with Vocabularies and Exercises.* 1955. Pp. xxiv+336. (Narod Press, London. Price : 15s. 0d.)

This grammar will probably be successful in one of its aims, that of providing Jewish schoolchildren with a working knowledge of Hebrew Grammar as a background to the Old Testament and to Modern Hebrew. The paradigms and other grammatical details are set out clearly and objectively without being encumbered with detailed explanatory notes.

In its other aim, that of preparing scholars for examination at G.C.E. Ordinary level it will be less successful, for, although it is at pains to mention which words and idioms are non-Biblical, its exercises, with the exception of 48-62 (where Modern and Biblical Hebrew are printed separately), make no attempt to distinguish between Biblical and Modern Hebrew. Its users will have no clear idea of Biblical Hebrew as a classical language. L.H.B.

GARBINI, G. : *L'Aramaico Antico*. (Classe di Scienze morali, storiche e filologiche, Serie viii, Vol. vii, Fasc. 5.) 1956. Pp. 50. (Accademia Nazionale dei Lincei, Rome. Price : Lire 700.)

This fascicle compares, on the basis of inscriptions, the Aramaic used at various centres, such as Damascus, or in regions, such as Assyria, under the headings of orthography, phonology and morphology. The different dialects, for such they are seen to be, are characterized, and the influences, for example Phoenician and Assyrian, made clear. From the analysis it is concluded that one cannot speak of a common Aramaic before the beginning of the seventh century, for the end of the eighth century marks the end of the ' ancient ' Aramaic and the beginning of the ' imperial ' Aramaic. This is an important study in that the author breaks new ground and offers criticism of previous theories of the development of Aramaic, especially the theories advanced by Ginsberg and Dupont-Sommer. W.D.M.

GOTTSTEIN, M. H. : *A List of some Uncatalogued Syriac Biblical Manuscripts*. (Reprinted from the *Bulletin of the John Rylands Library*, xxxvii, No. 2, March, 1955.) 1955. Pp. 20. (John Rylands Library, Manchester, and the Manchester University Press. Price : 2s. 6d.)

Dr. Gottstein's list of uncatalogued manuscripts in Manchester, Paris, London, Oxford and Cambridge is most welcome. The descriptive notes were made originally for Dr. Gottstein's own reference, and so they are often not so full or so precise as one would have wished. Those interested in the subject may supplement the descriptions of the manuscripts in the Jenks Collection at Cambridge from the list published by A. E. Goodman in the *JRAS*, October, 1939, pp. 581-600. Note that Mss. Or. 1292, 1293 and 1295 in Dr. Gottstein's article correspond to Mss. Or. 1297, Or. 1292 and Or. 1293 in Mr. Goodman's list. W.D.McH.

HARRISON, R. K. : *Teach Yourself Hebrew*. 1955. Pp. x + 216. (English Universities Press, London. Price : 10s. 6d.)

Whoever writes an elementary Hebrew Grammar should be pachydermatous, as he is sure to be criticized for being either too inclusive or too elementary. Certainly most critics of the present book will put it into the latter class. On my reckoning, this book offers about two fifths of the grammatical information contained in Davidson-McFadyen, which seems to be insufficient to provide an adequate grounding in the language. Apart from the omission of highly desirable, not to say necessary, information, there is an inexactness of phrase and occasional misstatement such as to befog the self-taught and exasperate the class teacher. The Hebrew type is clear and readable ; and the set-up is attractive, though not always marking off unrelated paragraphs clearly enough. A good deal of space is wasted in the paradigms ; where the Hithpa'el follows the causatives, and the use of *etc.* may sometimes leave doubt in the beginner's mind. The exercises to each lesson, with vocabularies and key, appear to be good ; and a commendable feature is the reference to passages to be attempted from the Hebrew Bible direct. The proportion of misprints is not unduly high for a first edition, though some are surprising.   D.R.Ap-T.

HOLLENBERG-BUDDE (ed. W. BAUMGARTNER) : *Hebräisches Schulbuch*. 21st ed. 1955. Pp. 230. (Helbing & Lichtenhahn, Basel. Price : Swiss Fr. 7.80, DM. 7.50.)

W. Hollenberg's *Schulbuch* appeared first over a century ago. It was later edited successively by his brother J. Hollenberg, K. Budde, and since 1935 by W. Baumgartner. In this new edition some significant alterations have been made, the chief being a fresh treatment of certain paragraphs on vocalization, the removal of some difficult passages for reading, the provision of a larger choice of unvocalized passages for reading, and the inclusion of some extra-Biblical Hebrew texts (the Siloam inscription, and two short passages from the Manual of Discipline and the Hymns from Qumran). The four main sections are devoted to grammar and syntax, exercises, reading selections, and vocabularies. The main essentials of Hebrew grammar and syntax are clearly and succinctly presented, the exercises are well planned, and the selection of pieces for reading is excellent. The work is generally to be relied upon, and its usefulness has been proved over a long period. It deserves to be better known in this country than it is.   D.W.T.

MIEROWSKY, D. : *Hebrew Grammar and Grammarians throughout the ages*. 1955. Pp. 210. (D. Dainow, 33 Hunter Street, Yeoville, Johannesburg. Price : 63s. 0d.)

This work, which is duplicated in typescript, is a doctoral thesis submitted to the University of the Witwatersrand. The author became a professional scholar only late in life. His book, which was published after his death, consists of twenty-three short chapters, in which he gives a somewhat sketchy account of the development of the study of Hebrew grammar, beginning with the origins of it traceable in the Massorah and in Talmudic and Midrashic literature, and ending with the study of it in Palestine today. The author leans heavily upon the work of others ; there are a number of inaccuracies; some of the views expressed are antiquated; and there is little attempt at a critical evaluation of the material used. There are some things of interest in the work, for example, a number of works by Palestinian scholars on Hebrew grammar are referred to which will probably be unfamiliar to many Hebraists in this country.   D.W.T.

THACKERAY, H. St. J. and MARCUS, R. : *A Lexicon to Josephus*. Part IV. *Egeirein to Emphilochōrein*. (Publications of the Alexander Kohut Memorial Foundation.) 1955. Pp. 48. (Librairie Orientaliste P. Geuthner, Paris.)

The resumption of publication of this most valuable work (fasc. iii appeared in 1948, i and ii in 1930 and 1934) is hailed with gratitude and satisfaction. This is not a mechanical index of the kind which anyone able to spell Greek and blessed with a painstaking secretary may produce—the kind of which we are getting too many samples of late. Here is a proper lexicon. Every entry is based upon penetrating interpretation ; every article constructed in logical order ; the obvious is not enlarged upon, the significant is duly illustrated. The peculiarities of Josephus' various amanuenses stand out at a glance. In a field where such help is as rare as it is necessary, theologians, historians and Greek scholars are here offered an invaluable tool.   G.Z.

TUR-SINAI, N. H. : *The Language and the Book : Beliefs and Doctrines*. Vol. 3. (in Hebrew). 1955. Pp. vi+440. (Bialik Institute, Jerusalem.)

This, the third and last volume of Professor Tur-Sinai's Hebrew work, does not, as suggested by the sub-title, deal with abstract ideas but consists in the main of philological studies, many of which had been published before and appear here in a revised form. The book is divided into 5 sections, the last of which contains supplements to the previous volumes, and the last but one is devoted to Talmudic and mediaeval Hebrew, philological and literary problems. The first and largest section ' The Ark of God and its History in the Religion of Israel,' is a revision of the author's well-known German work on the subject. In the miscellaneous essays of the other two sections the author arrives among others at the following derivations : Urim from the root *'rr* (following D. H. Müller) ; Azazel from Heb. *'z* (goat) and Acc. *azlu* (wild) ; Ob (necromancer) from *'b* (skin bottle), necromancers having used skin blowers for producing noises ; Satan from *shwt* (to rove about, hence spy after) ; *nṣḥ* in connection with building has the same meaning as in the psalm titles, work having been accompanied by music ; the names for sky *shaḥaq* and *rāqia'* derive from *shḥq* (worn) and *rq'* (to patch), the clouds need mending after having been torn by the rain ; the names for rain and dew, *s'irim*, *rbibim* and *tal*, are connected with the names for goats and sheep, *sā'ir*, *rbb* (Ps. cxliv, 13) and *ṭleh*, the clouds having been pictured as herds of sheep. The work is marked by Prof. Tur-Sinai's well-known ingenuity. P.R.W.

KEY TO INITIALS
UNDER BOOK NOTICES

G.W.A.—G. W. Anderson
W.F.A.—W. F. Albright
D.R.Ap-T.—D. R. Ap-Thomas

A.B.—A. Bentzen
F.F.B.—F. F. Bruce
J.M.T.B.—J. M. T. Barton
L.H.B.—L. H. Brockington
M.B.—M. Burdess
P.A.H. de B.—P. A. H. de Boer
S.G.F.B.—S. G. F. Brandon
W.B. or W.Bg.—W. Baumgartner
M.Bl.—M. Black

D.D.—D. Daube
G.H.D.—G. H. Davies
G.R.D.—G. R. Driver
H.D.—H. Danby
M.D.—M. Delcor

I.E.—I. Engnell
O.E.—O. Eissfeldt

T.F.—T. Fish

A.G.—A. Guillaume
C.J.G.—C. J. Gadd
J.G.—J. Gray

A.S.H.—A. S. Herbert
E.H.—E. Hammershaimb
H.St.J.H.—H. St. J. Hart
S.H.H.—S. H. Hooke

A.R.J.—A. R. Johnson

A.S.K.—A. S. Kapelrud
H.K.—H. Knight

R.J.L. or R.L.—R. (J.) Loewe
A.La—A. Lauha

J.M.—J. Mauchline
T.W.M.—T. W. Manson

W.D.McH. or
W.D.M.—W. D. McHardy
J.Mu.—J. Muilenburg

C.R.N.—C. R. North

A.P.—A. Parrot
A.F.P.—A. F. Puukko
J.P.—J. Pedersen
J.v.d.P.—J. van der Ploeg
J.W.P.—J. W. Parkes
L.A.P.—L. A. Poore
N.W.P.—N. W. Porteous

B.J.R.—B. J. Roberts
B.K.R.—B. K. Rattey
E.R.—E. Robertson
H.R.—H. Ringgren
H.H.R.—H. H. Rowley
O.S.R.—O. S. Rankin
T.H.R.—T. H. Robinson

H.S.—H. Stock
I.L.S.—I. L. Seeligmann
J.N.S.—J. N. Schofield
N.H.S.—N. H. Snaith
S.S.—S. Stein
F.St.—F. Stummer

D.W.T.—D. W. Thomas
J.L.T.—J. L. Teicher
T.W.T.—T. W. Thacker

A.G.U.—A. G. Ulecia
E.U.—E. Ullendorff
W.C.vanU.—W. C. van Unnik

Th.C.V.—Th. C. Vriezen

C.J.M.W.—C. J. Mullo Weir
J.W.—J. Weingreen
M.W.—M. Wallenstein
P.R.W.—P. R. Weis

G.Z.—G Zuntz

SUBJECT INDEX

AUTHOR INDEX

AUTHOR INDEX

AUTHOR INDEX

van Ruler, A. A., 759
Russell, R., 488
Rust, E. C., 516
Rüthy, A. E., 104
Ryckmans, G., 471
Rylaarsdam, J. C., 94
Rypins, S., 481
Ryser, F., 687

Sachs, W., 683
Sainte Fare Garnot, J., 238
de Sainte-Marie, H., 660
Salomies, I., 551
Sanders, J. A., 760
Sauber, K. R., 607
Scarpat, G., 565
Schaeffer, C. F. A., 177, 238, 317, 722
Scharff, A., 323
Schauer, A., 604
Schedl, C., 249, 285
Scheiber, A., 118, 225
Schempp, P., 285
Schildenberger, J., 76, 83, 430
Schilder, H. J., 765
Schilling, O., 516, 782
Schmauch, W., 460
Schmidt, H., 126
Schmidt, J., 94
Schmidt, K. L., 348
Schmidt, M., 211
Schmidtke, F., 479
Schmitt, E., 608
Schmitz, O., 548
Schneider, H., 491, 580, 661
Schoeps, H. J., 290, 361
Schofield, J. N., 51, 390
Schönbächler, V., 94
Schott, S., 390, 391
Schötz, D., 189
Schousboe, J., 57
Schrade, H., 361
Schreiner, H., 548
Schrenk, G., 422
Schrey, H. H., 760
Schroeder, F. J., 687
Schulz, A., 84
Schumpp, M., 258
Schunck, K. D., 701
Schwab, R., 328, 732
Schwabe, M., 638
Schwarz, W., 728
Schwarzenbach, A., 707

Schweitzer, U., 238
Schweitzer, W., 428
Scott, R. B. Y., 51, 772
Seele, K. C., 19, 128
Seeligmann, I. L., 183
Segal, J. B., 633
Segal, M. H., 627
Seierstad, I. P., 159
Seligson, Miriam, 452
Sellers, O. R., 536, 558
Sellin, E., 346
van Selms, A., 139, 617
XIV Semana Bíblica Española, 716
Semirin, S., 657
Semitica, 171, 228, 379, 548, 717
Septuagint Bible, The, 729
Seventh-Day Adventist Bible Commentary, 669, 738
Seynaeve, J., 608
Ben Shammai, M. H., 18
Shipton, G. M., 175
Shohet, A., 463
Short, A. R., 391
Simon, H., 308
Simon, M., 290
Simon, U. E., 580
Simons, J., 475
Simpson, C. A., 159, 198
Sjöberg, E., 57, 114, 160
Skoss, S. L., 104
Slotki, I. W., 259, 331, 401
Slotki, J. J., 32, 331, 401
Smal, P. J. N., 761
Smalley, Beryl, 9, 415
Smart, J. D., 272
Smart, W. A., 285
Smick, E. B., 692
Smit, J. O., 249
Smith, C. Ryder, 52, 198, 429, 517
Smith, D. H., 211
Smith, M., 444
Smith, S., 18
Snaith, N. H., 37, 52, 160, 192, 230, 337, 415, 591, 671
Snell, H. C., 285
Snijders, L. A., 633
Snowman, J., 163
von Soden, W., 614, 692
Søe, N. H., 265, 294, 299
Soisalon-Soininen, I., 397, 566
Somogyi, J., 222
Sorg, R., 761